Communicating
IN THE 21st CENTURY
3rd Edition

Communicating
IN THE 21st CENTURY
3rd Edition

Baden Eunson

WILEY
John Wiley & Sons Australia, Ltd

Third edition published 2012 by
John Wiley & Sons Australia, Ltd
42 McDougall Street, Milton Qld 4064

First edition published 2005
Second edition published 2008

Typeset in 10/12 pt Agfa Rotis Serif

© Baden Eunson 2005, 2008, 2012

The moral rights of the authors have been asserted.

National Library of Australia
Cataloguing-in-Publication entry

Author:	Eunson, Baden.
Title:	Communicating in the 21st century / Baden Eunson.
Edition:	3rd ed.
ISBN:	9781742166179 (pbk.)
Notes:	Includes bibliographical references and index.
Subjects:	Communication — Social aspects — Australia.
	Communication — Research — Australia.
	Business communication — Australia.
	Knowledge management — Australia.
	Communication in personnel management — Australia.
Dewey Number:	302.20994

Internal design images: © John Wiley & Sons, Australia/Photo by Renee
Bryon; © iStockphoto.com/Mlenny Photography; © Shutterstock/Sandra
Gligorijevic, /Yuri Arcurs, /Andrejs Pidjass, /auremar, 2011.

Typeset in India by diacriTech

Printed in China by
1010 Printing

10 9 8 7 6 5 4 3 2 1

For my parents

BRIEF CONTENTS

CONTENTS

4 Letters, emails and memos 110

5 Reports and proposals 152

6 Online writing 196

7 Academic writing: the essay 222

11 Oral communication 338

12 Argument: logic, persuasion and influence 376

13 Negotiation skills 404

14 Conflict management   442

15 Intercultural communication   470

16 Organisational communication   508

17 Public communication   550

18 Team communication   578

19 Communicating in meetings 622

20 Employment communication 664

21 Social media 702

PREFACE

How employable are you? If you are currently studying in X, Y or Z studies (pharmacy, dance, economics, arts, business, IT ... the list is endless), you've probably made the very sensible decision to study in the field or discipline that feeds into the industry or area of employment that is your goal. You've done this because you have assumed the conventional wisdom that the better your marks (showing your command of your discipline), the more likely you are to be employed. This seems logical – too logical to query, in fact – but you would be wrong. Our whole education system, and most of the administrators and course designers within it, also works under this fallacy.

Assertions need proofs, and there are ample. For example, Australian employers have been surveyed to find out what qualities they are looking for in graduates. Recent annual results from these surveys are shown in the next table.

TABLE Selection criteria by rank order for Australian organisations

	Selection criteria	2007	2008	2009	2010
1	Interpersonal and communication skills (written and oral)	1	1	1	1
2	Passion; knowledge of industry; drive; commitment; attitude	3	2	2	2
3	Critical reasoning and analytical skills; problem-solving; lateral thinking; technical skills	2	3	3	3
4	Calibre of academic results	5	6	4	4
5	Teamwork skills	6	5	5	7
6	Work experience	8	8	6	6
7	Cultural alignment; values fit	4	4	7	5
8	Emotional intelligence (including self-awareness, confidence, motivation)	7	7	8	8
9	Leadership skills	10	9	9	9
10	Activities (including intra- and extra-curricular activities)	9	10	10	10

Source: *Graduate Outlook 2010.* © Graduate Careers Australia.

The 'calibre of academic results' – the 'Bachelor of X' studies, the 'Diploma of Y Science' – has come in at a second or third priority in rankings of these criteria over the past few years. In contrast, interpersonal and communication skills (written and oral) have beaten the field every time (being ranked as the most important selection criterion for four consecutive years up to 2010) (Graduate Careers Australia 2010). These skills are discussed in this book in numerous chapters on different types of writing (including grammar and punctuation) and oral communication. Other topics covered in this book – critical reasoning, problem solving, lateral thinking, organisational culture, emotional intelligence, and leadership skills – also ranked highly on employers' wish lists for employee skills.

Practice is matched by theory, and instructors can draw on supporting expansion material in instructor resource guides for the chapters. These skill sets have been called employability skills, graduate skills, generic skills, interpersonal skills, soft skills, people skills, and transferable skills. Similar graduate skill preferences have been noted by employers in countries all over the world. Surprising as this may seem, it's old news. In 2000, the Australian Government published a report entitled, 'Employer satisfaction with graduate skills' (this should be available online). While generally satisfied with the calibre of academic results, the same old story was occurring. Consider this extract from the report (Commonwealth of Australia 2000, p. 9):

> *In saying that recruiters are satisfied, however, we should note that there is an apparent over-supply of graduates, and employers can pick from among them. Many graduates appear to miss out on job opportunities because of the lack of skills in basics such as literacy or numeracy. If there is dissatisfaction with graduate skills as such, it probably lies in the area of written communication, because the majority of students are not taught to write in a manner appropriate to business communications.*

So what has gone wrong? If we were to follow the strict logic and implications of this list of employability skills, then our sites of learning – universities, institutes of technical and further education, colleges and polytechnics – would devote a large part of their curriculum to communication. In reality, most higher learning courses conducted today might devote 5 per cent or less of course time to this area, and many courses would allocate no time at all. Professional communication, in other words, is often marginalised, held in contempt or ignored, despite what the outside world wants. What is demanded is rarely supplied.

Course designers in X, Y and Z studies are overwhelmed with new information to teach in their own disciplines, and don't often see the value of employability skills. Yet surely – or at least hopefully – more than a decade of the same message about priorities for graduates must eventually be confronted.

What is needed then is to move the communication skills part up the list of priorities for educators. How? By firstly recognising communication as a valid subject area, putting it on the curriculum, and then teaching it in its various forms and giving students qualifications in it. One or two communications subjects, units or modules in a qualification or on a resumé may be precisely what will help differentiate one person in search of a job or a role from others who do not have such qualifications. You deserve to have the communication advantage.

Such abilities are now universally recognised in the world of work as the means by which we understand ourselves and others, and as vitally important in helping us advance and grow in our careers and lives. This is true for various reasons:

- As technology becomes more dominant in many work processes, the human element of communication becomes more necessary as a counterweight and a reality-testing tool.
- As communication technologies proliferate, it becomes possible to be misunderstood in many more ways, so new strategies of communicating clearly become more important and more urgent.
- The majority of budget allocations in most organisations go on salaries, so the imperative is to see staff as human resources, and communication is the main way in which those resources can be tapped.
- As more learning goes online, much of it is convergent – that is, only one solution for any given problem is offered. In the real world, however, many problems are divergent – there are many solutions to the one problem. Communication concepts tend to be more divergent than convergent.
- Communication skills have very long shelf lives, remaining relevant for decades and being transferable between jobs and careers, while most technical learning is obsolete in a shorter time frame and is not usually transferable.

Yet the non-response, or limited response, of course designers and learning managers to such views shows that perhaps their own communication skills – listening skills, in particular – may be in need of a tune-up. The belief persists that 'all this soft skills stuff' can just be picked up along the way, presumably by some mysterious process of osmosis or by 'embedding' the content in mainstream curriculum. Such a belief is demonstrably wrong. It is common to hear academics and trainers argue, for example, that team or group skills can be acquired simply by setting team assignments for students. Nothing could be further from the truth. Students need to study group interaction as a separate and pedagogically valid set of content before embarking on team assignments. Such study, properly done, will reveal that:

- Group/team decision making can be faulty if its dynamics are not understood.
- 'Free riders' or work-shy members may unethically grab credit and marks/grades – defeating the purpose of team assignments, and creating cynicism and conflict – unless they can be induced to follow shared norms and act out appropriate roles.
- The concept of teams may be inappropriate and even dysfunctional for some real-world tasks.
- The very concept of teams may need to be challenged; while it implies empowered democratic decision making, in too many real-world situations it may be little more than a smokescreen or con to mask disempowering and autocratic decision making.

This broader context means that not only *skills* in communication, but also critical *knowledge* about communication and its environment, need to be acquired.

Of course, all of these faults of team-based working occur in the real world, but it is always better to know how to manage them than not to. Communication – focusing on written; visual; interpersonal; group or team; organisational; intercultural; inter-gender; public, customer or client; verbal or non-verbal; persuasive; online; information retrieval; and conflict and negotiation dynamics – is now a mature, research-based discipline that should be factored in to all courses of study. Slowly, very slowly, that is beginning to happen.

'Must have good communication skills' is almost a cliché in job advertisements and job descriptions these days. But where can we acquire such skills? And how can we prove we have them? Courses in communication, supported by books like this one, can help. Of course, the skills are not enough; we need theory to provide a foundation for the skills, just as we need skills to demonstrate that the theories work. We need to translate ideas into action, achieving *praxis* in communication. Yet too many of the communication techniques and theories sold in the marketplace are superficial, trite, gimmicky, self-serving or biased in presentation; too often they present a management-only perspective in organisational settings, or a naïve and narcissistic approach to personal development. Too often professional communication is presented either as a grab-bag of slick training formulas shot through with psychobabble or as an opaque research area with limited connection to the real world. It doesn't have to be like that, and it's not like that in the book now in your hands.

What's new in this third edition of *Communicating in the 21st century*? A new chapter has been created, all chapters have been updated, and you will find that a number have been substantially expanded to include the following material:

- Chapter 1: consideration of new technological channels (blogs, wikis); a new RSVP model of integrating messages with technology
- Chapter 2: the 'eye candy' model of breaking up text with graphic material to arrest the attention of readers; Microsoft Office 2010; updated data on graphics
- Chapter 3: a new screenshot of research engines; internet searching; expanded treatment of Harvard citation methods
- Chapter 4: integration of letters, memos and emails as genres
- Chapter 5: new material on pitfalls of using academic essay style in business reports and perils of tendering in corrupt situations
- Chapter 6: new Australian material in web design section
- Chapter 7: complete updates of 'good' and 'bad' model essays
- Chapter 8: new examples of non-verbal behaviour with biological bases
- Chapter 9: update on emotional intelligence; new four-way model of self-talk; new assertiveness diagrams
- Chapter 10: new material on listening processes, listening and technological overload

- Chapter 11: material on new technologies to aid speaking and presentation
- Chapter 12: new presentation of inductive and deductive logic; new collection of fallacies
- Chapter 13: 'winner's curse' concept; new list of tactics
- Chapter 14: expansion of conflict diagnostic model
- Chapter 15: new material on conflict between cultures and controversies about differing intercultural models
- Chapter 16: new material on knowledge management
- Chapter 17: new material on limiter publics; examples of situation analyses and matching solutions; position papers; profiles
- Chapter 18: techniques for controlling student team assignment participation; group-think and the global financial crisis; variations in stages of group development; critique of outdoor teambuilding; competition versus cooperation
- Chapter 19: meeting failure checklist; problems with videoconferencing; topless meetings
- Chapter 20: new material on finding jobs; warning regarding employers vetting potential employees via Facebook and other new media; handwritten resumes, new material in 'Job seeking: the funny side'; new arguments for superiority of manual work over office work
- Chapter 21: new chapter on social media (blogs, Twitter, Facebook and so on); a critical examination of the technical, social and interpersonal aspects of this new mode of communication on Web 2.0.

The 'Leadership and communication' and 'Communicating with customers' chapters have been moved online to keep the book size manageable, joining the other eight already there: 'Writing skills 1 (grammar)', 'Writing skills 2 (Punctuation, spelling and usage)', 'Writing skills 3 (Style)', 'Writing skills 4 (Plain English)', 'Writing skills 5 (How to write)', 'Writing for science and technology', 'Gender and communication', and 'Media and communication'.

Of course, there is a difference between simply reading and learning about something and putting it into practice. If we personally and individually master all, some or most of this content, and put it into practice in an ethical way, then we will be more likely to be employable and appreciated, as well as less likely to feel the pain of communication breakdowns in both our professional and personal lives. Soft skills are deceptively hard to master, but they have tangible, and pleasant, payoffs.

Baden Eunson
June 2011

HOW TO USE THIS BOOK

Each chapter in this book is a tightly structured learning unit that includes the following features.

Margin definitions Word snapshots of key concepts discussed in the text

Learning objectives Ideas you will have control over by the end of the chapter

Primary data: original unpublished material or material published in an original form

Secondary data: material that interprets primary material, published after primary data is published

Tertiary data: material that synthesises and summarises primary and secondary material, usually published well after primary and secondary sources

Primary data consists of ori[...] or writers or other individua[...] of primary data include exp[...] observations, databases, arch[...] meetings, company records, p[...]

Secondary data is material t[...] created, and is not original. Se[...] primary data. Examples inclu[...] in paper or electronic format,[...]

Tertiary data is material pub[...] comprises syntheses, summar[...] cally, tertiary material include[...] and abstracts.

It is a slight over-generalis[...] credit you will get for it. A[...] encyclopedia entries would [...] substantially on primary so[...] sources, and with only a sm[...] quality of information, and [...] problems with many online[...] largely true that the primary[...] all knowledge is created in t[...] mented on and interpreted i[...] in tertiary material.

LEARNING OBJECTIVES

After studying this chapter you should be able to:

- Explain why negotiation is not always the preferred mode for resolving a situation of conflict or disagreement
- Explain the nature of win-lose and win-win dynamics in conflicts
- Understand the value of research
- Define goals and bottom lines, and concessions, positions and interests
- Determine whether territory and time scarcity or abundance is relevant in negotiation
- Assess the role of publics or stakeholders in negotiation
- Understand how to package offers in negotiation
- Work better as an individual or as a member of a team in a negotiation situation
- Understand the role of nonverbal communication and signalling in negotiation
- Use listening skills, questioning skills and persuasive skills in negotiations
- Understand the role of culture and gender in negotiations
- Understand the importance of personal styles in negotiation
- Identify and use strategies and tactics in negotiations
- Identify and effectively use communication channels in negotiation situations
- Create an effective plan for a variety of negotiation situations

What would you do? Mini case studies promote higher order thinking by applying chapter content to real-life situations.

WHAT WOULD YOU DO?

In Victoria, Australia, in 2009, 173 people died in what soon became Australia's worst peace-time disaster (AAP 2009). There were many reasons why the Victorian bushfire disaster occurred. One that stands out was the sheer, almost unbelievable lack of communication between the trained professionals in charge of the operation.

The essence of any counter-disaster operation is effective coordination. This proved to be impossible to achieve with the disaster, with rural fire-fighting authorities and metropolitan emergency services operating on incompatible communications systems during the crisis. The rural fire-fighting authorities were operating on analogue radio, while the metropolitan emergency services were operating on digital radio. There were no digital communication towers in rural Victoria at the time of the fires. People who were on the fringe between a metropolitan area and a bush area usually had both systems (Caldwell 2009).

During an investigation that followed, Victorian Police Deputy Commissioner Kieran Walshe told the investigating body, the Bushfire Royal Commission, that a 'single integrated radio

KEY TERMS

backgrounder *p. 563*
campaign *p. 557*
crisis communication *p. 566*
environmental scanning
   p. 567
fact sheet *p. 565*
grabspeak *p. 570*
high-transparency
   organisation *p. 568*
issue *p. 566*

low-transparency
   organisation *p. 568*
media kit *p. 565*
media release *p. 560*
position paper *p. 564*
profile *p. 565*
pseudo-event *p. 553*
public information
   model *p. 553*
publicity model *p. 553*

public *p. 556*
shoot-the-messenger climate
   p. 567
spin *p. 552*
tools *p. 560*
two-way asymmetric
   model *p. 554*
two-way symmetric
   model *p. 554*

Key terms are listed at the end of each chapter.

Assess yourself
In-chapter exercises that allow you to pause and consolidate your learning up to that point

Review questions
Opportunities to check and refresh your understanding of concepts discussed in the chapter

REVIEW QUESTIONS

1. '"Information design" is just a piece of pompous jargon. Why not leave it at that?' Discuss.
2. List at least three typical usability problems encountered in docum
3. What problems can differing forms of justification of text present?
4. What are two strengths and two weaknesses of visuals?
5. What does VOYD-HAXI stand for?
6. What type of data set would you *not* represent using a pie graph?
7. What type of data set would you *not* represent using a pie graph?
8. What problems are involved in the use of 3D graphs?
9. Why should you consider how a colour visual might look in black

APPLIED ACTIVITIES

1. Find some old textbooks, preferably written 30 to 60 years ago. N with modern examples. In what ways are the modern books superi they inferior?
2. Find examples of *Idiots*, *For Dummies* or *For Beginners* guide book treatment of topics with the treatments given in conventional text advantages of the more graphic approach? What are the disadvant
3. Select a sample of about 1000 words of text. This can be:
   - text you write yourself, describing a product or process
   - existing text written by you or someone else and stored electronically an essay or an article
   - material scanned electronically (using optical character recognition so word processor from a book or other source.

Chapter 2 Document design and grap

Applied activities provide opportunities for higher order thinking skills to be displayed via more in-depth analysis and practical exercises.

ASSESS YOURSELF

The feedback model gives us a structure for controlling our stress when giving negative feedback (as well as helping us avoid counterproductive aggressive, passive or manipulative mind games). When you first start to use it, it may feel artificial and silly, but persevere and you may find it a very useful tool of assertive communication.

Write a 'script' that covers the specifics of the negative feedback you need to give. Then rehearse in front of a mirror, video camera and/or friends. This can improve your technique and also make you feel a good deal more comfortable with it.

Rehearsal also means that in the real or perceived stress of a confrontation with the target of your feedback, you can put some of your thinking brain on automatic pilot while playing back your new memories of the sequence. When you run through the sequence, look directly at the target; if you avert your gaze, you are sending out mixed, contradictory messages. Remember, you are expressing the way you feel based on what you think, not the ways others might feel or think. You have a perfect right to express this, just as others have the right to use the sequence when talking to you.

It sometimes helps to do a background analysis of the situation in which you find yourself. Have a go at completing this in the following form, or simply type or write it up on a larger sheet of paper. Once you have done this, write a script using the feedback sequence, and then rehearse it. If you feel it has potential to change a real-world situation, take the plunge and try it.

Background analysis

The situation is:	
The target person is:	
The main problems you have in communicating with the target person are:	

Feedback sequence and scripting

Phase	Cue words	Your script
1	When you …	
2	This happens …	
3	And I feel …	
4	Would you …	
5	Because/That way/This would mean …	
6	I/You/They would feel …	
7	So what do you think?	

References support the text and provide a starting point for further research.

REFERENCES

Anderson, Paul 2011, *Web 2.0: principles and technologies*, Chapman and Hall, United Kingdom.

Abaya, Eleanor & Gilbert, Fred 2008, 'Lakehead says no to WiFi: Lakehead University takes a precautionary approach to the widespread application of WiFi technology', *Lakehead University Magazine*, http://magazine.lakeheadu.ca.

Abram, Carolyn & Pearlman, Leah 2008, *Facebook for dummies*, John Wiley & Sons, New York.

Angwin, Julia 2009, *Stealing MySpace: the battle control the most popular website in America*, Random House, New York.

Bauerlein, Mark 2009, *The dumbest generation: how the digital age stupefies young Americans and jeopardizes our future*, Tarcher/Penguin, New York.

Bingham, John 2009, 'MI6's chief's security 'compromised' by wife's Facebook postings', *The Telegraph*, 6 July, www.telegraph.co.uk.

Blossom, John 2009, *Content nation: surviving and thriving as social media changes our work, our lives, and our future*, John Wiley & Sons, Indianapolis, IN.

Brake, David 2008, 'Shaping the "me" in MySpace: the framing of profiles on a social network site', in Lundby, Knut (ed.) *Digital storytelling, mediatized stories: self-representations in the new media*, Peter Lang, New York.

Burroughs, Benjamin 2007, 'Kissing Macaca': blogs, narrative and political discourse', *Journal for Cultural Research*, vol. 11 no. 4, pp. 319–35.

Bruns, Axel 2009, *Blogs, Wikipedia, Second Life, and beyond: from production to produsage*, Peter Lang, New York.

Canning, Simon 2009, 'Social websites help to broadcast news', *The Australian*, 3 August, p. 38.

Cashone, Josh 2009, 'Top 5 business mistakes and how to avoid them', *Open Forum*, 17 September, www.openforum.com.

a case of 'you show me yours, and I'll show you mine', *International Journal of Information Management*, vol. 29 pp. 255–61.

Dudley-Nicholson, Jennifer 2009, 'Facebook, MySpace social networking bigger than email', *The Courier Mail*, 10 March, www.news.com.au.

Dobbin, Marika 2010, '$78,000 to tweet for city council', *The Age*, 18 November, p. 3.

Evans, Kathy 2010, 'This is our life', *The Sunday Age*, 28 November, p. 11.

Facebook 2009. *Facebook phishing scam awareness*, www.facebook.com.

Fitton, Laura, Gruen, Michael, & Poston, Leslie 2009, *Twitter for dummies*, John Wiley & Sons, Hoboken, NY.

Fixmer, A & Rabil, S 2011, 'News Corp.'s MySpace cuts staff by 47% amid reports website may be sold', *Bloomberg*, 12 January.

Fogel, Joshua & Nehmad, Elham 2009, 'Internet social network communities: risk-taking, trust, and privacy concerns', *Computers in human behavior*, vol. 25 pp. 153–60.

Foster, Rusty 2001, 'The utter failure of weblogs as journalism', *Kuro5hin*, 11 Oct, www.kuro5hin.org.

Gardner, Susannah & Birley, Shane 2008, *Blogging for dummies*, 2nd edn, John Wiley & Sons, Hoboken, NJ.

Gaudin, Sharon 2009a, 'Facebook, Twitter users are affluent and urban, study shows', *Computerworld*, 28 September, p. 7.

Gaudin, Sharon 2009b, 'Study: Facebook linked to lower grades in college', *Macworld*, 14 April, p. 4.

Gauvin, W. et al. 2010, 'Measurement and gender-specific analysis of user publishing characteristics on MySpace', *IEEE*, vol. 24 no. 5, pp. 38–43.

George, Alison 2006, 'Things you wouldn't tell your mother',

Suggested reading
Comprehensive, up-to-date resources that can help you research further into content areas

Annotated guides provide clear, helpful pointers to good and bad communication techniques.

SUGGESTED READING

Baker, Stephen 2009, 'Beware social media snake oil', *Business Week*, 14

Brown, Rob 2009, *Public relations and the social web: how to use socia communications*, Kogan Page, London/Philadelphia.

Bruns, Axel & Adams, Debra 2009, 'Mapping the Australian blogosphere Echchaibi, Nabil (eds.) *International blogging: identity, politics and ne New York.

Cass, John 2007, *Strategies and tools for corporate blogging*, Butterworth Oxford, UK.

Falkner, Xristine & Culwin, Fintan 2005, 'When fingers do the talking: a *Interacting with Computers*, vol. 17, 167–85.

Fortunati, Leopoldina 2005, 'Mobile telephones and the presentation of Per E. (eds.) *Mobile Communications: Re-negotiation of the social sph

Hay, Deltina 2009, *A survival guide to social media and web 2.0 optimi tools for succeeding in the social web*, Wiggy Press/ Dalton Publishing

Kraynak, Joe & Belicove, Mikal E 2010, *The complete idiot's guide to Fa Books/Pearson.

Li, Charlene & Bernoff 2008, *Groundswell: winning in a world transform Harvard Business School Press.

Licoppe, Christian 2004, 'Connected presence: the emergence of a new r relationships in a changing communications technoscape', *Environme Space*, vol. 22, pp. 135–56.

Ling, Rich & Donner, Jonathan 2009, *Mobile communication*, Polity Pres

MacArthur, Amber 2010, *Power friending: demystifying social media to Penguin, New York.

Mahar, Sue Martin & Mahar, Jay 2009, *The unofficial guide to building Life® virtual world: marketing and selling your product, services and Amacom, New York.

Marshall, Michael 2009, 'Facebook is good for you', *New Scientist*, 7 Ma

Myers, Greg 2010, *Discourse of blogs and wikis*, Continuum, London/Ne

Parsons, Claudia 2009, 'Hate goes viral on social networking sites', *The

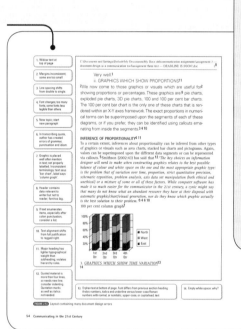

FIGURE 2.11 Layout containing many document design errors

Clear layout provides lucid overviews of salient points.

TABLE 19.1 Types of meetings

Meeting type	What happens?	Who runs it?	Who else attends?
Public meeting	■ Issues of public concern are discussed ■ A forum is provided to hear information	■ Public action/pressure groups ■ Commercial companies ■ Local councils	■ Members of the public ■ Shareholders
Private meeting	■ Issues of concern to a particular group, association or organisation are discussed	■ Executives or committees of service clubs (Rotary, Lions), unions, hobby groups	■ Members of associations, unions, clubs
Briefing meeting	■ Information is given out about new policies, procedures, daily routines ■ Downward flow of information	■ Managers, team leaders in private and public sector organisations	■ Staff of teams, departments
Feedback meeting	■ Information and opinions are sought ■ Upward flow of information	■ Managers, team leaders in private and public sector organisations	■ Staff of teams, departments
Board meeting	■ Company directors monitor developments within an organisation (often monthly)	■ Board chairperson	■ Board members
Annual general meeting (AGM)	■ Company directors report on developments (usually annual) ■ Shareholders get chance to question directors	■ Company directors/board members	■ Shareholders
Extraordinary general meeting (EGM)	■ Same as an AGM, except held between normal AGMs ■ May be in response to a crisis ■ May be in response to shareholder initiative	■ Company directors/board members	■ Shareholders

Practical learning tools allow you to get clear feedback on your communication strengths and weaknesses.

Visual approach uses incisive diagrams to provide graphic insight into the concepts being examined.

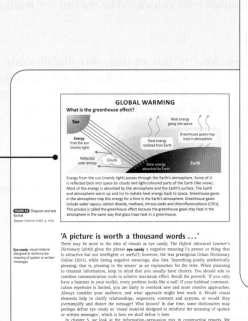

GLOBAL WARMING
What is the greenhouse effect?

FIGURE 2.6 Diagram and text format
Source: Schriver (1997, p. 415).

Eye candy: visual material designed to reinforce the meaning of spoken or written messages

Energy from the sun (mainly light) passes through the Earth's atmosphere. Some of it is reflected back into space by clouds and light-coloured parts of the Earth (like snow). Most of the energy is absorbed by the atmosphere and the Earth's surface. The Earth and atmosphere warm up and try to radiate heat energy back to space. Greenhouse gases in the atmosphere trap this energy for a time in the Earth's atmosphere. Greenhouse gases include water vapour, carbon dioxide, methane, nitrous oxide and chlorofluorocarbons (CFCs). This process is called the greenhouse effect because the greenhouse gases trap heat in the atmosphere in the same way that glass traps heat in a greenhouse.

'A picture is worth a thousand words . . .'

There may be more to the idea of visuals as eye candy. The *Oxford Advanced Learner's Dictionary* (2010) gives the phrase **eye candy** a negative meaning ('a person or thing that is attractive but not intelligent or useful'; however, the less prestigious Urban Dictionary Online (2011), while listing negative meanings, also lists 'Something purely aesthetically pleasing; that is, pleasing to the senses' as an explanation for the term. When planning to transmit information, keep in mind that you usually have choices. You should aim to combine communication tools to achieve maximum effect. Recall the proverb: 'If you only have a hammer in your toolkit, every problem looks like a nail'. If your habitual communication repertoire is limited, you are likely to overlook new and more creative approaches. Always consider your audience, and what approach might best reach it. Would visual elements help to clarify relationships, sequences, contexts and systems, or would they oversimplify and distort the message? Who knows? In due time, some dictionaries may perhaps define eye candy as 'visual material designed to reinforce the meaning of spoken or written messages', which is how we shall define it here.

In chapter 5, we look at the information–persuasion mix in constructing reports. We also mention the entertainment value of a document. This is a tribute to that great cliché that a picture is worth a thousand words. When composing documents, even short ones, use your word processing software to get a multi-page view of how the document is progressing. If appropriate to the genre, try to ensure that there is least a piece of eye candy – a graph, a table or a photo – on every second page. Chances are that, in this age of nonreaders who simply skim and scan (and thus lose the intricate thread of your words), the eye candy will arrest their attention. Stick the pages to a wall or look at a multi-page view: you might be surprised at how your exposition is, or is not, turning out. Edit, edit,

ASSESS YOURSELF

In the following questionnaire, mark the appropriate response. Consider the questions either generally or in relation to one particular part of your life (e.g. as a member of a work group or family, or as a student attending classes). In a sense, this questionnaire is impossible to complete accurately, because many of the communication patterns described here are unconscious, or only partly conscious. Complete it anyway, however, and perhaps consider:
■ doing it again in a few days' time, when you have had time to reflect on it and observe your own behaviour more closely
■ having someone else complete a copy of it, rating you as a listener. You may be interested to discover how others evaluate your abilities (and you can, of course, return the favour).

		Nearly always	Often	Not often	Almost never	SCORE
1.	Do you only pretend you are listening to someone speaking, when in fact your mind is far away?					
2.	Do you concentrate on the dress, grooming and gestures of the speaker rather than on what is being said?					
3.	Do you continue multitasking or doing other things (e.g. signing papers, performing calculations, working on equipment) while others are talking?					
4.	Are you distracted by other things (e.g. your watch, a newspaper or a book, other conversations, the television, the radio, a telephone ringing, a computer screen) while someone else is talking?					
5.	Do you operate in an environment in which physical barriers (e.g. noise, heating, comfort) distract you from listening to others?					
SUBTOTAL A						
6.	Do you believe 'boring' people have nothing useful to say?					
7.	Do you interrupt others?					
8.	Do you believe that facts (not emotions, values and opinions) are the only things worth listening for?					
9.	Do you periodically paraphrase (put into your own words) a speaker's words back to him/her to confirm you understand each other?					
10.	Do you get so angry with a speaker that you spend time thinking of your response — and thus lose track of the rest of the conversation?					
SUBTOTAL B						
11.	Do you look directly at the speaker?					
12.	Do you forget what a speaker has only just said?					
13.	When listening, do you fail to give nonverbal feedback (e.g. head-nods, 'friendly grunts') while maintaining a blank stare and immobile face?					
14.	Do you 'tune out' when someone starts talking, because you know the rest of their talk is totally predictable?					
15.	Do you relax and listen uncritically when the speaker seems to reflect your values and uses jargon and buzz-phrases you are comfortable with?					

ADDITIONAL RESOURCES

For instructors

- Learning management system resources are available to suit a variety of online course delivery platforms, such as BlackBoard/WebCT and Moodle. John Wiley & Sons provides content that integrates seamlessly with the textbook. Instructors have the option of uploading additional material and customising existing content to meet their needs.
- An Instructor's Resource Guide, prepared by text author Baden Eunson, is available that contains a range of additional resources, including:
  - chapter synopses
  - lecture stops
  - sample assignments
  - class exercises
  - suggested answers to text questions
  - additional questions and exercises.
- PowerPoint teaching slides, prepared by Helene Strawbridge, Deakin University, outline key concepts from each chapter and contain data, tables, charts and diagrams from the text. Instructors can easily customise the slides to suit course requirements.
- A Computerised Test Bank, prepared by Gregory Nash, University of the Sunshine Coast, contains page-referenced multiple choice questions to test student knowledge and understanding, as well as short answer/mini-essay style questions to test higher order thinking skills. Customised tests can easily be created for multiple classes.

For students

- *iStudy Communication.* New to this edition, this digital study guide contains a range of interactive modules, skills assessment exercises and template documents. This study guide facilitates the understanding and application of key communication concepts.
- *Chapter practice quizzes and self-marking key term exercises.* These are provided for university learning management systems with this edition.
- *Wiley 'DeskTop' edition e-book.* A full electronic version of the text is available as a cheaper alternative to the printed text. The e-book runs on devices such as iPads, iPhones and computers.
- *10 additional chapters.* These chapters are available free online and/or in the e-book version of the text, covering the following topics:
  - Grammar
  - Punctuation, Spelling and Usage
  - Style
  - Plain English
  - How to Write
  - Scientific and Technical Writing
  - Gender and Communication
  - Media and Communication
  - Communicating with Customers
  - Leadership and Communication.

ACKNOWLEDGEMENTS

I would like to thank Helene Strawbridge from Deakin University for her work on the PowerPoint slides to accompany the text, and also Gregory Nash from the University of the Sunshine Coast for his work on the Test Banks and Practice Quizzes.

Thanks also to the editorial team at John Wiley & Sons, Australia, for their assistance. Their author training and management skills were excellent, and the team helped me to deliver this comprehensive resource without going through too many deadlines.

Finally, thanks to Annette, Ben and James, who tolerated all this with 'saint-like' patience for a third time.

Baden Eunson

The authors and publisher would like to thank the following copyright holders, organisations and individuals for their permission to reproduce copyright material in this book.

Images
- © Shutterstock: 4 (top left) /Dmitriy Shironosov; 13 (bottom left) /Diego Cervo; 18 (middle left) / Yuri Arcurs; 27 (top left) /gary718; 79 (bottom left) /Robert Kneschke; 108 (middle left) /StockLite; 150 (bottom left) /Yuri Arcurs; 219 (middle left) /AVAVA; 231 (top left) /Monkey Business Images; 252 (middle left) /Kuzma; 256 (bottom left) /Yuri Arcurs; 261 (middle left) /Supri Suharjoto; 271 (top left) /Yuri Arcurs; 277 (middle left) /Chris Howey; 284 (bottom left) /Yellowj; 284 (bottom right) /Blaj Gabriel; 284 (middle left) /Dmitriy Shironosov; 284 (middle right) /Diego Cervo; 290 (middle left) /bikeriderlondon; 299 (top left) /micro10x; 305 (middle left) /Deklofenak; 310 (middle left) /Marcel Mooij; 311 (top left) /Losevsky Pavel; 336 (middle left) /HYPESTOCK; 378 (bottom left) /Gladskikh Tatiana; 396 (bottom left) /Liv friis-larsen; 406 (bottom right) /Losevsky Pavel; 406 (bottom right middle) /Monkey Business Images; 406 (middle left) /Monkey Business Images; 423 (middle left) /Benis Arapovic; 467 (top left) /Piotr Marcinski; 519 (top left) /JustASC; 555 (bottom left) /Picsfive; 581 (bottom left) /Ximagination; 581 (bottom right) /wavebreakmedia Ltd; 581 (middle left) /max blain; 581 (middle right) /auremar; 616 (middle left) /auremar; 693 (top left) /Adam Gregor • © Cengage Learning: 10 (top) /Berlo D 1960, *Process of communication*, 1st edn, Wadsworth, a part of Cengage Learning, Inc • © Transaction Publishers: 11 (top) /Lievrouw LA & Finn TA 1990 'Identifying the common dimensions of communication: The communication systems model' in Ruben BD & Lievrouw LA 1990 *Mediation, Information and Communication: Information and Behaviour*, vol. 3, p. 54, Transaction Publishers • © Davis Foulger: 12 (middle) / Foulger D 2004, 'Models of the communication process' • © Newspix: 32 (bottom left) /Alex Coppel; 257 (top left) /News Ltd; 378 (bottom left) /Fiona Hamilton; 553 (top left) /News Ltd; 723 (bottom left) /Alan Pryke • © ASTD: 33 (bottom) /Galpin T 1995, 'Pruning the grapevine', *Training and Development*, vol. 49, no. 4, April • © John Wiley & Sons, Inc: 42 (bottom) /Schriver KA 1997, 'Dynamics in document design: creating text for readers'; 43 (middle) /Schriver KA 1997, 'Dynamics in document design: creating text for readers'; 43 (top) /Schriver KA 1997, 'Dynamics in document design: creating text for readers'; 44 (top) /Schriver KA 1997, 'Dynamics in document design: creating text for readers'; 213 (top) /Hammerich I & Harrison C, 'Developing Online Content'; 330 (bottom) /Hanson PC, 'The Johari window: A model for soliciting and giving feedback' in *The 1973 Annual Handbook for Group Facilitators*, Jossey-Bass Pfeiffer, p. 115; 332 (middle) /Hanson PC, 'The Johari window: A model for soliciting and giving feedback' in *The 1973 Annual Handbook for Group Facilitators*, Jossey-Bass Pfeiffer, p. 115 • © William DuBay: 42 (top) /Dubay WH 2004, 'The principles of readability', Impact Information, Costa Mesa, p. 18 • © Janice C. Redish: 45 (bottom) • © Australian Bureau of Statistics: 61 (bottom middle) /Commonwealth of Australia; 668 (top) / Commonwealth of Australia • © Queensland Treasury: 62 (bottom) /Queensland Treasury, Australian Gambling Statistics • © Reserve Bank of Australia: 62 (top) • © Department of Climate Change: 68 (top) /Information courtesy of the Department of Climate Change and Energy Efficiency • © Ian Plimer: 68 (bottom) /Ian Plimer, *IPA Review*, December 2002 • © Google Inc: 87 (bottom) • © John Wiley & Sons, Australia: 99 (top left) /Renee Bryon; 209 (top left) /Renee Bryon; 565 (bottom left) /Renee Bryon; 717 (top left) /Renee Bryon; 728 (top left) /Renee Bryon • © Roberts Management Concepts: 193 (middle) /Jean Roberts, Director, Roberts Management Concepts Pty Ltd • © Robert H Zakon: 198 (middle) /Hobbes' Internet Timeline, 1993–2006 www.zakon.org/robert/internet/timeline/

• © Elsevier: **203** (middle) /Gimenez JC 2000, 'Business e-mail communication', *English for Specific Purposes*, vol. 19, no. 1, p. 240; **239** (top) /Tang R & John S 1999, 'The "I" in identity: Exploring the writer identity in student academic writing through the first person pronoun', *English for Specific Purposes*, vol. 18, supp. 1, p. S23–S39; **475** (bottom middle) /Hammer, Bennett & Wiseman 2003, 'Measuring intercultural sensitivity: The intercultural development inventory', *International Journal of Intercultural Relations*, vol. 27, iss. 4, p. 421–43; **542** (bottom) /Gottschalk P 2006, 'Expert systems at stage IV of the knowledge management technology stage model: The case of police investigations', *Expert Systems with Applications,* vol. 31, p. 617–28 • © iStockphoto: **264** (bottom left) /Steve Cole; **359** (middle left) /Aldo Murillo; **534** (top left) /Susanna Fieramosca Naranjo; **704** (top left) /franckreporter; **716** (top left) /Giorgio Fochesato • © Slattery Media Group: **297** (bottom left) / AFL 2010; **605** (bottom left) /Greg Ford/ GSP Images • © AAP Image: **378** (middle right) /Dean Lewins; **386** (top left) /Tracey Nearmy; **406** (bottom left) /Susan Walsh; **566** (top left) /Gerald Herbert • © Photolibrary: **378** (middle left) /Imagesource; **473** (middle left) /Cusp; **545** (bottom left) /Brand X Pictures • © Team Publications Pty Ltd: **429** (top) /Warner J 2000, 'Negotiating skills', Team Publications Pty Ltd, p. 35 • © Copyright Clearance Center: **449** (bottom middle) /Thomas KW 1977, 'Towards multi-dimensional values in teaching...', *Academy of Management Review*; **481** (middle) /Based on Hofstede's five dimensions of national cultures from, G. Hofstede 1993, 'Cultural constraints in management theories', *The Academy of Management Executive*, vol. 7; **493** (top right) /Joshi A 2006, 'The influence of organizational demography on the external networking behaviour of teams', *Academy of Management Review*, vol. 31, no. 3, p. 583–95; **537** (bottom) /Thomas KW 1977, 'Towards multi-dimensional values in teaching...', *Academy of Management Review*; **722** (bottom) /Kaplan AM & Haenlein M 2009, 'Users of the world, unite! The challenges and opportunities of Social Media', *Business Horizons*, vol. 53 • © Pearson Education US: **464** (middle) /Robbins, Stephen; Coulter, Mary 2005, 'Management', 8th edn, p. 381 • © Sage Publications USA: **476** (bottom) /Deardorff DK 2006, *Journal of Studies in International Education*, vol. 10, iss. 3, p. 241–66 • © PureStock: **497** (bottom left) • © Emerald Group Publishing Ltd: **535** (top left) /Igo T & Skitmore M 2006, 'Diagnosing the organisational culture of an Australian engineering consultancy using the competing values framework', *Construction Innovation*, vol. 6, no. 2, p. 121–39 • © Penguin Group (USA) Inc: **540** (bottom) /'SECI knowledge spiral', from *The complete idiot's guide to knowledge management* by Melissie Clemmons Rumizen, 1998 by Alpha Books • © Picture Media: **570** (top left) /Picture Media/ Reuters/Andrew Meares • © Baden Eunson: **593** (middle) /Coch Land French J 1948, 'Overcoming resistance to change', *Human Relations*, vol. 2, no. 4; **645** (top) /*Behaving: managing yourself and others*, McGraw-Hill Education • © The Kobal Collection: **610** (middle left) /Chris Haston • © Digital Vision: **656** (top left) • © Linkedin: **673** (bottom left).

Text

• © Commonwealth Copyright Admin: **88–9** /Department of Education, Science & Training 2002, *Employability Skills for the Future*, Commonwealth of Australia reproduced by permission • © Tender Search: **192** /TenderSearch • © Nielson Norman Group: **214–15** /Dr. Jakob Nielson • © Elsevier: **224** /Blattner & Frazier 2002, 'Developing a performance-based assessment of students' critical thinking skills', *Assessing Writing*, vol. 8, no. 1, p. 47–64; **485** /Javidan & House 2001, 'Cultural acumen for the global manager: Lessons from project GLOBE', Reprinted from *Organizational Dynamics*, vol. 29, no. 4, pp. 302–03; **528** /Anand N & Conger JA 2007, 'Capabilities of the consummate networker', Reprinted from *Organizational Dynamics*, vol. 36, iss. 1, p. 13–27; **612** /Yauch CA 2007, 'Team-based work and work system balance in the context of agile manufacturing', *Applied Ergonomics*, vol. 38, iss. 1, p. 19–27 • © Cambridge University Press: **248–50** /King C, *Battling the six evil geniuses of essay writing*, Cambridge University Press; **552** /Turner G, Bonner F & Marshall D 2000, *Fame games*, Cambridge University Press • © John Wiley & Sons, Inc: **320** /Burley-Allen M 1995, 'Listening: the forgotten skill', John Wiley Inc • © John Wiley & Sons, UK: **399** /Morand DA 2000, *Journal of Organizational Behavior*, vol. 21, pp. 235–48 • © Wiley Blackwell Publishers: **419–20** /Salacuse J & Rubin JZ 1990, 'Your place or mine: site location and negotiation', *Negotiation Journal*, January, Blackwell Publishers • © Copyright Clearance Center: **450** /Thomas KW 1977, 'Towards multi-dimensional values in teaching...', *Academy of Management Review* • © California Management Review: **463** /1978, The Regents of the University of California, *The California Management Review,* vol. 21, no. 2 • © Geert Hofstede: **477** /Hofstede G 2001, 'Culture's consequences', p. 436 • © ABC-CLIO LLC: **498** /Hendon, Hendon & Herbig 1990, 'Cross-cultural business negotiations'; **499** /Hendon, Hendon & Herbig 1990, 'Cross-cultural business negotiations' • © Emerald Group

Publishing Ltd: **554** /Grunig JE & Grunig LA 2002, 'Implications of the IABC excellence study for PR education', *Journal of Communication Management*, vol. 7, no. 1, Emerald Group Publishing Limited • © ACCC: **561** /2010 • © Caruba Organization: **563** /Alan Caruba, www.caruba.com • © Jon Warner: **566** /Eunson B & Warner J 2000, 'Dealing with the media and external stakeholders', Team Publications • © Pearson Education: **585** /Seta CE, Paulus PB & Baron RA 2000, *Effective Human Relations: A Guide To People At Work*, 4th edn, Allyn and Bacon, Boston, MA • © News Ltd: **601–2** /Sinclair A 1990, 'Myths about teamwork', *The Weekend Australian*, 7–8 April • © Till Schümmer: **636** /Schümmer T & Tandler P, 'Patterns for technology enhanced meetings', http://living-agendas.de • © Graduate Careers Australia: **671** /Graduate Careers Australia, from the 2010 Graduate Outlook Survey of graduate employers in Australasia. www.graduatecareers.com.au • © World Future Society: **666** /Originally published in the Jan–Feb 1995 issues of *The Futurist*. Used with permission from the World Future Society, 7910 Woodmont Avenue, Suite 450, Bethesda, Maryland 20814. Telephone: 301/6568274; Fax: 301/9510394; www.wfs.org • © NCVER: **670** /Werner 1995, first published by NCVER. Adapted for 'Employability skills for the future, 2002', Commonwealth of Australia; • © Springer: **296** /Galassi 1977, 'Assertiveness matrix' from *Assert yourself! How to be your own person*, Human Sciences Press, New York, 1977, p. 9 • © Gerry McGovern: **709** /www.corporateblogging.info • © Mike Krieger: **711** /www.mkrieger.org

Every effort has been made to trace the ownership of copyright material. Information that will enable the publisher to rectify any error or omission in subsequent editions will be welcome. In such cases, please contact the Permissions Section of John Wiley & Sons Australia, Ltd.

1

Communication today

LEARNING OBJECTIVES

After studying this chapter you should be able to:

- Explain the difference between communication and communications
- Discuss the strengths and weaknesses of various communication models
- Explain why communication breaks down and why it succeeds
- Explain the limitations of communication processes

One communication, two communications

Communication is a challenging concept, with a search on 'communication' likely to bring up topics as diverse as team communication, body language and electronics.

Communication: the study of the transfer of meaning

Communications: the study of the transfer of data

What is communication? Look it up in a library catalogue or an online bookstore and you could easily become confused. For example, you might be interested in finding out about public speaking or body language or journalism but find that your search is impeded by numerous entries for books on electronics. Or you might be researching the physics of the internet or telephones but instead find countless entries for books on negotiation, public relations and writing skills. So what's going on?

Right from the start – ironically enough – we find confusing communications about communication. The first task, then, is to establish the differences between these two concepts.

Communication (singular), as applied to human interaction, includes:

- body language or nonverbal communication
- public speaking and presentation skills
- journalism or writing for the mass media
- graphic communication
- leadership, power and managing skills
- debate, logic, persuading and influencing skills
- negotiation and conflict resolution skills
- interpersonal skills (such as listening, assertiveness, questioning and giving feedback)
- intrapersonal communication (self-talk, affirmations, distorted thinking)
- organisational communication skills
- intercultural communication
- writing skills
- communicating with customers
- public relations communication
- communicating in teams and meetings
- job-seeking communication.

The list is endless. Virtually all these areas of skill and knowledge relate to the humanities or social sciences – although increasingly they are being classified as transferable skills, soft skills or generic skills – and they are recognised as essential by employers in all sectors. A general definition of this type of communication might be *the study of the transfer of meaning.*

We can visualise these different types of communication interconnecting in a systematic way (figure 1.1). We see here that there are six levels or concentric spheres or arenas or fields of communication enquiry. This could well be a map of communication enquiry, as well as a map of the contents of this book (could we perhaps have a seventh circle of inter-species communication, which might run from communicating with animals to communicating with whatever aliens there might be in space?).

Communications (plural), as distinct from communication, usually relates to the physics and mechanics of telecommunications systems such as telephone networks, satellites and the internet. These areas of skill and knowledge fall into the fields of engineering and the sciences. A general definition for these types of communications might be *the study of the transfer of data*.

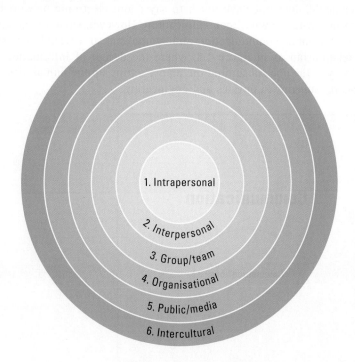

FIGURE 1.1 A concentric model of fields of communication

These are not absolute distinctions: you will encounter cases of 'communications' clearly referring to the transfer of knowledge and you may encounter instances of 'communication' relating to the engineering application. The confusion can be annoying, but perhaps it is understandable in an age in which so much human communication is **technologically mediated**; that is, it uses mechanical or electronic means or media to transfer meanings. Such means, or media, can also be referred to as *channels of communication* (we explore this concept further later in the chapter).

A useful way of conceiving the difference between the singular and the plural usages of communication is to think of the plural *encompassing* the singular — that is, mechanical transmission enables the transfer of meaning or content (figure 1.2).

Technologically mediated communication: human communication that uses mechanical or electronic means to transfer meaning

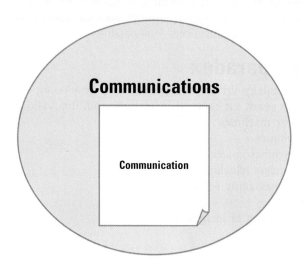

FIGURE 1.2 Communication within communications

Of course an engineer or physicist might suggest that this conception clearly demonstrates that the many subsume the one, and therefore demonstrates the superiority of engineering and physics over the social sciences, but this is not necessarily true. This book, for example, does not have much to say about electronic networks or technology (being concerned with 'singular' communication). However, some of the concepts we explore do relate to graphic communication and symbolism, so it would be perfectly viable to render the relationship as in figure 1.3, where the design of information suggests the opposite tendency – the one subsuming the many, setting up the humanities and the social sciences as clearly superior to physics and engineering.

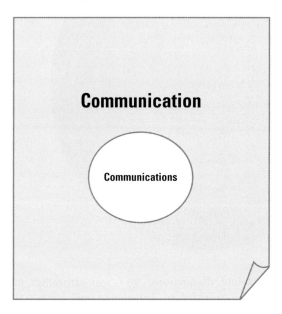

FIGURE 1.3 Communications within communication

Such a debate is ultimately futile or an example of a false dilemma fallacy: communication and communications are both vitally important and increasingly interact with one another.

As we learn more about human communication and as the technology of communications seems to accelerate in development every day, it would certainly be a good idea for communication specialists (and that includes all human beings) to know more about communications, and it would be an equally good idea for technologists, or communications specialists (who are also part of humanity) to know more about human communication.

Meta-communication: communication about communication and communications

We need, in other words, to have as much **meta-communication** – communication about communication and communications – as possible.

Priestley's paradox

Mediated or technology-driven communication is developing and expanding all the time. In the past thirty years, for example, communication innovations have included:
- facsimile or fax machines
- cordless telephones
- answering machines/voicemail
- mobile/cell/wireless telephones
- SMS, or short messaging service
- pagers
- satellite transmission of images and sounds
- cable television
- interactive television

- the internet
- email
- online chat rooms
- online instant messaging
- blogging (web logging)
- podcasting
- texting
- wikis.

More technological innovations in communications technology are in the pipeline. Surely all these innovations in communications enhance communication? Surely such a rise in the *quantity* of information transferred leads to an increase in the *quality* of communication and understanding? Again, this is not necessarily true. More than half a century ago, the British writer JB Priestley had this to say about the innovations of TV and communications technology:

> Already we Viewers, when not viewing, have begun to whisper to one another that the more we elaborate our means of communication, the less we communicate. (Priestley 1957)

In other words, the quantity of channels of communications may actually be diminishing the quality of our communication. This may mean that people living in low-technology societies and situations could have a richer experience of interpersonal communication than people living in high-technology cultures. This is **Priestley's paradox**. In particular, technologically mediated communication is increasingly driving out face-to-face communication. Thus, the idea that improvements in technology can bring about an increase in the quality of communication may in practice be contradicted by Priestley's paradox (figure 1.4).

Priestley's paradox: the more we elaborate our means of communication, the less we actually communicate

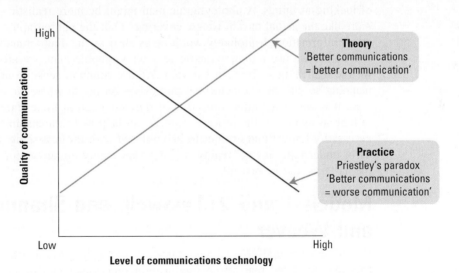

FIGURE 1.4 Priestley's paradox

We are only beginning to perceive the dynamics operating between communication and communications. What if, as has been suggested, communications technologies are not simply neutral and instrumental means to facilitate communication, but in fact addictive systems that create **dataholics** who become emotionally dependent on mobile phones, the internet and other technologies (Klimkiewicz 2007; Cao & Su 2007; Aoki & Downes 2003; Moskowitz 2001; Gottlieb & McLelland 2003)? Perhaps we can go even further and speculate that some people may in fact use communications technology – computers, the internet, television, radio and telephones – to avoid engaging in personal, face-to-face communication with others.

Dataholic: a person who is emotionally dependent on communications systems such as mobile phones and the internet

During the 11 September 2001 terrorist attacks in the United States, hijackers used mobile phones to coordinate the attacks, while passengers on the doomed aeroplanes used the same technology to say goodbye to their relatives (Dutton & Nainoa 2002). In light of this, how do we reconcile the potential for good and bad of the new technologies?

Communication: models for understanding

When we travel to unfamiliar places, we use a road map to help us arrive at our destination. When we look at a map, we accept that it is a diagram; a simplified schematic way of looking at things. A photographic map might be more realistic — that is, it might look more like the actual terrain we are covering — but the photographic map might give us too much information. It probably won't be as clear as the diagrammatic map.

Whether we use a diagrammatic or a photographic map, we are unlikely to confuse it for the real thing — the actual terrain. We use common sense to accept the limitations of mapping so that we can achieve a purpose — getting to where we want to go.

So it is with communication. One of the best ways of understanding communication is to look at models of the process. Models can help us to understand, even though they are necessarily limited and are not to be confused with the real thing. Maps and models help us to understand or 'see' reality in ways that reality alone cannot, because reality masks the patterns that lie beneath.

Models 1 and 2: Lasswell, and Shannon and Weaver

The systematic analysis of communication began in earnest after World War II. Harold Lasswell suggested that all communication processes could be understood in terms of a simple process (table 1.1). (We might compare this model with the mnemonic used by journalists when covering a news story — 5W-H, or What, When, Where, Why, Who and How — see online chapter 8 'Media communication'; note also the discussion of communication models in chapter 17 'Public communication').

TABLE 1.1 Lasswell's model of communication

Who	What	Channel	Whom	Effect
Who?	Says what?	In what channel?	To whom?	With what effect?

Source: Adapted from Lasswell (1948).

Shannon and Weaver developed a more mechanical or technological perspective on the communication process, introducing the concept of noise (figure 1.5). In physics and telecommunications, 'noise' is a disturbance that obscures or reduces the clarity of a signal (e.g. static, 'visual confetti' or echo). Thus, the clarity of a TV picture or radio signal or phone line is sometimes measured using a signal-to-noise (S/N) ratio: a high ratio suggests that the TV picture or radio sound or telephone signal will be of high quality, because there is much more signal than noise.

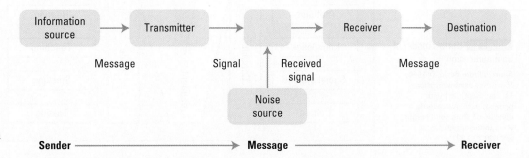

FIGURE 1.5 The Shannon–Weaver model

Source: Adapted from Shannon and Weaver (1999 [1949]).

Sender–Message–Receiver (SMR) model: a model showing a one-way path or pattern of communication

Communication breakdown: a misunderstanding or failure to communicate

Communication success: achievement of understanding between interacting individuals and groups

Shannon and Weaver's **Sender–Message–Receiver (SMR) model** has been very influential in the communication sphere (Maras 2000). It helps simplify the complexities of communication and makes it possible to analyse communication processes to see where, for example, barriers to communication might be erected or where **communication breakdown** might take place, as well as how barriers to communication might be dismantled so that **communication success** can occur.

The Shannon–Weaver model, however, has also received the following criticisms (Chandler 1994):

- It embodies a bad metaphor – that of information as a packet or container being transported, as if meanings were neutral rather than constructed and liable to subjective reading, or decoding. In reality, different individuals will interpret the same information in different ways.
- It is linear – that is, it sees communication as a one-way process, the receiver being passive, whereas communication usually occurs in both directions, involving a response or feedback from the receiver, who then becomes a sender, with the original sender becoming the receiver.
- It presumes that all communication is intentional and transparent, but some communication is unintentional, such as body language that contradicts what is being said, and some is nontransparent (its meaning is hidden).
- It ignores the social context in which communication occurs: the context comprises spoken and unspoken social rules and norms, cultural patterns, gender differences and other factors that potentially could radically transform the meanings of messages.

Models 3, 4 and 5: Berlo, Lievrouw/Finn and Foulger

Let's now build on the basic models we have considered and look at more complex (and perhaps more effective) models.

Berlo's SMCR model

Berlo (1960) developed his SMCR model of communication (figure 1.6) after contemplating the shortcomings of earlier models. He analyses communication in terms of four phases: S (= Source), M (= Message), C (= Channel) and R (= Receiver).

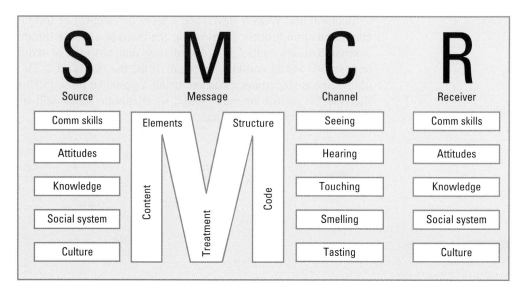

FIGURE 1.6 Berlo's model of communication

Source: From Berlo, D 1960, *Process of communication,* 1st edn. Reprinted with permission of Wadsworth, a division of Thomson Learning, www.thomsonrights.com, fax 800 730 2215.

The source and the receiver are, of course, human beings, and the messages they send will be a function of communication skills: encoding skills (writing and speaking), decoding skills (reading and listening) and an encoding–decoding skill (thought or reasoning). Senders and receivers will also be affected by their own attitudes, knowledge, social system and culture.

The message itself is characterised by elements and structure. In art, elements are the substance, while the structure is the form; in communication, having good ideas would comprise elements, while having good organisation would comprise structure. The two should ideally be inseparable. The message is also characterised by codes, content and treatment. A code is anything 'which has a group of elements (a vocabulary) and a set of procedures for combining those elements meaningfully (a syntax). If we want to know whether a set of symbols is a code, we have to isolate its vocabulary and check to see if there are systematic ways (structures) for combining the elements' (Berlo 1960, p. 57). Languages are codes, but so also are dance, radio and television, advertising and headline writing. Content is the material selected by the source to express a purpose. The treatment of a message comprises the decisions which the communication source makes in selecting and arranging both codes and content. A channel comprises the senses through which a decoder–receiver can perceive a message which has been encoded and transmitted by a source–encoder.

Berlo stressed the complex and dynamic nature of communication and the SMCR model was thus a significant advance upon the Shannon–Weaver model. Nevertheless, it is still relatively static and one-way in flow: Berlo did in fact consider feedback processes, but they are not immediately obvious in figure 1.6.

Lievrouw and Finn's communication systems model

We have mentioned before that communication can be mediated – that is, messages can be transferred by technological, and not simply human, means. In terms of the study of the field of communication, this has often meant in practice that there is a vast gulf between the study of interpersonal communication and the study of mass communication. Lievrouw and Finn (1990, 1996) have created a model of communication modes that attempts to bridge this gap (figure 1.7). The three dimensions of the model are control, involvement and temporality, and they help to explain the properties of different modes and channels of communication.

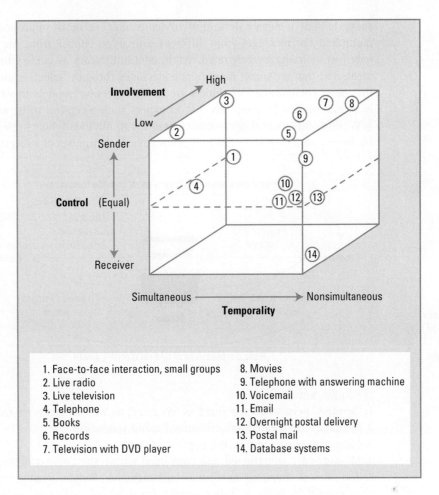

1. Face-to-face interaction, small groups
2. Live radio
3. Live television
4. Telephone
5. Books
6. Records
7. Television with DVD player
8. Movies
9. Telephone with answering machine
10. Voicemail
11. Email
12. Overnight postal delivery
13. Postal mail
14. Database systems

FIGURE 1.7 Lievrouw and Finn's communication systems model

Source: Adapted from Lievrouw and Finn (1990, p. 54).

Senders and receivers figure in the model, but the linear progression of messages assumes less importance here. What is most significant is the balance of control between senders and receivers. Involvement refers to distance – both physical and psychological – and the extent to which such distances are low or high. Finally, the experience of the message can be understood in terms of whether things happen simultaneously or not. Thus, face-to-face interaction between two individuals or members of a group can be characterised as equal control/high involvement/simultaneous, while email can be characterised as control slightly in favour of sender/low involvement/mainly nonsimultaneous.

For Lievrouw and Finn, the mediated/nonmediated dichotomy is a false dilemma: they assert that all communication is mediated, even interpersonal, because interpersonal communication cannot take place without the mediation of five senses and channels such as air and light.

The model helps us to compare apples with oranges – modes of communication that are normally not compared. While the assertion that senses are media and that channels are air and light is problematic for some, the model nevertheless helps us to see that variables such as control, involvement and temporality may be as important as left-to-right sequences in diagrams in our quest to understand communication processes.

Foulger's ecological model of communication

Foulger (2004) notes that considerable progress has been made in our understanding of communication processes. Rather than simply define message users as receivers, he suggests that a newer definition of 'consumer' is more appropriate, as we all have a multiplicity of messages from different sources to choose from. He also notes that 'noise' may just as easily be generated within communicators as come from the outside environment, and that we sometimes engage messages through 'selective attention'. He also argues that most communication models are really 'injection' models in which message reception is automatic, but he contends that to expect such reception to be automatic is unrealistic.

While Foulger's ecological model (figure 1.8) obviously bears resemblance to the models we have considered thus far, it is innovative in a number of aspects.

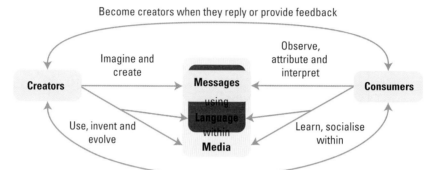

FIGURE 1.8 Foulger's ecological model of communication
Source: Foulger (2004).

Foulger argues that:
1. 'Senders' need to be redefined as 'creators', as well as receivers redefined as 'consumers'.
2. Messages are created and consumed using language.
3. Language occurs within the context of media.
4. Messages are constructed and consumed within the context of media.
5. The roles of consumer and creator are reflexive. People become creators when they reply or supply feedback to other people. Creators become consumers when they make use of feedback to adapt their messages to message consumers. People learn how to create messages through the act of consuming other people's messages.
6. A consumer's interpretation of a message necessarily attributes meaning imperfectly. Consumers interpret messages within the limits of the languages used and the media those languages are used in. A consumer's interpretation of a message may be very different than what the creator of a message imagined.
7. People learn media by using media. The media they learn will necessarily be the media used by the people they communicate with.
8. People invent and evolve media. While some of the modalities and channels associated with communication are naturally occurring, the media we use to communicate are not. (Adapted from Foulger 2004)

Foulger's model then notes the role shift we are all undertaking in a world bombarded with messages, it links language use to message formation, and it stresses the subjectivity and synergy of message creation and consumption.

Model 6: an expanded model of communication

Building upon what we have learnt by looking at the five previous models, figure 1.9 suggests another – although not necessarily perfect – model of communication (Eunson 2007). Let's see how it might work.

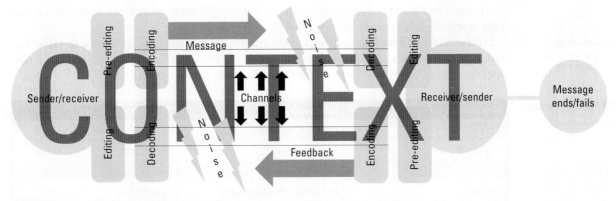

FIGURE 1.9 An expanded model of communication

Senders and receivers

The message sender does not stay in that one role for long: in most cases, communication is two-way, with sender and receiver switching roles. As shown in table 1.2, receivers are known by different names, depending on the type of communication.

TABLE 1.2 Message receivers in different fields of communication

Communication field	Receivers
Interpersonal communication	Listeners
Public relations	Publics
Mass media	Audiences, demographics, viewers, listeners, targets (see online chapter 8)
Organisational communication	Customers, clients, stakeholders
Presentations, public speaking	Audiences, auditors
Online communication	Users, participants

Sources: Adapted from Seitel (2011), McQuail and Windahl (1995), Wood (2011).

Message: information conveyed by any means from one person or group to another person or group

Messages may be written, spoken, nonverbal, graphic or visual. A simple handshake can convey several messages all at once.

Messages

Human communication is varied and often complex. **Messages** may be written, spoken, nonverbal, graphic or visual. A message may involve a simple greeting ('Good morning, can I help you?') or warning ('Stop!'); a nonverbal communication (a smile, a frown); a transmitted text message (a letter or email); or a verbal presentation (a radio broadcast, a speech or a declaration of war) (Gozzi 2004a; Gozzi 2004b; Gozzi 2005). Message production can be analysed in terms of qualities such as directness and listener adaptedness; specific word choices (e.g. 'can you' versus 'will you'); and para-verbal aspects such as filled pauses; and in terms of strategies, such as goal-seeking behaviour, persuasion and politeness (Wilson 1997).

Messages are also carried via cultural products such as songs and films: 'message songs' or 'message films' may be socio-political discussions rather than mere vessels of entertainment. Such messages are not always popular: Hollywood producer Samuel Goldwyn, noted for his cynicism, once remarked: 'If I want to send a message, I'll call Western Union [the US telegraph company]'.

Pre-editing, encoding, decoding, editing

In war or any situation involving conflict, messages are sometimes sent in secret codes, which can then be decoded by recipients who know what the code is. A similar process can happen in everyday communication, with messages often edited and encoded (i.e. the 'pure' message is transformed or masked in some way).

Typical ways of **encoding** or qualitatively transforming messages are shown in table 1.3. Although these types of encoding are, for the sake of clarity, classified here into three distinct categories, in reality they commonly spill across these categories.

Encoding: qualitatively transforming or masking a message in some way

TABLE 1.3 Types of message encoding

Mechanical	Behavioural	Systematic
Accent	Compassionate tone	Jargon or technical language
Inflection	Sarcastic tone	Secret code
Pitch	Hinting/innuendo	Sign language
Pausing	Secretive body language	Semaphore
Emphasis	Directness	Puns
Pronunciation	Aggressive tone	Double entendres
Garbled speech	Hesitation	Irony
Quiet speech	Stressed demeanour	Style or register

Of course, if the encoded message is to get through, the receiver must have the knowledge and skills needed for **decoding** or interpreting the message, and this is far from guaranteed.

However, while the encoding–decoding metaphor makes sense for most of the messages we might send and receive, we need to consider other factors and situations. What if, for example, a message is never sent? What if a message is sent, but it is substantially modified or engineered before it is sent? Table 1.4 compares encoding with pre-editing.

Decoding: qualitatively transforming or converting a message from a coded form into a plain form

TABLE 1.4 Encoding versus pre-editing

Pre-editing	Encoding
Transforming the message content quantitatively	Transforming the message content qualitatively

Pre-editing: consciously or unconsciously choosing to quantitatively transform or limit the content of a message before it is sent

Sometimes messages are pre-edited or shaped or filtered. Like encoding, **pre-editing** involves transforming the message content, but whereas encoding involves *qualitative* transformation, pre-editing involves *quantitative* transformation.

After pre-editing, what remains of the message is then encoded and sent. This is not always the case – in fact, it may be the mark of authenticity, honesty, transparency and effectiveness in communication if the message is not shaped or pre-edited in any way – but it happens often enough for us to need to pay attention to the process. Table 1.5 shows how this pre-editing of messages sometimes happens in different areas of communication (note that some strategies may overlap in some contexts).

TABLE 1.5 Types of message pre-editing

Pre-editing strategy	Communication field	Explanation/example
No pre-editing	All	Complete openness in message sending
Denial	Intrapersonal, interpersonal	Psychological defence mechanism, sometimes operating unconsciously. A person in denial simply refuses to acknowledge certain facts (Freud 1971; Ewen 2003; Seeley & Murphy 2009; Townsend, Markus & Bergkieker 2009; Vos & de Haes 2007).
Topic avoidance	Interpersonal	Couples in developing romantic relationships may avoid particular topics according to levels of intimacy and relationship uncertainty (Knobloch & Carpenter-Theune 2004); certain topics, such as religion, may be avoided in some relationships (Mikkelsen & Hesse 2009).

Pre-editing strategy	Communication field	Explanation/example
Self-silencing	Interpersonal	Women who have contracted AIDs via sexual activity may silence their own feelings, thoughts and actions to avoid conflict and maintain a relationship (Jacobs & Thomlison 2009).
Chilling effect	Interpersonal, group	Family members may suppress information and conceal secrets because of fears of recrimination (Afifi & Olson 2005); researchers may draft grant requests, leaving out 'controversial' research objectives (Kempner 2008).
Contextomy	Interpersonal, organisational, public	Words when quoted are taken out of their original linguistic context in order to give a false impression (McGlone 2005).
Self-censorship	Group	In the groupthink model, members of cohesive groups contribute to ineffective decision making by deciding not to bring controversial material into the discussion (Janis 1982; Halbesleben et al. 2007; Maharaj 2008: Adler 2009).
	Organisational	Academics in a Chinese university self-censor expression of ideas because of political pressure, while academics in a North American university self-censor because of corporate sponsorship of research and political pressure caused by anti-terrorist sentiment (Bowen 2005).
	Public	Individuals withhold their true opinions from an audience perceived to disagree with those opinions; media editors suppress material because of perceived threats from religious extremists and authoritarian governments (Hayes, Glynn & Shanhan 2005; Jacoby 2006; Chan 2009).
Spin	Public	Some public relations techniques may be used to manipulate the truth (Stauber & Rampton 1995; Miller & Dinan 2008).
Agenda setting	Public/media	Media may not be successful in telling people what to think, but may be more successful in telling people what to think about; some issues are focused on, while others are not (McCombs, Shaw & Weaver 1997; Shaw et al. 1999; Kim, Scheufele & Shanahan 2002; Kiousis, McDevitt & Wu 2005; Walgrave, Soroka & Nuytemans 2008; see online chapter 8).
	Group	Items may be arranged on a meeting agenda to emphasise and de-emphasise certain issues; there may also be a 'hidden agenda' or concealed strategy of control (Roessler 2008).
Framing	Interpersonal	Mediators in conflicts may choose to re-phrase words and concepts in order to make agreement more likely. Females may cast themselves in a particular inferior role to conform to social expectations (Bloch & Lemish 2005; Livinwood 2003; Roessler 2008).
	Public/media	Media editors and proprietors may emphasise and de-emphasise certain issues and approaches (Kendall 2005; Greenberg & Knight 2004; Scheufele 1999; Zillman et al. 2004); environmental issues can be framed in different ways (Hansson and Bryngelsson 2009).

(continued)

TABLE 1.5 *(continued)*

Pre-editing strategy	Communication field	Explanation/example
Spiral of silence	Interpersonal, group, public	People may experience pressure to conceal their views when they think they are in the minority — public opinion is our 'social skin' and comprises attitudes one can express without running the danger of isolating oneself (Noelle-Neumann 1993; Neuwirth & Frederick 2004; Drake 2008).
Shyness	Intrapersonal, interpersonal	Shyness may be biologically determined, but is certainly a restricting role that may inhibit an individual from expressing true feelings and thoughts (Scott 2004; www.shyness.com 2006).
Muted group theory	Interpersonal, group, public	Women and other marginalised or minority groups may have their opinions discounted: their gender, ethnic and sociopolitical roles mean that they are not taken seriously (Kramarae 1981; Wall & Gannon-Leary 1999; Hagan 2008; see online chapter 7).
Gender-based withholding	Interpersonal	Males may withhold emotional support from other males because empathy may be seen as unmasculine (Burleson, Holmstrom & Gilstrap 2005).
Tactful omission/ deafening silence	Interpersonal	Individuals may try to spare the feelings of others by deliberately not talking about certain issues; the same thing might be attempted with manipulative and hostile intent. The undiscussed issues may be the 'elephant in the living room' that sooner or later will demand attention (Zerubavel 2006; Kostigan 2009).
Taboo	Public, intercultural	Certain issues and topics are off-limits because of spiritual and/or social precepts (Douglas 2002; Freud 1962 [1913]).

Editing: consciously or unconsciously choosing to quantitatively transform or limit the content of a message after it is received

Also, what happens if a message is sent and decoded, but is then reacted to in such a way that the message content is further modified? In such circumstances, it may be that **editing** takes place (table 1.6).

TABLE 1.6 Types of message editing

Editing strategy	Communication field	Explanation/example
Selective perception/ recall	Intrapersonal, interpersonal	People may not recall all of the content of a message because of ineffective psychological processing or conscious or unconscious bias; they may be so hyper-vigilant in perceiving some things that they fail to notice other things (Bronner 2003; Catt, Miller & Hinds 2005; Colman & Kardash 1999; Higgins, Herman & Zanna 1982; Mogg, Philpott & Bradley 2004; Toch & McLean 1970; Eckstein 2005; Wojcieszak & Price 2009; Green, Sedikides & Gregg, 2008).
Cognitive dissonance	Intrapersonal, interpersonal, public	Individuals have drives that motivate them to avoid or discount information that conflicts with their values and attitudes, and that motivate them to seek out information that reinforces those values and attitudes (Festinger 1957; Zajonc 1970; Mullainathan & Washington 2009).
Self-reinforcing media selection/social dissonance; agenda melding	Intrapersonal, interpersonal, group, public, media	Individuals will pay more attention to messages that reinforce their basic personalities and discount other types of messages; they will give preference to media that reflect the values and attitudes of the groups that individuals belong to (Slater et al. 2003; Shaw, McCombs, Weaver & Hamm 1999; Roessler 2008).

Editing strategy	Communication field	Explanation/example
Inoculation and reactance	Intrapersonal, interpersonal, public	Individuals may resist accepting new ideas because of underlying belief systems and hostile attitudes (Pfau et al. 2005; Dillard & Shen, 2005; Breen, Gerald-Mark & Matusitz, 2009; Veil & Kent 2008).
Hostile media effect	Public, media	Individuals may see unbiased media coverage as biased against their interests (Schmitt, Gunther & Liebhart 2004; Choi, Yang & Chang 2009; see online chapter 8).
Knowledge gap	Interpersonal, public	As information flows into a social system, members of one socioeconomic status group are more likely to acquire information at a faster rate than members of other socioeconomic status groups (Rucinksi 2004; Gaziano & Gaziano 2008).

Pre-editing and editing, therefore, deal with quantitative transformation of messages, while encoding and decoding deal with qualitative transformation of messages (table 1.7).

TABLE 1.7 Encoding versus pre-editing

Pre-editing, editing	Encoding, decoding
Transforming the message content quantitatively	Transforming the message content qualitatively

The categories are not hard and fast, and in some communication transactions, the different terms might simply embody distinctions without differences. Indeed, it might be possible to do away with the editing concepts and simply say that message distortion or suppression can be explained by the concept of noise in communication models. If, however, we are to speculate on why some messages don't get sent in the first place, or if received and decoded still do not seem to get through, then the editing concepts might have some value.

ASSESS YOURSELF

Working by yourself or with others, brainstorm different ways in which communicators might pre-edit or edit different messages. Use the explanations listed in tables 1.5 and 1.6 or invent new explanations drawn from your own experience and knowledge.

Noise

Noise: anything that interferes with or distorts a message, or creates barriers to communication

Noise is anything that distorts the message or creates barriers to communication. Typical sources of noise in communication include:

- sounds, noise
- static, echo
- hearing impairment
- faulty eyesight
- imperfect transfer of information (e.g. a telephone message is passed on inaccurately)
- poor concentration
- incomplete message transfer
- information deliberately withheld
- message misinterpretation (e.g. as a result of fatigue, false assumptions or prejudices)
- mispronunciation
- nonverbal behaviour that appears to contradict message content
- misperception of situations and people.

Feedback

Feedback: response from message recipient, turning one-way into two-way communication

Feedback (a term that originated in the field of telecommunications but has come to be understood as any response to a message) may entail a raised eyebrow, applause, laughter, disagreement, a spoken response ('Yes', 'No', 'I do'), a physical response (a punch, a kiss, a confused look), a written response (a reply to a letter, memo or email), or a change in social behaviour (an increase in TV ratings, a consumer decision to buy something, a bid at an auction).

Feedback transforms a one-way message into two-way communication.

Feedback, then, transforms a one-way message into two-way communication, by allowing the participants in the communication process to switch the roles of sender and receiver. 'Feedback', as a term, reveals its history in the telecommunications engineering discourse of Shannon and Weaver and the later discourse of computer science. As such, it strikes some as being a piece of jargon, and suggests a dehumanised, mechanical and unrealistic way of describing human communication. A North American university senior administrator once created a policy whereby any administrator using the terms 'feedback' or 'input' would be fined a small but symbolic amount (Dickson 1992). It is nicely ironic that a term that has become a key concept in communication is seen by many as jargon — the antithesis of good communication. The paradox may be that the very 'jargon-ness' of the term may create a comfortable distance in communication processes for some people, helping to negate threatening perceptions of criticism and/or intimacy in human interaction — 'Can you send me some feedback on my report?'

Channels

Channel: the medium or means of sending messages

Mediated communication: communication that takes place by means of a technological channel

Synchronous communication: communication that is sent and received at virtually the same time

Asynchronous communication: communication that is sent at one time and received at another time

Channels are the means by which messages are conveyed. (Communication analysts sometimes use the terms *channels* and *media* interchangeably, as we do here.) To help make the concept less abstract, let's consider the channels frequently used in the workplace.

There are many channels, both traditional and new, by which messages can be communicated around workplaces or organisations. Such channels can be:

- one-way, two-way or multidirectional
- technologically **mediated** (e.g. via telephone, internal/external mail, computer or video) or unmediated (delivered personally)
- **synchronous** (sent and received virtually simultaneously) or **asynchronous** (received at a later time)

- individual (involving a **dyad,** or two people) or group (involving more than two people). (Note that communications may be characterised as *Individual ↔ Individual, Individual ↔ Group, Group ↔ Individual, Group ↔ Group.*)
- hard copy (taking a physical form, such as a letter or printed report) or electronic (viewed and/or stored using an electronic device)
- permanent or transient (can the message be stored or not?)
- formal or informal (is the message official or unofficial?)

- **lean** or rich (a **rich medium** transfers a range of verbal and nonverbal information, including colour, auditory and visual elements).

Traditional communication channels include memos, formal meetings, suggestion boxes, plenary or large-scale official briefings, team or department briefings, newsletters, charts and posters. Current approaches include:

- email
- websites — the internet (accessible by all) and intranets (accessible only by those inside the organisation (e.g. formally laid out web pages, wikis, podcasts and blogs)
- 360° feedback (in which a person is appraised or evaluated by those above, below and at the same level in an organisation)
- MBWA (Management By Walking Around), a management approach that entails leaders simply walking through work areas, making themselves available to listen to all staff members, rather than remaining inaccessible in management offices
- closed-circuit telecast — private TV programs broadcast via cable or satellite throughout an organisation
- video recordings and DVDs — e.g. briefings or training programs
- position papers — documents outlining organisational policy
- focus groups — small groups brought together to discuss particular issues
- instant messaging — real-time messages sent via computer networks, often viewed on screen on an ongoing basis
- ombudsman or ombudswoman — a person whose role is to mediate conflicts and communication problems within an organisation.

Other, informal channels of communication within organisations are not controlled by management. These include informal meetings and the grapevine, or rumour mill. All these approaches to communication have their strengths and weaknesses (table 1.8).

TABLE 1.8 Strengths and weaknesses of different information channels

Information channel	Strengths	Weaknesses
Memos	■ Provide hard-copy documentation of events, situations and problems ■ Can ensure that the same message reaches everyone ■ Can impose discipline upon the writer to describe a situation accurately ■ Can be used to send attachments (graphics etc.) that provide real information	■ May be unnecessary and irksome ■ If sent too frequently, will not be read or taken seriously ■ May be an excuse for some writers to avoid face-to-face communication with others ■ Slower than email; becoming used much less often than email
Facsimile	■ Provide hard-copy documentation of events, situations and problems ■ Can provide a more rapid response to those outside the organisation than channels such as letters ■ Can provide basic, hand-drawn visuals	■ Dependent on recipient having similar hardware in order to receive message ■ Older models use paper that does not retain images well ■ Increasingly being ignored in favour of email

(continued)

TABLE 1.8 *(continued)*

Information channel	Strengths	Weaknesses
Noticeboards	■ Cheap, low-tech ■ Democratic — everyone has equal access to information ■ Traditional	■ Physically fragile ■ Can easily get lost under notice overload ■ Can easily be defaced, removed ■ Readers need to be motivated to read
Emails	■ Provide documentation of events ■ Can ensure that the same message reaches everyone ■ Asynchronous — that is, sender can send them out at one time and receivers can receive them at another time ■ Can impose discipline on the writer to describe a situation accurately and in detail ■ Can be used to send attachments (graphics etc.) that provide real information more dramatically than memos can ■ May encourage more upward and lateral communication ■ Faster than paper-based memos	■ May be unnecessary and irksome ■ If sent too frequently, will not be read or taken seriously ■ May be an excuse for some writers to avoid face-to-face communication with others ■ If created in a hurry (as many are), may convey impression of sloppiness and lack of professionalism ■ May prove difficult to store, file and access ■ Might be lost if hardware and/or software crashes ■ Might not be taken as seriously as a hard-copy document
Voicemail	■ Asynchronous — we can leave the message when it suits us ■ Can convey personal touch ■ Can convey nonverbal messages	■ Can be done badly (insufficient details left, poor diction, unclear message) ■ Lean — lends itself to simple messages, not detail ■ Can lead to 'message ping-pong', in which two people leave messages for each other but never get to talk
Formal meetings	■ Personal ■ Easy to observe nonverbal behaviour ■ Conversational pacing/interchange cues clear ■ Formal record kept (minutes) ■ Easy for observers, media to monitor ■ Familiar set structure for handling rituals of conflict and agreement	■ Formality may inhibit free flow of information, opinions, hunches, gossip ■ Hampered by fear of going 'on record' in meeting minutes ■ Tendencies to ritual posturing ■ May suffer from 'hidden agenda' ■ May be too stressful or uncomfortable for shy individuals, who are inhibited from contributing ■ Subject to pressure to reach decisions merely because of time, agenda pressures
Informal meetings	■ Fewer inhibitions on free flow of information, opinions, hunches, gossip ■ No fear of going 'on record' in meeting minutes	■ Trust may be betrayed ■ Some don't feel bound to honour commitments because of informality — there may be good talk but little follow-up
Suggestion boxes	■ Encourage anonymous suggestions, which removes inhibitions and might help some write down their thoughts ■ Give opportunity for considered views — conveyed with more discipline than 'just talking'	■ Might not be taken seriously by management or staff unless follow-up is clearly demonstrated ■ Some may hide behind anonymity to express unconstructive, malicious views

Information channel	Strengths	Weaknesses
360° feedback	■ Can break down barriers restricting free flow of information and opinion imposed by hierarchy ■ Can impose discipline upon subordinates to take a wider view of tasks and teams in the organisation	■ Can be exercises in hypocrisy unless anonymous or managed by third parties ■ Can slow down decision processes with paperwork ■ Can as easily increase conflict as decrease it
Focus groups	■ Provide a structure for drawing out opinions and facts ■ Facilitator can ensure that group moves beyond 'pet peeve' anecdotes to structured responses ■ Can be repeated around workplace to build up database	■ May not be typical of the larger group (i.e. not a statistically valid sample) ■ May simply legitimise complaining, without constructive suggestions or rationales for opinions given
Plenary briefings	■ Ensure same message gets out to everyone ■ Everyone sees everyone else — common purpose of larger workplace dramatically emphasised ■ Good occasions for executives skilled in communication to inform, persuade and motivate	■ Depend critically on communication skills of speakers — cannot always be guaranteed ■ Little opportunity for two-way communication, questions, back-and-forth conversations ■ Unless rich in facts and overviews, can lead to cynical and confused responses from staff
Briefings by supervisor/team leader	■ Message has high credibility ■ Give local details, feedback ■ Can show how local efforts fit into bigger picture ■ Can be focus of two-way communication, feedback going back up the organisation	■ Depend critically on supervisor's communication skills ■ May lead to overemphasis on local issues as opposed to big picture ■ Can lead to 'us against them' paranoia and excuse making
Closed-circuit telecasts	■ Ensure same message gets out to everyone ■ Everyone sees same message, irrespective of location in organisation — dramatically promotes common purpose of larger workplace ■ Opportunity for executives skilled in communication to inform, persuade and motivate ■ Can feature visually rich material in cutaway and intro shots as examples or case studies (see podcasts)	■ Depend critically on communication skills of speakers ■ Little opportunity for two-way communication, questions, back-and-forth conversations ■ Can be expensive ■ Subject to technical glitches ■ Unless rich in facts and overviews, can lead to cynical and confused responses from staff
Teleconferencing 1: audio-conferencing	■ Can cut travel costs ■ Can make meetings happen that might not have happened at all ■ Cheaper than video/webcam-based systems	■ Can still be expensive ■ Cannot show nonverbal communication ■ Cannot display data as basis for discussion
Teleconferencing 2: video-conferencing	■ Can cut travel costs ■ Can make meetings happen that might not have happened at all ■ Can display nonverbal communication of participants	■ Can be expensive ■ Can be impersonal: face-to-face communication is valuable ■ Technical problems may mean that all participants cannot be seen

(continued)

TABLE 1.8 *(continued)*

Information channel	Strengths	Weaknesses
Teleconferencing 2: video-conferencing *(continued)*	■ Can incorporate data displays — enrich content	■ Can be expensive to set up and maintain ■ May inhibit interaction because of technological artificiality
Teleconferencing 3: web-conferencing	■ Individuals and groups physically distant from each other can confer ■ Can be cheap if savings on transport and accommodation are great ■ Technological artificiality may damp down conflict dynamics ■ Cheaper than videoconferencing	■ Excludes those who do not have access to technology ■ Computer-based conferencing is limited in the number of images that can fit on a computer screen
Video recordings/ DVDs	■ Ensure same message gets out to everyone ■ Everyone sees same message, irrespective of location in organisation — dramatically promotes common purpose of larger organisation ■ Opportunity for executives skilled in communication to inform, persuade and motivate ■ Easier than with broadcasts to feature visually rich material in cutaway and intro shots as examples or case studies ■ Staff can secure their own copies ■ Message can be replayed as required	■ Depend critically on communication skills of speakers ■ No opportunity for two-way communication, questions, back-and-forth conversations ■ Can be expensive, especially if complex production techniques are used to escape 'talking heads' effect ■ Subject to technical glitches ■ Unless rich in facts and overviews, can lead to cynical and confused responses from staff ■ May not be played
Newsletters	■ Hard copy, semi-permanent ■ Can show examples of a change program ■ Can personalise a change program with interviews and photos	■ May not be kept as record ■ Unless approach is professional, showing problems as well as successes, may be dismissed as management propaganda
Charts and posters	■ Hard copy, semi-permanent ■ Good for showing progress, relationships between goals or units ■ Relatively cheap, can be displayed in numerous locations	■ Can be relatively expensive, depending on production values ■ Unless kept up to date, can quickly become irrelevant ■ Unless approach is professional, showing problems as well as successes, may be dismissed as management propaganda
MBWA	■ Gets bosses out from behind desks to the 'sharp end' ■ Gives managers higher quality, fresher, unfiltered information ■ Can motivate staff to see bosses taking a direct interest and listening	■ May tempt 'short concentration span' bosses to avoid detailed paperwork and other obligations ■ Unless data unearthed is recorded in some way, may not lead to follow-through — 'all talk, no action' perception
Grapevine	■ Often correct ■ May be only source of information in low-transparency organisations	■ Often incorrect ■ May be a sign of lack of transparency in organisation
Position papers	■ Can provide detailed rationale of change process for those who want it ■ Hard copy, permanent ■ Can be put on intranet	■ Unless well written and laid out, and discussing problems as well as good news, may be ignored ■ May be too much information if other sources are available

Information channel	Strengths	Weaknesses
Websites/ intranets	■ Easy to access ■ Can contain solid, valuable information if hyperlinking is used intelligently ■ Can be updated quickly, reflecting new developments in change program ■ (see wikis, podcasts and blogs)	■ Require a lot of resources to set up and maintain ■ Unless approach is professional — showing problems as well as successes — may be dismissed as management propaganda
Ombudsman or Ombudswoman	■ Can provide impartial advice ■ Has some authority to follow through ■ Can alert management to brewing problems	■ Impartiality may be compromised if paid by management, unless guarantees are put in place ■ May simply become a conduit for a torrent of complaint
Instant messaging	■ Real-time communication ■ Presence detection (target is always aware message is coming through) ■ Immediate priority can be given	■ Technical problems (e.g. computer viruses) ■ Considered by some to be immature technology ■ Often seen as simply a tool for gossip
Texting	■ Useful for short messages ■ Can be used to send messages quietly	■ As with instant messaging, can be considered by some to be immature technology ■ Often seen as simply a tool for gossip ■ Not ideal for lengthy messages ■ Problems with storage, getting hard copy
Podcasts	■ A form of narrowcasting (based on the words 'broadcast' and 'iPod' (an Apple device for storing and receiving audio and video files), it shares virtues of closed-circuit telecasts ■ Allows portability — listener/viewer can receive messages anywhere on hand-held devices (not only those made by Apple) or on computers	■ Requires special technology to receive ■ One-way medium of communication ■ May lead to deterioration in human interaction and rapport
Wikis	■ A group or 'patchwork quilt' of web pages that allows collaborative documents on internet or private intranets to let many contributors build knowledge and exchange ideas ■ Encourages 'piggy-backing' of ideas, as in brainstorming, allowing synergy and inspiration to create new knowledge management database ■ Helps build teamwork	■ Depends critically upon trust and nonmalicious behaviour of contributors ■ Many items or sections are amateurish, as the peer review process of print-based encyclopedias is lacking (although this is changing with internet-based wikis such as Wikipedia and Citizendium) ■ Editors may interfere in editing of contributions ■ May be seen as management propaganda ■ Items contributed may suffer same problems as many knowledge management programs

(continued)

TABLE 1.8 *(continued)*

Information channel	Strengths	Weaknesses
Blogs	<ul><li>Web logs or blogs can be seen as part of 'social media' of 'user-generated content' as opposed to official messages through mainstream media</li><li>Can be used internally in an organisation to provide updates, generate discussions, foreshadow new developments via 'posts'</li><li>Can be used externally to maintain contact with customers, foreshadow new products and services and invite feedback</li><li>Can act as ongoing 'window' or press release or position paper of an organisation</li></ul>	<ul><li>Can be seen as amateurish, egocentric diary-like 'vanity publishing'</li><li>Many blogs are not read or maintained</li><li>Many are seen as too informal/sloppy in use of language, which gives an impression of amateurism</li><li>May give away too much of internal information, culture</li><li>May give the impression that writer has too much time on their hands</li></ul>

Sources: Adapted from Eunson (1994); Osterman (2003); Lewis (1999); Te'eni, Sagie, Schwartz and Amichai-Hamburger (2001); Timmerman (2003); Modaff, DeWine & Butler (2008); Harris (2002); Mitchell (2000), Myers (2010), Hussey (2009), Crystal (2008).

Communicating effectively using channels

There are four main criteria we need to bear in mind when choosing the medium of communication. This is shown in the RSVP model of communication channels in figure 1.10. (RSVP is a standard abbreviation, often written on invitations, taken from the French *répondez s'il vous plaît*, or reply if you please.) Your messages will get more replies if you follow the model, so let's now explore it in more detail.

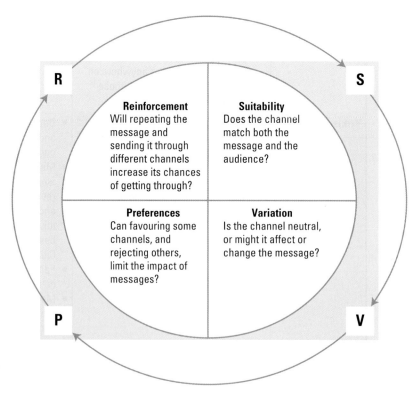

Reinforcement
Will repeating the message and sending it through different channels increase its chances of getting through?

Suitability
Does the channel match both the message and the audience?

Preferences
Can favouring some channels, and rejecting others, limit the impact of messages?

Variation
Is the channel neutral, or might it affect or change the message?

FIGURE 1.10 The RSVP model of communication channels

1. Reinforcement

Reinforcement: sending the same message through different channels

The surest way to get a message across to others is to use more than one channel. This means the message may have to be tailored to different channels, exploiting the strengths of a particular channel while avoiding its weaknesses. Communication effectiveness may therefore depend on saying something more than once, and on saying it in different ways. **Reinforcement** and repetition, applied through different channels, will increase the chances of the message getting through.

2. Suitability

Channel suitability: matching the channel to the message and the receiver, audience or target

Match the channel to the message itself and the receiver, audience or target. **Channel suitability** simply means that you choose a channel whose strengths are greater than its weaknesses in terms of the nature of the message and the audience or target (see figure 1.11).

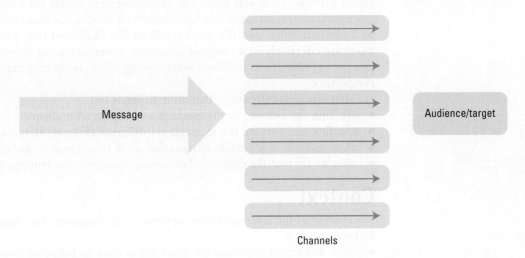

FIGURE 1.11 Choosing the appropriate channel: first consider the message type and the audience or target

Message

Audience/target

Channels

3. Variation

Variation: the possible tendency of media or message processes to vary or transform or change the content of a message

We cannot assume that the channels or media we use will necessarily convey a message in a neutral and mechanical way: they may affect or **vary** the content of the message in subtle or significant ways, and these effects may be positive or negative. Indeed, we may, consciously or unconsciously, send out quite different messages, depending on the channels we use (Chandler 2002). In effect, this is another type of noise in the communication process. Media theorist Marshall McLuhan once famously claimed 'the medium is the message' – in other words, media are not neutral, but actually vary or transform messages and, ultimately, human institutions; see McLuhan (2004 [1964]) and Griffin and Park's discussion of McLuhan's 'technological determinism' (Griffin 2011, p. 357; Griffin & Park 2006). Thus, one group listening to a debate on radio and another watching the same debate on television may disagree on who actually won the debate, even though they heard exactly the same words.

4. Preferences

Preferences: the inclination or bias towards one particular communication channel rather than another

While being aware of our own **preferences** in communication style, in order to choose channels we can work with we should not reject other channels that are effective but with which we may not be as comfortable. For example, a workplace manager who feels uncomfortable interacting directly with her people may keep them at arm's length with a stream of emails and memos, most of which are ignored by her staff, who feel demoralised and unsupported. She might well be more effective if she were to hold informal meetings or begin to trust her area supervisors to brief staff on important matters.

By contrast, another manager who depends too much on informal meetings and random conversations may confuse his staff with inconsistent messages and policy, and could perhaps benefit from sending out electronic and paper documents setting out policy in a consistent way. If we practice using new or unfamiliar channels, we may become more effective in getting our messages through.

Effective communication depends on being able to match strategies, messages, channels and audiences. The same message may need to be repackaged for different audiences and for different channels of communication. Quinn, Hildebrandt, Rogers and Thompson (1991), for example, suggest that an effective communicator will exploit different communication strategies when, say, making a keynote presentation at a convention or writing a technical or instructional manual. One channel or strategy is not inherently better than another, although it may offer different opportunities. Transformational communication stimulates change, instructional communication directs action, informational communication provides facts and relational communication builds trust (Quinn et al., 1991). The more communication skills and knowledge you master, the more versatile you will become as a communicator, and the greater will be the likelihood that you will be able to communicate effectively in a range of situations. Communicating differentially not only gives you the opportunity to reinforce your message, but also demonstrates your versatility and competence.

Using channels effectively, therefore, depends on:
- matching the channel to the message and the target audience
- repeating and varying the message via different channels to reinforce the message
- being ready to step outside our comfort zone to use new or unfamiliar channels
- being aware that the channel chosen may transform the content of the message.

Context

The context of the communication process is also important (see figure 1.9). Context issues include:
- *power and status relationships*. Who has control or influence over whom, and what are people trying to achieve in sending a particular message?
- *cultural factors*. Do the message sender and receiver understand each other's cultural programming, which affects their choice of words and their nonverbal communication?
- *interpersonal relationships*. What dynamics of empathy/lack of empathy, assertiveness/ lack of assertiveness, confidence/lack of confidence, openness/lack of openness exist between receiver and sender?
- *time*. How does time affect the message? Is it still relevant? Was the response too quick? For example, did a hesitation undercut the impact of the response? How does the communication pattern between people change over seconds, minutes, hours, days, months, years?

Message termination and failure

We have touched briefly on communication breakdown and success. Part of the beauty of communication models is that they help us to remember that so much communication is transactional or interactive: one message begets another, which in turn begets another, and so on. This dynamic aspect of communication is important, not least because knowing about such dynamism might help us to try harder to see that communication is still going on — for example, via nonverbal gestures, facial movements and postures. Nevertheless, sometimes communication does break down, and there may be no pleasing circularity to the way in which we interact with others. **Messages** may simply **terminate**, and communication **fails** as a result (see figure 1.9). People may simply never return our calls or answer our letters, and so we give up. Public relations and advertising campaigns may

Message termination and failure: when messages are terminal and when there is no reciprocal response from the message receiver switching into the role of a message sender

Message termination and failure can occur in a variety of different ways. Advertising campaigns, such as the campaigns on these bright billboards at Times Square in New York, may fail simply because the public does not care. They can also fail because consumers feel burdened by information overload — a perception of sensory overload caused by overexposure to communication messages.

be complete failures as the public simply does not care. Negotiators may walk out, perhaps never to return. A loved one may die without our saying things we wanted to say. Various types of extreme messages may simply leave us speechless, at least for the time being (Berger 2004).

Time and simultaneity

Looking at the various communication models in this chapter, we can see that it sometimes makes sense to try to break communication down into various phases. It also makes sense in the real world to respect such phases – for example, by patiently listening to another person until they have stopped talking, at which point we reciprocate. However, it is wise not to impose too static and ritualised a view of communication, because we might miss out on certain things happening in certain circumstances, and we might also unnecessarily limit our own repertoire of communication skills and strategies. For example, if person A is talking, person B may be nonverbally reacting at the same time or with a minor time lag. Person A may decide – based on observation of person B – to change the content and delivery of the message in order to be more effective. The situation becomes even more complicated – and interesting – when members of a group are communicating with each other. Communication models thus help us to slow down and analyse communication patterns, but we should try to then use the learning we get from that analysis to allow us to speed up and analyse the complex patterns of interaction in real time, in the real world.

ASSESS YOURSELF

Pair off and ask your partner to think of an example in his or her life of:
- communication breakdown
- communication success.

Swap roles. Use different communication models to explain what happened. Each person should then introduce his or her partner to the larger group and then recount the shared experiences to the group.

Communication: always a good thing?

Communication is sometimes seen as a panacea: 'If only we could communicate more, then things would be better'. This is not necessarily the case. To begin with, some people confuse communication with agreement with their views: 'If only you would agree with me, then things would be better'. The same assumption sometimes underlies people's understanding of listening: 'If only you would listen to me . . .' The outcome of real communication may in fact be disagreement rather than agreement, and to merely 'talk' or to see communication as a metadiscourse of 'talking about talking' (Craig 2005) may not be enough (see the discussion of meta-communication earlier in the chapter).

Within organisations, communication is sometimes overrated as a source of conflict. Conflict may also be due to objective factors such as unit, divisional or team goals, role requirements, organisational structures, personalities, performance criteria, resource allocation and different value systems (Robbins & Judge 2010).

More communication, rather than less, can also backfire when

- we 'talk a problem to death', going over the same ground again and again without making headway
- a salesperson doesn't shut up and let the customer think about the product and purchase decision
- two people engaged in heated argument say things they later regret (Adler, Rosenfeld & Proctor 2009).

In other words, we can all learn to be more effective in our communication with others, but sometimes the most effective communication is to say nothing at all, and sometimes we miss the point if we think that a problem is solely or even partially due to communication difficulties.

Communication and ethics

As communicators, we are often faced with ethical dilemmas, and in this book, we consider many situations in which such dilemmas are presented, such as:

- Should I embellish my résumé or curriculum vitae with 'half-truths' in order to get a job?
- Should I 'lie with statistics' when using graphs or charts in documents or presentations to make my arguments more persuasive?
- Should I pass on, and perhaps embellish, rumours on the organisational grapevine?
- Should I plagiarise material to pad out documents I am writing?
- Should I use dubious tactics (attack the person, divide and conquer) when negotiating with others?
- Should I censor or filter or block information getting to others?
- Should I censor myself or remain silent when the group I am in is making important decisions?
- Should I contribute to a 'shoot-the-messenger' culture by coercing those who bring bad news or those who are 'whistleblowers' or want to speak out about organisational malpractice?
- Should I create 'spin' or deceptive impressions when communicating with the public?
- Should I use knowledge about human behaviour (body language, emotional intelligence, neurolinguistic programming) to more effectively manipulate others? (See chapters 8–10.)
- Should I deliberately distort the situation analysed in a report I am writing in order to create further work opportunities for myself?
- Should I manipulate meetings so that a hidden agenda, rather than the written agenda, is followed?

These are not easy questions, and the realities of the workplace and the wider world often make decisions more difficult than we might think. Marcoux (2006), for example, has argued that, in certain circumstances, it might be right to embellish a résumé, and indeed it might be necessary to do so as a matter of self-defence (the circumstances include those where former employers might not divulge job position details because of legal constraints and where future employers use selection methods apart from simply perusing résumés). However, as with all ethical questions, we must tread warily on such an issue.

Ethics and rationalisation

We need to be aware of rationalisations we might indulge in to come up with reasons for conduct that is not ethical. Such rationalisations include:

'Everybody's doing it, so why shouldn't I?'

This is the argument from democracy: numbers determine what is right. A cliché image of blind conformity is that of lemmings jumping off a cliff: if, however, you are smarter than the average lemming, should you go over the cliff too, along with the rest of the herd? Also, if everyone else around you believes that the world is flat, but you can see that the horizon is curved, should you go along with what they are saying? In fact, in many circumstances, it does make sense to go along with a lie or delusion if the consequences of not doing so are too negative (e.g. being burnt at the stake for affirming that the world is not flat). As the old saying goes, there is no greater sin than to be right at the wrong time. Nevertheless, if the consequences are not too negative, it pays to speak out and speak the truth. Later on, you will be hailed as a leader rather than a heretic. When in doubt, apply the hostile lawyer or courtroom test. Imagine that you are on trial; you give this rationalisation as your excuse for your conduct, and you are cross-examined by a hostile lawyer who says: 'Do you really expect this court to accept that you did what you did merely because the other defendants did it as well?' If such a situation makes you think twice, then you should resist group pressure and the siren call of this rationalisation.

'It's not illegal.'

True, but is it right? As US Supreme Court judge Potter Stewart (1915–1985) put it: 'Ethics is knowing the difference between what you have a right to do and what is right to do'.

'They did it to me, so I'm going to do it to them.'

Very seductive logic with this rationalisation, but a tit-for-tat dynamic rarely works as a mechanism for resolving conflict, not least because both parties to a dispute will rarely agree on who started it or the actual quantitative measure of action and reaction. The counter to this is 'two wrongs don't make right'.

'If I don't do it, somebody else will.'

Ah, but sometimes they don't. And even if they do, what if what they do is killing people or some other unacceptable action? Are you constrained by circumstances to pre-empt them? Of course not. (For more on ethical rationalisations, see the 'Ethics scoreboard rule book: ethics fallacies, myths, distortions and rationalizations' at www.ethicsscore board.com.)

Schermerhorn (2007) has described the way in which organisations try to come to terms with ethical dilemmas in meeting social responsibilities. He argues that there are four strategies that organisations can adopt. These are shown in table 1.9.

TABLE 1.9 Ethical strategies for organisations

Strategy	Nature of strategy
Proactive	This is the top-level approach. Here, the organisation's managers and/or staff meet economic, legal and ethical responsibilities, but also actively consider discretionary performance. Problems are anticipated and sought out, and maximum transparency and flow of information within the organisation and at its boundaries with its stakeholders are central to its transactions with the world.
Accommodation	This is the third-level approach. Here, the organisation's managers and/or staff decide to meet their economic, legal and ethical responsibilities. The ethical response, however, is only because of outside pressures. Thus, a company may move to rectify the damage of an oil spill, but respond to the crisis slowly, and only out of fear of bad publicity.

(continued)

 **TABLE 1.9** *(continued)*

Strategy	Nature of strategy
Defensive	This is the level above obstruction. Here, the organisation's managers and/or staff decide to meet their economic responsibilities but also their legal responsibilities by meeting, but not exceeding, minimum legal requirements.
Obstructionist	This is the lowest level strategy. When an organisation is confronted with ethical dilemmas, its managers and/or staff simply decide to meet their economic responsibilities (e.g. to shareholders and other stakeholders) and then fight social demands.

Communicators need to keep these four levels in mind and try to operate at the proactive level wherever possible.

When confronted with the ethical dilemmas we have considered, from embellishing résumés to manipulating meetings, we should always check our conduct and thoughts with these tests:

- *Are we rationalising?* We should be familiar with the ethical rationalisations we have considered, as well as numerous others, and see if these are motivating us.
- *What about the Golden Rule?* The Golden Rule is 'do unto others as you would have them do unto you'. How would you feel if what you are contemplating was done to you? If you wouldn't feel good, then don't do it.
- *What about short-term consequences?* Will someone get hurt? What will happen if you get caught? Are you ready to look a hostile lawyer in the eye?
- *What about long-term consequences?* If you believe in an afterlife, what about karma, or the sundry other punishments religions have promised us? Are you ready for those?
- *What about the mirror?* Can you look at yourself in the mirror and not blush, nervously scratch or look away? Can you look into your conscience and not blink?
- *What about action?* We can talk the talk about ethics in communication, but can we walk the walk? As Mason Cooley, the North American aphorist, put it: 'Reading about ethics is about as likely to improve one's behavior as reading about sports is to make one into an athlete'. Of course, sometimes what is required is *in*action: not doing or saying something.

More dilemmas, ethical and otherwise, are presented at the end of each chapter with the 'What Would You Do?' section.

Communication: the next frontier

Communication is emerging as a new and exciting discipline. While there are many subfields in the area, stretching from intrapersonal communication to intercultural communication and beyond, the underlying similarities are usually greater than the differences. In the next few decades, we may see the development of trends already apparent, such as communibiology (the study of the biological bases of communication) (McCroskey 1998; Paulsel & Mottet 2004; Wahba & McCroskey 2005; Mildner 2008) and critical communication theory (the radical analysis of power structures underlying types of discourse) (Jansen 2003; Ganesh, Zoller & Cheney 2005; Kuhn & Deetz 2008).

Right here and right now, however, we have, at the end of this chapter, a good foundation for moving out and sampling other chapters dealing with many areas of communication. Please enjoy the journey.

STUDENT STUDY GUIDE

SUMMARY

In this chapter we considered the differences between communication (or the transfer of meaning) and communications (or the transfer of data). We examined the strengths and weaknesses of various communication models and channels. We looked at the ways in which communication can break down and how it can succeed. Finally, we considered some of the limitations of communication processes.

KEY TERMS

asynchronous communication *p. 18*
channel *p. 18*
channel suitability *p. 25*
communication *p. 4*
communication breakdown *p. 9*
communication success *p. 9*
communications *p. 4*
dataholic *p. 7*
decoding *p. 14*
dyad *p. 19*

editing *p. 16*
encoding *p. 14*
feedback *p. 18*
lean medium *p. 19*
mediated communication *p. 18*
message *p. 13*
message termination and failure *p. 26*
meta-communication *p. 6*
noise *p. 17*
pre-editing *p. 14*

preferences *p. 25*
Priestley's paradox *p. 7*
reinforcement *p. 25*
rich medium *p. 19*
Sender–Message–Receiver (SMR) model *p. 9*
synchronous communication *p. 18*
technologically mediated communication *p. 5*
variation *p. 25*

REVIEW QUESTIONS

1. What is the fundamental difference between 'communication' and 'communications'?
2. What are the six levels of communication enquiry?
3. What is Priestley's paradox?
4. How does Lasswell's model of communication differ from that of Shannon and Weaver?
5. List at least two limitations of the Shannon–Weaver model.
6. Give three examples of your own of each of the following: (a) encoding (b) messages (c) noise (d) feedback.
7. What are the advantages and disadvantages of asynchronous communication when compared with synchronous communication?
8. Identify two strengths and two weaknesses of at least two channels of communication.
9. What are the four aspects of the RSVP model of communication channels?

APPLIED ACTIVITIES

1. Analyse a communication interchange between two real or imaginary people. Use this chart or an enlarged copy to analyse the nature of the communication.

	PERSON A	PERSON B
ENCODING		
MESSAGE		
CHANNELS		
NOISE		
DECODING		
CONTEXT		

2. Analyse the strengths and weaknesses of the seven communication models discussed in this chapter. Use this chart or an enlarged copy to conduct your analysis.

MODEL	STRENGTHS	WEAKNESSES
Lasswell		
Shannon–Weaver		
Berlo		
Lievrouw/Finn		
Foulger		
Expanded		

3. Using print and internet sources, find at least two other models of communication (e.g. those of Jakobson, Barnlund, Aristotle, Gerbner, Osgood and Schramm, Maletzke). Assess their advantages and disadvantages when compared with those discussed in this chapter.
4. Create your own communication model. Be prepared to describe how it works and its weaknesses and strengths.
5. Using print and online sources, find at least three quotations on the subject of communication. Prepare a three-minute talk based on these quotations.
6. Using print and online sources, research Wiio's Laws of Communication. Describe how at least one of the laws could be reversed using good communication practices.
7. 'Pre-editing is just another form of encoding and post-editing is just another form of decoding. There is really no need for four terms when two will do.' Discuss.
8. Imagine you are a lecturer in communication. You have just looked at figure 1.1 and decide to prepare a lecture on the next level — inter-species communication. Prepare a ten-slide bullet-point presentation/lecture on the topic.
9. 'Better communication is the solution to all human problems.' Discuss.

WHAT WOULD YOU DO?

In Victoria, Australia, in 2009, 173 people died in what soon became Australia's worst peace-time disaster (AAP 2009). There were many reasons why the Victorian bushfire disaster occurred. One that stands out was the sheer, almost unbelievable lack of communication between the trained professionals in charge of the operation.

The essence of any counter-disaster operation is effective coordination. This proved to be impossible to achieve with the disaster, with rural fire-fighting authorities and metropolitan emergency services operating on incompatible communications systems during the crisis. The rural fire-fighting authorities were operating on analogue radio, while the metropolitan emergency services were operating on digital radio. There were no digital communication towers in rural Victoria at the time of the fires. People who were on the fringe between a metropolitan area and a bush area usually had both systems (Caldwell 2009).

During an investigation that followed, Victorian Police Deputy Commissioner Kieran Walshe told the investigating body, the Bushfire Royal Commission, that a 'single integrated radio communications network' was needed to ensure that a similar communications breakdown did not occur again in the future. When the Commission Chairman described the dual system approach as a 'major disability' in a situation in which resources needed to be deployed quickly, Deputy Commissioner Walshe agreed (Caldwell 2009).

At one time during the crisis, the same problem existed for the metropolitan fire brigade and the metropolitan ambulance service. One resident who testified said:

> It's important for them to be able to communicate with each other so they can mass resources and let people know what's happening and call in other resources if it's necessary. And if they have trouble communicating, it's going to cause delays (Caldwell 2009).

More than two decades earlier, another communications breakdown contributed to a different serious event in the United States. On December 11 1988, the Mars Climate Orbiter spacecraft lifted off from Cape Canaveral in Florida. The Orbiter's main mission was to monitor weather patterns on Mars, and its total cost at the time was US$328 million. A few months later, the Challenger crashed on the moon. What was the cause? One team at NASA had been working in metric units, while another team had been working in imperial units.

'People sometimes make errors', said Dr Edward Weiler, NASA Associate Administrator for Space Science. 'The problem here was not the error, it was the failure of NASA systems engineering, and the checks and balances in our processes to detect the error. That's why we lost the spacecraft' (quoted in Oberg 1999).

Miller and Rosenfeld (2009) call this type of faulty decision making and non-communication 'intellectual hazard', or 'the tendency of behavioural biases to interfere with accurate thought and analysis within complex organisations'. They argue that 'Intellectual hazard impairs the acquisition, analysis, communication and implementation of information within an organisation and the communication of such information between an organisation and external parties' (p. 1).

Questions

1. Discuss how poor communication played a role in the Victorian bushfire crisis. What might have been done in response to the communication breakdown during the crisis?
2. Discuss how poor communication played a role in the Challenger crash during the late 1980s. What might have been done to avoid the communication breakdown?

SUGGESTED READING

Beck, Andrew & Smith, Roger 2010, *Communication skills and social work*, McGraw-Hill, New York/ London.

Baldwin, John R, Perry, Stephen D & Moffitt, Mary Ann 2004, *Communication theories for everyday life*, Allyn & Bacon, Boston, MA.

Barnlund, DC 1970, 'A transactional model of communication', in KK Sereno and CD Mortensen (eds), *Foundations of communication theory*, Harper and Row, New York.

Cobley, Paul 2010, *Communications: an introduction*, Routledge, New York/ Milton Park, UK.

Craig, Robert T & Muller, Heidi L 2007, *Communication theory as a field: essential readings*, Sage, Thousand Oaks, CA.

DeVito, Joseph 2009, *Human communication: the basic course*, 11th edn., Allyn & Bacon, Boston, MA.

Flatley, Marie E & Rentz, Kathryn 2010, *Business communication*, 11th edn., McGraw-Hill, New York.

Forey, Gail & Lockwood, Jane (eds.) 2010, *Globalization, communication and the workplace: talking across the world*, Continuum, New York/London.

Waller, David S & Polonsky, Michael J 1998, 'Multiple senders and receivers: a business communications model', *Corporate Communications*, vol. 3, no. 3, pp. 83–91.

Walther, Joseph B 1996, 'Computer-mediated communication: impersonal, interpersonal, and hyperpersonal interaction', *Communication Research*, vol. 23, no. 1, pp. 3–43.

Watzlawick, Paul, Beavin, Janet Helmick & Jackson, Don D 1967, *Pragmatics of human communication: a study of interactional patterns, pathologies, and paradoxes*, W.W. Norton & Co., New York.

West, Richard B & Turner, Lynn H 2010, *Introducing communication theory: analysis and application*, 4th edn., McGraw-Hill, New York.

Wood, Julia T 2009, *Interpersonal communication: everyday encounters*, 6th edn., Wadsworth, Belmont, CA.

REFERENCES

AAP 2009, 'Bushfire death toll revised down', 30 March, www.news.com.au.

Adler, Ronald B, Rosenfeld, Lawrence B & Proctor, Russell F 2009, *Interplay: the process of interpersonal communication*, 11th edn., Oxford University Press, New York/Oxford.

Adler, Stephen J 2009, 'Beware groupthink on the economy CEO pay: Obama's Reagan moment: his attack on executive salaries recalls Reagan's hard line on striking air-traffic controllers', *Business Week*, 16 February, p. 16.

Afifi, Tamara D & Olson, Loreen 2005, 'The chilling effect in families and the pressure to conceal secrets', *Communication Monographs*, vol. 72, no. 2, pp. 192–216.

Aoki, Kumiko & Downes, Edward J 2003, 'An analysis of young people's use of and attitudes towards cell phones', *Telematics and Informatics*, vol. 20, pp. 349–64.

Berger, Charles R 2004 'Speechlessness: causal attributions, motional features and social consequences', *Journal of Language and Social Psychology*, vol. 23, no. 2, pp. 147–79.

Berlo, David K 1960, *The process of communication: an introduction to theory and practice*, Holt Rinehart and Winston, New York.

Bloch, Arthur 2004, *Murphy's law*, Perigee, New York.

Bloch, Linda-Renee & Lemish, Dafna 2005, '"I know I'm a *Freiierit*, but … ": how a key cultural frame (en)genders a discourse of inequality', *Journal of Communication*, vol. 55, no. 1, pp. 38–55.

Breen, Gerald-Mark & Matusitz, Jonathan 2009, 'Preventing youths from joining gangs: how to apply inoculation theory', *Journal of Applied Security Research*, vol. 4, nos. 1 and 2, pp. 109–28.

Bowen, Roger W 2005, 'Academic freedom undermined: self-censorship', *Academe*, vol. 91, no. 4, p. 72.

Bronner, Rolf 2003, 'Pathologies of decision-making: causes, forms and handling', *Management International Review*, vol. 43, no. 1, pp. 85–101.

Burleson, Brant R, Holmstrom, Amanda J & Gilstrap, Cristina M 2005, '"Guys can't say *that* to guys": four experiments assessing the normative motivation account for deficiencies in the emotional support provided by men', *Commmunication Monographs*, vol. 72, no. 4, pp. 468–501.

Caldwell, A 2009, 'Communication breakdown in Vic fires', radio transcript, *AM*, 19 May, www.abc.net.au.

Cao, F & Su, L 2007, 'Internet addiction among Chinese adolescents: prevalence and psychological features', *Child: Care, Health and Development* vol. 33, no. 3, pp. 275–81.

Catt, Stephen E, Miller, Donald S & Hinds, Nitham M 2005, 'Don't misconstrue communication cues', *Strategic Finance*, vol. 86, no. 12, pp. 50–5.

Chan, Joseph 2009 'Organizational production of self-censorship in the Hong Kong media', *The International Journal of Press/Politics*, vol. 14, no. 1, pp. 112–133.

Chandler, Daniel 1994, 'The transmission model of communication', www.aber.ac.uk.

—— 2002, *Semiotics: the basics*, Routledge, London.

Clampitt, Phillip G 2000, *Communicating for managerial effectiveness*, Sage, Thousand Oaks, CA.

Choi, Jounghwa, Yang Myengja & Chang, Jeongheon J C 2009, 'Elaboration of the hostile media phenomenon: the roles of involvement, media scepticism, congruency of perceived media influence, and perceived opinion climate', *Communication Research*, vol. 36, no. 1, pp. 54–72.

Colman, Janet M & Kardash, Carolanne M 1999, 'Encoding and retrieval of ambiguous and unambiguous information by aggressive and nonaggressive elementary boys', *Child Study Journal*, vol. 29, no. 2, pp. 133–56.

Craig, Robert T 2005, 'How we talk about how we talk: communication theory in the public interest', *Journal of Communication*, vol. 55, no. 4, pp. 659–67.

Crystal, David 2008, *Txtng: the gr8 db8*, Oxford University Press, New York/London.

Dickson, Paul 1992, *Dickson's word treasury: a connoisseur's collection of old and new, weird and wonderful, useful and outlandish words*, John Wiley & Sons, New York.

Dillard, James Price & Shen, Lijiang 2005, 'On the nature of reactance and its role in persuasive health communication', *Communication Monographs*, vol. 72, no. 2, pp. 144–68.

Douglas, Mary 2002, *Purity and danger: an analysis of concepts of pollution and taboo*, Routledge, London/New York.

Drake, Jessica 2008, *Spiral of silence and the Iraq War*, Dissertation, Rochester Institute of Technology, Rochester, New York, https://ritdml.rit.edu.

Dutton, William H & Nainoa, Frank 2002, 'Say goodbye … let's roll: the social dynamics of wireless networks on September 11', *Prometheus*, vol. 20, no. 3, pp. 237–45.

Eckstein, Jessica J 200 'Conversion conundrums: listener perceptions of affective influence attempts as mediated by personality and individual differences', *Communication Quarterly*, vol. 53, no. 3, pp. 401–19.

Eunson, Baden 1994, *Negotiation skills*, John Wiley & Sons, Brisbane.

—— 2007, 'Communication models: can pre-editing and post-editing of messages help improve basis models?', paper presented at Australian New Zealand Communication Association 2007 conference, University of Melbourne, 5–6 July.

Ewen, Robert B 2003, *An introduction to theories of personality*, Lawrence Erlbaum Associates, Mahwa, NJ.

Festinger, Leon 1957, *Theory of cognitive dissonance*, Stanford University Press, Stanford.

Foulger, Davis 2004, 'Models of the communication process', http://foulger.info/davis.

Freud, Anna 1971, *The ego and the mechanisms of defense*, International Universities Press, New York.

Freud, Sigmund 1962 [1913], *Totem and taboo: some points of agreement between the mental lives of savages and neurotics and other works*, W.W. Norton, New York.

Ganesh, Shiv, Zoller, Heather & Cheney, George 2005, 'Transforming resistance, broadening our boundaries: critical organizational communication meets globalization from below', *Communication Monographs*, vol. 72, no. 2, pp. 169–97.

Gaziano, Cecilie & Gaziano, Emanuel 2008, 'Theories and methods in knowledge gap research', in Stacks, Don W. (ed.) *An integrated approach to communication theory and research* (2nd edn), Routledge, London/New York.

Gottlieb, Nanette & McLelland, Mark 2003, *Japanese cybercultures: Asia's transformations*, Routledge, London/New York.

Gozzi, Raymond Jr 2004a, 'Where is the "message" in communication models?', *et Cetera*, vol. 61, no. 1, pp. 145–6.

—— 2004b, 'Who is the "source" in communication models?', *et Cetera*, vol. 61, no. 2, pp. 274–5.

—— 2005, 'From linear myths to musical models of communication', *et Cetera*, vol. 62, no. 1, pp. 89–90.

Green, Jeffrey D., Sedikides, Constantine, & Gregg, Aiden P. 2008 'Forgotten but not gone: the recall and recognition of self-threatening memories', *Journal of Experimental Social Psychology*, vol. 44, no. 3, pp. 547–561.

Greenberg, Josh & Knight, Graham 2004, 'Framing sweatshops: Nike, global production and the American news media', *Communication and Critical/Cultural Studies*, vol. 1, no. 2, pp. 151–75.

Griffin, Em 2011, *A first look at communication theory*, 8th edn, McGraw-Hill, New York.

Griffin, Em, & Park, EJ 2006, 'Media ecology of Marshall McLuhan', online chapter supplement to Griffin 2006, www.afirstlook.com.

Hagan, Martha 2008 'Contested playgrounds: e-mail harassment in the academy', Paper presented at the annual meeting of the NCA 94th Annual Convention, TBA, San Diego, www.allacademic.com.

Halbesleben, Jonathan RB, Wheeler, Anthony R & Buckley, M Ronald 2007, 'Understanding pluralistic ignorance in organizations: application and theory', *Journal of Managerial Psychology*, vol. 22, no. 1.

Hansson, Anders, & Bryngelsson, Mårten 2009 'Expert opinions on carbon dioxide capture and storage — a framing of uncertainties and possibilities', *Energy Policy*, vol. 37, no. 6, pp. 2273–91, 65–83.

Harris, Thomas E 2002, *Applied organizational communication: principles and pragmatics for future practice*, 2nd edn, Lawrence Erlbaum Associates, Mahwah NJ.

Hayes, Andrew F, Glynn, Carroll J & Shanahan, James 2005, 'Willingness to self-censor: a construct and measurement tool for public opinion research', *International Journal of Public Opinion Research*, vol. 17, no. 3, pp. 298–323.

Henningsen, David Dryden, Henningsen, Mary Lynn Miller, Eden, Jennifer & Cruz, Michael G 2006, 'Examining the symptoms of groupthink and retrospective sensemaking', *Small Group Research*, vol. 37, no. 1, pp. 36–64.

Higgins, E Tory, Herman, C Peter & Zanna, Mark P 1982, *Consistency in social behavior*, Lawrence Erlbaum Associates, Hillsdale, NJ.

Hussey, Tris 2009, *Create your own blog: 6 easy projects to start blogging like a pro*, SAMS, New York.

Jacobs, Robin J & Thomlison, Barbara 2009, 'Self-silencing and age as risk factors for sexually acquired HIV in midlife and older women', *Journal of Aging and Health*, vol. 21, no. 1, pp. 102–28.

Jacoby, Jeff 2006, 'We are all Danes now', *Boston Globe*, 5 February, p. E11.

Janis, Irving L 1982, *Groupthink*, 2nd edn, Houghton Mifflin, Boston.

Jansen, Sue Curry 2003, *Critical communication theory: power, media, gender and technology*, Rowman & Littlefield, Lanham, MD.

Kempner, Joanna 2008, 'The chilling effect: how do researchers react to controversy?' *PLos Medicine*, vol. 5, no. 11, pp. 1571–8, www.plosmedicine.org.

Kendall, Diana 2005, *Framing class: media representations of wealth and poverty in America*, Rowman & Littlefield, Lanham, MD.

Kessler, Michelle, 2007, 'Fridays go from casual to e-mail-free', USATODAY.com, www.usatoday.com.

Kim, Sei-Hill, Scheufele, Dietram A & Shanahan, James 2002, 'Think about it this way: attribute agenda-setting function of the press and the public's evaluation of a local issue', *Journalism and Mass Communication Quarterly*, vol. 79, no. 1, pp. 7–26.

Kiousis, Spiro, McDevitt, Michael & Wu, Xu 2005, 'The genesis of civic awareness: agenda setting in political socialization', *Journal of Communication*, vol. 5, no. 4, pp. 756–74.

Klimkiewicz, Joann 2007, 'Internet junkies hooked online: one in eight Americans find it hard to log off', *Knight Ridder Tribune Business News*, 26 January, p. 1.

Knobloch, Leanne K & Carpenter-Theune, Katy E 2004, 'Topic avoidance in developing romantic relationships', *Communication Research*, vol. 31, no. 2, pp. 173–205.

Kostigan, Thomas 2009, 'The $700 trillion elephant', *Marketwatch.com*, www.marketwatch.com.

Kramarae, Cheris 1981, Women and men speaking, Newbury House, Rowley, MA.

Kuhn, Timothy & Deetz, Stanley 2008, 'Critical theory and corporate social responsibility: can/should we get beyond cynical reasoning?' in Crane, Andrew, McWilliams, Abagail, Matten, Dirk & Moon, Jeremy (eds.), *The Oxford handbook of corporate social responsibility*, Oxford.

Lasswell, Harold D 1948, 'The structure and function of communication in society', in Lymon Bryson (ed.), *The communication of ideas*, Harper & Row/Institute for Religious and Social Studies, New York.

Lewis, Laurie K 1999, 'Disseminating information and soliciting input during planned organizational change: implementers' targets, sources, and channels for communicating', *Management Communication Quarterly*, vol. 13, no. 1, pp. 43–76.

Lievrouw, Leah A & Finn, T Andrew 1990, 'Identifying the common dimensions of communication: the communication systems model', in BD Ruben and LA Lievrouw (eds), *Mediation, information and communication: information and behavior*, vol. 3, Transaction Books, New Brunswick, NJ, pp. 37–65.

—— 1996, 'New information technologies and informality: comparing organizational information flows using the CSM', *International Journal of Technology Management*, vol. 11, no. 1–2, pp. 28–42.

Livinwood, John W 2003, 'Mediation: reframing and its uses', *Dispute Resolution Journal*, vol. 57, no. 42, pp. 12–23.

Maharaj, Rookmin 2008, 'Corporate governance, groupthink and bullies in the boardroom', *International Journal of Disclosure and Governance*, vol. 5, no. 1, pp. 68–92.

Maras, Steven 2000, 'Beyond the transmission model: Shannon, Weaver and the critique of Sender/Message/Receiver', *Australian Journal of Communication*, vol. 27, no. 3, pp. 123–42.

Marcoux, Alexei M 2006, 'A counterintuitive argument for résumé embellishment', *Journal of Business Ethics*, vol. 63, no. 2, pp. 183–94.

McCombs, Maxwell, Shaw, Donald L & Weaver, David 1997, *Communication and democracy: exploring the intellectual frontiers in agenda-setting theory*, Lawrence Erlbaum, Mahwah, NJ.

McCroskey, JC 1998, *Why we communicate the way we do: a communibiological perspective*, Allyn & Bacon, Boston, MA.

McGlone, Matthew S 2005, '"Quoted out of context": contextomy and its consequences', *Journal of Communication*, vol. 55, no. 2, pp. 330–46.

McLuhan, Marshall 2004 [1964], *Understanding media: the extensions of man*, critical edn, ed. W Terrence Gordon, Gingko Press, Corte Madera, CA.

McQuail, Dennis & Windahl, Sven 1995, *Communication models for the study of mass communications*, 2nd edn, Pearson, London/New York.

Mikkelson, Alan C & Hesse, Colin 2009, 'Discussions of religion and relational messages: differences between comfortable and uncomfortable interactions', *Southern Communication Journal*, vol. 74, no. 1, pp, 40–56.

Mildner, Vesna 2008, *The cognitive neuroscience of human communication*, Lawrence Erlbaum Associates, Mahwah, NJ.

Miller, David, & Dinan, William 2008, *A century of spin*, Pluto Press, London.

Miller, Geoffrey P & Rosenfeld, Gerald 2009, *Intellectual hazard: how conceptual biases in complex organizations contributed to the crisis of 2008*, New York University Law and Economics Working Papers, New York University School of Law, 11 January, no. 2529.

Mitchell, Christopher 2000, *Gestures of conciliation: factors contributing to successful olive branches*, Macmillan, London.

Modaff, Daniel, DeWine, Sue & Butler, Jennifer 2008, *Organizational communication*, 2nd edn, Allyn & Bacon, Boston, MA.

Mogg, Karin, Philpott, Pierre & Bradley, Brendan P 2004, 'Selective attention to angry faces in clinical social phobia', *Journal of Abnormal Psychology*, vol. 113, no. 1, pp. 160–5.

Mortensen, C David 1972, *Communication: the study of human communication*, McGraw-Hill, New York.

Moskowitz, Eva S 2001, *In therapy we trust: America's obsession with self-fulfillment*, Johns Hopkins University Press, Baltimore, MD.

Mullainathan, Sendhil & Washington, Ebonya 2009, 'Sticking with your vote: cognitive dissonance and political attitudes', *American Economic Journal: Applied Economics*, vol. 1, no. 1, pp. 86–111.

Myers, Greg 2010, *Discourse of blogs and wikis*, Continuum, New York/London.

Neuwirth, Kurt & Frederick, Edward 2004, 'Peer and social influence on opinion expression: combining the theories of planned behavior and the spiral of silence', *Communication Research*, vol. 31, no. 6, pp. 669–703.

Nightly Business Report, Friday, 5 October, 2007 '"Last word"– e-mail free Friday', www.pbs.org.

Noelle-Neumann, Elizabeth 1993, *The spiral of silence: public opinion – our social skin*, 2nd edn, University of Chicago, Chicago.

Oberg, James A 1999, 'Why the Mars probe went off course', *Spectrum*, December, vol. 36, no. 12.

Osterman, Michael D 2003, 'Instant messaging in the enterprise', *Business Communications Review*, vol. 33, no. 1, pp. 59–62.

Paulsel, Michelle L & Mottet, Timothy P 2004, 'Interpersonal communication motives', *Communication Quarterly*, vol. 52, no. 2, pp. 182–195.

Pfau, Michael, Ivanov, Bobi, Houston, Brian, Haigh, Michel, Sims, Jeanette, Gilchrist, Eileen, Russell, Jason, Wigley, Shelley, Eckstein, Jackie & Richert, Natalie 2005, 'Inoculation and mental processing: the instrumental role of associative networks in the process of resistance to counterattitudinal influence', *Communication Monographs*, vol. 72, no. 4, pp. 414–41.

Priestley, JB 1957, 'Televiewing', in *Thoughts in the wilderness*, Heinemann, London.

Quinn, Robert E, Hildebrandt, Herbert W, Rogers, Priscilla & Thompson, Michael P 1991, 'A competing values framework for analyzing presentational communication in management contexts', *Journal of Business Communication*, vol. 28, no. 3, pp. 213–32.

Robbins, Stephen P & Judge, Tim A 2010, *Essentials of Organizational behaviour*, 10th edn, Prentice Hall, Upper Saddle River, NJ.

Roessler, Patrick 2008, 'Agenda-setting, framing and priming', in Donsbach, Wolfgang, and Traugott, Michael W. (eds.), *The SAGE handbook of public opinion research*, Sage, London.

Rucinksi, Dianne 2004, 'Community boundedness, personal relevance, and the knowledge gap', *Communication Research*, vol. 31. no. 4, pp. 472–95.

Schermerhorn, John R Jr 2010, *Management*, 10th edn, John Wiley and Sons, New York.

Scheufele, Dietram A 1999, 'Framing as a theory of media effects', *Journal of Communication*, vol. 49, no. 1, pp. 103–22.

Schmitt, Kathleen M, Gunther, Albert C & Liebhart, Janice L 2004, 'Why partisans see mass media as biased', *Communication Research*, vol. 31, no. 6, pp. 623–41.

Scott, Susie 2004, 'The shell, the stranger and the competent other: towards a sociology of shyness', *Sociology*, vol. 38, no. 1, pp. 121–37.

Seeley, Ken and Murphy, Myatt 2009, *Face it and fix it: a three-step plan to break free from denial and discover the life you deserve*, HarperOne, New York.

Seitel, Fraser P 2011, *The practice of public relations*, 11th edn, Prentice Hall, Upper Saddle River, NJ.

Sereno, KK & Mortensen, CD (eds) 1970, *Foundations of communication theory*, Harper and Row, New York.

Shannon, Claude E & Weaver, Warren 1999 [*1949*], *The mathematical theory of communication*, University of Illinois Press, Chicago, IL.

Shaw, Donald, McCombs, Maxwell, Weaver, David & Hamm, Bradley 1999, 'Individuals, groups, and agenda melding: a theory of social dissonance', *International Journal of Public Opinion Research*, vol. 11, no. 1, pp. 2–24.

Slater, Michael D, Henry, Kimberly, Swaim, Randall C & Anderson, Lori L 2003, 'Violent media content and aggressiveness in adolescents', *Communication Research*, vol. 36, no. 1, pp. 713–36.

Stauber, John & Rampton, Sheldon 1995, *Toxic sludge is good for you! Lies, damned lies, and the public relations industry*, Common Courage Press, Monroe, ME.

Te'eni, Dov, Sagie, Abraham, Schwartz, David G & Amichai-Hamburger, Yair 2001, 'The process of organizational communication: a model and field study', *IEEE Transactions on Professional Communication*, vol. 44, no. 1, pp. 6–20.

Timmerman, C Erik 2003, 'Media selection during the implementation of planned organizational change', *Management Communication Quarterly*, vol. 16, no. 3, pp. 40–54.

Toch, Hans & McLean, Malcolm S Jr 1970, 'Perception and communication: a transactional view', in KK Sereno and CD Mortensen (eds), *Foundations of communication theory*, Harper and Row, New York.

Townsend, Sarah SM, Markus, Hazel R & Bergkieker, Hilary B 2009, 'My Choice, Your Categories: The Denial of multiracial identities', *Journal of Social Issues*, vol. 65, no. 1, pp. 185–204.

Veil, Shari R & Kent, Michael L 2008, 'Issue management and inoculation: Tylenol's responsible dosing advertising', *Public Relations Review*, vol. 34, no. 4, pp. 399–402.

Vos, MS & de Haes, JCJM 2007, 'Denial in cancer patients: an explorative view', *Psycho-Oncology*, vol. 16, pp. 12–25.

Wahba, Jodi Sauders & McCroskey, James C 2005, 'Temperament and brain systems as predictors of assertive communication traits', *Communication Research Reports*, vol. 22, no. 2, pp. 157–64.

Wakefield, Jane 2007, 'Turn off e-mail and do some work', http://news.bbc.co.uk.

Wall, Celia J & Gannon-Leary, Pat 1999, 'A sentence made by men: muted group theory revisited', *European Journal of Women's Studies*, vol. 6, pp. 21–9.

Wilson, Steven R 1997, 'Developing theories of persuasive message production: the next generation', ch. 2 in John O Greene (ed.), *Message production: advances in communication theory*, Lawrence Erlbaum Associates, Mahwah, NJ.

Wood, Julia T 2011, *Communication mosaics: an introduction to the field of communication*, 6th edn, Wadsworth, Belmont, CA.

www.shyness.com 2006, 'The shyness home page: an index to resources for shyness', www.shyness.com.

Zajonc, Robert B 1970, 'The concept of balance, congruity and dissonance', in KK Sereno and CD Mortensen (eds.), *Foundations of communication theory*, Harper and Row, New York.

Zerubavel, Eviatar 2006, *The elephant in the room: silence and denial in everyday life*, Oxford University Press, New York.

Zillman, Dolf, Chen, Lei, Knobloch, Silvia & Callison, Coy 2004, 'Effects of lead framing on selective exposure to Internet news reports', *Communication Research*, vol. 31, no. 1, pp. 58–81.

2

Document design and graphic communication

LEARNING OBJECTIVES

After studying this chapter you should be able to:

- Define document design, information design and information architecture
- Explain basic techniques of text layout and choice of type, colour, headings and white space
- Construct different types of visual aids
- Recognise the strengths and weaknesses of different types of visual aids
- Explain how graphic communication can be used to convey or distort facts

Document and information design: an introduction

Messages on paper and computer screens comprise text and nontext elements. If we communicate primarily through words, however, why should we be concerned with other message elements? Why not simply present written documents, web pages, letters — this text you are reading now — without bothering with design or graphic elements?

The answer to this question is complex. A good place to start is a newspaper archive. You will find that most newspapers from a century ago overwhelmingly feature plain text, with very little graphic information in the way of photographs, figures, colour or strongly differentiated headlines. The contrast with today's newspapers is stark.

Most readers, or information consumers, would say that modern newspapers and web pages are much easier to read and extract information from when compared with the earlier, all-text layouts. The same might be said of other communication forms: try comparing a modern annual report, technical paper or textbook with examples of a century ago; even contrast a document produced by an early-generation computer with today's output. We are confronted, in short, with a pervasive movement from the simple linear presentation of information to a far broader, more flexible 'mosaic' presentation (see 'Online writing: mosaic and 3D' in chapter 6).

These changes have been made possible by the rapid developments in printing and computer technology, and design philosophies have reflected the shifts. Today we cope with an ever increasing flood of information, while advertising and entertainment media such as television have changed our expectations about the presentation of this information.

Of course, a less charitable view of this evolutionary process is that modern presentation of information to a large extent trivialises, distorts and 'dumbs down' these communications for audiences with such diminished concentration spans that they need a never-ending stream of 'eye-candy', or somewhat trivial visual stimulus, to keep them amused, having lost the gift of closely reading extended text solely for its information content.

Information design: a process focusing on the fusion of content, structure and appearance of documents

Document design: a process focusing on the appearance and navigability of documents

Information architecture: a process focusing on the structure of content, especially that of websites

Some definitions

In recent years many new terms have emerged to define these innovative forms of presenting information in print and nonprint modes of communication. Three central concepts are **information design**, **document design** and **information architecture** (figure 2.1).

Document design
Focuses on the appearance and navigability of documents

Information architecture
Focuses on the structure of content, especially that of websites

Information design
Focuses on the fusion of content, structure and appearance of documents

FIGURE 2.1 Interaction of document design, information design and information architecture

Source: Adapted from Carliner (2002).

The definitions of these terms – which may refer either to print text, or to text in electronic sources such as web pages – point to some interesting trends. These trends include:

- the convergence of technologies (computers, the internet, television) and the interaction of these technologies with emerging print technologies
- innovations in computer software, which mean that office suite applications, in word processing and presentations in particular, offer novel and creative ways of presenting information (and indeed, the design principles of word processing and presentations cross-fertilise each other)
- the skills redeployment apparent in workplaces, with the decline of formally qualified secretaries, trained in document presentation, and the rise of the semiskilled clerk or executive who needs to be able to draft, create/design/type, lay out, edit and print/send complete documents to different audiences
- a shift in the presentation of physical and electronic/online documents or texts away from linear, static and monochrome values to mosaic, dynamic/animated and colour values.

This means that as well as being a writer when you communicate on paper or via a computer screen, you will be an editor, a designer, a typographer and a graphic artist. Can you be an expert in all these fields? This is unlikely, and the more important the document, the smarter it may be to bring in trained professionals from these areas to help you.

Crossovers and connections

Much of the document design research that took place from the late 1970s derived its impetus from the plain language or plain English movement (Redish 2000), and new insights are now emerging with the convergence of linear print text writing and online writing (Klanten et al. 2010; Wright 2004). Popular modes of book publishing, for example, are beginning to incorporate design elements from comic books (see the *For Dummies*, *Idiots* and *For Beginners* guide series). Some of these values are now apparent in formerly staid areas such as textbook publishing, where the competition for the reader's attention may not be another textbook but a television program, website or computer game. Rather than simply reading a prepared paper, speakers at academic conferences are increasingly presenting their work in poster form, so that it can be absorbed visually (Nicol & Pexman 2010).

Information design and readability

The readability of documents usually relates to statistical counts of word length (semantic complexity) and sentence length (syntax complexity) within documents. It is common, for example, to rate a piece of text according to readability scores and on how many years of education a reader may need before understanding it (see online chapter 3).

Dubay (2004), however, argues that readability, or understandability of documents (online as well as paper-based), is only partly related to word and sentence length, or style. He suggests that three other areas are just as important (see figure 2.2):

- *content* (relating to the propositions advanced by the writer, the way in which the material is organised, and the coherence or lack of it in the material)
- *structure* (the way in which the material is laid out in chapters or sections, the use or nonuse of cues such as headings, and the ease with which the document can be navigated or explored)
- *design* (the way in which the material is laid out in types or fonts, the use of formats or pre-determined styles of fonts and spacings in word processors, and illustrations or graphics).

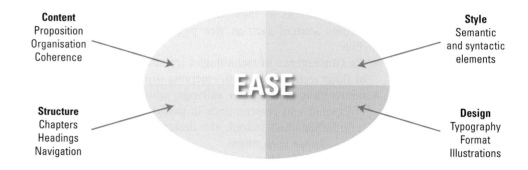

FIGURE 2.2 A model of readability
Source: Dubay (2004, p. 18).

Thus, any strategies we learn in this chapter about laying out text and presenting data can help reinforce our written style and our overall ability to communicate ideas to our audiences (just as surely as they can help to undermine and contradict our ideas if we use them badly).

Designing information: how do you do it?

Usability: the extent to which a document or process or product can be understood and used

Information design encompasses an approach to the total look and '**usability**' of a document that considers the full panoply of text, typefaces or fonts, use of colour, white space or background, graphics, headings, bullet points and lists, and layout (the arrangement of elements of text and graphics on a page or screen in lines, paragraphs, columns, boxes, tables/matrices, hypertext, notes and other patterns) (Barnum 2002).

Mixing and matching for maximum effect

The ways in which these communication tools are mixed and matched will help determine how effectively you get your message across. A successful mix will increase the motivation of your audience to consider your message and help them understand and recall it later.

Consider, for example, how you might best communicate a basic idea such as the greenhouse effect. Figures 2.3 to 2.6 show four different treatments of the topic, using varying mixes of linear text, lists, charts and diagrams.

GLOBAL WARMING
What is the greenhouse effect?

Energy from the sun (mainly light) passes through the Earth's atmosphere. Some of it is reflected back into space by clouds and light-coloured parts of the Earth (like snow). Most of the energy is absorbed by the atmosphere and the Earth's surface. The Earth and atmosphere warm up and try to radiate heat energy back to space.

Greenhouse gases in the atmosphere trap this energy for a time in the Earth's atmosphere. Greenhouse gases include water vapour, carbon dioxide, methane, nitrous oxide and chlorofluorocarbons (CFCs). This process is called the greenhouse effect because the greenhouse gases trap heat in the atmosphere in the same way that glass traps heat in a greenhouse.

FIGURE 2.3 Continuous text format
Source: Schriver (1997, p. 414).

GLOBAL WARMING
What is the greenhouse effect?

GLOBAL WARMING
What is the greenhouse effect?

- Energy from the sun (mainly light) passes through the Earth's atmosphere.
- Some of it is reflected back into space by clouds and light-coloured parts of the Earth (like snow). Most of the energy is absorbed by the atmosphere and the Earth's surface.
- The Earth and atmosphere warm up and try to radiate heat energy back to space.
- Greenhouse gases in the atmosphere trap this energy for a time in the Earth's atmosphere. Greenhouse gases include water vapour, carbon dioxide, methane, nitrous oxide and chlorofluorocarbons (CFCs).
- This process is called the greenhouse effect because the greenhouse gases trap heat in the atmosphere in the same way that glass traps heat in a greenhouse.

FIGURE 2.4 Itemised list format

Source: Schriver (1997, p. 414).

GLOBAL WARMING
What is the greenhouse effect?

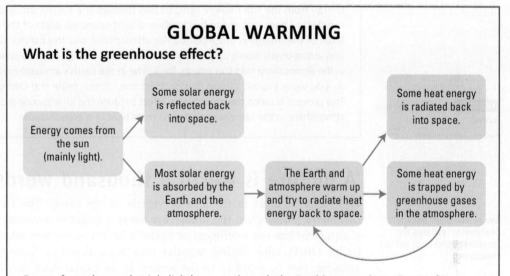

Energy from the sun (mainly light) passes through the Earth's atmosphere. Some of it is reflected back into space by clouds and light-coloured parts of the Earth (like snow). Most of the energy is absorbed by the atmosphere and the Earth's surface. The Earth and atmosphere warm up and try to radiate heat energy back to space. Greenhouse gases in the atmosphere trap this energy for a time in the Earth's atmosphere. Greenhouse gases include water vapour, carbon dioxide, methane, nitrous oxide and chlorofluorocarbons (CFCs). This process is called the greenhouse effect because the greenhouse gases trap heat in the atmosphere in the same way that glass traps heat in a greenhouse.

FIGURE 2.5 Flowchart and text format

Source: Schriver (1997, p. 415).

You need to give thought not only to objective factors such as comprehension and recall, but also to how you will motivate your audience to even consider your message. In test samples of readers, Schriver (1997, pp. 414–15) found all four approaches shown in figures 2.3 to 2.6 to be equal in terms of communicating comprehensible content, but that the same readers overwhelmingly expressed a preference for the last approach — the diagram and prose format. Given this finding, is there any benefit in presenting documents incorporating more complex information design? Schriver suggests that there might be: 'what people may prefer to read may offer them no better information, but may keep them reading long enough to get the most from a document' (Schriver 1997, pp. 414–15).

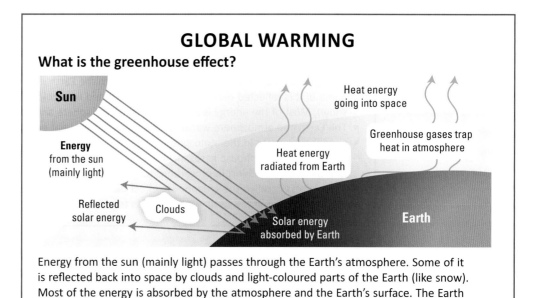

GLOBAL WARMING

What is the greenhouse effect?

Energy from the sun (mainly light) passes through the Earth's atmosphere. Some of it is reflected back into space by clouds and light-coloured parts of the Earth (like snow). Most of the energy is absorbed by the atmosphere and the Earth's surface. The Earth and atmosphere warm up and try to radiate heat energy back to space. Greenhouse gases in the atmosphere trap this energy for a time in the Earth's atmosphere. Greenhouse gases include water vapour, carbon dioxide, methane, nitrous oxide and chlorofluorocarbons (CFCs). This process is called the greenhouse effect because the greenhouse gases trap heat in the atmosphere in the same way that glass traps heat in a greenhouse.

FIGURE 2.6 Diagram and text format

Source: Schriver (1997, p. 415).

'A picture is worth a thousand words ...'

Eye candy: visual material designed to reinforce the meaning of spoken or written messages

There may be more to the idea of visuals as eye candy. The *Oxford Advanced Learner's Dictionary* (2010) gives the phrase **eye candy** a negative meaning ('a person or thing that is attractive but not intelligent or useful'); however, the less prestigious Urban Dictionary Online (2011), while listing negative meanings, also lists 'Something purely aesthetically pleasing; that is, pleasing to the senses' as an explanation for the term. When planning to transmit information, keep in mind that you usually have choices. You should aim to combine communication tools to achieve maximum effect. Recall the proverb: 'If you only have a hammer in your toolkit, every problem looks like a nail'. If your habitual communication repertoire is limited, you are likely to overlook new and more creative approaches. Always consider your audience, and what approach might best reach it. Would visual elements help to clarify relationships, sequences, contexts and systems, or would they oversimplify and distort the message? Who knows? In due time, some dictionaries may perhaps define eye candy as 'visual material designed to reinforce the meaning of spoken or written messages', which is how we shall define it here.

In chapter 5, we look at the information–persuasion mix in constructing reports. We also mention the entertainment value of a document. This is a tribute to that great cliché that a picture is worth a thousand words. When composing documents, even short ones, use your word processing software to get a multi-page view of how the document is progressing. If appropriate to the genre, try to ensure that there is least a piece of eye candy – a graph, a table or a photo – on every second page. Chances are that, in this age of nonreaders who simply skim and scan (and thus lose the intricate thread of your words), the eye candy will arrest their attention. Stick the pages to a wall or look at a multi-page view: you might be surprised at how your exposition is, or is not, turning out. Edit, edit, edit. Don't believe me? Wait and see the sheer dramatic communicative power of graphics in the rest of this chapter.

Structure and analysis

The ways in which we present ideas, then, are clearly important if we want to communicate those ideas successfully. Of course, we often want to do more than simply inform others; we want to persuade them, and sometimes also entertain them. Good information design is essential here, and not something that should be considered as an afterthought. You might have an excellent message, but if no-one in your audience is motivated to receive it, then the quality of your ideas becomes quite immaterial.

More on planning

Many aspects of planning and design need to be considered. For example, what is it we are trying to achieve? How well will the document connect with and communicate to the target audience? How 'usable' is it? Figure 2.7, which shows a model of information design, outlines some of the essential steps in planning, designing and drafting documents.

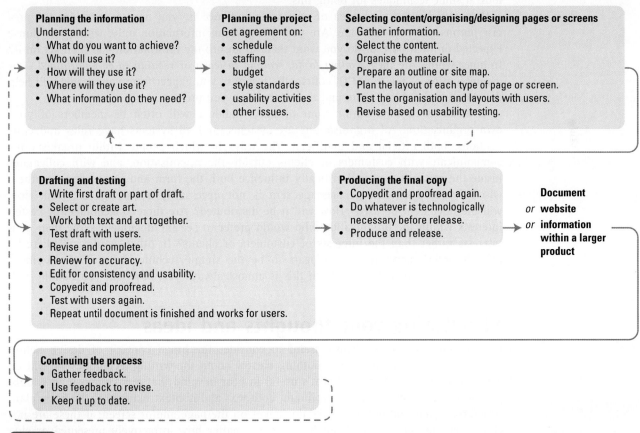

Planning the information
Understand:
- What do you want to achieve?
- Who will use it?
- How will they use it?
- Where will they use it?
- What information do they need?

Planning the project
Get agreement on:
- schedule
- staffing
- budget
- style standards
- usability activities
- other issues.

Selecting content/organising/designing pages or screens
- Gather information.
- Select the content.
- Organise the material.
- Prepare an outline or site map.
- Plan the layout of each type of page or screen.
- Test the organisation and layouts with users.
- Revise based on usability testing.

Drafting and testing
- Write first draft or part of draft.
- Select or create art.
- Work both text and art together.
- Test draft with users.
- Revise and complete.
- Review for accuracy.
- Edit for consistency and usability.
- Copyedit and proofread.
- Test with users again.
- Repeat until document is finished and works for users.

Producing the final copy
- Copyedit and proofread again.
- Do whatever is technologically necessary before release.
- Produce and release.

Document
or **website**
or **information within a larger product**

Continuing the process
- Gather feedback.
- Use feedback to revise.
- Keep it up to date.

FIGURE 2.7 A model of information design

Source: © 1999 Janice C Redish; based on versions of a similar model developed between 1976 and 1999 at the American Institutes of Research and at Redish & Associates, Inc. Reproduced with permission.

Means, ends, assumptions and audiences

Planning communications requires us to weigh up means and ends. Certain documents (e.g. works of art such as novels or poems) may be ends in themselves. However, most business documents – reports, letters, emails, web text and instructional manuals – are a means to an end. Here usability is an important consideration, because it helps us avoid making assumptions – we know what they want and how to communicate with them without being misunderstood – and constrains us to find out through testing processes what could be understood.

All communicators must first identify their audience, and always keep this audience in mind, conveying the message clearly and effectively while helping readers avoid information overload. Our audiences do not want us simply to project our assumptions and jargon onto them; they do expect us to take seriously their frustrations when ideas are not clearly communicated. If we do not respond to these needs, then communication does not take place. Remember the maxim:

> More work for the writer, less work for the reader; less work for the writer, more work for the reader.

In many cases we cannot assume that the audience will actually read extended text. (Indeed, the audience's actual reading ability may be substantially lower than we might expect). Audiences often skim and scan, so we may have to package our message in 'layers', capable of being absorbed in small portions (Delin & Bateman 2002). We will soon look at some techniques for doing this.

Once you have a clear idea of who your audience is, you need to consider the precise purpose of your message. Are you giving them information only, with no response expected on their part, or do you want them to absorb the information and then act on it? In other words, are they *reading to do*, *reading to learn* or *reading to be entertained* – or a combination of the three? Of course, the response you expect from your reader will help determine the way you write and the information you present.

In business communication your primary audience will often be members of your own organisation. All organisations are systems, and all systems have rules and conventions, both official and unofficial. The ways in which people within organisations communicate with customers or clients outside the organisation, and with colleagues inside the organisation, will critically influence both the form and the success or otherwise of your document. A message sent is not necessarily a message received. How will the document be used? How will it be distributed? Are there stakeholders or vested interests within the organisation who would prefer to see the document serve their own interests rather than the interests of customers or clients? In other words, will there be political interference in what appears to be the simple technical matter of document creation? Given that the answer to this is almost always yes, how will you handle such interference?

Structuring your thoughts and ideas

In communication it is always useful to consider the broad concept of design before approaching the writing. There's nothing narrow about the writing techniques we will be considering in later chapters, but it's useful to bear in mind that text composition is only part of document creation. Underpinning both text and nontext material is the basic plan, structure, layout and outline of the document on the page and/or screen: if these are not clear, then the message will not be clear, no matter how attractively presented or eloquently expressed. Without structure, your message will be lost in a wilderness of muddle and good intentions.

Drafting and testing

Your first draft will not be, or should not be, your final draft. You may need to push your document through a number of versions. A critical part of usability testing is finding out what others think of what you are trying to communicate. Remember, we all tend to be too close to our own creation, which will always benefit from an objective review. We need to be able to recognise and act on good advice while rejecting views that our common sense tells us are unsound. One useful source of advice, the **expert user review**, draws on the experience of informed individuals who can make well-founded suggestions for improvement. These people might be:

- colleagues who talk to customers at the counter or on the telephone
- data processors who transfer data from completed forms
- sales personnel who talk to customers in the field
- graphic artists
- professional or technical writers
- 'expert customers' – customers who know existing products, processes and documentation, and who participate in testing in a paid or unpaid capacity.

The beauty of expert testing is that you can benefit from the experience of others. But are experts always right? They will tell you they are, but of course they are not, and their advice may not always be sound. A **naïve user review** can be extremely useful here. This type of review involves someone who knows little or nothing about your world, your ideas or your specialised audience. Many problems not immediately obvious to the writer or an expert reviewer – assumptions about technical language or jargon or prior knowledge, misleading instructions, ambiguous or confusing phrasing and visuals, ineffective cross-referencing, inefficient layout – can be revealed in this way.

Such testing is used extensively in testing new products or processes. Experts sometimes object to naïve user tests: 'What could *they* possibly know about it?' But this discounts the process known as *educated incapacity*, or the tendency of technically specialised groups to have blind spots and misperceptions about their own field. Naïve user opinion and information doesn't replace expert opinion; it complements it.

Feedback from expert and naïve user reviews can therefore contribute to the composition of a second draft. Indeed, you may consider going through several cycles, or iterations, of such reviewing before publishing your final draft. This review process should be combined with your own editing and proofreading. It is sometimes useful to keep the loop open on certain types of reviewing or feedback processes. Product evaluation, for example, may be ongoing, in a process called *strategic listening* (see chapter 17). Table 2.1 highlights some problems in instruction manuals identified by expert and naïve users, but many of the comments are equally relevant to other documents.

Expert user review: a process in which a draft document is appraised by experts

Naïve user review: a process in which a draft document is appraised by individuals who have no specific expertise in the area

TABLE 2.1 Some usability problems with documentation found through usability testing

Major problems	Specific problems
Cannot understand what can be done with the product because ...	- No introduction that describes the product and its features - No description of audience(s) for manual - Introductory material filled with jargon
Cannot find the information I need because ...	- No tabs separating sections or parts - Table of contents organised around system, not tasks - No parallel sentence structure in the table of contents - No index - Index entries not cross-referenced - Levels of headings not shown consistently - Levels of headings not visually distinct - Not enough white space on a page - Too much text — not enough lists, tables and graphics - Typeface not readable

(continued)

TABLE 2.1 *(continued)*

Major problems	Specific problems
Cannot understand information when I find it because...	■ Ineffective or missing brief overviews of sections describing tasks ■ Tasks described from the system's point of view ■ Not enough examples ■ Illustrations not near the text they relate to ■ Technical terms not defined ■ Too much jargon ■ Instructions in the past tense ■ Instructions in the passive voice ■ Too many steps in procedures

Source: Adapted from Dumas and Redish (1993, pp. 328–30).

Layout: how does it look?

HATS: an acronym standing for headings, access, typography and spacing

Baker (2001) suggests a useful starting point from which to approach business document design in his acronym **HATS**, which stands for Headings, Access, Typography and Spacing.

Headings break up blocks of text, making them easier to read and digest, while also acting as navigational tools, signposting the section or subsection that follows. A logical hierarchy for headings and subheadings improves accessibility and can aid the reader's understanding considerably. Take a look at the system of headings and subheadings used in this book. Good access to documents facilitates the reader's task of finding and mentally digesting important information (Baker 2001, p. 66). Access is also greatly facilitated by the careful use, where appropriate, of bullet points and numbered lists, along with graphics such as tables, graphs, charts and photographs. Careful use of paragraphing, transitional words and phrases, and grammatical parallelism (see online chapter 3) are also important.

Types and fonts

There are two main families of type, or typefaces – serif and sanserif. The word *serif* literally means 'line'; thus serif typefaces are those that feature small lines that finish off the main strokes of each letter, while sanserif types lack these lines (see figure 2.8).

M	M
The letter 'M' in Times New Roman 24 point. Times New Roman is a serif typeface.	The letter 'M' in Arial 24 point. Arial is a sanserif typeface.

FIGURE 2.8 Serif and sanserif typefaces

People tend to hold strong views on the relative merits of serif and sanserif typefaces. Serif typefaces are more traditional, and are generally considered easier to read, especially in long passages of text. Serif letters vary in thickness more than sanserif letters, and so may offer the eye more variety. Sanserif typefaces, on the other hand, may appear cleaner and more modern. They have some legibility advantages (e.g. in reversed type), but also present some legibility problems (e.g. in words such as 'Ill' and 'Illustrate').

Size

Type size is measured in imperial or nonmetric units. In printing there are 72 *points* to an inch, and 12 points to a *pica*. Figure 2.9 shows different point sizes for Times New Roman and Arial fonts. Try not to use font sizes below ten point in written documents, and below 15 point in slide presentations.

This (Times New Roman 48 pt)	This (Arial 48 pt)
This is Times (Times New Roman 28 pt)	This is Arial (Arial 28 pt)
This is Times New Roman (Times New Roman 16 pt)	This is Arial type. It is a (Arial 16 pt)
This is Times New Roman. It is a (Times New Roman 12 pt)	This is Arial type. It is a (Arial 12 pt)
This is Times New Roman. It is a serif type. (Times New Roman 9 pt)	This is Arial. It is a sanserif type. Some (Arial 9 pt)
This is Times New Roman. It is a serif type. Some people prefer serif (Times New Roman 6 pt)	This is Arial. It is a sanserif type. Some people prefer a (Arial 6 pt)

FIGURE 2.9 A serif series and a sanserif series

Font: the complete assortment of letters, numerals, punctuation marks and other characters of a specific typeface

Strictly speaking, a **font** is the complete assortment of letters, numerals, punctuation marks and other characters of a specific type or typeface. Figure 2.10 shows an example of an Arial font so defined.

ABCDEFGHIJKLMNOPQRSTUVWXYZ
abcdefghijklmnopqrstuvwxyz
1234567890;'.,?

FIGURE 2.10 An Arial font

Figure 2.9 shows two *type series*, or typefaces at different point sizes. Word processing programs, however, tend to ignore the distinction between 'typeface' and 'font', and generalise the word *font* to cover both meanings. To the displeasure of some old-school printers and typographers, this generalised meaning now dominates.

The market leader in software office packages, Microsoft, originally had Times New Roman as the default font for Word, and Arial was the default on PowerPoint, Outlook and Excel. From the Office 2007 and 2010 releases onward, a new sanserif font, Calibri, replaced both older fonts. (An example of Calibri can be seen in figure 2.3. It is more curvilinear than Arial, and opinion is still divided on it.)

Fonts can be further characterised according to whether they are set in bold, italic, bold italic, light, medium or condensed type, as illustrated in figure 2.11.

| **Arial** bold | *Arial* Italic | ***Arial*** Bold italic | **Arial** Black |
| Arial light | Arial medium | Arial condensed | ***Arial*** Black italic |

FIGURE 2.11 Type treatment

Typefaces of different weight and size can be used to distinguish different levels of hierarchy in your headings, with main headings given bolder treatment, and subheadings using less dominant fonts.

Where once such technology was available only to printers and graphic artists, word processing and desktop publishing packages now offer all personal computer users a wide range of fonts and text effects. It is a mistake, however, to be tempted to use them extravagantly simply because they are available. Good designers will use no more than three fonts in a document; any more and the result tends to look messy and amateurish, like a painting executed by an enthusiastic amateur who has just been given a big new box of paints and wants to try them all.

As with type, so with all other aspects of information design: when in doubt, get a professional to do it. We often don't notice the work of professionals – that's why they're professionals; the work of amateurs is usually painfully apparent.

Margins, spacing and alignment

A **margin** is the point at which white space ends and text begins. There are top, bottom, left and right margins. The default setting for a page margin in most word processors is 2.54 cm or one inch. If you are printing on one side of the paper only, then binding the pages, make sure that the left-hand margin is wide enough so that when the reader opens any page, information on the left-hand side is visible. If you are printing back-to-back pages, check this for right-hand margins as well. Keep margins consistent within documents and sections of documents.

Spacing between lines of text can help or hinder your readers understand your text.

Single spacing may present too cramped a view of your words, although this might be useful for blocks of quoted material, helping to differentiate it from your primary text. Triple spacing may be too much, except for specialised document types such as legal documents or a rough edit version of text you want to mark up manually. Try for 1.5 or double spacing for most documents (although if you are trying to lay out text so that only a certain amount appears on one page, you might try fractional or decimal spacing).

Alignment refers to the position of your text lines in relation to the left and right margins. There are four types of alignment offered by most word processors. Figure 2.12 shows examples of all four. As with so much of document layout, views differ on the merits of different forms of alignment, although each can be useful, according to context.

Here is an example of **justified** text. There's not much you can say about this text, except that it contains some quite short words, such as *I*, *me*, *a* and *is*, as well as some extraordinarily long words, such as *supercalifragelisticexpialidocious* and *antidisestablishmentarianism*. The main thing to note with text of this kind, and indeed with text of any kind, is that the reader should not be distracted from the content of the words — the message — by the look or arrangement of the words.	Here is an example of **left-aligned** text. There's not much you can say about this text, except that it contains some quite short words, such as *I*, *me*, *a* and *is*, as well as some extraordinarily long words, such as *supercalifragelisticexpialidocious* and *antidisestablishmentarianism*. The main thing to note with text of this kind, and indeed with text of any kind, is that the reader should not be distracted from the content of the words — the message — by the look or arrangement of the words.
Here is an example of **centrally-aligned** text. There's not much you can say about this text, except that it contains some quite short words, such as *I*, *me*, *a* and *is*, as well as some extraordinarily long words, such as *supercalifragelisticexpialidocious* and *antidisestablishmentarianism*. The main thing to note with text of this kind, and indeed with text of any kind, is that the reader should not be distracted from the content of the words — the message — by the look or arrangement of the words.	Here is an example of **right-aligned** text. There's not much you can say about this text, except that it contains some quite short words, such as *I*, *me*, *a* and *is*, as well as some extraordinarily long words, such as *supercalifragelisticexpialidocious* and *antidisestablishmentarianism*. The main thing to note with text of this kind, and indeed with text of any kind, is that the reader should not be distracted from the content of the words — the message — by the look or arrangement of the words.

FIGURE 2.12 Four different types of text alignment

Justification: the equal spacing of words and lines according to a given measure

Justification is the equal spacing of words and lines, particularly in relation to margins. Justified text uses variable spacings between words and letters in order to fill the line to both left and right margins. This can be attractive, but unless hyphenation is used, justification can leave blank spaces in text.

Left-aligned, left-justified, flush left or ragged right alignment means that the spacings between words and letters are not variable, and because each line has a different number of letters each is of a different length – hence the 'ragged' right margin. It has the visual advantages of consistent spacing between words and less (or no) hyphenation, and is perhaps more informal. Most books, magazines and newspapers, on the other hand, use fully justified text, so more readers are probably accustomed to this layout. What convention has been followed in this book?

Centrally aligning your text may have some virtue for certain types of documents, such as posters and flyers, but may be distracting in more routine documents.

Right-aligned, right-justified, flush right or ragged left alignment is rarely used in written English, except for novelty effects. It is the mirror image of left-aligned text.

White space

Returning to Baker's HATS (Baker 2001), the last principle to examine is space. White space on a page refers to the area not taken up by text or other features. This means space around the text (margins) and within the text (influenced by the kerning, or horizontal letter spacing, and leading, or vertical spacing between lines). It also refers to space around blocks of text, such as between paragraphs and sections:

> Space gives visual relief, preventing reader fatigue, and enhances reader friendliness, encouraging readers to engage the content. Space also divides and frames elements on a page. For example, white space around a graph divides the graph from neighboring elements and provides a white frame. (Baker 2001, p. 69)

It is functionally important, of course, to ensure the left and right margins are sufficiently wide if the pages are to be bound together; otherwise there is a risk of the text disappearing into the central fold or gutter. But other usability issues must also be considered. Squeezing text up to save space and paper is a false economy, as cramped text puts most readers off and may indeed discourage them from reading your message at all. Just as a composer mixes sound and silence in a musical work, a page should offer a balance between white space and text or image.

Response space

In business forms, if you want your readers to respond within the document – for example, entering their name, address and other details – then it is important that you give them plenty of space to do this. Some people have long names and/or addresses, and some people's handwriting or printing takes up more space than others. As with white space, don't resort to false economy by restricting the space you provide to the needs of an 'average' respondent. Cramping the response space risks not only irritating readers; it may lead them to make illegible, inappropriate or inadequate responses.

The shape of the page

Portrait: a text block, page or image having a height greater than its width
Landscape: a text block, page or image having a width greater than its height

Most text pages have proportions similar to the one you are reading now: following the language of painting, this page – a tall rectangle – is described as having a **portrait** orientation or setup. Depending on the nature of the text, data and graphics you want to display in a document, you may occasionally choose instead a flat rectangle, called a **landscape** orientation. In a document, this may mean that your reader will have to rotate the document through 90 degrees, but if the landscape orientation helps the exposition of your content, then that is not too great a problem, and in fact may add to the professional look of your document.

In some contexts it makes sense to try to ensure that the text flows from one page to the next naturally although, depending on the effect you are trying to achieve, you may decide to use fractional spacing to keep text from spilling to another page. You may chose to use such word processing techniques, or rewrite your text, to avoid creating an **orphan** (the first line of a paragraph at the bottom of a column or page, which then spills onto the next column or page) or a **widow** (the last line of a paragraph at the top of a column or page).

To reinforce the unity of the text, and help your reader navigate around it, you may consider using **headers** or **footers** – signifiers at the top or bottom of the page giving details such as the document name, chapter and/or section heading, page number and/ or author name. These features are clearly set off from the main text, and may be further differentiated by being set in a smaller and/or different font.

Page orientation, text fitting, and headers and footers can all be controlled from within a word processing program, and you should make it your business to find out how to use such features to create more attractive and functional documents.

Paragraphs, lists, columns

Give thought also to how you present the exposition of your theme. Break up blocks of writing using **paragraphs**. Distinguish paragraphs by indenting their opening line from the left-hand margin, or else by leaving a line of spacing between them. Think carefully about running paragraphs more than ten lines long. Sometimes your argument merits it, but you have to keep your reader interested, and white space can help that.

If your text contains a long and repetitive sequence of ideas, consider breaking that sequence out into a **list**, using either bullet points or numbering.

For variety – and if your audience is comfortable with such layout – consider presenting your texts in **columns**. In standard A4 paper format, it might be unwise to attempt more than two columns (putting your work temporarily into column format, or into some of the more bizarre fonts, can help you edit your work by 'making it strange' so that you can see it with more objective eyes).

Colour

Colour/color[1] in documents costs money, although printing costs are falling as new technology advances. Even if you can afford to print in colour, however, you should consider the wisdom of the maxim 'less is more' (Zelanzny 2007). As with fonts, it is often tempting to use lots of colours simply because they are available, but that could be a mistake. In text documents, use colour sparingly; for example, to give your readers cues to headings, fill-in boxes and other significant areas. Also, bear in mind that your colour masterpieces may well be reproduced subsequently in monochrome or black and white, so you would be wise to test print (in black and white) all documents that include colour before delivering them. They may be illegible printed in one particular colour or in several colours. This advice applies as much to on-screen documents as to print pages. Exercise restraint when creating web pages and presentation slides.

Orphan: the first line of a paragraph at the bottom of a column or page, which then spills onto the next column or page

Widow: the last line of a paragraph at the top of a column or page

Header: text at the top of the page set off from the main body of text and containing details about the document

Footer: text at the bottom of the page set off from the main body of text and containing details about the document

Paragraph: block of text dealing with one topic

List: vertical array of related ideas

Column: vertical layout of text in blocks

---

1. All major word processors use American spelling for commands and tools. The US spelling (color) is derived directly from the Latin *color*, while the British/Australian/Canadian spelling (colour) is derived from an Old French variation of the Latin spelling (see online chapter 2 for international variations in spelling).

Document design and structure

The major word processors available today allow you to control the consistency of your page look via 'styles' subprograms and tools such as format painters. Spend some time learning to use these features, and you will gain more control over the look of your documents. You might also consider looking at more high-powered desktop publishing programs to learn more about design.

You can, of course, get a good overview of how your pages and the flow of your ideas are shaping up by using 'print preview' and 'show multiple pages' commands. Bear in mind that word processors may fail to give you the formatting or design you might want.

Typical problems may emerge in a variety of instances. For example, problems can emerge when you experiment with:

- bullet points
- numbering
- vertical and horizontal spacing
- text alignment
- section breaks, page breaks and column breaks
- text wrapping
- fonts
- page borders
- headers and footers
- margins
- design features (e.g. using drop caps)
- tables
- graphics (e.g. using charts, clip art and word art)
- pictures.

Some word processors (e.g. Word Perfect, with its 'reveal codes' feature) allow you to troubleshoot your document structure by giving you an 'X-ray' view of what lies beneath the screen or page.

ASSESS YOURSELF

1. Gather together a range of documents or publications — letters, newsletters, magazines, books, reports, advertisements. Compare and contrast the ways in which they have been designed (headings, numbering, bullet points, consistency, font, leading, kerning, justification, use of white space and colour). How successful do you think they are in conveying their message or information? Would you have designed them differently? If so, how?
2. Find a block of solid text; for example, a long encyclopedia entry. Restructure it by introducing paragraphing, headings of different levels and bullet points. Compare the original against your new document.

Layout/document design: from before to after

Practically, what do all of these concepts and terms mean to you, as a document originator? Figure 2.13 shows a 'horror' page, containing many errors of document design, while figure 2.14 shows a cleaned-up version of the same page. Ensure that your pages contain as few horrors as possible. Let the form and design of your pages subtly reinforce the content of your message, not distract from it and undermine and contradict it.

1. Header contains data relevant to writer but not to reader; font too big.

Very well.[2]

2. Widow text at top of page

ii. GRAPHICS WHICH SHOW PROPORTIONS[3]

We now come to those graphics or visuals which are useful for[4] showing proportions or percentages. These graphics are:[5] pie charts, exploded pie charts, 3D pie charts, 100 and 100 per cent bar charts. The 100 per cent bar chart is the only one of these charts that is rendered within an X-Y axes framework. The exact proportions in numerical terms can be superimposed upon the segments of each of these diagrams, or if you prefer, they can be identified using callouts emanating from inside the segments.[6][7][8]

3. Major heading has lighter typographical weight than subheading; violates hierarchy rules.

4. Margins inconsistent; some are too small.

INFERENCE OF PROPORTIONALITY[3][7]

To a certain extent, inferences about proportionality can be inferred from other[4] types of graphics or visuals such as area charts, stacked bar charts and pictograms. Again, values can be superimposed upon the different data segments or can be represented via callouts. [9]Smithson (2002:43) has said that [10]*"The key choices an information designer will need to make when constructing graphics relates to the best possible balance of colour and white space on the one and the most appropriate graphic type: is the problem that of variation over time, proportion, strict quantitative precision, schematic exposition, problem analysis, axis data set manipulation (both ethical and unethical) or a mixture of some or all of these factors. While computer software has made it so much easier for the communicator in the 21st century, a cynic might say that many do not know what an abundant resource they have at their disposal with automatic graphic/chart/visual generation, nor do they know which graphic actually is the best solution to their problem."*[6][7][8][11]

100 per cent column graph[12]

5. If text enumerates items, especially after colon punctuation, consider a list.

6. Line spacing shifts from double to single.

7. Font changes; too many fonts; some fonts less legible than others.

8. Text alignment shifts from full justification to ragged right.

9. New topic; start new paragraph

10. Quoted material is more than four lines, so needs new line; consider indenting. Quotation marks as well as italics not needed.

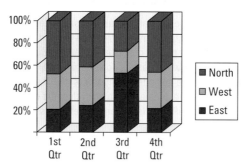

3. *GRAPHICS WHICH SHOW TIME VARIATION*[13]
[14]

11. In transcribing quote, author has created errors of grammar, punctuation and idiom.

12. Graphic is placed well after mention in text; not properly labelled. Inconsistent terminology; text says 'bar chart', label says 'column graph'.

13. Orphan text at bottom of page. Font differs from previous section heading: Arabic numbers, italics and underline versus lower-case Roman numbers with normal, or nonitalic, upper-case, or capitalised, text.

14. Empty white space: why?

FIGURE 2.13 Layout containing many document design errors

The callout boxes on the left margin (numbered):

1. More appropriate header; font more subtle. Don't forget pagination.

2. Widow text —'very well' — has been edited and re-set to bottom of previous page, allowing clean beginning for section 2 heading.

3. Colon punctuation deleted. Writer has gone for sentence exposition, but could have used a list.

4. Uniform font/typeface. Headings in bold, 1–2 points heavier than body text; heavier weight capital case for major headings, reinforcing hierarchy of ideas in writer's text

5. Uniform spacing, except for quoted material

6. Graphic placed near text where mentioned. Labelling consistent. Self-created graphic; if from another source, source details would be needed.

7. Alignment (left alignment–ragged right) is uniform. Margins consistent. Indented subsection 2.a OK, or remove indent? Keep or remove capital in preposition 'of'?

8. New idea in separate paragraph

[2]2. GRAPHICS WHICH SHOW PROPORTIONS

We now come to those graphics or visuals which are useful for showing proportions or percentages. These graphics are[3] pie charts, exploded pie charts, 3D pie charts, and 100 per cent bar charts. The 100 per cent bar/column chart is the only one of these charts that is rendered within an X-Y axes framework (see Fig. 6.2)[4][5]

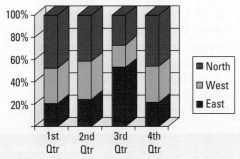

Fig. 6.2: 100 per cent bar/column chart[6]

The exact proportions in numerical terms can be superimposed upon the segments of each of these diagrams, or if you prefer, they can be identified using callouts emanating from inside the segments.

2. a. Inference Of Proportionality[7]

To a certain extent, inferences about proportionality can be drawn other types of graphics or visuals such as area charts, stacked bar charts and pictograms. Again, values can be superimposed upon the different data segments or can be represented via callouts.[4][5]

Smithson (2002:43) has said that[7][8]

The key choices an information designer will need to make when constructing graphics relate to the best possible balance of colour and white space on the one hand and the most appropriate graphic type on the other: is the problem that of variation over time, proportion, strict quantitative precision, schematic exposition, problem analysis, axis data set manipulation (both ethical and unethical) or a mixture of some or all of these factors? While computer software has made it so much easier for the communicator in the 21st century, a cynic might say that many do not know what an abundant resource they have at their disposal with automatic graphic/chart/visual generation, nor do they know which graphic actually is the best solution to their problem.[9][10]
[11]

9. Quoted material more than four lines, so set as separate text. Italics only; quotation marks not needed. Single spacing has been used to differentiate from body text. Consider indenting quoted material.

10. Pleasing use of white space allows text and graphics to 'breathe' and stand out clearly. Spacing allows avoidance of widow and orphan text.

11. Next section heading — 3. GRAPHICS WHICH SHOW TIME VARIATION — spilled to next page, to avoid creating orphan text.

FIGURE 2.14 Layout showing good design features

Every picture tells a story: graphic communication

We now have a clearer idea of the role of planning and layout in documents. Successful communication is critically affected by the way in which you present data, or its *look*. Some ideas can be conveyed more effectively using graphic or visual communication techniques. The software revolution of the past few years has meant that complex graphic tools, such as charts or diagrams of various kinds, can now be simply created by anyone with a basic word processor. But care must be exercised when communicating information visually – for example, in graphs, charts or tables.

Each visual form has its strengths and weaknesses. Again, the first questions to ask are: 'What is our purpose here? What is it we are trying to show?' We must avoid being so carried away by the decorative potential of visual effects that we end up creating **chartjunk**, or unnecessary and distracting graphics that 'dumb down', rather than clarify, our message (Tufte 2001; Tractinksy & Meyer 1999; Prosser & Loxley 2007). (Note that Bateman et al. [2010] includes a defence of alleged chartjunk.)

Table 2.2 summarises the pros and cons of visual effects.

Chartjunk: unnecessary and distracting graphics

TABLE 2.2 Visuals — the good and the bad (a visual aid for visual aids)

Good visuals can ...	Bad visuals can ...
■ Summarise ■ Back up your words ■ Clarify and reveal ■ Reduce space and time needed to communicate message ■ Add variety ■ Entertain ■ Permit visual processing of information ■ Stimulate the discovery of trends, comparisons and possibilities ■ Convey ideas cheaply and/or cost-effectively ■ Demonstrate professionalism	■ Confuse and distort ■ Trivialise ■ Distract from the primary message ■ Increase space and time needed to communicate message ■ Be expensive and bothersome ■ Demonstrate amateurism

Visuals: what they are and how to use them

The strengths and weaknesses of the various modes of visual presentation depend on the type of communication problem you are trying to solve. Having established the nature of your data, or raw information, consider what it is you are trying to convey. For example, are you trying to describe a trend, a phenomenon that happens over time – such as the growing cycle of a garden plant? Or are you trying to draw a comparison between different parts of something, where time is not of primary relevance – such as the different departmental budget allowances within an organisation, expressed as proportions or fractions of the total budget?

Constants, variables, continuous/discrete, correlation/causation

Are you trying to measure a constant (something that doesn't change) or a variable (something that does)? Perhaps you are measuring a *continuous* variable, which is one that can theoretically fall anywhere between two given values – for example, the height of an individual (height might be measured as, say, 1.7 metres, 1.71 metres or 1.7111 metres). Or perhaps you are measuring a *discrete* variable, which cannot assume a fractional value between two given whole values – for example, the number of children in a family (the number might be 3 or 4, but cannot be 3.56).

If you are trying to show the relationship between two sets of data, remember that *correlation is not causation*; that is, merely because there seems to be a relationship between two sets of data does not mean such a relationship exists. If, for example, you attempt to show a relationship between red hair and sunspots, you might just pull off a scientific breakthrough, but it is more likely you will produce a false hypothesis that is subsequently strongly criticised.

Labels, callouts, legends, keys, graphs/charts

Within the visual itself, different parts – lines, slices of a pie – can be labelled using words placed within the graph or figure, or using lines from different parts leading to explanatory words (called callouts). Alternatively, they can be identified in a *legend or key* – an explanatory table or list of symbols (by colour or shape) placed next to the graph. Place the key where you think it will be most helpful (e.g. if the visual is large, consider placing the key below or above rather than alongside it).

The terms *graph* and *chart* are sometimes used interchangeably to refer to pie charts, bar graphs, line graphs and so on. The convention adopted here will be to refer to all such features as graphs, while charts will refer to organisation and flowcharts.

The X–Y system (some painless maths)

Several types of visuals use the X–Y or Cartesian system of structuring and displaying data. In this system the vertical line is the Y axis (or *y*-axis), sometimes called the *ordinate*, which is used to show dependent variables (data that changes according to changes in another data set). The horizontal line in this system is the X axis (or *x*-axis), sometimes called the *abscissa*, and is used to show independent variables (data varied by researchers to measure changes). The point at which the X axis and the Y axis meet is called the *origin*, and usually takes a value of zero for both axes.

A useful mnemonic for remembering the function of each line is VOYD HAXI (see figure 2.15). When we use a graph with two Y axes, the second is called the Y2 or RHS (right-hand side) axis. When a third dimension is shown, the third dimension axis is called the Z axis.

V	Vertical
O	Ordinate
Y	Y axis
D	Dependent variable

Origin

H	Horizontal
A	Abscissa
X	X axis
I	Independent variable

FIGURE 2.15 The X-Y system of structuring graphs

Let's now turn our attention to various modes of visual presentation.

Pie graphs

Pie graphs (figures 2.16 to 2.18), also known as circle graphs, are very useful for showing the relative proportions of components or parts of one particular set of data. The different components should always add up to 100 per cent. The largest slice or component is placed at the 12 o'clock position on an analogue clock, with other, progressively smaller 'slices' arranged in a clockwise direction.

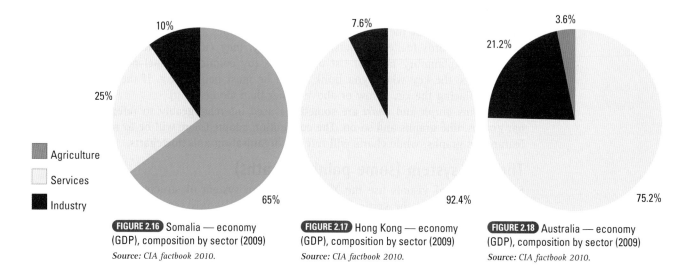

FIGURE 2.16 Somalia — economy (GDP), composition by sector (2009)
Source: CIA factbook 2010.

FIGURE 2.17 Hong Kong — economy (GDP), composition by sector (2009)
Source: CIA factbook 2010.

FIGURE 2.18 Australia — economy (GDP), composition by sector (2009)
Source: CIA factbook 2010.

If you need to draw a pie chart by hand, remember: there are 360 degrees in a circle; therefore 3.6 degrees equals 1 per cent, and percentage values of pie slices need to be multiplied by 3.6 to determine the arc or size of the slice (e.g. *20 per cent × 3.6 = 72*). To measure degrees precisely, you need to use a protractor.

Pie charts are very useful for showing proportional relationships, but don't overload them. If you need to show more than six values, a pie chart can be cluttered. This problem can sometimes be minimised by simply combining a number of the smaller values into a miscellaneous or 'other' slice, or else by using another visual method entirely — for example, a 100 per cent bar graph or a table.

Comparisons with other, similar sets of data — for example, economic patterns in different countries, or budget allocations in different years — may require the use of multiple pie charts. If you need to use more than four sets of data, it might be better to use a multiple line graph.

Pie charts can be rendered in two dimensions or in three. Three-dimensional pie charts are more visually effective, but they can prove harder to read if precise data is being used. If real precision is needed, however, use a table. Also, pie charts are not good for showing variation over time or for showing negative values.

Bar graphs

Bar and line graphs use X and Y axes. There are numerous types of bar graphs. Most of them are used to show discrete values, usually varying over time. For some people, bar graphs mean graphs in which the bars are arranged horizontally, as opposed to column graphs, in which the bars are displayed vertically. For others, the term bar graph may refer to either arrangement. We will use this broader definition. Note that all Microsoft software refers to all visuals or graphs as charts (e.g. vertical bar graphs are called column charts).

Simple bar graphs are useful for showing data such as annual sales – a discrete figure. If you need more precision – for example, monthly, weekly or daily sales – you should consider a line graph or table. A simple bar graph, however, can make a clear, bold statement about trends.

Multiple bar graphs (figure 2.19) can be useful for comparing sets of discrete data – say, sales of four products over a number of years, or the population patterns of five species. Displaying more than five or six variables on a single graph can lead to visual confusion, and a multiple-line graph – a series of graphs showing different parts of the same data set – or a table might be more useful in such cases.

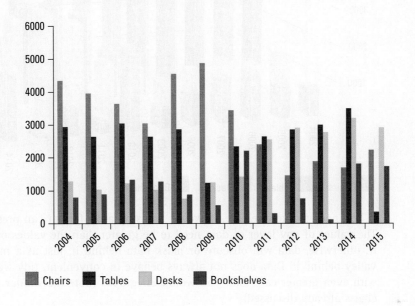

FIGURE 2.19 Multiple bar graph

Chairs   Tables   Desks   Bookshelves

The 100 per cent bar graph (figure 2.20) does not show absolute quantities, but rather proportions. In that sense, it is similar to the pie chart. Note that time values switch to the vertical or Y axis for this type of graph.

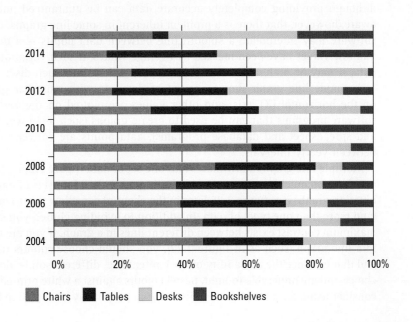

FIGURE 2.20 100 per cent bar graph

Chairs   Tables   Desks   Bookshelves

Three-dimensional graphs offer dramatic and attractive effects, and the 3D bar graph is no exception (figure 2.21).

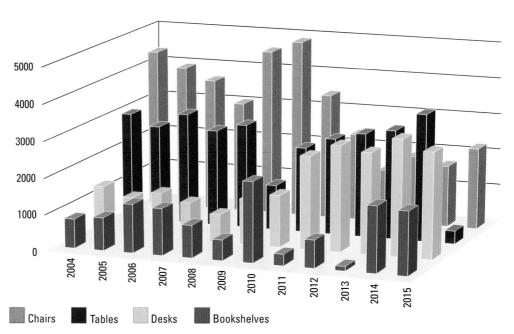

FIGURE 2.21 Three-dimensional bar graph

Chairs   Tables   Desks   Bookshelves

You need to exercise care, however, as using a 3D format can present unique problems. The values of any layer of data need to be greater than the values of the layer in front of it; otherwise, data will obscure or mask data behind it, just as a mountain will hide the valley behind it. Data does not always behave in convenient, tidy ways, so edit 3D graphs with even greater care than you would 2D graphs (note the similar problems with 3D pie charts already discussed).

Line graphs

Line graphs are most useful for showing trends and comparisons in large amounts of continuous data. They are more useful than bar graphs for showing subtle and frequent changes, although providing completely accurate data can be guaranteed only by using tables. Be aware, however, that there is a problem inherent in some line graphs: our eyes and computer software may interpolate a smooth line between data points – a deceptive effect if high and low values have been masked by average values. If such variation does exist in the raw data, it may be preferable to use bar graphs, which show such discrete points.

A simple line graph shows one set of data. As with most bar graphs, time is plotted on the horizontal (X) axis, and other values are plotted on the vertical (Y) axis. In most software programs that can be used to create graphs (such as in word processing programs and spreadsheet and database programs), data points are conventionally plotted midway between yearly intervals.

Multiple line graphs show more than one set of data (figure 2.22). Multiple line graphs can get cluttered quickly, so try to avoid plotting more than four sets of data on one graph. Combination graphs (see figure 2.25 later in the chapter) can allow you to plot more than four sets (and more than one type) of data. In addition to avoiding clutter, you should also ensure that maximum contrast exists between different lines in a graph. If you are using different colours in a line graph (such as in figure 2.22), you should choose colours that are not too similar and that enhance the readability of the content (e.g. different solid colours are usually a good choice and are preferable to light, pastel colours against a white printed page). You might also consider using dotted and dashed lines if your graph may be copied in black and white.

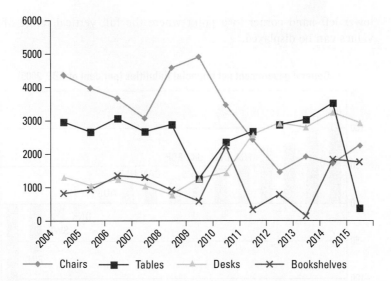

FIGURE 2.22 Multiple line graph

Dot graphs

Dot graphs can show trends clearly, and can show some comparative trends clearly. They are very cheap to produce, lending themselves to monochrome or black and white reproduction, and occupy less surface area than bar charts. However, some people find them difficult to read and also find them lacking in visual interest – there is very little eye candy or entertainment value (from another point of view, this can be seen as an advantage). Nevertheless, more dot graphs are appearing in colour, which, while making them more expensive to reproduce, also makes them clearer. As with bar charts, dot graphs do not readily reveal trends, such as when one data set cuts across another. This is illustrated by the data shown in figure 2.23. Trends may be one of the very things that researchers need to be able to rapidly detect.

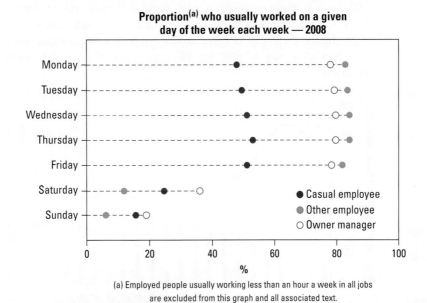

FIGURE 2.23 Dot graph

Source: Australian Bureau of Statistics (2010).

Deviation graphs

It is often necessary to express negative values, and the variation or deviation bar graph (figure 2.24) can help you do that. The origin (zero) shifts upwards from its traditional lower left-hand corner to a point where the full vertical range of positive and negative values can be displayed.

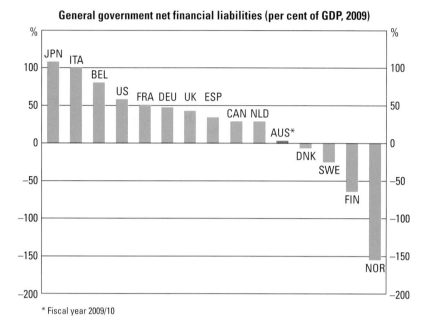

General government net financial liabilities (per cent of GDP, 2009)

FIGURE 2.24 Deviation graph

Source: Reserve Bank of Australia (2010).

* Fiscal year 2009/10

Combination graphs

Sometimes it is necessary to plot two sets of data, with each data set referring to a different type of variable. In this case, it becomes necessary to use the right-hand Y axis or Y2 axis, sometimes referred to as RHS (right-hand side), in contrast with LHS (the left-hand side or standard Y axis).

While it is quite possible to plot these different sets of data using just one type of visual — a multiple line graph, for example — this can lead to confusion. A combination graph (figure 2.25) can remove confusion and make comparisons clearer. Such a graph also gives us a way of plotting different types of data (e.g. continuous and discrete) in one figure.

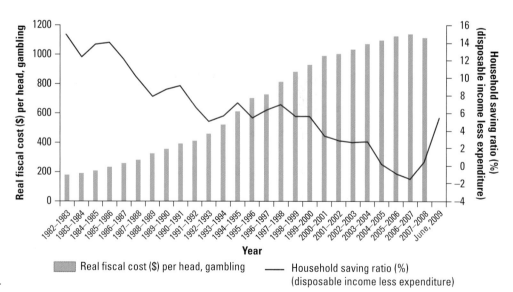

FIGURE 2.25 Combination graph — real gambling expenditure (1972–2005); household savings (1972–2005)

Sources: Australian Bureau of Statistics, Tasmanian Gaming Commission, Queensland Treasury Office of Economic and Statistical Research, *Australian gambling statistics* 2009, Australian Parliamentary Library.

Care is needed when plotting combination graphs. We must be sure of the validity of plotting two sets of data against each other. Other factors may need to be taken into account to give the full picture. In relation to savings levels, these factors may include compulsory saving (superannuation), the global financial crisis and housing prices; and in relation to gambling levels, they may include online gambling – the levels for which are rising fast.

Pictograms

Pictograms are symbols used to convey information, such as quantities. For example, numbers of passengers carried on an airline might be shown as in figure 2.26, while changes in oil consumption occurring over a period of time might be shown as in figure 2.27(a) (barrels shown in two dimensions) or figure 2.27(b) (barrels shown in 3D).

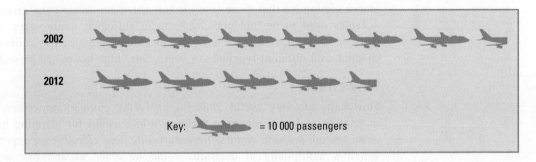

FIGURE 2.26 Passengers carried by Acrophobia Airlines, 2002 and 2012

Pictograms are attractive and can capture the imagination of the viewer. They do not permit much accuracy, though. With each aeroplane representing 10 000 passengers, for example, it would be impossible to extract from the final partial pictogram in figure 2.26 the total of 5341 passengers.

Pictograms can be misleading as well as inaccurate. In both figures 2.27(a) and 2.27(b), for example, the pictogram for 2012 is constructed by simply doubling the height of the pictogram for 2002. This is not valid, however. In figure 2.27(a) the two-dimensional 2012 barrel is twice the height of the 2002 one, but it is also four times as big in area; in figure 2.27(b), the three-dimensional 2012 barrel is twice as tall as the 2002 one, but it has eight times the volume.

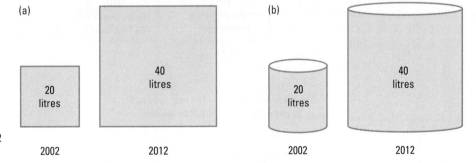

FIGURE 2.27 **(a)**: Daily oil consumption per head in Greedonia, 2002 and 2012; **(b)**: Daily oil consumption per head in Greedonia, 2002 and 2012

Tables

Tables display data numerically, with numbers arranged in rows and columns. Most statistical information is presented in tabular form, as is data displayed in spreadsheet and database software. Tables are most useful when you need to display precise quantities; they will always be more accurate than graphs. Table 2.3 (see overleaf) is the database used to construct some of the previous figures. Most graphs are based on tables, but very few tables are based on graphs.

	2004	2005	2006	2007	2008	2009	2010	2011	2012	2013	2014	2015
Chairs	4354	3965	3654	3054	4562	4892	3452	2412	1462	1902	1702	2245
Tables	2951	2653	3056	2656	2871	1245	2349	2659	2866	3012	3512	361
Desks	1297	1045	1234	1032	764	1256	1431	2563	2910	2777	3211	2921
Bookshelves	805	905	1342	1287	895	567	2211	314	768	129	1821	1743

TABLE 2.3 Sales of four main product lines at Juggernaut Manufacturing

Trends and comparisons are not always immediately apparent in tables, however, so important developments may be missed if you rely solely on tabular presentation. Ideally, both graphs and tables should be used – graphs for broad treatments of the topic, and tables to back up your arguments. For example, use graphs in the body of a document, web page or presentation, and include the tables they are based on in an appendix or reference section (so that those who are interested can inspect the precise figures).

Tables need to be laid out clearly, with sufficient white space around the table and between rows and columns. Clarity can be enhanced by the use of lines, double lines, colour shading, and different typefaces or fonts. Note how tables are presented in this book.

Flowcharts

Flowcharts are very useful tools for analysing complex processes, whether mechanical or relating to human decision making. While useful for mapping processes that involve clear yes/no decision points, flowcharts are less effective in representing processes in which a multiplicity of decisions could be made at any one point (yes/no/perhaps/ perhaps [2]/perhaps [3] and so on). Figure 2.28 (James 2009) illustrates a flowchart for receiving evidence during a legal trial. Factors including relevance, admissibility and weight affect whether or not evidence is considered during a trial, as shown in the flowchart.

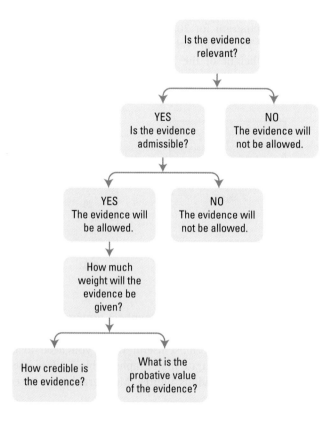

FIGURE 2.28 The receipt of evidence in a legal trial

Flowcharting usually involves the use of specific symbols from the world of information technology. Many so-called flowcharts, however, are really visual mappings of sequences and relationships. There is nothing wrong with these, of course; if writers and information designers are challenged to render complex processes in visual ways (without distorting the content along the way), then the cause of clearer communication is well served. Highly complex concepts are sometimes buried in a morass of text, and an imaginative visual rendering can sometimes represent a real breakthrough in the exposition of ideas.

Gantt/project charts

Henry Laurence Gantt (1861–1919) was a North American engineer and management consultant who invented and developed the Gantt chart between 1910 and 1920. The chart is usually used to track progress in a project over time, showing linkages between tasks and critical milestones that need to be observed. An example of a simplified Gantt chart is shown in figure 2.29. Over-use of such charts can lead to an emphasis on rational planning at the expense of human factors, but this is not always a bad thing.

Task	Start	End	Time (days)	22-Jan	29-Jan	5-Feb	12-Feb	19-Feb	26-Feb	5-Mar	12-Mar	19-Mar
Prepare survey	22-Jan	24-Jan	3	■								
Determine sample	22-Jan	25-Jan	4	■								
Distribute survey	29-Jan	31-Jan	3		■							
Receive responses	5-Feb	23-Feb	15			■	■	■				
Filter responses	12-Feb	2-Mar	15				■	■	■			
Analyse responses	19-Feb	9-Mar	15					■	■	■		
Prepare report	12-Mar	16-Mar	5								■	
Report findings	19-Mar	19-Mar	1									■

FIGURE 2.29 A simplified Gantt chart (data collection, analysis, reporting)

Maps, photographs and diagrams

A *map* is a visual representation of a space or area. Maps can use gridlines such as longitude and latitude or simple alphanumeric gridlines, as in road maps and directories. Maps can show topographical features such as high and low surfaces using line systems; and features such as rivers, streets and parks. The scale of the map is always an important factor for extracting maximum information from it. Maps can depict an area schematically, although obviously they cannot provide the full information that photographs of the same area can (although some maps now incorporate photographic images taken from satellites and aircraft).

Photographs can show what an object, area or person actually looks like. Digital photography has made it much easier to incorporate such images into documents. However, care has to be taken to minimise the data file size of the image. If care is not taken, the file size of the total document may become unmanageable. Photographs can provide details, but this strength can also be a weakness, if there is so much detail that an objective view cannot be obtained. Thus, a photograph of an area may not be as revealing as a more schematic image, such as a map, which may simplify and concentrate salient aspects of the area for us to analyse.

In the same way, *diagrams* can provide a schematic view of objects, areas or persons. Diagrams can show sequences, and can 'show' the interiors of objects and persons in exploded, cross-sectional or cutaway views. Many diagrams, such as those used in other chapters in this book, can show linkages and relationships between complex sets of factors in situations (care must be taken to ensure that over-simplification does not occur).

Overview: which graphic do I use for which situation?

So which graphic should you use for different communication situations? This depends on the data you are working with, and what you are trying to emphasise. Figure 2.30 shows the properties of a number of graphic tools evaluated across different criteria. Use only as many of these tools as are needed to add value to a document.

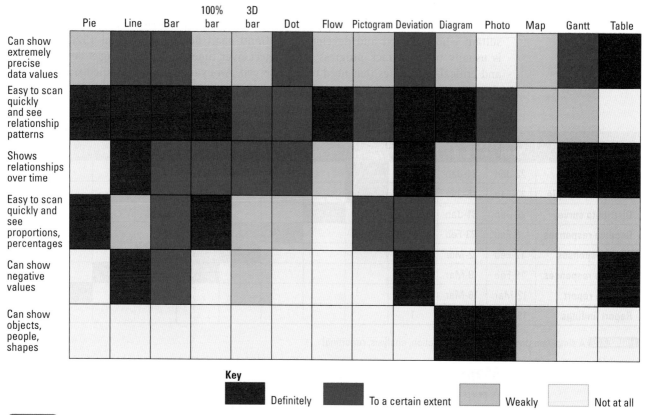

FIGURE 2.30 Properties of different graphic tools

Graphics can provide insight and visual relief in a document, but an overuse of graphics can detract from the written word. The same consideration applies when you are presenting images in a slide presentation. Also remember to test images if you are using them in more than one communication mode or channel: a graphic that works well on paper will not necessarily work when projected from a computer, and vice-versa (see 'Using audiovisual aids' in chapter 11).

Data and the scale of things: the use and abuse of graphic communication

Mark Twain once famously said: 'There are lies, damned lies and statistics'. Graphic communication depends critically upon statistics, so you need to approach statistical data with care, especially when it is being used to persuade as well as inform (Dilla & Steinbart 2005).

Consider, for example, figures 2.31 and 2.32. Although they appear to show quite different sets of data, this is not in fact the case. The only differences are that the Y axis has been narrowed in range and the origin has been moved from 0 to 77 in figure 2.31

(note the truncation mark showing a broken axis); in this way the graph has been squeezed from the right margin to make it appear more compact – a portrait orientation, rather than a landscape one.

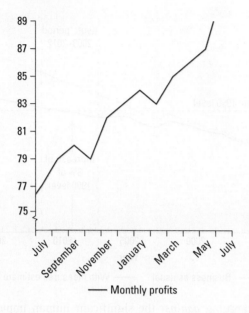

FIGURE 2.31 Graph — portrait

—— Monthly profits

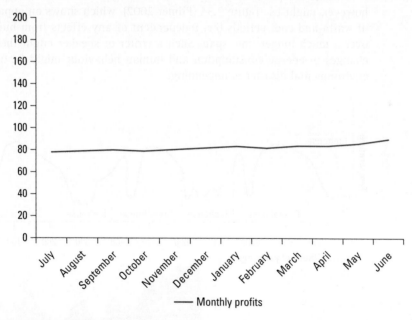

FIGURE 2.32 Graph — landscape

—— Monthly profits

An ethically suspect board of management might choose to display figure 2.31 in an annual report to stockholders (demonstrating success) and figure 2.32 to union negotiators when negotiating wage claims (demonstrating that times are tough, and poor profit performance means little or no wage increases are possible). Of course, the union negotiators might counter this strategy by tabling the annual report (Arunachalam, Buck, Pei, & Steinbart, 2002).

Similar data can be used to produce quite different outcomes. Thus, a writer or speaker arguing *for* the significant impact of human activity on climate change might use figure 2.33 to support their case. Figure 2.33 shows projections of greenhouse gas emissions in Australia through the Kyoto period, both with and without actions to reduce emissions over time. The figure suggests that an absence of action during the Kyoto period would correspond with dramatically higher national emissions levels.

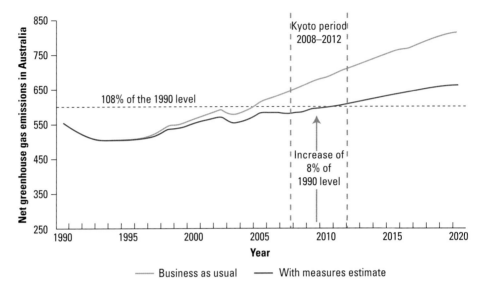

FIGURE 2.33 Australian greenhouse gas emissions projections to 2020 with an analysis of the Kyoto period impact

Source: Department of Climate Change 2007, *Tracking to the Kyoto target*, February.

A writer or speaker arguing *against* the significant human impact on climate change, however, might use figure 2.34 (Plimer 2002), which shows an apparent natural oscillation of warm and cool periods (i.e. independent of any effects from human industrial activity) over a much longer time span. Such a writer or speaker might then infer that large-scale changes in energy consumption and human behaviour might be quite unnecessary as no environmental disaster is impending.

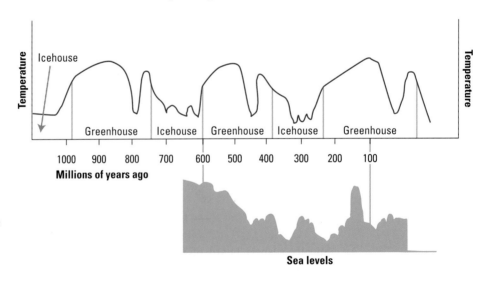

FIGURE 2.34 Climate change phenomena and scale over time showing varied temperature levels

Do all these differing perspectives then suggest that the truth is impossible to find? Not at all. They simply indicate that the truth is harder to pin down than some of us realise, but it can be done, usually through healthy debate. Such debate can be supported and may be most productive when we understand the best (and worst) ways to present data in visuals.

STUDENT STUDY GUIDE

SUMMARY

In this chapter we have explored the meanings of the terms document design, information design and information architecture. We have investigated the basic principles and techniques of text layout, including the roles of choice of type, colour, headings and white space, and how these affect the look and usefulness of document pages and screens. We have considered different types of visual aids such as graphs, charts and tables, and have assessed the strengths and weaknesses of these visual aids. We have seen how graphic representation can be used to clarify or distort facts and ideas, and how knowledge of graphic communication can enhance both our ability to convey information and our critical capabilities as readers.

KEY TERMS

alignment *p. 50*	HATS *p. 48*	naïve user review *p. 47*
chartjunk *p. 56*	header *p. 52*	orphan *p. 52*
column *p. 52*	information architecture *p. 40*	paragraph *p. 52*
document design *p. 40*	information design *p. 40*	portrait *p. 51*
eye candy *p. 44*	justification *p. 51*	spacing *p. 50*
expert user review *p. 47*	landscape *p. 51*	usability *p.42*
font *p. 49*	list *p. 52*	widow *p. 52*
footer *p. 52*	margin *p. 50*	

REVIEW QUESTIONS

1. '"Information design" is just a piece of pompous jargon. Why not just say "layout" and leave it at that?' Discuss.
2. List at least three typical usability problems encountered in documents.
3. What problems can differing forms of justification of text present?
4. What are two strengths and two weaknesses of visuals?
5. What does VOYD-HAXI stand for?
6. What type of data set would you represent using a pie graph?
7. What type of data set would you *not* represent using a pie graph?
8. What problems are involved in the use of 3D graphs?
9. Why should you consider how a colour visual might look in black and white?

APPLIED ACTIVITIES

1. Find some old textbooks, preferably written 30 to 60 years ago. Now compare these with modern examples. In what ways are the modern books superior? In what ways are they inferior?
2. Find examples of *Idiots*, *For Dummies* or *For Beginners* guide books. Compare their treatment of topics with the treatments given in conventional texts. What are the advantages of the more graphic approach? What are the disadvantages?
3. Select a sample of about 1000 words of text. This can be:
   - text you write yourself, describing a product or process
   - existing text written by you or someone else and stored electronically; for example, an essay or an article
   - material scanned electronically (using optical character recognition software) into a word processor from a book or other source.

Using the approaches described in this chapter, lay out the text in at least two different forms. If possible, get at least one other person to undertake the same exercise. Compare the results, and reflect on what makes for effective layout and information design.

4. Create a list of the various graphs, tables and charts discussed in this chapter. List the strengths and weaknesses of each of them.

5. Using print and online research, investigate the uses, strengths and weaknesses of the following graphic tools: Gantt chart; Pareto chart; break-even chart; exploded view; cutaway/cross-sectional diagrams/views; organisation chart; dot graph; map; area graphs; stacked bar charts; logarithmic charts; icon plots; fishbone/cause – effect charts; critical path diagrams; PERT (program evaluation and review technology) charts; doughnut charts; radar charts; surface charts; schematic drawings in electronics; scatter charts; bubble charts; stock charts; outliers.

6. Using the image search function of an online search engine, create a gallery of good and bad examples of various types of visual presentation. Write brief notes on each, explaining why the sample is effective or not.

7. Investigate at least two vocabulary, graphic, project management or data mining programs (e.g. Thinkmap Visual Thesaurus, Microsoft Visio, Popplet, SmartDraw, Corel Smart Graphics, Statistica, Microsoft Project, SPSS, IBM DB2). What value might they have in helping or hindering communication processes?

8. Using a spreadsheet or database function of a word processing program, create a table of nonsense data, copy the data in table 2.3 or find a table of real data. Open up the graphics/chart function in the application and use this data to create a series of graphics. Work through the menu of graphics/charts available. What do you learn about the different graph or chart types (standard and custom) from this exercise?

9. Using a word processor, re-create figure 2.30. Create new criteria, and evaluate the graphic tools considered in figure 2.30, or evaluate other graphic tools.

10. Using multiple sets of data can sometime present problems, as is combination graphs. Track down the primary sources of data for figure 2.25, especially those from the Australian Bureau of Statistics and the Queensland Treasury, and analyse the properties of the two sets of data.

11. Create at least two graphics that are deliberately distorted, and then produce corrected versions. If possible, do this exercise with someone else, having them perform the same exercise. Compare results, and reflect on how we can best defeat 'lies, damned lies and statistics'.

12. The figures in table 2.3 are used to create figures 2.19, 2.20, 2.21 and 2.22. Re-create them yourself in a word processor or spreadsheet to better compare the properties of tables versus graphs.

WHAT WOULD YOU DO?

Your division's performance over the past two quarters has not been good. Several product lines have performed badly – not least because quality faults have caused a number of major customers to return items and demand full refunds. Raj, your team leader, has been asked to speak to the board about performance problems, and he has asked you to come along to answer any technical questions. Since you have the most technical experience in the team, this seems to make sense to you. All the same, you feel uncomfortable, as you have had numerous conflicts with Raj about quality problems, and you feel that he just doesn't listen. You believe Raj cuts too many corners, and has avoided a reckoning on problems in your area only because he turns on the charm and baffles superiors with jargon and fancy number-crunching. In fact, the main reason for the problems in your division, you feel, is Raj himself.

At the presentation, you become somewhat alarmed as Raj gives an overview of the division's situation using graphics. In one 3D bar chart, low-performing products have been put in the back row so that they don't even appear. Another graphic has a broken Y axis (although the break is not shown) and has been squeezed so as to represent a fairly flat curve of performance as an (unjustifiably) steep curve. Yet another graphic shows a growth in profits, but the data is in current dollars over the past ten years, rather than in constant dollars (when inflation is taken into account, the 'profits' are seen to be losses). Raj finishes his presentation with a flourish, and then asks for any specific questions to be addressed to you.

What will you do now?

SUGGESTED READING

Baer, Kim 2010, *Information design workbook: graphic approaches, solutions, and inspiration + 30 case studies*, Rockport Publishers, Beverley, MA.

Campbell, Nittaya 2006, 'Communicating visually: incorporating document design in writing tasks', *Business Communication Quarterly*, vol. 69, no. 4, pp 399–403.

Gaugin, Jan & Marcus, Aaron 2011, *Designing diagrams: making information accessible through design*, BIS Publishers, Amsterdam.

Glaser, Jessica & Knight, Carolyn 2010, *Diagrams: innovative solutions for graphic designers*, Rotovision, Hove, East Sussex.

Jones, Gerald Everett 2007, *How to lie with charts*, 2nd edn, La Puerta, Santa Monica, CA.

Kirkham, Harold & Dumas 2010, *The right graph: a manual for technical and scientific authors*, John Wiley & Sons, Chichester.

Miller, T 1998, 'Visual persuasion: a comparison of visuals in academic texts and the popular press', *English for Specific Purposes*, vol. 17, no. 1, pp. 29–46.

O'Rourke, James S, Sedlack, Robert P, Shwom, Barbara L & Keller, Karl P 2007, *Graphics and visual communication for managers*, South Western College Publishing, Mason, OH.

Tiffen, Rodney & Gittins, Ross 2010, *How Australia compares*, 2nd edn, Cambridge University Press, Cambridge.

Zelazny, Gene 2007, *The say it with charts complete toolkit*, McGraw-Hill, New York.

REFERENCES

Arunachalam, Vairam, Buck, KW Pei & Steinbart, John 2002, 'Impression management with graphs: effects on choices', *Journal of Information Systems*, vol. 16, no. 2, pp. 183–202.

Australian Bureau of Statistics 2010, 'Patterns in work', 4102.0 – Australian Social Trends, Dec 2009 (revised 15 March, 2010), www.abs.gov.au.

Baker, William H 2001, 'HATS: a design procedure for routine business documents', *Business Communication Quarterly*, vol. 64, no. 2, pp. 65–77.

Barnum, Carol M 2002, *Usability testing and research*, Allyn & Bacon, Needham Heights, MA.

Bateman, S, Mandryk, RL, Gutwin, C, Genest, AM, McDine, D, Brooks, C 2010, 'Useful junk? The effects of visual embellishment on comprehension and memorability of charts', paper presented at CHI (Computer-Human Interaction) 2010, ACM Special Interest Group on Computer Human Interaction (SIGCHI), 10–15 April.

Carliner, Saul 2002, 'Designing better documents', *Information Management Journal*, vol. 36, no. 5, pp. 42–50.

Central Intelligence Agency 2010, *World fact book*, CIA, Washington, D.C., www.cia.gov.

Crystal, David & Ben Crystal 2004, *Shakespeare's words: a glossary and language companion*, Penguin Books, London.

Delin, Judy & Bateman, John 2002, 'Describing and critiquing multimodal documents', *Document Design*, vol. 3, no. 2, pp. 141–55.

Dilla, William N & Steinbart, Paul John 2005, 'Using information display characteristics to provide decision guidance in a choice task under conditions of strict uncertainty', *Journal of Information Systems*, vol. 19, no. 2, pp. 29–55.

Dubay, William H 2004, *The principles of readability*, Impact Information, Costa Mesa, CA.

Dumas, Joseph S & Redish, Janice 1993, *A practical guide to useability testing*, Ablex Publishing Company, Norwood, NJ.

James, Nickolas 2009, *Business law*, John Wiley & Sons, Milton, QLD.

Klanten, Robert, Bourquin, N, Ehmann, S & Tissot, T (eds.) 2010, *Data flow 2: visualising information in graphic design*, Die Gestalten Verlag, Berlin.

Nicol, Adelheid AM & Pexman, Penny M 2010, *Displaying your findings: a practical guide for presenting figures, posters and presentations*, 6th edn, American Psychological Association, Washington, DC.

Oxford Advanced Learner's Dictionary, www.oup.com.

Plimer, Ian 2002, 'The past is the key to the present: greenhouse and icehouse over time', *IPA Review*, December, p. 21.

Prosser, Jon & Loxley, Andrew 2007, 'Enhancing the contribution of visual methods to inclusive education', *Journal of Research in Special Educational Needs*, vol. 7, no. 1, pp. 1–68.

Queensland Treasury Office of Economic and Statistical Research 2009, *Australian gambling statistics 1982–83 to 2007–08*, Queensland Government, Brisbane.

Redish, Janice C 2000, 'What is information design?', *Technical Communication*, vol. 47, no. 2, pp. 45–61.

Reserve Bank of Australia 2010, *Graphs on the Australian economy and financial markets (Chart pack)*, 29 April, www.rba.gov.au.

Schriver, Karen A 1997, *Dynamics in document design: creating texts for readers*, John Wiley & Sons, New York.

Tractinsky, Noam & Meyer, Joachim 1999, 'Chartjunk or goldgraph? Effects of presentation objectives and content desirability on information presentation', *MIS Quarterly*, vol. 23, no. 3, pp. 397–420.

Tufte, Edward 2001, *The visual display of quantitative information*, 2nd edn, Graphics Press, Cheshire, CT.

Urban Dictionary 2011, www.urbandictionary.com.

Wright, Patricia 2004, *Document design*, Cambridge University Press, Cambridge, UK.

3

Doing and using research

LEARNING OBJECTIVES

After reading this chapter you should be able to:

- Explain the difference between primary, secondary and tertiary sources of information
- Identify the major strengths and weaknesses of paper-based and electronic sources of information
- Discuss different approaches to obtaining information from libraries, databases and the internet
- Explain approaches to note taking
- Explain approaches to referencing
- Distinguish between legitimate citation of sources, paraphrasing and plagiarism
- Design and carry out surveys and questionnaires to derive primary data

Research skills and the knowledge-based society

Knowledge and information are some of the most important social and economic commodities in modern society. It is a commonplace to hear that we are all struggling from information overload: we have too much data and not enough information, too much information and not enough knowledge, too much knowledge and not enough wisdom.

Knowledge management is of first importance in many organisations today. The ability to discover information has become one of the most important survival skills. In this chapter we will briefly survey this area, examining research skills that will help us become more adept at locating and using print, online and other information materials, and creating our own knowledge resources.

The research process

How do we approach the process of research? Figure 3.1 offers a model of the kinds of steps we usually follow.

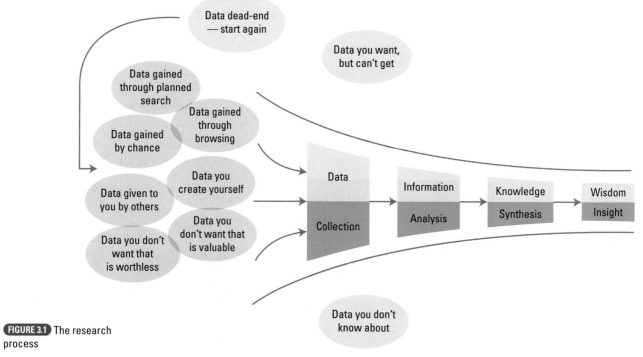

FIGURE 3.1 The research process

We tend to move through a series of phases in the research process:

- the collection or acquisition phase, in which we focus on actually finding data
- the analysis phase, in which we focus on turning our data into information, sifting out the rubbish (or is it all rubbish?)
- the synthesis phase, in which we process our information so that interconnections are revealed
- the insight phase, in which our knowledge becomes wisdom: we stand on the shoulders of those researchers who have come before us and develop our own original perceptions.

As figure 3.1 suggests, the process can be depicted as a funnel: we begin with a very large body of data and gradually narrow it down in order to produce something specific that meets our particular needs.

Among the different types of data we encounter along the way are:

- data we want but can't get (we don't have time, or we can't afford it)
- data gained through planned search
- data gained by simply browsing print and electronic sources
- data gained by chance
- data given to us by others
- data we create ourselves (e.g. through interviews, questionnaires or laboratory experimentation)
- worthless data we don't want
- valuable data we don't want
- data we don't know about.

Sometimes we will strike dead ends and will need to start our search afresh. But following this research path in a disciplined way will lead us to high-quality information, knowledge and wisdom that we can use in communicating with others. Research, at one level or another, is a vital part of planning all of our communications.

A useful way to focus our research is by beginning with a hypothesis or thesis statement. The **thesis statement** sets out the goal of our research, or what it is we are setting out to discover or prove. A thesis statement or hypothesis may offer valuable direction; but, if along the way we discover information that does not fit the frame, we must be prepared to modify or abandon it.

Thesis statement: statement of research goal

Researching sources: primary, secondary and tertiary sources

In doing research, we need to distinguish between primary, secondary and tertiary sources of data (table 3.1).

TABLE 3.1 Primary, secondary and tertiary sources of data

Data type	Properties	Examples	Published as
Primary	■ Original ■ Evidence of facts, happenings ■ Contemporary with what is being described — from the same time period ■ Has not been interpreted or changed by others who are not data creators	■ Experimental findings ■ Observations ■ Questionnaires ■ Interviews ■ Investigations ■ Databases ■ Archives ■ Correspondence, email ■ Works of art, literature ■ Manuscripts ■ Meeting records ■ Company records, files ■ Patents ■ Conference papers ■ Theses/dissertations ■ Documents (birth, marriage, death certificates, tax records) ■ Genealogies ■ Photographs, video ■ Diaries, blogs, tweets, personal/organisational web pages ■ Autobiographies ■ Testimony, oral histories	■ Research articles in refereed journals ■ Conference papers ■ Theses/dissertations ■ Reports ■ Monographs/books treating hitherto unpublished matter ■ Transcripts ■ Internet blog sites ■ Journalism — original or 'exclusive' matter ■ (Remains unpublished)

(continued)

TABLE 3.1 *(continued)*

Data type	Properties	Examples	Published as
Secondary	■ Not original ■ Not evidence, but analysis, summary, re-packaging, distillation of primary matter ■ Occurs after creation of primary matter	■ Interpretations, accounts of primary matter, citation/quotation	■ Review articles in journals ■ Journalism, news stories ■ Conference proceedings ■ Monographs/books (by single and multiple authors, edited collections) ■ Theses/dissertations ■ Biographies ■ Textbooks
Tertiary	■ Not original ■ Not evidence, but analysis, summary, re-packaging, distillation of primary and secondary matter ■ Occurs well after creation of primary matter	■ Interpretations, accounts of primary and secondary matter, citation/quotation	■ Encyclopedias ■ Almanacs ■ Year books ■ Hand books ■ Chronologies ■ Manuals ■ Dictionaries ■ Directories ■ Bibliographies ■ Indexes ■ Databases — print and online ■ Library catalogues — print and online ■ Abstracts ■ Literature searches

Primary data: original unpublished material or material published in an original form

Secondary data: material that interprets primary material, published after primary data is published

Tertiary data: material that synthesises and summarises primary and secondary material, usually published well after primary and secondary sources

Primary data consists of original unpublished material, or material created by researchers or writers or other individuals and groups and published in an original form. Sources of primary data include experimental findings, questionnaires, interviews, experiments, observations, databases, archives, correspondence, works of art, manuscripts, minutes of meetings, company records, patents, photographs and autobiographies.

Secondary data is material that has been published after the time when primary data was created, and is not original. Secondary data tends to be an examination or re-examination of primary data. Examples include books, newspapers, periodicals, government documents — in paper or electronic format, or on websites.

Tertiary data is material published well after the time when primary data was created, and comprises syntheses, summaries and accounts of primary and secondary material. Typically, tertiary material includes encyclopedias, dictionaries, handbooks, manuals, databases and abstracts.

It is a slight over-generalisation, but usually, the more original your work is, the more credit you will get for it. An essay or report, for example, based largely or totally on encyclopedia entries would not be as credible, or credit-worthy, a piece as one based substantially on primary sources, backed up with excellent material from secondary sources, and with only a small component of the piece based on tertiary sources. (The quality of information, and the prestige and reliability of the source, are some of the problems with many online, as distinct from print, sources; see table 3.2.) It is also largely true that the primary – secondary – tertiary sequence is not just a coincidence: all knowledge is created in the first instance as primary material, then re-worked, commented on and interpreted in secondary material, and finally ends up being synthesised in tertiary material.

TABLE 3.2 Print versus electronic sources

	Advantages	Disadvantages
Print (hard copy): books, journals, reference texts	■ Permanent ■ Tangible ■ Portable ■ Can be annotated easily ■ No technology required ■ Full text always available ■ Easy to concentrate on for prolonged periods ■ Quality of content sustained by editorial/publishing oversight	■ Difficult to perform rapid large-scale searches ■ Cross-referencing can be slow ■ Take up a lot of space ■ Not available at certain times
Electronic: electronic databases, the internet	■ Easy to perform rapid large-scale searches ■ Take up less physical space than paper ■ Always accessible ■ May be accessed anywhere ■ Can display material in draft form ■ Can incorporate colour, motion, sound ■ Can exploit hyperlinking for rapid cross-reference	■ Not permanent unless printed out ■ Not tangible unless printed ■ Technology required to access ■ Not as easy to concentrate on ■ Vulnerable to technology failure ■ Generally less portable ■ Full text not always available ■ Most older texts (pre-1995) not available ■ Full duplication/digitisation of existing print resources not always possible ■ Difficult to search if text not digitised ■ Quality variable (especially websites)

When conducting research, it makes sense to begin with the secondary and tertiary research already completed. If excellent and exhaustive research already exists, then there may be no need for you to continually go back to basics by duplicating the efforts of others; if there are gaps in the primary data, then you can concentrate your efforts on these, thereby conserving valuable time and resources. One course is to conduct a **literature search or survey** before commissioning original research, and then to budget or plan for research on the basis of whatever shortcomings are revealed by the search.

Literature search or survey: review of published work in a given field

Secondary and tertiary data

Traditionally, the place to find most secondary data has been a library. Here information can be retrieved from books, journals, electronic databases and clippings files and via audio-

visual media. With the growth of electronic databases and the internet, however, it is now possible for you to access vast resources of information directly from your home or office computer. The two approaches should be seen as complementary, not mutually exclusive.

It is important to remember that print and electronic data have different strengths and weaknesses; good researchers exploit the strengths of the different approaches, and steer clear of the traps inherent in their weaknesses (refer back to table 3.2).

In the following sections we will consider how to locate books and other resources in libraries, how to use electronic databases, and how to search the internet for information.

Organising information

Dewey decimal classification system: a numeric system of classifying published materials into subject-classes and divisions

Library of Congress classification system: a library classification system using both numbers and letters

The non-fiction resources in about 85 per cent of the world's libraries are organised according to the **Dewey decimal classification system** (see figure 3.2), while the remaining 15 per cent are organised around the US **Library of Congress** and other more specialised cataloguing systems, such as the UDC (Universal Decimal Classification) system.

Such systems represent attempts to systematically organise and classify all books and other published materials into subject-classes and subcategories, identified by numeric and/or letter codes.

000	**GENERAL**	290	Other religions and comparative religion
010	Bibliographies and catalogues	**300**	**SOCIAL SCIENCES**
020	Library science	310	Statistical methods and statistics
030	General encyclopedic works	320	Political science
040	(not yet assigned)	330	Economics
050	General periodicals	340	Law
060	General organisations	350	Public administration
070	Newspapers and journalism	360	Welfare and association
080	General collections	370	Education
090	Manuscripts and book rarities	380	Commerce
100	**PHILOSOPHY/RELATED SUBJECTS**	390	Customs and folklore
110	Ontology and methodology	**400**	**LANGUAGE**
120	Knowledge, cause, purpose, man	410	Linguistics and non-verbal language
130	Pseudo- and parapsychology	420	English and Anglo-Saxon
140	Specific philosophic viewpoints	430	Germanic languages
150	Psychology	440	French, Provençal, Catalan
160	Logic	450	Italian, Romanian etc.
170	Ethics (moral philosophy)	460	Spanish and Portuguese
180	Ancient, mediaeval, Oriental philosophies	470	Italic languages
190	Modern Western philosophy	480	Classical and Greek
200	**RELIGION**	490	Other languages
210	Natural religion	**500**	**PURE SCIENCE**
220	Bible	510	Mathematics
230	Christian doctrinal theology	520	Astronomy and allied sciences
240	Christian moral and devotional theology	530	Physics
250	Christian pastoral, parochial etc.	540	Chemistry and allied sciences
260	Christian social and ecclesiastical theology	550	Earth sciences
270	History and geography of Christian church	560	Palaeontology
280	Christian denominations and sects	570	Anthropological and biological sciences

FIGURE 3.2 The Dewey decimal system of classification

580	Botanical sciences	790	Recreation (recreational arts)
590	Zoological sciences	**800**	**LITERATURE AND RHETORIC**
600	**TECHNOLOGY (APPLIED SCIENCES)**	810	American literature in English
610	Medical sciences	820	English and Anglo-Saxon literature
620	Engineering and allied operations	830	Germanic languages literature
630	Agriculture and agricultural industries	840	French, Provençal, Catalan literature
640	Domestic arts and sciences	850	Italian and Romanian literature
650	Management and auxiliary services	860	Spanish and Portuguese literature
660	Chemical technology etc.	870	Italic languages literature
670	Manufactures	880	Classical and Greek literature
680	Assembled and final products	890	Literature of other languages
690	Buildings	**900**	**GENERAL GEOGRAPHY AND HISTORY ETC.**
700	**THE ARTS**	910	General geography
710	Civic and landscape art	920	General biography and genealogy
720	Architecture	930	General history of ancient world
730	Sculpture and the plastic arts	940	General history of modern Europe
740	Drawing and decorative arts	950	General history of modern Asia
750	Painting and paintings	960	General history of modern Africa
760	Graphic arts	970	General history of North America
770	Photography and photographs	980	General history of South America
780	Music	990	General history of the rest of the world

Figure 3.3 shows the Library of Congress system of classification.

A	General works	M	Music
B	Philosophy, psychology, religion	N	Fine arts
C	History, related subjects	P	Languages and literature
D	History and topography, not including US	Q	Sciences
E	American history	R	Medicine
F	American history, individual states	S	Agriculture, plant and animal husbandry
G	Geography, anthropology	T	Technology
H	Social science	U	Military science
J	Political science	V	Naval science
K	Law	Z	Bibliography and library science
L	Education		

FIGURE 3.3 The Library of Congress system of classification

Drilling down to find specific resources

These systems further classify library resources according to a specific set of subcategories. Say, for example, you needed a book on customer relations. The Dewey code for customer relations is 658.812. This is arrived at by taking the broad Dewey subject-class of 650 (Management and auxiliary services) and refining it through various sublevels (see figure 3.4). The Dewey code can then be still further refined by appending the first letter or first three letters of the author's family name. This system means you can, at least in theory, search for information in a library without needing to consult a catalogue or index; armed with the Dewey number, you can readily locate a given book or section in any library.

```
600   Technology (applied sciences)
   650   Management and auxiliary services
      658   General management
         658.8   Management of distribution (marketing)
            658.81   Sales management
               658.812   Customer relations
```

FIGURE 3.4 Drilling down through the Dewey decimal system

Using catalogues

Information about the library holdings can, of course, also be found in the catalogue.

Catalogues can be of three types:

1. card
2. microfiche
3. computer.

Technology has largely overtaken card and fiche systems, and today most catalogues are computer-based.

Computer catalogues usually permit library searches according to author, title, subject, keyword (identifying word or concept found in title or bibliographic description), call number (the Dewey, Library of Congress or other catalogue number), nearby filings (other resources located close to the one in question) or physical location (collection, campus etc.) In a search on customer relations, for example, the catalogue of a particular library would list all relevant entries. Note that different libraries present information in different ways.

Most people use only a small amount of the available data-crunching power of the catalogues, and it is worth spending some time acquainting yourself with the capabilities of the catalogues you use.

Other information contained in catalogue entries may include:

- ISBN (International Standard Book Number), a unique library identification number (note that different numbers are allocated for hardback and paperback editions)
- accession number (another unique library number used as an internal housekeeping tool)
- edition number
- contents details (chapter headings, names of contributors to edited volumes, etc.)
- whether a book is illustrated
- whether it contains a bibliography
- number of pages of frontmatter (preface, introduction, table of contents etc.), given as lower-case roman numerals (e.g. *xxiii*)
- its physical dimensions (usually in centimetres)
- the author's birth date.

You can glean even more information about a resource from a physical inspection. With a book, for example, the imprint or copyright page (normally the left-hand page immediately following the title page) will often contain such details as the year of publication, previous editions and reprints, library cataloguing data, publisher information, copyright ownership, design and illustration credits, and printing and typesetting particulars (see figure 3.5) (Kralik & van Loon 2011). You will need some of this information when constructing a reference list or bibliography.

Second edition published 2011
by John Wiley & Sons Australia, Ltd
42 McDougall Street, Milton Qld 4064

Typeset in 10.5/13.5 pt Adobe Garamond LT

© John Wiley & Sons Australia, Ltd 2011

The moral rights of the authors have been asserted.

National Library of Australia
Cataloguing-in-Publication entry

Title:	Community nursing in Australia/edited by Debbie Kralik and Antonia van Loon.
Edition:	2nd ed.
ISBN:	9781742168067 (pbk.)
Notes:	Includes index.
Subjects:	Community health nursing — Australia.
Other Authors/ Contributors:	Kralik, Debbie, 1961– Van Loon, Antonia, 1956–
Dewey Number:	610.73430994

Reproduction and Communication for educational purposes
The Australian *Copyright Act 1968* (the Act) allows a maximum of one chapter or 10% of the pages of this work, whichever is the greater, to be reproduced and/or communicated by any educational institution for its educational purposes provided that the educational institution (or the body that administers it) has given a remuneration notice to Copyright Agency Limited (CAL).

Reproduction and Communication for other purposes
Except as permitted under the Act (for example, a fair dealing for the purposes of study, research, criticism or review), no part of this book may be reproduced, stored in a retrieval system, communicated or transmitted in any form or by any means without prior written permission. All inquiries should be made to the publisher.

Cover and internal design images: © Phase4Photography/Used under license from Shutterstock; © Royal District Nursing Service of SA Inc; © John Wiley & Sons, Australia. Photo by Jen Walter; © Lisa F. Young/Used under license from Shutterstock; © Alexander Raths/Used under license from Shutterstock; © Flying Doctors/Photo by Longshots, www.longshots.com.au; © iStockphoto/Charles Schug; © jordache/Used under license from Shutterstock; © iStockphoto.com/Gary Raddler; © ZTS/Used under license from Shutterstock.

Typeset in India by diacriTech

Printed in Singapore by
Toppan Security Printing Pte Ltd

10 9 8 7 6 5 4 3 2 1

FIGURE 3.5 An imprint page containing publishing data

Note that some journals are beginning to print partly edited or peer-reviewed articles – to give readers a glimpse of what is coming up. But such articles necessarily cannot have a volume, number or issue number, so how would you cite such an article? A new system called the Digital Object Identifier (DOI) has been set up, assigning a unique number to an article or object. You will find this on the cover. When the article is finally published, it will have the normal volume and number/issue data. DOIs are more permanent than URLs – the 'www' addresses of items on the internet.

Here are some other search tips you may find useful:

- In some libraries larger format books, sometimes called folios, are often held on separate shelves.
- What may seem to you an obvious subject heading may not correspond to the one used by the librarian responsible for cataloguing material. Try to think of as many alternative descriptors as possible for the topic you are researching, and check each of these in the subject catalogue.
- Use the pool of expert researchers already available – the library staff. They can often alert you to resources you never dreamed existed.
- After locating the book you want, examine it briefly to determine how useful it may be to you: check the table of contents and the index; look for keywords and phrases. If it contains a bibliography, this may be a valuable source of information about other publications.
- Sometimes it's useful to use the old-fashioned, no-tech strategy of simply browsing bookshelves. Indeed, you may find books even more suited to your purpose than the one you originally had in mind.
- If the book is not on the shelves, it may be out on loan; alternatively, it may be being held by library staff on a reserve shelf or in another collection in the library. If it is out on loan, reserve the book by placing it 'on hold'. If it is already on reserve, you may still wish to borrow it for the limited time available.
- Don't restrict yourself to one library. Be prepared to travel to other libraries, or at least to borrow from other libraries by interlibrary loan.
- Don't neglect alternative sources such as encyclopedias, almanacs, yearbooks, video-tapes, atlases, dictionaries, audiotapes, slides, manuscripts, theses or dissertations, rare books, government company registers and other government publications. Some of these may be found in the library's separate reference section; these resources are normally not for loan and must be consulted in the library.

Other sources of information

Other useful leads include:

- the bibliographies of the books you already have
- book reviews in journals
- websites of online bookstores (e.g. Amazon, Barnes and Noble, Blackwell)
- searchable full-text book databases sold on subscription (Questia.com, HighBeam, High-Wire)
- electronic book libraries (E-books.com, ebrary.com, netbooks.com)
- free online text services (Project Gutenberg, The Online Books Page, Classic Bookshelf, E-Text Archives, Bartleby.com, LibrarySpot.com, Electronic Journal Miner).

Electronic databases

Databases: large collection of information stored electronically and organised in categories for ease of retrieval

Electronic **databases** have boomed over the past few years. Writers and researchers can now access extraordinarily large volumes of information almost instantly. Well-constructed databases contain summaries or abstracts and/or full text and images of journal articles indexed and cross-referenced by topic. Some are available on CD-ROM, but most are available online. A small proportion may be accessed without charge on the open internet; the majority are available only via an institutional library network or intranet, and accessible only through subscription, usually paid by libraries on behalf of users.

Large numbers of databases covering a wide range of topic areas are now available (a short, representative list is offered in figure 3.6), and new ones are emerging all the time. Databases are superb resources, but they are not perfect as sources of information, and you should bear in mind their limitations, as noted in table 3.2.

- Academic Research Library (via ProQuest): multidisciplinary index of selected, full-text journals
- ABI/Inform (via ProQuest): all aspects of business, selected full text
- APAIS (via Informit Online): Australian Public Affairs Information Service
- Applied Science & Technology PlusText (via ProQuest): index, some full-text journals
- Business Source Premier: management, industries
- Current Contents (via OVID): multidisciplinary current awareness database
- Dissertation Abstracts: abstracts of master's and doctoral theses
- Early English Books Online
- ERIC (via CSA): education database
- Infotrac Expanded Academic ASAP: general and academic publications
- Ingenta: full-text journals
- JSTOR: full text of back issues of scholarly journals online
- LexisNexis: news, business, legal and public records information
- LION — Literature Online
- LISA — Library and Information Science Abstracts
- MLA: literature, language, linguistics, folklore
- ODS Online: full-text United Nations documents
- Oxford English Dictionary online
- ProQuest Religion (via ProQuest): selected full-text journals
- PsycINFO: psychology; incorporates PsycLit
- Refworld 2000 (CD-ROM): information on refugees and human rights from United Nations
- ScienceDirect: sciences, technology, engineering, economics
- Scopus: sciences, social science and humanities
- Sociofile (via OVID): sociology; includes Sociological Abstracts
- SPORTDiscus (via OVID): physiology, sports medicine, coaching and psychology
- Web of Science (via ISI Web of Knowledge)
- Wiley InterScience: science journals and reference works

FIGURE 3.6 Some online databases

The internet: treasure trove or junk pile?

The internet presents us with a vast fund of information, but as a communication medium it is still in a development phase. Surfing the net for hard information you can use in research can be like going to a library where each shelf contains only a few good books, with much of the shelf taken up by a chaotic pile of junk mail, product brochures, transcripts of meaningless conversations conducted by people you will never meet (and probably have no desire to meet) and pornography. In other words, the quality of internet information varies wildly, and you need to be actively sceptical in order to be able to discriminate the real deal from the shonkiness (low quality), nastiness and lies.

In assessing a website, ask the following questions:
- When was this site last updated?
- Do you know who created the site?
- Is this site selling something?
- Does the site contain multiple, competitive opinions, or is only one point of view presented?
- What are the credentials or qualifications of the people who created the site?

One free database that deserves special mention is a sub-program of Google, Google Scholar. So far, it appears to be the only database that features peer-reviewed articles, references to peer-reviewed articles that can be tracked down through other library databases (or, can be used for the basis of an inter-library loan or be purchased online immediately), and also generally high-quality, self-published articles by scholars themselves. Articles can be arranged by date of publication and other characteristics. Alert: commercial publishers are beginning to use Scholar as a way of promoting new books, although that may not be such a bad thing if you can afford it yourself or you can request your library to buy it. It's convenient to have so many sources grouped in the one place, but don't neglect other methods of research.

The brutal reality of the internet is that of the rest of the cruel world: you often get only what you pay for, and when information is in the public domain – something you do not have to pay for – it will often be of questionable quality. It is true that there are high-quality free sites, and poor quality pay-per-view sites, but these tend to be the exception rather than the rule. Intellectual property is the stock in trade of the new knowledge-based economy, and we often need to pay for it, just as consumers in previous areas paid for sickles and hoes and turbines and typewriters.

Search engines, directories, groups and chat, and images

The two main ways of searching the internet are by keyword searches and directories. Keyword searches and some directories are accessed by search engines, while other directories have their own websites.

Search engines are automated processes, using 'dumb' search software known as 'spiders'. A **metacrawler** is a search engine, or a software program, that displays results from multiple search engines. Search engines will search documents and files on the internet for matches to the keywords we supply. When we conduct automated searches, we are provided with lists of 'hits' (useful references) and 'misses' (sources we can't use). To maximise our chances of getting more hits than misses, it is useful to narrow or refine the search by using search operators or symbols: these allow you to locate a phrase or concept containing particular words, while excluding irrelevant material relating to other meanings of those words (see table 3.3).

Metacrawler: a search engine, or a software program, that displays results from multiple search engines

TABLE 3.3 Some basic search operators

Operators	Function	Example	Used to
+ AND	Find examples of these keywords used together	Fish + chips Fish AND chips	Locate references to food but exclude reference to live fish and wood chips and microchips
– NOT	Find keyword and exclude other keyword	Chips – fish Chips NOT fish	Locate references to wood chips and microchips but exclude food
" "	Exact phrase	"to be or not to be"	Locate exact phrase
Combinations		Grapevine + gossip – wine	Locate references to organisational grapevines or rumour mills but exclude references to physical grapevines

Some operators are generic to all search engines; others are unique to a particular search engine. No commands are foolproof, and you will inevitably get misses.

Like library catalogues, directories are compiled by people and offer ways of organising information in categories and various levels of subcategory, through which you need to drill down to find the data you need.

With experience you will find that different search engines and directories are best suited to different kinds of research tasks (figure 3.7). Each has different strengths and weaknesses. The more you know about searching, the more your searches will uncover, and search engine management tools can help you here.

Search engines	Google/Google Scholar/CrossRef Google, Alta Vista, Lycos, Excite, HotBot, Yahoo, Askjeeves, Infoseek, Northern Light, Looksmart, Blekko, Mooter, Bing and MIVA
Metacrawlers (multiple search engines)	Mamma, MetaCrawler, Dogpile, IXquick, Vivisimo and Kart00
Search engine management tools	Searchenginewatch.com, Searchenginecolossus.com. Amnesi.com, Allsearchengines.com, Beaucoup.com, Spider's Apprentice and Searchengines.com
Directories	Yahoo, About.com, Experts.com, Globaldirectories.com, Academicinfo.net, Digital Librarian, Google Directory, Best of the Web, About.Us.org and Joe Ant

FIGURE 3.7 Some search engines, metacrawlers, management tools and directories

Other aspects of internet resources accessed through search engines should be touched on here – groups and chat, and images. Groups are networks of people who communicate via the net, posting their conversations. Some of these are accessible to all (usenet groups) and some are semi-private (listserv or discussion mailing lists). Such communication occurs in real time in chat rooms, or areas set aside in a computer network or web page where users can conduct online conversations. Sometimes groups pages will provide you with useful information, or at least offer insights into the current issues and controversies in a given field. Images are simply databases of images found somewhere online and accessed by keyword. Although many are subject to the rules of copyright, such images can be helpful in compiling presentations and documents, as well as providing new perspectives on subjects (see figure 3.8). As with all aspects of the internet, the quality of group, chat and image sites vary widely, so exercise discretion.

FIGURE 3.8 Google image search results for 'search engines'

Managing your research catch

Working with print sources, it is fairly easy to organise our 'catch' or raw data – we just take copies of what we want to use and file them in folders. With electronic material, it's not quite that simple; indeed, it's easy to get lost, to forget where we found that really good web page, or simply to fail to cognitively process the volume of data we have found. The following strategies can be helpful:

- Within your internet browser (Netscape, Internet Explorer, Mozilla Firefox, Opera, Safari, Chrome), bookmark useful sites or add them to your Favourites file.
- Create topic folders within your browser where you can 'park' useful pages, saving them as HTML files.
- Track your accessing of pages using the history function within your browser.
- Create folders within your word processor, and save web pages as HTML files (these cannot be opened easily from within the processor, and you may have to open them through your Windows, Apple or Linux operating system).
- Save PDF files to your folders, and use thumbnail, bookmark and internal search functions (e.g. Google Desktop or Windows 7.0 desktop search) to locate and manage data.
- Access text for quotation and images from inside PDFs by using selection tools.
- Set up files containing groups of URLs (web addresses), which can be simply copied from a browser window into a word processing file. Make sure the URLs are 'hot', or blue, so that you can simply click on one to open the site through a browser.
- If necessary, print out your material. Many web pages now offer a printer-friendly version of documents, which gives you text plus main graphics, but excludes the 'eye candy' or visual attractiveness of HTML layout features. Try not to use up too much paper in doing this, of course.

Taking notes: paper and electronic

Now that you have located your secondary data, what are you going to do with it? First you need to get records of the data you can take away with you and study. There are several ways of doing this. New electronic approaches to taking and organising notes are emerging, such as the bibliographic software packages EndNotes, Biblioscape and RefWorks. You can also scan sources and file them, or use optical character recognition programs (e.g. Omnipage, Anydoc), which are like scanning but actually allow you to digitally search and manipulate print text, handwriting and faxes. The plagiarism temptation rating is high, but then again, plagiarism detection software is not far behind; in some cases, it is in front).

More traditional approaches still, however, have much to recommend them. By simply photocopying or printing out the relevant data, you create a permanent record you can take with you and consult later when you need it. Identify all useful information by means of underlining or marginal notation.

Note taking means just that: unless you want a word-for-word quote, you simply need to extract the essence of a source (figure 3.9) (Department of Education 2002).

Employers see communication skills as critical to <u>customer service and workplace harmony,</u> <u>effective operations and productivity</u>.

In a number of large enterprise case studies reference was made to the importance and more sophisticated use of communication skills in workplaces enabled by <u>Information and Communications Technology (ICT)</u>.

The elements provide a broad definition of communication with an emphasis on the <u>two-way nature of communication</u> that was underpinned by the need to respond to people from all walks of life. These broad expectations are typical across all industry areas and enterprises whether small, medium or large.

The <u>need for a second language was confined in this study to some higher level jobs</u> in the large enterprises, many of which are part of global corporations, or are focused on the international marketplace.

FIGURE 3.9 Note taking — extracting core information from a published source

Enterprises did not differentiate their need for communication skills between entry-level and ongoing employees, but some noted that there were particular jobs at particular sites that might require more or higher application of certain elements.

Many enterprises did, however, reflect that they no longer wanted technical 'boffins' or operators who could not communicate with their work peers and clients.

Enterprises with large customer service functions — for example, enterprises with call centres — stressed that effective application of the communication skill would require a strong listening element. Other enterprises stressed the importance of this element in terms of receiving feedback and understanding the requirements of peers, supervisors and customers.

This quick-and-dirty, or hasty but superficial, approach works well in certain circumstances, but there are problems associated with it. Firstly, once you have collected more than a few references, you will need a photographic memory to recall where all the important points are. Secondly, you may have difficulty in bringing together similar points from different sources. As a result, when you come to write, your writing may have a crude cut-and-paste, half-formed feel to it. In other words, this piecemeal approach does not provide a framework around which to organise your material or ideas.

Note taking and tactile thinking

Such a framework is available when you actually take notes. Taking notes takes more time than simply marking up photocopies, but it is usually time well spent. You may in fact photocopy your original sources, and then take notes from the photocopies (but don't forget the trees: don't take copious photocopies solely to avoid having to take notes). Is taking notes old-fashioned, and a waste of time? Not at all. By taking notes, you put your brain to work on the ideas you are considering. You are actively (rather than just mechanically) involved with your topic, analysing and comparing ideas and arguments as presented in different sources, and in the process synthesising your own ideas – expressed in your own words. You are engaging in **tactile thinking** – the process of stimulating cognitive processes through physical movement (Chandler 1992). Chandler quotes a gallery of great writers to prove his point:

Tactile thinking: the process by which the physical activity of writing by hand (as opposed to using a keyboard) can trigger thought patterns

> I choose to believe that there is some kind of mystic connection between the brain and the actual act of writing in longhand. (Faye Weldon)

> Some authors type their works, but I cannot do that. Writing is tied up with the hand, almost with a special nerve. (Graham Greene)

This kind of thinking can help you to produce a structure or pattern in the way you approach the problem you are considering.

When taking notes, do so methodically, clearly separating your own ideas and words from those of others, whether paraphrasing, summarising or quoting. This will ensure you do not inadvertently plagiarise the ideas and words of others. You need to clearly record both substantive content and bibliographic information as part of any note taking. Along with bibliographic information, it is useful to record the library call number or URL of the reference, in case you need to consult the specific source again.

On-screen note taking

Aside from specialised bibliographic software, some word processing programs offer simple outliner and diagramming features to facilitate note taking (see online chapter 'Writing skills 5: how to write'). This technique takes a bit a practice, but it can be very effective. The outliner feature helps provide structures for your thoughts. You can key in notes directly using this facility, then when it comes time to draft your document you will find that you have already keyed in much of the text, and that it will be a semi-organised, hierarchical state. Stand-alone note-taking programs that have note-taking capability include Evernote, Windows One Note and Google Docs.

Referring to secondary and tertiary sources

We consult secondary sources in order to unearth ideas, especially when we are writing documents such as reports and essays. It is often useful to consult and refer to published work, and sometimes to quote directly from it. Referring and quoting are specific skills, and you should try to master them. What is the difference between referring and quoting? Referring to, or citing, a source means you identify a published work, whether or not you quote or reproduce words directly from that source.

Note here also the distinction between a reference list and a bibliography. A bibliography is a list of works relevant to the topic area; it is not necessary to have specifically referred in your work to every item in a bibliography. A reference list, or list of works cited, is a list of works you actually refer to or quote from in your document. You may choose to include both in your work, drawing the reader's attention to works cited and to other works of interest. Reference lists and bibliographies can be placed at the end of the document or at the end of sections or chapters within the document.

Referencing systems

In a personal letter, a writer will convey primarily his or her own thoughts and perspective. Perhaps the letter writer will refer to the thoughts and opinions of others, but this will be done in an informal way. Personal letters tend to follow the natural flow of the writer's thoughts, with digressions from the main theme often placed in brackets or parentheses so as not to disturb the flow. In a professional document, where logical structure is more important, the writer can use specific tools to direct the reader's attention beyond the body of the main text. Writers use referencing systems to:

- support an argument by providing a reference to an authoritative piece of writing or research
- provide readers with the information they need to independently check the cited work
- shorten the document by referring the reader elsewhere for details
- introduce related thoughts or opinions without disturbing the flow of the main text
- demonstrate their familiarity with the topic area.

When a writer documents a source so that a reader may consult that source, the documentation provides, if you like, the 'address' of the source. In the two main types of print sources you will probably be concerned with – books and articles – the minimum documentation required is as follows:

1. *Book.*
   - Name of author(s)
   - Title of work
   - Place of publication
   - Publisher
   - Year of publication
2. *Article in newspaper, magazine or journal.*
   - Name of author(s)
   - Title of work/article
   - Title of publication
   - Date of publication/volume and number or issue/page numbers.

Other documentation is needed for other types of sources, as discussed later in this chapter.

The two main referencing systems used to cite other works are the Harvard (or author–date) system and the documentary-note system. Other specialised systems include the Vancouver system, and the MLA (Modern Language Association) and APA (American Psychological Association) styles. These systems take different approaches to matters such as order of information, name treatment, punctuation, capitalisation and abbreviations.

Different academic disciplines have adopted particular publication styles over time. If you are writing documents for different audiences in academia or industry, you may need to use different styles of citation for each. Even different lecturers in the same department may have slightly different requirements for citations. It is important that you find out exactly which system is required in each case. As barriers break down between disciplines, new syntheses of styles may yet emerge.

Harvard system and documentary–note system

Let's now look at the two main systems of citation, Harvard and documentary-note (compared in figure 3.10).

HARVARD/AUTHOR–DATE	DOCUMENTARY-NOTE
. . . Too many of our managers are good with things but not with people. It is a phenomenon that has been noted all over the world. As Douglas observes of British managers, '. . . experience shows that there is often an inverse correlation between the extent of a particular individual's technical expertise and that person's ability to manage people' (Douglas 2002–2003, p. 34). Alsop (2002, p. R11) notes that US employers are complaining about graduates who are primarily 'number-crunchers' but who communicate poorly with clients and staff. Australian business and government surveys show that employers across the board are dissatisfied with the abilities of graduates to communicate in team and face-to-face situations (Department of Education, Science and Training 2002, p. 12; Business Council of Australia 2006).

So do we simply replace our existing managers? No, but we do need to start to change our training and recruitment priorities. Communications training, employing off-the-shelf resources already being used in a limited way by our training departments (e.g. Biech 2010), may help us improve on our turnover reduction and conflict management objectives. | . . . Too many of our managers are good with things but not with people. It is a phenomenon that has been noted all over the world. As Douglas observes of British managers, '. . . experience shows that there is often a definite inverse correlation between the extent of a particular individual's technical expertise and that person's ability to manage people'.[6] Alsop[7] notes that US employers are complaining about graduates who are primarily 'number-crunchers' but who communicate poorly with clients and staff. Australian business and government surveys show that employers across the board are dissatisfied with the abilities of graduates to communicate in team and face-to-face situations.[8]

So do we simply replace our existing managers? No, but we do need to start to change our training and recruitment priorities. Communications training, employing off-the-shelf resources already being used in a limited way by our training departments,[9] may help us improve on our turnover reduction and conflict management objectives. |
| **References**
Alsop, Ronald 2002, 'The top business schools (a special report) — playing well with others: recruiters say the "soft" skills, such as leadership, communication and the ability to work in teams, are just as important as the hard stuff; and a lot harder to teach', *The Wall Street Journal*, 9 September, p. R11.
Biech, Elaine 2010, *Pfeiffer Annual Set: Training and Consulting*, John Wiley & Sons, New York. | [6] Michael Douglas, 'Why "soft skills" are an essential part of the hard world of business', *British Journal of Administrative Management*, Christmas/New Year, 2002–2003, pp. 34–5.
[7] Ronald Alsop, 'The top business schools (a special report) — playing well with others: recruiters say the "soft" skills, such as leadership, communication and the ability to work in teams, are just as important as the hard stuff; and a lot harder to teach', *The Wall Street Journal*, 9 September 2002, p. R11. |

FIGURE 3.10 A comparison of Harvard and documentary-note referencing styles

(continued)

FIGURE 3.10 *(continued)*

Business Council of Australia 2006, *New concepts in innovation — the keys to a growing Australia*, viewed 11 January 2011, http://www.bca.com.au/Content.aspx?ContentID=99787.
Department of Education, Science and Training 2002, *Employability skills for the future*, http://www.dest.gov.au/sectors/training_skills/publications_resources/other_publications/.
Douglas, Michael 2002/2003, 'Why "soft skills" are an essential part of the hard world of business', *British Journal of Administrative Management*, Christmas/New Year, pp. 34–5.

[8] Department of Education, Science and Training, *Employability skills for the future*, http://www.dest.gov.au/sectors/training_skills/publications_resources/other_publications/, 2002. Business Council of Australia, *New concepts in innovation — the keys to a growing Australia*, http://www.bca.com.au/Content.aspx?ContentID=99787
[9] For example, Elaine Biech, 2010, *Pfeiffer Annual Set: Training and Consulting*, John Wiley & Sons, New York.

Harvard system: system for citing sources using author names and the year of publication

In the **Harvard system**, the writer refers at the appropriate place in the text to a source by providing (in parentheses) the author's family name, the year of publication, and in certain circumstances, the page number. Some prefer to separate the name, date and page by a comma, some by a colon: (Smith, 2011, p. 6); (Smith, 2011:6).

A page number or number range (e.g. pp. 123–26) should be included if the writer refers to, or quotes from, a specific part of the source, and is sometimes included even for paraphrased citations. The reader can then find the full source details of the publication by referring to the reference list or bibliography.

This will mean (in order) family name of author, first name initial or name, date of publication (sometimes in round brackets), title (often in italics; the current trend is to capitalise the first letter of the title, and then put the rest in lowercase), city of publication, which edition (2nd? 5th? – ignore if the book is in its first edition), and then the publisher's name.

(Ask your lecturers about referencing requirements for your particular course: there are general rules for writing citations, but it is surprising how this varies according to the 'house style' of a department or lecturer.)

The following specific conventions are used in the Harvard system to document different types of sources:

BOOK BY ONE AUTHOR

Baggott, Jim 2008, *The first war of physics: the secret history of the atom bomb*, 1939–1949, Pegasus/Norton, New York.

BOOK BY TWO OR THREE AUTHORS

Sadri, Houman A & Flammia, Madelyn 2011, *Intercultural communication: a new approach to international relations and global challenges*, Continuum Books, London.

BOOK BY MORE THAN THREE AUTHORS – ABBREVIATED FORM

Turabian, Kate L et al. 2007, *A manual for writers of research papers, theses, and dissertations: Chicago style for students and researchers*, 7th edn, University of Chicago Press.

TWO OR MORE BOOKS BY THE SAME AUTHOR

Tannen, Deborah 2011, *That's not what I meant!: How conversational style makes or breaks relationships*, Harper, New York.

—2010, *You were always mum's favourite!: sisters in conversation throughout their lives*, Random House, New York.

TWO OR MORE WORKS BY THE SAME AUTHOR IN THE SAME YEAR

Crystal, David 2011a, *Evolving English: one language, many voices*, British Library, London.

—2011b, Internet linguistics: a student guide, Routledge, London.

BOOK BY GROUP OR CORPORATE AUTHOR

World Health Organization 2010, *The World Health Report 2010 – Health systems financing: the path to universal coverage*, Geneva, Switzerland.

BOOK WITH NO AUTHOR NAMED

The Economist style guide 2010, 10th edn, The Economist Press, London.

ANTHOLOGY OR EDITED BOOK

Harkin-Jones, E & Rajeev, RS (eds.) 2011, *Nanomaterials and polymer nanocomposites: characterisation and techniques*, CRC Press, Boca Raton, FL.

CHAPTER IN BOOK

Wills, Frances 2011, 'Variation and forensic linguistics', in M Maguire, T Warren and J McMahon (eds.), April, *Analysing Variation in English*, Cambridge University Press.

ARTICLE IN A JOURNAL WITH CONTINUOUS PAGINATION

Sad, Gaad 2010, 'Munchausen by proxy: The dark side of parental investment theory?', *Medical Hypotheses*, vol. 75, no. 6, pp. 479–81.

ARTICLE IN A JOURNAL THAT PAGES EACH ISSUE SEPARATELY

Greengard, Samuel 2001, 'Gossip poisons business: HR can stop it', *Workforce*, vol. 80, no. 7, pp. 24–8.

UNSIGNED MAGAZINE/NEWSPAPER ARTICLE

'Transplanting a face is only half the challenge', 2009, *New Scientist*, vol. 10 no. 4, March, p. 5, doi: 10.1134/n.scientist.2009.24.111.

PAPER PRESENTED AT A MEETING OR CONFERENCE

Eunson, Baden 2007, 'Communication models: can pre-editing and post-editing help improve basic models?', paper presented at the Australian New Zealand Communication Association 2007 Conference, University of Melbourne, 5–6 July.

INTERVIEW

Whipsnade, LE, Director of Public Relations, Juggernaut Manufacturing Pty Ltd. Telephone interview. 4 April 2011.

GOVERNMENT DOCUMENT

AC Nielsen Research Services 2000, *Employer satisfaction with graduate skills – research report*, Department of Education, Training and Youth Affairs, Canberra.

FILM/VIDEOTAPE/DVD

The customer relationship 2009, video recording, BBC for Business/Centre for Tomorrow's Company, London. Produced and directed by Donald Leggatt.

ONLINE ARTICLE

Joy, B 2000, 'Why the future doesn't need us', *Wired*, April, accessed 8 February 2011, http://www.wired.com/wired/archive/8.04/joy.html.

Documentary–note system

Documentary-note system: referencing system using in-text superscript numbers or symbols rather than author name and year of publication

The **documentary-note system** is widely used in the humanities, although it seems to be losing ground to the Harvard or author–date system. The Harvard and documentary-note systems vary stylistically in various ways, as outlined in figure 3.10. The main distinction between the two systems is that in the documentary-note system an in-text citation or comment is marked by the insertion of a superscript number or symbol. Symbols include the asterisk (*), the dagger (†), the double dagger (‡), the section mark (§), the blind P or paragraph mark (¶) and the parallel mark (||). The reader then refers to the foot of the page (*foot* notes) or to the end of the report, article, chapter or book (*end* notes).

Notes may be *content* notes (which provide comment on the text or a cross-reference to another source or section of the main text) or *source* notes (which simply provide the bibliographic details of the source cited). The notes in the right-hand column of figure 3.12 might optionally be run at the end of the document.

The numbering of footnotes may begin anew on each page, or it may be continued sequentially until the end of the essay, chapter or book. The numbering of endnotes may begin anew for each chapter or section, or a single sequential listing may be given at the end of the document. If a document requires both endnotes and footnotes, symbols should be used for footnotes and numbers for endnotes. In documents that feature mathematical notation, superscript reference numbers risk being confused for superscripts in formulae and equations. In such circumstances, symbols might again be less distracting in footnotes.

Vancouver system

Vancouver: system for citing sources using superscript numbers instead of names and dates, and often grouping several cross-reference numbers at the same point in the text

The **Vancouver** or citation-sequence system is used mainly in scientific and medical writing. As in the documentary-note system, items in the reference list are numbered and text citation is made either by a superscript number or a number in brackets. A semi-colon is used to separate the volume or issue numbers from the page numbers with the Vancouver system. This system's primary distinctions are in the presentation style of the reference list, and that several superscript cross-references can appear at the same point in the text. For example:

> We need to distinguish between studies which focus on biomedical impacts of wireless phones [1,2,3,4,5] and those which focus on behavioural impacts [6,7,8].

In the reference list, we would then find:

1. Sato, Yasuto, Akiba, Kubo, Osami & Yamaguchi, Naohito. A case–case study of mobile phone use and acoustic neuroma risk in Japan. Bioelectromagnetics 2010;65(2):222–34. doi: 10.1186/bem.a2546.

2. Repacholi M. Health risks from the use of mobile phones. Toxicology Letters 2001;12(3): 323–31.

3. No link between cellular phone use and brain cancer. Trends in Neurosciences 2001(March);24(3):138.

4. Hardell, Lennart O. et al. Long-term use of cellular phones and brain tumours – increased risk associated with use for > 10 years. Occupational and Environmental Medicine 2007 April 4, doi:10.1136/oem.2006.029751.

5. Christ A, Kuster N. Differences in RF energy absorption in the heads of adults and children. Bioelectromagnetics 2005;26:S7,S31–S44.

6. Gittleman, Ann Louise. Zapped: why your cell phone shouldn't be your alarm clock and 1268 ways to outsmart the hazards of electronic pollution, New York: HarperOne, 2010.

7. Hosking, Simon G, Young, Christie L & Regan, Michael A. The effects of text messaging on young drivers. Human factors: the journal of the human factors and ergonomics society 2009;51(4):582–92.8.

8. Charette, Robert. Collision risk while driving a truck and texting 23 times higher than when not texting. IEEE Spectrum 2009 July 29, Available from: http://spectrum.ieee.org/riskfactor/computing/it/texting-while-driving-a-truck-collision-risk-23-times-greater-than-when-not-texting.

Page numbers should be included in references if the citation is specific. Individual in-text cross-references are separated by commas. Numbers in a sequence may be cited as ranges [26–31]. It is also conventional to cite non-consecutive references [3,14,28].

Electronic citing

As the differences between paper documents and electronic documents become greater, so to do the opportunities to explore processes of citation and connection. Most major word processors now feature the ability to hyperlink; that is, to link one underlined and/or differently coloured word with another document, file or website. This is 'three-dimensional' writing as discussed in chapter 6, and it can be very useful for the reader. With the rise of social media like Twitter, it becomes almost impossible to write in a URL internet address (because they take up so much space), but programs exist that 'squeeze' the length of the URL, like Tiny URL, Doiop or bit.ly.

Style variations in reference systems

You will encounter stylistic variations in the ways in which each of these systems is applied. Individual authors and editors may use different punctuation, capitalisation, underlining, italicising, use of quotation marks, abbreviations, ordering and so on. They may decide to include personal communications (letters) in a bibliography, or exclude them.

Style conventions will be found to vary considerably between departments, organisations, publishing houses, industries and professions. When in doubt, always ask if the department or organisation has a house style guide you can consult. It is important that you present your communications according to conventions your audience feels comfortable with.

May we quote you? Citing, quoting, paraphrasing and plagiarising

Let's now turn from referencing to examine the related process of quotation. Quotations, a major element in referencing, are used primarily to support the writer's argument through substantive reference to the published work of another writer or researcher. Another writer's exact words may be particularly expressive and therefore better quoted than summarised. You need not use quotation conventions when:

- the ideas and the words used to express them are common knowledge
- the words used are your own.

If you are not sure whether or not words and ideas are common knowledge, it is best to err on the side of caution, seek out a reference and quote it, giving full documentation. Illegitimate use of others' ideas includes **plagiarism**, which means passing off someone else's ideas, and the way in which they are expressed, as your own. Plagiarism has always been with us, but it is more widespread these days because of the availability of so much material on the internet (DeVoss & Rosati 2002; Buranen 1999). 'Material' here includes not only words but concepts, diagrams, images and any other type of intellectual property (as some samplers of music have discovered to their cost). In a global knowledge-based economy, intellectual property becomes both more important and highly valued – and more vulnerable to illegitimate use. Issues concerning intellectual property therefore need to be handled with care.

Plagiarism: passing off someone else's ideas, and the way in which they are expressed, as your own

Legitimate quotation: fair dealing

If you are quoting more than four lines of text:

- lead into the quotation with a colon, if appropriate (not a semicolon)
- indent the quoted lines (use the computer tab key) sometimes from both the right and left margins
- run the quotation as a block set off from the main text by a line space above and below
- don't use quotation marks around the quoted block, although you may, in some circumstances, choose to further highlight it by using another type treatment, such as italics. Here's an example:

> Plagiarism is widespread in universities and colleges, and it has become worse in the past few years with the vast increase of online material, as observers of the academic scene such as DeVoss and Rosati point out:
>
> > *Online plagiarism is just as complicated as any other form of plagiarism, and these same – and different – complications apply to research and writing in online realms. Students may plagiarize from online research spaces because it's easy to do so; cutting and pasting is a common virtual text manipulation trick. Students may plagiarize from virtual realms because they lack sophistication in searching and evaluating sources within this realm and, frustrated, resort to stealing texts.* (DeVoss and Rosati 2002, p. 196)
>
> With these developments in mind, we need to ensure that none of our staff are tempted by such bad habits.

If you are quoting less than four lines of text, simply incorporate the quote into the body of your own material, setting off the quoted material within quotation marks.

> The bad habits that some our staff members have of stealing intellectual property may have developed in their student days. Some observers of the academic scene have noted an increase in situations in which students 'plagiarize from online research spaces because it's easy to do so' and 'because they lack sophistication in searching and evaluating sources within this realm' (DeVoss & Rosati 2002, p. 196).

If you cut out any of the original text from within a quotation, be sure to indicate the omission by using an ellipsis.

> Students may plagiarize from online research spaces because it's easy to do so ... Students may plagiarize from virtual realms because they lack sophistication in searching and evaluating sources within this realm and, frustrated, resort to stealing texts (DeVoss & Rosati 2002, p. 196).

If you need to make a change within the quotation so that it fits in with your wording, place your own material in square brackets.

> A recent study pointed out that today's students sometimes succumb to the temptation to use material accessed on the internet. '[They] may plagiarize from online research spaces because it's easy to do so; cutting and pasting is a common virtual text manipulation trick' (DeVoss & Rosati 2002, p. 196).

Ensure that your introductory text and the quotation are grammatically matched. Be alert for the obvious mismatches of subject and verb, pronouns and antecedents, punctuation and tense.

Illegitimate quotation: plagiarising

Plagiarism is the unacceptable face of quotation. It may entail lifting a couple of lines without identifying them as from another source, as in the following example (the plagiarised section underlined):

> The pressing deadline, the convenience of computer technology, the sheer abundance of so much material on the internet may seduce some of us into plagiarising <u>from online research spaces because it's easy to do so; cutting and pasting is a common virtual text manipulation trick.</u>

In more extreme cases it may entail stealing entire paragraphs or pages. Sometimes writers plagiarise unconsciously as a result of sloppy research methods – for example, confusing the notes they have taken from other sources with their own thoughts. Techniques used to prevent such errors include:

- using different coloured ink for direct quotation, summary, paraphrase and your own thoughts
- using circles, asterisks, arrows or underlining to distinguish quoted text
- printing out online source material and keeping hard copies
- keeping careful bibliographic records of print and online publication details.

Good note-taking practice will also help prevent such errors occurring.

Illegitimate quotation again: 'biblio–dumping'

Biblio-dumping: the unprofessional practice of simply listing your sources in the bibliography, but not citing them directly even though the sources have been quoted from or paraphrased

'**Biblio-dumping**' is not a real word, and let's hope it never becomes one. It describes the unprofessional practice of writers using material from other sources, but not citing the sources when reference is made to them in the text. Instead, the source is listed in the bibliography or reference list. In other words, it is simply another form of plagiarism. It is, of course, normal – not to mention necessary – to list sources in your bibliography or reference list. If, however, you are accused of plagiarism, and try to defend yourself by saying that the material used was not cited directly but the source is listed in the bibliography, then you will be in the wrong, and your assessors will have no choice but to interpret your technique as one which employs plagiarism. You *must cite* your sources in the body of your work when you use source material. It is not adequate to simply list your material at the end of the document. It doesn't matter what citation system you use – whatever you are using, use it properly. By not following professional practice, you are asking your reader/assessor to hunt through your document, trying to match up items in the bibliography with points made in the body of the document. It is not the job of your reader/assessor to do this. Unethical people – plagiarisers – will sometimes use this as a technique, working other people's material into their own words. Don't biblio-dump – it's unprofessional, and it will damage your reputation (see Howard 2007).

Paraphrasing

Paraphrasing: recasting someone else's words in your own

Paraphrasing means recasting someone else's words in your own. A paraphrase usually involves summarising, but it may be as long as, or even longer than, the original text. Use synonyms and rephrasing to get away from the original wording, so that the passage you write sounds like you. (Sudden changes in vocabulary and tone are the usual giveaway signs that the writer has just switched from his or her own words to those of someone else.) If the writer you are drawing on uses very particular and apposite expressions, it is often better not to attempt to create synonyms but rather to quote them directly, using quotation marks. Even if you do not quote a single word, however, a paraphrase still requires source acknowledgement. Changing some words does not make the thought your own.

Here's an example of an unacceptable paraphrase (compare the source wording with the wording of the example under the 'Illegitimate quotation: plagiarising' section):

> Copying words from internet sites without acknowledgement comes easily to some because it is simply cutting and pasting – a common virtual-text rearranging trick. Some of our staff may be unethically borrowing material from internet sites because they are simply not sophisticated enough when it comes to scanning and judging sources in cyberspace, and when this gets too much for them they just decide to steal.

Here is an example of an acceptable paraphrase:

> Copying text from internet sites may be simply a bad habit that some of our staff picked up in their student days. This habit springs partly from the sheer ease of cutting and pasting web text, and partly from the lack of sophistication of some students in searching and evaluating sources, which can cause frustration and may predispose some to copy others' work, irrespective of the consequences (DeVoss & Rosati 2002, p. 196).

Sources: success and failure

You can demonstrate your professionalism or lack of it in the way you use sources, or other people's intellectual property.

The rule of the academic jungle, and the world outside it, is brutally simple:

- Use sources well, and you will achieve recognition for your professionalism, be rewarded, and have your reputation enhanced.
- Use sources badly and/or unprofessionally, and you will feel pain, and have your reputation damaged or destroyed.

ASSESS YOURSELF

Select a passage of text from a published source. Now create:
- a paragraph in which you legitimately quote the text
- a paragraph in which you legitimately paraphrase the text
- a paragraph in which you illegitimately paraphrase the text
- a paragraph in which you plagiarise the text.

Learn to differentiate the four forms of usage, and to avoid the last two.

Getting the facts: primary sources of data

Once we have completed our review of the secondary data, gaps or weaknesses in the published record may have become apparent. Here is where we need to create our own primary data.

Primary data

Sources of primary data may include experiments, observations and organisational records. Two major sources of primary data are the survey methods of interviews and question-naires. Interviews are preferable to questionnaires in some circumstances, because as the researcher you have the flexibility to vary the nature of your enquiry according to the person you are interviewing. On the other hand, questionnaires can be cheaper and the data extracted from them can be more easily quantified. Questionnaires and interviews both have advantages and disadvantages that can affect the reliability and success of data collection in different circumstances.

Although interviews can be varied to suit the occasion, it is important to ensure that you maintain a consistent structure and sequence of questions from interview to interview. In interviewing a number of people for a job, for example, it is essential, for the sake of both fairness and effectiveness, that similar questions be asked of all interviewees; otherwise it becomes impossible to make a legitimate choice between the applicants. Similar considerations apply when conducting survey interviews in order to gather social data. Indeed, in some circumstances, depending on the nature of the questions asked and the manner of recording the responses, the line between conducting an interview and administering a questionnaire may blur.

Surveys, of course, do not necessarily produce reliable results. There is no guarantee that the interviewees will tell the truth. They may say one thing but do another. They may have contradictory beliefs and opinions. They may be trying to create a good impression or seek to give the response they think the questioner wants. They may give any response they think will persuade the questioner to go away quickly. They may even work to undermine the survey with false responses. Ensuring anonymity can help, but even this is no guarantee of totally reliable responses. These factors may impose limitations on the value of the data you gather, but if you are realistic about such limitations you may still make good use of the data.

The survey methods of interviews and questionnaires are two major sources of primary data. Face-to-face interviews give researchers the opportunity both to build rapport and to observe the nonverbal behaviour of respondents.

Interviewing

The two primary methods of interviewing are the face-to-face and telephone approaches.

Telephone interviewing

Telephone interviewing has obvious practical advantages – both in terms of time and access – that save the researcher money. Some people may respond more frankly on the telephone than they would in a face-to-face situation. Others, however, are inhibited by the medium, finding it artificial and even suspect (is the exchange being overheard or recorded?).

When we conduct a telephone interview we are deprived of the advantage of observing the respondent's non-verbal responses. Such non-verbal behaviour can sometimes be important, not least when it appears to contradict what is said. The telephone researcher is thus deprived of valuable clues to the respondent's true feelings on an issue.

It is also much easier for a respondent to terminate a telephone encounter, either by simply hanging up, or by inventing pressing circumstances. Telephone interviewing is not always as time-saving as it might first appear, either: much time can be lost in simply getting through to the appropriate person, particularly at a time suitable to the researcher.

Face-to-face interviewing

Face-to-face interviewing has the advantage of allowing you to observe the non-verbal behaviour of the respondent. Should you detect inconsistencies between what is being said and what is being expressed non-verbally, for example, you can adapt the flow of the interview accordingly to ensure you are getting accurate responses. It may also be easier to establish a rapport with a person face to face than over the telephone.

Face-to-face interviewing will probably be more expensive than telephone interviewing, and will involve more time and inconvenience for the researcher. Also, although some people will be more relaxed and open in their face-to-face responses, others will be more inhibited, preferring the semi-anonymity of the telephone encounter.

Questionnaires

The two primary methods of administering questionnaires are face to face and by mail.

Administering questionnaires in person

The great advantage of administering a questionnaire in person is that any misunderstandings or uncertainties on the part of the respondent can be clarified on the spot. This will undoubtedly improve the quality of the responses you receive. Another advantage is that the situation creates an obligation in the mind of the respondent to complete the questionnaire. Unmotivated respondents may fill in the document in a desultory or unhelpful way, but they will still fill it in. This is not always the case with mail questionnaires.

Administering questionnaires face to face, however, is relatively expensive and may entail considerable organisation simply to ensure that respondents show up at the agreed time and place.

Administering questionnaires by mail

Administering questionnaires by mail is usually much cheaper than administering them in person. This approach allows the researcher to contact large numbers of people, including those in distant locations and those who, for whatever reason, cannot be interviewed effectively over the telephone. Mail questionnaires are the most effective means of sampling broad opinion.

The main problem with mail questionnaires is a low response rate. Sometimes people don't have the time or the inclination to respond, or have good intentions but never quite get around to it. There is also the possibility that those who do respond are not representative of the group you are trying to survey, so that any data you gather is misleading. You can improve your chances of getting a high response rate by:

- keeping the questionnaire short
- providing a reply-paid and pre-addressed envelope
- providing incentives for returning the questionnaire
- demonstrating that the data gained will benefit the respondent in the future.

Types of questions

Questions that can be asked in interviews and questionnaires may be meaningfully grouped under three headings: open search strategies, closed search strategies and mixed search strategies.

Open search strategies

Open search strategies: approaches to creating primary data that provide for an unlimited range of responses from respondents

Open search strategies, which provide for an unlimited range of responses from respondents, depend on asking open questions.

Open questions

An open question allows respondents to answer in any way they please: you do not limit the menu or range of responses they can give. Examples of open questions are:

> What do you think of the new productivity agreement?

> Why did you apply for this job?

Open questions allow respondents to speak their mind and give opinions; a simple 'yes' or 'no' is insufficient. This makes some respondents happy, while it is a source of stress to others. The researcher can observe respondents' particular reactions to the issues raised by the question.

The data obtained from surveys eventually has to be organised and quantified so that an overall view can be obtained. With a small pool of respondents this is usually not difficult, but it becomes a major exercise with a large sample pool. Closed questions, as we shall see, are simple to quantify, as all respondents are asked to respond in a strictly limited number of ways. With responses to open questions, however, the researcher must try to find patterns that can be meaningfully summarised.

Mirror questions

Another open search strategy, the mirror question, is useful in interview situations where a respondent has raised an issue but has not provided a clear resolution to it. A direct question from the researcher may, in some circumstances, provoke a defensive response. The mirror question is a more subtle way of drawing out the respondent by simply repeating the significant word or words:

> *Respondent:* I quite like the powder for hot water washes, but I always get that problem with the bubbles in cold water washes.

> *Researcher:* Bubbles?

> *Respondent:* Oh yes, I often find there are bubbles left in the machine, but not of course with synthetics.

Silence

Sometimes it may be useful to pause, rather than to go on to the next question. Respondents may indicate non-verbally that they are still thinking through the implications of what they have just said. Your silence relieves them from the pressure of finishing quickly and preparing for the next question. Of course, too long and the silence can discomfit them, so be alert to this.

Closed search strategies

Closed search strategies: approaches to creating primary data that restrict respondents to a limited range of responses

Closed search strategies restrict respondents to a limited range of responses. Although this can inhibit responses in some ways, it can also lead some people to respond in ways that they had not previously considered. Closed strategies are much easier to quantify than open strategies: many responses can be meaningfully aggregated with a minimum of effort.

Dichotomous questions

Dichotomous questions are questions to which there are only two answers (yes/no, agree/disagree, true/false). Care has to be taken to ensure that there really are only two alternative responses to every such question.

Rank order questions

With a rank order question, respondents are asked to place multiple alternatives in a sequence. For example:

> What influenced your decision to come to this college? Rank the following five items in order of most important (1) to least important (5).
>
> _____ The academic reputation of college is high.
>
> _____ My social life should improve.
>
> _____ The college is easy to get to.
>
> _____ The qualification I receive will help me get a job.
>
> _____ The flexibility of the program suits my lifestyle.

Again, it is important to consider whether the range of alternatives you provide is exhaustive. In this case, there may well be a sixth, seventh or thirty-fourth alternative that is the really important one. Of all the closed search strategies, the rank order question is the one that can most easily be adapted to give a measure of openness: thus, a blank alternative such as

> _____ Other (please specify in space provided)

might be added. This will provide quantification problems, of course, but the inconvenience of that quantification may well be a lesser evil than an inadequate range of choices.

Scale questions

Attitude or Likert scales permit respondents to position themselves at a point across a range. In contrast to the rank order question, the scale question requires the respondent to make only one choice. For example:

> The food in the bistro is of a high standard.

The respondent places a mark on the scale or continuum; it is simple for the researcher to collate the results from any number of responses.

Mixed search strategies

Many effective questionnaires take a mixed approach, using both open and closed questions. One technique which employs a mixed approach is the ' … or other' type of question.

' … or other' questions

This type of question lists a number of specific, or closed, options or choices, with a last, open option represented by the word 'other'. This strategy allows respondents to contribute their own viewpoints and choices, and also permits the range of options given to be less than exhaustive. Figure 3.11 shows part of a sample questionnaire.

---

1. Where do you normally have lunch? (tick one box)
   a. ❑ Company cafeteria
   b. ❑ Wellins Park
   c. ❑ Danny's Bistro
   d. ❑ Clean Food Company Health Foods
   e. ❑ Rose Street Subway
   f. ❑ Other (please specify venue and type of food)

   _____

   _____

FIGURE 3.11 Part of a sample questionnaire

2. Please rank in order of importance the factors that influence your choice of venue for lunch
(1 = most important; 2 = next most important and so on, until all factors are listed)
- ❏ Price
- ❏ Food quality
- ❏ Pleasant environment
- ❏ Music
- ❏ Variety of food
- ❏ Other (please specify) _____

3. If you have used the company cafeteria, how do you respond to this statement:

The food in the cafeteria is of quite a high standard.

| Strongly agree | Agree | Neutral | Disagree | Strongly disagree |

(Please place a cross on the scale showing your opinion.)

Collating data

The raw data you collect from a survey is relatively meaningless until it is analysed. First the results must be organised into meaningful categories, which can then be tabulated (see chapter 2). If you have designed your survey document well, you should be able to collate data from different questions in discrete categories. Tabulation and analysis can be done manually or using specialised computer software packages. If you are handling data manually, it is most easily aggregated using a tally sheet (figure 3.12) (Eunson 1994).

Question 1			
NO.	PLACE	TALLY	TOTAL
a.	Company café	ⅢⅢ |||	8
b.	Wellins Park	||||	4
c.	Danny's Bistro	ⅢⅢ	5
d.	Clean Food Company	ⅢⅢ |||	8
e.	Rose Street Subway	|||	3
f.	Other — eat at desk — don't have lunch — Beefeater pub			
		 ⅢⅢ	3 3 5
	No answer			1
	Total		40

FIGURE 3.12 Part of a tally sheet

Beware of confused responses resulting from respondents' misinterpretation of questions. It may be that you have written a confusing question. Note also questions that a number of respondents don't answer. Perhaps the question was inappropriate, potentially embarrassing or had some other negative connotation.

You may have to make some executive decisions. With open questions, it will help if you can see a pattern in the responses and can categorise them accordingly. You may also find that some respondents have answered in such a way that it is clear they have misinterpreted the question. You will have to decide whether simply to disregard these responses or to adjust them, honestly and professionally, to reflect what you believe would have been their likely response had they understood the question.

Testing your survey: don't open the show without a rehearsal

Pilot or test your survey with a small group of people before undertaking the full-scale exercise. You might be surprised to discover that some people find the wording of certain questions ambiguous, confusing, over-technical, patronising, insulting, meaningless or possessing meanings quite different to the meanings you thought you had communicated. You might discover that there are factual and typographical errors present. You might find that the layout of the survey document is not ideal — certain items are difficult to score or collate, other items require a lot of shuffling back and forth between pages, and so on. Consider using both 'expert' and 'naïve' testers (see chapter 2).

Introducing the survey

With questionnaires, it is always wise to attach some type of written explanation to the document. Such a cover letter should contain details about who you are and what the purpose of the exercise is: it should also motivate the respondent to respond. In other words, you have to show people what's in it for them. You might, for example, pose a question such as *How can completing this questionnaire help you?* and answer it yourself according to the nature of your survey. Some of the responses might include:

Pay scales may be revised upward.

Public transport schedules might be reclassified to take account of new passenger demands.

The café may begin to sell organic food if sufficient demand can be demonstrated.

Try to make the cover letter reasonably personalised, and not too mass-produced. Include details of how you can be contacted, should respondents need clarification on question wording or other matters. Few people make such contacts, but all people like to know that they can contact you if need be. Those few who do contact you may be a valuable source of feedback. If you are asking for information that in any way might be sensitive, give assurances about the confidentiality of the data.

When professional interviewers conduct interviews or administer questionnaires, they know it is important to ensure that they are as consistent as possible when interacting with large numbers of people. If an interviewer introduces a questionnaire or a sequence of interview questions in different ways to different people, then the responses may not be strictly comparable — in other words, distortion of data may occur. This effect can be overcome, or at least reduced, if a standard preamble or set of introductory remarks is created for interviewers. Such a preamble functions in a similar manner to a cover letter — the potential respondent finds out who is talking, what he or she wants, and why the respondent should bother cooperating.

Ensure that your sampling is accurate

When conducting surveys, you need to distinguish between a *sample* and a *population*. A *population* is understood here in a technical sense as meaning all people in a particular target group, while a *sample* is understood to mean a small part or fraction of that target group. If you want to find out the opinions of everyone in the marketing department, and there are 22 people in the department, if you survey all 22, then you have surveyed a population. If you want to find out the opinions of everyone in an organisation (or suburb, or state, or nation, or socioeconomic class, or the group of all red-haired, left-handed people), then it will probably be impractical to survey the population, and you will therefore have to survey a sample.

Sample size

Sample size is important. Generally speaking, the nearer your sample size approaches the size of the population, the more meaningful your results will be. Strive to get the biggest sample your budget and stamina will allow. Accurately calculating sample sizes and ensuring true randomness will involve some fairly complex number-crunching, but table 3.4 gives an idea of how large a sample needs to be in relation to a population to produce meaningful results. 'Meaningful' does not mean 100 per cent accuracy; it means 95 per cent accuracy – in other words, the data obtained from the sample has one chance in twenty of being an inaccurate reflection of the real situation within the population.

TABLE 3.4 Determining sample size for a given population

Population	Sample	Population	Sample
10	10	800	260
15	14	900	269
20	19	1 000	278
25	24	2 000	322
30	28	3 000	341
35	32	4 000	351
40	36	5 000	357
45	40	6 000	361
50	44	7 000	364
100	80	8 000	367
200	132	9 000	368
300	169	10 000	370
400	196	20 000	377
500	217	50 000	381
600	234	75 000	382
700	248	1 000 000	384

Source: Adapted from Sekaran and Bougie (2010).

Sample randomness

It is vital that your sample be typical of the population, rather than atypical. Your sample therefore needs to be what statisticians call a *random* sample; that is, one that is not biased or atypical in any way. Randomness can be achieved, or at least approximated, in a number of ways:

- Names of everyone in the population to be surveyed could be written on pieces of paper, placed in a container, mixed up, and then a number of these pieces could be drawn out. Or, you might interview every twentieth person who walks by a street corner.
- You might knock on the door of every fourteenth house of every street in a suburb.
- You might give a number to every person in your population, and then consult a list of random numbers in a mathematics or statistical textbook, reading off the numbers in the list to select the numbers from your population.

Sample stratification

You might need to *stratify* your sample. For example, say you wished to conduct a survey in an organisation of 1000 people, and that organisation had three major divisions: Division A (300 staff), Division B (500 staff) and Division C (200 staff). If you wanted to sample 10 per cent of the entire organisation, it would make sense to work with three strata or sections of 10 per cent or 100 people: 30 from Division A, 50 from Division B, and 20 from Division C. Respondents within those strata or sub-samples could then be randomly selected. Stratification in this or other situations could also be based upon factors such as age, sex, income and geography.

Convenience sampling and judgement sampling

Convenience sampling: asking questions of whoever happens to be available when data is required, with no guarantee that those asked will be typical of the broader population

Judgement sampling: asking questions of experts rather than people who have been randomly sampled

Two non-statistical methods of sampling should be mentioned – convenience sampling and judgement sampling. **Convenience sampling** means simply asking questions of whoever happens to be available. For example, you may ask members of your own workplace department what they think about a range of issues. But your colleagues might be a quite atypical sample of the population of the workplace. Convenience sampling, therefore, while usually quick, convenient and cheap, is also often misleading.

Judgement sampling means asking questions of experts rather than people who have been randomly sampled. For example, if you wanted to obtain detailed information about workplace accidents rather than the distribution of accidents throughout the population under consideration, it might be better to go straight to those people who are known to have had accidents rather than seek out a random sample of the population. Experts are not always right, but sometimes they are the first logical source of data.

STUDENT STUDY GUIDE

SUMMARY

In this chapter we examined the major sources of research information – primary, secondary and tertiary data. We learned that good researchers need to be able to exploit the strengths of both paper-based and electronic resources. We explored different approaches to research using library catalogues, databases and the internet. We considered approaches to note taking and learned about different paper and electronic methods of referencing our sources. We learned the critical distinctions between legitimate citing of sources, paraphrasing and plagiarism and biblio-dumping. Finally, we investigated differing approaches to creating our own primary data through conducting surveys and questionnaires using open, closed and mixed research strategies.

KEY TERMS

biblio-dumping *p. 97*
closed search
  strategies *p. 101*
convenience sampling *p. 106*
database *p. 84*
Dewey decimal classification
  system *p. 80*
documentary-note
  system *p. 94*

Harvard system *p. 92*
judgement sampling *p. 106*
Library of Congress
  classification system *p. 80*
literature search or
  survey *p. 79*
metacrawler *p. 86*
open search strategies *p. 100*
paraphrasing *p. 98*

plagiarism *p. 96*
primary data *p. 78*
secondary data *p. 78*
tactile thinking *p. 89*
tertiary data *p. 78*
thesis statement *p. 77*
Vancouver *p. 94*

REVIEW QUESTIONS

1. Name three types of data collected in the research process.
2. What are three limitations of electronic data?
3. What is a metacrawler?
4. What are the main differences between documentary-note citation and Harvard or author–date citation?
5. What is tactile thinking?
6. How does plagiarism differ from paraphrasing?
7. What are the advantages of URL compactors like tiny url, bit.li or doiop?
8. What is open about an open search strategy?
9. Name two advantages of using open '… or other' questions.
10. What might be the strengths and weaknesses of judgement sampling?

APPLIED ACTIVITIES

1. Create a plan for researching the market potential of a new product. What secondary and primary research might be necessary? Render your search strategy as a diagram or flowchart.
2. Pick out two topics that interest you. Using a library catalogue, locate books about these topics. Either by yourself or with a librarian's assistance, determine why the books have been given the call numbers they have. Determine whether other sources of data (periodicals, theses, government publications and so on) have the same call numbers, or whether they have been classified in a different way.
3. Either by yourself or with a librarian's assistance, undertake a database search to locate articles in periodicals.

4. Find an article, chapter or section of a book referenced in a particular style (e.g. Harvard or documentary-note). Photocopy it. Using a coloured pen, re-edit the piece applying a different style of referencing. Rewrite the article by hand or via a keyboard using the different system. Which do you think is the better referencing system? Why?

5. Create a simple ten-question questionnaire on a topic you are familiar with. Use:
   (a) two open questions
   (b) two dichotomous questions
   (c) two rank questions without an 'other' option
   (d) two rank questions with an 'other' option
   (e) two scale questions.

   You may place these in whatever sequence you choose. What advantages and disadvantages are there in constructing a questionnaire according to such a formula?

6. Create a tally sheet for the questionnaire. What problems might there be in tallying different types of data, and how could these problems be overcome?

7. Design a sample for the questionnaire. What considerations will guide you?

8. Test the questionnaire. What modifications (if any) need to be made? Why?

WHAT WOULD YOU DO?

You supervise a department that produces all publications for your organisation. Today, Charlie Vance of the legal department telephones you. 'Are you aware that our new brochure for the LD-90 model has wording that is lifted straight from a website of Golem Inc., our chief competitor?' That can't be right, you reply. Your people are completely professional – they wouldn't do that. Charlie persists: 'Golem not only are threatening legal action, but also plan to hold a media conference, comparing the two texts. If they can make a case, they'll humiliate us in the marketplace, make us a laughing stock. This could lose us some of our biggest customers! Check it out as a top priority, ok?' Of course, you say yes. You walk across to the office of Manny Tone, the copy-writer for the brochure in question. You ask him if all the copy was his, or did he get some from other sources? 'It's mainly my stuff,' he says, 'but I checked out our competitors, as you suggested we do at last month's staff meeting. But don't worry – it's ok: I swiped some stuff from an obscure Golem website, and then rewrote it completely in our style. Is there a problem?'

How will you respond to Manny and Charlie?

SUGGESTED READING

Garrison, D Randy 2011, *E-Learning in the 21st century: a framework for research and practice*, 2nd edn., Routledge, London/New York.

Northey, Margot 2010, *Making sense: a student's guide to research and writing*, 6th edn., Oxford University Press, USA.

Saris, Willem E & Galhofer, Irmtraud N 2008, *Design, evaluation, and analysis of questionnaires for survey research*, John Wiley & Sons, New York.

Style manual for authors, editors and printers 2002, 6th edn, rev. Snooks & Co., John Wiley & Sons, Brisbane.

Turabian, Kate L, Williams, Joseph M, Colomb, Gregory G, and Booth, Wayne C. 2007, *A manual for writers of research papers, theses, and dissertations: Chicago style for students and researchers*, 7th edn., University of Chicago Press.

Woods, Geraldine 2002, *Research papers for dummies*, John Wiley & Sons, New York.

REFERENCES

Buranen, Lise 1999, '"But I wasn't cheating": plagiarism and cross-cultural mythology', in Lise Buranen and Alice M Roy (eds.), *Perspectives on plagiarism and intellectual property in a postmodern world*, State University of New York Press, New York.

Chandler, Daniel 1992, 'The phenomenology of writing by hand', *Intelligent Tutoring Media*, vol. 3, no. 2/3, pp. 65–74.

Department of Education, Science and Training 2002, 'Employability skills for the future', www.dest.gov.au, DEST, Canberra.

DeVoss, Danielle & Rosati, Annette C 2002, '"It wasn't me, was it?" Plagiarism and the web', *Computers and Composition*, vol. 19, pp. 191–203.

Eunson 1994, *Communicating for team building*, John Wiley & Sons, Brisbane.

Howard, Rebecca Moore 2007, 'Understanding "internet plagiarism"', *Computers and Composition*, vol. 24, no. 1, pp. 3–15.

Kralik, Debbie & van Loon, Antonia (eds.) 2011, *Community nursing in Australia*, 2nd edn., John Wiley & Sons, Brisbane.

Uma, Sekaran & Bougie, Roger 2010, *Research methods for business: a skill building approach*, 5th edn., John Wiley & Sons, New York.

4

Letters, emails and memos

LEARNING OBJECTIVES

After studying this chapter you should be able to:

- Discern when to write letters and when to use other channels of communication
- Apply the 8 Cs of written communication
- Identify the merits of direct versus indirect approaches in writing
- Explain factors involved in the layout of letters
- Create effective good news letters
- Create effective bad news letters
- Write effective persuasive letters
- Write effective emails and memos

Who's writing what?

To state the obvious, we live in a time of rapid change, as is clearly seen in the world of communication. In a relatively short historic time, older forms of communication, such as letters and memos, have been challenged by newer forms, such as emails and social media, including texting and forums such as Facebook and Twitter (see chapter 21). 'Challenge', however, does not mean 'defeat', and just as surely as radio was not 'defeated' by television, or television by video recordings and DVDs, so too letters and memos have not been defeated by emails and Twitter. We choose the medium of communication that will maximise the strengths and minimise the weaknesses of that medium.

Letters: when, why and how

Letters are one of a number of genres we use as communicators. As we have just noted, with the rise of email, it is commonplace to hear about 'the death of letter writing' in relation to both personal and professional communication. In spite of this, the letter is still very much alive, primarily because its advantages still outweigh its disadvantages (figure 4.1).

Advantages	Disadvantages
■ **Official status:** A letter, especially on letterhead, will be taken more seriously than a fax or email by many recipients. ■ **Touch and keep:** A letter can be handled, filed and stored without loss of quality. ■ **The personal touch:** A signed or handwritten letter carries more weight and consequence for many recipients than a fax, email or telephone call. ■ **Slow delivery:** The weakness of relatively slow delivery can be a strength if the creation process leads us to take more care in the message's production, putting more thought into the words, ideas, grammar, punctuation and style on the page.	■ **Time cost:** It takes longer to plan, draft, write, edit and send a letter, via mail or courier, than to use email. ■ **Financial cost:** Letters involve costs in labour, materials (printed letterhead is costly), postage/delivery costs, and creation and storage of copies. ■ **Slow delivery:** Letters sent via 'snail mail' involve longer delivery times than faxes or emails. ■ **Slow response:** A rapid response to a situation may be required, and a letter may be simply too slow when compared with email.

FIGURE 4.1 Advantages and disadvantages of letters as a channel of communication

Technologies change, and while we may become bewitched by some to the exclusion of others, certain principles of communication remain constant. Table 4.1 sets out the 8 Cs of written communication.

TABLE 4.1 The 8 Cs of written communication

As writers, we need to be …	How?
1. Clear	■ The document should send a plain and unambiguous message. ■ It should not confuse or patronise the recipient. ■ It should aim to prevent or fix, not cause, communication breakdowns.
2. Correct	■ The message should contain no factual errors. ■ All words, especially proper names, should be correctly spelt. ■ Grammar and punctuation should be perfect.
3. Comprehensive	■ The message should include all critical information. ■ The recipient should not need to seek clarification because the writer made assumptions about the recipient's knowledge.
4. Concise	■ The message should be only as long as it needs to be. ■ The message should be only as complex as it needs to be.

As writers, we need to be ...	How?
5. Credible	■ The message should be conveyed in a professional way. ■ Any opinions should be supported by facts.
6. Considerate	■ The message should reflect the **'you' attitude** (i.e. a concern for the reader's needs and interests, rather than the writer's). The 'you' attitude is: 　■ polite — demonstrating good manners and tact 　■ practical — answering the recipient's question 'What's in it for me?' (i.e. it gives the recipient an incentive to respond to, rather than ignore, the message) (see online chapter 5).
7. Courteous	■ The message should reflect respectful and civilised values. ■ It should not give the reader cause to take offence or to take legal or retaliatory action.
8. Conscientious	■ The message should meet the highest ethical standards. ■ It should contain no material unethically taken from other sources.

'You' attitude: approach to writing that prioritises the needs and interests of the reader

Approaches to writing letters

Different approaches may be taken when writing letters, depending on their purpose. For example, it's useful to distinguish between direct and indirect approaches to the topic (table 4.2). Each pattern has its strengths and weaknesses. The direct approach in a business letter is appropriate, for example, when we are able to give our readers what they want, while a more indirect approach might be taken when we are unable to do so or when conditions apply. We need to keep the direct/indirect distinction in mind when creating documents for different situations and recipients.

TABLE 4.2 Direct and indirect patterns of letter organisation

Pattern	Approach	Strengths	Weaknesses
Direct	States primary message right away	■ Quick ■ Honest ■ Straightforward	■ Can seem abrupt ■ Can alienate reader before writer has time to convey other messages
Indirect	Leads gradually towards primary message, which is couched within a sequence of minor messages	■ Can be a sensitive way of preparing reader for bad news ■ Can be used to convey other messages before primary message	■ Can lead to waffle, evasion ■ Can be seen as dishonest, manipulative

Before we turn to some of the techniques involved in composing letters, we will briefly look at matters of process — presentation, layout, formatting or information design, and conventions of wording and expression.

The elements of a letter

There are various parts to a letter that you need to know about. Some of these parts are essential, while others are optional (table 4.3; see overleaf). What is 'essential' and what is 'optional', however, tends to vary from organisation to organisation. House style — 'the way we do things around here' — is everything in these matters. Conventions develop over time and vary according to place: 'what everyone around here knows is correct form' will vary considerably according to whether we are in London in 1955, Singapore in 1995, Los Angeles in 2005 or Adelaide in 2025. People within organisations are usually unaware of the uniqueness (or dysfunctionality) of house style until:

- someone decides it would be a good idea to write a house style manual
- the organisation merges with another and is confronted with a different culture and conventions that differ slightly or radically
- technological changes prompt writers to challenge current conventions.

TABLE 4.3 Essential and optional parts of a letter

Essential	Optional
Sender's address	Subject line
Date	Attention line
Recipient's name and address	Security heading
Salutation	Reference details
Body of letter	Document initials
Close	Sender's contact details
Signature block	Enclosure details
	Copy details
	Headers/footers

Much of this section on document conventions is concerned with details. Details can be boring, but when writers get one or several details wrong, the impact and effectiveness of the document may be compromised. Attention to, or neglect of, detail sends out a message of its own, separate from but linked to the main content of the communication, and it's not a good message.

Laying out a letter using a word processor conceals a conflict between differing systems of paper sizes and measuring systems. For example, most people now use A4 size paper for letters, usually with default margins of 2.54 cm. A4 is a metric paper size measuring 21 cm (210 mm) × 29.7 cm (297 mm). The margin of 2.54 cm, however, is a simple conversion of the imperial measure of one inch. Although most of the world now uses the metric SI (*Système International [d'Unités]*, or International System [of Units]) paper size system developed by the International Standards Organisation, the US tends to stick with imperial measures, and most word processors are made in the US (Nationmaster.com 2011). It is a tradition in the US (as it was in most of the English-speaking world) to use margins of one inch — hence the default setting in word processors. Note that margins can also be set in other units, such as picas and points. Note also that you can set any margins you choose, according to the layout or document design effect you are trying to achieve. Margins, of course, will need to be adjusted if letterhead is used. Letterhead — paper carrying a preprinted heading giving the organisation's name together with full address and contact details — is primarily a form of marketing and corporate image making. It is also relatively expensive to produce. For these reasons, most individuals don't use letterhead in personal communications (although some choose to have a personal letterhead printed to emphasise individuality and style).

On letterhead the sender's details (name, addresses and other organisational information) are usually printed at the top of the page and centred, with the date entered at top left. In personal letters on nonletterhead the sender's details are usually positioned at the top right, 3 cm to 4 cm from the top, with the date beneath (figure 4.2).

1. Letterhead: contains sender's details	**CLEAN FOOD COMPANY Ltd.** 32 Ozone Way, Seaspray Park 8902 Telephone 06.4921.3200 Facsimile 06.4921.3201 www.cleanfood.com[1]
2. Date	
	14 August 2012[2]
3. Recipient's name and address	Dr Martita Clemens, Chief Executive Officer, Acme Warehousing Systems, 6 Enterprise Court, SEASPRAY PARK 8901[3]
4. Salutation	Dear Dr Clemens:[4]
	CLEAN FOOD AT ACME?[5]
	Congratulations on moving into the Seaspray Coast Industry Park.
5. Subject line	Setting up a new operation means many worries and challenges, so food catering may not be your top priority at the moment.
	However, when you have time to breathe, I urge you to think about getting your meals custom catered through Clean Food Company. Ten other businesses in Seaspray do, and they are all happy with the service we provide. Five of these companies are big enough to have their own cafés, but choose to outsource their food and drink requirements through us.
	So what do we provide? I attach a list and brochure of our wares, but, in brief, we can supply you and your staff with cost-effective and nutritious food, 24 hours a day, seven days a week if needed.
6. Body of letter	Just imagine being able to choose from a variety of hot and cold foods at any time — and what foods! Our specialties include gourmet hamburgers, sushi, wholemeal pizza, cashew loaf, soy salads, fruit smoothies, exotic fruit salads, 32 varieties of cakes and biscuits, and 15 types of coffee and tea. Over 50 per cent of our food and drink is organic in origin, and over 80 per cent is from nongenetically modified sources. We also go easy on the sugar, fat and salt.
7. Close	We can provide biodegradable, use-only-once plates, cups and utensils, or full-grade crockery, glassware and utensils, which we clean for you. We can cater into your premises, or your people can simply walk to one of our food wagons, which are stationed throughout Seaspray at various times of the day. You can order a custom menu for one or one hundred just by ringing us or logging on to our website. Most people spend less than ten dollars a day on a main meal plus dessert, and many use us for morning and afternoon breaks, as well as shift work meals. Need multiple courses of fine foods, with wines, silver service and waiting staff for entertaining your special clients? Not a problem.
	Don't take my word for it, though. I'm biased! Talk to our satisfied clients and find out what they think. I attach a list of our contacts at businesses in Seaspray. I also enclose 20 ten-dollar-value tokens, which can be used at any of our wagons. Enjoy!
8. Signature block	Please ring me if you have any queries about Clean Food Company's operation. I hope you find Seaspray is exactly what you need to make your business thrive.[6]
	Yours sincerely,[7]
9. Document initials	*Charlie Renton*[8]
	Charlie Renton, Manager
10. Enclosure details	CM/zr[9] Encs. Price list, brochure, Contacts list, 20 × tokens[10]

FIGURE 4.2 Elements of a professional or letterhead letter

Using the model letter in figure 4.2, let's analyse the various parts of letters.

Sender's address

The sender's address should include street name and number, or post office box or private bag number, suburb/city and postcode or other coding details required by postal authorities. If the letter is being sent interstate or overseas, state and national details should be included.

If you are using letterhead, then the address and contact details are already given.

Date

Confusion sometimes arises about appropriate date styles, as varying conventions apply in different parts of the world. As global communication increases, professional communicators increasingly encounter different forms and conventions. Thus, the date style '11-12-13' can mean different things to different people (table 4.4).

TABLE 4.4 Variations in dating systems

System	Countries using	'11-12-13' means
year-month-day	China, Japan, Korea, Hungary, Sweden	The thirteenth day of December, 2011
month-day-year	United States	The twelfth day of November, 2013
day-month-year	United Kingdom, Australia, New Zealand, France	The eleventh day of December, 2013

The International Standard ISO 8601 gives preference to the year-month-day (yyyy-mm-dd) system, but with the full year given, numbers less than ten starting with a zero, and separation made by dashes (e.g. '2009-08-07' means the seventh day of August, 2009). This helps avoid day/month confusion and establish that 2009 and not 1909 is meant. The simplest way of avoiding such confusion, of course, is to write out the date in full (e.g. '7 August 2009' or '11 December, 2013').

Recipient's name and address

The recipient's name and address are placed below the date, normally on the left-hand side of the page. In some cases a courtesy title or honorific will precede (Mr, Ms, Dr) or follow (MD, PhD, Esq., MP) the name (see figure 4.3). Role titles usually take capitals for major words.

Abbreviated courtesy titles or honorifics	Role titles
Mr, Ms, Mrs, Master, Dr, Professor, Monsignor, The Right Honourable, Reverend, Rabbi, Senator MD, PhD, Esq., MP	Coordinator of Student Activities Manager, Operations Team Facilitator Pastoral Care Advisor Minister for the Environment

FIGURE 4.3 Abbreviated courtesy titles/honorifics and role titles

Accuracy in relation to titles, names and addresses is vital. This is not only because accuracy will help a letter reach its destination, but because people are very sensitive about their personal details — they do not appreciate it when correspondents are careless over these particulars. This is especially true for people with unusual names; so when in doubt, check. (Remember that, like dates, name sequences vary from culture to culture.) Think about how you feel when you receive a document that:

- gets your courtesy title wrong
- gets your gender wrong
- misspells your name

- confuses your first name with your last name
- gets your role title wrong.

Don't hesitate to make a simple telephone enquiry to confirm these personal details. Any possible embarrassment or inconvenience this may cause you is more than outweighed by the positive impact that your having taken the trouble to get it right has upon your reader. You have passed the first test: you have shown courtesy, consideration and care. You may well be the only correspondent this week or month to have done so.

Similarly, if a courtesy title is appropriate and your reader is female, find out whether she prefers to be addressed as Ms, Miss or Mrs. Alternatively, avoid such titles altogether. If unsure of the gender of the target reader, or the cultural conventions governing the name sequence, use the full name (e.g. 'Dear Lee Hoh').

Salutation

Whether or not the person you are writing to is the object of your affection, it is conventional to open letters with the salutation 'Dear [*name*]'. If your relationship is formal, or if this is the first time you have communicated, use the recipient's surname or family name. Once you have some familiarity or rapport it is usual to use personal or given name. If unsure of the reader's gender, use the (only partly satisfactory) greeting 'Dear Sir/Madam' or 'Dear Madam/Sir'.

Body of letter

The body of the letter contains the substance of the communication – your message. Its style and structure are largely determined by the kind of letter you are sending. Various types of letters are discussed in this chapter.

Close

Closes, or complimentary closes, are a way of terminating your letter with courtesy. Again, the wording you choose will vary according to the situation, and the tone appropriate to that situation (figure 4.4). As with the salutation, you may feel slightly uncomfortable or even hypocritical in using the customary forms, especially to people who are not dear to you and for whom you have no sincere, faithful, respectful or true feelings. Unless you wish to dispense with such customs, however, you should persevere, seeing salutations and closes as marks of respect and civility in a world too often devoid of these qualities.

Signature block

The signature block contains the writer's signature. In business correspondence, it is usual to place this above the typed name (and title) of the writer. Sometimes a secretary or colleague may be empowered to sign on the writer's behalf. In these cases, this person signs:
1. the writer's name
2. the initials *p.p.* (Latin for *per procurationem*, meaning 'by proxy')
3. his or her own name.

Use this convention only when necessary. In some situations (e.g. when the letter is personal or its impact profound), your reader may interpret this signature convention negatively ('He's so arrogant and insensitive he won't even take the time to write it himself').

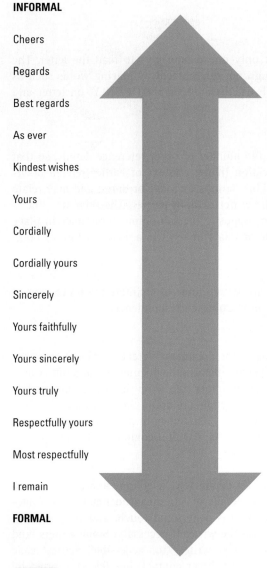

INFORMAL

Cheers

Regards

Best regards

As ever

Kindest wishes

Yours

Cordially

Cordially yours

Sincerely

Yours faithfully

Yours sincerely

Yours truly

Respectfully yours

Most respectfully

I remain

FORMAL

FIGURE 4.4 Continuum of informal to formal closes

Sources: Adapted from Chesterton (1992, p. 147); Blake and Bly (1992, p. 129); Wilson and Wauson (2011).

Subject line

The subject line is a way of instantly telling the reader what the letter is about. It is placed between the salutation and the body, and is sometimes underlined or set in a different font. Email software packages have successfully borrowed this print document convention. Make sure the subject line accurately describes the message's content. Treat it as if you were writing a headline for a news story – to get your reader's attention without misrepresenting the message.

Attention line

In a large organisation it is not always clear who should handle a particular piece of correspondence. An attention line (e.g. 'ATTENTION: JOE SMITH') is a way of increasing the probability of the letter reaching the right person. It is also useful if the role or position of the reader is the more significant factor (e.g. 'ATTENTION: STATIONERY PURCHASING MANAGER'). Attention lines are often centred and set in a highlighted font – italics, bold or underlined.

Security heading

Occasionally a writer wishes to ensure that only one person gets to read the letter. The probability of this can be maximised (although not guaranteed) by placing words such as 'PRIVATE AND CONFIDENTIAL' or 'FOR THE EYES OF JANE SMITH ONLY' on letter and envelope.

Reference details

It is sometimes useful to mention a specific file number or other reference details, so that the reader can place the current communication in the context of earlier related documents. These details may take the form of abbreviations or codes or dates, and may relate to a reference system used by the reader, the writer or both parties. The reference line is normally placed above the body and after or opposite the salutation, sometimes in place of the subject line. It is common to underline this data or set it in a different font or both:

Your Ref. As/ceZZ/2. Our Ref. QWE/04

The subject, attention and reference lines are simple tools to facilitate the processing of information and are particularly convenient in ongoing correspondence.

Document initials

A common convention is to place the initials of the document's creator or creators at the bottom left-hand corner of each page. If one person dictates the document and another produces it, the initials of the principal are often set in upper case, with the typist's initials following in lower case (e.g. 'CFR/sw'). Increasingly, people are doing their own keyboarding, and this means that they will either dispense with this altogether, or place their own initials in the conventional lower left position, together perhaps with a computer file name.

Sender's contact details

Senders will sometimes include their own contact details (e.g. telephone and fax extension numbers, email address, mobile number). Such details in letterhead documents are sometimes placed just below the signature block. This is a personal touch, and readers often appreciate the fact that they can quickly contact the writer if necessary. Some writers (and organisations) are loath to do this, as it might make writers 'too accessible'. Setting aside the fact that most recipients do not actually make direct contact (but feel comforted by the fact that they could if they wanted to), it should perhaps be asked just what is wrong with the culture of an organisation that feels that it is indeed possible to be 'too accessible'.

Enclosure details

If other documents are attached or enclosed in the envelope, it is conventional to alert the reader to this fact with an abbreviation ('Enc.' or 'Encs.') in the lower left-hand corner of the last page of the letter. Sometimes a brief description of the enclosed material is added. With email, additional materials are usually called attachments.

Copy details

If copies of the current document are being distributed to others, it is conventional to indicate this using the abbreviation *c.c.* (for 'carbon copy', a reference to the days when copies were made using carbon sheets in typewriters), followed by the names of those receiving copies (e.g. 'c.c.: John Shana, Lara Maxton').

Occasionally blind copies of a document are made. This means that copies are distributed without the knowledge of the person to whom the document is addressed. In this case, the initials *b.c.* or *b.c.c.* are added to the copies, although not to the original. Again, email packages provide for this feature.

Be careful when using blind copies. If the principal reader is alerted to their existence by the writer's inadvertence, it can make a very poor impression. It may often be safer simply to photocopy the document to send to your confidential audience.

Headers/footers

Occasionally writers will include a header or footer (an identifying line at the top or bottom of the page) on each page. These are particularly useful if the document is long. They may contain a coded summary of the content, the date, the writer's name and the page number. A typical header or footer might look like this:

> Smythe insurance claim/4 May 2011/p. 2

A header or footer will not usually be included on the first page of printed letterhead.

Letter formats

Full block format: layout style in which all elements of a letter are justified to the left margin

The format used in letters is sometimes determined by an organisation's house style, which in turn reflects a consensus or officially prescribed perception of what 'looks good'. The major formats are given in table 4.5.

TABLE 4.5 Common letter formats

Format	Features	Remarks
Full block	Each line begins at the left margin (i.e. it is left justified). This includes date, address and signature details. **Full block format** can be typed rapidly, because the typist simply has to start from where the return or cursor is automatically placed after each line is completed.	Some dislike full block because (to their eyes) the document seems to lean to the left — in other words, it looks visually unbalanced.
Modified block	The date, close and signature block are centred. Full justification (words spaced to fill entire line) may be used to avoid perception of 'lop-sided' left justification.	Some believe this looks more balanced. Others prefer the simpler look of the full block. Centring is an automatic option with word processing software.
Traditional	Similar to full block or modified block, except that the first line of each paragraph is indented about 4–6 letter spaces.	Vertical spacing between paragraph blocks often not used. More text can, therefore, be fitted onto a page, but it can look cramped.
Simplified	Similar to full block, with all lines left justified. The salutation and close are dropped, however, with emphasis falling on the subject line.	Clean and modern to some eyes, especially writers uncomfortable with traditional salutation and closes. To other eyes, however, it can seem impersonal. Often uses open punctuation.

Paragraphing

Some writers prefer to mark the beginning of a new paragraph by indenting from the left margin, while others prefer to leave the new paragraph flush with the left margin, but separated from the previous paragraph by a line space. Some choose to combine these approaches, although this duplication tends to annoy some readers.

Punctuation

A letter writer using a traditional punctuation style will include commas after each line of name and address details, full stops or periods after abbreviations, and a comma or colon after the salutation. The open punctuation style dispenses with these punctuation marks, while sometimes maintaining normal punctuation in the body (figure 4.5). Some writers choose to mix traditional and open punctuation styles (see online chapter 2).

Traditional punctuation	Open punctuation
Dr. J. A. Smith,	Dr J A Smith
44, Carroll's Way,	44 Carroll's Way
Middletown, 7451	Middletown 7451
Dear Dr. Smith:	Dear Dr Smith

FIGURE 4.5 Traditional versus open punctuation

With traditional punctuation, opinions vary as to whether the opening salutation should be followed by a comma or a colon. Generally speaking, US usage has been to use a comma in an informal letter or note ('Dear Betty,') and a colon for a formal business letter, with a comma for the close ('Yours sincerely,') (Troyka & Hesse 2010). The UK/Commonwealth usage has been to use a comma after the salutation, irrespective of whether the letter is formal or informal, and a comma after the close. Both systems use an uppercase letter for the first part of the close, and a lowercase letter for the second word in the close ('Yours sincerely,/faithfully,/truly,'). These 'rules' have grown up haphazardly over the centuries, and there is not much logic behind any of them ('proper style' would have us write 'Dear Mr Hitler,' when he is by no means dear to us). That does not mean that the person you are writing to will not become upset if the conventions they have followed for a long time are ignored in your letter, which perhaps explains why the simplified form of letter layout has not been wildly popular. The conventions adopted here are US ones, with a colon adopted for the opening, but use what style you feel might match the expectations of your audience.

Letter look: corporate identity and marketing tool

Many organisations take the look of their correspondence, both external and internal, very seriously. They believe — not without justification — that the appearance of their correspondence sends powerful messages about the professionalism of the organisation. House style guides for employees are designed to introduce a consistent standard to all correspondence.

ASSESS YOURSELF

1. Collect a range of letters — business correspondence, junk mail and so on. Analyse them in terms of the various elements we have considered. How effective are they? If you were to reformat them, what changes would you make?
2. If you ran your own business, or held a position within an organisation, how would you choose to lay out your letters? What formatting, paragraphing and punctuation would you use? Why?

Letters: the message

We have considered various letter formats. Now let's explore some different categories of business letters.

Routine messages

Organisations have developed a number of ways of conveying routine messages to customers or clients. These include form letters, postcards, acknowledgement slips, and the 'compliments' slip or business card that accompanies pamphlets, brochures or other promotional literature. Form or 'canned' letters are standard letters fitting into a template that are 'personalised' via word processing software. Sometimes this process is undetectable; at other times, particularly in much 'junk' or 'spam' mail, it is all too detectable. Many people don't ordinarily appreciate receiving junk or canned letters, so such communications often do more damage than good to the organisation that sends them. Why do organisations persist in using such means? Simple: it's cheaper (or it appears to be cheaper): it costs the organisation time and money to personalise letters to prospective customers or clients, or even to modify a form letter.

The nonroutine: giving the news

Nonroutine letters are often sent in situations in which routine replies are not expected. Again, these documents cost time and money, but if they are well designed, this investment will pay off. This is because, in a real sense, *every letter is a sales letter*. That is, every document that an organisation sends out is a marketing tool for that organisation, conveying more than the mere facts of the communication. For example, it sends a message about whether the organisation is courteous or rude, competent or derelict, up to date or obsolete. So there is no such thing as 'just a letter': letters can make or break the good name of an organisation or individual.

Good news letters

Good news letter: a letter in which the writer conveys news that the reader will probably be happy to read

Bad news letter: a letter in which the writer conveys news that the reader will probably not be happy to read

Good news letters convey positive messages to readers (we can help you), while bad news letters convey negative messages. **Bad news letters** are often more challenging to write, but that does not mean good news letters cannot be written badly.

Good news: using the direct approach

The ideal structure of the good news letter is as follows:

- Give the good news right away.
- Background the good news; if appropriate, use the letter to promote other products or services of the organisation.
- Close in an upbeat way.

Applying an indirect structure by burying the good news within other material risks irritating the reader. This irritation is compounded if the writing style is obscure or waffly. Overlong business letters of this type are usually ineffective (figure 4.6).

Be wary, however, of committing the opposite sin − that of being direct to the point of abruptness, failing to place the message in context, and therefore communicating ineffectively because too few words are used − not so much 'plain English' as 'pain English'.

Opening words thanking the reader for his or her letter, phone call, fax, email or other communication are not simply ritual courtesies (although in the modern world such courtesy has much to recommend it); they remind the reader of the nature of the original enquiry. This is not to suggest readers are idiots who need to be reminded of everything they have written or said. The point is they may have made five, ten or 50 enquiries within a week, on numerous matters, to many organisations and individuals. It is inappropriate and potentially confusing, then, to respond as though in a real-time conversation.

Ineffective opening: too wordy	Effective opening	Ineffective opening: too brief

'Dear...
Thank you for your valued letter of the 19th inst. It is always a pleasure to hear from our customers, and your letter was no exception. Since the foundation of this august institution in 1895, customer service has been our watchword.
    I refer to your letter, in which you ask whether we at Protector Insurance allow incremental or fractional payments of premiums. We calculate our premiums according to various formulae...'
	'Dear...
	Thank you for your letter of 19 June, in which you enquire whether Protector offers alternatives to single annual premiums.
	    Yes, we do offer a range of payment options. These are...'
		'Dear...
		Yes, we do offer monthly payment of premiums. Details are in the attached brochure.'

FIGURE 4.6 Ineffective and effective openings

Indeed, there is no guarantee that the letter will be opened by the person who made the first contact. In some organisations, it is standard practice for one individual – someone in the mail office or central registry, a secretary, a personal or administrative assistant – to open mail addressed to another person.

The introductory comments, therefore, should briefly orientate the reader to the issue at hand, before setting out the substantive message. The writer who neglects this introduction may be perceived as discourteous, impatient, rude or simply disorganised.

An effective way of reconciling the need to orientate the reader with the need to convey the good news as soon as possible is to use a subject line:

Dear...

Your letter 19 June: Protector premium rates

Yes, we do offer monthly payment of premiums...

Bringing good news: what not to do

Good news should be conveyed with speed, empathy and good grace. Such messages can be compromised by:

- lateness
- communication of the writer's boredom or lack of empathy
- communication of resentment or a grudging attitude.

Bad and good examples of a good news letter are provided in figures 4.7 and 4.8.

1. Self-centred approach: 'we' attitude, not 'you' attitude

2. Suspicious, hostile attitude — inference that the customer is wrong

3. No preamble identifying what situation is

4. Detail that is irrelevant to customer

5. Finally, the good news — expressed abruptly, ungraciously

CLONE POWER

Suite 39, Rintrah Industrial Park Claymore 23121 Freedonia
Telephone (61[5]) 1233.4352 Facsimile (61[5] 1233.4354
www.clonepower.com Customer service info@clonepower.com

March 14, 2011

Ms Monica Zalecki,
Supervisor,
Administration Services,
Cogito University,
Smithfield 20114

Dear Ms Zalecki:

[1]We often get complaints from customers, although very few of them, we find, have any foundation.[2]

We subjected your *Quill* packages to intensive scrutiny, with two software engineers working on it for four hours to determine whether the packages were in the same condition as they were when they left our premises.[3] We installed the packages onto four machines we keep especially for this purpose (each machine has a particular combination of hardware and operating system faults). Two of the machines replicated the faults you described in your letter (files lock up after 33,000 bytes, endnotes are unstable), while two did not.[4] We then installed the packages on two new, optimally functioning machines, and found that the faults appeared intermittently.

Your cheque for $1296.00 is enclosed. Please ensure that it is banked within 5 working days.[5]

Yours sincerely,

Malcolm Bickstaff,
Service Manager

Enc.

FIGURE 4.7 An ineffective good news letter

CLONE POWER

Suite 39, Rintrah Industrial Park Claymore 23121 Freedonia
Telephone (61[5]) 1233.4352 Facsimile (61[5] 1233.4354
www.clonepower.com   Customer service info@clonepower.com

March 14, 2011

Ms Monica Zalecki,
Supervisor,
Administration Services,
Cogito University,
Smithfield 20114

Dear Ms Zalecki:

Thank you for your letter of 3 February, enclosed with the four copies of our *Quill* multi-user word processing package.

I am pleased to offer you two options:[1]

(1) A refund cheque for $1296.00

(2) Replacement copies of your Quill packages, all four having been bench-tested by our software engineers, together with 12 months' free on-line help on our *Quill* toll-free number.[2]

The replacement copies or the cheque will be sent to you, by courier, at no charge to you. Just ring me direct at 1500.419.2331 and tell me how I can best help you.

The faults discovered by you were most extraordinary, and will help us to refine Version 3.3, scheduled for release in June. (Should you choose to accept replacement copies of the Version 3.2 packages, we will give you free upgrades.)[3]

I apologise for the delays in your workload that have been caused by this glitch.[4]

In your letter you mentioned that one of the faults encountered in the *Quill* packages was the instability of templates for forms — an important factor, as you need to design many forms. The *Quill* package is good for designing forms, but specialists such as yourselves may need a more high-powered package, such as *QuillFormz*. This package gives you over 200 templates, 92 more fonts and electronic form-filling capacity linking to databases. I attach a brochure for your interest. A demonstration version of Quillformz can also be downloaded from our website.[5]

Thank you for your interest in Clone Power products.

Yours sincerely,

Malcolm Bickstaff,
Service Manager

Enc.

FIGURE 4.8 An effective good news letter

1. Assume that you are the manager of a sporting goods store. In reviewing your monthly accounts, you find that 24 of your customers have been wrongly charged a $25 accounting fee. Write a standard letter, telling them of the good news of a refund.
2. Assume that you work in the Shareholder Communications branch of Gigabank. Gigabank has performed well this year, so shareholders will receive a record dividend of 12 per cent and a bonus of 2 per cent. Write a good news letter that can be signed by the general manager. This letter will become a template for all such communications mailed out with dividend payments.

Communicating bad news

One of the shortest words in the English language, *no*, is a word many of us have difficulty saying. It may suggest negativity, inadequacy, unhappiness, anger or conflict, and few of us are happy with such situations or emotions. In writing workplace documents, we sometimes have to break bad news to our readers, and say no. Such situations might involve any of the following scenarios:

- Someone has asked for credit or for an increase in credit.
- Someone has applied for a job.
- Someone has requested an adjustment, such as a refund or product return.
- Someone has ordered a product or service that is no longer available.
- Someone has requested a donation to a cause.
- Someone has asked us to attend or speak at a social gathering.
- Someone seeks approval for an idea or project.
- Someone has submitted work (a working model, a pilot study, a manuscript) in the hope that we will develop, produce or publish such work.

Letting them down gently: the indirect approach

Conveying a bad news message often requires the formality of a mailed letter. Sometimes the news is sent by fax or email, but this channel choice does not excuse a rushed, garbled or inconsiderate communication. The communication principles for letters we will examine here are equally valid for messages transmitted electronically, and indeed for bad news conveyed verbally.

To convey bad news effectively, whether delivering the message in writing, over the phone or in person, it is useful to write out a 'script' to help you navigate a potentially unpleasant situation.

Most bad news messages are best conveyed using the indirect approach, which means the bad news is initially withheld. Why should we use such an approach? In the interests of clear, honest and time-effective communication, why not just tell it like it is, in a few brief, polite words, and get on with other things? Such honesty has much to recommend it, but the bringer of bad news has to be careful. In workplace documents, we break bad news to people in an indirect way for a number of reasons:

- *Common courtesy and empathy.* Sensitive communicators put themselves in the place of the recipient, asking the question: how would *I* feel if I received this?
- *Tact and taking it personally.* One of the most futile pieces of advice we can ever give anyone is 'don't take this personally'. We tend to take most things personally, and this is particularly the case with bad news. Many of us will take a denial of credit or news that we didn't get the job we applied for as a sign of personal failure or rejection. In other words, bad news messages can easily provoke powerful emotional reactions.

Such situations call for considerable tact, bearing in mind the old definition of tact as 'making a point without making an enemy'.

- *Maybe there is some good news.* Bad news is not always a catastrophe. Merely because we cannot give the reader what he or she wants to hear at this time does not mean we cannot offer *something*, either now or in the future. If, however, we place this offer *after* a brutally direct bad news opening, the reader may be so upset as to be in no state of mind to grasp the consolation. Hot blood and understanding tend to be inversely related.

With bad news messages, then, we use the indirect approach because it is courteous and sensitive, and because it is a practical way to ensure that our total message gets through, undistorted by premature negative emotional reactions.

If you want their business, don't give them the business

We also need to consider the longer-term effects of such emotional reactions. As already noted, in a very real sense, all documents are sales documents. We send letters and emails to customers or others outside our workplace, and we send memos and emails to people who can be thought of as internal customers (see online chapter 10). When we write to our customers or stakeholders, both internal and external, we are in fact sending not one but two messages:

- *the explicit or surface message.* 'Here is my presentation of facts and opinions about the situation/problem we are both familiar with.'
- *an implicit or hidden message.* 'I am a competent person: I solve problems well.' (Or 'I am an incompetent person: I solve problems badly.') Also, 'I am a sensitive person: I am sympathetic to your needs.' (Or 'I am an insensitive person: I am unsympathetic to your needs.')

If we are unaware of the implicit, hidden messages we send, then our current communication with this customer may be our last. This is what is meant by the idea that *all documents are sales documents*: we may not think we are selling something when we write documents that are not specifically sales oriented, but in fact we are: implicitly we are selling ourselves, and the organisation we represent. And if you have to sell yourself, don't sell yourself short.

In this selling process, if we do not create and preserve customer goodwill, then we must surely create ill will. Many of the customer's impressions of an organisation — both good and bad — come not from face-to-face or telephone transactions, but through correspondence, and a good deal of that correspondence consists of bad news letters. A rule of thumb is to presume that any business communications you write may be handed around, photocopied, pinned up on a noticeboard, faxed — in short, they may reach an audience much wider than that of the one person to whom they were sent. You should aim to be the instigator of a chain of good impressions, rather than that of a succession of bad impressions.

Being the bearer of bad news: how to do it well

Certain patterns of expression can be used in responding to a range of bad news situations. These patterns offer ways of conveying the bad news indirectly, with tact and sensitivity. Be wary, however, of adopting an unthinking, formulaic approach: many readers will detect such insincerity, and will find it as offensive as a blunt, rude one-line note.

Kisses, kicks, buffers, sandwiches

As has been noted, it is good elementary psychology to embed a bad news message inside a more positive communication. This means opening, and probably closing, your letter with good news or neutral information. This approach is sometimes called the **bad news sandwich** approach, in which the bad news is surrounded or buffered by other material, or the blow or *kick* you deliver is softened by the *kisses* that precede and follow it (figure 4.9).

Buffer	Kiss
Bad news	**Kick**
Buffer	Kiss

FIGURE 4.9 The bad news sandwich

A buffer of more positive words and ideas will help soften the blow of bad news. Opening buffers:

- express appreciation
- restate the situation
- explore common areas of agreement
- offer reasons or explanations
- offer alternatives.

Buffers can be used separately and sequentially, or can be combined in a variety of ways, depending on your style preferences.

Appreciation buffers

Appreciation is usually expressed in the opening remarks (table 4.6).

TABLE 4.6 Expressions of appreciation

What is appreciated	How expressed
Efforts of recipient in having written/made contact	'Thank you for taking the time to notify us of the difficulties you have been experiencing with your . . .'
Good taste of recipient in having chosen our product	'We appreciate your interest in the Excelsior range of marine insurance policies . . .'

Restatement buffers

Restating the situation allows you, the writer, not only to put off the bad news but also to define the parameters of the issue, or just what it is that you and the reader are concerned with. Perceptions of a situation can vary from individual to individual, and your reader may see things differently from you, so it is worth going through this exercise. The details of a situation may, of course, already be summarised succinctly in the subject line, but a restatement in the text of the letter will further clarify the matter. Restatements are often combined with appreciations:

> 'Thank you for contacting us regarding your order of 6 June for 32 gross of our Kaylite S30 metabolic transducers . . .'

Agreement buffers

It is useful for the writer to express some type of agreement in the opening of a bad news letter, even though *all bad news letters are ultimately about disagreement* (i.e. the writer disagrees with the recipient about what should finally be done in a particular situation).

Disagreement is about people having differing views or areas of interest, and it often involves a measure of unpleasantness. Finding an area of agreement means finding some common interest between writer and reader; if this can be achieved, then the unpleasantness can be neutralised. Typical agreement statements are:

> 'We agree that account fees can initially be quite irritating to our customers, as savings account banking has always been a "free" service in this country ...'

> 'You are right to expect that our drill bits, when operated within normal tolerances, will deliver the performance people have come to expect from this outstanding market leader product ...'

Such statements aim to establish rapport with readers, demonstrating that the writer is on the same side as the reader. This can create a foundation of trust that can perhaps be used to explore alternative solutions to the reader's problem.

Notice that these statements offer partial or conditional rather than total agreement. Almost certainly the bank customer does not think of bank fees as 'initially ... quite irritating' but rather as permanently infuriating and something that should be abolished forever. Similarly, the astute drill user (or abuser) will have detected the hedging or qualification in the words 'when operated within normal tolerances', which may well form the basis of the 'no' message to come. The writers of such statements have probably taken the initial customer comments or complaint and have edited them or modified them to convey a specific sentiment.

When using appreciation and agreement buffers, it is important that writers:

- convey cordiality, but do not give the false impression that good news is to come (unless it is)
- do not come across as sycophantic or crawling, dishonest or sarcastic
- do not twist the readers' own words in such a way that readers feel manipulated or suspect that the writers are being hypocritical and devious (lying through their smiles).

Explanation buffers

It is best to give your personal reasons for saying no before actually saying it. Not only can this help to soften the blow, but it helps to create a context in which the refusal will seem more reasonable.

When giving explanations or reasons, consider the following guidelines:

1. *Don't over-rely on official or company policy.* This position translates as 'we won't because we don't'. There may be good reasons for the policy, but applying it arbitrarily and unconditionally comes across as impersonal and bureaucratic. Each person believes that he or she is an exception to the rule, rather than an obedient, unthinking cog in a vast machine. Always put yourself in the shoes of the recipient: how would *you* feel if you read this?
2. *Don't use jargon and/or adopt an 'in-house' perspective.* Don't assume that your reader understands the intricacies of your products or processes. That's not their job — it's yours. They are paying your salary, and they have no desire to be bamboozled, humiliated or excluded.
3. *Don't make the explanation overlong.* The reader may feel that you are beating about the bush or waffling rather than getting to the point, and it may well be a correct perception. Therefore cut a long story short, and use the explanation as a transition to the bad news.
4. *Try to demonstrate some benefit of the policy.* It's a cliché to say that 'rules benefit us all', but sometimes this can be clearly demonstrated in a nondogmatic way. If this can be done (and it won't always work), then do it. Some sample rules and applications are shown in table 4.7.
5. *Don't talk down to the reader.* A patronising tone, like the 'company policy only' approach, demeans the reader. Assertions such as 'our vast experience over 26 years has shown us that this is the correct course' and 'we know what's best for our customers' may be true, but they should be demonstrated rather than declared.

TABLE 4.7 Rules and applications

Rule	Unacceptable action sought by customer	Benefit for customer by observing rule
Every car should be brought in for a service inspection regularly (every six months); if this is not done, then the insurance contract ceases to provide coverage.	Payment for repairs, even though the car has not been brought in for regular inspection	Regular inspections help to identify problems early, meaning minor faults do not develop into major ones requiring expensive repairs.
Any clothing returned must be in perfect condition.	Return of suit with food stains on it	The store can be trusted to sell only garments that have not been worn or damaged by others.

Source: Adapted from Lahiff and Penrose (1997, p. 205).

6. *Don't apologise.* Or at least keep apologies to a minimum. An apology may form part of the rituals of courtesy, but it can also sound defensive, suggesting the writer is not completely sure of his or her ground, and that the situation may therefore still be open to negotiation (the *no* that might mean *yes*). An apology emphasises the negative rather than the positive aspect of the communication; it can also widen the gulf between writer and reader — sympathy is a poor substitute for problem solving. Don't apologise — explain.

7. *Loose lips sink ships.* Be careful not to reveal commercially sensitive information, or information that could demonstrate culpability or inconsistency on the part of your organisation.

The meat of the sandwich: telling the bad news

The inevitable cannot be delayed any longer. There comes a time when you really have to tell the bad news, and this is it. If the explanation buffer has been well developed, of course, then the shock will not be so great.

When saying no, consider the following guidelines:

1. *Avoid predictable negative transitional words.* These signal words ('however', 'but', 'nevertheless' and so on) almost always provoke a powerful negative response from readers, and can often undo all the good work that you have done in developing the explanation buffer (see online chapter 3).

2. *Put a sandwich in a sandwich.* Place the 'no' sentence in the middle of a paragraph — as a sandwich within a sandwich, if you like, in the middle of the middle section of the letter.

Complex sentence technique: a way of de-emphasising bad news by placing it in a subordinate clause of a complex sentence

3. *Use the* **complex sentence technique.** Complex sentences comprise one main or independent clause, and one or more subordinate or dependent clauses (see online chapter 1). The bad news is linked with other material — reasons, perhaps, or more positive alternative outcomes (Wells 1988, pp. 307–8). People usually pay most attention to the main clause in a sentence. Messages tend to have a diminished impact if buried in subordinate clauses, so it makes sense to put the bad news in the subordinate clause, and give greater emphasis to the more positive main clause (figure 4.10).

4. *Avoid 'hot-button' words.* All words have various connotations or meanings. Words that sound harmless enough to you may in certain circumstances cause offence to others. Try to be sensitive to such possibilities. Of course, some words are unequivocally disrespectful or 'hard' and should be avoided. Not only is it bad manners to use such words, but it may also give cause for legal action to be taken against you. At the least, strong language will have negative public relations payoffs for your organisation. Always try to consider respectful, 'soft' alternatives (table 4.8; see overleaf).

LESS EFFECTIVE COMPLEX SENTENCE:
bad news in main clause; other material in subordinate clause

Main clause

We cannot extend credit facilities to you at this time, although we will be able to review this decision if you can obtain long-term employment.

Subordinate clause

Main clause

Your order cannot be processed at this time, although we may be able to supply you with a generator on a temporary basis.

Subordinate clause

MORE EFFECTIVE COMPLEX SENTENCE:
other material in main clause; bad news in subordinate clause

Subordinate clause

While we cannot extend credit facilities to you at this time, we will be able to review this decision if you can obtain long-term employment.

Main clause

Subordinate clause

Although your order cannot be processed at this time, we may be able to supply you with a generator on a temporary basis.

Main clause

FIGURE 4.10 The complex sentence technique in bad news letters

TABLE 4.8 Soft words and hot-button words: becoming sensitive to connotations

Hot-button word	Soft word
Crisis	Problem, situation
Refuse	Decline
Abandon	Relinquish
Cancel, quit	Forgo
Prevent	Preclude
Delayed	Are not yet available, Will now not be available until …
Bad risk	Do not satisfy all of our current criteria
Not good enough, inferior	Do not match our immediate requirements
Abused, wrecked	When tested, showed an extraordinarily high degree of wear and tear
Desperate	Concerned
Terrible, pathetic, outrageous, disgusting	Unacceptable

5. *Avoid euphemisms.* At the other extreme from 'hot button' words are euphemisms. Euphemisms are used to describe unpleasant things in the most pleasant, 'diplomatic' way possible. Thus a euphemism for *dead* is 'passed away', while a euphemism for *unemployed* is 'between contracts'. Euphemisms can sometimes be tactful, but they can all too easily be perceived as hypocritical gobbledegook. Wherever possible, choose plain English alternatives to euphemistic constructions (table 4.9).

6. *Refer to groups or situations rather than to individuals.* Referring to the reader using second-person pronouns ('you', 'your') can sometimes convey an accusatory tone. It also emphasises the isolation of the reader from the writer, or even from the community

in general. Whenever possible, include rather than exclude. Readers will often feel less threatened if you refer to them as part of a wider group ('you and other retailers', 'in fairness to all our retailers', 'in everyone's best interests') or as participants in wider situations ('in the current economic circumstances'). Misery loves company, so make it work for you.

Euphemisms and plain English alternatives

Euphemism	Plain English alternative
'It is not possible at this juncture to facilitate reimbursement...'	'We cannot give you a refund...'
'It is not possible for the current employer–employee relationship to be sustained in the immediate future...'	'Your employment with us is terminated...' 'You are dismissed from your position...'
'inflation-driven retail charge adjustment'	'price increase'
'appears to have experienced a retrogradation in optimal performance parameters'	'has been damaged'

7. *Use the passive voice.* When a person uses the evasive passive voice, we have every reason to believe they are seeking to avoid responsibility (see online chapter 1). The active voice is more direct and personal, and so usually to be preferred. Sometimes, however, the active voice may seem confrontational, and a passive construction, particularly an impersonal or agentless one, will help to soften the blow of the bad news (table 4.10).

Active versus passive constructions

Active voice	Passive voice
'I found that...'	'It was discovered that...'
'You have not maintained the equipment correctly...'	'The equipment has not been maintained correctly...'
'We cannot refund the amount...'	'A refund cannot be made...'

8. *Use subjunctive mood.* Mood is a property of verbs (see online chapter 1). Unlike the indicative and imperative moods, the subjunctive mood conveys types of conditionality, such as wishes, recommendations, indirect requests and speculations. The subjunctive mood is less confrontational than other moods and, like the passive voice, can help to make expression more indirect (table 4.11).

Use of mood

Imperative/indicative mood	Subjunctive mood
'Pay by the 10th June...'	'We would be able to process this if you were able to pay by 10 June...'
'I cannot reverse this decision...'	'I wish that I were able to reverse this decision...'

Kisses and buffers again: creating silver linings

We have already noted the benefits of offsetting bad news by more positive information. Bad news relates to what you *cannot* do for the reader; good news relates to what you *can* do. Is there anything positive you can extract from an unpleasant situation? What silver linings can be found in the clouds hanging over your reader?

- If you cannot give a person credit facilities, can you give details of alternatives, such as lay-by/layaway plans or discounts for cash purchases?
- If you cannot give a refund on an item, can you offer a trade-in allowance on another item or a discount on a further purchase?
- If you have to dismiss someone, can you offer them retraining or at least facilities (desk, phone) so they can hunt for another job?

It is not always possible to create options or alternatives, but whenever it is, be creative. Sometimes the alternative may prove to benefit the customer even more than the original outcome sought — one door closes, another opens.

Writing technique and the bigger picture: silver linings and top brass

Here we leave letter-writing technique for the moment to enter the realm of organisational policy. It is vital that management recognise the importance of offering options to both customers and staff. Silver linings can only be created by senior management, or 'top brass'. This is a crucial policy area for several reasons:

- Offering options is an ethical and compassionate strategy.
- It helps to avert negative public relations outcomes for the organisation.
- It gives the organisation a strategic marketing edge over its competitors who fail to recognise the wisdom of such an approach.

Bad news: an overview

Figure 4.11 summarises different techniques for conveying bad news. Evidently, there are several ways that this information can be communicated.

Letter	Use buffers, sandwich, kiss–kick–kiss approach (appreciation, restatement, agreement, explanations).
Paragraph	Embed bad news in central paragraph (sandwich approach).
Sentence	Use complex sentence technique — bad news in subordinate clause, alternative in main clause: 'Although your order cannot be processed at this time, *we may be able to supply you with a generator on a temporary basis.*'
Words	Avoid 'hot button' words and euphemisms. Refer to groups or situations rather than individuals.
Voice	Use passive rather than active voice to convey bad news (impersonal passive best in some cases): 'Your request cannot be granted' rather than 'I cannot grant your request'.
Mood	Use subjunctive, rather than indicative or imperative: 'If you were able to . . .'

FIGURE 4.11 Techniques for conveying bad news

Table 4.12 provides an overview of various bad news situations and suggested approaches. You may find it helpful to use the table as a content generator/writer's block unblocker when you are having difficulty with this less-than-pleasant communication task.

TABLE 4.12 Approaches to bad news situations: a bad news content generator

Situation	Possible appreciation, restatement, agreement buffers	Possible explanation buffers	Possible expressions of bad news	Possible alternatives
Credit refusal	'Thank you for choosing to shop at Hellier's.'	'We feel that it is unfair and unwise to ask customers to commit more than 12 per cent of their income to account repayments.'	'In these circumstances, we would be unable to offer you account facilities.'	▪ Offer lay-by/layaway scheme. ▪ Offer discount for cash payment. ▪ Suggest customer reapply when financial situation improves.
Loan refusal	'We agree that a reliable line of credit is extremely helpful for all start-up businesses.'	'It would, of course, be unwise for you to over-commit yourself at this time, given the unstable nature of your market.'	'We feel that it would be unwise to proceed at this time with the line of credit we have been discussing.'	▪ Offer smaller loan. ▪ Suggest customer reapply when market situation improves.
Adjustment	'Thank you for your letter and package of 4 September containing a returned copy of *Quill* software.'	'The software envelope appears to have been opened and re-glued. Unfortunately this voids the *Quill* warranty and ...'	'... your package is returned herewith.'	▪ Offer good trade-in/upgrade allowance. ▪ Offer discount on future purchase. ▪ Give information about other products.
Item not in stock	'Your order (18 January 2012) for 12 Waveform AA2 speakers shows you to be a true connoisseur of sound.'	'Recent favourable publicity has caused a rush on our stocks, and we have had to increase production to meet orders.'	'Your Waveform speakers will be delivered to you on the amended date of 4 May.'	▪ Promise a specific (amended) delivery date. ▪ Offer reduced charges (e.g. on delivery).
Item discontinued	'Your order (18 January 2012) for 12 Waveform speakers shows you to be a true connoisseur of sound.'	'To meet our commitment to stay at the cutting edge of innovation, we have now produced the AA3 series, which supersedes the AA2 model ...'	'... production of which has been discontinued.'	▪ Offer superior alternative or substitute on sale/loan/rental/lease. ▪ Offer new product at old price. ▪ Offer old product at old/reduced price (to clear stock). ▪ Offer smaller quantities of new product, so customer does not have to pay any more.
Price increase	'Thank you for being a long-term Waveform customer. Your commitment to excellence in sound allows us to do what we enjoy doing most — produce the world's top speaker systems.'	'As a professional, you know that research and development and state-of-the-art materials don't come cheap. If you wanted the cheapies, you wouldn't be listening to Waveform!'	'Accordingly, Waveform prices will need to rise by 8 per cent as of 1 June (see attached list).'	▪ Offer choice in terms of payment. ▪ Mention other, cheaper alternative products/services/models/lines.

(continued)

TABLE 4.12 *(continued)*

Situation	Possible appreciation, restatement, agreement buffers	Possible explanation buffers	Possible expressions of bad news	Possible alternatives
Unsuccessful job application	'We are gratified that you were interested enough in DayCo to approach us.'	'Your qualifications, experience and references, while impressive, . . .'	'. . . do not match our requirements at this time.'	■ Suggest other possible employers. ■ Offer to keep application on file.
Money solicited	'I admire the work you have done with homeless children and the non-English-speaking unemployed.'	'We make large corporate donations each year to the Wider Community Benefit Fund . . .'	'. . . and thus cannot provide you with a direct donation this financial year.'	■ Mention other organisations (e.g. general charities) to which money has been given and to which solicitor might apply.
Unsuccessful funding application	'Thank you for your excellent submission to the 2012–13 budget for your team's Mantra project.'	'The ideas presented are exciting, but given the pressure we are under to deliver short-term payoffs . . .'	'. . . we cannot fund you this year.'	■ Offer reduced funding for pilot project. ■ Offer counselling on better submission writing strategies. ■ Offer to give high priority to submission in next funding round. ■ Offer to partially or totally fund if other funded program can be sacrificed. ■ Suggest other funding sources.
Request to speak	'Thank you for your kind request for me to speak to your senior year science students about our new "green chemistry" production plant.'	'The new model production process is out of the prototype stage, and all of our staff, myself included, are working intensively on getting it to a routine operational status.'	'This means, unfortunately, that we cannot spare anyone at the moment to come to the school and speak. We do have public affairs staff who could present an overview, but I understand that your science students would like more technical details, and that is what we would like to deliver down the track.'	■ Offer to send specialist speakers at a specific later date. ■ Provide materials, such as brochures, position papers, website references. ■ Mention upcoming public events, such as open days. ■ Offer work experience programs for students.

Let's now apply some of these ideas to a sample bad news letter. Figure 4.12 presents an ineffective bad news letter, in which the writer demonstrates aggression and insensitivity. Figure 4.13 illustrates the opposite, equally ineffective tendency: the writer is simply too passive, and in fact indiscreet. Both these extremes are of course exaggerated for effect; only a thoroughly incompetent writer would send out letters as inept as these. Figure 4.14 presents a more effective bad news letter, in which many of the techniques we have considered are applied.

PLASMAVID SYSTEMS Inc.
1 Proton Drive, Erewhon 9127
Telephone 1500.321.321 Facsimile 1500.321.322
www.plasmavid.net

1. Evidence of poor editing; writer changes title and spelling of receiver's name, insulting to receiver

24 June 2011
Ms Julia Crosson[1]
23 Poling Road
Morristown 4288

2. No restatement of situation

Dear Mrs Crossong:[1]

3. Brutally direct approach

Under no circumstances can you have a replacement for your PlasmaVid TV screen.[2] [3]

4. Accusations might have legal implications

Our technicians have inspected the screen and have evidence that you, or someone in your household, has subjected the unit to wilful abuse. There is no way known that the picture quality on such a state-of-the-art system could have deteriorated to the extent that it has through normal wear and tear.[4]

5. Officious, lecturing resort to company policy

It is strict PlasmaVid policy that exchanges are not possible under such circumstances (see section 9.2.6 of the PV3000 Information booklet).[5]

6. Clichés

In our nine years of operation, we have found that very few of the claims made against our superior products have any basis in fact. Our tradition of excellence is one that we carry on today and we will continue to do so in the future.[6] [7]

7. 'We', not 'you', attitude

Your claim is rejected. Your PV3000 will be returned to the Staunton Megalectrix store where you bought it, and you may pick it up there after the 28th of this month.[8]

Cordially,

8. Cold, off-hand approach

Hector Roth

CUSTOMER SERVICE

FIGURE 4.12 An ineffective bad news letter: too aggressive

1. No restatement of situation

2. Effusive style inappropriate; it might be interpreted as the writer taking pleasure in the reader's problems

3. Wrongly raises reader's expectations; false impression is given that good news is coming

4. Indiscreet to reveal this confidential information; irrelevant for some readers, while for others it constitutes a documented admission of low quality standards

5. Waffle, jargon; bad news is buried in impersonal passive construction; may confuse reader

6. Inappropriate expression of writer's disagreement with policy in misguided attempt to show solidarity with reader; disagreements should have been settled prior to letter being written

7. Encouragement of correspondence is counter-productive.

PLASMAVID SYSTEMS Inc.
1 Proton Drive, Erewhon 9127
Telephone 1500.321.321 Facsimile 1500.321.322
www.plasmavid.net

24 June 2011
Ms Julia Crosson
23 Poling Road
Morristown 4288

Dear Ms Crosson:

I was so very pleased to take your call after your being referred to us by Mr Rowland of the Staunton Megalectrix Store. We always take great pleasure in hearing from our customers, and we in turn take the greatest pains imaginable to ensure that our customers are satisfied with PlasmaVid products.[1] [2] [3]

The PV3000 model has suffered a few teething pains, but the standard has definitely been rising, as shown by the diminishing number of complaints we have been receiving. Our Quality Control section estimates that fully 97.6 per cent of screens shipped are completely fault-free.[4]

We have had occasion in the past to issue some customers with a substitute screen, or to undertake repairs upon units at no cost. Upon consideration of all of the appropriate facts to hand at this point in time, it is not immediately apparent that this eventuality can be replicated in this particular situation.[5]

I do most sincerely apologise for this, being personally sympathetic to your predicament, and would authorise a replacement if I could, but unfortunately my hands are tied in this particular instance.[6]

If there is anything further I can do to help, please do not hesitate to contact me at the above number.[7]

Yours most sincerely,

Selena Cringe,
CUSTOMER SERVICE

FIGURE 4.13 Another ineffective bad news letter: too passive

PLASMAVID SYSTEMS Inc.

1 Proton Drive, Erewhon 9127
Telephone 1500.321.321 Facsimile 1500.321.322
www.plasmavid.net

24 June 2011
Ms Julia Crosson
23 Poling Road
Morristown 4288

Dear Ms Crosson:

Thank you for taking the trouble to return your PV3000 television unit to the Staunton Megalectrix store. Mr John Rowland of Megalectrix has conveyed your views to me via email and telephone.[1]

We are always concerned when one of our products does not meet the requirements of our customers, and automatically subject any returned items to stringent laboratory tests.[2]

On this occasion, it was discovered that the back seals have been breached, and the central input unit appears to have been removed, subjected to strong distorting impact pressure, and reinserted into the custom plug array with pressure that has led to the yellow pickup pins being bent. This type of damage is sometimes seen when unauthorised attempts are made to insert illegal game console emulation chips and illegal cable programming chips. I attach a copy of the report, incorporating digital photographs used in the inspection.[3] [4]

The PlasmaVid Warranty does not cover such circumstances, and thus it is not possible to issue a full refund on the price or to provide another model free of charge.

I can, however, offer you a number of options:[5]

(1) Expert factory repair of plug/pin unit (cost $154.00)
(2) A voucher (convertible at any store) which will guarantee you a trade-in price of $5050 on a new PV3000 (recommended retail price: $8555) or an approved second-hand PlasmaVid product.

Please telephone me at 1500.321.916 (direct) and advise me how we can best help you.[6]

Yours sincerely,

Jane Carruthers
CUSTOMER SERVICE

Enc.

FIGURE 4.14 An effective bad news letter

Persuasive letters

Persuasive letter: a document sent to an organisation or individual to influence or effect a change in behaviour

Letters are one of the most important channels we can use to **persuade** others. In chapter 12 various approaches to persuasion are reviewed. These include:

- establishing your own credibility (e.g. via power bases such as expert power and referent power)
- convincing yourself of the validity of the message you are sending
- the rhetorical mix of *logos* (appeal to logic), *pathos* (appeal to emotions) and *ethos* (appeal to credibility) (see Myers 2007)
- the mix of features (the characteristics of an idea, product or process) and benefits (the advantage or relevance of a feature)
- the demonstration of proofs
- the language used in the construction of the message
- sending messages using appropriate techniques (foot-in-the-door versus door-in-the-face, central versus peripheral processing, persuasion or propaganda sequences)
- tapping into motivational patterns in target persons or *persuadees*
- being aware of, and perhaps affecting, the social context of the target persons so that behavioural mechanisms (such as conformity) are brought into play
- monitoring responses to the persuasive messages sent.

All these approaches can be applied to a variety of spoken and written communication situations. Let's now zoom in on the genre of persuasive letters, and see how some of these persuasive techniques can be used in the documents you provide.

Structuring persuasive documents: the AIDA sequence

Persuasion implies that the target person disagrees with you or has no opinion on the topic, and it is your job to bring them around to your point of view. Some people seem to be more successful in persuading others, and are credited with having 'the gift of the gab'. The 'gift of the gab', however, can be learnt. Similarly, approaches for developing persuasive written materials can also be learnt, and we will now consider one of these techniques in greater detail.

AIDA sequence: an approach to structuring persuasive documents (acronym for Attention–Interest–Desire–Action)

A useful way of structuring persuasive documents is to apply the **AIDA sequence** (for Attention–Interest–Desire–Action) (figure 4.15) (see also online chapter 5). The AIDA model allows the writer to lead a reader through a sequence of steps involving both rationality and emotion.

OCEAN VIEW ESTATE INC.
44 Vista Boulevard, Ocean View 41920
Phone 1800.321321 Facsimile 1800.322.322
Email info@oceanviewnow.net
Internet: www.oceanviewnow.net

Dear_____

1. GET ATTENTION

As you well know, housing has never been less affordable. Today you could face a debt load three times higher than the one your parents took on, just for a roof over your head!

2. STIMULATE INTEREST

But don't despair — Ocean View Estate on the north coast is based on a new release of government land, at zero cost to you. Power, gas, water, sewerage and data/TV cabling have been provided at no cost by the state government, and there's a 35-minute, high-speed rail link to the city centre. Best of all, our new sustainable energy house models are priced from an ultra-low $79,999!

3. CREATE DESIRE

You'll love the price, and you'll love the ocean view and the fresh air. You'll save heaps, live the life usually available only to millionaires, and be in touch with the heart of the city.

4. ELICIT ACTION

For a free brochure showing everything Ocean View Estate has to offer, call 1800- 321321 now, or visit our website at www.oceanviewnow.net.

FIGURE 4.15 The Attention–Interest–Desire–Action (AIDA) sequence in structuring persuasive documents

Getting attention

Persuasive communications can be either solicited or unsolicited. A solicited communication is one requested by the receiver: there has been prior communication between sender and receiver (perhaps a telephone call). In solicited communications, there is no need to grab the attention of the reader or audience (although it should never be taken for granted).

In unsolicited persuasive communications (e.g. a sales letter), it is essential to grab the attention of the reader or audience right away. Readers of unsolicited communications often make up their minds very quickly, sometimes too quickly. First impressions are often final impressions. Figure 4.16 outlines some of the ways this all-important initial interest may be sought.

Interesting statistics	'Most of our staff admit to losing at least 40 minutes a day handling junk emails, wrong telephone numbers and telemarketers, and redirecting customers. If we could free up that time, that's the equivalent of getting a thirteenth or bonus month of productivity each year.'
Rhetorical question	'Would you like to make $5000 tax free in the next three months?'
Quotations	'"Isn't it better to have men being ungrateful than to miss a chance to do good?" (Denis Diderot, 18th-century French philosopher). Many of us are sceptical about giving to charity because we feel that it doesn't do any good, but have you ever thought that the greatest beneficiary of giving is to yourself, and your own peace of mind?'
Unusual facts	'The average person will spend four years of their lives watching television commercials.'
Humour	'Did you know that income tax has made more liars out of people than fishing and golf combined?'
Pointed questions	'Will you have enough money to retire on?'
Anecdote	'A young man started a magazine in 1956, selling only 32 copies of the first issue. That magazine now sells over 1.2 million copies per issue in the Asia–Pacific region alone.'

FIGURE 4.16 Ways of attracting reader interest

Stimulating interest

Having gained the reader's attention, the next task is to create an interest in, and a desire for, the product, process or idea. Features (or characteristics) and proofs (e.g. statistics, samples, guarantees) are critical here (see 'Features–benefits mix' in chapter 12). By stressing features and proofs, you hope to be able to engage the logical decision-making faculties of your reader.

Creating desire

We don't always make decisions with the head only, of course; often we are guided by the heart and by our own self-interest. To create desire in the reader or audience we need to keep the *'you' attitude* in mind, addressing the question 'What's in it for you?' We can answer this question by stressing the benefits as distinct from features, and by tapping into the motivational patterns of our reader or audience.

Elicit action

Once the reader's attention has been gained, and interest and desire stimulated, it is necessary to elicit an action response. Action can be stimulated by making a response easy for the reader. Such stimulants include:

- enclosing prepaid envelopes
- enclosing reply-paid forms that are simple to complete
- giving toll-free telephone and fax numbers
- allowing payment by credit card
- offering deferred payment (send nothing now – we'll bill you later).

Proofs such as guarantees, samples and trial periods should be mentioned now if not already covered earlier in the document. Incentives for prompt response may include discounts, free entry in a lottery or gifts. Postscript (P.S.) messages at the end of such letters are, perhaps surprisingly, the most often read part of some sales letters (Ober 2007, p.151).

Message plus . . .

The overall appearance of the persuasive message can be vital to its reception, as can the presence of other material enclosed with the message. Letterheads, embossing, the quality and colour of paper used in envelopes and letters – all can convey powerful nonverbal messages to the reader. Ensure that they are positive messages rather than negative ones.

Various items can be enclosed with your primary document so that a 'document mix' is created. The most common of these is a brochure of some kind. A brochure or similar document 'takes the pressure off' the main document: the writer does not have to cram all information into a single text letter and can simply refer the reader to appropriate sections of the brochure. Most readers will not read the full message anyway but will skim and scan, while their eye will be drawn to an attractive detail in a colour brochure. (For other document mixes, see 'Public communication documents' in chapter 17 and 'The document mix' in chapter 20.)

Other enclosures include proofs (such as samples) and gifts. Pens, rulers, mouse pads and such inexpensive gifts, suitably inscribed with logos and other advertising devices, may well outlast kilos of paper communications, and may eventually get your message across by dint of pure physical survival.

Collection letters

When we study persuasion processes, we usually focus on those situations involving efforts to 'sell' products, processes or ideas. Certainly, the area of sales and marketing relies heavily on the effective use of persuasive techniques in written and spoken communication. We will now consider a very different situation that arises after such persuasion has been successful – sometimes too successful.

Collection letters are sent when purchasers are late with payment. Normally sent by organisations to individuals or other organisations, the writers have two objectives:

1. to secure the money owed
2. to preserve the goodwill and reputation of both parties.

Why not simply send a debtor a one-line letter reading 'Pay up or else.' as soon as a bill or invoice is overdue? This would be ill-advised, for a number of reasons:

- It's illegal to make threats.
- It's unethical.
- It's insensitive: there may be very good reasons why payment has not been forthcoming.
- It may be counterproductive, evoking an aggressive and hostile response from recipients, making them even less likely to pay.
- It may have significant negative public relations payoffs. If the collection process is handled sensitively, the recipients' goodwill will be retained (it may even be strengthened), and they may relay positive word-of-mouth perceptions about the sender through their personal networks. If the collection process is handled badly, the recipients' goodwill will be lost, and negative perceptions of the sender may be passed on through the recipients' personal networks.

Writers of collection letters normally calibrate their messages to reflect the urgency of different situations. As the period of nonpayment becomes longer, collection letters become progressively less indirect and more direct, less about persuasion and more about demand.

Typically, collection letters are created in response to three or four different phases or situations (table 4.13). Each of these phases lasts 14 or 30 days. Letters may be accompanied and reinforced by telephone calls and, on occasion, personal meetings.

> **Collection letter:** a document sent to an organisation or individual seeking overdue payment for goods or services

TABLE 4.13 Different types of collection letters

Phase	Days overdue	Approach	Sample wording
1 Reminder	14–30	Indirect approach Assumption: simple misunderstanding, oversight	'We appreciate your custom, and attach details of next week's sale.' 'We understand it is often easy to overlook payments of accounts in today's busy world. Please attend to the attached bill in order to avoid unnecessary interest payments.'
2 Enquiry	28–60	Indirect approach Assumption of misunderstanding dropped New assumption: there is a legitimate reason preventing payment.	'We note that this account has not been paid for some time. Is there something wrong? If you are experiencing difficulties meeting this payment, please contact us and we can discuss other payment options.'
3 Appeal	42–90	More direct approach Assumption: there is a growing danger of complete default. Appeals to equity/fair play, pride, fear, self-interest	'You have built up a good reputation as a reliable customer of ours over a number of years. We would be sorry to see that reputation suffer, and your credit rating along with it. Please attend to this outstanding payment as soon as possible.'
4 Ultimatum	56–120	Direct approach Assumption: preservation of goodwill is still important, but getting payment is now paramount.	'If we have not received your payment of $495.95 by 11 June, we will have to place this matter with the Nemesis Debt Collection agency.'

Phase one: reminder

A reminder is sent out on the assumption that the recipient has merely overlooked the payment. This assumption is often correct, and sometimes the reminder letter will cross the payment in the mail.

Phase two: enquiry

In this phase the writer no longer assumes oversight on the part of the debtor, but rather infers that special circumstances are creating a legitimate barrier to payment. The benefit of the doubt is extended to the debtor, giving him or her an opportunity to rectify the situation, either through full payment or via a negotiated schedule of part-payments. When writing request letters, enquire about the recipient's circumstances, but don't ask whether the product/process was unsatisfactory. This risks simply prolonging matters.

Phase three: appeal

If there is still no reply, matters proceed to phase three. Hitherto positive approaches have been tried (empathy, concern, problem solving). Now it is time to introduce greater resolution. The writer may try a number of appeals to the reader.

The first appeal may be to equity or fair play: the recipient has benefited by using the product or process – surely it's only ethical that he or she pay for it. Another appeal may be to fear: vague or oblique references may be made to legal action. A third appeal may be a mixture of pride, fear and self-interest: the recipient's hard-won credit rating may be damaged.

Phase four: ultimatum

Having exhausted all other options, the writer is now no longer requesting but demanding action by the debtor. Specific consequences of continued dereliction need to be spelt out, along with specific deadlines. For example, unless payment is received in a nominated number of days, the account will be turned over to a collection agency (we're not nasty, but they are). The writer must be careful not to overstep the mark legally in *all* collection letters, but should be particularly careful with ultimatum or final demand letters: know what you can legally demand, and go no further. If necessary, seek legal advice.

Ultimatum letters are given additional weight by being sent by special mail or being signed by someone more senior in the organisation than the writer of the previous letters. If possible, hold out some hope that the damage can be undone if payment is made: this is not only ethical and pragmatic, but sound public relations too. Some organisations, in fact, only go through the motions with letters of this kind, preferring to write off a relatively small proportion of bad debts rather than risk negative public relations impacts.

Emails and memos

Memo/memorandum: paper or email document sent to one or more recipients within an organisation

Most letters are sent to recipients outside the writer's organisation. Emails and **memos**, or **memorandums** (from the Latin *memorandus*: thing to be remembered), are usually transmitted within an organisation, although it is quite routine to send emails externally to other organisations. Most memos are now sent as emails because of their speed and convenience. But, as we shall see, there are still some occasions where paper memos are more effective.

Examples of a typical letter and a typical email, highlighting the differences between the two forms of documents, are shown in figures 4.17 and 4.18.

JUGGERNAUT MANUFACTURING INC.

1000 Eastmore Road, Newtown 68113 Freedonia[1]
Telephone (61.2) 419 6911.Toll-free (61) 008.420.4322
Facsimile (61.2) 419.6924
www.juggernautfacture.com

11 September 2011

Ms Joanne Ajogalu,
Production Manager,
Close Shaves Company,
11 West Place,
Tiriel Industrial Park 91233[2]

Dear Ms Ajogalu:[3]

Ceramic Razor Blade Strip

Following our phone conversations, I am writing to you to apologise for the nondelivery of your order of 40 80KG reels of 3mm ceramic razor blade strip. Delivery will now occur on 18 September at 9:30 AM at your No. 3 Bay.

The volatility of production of new materials such as ceramic strip is notorious, but we at Juggernaut and Close Shaves entered into this production mode with our eyes open, because we both believe in the product's ability ultimately to give Close Shaves a market advantage over other companies using conventional metal strip.

We are satisfied the problems with the thermoelectric kilns have now been eliminated, and would be happy to have Mr Percy and his quality people from Close Shaves drop over at any time to confirm this.

As I mentioned in our conversation, Juggernaut's plastics division might be able to provide you with a better product, both in terms of price and quality, than those made by your current suppliers. If we were able to supply both the razor strip and the plastic handles for your razors, I am sure that Shane DiMeola of our Plastics Division and I could make the total pricing package even more attractive.[4]

Please take this up with your management group, as discussed, and get back to me. Should you require any further information, please call me direct on 8419.6111.

Yours sincerely,

Brian McLeod[5]

Brian McLeod,[6]
Chief Executive Officer,
Ceramics Division

BmcL: lh

FIGURE 4.17 Letter format and style

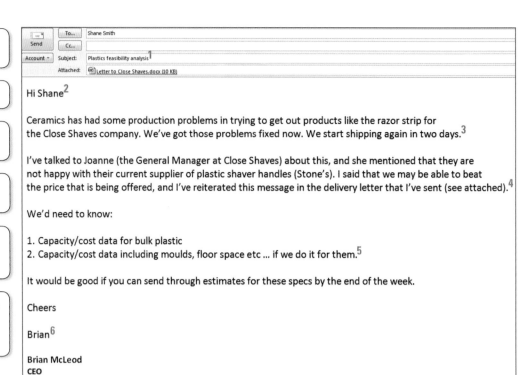

| 1. Subject details always provided |
| 2. Salutation |
| 3. Informal and casual writing style |
| 4. Cross-reference attachments |
| 5. Numbered and bulleted lists acceptable in genre |
| 6. Sign-off and signature may be formal or casual to suit correspondence |

To... Shane Smith
Cc...
Subject: Plastics feasibility analysis[1]
Attached: Letter to Close Shaves.docx (10 KB)

Hi Shane[2]

Ceramics has had some production problems in trying to get out products like the razor strip for the Close Shaves company. We've got those problems fixed now. We start shipping again in two days.[3]

I've talked to Joanne (the General Manager at Close Shaves) about this, and she mentioned that they are not happy with their current supplier of plastic shaver handles (Stone's). I said that we may be able to beat the price that is being offered, and I've reiterated this message in the delivery letter that I've sent (see attached).[4]

We'd need to know:

1. Capacity/cost data for bulk plastic
2. Capacity/cost data including moulds, floor space etc ... if we do it for them.[5]

It would be good if you can send through estimates for these specs by the end of the week.

Cheers

Brian[6]

Brian McLeod
CEO
Juggernaut Manufacturing Inc.
PO Box 194, Sydney NSW
Mobile: 0323 354 123
E: bmcleod@juggernaut.com.au

FIGURE 4.18 Email format and style

Emails: what are they for?

Don't send emails when face-to-face or telephone interaction will solve your communication problem more quickly and directly. Nevertheless, if there is a case for putting it in writing, do so. Bear in mind that everything we have considered about letters in terms of general communication principles still holds true: email recipients, like letter recipients, have basic needs for information and respect.

Many types of emails are used in organisations. Some of the most common ones deal with:

- requests
- announcements
- instructions
- self-protection.

Request emails

Request email: a document, sent within an organisation, asking for solutions and action

Request emails are a particularly common form. Such emails go beyond information-only documents: the writer expects the recipient to take action, and to communicate that action either in person, by telephone or via another email. This type of document carries a strong element of accountability. Figure 4.18 shows a request email.

Announcement emails

Annoucement email: an email sent to all persons in an organisation. A reply is usually not called for, and thus it is usually a one-way communication

Announcement emails (figure 4.19) usually have large audiences. Rather than being addressed to one person, perhaps with copies to several others, announcement emails are addressed to, say, a group, a department or the whole organisation. The interests of everyone are affected by the content of the email, and it is thus more efficient to send out a single announcement email than to personalise it many times over. Announcement emails are sometimes referred to as 'broadcast' or 'block' emails. Such emails are often addressed by copying individual addresses from a mailing list or spreadsheet and pasting them into the blind copy window of an email. Alternatively, a mailing list might be automatically cued by a created general address (e.g. allstaff@megabank.com). Such messages may be sent through internal paper mail, displayed on noticeboards or sent as emails.

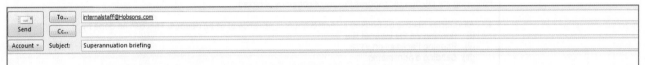

Send	To...	internalstaff@Hobsons.com
	Cc...	
Account ▾	Subject:	Superannuation briefing

Compulsory deductions — superannuation

There has been ongoing discussion about the government's plan to adjust compulsory superannuation levels for all private sector staff. If the proposal is implemented, it will have a direct effect on our employees. There will be briefing sessions about this proposal for all staff on Tuesday 4 October.

TIMES: 10 am, 1 pm and 3 pm
DURATION: 30 minutes
VENUE: Conference room B

Supervisors need to ensure that all staff have an opportunity to attend one of these sessions. A DVD of the briefing will also be available on the intranet next week.

FIGURE 4.19 Announcement memo

Layout is perhaps of more importance in announcement emails than other types of emails, as people may not scan an announcement email with the care they would give to one addressed personally. Thoughtful composition and design involving different fonts, subheadings and bulleted lists will help this type of memo communicate effectively. Like instruction/procedures emails, announcement emails are information-only documents: readers are usually not expected to respond directly.

Instruction emails

Instruction email: a document, sent within an organisation, setting out information about procedures or operating routines

An **instruction email** (figure 4.20) sets out information about procedures or operating routines. Like announcement emails, they tend to be given wider distribution, and a reply from recipients is not normally expected. Writing instructions, procedures and policy, however, is not necessarily as easy as it looks. These emails place a heavy emphasis on facts, sequences and covering all possibilities and options (see online chapter 6). If writing, for example, on how to operate a machine or system, it is important that a logical sequence be followed, without assuming that certain intermediate steps are so obvious that such details can be omitted.

Instruction emails are sometimes issued when procedures in a certain area have become so complex that commonsense understandings are no longer adequate. They may also be issued to neutralise controversies over scarce resources, or misuse of facilities and equipment.

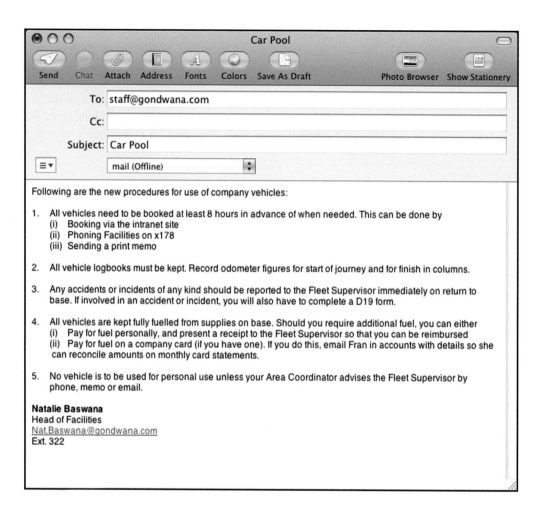

FIGURE 4.20 Instruction memo

The following appears inside the figure:

> **Car Pool**
>
> Send · Chat · Attach · Address · Fonts · Colors · Save As Draft · Photo Browser · Show Stationery
>
> To: staff@gondwana.com
> Cc:
> Subject: Car Pool
> mail (Offline)
>
> Following are the new procedures for use of company vehicles:
>
> 1. All vehicles need to be booked at least 8 hours in advance of when needed. This can be done by
>   (i) Booking via the intranet site
>   (ii) Phoning Facilities on x178
>   (iii) Sending a print memo
>
> 2. All vehicle logbooks must be kept. Record odometer figures for start of journey and for finish in columns.
>
> 3. Any accidents or incidents of any kind should be reported to the Fleet Supervisor immediately on return to base. If involved in an accident or incident, you will also have to complete a D19 form.
>
> 4. All vehicles are kept fully fuelled from supplies on base. Should you require additional fuel, you can either
>   (i) Pay for fuel personally, and present a receipt to the Fleet Supervisor so that you can be reimbursed
>   (ii) Pay for fuel on a company card (if you have one). If you do this, email Fran in accounts with details so she can reconcile amounts on monthly card statements.
>
> 5. No vehicle is to be used for personal use unless your Area Coordinator advises the Fleet Supervisor by phone, memo or email.
>
> **Natalie Baswana**
> Head of Facilities
> Nat.Baswana@gondwana.com
> Ext. 322

Warning memos

So then, is the paper-based message of the memo obsolete? Not at all. In fact, in some communication situations, a paper-based message has distinct advantages over an electronic message, such as when we need to send a warning to someone. Depending on the integrity of the systems and of your colleagues, a sealed envelope may guarantee more confidentiality than an email. The **warning memo** is concerned with the dark side of organisational life, and critically depends on hard-copy paper writing and delivery. Warning memos are sent when there is a perception that someone is not doing the right thing, The warning may be low-key and confidential, with perhaps no copy going to anyone else. This is the type of communication that might be written if a writer thought that verbal hints or warnings were not hitting their mark by changing the behaviour of the target person. As the gravity of the warning increases, the likelihood of copies being sent to others increases. In the first instance, however, the warning memo may be sent in hard copy only – to maintain confidentiality, by using a paper document only, but with the message conveying a threat that other channels will be used if this one doesn't work.

Warning memos may form part of a formal discipline procedure, perhaps leading to dismissal or termination. Care has to be taken in the wording of warning memos, primarily due not just to the feelings of the target person, but also because if the content is not factually incontrovertible, then there may be legal repercussions (see figure 4.21). Do not make accusations you cannot substantiate, and do not use abusive or demeaning language.

Warning memo: a document sent when there is a perception that someone is not doing the right thing

While there is still hope of a negative situation being turned around, try and accentuate any positives there are.

To: Mitch Presbury, Welfare Clients/North Zone Management Team

From: Zach Warrell, Welfare Clients Division Manager

Subject: Download Problems

Date: 19 September 2011

Further to our brief conversation today, I thought it useful to document my views on this situation.

An IT professional like yourself knows the cost involved in running a corporate broadband service, and is also aware of company policy on downloading personal and/or offensive material.

Despite your protestations that neither you nor anyone in your department is involved in inappropriate use of the system, the new security tracking software I have been using suggests otherwise, as do total download figures for the past two months.

You are responsible for usage in your area, just as I am responsible for usage in the broader division. We are presumed by head office to be completely in control of electronic traffic and that extends to legal liability as well. As I mentioned to you in our conversation, recent local and interstate legal actions involving the downloading of inappropriate material (games, pornography, etc.) demonstrate that we all need to be vigilant in this regard.

This paper memo has not been copied to anyone, and I see no need for this matter to proceed any further right now. However, if I do become aware of further problems arising in this area, I will send you an email memo as a formal warning with copies to HK and BLJ in head office, with a date-stamped copy of this memo attached.

You are a skilled person, Mitch, and we do not want to lose such skills if it can be helped. Let's work together on this, and not against each other.

FIGURE 4.21 A warning memo

STUDENT STUDY GUIDE

SUMMARY

Letters can be a remarkably effective means of communication in a variety of situations. The 8 Cs of written communication (being clear, correct, comprehensive, concise, credible, considerate, courteous and conscientious) can again be usefully applied in this genre. We also need to ensure that we choose an effective layout for our documents. We may use a direct or indirect approach to structuring letters, depending on their purpose. Good news letters, relating to situations in which we can give our readers what they want, usually call for the direct approach. Bad news letters, relating to situations in which we cannot give our readers what they want, often require the indirect approach. Persuasive letters are written when we want to influence our readers' behaviour. All types of letters require the adoption of specific techniques of expression to convey their meaning effectively. Emails, which also vary widely according to their purpose, need to be crafted with an internal audience in mind, although they are increasingly being used for external audiences. The paper-based, hard-copy memo still has some uses in certain situations, and has not become obsolete.

KEY TERMS

AIDA sequence *p. 138*
announcement email *p. 144*
bad news letter *p. 121*
bad news sandwich *p. 127*
collection letter *p. 141*

complex sentence
   technique *p. 129*
full block format *p. 119*
good news letter *p. 121*
instruction email *p. 145*

memo/memorandum *p. 142*
persuasive letter *p. 138*
request email *p. 144*
warning memo *p. 146*
'you' attitude *p. 113*

REVIEW QUESTIONS

1. What are the 8 Cs of writing?
2. List three optional parts of letters.
3. Identify at least three ways in which good news letters can be mishandled.
4. In what circumstances should the direct approach be used in bad news letters?
5. Identify at least three techniques that can be used in creating bad news letters.
6. List at least three different ways of getting the reader's attention when writing a persuasive letter.
7. Consider the strengths and weaknesses chart in chapter 1 (table 1.8), and then perform the same type of analysis for letters, emails and memos. For each of the three communication channels, try to generate at least two strengths and weaknesses not listed in chapter 1.

APPLIED ACTIVITIES

1. Assume that you are the marketing manager for Perennial Insurance. You have been unhappy with your long-time advertising agency and have been privately interviewing representatives of six other agencies. Perennial is trying to build up its customer base with younger clients, and is developing new products in health insurance, accident insurance, employment interruption insurance and computer equipment insurance. After much deliberation, you and your colleagues have finally opted for JJC, an energetic outfit that specialises in television advertising featuring computer-generated special effects. Write to Miranda Styles, CEO of JJC, telling her of the good news of their being given a two-year contract to do all of Protector's advertising business. The contract with your current advertising firm has only another four months to

run, and you want to get together with representatives of JJC as soon as possible to start planning campaigns for the 12-month period starting on the completion of that four months.

2. You are still marketing manager for Perennial Insurance. Write a bad news letter to Maurie Chen, Managing Director of AdverTies, the agency that has handled Perennial's advertising for the past seven years. Their contract is up for review in four months, and you are not going to renew it.

3. You are the manager of The Sound Studio, a shop that specialises in up-market home entertainment systems. A customer, Elisabeth Frankel, recently returned a Technor 4000 surround sound television set, claiming it was faulty. She had purchased the set only last month, and you offer a 48-month warranty on everything you sell. Your technician, Brian, has tested the Technor, and found that the appliance has been subjected to extremely high volumes, thus deforming two speakers, and a large quantity of liquid, possibly water from a flower vase, has been spilled on the top casing and has leaked into the inside cavity. Write a letter to Frankel, explaining why you cannot repair the set or replace it free of charge. Invent whatever details you feel are necessary.

4. You work as assistant to the manager in World of Paint, a paint store. Jacek Lewicki, a painter, has recently applied for a $5000 credit account with the store. Lewicki has only recently launched his business, and you have doubts that he will be able to find many customers, given that the local area is already over-serviced with painters. Write a letter of refusal. Invent whatever details you feel are necessary.

5. Assume that you are the general manager of a new branch of the community bank VillageBank. You are overseeing the fitting out of the office space on the main street of the suburb of Eastleigh. You have ample supplies of VillageBank brochures but decide to do a mail-out of letters to every household in a five-kilometre radius of the bank. VillageBank head office has purchased the mailing list database for you from a commercial service and is interested in seeing whether a local mail campaign will have any impact on customer growth. The major banks have created much ill feeling in the past few years by increasing existing fees and creating new ones for personal and business customers. They have also alienated many of their older customers by forcing the pace on inducing people to use automatic tellers and internet banking. Write a letter to each household and business in your target area endeavouring to persuade them to set up at least one new account at the VillageBank branch or to consider taking out a loan for personal, housing or business purposes.

6. You are finance manager of Green Energy, a company that specialises in generating and selling sustainable power to domestic and business customers. You notice that a number of your corporate clients have overdue bills. Write a series of collection letters that can be used as templates by your staff in extracting payment from these corporate clients.

7. You have been assigned the duty of running the annual Christmas party in an organisation you are familiar with. Write an announcement memo to all staff, setting out details of time, venue, entertainment, costs and any other details you feel are relevant.

8. You are the general manager of welfare services at the local council. You supervise 322 staff, who run five different child day-care, disabled industry training and aged-care facilities. Last year two highly favourable articles were written in national newspapers about your operations, and the articles have since been reproduced overseas. You have just been notified that a delegation of federal politicians and overseas journalists will be visiting your offices in three weeks' time. You decide to organise a team presentation about all the operations in your areas. Send out a request memo to all five facilities' team leaders, asking for current information about their operations.

What case study material can they provide? What visual content (diagrams, digital photographs) could be used in the presentation? Invent whatever details you need.

9. Consider something (an item of equipment, a software package, a recipe) you are familiar with. Write an instruction memo to another person, real or fictitious.

10. Assume you are the head of sales at Juggernaut Manufacturing. Angela Hayes, one of your best sales representatives, has arrived smelling of alcohol several times in the past week, and apparently affected by her alcohol intake. You have attempted to raise the matter in a half-joking way, but Angela has taken offence at your remarks. She is a competent professional, in fact one of your rising stars, but you cannot ignore the situation in case it worsens. You spoke with her today in the corridor, trying to strike a more serious note, but she dismissed your concerns, affirming that her private life was hers and hers alone. You know that she has been involved in two minor accidents in the car park in the past fortnight, and graffiti about her condition is now appearing in both the male and female toilets on the floor you both work on. Write a warning memo to Angela.

WHAT WOULD YOU DO?

The new boss of your organisation, Josephine Hoo, arrived a few days back, but not many staff have met her yet, not even team leaders such as yourself. This morning she sent everyone an email that covered a number of matters, but it was the final paragraph that has everyone talking:

We are now well into the twenty-first century, and that means that we have got to start looking like a twenty-first century corporation. As of the first of next month, we will be doing away with all paper-based communication, for both internal and external purposes. I see no reason why all communication should now not be conducted by email. Only in exceptional circumstances will communications be mailed. I attach letterhead templates. Please install them in your email systems, and use them from now on. I believe that this will dramatically differentiate us from our competitors, and that our clients will be impressed with our commitment to contemporary communication practices.

Some people in your area are impressed by this new approach, but most are uncomfortable with it, finding it high-handed and impractical. Jane, never at a loss for words, comments, 'Oh yeah, this is *really* going to impress our top customers – I don't think!' A delegation of people, led by Jane, soon approaches you. After almost an hour of agitated discussion, Jane requests that you go and speak to Josephine personally and ask her to reconsider this new policy. What will you do?

SUGGESTED READING

Cyphert, Dale, Guffey, Mary Ellen & Stancill, James McNeill 2006, *Communicating at work*, South-Western, Mason, OH.

Kimball, Cheryl & Van Gelder, Joni 2007, *The ultimate book of business letters*, Entrepreneur Press, New York.

Lindsell-Roberts, Sheryl 1999, *Writing business letters for dummies*, John Wiley & Sons, New York.

Locker, Kitty O 2011, *Business communication: building critical skills*, 5th rev. edn., McGraw-Hill Higher Education, New York.

Oates, Laurel Currie & Enquist, Anne 2003, *Just memos*, Aspen, New York.

Poe, Roy W 2009, *The McGraw-Hill handbook of more business letters*, 4th edn., McGraw-Hill, New York.

Shipley, David & Schwalbe, Will 2009, *Send: why people email so badly and how to do it better*, rev. edn., Knopf, New York.

Smith, Helen 2004, *Letter writing, email and texting: essentials*, Foulsham, Slough, UK.

Taylor, Shirley 2004, *Model business letters, e-mails and other business documents*, Financial Times/Prentice Hall/Pearson, London.

REFERENCES

Blake, Gary & Bly, Robert W 1992, *The elements of business writing: a guide to writing clear, concise letters, memos, reports, proposals, and other business documents*, Longman, New York.

Chesterton, Laura (ed.) 1992, *Effective business communication*, Houghton Mifflin, Boston, MA.

Eunson, Baden 1995, *Communicating with customers*, John Wiley & Sons, Brisbane.

Lahiff, James & Penrose, John 1997, *Business communication: strategies and skills*, 5th edn, Prentice Hall, Upper Saddle River, NJ.

Maslow, Abraham 1970, *Motivation and personality*, 2nd edn., Harper & Row, New York.

Myers, Marshall 2007, 'The use of pathos in charity letters: some notes toward a theory and analysis', *Journal of Technical Writing and Communication*, vol. 37, no. 1, pp. 3–16.

Nationmaster.com 2011, 'Encyclopedia – paper size', www.nationmaster.com.

Ober, Scott 2007, *Contemporary business communication*, 7th edn., Houghton Mifflin, Boston, MA.

Troyka, Lynn Q & Hesse, Doug 2010, *Quick access: reference for writers*, 6th edn, Longman, New York.

Wells, Walter 1988, *Communications in business*, 5th edn., PWS-Kent, Boston, MA.

Wilson, Kevin & Wauson, Jennifer 2011, *The AMA handbook of business writing: the ultimate guide to style, grammar, punctuation, construction and formatting*, American Management Association, New York.

5

Reports and proposals

LEARNING OBJECTIVES

After studying this chapter you should be able to:

- Explain the differences and similarities between formats, types and subgenres of reports
- Explain the differences and similarities between reports and essays
- Explain why documents need to contain an appropriate balance of information and persuasion
- Demonstrate competence in writing a longer, analytical research report
- Explain the differences between reports and submissions, and proposals and tenders

So you've got to write a report ...

The ability to write reports is one of the most useful writing skills you can acquire. To be a good report writer means you must be competent at describing and analysing situations and people. However, the main complaint of employers is that graduates' writing is too 'essay-like'; often verging on the illiterate, and with limited relevance or effectiveness to the real world:

> If there is dissatisfaction with graduate skills as such, it probably lies in the area of written communication, because the majority of students are not taught to write in a manner appropriate to business communications. (Nielsen, 2000, p. 9)

As Kuiper (2009, p. 1) points out,

> For many students the word *report* suggests a term paper, a book review, or a case analysis. But those documents differ from on-the-job reports in many respects. Whereas you may write a term paper to demonstrate your knowledge of a subject, you will write business reports to influence the actions of other people. Although school reports usually flow upward (from student to instructor), business reports move up, down, and across the formal organizational structure. You may use the Internet or books and journals from your university library as the major data sources for a term paper, but your business reports will frequently contain data from the company files or your experience and observations, as well as from print and electronic media. The quality of a term paper may affect your course grade, but the quality of a business report can determine the success or failure of your career – and that of your company.

There are many types of reports, but in this chapter we will focus primarily on analytical or research reports. We will also consider some types of documents that bear a strong resemblance to reports – namely, submissions, proposals or tenders. Table 5.1 sets out some of the key features of differing types of reports.

TABLE 5.1 Some report/proposal formats

Report type	Function	Audience	Format and features
Computer or data report	Gives quick visual overview of data	■ Mainly internal ■ Decision makers and process monitors	■ Mainly graphic renditions of tabular data from databases and spreadsheets ■ Minimal amount of descriptive and analytical text ■ Often created with specialised software (e.g. Crystal Reports) ■ Rarely involves conclusions or recommendations
Incident report	Gives quick overview of event not associated with human injury	■ Mainly internal ■ Decision makers and process monitors	■ Strongly fact-based: what, where, why, who, when, how ■ Created to document nonroutine situation ■ May be used to detect emerging problems ■ May use standard format print/online document ■ Occasionally will give conclusions and recommendations
Accident report	Gives quick overview of event associated with human injury	■ Mainly internal ■ Decision makers and process monitors	■ Strongly fact-based: what, where, why, who, when, how ■ Created to document nonroutine situation ■ May be used to detect emerging problems ■ May use standard format print/online document ■ Occasionally will give conclusions and recommendations ■ Critical part of occupational health and safety/legal regimes
Periodic report	Gives quick picture of routine processes and situations	■ Mainly internal ■ Decision makers and process monitors	■ Documents routine situations ■ Standardised format is used across time and space to facilitate comparability and monitoring ■ Does not include conclusions or recommendations

Report type	Function	Audience	Format and features
Progress report	Gives picture of nonroutine processes and situations	• Mainly internal, but can be for external, such as clients • Decision makers and process monitors	• Documents nonroutine situations, such as projects • Key function is to inform whether project is on schedule, and if not, why not • Sometimes has standardised format • May give conclusions and recommendations
Memo report	Gives picture of nonroutine processes and situations	• Mainly internal • Decision makers and process monitors	• Longer than a standard memo • More structured than a standard memo — will have sections with headings • May involve conclusions and recommendations
Letter report	Gives picture of nonroutine processes and situations	• Mainly external • Decision makers	• Longer than a standard letter • More structured than a standard letter — will have sections with headings • May involve conclusions and recommendations
Justification report	Presents a case for change (e.g. a purchase, a new system and/or staffing)	• Mainly internal • Decision makers	• Needs to establish a rationale for change in status quo • Case needs to be established based on research, costings • Will involve conclusions and recommendations • In effect, a short proposal
Accountability report	Gives quick picture of routine processes and situations	• Mainly external • Regulators, often in public sector	• Examples include tax reports, environment/equal opportunity/health and safety/industry compliance documentation • Usually on a periodic basis • May use standard format print/online document • Rarely gives conclusions and recommendations
Research or analytical report	Gives detailed analysis of a situation	• Mainly internal • Decision makers	• May be long (1000+ words) • May involve considerable research • Involves analysis as well as description • Format and structure are created by writer, usually in accordance with conventions • Will give conclusions and (usually) recommendations
Proposal/ submission/ tender	Presents a case for change (e.g. a purchase, a new system and/or staffing)	• Can be internal or external • Decision makers	• Similar in many respects to analytical report • Used in competitive bidding situations
Annual report	Gives account of year's operation of organisation	• Mainly external: shareholders and stakeholders • Staff	• May be elaborately designed, with high production values • Meets legal requirements for accountability • May not include any conclusions or recommendations

Information and persuasion: getting the mix right

The purpose of some report types is purely to provide specific information to their audiences — just the facts and nothing else. Others are intended to be persuasive: their object is to convince decision makers, for example, to adopt a course of action or to buy a new piece of equipment. Figure 5.1 shows how different document types can be placed on a continuum, according to the **information/persuasion mix**. Does this mean that some documents are purely persuasive, while others are exclusively informative? Not necessarily. A persuasive document needs to contain proof as a basis for persuasion (see chapter 12), while even the most basic informative document — for example, a simple data report showing a graphic

Information/persuasion mix: the synthesis of fact and opinion in a report; information is concerned with fact; persuasion is concerned with opinion

rendering of data from a spreadsheet — may prove more persuasive than a long but unconvincing and poorly presented analytical report on the same topic.

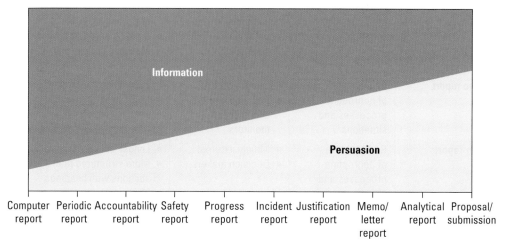

It follows, then, that while report writers can often get away with filling in a few boxes in routine report documents, they may need to become more versatile in order to create nonroutine reports based on a synthesis of fact and opinion. Indeed, the more we progress in our careers, the more we will be required to produce documents dealing with nonroutine situations.

Information, persuasion, entertainment, talk and lobbying

We need, therefore, to get the information/persuasion mix of our documents under control. To be really effective, however, we must consider three other factors too.

Firstly, we need to consider the *look* of the document, or the document design (see chapter 2). Although reports are work-based documents, most of their readers will still appreciate a striking-looking, colourful design rather than a conventional, unimaginative black-and-white one. While most of us are not trained graphic designers, we should recognise that a well-designed, attractively presented document is likely to communicate a message more effectively.

Secondly, we need to consider that sometimes a written document marks the beginning of a communication process rather than the end. Increasingly, document writers are asked to give a spoken presentation — in effect, an oral report — to back up, or sometimes substitute for, a written report. Office suite software makes this task a lot easier although sometimes it still makes sense to seek the help of a professional graphic designer, especially when we consider that words and images that look good on a page do not necessarily look as good on a screen — and vice versa (see 'Using audiovisual aids' in chapter 11). Be prepared, therefore, to deliver your report verbally as well as in writing. In some circumstances, your audience may not read a word of what you have written unless a spoken presentation from you piques their interest (see chapter 11).

Finally, we need to consider to what extent the communication process reaches beyond the delivery of written and oral reports. Neither guarantees that your message is conveyed; one message may have to reinforce the other (see 'Communicating effectively using channels' in chapter 1). Sometimes you need to lobby or attempt to influence members of your audience so that they will act on your recommendations. In other words, you have to write it, pitch it and sell it (lobbying will be considered later in this chapter).

The big leap: writing essays and writing reports

The report is a specific genre of writing, like the novel, poetry, email or journalism. Within the report genre are subgenres, such as memo reports and research reports. When asked to prepare a report for the first time, many writers draw inspiration from the genre they have had most experience with in their formal education – the **essay**. Essay writing requires a complete set of skills (see chapter 7), and many of these skills are different from those required for writing reports. *The most common complaint made about reports written by inexperienced writers is that the report 'reads like an essay, not a report'.* Study the similarities and differences between the two genres in table 5.2, and respect them.

Essay: a document type that is concerned primarily with analysis rather than problem solving, and which rarely contains recommendations

TABLE 5.2 Reports and essays compared

Genre/attributes	Essay	Report
Approach	Tends to concentrate on analysis of a situation or problem, without necessarily providing solutions	Tends to be problem focused and action oriented
Topic/focus	Usually set by others as topic to be answered	Usually set by others as a brief or with terms of reference
Table of contents	Not often included	Common in longer documents
Context	Academic world: submitted for marks; one of many submitted	World of work: submitted to aid decision making and problem solving, but will attract compliments, criticism or both; usually only one submitted.
Summary	Not often included	Usually given, often mentioning key conclusions and recommendations
Audience reading style	Likely to read all the way through; unlikely to reread	Likely to skim; may reread for reference
Introduction	Usually included; sets scene for what is to come	Always included; sets scene for what is to come
Discussion/analysis	Yes — the main body of writing	Yes — the main body of writing
Conclusion	Yes — sums up the situation, gives an overview	Yes — sums up the situation, gives an overview
Recommendations	Not usually made	Usually made — suggest specific course of action that report reader may choose to take
Layout techniques	■ Paragraphs tend to be longer ■ Sections and subsections not often numbered ■ Bullet points not often used	■ Paragraphs tend to be shorter ■ Sections and subsections often numbered, giving clear signposts to structure ■ Bullet points sometimes used
Tables, graphics	Not always used	Often used to show data
Expression of opinion	Opinions are often expressed throughout	Opinions tend to be reserved for conclusions and recommendations
Style	■ May be impersonal and objective, or personal and subjective ■ Sentences and words tend to be longer ■ Tends to have high readability scores because of academic jargon/formal register	■ Tends to be impersonal and objective ■ Sentences and words tend to be shorter ■ May sometimes have high readability scores because of professional jargon
Referencing, quotation	May be extensive; secondary data tends to predominate	Usually light; primary data may be used as much as secondary data
Authoring	Usually individual	Often collective
Relationship to spoken presentation	Does not often lead to spoken presentation	Can often lead to oral presentation

Simply being aware that a document is an example of a particular genre, with a specific set of conventions, may help you become a better writer not only in that genre, but in others as well, because you may now have a better grasp of the distinctive structures of genres and thus move more adeptly between them. For example, although the essay is primarily concerned with analysis, the report is usually more concerned with problem solving, although analysis necessarily forms the basis of that problem solving. It is also common for reports to contain recommendations.

ASSESS YOURSELF

Examine samples of essays you have written and consider what would be needed to turn them into reports.

What are reports for?

Table 5.1 catalogued different types, or subgenres, of reports. What are the main purposes of reports? A report can be used:
- to record routine events
- to record nonroutine events
- as the basis for making decisions
- as a basis for avoiding decisions

Reports can be purely descriptive or informative, recording routine events such as:
- monthly sales
- daily catches of fish
- the weather forecast for the next four days
- national balance of payment figures.

Descriptive or informative reports can also describe nonroutine events, such as accidents. They tend to be short (e.g. one page), are often set out on pre-printed forms, and rarely contain sections on conclusions or recommendations. Computer reports are among the most frequently requested descriptive or informative reports. They mainly present data drawn from software databases or spreadsheets.

More analytical or persuasive reports can be used as the basis for making decisions. These reports usually present a large amount of information on topics such as the following:
- Should we seek to open up new export markets?
- Should we hire four more staff for the legal department, or should we contract the work out to independent specialists?
- Why has the northern region consistently outperformed the other three offices?
- Are we happy with our existing software, or could rival packages do a better job?
- Should we use some of our scarce resources to set up an in-house fitness facility?
- Are existing government broadcasting regulations on censorship adequate?

Analytical or persuasive reports may be short (e.g. a memo or letter) or long, depending on the scope of the problem they seek to address.

Reports are vital decision-making tools, but in some situations they may be used as a basis for *avoiding* decisions. Researching and writing a report can take up a lot of time, and even when complete there is no guarantee that the recommendations made will be implemented. Some people who commission reports are concerned to bring about change, while others are concerned to maintain the status quo while giving the *impression* of being open to change.

Many a report languishes unheeded, gathering dust on a shelf. This may be for good reason. Perhaps the report was no good; perhaps the recommendations were impractical, or at least currently unrealistic. On the other hand, good reports are sometimes shelved because the individuals who commissioned them never had any intention of following them up. So if you believe in your report, and want it to have some impact, then writing it may be only the beginning. As we have noted, not only may you need to speak to it in a formal presentation or oral report, but you may also have to lobby for it, perhaps going behind the scenes to try to persuade decision makers of the wisdom of your analysis. In other words, after you write, you may need to fight.

Don't be discouraged by this. Firstly, your audience may already be suffering from information overload, and you will need to get your message across to them with care. Secondly, no matter how long your report document is, almost certainly you will not have been able to get everything in it that you wanted to. Talking about it in a formal presentation or an informal lobbying situation allows you to get across your total message. As we saw in chapter 1, total communication effectiveness often involves using multiple channels and repetition and reinforcement of the message, so why should the report genre be any different? This sounds like a lot of work, and it is. But try to see it as less a chore than an opportunity to strut your stuff – to show your audience that you have exceptional problem-solving and communication skills. That can't be bad for your career.

Who are reports for? Know your audience

Once you have decided *what* your report is for, you need to decide *who* it is for. Who is your audience? If you need to deliver an oral report, who will you be speaking to? Is there an unofficial as well as an official **audience**? (Note that in chapter 1 we saw that audiences in different fields of communication are known by different names – listeners, publics, demographics, viewers, customers, clients, stakeholders, auditors, users and participants.)

Audience: the reader(s) of the report; the audience may be larger than you expect, including both official and unofficial components

Nonroutine reports are normally commissioned or authorised by a person or persons further up the organisational pyramid. If the culture of your organisation encourages initiative, you may find it useful to volunteer to write and present a report, perhaps even suggesting the topic yourself.

You need to know certain things about your audience. Once you know these things, you can respond appropriately. Some questions about your audience, and your appropriate responses, are set out in table 5.3. Note that these questions and considerations may apply to audiences for routine as well as nonroutine documents.

TABLE 5.3 Analysing your audience

Factor	Question	Response
Personal style	Is the audience made up of people who prefer hearing rather than reading about something?	Put more effort into preparing the oral report than the written report.
	Is the audience made up of people who prefer reading rather than hearing about something?	Put more effort into the written report than the oral report.
	Is the audience made up of people who prefer detail rather than the big picture?	Concentrate on detail, but be ready to show how details fit into the big picture.
	Is your audience made up of people who prefer the big picture rather than the detailed approach?	Give the big picture, but be ready to supply details to fill in the big picture.

(continued)

TABLE 5.3 *(continued)*

Factor	Question	Response
Technical background	Is your audience made up of people who are familiar and comfortable with the area's key ideas, assumptions and jargon?	Don't waste time on background explanations, as your audience might feel insulted. Jump straight in at the technical level, but be on guard against in-group complacency or groupthink (which occurs when a group is cut off from reality in its world of comfortable and nonthreatening assumptions).
	Is your audience made up of people who are *not* familiar and comfortable with the area's key ideas, assumptions and jargon?	Define terms, assumptions and key ideas. Make it easy for them with glossaries, simplified visual models, analogies, demonstrations and historical overviews. Don't patronise people, but put them at their ease so they feel confident enough to ask questions. Remember that everyone — even you — has different areas of expertise, and that preparing a basic view of the subject may in fact give you insights that you would otherwise have missed (because you have been too close to the action to see it in perspective).
Status	Does the audience value formality?	Keep it formal.
	Does the audience value informality?	Keep it informal.
	Is it possible that people outside the official audience will read or hear the report?	The answer to this is always *yes* — or you should at least take it that it's *yes*, and act accordingly. It pays to be paranoid. So beware of sweeping generalisations, unsupported assertions, libellous statements, cheap jokes at the expense of others not present. Let your report help, not haunt, your career.
Initial attitude	Positive	Good. Don't lose it by being complacent. Work on it (by paying attention to the listed factors, questions and responses) to make it still more positive.
	Neutral	Good. Work on it to make it positive.
	Hostile	Not so good, but not necessarily disastrous. Pay attention to the listed factors, questions and responses. Are the audience's vested interests threatened by what you are saying? Are you in competition with them for the same scarce resources? Can you show them a mutually beneficial outcome?

Unfortunately, the answer to the questions posed in table 5.3 is usually 'All of the above', and your responses should reflect this. Remember, the difficult takes some time, and the impossible takes a little longer.

What is involved in preparing a report? A production model

All reports have some similarities in the way in which they are produced. Figure 5.2 shows a model of production that will help us to understand just how a report should — and should not — be produced.

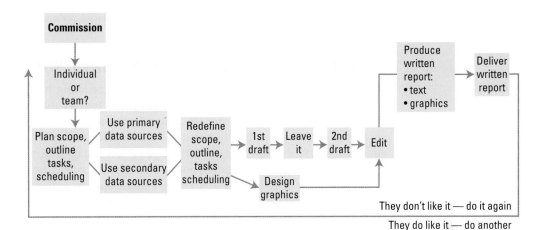

Commissioning the report

Routine reports do not require commissioning: the normal flow of work provides a structure of trigger points for report generation. Nonroutine reports, however, require a specific commissioning decision. The person who commissions the report is normally part of your audience. The actual commissioning may be informal and verbal — 'Oh, Joe, can you do me a report on your monthly sales figures?' — or formal and written, set out in a letter or memo.

The **scope** or focus of the report (its *terms of reference*) is defined at the time of commission.

Scope: the terms of reference of a report; what the document is about, and what it is not about

Individual or team?

A decision needs to be made as to whether the report will be generated by an individual or a team. This will be determined by the complexity of the task and the mix of skills required. Sometimes, especially with nonroutine documents, you will need to put together a writing group; sometimes, especially with routine documents, you will need simply to contact individuals in a loose network around you to get figures and facts (see chapter 18).

Plan scope, outline, tasks, scheduling

What is the report about? What is it *not* about? In nonroutine documents, questions of scope will have a strong influence on the title of the report. The scope will determine the structure of the report. At this stage, a detailed structure is not required, but an outline is. Such an outline will set out the sections, headings, points and subpoints of the overall document. The outline of your report will bear more than a passing resemblance to the table of contents of the final document.

The scope and outline will help to determine the tasks of research and production, and the time frame or schedule within which such tasks need to be achieved. At this stage the types of questions that need to be asked include: How long do I have to complete the report? What resources do I have? What specific subtasks can the report be broken down into? How much more to the writing of a report is there than the actual writing? Such time and task planning is not trivial (see also online chapter 'Writing skills 5: how to write'):

> The first rule is to give yourself time to write your report. You will need to investigate the topic and gather the information, and then plan and structure your report, form your conclusions, write it and revise it. Writing the report actually accounts for quite a small percentage of the overall process. (Thornbory & White 2007)

Primary, secondary and tertiary sources of data

Once decisions about scope, structure, tasks and scheduling have been made, primary data can be collected and analysed, and secondary and tertiary data can be studied. Sources of primary data include questionnaires, interviews and company records. Primary data does not exist until it is created by researchers or people who collect data as part of their jobs. Once such data exists, it can form the basis of secondary and tertiary data, which is published in various forms, including books, journals, electronic databases and encyclopaedias.

Secondary and tertiary data is easier and cheaper to collect than primary data, but it may be too general or out of date. Much will depend on the situation, the problem to be studied, the nature of existing data, and the availability of resources to create new data and retrieve existing data. Nevertheless, it makes sense to check secondary and tertiary data first: if this information is good enough, there will be no need to go to the trouble of creating primary data.

Redefine scope, outline, tasks, scheduling

Once primary, secondary and tertiary data have been collected and studied, it may be that the report needs to be changed. Now, you may discover that:

- what you thought was going to be a general study will simply be too big, and you now need to narrow the focus
- what you thought was a small-scale phenomenon has much wider ramifications, and a broader approach is needed
- the data provides answers but also raises new questions
- promising areas turn out to be dead-ends
- initially unpromising areas turn out to be gold mines
- some data proves to be unavailable
- some data proves to be so rich that it is difficult to manage
- some areas are interesting, but the time to explore them is not available
- your enthusiasm for some areas declines
- your enthusiasm for other areas increases (see 'Research skills and the knowledge-based society' in chapter 3).

A redefinition of scope is a fairly normal occurrence and nothing to worry about. Of course, it may also entail a redefinition of the report's outline structure, and of the appropriate tasks and scheduling.

Design graphics

Once the outline is clear, decisions can be made about what type of graphic communication needs to be included in the document. You may have to speak to your report — in effect, to deliver it orally — so keep in mind that graphics prepared for the page might not necessarily work as projected graphics in a presentation.

Draft, set aside, redraft

Drafting: writing multiple versions of a document, allowing time to reconsider, reconceptualise and re-edit each version until a final draft is achieved

Now the **drafting** begins. Remember that what you write now will not necessarily be what your audience eventually reads or hears. Very few of us can write so flawlessly that our first draft can be used as the final draft. Expect to complete at least two drafts (more if the need arises). If time permits, and you should try to schedule the work so that it does, set the draft document aside before rereading it and attempting the next draft. You can get too close to a piece of work and lose perspective.

All your ideas and insights will not simply appear, fully formed, in your first draft. Once your mind is set loose on a problem, it will produce all kinds of straightforward and quirky perspectives over time (see online chapter 'Writing skills 5: how to write'). It's not uncommon to have a blinding insight into a problem analysed well after a document has been finished. Preparing reports is rarely associated with creativity, but the analysis involved in preparing reports is part of the wider problem-solving process, and that process is often a creative one. Work with the creative impulse by allowing time to pass while you turn your attention to other matters, returning to start the second draft with a refreshed mind and, with luck, new perspectives.

Edit, produce, deliver

Once you have completed your final draft, you can edit it more closely. Editing entails checking the logical flow of information, the clarity of expression, the language mechanics, the layout, the conventions of citation and so forth. If you are required to prepare an oral as well as a written report, this is an opportune time to edit or repackage the content of the written report so that it is more suitable for spoken delivery (see online chapter 'Writing skills 5: how to write'). Office software packages appear to simplify this content repackaging task, but be careful: what works well on the printed page will not necessarily work well on a computer slide, and vice versa.

The production of the document is no minor task. Aesthetic decisions about layout design and overall look have to be made and then executed professionally. As mentioned, the report's visual appeal can substantially influence its acceptance. Make sure that any graphic illustrations enhance your message, rather than detract from it.

Delivery of a written report may be a straightforward process, without much ritual. A paper document may be sent through an organisation's internal mail, or it may be sent by email, usually as an attachment. However, the ritual of physically handing over a document to the person who commissioned it may be worth retaining, as it constitutes a lobbying act in itself. Presenting an oral report tends to be more ritualised.

Evaluate

Do they like it? Do they hate it? Either outcome may point to further report writing in the future. If your audience responds negatively, you may be asked to go back and do it again. If the audience likes it, you may be asked to do others. It won't do your career any harm to be known as someone who can be relied on to produce a useful report.

Analytical reports

Let's now apply what we have learned about reports by looking at 'the big one' – the analytical or research report. Most formal analytical or investigative reports have a standard structure, although some individual writers and organisations have developed their own variations. This type of report has three main sections, with items in each section being either essential or optional (table 5.4). Let's consider what may be involved in this large document, and then look at what such a document might look like.

TABLE 5.4 Structure of an analytical report

Section	Essential	Optional
Front matter	■ Title page ■ Summary/synopsis ■ Table of contents	■ Cover ■ Terms of reference ■ Memo/letter of transmittal ■ List of figures ■ List of tables
Body	■ Introduction ■ Discussion ■ Conclusions ■ Recommendations	■ Figures (diagrams) ■ Tables (data arrays) ■ Plates (photographs)
End matter	■ References/bibliography	■ Index ■ Glossary ■ Appendices

Good news and bad news: structure and the politics of persuasion

Direct structure: used to deliver a 'good news' message in a straightforward manner at the beginning of the report

Indirect structure: used to defer the major impact of a 'bad news' message until later in the report

A report can have either a **direct structure** (in which you state the gist of your message at the start) or an **indirect structure** (in which you defer this statement). Which structure you choose will often depend on the reception you expect from your audience: if you expect them to be happy to receive your message, this is a 'good news' situation and a direct approach should be used. If you expect them to be unhappy to receive your message, or to have reservations about it, this is a 'bad news' situation and the indirect approach is preferred.

The indirect approach may be used when you are describing a complex situation, with a number of challenging but nevertheless soluble problems, and you simply need to introduce your audience to such solutions before they react prematurely to the potentially negative aspects of the message. Writing in this form will stretch your abilities as a writer, but that is also challenging.

When deciding whether to use a direct or indirect structure, you need to consider the sequence in which you will present your argument, paying particular attention to your summary or synopsis. Choose your words carefully according to what you are trying to achieve: when using the indirect structure, you do not aim to be dishonest, but rather to create a context that will stimulate considered rather than impulsive and reactive decision making (figure 5.3).

Direct structure: summary section wording	Indirect structure: summary section wording
This report examines the need for policy measures to cope with new budget constraints, particularly in the area of salaries. 　It is recommended that: ■ band A staff take a pay cut of 12 per cent ■ band B staff take a pay cut of 6.5 per cent, with all overtime eliminated ■ no expenses be allowable unless given prior approval by DOF.	This report examines the need for policy measures to cope with new budget constraints, particularly in the area of salaries. 　Various issues are examined, including the possibility of: ■ pay cuts ■ reducing or eliminating overtime ■ changing approval mechanisms for expenses.

FIGURE 5.3 Direct and indirect report structures

Source: Adapted from Anderson (2010, p. 132).

Cover

The document may be secured in a folder or even professionally bound as a book. The line between 'professional' and 'nonprofessional' document production has been blurred in the past few years with the increased availability and sophistication of computer word processing packages. All but the briefest reports are likely to have a cover. It is not difficult for a report writer today to design and create a cover featuring stylish typography and images. People do judge books by their covers, and it is important that the cover of a report is inviting enough to motivate the prospective reader to look further.

A folder or binding will protect the report and give the document a stronger identity, making it less likely to be lost in the paperwork that builds up on many people's desks. Durability and visibility may help ensure that it is placed on a shelf, where it can be easily retrieved, rather than filed away where it may sink without trace. An attractive cover will help; if possible, ensure that the report title is on the front and on the spine.

As with all organisational communications, house style and organisational culture are paramount: if your cover is likely to be regarded by the organisation as too radical, distracting or wasteful, then follow the accepted conventions.

Letter of transmittal: introductory or covering document for a report, used when the audience is outside the organisation

Memo of transmittal: introductory or covering document for a report, used when the audience for your document is within the organisation

Letter/memorandum of transmittal

You may be required to compose a **letter** or **memo of transmittal** for a report. This is the most personal part of the communication exercise. It is the most direct message from writer to reader. Table 5.5 shows typical wording of such a letter or memo.

TABLE 5.5 Typical wording used in a letter or memo of transmission

Letter/memo of transmittal section	Typical wording
Salutation to the person who commissioned or authorised the report	*'Dear Mr/Ms Smith . . .'*
Statement of purpose of letter/memo	*'Here is the report on . . . you requested. . .'*
Brief overview or summary of report	*'In this report you will find . . .'*
Acknowledgements to people who helped you with your investigations	*'Several people proved to be of great assistance to me . . .'*
Courteous close	*'Thank you for the opportunity to investigate . . . If you have any questions about the report, please contact me . . .'*

Some writers will include a brief mention of their recommendations in the letter or memo. Whether you decide to do so will depend on factors such as whether your recommendations are controversial and you would prefer the reader to read the rationale behind them before being confronted with them, as well as on space constraints.

If the report is transmitted internally, within the organisation, then a memo of transmittal, in standard memo format, is used. If a report is transmitted to someone in another organisation, then a letter of transmittal, in standard letter format, is used.

Title

The title of the report should clearly describe to the reader what the report is about. Remember, what is obvious to you in a title may not be obvious to your reader: you may be too close to the issue, taking for granted a knowledge of certain concepts or jargon that may not be familiar to your reader. Try out a number of titles on people who are more removed from the problem.

If the report has a cover, the wording of the cover title and the title page should be identical. Your title is a promise to the reader, and the report itself should fulfil that promise. The promise will not be realised, for example, if the scope of the report, as represented by your original title, has since shifted. It is perfectly normal for the scope of a report to shift several times in the course of the document's preparation, for instance when new information leads to different perspectives or conclusions. One of the most often overlooked tasks in editing a report is ensuring that the title actually sums up the content of the final document. Make sure you promise what you deliver and deliver what you promise.

Contents page

On the contents page you will list each element in the front matter, the body of the report and the end matter – with the exception of the letter or memo of transmittal (which should be attached to the front of the report), the cover, the title page and the table of contents itself. All sections and subsections of the report are listed, with their respective page numbers. The table of contents, which will probably be similar to the outline you developed in the report planning process, is the reader's roadmap. The bigger and more complex the report, the more important a table of contents becomes.

List of illustrations

A list of illustrations may be helpful for larger reports with a substantial number of graphics. For more complex documents it may also be useful to provide separate lists for figures and tables (see 'Every picture tells a story: graphic communication' in chapter 2). Note that photographs are sometimes referred to as 'plates' or 'figures'.

Summary/synopsis/abstract

Summary: briefly sums up the content of the document; sometimes the only part of a report that is properly read

Summary, synopsis and abstract are three terms sometimes used interchangeably in report writing. *Synopsis* and *abstract* tend to be used in more academic and scientific documents, while *summary* is the less academic, more general usage. The term *executive summary* is also common. In this brief section you need to summarise the entire content of the body of the report, including the introduction, the main discussion, and your conclusions and recommendations. Keep in mind the considerations of direct versus indirect approach.

At the risk of a bruised ego, you should recognise that the summary is as far as many of your readers will get in your report, or indeed will want to get. They want the quick version, so you must ensure your summary is good. Write your summary last, not first. This may sound paradoxical, but it makes good sense – taking into account sound editing and revision practices as well as compensating for our own shortcomings in human perception when we try to establish a true perspective on our work. After you have completed the first draft of a document you will have a reasonable overview of what it should contain and you will be able to write an accurate summary. At this interim stage, a good summary will confirm what is already present in your document and reveal what is missing. You may need to revise your scope and approach as a result. While this may be annoying, it is better than discovering major errors or omissions after the document has gone out to its audience.

Introduction

The introduction should inform the reader about some or all of the following:
- Background. Why was the report commissioned? What circumstances led people to believe that a report was needed?
- Purpose. What is the purpose of the report?
- Scope. What issues are discussed in the report? What issues are not covered? (This is also known as the brief or terms of reference.)

- Research methods. How was the data in this report obtained? What types of primary, secondary and/or tertiary data were used? Does the data limit the report in any way (see limitations that follow)?
- Definition of terms. What specific terminology is used that the lay reader may not be familiar with? (If there are more than five or six such terms, you should consider including a separate glossary of terms in the end matter of the report.)
- Limitations. What constraints (e.g. time, resources, data) were there on the exercise?
- Assumptions. What has the writer assumed about background, concepts, language and reader awareness?

Discussion

The main discussion, body or findings section is the real meat of the report. It will almost certainly be the largest section, and its preparation will entail the most work. Ensure that your argument is developed clearly, and is broken up logically into sections and subsections, with appropriate headings and subheadings (see online chapter 'Writing skills 5: how to write').

Table 5.6 lists some of the many ways in which to develop an argument. It is possible to combine some of these methods. Given that they all have their limitations, this is sometimes desirable. However, be sure you do not confuse your reader (and possibly yourself).

TABLE 5.6 Some argument development methods

Argument development method	Approach
Chronological	From then to now, and on into the future
Inductive	From the particular to the general
Deductive	From the general to the particular
Geographical	From one area/section/state/country/planet to another
Topical	From one subject to another
Problem/solution	The problem is ... The solution/options are ...
Pros/cons	The advantages are ... The disadvantages are ...
5W/H	Explanation of what, where, when, why, who, how
Ideal/reality	What we would like is ... What we are stuck with is ...

After outlining the problem, it is quite valid to discuss a range of options or alternative responses (the problem–solution approach to developing an argument lends itself particularly to this method). These alternatives can then be referred to when making recommendations. Remember to confine yourself to facts in the discussion section of your report. If you have opinions, you should reserve them for the conclusions and recommendations sections.

Balanced approach: an even-handed writing approach that avoids bias in what is presented or omitted

Some ways in which reports can be broken rather than made include:
- *Preconceived bias.* Make sure that you take a **balanced approach** in your discussion, covering all points of view and options, or at least as many as possible. A common mistake committed by report writers is to come to a topic with preconceived views, and then create a biased document in support of those views. There will always be someone in your audience who can, and will, challenge your preconceived bias, with the result that your reputation will suffer and any good material in your document can more easily be dismissed.

(continued)

(continued)

Topic loyalty or capture: the process by which researcher/writers become so involved with an idea they are reporting on that they lose objectivity and recommend implementation even when some of the evidence suggests this would be inadvisable

Job creationism: the process by which researcher/writers present the outcome of a report in such a way that they become the most likely candidates to implement its recommendations

Timidity: a characteristic of reports that do not confront or tackle the real issues of a situation

Whitewash: a characteristic of reports that avoid apportioning blame where it is due

Vendetta: a characteristic of reports that unfairly ascribe blame to innocent parties

Indiscreet insiderism: a characteristic of reports full of in-group jargon and often unjustified hostility to out-group others

Boosterism: a characteristic of reports that focus only on positive aspects of a situation, unrealistically ignoring negative aspects

Flag-waving: a characteristic of reports that overemphasise the value of the writers' own department, team or section

Hobby horse: a pet project or idea given undue prominence in a report

Sloppiness: a characteristic of reports written in a superficial and unprofessional manner

Reactivity: a characteristic of reports that focus only on the past

Decision avoidance: the behaviour of those who commission reports in order to avoid solving a problem

Conclusions: section of a report in which writers set out their opinions about the facts presented in the report body

- *Acquired bias.* A related pitfall is that of acquired bias, which occurs when **topic loyalty or capture** sets in. A report involves a lot of work, and there is a tendency for some researcher/writers to invest so much time, energy and resources into the document that they become intellectually and emotionally committed to the ideas they are presenting, perhaps to the point of turning a blind eye to the ideas' weaknesses, and find it impossible to reach a negative conclusion.
- *Job creationism.* Topic loyalty or capture also occurs when researcher/writers begin to sense that their recommendations could enhance their own career paths. **Job creationism** may be human nature, but be careful not to fall into the trap, or at least do so with such subtlety that no-one is aware you are doing it.
- *Timidity.* **Timidity** is a problem when report writers present an unchallenging document even when the evidence suggests that faults need to be pointed out and radical changes recommended. Timidity often occurs in organisations with a 'shoot the messenger' culture, where groupthink is prevalent.
- *Whitewash.* A **whitewash** occurs when a report writer conceals the true (and unpleasant) nature of the problem the report was meant to investigate. The guilty parties (problem-creators) escape judgement.
- *Vendetta.* The opposite of a whitewash is a **vendetta**, or witch hunt, which occurs when a report writer aggressively ascribes guilt or responsibility for a problem, sometimes to those who do not deserve it. Note that a report can be both a whitewash and a vendetta.
- *Indiscreet insiderism.* **Indiscreet insiderism** occurs when the writer presumes that only a limited audience of like-minded people will see a document. It may be laden with in-group jargon, and may make hurtful remarks about others outside the in-group. There is no such thing as a totally private and confidential document: write every document so that you could defend it in a court of law.
- *Boosterism.* **Boosterism** means writing propaganda and public relations rather than analysis. For example, a report writer may simply sing the praises of the organisation's products without realistically assessing rival products and the wider market.
- *Flag-waving.* A **flag-waving** report is self-serving in that it overemphasises the virtues and importance of one section of the organisation — the report writer's section.
- *Hobby horses.* **Hobby horse** are pet projects or ideas of report writers that are given undue prominence in a report.
- *Sloppiness.* **Sloppiness** in report writing is often shown by poor research, overdependence on low-quality sources, and signs of plagiarism and cut-and-pasting of pre-existing documents.
- *Reactivity.* **Reactivity** is a characteristic of report writers who produce post-mortems on situations but offer very little in the way of future orientation, proactive planning or fresh thought.
- *Decision avoidance.* Reports are sometimes commissioned in order to avoid decisions, rather than to aid them. Less-than-ethical report commissioners may hope a problem will go away if they engage in **decision avoidance** and ask someone to engage in time-wasting research and writing.

Conclusions

In the **conclusions** section, you provide an overview of the content of the report. Here you can provide your own interpretation of the information that has been set out, answering the question 'What does all this mean?' You can also provide a specific context for the recommendations you are about to make. Typical conclusions might take the following form:

It is clear that the photocopying centre cannot cope with certain peak work loads, particularly when we are conducting audits of large clients ...

Options 2 and 6 are attractive if solely financial criteria are applied, but would be unpopular with staff in the eastern zone plant. Options 1, 3, 4 and 5 would be less unpopular, but clearly would entail greater expense, particularly if we buy rather than lease ...

Recommendations

In the final, **recommendations** section of the report you propose specific actions that should flow from the conclusions. Keep in mind that just as recommendations are based on conclusions, so conclusions are based on the information discussed in the body of the report.

You should not introduce new material in the conclusions or recommendations sections. It is common for report writers to reach conclusions and recommendations whose foundation has not been demonstrated in the body of the document. It's only natural: your mind, turning over the problem, delivers up novel solutions that may be unconnected to the facts as you have presented them. Don't maroon your good ideas, however; rather, grasp the perhaps unpleasant fact that you may now need to go back and revise the body, creating a foundation for your new conclusions and recommendations.

If the introduction, discussion and conclusions are part of the problem-solving process, then the recommendations are part of the decision-making process. Because of this, some commissioners of reports exclude recommendations from the scope, brief or terms of reference of the report, believing that they can produce their own action plans based on what they have read.

It may be useful to number your recommendations. This will make discussion of them easier. You may also choose to place recommendations in priority order.

Some writers prefer to give recommendations in the body of the report, at the end of each section. This style is adopted particularly with large reports. It can be a useful way of linking a response directly to the problem discussed. If you choose to do this, it is still helpful to list all of the recommendations together, and the best place for such a list is where most readers would expect to find them – at the end of the report, following the conclusions.

Typical recommendations might take the following forms:

It is recommended that all systems continue operating the Microsoft operating system for the next six months. At that time, Data Processing will report on options to convert systems to an alternative operating system.

3. Option 3 (subcontract new accounts to external consultants via competitive tendering) should be trialled for 12 months.

References, bibliography, endnotes

With your conclusions and recommendations, you have completed the main parts of the report. All that remains is the end matter. Here the reference list usually comes first. This section lists all the materials you have referred to in your research and used in the report.

Appendices or attachments

You may wish to include material with your report that does not belong in it (perhaps it is too large, or would be of interest to only part of your audience) but still might be useful for the reader to refer to. Such material is included at the back of a report as an **appendix**.

If you have more than one set of such material, then each should be separately identified (e.g. Appendix A, B, C or Appendix I, II, III and so on). This material might include raw data, copies of questionnaires used, interview transcripts, maps, copies of legislation appropriate to the topic, detailed historical background, complex graphics, computer software demonstrating what you are talking about, a video recording – in short, anything that does not fit tidily into the structure of the written report.

Glossary, list of abbreviations and index

If your report is particularly complex, involving terminology that may be unfamiliar to some of your audience, consider creating a glossary in which you list and define these terms. Similarly, create a list of, or key to, possibly confusing abbreviations (acronyms, initialisms or shortened words). If your glossary or list of abbreviations extends beyond about ten entries, perhaps you should consider whether you are in danger of losing your audience.

If your report is extensive (say, over 20 pages), consider creating an index. Indexing can be time-consuming, but word processing software has taken much of the labour out of it. An index will sometimes provide your audience with a more detailed 'navigation map' than is possible with the table of contents.

A checklist for ensuring that your analytical or research report has the minimum number of weaknesses and the maximum number of strengths follows.

An editing checklist for analytical reports

Report title: **Report author:**

Feature	Detail	
Cover (where separate from title page)	Durability	
	Attractiveness	
	Identification (title)	
Letter/memo of transmittal	Salutation	
	Statement of letter's/memo's purpose	
	Brief overview of report	
	Acknowledgements	
	Courteous close	
Title	Accurate description of scope/contents	
	Same as on cover	
Contents page	Accurate reflection of structure	
	Accurate reflection of pagination	
List of illustrations (optional)	Accurate reflection of sequence	
Synopsis/summary/abstract	Accurate summary of body, end matter	
Introduction	Background given	
	Purpose described	
	Scope defined	
	Research methods described	
	Terms defined	
Discussion	Argument developed logically	
	Factual approach — no opinions yet	
	Balanced approach — not biased in what is presented or omitted	

Feature	Detail	
Conclusions	Based on matter discussed	
Recommendations	Based on matter discussed and conclusions	
References/bibliography	Complete	
	Consistent use of citation system	
Appendix/appendixes	Complete	
Glossary (optional)	Complete	
Index (optional)	Complete	
Structure	Clear and consistent	
	Headings accurate	
	Hierarchical structure reflects correct exposition of argument	
	Headings grammatically parallel	
Layout/document design	Adequate white space	
	Fonts — minimal variation	
	Fonts — consistent use	
	Graphics placed appropriately	
Graphics	Appropriate	
	Identified	
	Referred to in text close to graphic	
Pagination	Accurate	
Referencing	Correct	
	Consistent	
Quotation	Correct	
	Consistent	
	Legitimate — no plagiarism or distortion	
Language	Clear, readable style	
	Style consistent between sections	
	Grammar correct	
	Spelling correct	
	Punctuation correct	
	No unnecessary jargon	
	No cliché	
	No redundancies	
	More concrete than abstract	
	No repetition	
	Paragraphing clear	

A sample analytical report

Here is an example of what a 4000-word analytical report can look like. Use it as a model to refer to when you need to undertake such a project.

1

Filling the void: What is the best use for the vacant space on the ground floor of the Greenfields building?[2]

3

Report prepared for Rocco Marcolino,
Chief Executive Officer, Agenda21[4]

Prepared by Fran Powers, Manager, Operations, Agenda21[5]

November 6, 2012

1. Or memorandum of transmittal. If the report is going to an external audience, consider making this a letter of transmittal.

2. Personal style, as befits a memo

3. Upshot of report is foreshadowed

4. Courteous acknowledgement of others who helped out

5. Thanks to report commissioner, invitation to follow up with discussions

MEMO OF TRANSMITTAL[1]

TO: Rocco Marcolino, Chief Executive Officer
FROM: Fran Powers, Manager, Operations
DATE: November 6, 2012
SUBJECT: <u>Options for allocation of vacant space in Greenfields building</u>

Attached please find the report you asked me to undertake on best uses of vacant space in the main building.[2]

I looked at a number of options, including the option that has been informally discussed for some time — namely, using the space to establish a fitness/wellness facility. On balance, I think this is the best option.[3]

The costs are potentially high, but then so are the benefits. I have tried to recommend a pathway that will minimise risk and maximise positive outcomes.

Max Franks in Operations and Jai Cellisi in Finance were very helpful in putting data together for this project, as was the Information Desk at West Pacific College library.[4]

This assignment was like no other I have tackled before, involving as it does so many intangibles, but it was a bracing and challenging one for the same reasons. Thanks for giving me the opportunity to come to grips with it.[5]

If you want to discuss any of this material, please call me at any time (X6112).

TABLE OF CONTENTS

3

Sidebar notes:

1. Identify pages as you see fit. The scheme here is to use lower-case Roman numerals for all material prior to the introduction, from which point Arabic numerals are used. The cover is presumed to be p. i and the memo of transmittal is presumed to be p. ii, but they are not identified as such. The table of contents page does not refer to itself.

2. Indent different levels of report's hierarchical structure appropriately; this allows the reader to see structure more clearly. As you prepare the report, this exercise may help you see for the first time whether the structure makes sense, or whether changes might be needed. For example, is a subsection really a new section by itself? Is the sequence logical?

3. Index needed? Possibly not for a document this short, but consider for longer documents.

1. Obviously not needed if you have no tables or figures. It is better to have a good document without them than a bad document with them.

2. It may make things clearer for your reader if figures and tables are listed separately.

LIST OF ILLUSTRATIONS[1]

1. Remember, that this may be the only section of your masterpiece that your audience will actually read. Forget about bruised egos and feelings of rejection — just make sure that you deliver a credible and persuasive message on this page.

2. Writer shifts from personal style of memo of transmittal to more formal and impersonal style. Match your style to the expectations of your reader(s) — for example, use personal pronouns if your reader(s) are comfortable with that.

3. Conclusions and recommendations are presented clearly. If you expect a hostile or critical response, it might pay to word this section less directly, trusting in the force of your argument to persuade your readers to accept conclusions and recommendations.

SUMMARY[1]

This report examines various uses for the empty space on the ground floor of Agenda21's Greenfields building.[2]

Four major options for use are considered: move out; stay and sublease the area; stay and use the area for warehousing; stay and use the area for the establishment of a fitness/wellness facility for the use of Agenda21 staff.

Option four is the most complex, and thus most of this report is taken up with the analysis of the pro's and cons of such a project.

It is concluded that, while there are some positive features of the first three options, the best option is the fourth one.

It is recommended that a medium- to high-expense version of such a fitness/wellness facility be created. The venture should be reviewed after a three-year trial period.[3]

1.0 INTRODUCTION[2]

1.1. PURPOSE[2]

The purpose of this report is to consider various options for using vacant space in the Agenda21 building.[3]

1.2. SCOPE[4]

This report considers a number of options, including the option of converting the vacant space to a fitness/wellness facility. Only internal management of such a facility is considered; other options, such as outsourcing the management of the facility, or simply subsidising staff to attend commercial gymnasiums, are not considered.

1.3. SOURCES AND METHODS[5]

Information was collected from books, professional journal articles, the business press, newspapers, websites, an in-house survey, and brochure and quotation material from commercial vendors of fitness equipment.

1.4. LIMITATIONS AND ASSUMPTIONS[6]

There was some urgency in the preparation of this report, primarily because of the possibility of other tenants making firm offers on subleasing the space, but this has not compromised the analysis. All figures quoted from commercial vendors and other sources are assumed to be accurate, and survey responses of staff are taken to be a fair indicator of actual behaviour.

1.5. BACKGROUND[7]

The move to the Greenfields Industrial Estate building has been, on balance, a positive one for Agenda21. Our new building at 6–12 Main Street is attractive, and is easily the best facility we have worked in. We took on the lease at 6–12 knowing the building was too big for our current needs, but recognising the quality and ambience of the facility. The unexpected competitive pressure of bidding for the lease, combined with what appeared to be the certainty of a reliable and desirable sublease tenant, meant we signed off on the site before we normally would have. The sudden and unexpected financial collapse of our prospective tenant, Meridian, has occasioned a rethink about the best use for our facility, or indeed whether we should stay at this address.

1.5.1. The current situation at Agenda21's Greenfields building

Figure 1 shows the layout of the typical floor of the building at 6–12 Main Street.[8] The building is 48×32 metres/157×105 feet in size, giving a floor area of 1536 m^2/16 534 ft^2, with all three floors (excluding basement parking and rooftop) adding up to approximately 4608 m^2/49 600 ft^2.

---

1. Arabic numeral pagination begins.

2. Hierarchical structure reinforced by use of different fonts

3. Statement of purpose: what is this document about? Keep it brief.

4. Statement of scope, or terms of reference: what report is about, and what it is not about

5. Sources and methods are combined here, but they can be treated separately if you prefer, or simply not considered at all if not appropriate.

6. Limitations and assumptions are combined here, but they can be treated separately if you prefer, or simply not considered at all if appropriate to ignore.

7. Statement of background, useful for setting the scene; can be a statement of the obvious, but sometimes that needs to be done.

8. Position all figures and tables close to the point in the text where they are referred to. Don't forget to refer to them in your text.

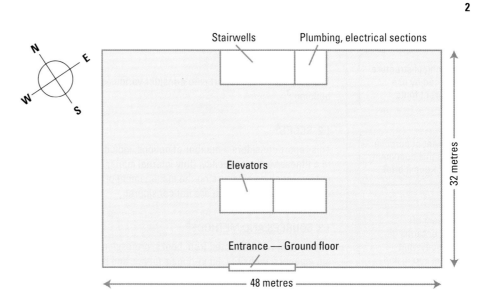

Figure 1: Floor plan layout for all three floors of 6–12 Main Street block[1]

Currently we have 286 staff, with no plans for substantial growth above this level for the next few years. Our typical workspace requirements have been for an average of 9 m²/97 ft² per person, with approximately another 1200 m²/12,917 ft² allowed for corridors/walkways, warehousing, cafeteria, library and utilities (elevators, stairwells, toilets, air conditioning, cabling, pipes etc.). Allowing for a small growth in staffing needs, this leaves us with approximately 700 m², or approximately half a floor, on the ground floor, unaccounted for (Table 1).

Table 1: Space needs at 6–12 Main Street block

(1) Total floor space	4608 m² / 49 601 ft²
(2) Space needs of approx. 300 staff @ 9 m² per person	2700 m² / 29 063 ft²
(3) Other space needs (corridors/ walkways, warehousing, cafeteria, library and utilities (elevators, stairwells, toilets, air conditioning, cabling, pipes, etc.)	1200 m² / 12 917 ft²
Spare space = 1 – (2 + 3)	700 m² / 7534 ft² (approx.)

2

1.6. APPROACH TAKEN IN THIS REPORT

This report considers four major options for Agenda21:

(1) Move out to a smaller facility.

(2) Stay, and sublease the vacant space.

(3) Stay, and warehouse stocks in vacant space.

(4) Stay, and set up corporate fitness/wellness facility in vacant space.[3]

1. Figure captions should explain succinctly just what the reader is looking at.

2. There is no point 1.5.2. Some readers prefer that each section should have more than one subsection. Don't, however, create a subsection just for the sake of symmetry.

3. Clear setting out of alternatives creates a context for decision making.

1. Definitions might also be placed in introduction section, or in a separate glossary, depending on what you are trying to get across to your reader.

2. Writer mixes documentary-note and author–date (Harvard) citation systems. Avoid this if audience has expectations of consistent style.

3. Proof that verifiable data is being cited here

2.0. OPTION #1: MOVE OUT

This is not really a viable option. We are legally bound to a seven-year lease, and the vendors, Imperia, are not sympathetic to our predicament. Legal action and penalties would cost us several hundred thousand dollars. Apart from these considerations, staff appear to have become strongly attached to the high-quality built environment, and a shift might have negative impacts on morale.

3.0. OPTION #2: STAY, AND SUBLEASE THE AREA

We can sublease the vacant space to other tenants. Rates for rental/leasing of commercial property of this quality in this area are in the $180–$220/m^2 / $17–$20/ft^2 range.[1] This means that we could recoup approximately $126 000–$154 000 per year.

Initial preparation would entail only partitioning costs of $2000 approx. The main advantage of this is that we would receive a substantial cash flow from tenants. Disadvantages might be that we lose control of some of our space, there might be security problems with noncompany personnel in the building, and there might be territorial frictions (which commonly occur with leasing/landlord relationships).

4.0. OPTION #3: STAY, AND WAREHOUSE STOCKS IN AREA

We are already warehousing some of our more valuable stock lines (Aegis 202, Aegis 303), but even now the rationale for this is tenuous. This facility is really an office facility, and secure warehousing for even our premium lines can be obtained elsewhere. This would save us $17 000–$19 000 per year. The public relations benefits of being able to take clients through the warehouse section are considerable, but not decisive.

5.0. OPTION #4: STAY, AND SET UP CORPORATE FITNESS/WELLNESS FACILITY IN AREA

Many private and public sector organisations have in the past few years set up in-house fitness facilities, and perhaps the spare floor space could be used to accommodate such a facility.

5.1. FITNESS AND WELLNESS: DEFINITIONS[1]

Some terminology definitions may be useful at this point. 'Fitness' is used here to describe exercise programs, which may entail weight training, aerobics, callisthenics/stretching, indoor sports such as table tennis, and cardiovascular routines such as cycling, stepping, walking and running. Many of these activities involve specialised equipment and (obviously) significant physical exertion.

---

[1] Sources: Max Franks, Operations Management, and newspaper and internet real estate sources[2,3]

4

1. A list or sequence could also be treated in a sentence, with items separated by commas, or else in a table.

2. Sources, with dates, help to establish credibility of assertions.

3. Informal style of heading. A more formal version might be: 'Effectiveness of Fitness/Wellness Programs'.

4. Balanced approach, showing that all pros and cons will be considered, rather than a biased and unprofessional approach in which only one point of view is pushed

'Wellness' is a broader concept, embracing all aspects of fitness set out, but also encompassing programs such as:

- smoking cessation
- second-hand tobacco smoke control
- stress management
- weight management
- nutrition programs
- alcohol and substance counselling
- ergonomic analysis of work practices
- occupational health and safety — injury prevention and rehabilitation
- corporate sporting teams
- time management
- assertiveness training
- interpersonal and communication skills training
- yoga
- massage
- meditation.[1]

(Grant & Brisbin 1992; Wolf 2011)[2]

5.2. FITNESS/WELLNESS PROGRAMS: DO THEY WORK?[3]

The evidence on whether fitness/wellness programs work is mixed.[4] Those who argue that the benefits of fitness/wellness programs outweigh the costs suggest that such programs lead to:

- declines in absenteeism
- declines in staff turnover
- declines in injury rates (including work-related injuries and compensation claims)
- improvements in job performance and productivity
- improvements in morale and team spirit
- reductions in stress levels
- reductions in health care and insurance costs
- increased recruitment of employees with a favourable attitude to both work and health
- cumulative benefits of $500–$700 per employee per year.

(Shephard 1999; Dinubile & Sherman 1999; Baicker, Cutler, David, & Song, 2010)

On the downside, the following negative aspects of fitness/wellness programs have also been noted:

- Capital, resource allocation and recurrent costs of programs can be very high.

1. More formal phrasing in heading. Less formal wording might be: 'Blood, Sweat and Tears: How Much Bang Would We Get for Our Buck in a Fitness/Wellness Program?'

2. Argument shifts to third level of hierarchy.

3. Rather than clutter up body text with these details, the writer refers readers to an appendix section.

4. Sources for data given

- In many programs, only a minority of enthusiasts participate (and many of these were fit to begin with).
- In some programs, an initial wave of enthusiasm is followed by high drop-out rates.
- Health claim costs might increase rather than decrease if relatively unhealthy individuals self-select into the program.
- Costs might increase owing to exercise-related injuries.
- Productivity might decline, and discipline issues rise, if staff use fitness/wellness programs to avoid doing real work.

5.3. FITNESS/WELLNESS PROGRAMS: FINANCIAL CONSIDERATIONS[1]

In looking at the costs and benefits of a fitness/wellness program, we need to consider the positive and negative cash flows associated directly with a program, and the flows associated with the broader picture.

5.3.1. Program costs and benefits[2]

The setup costs of a fitness/wellness facility depend on what we are trying to achieve. Alternatives might include a rock-bottom, no-frills, unsupervised exercise area and a fully staffed and extensively equipped facility offering a range of services. Table 2 shows six scenarios that could be pursued (full details of these costings are given in Appendix A).[3] A critical part of costing is staffing, and Figure 2 shows some factors affecting the staffing costs of a fitness/wellness facility.

- Casual trained staff (e.g. aerobics/yoga instructors, masseurs): ~$40/hour.
- Four hours of aerobics classes/day = $160/day × 5-day week = $800/week × 52 weeks = $41 600
- Full-time (40-hour week, 40 weeks/year) fitness coordinator/director (with, e.g., bachelor's degree in fitness/physical education): market rate seems to be ~$35 000–$40 000/year, plus on-costs (superannuation, insurance etc.) of 15% = $40 250–$46 000; median: $43 125

  Full-time (40-hour week, 40 weeks/year) medically qualified fitness coordinator/director (with, e.g., MD/MBBS degree): market rate seems to be ~$40 000–$50 000/year, plus on-costs (superannuation, insurance etc.) of 15% = $46 000–$57 500; median: $57 150

Figure 2: Some costs associated with fitness/wellness programs

(Sources: *Daily Standard* and www.workplacehealth.net, Internet job advertisements in health care/sports medicine)[4]

1. Tabular presentation good for complex and interrelated data sets

2. 'Scenario' is used to distinguish choices from 'Options', but other terms such as 'Alternative' or 'Model' could also be used.

Table 2: Six scenarios for fitness/wellness programs[1]

Scenario[2]	Program	Staffing	Facilities	Setup costs ($) (approx.)	Recurrent costs ($) (approx.)
A	Simple exercise	None — unsupervised	Basic equipment (8 unmotorised workout stations, plus free weights in racks) No change rooms, showers, lockers	7000	200
B	More complex exercise, including four hours/day group exercise	Casual staff (e.g. aerobics) — 20 hours/ week	Basic equipment (8 unmotorised workout stations, plus free weights in racks) Change rooms, showers, lockers, reinforced flooring, glass partitioning, stereo	16 000	48 000
C	More complex exercise, including 4 hours/day group exercise	One full-time manager (nonmedical) + 20 hours/week casual	Basic equipment (8 unmotorised workout stations, plus free weights in racks) Change rooms, showers, lockers, reinforced flooring, glass partitioning, stereo	16 000	92 000
D	More complex exercise, including 4 hours/day group exercise	One full-time manager (medical) + 20 hours/week casual	Basic equipment (8 unmotorised workout stations, plus free weights in racks) Change rooms, showers, lockers, reinforced flooring, glass partitioning, stereo/PA	16 000	105 150
E	More complex exercise, including 8 hours/day group exercise	One full-time manager (medical) + 40 hours/week casual	More advanced equipment (20 unmotorised workout stations, 12 motorised workout stations (treadmills, steppers etc. plus free weights in racks) Change rooms, showers, lockers, reinforced flooring, glass partitioning, stereo/PA	74 000	147 000
F	More complex exercise, including 8 hours/day group exercise, plus programs in nutrition, weight control, smoking reduction, stress management, massage, meditation	One full-time manager (medical) + one assistant manager (nonmedical) + 80 hours/week casual/ contract	More advanced equipment (20 unmotorised workout stations, 12 motorised workout stations (treadmills, steppers etc. plus free weights in racks) Change rooms, showers, lockers, reinforced flooring, glass partitioning, stereo/PA, massage benches	86 000	216 000

(Sources: brochures from three corporate fitness companies, three sporting equipment manufacturers. Full details of costings in Appendix A)

5.3.2. Purchase versus lease/rent costs

Facilities costs here relate to outright purchase. These costs can be offset by depreciation (20 per cent per year), which can improve our overall tax situation. The lease/rent options can also be explored. Generally, leasing/rental works out at 23 per cent per year of outright purchase costs, and 40 per cent of these costs can be written off against tax.

5.3.3. 'Low cost' options not necessarily cheap

Scenario A has the attractiveness of low cost, but the unsupervised nature of the program might mean that the company is neglecting its duty of care, which has negative ethical and legal implications. It is likely that such a program would also be 'preaching to the converted'; that is, it would appeal to those staff members who are already committed to fitness and not to those most in need of a program. (There is also the possibility that such an unenriched setup might not appeal even to fitness enthusiasts, who might well prefer to exercise elsewhere, carrying the costs themselves.)

5.3.4. Skill levels of staff: a doctor in the house?[1]

Supervision is probably essential, not only from ethical and legal standpoints, but from the point of view of giving confidence to those contemplating joining a program. Research on industry websites suggests that some workplace fitness/wellness facilities are hiring medical doctors, with or without sports medicine training. There is a salary premium involved here, but the presence of a qualified medical practitioner may add prestige and credibility to a program, and would obviously allow production of high-quality diagnostic information about health and wellness in general. Such a person could also contribute considerably to occupational health and safety programs already in place.

5.3.5. Possible impacts on key factors

It is difficult to come up with exact figures about what impacts, positive or negative, a fitness/wellness program might have on our workplace. Nevertheless, it is useful to work from the optimistic but prudent data offered in some of the literature (e.g. Grant & Brisbin 1992; Kerr, Cox & Griffiths 1996) and factor in some our key figures, such as sick leave, absenteeism, workplace-related injury costs and productivity. Approximate estimates of potential improvements in these figures, as a direct result of the establishment of a fitness/wellness facility, are shown in Table 3. These figures are based on median percentage changes possible; that is, the picture could be even brighter if, for example, productivity gains were greater than 5 per cent. Then again, the real situation might well not be so rosy.

---

1. Thought-provoking argument; don't use if house style is very formal

Table 3: Possible impacts of a fitness/wellness program on key figures

Category	Details	Approx. cost ($)	Median change possible, according to literature	Approx. benefit ($)
Sick leave (noninjury) taken in past 12 months	Average 6.3 days × 286 staff = 1802 days. Average cost (productivity loss, replacement staff) = $169/day	304 500	−5%	15 225
Absenteeism (when not sick leave related)	Average 3.4 days × 286 staff = 972 days. Average cost (productivity loss, replacement staff) = $169/day	164 335	−4%	6 573
Workplace-related injury compensation costs (above insurance reimbursement)	Rehabilitation, legal	221 500	−5%	11 075
Productivity gain	Current output produced by total salary bill (average total salary plus costs = $50 000)	Salary bill = $14 300 000	+5%	715 000
TOTAL				747 873

It needs to be stressed that these figures are hypothetical. In the real world, there might well be a negative outcome if a fitness/wellness facility were to be set up here at Agenda21. It may be of interest, however, to look at a very optimistic projection of outcomes to try to reconcile some of these figures. For example, Figure 3 shows the costs of the most expensive scenario (Scenario F — equipment costs annualised at 23 per cent, with no adjustments for depreciation or tax benefits) against the figures from Table 3 and the State and Federal tax and insurance benefits discussed earlier.

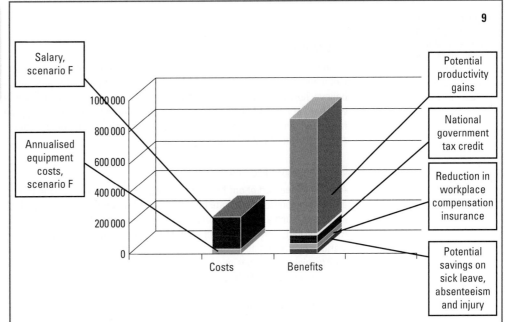

Figure 3: An optimistic projection of costs and benefits of a fitness/wellness facility

5.3.6. Nonprogram costs and benefits

Our general insurance covers any additional liabilities associated with exercise-related injuries. There are several positive factors in relation to government-associated costs. Under new (2008) State government legislation, we are eligible for a 25 per cent reduction in our workplace compensation insurance, which amounts to 25% × $56 000 per year = $14 000 per year. Under proposed Commonwealth legislation, we can claim $300 tax credit per year for each person who participates fully in a workplace fitness/wellness program. If everyone were to participate, we could claim 286 × $300 = $85 800.

5.4. FITNESS/WELLNESS PROGRAMS: NONFINANCIAL CONSIDERATIONS

There are other considerations that may be important in considering such a project, although it is difficult to quantify them.[1]

5.4.1. Corporate Olympics

Each year we participate in the Corporate Olympics, although not with great success. A number of staff members have commented on the relative success of our competitors, Gigantic Technologies and Ramified Systems, in this contest, and in particular how Ramified's achievements last year led to substantial coverage of its team in the general, business and trade media. It is difficult to say whether such success really pays off in bottom-line terms, but it is not in contention that a number of our customers raised the Ramified success unprompted in negotiations with our reps. Both Ramified and Gigantic have in-house exercise facilities, which feature on their websites and in their recruitment literature.

1. Reference to second appendix directs reader's attention to detailed data without breaking up flow of text.

5.4.2. Netball

We also sponsor the Hummingbirds netball team. The Hummingbirds have had some success, a number of the team having had interstate and international experience in the sport. Members believe, however, that it is difficult for them to maintain a high level of fitness as well as perform well here at the workplace, and have anecdotally expressed a strong preference for an in-house facility, which might lead to an improvement in their performance — decked out, of course, in Agenda21 Hummingbird uniforms.

5.4.3. Corporate sport and networking

A little-noticed part of our business strategy is informal networking through industry golf days and golf in general. Corporate golf is an important part of the culture of this industry, while other industries, such as IT, see sports such as hockey as nontrivial parts of team-building efforts (O'Keefe 2001; Colvin 2001). Anecdotal feedback suggests that our performance in these arenas of 'serious play' is not all it could be. It is not guaranteed, of course, but an in-house fitness/wellness facility might have a positive impact on the performance of staff members engaged in these 'off-duty/on-duty' activities.

5.4.4. Morale and teamwork

The workplace fitness/wellness literature also notes how programs lead to boosts in morale and teamwork, and some writers speculate that a reduction in staff turnover may be due to the perception of staff that a fitness/wellness facility, membership of which they do not pay for, is a perk, or benefit, that they might not get elsewhere (Grant & Brisbin 1992; O'Donnell 2001).

6.0. IN-HOUSE SURVEY OF POTENTIAL DEMAND FOR FITNESS/WELLNESS PROGRAMS

If an in-house fitness/wellness facility was created, would anyone use it? The research data is sometimes pessimistic about short-, medium- and long-term attendance figures.

A survey form was created and distributed via the corporate intranet (see Appendix 2 for the full text and results of the survey[1]), using the question format 'If the following activity was available in-house throughout the day, how would you feel about it?' Some of the responses are shown in Figure 4. On the one hand, merely because people say they want something or are going to do something is no real indication that they will actually do it; on the other hand, we received responses from 235 people (an 82 per cent response rate), which is the highest response we have ever had for a survey. (There is also the possibility that the true interest is even greater than the figures suggest, given that some staff might be embarrassed to respond positively to some activities, but would be interested in quietly taking up the option if the opportunity arose and others were going, or not going.)

1. Data presentation problem is to show proportions of responses across multiple items. Stacked bar chart is probably the best graphic to achieve this.

On the basis of the responses, it is reasonable to conclude that a fitness/wellness facility would be well patronised.

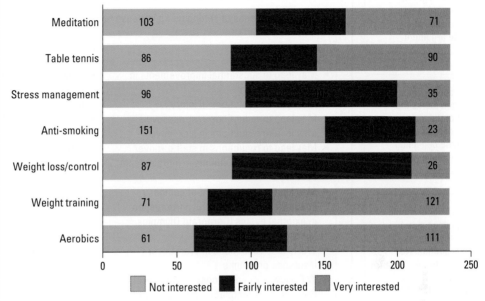

Figure 4: Some responses from the Intranet Survey, October 16, 2011. N = 235 responses[1]

7.0. THE WORST-CASE SITUATION: WHAT IF IT DOESN'T WORK?

Setting aside the possibility of catastrophic injuries being caused by participation in programs, the financial pain of a failed exercise would be considerable but not disastrous. If, for example, a three-year trial period was set, based on a moderate-to-high cost scenario, then approximately 60 per cent of equipment and hardware cost could be recouped by sales. Salaries, of course, would be nonrecoverable.

1. Some readers like an overview section, some don't. This could have appeared at the opening of section 5, but that might be premature in terms of the exposition of the argument.

2. The conclusions section marks the end of the main part of the report, and the beginning of the end matter.

3. Conclusions should be built on matter in discussion in body section. No new material, ideas, options or choices should be introduced here.

4. Number conclusions either as subnumbers of section, or independent numbers (1, 2, 3, . . .), or don't number at all, as taste dictates.

8.0. OVERVIEW[1]

Table 4 summarises the pros and cons of setting up an in-house fitness facility.

Table 4: Pros and cons of setting up an in-house fitness/wellness facility

For	Against
■ May lead to substantial improvements in personnel health ■ May lead to reductions in injury ■ May lead to reductions in stress levels ■ May lead to reductions in sick leave ■ May lead to reductions in staff turnover ■ May lead to improvements in morale, team building ■ May lead to improvement of company image via more successful participation in external events (Corporate Olympics, sponsored netball team) ■ Will lead to reductions in WorkCover insurance premiums ■ Will allow tax deductions under Federal Government Workplace Wellness plan ■ May be attractive to future staff hires ■ May help to limit company liability in event of future 'unhealthy work practices' claims	■ Only 'activists' may participate, or continue to participate ■ Quite expensive to set up and maintain ■ Improvements in health not always guaranteed ■ Link between health and productivity not always strong ■ Might be expensive if less healthy staff participate and drive up costs ■ Might backfire if staff begin to sustain exercise-related injuries ■ Might reduce productivity and introduce discipline and coordination problems caused by staff exercising at inappropriate times

9.0. CONCLUSIONS[2][3]

9.1.	Options 1 (Move out to a smaller facility), 2 (Stay, and sublease the area), and 3 (Stay, and warehouse stocks in area) are not as attractive as Option 4 (Stay, and set up corporate fitness/wellness facility in area).

9.2.	There is conflicting evidence about the financial viability of such facilities, but the balance of evidence seems to be in their favour.

9.3.	There may also be a range of nonfinancial reasons to favour such a facility.

9.4.	There seems to be considerable support among staff for such a facility.

9.5.[4]	In light of the range of uncertainties about such a venture, it might be wise to set up a pilot project, costed at a medium-to-high level, for a period of three years, and then evaluate it at the end of that period.

10.0. RECOMMENDATIONS[1][2][3]

10.1.   It is recommended that 400 m²/4306 ft² of the vacant space on the ground floor of 6–12 Main Street be set aside for the development of a fitness/wellness facility.

10.2.   It is recommended that the Scenario E funding level be implemented. This entails the hiring of a full-time manager, with medical qualifications, and the hiring of casual/contract staff for 40 hours per week. The facility will be equipped with 20 unmotorised workout stations, 12 motorised workout stations (treadmills, steppers etc. plus free weights in racks), change rooms, showers, lockers, reinforced flooring, glass partitioning and a stereo/PA system. Salary costs will be $147 000 per annum (approx.), and a leasing agreement for equipment (rated at 23 per cent of $74 000 purchase price, or $17 020 per annum) will be negotiated by competitive bidding from equipment vendors.

10.3.   It is recommended that the facility should run for a trial period of 36 months, and be re-evaluated against financial and nonfinancial criteria at that stage.

11.0. REFERENCES[4]

Baicker, Katherine, Cutler, David & Song, Ziruii 2010, 'Workplace wellness programs can generate savings', *Health Affairs*, vol. 29. no. 2, pp. 304–11.

Colvin, Geoffrey 2001, 'Why execs love golf', *Fortune*, April 19.

DiNubile, Nicholas A & Sherman, Carl 1999, 'Exercise and the bottom line', *The Physician and Sportsmedicine*, vol. 27, no. 2, February.

Grant, Carol Bayly & Brisbin, Robert E 1992, *Workplace wellness: the key to higher productivity and lower health costs*, John Wiley & Sons, New York.

Haynes, George, Dunnagan, Tim & Smith, Vince 1999, 'Do employees participating in voluntary health promotion programs incur lower health care costs?' *Health Promotion International*, vol. 14, no. 1.

Kerr, John H, Cox, Amanda & Griffiths, Tom (eds) 1996, *Workplace health: employee fitness and exercise*, Taylor & Francis, London.

O'Donnell, Michael P 2001, *Health promotion in the workplace*, Delmar Learning, Clifton Park, NY.

O'Keefe, Brian 2001, 'Corporate sports: is hockey the new golf?' *Fortune*, May 2.

Ontario Health Quality Council 2010, A framework for public reporting on healthy work environments in Ontario healthcare settings, Toronto, Ontario Health Quality Council.

Shephard, Roy J 1999, 'Do work-site exercise and health programs work?' *The Physician and Sportsmedicine*, vol. 27, no. 2, February.

1. Recommendations are action steps based upon conclusions.

2. Recommendations should be built on matter in discussion in body section and conclusions. No new material, ideas, options or choices should be introduced here.

3. Formal, impersonal style used. If house style allows, simply rephrase to read 'I/We recommend that . . .'

4. References listed alphabetically by first author. Author, date, title, publisher, place of publication given for books; author, date, article title, journal title, volume and issue details given for journals.

Proposals and submissions

A document quite similar to the report is the proposal or submission. People write proposals or submissions to obtain funding or resources to achieve certain goals. The goals might involve, for example:

- winning a contract from a company to deliver goods and/or services
- obtaining government funding to set up and manage a program or enterprise.

Proposal is generally the preferred term in North American business and government circles, while *submission* tends to be used in British and Commonwealth business and government circles. Bid documents for public sector program and private sector philanthropic funding tend to be called *grant applications* in North America. *Procurement* is a term sometimes used to describe bidding for contracts in various areas.

Some government departments and agencies disbursing funds no longer call for submissions but for *business plans*. Within the British/Commonwealth culture, the term *tender* is sometimes applied to a document used to bid for a public or private sector contract to provide goods and/or services.

A *submission* can also be a document containing information and opinion that is submitted or given to a government committee of inquiry into a particular issue (with the committee usually producing a report, based in part on submissions from various concerned parties).

Proposals, tenders, submissions, bids, grants and quotations: persuasive documents often used in situations of competitive bidding for scarce resources

Because **proposals, tenders, submissions, bids, grants and quotations** usually require more in the way of documentation to demonstrate credibility (e.g. documentation about staffing, costings and project timelines), writers often use not only word processing software but also project management software to create the final body of documentation.

Submissions or proposals often have a similar structure to reports, but there are some notable differences (see table 5.7).

TABLE 5.7 Reports versus proposals/submissions

	Reports	Proposals/submissions
Role of writer?	Apparently neutral; makes disinterested choice among possible solutions	Interested party; pursues advocacy of one solution
Is present writer same as future implementer?	Not necessarily	Usually

	Reports	Proposals/submissions
Pattern?	Recommendations mentioned briefly at beginning, then in detail at conclusion	Entire document can be a recommendation
Nature of persuasion?	Implicit, low profile	Explicit, high profile
Message?	... needs to be done about ...	Let us do ... about ...
Focus?	Phenomenon, problem	Project, solution
Are action plan, budget, schedule, staffing details, details of writers included?	Not necessarily	Yes
How many per situation?	Usually only one	Often more than one
Software used in preparation	Word processing, perhaps presentation	Word processing, perhaps presentation and project management
Relationship between writer and reader?	Patron/artist; research commissioner/ researcher	buyer/seller
Action stance?	Usually reactive	Proactive and reactive
Comes from?	Usually from inside the organisation	Inside and outside the organisation
Organisational culture?	More routine; less competition-driven	Less routine; more competition-driven
Formalised structure?	Medium	High, medium, low
Lobbying likely after delivery of document?	Less likely	More likely

Most of these differences and similarities are self-evident, but special mention should be made of the process of lobbying. Decision makers can be influenced by the documents presented to them, but lobbying or active persuasion can also influence them after the document has been presented. Such lobbying may take the following forms:

- Making continual phone calls to an administrator who is considering a number of submissions
- Arranging an 'accidental' social encounter with a manager who helps choose proposals for an organisation
- Talking to politicians who may influence a submission/proposal process
- Providing free transport, accommodation, hospitality and an inspection tour for influential decision makers.

Writers of proposals and submissions tend to be more involved with lobbying than writers of reports, but it would be wrong to think that report writers are not involved in lobbying. All organisations — indeed all human communication — is political to some extent. Such projects can be open to corruption and bad practice, and due diligence on all bids should be carried out before document planning begins (Transparency International, 2010; Overton, 2003). Honesty is the best policy, and not just for ethical reasons. If you use a computer browser to search for combinations of 'tender', 'corruption', 'proposal', 'bid' and 'bribery' and you will see interesting results. If tendering internationally, be very wary of 'local practices' of bribes being expected. Scandals in the past few years, both international and national, have shown that it is just too dangerous: the damage done to your reputation, and indeed to organisational survival, will almost certainly outweigh any profit to be made on such a basis.

Some recommendations for preparing these documents are set out in figure 5.4.

Tenders/proposals/submissions — dos and don'ts

Dos	Don'ts
Always address the question asked.	Include information, pricing or details in your tender document until you are sure that it is correct.
Follow the protocol of the document and structure each sub-section within your response with an introduction, middle and conclusion.	Leave the reader to reach their own conclusion about the point you are making.
Ensure you can deliver what you say in the document.	Presume that because you are the incumbent supplier or you have a good relationship with the buyer that you 'have it in the bag'.
Use a compliance table to demonstrate your ability to meet the client's requirements.	Don't think as yourself or your business when preparing: always have the client's perspective in mind.
Have an independent person review the document; a fresh pair of eyes may identify things you have missed because of your narrow focus.	Never underestimate the competition.
Read the client's document thoroughly to ensure you understand what they need.	Don't include irrelevant content or extensive marketing material.
Always keep the client's specific requirements in mind — you must demonstrate your understanding of what the client requires.	Don't treat questions in isolation — they are part of a larger response.
Always ask questions to make sure you understand.	Don't be afraid to ask questions: the more information you have, the better prepared you are.
Schedule time to allow for a full review and redraft of your completed tender response.	Never deliver a document that has not been reviewed and/or edited.
Have a legal representative or someone with an understanding of contracts review the request for tender documents and your response prior to submission.	Commit to any conditions that you are unable to meet. You will not have the opportunity to negotiate them later on if you agree to them in the tender.
Ask questions of the buyer. This shows that you are eager about the tender and can show insight into the buyer's needs.	Ask questions that reveal your strategy or solution — especially if you are preparing an alternative solution to the tender.
Provide contact details including name, phone number, email, office address.	Use words that have a negative connotation, such as 'but', 'can't' and 'won't'.

FIGURE 5.4 Dos and don'ts for tenders/proposals/submissions

Source: Adapted from TenderSearch, © 2011 TenderSearch www.tendersearch.com.au. Reproduced with permission.

How to do it: a sample tender/submission

Roberts (2009) suggests a hierarchical model in writing documents for funding project development:

- Level one covers the aim of the project
- Level two covers the key objectives
- Level 3 covers the specific objectives.

Aims need to give an indication of the benefit, an outline of what you want to do and reference to the total budget figures. Thus, a submission or proposal (one that is internal to an organisation) could be planned like a tree diagram (figure 5.5). It is likely, of course, that there would be more than one 'branch' descending from the level above, but this version shows the necessity to plan in sequence.

FIGURE 5.5 A hierarchical model of planning a sample tender/submission

Source: Adapted with permission from Roberts (2009).

STUDENT STUDY GUIDE

SUMMARY

In this chapter we considered the differences and similarities between different formats, types or subgenres of reports. We examined the differences and similarities between the report and the essay. The information–persuasion mix was examined, as were visual attractiveness, the related idea of the oral report or presentation, and the possibility of having to lobby the report's audience to consolidate its impact and encourage implementation. We looked at the analytical or research report format, noting aspects of structure and style. Finally, we looked at related document types such as proposals, submissions, tenders, bids, procurement and quotations.

KEY TERMS

appendix *p. 169*
audience *p. 159*
balanced approach *p. 167*
boosterism *p. 168*
conclusions *p. 168*
decision avoidance *p. 168*
direct structure *p. 164*
drafting *p. 163*
essay *p. 157*
flag-waving *p. 168*
hobby horse *p. 168*

indirect structure *p. 164*
indiscreet insiderism *p. 168*
information/persuasion mix *p. 155*
job creationism *p. 168*
letter of transmittal *p. 165*
memo of transmittal *p. 165*
proposals, tenders, submissions, bids, grants and quotations *p. 190*
reactivity *p. 168*

recommendations *p. 169*
scope *p. 161*
sloppiness *p. 168*
summary *p. 166*
timidity *p. 168*
topic loyalty or capture *p. 168*
vendetta *p. 168*
whitewash *p. 168*

REVIEW QUESTIONS

1. What factors apart from information and persuasion need to be taken into account when writing a report?
2. Name two ways in which a report differs from an essay.
3. How can a report be used to avoid making a decision?
4. Name two factors that need to be borne in mind when analysing audiences for reports.
5. Why might the scope of a report change while the document is being written?
6. Why would you use an indirect structure in a report?
7. Why is the summary of a report so important?
8. Name three methods of argument development in a report.
9. Why should no new material be placed in conclusions and recommendations?
10. Why would you place report material in an appendix?
11. Why is a balanced and unbiased approach vital in writing documents?
12. Name two ways in which reports differ from submissions/proposals/tenders
13. Why, apart from ethical considerations, should you avoid any corrupt practices (such as bribery) when submitting a tender or proposal?

APPLIED ACTIVITIES

1. Using print or internet sources, obtain copies of reports created in different industries or academic disciplines. Compare and contrast them. What conventions of structure and style are used?
2. Identify one private sector and two public sector organisations that grant funding to individuals and organisations on the basis of proposals, submissions, tenders or business plans. Obtain copies of the guideline documentation issued by the funding

organisations, and compare them. If time is available, prepare a proposal, submission, tender or business plan. Invent details where necessary.

3. Consider how essays might be better written if report-writing guidelines were observed.
4. Consider how reports might be better written if essay-writing guidelines were observed.

WHAT WOULD YOU DO?

You have been asked to write a report on the progress of a major project in the Finance department. You work as a team leader in Finance, and report to Cynthia Wan, the general manager of the area. In doing research for the report, you begin to perceive that all is not well with the project. Where the data is clear, it is apparent that some major milestones have been missed, and in a number of other cases the data appears to have been deliberately recorded in an ambiguous or confusing way, or not at all.

You complete your final draft, and email a copy to Cynthia for approval. Later that night Cynthia rings you at home, a most unusual occurrence. She doesn't make herself clear for some time, chatting aimlessly, then, out of the blue, she asks you – in fact, pleads with you – to rewrite the report so it is not quite so negative.

'What do you want me to do?' you ask. 'Make it more indirect in style?'

'No', she says, 'not just a cosmetic style makeover, but a rewrite that passes over those problems you've identified. Please do this for me. I have had some personal problems lately and haven't been able to concentrate properly on the project, but I promise I will focus on it now. By the time you need to write the next progress report, there'll be no need to "reinterpret" the situation.'

How will you respond to Cynthia's request?

SUGGESTED READING

Coley, Soraya M & Scheinberg, Cynthia A 2008, *Proposal writing: effective grantsmanship*, 3rd edn, Sage, London/Thousand Oaks/New Delhi.

Karsh, Ellen & Fox, Arlen Sue 2009, *The only grant-writing book you'll ever need: top grant writers and grant givers share their secrets*, Basic Books, New York.

Lewis, Harold 2009, *Bids, tenders and proposals: how to win business through best practice*, 3rd edn, Kogan Page, London.

Robinson, Andy 1996, *Grassroots grants: an activist's guide to proposal writing*, Jossey-Bass, San Francisco, CA.

REFERENCES

A.C. Nielsen Research Services 2000, *Employer satisfaction with graduate skills: research report*, Department of Education, Training and Youth Affairs, Canberra.

Anderson, Paul 2010, *Technical writing: a reader-centered approach*, 7th edn, Wadsworth/Cengage, Florence, KY.

Baicker, Katherine, Cutler, David & Song, Ziruii 2010, 'Workplace wellness programs can generate savings', *Health Affairs*, vol. 29. no. 2, pp. 304–11.

Couzins, Martin & Beagrie, Scott 2003, *Personnel Today*, 9 February, p. 23.

Eunson, Baden 1994, *Writing and presenting reports*, John Wiley & Sons, Brisbane.

Kuiper, Shirley 2009, *Contemporary business report writing*, 4th edn, South-Western/Cengage Learning, Mason, OH.

Overton, Rodney 2003, *Writing tenders and proposals: a planning kit*, Sydney Business Centre/Martin Books, Sydney.

Roberts, Jean 2009, *Successful submission writing for business and nonprofits*, Roberts Management Publications, Wilkinson Publishing, Melbourne.

Thornbory, Greta & White, Claire 2007, 'How to ... write reports effectively', *Occupational Health*, vol. 59, no. 2, pp. 20–1.

Transparency International 2010, *Anti-corruption plain language guide*, Transparency International, Berlin.

6

Online writing

LEARNING OBJECTIVES

After studying this chapter you should be able to:

- List at least three advantages and three disadvantages of nonlinear writing
- Discuss the changing nature of style in the composition of email
- Apply the MADE (message, action, details, evidence) model when writing email
- Explain problems involved in editing email and identify solutions to those problems
- Explain problems involved in laying out and formatting email, and identify solutions to those problems
- Explain different methods of attaching supplementary materials to email
- Apply the DRAFS (delete, reply, act, forward, save) model to the management of email
- Explain the phenomenon of email addiction
- List at least four attributes of effective websites
- Explain the value of meta-tags

The offline world goes online

The online world began in 1969, when the Advanced Research Project Agency (ARPA) of the US Department of Defense developed ARPANET, a computer network that facilitated communication between researchers at dispersed locations and also provided a communication system decentralised and robust enough to take over, in the event that a nuclear attack disrupted conventional, centralised systems. Email addresses using the @ symbol were used for the first time in 1972. The world wide web, which constitutes a large part of the internet as we know it today, was developed in 1989 at CERN (Conseil Européen pour la Recherche Nucléaire, or the European Organization for Particle Physics Research) in Switzerland. Since 1969 the growth in online communication has been phenomenal (figure 6.1).

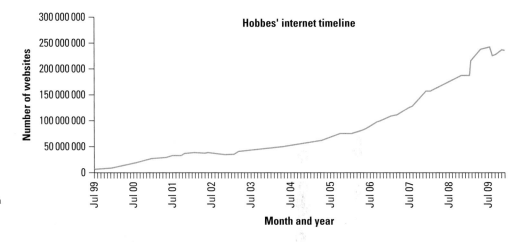

FIGURE 6.1 Growth of the internet (measured in terms of websites, logarithmic scale)

Source: Adapted from RH Zakon 2010, Hobbes' internet timeline, www.zakon.org.

Because of this rapid growth, the internet and the modes of communication it has made possible are still very much evolving, and the web environment is simultaneously both highly structured and anarchic.

The **internet**, which is in fact a network of networks, facilitates a number of forms of electronic communication, including:

- electronic mail (or email)
- the world wide web
- newsgroups, or online discussion/chat groups
- file transfer protocol (FTP) (links to data files)
- instant messaging (im) (real-time chat between identified individuals)
- social media (e.g. Facebook, MySpace, Twitter, RSS feeds) (see chapter 21).

Two offshoots of the internet are intranets and extranets. An **intranet** is a computer network that serves the internal needs of an organisation, creating a virtual space that allows local email exchange and use of web pages not available to the general public. An **extranet** is a network, external to an organisation, that links two or more intranets and creates a virtual space for communication between them. Extranets support B2B (business-to-business) communication, facilitating the secure interchange of information between organisations such as procurement/ordering details, maintenance requests and inventory checks (see online chapter 10).

People and organisations access various electronic communication channels via different types of hardware. In medium to large organisations powerful mainframe computers act as servers, providing resources to the desktop or portable computers of individual staff members. Network access is obtained through telephone lines, or cable, wireless or satellite

Internet: a network of computer networks allowing the transfer of data and information between remote computer users

Intranet: a private computer network operating within an organisation

Extranet: a linked system of intranets that facilitates B2B (business-to-business) communication

Modem: a device that allows computers to talk to each other in the same way that a telephone allows humans to talk to each other

Broadband: high-capacity transmission channels that can carry multiple simultaneous transmissions

Wireless transmission: transmitting data as a broadcast signal in the electromagnetic spectrum

connections. An essential linking technology is the **modem**, which enables a computer to transmit and receive information over a telephone line or cable. The channel or medium of transmission (whether phone line, high-capacity cable or satellite) defines the bandwidth of the signal that can be carried. Fibre-optic cable, satellite and ISDN (integrated services digital network) are **broadband** channels, which can carry multiple messages simultaneously; conventional telephone lines, which have much lower capacity, can carry only one message at a time. Signals can also be sent by **wireless transmission**, which simply means that no wires or cables are needed to physically transmit data. Instead, data are transmitted like radio or television signals (for concerns about the potential negative health impacts of wireless systems, see chapter 21).

The lower the capacity of your modem and transmission channel, the slower and less capable your internet connection will be. Such constraints have implications for the size of emails and attachments that can be sent, and for the loading times of web pages (the more complex the page, the slower the loading). Web pages are viewed through enabling computer programs called browsers, and can be located via search engines.

Writing on the net

In chapter 4, we saw how emails have, for the most part, taken over from paper-based memos, and the focus there was on communicating in different situations. In this chapter we will examine writing approaches for email and websites. Writing for social media is looked at in chapter 21.

Emails, which are generally informal, unstructured and unformatted plain text, are perhaps closer to the memo genre than to the letter. They are a quick and cheap means of exchanging messages – virtues that have begun to cause problems, with junk or spam email increasing exponentially since about 2002.

As a communication form, websites may be usefully compared to advertising brochures, magazines and journals. Web documents, however, vary wildly in quality, with the substantial and enduring existing alongside the trivial and ephemeral. Content is, for the most part, unregulated, so that problematic material (hate sites and on on) exists side by side with more mainstream coverage. Both email and websites may carry viruses and other types of destructive programming that can harm your computer.

There is much contention about what this all means. Some web enthusiasts see spam, social networking and junk information as signs of a vibrant entrepreneurial culture that will help develop e-commerce (electronic commerce) and hasten the day when the whole planet communicates online. Others are more pessimistic, seeing these developments as counterproductive and likely to strangle online communication before it goes much further.

Online writing: mosaic and 3D

Traditional writing in paper texts is by definition linear and narrative; that is, we most often start at the beginning and proceed to the end. This is the case with most works of fiction, in which creative writing is an end in itself. The linear approach is also fairly standard in documents such as essays, letters, memos and reports, although they may include endmatter or attachments (appendices, bibliographies and so on) that go beyond the nominal end of the document and that we may choose to look at or not. (Report readers may get no further than the summary.)

In other areas of non-fiction publication, the words are more likely to be a means to an end, with the end usually being to obtain specific information. We may choose to skim and scan workplace documents, reading relevant material rather than every deathless word (except in certain circumstances, where legality or safety is concerned). In the case of textbooks, we may use the table of contents, index or other navigation tools to locate the information we need, while ignoring the rest. With a phone book, directory, catalogue or other reference book, we will also consult only that information we need, disregarding the rest. We read instruction manuals in order to *do* rather than to *learn*, and so may pick only the content most immediately relevant (a strategy not without peril, of course). In all such texts, although we may not always read them from beginning to end, but rather select the information we need, the documents are in most cases constructed in a linear way.

Online writing, on the other hand, while it developed from traditional writing, tends more to nonlinear or **mosaic forms** than traditional print-based narrative and descriptive text (Van der Geest 2001). Conventional writing is two-dimensional: a page has horizontal and vertical dimensions. In most language traditions, the reader starts at the top left of the page, moves across the line to the right margin, then repeats the process, moving down the page, turning the page when necessary. Online writing adds a third 'dimension' within the screen space with hypertext, or electronic links to other parts of the document or to other documents or websites (figure 6.2). Thus, a book on animals may be constructed as indicated in figure 6.3.

Mosaic form: a nonlinear approach to information design facilitated by hyperlinking around and between web pages

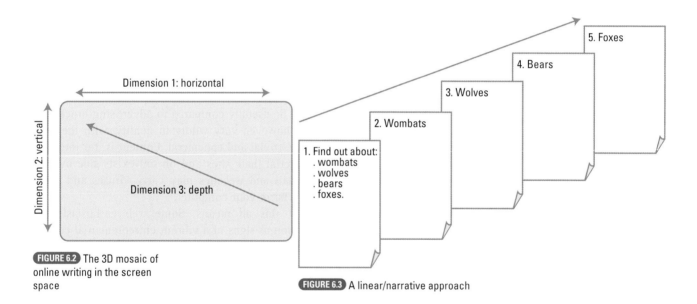

FIGURE 6.2 The 3D mosaic of online writing in the screen space

FIGURE 6.3 A linear/narrative approach

On the other hand, a website on the same topic may be constructed as shown in figure 6.4. In the nonlinear approach, hypertext links are indicated by underlined text, often in a different colour to indicate that the words are 'hot' — that is, electronically linked to other pages or sites.

Figure 6.4 indicates how the reader can access online information (here the second-level pages are labelled 2A, 2B, 2C and 2D) in any sequence, rather than being constrained by the linear approach most often followed by a book treatment of the same content. The reader may choose to 'drill down' through multiple structural levels of information or follow a different sequence entirely. This type of branching structure is common in online games and learning modules. The process has much in common with flow-charting, where IF-THEN logic is used to cover a variety of permutations and combinations of events.

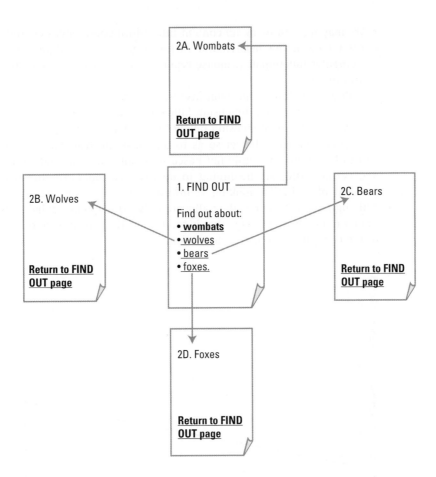

2A. Wombats

Return to FIND OUT page

1. FIND OUT

Find out about:
• **wombats**
• wolves
• bears
• foxes.

2B. Wolves

Return to FIND OUT page

2C. Bears

Return to FIND OUT page

2D. Foxes

Return to FIND OUT page

FIGURE 6.4 A nonlinear/ mosaic approach: hyperlinking is two-way

The online screen, then, has advantages and disadvantages when communicating information (figure 6.5).

Advantages	Disadvantages
▪ Able to hyperlink areas of content ▪ Gives the reader more control when interacting with the content and determining the sequence in which the content will be explored or navigated ▪ Able to show movement or animation ▪ Able to convey sound	▪ Less information can be contained in a typical single screen than in a typical printed page ▪ Screen text may not be as legible as printed page ▪ More reader effort is needed to scroll horizontally and vertically through screen text than to look at different parts of a printed page ▪ Readers navigating via hot links can miss vital, logically prior material when they choose their own pathway through content ▪ Lack of tactility ▪ Possible time lags, especially when low-powered modems or slow computers are used

FIGURE 6.5 Advantages and disadvantages of online/ mosaic over linear/narrative exposition

Implications for online writing when compared with conventional writing include the following:
▪ We may have to use fewer words on a screen than on a page.
▪ We have to reconceptualise the screen page, where the text may be closer to a printed paragraph than a printed page.

- We may have to break up content into information blocks connected by hypertext links.
- After considering behavioural factors (impatience, fatigue) and technological factors (computer functionality, mouse type), we may need to arrange our content according to priority:
  - Priority 1: third dimension (use hypertext)
  - Priority 2: second dimension (allow vertical scrolling)
  - Priority 3: first dimension (allow horizontal scrolling).

Page size needs to be set so as to minimise the reader's need to scroll horizontally or vertically. Figure 6.6, while not based on empirical data, underlines this message. Nielsen and Pernic (2010) are beginning to develop real data, arguing that web users spend 80 per cent of their time looking at information above the page fold or first screen image. Although users do scroll, they allocate only 20 per cent of their attention below the fold. Rather than creating a page that is too big for the screen, seek other solutions; one may lie in the third dimension, with hot links.

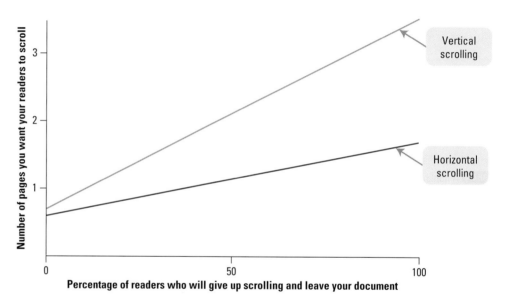

FIGURE 6.6 Considering readers' scrolling tolerance in web page design

ASSESS YOURSELF

Compare the online and print versions of a publication such as a newspaper. How is the same content handled in different ways in the different versions?

Email

Email: electronic text messages sent over a communications network between computers

Email, electronic text messages sent over a communications network between computers, has become the principal means of communicating in many organisations and among many individuals. Let's now consider different aspects of email, including the style or register of language used, design and layout factors, the use of attachments, some general writing and document management guidelines, and warnings about some of the hazards of the genre.

Email style

The writing style or register used in email tends to be more informal than that used in letters and even memos. For example, email frequently dispenses with formal salutations

('Dear . . .') and closes (e.g. 'Yours sincerely'), while contractions ('I'm', 'it's'), abbreviations, colloquialisms, slang and jargon are common. Gimenez (2000) compares the development of the email and facsimile with that of the telex, an obsolescent technological system of linked teletypewriters, and concludes that, whereas telex evolved in a fairly planned way, with well-established language norms set out in user's manuals, email and fax transmission developed in a more haphazard fashion, using language closer to that of speech than conventional writing forms (figure 6.7).

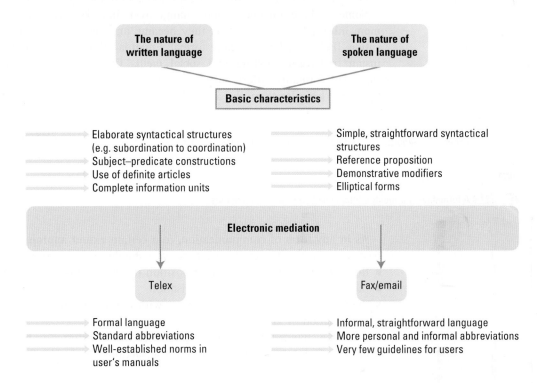

FIGURE 6.7 The origins of electronically mediated modes of communication

Source: Gimenez (2000). Reproduced with permission.

Baron (2000, 2010) also concludes that email:

- is in some ways like speech (use of first- and second-person pronouns, present tense, unedited) and in other ways closer to more formal writing (high use of adverbial subordinate clauses)
- is helping to develop a level conversational playing field (hierarchical distinctions within organisations, preserved by the mechanics of formal written communication, begin to break down, with people at junior levels communicating directly but informally with people at senior levels)
- encourages personal disclosure (sometimes email writers will reveal opinions and information online that they would not in face-to-face conversation or in a more formal document)
- can become emotional (some email writers indulge in 'flaming' – strongly worded expressions (e.g. of outrage or abuse) that they would not necessarily use in face-to-face conversation)
- may be leading to a decline in writing skills: this is not just because textspeak (such as '2' for 'to', 'too' or 'two', or 'BTW' for 'by the way') is appearing in more formal documents, nor only because such textspeak involves sloppy spelling and punctuation, but because by using email so much, we withdraw from spoken encounters, and encourage the notion that the quality of our writing matters less.

One reason why email style often reflects the informality of conversation is that users recognise the impermanence of the form. Other significant factors include:

- Emails are commonly unformatted plain text (without varying fonts, type treatment, colour and design features). Even when complex formatting of messages is attempted, there is no guarantee that with current technology your reader will receive your message in the form you sent it.
- Spell-checking and grammar/style checking features of email software generally lag behind those of word processing programs (although post-2007 versions are not bad).

Some of these tendencies may change over time. Twenty years ago faxes tended to be more informal in style, but as they became an accepted part of professional communication, their style became more formal. Email is following that path now, with chatrooms, instant messaging texting and social media filling the more informal communication roles. The formality–informality continuum in communication style today is suggested in figure 6.8 (see also 'You, the author' in chapter 7).

| Legal documents | Reports | Letters | Faxes | Memos | Emails | Chat/instant messaging | SMS text messaging | Facebook | Twitter |

Formal   **Informal**

FIGURE 6.8 A formality–informality continuum of communication modes

As in any form of communication, to a certain extent appropriate style depends on the receiver or reader. Generally speaking, you should use a more formal style when:

- the receiver holds a more senior position in the organisational hierarchy than you
- the receiver is outside your organisation
- the receiver is unlikely to be familiar with jargon or terminology used in your industry, organisation or area
- there is a chance that your correspondence will be referred to by others, will be archived or will form a part of important transactions (and all of these considerations are becoming more, not less, likely).

Writing email: what structure?

The structuring or sequencing of information critically influences the effectiveness of these communications. In other chapters in this book, we consider the AIDA and direct versus indirect methods of structuring messages. In email, direct structuring, getting your message up front, is usually the most suitable approach (Munter, Rogers & Rymer 2003). Booher (2001) proposes the **MADE** formula for structuring emails:

MADE: formula for structuring emails (acronym for Message, Action, Details, Evidence)

Message

Action

Details (apply the 5W2H principle: What, Where, When, Why, Who, How, How much?)

Evidence (optional enclosures or attachments).

The MADE approach is direct: it begins with the core of the message, creating a context and rationale for action and problem solving. Following this approach will help the writer avoid the common pitfalls of many emails, as characterised by:

- rambling, not getting to the point
- inadequate exposition of background circumstances
- inadequate definition of problem
- inadequate definition of actual and expected roles of receiver
- inadequate provision of supporting and explanatory material.

Figure 6.9 shows an email created using the MADE approach.

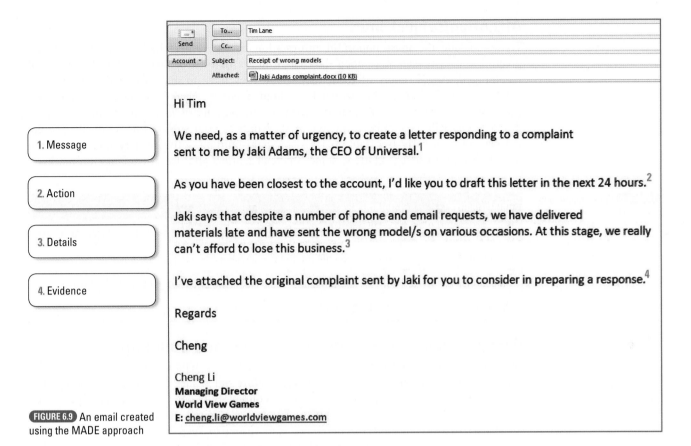

1. Message

2. Action

3. Details

4. Evidence

FIGURE 6.9 An email created using the MADE approach

Editing email

Email programs are only now beginning to carry such standard features of word processing packages as spelling and grammar checkers. These checkers are still quite primitive, but they serve a purpose, helping to improve the quality of your communication. If your email program lacks these functions, it may be useful to copy a draft of a more important email into a word processor, simply to check for grammatical and spelling errors. Alternatively you might compose the email from inside a word processor and, once you are satisfied with the quality of the text, copy it into an email document.

You may also find it useful to print out a draft of your email and edit and proofread it as you would a conventional, paper-based document. You can get maximum control over your writing by getting some distance from it, and a good way to do this is by printing it out and physically marking it up with a pen (resetting your text in a different, perhaps more legible font can also help).

Layout and appearance

Fonts

In email it is wise to limit your use of fonts to one of a basic four: Courier, Times New Roman, Arial or Calibri. If you are using plain text formatting, you may be limited to the default font, without bold, italic or underline functions. If you use HTML or rich text formatting, you will be able to introduce variety and symbols, but bear in mind that, depending on their own software functionality, your readers may not be able to open up your email and see it exactly as you sent it.

Attention/subject lines

Try to include the most important information in the subject line. Remember, on any given day your readers may open their email inbox to a list of dozens, even hundreds, of incoming messages (many of them spam), and they have to make quick decisions about what to open first (and what to delete without opening). Your aim, then, is to motivate them to open yours first. Remember, with the limitations of most email package inbox displays, you will have only about five or six words of your subject line on display, so get the keywords in early (see table 6.1). Also, spam-hunting software may target attention lines that refer to sexual matters, some financial matters and use of exclamation marks.

Uninformative	Informative
Meeting	Team 4 — Special meeting, Thursday 6 June re: poor results Prototype 5 test
Get together?	Thursday Social Tut group — meeting/meal to plan assignment?
Client report	Universal Bearings — complaints from CEO — urgent draft response
Old faces	Pacific City High reunion — 11 Feb

Paragraphing, white space, numbering and bulleting

Our 3D model of screen content (refer back to figure 6.2) tells us we have not got much vertical space in which to display a message before our reader has to start scrolling. The temptation, therefore, is to squeeze as much content into one screen as possible, which leads to a congested and cramped screen of text. Try to resist this temptation, and rely on the clarity of your message to encourage your reader to keep reading. Readers are more likely to scroll down a screen that is clearly laid out than to read and absorb information that is cramped and uninviting.

Accordingly, use paragraphing to separate key concepts, leaving a line space between them. In longer messages, consider using page numbering (perhaps using the format '2 of 6', '3 of 6' etc.) to help your reader. Dot point lists and headings can also help.

Attachments and links

Avoid trying your reader's patience with very long email messages. **Attachments**, such as those in PDF format, allow you to send more information by creatively exploiting the 3D space in the email zone. Normally, attachments play much the same role as appendices in reports. Report appendices are usually 'parked' at the back of a report: they contain useful information, but they are often too bulky and distracting to include in the body of the report.

Although technology is advancing and bandwidth capabilities are ever increasing, it is generally unwise to attach files with a size of more than 2 or 3 megabytes (MB), as not all servers or computers that transmit and receive electronic messages have the capacity to handle larger files. This limitation may be partly circumvented by:

- 'parking' supplementary files on a website, and creating a pathway to those files using a **file transfer protocol (FTP)** hyperlink embedded in the email
- sending multiple messages with individual attachments
- saving the file material to a shared hard drive
- using compression technology, such as ZIP files, to reduce the file size
- using traditional delivery methods (post, courier) to send high-capacity storage units such as DVDs or USBs/flash drives/memory sticks.

Figure 6.10 illustrates an unsent email containing attachments and a hyperlink. You should always check that attachments are included, if they are required, before sending an email.

Attachment: a data file electronically attached to an email. It can contain text, graphics, video or audio in a compressed or uncompressed format

File transfer protocol (FTP): a process that allows uploading and downloading of files on a network

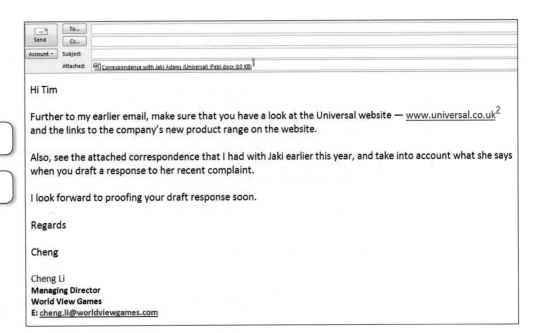

1. Attachment/s

2. Active URL

FIGURE 6.10 An email with attachments and a link

Identity details

Ensure that your readers know who you are. Remember, when your email arrives, the sender details may give your name, but not much else. You may decide to create an electronic business card and attach this to all your outgoing email. This is a type of attachment that can be transferred straight into your reader's contacts directory. These do not, however, always work well; an alternative strategy is to create your own signature block, which you can insert into each email. When using a card or signature insert, include your:

- full name
- title or position
- organisation name
- other contact details (postal address, landline telephone number, fax number, mobile telephone number, URL of company home page).

You may decide to use more than one signature block — say, one for official business to recipients outside the organisation, one for business communications within the organisation, and one for personal messages. Examples of formal and casual signature blocks are shown in the next figure.

SIGNATURE BLOCKS

Signature blocks can be casual or formal, depending on the circumstances. Two examples are shown below, with a formal signature block on the left and a casual signature block on the right.

John Smith
Chief Executive Officer
Daintree Corporation
19 Gully Avenue, Stoneleigh NSW 5646, Australia
(PO Box 2424, Stoneleigh NSW 5646, Australia)
Tel: +61 (0)2 3543 3535
Fax: +61 (0)2 4646 2546
Mobile: +61 (0)456 256 000
Email: jsmith@daintree.com

John Smith
Chief Executive Officer
Daintree Corporation
Tel: +61 (0)2 3543 3535
Email: jsmith@daintree.com

The following feature provides some background to addresses in cyberspace. These addresses, often differentiated with domains, are a form of identity for the multitude of organisations, government bodies, individuals, networks and other groups that have a web presence.

ONLINE ADDRESSES

Every website has an address, just like a street address. The web address is called a Uniform Resource Locator, or URL. URLs are based on domains, which are sections of cyberspace devoted to specific types of activities and are identified by suffixes within a URL, preceded by a full stop.

Top-level domains include:

- .com — commercial or business organisations
- .biz — commercial or business organisations
- .net — organisations running a computer network
- .org — nonprofit organisations
- .gov — government bodies
- .edu — educational institutions
- .mil — military organisations
- .name — personalised domain name
- .coop — cooperative business organisations
- .info — mainly commercial or business organisations
- .museum — museums

These domain suffixes are often followed by a country code; for example, .uk (United Kingdom), .au (Australia) and .cn (China).

A further domain level will often identify the organisation's region, province or state; for example, .vic.au (Victoria, Australia) and .sh.cn (Shanghai, China).

Email addresses tend to be associated with websites (e.g. customers wishing to learn more about www.thebestsite.com can email them at info@thebestsite.com).

When choosing a website URL and/or an email address, there is always a trade-off between the simple and concise and the definitive but long-winded. Long URLs and email addresses are specific, but they can be easily forgotten, or misspelled — and, on the net, a single wrong letter, number or punctuation mark will mean a failure to connect. Educational and government bodies are often guilty of overlong URLs and email addresses.

The first country to go online was the United States, so most US organisations do not require a country code. There is now a .us domain name, but it is not widely used. If you want your email and/or website to appear global rather than parochial, and to have the marketing advantage of being easily remembered, keep the address short. There are obvious advantages to having the email address kinross.bj@manitoba.gov (24 characters) rather than bertrandj.kinross@clientsupport.socialservices.metro.mb.gov.ca (63 characters).

Email management

DRAFS: an email management system (acronym for Delete, Reply, Act, Forward, Save)

Manage your email by using the **DRAFS** (Delete, Reply, Act, Forward, Save) system (Arnold 2002).

Delete as many unwanted or redundant messages as you can. Install spam filters to delete incoming junk mail even before you see it. Use your email package functions to set up rules to delete emails from people you don't want to hear from again. This usually means setting up a 'junk' folder and redirecting all unwanted emails into that folder, which you can clear with a simple block delete every week or month. Don't respond to junk emails by asking the senders to delete you from their mailing list. Response indicates to the unscrupulous that your address is 'live', and you risk receiving more, rather than fewer, messages from that sender and others to whom the sender has supplied your address.

Reply to emails as soon as you can, simply to clear the decks, but not too quickly, and not too often. As Arnold (2002) suggests, 'Generally speaking, people who respond to every message within five or ten minutes are paying more attention to their email than to their jobs. When email has been lobbed back and forth (like a tennis ball) for more than three volleys, it's time to pick up the phone and go face to face'.

If a detailed response is required, and you do not have the time to do so within 48 hours, simply send a brief response saying you are working on it. When replying to an email, ensure that your reader understands clearly what it is about. Usually, there is a 'thread' or sequence of previous correspondence to place the email in context. Your email program may allow you to append your reply to your correspondent's message. If there is no such thread, set the context for your reader by recapitulating the circumstances of the correspondence. If the thread goes on at unnecessary length, delete or edit, or simply save the previous correspondence as a file and attach it.

Act on email using good time management practices. Just as it is useful (if not always possible) to handle each piece of paper only once, it makes sense to use email as a tool for action rather than procrastination. Check out your email package's capacity to flag each item, so that your attention will automatically be drawn to it within a set time.

Forward email to those who need to know about it. If the content is sensitive, check with the sender before conveying it to others.

Save important email just as you would save paper mail. Investigate the filing capacity of your email package. You will find that you can create folders and subfolders in which to organise your emails. You can also archive your communications either within the email package or to your computer hard drive. Establish similar electronic filing structures to those you use for your physical files and filing cabinets. Consider printing out hard copies of important emails.

Email: problems and opportunities

Email has had a number of positive impacts on communication. Within organisations, it has helped to flatten hierarchical relations, breaking down barriers to communication based on position. People working at lower levels are more inclined to send an email than they would a memo or letter to someone of higher office. Email has increased the speed of communication, which is often a good thing in bureaucracies drowning in paper. It allows the transfer of types of information (visual, audio) that cannot be transferred via paper-based correspondence. Email also allows *asynchronous* communication – that is, senders send messages when it suits them; receivers open messages when it suits them. It can thus circumvent 'telephone ping-pong' (see table 1.8 in chapter 1 and 'Communication channels' in chapter 16).

Email, however, also has several disadvantages. It has been said that the greatest cause of problems are solutions, and email may be a case in point. Some organisations have found that email traffic has exploded so dramatically that it has placed an intolerable burden on their networks, with the result that they have been forced to place restrictions on traffic to minimise email overload ('The User Group' 2000). Thus, some organisations have implemented 'quiet time' regimes (no email or phones for the first four hours of the day) and **no email Fridays**, often with considerable success: people are forced into using richer forms of communication – such as face-to-face or the telephone – building rapport, reducing frustration and boosting productivity. Of course, information overload – too many emails, or supply or push dynamics – needs to be differentiated from internet addiction, which is a demand or pull dynamic. As Thomas, King et al. (2006, p. 278) observed:

No-email Fridays: policy of some organisations to cut down on too many emails and promote face-to-face communication

> With a rapid flow of information, individuals may feel pressured to respond even if they are on sick leave or vacation. More and more, we find individuals who answer e-mail while they talk on the phone or who respond to e-mail as they sit in meetings. Clearly, multitasking increases the complexity of the work. ... e-mail talk may both affect and create overload, a problem common in many organizations today.

With a rapid flow of information and pressure to be accountable, many employees respond to emails during their holidays and even when they are on sick leave.

Many people are more likely to ignore an email than they would a letter or paper memo. As distinct from the sheer number of emails that arrive, there is the question of email interruption. By disturbing the flow of concentration, emails may take more time to 'recover from' than a telephone interruption (Jackson, Dawson & Wilson 2001).

Email sometimes deceives people by its apparent informality, privacy, impermanence and speed: some email users will write things that they would never say in face-to-face conversation. But email is not private: legal decisions around the world have confirmed that the content of an email sent from the workplace belongs to the employer, not the sender. You should, therefore, be careful what you write: don't write anything in an email that you wouldn't write on a postcard, and don't write anything that you would not want to appear in a newspaper or be quoted in a court of law. Remember, even if you delete an email, the 'data shadow' of the email may be restorable on the network server (Smith 2002; Brake 2004).

Like the fax before it, email is sometimes *too* fast: it is easy to write things you might come to regret once you have given an issue more thought. Just as we can shoot our mouth off with intemperate words, we can shoot our fingers off with intemperate writing. As the proverb has it, 'Four things come not back: the spoken word, the spent arrow, the past, and the neglected opportunity' (Omar Idn Al-Halif). Byron (2008) argues that because of its asynchronous nature (the recipient is not always there to respond, as in face-to-face encounters) and the lack of nonverbal cues inherent in email, the communication of emotion is often misunderstood.

In 1999, the Canadian company Research in Motion released the BlackBerry smartphone, which, among other things, could be used to send and receive emails and texts. In 2006, the Webster's New World College Dictionary announced that its Word of the Year was 'crackberry' – a play upon the crack-cocaine-like addictive power of the Black-Berry, while Webster's Word of the Year in 2009 was 'distracted driving' – a reference to the dramatic upsurge in many countries of drivers using mobile phones, and smart or enhanced phones such as the BlackBerry, iPhone and Palm devices (Talmazan 2009; Michaluk, Mazo & Trautschold 2008). Users that check their email far more frequently than is necessary, and in a compulsive way, may be suffering from **email addiction**. Some addicts struggle to look away from their inbox for more than a few minutes at a time. Freeman quotes neurologists comparing the brain 'hit' email addicts get to that which slot machine gamblers get – the intermittent payoff keeps them coming back. Indeed, some psychologists are arguing for 'internet addiction' to be broadly classified as a clinical disorder (Freeman 2009).

Email addiction: the apparently compulsive behaviour of people who check their email far more frequently than is necessary.

This 'always on' mentality means that the barrier between our personal and professional lives breaks down, with addicts checking their email at 3 am and while they are on holidays. This means that they can never relax: their stress levels rise, and there are negative impacts on the home front as well as at work. In fact, for email addicts, the barrier between work and life dissolves (Chalofsky 2010). Schroeder (2010) points out the paradox of 'untethered devices' such as wireless smartphones and computers: they tether us closer to the tyranny of work, even when we are not physically there. Turke (2008) points out that these 'prosthetic devices' have changed social space, making behaviour which would have been considered rude 15 years ago – such as talking on a mobile phone in public places or 'multitasking' by writing emails while in meetings – suddenly seem routine (see online chapter 5 and the discussion about 'topless meetings' in chapter 19). Oquist (2009) points out the strong potential for us to lose privacy because of insecure wireless systems. Whether sending emails or using social networks, we risk losing our privacy by using these systems, because data is being gathered about us on them in much the same way that occurs through government databases and online shopping ventures and loyalty cards.

As a note, remember also that email is a relatively recent technology: twenty years ago most people didn't have it (and if spam and other toxic internet phenomena get any worse, ten years from now most people may no longer use it). Don't leave offline people out of the loop. Fax your message to them, send them a letter or telephone them.

Your career as an email guru

It is commonplace that most people only ever access a few per cent of the features of the computer software packages they use. Indeed, software companies have been criticised for producing *bloatware*, software packages that take up large amounts of space on a computer hard disk because they contain many irrelevant features.

Nevertheless, it may pay you to spend a few minutes each day simply familiarising yourself with the features of your email program. Study a print-based manual or a commercially available user's guide (the *Idiots'* and *For Dummies* guides are good places to start), or simply work through the help screens in your program. Even if you know only 20 per cent of what your program can do, you are way ahead of most users; you will be able to achieve much more in your use of email, your productivity will increase, and you will become known as a software guru – and that can't be bad for your career! Gurus in any area, of course, need to speak the language; the following feature introduces some of the jargon relating to online communication.

ONLINE JARGON ALERT

bcc (blind carbon copy): copy of an email sent to someone else without the knowledge of the primary recipient

.bmp: file extension for files stored in bit map graphic format

cc (carbon copy): copy of an email ('carbon copy' is a legacy from the days of typewriters)

.doc or *.docx:* suffix on file name (file extension) indicating it is a Microsoft Word document

download: move a copy of a file from a remote computer to the requesting computer via a modem or network

ftp (file transfer protocol): protocol used for copying files to and from remote computer systems on a network

.gif (Graphics Interchange Format): file extension of graphic file format, used for storing low-resolution 'bit map' graphic files

HTML (hypertext markup language): computer code language used in the construction of text and graphics on web pages

http (hypertext transfer protocol): coding protocol used to access information on the internet

.jpg: file extension of JPEG (Joint Photographic Expert Group) static graphic format, used for storing high-resolution images in compressed form

.mpg: file extension of MPEG (Motion Picture/Multimedia Expert Group) dynamic graphic format, used for storing compressed audio and video files

.ppt or *.pptx:* file extension used for Microsoft PowerPoint documents

upload: move a copy of a file from a local computer to a remote computer

URL (uniform resource locator): a website address

.xls or *.xlsx:* file extension used for Microsoft Excel documents

.zip: file extension indicating the file is compressed

---

1. If you have not already done so, set up a series of folders and subfolders in your inbox. Coordinate the categories of these with your paper filing system. If you already have an organised inbox, evaluate how effective the current system is; if you can think of improvements, make them.
2. If you have not already done so, create a series of rules for incoming emails to ensure deletion of spam and automatic redirection of emails into relevant folders (if that is a useful management strategy for you). If you already have rules set up, evaluate the effectiveness of those rules.
3. Print out the last ten emails you sent. Do they follow the MADE (Message, Action, Details, Evidence) formula? How effective/ineffective are they because of that?
4. Compare your current email software package with at least one other. What are the strengths and weaknesses of each package?

Writing for the web

Writing for the web requires a number of specific skills. One useful skill, of course, is technical writing of code such as HTML (Hypertext Markup Language), although WYSIWYG (what-you-see-is-what-you-get) website building tools such as Macromedia's Dreamweaver or Microsoft's Front Page now allow the construction of complex web pages without technical knowledge. Here, though, we are primarily concerned with online writing as a style best suited to communicating with audiences through **web pages**.

Web page: a document on the world wide web consisting of an HTML file and associated graphics and script files; a website may comprise a number of web pages

You as web writer

Web writing presents different challenges from those of other documents, such as letters and reports. In fact, web writing probably has more in common with scriptwriting for film, television or radio. Like scriptwriters, web writers are often part of a team putting together a complex artefact. The process can be involved, and your sanity may depend on your understanding of the roles played by different individuals in it. As writer, for example, you may be involved in collecting client information from which to create the copy that will form the basis of the text. You will be involved in editing and proofreading tasks too.

Web writers tend to have more control over technical processes than film/TV/radio scriptwriters, who work only with text, with the creation of visual and sound images left to others. In contrast, web writers may need to be involved with the form and structure of the web page because of the objective needs of the text. For example, a web writer might need to establish the following sorts of guidelines:

- In this website, it makes sense for pages to be linked in this manner, because that is the way users will drill down from a particular link or image.
- In this online learning program, users will need to know about these three interlinked concepts if they are to acquire the desired competencies.
- In this virtual game, players will need to know this information at this point, because otherwise they will not be able to proceed to the next level.
- In this website, returning to the home page should be a clear and simple navigating task.
- In this website, there needs to be a truly effective search function.
- In this website, there needs to be a truly effective plain text print function (just the words, and no graphics).

Figure 6.11 illustrates the role of writers in the development of a website, and how the tasks of writers and editors fit into this process.

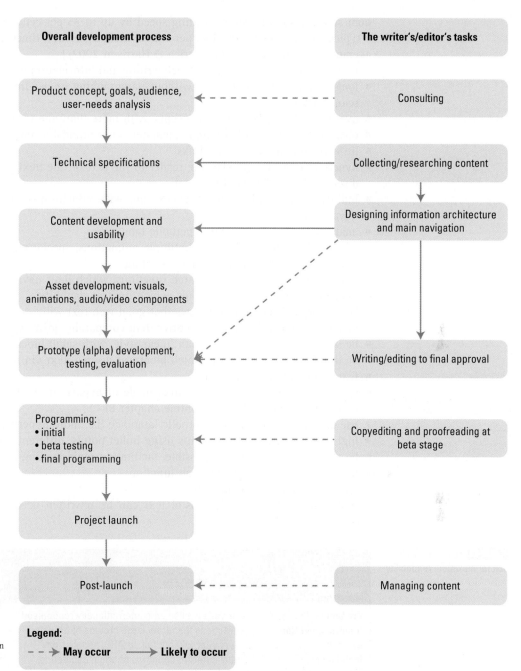

FIGURE 6.11 Website development: how the tasks of writers/editors fit into the process

Source: Hammerich and Harrison (2002, p. 14). Reproduced with permission.

Who are the readers, and why don't they read?

Any writing requires consideration of the audience. How do people read online documents? Do they read web text in the same way they read traditional print text? Nielsen (2010) suggests that users of the web do not read at all – they merely skim and scan, picking out salient pieces, rarely reading extended text blocks. This may be partly because the experience of reading computer text is closer to that of watching television than reading print on a page. Kilian (2000) proposes that readers of websites are in a 'cognitively hyperactive state', a state in which they are simultaneously 'revved up', looking for 'jolts' or sensory rewards (click on this and see animation and hear music), and 'dumbed down', because the poor screen resolution slows reading speed by up to 25 per cent. (The visual resolution of a typical book is 1 440 000 dots per square inch, up to 277 times sharper than that of an average computer screen (Hammerich & Harrison 2002).)

Nielsen (1997a) argues that bad web writing and information design are characterised by:

- long blocks of narrative text, without paragraphing or headings, making it difficult to scan quickly
- overly wordy expositions of concepts, with more than one idea per paragraph
- obscure or 'clever' (rather than immediately understandable and informative) subheadings
- little or no hypertext or hot links
- hypertext that merely takes the reader to the text on the next page, rather than linking discrete blocks of related material
- indirect or delayed mode of exposition, with conclusions and payoffs offered only towards the end
- 'marketese', or inflated and hyperbolic language
- technically complex elements (multiple animations, special effects, 'bells and whistles') that inflate file size and slow page loading
- inadequate/nonexistent site search functions, which limit navigability
- inadequate/nonexistent site maps, which limit navigability.

Using Nielsen's criteria, it follows that good web text will:

- be concise (up to 50 per cent shorter than comparable print text)
- be laid out in mosaic rather than linear style, with small blocks of text and headings
- be linked to other levels of related blocks of discrete text via hyperlinks
- feature one idea per paragraph
- be expressed according to the direct mode of exposition, with conclusions first (in the inverted pyramid style – see online chapter 8)
- use objective rather than hyperbolic language (i.e. more hypertext than hype)
- highlight and differentiate points using bullet points, different fonts and colour
- be as technically simple as possible, facilitating rapid loading of page
- be supported by good site search function
- be supported by good site map.

An example of how unsuccessful text can be rewritten according to these criteria is given in table 6.2.

TABLE 6.2 Rewriting web text for maximum readability

Version	Sample paragraph	Usability improvement (relative to control condition)
Promotional writing (control condition): using the 'marketese' found on many commercial websites	Australia is filled with internationally recognised attractions that draw large crowds of tourists every year without fail. In 2010, people from many different countries of origin decided to visit the beautiful country that is Australia. There were 5.7 million visitor arrivals during this year that decided to come and discover this amazing country. More than 97 000 New Zealanders came over to Australia during June 2010 and more than 41 000 visitors came from the United States during this month. More than 22 000 visitors came from Japan during this period, while over 30 000 Singaporeans decided to venture across to our stunning, dramatic country. High numbers of visitors also came to Australia from a variety of other countries.	0 per cent (by definition)

Version	Sample paragraph	Usability improvement (relative to control condition)
Concise text: about half the word count of the control	In 2010, 5.7 million visitors arrived in Australia from different countries of origin. Some of the highest visitor numbers during June 2010 were recorded by New Zealand, the United States, Singapore and Japan.	58 per cent
Scannable layout: using the same text as the control condition in a layout that facilitates scanning	Australia is a very popular destination choice with so many overseas travellers, with 5.7 million visitors arriving in the beautiful country during 2010. Some of countries that recorded the highest visitor numbers during June 2010 were: ■ New Zealand ((97 200) ■ the United States ((41 200) ■ Singapore (30 200) ■ Japan (22 200).	47 per cent
Objective language: using neutral rather than subjective, boastful or exaggerated language (otherwise the same as the control)	In 2010, 5.7 million visitors arrived in Australia. Visitors arrived in Australia from many different countries of residence. During June 2010, there were 97 200 visitors from New Zealand, 41 200 visitors from the United States, 30 200 visitors from Singapore and 22 200 visitors from Japan.	27 per cent
Combined version: combining the three improvements in writing style: concise, scannable and objective	In 2010, 5.7 million visitors arrived in Australia. In June 2010 some visitor numbers recorded were: ■ New Zealand (97 200 visitors) ■ the United States (41 200 visitors) ■ Singapore (30 200 visitors) ■ Japan (22 200 visitors).	124 per cent

Source: Adapted from Nielsen (1997a), www.useit.com; Tourism Australia (2010), 'June 2010', Visitor arrivals, www. tourismaustralia.com.

Microcontent: don't forget the tags

Keyword: a word or phrase, highlighted by a meta-tag, used by search engines to identify and classify web pages

Although we are not covering the technical writing or construction of websites here, mention does need to be made of tagging and **keywords**. Given that there are billions, soon to be trillions, of web pages out there, and you want at least some of these web users to visit yours, how will they find out about it? The most likely way will be via a computer program called a search engine. A search engine will undertake an automated search of virtual space, using information robots or 'spiders' to identify and classify web pages meeting the criteria of the search request (see 'Search engines, directories, groups and chat, and images' in chapter 3). Search engines do this identification and classification by reviewing data below the visible surface of your web page. The first things they look for are the page title and what are called meta-tags. **Meta-tags,** simply a few lines of HTML code that identify keywords, make it easier for search engines to find and classify your pages.

Meta-tag: a few lines of HTML code that identify keywords and make it easier for search engines to search and classify web pages

McAlpine suggests that without highlighted keywords your site is likely to be generally ignored, while too many keywords may lead to your site being classified by search engines as spam.

As a rule you can safely list up to 25 key phrases or keywords, each separated by a comma. Here's a list of 21 keywords [for a Canadian florist] *in a meta keyword tag. In this particular list, the most important key phrases are listed first (of course), and repeated toward the end:*

pink peonies, ontario, order peonies online, peony plants, peony nursery, canada peonies, cut flowers, pink paeonies, online, plants, flowers, credit cards, visa, mastercard, florist canada, toronto, vancouver, pink peonies, ontario, order peonies online

Vary the number of keywords you use for different pages. On one page, try using just three or four keywords. Some search engines give higher relevancy to keywords in a short list. (McAlpine 2001, p. 23)

Note that some page designers have ceased to employ meta-tags because unscrupulous operators, such as porn site designers, use meta-tags to trick search engines into bringing up porn site links in searches on innocuous topics; they have also hacked into legitimate websites, using their meta-tags to redirect searchers to porn sites.

ASSESS YOURSELF

1. Go to a website using a browser. Using the Print Screen>Paste commands, print out a number of pages from the site, drilling down through hyperlinks to create a sequence. Create a full-scale model of the site by arranging screenshots on a board or the floor and connecting them with ink lines or paper strips. Evaluate the structure of the sequence. Does it make sense? Would you have done it differently? In your opinion, what is missing from the site?
2. Using the View>Source or View>Page Source commands on your browser, identify the meta-tags in a number of sites. Compare and evaluate three sites selling the same product.

So what's on the horizon?

In spite of the good advice given about web pages, something rather strange has happened in the past few years – a counter revolution in favour of reading online narrative text, usually without the bells and whistles and garish effects designed to get us to buy something. This is tied up with the ugly but real jargon concept of 'monetisation' on the net: how might money be made out of sites or products when everything is virtually free (Keane 2009)?

E-book: electronic book, or book that can be read and/or interacted with on computers

A number of key commercial players (as distinct from bloggers, 'citizen journalists' and self-publishers) have entered the ring, usually selling electronic books or **e-books** downloadable to computers. These can be simple PDFs, scanned facsimiles of existing books, or digital books, with the capacity for text and graphics to be rearranged on the page, hyperlinking to other sections, overlining of text capacity, and the writing of 'sticky note' graphics to remind the reader of something. These books are sometimes sold virtually free with conventional books, especially textbooks, giving two books for the price of one, or stand-alone versions that are usually cheaper than the paper book.

Amazon, the world's biggest online bookshop, has introduced the Kindle, an electronic reader in tablet shape (currently only able to read black and white across a grey scale). The initial device is fairly expensive, but Amazon offers e-books for prices well below those of conventional paper books – often of the same title. Numerous books can be stored on the device. Various models are available, rotating images between portrait and landscape orientations (see chapter 2), which is particularly suitable for newspapers and textbooks. As well as books, it is possible to subscribe to blogs, newspapers and magazines, thus partially satisfying the monetisation problem. Clark, Goodwin, Samuelson and Coker (2008) found that Kindle was acceptable to users for reading fiction, but its use in an academic setting was limited due to content availability and licensing issues, graphic display capabilities, organisational issues, and its prohibitive cost. A summary of some other changes follows:

- *Google.* Google has plans to create the world's biggest online library, and has had staff working for the past several years scanning out-of-print and in-print titles. Google's motivation in doing so is not absolutely clear: is it altruism, bringing all knowledge to anyone who wants it via a computer screen, or is the beginning of a partial monetisation program, whereby books can be bought after seeing 'teaser' sections? Google has had – predictably enough – problems with publishers and authors over copyright. Agreements have been hammered out about profit sharing, but the final outcome is not yet clear (Skidelsky 2009).

- *Apple iTunes U.* Apple have taken their successful downloadable music format, iTunes, and are creating an online university, with more than 300 universities contributing lecture slideshows (as podcasts or videocasts) and other content. The US Museum of Modern Art and the New York Public Library have also contributed content (McKinney, Dycka & Lubera 2009).

- *Apple iPad.* In 2010, Apple launched a tablet PC, with the keyboard able to be called up on the screen, no mouse, and all manipulation and user navigation done by touch. The iPad has a bigger screen than the Kindle, an animated page-turning effect and the ability to handle colour. There were initial concerns that Apple might not have the software (i.e. the books) that Kindle/Amazon has access to, apart from free and for-payment newspaper subscriptions. However, Apple was working to resolve this issue after the release of the product.

Yet, doubts remain about reading on screen, such as: Will it fatigue the eyes? Is it worth it? Is it just a gimmick? A US-student Public Interest Research Group complained about the price of textbooks, and considered other options, such as renting texts and considering high-tech options such as e-books. Surprisingly, in assessing e-books over paper books, a majority of students preferred paper (Student Public Interest Group 2009; Eunson 2009). Such results may simply be due to the pleasant tactility of handling the text, or perhaps just simply because paper books are what we are used to.

While some suggest that paper books are doomed, the linear and the mosaic, the electronic and the products of trees, will likely co-exist – albeit uncomfortably – for some time yet. It is going to be interesting to see how it all turns out. It may well be that the two can be blended, with a linear version of a novel, like enhanced textbooks, having clickable features such as maps, glossaries, critical articles, video segments of film adaptations, photos of original locations, documentary information about the novel's characteristics, links to discussion forums, facsimiles of original versions, interviews with authors, and so on.

All of these issues overlap, of course, with the rapid rise of social media such as Facebook and Twitter, and with newer communication technologies that are rapidly appearing on the horizon (see chapter 21).

STUDENT STUDY GUIDE

SUMMARY

Online writing requires a nonlinear or mosaic structure, with the text layout or information design as important as the text itself. Email has evolved rapidly into an important communication medium. At its current stage of development, email has more in common with informal conversation than with most genres of writing, although it is gradually becoming more formal and structured. The direct structuring pattern is preferred for emails, and here the MADE (Message, Action, Details, Evidence) model is useful. Email technology still lags behind word processing technology, and this contributes to grammatical and spelling problems. Emails are generally presented as unformatted plain text, and this emphasises simplicity and clarity of communication.

Email technology allows us to send associated data files as attachments, but there are constraints on this feature, just as there are alternatives to communicating the content of attachments. For best results, email use needs to be carefully managed, and the application of the DRAFS (Delete, Reply, Act, Forward, Save) model can help us to become better managers. There are many advantages to email as a mode of communication, but there are also downsides, such as information overload and email addiction.

Writing for websites is not as simple as it might appear. There are a number of criteria for effective web writing. If followed, these techniques will increase the probability that the site will reach its audience and perhaps draw responses from it. Meta-tags are a useful means of identifying websites, allowing search engines to locate sites and direct potential readers, users and customers to the sites. New developments in software and hardware may mean that plain narrative text may stage a renaissance via new hardware and software.

KEY TERMS

attachment *p. 206*
broadband *p. 199*
DRAFS *p. 208*
e-book *p. 216*
email *p. 202*
email addiction *p. 210*
extranet *p. 198*

file transfer protocol
  (FTP) *p. 206*
internet *p. 198*
intranet *p. 198*
keyword *p. 215*
MADE *p. 204*
meta-tag *p. 215*

no-email Fridays *p. 209*
modem *p. 199*
mosaic form *p. 200*
web page *p. 212*
wireless transmission *p. 199*

REVIEW QUESTIONS

1. Why do we need to consider technical factors such as bandwidth when writing emails or creating websites?
2. List three advantages and three disadvantages of mosaic exposition when compared with linear/narrative exposition in online writing.
3. Is it inevitable that email will over time become more formal in style?
4. Name at least two alternatives to attaching files to emails as a means of communicating large amounts of information to readers.
5. List three advantages and three disadvantages of email as a communication medium.
6. List at least three desirable characteristics of websites identified by Nielsen.
7. Why is it important to insert meta-tags in a website?
8. In what ways is the experience of reading website text different from the experience of reading print-based text?
9. Evaluate Vincent Flanders' website 'Web pages that suck' at www.webpagesthatsuck. com. Do you agree or disagree with Flanders' judgements?

APPLIED ACTIVITIES

1. Analyse five websites and rate them from best to worst. What criteria are you applying? Create a table showing the criteria and the website names, or photocopy the one provided below.

	Criterion 1	Criterion 2	Criterion 3	Criterion ...	Criterion *n*	Ranking
Site 1						
Site 2						
Site 2						
Site 4						
Site 5						

2. Imagine you are setting up a business. Consider the reasons for and against creating a website to promote the business.
3. Compare and contrast at least two web browsers. To help your analysis, create a comparison table similar to the one supplied in question 1. What impact might browsers have on the future of online communication?
4. Compare and contrast at least four web search engines. To help your analysis, create a comparison table similar to the one in question 1. What impact might search engines have on the future of online communication?
5. Consider figure 6.8. How might the various genres identified affect each other over the next ten years?

WHAT WOULD YOU DO?

You receive two emails from a good friend working in the same organisation. One of them is a chain letter, with several thousand names on it. The second one contains a link to an adult website. You cannot remember your organisation's policy on chain emails and visiting 'undesirable' sites, but you are reasonably sure that all your movements on email and the web can be tracked. What will you do with these emails? Will you send on the chain letter or delete it? Will you open the web link or delete the email? What will you say to your friend, whom you are meeting for lunch?

SUGGESTED READING

Barr, Chris 2011, *The Yahoo! style guide: the ultimate sourcebook for writing, editing and creating content for the digital world*, St Martin's Griffin, New York.

Hoogeveen, Jeffrey & and Blakesley, David 2011, *Writing: a manual for the digital age*, 2nd rev. edn., Heinle, New York.

Nielsen, Jakob & Pernic, Kara 2010, *Eyetracking web usability*, New Riders Press, Indianapolis.

Oickles, Jason 2011, *Email: email marketing secrets. How to write killer promo emails that get massive results* [Kindle Edition], Amazon Digital Services, Seattle.

Song, Mike, Halsey, Vicki & Burress, Tim 2009, *The hamster revolution: how to manage your email before it manages you*, Berrett-Koehler, San Francisco.

Warner, Janine 2010, *Do it yourself: Web sites for dummies*, 2nd edn, John Wiley and Sons, Hoboken.

REFERENCES

Arnold, Kristin J 2002, 'Email basics: practical tips to improve communication', in Elaine Biech (ed.), *The 2002 annual handbook, vol. 1, Training*, Jossey-Bass, San Francisco, CA.

Baron, Naomi S 2000, *Alphabet to email: how written English evolved and where it's heading*, Routledge, London/New York.

—— 2010, *Always on: language in an online and mobile world*, Oxford University Press, New York.

Booher, Dianna 2001, *21st-century tools for effective communication*, Pocket Books, New York.

Brake, David 2004, *Dealing with e-mail*, Dorling Kindersley, London.

Byron, Kristin 2008, 'Carrying too heavy a load? The communication and miscommunication of emotion by email', *Academy of Management Review*, vol. 33, no. 2, pp. 209–327.

Chalofsky, Neal E 2010, *Meaningful workplaces: reframing how and where we work*, Jossey-Bass, San Francisco.

Eunson, Baden 2009, 'Vexed future for set texts', *The Australian*, 25 February, www.theaustralian.com.au.

Freeman, John 2009, *Shrinking the world: the 4000-year story of how email came to rule our lives*, Text Publishing, Melbourne.

Gimenez, Julio C 2000, 'Business e-mail communication: some emerging tendencies in register', *English for Specific Purposes*, vol. 9, 237–51.

Hammerich, Irene & Harrison, Claire 2002, *Developing online content: the principles of writing and editing for the web*, John Wiley & Sons, New York.

Hogg, Clare 2000, *Internet and e-mail use and abuse*, CIPD, London.

Holtz, Shel 1999, *Writing for the wired world: the communicator's guide to effective online content*, IABC, San Francisco, CA.

Jackson, Thomas, Dawson, Ray & Wilson, Darren 2001, 'The cost of email interruption', *Journal of Systems and Information Technology*, vol. 5, no. 1, pp. 81–92.

Keane, Meghan 2009, 'Murdoch's new monetization plan: somebody had to do it', 6 August, http://econsultancy.com.

Kilian, Crawford 2000, *Writing for the web*, Self Counsel Press, Bellingham, WA.

McAlpine, Rachel 2001, *Web word wizardry*, Ten Speed Press, Berkeley, CA.

McKinney, Dani, Dycka, Jennifer L & Lubera, Elise, S 2009, 'iTunes University and the classroom: can podcasts replace professors?' *Computers and Education*, vol. 52, no. 3, pp. 617–23, http://dme.medicine.dal.ca.

Mazmanian, Melissa A, Orlikowski, Wanda J & Yates, JoAnne 2005, 'CrackBerries: the social implications of ubiquitous wireless e-mail devices', *IFIP International Federation for Information Processing*, vol. 185, pp. 337–43, Springer, Boston.

Michaluk, Kevin, Mazo, Garyk & Trautschold, Martin 2008, *Crackberry: true tales of Blackberry use and abuse: tips, tricks and strategies for responsible Blackberry use*, CMT Publications, Ormond Beach, FL.

Munter, Mary, Rogers, Priscilla S & Rymer, Jane 2003, 'Business e-mail: guidelines for users', *Business Communication Quarterly*, vol. 66, no. 1, March.

Nielsen, Jakob 2007a, 'How users read on the web', *useit.com: Jakob Nielsen's website*, www.useit.com.

—— 2007b, 'Top ten mistakes in web design', *useit.com: Jakob Nielsen's website*, www.useit.com.

—— 2010, 'Scrolling and attention', *useit.com: Jakob Nielsen's website*, www.useit.com.

Nielsen, Jakob & Pernic, Kara 2010, *Eyetracking web usability*, New Riders Press, Indianapolis, IN.

Oqvist, Karen Lawrence 2009, *Virtual shadows: your privacy in the information society*, British Informatics Society, Swindon, Wiltshire.

Robinson, Joe 2010, 'E-mail is making you stupid', *Entrepreneur*, March, www.entrepreneur.com.

Schroeder, Ralph 2010, 'Mobile phones and the inexorable advance of multimodal connectedness', *New Media and Society*, vol. 12, no. 1, pp. 75–90.

Skidelsky, William 2009, 'Google's plan for world's biggest online library: philanthropy or act of piracy?' *The Guardian*, 30 August.

Smith, Lisa A 2002, *Business e-mail: how to make it professional and effective*, Writing and Editing at Work, San Anselmo, CA.

Student Public Interest Research Groups 2009, 'New report suggests technology could reverse skyrocketing textbook prices', press release, www.studentpirgs.org.

Talmazan, Yuliya 2009, '"Distracted driving" is Webster's 2009 word of the year', *NowPublic* website, www.nowpublic.com.

'The User Group: three hours a day wasted on irrelevant emails; research from the User Group shows information overload is a threat to the economy' 2000, *M2 Presswire*, 6 June, p. 1.

Thomas, Gail Fann, King, Cynthia L, Baroni, Brian, Cook, Linda, Keitelman, Marian, Miller, Steve & Wardle, Adelia 2006, 'Reconceptualizing email overload', *Journal of Business and Technical Communication*, vol. 20, no. 3, pp. 252–87.

Turkle, Sherry 2008, 'Always-on/Always-on-you: the tethered self', in Katz, James E & Castells, Manuel (eds.) *Handbook of Mobile Communication Studies*, Cambridge, MA: MIT Press.

Van Der Geest, Thea M 2001, *Web site design is communication design*, John Benjamins, Amsterdam/Philadelphia, PA.

Whelan, Jonathan 2000, *E-mail@ work: get moving with digital communication*, Financial Times, London.

7

Academic writing: the essay

LEARNING OBJECTIVES

After reading this chapter you should be able to:

- List at least three criteria of excellence in critical thinking as expressed in academic writing
- Explain the difference between fact and opinion, and explain why it is necessary to use both in essay writing
- Identify sources of bias and imbalance in the presentation of an argument
- Explain structural and layout features of the essay form
- Explain the importance of thesis statements and topic sentences
- Identify several major faults in poor essay writing

Essay writing

'The essay is a form of refined torture. Discuss.' You almost certainly will never encounter such an essay topic, but you might think it. Don't. The essay is simply a document that adheres to certain rules, strategies and stylistic conventions, all of which can be learnt and mastered.

Let's get down to basics. Almost certainly, you want to write not merely satisfactory essays but exceptional ones that score high marks. What is it, then, that your audience or reader wants (given that in academic situations your work is likely to be read by just one person – your lecturer or tutor)? What criteria will this reader apply when allocating marks or grades?

What makes a good or bad essay?

Table 7.1 offers an insight into the criteria for success or failure in essay writing. If you are scoring fours in your work, then you are more or less satisfying the criteria; if you are scoring ones, twos or threes, then you are not satisfying the criteria.

TABLE 7.1 Critical thinking scoring guide

Score	Criteria
4	Consistently does all or almost all of the following: ■ Accurately interprets evidence ■ Identifies the salient arguments for and against ■ Thoughtfully evaluates alternative points of view ■ Draws justified conclusions based on clearly explained reasons ■ Accurately and appropriately uses and/or cites source material ■ Presents ideas in a coherent, clear and technically correct manner.
3	Does most or many of the following: ■ Accurately interprets evidence ■ Identifies relevant arguments pro and con ■ Offers evaluations of alternative points of view ■ Draws justified conclusions based on some evidence ■ Accurately and appropriately uses and/or cites source material ■ Presents ideas in a coherent, clear and technically correct manner.
2	Does most or many of the following: ■ Misinterprets evidence ■ Fails to identify salient arguments for and against ■ Superficially evaluates alternative points of view ■ Draws unjustified conclusions based on little evidence ■ Maintains or defends views based on self-interest or preconceptions, regardless of the evidence ■ Inaccurately or inappropriately uses and/or cites source material ■ Fails to present ideas in a coherent, clear and technically correct manner.
1	Consistently does all or almost all the following: ■ Offers biased interpretations of evidence ■ Fails to identify or dismisses relevant arguments for and against ■ Ignores alternative points of view ■ Draws irrelevant or unjustified conclusions ■ Exhibits closed-mindedness or hostility to reason ■ Inaccurately or inappropriately uses and/or cites source material ■ Fails to present ideas in a coherent, clear and technically correct manner.

Source: Blattner and Frazier (2002, p. 63).

These criteria for success are not arbitrary, or simply tools of torture to make life hard; rather, they are effective benchmarks against which a sustained argument can be tested – helping us to evaluate the mix of fact and opinion advanced in an effective piece of writing (or for that matter in an effective oral presentation). Switch roles for a minute: imagine that it is you who comprises the audience, and that someone else is trying to persuade you to:

1. change your mind and agree with them
2. give them money
3. help them out.

It probably makes sense for you, in the role of critical evaluator, to impose criteria upon which to assess what you are reading or hearing, and your criteria would probably be quite similar to those listed in table 7.1.

Essays: form and content

Essays are documents on specific topics that contain a mix of fact and opinion, laid out in logical sequences and employing appropriate strategies of expression. An essay comprises both content (what is said) and form (the way in which it is said). These aspects are separate, but not unrelated.

Let's take an example of an essay. Francis Bacon, one of the earliest users of the essay form, tackled a wide variety of topics. Here's one he wrote on that most basic of human impulses, revenge. The language and punctuation is that of 1625, but a modern reader can follow it without too much difficulty, and even after almost four centuries most of us can recognise what he was writing about.

An example: Francis Bacon's essay on revenge

Revenge is a kind of wild justice; which the more man's nature runs to, the more ought law to weed it out. For as for the first wrong, it doth but offend the law; but the revenge of that wrong, putteth the law out of office.

Certainly, in taking revenge, a man is but even with his enemy; but in passing it over, he is superior; for it is a prince's part to pardon. And Solomon, I am sure, saith, 'It is the glory of a man, to pass by an offence.' That which is past is gone, and irrevocable; and wise men have enough to do, with things present and to come; therefore they do but trifle with themselves, that labor in past matters. There is no man doth a wrong, for the wrong's sake; but thereby to purchase himself profit, or pleasure, or honor, or the like. Therefore why should I be angry with a man, for loving himself better than me? And if any man should do wrong, merely out of ill-nature, why, yet it is but like the thorn or briar, which prick and scratch, because they can do no other. The most tolerable sort of revenge, is for those wrongs which there is no law to remedy; but then let a man take heed, the revenge be such as there is no law to punish; else a man's enemy is still before hand, and it is two for one. Some, when they take revenge, are desirous, the party should know, whence it cometh. This is the more generous. For the delight seemeth to be, not so much in doing the hurt, as in making the party repent. But base and crafty cowards, are like the arrow that flieth in the dark. Cosmus, duke of Florence, had a desperate saying against perfidious or neglecting friends, as if those wrongs were unpardonable: 'You shall read (saith he) that we are commanded to forgive our enemies; but you never read, that we are commanded to forgive our friends.' But yet the spirit of Job was in a better tune: 'Shall we (saith he) take good at God's hands, and not be content to take evil also?' And so of friends in a proportion. This is certain, that a man that studieth revenge, keeps his own wounds green, which otherwise would heal, and do well. Public revenges are for the most part fortunate; as that for the death of Caesar; for the death of Pertinax; for the death of Henry the Third of France; and many more. But in private revenges, it is not so. Nay rather, vindictive persons live the life of witches; who, as they are mischievous, so end they infortunate.

Explanatory notes

Solomon: Tenth century BC king of Israel. His willingness to forgive, and not take revenge, is shown in, for example, 2 Chronicles 1:11.

Cosmus: Cosimo de Medici or Cosimo 'the Elder' (1389–1464), first of the Medici family to rule the Italian city-state of Florence.

Job: Biblical character in the Book of Job, Job 2:10.

Caesar: Gaius Julius Caesar, 100–44 BC. Roman general and emperor, assassinated by Brutus and Cassius and others, who feared Caesar was intent on becoming a dictator of the Roman empire.

Pertinax: Publius Helvius Pertinax, AD 126–193. Roman emperor, who ruled for 87 days. Killed by his own soldiers over a controversy about soldiers' pay.

Henry III: 1551–1589, king of France (1574–89); son of Henry II and Catherine de' Medici. Involved in the religious wars between Catholics and Protestants in the sixteenth century, he was killed by a Dominican monk who feared that Henry would recognise a Protestant successor.

Bacon's approach

Many ideas are packed into the 454 words of this essay. In most writing, there is a link between content and form or style, and this is certainly the case with Bacon's essay.

He makes a number of key points, many of which are further broken down into sub-points that are dialectically linked — that is, he sets out opposing arguments (on the one hand this, and on the other hand that). Table 7.2 shows how this structure is created.

TABLE 7.2 Structure of Bacon's essay 'On revenge'

Key point	First part	Second part
Revenge is a kind of wild justice	The more man's nature runs to revenge . . .	. . . the more ought the law to weed out that tendency in man.
Relationship of original wrong to revenge for the wrong	The first wrong merely offends the law.	The revenge taken for the wrong undermines the authority of the law itself.
Taking revenge or not taking revenge: relationships with our enemies	By taking revenge, a man shows that he is on the same level as his enemy.	By not taking or by passing over revenge, man shows that he is superior to his enemy. Example of Solomon.
Revenge and time present, past and future	Wise men have enough to do worrying about the present and the future without being stuck in the past, which is what thinking about revenge does.	Those who are stuck in the past, preoccupied with revenge, waste their time.
Motivation for wrongdoing	No-one does wrong for wrong's sake.	Men do wrong because it will profit them, or give them pleasure, or save their honour, and for other reasons.
Futility of being angry with others	If another man merely loves himself better than he loves me, that is not a good enough reason for my being angry.	If a man should do wrong because it is his nature to do so, then he cannot help it.
Revenge and the law	Revenge is acceptable when the law does punish wrongdoers.	We need to be careful when we take revenge, because the law might punish us for doing so, and that would mean that our enemies would triumph.

	Key point	First part	Second part
1. Main antithesis has minor antithesis nested within it.	[1]Revenge-taking: open and concealed styles	Some take revenge openly, and this is the more worthy approach.	Some take revenge in a base and crafty way.
	Motivation of open-style revenge-takers	These revenge-takers seem to take more satisfaction in making the guilty party repent . . .	. . . than in inflicting pain on the guilty party.
2. Main antithesis has minor antithesis nested within it.	[2]Forgiveness and our friends	Cosmus advises us not to forgive our friends.	But Job advises us that we must take the evil with the good in our friends (to a certain extent).
	Cosmus's paradoxical maxim	The Bible commands that we forgive our enemies (e.g. Mark 11:26: 'But if you do not forgive, neither will your Father who is in heaven forgive your sins.') . . .	. . . but you never read that we are commanded to forgive our friends.
	Revenge and wounds	The man who studies revenge keeps his wounds green, or unhealed, and thus does badly.	The man who does not study revenge lets his wounds heal, and does well.
	Public and private revenges	Public revenges for the most part lead to good fortune: it made sense to kill Caesar (who was intent on becoming a dictator), Pertinax (who withheld his soldiers' pay) and Henry III (who it was feared would recognise a Protestant successor to the French throne).	Private revenges for the most part lead to misfortune.
	Vindictive people and consequences	Vindictive people are like witches . . .	. . . but the mischief caused by witches brings down consequences on them.

This approach serves a number of purposes:

1. It shows that extreme opinions can sometimes miss the point unless we become aware of the relationships between apparently opposed ideas.
2. It allows us to see the paradoxical nature of reality.
3. It sets up a pleasing rhythm in the exposition of ideas.

Bacon's essay can tell us much more about an effective approach to essay writing. For example:

- **Point of view.** Do we know what Bacon believes? Yes, we do. He takes a position, states his opinion and backs up that opinion with clear arguments. Bacon advocates a broad philosophical view: that not only is revenge unproductive, but it will hurt those who pursue it.
- **Assertions.** Bacon follows certain specific lines of reasoning, using specific arguments. He develops the viewpoint that certain acts of revenge or killing are justified, but that in most cases it harms both victim and perpetrator.
- **Proofs and examples.** Bacon draws on historical evidence and authorities to substantiate his assertions.
- **Expositional technique.** Bacon develops the structure of his argument by using an explicit pattern that the reader can follow without difficulty. He uses a double, or antithetical, structure at the main level of argument and occasionally branches into a subsidiary, or nested, level:

    Major point. Revenge-taking – open and concealed styles
    Minor point. Motivation of open-style revenge-takers

Point of view: a stance or position; the expression of an opinion and the backing up of that opinion

Assertions: a specific line of reasoning, using specific arguments or claims

Proofs and examples: evidence to substantiate assertions

Expositional technique: the development of a structure of propositions that can be easily followed by a reader

> *Major point.* Forgiveness and our friends
>> *Minor point.* Cosmus's paradoxical maxim

■ **Cumulative method.** Bacon constructs one argument upon another, creating momentum and building up a persuasive sequence of reasoning, using junction points or transitions ('for', 'certainly', 'therefore', 'but', 'else', 'nay') to set up cause–effect linkages, reinforcement points and contrasts.

ASSESS YOURSELF

Analysing the essay structure
Locate print or internet sources of great historical essayists such as Francis Bacon, Michel de Montaigne, Ralph Waldo Emerson, Samuel Johnson and Mark Twain. For the sake of analysis, try to restrict yourself to essays under 1500 words in length. Create photocopies or printouts of a single essay to begin with, or edit on screen. Deconstruct or dissect the composition of the argument into points, and attempt to see how the points are linked. Using a highlighter pen on hard copy, break up the text into blocks, or alternatively break it into paragraphs on screen. If appropriate, use the format of table 7.2 to assess the structure. If you find this is not an appropriate approach, that in itself is an interesting conclusion.

Essay method

A contemporary academic essay will necessarily take a different form from the essay that Bacon wrote in the seventeenth century. For example, typical academic essays today rely more on using quoted sources to bolster their arguments, and are expected to cite full details of those sources in a bibliography or reference list. Nevertheless, certain elements are timeless, such as the creation and sustaining of an argument that makes sense. Better to have an essay with a strong argument, but without a single reference, than an essay with an elaborate bibliography and extensive use of quotation that is, in essence, nonsense.

Fact versus opinion: just what is it you have to say?

Your audience wants to know what you think – that is, your point of view. It is not enough, however, simply to assert a series of opinions: as in a courtroom or a science symposium, you need to prove what it is you are asserting. That means that opinions must rest on a bedrock of facts and data. That, in turn, means that you need to research your topic. As Arthur Conan Doyle's creation Sherlock Holmes puts it, 'I never guess. It is a capital mistake to theorize before one has data. Insensibly one begins to twist facts to suit theories, instead of theories to suit facts' (Doyle 1994 [1892]). (Contrast this view with Drucker (2002), who suggests it is better to get people to state their opinions first, as we all have a tendency to twist and edit facts to suit our own prejudices and values.)

Does this mean that you should bombard your reader with nothing but facts? In a literature review of a particular field or topic, perhaps – but if you are writing any other type of essay, definitely not. Facts are a means to an end, not an end in themselves, and that end, for the essay writer, is the presentation of an argument. Your audience is looking for evidence of:

■ solid research in the area
■ insights, including into current controversies of the area
■ originality of thought.

Too many facts and not enough opinions can be as bad as too few facts and too many opinions. Striking a balance between information and persuasion means striking a balance between fact and opinion.

Critical analysis

Your essay or paper will be an example of argumentation – the presentation of a mix of fact and opinion. Argumentation is an underlying factor in most of the ways we communicate – in writing, in speech, via the media, and even in non-verbal communication.

In constructing your argument, you need to be aware of and use the tools of argumentation, such as:

- the power of paradigms, or dominant worldviews or belief systems; and the nature of paradigm shifts, or the processes of challenging those dominant world views or belief systems
- logical argumentation categories (premises and conclusions, syllogisms, and inductive versus deductive logic; distinctions of kind versus distinctions of degree, necessary versus sufficient conditions, and explanations versus excuses)
- avoidance of logical fallacies (begging the question, false dilemma, slippery slope, straw man and so on)
- lateral versus vertical thinking
- persuasive approaches (message senders, rhetorical mix, features–benefits mix, demonstration of proofs, persuasive language, foot-in-the-door versus door-in-the-face approaches, central versus peripheral processing, persuasion-propaganda sequences, motivational drives, conformity, cognitive dissonance and message responses)
- principles of influence (liking, reciprocity, consistency, social validation and so on) and tactics of influence (assertiveness, ingratiation, impression management, negative and positive politeness and so on).

All of these factors are considered in detail in chapter 12 'Argument: logic, persuasion and influence'.

Bias and balance 1

In presenting an argument in an essay, you need to demonstrate that you are willing to explore and consider all sources of fact and opinion, even those with which you may eventually disagree. This means, firstly, that you make yourself aware of a broad range of sources and are ready to cite them. Beyond this minimum requirement, you should be ready to take issue with other writers in the topic area – who almost certainly will be much more experienced and have greater authority on the subject than you – and give reasons for your contrary opinions. This can be daunting for the beginning writer, but it goes to the heart of the critical method that you need to master.

A vital part of that critical method is the ability to be balanced in your approach – that is, to avoid **bias**. Bias, or lack of balance, can be conveyed by:

Bias: a tendency in argument to ignore opposing opinion by using sources selectively or deceptively and/or by giving disproportionate weight to sources that support only one point of view

- ignoring major or minor sources of contrary data and opinion
- acknowledging such sources, but then simply ignoring them
- selectively or deceptively quoting from such sources
- giving disproportionate weight to sources that support your point of view.

Bias is ethically wrong, but it is also practically unwise: you will almost certainly be found out. Far better to take on the sources you disagree with, and attempt to rebut them honestly, or at least to cast doubt on some of their arguments. Threatening though the thought can be, you may be wrong and your opponents may be right. There is nothing to be gained from submitting a superbly presented and footnoted rationale for the Earth being flat when you can look out of the window and see that the horizon is curved.

Always be on the lookout for bias in others' writing too, for we all have blind spots. Conscious bias demonstrates intellectual dishonesty; unconscious bias, where we are not even aware of our selective manipulation of the topic, merely shows that we are not very bright.

Synthesis and originality

Let's go back and consider the vexed question of originality. There may be dozens, hundreds or even thousands of scholars and non-scholarly writers who have contributed to the field that you are interested in, so how can you possibly demonstrate originality in your work?

There are different kinds of originality. If you are undertaking your own research, then originality will be easily achievable. In well-examined topic areas, it is still possible to be original. You can do this by:

- reinterpreting the work of others in light of other more recent (or older) sources
- synthesising the arguments of various sources – showing linkages, similarities, patterns and synergies that may not yet have been detected.

This may sound intimidating, but it doesn't have to be. If you do the necessary research and reading in the topic area – taking notes, checking internet sources, and doing everything else you should do as a researcher – you may experience a sequence of responses to your reading and note taking that goes something like this:

1. *Amazement and exhaustion.* Wow, what a lot of ideas.
2. *Despair and paralysis.* I don't think there is anything else that could possibly be said about this area.
3. *Endurance.* Time passes; your brain stews on what you have read; you sleep on it; you discuss things with colleagues and friends, which provides further stimulus ...

Creative doubt: process in which study and synthesis of research may help a writer detect shortcomings in the literature and thus come up with original perspectives

4. **Creative doubt.** But now I think about it, authority A didn't have much say about topic X, and authority B seemed to have ignored phenomenon Z ...
5. *More creative doubt.* And authorities C, D and E seem to have come up with similar conclusions about topic Y, but no-one yet seems to have pointed out the interconnections between their projects.
6. *A lot of creative doubt.* Writers in this field have done wonderful work in detecting patterns, but I happen to be familiar with another, related (or apparently unrelated) field, and I can see the following similarities and differences ...

There are no guarantees that this process will work, but input often leads to output, and occasionally virtue and hard work are rewarded. Do the research and you might be pleasantly surprised by what your brain delivers.

Bias and balance 2: the other side

Every student needs to come to terms with the politics of assessment: should I be a sycophant and simply play back to my lecturer/tutor what I think he/she wants to hear, or should I strike out on my own and express my own views, irrespective of the consequences? It makes no sense to offer up a barrage of unsubstantiated prejudice to an audience with diametrically opposed prejudices, pet theories and preoccupations, but be careful about self-editing so much that there is nothing left of you in what you offer. Students need to learn not only about the content of their subjects, but also about the 'rules of the game' of essay writing and the 'codes' in which such essays are written – without losing their own voice in the process (see, for example, Francis & Robson 2001).

It is only a slight exaggeration to suggest that the rule 'Know what you are talking about, and then say what you like' is one you should adhere to. Be prepared to take up any issues of bias or unfair treatment with your audience of one, and if that doesn't work, then you need to proactively broaden that audience. It is ultimately a question of being assertive, demonstrating professional competence and reading the politics of a situation astutely. Demonstrating professional competence is of particular importance.

Sources and proofs

In his 1625 essay, Francis Bacon supported his opinions on revenge with biblical and historical references. It's possible to create an excellent essay today by using similar references, but generally you will need to cast a broader net if you want to get better than ordinary marks for your efforts. You need to research your topic thoroughly, and that means finding high-quality resources. You may help your cause by being able to cite or quote those sources in support of your assertions.

Using a wide range of credible and relevant source materials to support your opinions provides a solid foundation for a well-written essay.

When we use sources, we stand on the shoulders of those who have gone before us. At the very least, finding out what others think saves us the trouble of reinventing the wheel (doing unnecessary work) on a particular topic. Remember, however, that sources are a means to an end, not an end in themselves. Describe earlier work by all means, but then develop your own analysis and argument. It may be appropriate that you tell us that X thinks this, Y thinks that and Z thinks the other thing, but the real question is: What do you think? You use sources as a platform for your opinions, not as a substitute for them.

The correct use of sources is a complex matter, but a number of points need to be noted here in the context of essay writing. Your sources should be:

1. *Credible and authoritative.* Use sources from mainstream publishers, and choose articles from professional, refereed journals rather than general, unrefereed journals or magazines. Be wary about using material from internet sources, as much of it is ephemeral and biased. Online journal articles that are available via credible databases are an exception to this rule. Of course, if your purpose is to attack orthodox views, use any sources you like, but ensure that the material is solid and verifiable.

2. *Locatable.* Your audience needs to be able to track down and check your sources. This means observing professional referencing standards, such as providing author name, title of book or journal, year of publication, publisher and place of publication in the case of a book, volume and issue number in the case of a journal, and page numbers if appropriate. Electronic citations need full location details (i.e. URL) and if possible the date you accessed or viewed the source.

3. *Up to date.* Using the most recent references available shows you are aware of the latest developments in your area, which is one of the criteria of professional performance in academic writing. Keep abreast of the latest issues of journals and recently published books. Online databases make the task much easier than it used to be. There is an information explosion going on today, and if you can demonstrate that you are harnessing the energy of that explosion, then you will receive recognition for this. Of course, sometimes it pays to cite older, original sources to show you are familiar with the foundations of a field.

4. *Relevant.* There is no point in showing off your research skills in citing references if they are the wrong references. Merely because a source is new and/or prestigious does not mean it is appropriate to cite it in your work. Irrelevant citation will be marked down.

5. *Convincing.* Even when a reference is relevant, there is no guarantee that it will be convincing in the context of your essay – that is, that it will be the proof you need to support the point you are making. If it is not completely convincing on its own, might it be more persuasive in concert with material from other sources? As a professional, you need to make these hard judgements, and to decide when the material is simply not good enough. If you find yourself believing, 'I've got to use this quote – it's the only

one I've got', then the bad news is you probably haven't done enough research in the first place. It is always better to have too much material from which to pick and choose carefully than not enough, which might compel you to use rubbish when you run out of high-quality data.

6. *In proportion.* It is useful to bring in the voices of others to back you up, but we also need to hear your voice. Don't load your essay so heavily with quoted material that there is little room for your own views. It is difficult to come up with hard and fast rules about this, but if quoted material comprises more than 20 per cent of your total word count, think very carefully about the quality and quantity of what you want to cite, and what you should be citing.

7. *Ethically rigorous.* Don't plagiarise. Plagiarism is theft, and when (not if) discovered, it will bring nasty punishments.

8. *Matched to the context.* Quotations should be worked seamlessly into the flow of your argument, rather than simply plugged in to build up your word count. When introducing a quoted passage, be careful to match your lead-in text grammatically to the opening words of the quote.

Essay structure

Your essay needs to be structured in a particular way to maximise its effectiveness. A typical structure is shown in figure 7.1.

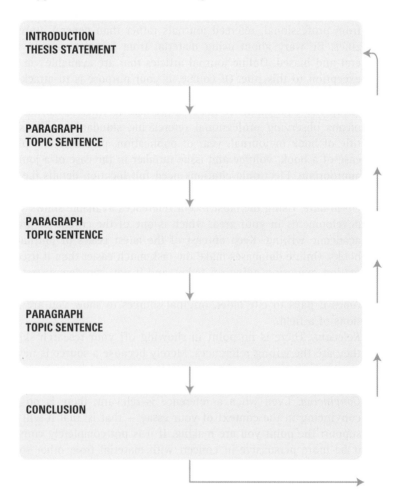

FIGURE 7.1 Structure of your essay

Structuring an essay requires planning so that you develop major and minor ideas and themes logically. Becoming more effective at writing means:

- analysing your audience or reader
- considering time management and priority settings
- considering strategies for breaking writer's blocks
- using structuring approaches to generate content and aid exposition (indirect versus direct approach, the 5W–H approach, question and answer techniques, diagramming or mind-mapping, and outlining using software tools)
- editing and proofreading.

All of these issues are considered in greater depth in online chapter 'Writing skills 5: how to write'.

The main components of an essay are:

1. Introduction
2. Body or argument
3. Conclusion.

In the introduction, you need to set down the topic question you will endeavour to answer. Here you set the scene, paying attention to the scope of what you are attempting — that is, you will define what you intend to talk about.

Thesis statements, summaries and drafting

Thesis statement: sentence or sentences, usually positioned at the beginning of an essay, that sum up the writer's argument and purpose in the discussion to follow

It is often useful to establish a **thesis statement** at the outset. The thesis statement is a succinct expression of how you will respond to the topic question. In it you inform your reader of the scope of your argument and the approach you will take. This declaration may be recapitulated in your conclusion, so that there is a clear, cohesive connection between your introductory statement of purpose and the conclusions you reach as a result of your arguments. The thesis statement, in effect, summarises the extended argument. If you are required to write a formal summary or abstract, your thesis statement will contain the gist of this summary or abstract.

Thesis statements, introductions and summaries or abstracts are often hard to write, but they are important in helping to clarify your purpose in writing the essay, which is not always easy to identify. For the following reasons, you may find it useful to write these sections *after* you have written the body of the essay:

1. You may arrive at your true opinion only once you have undertaken an exposition of the major salient points.
2. You may have unresolved conflicts about the issues in the essay, and may end up changing your mind as you write (a painful experience, involving more work, but not nearly as painful as handing in an assignment you don't really believe in, and being marked accordingly).
3. The scope of your argument may change as you expand on some ideas and reduce coverage on, or eliminate, others.

It is useful at the start to clarify the definitions of terms you will be working with. If you find yourself using a number of specialised terms, it may be helpful to collate a glossary of terms, which can be attached at the end of the essay.

Now you can begin to draft the main body of the essay. Each paragraph should cover one particular topic or subtopic. A paragraph can be one or a number of sentences long. Aim for a range of between 50 and 150 words. Keeping paragraphs relatively short helps your reader to more easily process your ideas, and to follow the linkages between your ideas.

It's hard work trying to separate out the ideas in such an undifferentiated lump of text. Great writing is sometimes defined as 'deathless prose', but *your* deathless prose may not be so deathless if your reader has to work too hard to extract your ideas, so give some thought to layout and document design.

Topic sentences

Topic sentence: usually the first sentence in a paragraph; introduces the main idea of the paragraph

You should also give serious thought to beginning each paragraph with a topic sentence. A **topic sentence** introduces the reader to the main idea of the paragraph. It usually takes the form of a statement, but it can also be a question (see figure 7.2).

There are five main factors to bear in mind in the management of intensive care patients, but they are not always listed in order of importance.

How ironic that, as the world was moving towards unanimity on the Kyoto Protocol, the global financial crisis should make many nations back off from commitments to lower carbon output when they perceived it would cost too much to meet the targets.

It is a mistake to think that Keynes was not aware of the monetarist theories being developed by the Chicago School in the 1930s.

The consensus method of group decision making has shortcomings, and I believe that these outweigh its apparent strengths.

At first glance, Drucker does not appear to give the marketing function much importance in the survival plans of the firm, but appearances can be deceptive.

FIGURE 7.2 Topic sentences: some samples

Topic sentences should flag what is coming, but like leads in news stories written by journalists, they should not only inform. Rather, they should also intrigue, making readers want to learn more. Some software summarising programs or functions (e.g. Autosummarize and Document Map in Microsoft Word) can skim the first sentence of each of your paragraphs and mechanically produce a meaningful summary of the entire document. It is possible, and sometimes desirable, to delay the topic sentence — for example, for dramatic effect — but don't push your reader's patience too far.

Writing topic sentences can help in the planning of your essay. Whether in full or summarised in note form, a list of your topic sentences can help you create a meaningful structure.

Make sure that your paragraphs are not simply unrelated blocks of text floating in a sea of white space. Link them logically and dynamically using words and phrases that define relationships, such as:

- In spite of this, ...
- Yet again, however, ...
- Secondly, ...
- Meanwhile, in another part of the battlefield, ...
- In contrast to this, ...
- The exception to this rule is ...

Such linkages help draw together your ideas in a coherent whole, and should not be regarded as trivial (for more on the expositional tools of paragraphing and transitional statements, as well as those of grammatical parallelism and rhetorical patterning, see online chapter 'Writing skills 3: style').

Your conclusion should sum up your argument, drawing all the threads together. In a real sense, the conclusion is the most important part of your essay, because it is the forum in which your authentic voice is heard. No new information is introduced at this stage; it's just you, summing up your arguments, recapitulating, giving your final response to the thesis statement, and spelling out the implications of this. You should not repeat the wording from the introduction, but there should be a symmetry between your introduction and conclusion. The three-part structure of your essay, therefore, should follow the form of a good spoken presentation:

1. Tell them what you're going to tell them.
2. Tell them.
3. Tell them what you've just told them.

Keeping on track

Don't lose sight of the focus of the essay. Remember, you have one purpose and one alone: to answer the question that has been set. Will the next sentence you write help to answer the question, or not? Apply this test to every sentence.

Don't wander from the main point, even if the material you have seems particularly interesting. If you have a lot of good ideas and good quoted material, maybe some of it is not for this essay, but for another one; don't waste it – store it in a notebook or a file and use it another time. If you feel you have to use it because you don't have anything else to say, then you are just going through the motions, and don't be too surprised or disappointed if you receive a low mark. It is your problem, not the assessor's, that you don't have enough material. Do something about it.

Don't **waffle** or pad out your writing. The only person you will be fooling by this approach is yourself.

At the other extreme, don't leave out what should be included. If you feel you run the risk of patronising your reader by stating the obvious, play it safe by putting linking and contextual material in footnotes or appendices.

Style and technique

Make sure your style is clear and easy to read. This does not mean that it should be mechanical and sterile, and devoid of personality; it does mean that the message should be at the forefront, with the medium (or the way in which you communicate the message) being secondary. If you know your stuff, then you should be able to put your ideas together in such a form that reading the essay will be a pleasant experience for your reader, and that won't do you any harm at all.

> Style matters. Some professors may even prefer essays that are well-structured and well-written but not particularly brilliant, to those that contain a truly original insight cloaked in language that would make Webster and Fowler turn in their graves. Writing a sonnet or a short one-act play is not usually a good idea, but a student should be encouraged to bring all his [her] skills as a writer to bear on the essay topic. After all, that is why the question is an essay question, rather than a true/false or short-answer. (King 1998, p. 63)

When quoting other sources, make sure you use the citing conventions appropriate to the subject or area in which you are writing. Use quoted material professionally: don't, for example, quote only part of a source to create a false impression of what that source is really saying. Whatever you do, don't plagiarise, or try to pass off someone else's work as your own (see chapter 3).

Time and technique

Writing is not really writing unless it involves some measure of rewriting. Drafting, redrafting and editing are all part of the grinding and stewing process that underlies the clear expression of your thoughts. Getting it right the first time is a good principle to follow in many areas of life, such as time management, but it is not an effective approach to producing a good piece of writing.

Having said that, it is also true that the most effective tool you have as a writer is time itself: time to stew on things, time to reconsider, time to rip it all apart and put it back together again in a better form, time to reluctantly edit out that superb phrase or witticism that doesn't quite fit, time for that flash of insight that reveals to you that you don't really believe in what you have just written, time to work through a second or third draft – it all takes time. The only way you can ensure you have that time is to plan, to avoid procrastination and to know your own weaknesses and strengths.

Say what you mean, and mean what you say

The more research and thought you put into a topic, the more confident you should be about expressing a view on the topic. Be direct, but avoid being dogmatic. Sweeping generalisations that are only weakly supported by your evidence (or perhaps not supported at all) do your cause no good at all. Let your arguments speak for themselves as you build and interconnect assertions and proofs, creating a momentum for your thesis or ideas.

Note that academic writers use certain linguistic strategies to hedge or to boost their ideas:

> Academic texts are most frequently characterised by a desire to avoid making claims and statements that are too direct and assertive, since academic discourse is often about theories, conclusions drawn from evidence, exchanging viewpoints, and so on, rather than hard, indisputable facts. Therefore hedging (making a proposition less assertive) is very important in academic styles. Less often, it is sometimes also necessary to assert a claim or viewpoint quite directly and more confidently, a process we shall refer to as boosting. (Carter & McCarthy 2006, p. 279)

Hedging: qualification of statements or claims

Boosting: assertion of statements or claims

Examples of **hedging** and **boosting** linguistic strategies are shown in figure 7.3 (for definitions of grammatical terms such as adverbs and prepositional phrases, see online chapter 'Writing skills 1: grammar').

Hedging strategies	Boosting strategies
■ Modal/auxiliary verbs (can, could, might, may, would) ■ Adverbs (arguably, generally, typically, probably) ■ Prepositional phrases (in a sense, in most cases, in principle) ■ Impersonal constructions (it is suggested, it is generally agreed)	■ Adverbs (clearly, inevitably, plainly, undoubtedly) ■ Other expressions (for certain, it was clear that)

FIGURE 7.3 Hedging and boosting writing strategies

Source: Adapted from Carter and McCarthy (2006, pp. 282–4).

Hedging can go too far, of course: you can set off a statement with so many qualifications that your original proposition is negated, and it becomes a mystery as to why you would have wanted to make such an assertion in the first place (see online chapter 6 'Scientific and technical writing').

Similarly, an over-use of boosting phrases may create the suspicion that you are trying to bluster or deceive your way around a weak argument. By all means, use 'clearly' and 'obviously', but in moderation: let your reader be the judge of what is clear and obvious. Use your common sense: be prudent but forthright in saying what you mean, and meaning what you say.

Rather than simply making sweeping and unsupported assertions, and trying to bluff your reader, it is better to make clear statements and then qualify those statements with a judicious use of hedging or riders (figure 7.4).

You can also use boosting strategies or locutions (figure 7.5), but in the academic arena, the reality is that you will end up hedging more than boosting.

These factors, taken together, **might seem** to present a strong case for much, if not all, gender-specific behaviour being socially conditioned, but it may be wise to consider the critique of the environmentalist position presented by sociobiological writers such as Stewart-Williams (2010) and Hardy (2011).

Beyond a certain point, however, we are **probably** in the realms of speculation; even though we may theorise on what Alexander's motivations were at this point in the move eastward, the reality is that we just do not know. The data does not exist, and all we have are the anecdotes of two historians of problematic reliability and integrity.

In principle, class action suits have much to recommend them, as much for reasons of social equity as for securing natural justice, but a number of caveats need to be borne in mind, especially by those in legal practice with large pro bono commitments and other activities that may have a negative impact on cash flow.

Therefore, it **would appear** to make sense for hospitality industry companies to walk away from exchange rate-related losses and shift preferred payment modes to credit card and electronic fund transfer. This policy change can be communicated through letters, brochures, advertising and web presence, but the most effective channel may be for counter staff to impart this directly to guests. It **might be** wise to retain minimal systems for cash in major currencies, however, as catastrophic system breakdown in computer systems cannot be ruled out permanently.

Consumer demand for plain and sateen weaves could well increase because of their well-publicised appearance in the recent Paris prêt-a-porter collections, but it is **generally agreed** that twill weaves may still have a place for the next few years, higher manufacturing costs notwithstanding, because the superior drape and wrinkle-free properties of twill may give designers more freedom and customers more satisfaction than those of plains and sateens.

FIGURE 7.4 Stating and hedging: sample wording

I believe, therefore, that there is overwhelming evidence for the case presented by the researchers. The parallels they draw are **clearly** compelling.

The four trial balance spreadsheet programs and templates available to firms therefore all have much to offer, and the market leader has certain features that **without doubt** justify its place in the market.

FIGURE 7.5 Stating and boosting: sample wording

You, the author

Hedging and boosting, but particularly hedging, are part of academic style, and that style often presents problems for writers trying to learn how to master style in post-secondary or post-school learning situations. While writers may have been encouraged to use personal styles of expression in school writing situations, they may find that there is a different culture of expectations in tertiary educational environments. This is the problem or matter of appropriate **authorial voice**.

Authorial voice: the style most favoured in a discipline, area or publication, usually involving use or non-use of first-person pronouns and use or non-use of passive voice, nominalisations and hedging

Academic writing, together with much scientific writing (see online chapter 6 'Scientific and technical writing'), often seems to be impersonal and abstract, making heavy use of passive voice – 'It is believed ... ' rather than 'I believe ... '.

Writing styles can be characterised as being on a continuum ranging from personal/direct style to impersonal/indirect style (see figure 7.6). The most personal and direct type of discourse involves the author – a person you are reading, or you, depending upon the role you play – using the first person singular pronoun and the active voice. Moving away from this point, authors may use the plural first person. This is literally true when there is more than one author, but sometimes sole authors will use it to refer to a broader community (see the footnote) or – in some circumstances – when they are not as confident as they might be, and invoke the authority of a plural.[1] Further along the continuum is the use of the agentless passive. This is often favoured in scientific writing, so that instead of saying 'I/we conducted experiments ... ' the tendency is to say 'Experiments were conducted ... ' Even further along the continuum comes the use of nominalisations (see online chapter 'Writing skills 4: plain English'), where simple verb constructions are replaced by noun/verb constructions. Finally, the most impersonal and indirect style may involve hedging, as well as nominalisations, in order to moderate the claims being made (the example given here is deliberately exaggerated).

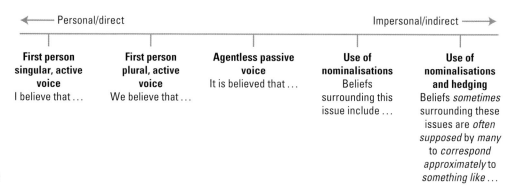

FIGURE 7.6 Personal/direct style versus impersonal/indirect style — a continuum

Even within the use of first person pronouns, however, there may be subtle variations. Tang and John (1999) suggest that there is a continuum of shades of usage for 'I' and 'we/us' (shown in figure 7.7) (see also Harwood 2005; Kuo 1999; Freddi 2005; Hyland 2002). These usages are:

- No 'I' (impersonal style)
- 'I' as representative ('In this sphere, we have words like ...' or 'We know that all dialects ...')
- 'I' as guide ('In example one, we see ...' or 'So far, we have said nothing about ...')
- 'I' as architect ('I will concentrate on ...' or 'In my essay, I shall ...)
- 'I' as a recounter of research process ('I recorded a conversation with ...' or 'All of the papers I read were ...')
- 'I' as opinion holder ('I would like to show that ...' or 'I agree with Fairclough [1992b] that ...')
- 'I' as originator ('Hence, I will examine the factors ...' or 'To me, the phrase embodies the whole process ...'). (Adapted from Tang and John, 1999)

So when should you use 'I'? This is not always clear. The traditional academic/scientific culture that shied away from personal pronouns and heavily favoured passive voice is changing, and there is a move towards a more personal and active style in a number of disciplines and publications. However, there is no uniform pattern here, and you may find that a style that is acceptable in one subject (or even for one lecturer in one subject) is not acceptable in another. You need to seek out clear guidelines on this. You have the right

---

1. In rhetoric, a distinction is sometimes drawn between *plural majestatis*, or 'royal we', sometimes used by royalty and popes (an individual saying 'we decree that ... ') and *plural modestiae* or *plural auctoris*, or authority's or author's plural, which includes readers and listeners.

The *plural majestatis* tends to get short shrift in modern democratic societies: Mark Twain once observed that 'Only kings, editors and people with tapeworm have the right to use the editorial "we"', while US Navy Admiral Hyman Rickover told a subordinate who used 'we' that 'Three groups of people are permitted that usage: pregnant women, royalty and schizophrenics. Which one are you?'.

to ask for guidelines or a style guide, and, in fact, the very act of asking may stimulate changes within the area you are studying in.

FIGURE 7.7 A typology of possible identities behind the first person pronoun in academic writing
Source: Tang and John (1999, p. S29).

No 'I'	'I' as representative	'I' as guide	'I' as architect	'I' as recounter of research process	'I' as opinion holder	'I' as originator

Least powerful authorial presence − −➤ − −➤ − −➤ − −➤ − −➤ − −➤ − −➤ − −➤ − −➤ Most powerful authorial presence

Academic writing versus workplace writing: match your style to your audience

The style or register you use when you are in the role of a student is not necessarily the same style or register you might use in other settings, such as a workplace. Note, for example, the styles of expression that are used in the chapters dealing with letters, emails and memos (chapter 4), reports and proposals (chapter 5), and online writing (chapter 6). Generally speaking, the differences between academic style and workplace style are clear (figure 7.8).

	Academic style	Workplace style
Vocabulary/lexis	Heavy use of Latin-derived words; longer words	Stronger use of Anglo-Saxon derived words; shorter words
Technical language/jargon	Often strong, although there are some attempts to simplify	Often strong, although there are some attempts to simplify
Syntax	Longer sentences	Shorter sentences
Passive voice	High use	Low use
Style	Usually impersonal; first person pronouns often discouraged	Can be impersonal or personal, depending upon documents, situation, stance of writer
Hedging	Substantial use	Low use; used when writing is exploring possibilities and/or is deceptive
Boosting	Low use; used when writing is exploring possibilities and/or is deceptive	Low use; used when writing is exploring possibilities and/or is deceptive
Readability scores	High (12+) (see online chapter 3)	Usually lower (8+)
Document design/layout	Long paragraphs; little/no use of bullet points, headings	Short paragraphs; frequent use of bullet points, headings
Use of reference/quoted material	Extensive	Light, non-existent

FIGURE 7.8 Academic and workplace styles compared

One of the major criticisms made by employers of graduates they have hired is that too much of the graduates' writing is 'essay-like'. Essays or papers are what get you good (or bad) marks when you are in your role as a student, but workplace documents such as reports and emails are what attract favourable (or unfavourable) attention when you are in your role as an employee. Be versatile: match your style to your audience.

Layout factors

Traditionally, essays were written without headings or graphics such as figures and tables. Now the genre of the essay is discernibly taking on features traditionally associated with documents such as reports. Nevertheless, in some areas and disciplines, essay markers are uncomfortable with such features. So before you begin, seek guidance on the format expected and keep that guidance in mind as you develop your work.

ASSESS YOURSELF

1. Photocopy pages from journal articles or from books dealing with your area of enquiry. Using highlighter pens, mark up the topic sentence in each paragraph. Now, respond to the following questions.
   (a) What function do these sentences play in the paragraphs?
   (b) Are topic sentences hard to find or non-existent?
   (c) Do these sentences help or hinder comprehension of the writer's argument?
2. Cut and paste into a word-processing file some pages from journal articles or books dealing with your area of enquiry. Now, use software-summarising tools to summarise or analyse the structure of the argument of your selection. What does it reveal to you about the topic sentence structure of the samples?
3. Look at textbooks and journal articles from 20 to 30 years ago and at those of today. Are there any differences in authorial voice or style?

Before we go any further, let's take stock of what we have learnt so far. We have looked at the criteria of good and bad essay writing. Looking at Bacon's essay, we have learnt the importance of:

- having a point of view
- making valid assertions
- giving solid proof and examples
- following a sound expositional technique
- using a cumulative approach to build the plausibility of what you want to persuade us of.

These goals remain the same after almost 400 years.

We saw that the most discouraging thing for essay writers – 'How can I say something original, when it's all been said before?' – can be partially overcome by processes such as creative doubt. We have also looked at structuring topic sentences, thesis statements, transitions, hedging and boosting, and authorial voice.

With concepts like these under our belt, let's now see them put to work (or ignored) by looking at two condensed sample essays that are both on the same topic.

Putting it together: sample essays

The samples shown on the next pages are not complete essays, but they may help us to understand what works and what does not work in the construction of an essay. The 'good' example is not perfect, but it presents a useful model to learn from.

Essay one: a bad example

PUBLIC POLICY 206

WHAT ARE THE POLICY IMPLICATIONS OF THE GREENHOUSE EFFECT?

Martin Plaistowe
ID No. 43211789
Tutorial Group: Wednesday 2–3 pm
Lecturer: Dr Rolf Birtles

The so-called[1] 'greenhouse effect' is nothing but a crock of hype.[2]

[3]Studies done by the Competitive Enterprise Institute show clearly that claims of global warming are false:

[4]There are three reasons why this claim is not valid, according to Dr Baliunas. First, most of the warming in the last 100 years occurred before the build-up of greenhouse gases. Second, the surface temperature record suffers from many confounding factors. The most important being the urban heat island effect, where growing cities surrounding thermometer stations bias the temperature record upwards.[5][6] Finally, the surface record suffers from inadequate global coverage. 'Good records', according to Dr Baliunas, 'with near-continual coverage of the last 100 years, cover only 18 percent of the surface.'

> *Computer models, which have been used to bolster the case for global warming, are also deficient, said Dr Baliunas. The assumption that water vapor will increase with a rise in man-made greenhouse gases, accounting for most of the predicted warming, has been 'challenged by developments in convection theory and new measurements.'* (http://www.cei.org/utils/printer.cfm?AID=1220)[7][8][9]

Many academics tend, predictably enough, to push a straight environmentalist or green line on 'global warming' (Botkin & Keller 2005; McElroy 2002; Stern, 2007; Oreskes & Conway, 2011), refusing to acknowledge that there are many reputable scientists who think that the whole thing is a lot of hot air.[10] In fact the very use of the term 'greenhouse' is wrong, as Harvey points out:

> The term 'greenhouse effect' is used to refer to the tendency of the atmosphere to create a warmer climate than would otherwise be the case. However the physical mechanisms by which the presence of the atmosphere warms the climate and the primary mechanism that causes a greenhouse to be warm are in fact quite different. A greenhouse heats up by day as the air within the greenhouse is heated by the sun. Outside the greenhouse, near-surface air that is heated through absorption of solar radiation by the ground surface is free to rise and be replaced with colder air from above. This cannot happen in a greenhouse, where the heated air is physically prevented from rising and being replaced with colder air. The so-called greenhouse effect does not prevent the physical movement of air parcels. (Harvey 2000)[11][12]

1. Sarcasm may be inappropriate.

2. Avoid use of slang.

3. No introduction to issues to be explored in essay

4. No lead-in to quote or explanation of who the expert is

5. Plagiarism: merely a cut-and-paste from website source

6. Grammatical error; sentence fragment (uncorrected)

7. Website text is ephemeral — a media release from 1998. The URL has since changed, as often happens on the net. It would have been better to seek out a more substantial and up-to-date reference from the same source, e.g. Bailey (2008).

8. Cited text is inconsistently laid out: indenting and fonts.

9. Invalid citation method for web document — try, wherever possible, to tie down to author surname: here, Georgia (1998).

10. But what, specifically, do they say? This is abuse, not argument.

11. Selective quotation; the source then goes on to say that there is, in fact, a similarity, and the entire reference accepts the notion of global warming.

12. Semantic quibbling; the essay writer is trying to show that, because an analogy is not perfect, the phenomenon being analysed cannot be real. This remains unproven.

(continued)

(continued)

Scientists have proven that 'Global warming' does not, in fact, exist (Milloy, 2009; Horner, 2009). Rather, global cooling is what we should be concerned about. Taylor (1999) has studied climate change and has proven[1] that another ice age is about to begin (Landscheidt, Theodor (2003) 'New Little Ice Age Instead of Global Warming?' *Energy and Environment*, Vol. 14, No. 2-3, pp 327–350).[2] [3]

Buydko[4] (1996) also points out that increased global warming would in fact be beneficial as increased levels of carbon dioxide would boost photosynthetic processes and increase agricultural productivity, thus ensuring that starving billions would not have to starve.[5] [6] The economic costs of succumbing to greenhouse hype are considerable, and may well be crippling, when all economic, fiscal, monetary, macro-economic, industrial, institutional and other factors are factored into any type of reasonable decision making and problem-solving process, or processes.[7] Any rational and ethical decision maker would need to weigh up, consider, ponder, contemplate and factor in every possible scenario of cost-benefit analysis to eventually arrive at reasonable policy outcomes that would be acceptable to the democratic majority that needs must provide (or withhold) the mandate needed in any democratic decision-making process. It is imperative that such a process not be held hostage by wild-eyed radicals with a hidden agenda,[8] as experts like Stott point out:

> Even if all 180 countries ratified the protocol and then actually met their greenhouse gas emission targets — a highly unlikely political scenario — we still might only affect temperature by between 0.07 and 0.2° Celsius, and even this could be thrown out by a couple of erupting volcanoes or altering landscape albedos. And what are the economics of this meaningless self-sacrifice demanded by Kyoto? According to recent models, implementing Kyoto will cost anywhere between $100b and $1000b, with a mean around $350b. Now that amount of money could pay off the public debt of the 49 poorest countries of the world and provide clean drinking water for all! Need one say more? (Stott 2001)[9]

The greenhouse effect is comprised of a number of synergistically linked processes such as radiative forcing, which is[10]

> ... due to the increases of the well-mixed greenhouse gases from 1750 to 2000 is estimated to be 2.43 Wm^{-2}. 1.46 Wm^{-2} from CO_2; 0.48 Wm^{-2} from CH_4; 0.34 Wm^{-2} from the halocarbons; and 0.15 Wm^{-2} from N_2O.[1] [11]

The hype surrounding the greenhouse effect cannot simply be shrugged off. If the widespread changes[12] advocated by greenhouse zealots were to be implemented, then the financial costs would be crippling. No responsible administrator or politician could rationally contemplate factoring in such pseudo-science when the real work of decision making needs to be undertaken in a democratic society, or for that matter, in an undemocratic society.[13] Just as surely as the so-called ozone layer crisis was proven to be another fantasy, so too will the greenhouse effect, so-called.[14]

The credibility of the whole idea has, anyway, been dispelled by Climategate and the destruction of the hockey stick graph of change.[15]

---

[1] Houghton, J.T. et al (Eds) (2001) *Climate Change 2001: The Scientific Basis* (Cambridge: Cambridge University Press), p. 7[16]

Margin annotations (left column):

1. Suggested, not proven

2. Sources cited tend to be sensationalist.

3. Second reference needs to be linked with first into broader point about cooling; full details should not be cited in text, but in reference list.

4. Author's name misspelled

5. Topic change: new paragraph required

6. Author suggests only that it might be possible.

7. Non sequitur; is the essay writer denying or affirming warming? The cited author also expresses concern about warming.

8. Padding, waffle

9. Quoted author is talking about the Kyoto Protocol — introductory wording setting this connection up is needed.

10. Lead-in text and quoted text not grammatically matched

Margin annotations (right column):

11. This is meant to be a general definition, but it contains extremely, even overly, specific and technically complex information, using undefined terms.

12. What are these proposed changes? Surely they would be a critical aspect of an essay on policy implications?

13. Repetition, padding

14. Unproven assertion

15. Both factors could strengthen the argument, but they are not explained or cited correctly (e.g. Montford 2010).

16. Reference details in footnote: citation system different from that of main style used

1. Several factual errors

2. Bizarre conclusion, shifting ground, and introducing new information

US President Obama walked away from a deal at the Kyoto conference, and we know why he did: the global financial crisis of 1995 meant that luxuries like carbon taxes would make industries uneconomic, and thus economics proved more important than spurious environmental ideas.[1]

The choice is then clear for all responsible decision makers, and that is to respond to global warming by implementing a range of low-impact technologies, from hydrogen-powered cars to nuclear power plants.[2]

REFERENCES

Milloy, Steven 2009 *Green Hell: How Environmentalists Plan to Control Your Life and What You Can Do to Stop Them,* Regnery Press, Washington, DC

Stott, Philip (2001) 'The Kyoto Protocol: Dangerous for both Science and Society?,' AntiEcohype, http://www.scidev.net/dossiers/index.cfm?fuseaction=dossierReadItem&type=3&itemid=8&language=1&dossier=4, Accessed 28 January, 2009[3]

Stern, Nicholas (2007) *The Economics of Climate Change: The Stern Review*, Cambridge University Press

Clark, Stuart 2010 "What's wrong with the sun, *New Scientist*, Issue 2764, http://www.newscientist.com/article/mg20627640.800-whats-wrong-with-the-sun.html?page=3

Harvey, L.D. Danny (2000) *Climate and Global Environmental Change* (Edinburgh Gate, Harlow: Pearson Education)

Oreskes, Naomi, and Conway, Erik. M.M. 2011 *Merchants of Doubt: How a Handful of Scientists Obscured the Truth on Issues from Tobacco Smoke to Global Warming*, Bloomsbury Press, London

Singer, S. Fred (2007) *Unstoppable Global Warming: Every 1500 Years* (Lanham MD: Rowman and Littlefield)

Zyrkowski, John (2006) *It's the Sun, Not Your SUV: CO2 Does Not Cause Global Warming* (South Bend, IN: St Augustine's Press)

Horner, Christopher C., 2009 *Red Hot Lies: How Global Warming Alarmists Use Threats, Fraud, and Deception to Keep You Misinformed* , Regnery Press, Washington, DC

Montford, A.W. 2010 *The Hockey Stick Illusion: Climategate and the Corruption of Science*, Stacey International, London

Georgia, Paul J. 1998 "Climate Science Briefings Debunk Greenhouse Scares," Competitive Enterprise Institute: Free Markets and Limited Government, Competitive Enterprise Institute, Washington, DC, October 1.[4]

3. URL address is out of date; access date is also very dated.

4. Reference list incomplete; uncited references given; not in alphabetical order; inconsistent reference style used.

Essay two: a better example

PUBLIC POLICY 206

WHAT ARE THE POLICY IMPLICATIONS OF THE GREENHOUSE EFFECT?

Martin Plaistowe
ID No. 43211789
Tutorial Group: Wednesday 2–3 pm
Lecturer: Dr Rolf Birtles

The greenhouse effect and the associated concept of global warming present great challenges to policy makers at local, state or provincial, national and international levels.

[1]The fundamental position of this essay will be that the responses of decision makers in public and private sectors to the greenhouse effect phenomenon have been mixed, and this has reflected the flawed consensus that exists within the scientific community. Trends may be emerging, however, which indicate that some actors are behaving as if the effect is real, no matter what. Because their actions may accord them strategic advantages in certain arenas, this may trigger a bandwagon effect, whereby many decision makers ignore underlying uncertainties in order to preserve commercial and national strategic positions.[2] [3]

There are, in fact, two greenhouse effects. The first is the 'natural' greenhouse effect, whereby radiation from the sun hits the earth, and is retransmitted back to space: part of that energy, however, is absorbed by certain greenhouse gases (carbon dioxide, methane, chlorofluorocarbons), which leads to a warming of the atmosphere — just like a glass greenhouse retains some of the sun's warmth to help stimulate plant growth within the greenhouse. The second effect is the 'enhanced' greenhouse effect, due to human activity such as burning fossil fuels and deforestation, which creates greenhouse gases (Houghton, 2009, p. 22).[4]

Many scientists argue that in the past few decades the planet has undergone unprecedented warming, and that this warming appears to have been caused by anthropogenic or human-caused activity. The prestigious Intergovernmental Panel on Climate Change (IPCC), in its early 2001 report, concluded that:[5] [6]

> In the light of new evidence and taking into account the remaining uncertainties, most of the observed warming over the last 50 years is likely [i.e., having a 66–90 per cent chance] to have been due to the increase in greenhouse gas concentrations. (Houghton et al. (eds.) 2001, p. 10) [7]

Such global warming could result in regional increases in floods and droughts, inundation of coastal areas, increase in high-temperature events and fires, outbreaks of pests and diseases, and significant damage to ecosystems (Jepma & Munansinghe 1998, pp. 28–34 ; Parks & Ellis 2005, pp. 4–11; Gore 2007, pp. 2–14).[8]

Concerns about global warming led to the international meeting on climate change in Kyoto in 1997, which led to the declaration of the Kyoto Protocol (McElroy 2002, pp. 232–51). The Kyoto Protocol has been signed by many countries, including Australia, and commits them to specific reductions in the production of greenhouse gases. A number of countries, including the United States, have still not signed the Protocol, arguing that committing to reductions would cause unacceptable damage to their economies (Koh 2009, p. 325). On the other hand, some scientists, such as Plimer (2009), argue that the greenhouse effect is a natural phenomenon alternating with ice ages over periods of thousands of years, with anthropogenic causes having little effect.[9]

1. References include recent peer-reviewed journals.

2. Cited references show wide reading, and ability to synthesise materials from different sources.

3. Writer now moves away from 'greenhouse effect' as main concept, using 'global warming' as a term covering both ideas. A good strategy, or not?

4. Balanced treatment of non-mainstream views

5. Use of print and online sources

6. New section raises other possibilities and trends, thus picking up approach foreshadowed in thesis statement.

7. Restatement of part of thesis statement, giving overview of previous point

8. Recapitulation demonstrates that original objectives of the essay have been met.

If it is believed that global warming is real, and if it is believed something should be done about it, then a number of useful policy shifts become apparent. These policies might include the mandating of reduction in CO_2 production of motor vehicles (such as in California — see Warnatzsch & Reay 2011, pp. 23–39[1]), shifting of production of electricity away from coal-fired methods to sustainable or 'green' methods (Tükay & Telli 2011), the setting up markets in energy credits, and allowing trading of these (Christiansen & Wettestad 2003, p. 14; Stern 2007, pp. 324–27[2]), the allocating of permits to emit gases based upon current efficiency data of individual power plants (Vesterdal & Svendsen 2004, p. 963), and the changing of land management practices, leading to less burning off of biomass and sequestration of carbon through creation of carbon sinks such as forests and better management of grasslands, soils and forests (Botkin & Keller 2005, pp. 481–83).[3]

Global warming skeptics see dangers in some or all of these policies (Zyrkowski 2006, pp. 2–16; Singer & Avery 2007, pp. 3–12). Wildavsky, for example, sees global warming as a myth created by environmentalists to engineer radical social changes such as lower growth rates, smaller populations, consuming less and sharing a much lower level of resources much more equally (Wildavsky 1992, p. xv).[4]

Budyko also argues that increased warming may lead to rises in productivity of crops, which will be necessary to feed another five billion people born in the next few decades (although he does also acknowledge potentially damaging effects of this) (Budyko 1996, pp. 113–119) (see also Stott 2001).[4][5]

Some writers have suggested, however, that it does not matter whether global warming exists or not, because if actors such as policy-makers and entrepreneurs act as if it does, then jobs and wealth can be created by developing renewable energy industries. Lovins, for example, states that the major controversy about uncertainties in climate science is immaterial because of this — money can be made from renewables, so why not do it anyway? (Amory Lovins, quoted in Hoffman 2009, p. 330)[6]

Further, Krause, Decanio, Hoerner and Baer (2002, p. 342) argue that there are 'co-benefits' to behaving as if global warming was real, such as cleaner air due to less pollution and healthier people.

Lomborg (2008, 2010, 2011) follows up on this line, arguing that carbon limitation is a lost cause, as international conferences on carbon reduction keep failing. This failure will be exacerbated by the global financial crisis, with there being no 'first mover' advantage in imposing carbon taxes — the opposite, in fact, is true. Lomborg notes that three US think tanks from opposite ends of the political spectrum have come to a consensus that creation of affordable alternative energy sources is the only way — the middle way — between proponents of no carbon and a 'deep green' return to basiclifestyles. Lomberg argues that this can be done for the cost of 0.2 per cent of global gross product, or roughly US$100 billion a year, to invent alternative energy technologies that everyone can afford.

If numerous political and industrial actors behave in this way, with a consensus to spend for such a program, their actions may accord them strategic advantages in certain arenas, and this may trigger a 'bandwagon effect', whereby many or most decision makers ignore underlying uncertainties in order to preserve commercial and national strategic positions.[7]

In conclusion, a number of points about global warming are now apparent. Is global warming real? Probably, but it may not matter anyway. Some actors are moving the goalposts by redefining business objectives and government policy to develop alternative industries, to improve public health and to reap conservation benefits.[8]

(continued)

(continued)

REFERENCES

Bailey, Ronald (ed). Competitive Enterprise Institute 2008, *The true state of the planet: ten of the world's premier environmental researchers in a major challenge to the environmental movement*, Free Press, New York.

Balling, Robert C Jr 1992, *The heated debate: greenhouse predictions versus climate reality*, Pacific Research Institute for Public Policy, San Francisco, CA.

Botkin, Daniel B & Keller, Edward A 2005, *Environmental science: Earth as a living planet*, 5th edn, John Wiley & Sons, New York.

Budyko, MI 1996, 'Past changes in climate and societal adaptations', in Smith, Joel B et al. (eds), *Adapting to climate change: assessment and issues*, Springer-Verlag, New York.

Christiansen, Atle & Wettestad, Jørgen 2003, 'The EU as a frontrunner on greenhouse gas emissions trading: how did it happen, and will the EU succeed?', *Climate Policy*, 101, pp. 1–16.

Georgia, Paul J 1998, 'Climate science briefings debunk greenhouse scares', Competitive Enterprise Institute: Free Markets and Limited Government, Competitive Enterprise Institute, Washington, DC, 1 October.

Gore, Al 2007, *An inconvenient truth: the crisis of global warming*, Viking, New York.

Houghton, JT et al. (eds.) 2001, *Climate change 2001: the scientific basis*, Cambridge University Press, Cambridge, UK.

Houghton, John 2009 *Global warming: the complete briefing*, 4th edn, Cambridge University Press, Cambridge, UK.

Jepma, Catrinus J & Munansinghe, Mohan 1998, *Climate change policy: facts, issues and analyses*, Cambridge University Press, Cambridge, UK.

Krause, Florentin, Decanio, Stephen J, Hoerner, Andrew & Baer, Paul 2002, 'Cutting carbon emissions at a profit (part 1): opportunities for the United States', *Contemporary Economic Policy*, vol. 20, no. 4, pp. 339–366.

Koh, Kheng-Lia, (ed.) 2009, *Crucial issues in climate change and the Kyoto Protocol: Asia and the World*, World Scientific Publishing Corporation, New Jersey.

Lomborg, Bjorn 2008, *Cool it: the sceptical environmentalist's guide to global warming*, Vintage, New York.

—— 2010, 'A rational take on warming', *The Australian*, 15 November, p. 14.

—— 2011, 'Harness resources to save the earth', *The Weekend Australian*, 29–30 January, p. 4.

McElroy, Michael B 2002, *The atmospheric environment: effects of human activity*, Princeton University Press, Princeton, NJ.

Manne, Alan & Richels, Richard 2004, 'US rejection of the Kyoto Protocol: the impact on compliance costs and CO2 emissions', *Energy Policy*, vol. 32, no. 4, pp. 447–54.

Parks, Peggy J & Ellis, Barbara G 2005, *Global warming: our environment*, Kidhaven, San Diego, CA.

Plimer, Ian 2009, *Heaven and earth: global warming: the missing science*, Taylor, London.

Rink, Deane 2007, *Global warming*, Facts on File, New York.

Singer, S Fred & Avery, Dennis T 2007, *Unstoppable global warming: every 1500 years*, Rowman and Littlefield, Lanham, MD.

Stern, Nicholas 2007, *The economics of climate change: the Stern Review*, Cambridge University Press, Cambridge.

Stott, Philip 2001, 'The Kyoto Protocol: dangerous for both science and society?', *The Chemical Engineer*, September.

Tükay, Belgin Emre & Telli, Yasin 2011, 'Economic analysis of standalone and grid connected hybrid energy systems', *Renewable Energy*, vol. 36, no. 7, pp. 1931–43, doi:10.1016/j.renene.2010.12.007.

Vesterdal, Morten & Svendsen, Gert Tinggaard 2004, 'How should greenhouse gas permits be allocated in the EU?', *Energy Policy*, vol. 32, no. 8, pp. 961–8.

Warnatzsch, Erika Alison & Reay, David S 2011, 'Cutting CO_2 emissions from the US energy sector: meeting a 50% requirement target by 2030', *Carbon Management*, vol. 2, no.1, pp. 23–39.

Wildavsky, Aaron 1992, 'Introduction' in Robert C Balling Jr, *The heated debate: greenhouse predictions versus climate reality*, Pacific Research Institute for Public Policy, San Francisco, CA, pp. xv–xxi.

Zyrkowksi, John 2006, *It's the sun, not your SUV: CO2 does not cause global warming*, St Augustine's Press, South Bend, IN.

Essay writing: dos and don'ts

Our two sample essays provide insights into what to do and what not to do when writing essays (note also the criteria listed earlier in table 7.1). Table 7.3 summarises the main principles.

TABLE 7.3 Essay writing dos and don'ts

Aspect	Do this	Don't do this
Position	Be even-handed, considering all sides of question.	Show bias, looking at only one viewpoint.
Statement of position	Use a thesis statement to introduce the direction you will take.	Jump straight into argument without creating a context for that argument.
Statement of scope	Clarify what issues are to be covered, and what will not be covered.	Avoid statement of scope.
Terminology	Define terms; if technical terms need to be used, explain them in first instance.	Avoid defining terms; switch between normal and technical language without notice.
Exposition of argument	Clearly set out paragraphs; use headings where appropriate; use topic sentences; link ideas to reinforce unfolding argument.	Avoid clear topic changes with paragraphing; use inappropriate or confusing headings; use no or few topic sentences; confuse reader with choppy exposition and development.
Structural integrity	In conclusion, recapitulate issues, showing how the topic question has been answered.	Don't provide a clear recapitulation of ideas in the conclusion; end without reference to topic question; introduce new material at the end.
Research	Use old and new material; show preference for reputable, peer-reviewed material; handle popular and internet sources with care; show evidence of understanding and synthesis of sources.	Use out-of-date material; use only popular material (such as journalism) and internet sources of problematic quality; show no evidence of understanding and synthesis of sources.
Quotation	Cite sources legitimately (i.e. don't quote selectively); lead into quotes with appropriate introductory text, matching grammatical structure of lead-in text with quoted material; if quoting, give page numbers; avoid plagiarism.	Selectively quote sources to give false impressions; insert quotes without (or with inappropriate) introductory text; ignore matching grammatical structure of lead-in text with quoted material; if quoting, don't give page numbers; plagiarise.
Original thought	Try to demonstrate original views.	Simply rehash the views of others, never stating your own.
Professional style	Use appropriate academic language; avoid waffle and padding.	Use slang, sarcasm and waffle to increase word count.

(continued)

TABLE 7.3 *(continued)*

Aspect	Do this	Don't do this
Referencing	Use appropriate referencing conventions: always cite source by using footnotes, endnotes or Harvard author-date system. Don't presume it is acceptable merely to list them in the bibliography.	Mix up referencing styles; forget to include all source details; list references out of alphabetical order; don't refer to sources by citing: only put them in the bibliography (let the reader work out where they are cited).
Layout	Use simple, clear layout; use fonts consistently; include graphics where appropriate.	Adopt confused, cluttered layout; use fonts inconsistently; omit graphics where they would help clarify; use confusing graphics or include graphics where none required.

Essay writing: a humorous approach

We have looked at what needs to be done when writing essays, but what about the things that shouldn't be done? King (1998), using a humorous approach, warns students writing in one discipline – political science – of the perils of the Six Evil Geniuses of essay writing. Every essay writer, no matter what the discipline, at times feels the presence of these evil spirits; table 7.4 shows what happens when such spirits take over honest writers. King's Evil Geniuses model of what not to do could be renamed 'games essay writers play (and usually lose)'. The chief antidote to an Evil Genius, King suggests, is intellectual honesty, and that is true no matter what discipline we are writing in. There is only one thing worse than writing like this, and that is being so misguided that you think you can do so and get away with it.

TABLE 7.4 The Six Evil Geniuses of essay writing

Evil genius	Motivation	Sample essay question	Sample essay response	Analysis
1. The Sycophant	The Sycophant thinks if she butters up the marker (e.g. by praising the lectures or the reading assignments), the marker will be likely to think better of the content of the essay itself.	Why are political scientists concerned with the concept of 'political culture'?	In their brilliant, ground-breaking work, Almond and Verba address the concept of political culture. As Professor Jones demonstrated in her excellent and stimulating lecture, the concept of political culture is important. By using it, as Professor Jones cogently argued, political scientists can explain a number of political phenomena ...	Sycophantism is, of course, a bad idea. Essays like this read more like the minutes of a Soviet Communist Party congress than a response to an exam question. The fact that a lecturer has assigned a particular reading during a course is no guarantee that he/she thinks that the author of the reading is 'right'. Indeed, testing the student's ability to engage critically with assigned readings, instead of merely accepting them as fact because they are written by professional academics, is one of the chief reasons for asking essay questions in the first place.

Evil genius	Motivation	Sample essay question	Sample essay response	Analysis
2. The Rakish Raconteur	The Rakish Raconteur is the first cousin of the Sycophant. The Raconteur feels that writing in a conversational style and using the essay as a way of 'conversing' with the lecturer will allow his innate wit and charm to mask his lack of knowledge.	Discuss the contrasting views of 'modernisation theory' and 'dependency theory'. Which one gives a better account of economic development?	Well, as I was thinking the other night, modernisation and dependency are really two sides of the same coin. I mean, after all, who can say who is more modern than someone else? But seriously (is this a trick question?), there are a couple of ways that one differs from the other. Modernisationists think that the world is linear and ordered (they should see my dorm room!) . . .	This student may have a great career selling used cars, but his prospects in any job that requires serious analytical skills are definitely limited. This style is guaranteed to turn off any marker. Essay questions are a tool lecturers use to assess a student's knowledge and ability to formulate a clear argument. They should not be viewed as a chance to hang out with that lecture dude, know what I'm saying?
3. The Sanitary Engineer	The Sanitary Engineer (known long ago, in a less politically correct age, as a 'garbage man') is an expert at mind-dumping. He has crammed a huge amount of facts, terms, typologies and other information into his short-term memory, and nothing — not even the essay question itself — will prevent him from getting it all down on paper.	What did Tocqueville mean when he wrote about the importance of 'associations' in American civic life?	Alexis de Tocqueville was a young (26 years old) French traveller and writer who visited America for 9 months in 1831–1832 and wrote a book on his travels, published in two volumes in French in 1835–1840, and in its English translation as *Democracy in America*. His purpose in coming to the young United States (in which he visited 17 of the 24 states of the time), which had engaged in a revolution with Great Britain over a half century before and had adopted an independent Constitution, was actually to write a report on the American prison system. He travelled with an associate, Gustave Beaumont (see map and sketch of Beaumont on next page) . . .	Of course, it is a good idea to let the marker know you have full command of the facts, but throwing in a congeries of irrelevant factoids (or non-facts) without addressing the question set is never helpful. The Sanitary Engineer has accumulated a great deal of information, and his ability to recall it all is certainly impressive. But while his skills might be useful in a game of Trivial Pursuit, they will not necessarily help him answer the essay question.
4. The Jargon-Meister	The Jargon-Meister attempts to blind the reader with science. Using an array of political science terms — most of which she probably does not understand — she hopes to so impress the marker that he/she will ignore the fact that the essay really says nothing at all.	What do theorists mean when they say that humans are 'rational actors'?	Rationality is an exogenous component of selective incentives. As such, and in direct contradiction to the concept of endogenising preferences, actors cannot be truly rational unless they have engaged in side-payments to rotating credit organisations.	The Jargon-Meister appears to make an argument, and a forceful one at that. But once one peels away the terminology, it is clear that the thesis really has very little content. Political science, like all academic disciplines, has its own particular language;

(continued)

TABLE 7.4 *(continued)*

Evil genius	Motivation	Sample essay question	Sample essay response	Analysis
4. The Jargon-Meister *(continued)*			This gives Mancur Olson a collective action problem from which he cannot reasonably be expected to recover ...	complex concepts and ideas are expressed through specialised terms that sometimes appear impenetrable to the uninitiated. Learning to wield these terms effectively is part of doing political science well, but their use should not get in the way of making a clear and accessible argument.
5. The Bait-and-Switch Artist	The Bait-and-Switch Artist is a master of prestidigitation. She engages in a sleight-of-hand in which she substitutes a new essay question for the one that appears on the page — and (poof!) the original essay question magically disappears. Her calling card is often the word 'while'.	Evaluate Theda Skocpol's argument on the origins of social revolutions.	While Theda Skocpol makes many interesting and important arguments about the origins of social revolutions, the concept of political culture is also extremely relevant. Political culture can be defined as the array of beliefs and norms in a given society relating to the legitimacy of political actors and political institutions ...	The Bait-and-Switch Artist may go on to write a brilliant essay, but not one that answers the question that was originally asked. Of course, highlighting your knowledge in particular areas is a useful strategy when writing exam essays, but if the response provided fails to address the question asked, even the most insightful essay will not receive much attention from the marker.
6. The Knee-Jerk Nihilist	The Knee-Jerk Nihilist is the most sophisticated, most dangerous, and most evil of the geniuses. He has probably taken an introductory course in literary theory, quantum physics or postmodernism, but has forgotten most of what he learned. The one thing he took away from these courses, though, was a fundamental conviction that the world around us is just too complicated and too contradictory for us to make any sense of it.	What makes a political system democratic?	Democracy is a relative concept. In fact, the concept of 'concept' is also relative. Words mean whatever we want them to 'mean', and this is especially true for 'democracy'. For some, it means 'free' elections. For others, it means keeping your own thugs 'in power' and keeping the enemy thugs 'out of power'. No-one can ever give a coherent definition, because it always depends on the context. And since the 'context' is always shifting, the 'concept' of 'democracy' also shifts ...	The Knee-Jerk Nihilist is smart. He has read a great deal and thought seriously about issues. He has become so disillusioned about the possibility of our arriving at any real understanding of the world, however, that he has mortgaged his powers of analysis for a modish slavery to intellectual scepticism. He also believes that because all our judgements are clouded by our own prejudices, anyone's opinion is as good as anyone else's. The Knee-Jerk Nihilist is often seen wearing black and reading Nietzsche. He is very fond of quotation marks.

Source: King (1998).

STUDENT STUDY GUIDE

SUMMARY

The essay is a particular genre of writing that is at the heart of academic writing today. Criteria of excellence in this genre have been identified, and should be observed. All essay writers want high marks, and there should be nothing, apart from not doing the hard preparatory work and not observing the codes and protocols of good essay writing, that should limit them from achieving these marks.

Good essay writing depends upon striking a balance between fact and opinion, and avoiding imbalance and bias. Solid research can create good foundations for the essay, and synthesis of data obtained in research can help writers obtain original perspectives. Sources and proofs should be credible and authoritative, locatable, up to date, relevant, convincing, in proportion, ethically clean, and matched to the context. Essays are structured in three parts: introduction, body and conclusion. Thesis statements can help clarify the writer's approach, and paragraphing, topic sentences, linking words and headings are effective means of laying out and structuring an argument. It is vital to stay focused – answering the question and not wandering or waffling along the way. Use clear style and make clear statements of argument – modifying the thrust of the argument where appropriate. Students should also remember to use the authorial voice and layout style most acceptable to assessors.

KEY TERMS

assertion *p. 227*
authorial voice *p. 237*
bias *p. 229*
boosting *p. 236*
creative doubt *p. 230*

cumulative method *p. 228*
expositional technique
  p. 227
hedging *p. 236*
point of view *p. 227*

proofs and
  examples *p. 227*
thesis statement *p. 233*
topic sentence *p. 234*
waffle *p. 235*

REVIEW QUESTIONS

1. Identify three criteria of failure in critical thinking.
2. What are the strengths and weaknesses of the structure used in Bacon's essay on revenge?
3. What is 'creative doubt'?
4. Identify four factors associated with worthwhile sources and proofs.
5. What role does the topic sentence play in a paragraph?
6. When is it appropriate to use 'I' in writing?
7. Identify three strategies for keeping focused when writing an essay.
8. What is the purpose of judicious hedging?
9. Identify four errors that an essay writer should avoid.
10. Identify and describe three Evil Geniuses of essay writing.

APPLIED ACTIVITIES

1. Examine some essays you have written, and reconsider the marks given and the comments made by the marker. Assuming the mark and comments are not grossly unfair, can you detect any trends apparent over a number of assignments submitted over time?
2. Consulting one or more books of quotations, find at least ten substantially different quotations on at least one topic: love; money; anger; a discipline or industry you are familiar with; a city you know or, in fact, anything you like. Now use these quotes in

a short essay (400–600 words), creating a structure and context for the quotes using appropriate transitions ('This view is reinforced by the view of . . . ', 'On the other hand, consider the opinion of . . . ').

3. Following the pattern of table 7.4, create writing samples from each of the Six Evil Geniuses for a discipline or area you are familiar with (i.e. create Evil Genius type, motivation, sample essay question, sample essay response and analysis).

4. Following the pattern of table 7.4, invent a Seventh, Eighth and Ninth Evil Genius of essay writing, giving Evil Genius type, motivation, sample essay question (in a field or discipline you are familiar with), sample essay response and analysis.

WHAT WOULD YOU DO?

Your studies are going well. In the past eighteen months you have received seven A grades for your essays. It's not easy surviving, though: you have found it difficult to make ends

meet while you are studying. Today you received a phone call from a cousin who lives interstate. She's doing a similar course, but is not doing as well as you. She offers you a healthy sum of money if you will email all your essays to her so that she can copy them and hand them in under her own name. She has promised that she will not show them to anyone else, but in the past she has actually forwarded sensitive emails you have sent to her on a confidential basis to her friends. Later today someone tells you that a new national anti-plagiarism database is going to be set up in the next few months. You are only six months away from graduating. The manager at the place where you work part-time rang today and told you that you no longer have the job.

How will you respond to your cousin's request?

SUGGESTED READING

Anderson, Jonathan 2001, *Assignment and thesis writing*, 4th edn., John Wiley & Sons, Brisbane.
—— 2003, *Academic writing: a practical guide for students*, Routledge/Taylor & Francis, London.
—— 2006, *Academic writing: a handbook for international students*, Routledge/Taylor & Francis, London.
Bailey, Stephen 2011, *Academic writing: a handbook for international students*, Routledge, London/New York.
Barry, Marian 2011, *Steps to academic writing*, Georgian Press, New York City.
Baumann, James F & Graves, Michael F 2010, 'What is academic vocabulary?' *Journal of Adolescent and Adult Literacy*, vol. 54, no. 1, pp. 4–12.
Behrens, Laurence M & Rosen, Leonard J 2007, *A sequence for academic writing*, 3rd edn., Longman, New York/London.
Bender, Sheila 2001, 'Personal essays: arguing your viewpoint', *Writers' Digest*, July, pp. 20–1.
Brittenham, Rebecca & Hoeller, Hildegard 2004, *Key words for academic writers*, Pearson, London/New York.
Cassell, Susie Lan & Moore, Kathleen Muller 2007, *Techniques for the thesis bound essay*, Longman, London/New York.
Davis, Lloyd & McKay, Susan 1996, *Structure and strategies: an introduction to academic writing*, Macmillan, South Melbourne.
Dwyer, Edward J 1992, 'Using a journalism model for teaching essay writing', *Journal of Reading*, vol. 36, no. 3, November, pp. 226–7.
McClain, Molly & Roth, Jacqueline D 1999, *Schaum's quick guide to writing great essays*, McGraw-Hill, New York.
Mulvey, Dan 2007, *Write on! Your easy-to-follow guide for writing essays and term papers*, Barron's Educational, New York.

Robson, Jocelyn, Francis, Becky & Read, Barbara 2002, 'Writes of passage: stylistic features of male and female undergraduate history essays', *Journal of Further and Higher Education*, vol. 26, no. 4.

Rosen, Leonard 2011, *Academic writer's handbook*, 3rd edn, Longman, London/New York.

REFERENCES

Baumann, James F & Graves, Michael F 2010, 'What is academic vocabulary?' *Journal of Adolescent and Adult Literacy,* vol. 54, no. 1, pp. 4–12.

Biber, Douglas & Grava, Bethany 2010, 'Challenging stereotypes about academic writing: Complexity, elaboration, explicitness', *Journal of English for Academic Purposes*, vol. 9, no. 1, pp. 2–20.

Blattner, Nancy H & Frazier, Christina L 2002, 'Developing a performance-based assessment of students' critical thinking skills', *Assessing Writing*, vol. 8, pp. 47–64.

Carter, Ronald & McCarthy, Michael 2006, *Cambridge grammar of English*, Cambridge University Press, Cambridge.

Doyle, Arthur Conan 1994 [1892], 'Scandal in Bohemia', in *The adventures of Sherlock Holmes*, Penguin, London.

Drucker, Peter 2002, *The effective executive revised*, HarperBusiness, New York.

Freddi, Maria 2005, 'Arguing linguistics: corpus investigation of one functional variety of academic discourse', *Journal of English for Academic Purposes*, vol. 4, pp. 5–26.

Georgia, Paul J 1998, 'Climate science briefings debunk greenhouse scares', *Competitive Enterprise Institute: Free Markets and Limited Government*, Competitive Enterprise Institute, Washington, DC, October 1.

Harwood, Nigel 2005, '"We do not seem to have a theory … the theory I present here attempts to fill this gap": inclusive and exclusive pronouns in academic writing', *Applied Linguistics*, vol. 26, no. 3, pp. 343–75.

Hyland, Ken 2002, 'Options of identity in academic writing', *ELT Journal*, vol. 56, no. 4, pp. 351–9.

King, Charles 1998, 'Battling the six evil geniuses of essay writing', *PS: Political Sciences and Politics*, March, vol. 31, no. 1.

Kuo, Chih-Hua 1999, 'The use of personal pronouns: role relationships in scientific journal articles', *English for Specific Purposes*, vol. 18, no. 2, pp. 121–38.

Read, Barbara, Francis, Becky & Robson, Jocelyn 2001, '"Playing safe": undergraduate essay writing and the presentation of the student "voice"', *British Journal of the Sociology of Education*, vol. 22, no. 3.

Tang, Ramona & John, Suganthi 1999, 'The "I" in identity: exploring writer identity in student academic writing through the first person pronoun', *English for Specific Purposes*, vol. 18, pp. S23–S39.

8

Nonverbal communication

LEARNING OBJECTIVES

After studying this chapter you should be able to:

- Explain the difference between body language and nonverbal communication
- Explain the importance of clustering and congruence for understanding –
  and avoiding misunderstanding – nonverbal communication
- Use a visual model to explain different aspects of nonverbal
  communication such as gesture, posture, body movement, touch,
  eye contact, paralinguistics, environment and time

What is nonverbal communication?

Nonverbal communication can be a very powerful tool in understanding ourselves and others. Are *nonverbal communication* and *body language* the same? No, they are not. Body language involves the physical behaviour of our bodies — eye contact, posture, gesture, orientation and so forth — while nonverbal communication embraces all body language communication, and also includes clothing and adornment, environmental factors and even the manner in which we use time. Nonverbal communication concepts feature heavily in other chapters in this book.

So what does nonverbal communication do for us that verbal communication and good old-fashioned words cannot do? Dickson and Hargie (2003, p. 50) suggest that we use nonverbal communication in order to:

1. replace verbal communication in situations where it may be impossible or inappropriate to talk
2. complement verbal communication, thereby enhancing the overall message
3. modify the spoken word
4. contradict, either intentionally or unintentionally, what is said
5. regulate conversation by helping to mark speech turns
6. express emotions and interpersonal attitudes
7. negotiate relationships in respect of, for instance, dominance, control and liking
8. convey personal and social identity through such features as dress and adornments
9. contextualise interaction by creating a particular social setting.

Tell: a nonverbal behaviour that reveals a person's true state of mind

Cluster: in relation to nonverbal communication, a group of different types of nonverbal behaviours or tells.

Nonverbal behaviours (e.g. a gesture or eye movements) are sometimes referred to as **tells** because they tell us about a person's true state of mind (Navarro 2008, 2011).

Nevertheless, nonverbal communication can be very ambiguous: we should not presume that we can 'read other people's minds' because of what we think they are 'saying' nonverbally. We may be right, but equally we may be wrong. To be more right than wrong, we should not seize upon one gesture or posture in isolation; rather, we need to recognise entire groups or **clusters** of nonverbal behaviour that suggest the same internal state of mind.

We should also not presume, as some do, that nonverbal communication is more important than verbal communication. It has become commonplace, for example, to hear that nonverbal communication comprises 70 to 90 per cent of our communication and that spoken words comprise only a small proportion of the totality of communication. This percentage approach is generally attributed to Mehrabian (1971), who based it on word-ambiguity experiments he conducted using US college students in the late 1960s. From this research he developed the idea that only about 7 per cent of meaning in communication could be extracted from the actual words spoken, while tone of voice accounted for about 38 per cent and body language about 55 per cent of conveyed meaning. This conjecture, based on experimental data that has often been challenged (Oestreich 1999), has wrongly been established in some minds as irrefutable fact relevant to all situations in all cultures. In some situations, of course, nonverbal communication comprises 100 per cent of the message being sent — for example, touching the hand of a grieving relative, or two lovers gazing into each other's eyes — but in others it might comprise only 10 per cent or less. The idea of applying percentages is misguided anyway. Some specialists in nonverbal communication use the illustration of a television set with the sound turned down: we can tell what is going on they suggest, merely by observing the nonverbal behaviour. This is

This young businesswoman is displaying several different types of nonverbal behaviours or tells. What might her nonverbal cues suggest about her internal state of mind?

Police officers are trained to interpret nonverbal cues, as well as to consider verbal feedback, in establishing the credibility of eyewitnesses and the accuracy of their testimonies.

Face of interviewee blurred for confidentiality reasons.

Congruence: the extent to which verbal and nonverbal messages reinforce or contradict each other

a dubious proposition: we might be able to work out, in general terms, what is happening, but we would certainly miss the specifics, and, more often than not, would get things totally wrong. An overemphasis on the previous percentages has been a useful corrective to our historical absorption in the verbal aspects of communication, but it's time the pendulum in the debate was wrenched back again.

Figure 8.1 presents a simple ten-part model of nonverbal communication.

In some respects, it is a false dichotomy to separate verbal and nonverbal communication (Jones & LeBaron 2002). Truly effective communication occurs when the two aspects are in harmony. When they are not **congruent** with each other – when, for example, a friend says 'I'm OK, really', but her mournful expression, slumped posture and teary eyes indicate otherwise – then we need to pay attention to the imbalance between the two channels of communication. Navarro (2008), for example, an FBI agent skilled in reading nonverbal communication, was interviewing a suspect in a rape case. The suspect denied involvement, saying that he had turned left and gone home, but his hand gestured to his right (he subsequently confessed). In many circumstances, therefore, it sometimes makes sense to give more credence to the nonverbal message than to the verbal message.

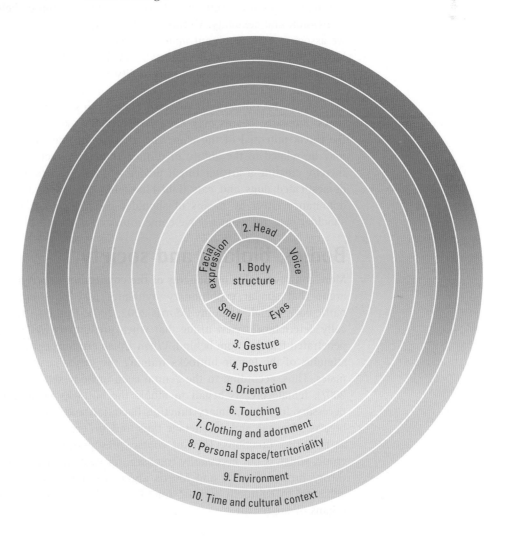

FIGURE 8.1 A model of nonverbal communication

Source: Adapted from Eunson (1987).

Body structure and deep behaviour: the medium is the message?

Some recent biological theories suggest that the body is not merely the medium used to convey meaning, but in fact may have itself been shaped by deeper forces, and that therefore much nonverbal communication can best be understood as the expression of basic biological drives. These controversial theories build on the pioneering work of Charles Darwin, who published a study in 1872 on 'the expression of emotions in man and animals' (Darwin 2002 [1872]).

Evolutionary psychology, for example, suggests that relatively minor characteristics such as physical attractiveness reveal deeper phenomena, with the 'survival of the prettiest' demonstrating that conventional physical attractiveness and symmetry (the tendency of both sides of the body and face to be balanced) may be adaptive. This implies that it is associated with physical robustness and thus more likely to lead to genetic survival and reproduction – not to mention the possibility that more 'attractive' people, even in a variety of human cultures, may be more likely to be successful in job hunting because of this 'lookism phenomenon' (Etcoff 2000; Wright 1995; Buss 2003; Geary 2004; Chiu & Babcock 2002; Warhurst, Van den Broek & Hall 2009).

Human anatomy itself may have evolved to express behavioural patterns such as aggression and sexuality. Guthrie (1976) suggests that many of the bodily characteristics we associate with dominant males – broad shoulders, wide, protuberant chin, heavy eyebrows and pronounced cheekbones – evolved to attract females (because such features suggested physical fitness and thus ability to provide and protect), and to dominate other, competing males. Certainly, the combination of these characteristics, particularly when associated with tall, heavily muscled males, can seem threatening, even in these 'civilised' times. Similarly, beards may have evolved not to keep the male face warm but to extend the threat potential of the chin. The 'tingling up the spine' felt in threatening situations may be related to the ability of proto-humans to erect hair or hackles on the shoulders, thereby creating a greater threat profile – a feature retained by many animals, including domesticated dogs and cats (Eibl-Eibesfeldt 2007). Nowadays males try to enhance this dominance effect by means of shoulder padding and epaulettes on uniforms (although shoulder pads for women have come into, and gone out of, fashion in recent decades).

Bodies, biology and society

More controversially, proponents of the connection between body structure and behaviour argue that similar evolutionary dynamics may have shaped human sexual anatomy, particularly female anatomy (Morris 2002, 2005; Guthrie 1976). Proponents of this biologically deterministic view argue that when prehumans walked on all fours, males sexually penetrated females from behind. When *Homo erectus* began to walk erect, the visual sexual stimulus of the female buttocks framing the genitalia was no longer readily available to males. Thus, according to the genital echo or body self-mimicry theory (Mick and Oswald 2007), female breasts began to mimic the buttocks by becoming much larger than was necessary for their primary function (lactation and suckling of young). In some cultures, breasts, cleavage and décolletage thus took on erotic or sexually cueing functions as well as nurturing functions. This, of course, presupposes that all cultures find female breasts erotic, which is not necessarily true; see, for example, Lattier (1998). Pursuing the mimicry theory further, Guthrie and Morris argue that the reddish lips of the female (sometimes enhanced by culturally specific amplifiers such as lipstick) imitate the labia or outer sexual organs of the female.

Obviously, to the extent that these phenomena are real, they would be the result of hereditary adaptation rather than environmental, socially conditioned behaviour (Pinker 2003). In explaining gender-linked behaviour and communication, such evolutionary psychology-based ideas are described as essentialist and stand in opposition to the constructivist view, which is that much or all sexual/gender behaviour and communication is influenced or determined by social factors rather than biological factors (see online chapter 'Gender and communication').

Some other possible aspects of biological bases of human behaviour are outlined in table 8.1.

TABLE 8.1 Some aspects of human behaviour that may have a biological basis

Phenomenon	Possible explanation
Contrary to the myth of the wicked stepmother, many parents invest more resources (e.g. teeth braces, cars, loans, weddings and homework help) in adoptive and stepchildren than in their own genetic children. In spite of this, adoptive children are far more likely to be assaulted or killed by a nongenetic parent, and are far less likely to succeed in academic testing and wealth accumulation over their lifespan.	Adoptive parents, or step-parents, invest more resources not because they love them more but because they need more help (and possibly because parents do not want to show the child that she/he is 'second class'). Poor life outcomes may be associated with genetic transmission from birth mothers who place or surrender their child, as such birth mothers tend to have higher incidences of addiction, mental health and domestic problems. Stepchildren may threaten the resources available to the genetic children of the step-parent. Canadian data shows that children living with step-parents are 40 times more likely to be abused and 120 times more likely to be killed by a live-in parent than those living with two genetic parents (Gibson 2008).
Dogs, when defecating, may turn around in circles, defecate and then kick dirt over their faeces.	In prehistoric times (and even today) an animal is most vulnerable to attack when defecating. Consequently, animals seek out long grass for cover, turn around in circles to create a space, and then kick dirt to cover their scent or spoor to prevent predators from tracking them (Morris 1998).
Dancers judged to be excellent also have more physically symmetrical bodies than other dancers (i.e. both halves of their bodies and faces are very similar).	Coordinated men and women hold and move their bodies in rhythmic ways, thus showing off their strong immune systems and genetic strength, while bodily and facial symmetry are associated with reproductive fitness (Fisher 2009)
Men in high-security hospitals and prisons were found to be 20 times more likely to have an XYY chromosomal pattern, as distinct from the normal XY pattern. XYY-pattern males were also said to be taller, to have lower IQs and to suffer from acne and personality disorders.	The height–chromosome correlation holds, but little else: most inmates were there for nonviolent crime and many XYY males lead normal, nonviolent lives (Rafter 2008; Malott 2007). Nevertheless, the 20 times factor remains intriguing.

(continued)

TABLE 8.1 *(continued)*

Phenomenon	Possible explanation
Some people seem to be able to detect when someone is staring at them, while some people claim that they can make people turn around or pets wake up just by looking at them. Some detectives are told not to look too long at the back of a person they are following, as the person may turn around and discover them. Some paparazzi and snipers claim that their targets seem to know when they are being looked at from afar.	Sheldrake (1995) suggests that animals, including humans, developed this ability through evolution in the context of predator–prey relationships: prey animals that could detect when predators were looking at them would probably stand a better chance of survival.
In Jane Austen's novels (and indeed, in much literature and other arts), females choose male mates, rather than vice-versa. Females are often poorer than males, but are often good conversationalists.	Darwinian literary theory (e.g. Barash & Barash 2005; Austin 2011; Boyd, Carroll & Gottschall 2011) explores beyond the socioeconomic and sex-role conventions of literary works to detect evolutionary strategies, showing that Austen's heroines are often confronted with a choice of males who have what biologists call $r^{3\cdot}$ 'reproductively relevant resources', which are usually wealth, health and fidelity, but also include skill in verbal repartee and mental agility — a signal of reproductive desirability.

Does this mean, therefore, that we are slaves to unconscious, evolutionary drives; that our bodies are merely machines driven by 'selfish genes' (Dawkins 2006) to create other bodies; that 'love' is merely an evolutionary trick; and that we have no free will? Not at all; rather, the more we learn about our biological programming, the more we will be in a position to go with it or challenge it — it is unconscious no more.

There is also the question of the model of reproductive sexuality we are considering here; namely the heterosexual model. What about homosexuals? Reuter (2002) argues for the existence of 'gaydar': a word formed from radar referring to the ability to pick up cues — many of which are nonverbal — that another person is homosexual. While the idea is popular in the gay community, the data backing it is not strong (Shelp 2002). Woolery (2007) points out that if gaydar exists, then it challenges, if not negates, the notion that 'you can never know' (the 'we are everywhere' slogan of the movement).

Head movements

Darwin (2002 [1872]) suggested that the 'yes' gesture (nodding the head up and down) derived from a baby moving towards the breast, while the 'no' gesture (moving the head side to side) derived from a baby rejecting the breast after it had drunk its fill. It may not be as simple as that, however, as we now know such nonverbal communication is often culture specific. While the positive head nod and negative head shake are commonly understood around the world, they are far from universal. In parts of Bulgaria and Greece, for example, nodding means no, while in parts of the former Yugoslavia and southern India, shaking the head signifies yes (Axtell 1998). Historically, nodding the head may be related to bowing, which was — and is — a way of showing submission to another's will.

In conversation, when people agree with the speaker, they tend to nod as the other speaks. If a person doesn't nod, we may deduce that he or she disagrees with the speaker. This impression will be borne out if this immobility is followed by a head shake. When

Backchanneling: in conversation, responding to a speaker with nonverbal and paraverbal feedback, such as nodding, smiling and 'friendly grunts'

we are listening effectively, we indulge in **backchanneling**; that is, we give nonverbal and paraverbal feedback by nodding, smiling and emitting 'friendly grunts' (e.g. 'Uh huh...', 'mmm...hmm...') (Kjellmer 2009).

In western cultures, individuals in conversation who wish to take over the speaking role may increase their rate of head-nods, move forward in their seats, increase the 'friendly grunts' and further 'bid' for attention with a raised hand, finger or pen. A tilted head may mean a number of things, including 'I am listening' (with thoughtful expression), 'I like you a lot' (with coy, smiling expression) or 'I am feeling angry' (with aggressive expression) (Fast 2002; Krumhuber, Manstead & Kappas 2007).

Facial expressions

The face reveals much of our emotional disposition, and there are strong cultural and social messages involved in suppressing or expressing those emotions. In Japanese culture, and to a lesser extent British culture, great value is placed on not revealing emotions, thereby demonstrating the desired characteristics of self-control (Morris 2002). In cultures characterised by more mobility of expression, such as the North American or Australian cultures, facial immobility is a clue to high-status individuals, whose behaviour contrasts with that of others, who have more plasticity in their expressions (traditionally, this was the case with individuals accorded lower status, such as children, slaves and women). High-status people thus rarely smile, but are smiled at by lower-status people or subordinates; their voices tend to be pitched lower, while those of their subordinates are pitched higher; they are looked at by but rarely look at their subordinates; and touch, but are rarely touched by, their subordinates (Henley 1986, 2002). There may be some relationship between these behaviours and those, first noted by Darwin, of apes in the wild: in a confrontation, the loser tends to smile, to propitiate or appease the winner (Darwin 2002 [1872]).

In the human world, of course, smiling does not necessarily signify submission, although it can. Smiling in many situations is a positive and spontaneous response. In the workplace, however, there is increasing pressure on staff to smile at customers and clients, whether or not they like those customers or clients. Hochschild (2003) calls this 'emotional labour', observing that in modern post-industrial economies, where the service sector predominates, such labour can be exhausting and stressful unless managed with regard to the dignity and stress levels of the workers involved.

Facial expressions are an important aspect of nonverbal communication and can vary between cultures.

A rigid or expressionless face is sometimes known as a 'poker face', after the card game that favours players with the ability to conceal their responses to the cards they are dealt. The capacity to void the face of telltale expression, to shut down any form of emotional leakage, can also be useful in situations involving negotiation, but in the long term such emotional suppression can lead to serious stress (Navarro 2011).

Eyes

Eyes, the 'portals of the soul', communicate fundamental messages, sometimes consciously, sometimes unconsciously. There are numerous messages in western culture relating to eye contact.

'Look me in the eye and say that!'
'It's rude to stare.'
'You can't hide your lyin' eyes.'

Eye contact, or direct gaze, means different things to different people. Euro-American, Saudi Arabian, Korean and Thai people tend to regard a direct gaze as a desirable characteristic indicating openness and honesty. Conversely, an averted gaze can be construed as suggesting dishonesty or shiftiness. In other cultures, however, such as Japanese, Mexican, West African and Puerto Rican, direct eye contact may be considered rude, while an averted gaze indicates respect (Morris 2002). There is obvious potential for misunderstanding here.

Gaze behaviour may also be linked to 'love at first sight', although Fisher takes a somewhat unromantic view of this phenomenon:

> Could this human ability to adore one another within moments of meeting come out of nature? I think it does. In fact, love at first sight may have a critical adaptive function among animals. During the mating season, a female squirrel, for example, needs to breed. It is not to her advantage to copulate with a porcupine. But if she sees a healthy squirrel, she should waste no time. She should size him up. And if he looks suitable, she should grab her chance to copulate. Perhaps love at first sight is no more than an inborn tendency in many creatures that evolved to spur the mating process. Then among our human ancestors, what had been animal attraction evolved into the human sensation of infatuation at a glance. (Fisher 1992, p. 51)

In many cultures, direct eye contact is the preserve of dominant individuals, while subordinates tend to avert their gaze and blink more frequently. In western groups eye contact is used to regulate conversation: a person who is speaking in a group may break eye contact with others while talking, refocusing on a person making 'bidding' signals only when ready to yield the floor (Argyle 1999). Similarly, listeners tend to look at speakers more than speakers look at listeners, but speakers will tend to re-establish eye contact at critical points while talking to seek reinforcement, feedback or approval from listeners; when each is looking at the other, a 'gaze window' is established (Bavalas, Coates & Johnson 2002).

In some cultures direct eye contact implies the listener is concentrating on what is being said, while in others (e.g. Japanese) concentration is indicated by an averted gaze, or closed or half-closed eyes (Axtell 1998). An apparently universal phenomenon is the 'eyebrow flash' – a lifting of the eyebrows when meeting or acknowledging someone (Eibl-Eibesfeldt 2007).

When we are interested in something, our pupils dilate, or expand. Although this is something western behavioural scientists have discovered only in the past few decades, elsewhere it has been known for centuries: Chinese and Arab traders have always watched for telltale dilations to reveal the motivations of their opponents during negotiations. Wearing dark glasses is a common strategy among modern hagglers.

Voice: it ain't what you say, but the way that you say it

The quality of our voices can surprise us. If you hear an audio recording of yourself, or watch yourself on video, what you hear (and see) may not be what you expect, but it does give you real feedback on the way you actually behave and how you may come across to others. Any strangeness you might feel in this self-perception is caused by:

- the fact that your voice resonates through your skull before it reaches your ears, which makes it sound slightly different from what you hear on playback or what others hear

- the fact that, before the invention of film and video, no-one in history had access to a moving representation of themselves. A few could afford a portrait, and many had seen themselves in a mirror, but a mirror is a 180° distortion of how you actually appear: stand, for example, in front of a mirror with someone you know, and you will see that their reflection – while accurate as far as it goes – is not what you see when you look at them directly.

Paralinguistics

Paralinguistics: the properties of voices, separate from the words being spoken, that can convey meanings

The meaning of the words we use – the words that can be reproduced in text, for example – can be modified substantially by **paralinguistic** changes. These changes include differences in emphasis, volume, pitch, inflection, nasality and articulation. Paralanguage can also give indications of geographical origins and socioeconomic class.

Silence and interruption behaviour also tell us much about what is going on in communication between people. We can change the meaning of what we say substantially by emphasising certain words and de-emphasising others:

'Who, *me*? Oh no – *never*.'
The *main* thing to be emphasized is that she was *nowhere near* the area when it happened.

Such emphases, sometimes shown in text by italics, can convey many meanings, including sarcasm, boredom, sexual suggestiveness or anger, or they may simply be a means of drawing attention to particular points or interpretations of word clusters.

The volume we use when we speak can indicate boldness, timidity, confidentiality or other states of mind. We will also change the volume according to the physical distance we are from others, and whether we are communicating in private or public settings. Voice volume can have significant cultural variations, as Hall notes:

> Personal status modulates voice tone, however, even in the Arab society. The Saudi Arabian shows respect to his superior – to a Sheikh, say – by lowering his voice and mumbling. The affluent American may also be addressed in this fashion, making almost impossible an already difficult situation. Since in American culture one unconsciously 'asks' another to raise his voice by raising his own, the American speaks louder. This lowers the Arab's tone more and increases the mumbles. This triggers a shouting response from the American – which cues the Arab into a frightened 'I'm not being respectful enough' tone well below audibility. (Hall 1977, p. 312)

We tend to pitch our voices higher when we are dealing with people we know (e.g. consider the change in pitch in most people's voices when they pick up the phone, say 'Hello', and then recognise a friend). We may pitch our voice lower as a warning signal, or out of defensiveness, when speaking to people we don't know, although we sometimes lower the pitch (along with the volume) when we wish to establish more intimate communication with someone we like (Guthrie 1976). Deception may be suggested in heightened pitch and in the use of non-word interjections ('Ah', 'uhh'), repetitions ('I, I, I mean I really ...') and partial words ('I rea- really liked it'). Generally, males pitch their voices lower than do females (Puts, Gaulin & Verdolini 2006). Female newsreaders may tend to pitch their voices lower than normal in order to sound more 'credible'.

Voice inflection is related to pitch. Upward inflection, or rising tone, is used conventionally when we ask questions: we are trying to cue a response. We may upwardly inflect or downwardly inflect when we are ready to stop talking and yield the floor to another person. This cue is often accompanied by eye contact. Continual high-rising tone tends to be associated with immaturity, lack of confidence or tentativeness: Crystal (1992) notes that Australian television programs such as Neighbours have had such influence in Britain that a high-rising tone — often used by Neighbours characters — is starting to be used in Britain as a tentativeness signal (see online chapter 'Gender and communication').

Nasality has negative connotations and tends to be inversely correlated with perceptions of persuasiveness. This can work to the detriment of females, who tend to have more nasal voices than males (Bloom, Zajac & Titus 1999).

Careful or exaggerated articulation can indicate confidence, overconfidence, precision, formality, pretentiousness or over-punctiliousness. Poor articulation or lack of articulation can indicate shyness, lack of confidence or sloppiness.

Accents, often in combination with vocabulary, can reveal where a person comes from geographically, and can also reveal socioeconomic status.

Interruptions can reveal interesting patterns of power and dominance or submission, and may also reflect on gender roles and listening behaviour — for example, men are more likely to interrupt women than vice-versa (Scheflen 1972; Dunbar & Burgoon 2005).

Silence can sometimes be more important than sound or words. Silence during conversation can mean many things, including:

- punctuating or drawing attention to certain words or ideas
- evaluating and judging another's words or behaviour; showing favour or disfavour, agreement or disagreement; attacking or 'freezing out' someone (e.g. not responding to a comment or greeting)
- disgust, sadness, fear, anger or love (Knapp and Hall 2010).

Bell suggests that silence can often be more effective than words for salespeople:

When asking for a decision, let silence fall after you've made your proposal. Don't weaken your position by tag-on comments and compromising chat. Successful salespeople live by the credo that, after they give the price of the item, the 'next one who speaks loses'. (Bell 1999, p. 166)

Paralinguistic behaviour may be influenced by the relative richness in the vocabulary of a language — we may compensate for the shortcomings of one channel by the strengths of another. Physically expressive people tend to rely more on paralinguistic behaviour, while people who are less physically demonstrative rely more on linguistic expression, as Poyatos has observed:

peoples who are more expressive kinesically, like Latins, Arabs or Mediterraneans in general, tend to use paralinguistic imitations in situations in which, for instance, we see English speakers utilize with great precision a legitimate onomatopoeic verb or noun from the particularly rich repertoire of their native tongue... When once at the beginning of my life in North America, I tried to explain to mechanics what happened to my car by imitating the sound it made, they would just say: 'You mean it whirs?' or 'It clatters?' (Poyatos 2002, p. 186)

Smell

Smell, too, is a form of nonverbal communication. Smell or olfactory communication is a major mode of communication in the animal world, and it would be surprising if there were not at least some residual manifestations in human communication (Hickson & Stacks 2004). Chemicals known as pheromones appear to be key signals in sexual behaviour, although the exact workings of such communication in humans is still not

Pheromones are sometimes expressed through perspiration. Do you think that sweat is sexy?

well understood (Wyatt 2003; Thornhill & Gangestad 1999). Pheromones are sometimes expressed through perspiration. Sweaty is sexy? In some circumstances, yes, but we must remember that the cultural inventions of the past few thousand years include clothes and artificial indoor environments (not to mention perfume and plumbing). There is evidence in some cultures of courting rituals in which young males wear handkerchiefs in their armpits during a dance, then take out the handkerchief and waft it beneath the noses of female admirers (Eibl-Eibesfeldt 2007).

In western societies, smell is virtually a taboo topic, because it is bound up with norms of cleanliness, health and attractiveness. Even those close to us may therefore be loath to let us know when we violate these norms ('even your best friends won't tell you'). Because it is often difficult to get feedback on our own body smell, many of us are persuaded to assume the worst and take corrective action. It should be noted that not all cultures share such norms. In some societies, perfumes and deodorants are frowned on because they mask the natural odours of the body, which are seen as sending messages about moods and states of mind. For similar reasons, some people prefer to smell the breath of the person they are talking to (Hall 1976).

NONVERBAL COMMUNICATION: THE POETS PRE-EMPT THE SCIENTISTS
Nonverbal communication is a relatively recent area of scientific study, yet writers have for centuries recognised its importance. Gesture and other aspects of nonverbal communication reveal much of our inner motivations without writers having to spell out those motivations (Portch 1985; Korte 1997; Hazard 2000). Here are some literary samples:

Fie, fie upon her!
There's language in her eye, her cheek, her lip,
Nay, her foot speaks; her wanton spirits look out
At every joint and motive of her body.

Shakespeare, *Troilus and Cressida* IV, v (1601)

Estella, pausing a moment in her knitting with her eyes upon me, and then going on, I fancied that I read in the action of her fingers, as plainly as if she had told me in the dumb alphabet, that she perceived I had discovered my real benefactor...

Charles Dickens, *Great Expectations* (1861)

The features of our face are hardly more than gestures which have become permanent.

Marcel Proust, *Within a Budding Grove, Remembrance of Things Past* (1919)

In her office, (Phoebe) sat at her desk, an imposing piece of ebony about a tennis-court wide. Her desk chair built up her height; wing chairs in front put visitors a foot below her head. I opted for one of the corner couches behind the desk. She swivelled and glared, angry at losing her barricade...
She pounded her right thigh in frustration... Phoebe frowned ferociously, her jaw jutting out far enough to cause permanent damage to her overbite... Her skin turned so pale that her freckles stood out like drops of blood against her skin... Tish was still planted at her computer as I came in. She shot me a resentful glance but closed her file and folded her hands with the exaggerated patience of one who has little.

Sarah Paretsky, *Tunnel Vision* (1994)

ASSESS YOURSELF

Research other examples of writers using nonverbal communication to describe characters and situations in novels, stories, poetry, plays, films and television programs.

Gesture

Gestures are movements of the body, especially the hands or arms, that express an idea or emotion. Again, there is considerable cultural variation in the repertoire, frequency and expressive range of gestures – some cultures are physically more expressive, while others are more subdued (Morris 2002; Kendon 2005; Hostetter & Alibali 2007).

Gestures are shorthand ways of communicating a whole range of states of mind or ideas, such as:

- *Insecurity.* When children are stressed they will often suck a thumb, which may conjure up for them the security they felt when being suckled on a real or artificial nipple. Later in life, adults may show insecurity by biting a pencil, the arm of their glasses or their fingernails, which may perform the same function. A person entering an open area may perform the barrier cross gesture, which entails crossing the body in some way (scratching, touching the body or other hand, or moving an object from one hand to the other). Self-touching, hair-stroking, playing with jewellery are other signs of insecurity.
- *Deceit.* When lying, people can show stress in many different ways, including scratching or rubbing the face or nose, covering the mouth with a hand, manipulating clothing (buttoning up a coat or blouse, tugging at a collar); erecting 'signal blunters' to hide behind, such as a purse, briefcase, folder or laptop computer; crossing and uncrossing legs.
- *Apathy.* Shrugging the shoulders, restricting movement and gestures, hands in pockets
- *Disapproval.* Picking off lint from clothing, moving items away, refusing eye contact, lowering voice
- *Approval.* Thumbs up, 'A-OK' finger gestures, 'you're the man' finger pointing, high-fives
- *Confidence.* Hands on hips, thumbs in belt or pockets, swaggering gait, erect posture
- *Arrogance.* Steepling hands (putting fingertips of two hands together in the shape of a church steeple), feet up on desk, dismissive waving
- *Despair.* Hand wringing, head in hands, head shaking
- *Hostility.* Bunched fists, waving fists, pointing fingers, obscene or taboo gestures
- *Courtship and affection.* People who are romantically interested in one another may engage in 'grooming' behaviour, which entails subtly adjusting one's appearance so that one looks better – adjusting and smoothing down clothing (ties, collars) and glasses, touching the hair, adornments or jewellery. In modern workplaces, suggest Knapp and Hall (2010), it may be necessary to train males and females in 'decourting' behaviour to shut down courting signals, so that potentially messy sexual entanglements and sexual harassment situations are less likely to occur.

Gestures are powerful tools of communication. When in conversation we rephrase others' words, we may find that we are also 'rephrasing' their gestures (Tabensky 2002).

Cultural variations on gestures are as great as in other aspects of nonverbal communication. Where a Vietnamese man might intend to send signals of respect by gazing directly and folding his arms across his chest, a North American might read the attitude as indicating defiance rather than respect. A perfectly innocent gesture in one culture can be profoundly insulting in another.

Posture

Posture relates to body movements and to height. Height, or tallness, still carries powerful messages of dominance. There is some evidence of height being positively correlated with success in leadership positions (Knapp & Hall 2010). Just as people are often unhappy with their overall body image, some are unhappy with their height and may try to compensate (very tall people may stoop, while short people may hold their bodies more erect to appear taller). To lower the body towards someone else – as in a shallow or deep bow – is a universal sign of respect and sometimes even defeat. Aggression can be shown by a rigid body, with shoulders raised, both signals of readiness for physical combat. Defeat or depression are indicated by a slumped posture, representing both humility and retreat to the helplessness but recalled security of the foetus.

Mirroring: consciously or unconsciously copying the nonverbal behaviour of someone admired

Admiration for another person can be manifested in a postural echo, or a **mirroring** of the admired person's posture. Indeed, other aspects of the admired person's nonverbal communication, such as gestural and vocal patterns, may also be knowingly or unknowingly copied. You can create empathy with another person by mirroring, but you can also create disquiet and even anger if the person perceives that you are mimicking or attempting to manipulate them. Mimicry, or the 'chameleon effect', may have evolved as a mechanism in early human groups to increase affiliation and build relationships with others (Lakin, Jefferis, Cheng & Chartrand 2003).

Body movement

Kinesics: the study of nonlinguistic body movement in relation to communication

The study of nonlinguistic body movement, or **kinesics**, is concerned with the way humans move their bodies in relation to communication. This involves processes such as *orientation* and *synchronisation*.

Orientation, or the attitude, inclination or body angle we adopt in relation to others, can send powerful nonverbal messages. If we are interested in someone, we tend to face him or her squarely. The less interested we are, whether through hostility or indifference, the more we tend to orientate ourselves away from the person. When males and females are in confined situations – for example, when brushing past each other – males will tend to face towards females, while females will tend to face away (Scheflen 1972).

Synchronisation, similar to postural echo, mirroring or mimicking is an interactive process that helps define relationships between individuals: the greater the rapport between them, the greater their synchronisation. It plays a critical part in courting rituals, and is in fact a form of dance, wherein females may be testing males for compatibility. Synchronisation is an important part of animal mating rituals (Remland 2000). Some synchronisation researchers have concluded that 'men typically don't realize that they are even involved in a courtship dance, or that they are typically very poor dancers' (Grammer, Kruck & Magnusson 1998, p. 23). Interpersonal conflicts can ensue when individuals are out of synchrony with one another – physically bumping into each other may sometimes be the nonverbal equivalent of verbal misunderstanding.

Touching

Haptics: the study of touch as a form of communication

The study of touch, or **haptics**, reveals much about human behaviour. It links gesture, posture and territory, or personal space. Touch is recognised as a basic human need, but the degree to which individuals touch one another varies considerably from culture to culture, as well as within cultures. Touch is critically allied to sensory integration and perhaps even psychological wellbeing: we probably need some degree of touching to survive and thrive, but for a variety of reasons we may not get enough of it (Field 2002). For example, displays of maternal warmth (touching, gaze) towards children may make those children develop a greater sense of internal control – that is, feelings that they can influence their surroundings and destiny, rather than feel powerless (Carton & Carton 1998). The touching involved in the grooming rituals of our prehuman ancestors may have been instrumental in developing conversation (in particular, gossip) and language (Dunbar 1998).

Touch can be usefully classified into five types (Johnson 1998):
1. Functional/professional
2. Social/polite

3. Friendship/warmth
4. Love/intimacy
5. Sexual/arousal.

In workplaces, most touching is of type 1 or type 2. Professional touchers include doctors, nurses, physiotherapists, masseurs, manicurists, hairdressers, dentists, priests and – occasionally – politicians. While there are strong taboos on various types of touching in different cultures, some people unconsciously or consciously feel deprived of types 2, 3, 4 and 5, and thus may seek out type 1 interactions at work (Montagu 1986). Professionals should not feel uneasy about this, as they are almost certainly performing a vital social-therapeutic role with some customers. Therapeutic touch from nurses in nursing homes has been associated with decreases in pain, increases in haemoglobin levels, decreases in sensory deprivation, increases in reality orientation and 'almost instantaneous calm' in aged persons (Simington 1993).

When cultural taboos on touching are strong – for example, male–male touching in Australia or England – then some may try to compensate by seeking touch through sporting rituals, immersion in crowds or violence (Kneidinger, Maple & Tross 2001; Canetti 2000 [1960]).

Perhaps the most common form of professional touching is the handshake. Darwin speculated that the handshake is in fact a 'relic gesture', an echo of a time when two men meeting for the first time would grasp each other's right forearm to prevent swords being drawn (2002 [1872]). The ritual is thus bound up with male dominance and may indicate that the initiator of the gesture is on home territory. (This may also help to explain the deeply rooted ambivalence towards left-handed people prevalent in some cultures.)

The western habit of shaking hands has been broadly adopted internationally, but any more demonstrative gesture – embracing or kissing, for example – needs to be approached with caution. High-contact cultures include Arab peoples, Latin Americans, Russians, most South-East Asians and southern Europeans. Low-contact cultures include people of Anglo-Saxon origin, Scandinavians, Japanese, Koreans and Chinese (Hall 1977).

Clothing and adornment

Clothes and bodily adornment are used primarily to protect us from the elements and to send social and sexual messages. 'Adornment' in this sense includes both physical decoration (hair styling, make-up, jewellery, wigs, suntans, shaving/not shaving, tattoos, body piercing) and body modification (plastic surgery, foot-binding), all social inventions by different cultures whose broad purpose is to emit messages of attractiveness, submission or dominance.

The ways we dress and adorn ourselves tell others whether we belong to a particular group, or which group or high-status individual we imitate out of admiration; they also carry messages about wealth, rank or class. Some clothing has a primarily functional purpose – say, to protect the wearer (e.g. a welder's gloves, apron and goggles; a mechanic's overalls; a diver's suit; underwear) or to protect the environment from the wearer (e.g. clean-room uniforms in computer chip manufacture; a surgeon's gown and gloves; cellophane gloves, hair covering and apron worn by delicatessen assistant). In other cases, clothing and adornment send nonverbal messages by performing functions such as:

- *an indication of sexual modesty or purity:* a nun's habit; concealing clothing (high necks and low hemlines); veils, burkas, chadors, hijabs (Killian 2003; McLarney 2009)
- *a display of sexual immodesty:* codpieces, figure-hugging or revealing clothing (low necks and high hemlines); transparent materials

- *an indication of leisurely life (without need to work):* delicate, light-coloured fabrics; long fingernails; suntan; tracksuits; sunglasses
- *a display of group identification:* uniforms; common clothing styles or bodily adornments; judges' gowns and wigs; sporting team insignia
- *a display of wealth/status:* brand-name clothes, jewellery; accessories; rank insignia
- *displays of dominance/threat/physical toughness:* shoulder pads, body piercing, tattoos, leather clothing, tight clothing, sunglasses, heavy boots, chewing gum, smoking
- *displays of compensation:* elevator/platform shoes, hair transplants, cosmetic surgery
- *displays of religious affiliation:* yarmulkes, crosses, clerical collars, turbans, beards.

Uniforms and nonuniforms

Some organisations require employees to wear a specific uniform, while in others uniforms are perceived as 'too military'. In those organisations that require uniforms to be worn, the shared identity they provide can lead to a more positive emotional response in customers and clients. Uniforms often convey powerful status and sex-role messages, too; as it is females and lower-status males who are most often required to wear uniforms, such dress codes may signal enforced conformity in less powerful people.

Of course, if we define the term more broadly, high-status people also often wear 'uniform': powerful dynamics of conformity ensure that executives dress and adorn themselves in narrowly prescribed ways (e.g. the traditional business suit). In this sense, well-paid executives wear uniforms just as surely as uniformed service staff in organisations or members of a street gang: they are all conforming to powerful norms, the violation of which will attract disapproval within the group.

Dressing down, dressing up

Some interesting debate on the question of uniform has emerged in the past few years. It has been traditional in the United States for schoolchildren not to wear uniforms, but there are now increasing demands for uniforms to be worn. Positions on the issue tend to gravitate to freedom of expression on the one hand and, on the other, to the perceived advantages of cheaper clothing (and less wealth display), the desirability of shutting down sexual and courting signals so that students can concentrate on their work, and the discouragement of too much individuality or too great a challenge to social norms (Remland 2000).

A similar debate is occurring in many workplaces, with the advent of 'dress-down Friday' or 'pre-weekend casual' initiatives, which allow many staff to avoid business dress for at least one day of the week. As with the school uniform debate, the arguments centre on issues of self-expression, freedom from conformity and a more relaxed work environment versus questions of whether 'casual clothes mean casual attitudes' and how such nonconformity affects the organisation's image of professionalism (McPherson 1997; Smith 1998; 'US companies averse to "dress down" Friday' 1995). Further debate rages about the acceptability of body adornment such as tattoos and body piercing (Smith 2003). There may be a correlation between the tendency of an individual to undergo tattooing and body piercing and the tendencies of that individual towards high levels of anxiety, self-mutilation, dysfunctional or violent social behaviour, suicide and risk-taking (Carroll, Riffenburgh, Roberts & Myhre 2002).

Fashionable dress, body piercing – for that matter most clothing and adornment phenomena – can be broadly seen as parts of a uniform. Indeed, all fashion can be seen as the ongoing creation and adaptation of uniforms for us all (Barnard 2001; Crane 2001). In counselling teenagers (a group that could well resist the idea of wearing business suits, in male or female versions) on survival in the real world, Brain has this to say: 'Many people ask, "But why? Why have people chosen this ridiculous outfit as the outward symbol of success, goals and intentions? It is expensive, cumbersome and absolutely worthless in any sort of inclement weather. Why? What possible purpose does a tie serve, for example?" The answer is simply BECAUSE. It is completely random. It makes no sense. But that is how it is. You can accept it and take advantage of the effect suits have, or you can reject it. By accepting it, you tend to accelerate your development' (Brain 1997, p. 34).

Personal space/territoriality

Proxemics: the study of the spatial relationships between individuals

Proxemics is the study of personal space or territoriality, or the way we create and cross spaces between ourselves and others.

Like animals, human beings exist within an invisible 'bubble' of personal space or territory, where we feel secure. We tend to feel anxious if others invade this space; for example, by standing too close or by touching us. Figure 8.2 illustrates this phenomenon. The four zones identified are:

1. *the intimate.* Within this zone we will be comfortable only with people we like and know very well – for example, family members and lovers.
2. *the personal.* Within this zone we will also be comfortable with people we know quite well – for example, friends and close colleagues.
3. *the social–consultative.* Within this zone we will also be comfortable with people we know only moderately well – for example, work colleagues in a meeting.
4. *the public.* Within this zone we will also be comfortable with people we know only slightly or not at all – for example, people in public places.

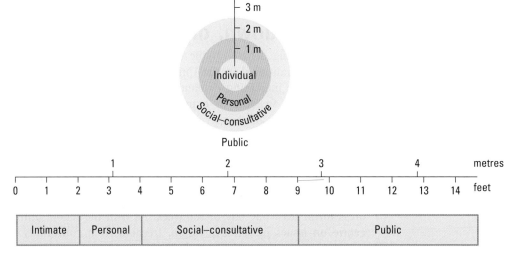

FIGURE 8.2 Personal space zones for a middle-class North American of northern European heritage

Source: Adapted from Hall (1966).

Note, however, that this personal space bubble is relevant only to a middle-class North American of northern European heritage. Personal space varies between cultures and classes, and even between the sexes. For example, researchers have reached the following conclusions:

- Many males demand more personal space than many females.
- People from rural areas may have higher personal space needs than people from city areas.
- Intercultural conflict can arise if norms about space and touch are not understood. For example, if a British negotiator (high space needs, low touch norms) meets a Saudi Arabian negotiator (low space needs, high touch norms), the Saudi may advance 'into' the British person's zone, and that person may step back; the Saudi may perceive this as coldness, or as a meaningless accident, and step forward again...and so on (Morris 2002; Pease & Pease 2006).

Personal space, unsurprisingly, is related to touching behaviour. People with lower space needs are more likely to use touch as a normal mode of communication; people with higher space needs are likely to practise social touching less. Having said this, it is often true that high-power, high-prestige people – who are rarely closely approached or touched by subordinates – will often assert their power by invading the personal space of subordinates and by touching them (Henley 1986).

Personal space needs may not be met when people are forced into close proximity, such as when business colleagues share a lift with a superior.

Personal space can be communicated by such means as a jacket left over a chair back, a cup left on a table, photographs and other personal items left on a desk, bumper stickers on cars ('Not so close – I hardly know you') or, more overtly, a 'Private' sign on a door. In extreme cases, violence may result from space violations in human encounters, but we are more likely to express anxiety and erect barriers in subtle, nonverbal ways – face rubbing, breaking eye contact, making the face expressionless, turning away, surrounding ourselves with objects, and so on. This happens when we are forced into close proximity in busy stores, in elevators, on public transport, at sporting events and in similar public situations. Road rage and parking rage may also be connected to territorial behaviour (Remland 2000).

Personal space can interact with orientation in interesting ways. Standing opposite someone can reinforce the idea that you are 'in opposition': meetings, negotiations and brainstorming can perhaps be facilitated if different parties sit side by side rather than face to face. Any controversy about who occupies a 'power seat' – for example, at the head of the table – is thus avoided. North American and North Vietnamese negotiators meeting in Paris in 1968 to negotiate an end to the Vietnam War spent several weeks arguing over the shape of the table before the two sides got down to more substantive matters (see 'Please be seated: chairs, tables and the curious habits of human beings' in chapter 19).

Environment

The physical environment in which we find ourselves can itself be a powerful mode of communication. As Winston Churchill said, 'We shape our buildings; thereafter they shape us'. A North American football coach understood the value of manipulating the environment to maximise his team's performance: at half-time players would rest in blue-painted rooms, but the coach would give his last-minute pep-talks in a smaller room painted in bright colours. The British Labour politician Aneurin Bevan observed that party conferences held in cheerful, bright-coloured rooms were significantly more successful than those held in dingy, depressing rooms. Building architecture, room size and shape, furniture, interior decoration and climate can all communicate strong messages to those who use or visit them.

Time and cultural context

Time and cultural context can also help us to understand nonverbal communication. The study of time use as a form of communication is called **chronemics** (Ballard & Seibold 2006; Turner & Reinsch 2007). Anthropologist Edward T Hall has made a useful distinction between 'high context' and 'low context' cultures. The high-context/low-context model incorporates variables such as chronemics (or the study of time use behaviour), the degree of sensory

Chronemics: the study of time use behaviour in relation to communication

involvement in a situation, the nature of messages sent and how they are sent or concealed in a given situation, and the extent to which identity is formed by affinity with individuals or groups. The context model thus has implications for intercultural communication and intra- and inter-group communication. The chief differences are shown in table 8.2.

TABLE 8.2 High context and low context cultures

	High context	**Low context**
Identification	Group	Individual
Sensory involvement	High (low personal space needs, high-contact touch behaviour)	Low (high personal space needs, low-contact touch behaviour)
Messages	Implicit: embedded in social context: ritual, personal relationships, personal word as guarantee	Explicit: words carry most information (emphasis on legal documents etc.)
Time sense/chronicity	Polychronic: multiple times. Time is circular. Events proceed at their own pace. Multiple events occur simultaneously (e.g. different people in room working on different tasks)	Monochronic. One time only. Time is linear. Events happen sequentially. Punctuality, scheduling, planning very important

Source: Adapted from Hall (1977).

As Hall (1977) explains:

> In some cultures, messages are explicit; the words carry most of the information. In other cultures, such as China or Japan or the Arab cultures, less information is contained in the verbal part of the message, since more is in the context. That's why American businessmen often complain that their Japanese counterparts never get to the point. The Japanese wouldn't dream of spelling the whole thing out... in general, high-context people can get by with less of the legal paperwork that is deemed essential in America. A man's word is his bond, and you need not spell out the details to make him behave...

> The German-Swiss are low-context, falling somewhere near the bottom of the scale. Next, the Germans, then the Scandinavians, as we move up. These cultures are all lower in context than the U.S. Above the Americans come the French, the English, the Italians, the Spanish, the Greeks, and the Arabs. In other words, as you move from Northern to Southern Europe, you will find that people move towards more involvement with each other. (p. 4)

Thus, for example, a German businessman trying to negotiate with a Latin American may not understand why the other person does not ascribe to the same sense of urgency to matters as he has (or indeed why there are other people in the room at the same time, apparently transacting other business). The differences between them are thus not purely a matter of language, but of culture; in particular, they experience quite different senses of time, or chronicity.

People from low-context cultures who want to understand high-context cultures probably need go no further than to talk to their grandparents or to relatives and friends living in country areas. Cultures that are low context now were once quite different: traditionally these communities were more oriented towards groups such as the family, the neighbourhood, the local church; the pace of life was more relaxed and commercial agreements were often based on verbal understandings – that is, they were (apart from factors relating to territorial and touching behaviour) classic high-context cultures. 'Low context' here is almost a code for 'modern urban', and even rural areas of low-context cultures tend to be relatively high-context in a number of ways.

Examples of new insights into context and chronemics are:

- It may be useful to distinguish between *monochrons* (people who prefer work to be structured in linear flows, with a minimum of interruptions) and *polychrons* (people who are happy to work on multiple projects at the same time and who don't get thrown by interruptions).
- Women may be more polychronic than men.
- Monochronic behaviour may be linked to stress-prone Type A behaviour.
- Vietnamese migrants to the United States may be more encouraged to use North American hospitals if a no-appointment, drop-in time zone is set up and if family members are encouraged to attend consultations.
- Chinese managers may make remarkably limited direct use of low-context tools, such as computer-based information systems, and western managers may need to bear this in mind.
- Within broad ethnic groupings, such as 'Asians', there may be significant variations: for example, Koreans may be considerably more low-context than Japanese.
- Southern European polychrons are under pressure to conform to Northern European mono-chronic time usage.

(Hall 1977; Houston 2002; Kaufman-Scarborough & Lindquist 1999; Martinsons & Westwood 1997; Frei, Racicot & Travagline 1999; Thomas 1998; Cunha & Cunha 2004)

Nonverbal applications A: applying the model

Figure 8.1 presented a model of nonverbal communication. Now let's try to apply that model to understanding different situations we might find ourselves in. We will ignore the physiological constant of body structure and use the remaining categories to analyse five behavioural states: respect, liking, hostility, distress and deceit. The brief analysis given in table 8.3 cannot, of course, hope to capture the full complexity of an individual's nonverbal behaviour, and its cultural bias is primarily Euro-American. Nevertheless, you may find it useful to analyse situations you have experienced and will find yourself in. Remember not to jump to conclusions with nonverbal communication: a gesture or posture or other manifestation in isolation may mean nothing. Groups or clusters of behaviours or tells may build up a more predictable picture. If, for example, you find yourself dealing with an individual exhibiting virtually every behaviour in one column of the table, then you can be reasonably sure that you would need no further words to identify and confirm the operation of that unique behavioural state.

TABLE 8.3 Nonverbal characteristics of five behavioural states

Expression	Emotion				
	Respect	Liking	Hostility	Distress	Deceit
Head movements	■ Head bow	■ Rapid nodding ■ Tilt	■ Jaw thrust forward ■ Tilt ■ Shaking of head (in disapproval)	■ Shaking of head (despair)	■ Nodding when saying 'no', shaking when saying 'yes'

(continued)

TABLE 8.3 *(continued)*

Expression	Emotion				
	Respect	**Liking**	**Hostility**	**Distress**	**Deceit**
Facial expression	■ Open expression ■ Mild smile	■ Smiling ■ Moistening lips	■ Scowling ■ Glaring ■ Bared teeth ■ Clenched teeth	■ Anguished expression ■ Rapid swallowing ■ Rapid biting, wetting of lips	■ Asymmetrical expression
Eyes	■ Averted gaze	■ Pupil dilation ■ Wide ■ Narrowing	■ Narrowing ■ Glaring ■ Rolling in disgust ■ Averted gaze	■ Rapid blinking ■ Darting ■ Downcast gaze	■ Rapid blinking ■ Pupil dilation ■ Averted gaze
Voice	■ Deferential tone ■ Silence	■ Higher pitch ■ Deeper pitch ■ Warmer tone	■ Deeper pitch ■ Loud	■ Shaking voice ■ Non-words, repetitions, partial words ■ Stumbling over words ■ Higher pitch ■ Sighs often	■ Shaking voice ■ Non-words, repetitions, partial words ■ Stumbling over words ■ Higher pitch
Gesture	■ Palms out	■ Grooming, preening ■ Mirroring	■ Shaking fist ■ Obscene gestures ■ Crossed arms ■ Hands on hips ■ Pointing finger ■ Picking lint from own clothing	■ Hands around mouth ■ Wringing hands ■ Jiggling legs ■ Feet turned in ■ Crossed arms ■ Fidgeting with adornments	■ Scratching ■ Finger under collar ■ Rapid crossing of legs
Posture	■ Bow ■ Standing at attention	■ Relaxed ■ Mirroring	■ Rigid ■ Shoulders raised	■ Slumped over ■ Rocking body	■ Nothing noticeable
Body movement	■ Sometimes oriented away ■ Synchronised	■ Oriented towards ■ Synchronised	■ Oriented away in disgust ■ Oriented towards in confrontation ■ Unsynchronised	■ Oriented away ■ Unsynchronised	■ Oriented away ■ Nothing noticeable
Touching	■ Touching clothing, feet, hands ■ Allowing oneself to be touched	■ Handshake ■ Hand-holding ■ Caress ■ Patting ■ Embrace ■ Kiss	■ Push ■ Elbow ■ Punch ■ Kick	■ Hand-holding ■ Self-touching	■ Nothing noticeable ■ Feigned liking gestures
Clothing and adornment	■ Imitation	■ Imitation ■ Sexually revealing	■ Rank display ■ Wealth display	■ Disorganised, ungroomed	■ Uncharacteristic clothing, display
Territoriality/ personal space	■ Maintain distance ■ Patient waiting (queues)	■ Come closer	■ Keep distance (disgust) ■ Invasive approach (aggression)	■ Keep distance (shame) ■ Invasive approach (seeking solace)	■ Nothing noticeable ■ Feigned liking gestures

	Emotion				
Expression	Respect	Liking	Hostility	Distress	Deceit
Environment	▪ Subdued colours ▪ Lack of noise	▪ Warm colours ▪ Quiet ▪ Soft furnishings ▪ Attention to physical needs (food, drink)	▪ Harsh colours ▪ Noise ▪ Uncomfortable furnishings ▪ Lack of attention to physical needs	▪ Disorganisation, untidiness	▪ Nothing noticeable
Time and cultural context	▪ Observing local chronicity patterns ▪ Matching time-use style to that of others	▪ Observing local chronicity patterns ▪ Generosity with time ▪ Matching time-use style to that of others	▪ Ignoring local chronicity patterns ▪ Being late ▪ Making people wait ▪ Stinginess with time ▪ Forcing others to adopt alien time style	▪ Confusion about local chronicity patterns ▪ Lateness ▪ Procrastination ▪ 'Hurry sickness'	▪ Nothing noticeable

Nonverbal applications B: becoming less dyssemic

Dyssemia: the condition of having difficulties in understanding or sending nonverbal information

According to Nowicki and Duke (2002), many people have difficulty fitting into social and professional situations because they are in fact **'dyssemic'**– that is, they experience difficulties in understanding or sending nonverbal information.

Dyssemic people, they suggest, tend to behave inappropriately in social situations. For example, they may:

▪ avoid eye contact when walking past people
▪ stare excessively at others
▪ stand too close to people when interacting
▪ spread their materials beyond their personal area when working
▪ speak in a monotone
▪ fail to alter their speech volume to suit the situation they are in
▪ maintain an expressionless face when discussing emotional topics
▪ not smile back when smiled at
▪ not care about their clothing or grooming
▪ persevere in actions or comments regardless of their adverse impact
▪ not check their appearance in mirrors or window reflections
▪ start talking before others have finished
▪ not listen to what others say
▪ arrive late for meetings
▪ finish eating long before or long after others (Nowicki & Duke 2002).

Exhibiting one or two of these behaviour patterns is unlikely to present overwhelming problems, but more than this may indicate that such individuals are socially 'out of synch' (Kranowitz & Silver 1998). If they were to study nonverbal communication in some depth and then try to apply what they have learned, such dyssemic people might find they fit in better with those around them, and experience fewer communication breakdowns, misunderstandings and conflicts (Wocadlo & Rieger 2006).

STUDENT STUDY GUIDE

SUMMARY

In this chapter we considered different aspects of nonverbal communication. Isolated nonverbal behaviours are not necessarily significant, but we may be able to make reasoned inferences about another person's behaviour or state of mind from consistent clusters of such behaviours. Nonverbal communication that is congruent with verbal communication suggests that the two channels of communication are reinforcing each other; where they are not congruent, we may be able to use that incongruence to make inferences about another person's behaviour and state of mind. Nonverbal communication and body language are not the same: body language is an element of nonverbal communication, but it has other aspects. We examined a visual model of nonverbal communication, looking at a number of (not mutually exclusive) categories, such as gesture, posture, body movement, touch, eye contact, paralinguistics, environment and time. We concluded that an understanding of the dynamics of nonverbal communication might offer us useful insights into our own behaviour.

KEY TERMS

backchanneling *p. 261*

chronemics *p. 271*

cluster *p. 256*

congruence *p. 257*

dyssemia *p. 275*

haptics *p. 267*

kinesics *p. 267*

mirroring *p. 267*

paralinguistics *p. 263*

proxemics *p. 270*

tell *p. 256*

REVIEW QUESTIONS

1. What is a cluster, and why is it important for understanding nonverbal communication?
2. What is congruence, and why is it important for understanding nonverbal communication?
3. Define 'backchanneling'.
4. What is meant by a poker face?
5. What is the relationship between synchronisation and mirroring?
6. List and explain three types of nonverbal communication that might suggest a person is lying or being deceitful.
7. List three ways in which a person might assert dominance over others.
8. What is a monochron?

APPLIED ACTIVITIES

1. A friend of yours is about to give a presentation but has not spent much time on researching the content. 'I'm not too worried about facts — a friend told me that people give only about 7 per cent of their attention to any words you use. So I'm spending most of my time in front of a mirror, working on my gestures and delivery.' Write a brief (100-word) memo or email in response to your friend's strategy.
2. Use the recording function on a smartphone or hire/use a traditional video camera for this activity: Working by yourself or with a partner, record (at least ten minutes) of yourself talking, walking, sitting, gesturing. If you are working with a partner, return the favour. If this is difficult, perhaps you can get access to some home movie video footage of yourself. Observe yourself on screen: is the sound and the image what you

expected? If not, why not? Might your observations cause you to change the way you behave? If so, why? If not, why not?

3. Conduct a debate on the topic 'Everyone wears a uniform'.

4. Create a list of at least six other aspects of nonverbal communication that could be perceived to be examples of dyssemia.

5. Select one scene, or several pages of dialogue, from a play script or screenplay. Write two sets of stage directions, specifying two completely different sets of nonverbal communication. Discuss the result with a partner.

6. The federal government has hired your advertising agency to create a television, radio and print advertising campaign. The purpose of the campaign is to sensitise people to becoming more polite in public spaces. Write a television or radio script, or copy for a newspaper/magazine advertisement, trying to persuade people not to conduct loud conversations in public: on mobile or cell phones; in native or non-native languages; in foreign countries using languages not native to those countries.

WHAT WOULD YOU DO?

Luis has transferred to your branch from the South American office, and is now manager of floor operations. He is strikingly handsome and tall, and is athletic in build. He moves quickly and has a deep, resonant voice. To make matters worse, as some of your male friends joke, he is both exceptionally intelligent and highly competent. He is also motivated and has excellent technical skills. You might expect, jokes aside, that many of the males in the building are envious of him.

He has a few personal habits, however, that are beginning to irritate people. He stands very close when talking, and when making a point he will often tap an index finger on the listener's forearm, irrespective of gender. His booming voice makes everyone turn around and look, which can embarrass the person he is talking to. He often simply bursts into people's offices and will go around to their side of the desk, sit on the desk and look intently at them while he is talking. He is also in the habit of making mock bows to a number of the female staff. In talking with staff members about problems, he will sometimes put his arm around their shoulder — again, irrespective of gender — and gesture strongly with his other hand. Your personal assistant, Marie, who is finely tuned at the best of times, has just come into your office and said this to you: 'Look, I'm sure he's well-intentioned, and he has really kicked the productivity figures up, but unless he lays off the touchy-feely stuff, Jen and Lisa and I will make a sexual harassment claim against him!'

What should you do about the situation?

SUGGESTED READING

Anderson, Peter A 2004, *The complete idiot's guide to understanding body language*, Alpha Books, New York.

Beattie, Geoffrey 2011, *Get the edge: see what they're saying: body language tips for a happier life*, Headline Book Publishing, Terra Alta, WV.

Bowden, Mark 2010, *Business body language: control the conversation, command attention, and convey the right message without saying a word*, McGraw-Hill, New York.

Drory, Amos & Zaidman, Nurit 2007, 'Impression management behavior: effects of the organizational system', *Journal of Managerial Psychology*, vol. 22, no. 3, pp. 290–308.

Hartley, Gregory & Karinch 2010, *The body language handbook: how to read everyone's hidden thoughts and intentions*, Career Press, Franklin Lakes, NJ.

Manusov, Valerie & Patterson, Miles, L 2006, *The Sage handbook of nonverbal communication*, Sage, Thousand Oaks, CA.

Richmond, Virginia Peck, McCroskey, James C & Hickson, Mark L 2011, *Nonverbal behaviour in interpersonal relations*, 7th edn, Allyn & Bacon, Boston, MA.

REFERENCES

Argyle, Michael 1999, *The psychology of interpersonal behaviour*, 5th edn, Penguin, London.

Austin, Michael 2011, *Useful fictions: evolution, anxiety, and the origins of literature*, University of Nebraska Press, Lincoln, NE.

Axtell, Roger 1998, *Gestures: the do's and taboos of body language around the world*, rev. edn, John Wiley & Sons, New York.

Ballard, Dawna I & Seibold, David R 2006, 'The experience of time at work: relationship to communication load, job satisfaction, and interdepartmental communication', *Communication Studies*, vol. 57, no. 3, pp. 317–40.

Barnard, Malcolm 2002, *Fashion as communication*, 2nd edn, Routledge, London.

Barash, David P & Barash, Nanelle R 2005, *Madame Bovary's ovarie: a Darwinian look at literature*, Delacorte/Random House, New York.

Bavelas, Janet Beavin, Coates, Linda & Johnson, Trudy 2002, 'Listener responses as a collaborative process: the role of gaze', *Journal of Communication*, vol. 52, pp. 562–80.

Bell, Arthur H 1999, 'Using nonverbal cues', *Incentive*, vol. 173, no. 9, pp. 162–6.

Boyd, Brian, Carroll, Joseph & Gottschall, Jonathan (eds.) 2010, *Evolution, literature and film: a reader*, Columbia University Press, New York, NY.

Brain, Marshall 1997, *The teenager's guide to the real world*, BYG Publishing, New York.

Burgoon, Judee K, Buller, David B & Goodall, W Gill 1995, *Nonverbal communications: the unspoken dialogue*, McGraw-Hill, New York.

Buss, David M 2003, *The evolution of desire: strategies of human mating*, Basic Books, New York.

Canetti, Elias 2000 [1960], *Crowds and power*, Weidenfeld & Nicolson, London.

Carroll, Joseph 2005, *Literary Darwinism: evolution, human nature, and literature*, Routledge, London/New York.

Carroll, Sean T, Riffenbergh, Robert H, Roberts, Timothy A & Myhre, Elizabeth B 2002, 'Tattoos and body piercings as indicators of adolescent risk-taking behaviors', *Pediatrics*, vol. 109, no. 6, pp. 1021–7.

Carter, JE Lindsay & Heath, Barbara Honeyman 2003, *Somatotyping: development and applications*, Cambridge University Press, Cambridge, UK.

Carton, John S & Carton, Erin ER 1998, 'Nonverbal maternal warmth and children's locus of control', *Journal of Nonverbal Behavior*, vol. 22, no. 1, pp. 77–87.

Chiu, RK & Babcock, RD 2002, 'The relative importance of facial attractiveness and gender in Hong Kong selection decisions', *International Journal of Human Resource Management*, vol. 13, no. 1, pp. 141–55.

Chopra, Deepak 2001, *Perfect health: the complete mind body guide*, Three Rivers Press/Crown, New York.

Crane, Diana 2001, *Fashion and its social agendas: class, gender and identity in clothing*, University of Chicago Press, Chicago, IL.

Cunha, Miguel Pina E & Cunha, Rita Campos E 2004, 'Changing a cultural grammar? The pressure towards the adoption of "northern time" by southern European managers', *Journal of Managerial Psychology*, vol. 19, no. 8, pp. 795–808.

Crystal, David 1992, 'The changing English language, NELLE Newsletter, vol. 2, no. 1, Reprinted in LEND: lingua e nuova didattica, 21, pp 13–17, www.davidcrystal.com.

Dawkins, Richard 2006 *The Selfish Gene*, 3rd edn., Oxford University Press, New York/London.

Darwin, Charles 2002 [1872], *The expression of the emotions in man and animals*, 3rd edn, ed. Paul, Ekman, Oxford University Press, Oxford, UK.

Dickson, David & Hargie, Owen 2003, *Skilled interpersonal communication: research, theory and practice*, Routledge, London.

Dunbar, Norah E & Burgoon, Judee K 2005, 'Perceptions of power and interactional dominance in interpersonal relationships', *Journal of Social and Personal Relationships*, vol. 22, no. 2, pp. 207–33.

Dunbar, Robin 1998, *Grooming, gossip and the evolution of language*, Harvard University Press, Harvard, CT.

Eibl-Eibesfeldt, Irenaus 2007, *Human ethology*, Aldine Transaction, Piscataway, NJ.

Ekman, Paul 2001, *Telling lies: clues to deceit in the marketplace, politics and marriage*, 3rd edn, WW Norton, New York.

—— 2003, *Emotions revealed: faces and feelings to improve communication and emotional life*, Times Books, New York.

Etcoff, Nancy 2000, *Survival of the prettiest*, Anchor, New York.

Fast, Julius 2002, *Body language*, rev. edn, M Evans & Co., New York.

Field, Tiffany 2002, *Touch*, MIT Press, Boston, MA.

Fisher, Helen E 1992, *The anatomy of love: the natural history of monogamy, adultery and divorce*, Norton, New York.

—— 2009, *Why him? Why her? Finding real love by understanding your personality type*, Henry Holt, New York.

Frei, RL, Racicot, B & Travagline, A 1999, 'The impact of monochronic and Type A behavior patterns on research productivity and stress', *Journal of Managerial Psychology*, vol. 14, no. 5, pp. 37–8.

Geary, David C 2004, *The origin of mind: evolution of brain, cognition and general intelligence*, American Psychological Association, Washington, DC.

Gibson, Kyle 2009, 'Differential parental investment in families with both adopted and genetic children', *Evolution and Human Behavior*, vol. 30, pp. 184–9.

Gottschall, Jonathan & Sloan Wilson, David 1995, *The literary Animal: evolution and the nature of narrative*, Northwestern University Press, Evanston, Ill.

Grammer, Karl, Kruck, Kirsten & Magnusson, Magnus S 1998, 'The courtship dance: patterns of nonverbal synchronization in opposite-sex encounters', *Journal of Nonverbal Behavior*, vol. 22, no. 1, pp. 3–29.

Guthrie, R Dale 1976, *Body hot spots: the anatomy of human social organs and behavior*, Van Nostrand Reinhold, New York. http://employees.csbsju.edu.

Hall, Edward T 1977, *Beyond culture*, Doubleday, New York.

—— 1996, *The dance of life: the other dimension of time*, Peter Smith, New York.

Hazard, Mary E 2000, *Elizabethan silent language*, University of Nebraska Press, Lincoln, NE.

Henley, Nancy 1986, *Body politics: power, sex and nonverbal communication*, Prentice Hall, Englewood Cliffs, NJ.

—— 2002, 'Response and afterword: body politics, psychology and oppression', *Feminism & Psychology*, vol. 12, no. 3, pp. 335–8.

Hickson, Mark L, Stacks, Don W & Moore, Nina-Jo 2004, *Nonverbal communication: studies and applications*, 4th edn, Roxbury, Los Angeles.

Hochschild, Arlie 2003, *The managed heart: commercialization of human feeling*, 20th anniversary edn, University of California Press, Berkeley, CA.

Hostetter, Autumn B & Alibali, Martha W 2007, 'Raise your hand if you're spatial: relations between verbal and spatial skills and gesture production', *Gesture*, vol. 7, no. 1, pp. 73–95.

Houston, H Rika 2002, 'Health care and the silent language of Vietnamese immigrant consumers', *Business Communication Quarterly*, vol. 65, no. 1, pp. 37–47.

Johnson, Kerry L 1988, 'The touch of persuasion', *Broker World*, April.

Jones, Stanley E & LeBaron, Curtis D 2002, 'Research on the relationship between verbal and nonverbal communication: emerging integrations', *Journal of Communication*, vol. 52, pp. 499–521.

Kaufman-Scarborough, C & Lindquist, JD 1999, 'Time management and polychronicity: comparisons, contrasts and insights for the workplace', *Journal of Managerial Psychology*, vol. 14, no. 34, pp. 28–51.

Kendon, Adam 2005, *Gesture: visible action as utterance*, Cambridge University Press, Cambridge.

Killian, Caitlin 2003, 'The other side of the veil: North African women in France respond to the headscarf affair', *Gender and Society*, vol. 17, no. 4, pp. 567–90.

Kjellmer, Göran 2009, 'Where do we backchannel? On the use of mm,mhm, uh huh and such like', *International Journal of Corpus Linguistics*, vol. 14, no. 1, pp. 81–112.

Knapp, Mark L & Hall, Judith A 2010, *Nonverbal Communication in human interaction*, 7th edn, Wadsworth, Florence, KY.

Kneidlinger, Linda M, Maple, Terry L & Tross, Stuart A 2001, 'Touching behavior in sport: functional components, analysis of sex differences, and ethological considerations', *Journal of Nonverbal Behavior*, vol. 25, no. 1, pp. 43–62.

Korte, Barbara 1997, *Body language in literature*, University of Toronto Press, Toronto.

Kranowitz, Carol Stock & Silver, Larry B 1998, *The out-of-sync child: recognizing and coping with sensory integration dysfunction*, Perigee, New York.

Krumhuber, Eva, Manstead, SR & Kappas, Arvid 2007, 'Temporal aspects of facial displays in person and expression perception: the effects of smile dynamics, head-tilt, and gender', *Journal of Nonverbal Behavior*, vol. 31. no. 1, pp. 39–56.

Lakin, Jessica L, Jefferis, Valerie E, Cheng, Clara Michelle & Chartrand, Tanya L 2003, 'The chameleon effect as social glue: evidence for the evolutionary significance of nonconscious mimicry', *Journal of Nonverbal Behavior*, vol. 27, no. 3, pp. 145–62.

Latteier, Carolyn 1998, *Breasts: the women's perspective on an American obsession*, Haworth Press, Binghamton, NY.

Leathers, Dale G 1997, *Successful nonverbal communication: principles and applications*, 3rd edn, Allyn & Bacon, Boston, MA.

McLarney, Ellen 2009, 'The Burqua in vogue: fashioning Afghanistan', *Journal of Middle East Women's Studies*, vol. 5, no. 1, pp. 1–20.

McKinnon, Susan 2005, *Neo-liberal genetics: the myths and moral tales of evolutionary psychology*, Prickly Paradigm Press, Chicago.

McPherson, William 1997, '"Dressing down" in the business curriculum', *Business Communication Quarterly*, vol. 60, no. 1, pp. 134–46.

Malandro, Loretta A, Barker, Deborah Ann & Barker, Larry Lee 1988, *Nonverbal communication*, 2nd edn, McGraw-Hill, New York.

Mallott, Richard W 2007, 'Opinion: notes from a radical behaviorist: Are women, people of color, Asians and southern Europeans inherently inferior to North-European males? A history of biological determinism – a cultural, spiritual, and intellectual disgrace – and the implications for understanding "mental illness", *Behavior and Social Issues*, vol. 16, pp. 134–69.

Martinsons, Maris G & Westwood, Robert L 1997, 'Management information systems in the Chinese business culture: an explanatory theory', *Information and Management*, vol. 32, pp. 215–30.

Mehrabian, Albert 1971, *Silent messages*, Wadsworth, Belmont, CA.

Mick, David Glen & Oswald, Laura R 2007, 'The semiotic paradigm on meaning in the marketplace', in Belk, Russell W (ed.), *Handbook of Qualitative Research Methods in Marketing*, Edward Elgar Publishing, London.

Montagu, Ashley 1986, *Touching: the human significance of the skin*, 3rd edn, Harper, New York.

Morris, Desmond 1998, *Ilustrated dogwatching*, Ebury Press, London.

—— 2002, *Peoplewatching: the Desmond Morris guide to body language*, Vintage, London.

—— 2005, *The naked woman: a study of the female body*, Thomas Dunne Books/St Martin's Press, New York.

Navarro, Joe 2011, *200 poker tells* (Kindle edition), Amazon Digital Services, Seattle, WA.

Navarro, Joe & Marvin, Karlins 2008, *What every body is saying: an ex-FBI agent's guide to speed-reading people*, HarperCollins, New York.

Nowicki, Stephen, Jr & Duke, Marshall 2002, *Will I ever fit in? The breakthrough program for conquering adult dyssemia. How to stop misunderstanding other people and learn to read and send signals vital to relationship success*, The Free Press, New York.

Oestrich, Herb 1999, 'Let's dump the 55%, 38%, 7% rule', *Transitions*, vol. 7, no. 2, pp. 11–14.

Pease, Allan & Pease, Barbara 2006, *The definitive book of body language*, Bantam, New York.

Pinker, Stephen 2003, *Blank slate: the modern denial of human nature*, Penguin, New York.

Portch, Stephen 1985, *Literature's silent language*, Peter Lang, New York.

Poyatos, Fernando 2002, *Nonverbal communication across disciplines. Vol. 1: culture, sensory interaction, conversation*, John Benajamins, Amsterdam.

Rafter, Nicole 2008, *The Criminal Brain*, New York University Press, Washington Square, New York.

Remland, Martin S 2000, *Nonverbal communication in everyday life*, Houghton Mifflin, Boston, MA.

Reuter, Donald 2002, *Gaydar: the ultimate insider guide to the gay sixth sense*, Crown Publishers, New York.

Scheflen, Albert E 1972, *Body language and the social order: communication as social control*, Prentice Hall, Englewood Cliffs, NJ.

Sheldrake, Rupert 2005, 'The sense of being stared at – Part 1: is it real or illusory?' *Journal of Consciousness Studies*, vol. 12, no. 6, pp. 10–31.

Shelp, Scott 2002, 'Gaydar: visual detection of sexual orientation among gay and straight men', *Journal of Homosexuality*, vol. 44, no.1, pp. 1–14.

Simington, Jane A 1993, 'The elderly require a "special touch"', *Nursing Homes*, April.

Smith, Mable H 2003, 'Body adornment – know the limits', *Nursing Management*, vol. 34, no. 2, pp. 22–3.

Smith, Stephen D 1998, 'Dress for success: are you compromising your credibility?' *Professional Safety*, vol. 43, no. 2, pp. 34–6.

Spence, Patric R, Westerman, David, Skalski, Paul D, Seeger, Matthew, Ulmer, Robert R, Venette, Steve & Sellnow, Timothy L 2005, 'Proxemic effects on information seeking after the September 11 attacks', *Communication Research Reports*, vol. 22, no. 1, pp. 39–46.

Tabensky, A 2002, 'Gesture and speech rephrasings in conversation', *Gesture*, vol. 1, no. 2, pp. 213–36.

Thomas, Jane 1998, 'Contexting Koreans: does the high/low model work?' *Business Communication Quarterly*, vol. 61, no. 4, pp. 9–26.

Thornhill, Randy & Gangestad, Steven W 1999, 'The scent of symmetry: a human sex pheromone that signals fitness?' *Evolution and Human Behavior*, vol. 20, no. 3, pp. 175–201.

Turner, Jeanine Warisse & Reinsch, N Lamar Jr 2007, 'The business communicator as presence allocator: multicommunicating, equivocality, and status at work', *Journal of Business Communication*, vol. 44, no. 1, pp. 36–58.

'US companies averse to "dress down" Friday' 1995, *Management Accounting*, July/August, vol. 73, issue 7, p. 70.

Wagner, Melissa & Armstrong, Nancy 2003, *Field guide to gestures*, Quirk Books, Philadelphia, PA.

Warhurst, Chris, Van den, Broek & Hall, Richard 2009, 'Lookism: the new frontier of employment discrimination?' *Journal of Industrial Relations*, vol. 51, no.1. pp. 131–6.

Wocadlo, Crista & Rieger, Ingrid 2006, 'Social skills and nonverbal decoding of emotions in very preterm children at early school age', *European Journal of Developmental Psychology*, vol. 3, no. 1, pp. 48–70.

Woolery, Lisa M 2007, 'Gaydar: a social cognitive analysis', *Journal of Homosexuality*, vol. 53, no. 3, pp. 9–17.

Wright, Robert 1995 *The moral animal: evolutionary psychology and everyday life*, Vintage, New York.

Wyatt, Tristram D 2003, *Pheromones and animal behaviour: communication by smell and taste*, Cambridge University Press, Cambridge, UK.

9

Interpersonal skills 1: emotional intelligence, self-talk and assertiveness

LEARNING OBJECTIVES

After studying this chapter you should be able to:

- Explain the concepts of emotional intelligence and emotional competence
- Identify various examples of negative and positive self-talk
- Describe a range of assertive behaviours
- Understand and use a range of assertive verbal skills
- Understand the cooperative principle and apply the Gricean Maxims in verbal communication exchanges

Interpersonal and intrapersonal skills: enlightenment, psychobabble or somewhere in between?

Interpersonal communication skills: processes that help, distort or block communication of messages between individuals

Intrapersonal communication skills: processes that help, distort or block communication messages within an individual

This is the first of two chapters examining interpersonal skills. In this chapter we will discuss emotional intelligence, intrapersonal communication or self-talk, and assertiveness. In the next chapter we will look at listening, questioning, reframing, feedback skills and the Johari Window tool of communication. **Interpersonal communication skills** are processes that help, but sometimes also distort or block, the communication of messages *between* individuals. **Intrapersonal communication skills** are processes that help, but sometimes also distort or block, communication messages within an individual.

These levels, as we have seen or will see, are part of a total system of communication. The field of communication is rapidly growing; its breadth is suggested by the many topics treated in this book. It draws from many older disciplines, such as psychology, sociology, anthropology, economics and linguistics. A search of 'communication' or 'interpersonal communication' in a library catalogue or online bookstore will unearth a range of texts that run the gamut from serious, arcane research scholarship to superficial and trite self-help books. This is not to say, however, that wisdom is only found in the former. Examining the trite and superficial can help us. It can give us a negative model of learning, so that we learn what best to avoid. It may also contain useful information, the value of which will emerge only with the passage of time and the benefit of hindsight.

Interpersonal and intrapersonal communication skills are both important within a person's total system of communication, and are relied upon in various contexts and settings.

Psychobabble: superficial and banal treatments of psychological theory

We need to be on our guard, however, against what has been called **psychobabble**, the superficial and banal treatments of psychology made popular in many self-help books (Rosen 1977; Tavris 2011). For example, self-esteem, which has been a central concept of social science for several decades, refers to feelings of self-worth and confidence – perceptions most people would agree are worthy of cultivation in all human beings. Critics of the concept, however, assert that it has been improperly reconceptualised as a panacea for all human ills, and its absence associated with all human shortcomings. This, they suggest, has led to undesirable outcomes such as a broad 'culture of narcissism' or 'cult of self-worship' throughout society, a 'dumbing down' of education (with some students being insulated from the real world of standards because of a fear that their 'self-esteem' might be damaged if they are permitted to fail), unrealistic expectations among students about the future world of work, and even a misunderstanding of criminal behaviour (some criminals may have unrealistically high rather than low self-esteem) (Lasch 1979; Rieff 1987; Vitz 1994; Dalrymple 1999; Stout 2001; Smith 2002; Twenge 2009).

Emotional intelligence (and other intelligences)

Intelligence is conventionally linked to the ability to solve logical problems, measured by standard IQ (intelligence quotient) tests (Sternberg & Prestz 2004). In the past few decades, however, models of intelligence have emerged that go beyond the purely logical. For example, Gardner (2000; Jie-Qi, Moran & Gardner 2009) proposes that there are multiple intelligences, including:

- logical–mathematical intelligence
- musical intelligence
- linguistic intelligence
- bodily–kinesthetic intelligence
- spatial intelligence
- interpersonal intelligence
- intrapersonal intelligence
- natural intelligence
- spiritual–existential intelligence.

Emotional intelligence: a person's basic underlying capability to recognise and use emotion to better communicate with others

Salovey and Mayer (1990) first proposed the concept of **emotional intelligence** (EI) in 1990, since which there has been considerable interest expressed in the idea (e.g. DuBrin 2008; Qualter, Gardner & Whitely 2007; Bar-On & Parker 2000; Goleman 1998; Matthews, Zeidner & Roberts 2003; Orme & Langhorn 2003; Singh 2003; Murphy 2006; Weisinger 1998; Bradbury & Greaves 2009).

Intelligence or competence?

There are some questions associated with the concept of EI. For example, is it inborn, and therefore unchangeable, or can it be manipulated – in other words, can we improve our EI? Also, can it be measured, in the way that IQ can be measured? These issues in turn raise further questions. One approach taken to working around such unresolved issues is to make a case for **emotional competency**, which can be broken down further into specific competencies (Goleman 1998; Gowing 2001). According to Gowing, '*Emotional intelligence* refers to a person's basic underlying capability to recognize and use emotion ... *Emotional competence* describes the personal and social skills that lead to superior performance in the world of work' (2001, p. 85).

Emotional competency: describes the personal and social skills that lead to superior performance in the world of work

Emotional competencies can be grouped into personal competencies (how we manage ourselves) and social competencies (how we manage our relations with others) (figure 9.1).

PERSONAL COMPETENCE: HOW WE MANAGE OURSELVES		
A. *Self-awareness:* knowing one's internal states, impulses and resources	**B.** *Self-regulation:* managing one's internal states, impulses and resources	**C.** *Motivation:* emotional tendencies that guide or facilitate achievement of goals
■ A1. *Emotional awareness:* recognising one's emotions and their effects ■ A2. *Accurate self-assessment:* knowing one's strengths and limits ■ A3. *Self-confidence:* one's sense of self-worth and capabilities	■ B1. *Self-control:* keeping disruptive emotions and impulses in check ■ B2. *Trustworthiness:* maintaining standards of honesty and integrity ■ B3. *Conscientiousness:* taking responsibility for personal performance ■ B4. *Adaptability:* flexibility in handling change ■ B5. *Innovation:* being comfortable with novel ideas and approaches	■ C1. *Achievement drive:* striving to meet or to improve a standard of excellence ■ C2. *Commitment:* aligning with the goals of the group or organisation ■ C3. *Initiative:* readiness to act on opportunities ■ C4. *Optimism:* persistence in pursuing goals despite obstacles and setbacks
SOCIAL COMPETENCE: HOW WE MANAGE RELATIONSHIPS WITH OTHERS		
D. *Empathy:* awareness of others' feelings, needs and concerns	**E.** *Social skills:* adeptness at inducing desirable responses in others	
D1. *Understanding others:* sensing others' feelings and perspectives, and taking an active interest in their concerns D2. *Developing others:* sensing others' development needs and bolstering their abilities D3. *Service orientation:* anticipating, recognising and meeting customers' needs D4. *Leveraging diversity:* cultivating opportunities through different kinds of people D5. *Political awareness:* reading a group's emotional currents and power relations	E1. *Influence:* employing effective tactics for persuasion E2. *Communication:* listening openly and sending convincing messages E3. *Conflict management:* negotiating and resolving disagreements E4. *Leadership:* inspiring and guiding individuals and groups E5. *Change catalyst:* initiating or managing change E6. *Building bonds:* nurturing instrumental relationships E7. *Collaboration and cooperation:* working with others towards shared goals E8. *Team capabilities:* creating group synergy in pursuing collective goals	

FIGURE 9.1 Emotional competencies as a basis for emotional intelligence

Sources: Adapted from Goleman (1998); Gowing (2001, pp. 88–9).

Looking at the competencies listed, we can see that in a real sense much of this book is about emotional intelligence, or emotional competence, dealing as it does with listening, conflict management and negotiation, group and team dynamics, working with customers, persuasion, diversity and intercultural communication. The applied or practical nature of emotional intelligence or competency is thus apparent. As one writer explains:

> emotional intelligence is the intelligent use of emotions: you intentionally make your emotions work for you by using them to help guide your behavior and thinking in ways that enhance your result.

> Let's say you have an important presentation to give and your self-awareness (a component of emotional intelligence) has pointed out to you that you're feeling extremely anxious. Your emotional intelligence then leads you to undertake a number of actions: you might take charge of any destructive thoughts; use relaxation to diminish your arousal; and cease any counterproductive behaviors, such as pacing about the room. In so doing, you reduce your anxiety sufficiently so that you can confidently make your presentation.

Applications of emotional intelligence in the workplace are almost infinite. Emotional intelligence is instrumental in resolving a sticky problem with a coworker, closing a deal with a difficult customer, criticizing your boss, staying on top of a task until it is completed, and in many other challenges affecting your success. Emotional intelligence is used both intrapersonally (helping yourself) and interpersonally (helping others). (Weisinger 1998, pp. xvi–xvii)

Emotional intelligence: problems and solutions

Emotional intelligence has been described as an indispensable suite of skills and abilities with real and immediate practical payoffs: 'IQ gets you hired, but EQ gets you promoted' (quoted in Matthews, Zeidner & Roberts 2003; see also Kappesser 2009). Yet the evidence on this is still limited, tending to the anecdotal or impressionistic, with only weak statistical clout: 'It is simply false to say that studies show that EQ is more predictive of real-life success than IQ …' (Zeidner, Matthews & Roberts 2009, p. 32). The testing of emotional intelligence (how do you measure it?) is still at a basic level, and much needs to be done to firm up some of the concepts (Grubb & McDaniel 2007; Conte & Dean 2006). There is contradictory evidence as to whether EI is solely a western cultural concept or whether it is universal (Suliman & Al-Shaikh 2007; Leung 2005), and allegations persist that EI is still an immature construct that has been prematurely adopted as just another management fad (Hogan & Stokes 2006). The ongoing turbulent state of emotional intelligence research and application has been well summed up by Sternberg:

> The positive side [of the emotional intelligence movement] is that it helps broaden our concept of intelligence and gets us away from the common fixation on IQ-based or IQ-related measures. The negative side of the movement is that it is often crass, profit-driven and socially and scientifically irresponsible. The same people who criticize the conventional psychometric testers for potentially making a mess out of the lives of people who have potential but do not score well on conventional tests do much worse in promoting what, for the most part, are largely unvalidated or poorly validated tests of emotional intelligence. (Sternberg 2003, p. xii)

Some of the fundamental ideas also present problems. For example, is commitment and alignment to group or organisational goals necessarily a desirable or wise behaviour? Might it not sometimes indicate an unwillingness or inability to challenge a coercive consensus or groupthink pattern in a group?

Broader ethical questions may need to be considered to expand the concept of EI. For example, the competencies listed in figure 9.1 on the previous page might as easily apply to a member of a criminal gang or terrorist cell as to an ethical person working in a legitimate organisation.

Learning and manipulation problem: knowledge of human nature may be used equally to enhance communication and as a tool of manipulation

There is also the **learning and manipulation problem**. The more successful we become in identifying subtle aspects of human communication (emotional intelligence, nonverbal communication, negotiation skills, listening skills and so on), the more likely we are to become better communicators; the same knowledge, however, can also be used for unethical and manipulative ends.

French writer and diplomat Jean Giradoux is perhaps most famous for his cynical maxim: 'The secret of success is sincerity. Once you can fake that you've got it made.' If we substitute 'emotional intelligence' for 'sincerity', the manipulation problem comes into sharper focus.

In spite of these problems, EI seems to have much to offer. At the very least, it gives us a context in which to describe the soft, interpersonal, transferable and communication skills that are increasingly seen as the key to both employment and personal success – reinforcing the point that soft skills have hard payoffs. Emotional intelligence is clearly highly prized by employers, and is an important lifelong skill that can be useful in many different contexts.

EI QUESTIONNAIRE

Complete the questionnaire, and then score your results. Remember, emotional intelligence is still a work in progress, and such scores are suggestive rather than scientifically precise.

		Strongly agree	Agree	Neutral	Disagree	Strongly disagree	SCORE
1	I am always fully aware of my emotions and the effect they have on me and others.	5	4	3	2	1	
2	I am not very good at knowing my strengths and limits.	1	2	3	4	5	
3	I have a strong sense of my self-worth and capabilities.	5	4	3	2	1	
4	I am good at keeping disruptive emotions and impulses in check.	5	4	3	2	1	
5	My standards of honesty and integrity are not as high as they could be.	1	2	3	4	5	
6	I always take complete responsibility for my personal performance in my life.	5	4	3	2	1	
7	I am not very flexible when confronted with change.	1	2	3	4	5	
8	New ideas and approaches to things and new information make me uncomfortable.	1	2	3	4	5	
9	I always strive to improve or to meet a standard of excellence.	5	4	3	2	1	
10	My personal goals are usually the same as those of my group or organisation.	5	4	3	2	1	
11	I get stressed if I take initiatives or act on opportunities.	1	2	3	4	5	
12	If I meet obstacles when pursuing goals, I find it easier just to give up.	1	2	3	4	5	

		Strongly agree	Agree	Neutral	Disagree	Strongly disagree	SCORE
13	I am good at sensing the feelings and perspectives of other people.	5	4	3	2	1	
14	I am not very good at working out when others need professional development.	1	2	3	4	5	
15	I am good at anticipating, recognising and meeting the needs of our customers.	5	4	3	2	1	
16	When I meet people different from me, I regard this as an opportunity, not a problem.	5	4	3	2	1	
17	I am hopeless at reading the emotional currents and power relations in groups.	1	2	3	4	5	
18	I am good at influencing and persuading people.	5	4	3	2	1	
19	I am not a good listener, and am also not good at sending convincing messages.	1	2	3	4	5	
20	I have had some success as a negotiator and in resolving disagreements.	5	4	3	2	1	
21	I don't think I could inspire or guide any individual or group.	1	2	3	4	5	
22	I am quite comfortable when I need to initiate or manage change.	5	4	3	2	1	
23	I am good at building relationships with people in professional settings.	5	4	3	2	1	
24	I am not very good at working with others towards shared goals.	1	2	3	4	5	
25	I can work as a team player, and can help others do the same.	5	4	3	2	1	
TOTAL SCORE							

(continued)

(continued)

This score ...	suggests you may have ...
101–125	Excellent EI
76–100	Good EI
51–75	Average EI
26–50	Weak EI
0–24	Very weak EI

Intrapersonal communication: self-talk

This chapter is primarily concerned with interpersonal communication – the types of communication that take place between individuals. But beneath this there may be a level of communication we each have with ourselves. There are some problems with the concept of intrapersonal communication. Firstly, we are considering here the totality of human experience rather than only people with medical conditions such as multiple personality syndrome. Secondly, how can such internal communication be measured?

In spite of such conundrums, the notion of intrapersonal communication remains an intriguing one. Schools of psychology such as psychoanalysis, with its consideration of ego defence mechanisms, and rational-emotive therapy (RET) or cognitive behavioural therapy (CBT), which analyses styles of distorted thinking, have delved deep in this area (Frosh 2003; Ellis 2001).

The idea of self-talk, or the conversations we have with ourselves, is applicable in many different settings. Just as elite sportspeople might benefit from establishing constructive thought patterns, so too might amateur sportspeople, such as this goalkeeper, benefit from reinforcing positive thoughts.

Self-talk: internal conversations we have with ourselves; a form of intrapersonal communication

The idea of **self-talk**, or the conversations we have with ourselves, has been used in speech therapy, sports training and motivation, and self-motivation through affirmations (Depape et al. 2006; Gammage, Hardy & Craig 2001; Hay 2004). Ostrow (2003) suggests that when we send negative and destructive messages to ourselves, we are addressing ourselves in a manner we simply would not tolerate from others.

Brinthaupt, Hein and Kramer (2009) suggest that there are four types of self-talk or conversations that we have with ourselves:

1. *Self-criticism.* For example, 'I should have done something differently – I'm really upset with myself'.
2. *Self-reinforcement.* For example, 'Something good has happened to me; I'm proud of something I've done'.
3. *Self-management.* For example, 'I need to figure out what to do or say and I'm giving myself instructions or directions about what I should do or say'.
4. *Social assessment.* For example, 'I try to anticipate what someone will say and how I'll respond to him or her'.

The self-talk literature has taken off in the past few years, suggesting that it's all about positive thinking making for success. But it may not be that simple: Heerey and Kring (2007) found that socially anxious individuals had negative self-talk (see table 9.1), while Hardy (2006) found that in sports, positive self-talk was by no means a guarantee of success. There is also the tricky methodological question of how to measure someone's self-talk.

You will remain the best judge of whether self-talk plays a significant role in your life.

An intrapersonal–interpersonal connection?

We might also consider the possible relationships between intrapersonal communication and interpersonal communication. Is it possible, for example, for an individual with predominantly negative self-talk patterns to adopt these patterns in her or his dealings with other people? Might, for example, the problems of a marriage in trouble or a low-performing work team be exacerbated by the negative self-talk of one or more individuals involved?

Similarly, might personal and professional relationships be made more effective and satisfying if one or more individuals involved practised more positive self-talk? Sporting coaches would give a resounding 'yes' to the last question, as they have for the past few decades been working on self-talk and group exhortation as mutually reinforcing strategies for boosting the performance of sporting teams. The sport and real world connection is not always clear-cut, of course, but the comparison is interesting and should not be dismissed out of hand.

TABLE 9.1 Types of self-talk

Self-talk pattern	Positive or negative?	Dynamic	Example
1A. Fallacy of change	(−)	You want to change others, even if they do not want to change. You impose high standards on others and become frustrated when they resist.	'I know he's hopeless, and he has so many appalling habits, but I know once we're married I'll be able to turn him into a real gentleman.'
1B. Achievable differences	(+)	You realistically assess the capacity of others to change, and perhaps challenge your own need to control others. Others will follow examples before orders.	'He's not perfect, and neither am I, but some things about him really worry me. I'll go into this marriage with eyes wide open, and with lots of love. But if he repeats some of his behaviour patterns frequently, I'm already gone.'
2A. Catastrophising	(−)	For you, all molehills become mountains: even routine problems seem overwhelming and insoluble.	'Oh no, I've lost my notes for the meeting . . . they'll all laugh at me . . . and that email didn't go through to Roger . . . he'll be furious . . . and I've probably missed all the best desserts in the café by now . . . why does this always happen to me?'
2B. Reality testing	(−)	You react to problems on their own terms, without panicking, trying to find short-term and permanent solutions.	'Oh no, I've lost my notes for the meeting . . . but I've still got half an hour . . . they might turn up in this mess, but I'll just jot down a few points now . . . hmm . . . that email to Roger hasn't gone through . . . better separate the attachments into separate emails and resend . . . this disorganisation is bad news . . . better stay back for an hour tonight and impose a bit of chaos control . . .'
3A. Shoulds	(−)	You feel that reality is constructed according to absolute standards, and we have no choice but to observe those standards. You tend to give sermons rather than advice.	'This is the second time that Daphne's report has been sloppy. She must not let this happen again. She simply has to take more care. She ought to see how this is just not good enough. I shouldn't roar at her in the open plan office, but I have no choice. She must shape up.'
3B. Flexible response	(+)	You judge each case on its merits, responding adaptively to situations and people, without walking away from judgement and consequences where necessary. You lead; you don't lecture.	'This is the second time that Daphne's report has been sloppy. I think I'll get her in and read her a gentle riot act. I'm not happy with this, and I presume she isn't either. I'll point out to her that if there's a problem, she can come to me before it gets any bigger.'

(continued)

TABLE 9.1 *(continued)*

Self-talk pattern	Positive or negative?	Dynamic	Example
4A. Denial	(−)	You refuse to face realities, preferring escapism and procrastination. You excel at lying to yourself.	'I don't need to see the dentist just now. That pain really doesn't bother me, and it will go away.'
4B. Confrontation	(+)	You are willing to face up to realities, even painful ones, and try to change them before they change you.	That pain in my tooth is quite bad. It may go away temporarily, but it's obviously a warning, I don't like it, but I'd better ring the dentist and make an appointment.
5A. Rationalisation	(−)	You invent reasons for doing something that you wanted to do anyway, making excuses for the inexcusable.	'I'll just steal some paper from the storeroom when Madge isn't looking. Everyone does it, so it's OK. No-one ever gets caught.'
5B. Thinking through	(+)	You resist the temptation to fabricate pretexts for unethical actions in order to minimise regrets.	'I really need some paper, and there's a whole storeroom full of it just over there, but I'd better not swipe it. I've seen Simon pinch some, but it's not right, and if I get caught it could do me a lot of damage with my next appraisal.'
6A. Fantasy	(−)	You cannot cope with unpleasant realities, and prefer to escape to a world of make-believe; not always harmful, but harmful often enough.	'Jack really wiped me out in that meeting today . . . he made me look a fool . . . yeah, but . . . in another world . . . I would have rebutted him . . . brought in that data I forgot to check . . . that'd fix him . . . and I would have looked more confident . . . and then I'd tell a brilliant joke to put him down . . . and now everyone's laughing with me, and at him . . . yeah . . .'
6B. Truth	(+)	Instead of dreaming your life away, you face facts and solve problems, learning from your mistakes.	'Jack really wiped me out in that meeting today . . . he made me look a fool . . . I'll be better prepared for next week's meeting, and I'll put it in my diary to check that data, rather than mess up like today . . . nobody's fault but mine . . . I'll order the data right now, and I'll try to smarten up my debating technique, which is pathetic right now . . . I'll ring my sister now and see if I can borrow her video camera so I can rehearse and learn not to come across like a moron . . .'

Sources: Adapted from David, Lynn and Ellis (2009), McKay, Davis and Fanning (2008); Frosch (2003); Knaus (2008).

ASSESS YOURSELF

Select several of the negative self-talk patterns listed in table 9.1 and create monologues reflecting those patterns. Now, write positive versions. After doing this, think of examples of situations in which the following self-talk strategies might be useful:
(a) achievable differences
(b) reality testing
(c) flexible response
(d) confrontation
(e) truth
(f) rationalisation.
Have you ever used some of these strategies without realising it, and, if so, did you find them useful?

Assertiveness

Some analysts of interpersonal communication (Back & Back 2005; Alberti & Emmons 2008) have found it useful to divide people's behaviour into one or a combination of four styles: (1) assertive, (2) passive, (3) aggressive, and (4) manipulative. Their communication styles and life positions or attitudes are shown in figures 9.2 and 9.3.

FIGURE 9.2 Assertiveness and other styles of communication

COMMUNICATION STYLES		
	Overt	**Covert**
Considers others	Assertive	Passive
Does not consider others	Aggressive	Manipulative

FIGURE 9.3 Life positions of different styles of communication

LIFE POSITIONS		
	I win	**I lose**
You win	Assertive	Passive
You lose	Aggressive, manipulative	

Assertiveness can be viewed as a defence system against the negative communication styles of others, such as the passive or timid style, the aggressive style, and the manipulative or devious style. We will explore in greater detail these four styles in the complementary chapter 10. Assertiveness can also be understood as a way of analysing your own communication styles, and as a system to increase your personal effectiveness. A good definition of assertiveness is: *Getting what you want from others without infringing on their rights.*

Assessing your assertiveness: behaviour patterns

Let's collect some basic data on how you communicate with a range of different people in different situations. For example, how do you stand up for your rights, make requests, express justified anger, and give and receive compliments?

Giving and receiving compliments

What do compliments have to do with assertive behaviour? Assertiveness is concerned with the full range of human communication, not just those parts relating to conflict and confrontation. Some people find it hard to express any type of feeling, positive or negative; others are more comfortable with expressing positive feelings than negative ones; still others are capable of expressing negative feelings, but not positive ones. As a complete person, you should be able to give expression to a complete range of feelings.

Many people feel uncomfortable giving compliments to others because they fear such praise might be interpreted as dishonest or manipulative. This fear, while understandable, is unfortunate and can lead to the impoverishment of human communication. Similarly, when complimented by others, we often either question their sincerity or adopt a charade of false modesty: 'It was nothing ... I was lucky, that's all.' We also fear that by accepting the compliment as our due, others will think us vain and egotistical.

Often people who pay sincere (non-manipulative) compliments to others do so because they feel secure and unthreatened in their personal and professional lives. In other words, they operate from a position of strength, and so feel confident that their words will not be misconstrued as sycophancy or 'crawling'. Frequently such individuals also receive compliments graciously, knowing that their acceptance does not signify pompous self-regard. Secure and competent people are often quietly self-confident and generous; that self-confidence is just another word for assertiveness. Assertive people receive compliments with a simple 'thank you', and without blushing or self-effacement.

Making requests: asking for favours or help

Often we do not make direct requests of others because we fear that such approaches will be seen as signs of weakness. We may take a very indirect path by:

- beating about the bush, using a series of qualifying phrases ('If you don't mind …', 'If it's not too much trouble …') (passive style)
- blustering, making statements that sound more like threats than requests ('See here, do you think you could get around to …') (aggressive style)
- beating about the bush, then slyly slipping in what we really want ('Oh, by the way …', 'Oh, just one more trifling thing …') (manipulative style).

These approaches not only are marginally dishonest, but they also waste a lot of time. By employing such indirect approaches, we are not communicating effectively: making requests is simply the first step in getting what you want, and in an increasingly interdependent world everyone needs something from others.

Expressing liking, love, affection

As we move into more personal expressions of feeling, we tend to encounter even greater degrees of avoidance and constraint. If you experience feelings of liking, love and affection, and you have the opportunity to express them, then it is usually best to do so. Without getting unduly morbid, it may be useful here to consider death as a defining point of human experience. When a friend, a relative, a lover or a colleague dies (particularly in unexpected circumstances), it is common to hear people say things like, 'I didn't even get a chance to tell her I loved her' or 'I never got the chance to tell him how much I respected and liked him'. Hindsight is 20–20. If you can think of no other reason for expressing respect, love or affection, then use the morbid argument – any one of us could die tomorrow. There are caveats. For example, Galassi and Galassi (1977) suggest it is usually inappropriate to express liking, love and affection to authority figures and business contacts. However, much assertive training is about taking risks in the messy, often uncontrollable realm of emotion, and here we are considering the most intense area of (positive) feeling. No risk, no reward.

Initiating and maintaining conversation

You've either got the 'gift of the gab' or you haven't, right? Wrong. Most human behaviour is learned rather than genetically transmitted from generation to generation, and what can be learned can be improved on. Social skills such as initiating and maintaining conversations comprise an important part of assertiveness: if we can control or at least influence the flow of words at relatively low levels of emotional intensity, then we stand a better chance of using words (means) to achieve our objectives (ends) at higher levels of emotional intensity.

Standing up for your rights

Your rights are under threat when your sense of fairness is jeopardised or ignored. Knowing that someone does not respect your legitimate rights is one thing; doing something about that person's behaviour is quite another. Sometimes the best you can do is lead by example.

Refusing requests

'No' is such a little word, yet many of us have great difficulty in saying it. When others make unreasonable requests of us, it should be simple to use this little word, but often we don't. Smith (2000) suggests we are often manipulated into granting unreasonable requests by the internal dialogue of self-talk. Manipulative requests may be anything from a boss asking you to work overtime when you don't want to, to someone trying to trick you into a sexual encounter. The usual self-talk in such situations is, 'When I say "no" I feel guilty, but if I say "yes" I'll hate myself.' To be able to say no in a firm, polite but effective way is an extraordinarily helpful skill. It is also quicker, more honest and less counterproductive than emotional responses such as:

'Get out of my way! How dare you ...' (aggressive)

'Oh all right, if that's what you want ...' (passive)

'Look, I'd love to help you out, but I've got to rush to catch a moon shuttle.' (manipulative)

We discuss verbal skills that can help us become more assertive, including saying no, later in the chapter.

Expressing personal opinions, including disagreement

There is a difference between having opinions and being opinionated, but many of us have difficulty in discerning that difference. In effective communication it should always be possible for you to speak out — to speak your mind; otherwise others will take your silence as consent. As with expressing liking, love and affection, use reverse hindsight to motivate you: don't be the one who says, 'What I should have said was ...' or 'I was going to say that ...'

Expressing justified displeasure and anger

Entering the territory of intense negative emotions, it is essential (as with positive feelings) that we feel able to express such feelings. If we suppress strong emotions, then our ill feelings towards others may turn inward against ourselves — dislike of others can become self-dislike, or self-hate.

With bottled-up feelings, particularly negative ones, there is a real danger that when we finally unburden ourselves, blurting out our feelings, we do so in an out-of-control way. At best, we will not achieve our objective; at worst, we may say and do things we later regret.

ASSESS YOURSELF

Fill in table 9.2 on the next page. In this table the columns show the people you might interact with in your personal and professional life; the rows list various assertive behaviours or communication strategies. By completing this table, you will produce a reasonably accurate picture of your assertive or nonassertive behaviours.

Complete the table by asking yourself, 'Do I [row heading] to/from/of/with [column heading] when it is appropriate?' For example, 'Do I [refuse requests] from [authority figures] (e.g. bosses, professors, doctors) when it is appropriate?'

Scoring the assertiveness self-assessment table

To complete the table, use these symbols and numerical ratings:
  U (usually) (3)
  S (sometimes) (2)
  R (rarely) (1).
Think carefully about each category, and apply the rating that you think applies for the majority of the time for you.

(continued)

(continued)

TABLE 9.2 Assertiveness matrix

Behaviours	Friends of the same sex	Friends of the opposite sex	Intimate relations (e.g. spouse, boyfriend, girlfriend)	Parents-in-law and other family members	Children	Authority figures (e.g. bosses, professors, doctors)	Business contacts (e.g. salespeople)	Co-workers, colleagues and subordinates	TOTAL SCORE
Give compliments									
Receive compliments									
Make requests, (e.g. ask for favours, help)									
Express liking, love and affection									
Initiate and maintain conversations									
Stand up for your legitimate rights									
Refuse requests									
Express personal opinions, including disagreement									
Express justified annoyance and displeasure									
Express justified anger									
TOTAL SCORE									

Source: Adapted with permission from Galassi and Galassi (1977, p. 9).

Assertiveness: some verbal skills

We now have a clearer idea of what is and what is not assertive behaviour. But how do you learn to communicate assertively? Here are nine verbal skills we can learn to help us to be more assertive.

1. Say no

Drug awareness programs have been built around the catchphrase, 'Just say no'. Players from leading AFL teams posed for this campaign, which led with the phrase 'AFL players say "no" to drugs'.

Helping people who are in genuine need can be a real pleasure. But sometimes when we grant, or give in to, the requests of others, we do so for the worst motives. We think to ourselves, 'When I say "no", I feel guilty, but when I say "yes", I hate myself'. This central behavioural trap was first analysed by Manuel Smith, one of the pioneers of assertiveness training (Smith 1975; Smith 2000; Smith 2002). When we think like this, we play into the hands of aggressive and manipulative people.

Drug awareness programs have been built around the catchphrase, 'Just say no'. We could usefully apply the formula to a range of interpersonal situations in which unreasonable demands are placed on us. Summon up your courage (first checking that you are not responding out of stress, or distracting yourself with negative self-talk, and that your body language is assertive), look the person in the eye and say forthrightly, politely and without strain, 'No. Sorry, I can't help you this time', 'Uh oh. Not possible, I'm afraid'.

Apologise when necessary, but do so with dignity – don't cringe. Don't fabricate excuses. Wherever possible, give reasons; wherever possible, give the other person something to go away with, so that at least some of his or her needs are met. Legitimate needs, that is: it's amazing how often when people are given a conditional 'no', they simply withdraw without exercising the option they are offered, suggesting that perhaps their needs were not so urgent after all, that you've simply called their bluff. Be a good role model of problem solving; don't respond to aggressive or manipulative mind games with mind games of your own.

2. Dismiss and redirect

Other people sometimes attempt to put us down, sidestep issues or introduce irrelevancies. This may be done in a deliberately manipulative way, or because they genuinely do not see the real issues in a situation (of course, we ourselves are not exempt from such failings). *Dismissing and redirecting* is a way of getting the conversation back on track. Be aware, however, that in conflict situations we have to listen and analyse carefully, not least because apparently irrelevant comments might point to the underlying causes of the conflict. The following examples show how the process works.

The fact that the homework is due tomorrow is not relevant right now. [DISMISS] *What is important is that this is the third time in two weeks that you've announced you have homework due tomorrow, and that you need someone to drop everything and rescue you by driving you to the library.* [REDIRECT] Let's talk about this, and see whether in fact you need to face the consequences of not handing it in on time.

The fact that it's the cheapest set in the range is beside the point. [DISMISS] *The point is that it is still covered by the guarantees of the manufacturer and this store, and that it shouldn't have died after only ten hours' use.* [REDIRECT]

3. Questioning to prompt awareness

We all need feedback on our own behaviour, even though we sometimes feel uncomfortable getting it, and giving it to others. If we could see ourselves through others' eyes, we would probably behave in different ways. *Questioning to prompt awareness* can help this process. Sometimes we can confront them directly with feedback about how they interact with us, but sometimes it is less threatening if we give them feedback about their interactions with third parties.

Have you ever noticed that when you talk to some customers, particularly women, they seem to be a bit in awe of you, perhaps even fearful? [QUESTIONING TO PROMPT AWARENESS] It may sound far-fetched, but if you check out their body language next time, I think you'll find they start to behave like school kids getting a lecture ... Just an observation ... See what you think.

Do you know that when you talk to me about our personal life, you seem to get quite tense and angry? [QUESTIONING TO PROMPT AWARENESS] You clench and unclench your fists, and you find it hard to look me in the eye. Tell me what you really feel. With what we've been through, I can take it.

4. Fogging

When people criticise us aggressively, they expect a reaction. Very few of us like criticism, so they are usually not disappointed. This can sometimes be useful: the air may be cleared by a frank exchange of words. Sometimes, however, a reaction is not useful, and we need to avoid getting trapped into riding a conflict spiral over which we have no control. In these circumstances, *fogging* may be useful. Fogging means calmly acknowledging that others' criticism may well be justified; when others then lash out, instead of connecting with something solid, they find it is like punching fog. Fogging helps to separate personalities from problems.

MARIA: You've mucked it up again? Are you completely useless?

FREDDY: *Yes, you're right. I do appear to have got it wrong.* [FOGGING]

5. Forcing a choice

Sometimes others pile work or demands on us. These may be legitimate demands, but all too often they are the result of others' thoughtlessness, aggression, manipulation and/or poor organisation. If we are unassertive, we can become:

- flustered
- guilty
- desperate to show that we can help
- desperate to show that we are competent.

Failing to act assertively in a work situation can lead to counterproductive responses such as stress and exhaustion.

These are all examples of counterproductive responses that can lead to stress, exhaustion and other negative consequences.

Sometimes the simplest solution to this situation is merely to say no. If this directness is inappropriate, then *forcing a choice* can be useful: it may be a skill with which you can switch responsibility for decision making back to the other party, force them to set limits, force them to get organised and stop dumping chaos onto others, and at the same time ensure that you are not overloaded with demands. You can do this without arguing or getting upset, by making it their problem, not yours.

BOSS: Tom, can you get me these figures ASAP? I need them for my 2 o'clock meeting.

TOM: You wanted me to finish drafting the proposal so that the meeting could look at it. *Which would you like me to finish first?* [FORCING A CHOICE]

JOAN: Oh, I'm running late again! Could you ring them and tell them I'll be there as soon as I can, and that I'm on my way?

BRIAN: I've almost finished this stew you wanted to take, but it takes some watching. *Do you want me to turn it off to make the call?* [FORCING A CHOICE]

6. Broken record

In the heat of confrontation we can sometimes forget our primary objective, particularly if we are interacting with people who are skilled in manipulating, provoking and distracting. Vinyl records used to scratch easily; this would often damage the playing surface so that one musical phrase would repeat again and again. When we use the *broken record* verbal skill, we repeat calmly again and again what we want, without getting upset, so that we can achieve our primary objective, without getting sidetracked or provoked.

CUSTOMER: Good morning. I bought this here last week, and it broke yesterday. I would like a refund, please.

SALESPERSON: Ah, well, I'm sure that we could repair that for you, or give you a replacement.

CUSTOMER: I'm sure that's possible, but I'm not happy with this model, and *I would like a refund, please* ... [BROKEN RECORD]

7. Ask for specifics

When someone is critical of us, often our first response is to wade in and give as good as we get. While this may feel satisfying, it seldom leads to meaningful conflict resolution. A better response to criticism is to ask for more specific criticism. This may sound paradoxical, but it has a number of benefits:

- It can help clarify what the problem is.
- It helps cool tempers and shift the focus away from subjective name-calling to objective problem solving.
- It can annoy the hell out of some people you dislike when you refuse to descend to their level!

You can ask them specifically which of your behaviours they do not like, and what behaviours they would prefer.

RANI: Your performance out there was pathetic, just pathetic!

JOE: *Can you tell me specifically what I did that you found pathetic?* [ASK FOR SPECIFICS]

CHRIS: Do you really have to spend so much time each day checking those damned spreadsheets?

LIM: *What would you have me to do instead, Chris?* [ASK FOR SPECIFICS]

8. Workable compromise

In resolving an impasse or conflict, it is often not enough merely to neutralise the ploys of aggressive, manipulative or passive people. We need to come up with practical solutions that will replace negativity with something positive. Both sides need a negotiated outcome that will move matters forward, give satisfaction and save face. Applying the skill of *workable compromise* can be very helpful here; the workable compromise is often the last of a number of techniques to be used.

BOSS: All right, if you won't do it, I'll do it myself!

TOM: No, don't go away mad. I said I couldn't do it now. *I can do it at three, and I can do it in about 40 minutes. That means it will be ready for your presentation at 4:15. Will that help?* [WORKABLE COMPROMISE]

9. Threats

Threats are often made by aggressive people, but occasionally assertive people also need to use them, or at least to make others aware of the consequences of their actions. This particular assertive skill should be used only as a last resort, when all other approaches have failed. You need to ensure that you are able to carry out any threats you make. It is also wise to link a threat to a more desirable outcome, thus giving the other person an option.

We think you are underperforming, and as a result the team's figures are down and we may miss out on the March bonus. *Unless you can get back to your old level of output, I will have to record the current variation, and then Jack Stilwell will have to discuss it with you.* [THREAT] Is there anything wrong? Can we help you with anything?

Unless you drop this continuous barrage of innuendoes, I will need to make an official complaint of harassment. [THREAT] I'd much prefer to settle this now, between the two of us. What do you think?

Verbal skills applied: a scenario

Let's now see how these verbal skills could be applied in a real-world situation. In this dialogue, Larry unethically tries to control Janice, who exerts counter-control through assertive verbal skills.

LARRY: Janice, you'll have to drop everything — we've got a major drama on our hands! I just got a call from a friend at head office, and he said that three bigwigs from head office will be dropping in unannounced tomorrow! We're all going to have to put in some overtime tonight just to make sure the books and our project figures look OK!

JANICE: *Sorry, Larry, but no.* [SAY NO] I can't do it. I'm going home to my family at 5:30.

LARRY: Well, that's just typical of a woman, isn't it? When the pressure is really on out here in the real world, you just can't handle it!

JANICE: *Perhaps you're right. Maybe pressure doesn't motivate me.* [FOGGING] *Nevertheless, I'm still going home to my family.* [BROKEN RECORD]

LARRY: Oh come on, Janice! I'm sorry about that pressure remark, but I really need your help. Everyone's staying back!

JANICE: Sorry, Larry, I just don't see what the problem is. The records in this section are just fine — we've got nothing to hide. *Sorry* [SAY NO], *but I'm going home.* [BROKEN RECORD]

LARRY: Yeah, well things may be OK for you here, where you've got it easy, but we've been completely snowed under in my area, and we've had to fall behind. You've got to help your mates out, just this once!

JANICE: *The fact that things are a bit messy in your area isn't the issue, Larry.* [DISMISS] *The real point is that this seems to happen all the time.* [REDIRECT] We are not underworked here; in fact my people have bailed you out twice in the past three months when crises like this occurred. *Excuse me, but I'm off.* [BROKEN RECORD]

LARRY: Please, Janice, I'm begging you! You're the best person in the building on these accounts!

JANICE: (Sighs) *Well ... I'm still going home* [BROKEN RECORD] *... the best I can offer you is that I can work on some of the accounts on my home computer, and I'll email it back to you. My husband can do the dishes, but I insist on reading to my sons. I can get stuff back to you by about 10 tonight, if you're still here. But I want something in return. I want the Metz account transferred to my area.* [WORKABLE COMPROMISE]

LARRY: That's not fair! You're taking advantage! Bob Jasper will hear about this tomorrow! In fact, I might ring him at home tonight! Yeah, you see if I don't! I'll fix you!

JANICE: *Yes, it might be unfair, mightn't it?* [FOGGING] *But that's my best offer, and that's where I stand on the issue.* [WORKABLE COMPROMISE, BROKEN RECORD] *Unless you calm down and focus on solutions, however, I'll let you stew in your own juice tonight and tomorrow, and I'll see Bob first thing tomorrow, and tell him how I see the situation.* [THREAT]

LARRY: Look ... you're being completely unreasonable about this!

JANICE: *What specifically do you find unreasonable about it?* [ASK FOR SPECIFICS]

LARRY: Surely you can help out just this once?

JANICE: *Larry, are you aware of what I pointed out to you before? That in fact it isn't just this once, but in fact the third time in three months?* [QUESTIONING TO PROMPT AWARENESS]

LARRY: I'm sure that can't be right, but if you insist, I'll try to help you out.

JANICE: Don't work too hard ... *I'm going home now.* [BROKEN RECORD]

LARRY: Yeah ... goodnight.

JANICE: Goodnight.

ASSESS YOURSELF

Think of a range of aggressive, passive and manipulative ploys that could be tried on you by others. Then devise a series of appropriate responses, using the nine verbal skills. Write out scripts for these scenarios, using the previous dialogue as a model.

Assertiveness: from theory to practice

If you feel you would like to become more assertive, then you may need to practise some of the skills and behaviours we have considered. Practice and rehearsal are invaluable here. If, for example, you have experienced problems with a particular person in a particular situation, and you think assertiveness skills might be useful, it makes sense to prepare a script incorporating the verbal skills we have discussed. Some feedback on your rehearsed performance might also help. This could include:

- the comments of a friend
- an audio recording of your rehearsal
- a video recording of your rehearsal
- rehearsing in front of a mirror.

As with presentations and speaking, the more you rehearse, the less stressed you should feel in the actual performance.

Limitations of assertiveness

Assertiveness, both as a set of skills and as a philosophy, has much to offer. However, we need to bear in mind a number of caveats:

- Skills such as fogging and broken record should not be tried in certain situations – for example, in legal situations or situations in which you are physically threatened (Smith 2000).
- Assertiveness is no good to anyone if it simply makes us more brash, overconfident and obnoxious – that is, if it simply makes us more skilled 'Aggressives' (Eglash 1980; Alberti & Emmons 2008; Ames & Flynn 2007).
- Most assertiveness training is offered to women, but this may be a 'blame the victim' approach that ignores challenging the power structures of workplaces and other situations: the emphasis on interpersonal tactics rather than on situational strategies relating to gender roles may miss the point (Crawford 1995) (see online chapter 'Gender and communication').
- Gender stereotyping may mean that women behaving assertively are seen as aggressive, while men behaving similarly are merely seen as assertive (Eagly & Karau 2002) (see online chapter 'Gender and communication').
- Assertiveness, like other social skills, is culturally specific – that is, in some cultures what we might consider assertive could be interpreted as rude and overbearing.
- It may not always be possible to communicate assertively with extremely aggressive, manipulative or passive people – that is, some individuals may be beyond the reach of even the most careful approach to assertive communication (McNeilage & Adams 1982).
- Assertive behaviour – calm, dignified, confident yet persistent – may simply not be understood by many, who may perceive assertiveness as rude, robotic or simply bizarre.

One of the main things to remember about assertiveness skills is that they are techniques to be applied when necessary. An effective communicator need not exercise them 24 hours a day, seven days a week. Assertiveness is a strategy, not a restricting role or a religion. 'If you *know how* to act assertively', Alberti and Emmons (2008) argue, 'you are free to *choose* whether or not you will. If you are *unable* to act assertively, you have no choices; you will be governed by others, and your well-being will suffer' (p. 260).

The cooperative principle

The cooperative principle is a principle that describes how people interact with each other that has relevance for contemporary interpersonal communication. The principle, which was proposed by philosopher Paul Grice, focuses on the need for listeners and speakers to cooperate in mutually accepting the purpose or meaning of what they say to each other. Grice (1975, p. 45) advises:

> Make your conversational contribution such as is required, at the stage at which it occurs, by the accepted purpose or direction of the talk exchange in which you are engaged. One might label this the COOPERATIVE PRINCIPLE.

Grice (1975) has established four categories of maxims that he suggests communicators can use to ensure cooperation in an exchange of dialogue. These maxims, known as the Gricean Maxims, are the Maxims of Quantity, Quality, Relation and Manner. Each Maxim includes a few key rules that communicators can use to improve their listening and speaking skills. The Maxim of Quantity relates to the amount of information that a speaker or listener provides, and includes two rules:

1. Make your contribution as informative as is required (for the current purposes of the exchange).
2. Do not make your contribution more informative than is required (p. 45).

The Maxim of Quality has an overarching supermaxim – 'Try to make your contribution one that is true', and includes two other rules:

1. Do not say what you believe to be false.
2. Do not say that for which you lack adequate evidence (p. 46).

The Maxim of Relation has a single rule: 'Be relevant', and the Maxim of Manner contains various guidelines, including:

1. Avoid obscurity of expression.
2. Avoid ambiguity.
3. Be brief (avoid unnecessary prolixity).
4. Be orderly (p. 46).

As a set, the maxims offer speakers and listeners a set of guidelines that can be applied in different contexts to facilitate cooperation in the dialogue exchange. This is the basis of the cooperative principle. By thinking carefully about what is communicated – including the amount, truthfulness and relevance of the information – as well as how this information is conveyed, speakers and listeners can facilitate an effective communication exchange.

STUDENT STUDY GUIDE

SUMMARY

Emotional intelligence and emotional competence are emerging concepts that help us understand the interpersonal and communication processes that take place between individuals. Intrapersonal communication is the process of communication that takes place within the consciousness of the individual. To become more effective intrapersonal communicators, and perhaps also interpersonal communicators, we need to challenge negative self-talk and convert it to more positive messages. Assertiveness can be defined as 'getting what you want from others without infringing on others' rights'. It involves identifying and practising a range of behaviours that may help to enhance personal effectiveness and interpersonal communication. There are at least four styles of behaviour we need to consider: (1) passive, (2) aggressive, (3) manipulative and (4) assertive. Assertive behaviour is the most effective and desirable of these four styles. We discussed nine verbal skills that can help us become more assertive communicators. The limitations of assertiveness were also discussed.

KEY TERMS

emotional competency *p. 285*
emotional intelligence *p. 285*
interpersonal communication skills *p. 284*
intrapersonal communication skills *p. 284*

learning and manipulation problem
 p. 287
psychobabble *p. 285*
self-talk *p. 290*

REVIEW QUESTIONS

1. Identify at least three emotional competencies associated with emotional intelligence.
2. Discuss at least two problems associated with the concept of emotional intelligence.
3. What is the learning and manipulation problem?
4. Describe at least five negative patterns of self-talk, and the positive versions of these.
5. Identify at least two possible connections between intrapersonal and interpersonal communication.
6. Describe at least five assertive behaviour patterns.
7. Give examples of at least four assertive verbal skills.
8. Identify at least two limitations of assertiveness.

APPLIED ACTIVITIES

1. Have at least one other person use the emotional intelligence questionnaire to rate you. How do their scores agree with or differ from your own?
2. The patterns of self-talk described in this chapter are based on the theory of distorted thinking developed by practitioners of rational-emotive/cognitive behavioural therapy and on ego defence mechanisms described by psychoanalysts. Conduct print and internet research to find out about at least five of these (e.g. mind reading, being right, personalisation, the heaven's reward fallacy, overgeneralisation, emotional reasoning, projection, repression, introjection, displacement, identification, compensation, regression, reaction formation, undoing, sublimation). What value do they have for explaining interpersonal and intrapersonal communication processes?

3. Begin to develop your assertiveness skills by role-playing a number of situations, such as:
   - speaking to a person who has jumped a queue
   - asking people in a theatre to stop talking
   - asking someone not to smoke
   - asking for a salary raise
   - pointing out to an authority figure that they are wrong on a matter of fact.
4. How might you combine the assertive verbal skills with the assertive feedback sequence (chapter 10)?
5. What other assertive verbal skills can you think of?
6. What relationships might there be between assertiveness and negotiation, conflict resolution and stress management?
7. What is the relationship between the interpersonal skills considered in this chapter and the skills (listening, questioning, feedback and the Johari window) considered in the next chapter?

WHAT WOULD YOU DO?

Tom met his work colleague Lee at the café just down the road from their office. As he walked in, Lee was organising material on his laptop.

'What are you doing?' asked Tom.

'Can you believe it? I'm being sent on an assertiveness course — what a waste of time,' Lee replied. 'As if I need to be any more assertive.'

Tom kept his thoughts on that to himself. He had actually done the course a few months earlier, and had suggested to their supervisor that she should fund Lee to do it as well. Lee's manner was often aggressive, but he didn't seem to notice that this often had a negative effect on those around him. In fact, Lee had recently annoyed two major customers with his phone manner, and complaints had been made — complaints that could do his career damage, and perhaps even lead to him being fired. Tom knew that for Lee's own good, he needed to learn what appropriate levels of assertiveness were, and felt that the course could potentially do him a lot of good.

'Maybe they want me for the inevitable role plays they do in these things,' mused Lee. 'You did this course, didn't you?' he asked Tom. 'What other point would there be for sending me on it?'

What would you say to Lee if you were Tom?

SUGGESTED READING

Bishop, Sue 2010, *Develop your assertiveness: change your behaviour, be more confident, get what you want*, Kogan Page, London.

Luciani, Joseph J 2007, *Self-coaching: the powerful program to beat anxiety and depression*, 2nd edn, John Wiley & Sons, New York.

Townsend, Anni 2008, *Assertiveness*, Palgrave Macmillan, London.

Wilding, Christine 2008, *Teach yourself emotional intelligence*, Teach Yourself Books, London.

REFERENCES

Alberti, Robert & Emmons, Michael 2008, *Your perfect right: assertiveness and equality in your life and relationships*, 9th edn, Impact Publishers, Atascadero, CA.

Ames, Daniel R & Flynn, Francis J 2007 'What breaks a leader: the curvilinear relation between assertiveness and leadership', *Journal of Personality and Social Psychology*, vol. 92, no. 2, pp. 307–24.

Anthony, Mitch 2003, *Selling with emotional intelligence: 5 skills for building stronger client relationships*, Dearborn Books, Chicago, IL.

Back, Ken & Back, Kate 2005, *Assertiveness at work: a practical guide to handling awkward situations*, 3rd edn, McGraw-Hill, London.

Bar-On, Reuven & Parker, James DA 2000, *The handbook of emotional intelligence: theory, development, assessment, and application at home, school, and in the workplace*, Jossey-Bass, San Francisco, CA.

Bradbury, Travis & Greaves, Jean 2009 *Emotional intelligence 2.0*, TalentSmart, San Diego, CA.

Brinthaupt, Thomas M, Hein, Michael B & Kramer, Tracey E 2009 'The self-talk scale: development, factor analysis, and validation preview', *Journal of Personality Assessment*, vol. 91, no. 1, pp. 82–92.

Cherniss, Cary & Goleman, Daniel (eds.) 2001, *The emotionally intelligent workplace: how to select for, measure, and improve emotional intelligence in individuals, groups and organizations*, Jossey-Bass, San Francisco, CA.

Conte, Jeffrey M & Dean, Michelle A 2006, 'Can emotional intelligence be measured?', in Kevin Murphy (ed.), *A critique of emotional intelligence: what are the problems and how can they be fixed?*, Lawrence Erlbaum Associates, Mahwah, NJ.

Crawford, Mary 1995 *Talking difference: on language and gender*, London/Thousand Oaks, CA/ New Delhi, Sage.

Dalrymple, Theodore 1999, 'Psychobabble that shields the seriously selfish', *New Statesman*, vol. 12, no. 568, pp. 24–5.

David, Daniel, Lynn, Steven & Ellis, Albert 2009 *Rational and irrational beliefs: research, theory, and clinical practice*, New York, Oxford University Press.

Depape, Anne-Marie R, Hakim-Larson, Julie, Voelker, Sylvia, Page, Stewart & Jackson, Dennis L 2006, 'Self-talk and emotional intelligence in university students', *Canadian Journal of Behavioral Science*, vol. 38, no. 3, pp. 250–61.

DuBrin, Andrew J 2008, *Human relations for career and personal success: concepts, applications and skills*, 8th edn, Prentice Hall, Upperl Saddle River, NJ.

Eagly, Alice H & Karau, Steven J 2002 'Role congruity theory of prejudice towards female leaders', *Psychological Review*, vol. 109, pp. 573–98.

Eglash, Albert 1980, *The case against assertion training*, Quest Press, Beverley Hills, CA.

Ellis, Albert 2001, *Overcoming destructive beliefs, feelings and behaviors: new directions for rational emotive behavior therapy*, Prometheus Books, Amherst, NY.

Eunson, Baden 1987, *Behaving: managing yourself and others*, McGraw-Hill, Sydney.

Eunson, Baden 1998, *Effective assertiveness skills*, Team Publications, West Burleigh, Qld.

Frosh, Stephen 2003, *Key concepts in psychoanalysis*, New York University Press, New York.

Galassi, MD & Galassi, JP 1977, *Assert yourself! how to be your own person*, Human Sciences Press, New York.

Gammage, Kimberley L, Hardy, James & Hall, Craig R 2001, 'A description of self-talk in exercise', *Psychology of Sport and Exercise*, vol. 2, no. 4, pp. 233–47.

Gardner, Howard 2000, *Intelligence reframed: multiple intelligences for the 21st century*, Basic Books, New York.

Goleman, Daniel 1998, *Working with emotional intelligence*, Bantam, New York.

Gowing, Marilyn K 2001, 'Measurement of individual emotional competence', in Cary Cherniss and Daniel Goleman (eds), *The emotionally intelligent workplace*, Jossey-Bass, San Francisco, CA.

Grice, HP 1975, 'Logic and conversation' in Cole, P & Morgan Jerry L (eds.), *Syntax and semantics 3: speech arts*, Academic Press, New York.

Grubb, W Lee III & McDaniel, Michael A 2007, 'The fakability of Bar-On's emotional quotient inventory short form: catch me if you can', *Human Performance*, vol. 20, no. 1, pp. 43–59.

Hardy, James 2006 'Speaking clearly: a critical review of the self-talk literature', *Psychology of Sport and Exercise*, vol. 7, pp. 81–97.

Hay, Louise L 2004, *I can do it: how to use affirmations to change your life*, Hay House Press, Carlsbad, CA.

Heerey, Erin A 2007, 'Interpersonal consequences of social anxiety', *Journal of AbnormalPsychology*, vol. 16, no.1, pp. 125–34.

Hogan, Robert & Stokes, Louis W 2006, 'Business susceptibility to consulting fads: the case of emotional intelligence', in Kevin Murphy (ed.), *A critique of emotional intellgence: what are the problems and how can they be fixed?*, Lawrence Erlbaum Associates, Mahwah, NJ.

Kapesser, Lisa Caldas 2009, *The smart new way to get hired: use emotional intelligence and land the right job*, Jist Works, St Paul, MN.

Knaus, William J 2008, *The cognitive behavioral workbook for anxiety: a step-by-step program*, New Harbinger, Oakland, CA.

Jie-Qi, Chen, Moran, Seana & Gardner, Howard (eds) 2009, *Multiple intelligences around the world*, Jossey-Bass, San Francisco.

Lasch, Christopher 1979, *The culture of narcissism: American life in an age of diminishing expectations*, Warner Books, New York.

Leung, Alicia SM 2005, 'Emotional intelligence or emotional blackmail: a study of a Chinese professional service firm', *International Journal of Cross Cultural Management*, vol. 5, no. 2, pp. 181–96.

Lorenz, Konrad 2002, *On aggression*, 2nd edn, Routledge, London.

McKay, Matthew, Davis, Martha & Fanning, Patrick 2008, *The relaxation & stress reduction workbook*, 6th edn, New Harbinger, San Francisco.

McNeilage, Linda A & Adams, Kathleen A 1982, *Assertiveness at work: how to increase your personal power on the job*, Prentice Hall, Englewood Cliffs, NJ.

Matthews, Gerald, Zeidner, Moshe & Roberts, Richard D 2003, *Emotional intelligence: science and myth*, MIT Press, Boston, MA.

Murphy, Kevin R (ed.) 2006, *A critique of emotional intellgence: what are the problems and how can they be fixed?*, Lawrence Erlbaum Associates, Mahwah, NJ.

O'Brien, Paddy 1997, *Positive management: assertiveness for managers*, Nicholas Brealey, London.

Orme, Geetu & Langhorn, Steve 2003, 'Lessons learned from implementing EI programmes – the cutting edge of emotional intelligence interventions', *Competency & Emotional Intelligence Quarterly*, vol. 10, no. 2, pp. 2–14.

Ostrow, Ruth 2003, 'A backbone to nurture change', *The Weekend Australian*, 19 April, p. B35.

Phelps, Stanlee & Austin, Nancy K 2002, *The assertive woman*, 4th edn, Impact Publishers, Inc., Atascadero, CA.

Qualter, Pamela, Gardner, Kathryn J & Whitely, Helen E 2007, 'Emotional intelligence: review of research and educational implications', *Pastoral Care in Education*, vol. 25, issue 1, pp. 25–3.

Rieff, Philip 1987, *The triumph of the therapeutic: uses of faith after Freud*, University of Chicago Press, Chicago, IL.

Rosen, Richard 1977, *Psychobabble: fast talk and quick cure in the era of feeling*, Scribner, New York.

Salovey, Peter & Mayer, John D 1990, 'Emotional intelligence', *Imagination, Cognition and Personality*, vol. 9, pp. 185–211.

Singh, Dalip 2003, *Emotional intelligence at work: a professional guide*, 2nd edn., Sage, Thousand Oaks, CA.

Smith, Manuel 1975, *When I say no, I feel guilty*, Bantam, New York.

—— 2000, *When I say no, I feel guilty, vol. II: for managers and executives*, A-Train Press, San Diego, CA.

—— 2002, *Here be dragons: the psychological problem, cause and cure: modernizing talk psychotherapy for both the self help and professional modes using the here be dragons coping model and verbal behavioral methods*, A-Train Press, San Diego, CA.

Smith, Richard 2002, 'Self-esteem: the kindly apocalypse', *Journal of the Philosophy of Education*, vol. 36, no. 1, pp. 87–100.

Sternberg, Robert J 2003, Preface to Gerald Matthews, Moshe, Zeidner & Richard D Roberts, *Emotional intelligence: science and myth*, MIT Press, Boston, MA.

Sternberg, Robert & Pretz, Jean (eds.) 2004, *Cognition and intelligence: identifying the mechanisms of the mind*, Cambridge University Press, Cambridge, UK.

Stout, Maureen 2001, *The feel-good curriculum: the dumbing down of America's kids in the name of self-esteem*, Perseus Publishing, New York.

Suliman, Abubakr M & Al-Shaikh, Fuad N 2007, 'Emotional intelligence at work: links to conflict and innovation', *Employee Relations*, vol. 29, no. 2, pp. 208–20.

Tavris, Carol 2011, *Psychobabble and biobunk: using psychology to think critically about issues in the news*, 3rd edn, Prentice Hall, Upper Saddle River, NJ.

Twenge, Jean M 2009, 'Generational changes and their impact in the classroom: teaching Generation Me', *Medical Education*, vol. 43, no. 5, pp. 398–405.

Ury, William 2001, *Must we fight?: from the battlefield to the schoolyard – a new perspective on violent conflict and its prevention*, John Wiley & Sons, New York.

Vitz, Paul C 1994, *Psychology as religion: the cult of self-worship*, Eerdmans Publishing, Grand Rapids, MI.

Zeidner, Moshe, Matthews, Gerald & Roberts, Richard D 2009 *What we know about emotional intelligence: how it affects learning, work, relationships, and our mental health*, Boston, MIT Press.

10

Interpersonal skills 2: listening, questioning and feedback

LEARNING OBJECTIVES

After studying this chapter you should be able to:

- Explain how listening differs from hearing
- Give at least three reasons why listening has value in personal and professional situations
- Explain the relationship between listening, interruption and agreement
- Name at least four barriers to effective listening
- Explain the concept of active or reflective listening
- Name at least four types of questions and explain the value of each of them in particular situations
- Identify at least three effective and three ineffective feedback strategies
- Use the feedback sequence to express evaluative views
- Use the Johari window concept to become more effective in communicating with others

Who's listening?

In the previous chapter we examined emotional intelligence, intrapersonal communication and assertiveness skills. In this chapter we will look at listening, questioning, reframing, feedback skills and a specific application of feedback — the Johari window.

Listening and hearing are not necessarily the same thing. Gamble and Gamble (2008, p. 182) define hearing as 'the involuntary, physiological process by which we process sound' and define listening as 'the deliberate, psychological process by which we receive, understand, and retain aural stimuli'. Locker and Kaczmarkek (2009, p. 307) make the same point: 'In interpersonal communication, hearing denotes perceiving sounds. Listening means decoding and interpretation them correctly.'

But there is more to it than that: we manipulate both processes. Stop right now and take note of the sounds aimed at you that you are not normally conscious of: air conditioning, a birdsong, a computer hum, people talking. We filter these out, just as we filter out or concentrate to listen. If we did not filter out or concentrate, then we would be deafened by a background of noise suddenly promoted to the foreground. We simply wouldn't cope.

If we were to define listening as 'paying attention', then a person with impaired hearing but excellent concentration, high motivation and good interpersonal skills could well be a better listener than someone with perfect hearing who has wandering concentration, poor motivation and weak interpersonal skills. The paradox of listening is this:

> Listening is the form of communication we practice most often. Yet because we rarely have formal training in it, it may be the one that we do most poorly. (Locker & Kaczmarkek, 2009, p. 306)

For example, some researchers estimate that most people spend 60 to 70 per cent of their waking hours communicating — with 9 per cent spent writing, 16 per cent reading, 30 per cent talking and 45 per cent listening (Rosenblatt, Cheatham & Watt 1982) (figure 10.1). Indeed, 'We listen more than we do any other human activity except breathe' (Montgomery 1984).

The ability to filter out background noise is essential to the productivity of employees, such as call centre workers and administration staff, who regularly deal with customers on the phone. This is particularly the case in open-plan offices.

These figures can vary considerably from individual to individual, of course, so we probably need to treat them circumspectly, just as we do figures used to suggest that more than 50 per cent of all communication is nonverbal.

FIGURE 10.1 Time spent on different communication processes

Source: Adapted from Rosenblatt, Cheatham and Watt (1982, p. 117).

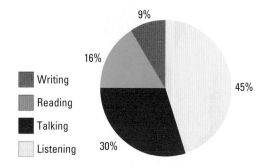

- Writing
- Reading
- Talking
- Listening

9%

16%

45%

30%

On the other hand, a survey found that 80 per cent of a sample of North American executives rated listening as the most important skill in the workforce, far above technical skills. Yet, 28 per cent of the same sample thought listening skills were also the most lacking in the workforce (Salopek 1999). Researchers at the University of Minnesota

Guffey suggests that people only listen at about 25 per cent efficiency: 'In other words, we ignore, forget, distort, or misunderstand 75 per cent of everything we hear' (Guffey 2008, p. 50). If this is true, it is likely several of these people are misinterpreting what the speaker is saying in this presentation.

concluded that nearly 60 per cent of misunderstanding in the business world could be traced to poor listening, and only 1 per cent to written communication (Montgomery 1984). Guffey suggests that people only listen at about 25 per cent efficiency: 'In other words, we ignore, forget, distort, or misunderstand 75 per cent of everything we hear' (Guffey 2008, p. 50). Research conducted in the Singapore insurance industry showed that the more experienced staff members were, the more likely they were to value listening above speaking as a communication strategy; and the more inexperienced staff members were, the more likely they were to interrupt and thus annoy customers (Goby & Lewis 2000). Does this mean the younger we are, the worse we are as listeners? Or is there more to the story?

We need to also bear in mind that:

- If listening is perceived as simply not talking, and if listeners are simply too scared or too uncertain to speak out, high listening figures might be bad, not good, for an organisation.
- Unassertive people such as Passives may be 'good listeners', but not because they want to, while Aggressives may hardly listen at all.
- There is a substantial gap between the rate at which most people talk (125–250 words per minute) and the 'thought rate' or rate at which information is processed in our minds (1000–3000 words per minute) (Guffey 2008, p. 50).
- The most effective way to exploit this gap is for the listener to analyse what is being said, anticipate what the speaker might be about to say and memorise what is being said by rote repetition or association with other concepts.
- Unfortunately, many people exploit the gap ineffectively, and begin to daydream and wander while the speaker is talking. While a surprising amount of these activities can be undertaken without losing the thread of what is being said, one daydream tends to lead to another, and all too often the listener is no longer paying attention. Yet, for all intents and purposes, the world believes the person is 'listening'.

Why, then, is listening so important in both professional and personal situations? Here's why:

- **Listening allows us to get the full picture.**
  Reading is superior to listening in a number of respects when it comes to gathering information. However, listening is sometimes superior to reading, in that it allows us not only to hear the views of others but to observe the full range of nonverbal behaviour that accompanies those views – the 'music' to the words. This accompaniment can sometimes make for more revealing and informative communication than if we simply read a transcript of the words. We can also observe the reactions of, and interact with, the speaker, opening up two-way communication to clarify the message.
- **Listening lets us learn and survive.**
  We have two ears and one mouth, and it often makes sense to use them in that ratio. By restraining our desire to talk, we sometimes learn from the talk of others. We do not always need to reinvent the wheel or think of things that have already been thought of, because we can learn from the experience of others. Instead of making fools of ourselves by jumping in before we have heard all the relevant information, the strategy of patiently listening often pays off, sometimes allowing us to look a lot smarter than we really are.
- **Listening lets us discover the truth.**
  Being known as 'a good listener' is not always a good thing. Overly aggressive talkers may intimidate others into silence, so that only one-way communication – and usually

ineffective one-way communication – takes place. Thus, an aggressive talker may describe someone else as a 'good listener' simply because they do not respond to the talker or engage in a two-way dialogue, or are intimidated into agreeing with the aggressive talker (although in private they may not agree with the talker at all). If we are assertive, however, this need not be the case. Being known as assertive – and also as someone who will listen – will pay off for us because so much more information will come our way. It is important that we listen to everyone, especially to people we do not particularly like. As Benjamin Franklin once observed: 'Love your enemies, for they tell you your faults'. This is a paradox reworked several centuries later by Stephen King: 'Only enemies speak the truth; friends and lovers lie endlessly, caught in the web of duty'. In other words, sometimes we will only hear the truth about ourselves from people who dislike us. Being known as a good listener may also mean that we are not – consciously or unconsciously – helping to create a 'shoot-the-messenger' ethos, wherein truth-tellers are punished for telling the truth, and soon learn to be quiet (with ultimately disastrous consequences for all). If we are known as someone who is willing to listen to bad news as well as good news, then we increase our chances of getting the full picture of a situation – and thus earning time to react to bad news. This means that we should go out of our way to actively solicit or request the opinions or feedback of others.

Nonlistening is often counterproductive, especially with individuals prone to interruptions and quick fixes. Doctors, often under time pressure, may do this. One study showed that some doctors only allowed patients 18 seconds of explaining their troubles before interrupting (Gamble & Gamble 2008, p. 184), while another study showed that doctors who put more time into listening were less likely to automatically prescribe antibiotics (Lundkvista et al. 2002). Perhaps listening is the best medicine for those who feel that no-one listens to them.

- **Listening to others lets them solve their own problems.**

Management by listening: allowing others to reach their own solutions by talking through their problems

We sometimes think that listening to others is a waste of our time, because the solution to their problems is pretty clear to us, and if they would only stop talking we could enlighten them. Iuppa (1986) suggests that this may be a serious misperception of the way human communication and problem solving really work, and that in fact **management by listening** has a lot going for it: on many occasions, if a manager simply listens to someone talking about a problem (perhaps interrupting briefly here and there to subtly nudge the monologue down one track rather than another), then the solution to the problem becomes apparent – a problem well defined is half solved, as the maxim goes. The speaker has unconsciously taken ownership of the problem, and solved it. If you interrupt the flow with a perfect solution, there is no guarantee that it will be embraced enthusiastically; indeed, there is a good chance that such an intrusion will make the speaker more motivated to arrive at his or her own, perhaps less-than-perfect solution.

The same principle applies well beyond the sphere of managers and organisations, of course. Sometimes by simply listening to someone else, they – and we – can reveal the truth. As novelist EM Forster (2000 [1927]) once put it, 'How do I know what I think until I see what I say?'. This revelation is especially likely to occur if you are the first real listener such a person has encountered in a world of nonlisteners. In this way people are given the chance to work through their thoughts aloud, perhaps in the process discovering linkages, synergies and contradictions that hitherto had not occurred to them. In interacting with others, therefore, we may not have to work so hard at providing solutions – we may need only to be a receptive listener.

- **Listening allows us to cope with distractions and to de-stress.**
We all sometimes suffer from information overload and feel pressured to do more to keep up with the frantic pace of life. We are surrounded by distractions, and it is very tempting to surrender to them, thereby shortening our concentration span. Conscious

listening, like any focused perception routine, permits us to slow down and process reality in a more meaningful way (Shafir 2003). We may also be prone to stress-inducing behaviour styles, such as the so-called Type A pattern – which drive us to interrupt others, to rudely change the subject, or to drift into other activities, such as keyboarding or reading email messages, while someone is talking to us. Consciously listening to others can help us avoid these bad habits (Clark 1999).

■ **Listening to others will probably mean they will listen to us.**

We tend to listen more to those people we think are intelligent. It follows, then, that those we listen to may well think that we are intelligent, and therefore worth listening to (Salopek 1999). Demonstrating politeness and empathy is, therefore, not only worthwhile, but also has high payoff values, setting up a reciprocal relationship. It comes down to the golden rule: do as you would be done by.

■ **Listening helps us to cope with technological overload**

Gamble and Gamble (2008) cite studies that show prolonged watching of television may shorten concentration spans, with this tendency worsened by shorter and shorter video images, music videos and radio newscasts. They also point out the overload of sound and messages we receive from mobile phones (and the breakdown of the concept of private space, with others conducting loud conversations on such phones in public places), CDs, videoconferences, beepers, voice mail, music players with headsets and computer phones. Perhaps the effects of such overload and shortened concentration spans can be overcome by becoming more effective listeners (see online chapter 5, 'How to write').

■ **Listening can give us an unfair advantage over others.**

The advantages of listening that we have considered so far are all entirely ethical. This one isn't; indeed, it can be manipulative and reprehensible (although perhaps useful in some circumstances). Just as listening compels us to keep quiet and sometimes saves us from embarrassing ourselves, patient listening can encourage speakers to insert both feet in their mouths (make fools of themselves). Interviewers sometimes set a trap for interviewees (called the 'pause pit'), wherein the interviewer simply says nothing, and the interviewee, uncomfortable with silence, is eventually spurred to say something – anything – to fill the silence (see online chapter 8, 'Media and communication'). This is the 'give people enough rope and they will hang themselves' view of the world. Perhaps you will never have to resort to **aggressive listening**, but at least you need to be able to recognise it. If it is used on you in an interview, just wait out the silence – after all, the interviewer is meant to be asking the questions.

Aggressive listening: patient listening with the primary purpose of spurring speakers to say things they might later regret

Listening: a vital workplace skill

Law-enforcement officers are learning that listening skills comprise a vital tool when managing highly stressful crisis situations, such as negotiating with hostage takers (Noesner & Webster 1997). Listening also seems to have payoffs in the mundane workplace situations many of us find ourselves in. Good listening habits are now recognised as critical in any selling role (Aggarwal, Castleberry & Ridnour 2005). Many nonsales roles, too, increasingly involve communicating with internal and external customers in a context very much like selling. Tom Peters (1991, 2002), for example, exhorts managers to see listening as strategically vital for helping to turn organisations around. He urges marketing staff to get out from behind their desks and spend at least 50 per cent of their time in the field; even manufacturing or operations managers, he argues, should spend at least 15 per cent of their time out listening to customers. Communicating with customers and stakeholders to find out what they really want should therefore be a top-level imperative in successful organisations. Leonard (2002) warns, however, that listening is not a panacea: customers familiar with products may give good advice, but not such good advice when questioned on new product recommendations or on areas in which they have little or no expertise.

Listening, power and gender

Listening behaviour can vary considerably according to gender and power relations. For example, high-status people tend to interrupt low-status people more than vice versa (just as high-status people often tend to invade the personal work space of low-status people more than vice versa) (Morris 2002). In practice, this means that some managers model bad listening behaviour, which – not surprisingly – is then emulated by employees. In this way bad listening habits can spread through organisations.

Sex roles are also a critical factor in understanding listening behaviour. One US survey revealed that when two men or two women were talking, the number of interruptions between partners was much the same, but when a man and a woman were talking, the man made about 96 per cent of the interruptions. About one-third of the time, women made 'retrievals', attempting to pick up the conversation from the point at which they were interrupted (Atwater 1991). This male behaviour was linked to the finding that males often simply 'tuned out' early in the conversation: some men, after listening for only a few sentences, switched from listening to the speaker (outward orientation) to 'self-listening' (inward orientation) – that is, concentrating on what they might add to the conversation – and then jumped into the conversation prematurely, without absorbing what the speaker had to say or first trying to draw the speaker out. This behaviour may be the result of sex-role conditioning, with males trained to dominant, problem-solving roles (Atwater 1991).

Some research suggests that males are superior to females in comprehension of factual material, whereas females are more sensitive to the nonverbal cues and expression of feelings that accompany the words (Hargie & Dixon 2010). The implication is clear: many males appear to have a listening problem when interacting with females, and it would not be surprising if this general pattern prevailed in both personal and professional situations (see online chapter 7 'Gender and Communication').

Listening and nonverbal communication

In most social encounters we need to 'listen' with our eyes as much as with our ears; that is, we need to observe the nonverbal behaviour that accompanies the words we are listening to. We need, for example, to be sensitive to any contradictions between the words and what a person is 'saying' nonverbally. This requires active listening and questioning to draw the person out. We also need to be aware of the ways in which our own nonverbal communication can help or hinder the process of effective listening. Listening responsiveness is associated with nonverbal behaviours, such as:

- head nods
- forward-leaning posture
- body oriented towards speaker
- visual attention (not being distracted by external tasks, events, people or internal thoughts)
- eyebrow raises
- smiling
- direct eye contact
- mirroring the facial expression of the speaker
- refraining from distracting mannerisms, such as doodling with a pen or fidgeting
- making appropriate 'friendly grunts' ('Mmm-hmm ... uh-huh') (Hargie & Dixon 2010; Bavelas, Coates & Johnson 2002; Aggarwal, Castleberry, Ridnour & Shepherd 2005).

In the following questionnaire, mark the appropriate response. Consider the questions either generally or in relation to one particular part of your life (e.g. as a member of a work group or family, or as a student attending classes). In a sense, this questionnaire is impossible to complete accurately, because many of the communication patterns described here are unconscious, or only partly conscious. Complete it anyway, and perhaps consider:

- doing it again in a few days' time, when you have had time to reflect on it and observe your own behaviour more closely
- having someone else complete a copy of it, rating you as a listener. You may be interested to discover how others evaluate your abilities (and you can, of course, return the favour).

		Nearly always	Often	Not often	Almost never	SCORE
1.	Do you only pretend you are listening to someone speaking, when in fact your mind is far away?					
2.	Do you concentrate on the dress, grooming and gestures of the speaker rather than on what is being said?					
3.	Do you continue multitasking or doing other things (e.g. signing papers, performing calculations, working on equipment) while others are talking?					
4.	Are you distracted by other things (e.g. your watch, a newspaper or a book, other conversations, the television, the radio, a telephone ringing, a computer screen) while someone else is talking?					
5.	Do you operate in an environment in which physical barriers (e.g. noise, heating, comfort) distract you from listening to others?					
SUBTOTAL A						
6.	Do you believe 'boring' people have nothing useful to say?					
7.	Do you interrupt others?					
8.	Do you believe that facts (not emotions, values and opinions) are the only things worth listening for?					
9.	Do you periodically paraphrase (put into your own words) a speaker's words back to him/her to confirm you understand each other?					
10.	Do you get so angry with a speaker that you spend time thinking of your response — and thus lose track of the rest of the conversation?					
SUBTOTAL B						
11.	Do you look directly at the speaker?					
12.	Do you forget what a speaker has only just said?					
13.	When listening, do you fail to give nonverbal feedback (e.g. head nods, 'friendly grunts') while maintaining a blank stare and immobile face?					
14.	Do you 'tune out' when someone starts talking, because you know the rest of their talk is totally predictable?					
15.	Do you relax and listen uncritically when the speaker seems to reflect your values and uses jargon and buzz-phrases you are comfortable with?					
SUBTOTAL C						

(continued)

(continued)

		Nearly always	Often	Not often	Almost never	SCORE
16.	Do you believe that, unless you interrupt the speaker, she or he will interpret your silence as agreement?					
17.	When someone uses jargon, slang, acronyms (initials) or specialised language, do you refrain from asking what they mean because you don't want to look a fool?					
18.	Do you change the subject of conversation when someone else is talking?					
19.	Do you find what is *unsaid* by a speaker (i.e. what is deliberately avoided, unstated or left out through ignorance) as instructive as what is said?					
20.	Do you forget the speaker's name?					
SUBTOTAL D						
21.	Do you welcome distractions and/or interruptions when someone is talking?					
22.	Do you believe that the solution to most people's problems is obvious, and that they need to be told about it sooner rather than later, before they waste any more of your time or theirs?					
23.	While a person is speaking, do you find yourself planning the 'more important' activities you want to do once they have gone?					
24.	Do you talk to others while someone is speaking?					
25.	Do you ask speakers to repeat themselves, even though your hearing is good and the speaker's diction is clear?					
SUBTOTAL E						
TOTAL (SUBTOTAL A + SUBTOTAL B + SUBTOTAL C + SUBTOTAL D + SUBTOTAL E)						

Score your answers to questions 1–5, 7–8, 10, 12–18 and 20–25 as follows:

Nearly always	Often	Not often	Almost never
1	2	3	4

Score your answers to questions 9, 11 and 19 as follows:

Nearly always	Often	Not often	Almost never
4	3	2	1

YOUR SCORE AND WHAT IT MAY MEAN

25–43	Sorry, you seem to be a bad listener. You need to do a lot of work on this communication skill.
44–62	You seem to be not too bad a listener, but your listening skills could do with considerable improvement.
63–81	Your listening skills are in reasonably good shape; now, would you like to try for perfection?
82–100	You seem to be an excellent listener. Congratulations.

Listening: developing our skills

The world outside your skin (and for that matter, inside your skin) can be seen as a gigantic information machine – a machine that bombards you with information all day and night. You neither need nor want all that information, so you filter most of it out, concentrating only on what interests you. For the most part, filtering out (and listening in) is a conscious process, but it can be partly unconscious, or at least not the focus of our attention: consider, for example, if you are in a group of people, all of them talking, and one of them says your name. The chances are you will hear it, separated out from the background hubbub, even though you were not focusing intently on the words of that particular speaker (in much the same way that your own name, or certain familiar or taboo words, might seem to 'leap off' a printed page).

The right to remain silent

So we need to 'focus our ears' to find out what is going on in the world. Listening means paying attention to others, even when we disagree with them or find them boring. In listening to others, you may note that what they are saying is wrong, and you will probably have the chance to point this out down the line. But you don't have to interrupt them in the mistaken belief that your silence signifies agreement (it doesn't). You have the right to remain silent without this implying that you agree with everything you are hearing. If others do not understand this, then persevere: if you become known as a person who listens nonjudgementally, then you will hear a lot more (a good deal of it to your advantage).

It is important that people do not abuse your good listening behaviour, either by interpreting your silence as agreement or consent, or by inferring poor listening skills: 'You're just not listening to me!' which, translated, means 'You're just not agreeing with me!' (see figure 10.2).

We need to think twice, therefore, about interrupting (although it may sometimes be necessary). We also need to ensure we are not 'interrupting ourselves' by switching off our concentration while we work out our response (the speaker's next sentence may pre-empt what we are planning to say).

Listening fallacy #1: 'You're not interrupting me; therefore you must be agreeing with me.'

Corollary to fallacy #1: If I am listening to you, and I find myself in disagreement with what you are saying, I must interrupt you; otherwise you will think that I am agreeing with you.

Listening fallacy #2: 'When you listen to me without interrupting, that must mean that you are agreeing with me.'

Corollary to fallacy #2: If after listening to me you mistakenly express disagreement with me, I will accuse you of just not listening. If I do this long enough, you will agree with me.

FIGURE 10.2 Listening fallacies

We need to be aware of the signs that warn us to improve our concentration, such as forgetting the speaker's name or forgetting what has just been said, or being distracted by the speaker's appearance or by other conversations or the TV set in the background, or 'tuning out' because we think the speaker is boring or predictable.

When specialised language, jargon or unfamiliar acronyms are obstructing the communication, we should ask for clarification without fearing that we will look foolish. Similarly, when we are part of an in-group, we must be alert for complacency or groupthink that leads us, for example, to an all-too-easy acceptance of 'our' jargon (as opposed to that used by out-groups). We also need to listen for what is *not* said: the conscious or unconscious omissions that may indicate an area of disagreement or a misperception of the situation.

Barriers to effective listening

A number of specific behaviour patterns that present barriers to effective listening are, in effect, mind games played by people who do not listen well. Some of these barriers are expressed in the words used by bad listeners. Some of them are invisible, comprising the 'self-talk' of intrapersonal communication explored in the previous chapter. Many are nonverbal, expressed in our body language: the 'go away' signal in the glassy stare, the sphinx-like immobile face, the drumming fingers, the glance at a watch or the computer screen, the pen held suspended over documents more interesting than your conversation, the body oriented away, lodged firmly behind the large desk – truly, the silent language of nonverbal communication can sometimes be deafening.

Most people are guilty of erecting such barriers every now and then; there is usually no malign intent involved and no great harm done. The real damage occurs when bad listeners erect one or several of these barriers all the time. Such barriers to effective listening are discussed in figure 10.3.

FIGURE 10.3 Barriers to effective listening

1. Subject changing	Occurs when a listener feels bored, embarrassed or threatened by what the speaker is saying, and shifts into speaking mode, rerouting the conversation.
2. Daydreaming	Occurs when a listener does not creatively exploit the gap between the speaking rate and listening rate by analysing speaker's words, but instead allows the speaker's words to trigger off an associated thought, and then drifts off through a progressively more remote series of associations, losing track entirely of what the speaker is saying. The Daydreamer's train of thought is a runaway train.
3. Distracted	We are barraged with information from a variety of sources in our environment. Effective listening (and good manners) means shutting out some of these sources. The Distracted person may appear to be paying attention to the speaker but is in fact drawn by more interesting things happening elsewhere. The Distracted person is like the Daydreamer, except that she or he *at least* gives the *outward* impression of following the conversation.
4. Just give me the facts (JGTF)	Facts are vital to understanding, but listeners also need information about feelings, values and implicit ('between the lines') meanings, some of which are conveyed through nonverbal behaviour, which may confirm or contradict the words. The JGTF listener feels that anything nonfactual is irrelevant, and thereby misses entire dimensions of meaning.
5. Mind-reading	Occurs when a listener attempts to read too much meaning into the speaker's words and nonverbal behaviour in a misguided attempt to detect and anticipate what the speaker is 'really saying' (the direct opposite of JGTF).
6. Rehearsing	Occurs when a person is angered by what he or she is hearing, and by concentrating too hard on a detailed rebuttal loses track of what is said. It also occurs when the listener is planning witty or profound responses. Such listeners may rehearse entire chains of responses: 'I'll say ... then she'll say ... then I'll say ...'
7. Comparing	Occurs when the listener is insecure, competitive, envious or jealous, or all of these. Loses track of or misinterprets what the speaker is saying because the listener continually compares their situations: 'I make more than that ...' 'What would I need to do to speak like that? ...' 'How can he afford those clothes?'
8. Push my buttons (PMB)	Many people lose their cool and objectivity and become extremely sensitive when certain topics (e.g. crime, abortion, capital punishment, terrorism, taxation, politics) are broached. Their reaction is so automatic and predictable that it is almost as if someone has just pushed a button in their brain. Fine for robots, but bad for effective listeners, conversationalists and problem solvers.

FIGURE 10.3 *(continued)*

9. Stereotyping	Similar to PMB, except that here the listener ignores the words being said because she or he takes exception to the speaker's hairstyle, clothes, sex, socioeconomic class, mannerisms, race, religion, sexual preference, approach to the topic, use of audiovisual aids or any one of a number of factors that do not have much to do with the ideas being expressed.
10. Quick fix	Some people are lucky enough to have the solutions to everyone's problems; they can detect a speaker's problem after only a few words or sentences — at which point they cut the speaker off and give him or her a detailed program of what to do. Such listeners ignore the feelings of speakers, and have not yet grasped the principle of management by listening; that is, if you are patient and let speakers talk about their problems, they will often discover solutions to their own problems (note also possible differences in gender styles of listening and interrupting).
11. Tuning out	When crises occur in organisations, you may hear talk such as 'We knew about it, but no-one would listen — it doesn't pay to shoot your mouth off around here'. All too often staff develop 'selective expectation' — if the boss isn't really going to pay attention, then staff learn to do likewise, and tune out. When this happens, daydreaming is understandable, and crises and problems which could have been prevented erupt.

Sources: Adapted from Adler, Rosenfeld and Proctor (2009); DeVito (2011); Hargie and Dixon (2010); de Janasz, O'Dowd and Schneider (2009); Flatley and Rentz (2010).

Active and effective listening

Active listening: a communication skill that requires concentration, attention and a minimal verbal response to help the speaker articulate his or her thoughts

When people erect barriers to effective listening, they sometimes move beyond the passive state of simply receiving a message and into the active role of speaker; this can be a sign of ineffective communication. Yet, an effective listener should be more than merely a passive receiver. Effective communication is not a one-way process, wherein the sender transmits a message and the receiver absorbs it like a sponge. Many messages are distorted in the sending and in the receiving, and unless the receiver checks back with the sender, communication may break down without one or both parties being aware of it. Good listeners abstain from passive listening to embrace the communication skill of active or reflective listening. The concept of **active listening**, pioneered by psychologist Carl Rogers, may initially seem to be a contradiction in terms, but effective listening involves concentration, attention and comprehension. Truly effective listening involves responding as well, not in the sense of entering into a dialogue, but in terms of prompting the speaker to help clarify and elaborate the message. As Mortimer Adler puts it:

> The most prevalent mistake that people make about listening is to regard it as passively receiving rather than as actively participating ... Catching is as much an activity as throwing and requires as much skill, though it is a skill of a different kind. Without the complementary efforts of both players ... the play cannot be completed. (quoted in Sigband & Bell 1989)

Active or reflective listening can perform the following functions:
- Clarify the speaker's meaning
- Check the accuracy of what the speaker has said
- Check the feelings of the speaker
- Summarise what the speaker has said
- Acknowledge what the speaker has said, without making any kind of commitment
- Open a door, prompting the speaker to continue.

Examples of these types of active listening or responding are summarised in table 10.1.

TABLE 10.1 Ways the listener can be in control: establishing and maintaining the flow of conversation

	Listening objective	Method	Listening technique
I. Clarifying check	When you want to clarify, you need more facts, you want to explore further or to check assumed meaning in order to understand message.	Ask a *what, how* or *when* question, then restate what you thought you heard.	1. 'Is this the problem as you see it?' 2. 'Will you clarify what you mean by …?' 3. 'What specifically do you mean by …?' 4. 'What I understand you to say is … Is that right?'
II. Accuracy check	1. To check your listening accuracy and encourage further discussion 2. To let the person know you have grasped the facts	Restate the person's basic ideas, emphasising the facts.	1. 'As I understand it, the problem is … [restatement]. Am I hearing you correctly?' 2. 'What I think you are saying is … '
III. Feelings check	1. To show you are listening and understanding the speaker 2. To reduce anxiety, anger or other negative feelings 3. To let the speaker know you understand how he or she feels	Reflect the speaker's feelings. Paraphrase in your own words what the speaker has said. Match the speaker's tone — whether light or serious. Ensure accurate communication of feelings.	1. 'You feel that you didn't get the proper treatment.' 2. 'It was unjust as you perceived it.' 3. 'It's annoying to have this happen.' 4. 'It seems to me you got turned off when your boss talked to you that way.' 5. 'I sense that you like the job but aren't sure how to go about it.'
IV. Summarising check	1. To focus the discussion and lead it to a new level 2. To focus on the main points and offer a springboard for further consideration 3. To pull together important ideas or facts 4. To review progress	Restate, reflect and summarise major ideas and feelings.	1. 'These are the key elements of the problem … ' 2. 'Let's see now, we've examined these factors … ' 3. 'These seem to be the key ideas you express … ' 4. 'To summarise, the main points, as I heard them, are … '
V. Noncommittal acknowledgement	To stay neutral but show you are interested	Don't agree or disagree. Use noncommittal words but in a positive tone of voice. Express noncommittal acknowledgement.	1. 'I see … ' 2. 'Uh-huh … ' 3. 'Mmm-hmm … ' 4. 'I get the idea … ' 5. 'I understand … ' (silence during the pause)
VI. Door opener	Acknowledge the problem.	Show willingness to discuss the problem.	1. 'Tell me about it.' 2. 'That does seem to be a problem.'

Source: Burley-Allen (1995, pp. 129–30).

When combined, passive and active listening perform a number of crucial functions:

- They allow the listener to learn patience.
- They allow the listener to gather all the facts and emotions involved in a situation, giving a sound basis for action – rather than encouraging the listener to jump in too soon.
- They help affirm the speaker's right to be heard.
- They give speakers a chance to contribute: they may have been ignored by the last five – or five hundred – people, yet they may have much to contribute.
- They allow speakers to solve their own problems: they may not have had the opportunity to think their way through a problem before.

- They allow speakers to make their own judgements about themselves. They realise you are not sitting in judgement of them: you grant them the compliment of understanding. This does not necessarily mean you agree with them; you may express disagreement later. As Atwater (1991) points out, 'Ironically, the less we judge speakers, the more apt they are to become self-critical, expressing their thoughts and feelings even more honestly than if they felt under scrutiny'.
- They allow the speaker to let off steam and thus become more amenable to rational problem solving.

ASSESS YOURSELF

Write a dialogue between two people, allowing it to descend rapidly into back-and-forth argument and abuse. Now rewrite it with one of the participants using active listening responses instead of participating directly in the back-and-forth exchange. Evaluate the result. Is the active listening approach effective? Is it realistic? Might it have some value for you?

Effective questioning

Active or reflective listening uses minimal forms of questioning to draw out the other person. It creates a 'one-and-a-half' speaker conversation, and in some situations can be very effective in cooling tempers and clarifying points of view. Let's now explore other types of questioning.

Questioning as an interpersonal communication 'soft skill' strikes some people as a nonsense or a strategy of weakness: why ask questions when, if you know what you are talking about, the stronger strategy is to make statements? Perhaps we need to examine more closely what we mean by 'weakness' and 'strength'. Perhaps, when interacting with others, asking questions is a more powerful approach than it first appears. Interviewing, for example, depends on questioning, and asking questions can also be a very effective technique when delivering presentations, sales pitches or briefings. In the world of negotiation, too, the efficacy of questioning techniques is increasingly acknowledged.

Consider the following observations:

> Statements generate resistance, whereas questions generate answers. Questions allow the other side to get their points across and let you understand them. They pose challenges and can be used to lead the other side to confront the problem. Questions offer them no target to strike at, no position to attack. Questions do not criticize, they educate ... (Fisher, Patton & Ury 1992, p. 117)

> We [North Americans] don't teach our students how to ask questions, how to get information, how to listen, or how to use questioning as a powerful persuasive tactic. Yet these latter skills are critical at the international negotiating table. Few of us realize that, in most places in the world, the one who asks the questions controls the process of negotiation and thereby accomplishes more in a bargaining situation. (Graham & Herberger 1990, p. 160)

(See 'Listening and questioning skills' in chapter 13.)

Questions also allow you to arrive at what is unsaid by others, which can often be more important than what is said. **Effective questioning** means knowing the different types of questions that can be asked, and matching them to the situations we find ourselves in and the personalities with whom we find ourselves interacting.

Table 10.2 lists the different types of questions that can be used in different communication situations (see overleaf).

Effective questioning: knowing the different types of questions that can be asked, and matching them to the situations we find ourselves in and the personalities with whom we interact

TABLE 10.2 Questioning approaches

Question type	Example	Analysis
1. Straightforward probe	'What do you want?' 'What's this really about?'	The direct and blunt approach is often refreshing, cutting through the tendencies of some of us to prevaricate and beat about the bush. This can be counterproductive, however, when we need to draw others out gently.
2. Open	'What is it that you dislike about her?' 'How can we improve the situation?'	Open questions cannot be answered with a yes or no; they require a discursive response. They are useful in the opening phases of a conversation to break the ice, build rapport and gain information. They pre-empt quick rejection and premature decision making. They are not useful when some type of closure or action is required.
3. Closed	'Is it her personality that irritates you?' 'Will this improve the situation?'	Closed questions require a yes or no answer. They are useful for establishing facts, forcing choices, getting others to take a stand and declare positions, making decisions, gaining commitments and achieving closure. They are not useful in the opening phases of a conversation, when rapport may need to be built patiently.
4. Objective criteria	'Can you suggest where we might find objective standards to help us resolve this question?'	Useful when conversations become heated exchanges of opinions. This question is a cue for seeking neutral facts whose legitimacy is accepted by both sides.
5. Testing	'What were the depreciation figures for the northern branch last year?'	A testing question is one for which you already know the answer: you are just trying to test the other's competence and honesty.
6. Softening up	'Would you say that last year was rougher than most?' 'Some plants are fairly sloppy at gathering data. Do you have any problems getting figures together at your place?'	Softening-up questions are questions to which it is hard to say no. They often have a flattering and rapport-building feel to them. This is the 'yes-able proposition' technique, with which the questioner tries to build rapport and make it more likely that the other person will agree to simple and nonthreatening things, and then go on to say yes to more complex and threatening things.
7. Hypothetical	'What if the workers in that section could increase output by, say, 8 per cent in two months — what type of reward would you consider then?'	These questions are a way of probing and exploring options, without locking either side into commitments. Often used as a negotiation tactic.
8. Reflective	'Your people might be unhappy with that figure, then?'	Such a question simply reflects back the other people's feelings, letting them know that you are listening and are sympathetic. It's a cue for them to explore their feelings further. A form of active or reflective listening.
9. Leading	'So your report should be on the intranet by 9:00 am tomorrow?'	The question is not neutral, as a closed one might be: the questioner is prompting the answer he or she wants to hear.
10. Rhetorical	'How many times have I told you?' 'How much of our miserable wages do you want us to give up?'	Self-answering questions, or questions that don't need an answer. Changing the subject or approach can help.
11. Stupid	'How do they actually put those little wheels on?'	There's possibly no such thing as a really stupid question. Questions like this can help to slow things down, distract, put others off their guard or get discussions back to basics.
12. Trick compliment	'These figures are very impressive. I bet it took quite a while to put together something this complex, right?' ['Well, actually, yes.'] 'Then I'm sure you won't mind if we take them away and put some time into them too.'	A strategy that buys time and gets others to back off, especially when they have you off balance and are trying to force you to accept a fait accompli. The question is a lure to the vanity of others.

Question type	Example	Analysis
13. Back on track	'Mary, can you apply the same insight you have shown for the overtime question to the redundancy package problem?'	Useful for shifting debate back to the agenda without being rude.
14. False dilemma	'So what are your people going to do: go on strike and starve, or take the redundancy money now?'	Also a logical fallacy. There may be more than two alternatives. A clever technique for limiting the menu, and probably provoking an aggressive response, but a real killer of rapport-building and creative, win–win solutions.

ASSESS YOURSELF

1. Take the rewritten active listening dialogue from the 'Assess yourself' feature on page 321 and rewrite it again, using this broader range of questioning approaches and matching the question type to the flow of the argument. How effective or ineffective might these questions be in real-life situations?
2. When working with people who want to overcome shyness and build up their social skills, counsellors sometimes advise the use of open rather than closed questions in social and professional encounters. Why might this be so?
3. 'The one who asks the questions is in control.' What does this mean?
4. Compare these concepts of listening with those of strategic or customer listening in online chapter 10, 'Communicating with customers'.

Feedback

Feedback: advice, support and critique provided in response by one person to another

If you had bad breath, or were performing badly at work, or were generally making a fool of yourself, could you count on others to gently point these things out to you? Or if others had such characteristics, would you gently point these things out to them? Gently, or sometimes not so gently, enlightening people about sometimes unpleasant truths is another way of describing the interpersonal skill of **feedback**. Will others give you feedback when you need it? Will you give feedback to others? Vazire and Mehl (2009) suggest that our self-knowledge is often wrong, and the perceptions of others are more correct in some circumstances. It makes sense, therefore, to rely on two sets of perceptions to get better self-knowledge — the perceptions of ourselves and others.

As the poet Robert Burns famously wrote:

O wad some Power the giftie gie us
To see oursels as ithers see us!
It wad frae monie a blunder free us,
And foolish notion.

These days, in fact, technology allows many of us to see ourselves as others see us. If you have seen yourself on video or heard a recording of your voice, you know what a shock it can be: is that *really* what I look/sound like? We can't, however, have permanent and ongoing video camera feedback of ourselves 24 hours a day (nor would we want it). Presuming that it is better to have knowledge about ourselves than to be without it, and presuming that those around us in our personal and professional worlds feel the same way, how can we improve the flow of feedback we get from others, and also begin to develop a network of interpersonal understandings with others so that it becomes more routine and acceptable for us to give feedback to others?

Feedback: what does it mean, and how might it work?

Feedback means different things to different people, but a good working definition might be *the advice, support and critique provided in response by one person to another*. It can be formal or informal, brief or lengthy. It can take place:

- downwards (from superior to subordinate)
- upwards (from subordinate to superior)
- laterally (from peer to peer)
- from outside to inside (from customers to organisation members)
- between friends
- between relatives.

Feedback can occur as:

- a spoken communication in private
- a spoken communication in a public situation, such as a meeting
- a written communication, such as a memo, letter or email, or an item on a noticeboard, or in a newsletter or an online medium
- an objective response, such as an award for achievement
- nonverbal communication, such as a frown, pat on the back or verbal inflection that reinforces or contradicts the words spoken.

In an ideal situation:

Feedback is effective when it is ...	Feedback is ineffective when it is ...
Fair	Unfair
Accurate	Inaccurate
Specific	Vague
Formally structured	Disorganised
Solution oriented	Problem oriented
Focused on behaviour, not personality	Focused on personality, not behaviour

Feedback is integrally linked to other issues, such as:

- listening, questioning and conflict resolution skills – giving and receiving feedback shares similar dynamics to these communication processes
- the recognition given (or denied) to dynamic constructs such as emotional intelligence, and the culture that supports (or suppresses) behaviour patterns such as assertiveness
- the culture and the formal and informal communication channels present (or absent) in any organisation
- the norms of openness or repression present in any group or team
- objectives, values and standards – feedback is often about the extent to which our colleagues, friends and relatives fall short of or exceed objectives, values, standards and goals (and the methods used to arrive at such objectives, values, standards and goals)
- the extent to which there are systems in place that are receptive to input from stakeholders external to the organisation
- the leadership, coaching, mentoring and motivation values and practices present in an organisation – feedback is a vital skill for working with others to achieve maximum productivity.

Why feedback?

Feedback is not a code word for punishment or a lecture on individual shortcomings. If there are negative aspects to the situation, then obviously they must be dealt with in an appropriate way. But feedback can also be positive. Sometimes you need to praise, to pay a compliment, to recognise or to reward. Sometimes good feedback involves both negative and positive reactions, and the way in which you combine and sequence the different types of feedback is crucial.

An organisation without systems of feedback of any kind is a vacuum, and all kinds of unpleasant and uncontrollable things will flourish there, including:

- undesirable and destructive work practices
- a demotivating climate of opinion – 'Nobody cares if we excel or fail; what's the point?'
- never-ending communication breakdowns – 'Nobody told us!'; 'Well, why didn't you say so?!'

Performance and potential

'How am I doing?' Everyone wants to know – it's a basic human motivation. People perform much better, achieving their full potential, if they are involved in an effective feedback program. As the CIRCLE model of feedback shows, feedback can inform, correct, reward and commend and lead to better things (figure 10.4).

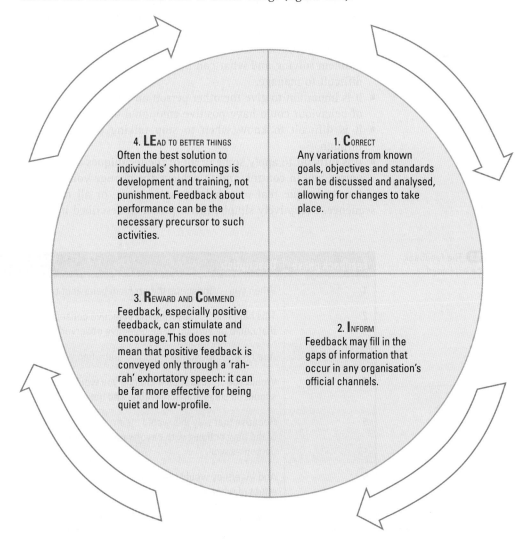

4. LEAD TO BETTER THINGS
Often the best solution to individuals' shortcomings is development and training, not punishment. Feedback about performance can be the necessary precursor to such activities.

1. CORRECT
Any variations from known goals, objectives and standards can be discussed and analysed, allowing for changes to take place.

3. REWARD AND COMMEND
Feedback, especially positive feedback, can stimulate and encourage. This does not mean that positive feedback is conveyed only through a 'rah-rah' exhortatory speech: it can be far more effective for being quiet and low-profile.

2. INFORM
Feedback may fill in the gaps of information that occur in any organisation's official channels.

FIGURE 10.4 The CIRCLE model of feedback

Feedback is not always welcome, of course. The target of our feedback may reject it for a number of reasons: they may believe it but not act on it, or they may be in denial (Folkman 2006, p. 2), or we might simply be wrong. The feedback or 'good advice' may also be conveyed with a hostile intent, as in the relational bullying phenomenon (see online chapter 7 'Gender and communication'), in which case the target of the feedback would be well advised not to take it. If feedback is not honestly given and not openly taken, then much of our human communication simply breaks down.

The feedback sequence: a verbal tool

Giving feedback to others, especially negative feedback, can give rise to a number of problems:

- The situation is often emotionally charged and stressful.
- It is important to try to change the behaviour of the target person by pointing out the objective consequences of what they are doing wrong, but this is often easier said than done.
- It is important to try to change the behaviour of the target person by pointing out the emotional or interpersonal impact or subjective consequences of what they are doing wrong, but this too is often easier said than done.
- It is important not to wallow in the diagnosis of what is wrong, but to move on to problem solving and what can be done to make things right, but this transition is often difficult to manage.
- It is important to give the other person an incentive to change, explaining how a change of behaviour could have positive emotional or interpersonal consequences.
- It is difficult to know when to stop talking to ascertain if your message is getting through.
- It is difficult to apply some or all of the techniques in a systematic way, remaining calm, poised and in control, and to achieve the change you are aiming for.

One technique that may help us solve some or all of these problems is the feedback sequence. Deceptively simple, the sequence is described in table 10.3.

TABLE 10.3 The feedback sequence explained

Feedback phase	Description
1	When you ... [describe the problem behaviour of the person you are talking to]
2	This happens ... [describe the objective consequences of their actions and words that could be verified by an objective observer]
3	And I feel ... [describe what you feel when you react to what they do or say]
4	Would you ... [describe a change you would like to see happen; such a change should be small and achievable, and not involve loss of face for the other person]
5	Because that way this would mean ... [describe wider positive consequences of the new actions, with payoffs not only for those around the person but for the person as well]
6	And I/we/they would feel ... [describe the subjective, emotional or interpersonal effect of what such a change in behaviour would achieve]
7	So what do you think? [turns the initiative back to the target person]

Using the feedback sequence assertively (and not so assertively)

In the previous chapter we considered the interpersonal skill of assertiveness. Assertiveness is one of a number of communication styles we can use. Three others are passivity, aggressiveness and manipulativeness. Of the four, assertiveness is the most effective.

Let's see how these four styles can be combined with the feedback sequence so we can get a better idea of how the sequence might work, and how it might fail (table 10.4).

TABLE 10.4 The feedback sequence — doing it right and doing it wrong

Feedback phase	Feedback: words to use	Example	Behavioural style	Analysis
1	When you ...	'When you lose one of my files, as you did today ...'	Assertive	Specific and descriptive: an impartial observer would be able to confirm that this behaviour occurred.
		'When you lost one of my documents last month ...'	Passive	Why procrastinate so long in complaining? Delaying means you have been stewing over the problem, and the other person has presumed that sloppiness is acceptable to you.
		'When you float around in the clouds and then leave one of my masterpieces there ...'	Aggressive	Sarcasm puts the other person on the defensive, and you send the message that you don't really want to solve the problem, merely to deliver abuse.
		'You're always losing things ...'	Aggressive	Absolutes like 'always' and 'never' polarise the situation: the other person either has nowhere to hide, and no way to save face, negotiate or solve the problem, or else will retaliate with nit-picking — 'I returned that report of yours last Tuesday ...' — which again leads away from problem solving.
		'People around here are getting pretty fed up with the situation ...'	Passive/ Manipulative	Are they? Have they been struck dumb? Let them speak for themselves, and you speak for yourself. These words are abstract too; how about keeping to specifics, like 'I' and 'you'?
		'You're totally useless ...'	Aggressive	Possible, but unlikely. Condemning people for their personality is like telling them that you don't like them because they're too short or too tall: there's nothing they can do to please you. It's an unconditional negative stroke. If, however, you refer to specific behaviour only, you give them freedom to move and the chance to change that behaviour.
2	This happens ...	'I can't deal with my best customer's enquiry ...'	Assertive	Specific and descriptive: shows impact or consequences of behaviour for you and your colleagues.
		'You've got to stop losing things or you will be punished ...'	Aggressive	Inflicting punishment, like taking revenge, is a cheap thrill that often proves to be very expensive. Why? Because punishment doesn't work that well as a strategy to change people's behaviour, and should be used only in extreme circumstances. Punishing an individual may draw resentment and retaliation from the individual, prolonging rather than solving conflict.
		'Things aren't going as well as they should.'	Passive	Evasive, pussy-footing and hopelessly vague. Again, the Passive's flight into the abstract and depersonalised.
		'You ought to be more reliable ...'	Aggressive	Yes, and we should all be perfect, but we're not. Moralising like this implies you are morally superior; it will block communication and lessen your influence. Aggressives really need to stop using 'should', 'ought' and 'must' so often; they need to stop wagging and pointing fingers.

(continued)

TABLE 10.4 *(continued)*

Feedback phase	Feedback: words to use	Example	Behavioural style	Analysis
3	And I feel …	'And I feel really frustrated because …'	Assertive	Clear statement of your feelings
		Silence	Passive	Passives will go silent here, because of their avoidance of 'I' statements. The stress they might feel at letting people know they have feelings is nothing compared with the stress they put themselves through in bottling up such feelings.
		'You make me feel stressed.'	Passive	Other people do not control us so much; they influence, but are not responsible for, our feelings. This is victim-talk. Use the 'I' word.
		More 'you have sinned' messages; no 'I' messages	Aggressive	'I' messages create an adult–peer relationship, and the other person is more likely to listen. 'You' messages invite defensiveness, with the other person less likely to hear what you are saying.
		'I'm a bit annoyed …' 'I'm just a little irritated by this …'	Passive	Don't be surprised, then, if the other person changes only 'a little' or 'a bit'. Modifiers are used here out of fear — presumably to appease the other person and avoid an angry response. However, they weaken your message, trivialise the issue (so what's the problem?) and are an exercise in self-humiliation.
4	Would you …	'Would you perhaps be able to work out a system of storing and recording details of material you borrow from me and others?'	Assertive	A positive solution is suggested, without the use of loaded language. The dignity of the other person is not compromised, so there's no need for defensiveness. 'Perhaps' helps soften the blow, but it should not be said as if it's a code for 'forget about this — I'm really not concerned'.
		'Would you be able to get your act together and remember what you actually do with things for a change?'	Aggressive	Have you stopped beating your wife? There are real questions, to which multiple responses are possible, and rhetorical or trick questions, to which no response can be given with dignity. This is not a real question, and sarcasm is the cheapest of thrills.
5	Because/ That way/ This would mean …	'This would mean that you could still borrow things from me and others, and we could look at them whenever we needed to.'	Assertive	Solution oriented. Answers questions everyone asks, or thinks: What's in it for me? What's the payoff for changing my behaviour?' This is the task-oriented incentive. 'still' contains enough threat to warn the offender.
		'That way we could at least stop others from grizzling about you. It's no skin off my nose, but let's not make waves.'	Manipulative	Compromise and politics have their place, but honesty and directness, not deviousness, are needed here. With Manipulatives, it's wise to remember that if they conspire with you, they may conspire against you; if they gossip to you, they will gossip about you.
6	I/You/They would feel …	'I would feel a lot better about the situation. So would the others. So would you, I'm sure.'	Assertive	This is the socio-emotional incentive. It's important to switch back from the logical, problem-solving dimension to the feelings dimension, to show that the drama and conflict being experienced can be resolved.
7	So what do you think?	'So, what do you think?'	Assertive	Neutral, nonconfrontational, an equal-to-equal expression. Shows you are willing to listen. The ball is now in their court. This is a dialogue, after all, not a monologue or sermon.

The feedback model gives us a structure for controlling our stress when giving negative feedback (as well as helping us avoid counterproductive aggressive, passive or manipulative mind games). When you first start to use it, it may feel artificial and silly, but persevere and you may find it a very useful tool of assertive communication.

Write a 'script' that covers the specifics of the negative feedback you need to give. Then rehearse in front of a mirror, video camera and/or friends. This can improve your technique and also make you feel a good deal more comfortable with it.

Rehearsal also means that, in the real or perceived stress of a confrontation with the target of your feedback, you can put some of your thinking brain on automatic pilot while playing back your new memories of the sequence. When you run through the sequence, look directly at the target; if you avert your gaze, you are sending out mixed, contradictory messages. Remember, you are expressing the way you feel based on what you think, not the ways others might feel or think. You have a perfect right to express this, just as others have the right to use the sequence when talking to you.

It sometimes helps to do a background analysis of the situation in which you find yourself. Have a go at completing this in the following form, or simply type or write it up on a larger sheet of paper. Once you have done this, write a script using the feedback sequence, and then rehearse it. If you feel it has potential to change a real-world situation, take the plunge and try it.

Background analysis

The situation is:	
The target person is:	
The main problems you have in communicating with the target person are:	

Feedback sequence and scripting

Phase	Cue words	Your script
1	When you …	
2	This happens …	
3	And I feel …	
4	Would you …	
5	Because/That way/This would mean …	
6	I/You/They would feel …	
7	So what do you think?	

Feedback: jargon we can do without?

'Feedback' – do we really need another piece of jargon? Why borrow a term from the worlds of computing and engineering when other, older, perfectly serviceable words such as 'advice', 'comment', 'response' and 'warning' could do the job? All those terms are useful and should be applied wherever possible. The term feedback might in fact be used by some to trivialise or downplay advice from others. However, in other circumstances it may have some value, especially for those of us who are uncomfortable with or suspicious of expressing emotions and opinions: the detached, arm's-length term allows some of us to transmit and receive perceptions and views without too much embarrassment or awkwardness. Sometimes people find it easier to say, in a low-key way, 'Can I give you some feedback on that?' or 'Can you give me some feedback on how I went?'

The same can be said of a related piece of jargon, again taken from the world of computing – 'input'. At one level, this use of the term ('Can we have some input from you on this?') is laughable, but again it may be the easiest way to get a response from certain people. In terms of transparent language and communication processes, it may well be that the only way we can communicate with some people – almost certainly heavy users of jargon themselves, with elaborate personal defence mechanisms in place – is to use jargon too. Our aim should then be to create a comfort zone for them from which we can gently begin to challenge their need for jargon in the first place (see online chapter 'Writing skills 4: plain English').

Receiving feedback

We should be willing to get as well as give feedback – if we can dish it out, we have to be able to take it too. We saw earlier that listening can let us discover the truth about ourselves and others, even if that truth is unpalatable. The repertoire of skills we have looked at in this chapter so far – listening and feedback – can thus be seen as intimately interconnected: the better we get at one, the chances are the better we will get at the others.

The Johari window

So far, we have considered the processes involved in giving feedback to others – the feedback being about those others. We have also considered the concept of receiving feedback through effective listening. What, however, about giving feedback to others about ourselves? Is this a wise thing – telling others about how we feel and what we think? And if it is a wise thing, are there limits to how much we should disclose to others?

Johari window: model for understanding communication interactions with others in terms of the extent to which we seek or solicit feedback (our capacity to listen) and the extent to which we are willing to give feedback about ourselves (our capacity to disclose)

A model which might prove useful in answering these questions is that of the **Johari window**, originally devised by Joseph Luft and Harry Ingham (Johari = JOseph + HAR(ry)I) (Luft 1969; Beck 1994; Shenton, 2007) (see figure 10.5). The Johari window is a model of the way we communicate or transact with the outside world. It works by categorising our interactions into:

- the extent to which we seek or solicit feedback from others – our capacity to listen
- the extent to which we are willing to give feedback about ourselves – our capacity to disclose.

The Johari window has four panes, but these panes can be of different sizes.

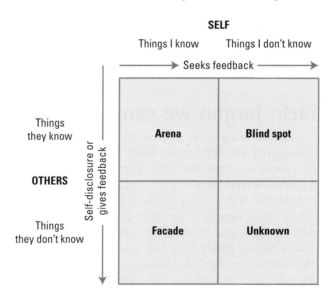

FIGURE 10.5 The Johari window

The first area is the *Arena*, which is the area known to ourselves and also known to others. This is the public domain: we have control over information and behaviour here, and we are comfortable with others knowing about such information and behaviour. These might be names, appearance, marital status, long-held and publicly-aired opinions, mannerisms we are aware of, and so on.

The second area is the *Blind spot*: in here we find information and behaviour that we are not currently aware of, but others are. On the downside, this might comprise factors such as bad breath, or displaying – via slips of the tongue and body language – our subconscious dislike of people whom we think we like; while on the upside, it might be our being not-so-blissfully unaware that other people really like us.

The third area is called the *Facade*: here, we find information and behaviour which we are aware of, but which we choose not to reveal to others. Here live our dark secrets, but also more innocuous facts, opinions and behaviour that we simply decide to suppress at certain times when dealing with certain people, but which we bring into the Arena area at other times and when dealing with other people.

Finally, we have the *Unknown* area: this is unknown to others, and also unknown to ourselves, and comprises information and behaviour which lies within our subconscious mind. Material within this pane may never move to the other panes at all, or else it may emerge when changed circumstances call forth hitherto unsuspected motives, feelings, opinions and behaviour.

Feedback and disclosure

The relative sizes of Arena, Blind spot and Facade – and to a lesser extent, Unknown – are determined by the way we interact with others. Our Blind spot pane can be made smaller, for example, by others giving feedback – observations, opinions – to us, but the extent to which others give us feedback usually is strongly influenced by the extent to which we send out signals ('vibes') that we are ready to listen to others and that we actively seek or solicit feedback. If others perceive us to be prickly and defensive, as someone who not only doesn't want to hear good or bad news, but in fact is ready to shoot the messenger or punish those who wish to tell the truth, then we won't hear much about ourselves from the outside world. 'And a good thing, too', you might respond – why should the opinions of others worry you? Feedback from others is the most important form of reality checking we have; to see ourselves as others see us is the most illuminating form of self-knowledge we can gain, and also cheap at the price – such reflected truth can save us a lot of the pain we would endure if we had to discover truth at first hand.

Our Facade pane can be made smaller by self-disclosure, or giving feedback. Why should you bother to do such a risky thing? For a start, self-disclosing may actually help you to clarify and formulate your own thoughts and feelings: 'How do I know what I think until I see what I say?' (Forster 2000 [1927]). Also, most people have a strong need to communicate with others, to 'get it off their chest' or to tell the truth. When this need cannot be met with actual interaction with others, people may self-disclose by keeping a diary, talking to a pet, or talking to God. Self-disclosure can be used to project a favourable impression, as when we selectively self-disclose when out on a date with someone we are trying to impress, or when we are being interviewed for a job or promotion. Further, when we self-disclose, this acts as a model for others, and may lead to more open communication – 'I'll lower my Facade if you lower yours'.

Finally, we should make a conscious effort to self-disclose because we may already be unconsciously self-disclosing through slips of the tongue and body language or other non-verbal communication.

Of course, while self-disclosure or giving feedback about yourself means expressing your opinions, feelings and thoughts in a manner appropriate to the situation, total truth in self-disclosure is not always necessary or even desirable. Sometimes even the frankest of communicators needs to tell white lies or practise deception (to save face, to reduce tension or conflict) or to equivocate ('Well, this food certainly is – different!') (Berger 2005). You need to make decisions about self-disclosure based upon your estimate of two inversely related quantities – risk and trust (Eunson 1994, pp. 72–4). We need to also bear in mind that the Johari window concept is very much a product of western, individualist, assertive, low context and low power–distance cultures (see 'Hofstede's model of communication' in chapter 15), and thus may not be appropriate for all cultures around the world.

Different windows: bulls, confessors and others

The Johari window can come in many different shapes. Different people have different windows, and indeed the one person might have different windows in different situations with different people (Hansen 1973). Some of these different windows are shown in figure 10.6.

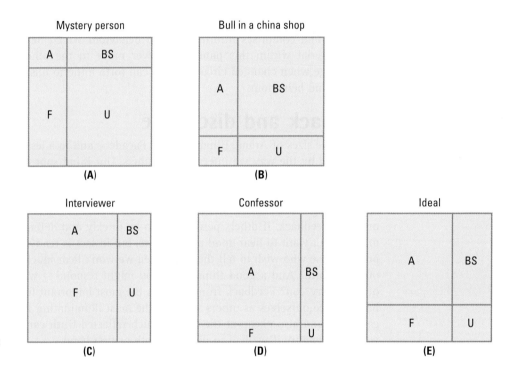

FIGURE 10.6 Five different types of Johari window

Source: Adapted from Hansen (1973).

Thus for example, Person A in figure 10.6 is a *Mystery person*: they don't give feedback about themselves, and they don't seek out feedback. Such a person may have perfect self-knowledge and therefore doesn't need to interact with the world, but this seems unlikely, to judge from the size of their Unknown area.

Person B is like a *Bull in a china shop*: they are very forward in giving feedback – opinions, feelings, thoughts – but they don't appear to be too ready to accept feedback. They may not listen well, they may have behaved in such ways in the past – getting angry, bursting into tears, threatening to leave – that others have learned not to try very hard in giving feedback. Thus their Blind spot is enormous. These persons tend to be Aggressive types and in nonverbal communication terms, they may be dyssemic.

Like Person B, Person C also indulges in one-way instead of two-way communication, but this time it is a different game: while this person asks for a lot of feedback ('What do you think?' 'How would you handle it if you were me?'), they give away very little about themselves. They want others to take risks, but do not wish to reciprocate. They play the role of an *Interviewer*, when in fact they should be playing the role of a conversationalist, who gives as well as takes. The Interviewer's Facade is thus very high.

Person D is very much into two-way communication, but at overkill levels. The *Confessor* self-discloses just about everything about themselves to others, and asks for continual feedback about themselves, but does not grasp that others are embarrassed or simply put off by such runaway feedback. They give out too much information, and do not have well-developed norms of tact and discretion. Their Blind spot is large, and their Facade is — for other people's liking — too low.

Person E has an *Ideal* window. Their Facade is low (but not too low) and while they still have a Blind spot, it is not large. As a consequence, their Arena is large and their Unknown area is small. Such a person is easy to communicate with, and others rarely have to read such people's minds to find out what they really think and feel. Their self-knowledge is considerable. The more we become aware of such different windows, the more self-aware we may become about our communication style and the way we interact — or don't interact — with others.

Windows: individual, group, organisational

The Johari window is usually used to analyse interpersonal and intrapersonal communication, but it has applications beyond those realms. It is sometimes meaningful to create a Johari window for a team or a group, in order to try to maximise the Arena or open area of communication. In teams or groups, for example, it is vital that norms of conformity (see 'Norms' in chapter 18) do not stifle a free flow of information. In fact, it can be very useful to establish a norm where the giving of such frank feedback is encouraged in a formal way; for example, a sound-off segment at the end of a team meeting when the formal business is concluded.

The Johari window model has also been expanded to help understand flows and breakdowns in organisational communication. Galpin (1995) uses the concept to talk about organisational grapevines or rumour mills (see 'The informal organisation: I heard it through the grapevine' in chapter 16). When communication consultants or change agents try to improve communication within an organisation, they may find it useful to use a Johari model (figure 10.7).

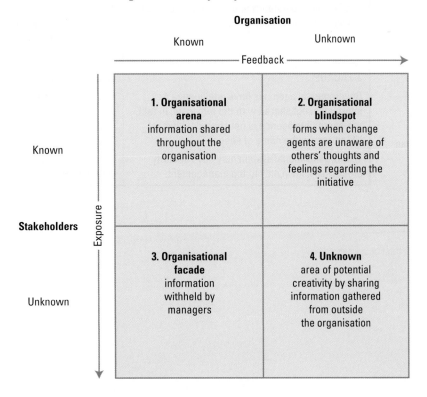

FIGURE 10.7 The organisational Johari
Source: Galpin (1995, p. 31).

In chapter 16, we explore the dynamics of organisational communication, noting that if upward communication is blocked or inhibited, messages will not get through. This is particularly the case if there is a 'shoot-the-messenger' ethos in place (see 'Bad culture 2: the culture of silence'), which means that anyone telling the truth may be punished for doing just that, even though the truth — about faulty products, health hazards, attitudes of resistance and hostility — may be precisely what is needed. In chapter 17, we explore the dynamics of public communication, and pay particular attention to crisis communication. Organisations which have a shoot-the-messenger ethos or culture tend to have a lot of crises because they have low levels of organisational transparency or information flow. Galpin's model suggests increasing the size of the organisational Arena quadrant to maximise information flow and trust, minimise or eliminate communication breakdowns and crises, and restrict the growth of the grapevine or rumour mill (see 'The information organisation: I heard it through the grapevine' in chapter 16; see also Hase, Davies & Dick 1999).

Davies (2005) has used the Johari model to analyse North American perceptions of extreme crises in or threats to US organisations (figure 10.8). Organisations, she argues, are now crucially dependent upon computer-based information systems, and yet these are uniquely vulnerable. Today, there are both threats posed from outside the organisation (e.g. by terrorists, industrial spies and hackers) and threats posed from inside the organisation (e.g. from disgruntled employees and computer criminals). (In the United States, the FBI estimates that 75 per cent of computer crime is committed by 'disgruntled insiders'.) In this model, while it may be preferred to decrease the size of the Blind spot and Unknown areas, it may not always be advisable to decrease the Facade (insofar as that is possible, of course).

1. ARENA	2. BLIND SPOT
The terrorists are threatened by the United States and feel we intrude into Middle East affairs much too often. Many feel the United States protects Israel at the expense of the Muslims.	The terrorists are living amongst us and living as one of us.
The insider understands your intranet and may be familiar with many pass codes.	The insider, if disgruntled, may have studied the company vulnerabilities and these vulnerabilities may not be a known for your corporate leadership.
3. FACADE	4. UNKNOWN
Governmental agencies have intelligence information not shared with the terrorists. In fact, top-secret intelligence is not shared with most US citizens in the name of security.	It is uncertain how the Israeli–Palestinian conflict will be resolved.
Your organisational system may have security processes known only to top management.	It is unknown how worldwide terrorism will affect your organisation's role in the global marketplace.

FIGURE 10.8 The Johari approach to analysing threats to North American organisations

Source: Adapted from Davis (2005, pp. 125–7).

STUDENT STUDY GUIDE

SUMMARY

Listening is not the same as hearing; rather, it is paying concentrated attention to the words and behaviour of others. The paradox of listening is that it is the form of communication we practise most often, yet because we rarely have formal training in it, it may be the one that we do most poorly.

Listening has considerable value in personal and professional settings: for example, it helps us to gain the full picture of a situation; it lets us learn and survive; it lets us discover the truth; it encourages others to solve their own problems; and it allows us to cope with distractions and stress. Simply listening to others does not necessarily mean we agree with them.

There are numerous barriers to effective listening, such as paying too much (or not enough) attention to facts, and being distracted by the appearance of and the values expressed by those we listen to. Active or reflective listening allows us to engage in two-way communication with others in order to clarify messages and reassure them. Effective questioning means using the right types of questions in different situations when interacting with different personalities. Feedback may mean advice, support or criticism. The feedback sequence offers us a script we can use to convey our thoughts without being distracted or undermined by the stress of confrontation. The Johari window model allows us to seek feedback about ourselves and to disclose feedback about ourselves to others so that we might gain better self-knowledge. We need to create an optimal mix of seeking and disclosing so that we learn but do not make ourselves too vulnerable in the process. The Johari model can also be applied usefully to understanding communication processes in groups and organisations.

KEY TERMS

active listening *p. 319*

aggressive listening *p. 313*

effective questioning *p. 321*

feedback *p. 323*

Johari window *p. 330*

management by listening *p. 312*

REVIEW QUESTIONS

1. What is the listening paradox?
2. Identify at least three reasons why listening is so important in both professional and personal situations.
3. What role does nonverbal communication play in listening?
4. What are the fallacies of listening?
5. Identify at least three different types of questioning.
6. Why is feedback sometimes ineffective?
7. What are the key phases in the script of the assertive feedback sequence?
8. What are the four different quadrants of the Johari window?

APPLIED ACTIVITIES

1. Write a dialogue in which both words and thoughts are set out. Create a scene in which two or more people interact with each other, with most or all of the barriers to listening erected. Comment on the communication problems this raises.
2. Why would closed questions be inappropriate at the beginning of some conversations, and why would open questions be inappropriate at the conclusion of some other conversations?
3. Consider a personal or professional situation you are familiar with. What effects might flow from not giving negative feedback in this situation?

4. Consider a personal or professional situation you are familiar with. What effects might flow from not giving positive feedback in this situation?
5. Consider a personal or professional situation you are familiar with. What effects might flow from one person disclosing feedback about themselves and the other person refusing to do the same?

WHAT WOULD YOU DO?

You work as a team leader in the Customer Accounts section of a large bank. One of your team members, Sylvia, comes to talk to you. A number of your team members have already confidentially made complaints about her, saying she has an aggressive style that is making things difficult not only with her colleagues but also with customers.

Sylvia has a number of gripes, all of which you listen to patiently, rarely interrupting and only occasionally responding with some active listening-type questions. You rapidly form the opinion that she is a very angry person, and possibly close to being out of control. This is going to take some fixing. She concludes by saying that because she has been looking after one of the bank's biggest customers, Mainline Informatics, she deserves a bonus over and above the standard bonus the team members – 'those slackers' – will be receiving in two weeks' time.

In fact, yesterday you received an email from the assistant manager at Mainline, complaining about Sylvia's poor attitude and requesting that she be replaced. You decide to broach these matters with Sylvia, but before you can get into this you need to veto the bonus request. You gently say no, meaning to go on to give your reasons. Sylvia suddenly yells: 'What do you mean, no? You've been standing there expressing complete agreement with me for the past five minutes! Are you crazy, or just a liar?'

How will you respond to Sylvia?

SUGGESTED READING

Bogaard, Lindsay 2006, 'Developing a stakeholder listening process', *Strategic Communication Management*, vol. 10, no. 2, pp. 18–21.

Fleenor, John W, Taylor, Sylvester & Chappelow 2009, 'Leveraging the impact of 360-degree feedback', *Personnel Psychology*, vol. 62, no. 1.

Goulston, Mark 2010, *Just listen: discover the secret to getting through to absolutely anyone*, AMACOM, New York.

Hathaway, Patti 1998, *Feedback: the breakthrough communication skill*, Crisp Publications, Menlo Park, CA.

London, Manuel 2009, *Job feedback: giving, seeking and using feedback for performance improvement*, 2nd edn., Lawrence Erlbaum Associates, Mahwah, NJ.

Maurer, Rick 2011, *Feedback toolkit: 16 tools for better communication in the workplace*, 2nd edn, Productivity Press, New York.

REFERENCES

Adler, Ronald B, Rosenfeld Lawrence B & Proctor, Russell F 2009, *Interplay: the process of interpersonal communication*, 11th edn., New York, Oxford University Press.

Aggarwal, Praveen, Castleberry, Stephen B & Ridnour, Rick 2005, 'Salesperson empathy and listening: impact on relationship outcomes', *Journal of Marketing Theory and Practice*, vol. 13, no. 3, pp. 16–30.

Atwater, Eastwood 1991, *I hear you: a listening skills handbook*, Walker and Co., New York.

Bavelas, Janet Beavin, Coates, Linda & Johnson, Trudy 2002, 'Listener responses as a collaborative process: the role of gaze', *Journal of Communication*, vol. 52, no. 3, pp. 566–80.

Beck, Charles E 1994, 'Perspectives on the self in communication: the cognition continuum and the Johari Window', *Technical Communication*, vol. 41, no. 4, pp. 753–4.

Berger, Charles R 2005, 'Interpersonal communication: theoretical perspectives, future prospects', *Journal of Communication*, vol. 55, no. 3, pp. 415–48.

Burley-Allen, Madelyn 1995, *Listening: the forgotten skill*, John Wiley & Sons, New York.

Clark, Thomas 1999, 'Sharing the importance of attentive listening skills', *Journal of Management Education*, vol. 23, no. 2, pp. 92–106.

Davis, Beverly J 2005, 'PREPARE: seeking systematic solutions for technological crisis management', *Knowledge and Process Management*, vol. 12, no. 2, pp. 123–31.

De Janasz, Suzanne C, O'Dowd, Karen O & Schneider, Beth Z 2009, *Interpersonal skills in organizations*, New York, McGraw-Hill, Irwin.

DeVito, Joseph A 2011, *Human Communication: the basic course*, 12th edn, Allyn & Bacon, Boston, MA.

Doherty, Nora & Guyler, Marcelas 2008, *The essential guide to workplace mediation and conflict resolution: rebuilding working relationships*, London/New York, Kogan Page.

Eunson, Baden 1994, *Communicating for team building*, John Wiley & Sons, Brisbane.

Fairhurst, Gail T 2005, 'Reframing the art of framing: problems and prospects for leadership', *Leadership*, vol. 1, no. 2, pp. 165–85.

Fairhurst, GT & Sarr, RA 1996, *The art of framing: managing the language of leadership*, Jossey-Bass, San Francisco.

Fisher, Roger, Patton, Bruce M & Ury, William L 1992, *Getting to yes: negotiating agreement without giving in*, 2nd edn., Houghton Mifflin, Boston, MA.

Flatley, Marie & Rentz, Kathryn 2010, *M: Business communication*, 2nd edn.. Boston, MA, Houghton Mifflin.

Folkman, Joseph R 2006, *The power of feedback: 35 principles for turning feedback from others into personal and professional change*, John Wiley & Sons, Hoboken, NJ.

Forster, EM 2000 [1927], *Aspects of the novel*, Penguin, London.

Galpin, Timothy 1995, 'Pruning the grapevine', *Training and Development*, vol. 49, no. 2, pp. 28–33.

Gamble, Terri Kwal & Gamble, Michael 2008, *Communication works*, 9th edn., McGraw-Hill, New York.

Goby, Valerie & Lewis, Justus 2000, 'The key role of listening in business: a study of the Singapore insurance industry', *Business Communication Quarterly*, June, vol. 63, no. 2, pp. 43–54.

Graham, John L & Herberger, Roy A Jr 1990, 'Negotiators abroad: don't shoot from the hip', *Harvard Business Review*, vol. 61, no. 4, pp. 160–9.

Guffey, Mary Ellen 2009, *Business communication: process & product*, 6th edn, Mason, OH, Cengage.

Hansen, Phillip C 1973, 'The Johari Window: a model for soliciting and giving feedback', in William J Pfeiffer and John E Jones (eds), *The 1973 annual handbook for group facilitators*, University Associates, Palo Alto, CA.

Hargie, Owen & Dixon, David 2011, *Skilled interpersonal communication: research, theory and practice*, 2nd edn, Routledge, London.

Hase, Stewart, Davies, Alan & Dick, Bob 1999, 'The Johari Window and the dark side of organisations', http://ultibase.rmit.edu.au, RMIT, Melbourne.

Iuppa, Nicholas V 1986, *Management by guilt, and other uncensored tactics*, Fawcett, New York.

Laughlin, Carol 2000, 'The trials, tribulations and traumas of feedback', *Training Journal*, April, pp. 4–6.

Leonard, Dorothy 2002, 'The limitations of listening', *Harvard Business Review*, vol. 80, no. 1, pp. 83–6.

Livingwood, John 2003, 'Mediation: reframing and its uses', *Dispute Resolution Journal*, vol. 57, no. 42, pp. 12–23.

Locker, Kitty O & Kaczmarek, Stephen Kyo 2009, *Business communication*, 4th edn, New York, McGraw-Hill.

Luft, Joseph 1969, *Of human interaction*, Natural Press, Palo Alto, CA.

Lundkvista, Jonas, Åkerlind, Ingemar, Borquist, Lars, and Mölstabd, Sigvard 2002, 'The more time spent on listening, the less time spent on prescribing antibiotics in general practice', *Family Practice*, vol. 19, no. 6, pp. 638–40.

Marigold, Denise C, Holmes, John G & Ross, Michael 2007, 'More than words: reframing compliments from romantic partners fosters security in low self-esteem individuals', *Journal of Personality and Social Psychology*, vol. 92, no. 2, pp. 232–48.

Montgomery, Robert 1984, *Listening made easy: how to improve listening on the job, at home, and in the community*, Amacom, New York.

Morris, Desmond 2002, *Peoplewatching: the Desmond Morris guide to body language*, Vintage, London.

Noesner, Gary W & Webster, Mike 1997, 'Crisis intervention: using active listening skills in negotiation', *FBI Law Enforcement Bulletin*, vol. 66, no. 8, pp. 13–20.

Peters, Tom 1991, *Thriving on chaos: handbook for a managerial revolution*, HarperCollins, New York.

—— 2002, 'What gets measured gets done', *Office Solutions*, November–December.

Rosenblatt, SB, Cheatham, TR & Watt, HH 1982, *Communication in business*, Prentice Hall, Englewood Cliffs, NJ.

Salopek, Jennifer J 1999, 'Survey says', *Training & Development*, vol. 53, no. 9, p. 16.

Shafir, Rebecca Z 2003, *The zen of listening: communications in the age of distractions*, Quest Books, Wheaton, IL.

Shenton, Andrew K 2007, 'Viewing information needs though a Johari Window', *Reference Services Review*, vol. 35, no. 3, pp. 487–96.

Shmueli, Deborah, Elliott, Michael & Kaufman, Sandra 2006, 'Frame changes and the management of intractable conflict', *Conflict Resolution Quarterly*, vol. 24, no. 2, pp. 207–18.

Sigband, Norman B & Bell, Arthur H 1989, *Communication for management and business*, 5th edn, Scott, Foresman, Glenview, IL.

Vazire, Simine 2009, 'Knowing me, knowing you: the accuracy and unique predictive validity of self-ratings and other-ratings of daily behavior', *Journal of Personality and Social Psychology*, vol. 95, no. 5, pp. 1202–16.

Wade, John H 1994, 'Strategic interventions used by mediators, facilitators, and conciliators', *Australasian Dispute Resolution Journal*, vol. 5, no. 4, pp. 292–304.

11

Oral communication

LEARNING OBJECTIVES

After studying this chapter you should be able to:

- List at least three types of oral communication that are important in our personal and professional lives
- Explain the differences between communicating a message in speech and in writing
- Recommend different strategies for communicating orally with different types of audiences
- Identify approaches to planning and structuring oral communication exercises
- Discuss at least five different approaches to managing stress in oral communication situations
- Describe nonverbal communication associated with effective speaking
- Describe effective voice production factors
- Recommend appropriate audiovisual aids to support oral communication performances
- Apply an evaluation model to effectiveness in oral communication performance

Speaking out and finding your tongue

Many people find public speaking stressful and thus avoid it whenever possible. We will shortly consider how best to manage stress when speaking. The ability to speak effectively to others in formal or informal settings is commonly regarded as something inborn ('the gift of the gab'), rather than as something that can be learned. Some abilities are to an extent inborn, but most of them can be acquired and improved with effort. Even if you are apprehensive about your own speaking abilities, working through the material in this chapter should help you become a substantially better communicator. Skills can be learned, so why not by you? You may also find that acquiring public speaking skills helps boost your self-confidence, so that you become a more competent communicator in a number of different areas.

Forms of oral communication

We often think of 'public speaking' or 'presentation skills' as referring to ourselves in a nightmare scenario: standing on a platform with a microphone and sweating with stress, with hundreds or even thousands of people listening to us — many of whom may have a skeptical or hostile look. But there are many situations in which we might be called on to speak, or where we may feel the need to speak, and they are not nearly so nightmarish.

For example, a survey of graduates who had recently entered the workforce identified the following oral communication situations (Crosling & Ward 2002):

- Presentations
- Informal work-related discussions
- Persuading colleagues
- Giving feedback
- Informal social conversation
- Listening
- Following instructions
- Networking
- Instructing, explaining and demonstrating
- Negotiating with clients and employers
- Conflict resolution
- Chairing/leading discussions
- Building relations with fellow team members.

Within the specific arena of meetings, for example, other important forms of communication besides presentations included participating in and leading discussions and persuading (figure 11.1) (Crosling & Ward 2002, p. 52). We may not even be in the same room with our audience, communicating instead by newer forms of communication, such as teleconferenced meetings.

Crosling and Ward (2002) concluded that to fully participate in the workplace and to achieve successful career outcomes, those yet to enter the workforce needed education or training in all of the generic skills listed, as well as:

- skill in participating in inductively structured communication situations (e.g. informal conversations) as well as in deductively structured communication situations (e.g. formal presentations and agenda-based meetings)
- rapport building and politeness
- awareness of gender, cultural, status-based and generational factors in interactions
- ability to approach issues critically
- ability to be assertive in presenting views.

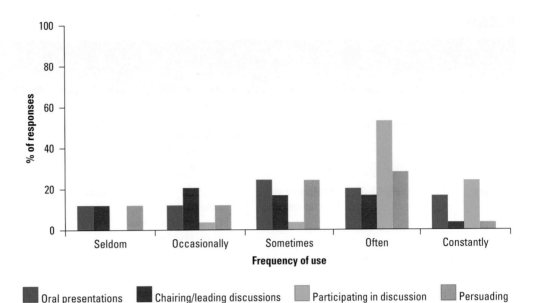

FIGURE 11.1 Frequency of forms of communication used in meetings

These *soft skills* are often not so much formally taught as picked up along the way; some are even thought to be inborn and, therefore, 'unlearnable'. The skills are learnable, of course, and need to be imparted in a systematic way in the context of the broader concept of communication.

Let's now look at the practicalities of oral communication, including different types of oral communication discourse, the distinctions between spoken and oral communication, how to understand and work with audiences, how to plan and structure a talk, how best to handle stress, some aspects of nonverbal communication, the use of audiovisual aids, and how to assess our performances.

Different types of oral communication discourse

Oral communication is not confined, of course, to the workplace. There are many situations in which individuals speak to others in nonconversational ways. These different situations can be analysed in terms of audience size, time taken, the intent or purpose of the speaker, whether there is a two-way communication with the audience, and whether audiovisual equipment or other props are needed (table 11.1).

TABLE 11.1 Speaking in different public situations

Discourse type	Audience size	Time taken	Speaker's intent	Two-way exchange?	Audiovisual equipment, props used
Impromptu speech	Any	Usually short	• To inform and persuade • To show mastery of content • To show verbal prowess	Sometimes (e.g. questions from audience, interjections, heckling)	Sometimes (e.g. microphone)
Wedding speech	Usually 30–200	Preferably short; sometimes long	• To celebrate ceremonial/ritual occasion • To entertain	Sometimes (e.g. interjections, heckling)	Sometimes (e.g. microphone)

(continued)

TABLE 11.1 *(continued)*

Discourse type	Audience size	Time taken	Speaker's intent	Two-way exchange?	Audiovisual equipment, props used
Work presentation	Usually 5–100; can be larger	Preferably short; sometimes long	■ To inform ■ To persuade ■ To challenge ■ Sometimes to entertain	Often (e.g. questions, sometimes hostile responses)	Often
Sermon	Usually 50–300	Preferably short; sometimes long	■ To inspire ■ To challenge ■ To present other values and perspectives	Rarely	Perhaps a public address (PA) system; ritual paraphernalia
Sport pep talk	Usually 5–30	Usually short	■ To inform ■ To persuade ■ To motivate ■ To challenge	Not much	Boards, charts, video
Work briefing	Usually 5–20	Preferably short; sometimes long	■ To inform ■ To persuade ■ To clarify roles and goals	Preferably yes (for feedback purposes)	Sometimes
Lift/elevator pitch	Usually 1	Very short	■ To inform ■ To persuade ■ To evoke interest	Preferably yes	Little opportunity (a business card?)

In each situation, we speak in order to inform, persuade or entertain, or a mix of these. In each case, the speaker takes on the role of principal communicator in the encounter between two or more people. In some situations, the speaker's intent is to please the audience, perhaps even to make them laugh; in others, the speaker may set out to provoke or challenge: the audience may be made angry, but if the object was to change the behaviour of others, this may have been part of the speaker's plan. In some circumstances, the audience will remain relatively passive, while in others it may be more active than the speaker would like. All oral communication involves two-way communication. Consider the circumstances surrounding a speaker addressing a crowd and an employee taking a problem to a manager: both speakers need to interact with 'the other', not just conduct a one-way transmission of information. All public speaking situations involve the types of dynamics we will explore in this chapter: audience analysis and management, planning and structuring, and getting the information/persuasion/entertainment mix right.

Perhaps surprisingly, the same principles apply to impromptu, off-the-cuff speeches. Some of the most accomplished speakers, who always seem to have a few apt words to say, have actually already planned their 'unprepared' speeches. Mark Twain once wrote, 'It usually takes more than three weeks to prepare a good impromptu speech'. Or, as the proverb goes, 'Luck is opportunity met by preparation'. Practice and preparation can help you not only to develop your speaking abilities, but also to master any stress you associate with public speaking situations. You may find it benefits both your career and your personal life to invest in preparation time now so you are not at a loss for words later; and to put in effort now so that others perceive you as speaking effortlessly later.

Spoken words and written words

Effective communication requires us to make the right channel choice, which is a jargon-ised way of saying that we need to work out what communication medium (an email? a private conversation? a written report? a phone call? an audiovisual presentation?) will best convey our message (see chapter 1). Oral communication may be ideal in certain situations and inappropriate in others. For example, in a professional or work setting we need to decide when it is better to communicate information and opinions in writing rather than verbally. In practical terms, this often boils down to the choice between writing a report or delivering a presentation (or an oral report) (see chapter 5, 'Reports and proposals'). In fact, they are not mutually exclusive: the large document you may have worked on may be ignored until your oral presentation piques the interest of your audience, and only then might they pick up the document.

Let's look at the differences between the channels or media of the written report and the oral report or presentation (table 11.2).

TABLE 11.2 Differences between written and oral reports

Written report	Oral report
Reader controls message: can reread difficult passages	Except in small group settings, speaker controls message: listeners must understand the first time
Reader's initial reaction is not known	Listener provides direct feedback, even in large groups
Reader sets the pace	Speaker sets the pace
Reader's attention span is usually longer	Listener's attention span is limited, although it may increase with the use of audiovisual aids
Content is often longer and developed in greater depth	Content is usually shorter with fewer points at more limited depth
Reader has fewer physical restrictions	Listener subject to physical limitations such as having to remain seated
Uses reader aids such as paragraphs and punctuation	Uses listener aids such as pauses, inflection, pitch and pace

(continued)

 **TABLE 11.2** *(continued)*

Written report	Oral report
Provides a written record	Provides no record unless recorded
Makes information retrieval relatively easy	Information retrieval from recorded speech more difficult
Writer must spell, punctuate and paragraph	Speaker must enunciate clearly and inflect and pause appropriately
Emphasis is on correctness because readers catch even small errors	Audiences are usually not so alert or critical of errors
Writer may not know all readers	Speaker usually can see who is listening

Source: Adapted from William V Ruch and Maurice L Crawford (1988), *Business reports: written and oral*, PWS-Kent, Boston, MA, p. 321. Reproduced with permission.

Control

With written reports, the message receiver – the reader – is in control of the communication process and has the freedom to reread difficult passages. With oral reports, control rests with the message sender – the presenter. Because of this, the receiver must understand the message the first time or else ask for clarification or repetition. With written reports it is the reader who sets the pace of the communication, whereas with oral reports it is the speaker who sets the pace.

Feedback and pacing

The creator of a written report does not know what the initial reaction of the reader is. Feedback may be forthcoming eventually, but there is a period of uncertainty for the writer. With oral reports, listeners (even when part of a large group) can usually provide immediate, direct feedback; the sender can often detect right away what people think by decoding the nonverbal messages they send (boredom, confusion, anger, sympathy, excitement), and can adjust the content and style accordingly. The speaker controls the pace at which the message is conveyed, while readers of a written document control the pace of communication.

Audience attention span and content depth

The reader of a written report generally has a longer attention span, and indeed is not obliged to absorb all the report's message in one sitting – having the option of reading it in sections and at convenient times and places. This is just as well, as written reports are usually considerably longer and developed in greater depth than oral presentations (just as a screenplay of a novel is usually substantially shorter than the novel itself). The attention span of a typical listener is shorter (although the use of audiovisual aids can provide additional stimulus), and the listener is physically more constrained than the reader.

Aids to comprehension

Effective communication is carefully planned. We choose our words carefully and use structure and pace to control the communication, giving cues to our audience on the meanings we wish to convey. These cues may be visual (e.g. the punctuation and paragraphing of a written document) or aural (a speaker's pausing, inflection, pitching and pacing).

To minimise ambiguity and communication breakdown, we need to observe the conventions appropriate to the communication channel we are using. Writers of all documents, including reports, need to spell, punctuate and paragraph with accuracy and care if their message is to be faithfully conveyed. Speakers need to enunciate clearly and inflect and pause appropriately. Different skills are used when delivering similar messages via different communication channels. At the same time, different standards of accuracy are applied by different audiences. Readers of a written document may detect the smallest typographical error. Written communication, therefore, places a high premium on correctness. Audiences listening to spoken presentations tend to be more forgiving; most people apply different standards to spoken and written English.

Record and recall

A written report provides a permanent, accessible record of the writer's communication. It is easy to retrieve information from it. An oral report, by contrast, provides no record, unless electronically recorded or transcribed. Even when recorded, it is difficult to retrieve information from it, just as it is more difficult for a musician to locate a musical passage from a record than from sheet music. Some oral presenters will distribute handout sheets covering the main points of the presentation. This can be useful as an aid to recall, although the text is usually very brief; for example, taking bullet-point form. A useful strategy is to put your professional details on the last slide of the handout, inviting members to email for a full electronic file of the presentation.

Who is the audience?

Finally, written and oral reports differ in terms of audience. A written report may ultimately have a much wider circulation than was originally intended. People quite unknown to the writer may read it. In contrast, presenters of oral reports can see their audience. Recordings of the oral report may go into circulation, but even this wider audience will probably remain relatively small.

So which is better — oral or written communication? The answer to this question, of course, depends on your audience, your message and the channels at your disposal. It may also be necessary and desirable to convey your message through more than one channel. Some members of your audience may prefer one channel over another; that is, they have different preferences and styles of processing information. Some channels have unique strengths you can exploit (and weaknesses to avoid); as such, you can send complementary messages through complementary channels, reinforcing and repeating your messages (see 'Communicating effectively using channels' in chapter 1). For example, even though you may have worked hard on a written report, your audience may not read it until their interest is triggered by a presentation from you on the same topic.

Office suite software may give you the capability to package similar and complementary units of information in different forms (e.g. a word-processed document, a presentation, a poster, a brochure, a website) — allowing you to develop a cost-effective and synergistic communication campaign that repeats and amplifies the message, and matches the format to the audience style and information processing preferences. Keep in mind that the visuals that work in a paper document may not work in a presentation, and vice versa (see 'Overview: which graphic do I use for which situation?' in chapter 2).

Audiences: targets for your message

As a public speaker, you may encounter audiences of one to 10 000 people (or even more!). Audiences differ enormously, but they also have things in common. Audiences, or specific audience members, may:
- be friendly, neutral or hostile
- prefer lots of audiovisuals or none at all

- prefer to hear the 'big picture' or want lots of detail
- have the power to make things happen or have no power at all.

It is useful to try to find out as much as possible about your audience beforehand. What are their preferences, shared values, likely prejudices and blind spots? How much technical background do they have? Will they understand the technical or specialised language or concepts you might use? All these issues need to be considered when preparing a written document too, and all of them need to be taken seriously.

Persuading your audience: a power map approach

A common oral communication situation is making a presentation or pitch to a small audience, group, meeting or panel. Perhaps you have never met the audience members before, or perhaps it is a group you are familiar with.

When you try to persuade people to adopt a particular course of action, you are dealing with the dynamics of authority and influence. These dynamics are not necessarily the same. In order to 'read' the political structure of an organisation, and the roles played by people within such structures, we need to distinguish between:

- the degree of *authority* a person has; that is, the power an individual has to make things happen
- the degree of *influence* a person has; that is, the effect an individual has on others (Flett 1996).

This distinction allows us to identify four types of people who will judge any presentation or pitch:

1. *Decision makers*. They have both authority and influence. Some individuals are 'rubber stampers', or people with authority but no influence (e.g. executives who send out emails that no-one pays any attention to).
2. *Influencers*. They have influence but no authority. Some (*key influencers*) are more influential than others.
3. *Collectors*. They have neither authority nor influence. They collect information, and act as a conduit to those with either influence or power or both. 'They can help you or hinder you, depending on the level of rapport or respect you share.'
4. *Socials*. They will be members of the group or panel, but will play no role (Flett 1996, pp. 126–7).

Using these categories, it is possible to create a 'power map' of those to whom you are speaking, in which the power wielded by each person is proportionally represented (figure 11.2).

The chief executive officer of an organisation may not always be the key decision maker; in some circumstances, the production manager or the marketing manager, or someone else entirely, may have greater influence. A relatively low-ranking technical expert may be deferred to in areas in which that person has expertise. A low-ranking assistant to a more powerful person may possess considerable clout in putting a positive or negative spin on a proposal.

It is not always possible to create a power map, but it is always a worthwhile exercise to attempt. In attempting to plan a power map, you will often have to do some detective work and call in a few favours. This is a reason, in addition to fulfilling a desire to be a good person, that you might consider performing favours for people in instances in which there is not an immediate reward on offer. Usually, people do not forget acts of kindness in the workplace, and such acts are often repaid. Technical specialists may also be able to help you to work out who you are dealing with in this regard. Such specialists often have industry connections and grapevines that they can draw on to identify power dynamics in an organisation (also see the boxed feature on 'Boundary spanners' in chapter 16). It is also worth remembering that such roles exist in both small and large audiences.

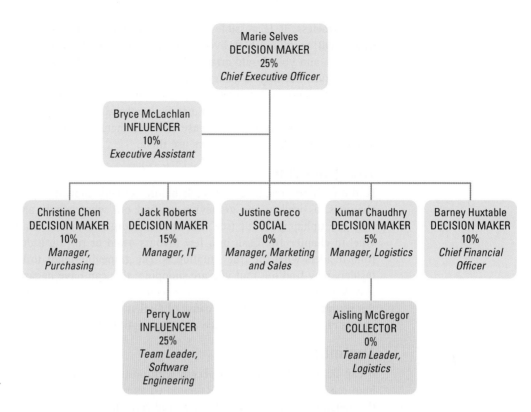

FIGURE 11.2 An organisational power map

Source: Eunson (1999, p. 224). Adapted from Flett (1996).

Analysing and working with problem audiences and audience members

Much of the fear and stress associated with public speaking comes from apprehension about the audience and its motives and behaviour. We sometimes fear the worst, worrying that the audience will be against us, but that is rarely the case. Most members of an audience generally want you to succeed, because:
- most people tend to be ethical and well intended
- even when people are neither ethical nor well intended, they don't want to have their time wasted by disruptions, and they want to hear what you have to say
- most people are fairly easily embarrassed and would prefer to avoid the embarrassment that might arise if you perform badly or if one or two members of the audience make things hard for you.

Nevertheless, it is possible that you will encounter hostility from audience members (Aziz 1998; Gordon 1984). Even then, all is not lost. In fact, if things break the right way for you – and you should arrange it so that things *do* break the right way – then you can actually turn hostility to your advantage.

Some techniques for managing a hostile audience follow. Before using any of them, bear in mind that some of them may be unethical or counterproductive in certain circumstances. Even if you choose to use none of them, however, you will still be in a better position to recognise when others use them.

The grapevine

Find out about enemies and friends before actually showing up and speaking. Use official channels, as well as the grapevine, to find out what people are happy about and what they are unhappy about (see 'The informal organisation: I heard it through the grapevine' in chapter 16). Cash in a few favours owed or run up a debt of favours to find out from insiders what the true situation is. The grapevine tends to be a two-way channel, so insiders may find out that you are snooping: this can have negative payoffs for you, but it may have positive payoffs if you are seen as someone who is concerned enough to check things out. The most common cause of audience hostility is a feeling that no-one is paying any attention (and the audience are often right to feel this).

The moderator

It can help considerably if a person with position or prestige, or someone who is held in high regard by the audience, is appointed as moderator or chair of the proceedings. Allow this person to nominate questioners, and rely on the moderator to give you a fair deal.

Mingling

It is strategic to arrive well before the scheduled time for your presentation. The time before the official talk begins is useful for getting to know people and finding out what their interests are; it is also helpful with the *Identification* tactic and may help you to manage your stress levels. Staying around afterwards allows you to debrief. It can be used as a tactic: if you are confronted with hostile individuals who take up too much airtime, you can, with justification, use the *Later* tactic – gently moving them into the post-question time period.

Knowing your stuff

Research the topic thoroughly and well in advance of the event, and be completely familiar with your material. Expertise, and the demonstration of expertise in a calm and modest manner (as opposed to an agitated and arrogant manner), will win you friends and perhaps the grudging respect of a few enemies.

Conceding ignorance

If you are asked a question to which you don't know the answer, don't try to bluff or lie – it will probably not come off, and even if it does it may come back to haunt you. It is far better to be honest and say that you don't know the answer to a question, and that you will get back to the person promptly with a response. It's a cliché, but your honesty, reputation and professionalism are among the best weapons you have, so don't throw them away.

Holding back

Don't reveal all of your information in your primary presentation or speech and be left with nothing new to say when people ask questions: new material is more likely to hold the attention of the audience and to distract them, if need be, from mulling over the content of the main presentation.

Listening with your eyes

Monitor the nonverbal reactions of your audience as you talk. Are they happy with what you are saying? Give them some more of it. Are they unhappy now? Move into another area.

Pulling the rug

Some audience members will expect you to be defensive. They will have expended considerable intellectual and emotional energy in developing critiques about what they imagine your position to be. The validity of such criticisms can be counteracted ('pulling the rug') by opening up with the concession of some points and the pre-emptive review (and, where possible, the rebuttal) of the arguments against your position. An agreement can be combined with a rebuttal by a 'changed circumstances' argument: this used to be the case, but that was then and this is now, and here are the reasons why circumstances have changed.

Avoiding arrogance

Use better information as a means of enlightenment, not as a power trip. Always show respect, especially towards those who least deserve it, and you will reap rewards in the longer term.

Multiple questioners

During question time, say you will take a question from this person with the green tie here, this person with the clipboard here, and this person with the red pen here. Strictly speaking, this reinforces your authority as the person in control. Also, if one questioner insists on turning the encounter into a dialogue, you can simply say that some good points have been raised here, but the next speaker deserves a go as well.

The recognition tactic

Set up a protocol or understanding at the start that you are more than happy to take questions, but that it might be useful for the rest of the audience if people asking questions first gave their names, and perhaps their role and organisation. Setting up such a protocol also reinforces your authority as ringmaster (the person in control), and makes for a more balanced situation.

The identification tactic

For this tactic to work, you need to know the names of those who oppose you. This is easy if you are speaking to a group you know, but not impossible in a group that you are encountering for the first time. This is why it can be very useful to arrive before show time and mingle. Make mental notes of people and their concerns, and when it comes to talking, identify them and their concerns. This lets people know that you have noted their anxieties and criticisms; it shows respect, personalises the talk and, when linked to the 'pull the rug' strategy, shows you are gracious enough to concede there is some merit in their point of view. Not incidentally, it also sets you up as the super-ringmaster who knows where people live, and can create apprehension on the part of those who haven't yet been named.

The later tactic

Here you simply point out the obvious: question and response time is limited, but you would be more than happy to talk to questioners after the formal conclusion of the session.

This should be quite acceptable for people who really do want more information, and it can be a discreet and diplomatic way of temporarily avoiding responding to people who either want to demonstrate their expertise or personal opinions, or who experience difficulty in framing suitable questions. As with conceding that you don't know some things, it is vital that you do actually make yourself available as promised. Don't be discouraged when many who agree to this course while all eyes are on them do not show up after all; this is the clearest demonstration of their true intentions when challenging you during question time.

The detox

Don't rise to the bait of loaded questions and loaded language. Simply reframe or restate the question in more neutral terms and then go on to answer it in those terms.

The filibuster

This is slightly unethical, but it can work (just as it can also backfire). When you are asked a question for which you can give a detailed response, do so in great detail. By using this approach, you will soon run out of time to answer other questions. This tactic is sometimes combined with the *Plant* tactic.

The plant

With this tactic, you simply arrange for someone to ask a nonhostile question or two, to which you respond – at length. Nonhostile here means also uncontroversial, so if there is contention in one area you might be quizzed on, but no contention in 19 others, you might receive so many perfectly innocent questions that there is no need to use a plant. Unless they are very convincing, plants tend to get 'monstered' by the audience, who accuse them of being flatterers.

The confidentiality tactic

This tactic means graciously declining to answer certain questions in detail and using an evasion, such as 'I am sure you would like to know the answer to that, and so would our competitors'. Offer to impart some kind of information privately. Sometimes confidentiality may be a genuine concern. As with most tactics, however, this one can be used only in moderation before it collapses into self-parody.

Telling the truth

Lying is very hard work. As Abraham Lincoln once remarked, 'No creature has a good enough memory to make a successful liar'. Before you face a hostile audience, it is vital that you honestly consider whether they have reason to be hostile. Finally, it doesn't matter how slick your words are or how glossy your delivery is, if you are lying. You have to look in the mirror each day, and if you do not believe what you are saying, then you should seriously reconsider your position.

Planning and structuring: what is your message?

Just what is it you want to say, and how can you best say it? What is it the audience wants to hear and not hear? What, in your judgement, does it need to hear? How can you make your message effective, standing out from other messages?

Time planning

Time is the best ally you can have, and haste your worst enemy, in any speaking situation – even those that are nominally spontaneous or impromptu. When planning an oral communication, you should factor in:

- at least twice the planned speaking time for rehearsal
- at least ten times the planned speaking time for planning and preparation (figure 11.3; see also online chapter 'Writing skills 5: how to write').

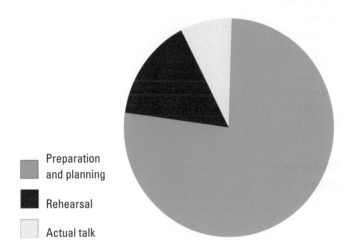

Preparation
and planning

Rehearsal

Actual talk

FIGURE 11.3 Time planning and speech preparation

Content planning

Planning the content of any communication is a demanding yet rewarding task. You need to consider the following factors:

- *Pattern of exposition.* Historical, geographical, inductive, deductive, problem solution, 5W-H (what, where, who, why, when, how).
- *Content quantity.* How many points can you make before you overload your audience? What is the minimum you can get away with so that your audience does not feel dissatisfied?
- *Focus.* What angle, emphasis or spin will you put on the content to accentuate certain aspects, concentrate attention and differentiate your approach from that of others?
- ***Spice.*** What material can you include that will add variety and insight, such as quotations, statistics, humour, an anecdote or story, analogies or metaphors, a dramatic visual, or a demonstration of a process, product, model, prop or sample?
- *The multiple audiences problem.* How can you best cater for subaudiences, such as technical versus nontechnical, visually oriented versus word oriented?
- *The multi-channel problem.* How can you best reinforce the spoken message through other channels or modes of communication and through one or several types of audio-visual aid?
- *Balance.* Have you been even-handed in considering opposing viewpoints? Do you have any blind spots or biases in your perspective that opponents or audience members will be able to point out? Have you supported your opinions with facts, or merely repeated personal prejudices?

Bearing these factors in mind, you can now plan what you are going to say, and how you are going to say it, by using the presentation structure model (figure 11.4; see overleaf).

Spice: variety added to a presentation, such as quotations, statistics, anecdotes, analogies or metaphors, dramatic visuals, demonstrations or humour

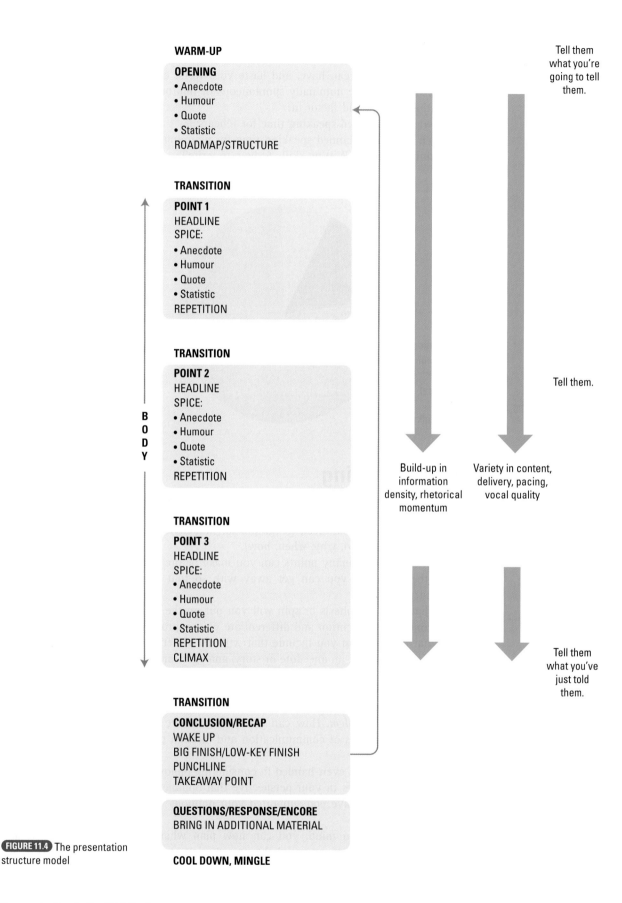

FIGURE 11.4 The presentation structure model

The model helps us stay focused on a number of factors that may help us succeed:

- If your audience is not familiar to you, get to know them beforehand by mingling and chatting. This will help warm you up to the task, sensitise you to some of the issues that concern them and help to reduce performance stress.

Three-part talk structure: Tell them what you are going to tell them; tell them; tell them what you have told them.

- Think of your oral communication as having a **three-part talk structure** like an essay — opening or introduction, body or main section, and conclusion or closing. The structure is common to many written documents. The three parts reflect one of the oldest models for speech communication:
  1. Tell them what you are going to tell them.
  2. Tell them.
  3. Tell them what you have just told them.

  A questions segment or phase would constitute a fourth part of the structure.
- Think about the need to cater to multiple or subaudiences. For example, should you plan to follow the main presentation with a formal or informal session at which you will present more specialised material?
- Try to make only three to five major points in the body or main section. Consider whether you need to make other points in other presentations or in documents, or by other means. Consider holding back some important material for release only when you are answering questions. This can help you in a number of ways. It can reduce pressure on you to cover everything, which, of course, probably will not be possible in the time allotted to you, and it can help reduce stress when you contemplate question time and interact with the audience. You can take comfort from the fact that you still have a lot of prime material with which to engage with the audience.
- Consider audiovisual presentation and other aids. What about handouts? Will computer projection work better than overhead transparencies or whiteboards? Is there a microphone, and if so, does it have any idiosyncrasies?
- Consider an attention-getting opening using 'spice' — an anecdote, statistic or quotation. This can be clichéd, but only if you let it be. Use humour if you feel comfortable with humour, but be aware that what is amusing to you may not be amusing to others.
- Let your audience in on your master plan by telling them what you are going to tell them. Consider a 'road map' graphic showing the structure of your talk.

Verbal headlining: using words like print headlines to give cues to content

- Use transitional words and phrases, rhetorical questions and **verbal headlining** to cue your audience to topic shifts, changes in perspective and summing-up sections:

  'So much for our wholesaling operations. Let's now look at retail ...'

  'What, however, can we offer our younger players who are hungry for experience in high-level games?'

  'I'll come back to these figures, but I want to turn now to the pay claim situation.'

  'At this point we can see that, on current figures, we are not going to make it. So what can we do?'
- Consider using repetition to drive points home. You can repeat one section once or several times for rhetorical effect, or you can rephrase it in a later setting.
- Increase the information density and rhetorical momentum of the talk so it builds to a climax at the end of the main or body section. Try to avoid a dull recitation of facts.
- Create variety in content, delivery, pacing and vocal range.
- In your conclusion, recapitulate material from the introduction and the body. This is not only to reinforce your argument but also to create a pleasing integrated structure for your thoughts. Consider a dramatic finish in order to 'wake up' the audience, as musical composers do. Alternatively, you might use a low-key finish that flows more seamlessly into a questions segment. Consider also whether you want to deliver a punchline or 'takeaway point' — a single word or phrase for your audience to recall 24 hours later.

- If there is a questions segment, stay at the same level of performance as you have maintained throughout your talk. Treat it as an encore, not an afterthought. You may find it useful to keep some important material in reserve, to be released only in question time.

Practice makes perfect: the value of rehearsal

As we have seen, you should spend *at least* twice the time you expect to speak on the task of rehearsing your oral communication. Rehearsal is essential because it helps you determine what material works and what doesn't; it is also a vital stress management strategy. Rehearsal may, however, be more complicated and time-consuming than it first appears. If, for example, you need to make a formal presentation, then the way to practise is to rehearse.

Rehearse:
- the full text of your presentation
- dressed and groomed as you will be during the real thing
- in the venue where you will deliver the real thing
- using the audiovisual aids you will be using in the real thing
- using video to record, play back and analyse your performance
- in front of a select audience.

Going through the *full text*, rather than rehearsing sections, will tell you the running time of the whole presentation, and help you and your select rehearsal audience determine how the communication holds together. Is it consistent? Are the transitions between sections smooth?

Familiar experiences tend to be less stressful for us, while strange experiences tend to be more stressful – not because they are necessarily unpleasant, but merely because they are unfamiliar and less predictable. The purpose of rehearsal is to make the strange more familiar and thus more manageable as an experience. You will be creating stress for yourself that you really don't need, and may give a performance far below what you are capable of if you:
- show up at a venue you are unfamiliar with
- have the intention of delivering a presentation you have never tried out before
- depend on audiovisual aids you have never worked with before
- are dressed and groomed differently from your normal everyday appearance
- do not have a clear idea of how you will look and sound.

Being *dressed and groomed as you will be* at the final event can be important. Theatre companies always have a full dress rehearsal because the artists find it easier to get 'inside' their roles than when they wear their everyday clothes. When you present, you are also playing a role different from the one you play in everyday life. Dressing up can help to habituate you to your performance clothing; it can also boost your self-image and thus – potentially – your performance. That's right – *performance*. Like it or not, you are a performer.

What about *the venue* where you will deliver the performance? It is useful to familiarise yourself with the venue. Where is it? How long does it take to get there? Is it big or small? Is it easy or difficult to work in? Where are the electrical controls (lighting, heating, cooling, power points)? How are the acoustics? Where are the exits?

Practise with the *audiovisuals* you propose to use. What works well in one venue will not necessarily work well in another. Be ready for disaster: have back-up hardware, software and spare parts (e.g. overhead projector bulbs). If travelling to the venue, whether across the corridor or across the planet, stay as close as possible to your hardware, software and spare parts.

Recording yourself in rehearsal is extremely useful, as the camera and recording device can simulate the audience's perception of you. Is your voice how you want it to sound, or will you need to modify it for this venue? Are you working well with the microphone here, or do you need to adjust it? How about your nonverbal communication? Is that how you want to look, or do you need to make changes? Is your clothing and grooming presenting you as you expected?

A *select audience* can help simulate the real performance. Having a few acquaintances in your rehearsal audience can provide you with useful feedback. They can offer suggestions on how you might modify your performance, and they can boost your confidence by telling you about the parts that went well. They can also give you practice in answering questions: sometimes your response to questions will be the most important part of your presentation. Some presenters find questions stressful because at that moment control shifts to the audience, but the best defence against aggressive questioning is to know your material; armed with such knowledge, control reverts to you. Familiarity with your material means you can repeat what you have already said in your presentation, give variations on that material and introduce new material you didn't have time to present in your presentation.

The ideal rehearsal, then, covers these six factors: reciting the full text, in the venue, in front of an audience, in front of a camera, using the audiovisual aids and dressed and groomed as for a full dress rehearsal. This, however, is normally an unattainable ideal, and you may be lucky to achieve two or three of these conditions. It would be unwise to settle for less.

'You're on now!' — managing your stress

Performance stress: anxiety related to performance; also known as *speaker anxiety* or *stage fright*

Speaking publicly is an experience many of us prefer to avoid. In fact, the very thought of it commonly induces **performance stress**: we experience 'speaker anxiety', 'stage fright', 'butterflies in the stomach' and so on (Bell 2008). Don't make the mistake of thinking only you endure such a response. Everyone, even the most experienced of speakers, feels stress before speaking. This is hardly surprising, as most of the stress reactions we undergo are biologically programmed in us. They are part of what is called the *fight, flight or freeze response* (Cannon 1932; Bracha 2004) which equips us to meet physical threats in our environment in one of three ways:

1. fight — to attack, meeting the threat head-on
2. flight — to run away from the threat
3. freeze — to 'play dead' so as to avoid becoming a target of the threat.

These responses are effective or adaptive when the threat we face is physical. They served our ancestors well, which is why we are here. The same responses can be ineffective or maladaptive, however, when the 'threat' is symbolic (e.g. an audience). For example, changes in blood structure, particularly if repeated often, can lead to cardiovascular disease (Pickering 1993).

Of course, they are still 'adaptive' to the extent that a controlled amount of stress or arousal can improve rather than detract from our speaking performance: we may be stimulated to perform better, in much the same way that actors or athletes can perform better with a certain amount of stress. In fact, this type of productive stress — 'eustress' rather than 'distress' (Selye 1983; McLean 2010) — can be a pleasurable experience, particularly when your presentation goes well and your audience responds warmly to your efforts.

Behnke and Sawyer (1998) suggest that there are four phases in public speaking:

1. Anticipation – the minute prior to starting the speech
2. Confrontation – the first minute of the speech
3. Adaptation – the last minute of the speech
4. Release – the minute immediately following the end of the speech.

Witt et al. (2006) tracked the gastrointestinal discomfort of speakers through these four phases and found that stressful reactions rose from phase one to phase two, declined in phase three, and rose again in phase four. However, not everyone in their research sample responded in the same way. They found that people could be characterised as either 'habituators' or 'sensitisers'. Habituators tend to have low trait anxiety and respond to initial stress ('I've got to do some public speaking?!') by managing their psychological and physiological reactions and acclimatising to the role. Sensitisers, by contrast, tend to have high trait anxiety and react apprehensively to the perceived threat of public speaking. Sensitisers experienced the same variation in gastrointestinal discomfort as habituators, but at a higher level.

So what can we do about stress? It cannot be eliminated, but to an extent it can be managed and can actually boost our performance. The essence of much stress management lies in understanding the fight/flight/freeze response and then working with it (table 11.3).

TABLE 11.3 Checklist on how to reduce your performance stress

Strategy	Details
1. Exercise.	Conducted some time before the presentation, this can be a good way of channelling off some of the energy of the fight/flight/freeze response.
	If vigorous exercise is not possible, isometric exercises (e.g. pushing against a wall in a nearby room or a toilet) can also help.
2. Yawn, stretch, roll head from side to side.	Useful ways of releasing energy.
3. Breathe deeply.	Breathe from the diaphragm when waiting to speak and when speaking. Try to resist, or at least modify, the fight/flight/freeze response of rapid and shallow breathing.
4. Relax.	Work through your muscle groups. Begin by clenching your toes as you breathe in slowly, and then unclench them as you breathe out slowly. Do this for feet, calves, thighs, buttocks, stomach, fingers, forearms, upper arms, shoulders and neck. Stretch the mouth and eyebrows in a similar way.
	Most of these exercises can be done unobtrusively, and some can be done while you wait to speak, or even while speaking.
	The essence of this effective relaxation routine, however, is that it should be second nature or habitual. In other words, practise this routine well before the time you are required to speak, so that your body and mind have 'learned' the behaviour in low-stress situations and thus will be able to 'remember' it in high-stress situations.
5. Meditate.	This is not simply allowing your thoughts to drift off — it is a particular skill, taught in a variety of religious and secular traditions. Many find it a powerful stress reduction approach that produces — among other physical and psychological effects — several relaxation outcomes but with much less effort.
6. Use music, laughter.	Listen to some favourite music or comedy to relax you.

Strategy	Details
7. Go to the toilet beforehand.	Anticipate the uncomfortable physical manifestations of the fight/flight/freeze response and manage it, rather than being managed by it.
8. Avoid stimulants.	Don't drink stimulating beverages such as coffee, tea or cola drinks beforehand. You already have one powerful arousal agent loose in your body — adrenalin — and it doesn't need any assistance. Overarousal can be distressing.
9. Avoid tranquillising agents.	Alcohol and pharmaceutical tranquillisers may seem to control anxiety, but they may also take the edge off your performance by inhibiting your thought processes and slurring your speech. If alcohol is a normal part of a pre-speech ritual (e.g. at a meal), then use it sparingly.
10. Avoid problematic foods.	Greasy foods may exacerbate the nausea you feel as a result of the fight/flight/freeze response. Dairy foods may curdle in your mouth and exacerbate mouth dryness.
11. Drink water.	Water can help offset the dry-mouth effect. Make sure a jug and a glass are nearby.
12. Build in a time cushion.	Leave for the venue early, and arrive early. Getting held up in traffic, or not having all of your material organised beforehand, can cause you unnecessary stress.
13. Make the strange familiar 1.	The familiar is less stressful than the strange. Check out the venue or location where you will speak. Walk all around the room or venue, familiarising yourself with it. Sit in various seats, looking towards where you will be speaking to reproduce the point of view of different members of your audience.
14. Make the strange familiar 2.	Practise speaking to informal groups before moving on to more formal groups. Practise speaking before small groups before moving on to bigger groups.
15. Make the strange familiar 3.	Mix and mingle with audience members before the presentation. If there are familiar faces at the venue, or outside it, seek them out and talk with them. It may help to be introduced to a few people so you can try out some of your material on them, and also so there will be some familiar faces in your audience.
16. Rehearse.	Another form of familiarisation. Do it often.
17. Revisualise.	Humanise your audience by thinking of them as individuals in other situations: wearing other clothes, at the beach, in a crowd at a sporting event, washing dishes. Revisualisation can make the situation less threatening.
18. Be overprepared.	Alternative name: build in a material cushion. Have more material than you need, reducing any fears about running out of material. If you have more than you need, edit ruthlessly as you go rather than rush to try to cram it all in. However, it pays to have some high-quality material prepared and placed several blank slides after the formal conclusion of your presentation. Audience members will often question you, and while you may not have the best answer in your main presentation, you can surprise them by going to this extra block of slides. You may have to sacrifice some good material by doing this, but any dissatisfaction will be offset by the appreciation given to you by your audience.

(continued)

TABLE 11.3 *(continued)*

Strategy	Details
19. Don't trust inanimate objects.	Inanimate objects, such as audiovisual equipment, can seem suspiciously animate and temperamental at times. Check them out beforehand, and have a Plan B if they fail. For example, have your materials prepared twice — each time using some of the audiovisual aids discussed shortly.
20. Redirect their gaze.	It sounds silly, but some people feel less stressed if their audience is not looking at them all the time. Use tools such as handouts, slides, overhead projectors and pointers to direct the gaze of audience members away from you.
21. Use props to prop.	Lecterns or podiums can help: you can lean on them, resting your hands (and sometimes feet) on them, which can help minimise muscular trembling. Organising your notes in a clear, sequential form on the lectern can be reassuring. A lectern also places a barrier between you and the audience, which may make you feel more secure.
22. Don't do it.	Fly, don't fight. If the previous 21 strategies don't work, seriously consider whether you can deliver the information in another way. Perhaps you don't need the stress in your life at this moment, and perhaps other communication channels would be more effective. Overcoming your fear of speaking can be an exhilarating and liberating experience, but you have to be ready for such an experience. Don't be bullied into it merely because some others think that it would be good for you; it may be, but equally it may not.

Understanding these responses can also help us to better understand the helpful and unhelpful nonverbal communication we display when speaking.

ASSESS YOURSELF

Consider how stress might be productive rather than destructive in helping us perform better when speaking. What strategies can we use to increase good stress and decrease bad stress?

Nonverbal communication

While speaking you are also communicating nonverbally. Your body language has as much effect on your audience as the words you use — in some cases, it has more. It's wise, then, to make sure you are sending out the nonverbal messages you want to send. Most of us, however, don't have a clue about our own body language. This is hardly surprising, as the means for capturing likenesses of ourselves as others see and hear us — via film, audio recording, video recording or smartphone — is rarely available to record what needs to be recorded: real-life, full-length, no-clowning-around-for-the-camera examples of ourselves speaking publicly (with attendant nonverbal communication) (see also chapter 8).

'Do I really look/sound like that?' Feedback on performance

When most people first play back a recording of themselves, they usually experience a strange mixture of fascination, embarrassment and horror. As a communicator, the more you watch and listen to recordings of yourself in action, the better. This is not an exercise in vanity (well, not much anyway); rather, it is an exercise in self-discovery. In seeing yourself as others see you, you can consciously re-engineer your communication style in order to send out the messages you want to send out (see 'Feedback' in chapter 10).

This technique can be taken too far, of course, and if you manipulate your own image excessively, you end up manipulating your audience – in other words, lying. A little manipulation, however, can assist in your self-knowledge.

Speaking: a two-way process

By becoming more attuned to your own nonverbal communication, you will also become more aware of the nonverbal communication of your audience. Communication is like dance: as a good dancer you respond, without words, to the movement of your partner – moving in harmony, now leading, now following, now acting, now reacting, in an ongoing, dynamic, fluid interaction. The more sensitive you are to your partner's signals, which express conscious and unconscious thoughts and emotions, the better you will be as a dancer.

Being a successful speaker requires willingness to both engage with, and respond to, the verbal and nonverbal cues of audience members.

So it is with communication in general, and speaking to an audience in particular. You need to learn to 'listen with your eyes' (Marchetti 1996). Speaking is not a mechanical process, a one-way flow of data, as if a recorder hooked up to a loudspeaker was sending out noises to a row of microphones, hooked up to other recorders. You are a living, responding organism, and so is your audience; you are responding to each other all the time, as in a dance. It's best, therefore, to ensure that the range of responses rests within your control rather than beyond it.

'Good' and 'bad' nonverbal communication

To determine how you should use appropriate nonverbal communication, put yourself in the position of an audience member. What is it you want from a speaker? What attitudes do you want to see conveyed by a speaker, and what do you dislike? In other words, what characteristics do you have in mind when you think of 'good' as opposed to 'bad' speakers?

When you think of a good speaker, you probably think of someone who is relaxed in approach, attentive to the audience's needs, interested in and informative about the topic. When you think of a bad speaker, you probably think of someone who is tense, oblivious to the audience's needs, bored by and uninformed about the topic. Well, your audience feels the same way.

Let's now look at the nonverbal characteristics of good and bad speakers. Various aspects of nonverbal communication or body language can have a positive or at least a neutral impact, while other aspects have a potentially or actually negative impact (table 11.4). Exhibiting any one of these behaviours in isolation will not make you a disastrous speaker. Combining a number of them, however, might well present serious problems for you. To reiterate, most of us are ignorant of our own nonverbal communication. Table 11.4 (see overleaf) will remain an interesting abstraction for you, unrelated to your own behaviour, unless you take practical steps to obtain recordings of your own speaking performance.

TABLE 11.4 Nonverbal communication when speaking

	Positive/neutral connotation	Potentially/actually negative connotation
Eyes	Contact with audience ■ Normal/slightly increased blink rate ■ Normal/slightly increased pupil dilation ■ Normal/slightly raised eyebrows	■ Minimal/no contact with audience ■ Rapid blink rate ■ Extreme pupil dilation (stress stare) ■ Raised eyebrows
Mouth	Open (clear projection)	■ Closed (mumbling) ■ Frequently wetting lips with tongue ■ Yawning
Head	■ Minimal movement ■ Tilted to show concentration when listening	■ Frequent movement, nodding ■ Tilted to show aggression
Shoulders	■ Lowered	■ Raised
Arms/ hands	■ Open arms ■ Hands beside body, on lectern/podium, around/on objects ■ Appropriate gestures	■ Folded arms ■ Figleaf position ■ Hands in pockets ■ Distracting gestures ■ Nervous touching, self-touching
Legs/feet	■ Minimal movement	■ Jiggling legs ■ Tapping toes ■ Bouncing on balls of feet ■ Pacing
Body	■ Erect posture ■ Relaxed posture	■ Slumped posture ■ Stiff posture
Orientation	■ Mainly towards audience	■ Mainly away from audience
Clothing	■ Appropriate for occasion ■ Neat	■ Inappropriate ■ Sloppy

Notice that many of the potentially or actually negative signals relate to stress responses. Very few people will condemn us for being anxious, but our being stressed may paradoxically cause our audience to become stressed: they feel embarrassed and concerned; they identify with our suffering. This can turn into a runaway feedback situation: we become stressed, which makes them stressed, and their display of stress makes us more stressed and so on. You may need to employ more strategies for reducing performance stress to prevent this happening. Keep in mind also that different cultures use not only different languages but different patterns of nonverbal communication too. The 'ideal' pattern of nonverbal communication given in table 11.4 pertains to Euro-American cultures, but not necessarily to others.

Eyes

We display fight/flight/freeze behaviour when we avert our gaze from people ('I'm not really here, not a threat' or 'I am being submissive when confronted with your fight behaviour, threat'), and when we dilate our pupils, raise our eyebrows, and blink more rapidly ('Where is the threat? I must protect myself from it'). In contrast, the more relaxed speaker shows lower, more manageable levels of stress arousal in his or her blink rate, pupil dilation and eyebrow elevation. Good eye contact with the audience is also an effective communication pattern. The message here is clear: don't read your notes or full text. Return to the text every now and then, but don't stay there.

Mouth

Dry mouth syndrome (often associated with rapid swallowing) can be a stress indicator and can be distracting. A ready supply of drinking water can manage this problem. Some speakers believe chilled water helps improve articulation. A mouth more closed than open, leading the speaker to mumble, may be a stress-related mannerism, but it may also be related to habitually poor diction. The more professional speaker speaks with an open mouth, which facilitates clear diction and voice projection. Using a clear speaking voice entails an aerobics workout for the lips, tongue and throat – make sure you get the exercise.

Head

The speaker who moves his or her head frequently may simply be exhibiting excitement or may be manifesting extreme agitation or stress. Either way, such a display can prove irritating to audiences.

Shaking the head from side to side might prove particularly irritating, and some body language analysts have suggested that head-shaking can be an unconscious signal indicating that the speaker really disagrees with what is being said – in other words, the nonverbal channel of communication is contradicting the verbal channel (see 'What is nonverbal communication?' in chapter 8).

Like much nonverbal communication, tilting the head can have different meanings in different contexts and in combination with other nonverbal behaviours. We tilt our heads, usually with a neutral or sympathetic expression, to indicate we are listening. We may also tilt our heads, accompanied by an aggressive expression, when we are angry. We see this type of nonverbal communication in hostile audience members asking questions, but equally it may be seen in speakers responding to hostile questioning. Effective speakers avoid being drawn into rancorous exchanges, preferring instead to respond with cool logic or defusing humour, and reserving head-tilting for listening situations. They will also keep head movements to a minimum, so as not to distract the audience. Some speakers will establish eye contact with various members of the audience at different times, and nod at them as they are making a point. This often evokes a nod in response and can thus be a useful method for building rapport, but don't overdo it.

Shoulders

Raised shoulders is a classic sign of strong stress. As a fight response, raised shoulders (commonly accompanied by hands on hips) increase our profile, presenting a greater threat to the enemy. As a flight response, in raising our shoulders we are imitating turtles, pulling our vulnerable heads into our body for protection. Neither attitude is recommended for effective speakers. Squared shoulders and erect posture are more appropriate, and they won't give you a headache or stiff neck and back, either.

Arms and hands

The arms and hands work together to create a repertoire of gestures, some of which are effective, and some of which are less so. People fold their arms across their bodies when they feel relaxed and comfortable, but also when adopting a defensive posture in which the arms protect the vulnerable areas of heart, lung and breasts. Stressed speakers are defensive speakers, and continually resorting to this gesture may send out messages that the speaker is ill at ease or has something to be defensive about. Don't avoid it, but try to minimise it.

Arm-folding is one solution to that age-old problem for speakers: *What do I do with my hands?* Some people will try anything to occupy their hands – even smoking. Gestural solutions include the figleaf position (hands clasped over the genital area), and standing with hands in pockets. The former tends to look overly formal, tense or both, while the latter can look casual, sloppy or arrogant, depending on the circumstances and other nonverbal communication of the speaker. Try to avoid these gestures.

To repeat, we are generally oblivious of our nonverbal communication, particularly that involving our arm and hand gestures. You may be unaware – until you see a playback of your performance – that you may have a repertoire of gestures that stand a chance of greatly irritating your audience. Some of these might include jingling coins in your pocket, snapping your fingers, drumming your fingers on the podium near the microphone, rattling your jewellery, twisting a ring on your finger, attacking the overhead projector or the projection screen with a pointer, and whacking the palm of your hand with the pointer. You have probably experienced presenters and teachers over the years with even more eccentric mannerisms. Such gestures distract from the message you are trying to impart. If they are an expression of pent-up stress, try to release this stress using other strategies.

The best source of stress management for an infant is its mother. When the environment threatens, and induces distress, mother is there to offer a nipple (real or synthetic) and to stroke and cuddle. When older children are subjected to stress they seek to recapture such oral and tactile gratification by sucking thumbs, biting nails, and patting and stroking their bodies and hair. Under stress, adults too will often play around their faces (particularly the mouth area), and stroke and twist their hair (see chapter 8). In isolation, such mannerisms are not necessarily offensive or distracting, or even indicative of great stress, but when they occur in groups or clusters they can distract an audience. Again, try to release your stress in other ways.

Effective speakers use nondefensive gestures, which means their arms are usually more open than closed. Hands can be placed beside the body or rested on the podium or lectern (a useful way of controlling stress-induced muscular trembling), or they can hold objects such as pointers, overhead transparencies, slide projector or DVD player remote controls or microphones.

The effective speaker uses gestures economically, untheatrically and with purpose – dramatising trends in graphics (sales *up*, raw materials *down*), and pointing (with fingers, pens or wooden or laser pointers) at audiovisual aids. Unless you are deliberately trying to provoke a reaction, think very carefully about pointing out at an audience.

Legs and feet

Certain nervous leg or feet movements (tapping the feet, jiggling the legs) can irritate audiences. A speaker may bounce up and down on the balls of his or her feet out of nervousness, boredom, haughtiness or just as an expression of the joy of life, but the gesture can prove distracting and even annoying to the audience. Similarly, pacing can be an amusing mannerism in some speakers but an intensely irritating one in others. As this varying response is not often within the speaker's power to control, it is wise to dispense with this behaviour. The effective speaker will minimise movements *in the brawn* and maximise activity *in the brain*.

Body

An infant who is depressed or stressed tends to slump over, to roll up into a ball, as if trying to recapture the feelings of security experienced as a foetus. Adults can manifest distress in similar ways. The speaker with slumped posture may be construed as being depressed or stressed, or simply as lazy and undisciplined. Taller speakers will sometimes stoop out of an unconscious desire to 'compensate' and appear of normal height, but a slumping posture never looks good. If you are hunching over simply because the microphone or overhead projector is positioned too low, then make the necessary adjustments to the equipment, not your backbone.

Then again, a stressed speaker may adopt an unusually stiff posture, as if braced for the blows life is about to mete out. Remember, the fight/flight/freeze response is a transient crisis mode for your body, not a response to maintain for hours or days. Keeping up any type of muscular rigidity for prolonged periods is unnecessary work and exhausting. Try to process the stress in other, more productive ways.

Standing up straight to impress others with your alertness and self-discipline has merit, but remember that there are no straight lines in the human body, so don't overdo it. The relationship you want to establish with your audience is that of someone having a conversation with peers. The effective speaker adopts a posture that is erect, but not unnaturally so. He or she is also relaxed, rather than stiff, which in turn usually relaxes the audience.

Orientation

Orientation refers not so much to the posture of the body as its direction. When we converse with someone, we typically face each other directly, our bodies parallel. So too with public speaking: typically, we prefer a speaker to face us directly for most of the time, using direct eye contact. When making a presentation, it is necessary from time to time to break eye contact and orientate away from the audience – for example, to attend to an overhead projector, to point to a projected image, or to read something. The ineffective speaker overdoes these interludes, however, and the impression develops that he or she is more interested in talking to the wall than to us. This orientating away may be stress-induced aversive behaviour, or it may be that the speaker is simply too absorbed in the details of the presentation and is not paying sufficient attention to the needs of the audience. Orientating away continually can also cause audibility problems, as the speaker's voice is not being projected towards the audience. Strive to be directly orientated towards your audience for at least 80 per cent of the time you are speaking.

Clothing

Clothing, our 'second skin', sends out a variety of messages to the world around us. Make sure you are sending out the appropriate messages. Casual or formal clothing that is obviously for social occasions is unsuitable for professional occasions. Similarly, delivering a presentation while wearing a sober, understated business suit may be inappropriate in certain settings – for example, if the culture of the organisation is more relaxed and most people wear casual clothes, or if casual wear is expected for this weekend workshop being conducted at a holiday resort. Generally speaking, use clothing as camouflage – to blend into the local environment, unless you want to make a particular statement about standing out from the crowd.

Eccentric geniuses can get away with being sloppy when they present to a group, but in most lesser mortals such eccentricity is unacceptable. If you dress sloppily, people may think you are sloppy in your work as well.

Body language meets content: you are a speaker, not a reader

Eye contact with the audience can be stressful, and stressed speakers tend to avoid eye contract. This usually means that the speaker becomes a reader. Some speakers who are not unduly stressed by speaking nevertheless read their notes. Whatever your stress levels, however, the message is the same: don't read.

The notes a speaker uses to deliver a presentation should be quite different from the text of a written document. Notes should contain key points only, not complete sentences or paragraphs. Let the sentences and paragraphs come from your brain as you talk. This may strike you as hard work, but it is not as hard as standing in front of a group of people, trying to find your place in a mass of finely printed text. For example, any notes or cue cards you use should more closely resemble the one in figure 11.5(b) than the one in figure 11.5(a). The hard work of creating sentences and paragraphs decreases in proportion to the amount of time you rehearse.

There is nothing so embarrassing for an audience or speaker as when the speaker rambles, saying something like 'Sorry, but I can't read my own writing ...'

So then, what do we do if the customer doesn't want the latest versions, such as the C6 or C7? It's all too easy to dismiss their misgivings, but sometimes their conservatism is based on bitter experience. Even though we know that the latest versions have some superb features that could really benefit their businesses, we know that some of our past products <u>have not been glitch-free</u>. This puts reps in a real dilemma: do they give them old product, or try to push the new stuff, no matter what? Firstly, you need to know just what our stocks of all models actually are> I find that the databases don't always tell the full story, so I make it my business to WALK THROUGH THE WAREHOUSE every few weeks, noting just what it is available, and what shape it's in. Next, if a client is really opposed to a new model, I make a point of getting them the older version, but <u>taking notes</u> on their problems with the new stuff. I then make a point of taking that <u>feedback</u> directly to

LARRY MITCHELL OR Vic

and let him know what's happening out there in the trenches.

<u>30 per cent discount VIPs — 33% TLK</u>

C4.2— big problem

FIGURE 11.5(a) Cue cards — a bad approach

Write, type or print out your notes on cards or paper. The typeface or font should be large. Paper sheets make more noise than cards when being handled near a microphone, but a computer–printer–paper system will give you larger, more legible fonts than a typewriter–card system. If necessary, use 'cheat sheets', or key words written on the frames of overhead transparencies or lightly written on flip charts. Software presentation programs allow you to create speaker notes to accompany individual slides (use large fonts for these). Remember, read your audience, not your notes.

5/12

Customers don't want latest version?

— Sometimes their fears are justified

— Problems with past models (C4.2)

— Dilemma: (1) Give them old stock?

(2) Push new stuff no matter what?

— Strategy: (1) Give old stock

(2) Take notes on their worries

(3) Report directly back to Larry Mitchell

(or Vic Carter)

(>6 Warehouse/databases)

FIGURE 11.5(b) Cue cards — a better approach

Video yourself. What are your impressions when watching yourself speaking? Are you happy or unhappy with what you see or hear? How might you improve your performance?

Using your voice

Let's turn now from nonverbal to verbal communication — specifically, voice production. The human voice is the most powerful communication tool we have, but it is often misused. To maximise its potential, you need to be aware of, and train yourself in, various aspects of verbal communication, such as pronunciation, enunciation, pitch, inflection and tone. All of these aspects of verbal communication are affected by performance stress, just as nonverbal communication is.

Articulateness and articulation: the hard work of speaking

Pronunciation: the act of producing the sounds of speech

Articulateness and **articulation:** articulateness (the ability to say meaningful words) can be helped considerably by articulation (the ability to say those words clearly)

Pronunciation is the act of producing the sounds of speech. **Articulateness** (the ability to say meaningful words) can be helped considerably by **articulation** (the ability to say those words clearly). We articulate vowels and consonants primarily by using tongue, lips and different parts of the vocal tract (table 11.5). Practise saying these sounds, taking note of the way in which the different parts of the vocal tract work together to produce the sounds. Speaking clearly can be hard work, but it is worth the effort to be understood and to sound credible (Mayer 2008).

TABLE 11.5 Formation of some consonants

Consonant category	Created by	Example	Voiced/unvoiced
PLOSIVES	Puff of air through lips	P	U
		B	V
	Tongue tip striking back of teeth	T	U
		D	V
	Back of tongue	K	U
		G	V
FRICATIVES	Lower lips + upper teeth	F	U
		V	V
	Tongue tip + gum	S	U
		Z	V
GLIDES	Tongue tip + gum	L	V
	Lips	W	V
	Tongue blade + palate	R	V
NASALS	Lips	M	V
	Tongue tip + gum	N	V
	Back of tongue + palate	NG	V

Many of us are not even aware that we mispronounce words. Recording devices can be of considerable assistance here. Read the following mispronunciations and correct pronunciations onto a recording, and play them back. If you feel more comfortable with the mispronunciations than the correct pronunciations, you may have a problem. The three major types of mispronunciation are elisions (omission of sounds), substitutions (replacing one sound with another) and intrusions (adding extra sounds). Examples of these are given in table 11.6.

TABLE 11.6 Types of mispronunciation

Fault category	Mispronunciation	Nature of fault	Correct pronunciation
Elisions	Strine	One syllable instead of four; medial glide L needed. More lip and tongue movement needed, less nasality	Australian
	Libary	Medial glide R needed	Library
	Febuary	Medial glide R needed	February
	Secetry	Medial glide R needed	Secretary
	Enviroment	Second medial nasal N needed	Environment
	Vunerable	Medial glide L needs to be used	Vulnerable
	Jool	Medial glide W needed	Jewel
Substitutions	Foopball	Medial plosive T next to medial plosive B replaced by medial plosive P	Football
	Choosdy	Initial plosive T needed, AY needed	Tuesday
	Arst	Final plosive K needed, not T	Ask
	Arks	K and S reversed	Ask
	Edjacation	D replaced by J	Education
	Jew	D replaced by J	Due/dew
	Wiv	TH replaced by V	With
Intrusions	Anythink	NG replaced by K	Anything
	Heighth	Final T has TH added	Height
	Stastistics	Medial S unnecessary: sound medial T	Statistics
	Athaletic	Medial vowel unnecessary	Athletic
	Fillum	Medial vowel unnecessary	Film
	Showen	Medial vowel unnecessary	Shown

The quickest way to solve your pronunciation problems is to study a good dictionary in which pronunciations are given in International Phonetic Script (IPS) or some other phonetic system. The English language is about 75 per cent phonetic (i.e. words being pronounced exactly as they are spelled), so check with a dictionary if you are unsure. Pronunciation also varies substantially according to nationality, region and socioeconomic background, and for many, is a matter of intense controversy and sensitivity. The main advantage of consistent pronunciation is to be understood by as many people as possible, anywhere, at any time.

It is possible to pronounce words correctly, but to enunciate them badly. Ensure that your enunciation, or diction, is clear: don't mumble or gabble. Record yourself reading various passages (newspaper articles, scenes from novels, a presentation you are working on), and identify any enunciation problems you find. If you are going to be using a microphone, pay close attention to words that contain plosive letters, in particular *p* and *b*: as the name suggests, these letters are created by little explosions of breath in the mouth, and can produce a harsh, popping sound from some microphones. Try reading the sentence

PerhaPs the ProPosed Parameters of this Project are Beyond our Brief.

into a recorder, or into the microphone you will be using for a presentation. If the effect is too harsh, modify your breath control or distance from the microphone.

Stress can also affect enunciation. Stressed speakers sometimes seem almost to strangle their words, primarily because their throat muscles are too tense.

Pitch

Voice pitch: height or depth of voice

Inflection: modulation of voice, changing pitch and/or loudness

Voice pitch can also be affected by stress. Stressed people often lift the pitch of their voice. Audiences, rightly or wrongly, tend to associate a deeper pitch with authoritativeness and formality. We usually raise the pitch of our voice at the end of questions, because such an **inflection** acts as a cue to elicit a response. Insecure speakers, in informal or formal situations, sometimes upwardly inflect, or modulate their voice, several times within one sentence, betraying a need to receive a continuous stream of approving responses from their listeners. Such a mannerism (called a *high rising tone*) can be irritating, and may detract from the credibility of the speaker (Crystal 2003).

A monotonous delivery may indicate stress on the part of the speaker, or it may simply show lack of interest or imagination. If people think the messenger boring, they will tend to discount the message too. Monotony can mean literally speaking in one tone all the time, or it can mean adopting a predictable, repetitive and irritating pattern of speech — for example, *rising tone/falling tone … rising tone/falling tone* (a common fault even among communication professionals, such as news presenters). Effective speakers convey the words and the music. They use clear but relaxed diction, appropriate inflection and medium to low pitch.

ASSESS YOURSELF

Record yourself on an audio device. What are your impressions on playing back the recording? Are you happy or unhappy with what you hear? How might you improve your performance?

Using audiovisual aids

Audiovisual aids: objects and mechanical and electronic systems used to communicate information

Audiovisual aids can help considerably in getting your message across. Research has shown that the audience is more easily persuaded when a presenter uses aids than when an unassisted oral presentation is given. Specifically, using visual aids such as software presentation slides boosts audience recall: some research has shown that while audiences remember only about 30 per cent of what they hear and only about 20 per cent of what they see, their retention of information rises to approximately 50 per cent when the two channels are combined (Hager & Scheiber 1992, p. 505). Other earlier research has shown that group agreement is reached about 80 per cent of the time when audiovisual aids are used in presentations and only 58 per cent of the time when they are not (Ruch & Crawford 1988, p. 358).

Visual aids can have drawbacks, but they also offer distinct advantages. They can help summarise an argument, clarify and illuminate, and add variety. Their use also indicates to audience members that you have gone to considerable trouble in your preparation, which can help motivate your audience and make them more receptive to your viewpoint.

Of course, what makes an excellent visual in a presentation may not work so well as a graphic in a written document, and vice versa. Generally, visuals used in presentations cannot convey as much detail as those used in written documents. Thus, a complex table may be usefully incorporated into a written document, but the same table might be disastrous as a slide or an overhead transparency. Then again, merely because a visual used in a spoken presentation is simple does not mean it is less dramatic or persuasive than a visual used in a written document. Sometimes the opposite is the case. You will be more effective in your oral (and written) communication if you understand the appropriate use of various types of graphic communication in documents and presentations (see chapter 2).

The pros and cons of various types of audiovisual aids are outlined in table 11.7. Remember that audiovisual aids are ultimately a means to an end, not an end in themselves: you need to match the message to the medium based on your evaluation of the various strengths and weaknesses of differing types of aids. Never depend completely on technology and always be ready — in a crisis — to continue your communication using different aids if one fails or, in the case of complete technology failure, to speak without aids.

TABLE 11.7 Using contemporary audiovisual aids

Medium	For	Against
Whiteboards	<ul><li>Widely available</li><li>No/low maintenance, recurrent cost</li><li>Flexible — presenter can change information displayed in response to audience</li><li>Immediacy — audiences tend to regard information displayed as more up-to-date than information displayed via other media</li><li>Relationships between key ideas easily shown</li><li>Audience participation can be encouraged by recording responses</li><li>Electronic boards allow hard copy</li><li>'Wow' special effects are available</li></ul>	<ul><li>Seen by some as boring</li><li>Can be slow</li><li>Depends on legible handwriting</li><li>May create 'teacher–student' feel</li><li>Easy for presenter to obscure information with body</li><li>Easy to lose eye contact, voice audibility</li><li>Limited visibility — not good for large audiences</li><li>Static — cannot show dynamic processes</li><li>Electronic boards expensive</li></ul>
Flip charts	<ul><li>Cheap</li><li>Easels, pads, markers widely available</li><li>Easy to transport</li><li>Can be prepared before presentation</li><li>Flexible — presenter can move back and forth between ideas</li><li>Information does not need to be erased</li><li>Provides permanent record</li><li>Progressive revelation easy</li></ul>	<ul><li>Sheets not robust, prone to wear and tear</li><li>Depends on legible handwriting</li><li>Difficult to show detailed information</li><li>Not good for large audiences</li><li>Easy for presenter to obscure information with body</li><li>Easy to lose eye contact, voice audibility</li><li>Limited visibility</li><li>Static — cannot show dynamic processes</li></ul>
CD-ROM/DVD	<ul><li>Can show dynamic processes</li><li>Flexible — fast forward/backward, freeze possible</li><li>Remote control possible</li><li>Easy, relatively cheap to produce archival, demonstration, interview material</li><li>Flexible presentation — easy to access specific sections</li></ul>	<ul><li>Expensive to produce professionally</li><li>Some machines not flexible</li><li>Inflexible presentation — difficult to alter sequence</li><li>Difficult to show detailed information</li><li>Problems with displaying to big audiences</li><li>May provoke 'relax — it's entertainment' behaviour</li><li>Potential compatibility/format problems</li></ul>

Medium	For	Against
Computer projection	■ Hardware and software becoming cheaper ■ Change of data/information displayed possible ■ Some dynamic displays possible ■ Smooth transitions/special effects between visuals	■ Cost still prohibitive for some ■ Computer screen only suitable for small audiences ■ Projectors for big audiences still have technical problems ■ Compatibility/ format problems
Models, props and samples	■ Three dimensions can be displayed ■ Senses other than sight and sound can be exploited ■ Creates audience involvement ■ Robust, long-lived	■ Can distract audience ■ Can be costly, involved to prepare ■ Usually only practical for small audiences
Handouts	■ Detailed information can be shown ■ Robust, long-lived ■ Can be taken away by audience ■ Can be produced in editing/production stages of written/oral reports	■ Can distract audience ■ Can be costly, involved to prepare ■ Can lead to audience confusion

AVOIDING 'DEATH BY POWERPOINT'

PowerPoint is a software program, usually bundled with Microsoft Office, that facilitates the presentation of text, images and sound in screens or slides. There are other presentation programs, such as Apple's Keynote, but, at this stage, PowerPoint has certainly achieved dominance. Death by PowerPoint refers to the mind-numbing tedium that takes over audiences subjected to an apparently infinite procession of slides in a PowerPoint presentation (Flocker 2007). For example, use a browser on the internet with the search term 'death by PowerPoint'. (Don't forget the quote marks to isolate that term only.) Several years ago, the entries were in the 20 000s — now, they have more than doubled.

PowerPoint presentations can degenerate into long and not very effective sessions, as the following two anecdotal reports indicate:

People are not listening to us, because they are spending so much time trying to understand these incredibly complex slides ... I would ban the presentations if I thought I could get away with it. For some of these guys, taking away their PowerPoint would be like cutting off their hands. (Former US Army Secretary Louis Calera)

PowerPoint briefings are only necessary for two reasons: if field conditions are changing rapidly or if the audience is functionally illiterate. In the Pentagon the second seems to be the underlying presumption. The idea behind most of these briefings is for us to sit through 100 slides with our eyes glazed over, and then to do what all military organizations hope for: to surrender to an overwhelming mass. (Former US Navy Secretary Richard Danzig, quoted in Jaffe 2000)

So should we avoid PowerPoint completely? Not at all. There is no doubt it is a powerful tool when used correctly. Visuals can inform and persuade (and entertain) in ways that written documents simply cannot. To make PowerPoint work, you need to consider the following guidelines:

■ Restrict your use of font types (use no more than two or three, and use fonts of 18 points or above).
■ Restrict the use of colours in fonts and backgrounds.
■ Keep backgrounds, templates and colours consistent, and be wary of special font effects (bouncing, rotating).
■ Restrict the types of transitions you use (no more than four or five), and resist using the flashier ones unless you really need to make a point. Dissolves are the least distracting.
■ Limit yourself to one idea (30–40 words) per slide. Compare this with the advice given in chapter 6 'Online writing', to use only the number of words on a web page that you find in a paragraph — not a page — of a book.

(continued)

(continued)

- Have no more than six lines per slide, and no more than six words per line.
- Use short words and sentences, and strong verbs, and favour the active voice (see online chapter 'Writing skills 1: grammar').
- Restrict the use of prepositions, adverbs and adjectives.
- Use clip art and animation for special effects sparingly.
- Restrict the size of graphic files — if a file size is unmanageable (possibly because of the inclusion of too many large images), and you try to email the file to others, their servers may not accept it.
- Consider printing out the presentation (e.g. six slides per sheet) and handing it out to your audience members. Although it alerts them to what's coming up, this potential loss of dramatic impact is often offset by the convenience and permanence of a hard copy that is also a take-away persuasive tool. If you are printing out in black and white, ensure that there is sufficient contrast between background and text.
- Plan the content rather than just throwing it together; ensure that it tells a story, and that the sequence of ideas makes sense. Test this out by changing views within PowerPoint (View>Normal>Outline, View>Slide Sorter, View>Notes) or even by printing out hard copies, pinning them to a wall, and then walking through it, checking sequence and rhythm.
- Edit your words carefully. Typos are easy to make with earlier versions of PowerPoint. Don't commit the signwriter's error of being so close to the text that you cannot see the context and thus miss mistakes.
- Inform your audience of the structure of the presentation by using a road-map slide at the start (coming back to it between sections if necessary), and use section headers.
- Rehearse the presentation in front of others, and listen to all negative and positive feedback they offer.
- Consider other means of getting your message across, either to provide variety to the PowerPoint presentation or as a substitute for it. These might involve whiteboards, flip charts, props or samples, a traditional written document, or a conversation or series of conversations.
- Beware of the entertainment relaxation response; when the lights go down, people settle down for a nice comfy break from work. Keep them alert, and let them know that this is still work.
- Keep the number of slides below 30–40, and consider taking breaks or breaking one large presentation into a number of smaller ones.
- Be wary about going online during a presentation unless you have rehearsed it, the systems are reliable and you can get your message across by other means if it all goes pear-shaped.
- Put your personal professional details — name, title, organisational position, email, phone and fax numbers — on your final slide and, depending on the audience, your contact details from social media websites such as Twitter and Facebook. Parts of such media are evolving from having a personal role to a professional role.
- Ask yourself: is this presentation really necessary?

The delivery: getting feedback on performance

The structure and planning of oral communication is, if you like, the theory, while the delivery is the practice. In an ideal world, the theory is close to the practice, and the more speaking practice we have, all else being equal, the closer theory and practice draw together.

We can usually judge our own performance reasonably well (especially if we are able to record and watch a rehearsal), but it still helps to have feedback from others about our delivery (see also chapter 10). When we speak, how do we come across? Are we using an effective mix of information, persuasion and entertainment? What about body language? Do we look as stressed as we feel? The speech checklist (figure 11.6) can be a useful tool for providing real feedback on performance.

Technique

1. Speed
Too fast 1—2—3—4—5 Just right 4—3—2—1 Too slow

2. Volume
Too loud 1—2—3—4—5 Just right 4—3—2—1 Too soft

3. Clarity/articulation
Too little (mumbling, slurring) 1—2—3—4—5 Just right 4—3—2—1 Too much (overprecise)

4. Pitch
Too high 1—2—3—4—5 Just right 4—3—2—1 Too low

5. Tone
Too monotonous (too little variety) 1—2—3—4—5 Just right 4—3—2—1 Too theatrical (too much variety)

6. Pausing
Too little 1—2—3—4—5 Just right 4—3—2—1 Too much

7. Use of notes
Too much (reads entire speech) 1—2—3—4—5 Just right 4—3—2—1 Not enough (loses place, gets off track)

Non-verbal aspect

8. Posture
Too rigid 1—2—3—4—5 Just right 4—3—2—1 Too relaxed

9. Gestures
Too extravagant 1—2—3—4—5 Just right 4—3—2—1 Too wooden

10. Eye contact
Too much (staring) 1—2—3—4—5 Just right 4—3—2—1 Not enough (looks at no-one)

11. Orientation
Bad (away from audience) 1—2—3—4—5 Good (towards audience)

12. Clothing
Inappropriate 1—2—3—4—5 Appropriate

Equipment/aids

13. Use of equipment item/aid (specify)
Poor 1—2—3—4—5 Good

14. Use of equipment item/aid (specify)
Poor 1—2—3—4—5 Good

Delivery

15. Vocabulary
Too specialised/too much jargon 1—2—3—4—5 Just right 4—3—2—1 Too general/vague

16. Content level
Too high for audience 1—2—3—4—5 Just right 4—3—2—1 Too low for audience

17. Style
Too formal 1—2—3—4—5 Just right 4—3—2—1 Too informal

18. Quantity of material
Too many points 1—2—3—4—5 Just right 4—3—2—1 Too few points

19. Fact/opinion
Too much fact, not enough opinion 1—2—3—4—5 Just right 4—3—2—1 Too much opinion, not enough fact

20. Humour
Too little 1—2—3—4—5 Just right 4—3—2—1 Too much

21. Examples, data used
Irrelevant 1—2—3—4—5 Relevant

22. Response to questioning
Ineffective 1—2—3—4—5 Effective

23. Even-handedness
Biased 1—2—3—4—5 Unbiased

24. Performance
Too slick 1—2—3—4—5 Just right 4—3—2—1 Amateurish

Structure

25. Beginning
Not interesting 1—2—3—4—5 Interesting

26. Ending
Too abrupt 1—2—3—4—5 Just right 4—3—2—1 Drags on

27. Linkages between sections
Disjointed 1—2—3—4—5 Smooth

Behaviour

28. Aggressive/passive
Too aggressive 1—2—3—4—5 Just right 4—3—2—1 Too passive

29. Stress/relaxation
Too tense 1—2—3—4—5 Just right 4—3—2—1 Too laid back

30. Sincerity
Insincere 1—2—3—4—5 Sincere

FIGURE 11.6 Speech evaluation checklist

Some of the assessment items shown in figure 11.6 are a simple 1–5 continuum, while some items are 'double-headers', with the scoring sequence running from 1 to 5 and then back to 1, depending on the aspect of performance being assessed. As part of this exercise, you will need to refer back to the checklist in figure 11.6. Now, using this checklist and copies of it if required, complete the following series of activities.

1. Team up with a friend or a classmate and take turns to rehearse an oral presentation and then to assess each other using the performance checklist. Reflecting on how you have measured your friend or classmate and their feedback towards you, consider:
   - the areas that you performed well in
   - the areas that you performed ok in
   - the areas, if any, that you did not perform well in
   - the areas in which you ranked your friend or classmate highly for their performance
   - the areas in which you ranked your friend or classmate less highly for their performance.
   Considering this information, what changes might you make with your next oral presentation to ensure that you receive a good overall mark? What recommendations do you have for your friend or classmate in terms of how they might improve the overall effectiveness of their performance if they present the same material again to a different audience?

2. Self-appraise your own performance against the checklist shown in figure 11.6. Is your self-appraisal about how you think you performed consistent with the feedback that you received from your friend or classmate?

3. Listen to a few short speeches delivered by high-profile identities such as politicians, celebrities or elite sportspeople that are available on a social media website such as YouTube. Reflecting on the different measures of performance that are listed in figure 11.6, consider the overall effectiveness of the presentations. Can you think of any ways in which these people might improve the effectiveness and impact of their oral presentations?

STUDENT STUDY GUIDE

SUMMARY

In our professional and personal lives we encounter many types of oral communication, including presentations and speeches, and persuading, conversing, negotiating, pitching and briefing situations. In this chapter we examined the differences between conveying a message in written and in spoken form, and saw how the effective communicator might choose to support a spoken communication with a written one. Given that different approaches are appropriate for different audience types, it is very useful to analyse our audience in advance. Planning and structuring are essential in order that we manage our time well in preparation and rehearsal and that we develop the content we need. Effective delivery of oral communication messages requires that we manage our stress and understand how to best use nonverbal communication and our voices. Audiovisual aids can increase the impact of our message, but we need to choose these with care. There are numerous criteria for excellence in oral communication, and the more we are aware of these, the more we will be able to improve our performance.

KEY TERMS

articulateness *p. 365*

articulation *p. 365*

audiovisual aids *p. 367*

inflection *p. 367*

performance stress *p. 355*

pronunciation *p. 365*

spice *p. 351*

three-part talk structure *p. 353*

verbal headlining *p. 353*

voice pitch *p. 367*

REVIEW QUESTIONS

1. What different forms of oral communication might we use in our professional and personal lives?
2. List three advantages of written communication when compared with spoken communication.
3. How much time should we set aside for planning and rehearsal of our presentation?
4. What audience analysis factors need to be borne in mind when preparing for a presentation?
5. Identify at least five strategies for managing stress when speaking.
6. Identify at least five tactics for managing hostile or difficult audiences.
7. What type of nonverbal behaviours do we look for in effective speakers?
8. How can we best improve our voice production?
9. What pitfalls are there in computer presentation, and how can these best be overcome?
10. What value might there be in putting your professional details on the last slide of a presentation?

APPLIED ACTIVITIES

1. How might you reinforce the message of a spoken presentation by creating a written document? What problems would you need to solve to ensure that the reinforcement was effective?
2. Prepare three different versions of the one presentation or speech for different audiences. What do you include or exclude in each of the versions? Why?
3. Working by yourself or with others, brainstorm at least two other tactics for dealing with difficult audiences.

4. Working by yourself or with others, brainstorm ideas on the best means to avoid bias or lack of even-handedness in oral communication.

5. In this chapter, a list is provided of various strategies that might help to reduce the stress a presenter might feel. Describe three more such strategies.

WHAT WOULD YOU DO?

Carl, your boss, needs to give a presentation to the budget committee tomorrow.

The chairman of the committee told you last week that your section's operations are considered to be among the most important for the overall national development strategy. You really need a budget increase to fund a program you have developed. You believe in the program, and if it goes well, you might just get a promotion out of here, and away from Carl. You and he do not get along well; in fact, you had a blazing row with him this morning about a major project whose deadline had passed (he blamed you, but you had sent him an email about it last week, which he now claims he didn't receive).

Carl has asked you to give a critique of his presentation. You have both gone to a meeting room, and he has run through his presentation, which depends heavily on Power-Point slides. His presentation is a shocker. The structure is confused, a number of technical terms are undefined, and the graphics don't make much sense. He has also included a number of ear-shattering and bizarre sound effects, and some migraine-inducing transitions. Carl stumbles over words, and mispronounces several, including the names of two of the committee members. He hasn't really established a convincing case for why your section should get the budget increase needed.

'Well?' snaps Carl at the end. 'Was it great, or was it great?'

What should you say to Carl?

SUGGESTED READING

Beebe, Steven & Beebe, Susan 2010, *Public Speaking Handbook*, Pearson, London/New York.

Grice, George L & Skinner, John F 2010, *Mastering public speaking: the handbook*, 2nd edn, Allyn and Bacon, Boston, MA.

Guffey, Mary-Ellen 2010, *Business communication: process and product*, 6th edn, South-Western College Publishing, Florence KY.

Howell, Lorraine 2010, *Give your elevator speech a lift!* Book Publishers Network, Bothell, WA.

Verdeber, Rudolph F, Verdeber, Kathleen S, & Sellnow, Deanna D 2011, *The challenge of effective speaking*, 15th edn, Wadsworth, Belmont, CA.

REFERENCES

Aziz, Khalid 1998, 'Defuse a hostile audience', *Management Today*, November.

Behnke, RR & Sawyer, CR 1998, 'Conceptualizing speech anxiety as a dynamic trait', *Southern Communication Journal*, vol. 63, no. 2, pp. 160–8.

Bell, Arthur A 2008, *Butterflies be gone: an 8-step approach to sweat-proof public speaking*, McGraw-Hill, New York.

Bracha, H Stephan 2004, 'Freeze, flight, fight, fright, faint: adaptationist perspectives on the acute stress response spectrum', *CNS Spectrums*, vol. 9, no. 4, pp. 679–85.

Campbell, Kim Sydow, Follender, Saroya I & Shane, Guy 1998, 'Preferred strategies for responding to hostile questions in environmental public meetings', *Management Communication Quarterly*, vol. 11, no. 3, February, pp. 401–21.

Cannon, Walter B 1932, *The wisdom of the body*, Norton, New York.

Crosling, Glenda & Ward, Ian 2002, 'Oral communication: the workplace needs and uses of business graduate employees', *English for Specific Purposes*, vol. 21, pp. 41–57.

Crystal, David 2003, *The Cambridge encyclopedia of the English language*, 2nd edn, Cambridge University Press, Cambridge.

Eunson, Baden 1999, *Corporate writing 1B*, TAFE Frontiers, Melbourne.

Flett, Neil 1996, *Pitch doctor: presenting to win multi-million dollar accounts*, Prentice Hall, Sydney.

Flocker, Michael 2007, *Death by PowerPoint: a modern office survival guide*, Da Capo Press, Jackson, TN.

Gordon F. Shea 1984, *Managing a difficult or hostile audience*, Prentice-Hall, New York.

Hager, Peter J & Scheiber, HJ 1992, *Report writing for management decisions*, Macmillan, New York.

Hahner, Jeffrey C 2002, *Speaking clearly: improving voice and diction*, McGraw-Hill, New York.

Jaffe, Greg 2000, 'What's your point, lieutenant? please, just cut to the pie charts', *Wall Street Journal*, April 26, p. 23.

Kerr, Cherie 2002, *Death by PowerPoint: how to avoid killing you presentation and sucking the life out of your audience. Your effective tip-kit for the effective use of PowerPoint*, Execuprov, Santa Ana, CA.

LeFevre, Mark, Matheny, Jonathan & Kolt, Gregory S 2003, 'Eustress, distress, and interpretation in occupational stress', *Journal of Managerial Psychology*, vol. 18, no. 7, pp. 726–44.

Liu, Helena 2010, 'When Leaders fail: a typology of failure and framing strategies', *Management Communication Quarterly*, vol. 24, no.2, pp. 232–59.

McLean, Jay 2010, *Psychological eustress: an exploratory regulated process: an empirical examination of positive stress — what it looks like and how to foster it*, Saarbrücken Germany.

Marchetti, Michele 1996, 'Speaking to a tough crowd', *Sales and Marketing Management*, November.

Mayer, Lyle V 2008, *Fundamentals of voice and articulation*, 14th edn, McGraw-Hill, New York.

Pickering, TG 1993, 'Blood platelets, stress and cardiovascular disease', *Psychosomatic Medicine*, vol. 55. pp. 483–4.

Pike, Bob & Arch, Dave 1997, *Dealing with difficult participants*, Jossey-Bass, San Francisco, CA.

Rees, Nigel 1980, *Quote, unquote*, Harper Collins, London.

Ruch, William V & Crawford, Maurice L 1988, *Business reports: written and oral*, PWS-Kent, Boston, MA.

Sawyer, Chris R & Behnke, Ralph R 2002, 'Behavioral inhibition and the communication of public speaking state anxiety', *Western Journal of Communication*, vol. 66, no. 4, Fall, pp. 412–22.

Selye, Hans 1983, 'The stress concept: past, present and future', in Cary L Cooper (ed.), *Stress research*, John Wiley & Sons, Chichester.

Shea, Gordon F 1984, *Managing a difficult or hostile audience*, Prentice Hall, Englewood Cliffs, NJ.

Smith, Terry C 1991, *Making successful presentations*, 2nd edn, John Wiley & Sons, New York.

Tracy, Lawrence L 1990, 'Taming the hostile audience', *Training and Development Journal*, February.

Wilder, Claudyne 2008, *Point, click and wow! a quick guide to brilliant laptop presentations*, 3rd edn, Pfeiffer, San Francisco, CA.

Witt, Paul L, Brown, Kennaria C, Roberts, James B, Weisel, Jessica, Sawyer, Chris R & Behnke, Ralph R 2006, 'Somatic anxiety patterns before during and after giving a public speech', *Southern Communication Journal*, vol. 71, no. 1, pp. 87–100.

12

Argument: logic, persuasion and influence

LEARNING OBJECTIVES

After studying this chapter you should be able to:

- Explain the different meanings of the word 'argument'
- Discuss the nature of facts and paradigms
- Explain the tools and the limitations of logic, including logical fallacies
- Explain the roles played by persuasive message senders and receivers
- Explain the nature of persuasive messages and the process of sending
- Discuss how social contexts may sometimes induce conformity
- Identify differing principles and tactics of influence

Arguing about argument

The word 'argument' can have a neutral meaning, conjuring up images of civilised discussions of issues, with little evidence of frayed tempers or aggressive mind-games. It can, however, also connote harsh conflict, abuse, bias, and verbal and physical aggression. Even when our sense of the word is more the former meaning rather than the latter, problems can still arise. For example, Tannen (1998) suggests that traditional modes of argument have become too deeply embedded in all societies, and that we prefer to debate rather than to engage in dialogue. This destructive 'argument culture' is seen in:

- law courts, where a polarisation of defence and prosecution inflames tempers and distorts truth
- the media, where issues are often trivialised in attempts to get 'both sides of the story'
- politics, where members are driven by ideology and the need to score points against opponents rather than create good policy
- personal relationships, where both genders often seem to have considerable difficulty understanding each other.

A destructive argument culture is sometimes seen in the law, the media and politics, as well as in personal relationships.

Seen in this light, the concept of argument is a multifaceted one, and one that has to be handled with care. It may also be that the aggressive cut-and-thrust of some arguments is not always a negative thing, if such dynamics can in fact act as a cauldron in which new ideas are forged, or as an arena where disputants are forced to test their beliefs.

The structure of arguments

Everybody knows that the process of discovering truth depends on uncovering facts, and that once those facts are uncovered and presented in a reasonable way, then others will become convinced of the ways things really are. Is it really that simple?

Get the facts before the facts get you

It used to be a 'fact' that the sun rotated around the earth, but it is now a fact that the earth rotates around the sun. How, then, did one fact supplant another? Kuhn (2003) argued that science is not a smooth and uncontroversial process of simply revealing facts, but rather a process fraught with conflict and discontinuity. He argued that 'normal' science proceeds by trying to accommodate a series of facts or data, but this is not always successful because not all facts or data fit comfortably into the dominant **paradigm** or pattern, or way of perceiving reality.

Paradigm: the most popular current view of an aspect of reality

The dominant paradigm holds sway for some period of time, but after a while the 'inconvenient' facts not explained by the paradigm multiply, triggering a crisis, and then a revolution or 'paradigm shift' occurs. Therefore the data gathered over time by astronomers diminished support for the idea that the sun rotated around the earth, until, after much scientific and theological controversy, the alternate view became the dominant one.

Facts, or at least points of view, that have not fared that well over time include:

- The Earth is flat.
- Flying machines are impossible.
- Smoking helps build up lung capacity and helps calm the nerves.
- Ulcers are caused solely by stress.
- Microsoft doesn't need to create a browser to match Netscape because the internet is just a fad.

To initiate a paradigm shift can be an uncomfortable experience, not least because so much energy has been invested in developing the old paradigm that there are numerous constituencies and vested interests that need to defend their investment of time and resources. However, facts are not as solid and incontrovertible as they might first appear.

- Sherlock Holmes, Arthur Conan Doyle's fictitious detective, remarks (in *A Scandal in Bohemia*) to his faithful companion, Dr Watson: 'I have no data yet. It is a capital mistake to theorise before one has data. Insensibly one begins to twist facts to suit theories, instead of theories to suit facts.'
- Drucker (2002) goes against the conventional wisdom of getting facts first and opinions second, and advocates a reversal of this order because fallible human beings will often simply adapt facts to serve opinions, so it makes more sense to get the opinions out in the open first before looking at 'the facts of the case'.
- Oscar Wilde (in 'The critic as artist') provoked uncertainty about facts, opinions and bias: 'It is only about things that do not interest one that one can give a really unbiased opinion, which is no doubt the reason why an unbiased opinion is absolutely valueless'.

To understand the structure of arguments, therefore, we need to know the facts, but we also need to be aware of other things, such as opinions, values, biases, prejudices and paradigms.

Logic and argument

Consider this sequence of words:

1. All men are mortal.
2. Socrates is a man.
3. Therefore, Socrates is mortal.

Sentences 1 and 2 are known as premises. A **premise** is a proposition or claim on which an argument is based, or from which a conclusion is drawn. Sentence 3 is a **conclusion**, or the outcome flowing from a premise or initial proposition.

We can often tell when premises or conclusions are being referred to by the language or cue words used (figure 12.1).

Premise: a proposition or claim on which an argument is based, or from which a conclusion is drawn

Conclusion: an outcome flowing from a premise or initial proposition

Cue words for premises	Cue words for conclusions
Assuming that	Therefore
Because	Hence
As	Thus
Since	It follows that
Imagine for the moment that	Consequently
If you accept that	We will see that
Given that	We have no choice but to see that
As shown by	Points to
Seeing as	Suggests that
In view of the fact that	Accordingly
If we take for granted that	As a result

FIGURE 12.1 Cue words for premises and conclusions

Inductive and deductive logic

Syllogism: a sequence of statements composed of premises leading to a conclusion

Deductive logic: logic that moves from the general to the specific

Inductive logic: logic that moves from the specific to the general

The sequence of ideas above is known as **syllogism**. Syllogisms are examples of **deductive logic** – that is, logic or problem solving that moves from the general to the specific. The opposite of deductive logic is **inductive logic** – logic or problem solving that moves from the specific to the general. These different processes are shown in figure 12.2.

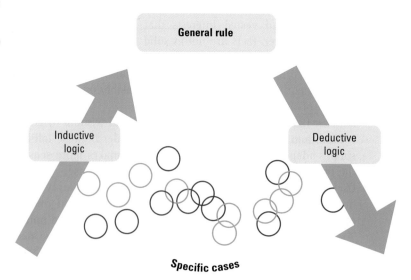

FIGURE 12.2 Inductive and deductive logic

Inductive logic is used in science when experiments are undertaken and data is created and recorded. That data can then be used to construct and prove or disprove hypotheses. Similarly, pollsters may sample public opinion about issues such as the popularity of politicians. In the real world, of course, both scientists and pollsters have ideas, hypotheses or general rules that they want to test, and there is an element of deduction in the induction, and vice versa. Both approaches have strengths and weaknesses (see figures 12.3 and 12.4). Use both, in a complementary fashion, to exploit strengths and avoid weaknesses.

Inductive logic: strengths	Inductive logic: weaknesses
■ It allows us to proceed from the known to the unknown. ■ It allows us to create predictive models of truth based on our everyday experience. ■ It allows us to save money and resources when trying to determine the beliefs and behaviours of a target population or large group by sampling only a fraction of that population or large group.	■ We may be tempted into over-generalising. ■ Our sampling methods may be flawed, producing wrong conclusions about the target population. ■ We may be tempted to ignore 'inconvenient' data because it does not fit into the dominant paradigm.

FIGURE 12.3 Inductive logic: strengths and weaknesses

Deductive logic: strengths	Deductive logic: weaknesses
■ It allows quick decisions to be made on the basis of experience and an accepted body of facts and understandings. ■ It allows us to move from the known to the unknown. ■ It allows us to make predictions about future events. ■ It provides us with models or sequences of premises and conclusions that discipline our thought and problem solving.	■ We may have assumed that our premises are correct, when in fact they are flawed. ■ We may proceed to conclusions that are not justified by the premises. ■ We may be trapped into restricted thinking, discounting other possibilities that do not fit comfortably into tidy syllogisms.

FIGURE 12.4 Deductive logic: strengths and weaknesses

Other tools of logic

Logicians use deductive and inductive logic to understand reality, but there are numerous other tools that can be deployed to help analyse ideas. These are sometimes dichotomies or opposites.

■ *Distinctions of kind versus distinctions of degree.* A **distinction of kind** marks the difference of two things of unlike kind or class by identity or quality; whereas a **distinction of degree** marks the difference of two things of like kind or class by extent or quantity. For example:
  – 'A foetus is a human being from the moment of conception' (distinction of kind) versus 'A foetus only gradually becomes a human being, probably at the moment the brain starts functioning' (distinction of degree)
  – 'Human beings are quite separate from species such as apes' (distinction of kind) versus 'Human beings are just another form of ape' (distinction of degree).

Distinction of kind:
a difference between two things of unlike or distinct kind or class, measured by identity or quality

Distinction of degree:
a difference between two things of the same kind or class, measured solely by extent or quantity

- *Necessary versus sufficient conditions.* A **necessary condition** provides a basis for something, but by itself is not adequate to make that something happen – for example, oxygen is a necessary condition for a fire, but by itself is not sufficient to make flames burst out of wood. A **sufficient condition** is one possible cause of a result, although not necessarily the only one – for example, the death of someone you love can serve as a sufficient condition for grief, but it is not a necessary condition, because other events can also cause grief (Cooper & Patton 1993).

- *Explanations versus excuses.* An **explanation** is a factual account of a situation usually expressed in neutral language, whereas an **excuse** is a justification usually expressed in biased language.
  - 'I had been drinking, so that when the fog came down my vision was impaired, and I ran the girl down before I could brake' (explanation), versus 'I had been fired and my wife had left me, so I drowned my sorrows, and when the fog came in, even though the weather bureau had promised that it wouldn't, I was operating under stress, and couldn't cope when that girl foolishly ran in front of me' (excuse).
  - 'The attacks on the World Trade Center by radical activists were motivated by dislike of North America and the processes of modernisation and globalisation' (explanation) versus 'The attacks on the World Trade Center by heroic freedom fighters were motivated by justified hatred of North America and the forces of modernisation and globalisation' (excuse).

When using these concepts, remember that it is wise not to confuse distinctions of kind with distinctions of degree, necessary with sufficient conditions, and explanations with excuses.

ASSESS YOURSELF

1. Think of two examples of deductive logic and two examples of inductive logic. Discuss these with at least one other person. Do others agree with your examples?
2. Think of two examples of distinctions of degree and two examples of distinctions of kind. Discuss these with at least one other person. Do others agree with your examples?
3. Think of two examples of necessary conditions and two examples of sufficient conditions. Discuss these with at least one other person. Do others agree with your examples?
4. Think of two examples of explanations, and then give the excuses that might be associated with those explanations.
5. Under what conditions might someone mistake an explanation for an excuse?

Fallacies

Logic, in its various forms, can be a powerful tool for analysis, problem solving and persuasion. It is fairly easy to go wrong when developing an argument, and this is when fallacies can occur. A **fallacy** is simply a false statement or belief. There are many fallacies in existence, but let's look at just ten (table 12.1). Ten fallacies are more than enough, but will demonstrate the wide range of false arguments and exemplify just how easy it is to fall into the habit of using bad arguments.

Fallacies are powerful aids to thinking, but remember that a little learning may be a dangerous thing. However, it should also be said that identifying fallacies can be fun, and can force us to be a bit more honest in the way we put arguments together.

Of course, it is important to bear in mind that fallacies are not always universally recognised as such. Just as surely as dominant paradigms are held to be the truth – and it may take centuries or millennia to demonstrate otherwise – so too are fallacies not always recognised as such by some. This is all the more true if a person has a strong emotional, lifestyle or cultural reason for not believing that a fallacy is fallacious.

TABLE 12.1 Ten common fallacies

Fallacy	Nature of fallacy	Example	Response
1. Two wrongs don't make a right/ Red Herring	Attempt to distract the other person with a red herring argument (red herrings were drawn across the path of hunting dogs to distract them). False attempt to assert that one immoral action is cancelled out by another.	*Here, have some photocopy paper. I pinched it from the storeroom.* *But I can't take it — that's stealing, and we both might get fired.* *Come on, everyone does it. Take it.*	I'd prefer not, thanks the same. (moral assertion) Hey, haven't they installed security cameras in the store? (motivation by fear)
2. Unrepresentative sample	'Samplings' of opinion, usually by newspapers, radio and TV programs. Inaccurate because audience is self-selecting (has not been randomly chosen), probably shares similar values and therefore may not be typical of general population, are more motivated to respond than most, and may be allowed to vote more than once. There may be corruption or bad faith involved if the opinion-gatherers harvest a payment for each call or text.	*Well, the figures are in, and you're hearing them first on the Black Death Soda Rockathon Show: 78 per cent of viewers have texted in that would prefer Johnny Bop as Prime Minister than the current real one.*	Challenge the logic. Get someone (preferably the claimants) to fund a true, large-scale randomly selected survey.
3. Argument from ignorance	A double argument: if you cannot show that something has not been proven false, it must be true; if you cannot show that something has not been proven true, it must be false.	*Since the body produced by the Prosecution cannot be identified by the trainee coroner, my client must be innocent.* *Since you cannot disprove that aliens exist, they must exist.*	Ask for more investigation; suspend judgment; refer to historical precedent. *(All once believed that the world was flat; were they right?)*
4. Anecdotal fallacy	Similar to false generalisation. The 'evidence' of one instance is taken to be conclusive. Especially effective if committed by prestigious person and/or in emotional terms.	*You're not going to buy that Gizmo Blu-Ray TV, are you? My cousin Danny's uncle bought one and it blew up the second night he had it. His daughter got scarred from the flying glass!*	Get factual evidence relating to all items in a class (TVs, cars, clothing, etc) and make a rational assessment. Usually, the further away the people 'it happened to' are, in geographical and/or genetic terms, the closer we get to urban myths.
5. Guilt by association	Similar to ad hominem fallacy (attacking someone's personal qualities rather than the argument). A link is established with an unpopular/ dangerous person to question the behaviour of someone else. Obverse is Honour by Association: *Charley belongs to the boy scouts. The scouts are really great guys, so Charley must be a great guy too.*	*You're not going vegetarian, are you? Hitler was a vegetarian, and so was my Aunt Minnie, who was the most miserable person you could meet.*	Cite counter-examples: *Yeah, but so was Gandhi, and my best friend Gus is one, and he's the happiest person I know.*

(continued)

TABLE 12.1 *(continued)*

Fallacy	Nature of fallacy	Example	Response
6. Appeal to popularity	Believing in something merely because the majority of people at that time believe it. People once believed that the world was flat, but that has since been disproven. The proposition may be true, but authenticated evidence must be produced.	*Look at this poll! 52 per cent of people believe in alien abduction! Therefore it's a fact!*	Ask for evidence, taking counter-arguments (e.g. 'hoax' websites) into account.
7. Special pleading	This occurs when a claim is made for something being an exception to the rule, but the linkage is weak or nonexistent. Often involves strong emotions and ethical dilemmas.	*I didn't know the gun was loaded, honestly? Can't you just cover it up? Come on, mate, we're in the same football team! Where's your loyalty?*	Ideally, special pleading should be ignored, but it sometimes isn't because of conflicting feelings, fear of being socially outcast if the pleading is ignored, and confusion about the differences between the spirit and letter of the law.
8. Appeal to wealth	Assumption that something that costs more than something else is better; also, the assumption that a person with more wealth is a better or more desirable person than less wealth.	*My anti-aging face cream cost 100 times what yours did, so it must be better.* *My car cost 20 times what yours did, so it is far less likely to break down.*	You get what you pay for, but not all the time. Obtain factual evidence (e.g. consumer reports) for things, and judge people according to their character, not their wealth.
9. Appeal to novelty	Assumption that newer is always better. While this is often the case, it is not always so. Opposite of appeal to antiquity (assuming that older is always better than new). Similar to the Bandwagon effect.	*My new mobile phone has a hands-free system, so I'm far less likely to have an accident when driving, unlike you with your old hand-held model.* *Well, I think we might just have a cure for your morning sickness — it's a brand new drug, called Thalidomide.*	Seek objective evidence, although this can be difficult in these cases because of incomplete data. Sometimes, it pays to be old-fashioned (the fashion industry depends partly on this fallacy, of course). (Hands-free phones are just as dangerous as hand-held phones when driving; Thalidomide was a drug distributed in the 1950s and early 1960s that caused over 10 000 serious malformations of babies.)
10. Appeal to flattery	Attempt to sidetrack rational evaluation by using flattery on the target person.	*'When we needed to have a personality who was popular with kids and was perceived to be honest — with the bonus of being beautiful — we thought of you. Sugarbomz cereal will be launched in two months and we want you to be the face of the campaign. It's all-natural, and perhaps your career could do with a bit more exposure.*	We all like flattery, but rationally consider why others are trying to persuade you on this basis.

Is logic enough?

There may be fundamental problems with the apparently clean and tidy process of logic. What if logic isn't enough? What if logic actually distorts reality rather than reveals it?

De Bono (1990, 2010) has argued for quite some time that traditional thinking, based on logical principles, sometimes misses the point and at other times leads us astray. He characterises traditional thinking as being 'vertical' thinking – that is, it depends on explaining reality by:

- looking for continuities in things
- breaking down processes into yes/no decision steps, as in computer programming and flowcharting
- trying to find absolutes and patterns of stability.

Against 'vertical' thinking, de Bono sets 'lateral' thinking or creativity, which explains reality by:

- looking for discontinuities in things
- avoiding 'right' and 'wrong' and looking for what is different or 'interesting'
- trying to find contingent or varying things and patterns of flux.

Traditional logical thinking has, he suggests, locked us into narrowly linear ways of seeing things. This means, for example, that in an argument, either I am right and you are wrong, or I am wrong and you are right. But what if things are more complicated, and interesting, than that simple binary logic outcome? What if, for example, the tidy yes/no decision points of a flowchart obscure 10, 17 or 93 possible outcomes of a particular decision point?

De Bono points an accusing finger at what he calls 'the gang of three' – Greek philosophers Socrates, Plato and Aristotle – who did so much to develop the logical theories we have been examining so far. He acknowledges that traditional logic has been an enormous force for good in aiding scientific discovery, but that it may also be an impediment when understanding human beings and their complexities.

This approach is also taken by Nisbett (2008), who looks at the philosophic approaches developed in both ancient Greece and ancient China. He characterises their divergent approaches as the difference between 'the syllogism and the Tao' – the Tao being an ancient Chinese philosophy of reality composed of opposites and contradictions, which stands in contrast to the linear and reductive premise–conclusion structure of the syllogism. Both approaches, he suggests, have their strengths as well as their weaknesses, and we would do well to try to combine both approaches to gain a better understanding of reality.

These ideas of de Bono, Nisbett and, for that matter, Tannen, have some interesting similarities with ideas of 'multiple intelligences' developed by Gardner (Chen, Moran & Gardner 2009: see also Gardner 2004). Just as traditional logic dictated that reality could be explained

The lead singer of former Australian band Powderfinger, Bernard Fanning, displays musical intelligence — one of several alternative intelligences that are becoming more widely recognised.

by syllogisms, so too did traditional approaches to intelligence testing suggest that there was only one true type of intelligence: the mathematical–logical type so effectively reflected in computer programming and IQ tests (Eysenck & Eysenck 2007).

The relatively new theory of multiple intelligences developed by Gardner and others suggests that the picture is more complex than that. Gardner suggests that there are at least eight intelligences that should be considered – linguistic, musical, logical–mathematical, spatial, bodily-kinaesthetic, interpersonal, intrapersonal and naturalist – and also argues that there may indeed be others, such as existential and spiritual intelligences (see chapter 9).

Persuasion

In considering the broader processes of argument, let's now move from logic to persuasion. How do we persuade people to do something, to buy something, to think something? How do they persuade us?

Think of the last time that you were persuaded to do, buy or think something. What set of factors induced you to move from one position to another? Some of these factors would have been logical and objective, and others would have been emotional and subjective. Persuaders may try to get others to:

- sample a particular product or process
- purchase that particular product or process
- adopt a particular course of action
- believe in a religious or political idea
- give a refund, apology or other response to a claim or complaint
- pay an overdue bill.

The persuasive process can be represented by a model (figure 12.5). As with most communication processes, there is a sender–message–receiver–feedback pattern (see chapter 1). Let's start with the message sender, the would-be persuader; and in so doing, we'll coin a barbarism by referring to the person at whom the persuasion is aimed not just as the message receiver or target person but also as the 'persuadee' (see 'Persuasion–propaganda sequences' later in this chapter).

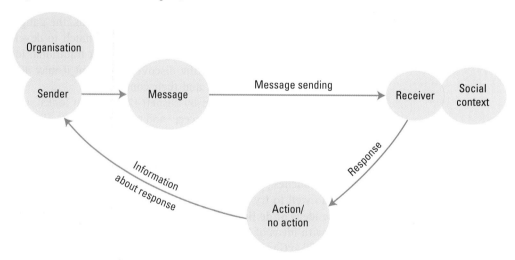

FIGURE 12.5 The persuasive process

The message sender

Before we discuss the persuasive message, we must consider the sender of that message. Why should someone be persuaded by you? What makes you so good as a persuader? We tend to believe people if we believe *in* them. Persuasion is about selling something – a commodity, an idea, a way of behaving – and in selling *something*, we need to sell *ourselves*. The credibility of the message is inextricably linked with the credibility of the messenger (see 'If you want their business, don't give them the business' in chapter 4).

If there are principles of persuasion, then they should be applicable across a wide range of fields. Rushkoff (1999), for example, points out that a CIA interrogation manual eschews vulgarities such as torture and is instead structured along the lines of Dale Carnegie's classic *How to Win Friends and Influence People* (Carnegie [1936] 1990). Mayo and Jarvis (1992) argue that the techniques of persuasion that are valid for commercial selling are also the same as those valid in politics. They suggest that effective sales people and successful politicians share qualities such as:

- being effective in establishing rapport, credibility and trust with their prospects before attempting to sell their product
- being articulate – having a good vocabulary, but knowing how to be brief
- creating a sense of togetherness with those to whom they speak (e.g. by using first-person plural pronouns such as 'we' and 'us') so that they join the customer as a full-fledged partner in the problem-solving process
- using nonverbal communication to reinforce verbal messages
- avoiding lying (or at least lying on a large scale) so as to avoid losing credibility
- listening to the needs of others and listening for crucial reality-testing feedback from others
- being effective in selling benefits, as distinct from features, and in overcoming resistance and closing a sale
- using the 'power of persuasion' rather than the 'persuasion of power' – that is, avoiding giving orders ('desk-pounding') and instead concentrating on the persuasive process. Former US President Harry S Truman said: 'The principal power that the President has is to bring people in and try to persuade them to do what they ought to do without persuasion'.

Advertisers spend considerable amounts of money paying famous people to endorse products. Often these famous people have no particular technical expertise in relation to the product or process they are selling; they have merely experienced it as lay people and may be as inexpert as the rest of us. Because we may have a high regard for the messenger or persuader – that is, have high regard for famous people and attribute considerable weight to their opinions – we also have a high regard for the message, and may well emulate the messenger or persuader by buying the particular product or process. Alternately, the messenger (famous person) may in fact have considerable technical expertise in relation to the product, process or idea being talked about, and we then attribute considerable weight to their opinions and endorsements.

The ability to persuade or influence because of expertise is known as *expert power*; whereas the ability to persuade or influence because of personality or charisma, irrespective of expertise and indeed sometimes despite a lack of expertise, is known as *referent power*. These power bases are critical components when we evaluate the credibility of others, and when others evaluate our credibility.

Credibility is not restricted to individuals, however. If you are employed by an organisation, big or small, then the credibility of the organisation has to be taken into account as well. What is its reputation? Good? Bad? Vague? Nonexistent? What is the organisation's expert power/referent power rating? In persuasion terms, the individual–organisation combination tends to be a package deal.

Convince yourself: you as expert

If you are selling something – an idea, a product, a process – then you need to know about it completely. You need to know, for example:

- What is the background, the historical context? How did it come into being?
- What are the characteristics and specifications? What can it do? What can't it do?
- How does it differ from previous models or versions? What changes might be expected with future models or versions?
- How does it stand with other products or processes in the market?
- What are the performance characteristics and specifications of competitors' processes or products?
- How does your organisation stand in backing up your process or product? Who are the key people you and your client need to know?

If you do not know these and other things, then your ignorance will become glaringly obvious – if not in the initial contact with the person you wish to persuade, then, inevitably, later on, in written or face-to-face communication.

But what if the something you are selling is complete and utter rubbish? This is an important ethical dilemma, and only you can resolve that. It is certainly true, however, that when you sell something, you not only sell yourself, but you must be sold *on* that something yourself. If *you* don't believe it, why should anyone else?

The message itself

The potency of the message a persuader sends depends on a number of factors, including the:

- rhetorical mix
- features–benefits mix
- demonstration of proofs
- language used in the construction of the message.

Rhetorical mix

Aristotle argued that the persuasive power of an argument depended on expertise in rhetoric (Aristotle 1992). The word 'rhetoric' these days can carry a negative meaning ('he was just talking rhetoric') but it refers to a collection of verbal techniques that are still quite effective (see online chapter 'Writing skills 3: style'). The three primary aspects of rhetoric are:

Logos: appeal to logic
Pathos: appeal to emotions
Ethos: appeal to credibility

- **logos,** or the appeal to logic
- **pathos,** or the appeal to the emotions
- **ethos,** or the appeal to credibility (see also Der Derian 2005; Myers 2007).

We have considered logos to a certain extent in our consideration of logical approaches, and we have discussed credibility as an important part of persuasion. Appealing to emotions is, of course, a time-honoured way of reinforcing, or stepping around, the appeals of logic and credibility. Aristotle's model can be applied in numerous ways. Figure 12.6 shows how a politician may announce a tax cut.

Logos emphasis	Pathos emphasis	Ethos emphasis
This tax cut will effectively put $15 per week back into the average pay packet.	*It will help struggling families save more, and buy more of the little luxuries that make life worthwhile.*	*We promised this at the last election, and now we are delivering on our promises.*

FIGURE 12.6 Rhetorical mix in politics

Winn and Beck (2002), for example, have used the three-part rhetorical model to evaluate websites in terms of:

- logos (price, variety, product information)

- pathos (entertainment potential of site, sensory appeal through visual, audio or other means, intuitiveness of navigation, and the extent to which the site can be personalised for users)
- ethos (privacy and security, corporate image and branding).

Features–benefits mix

Recall that the credibility of the message sender is bound up with his or her expertise, and that this expertise is demonstrated by knowing about the characteristics of the product, process or idea being communicated. Sometimes, simply listing the characteristics or features of something can be quite persuasive, without any explicit sales message being attached. This is often the case with specifications, particularly when the audience is a technically aware audience. Stating what something can do, or what it is, is a typical factual or logos-type appeal.

Features: the characteristics of an idea, product or process
Benefits: the advantages to, or relevance of, a feature

In many cases, however, features are not enough and it is necessary to show that there is a link between **features** and **benefits**. In communicating with the message receiver, the message sender has to ask, and then answer, the question: What's in it for you? How does this change your life? Message senders are often absorbed in the detail, assuming that message receivers share this concentration, awareness and enthusiasm.

Unless the message receiver sees the relevance of features, then no benefits can be perceived. Features are not an end in themselves, but they are a means to an end. Message senders need to keep in mind the 'you' attitude, and that means stressing benefits rather than features, or at least showing a link between the two. Harsh as it may seem, message receivers are sometimes not all that interested in a message about the trials and tribulations that went into producing something – that is, a message about the needs, wants or emotional states of the sender (an 'I/we' attitude). In rhetorical terms, persuaders may have to make the imaginative leap from logos appeal to pathos appeal. (See also online chapter 'Writing skills 5: how to write'.)

Successful persuaders will therefore tend to emphasise benefits rather than features (figure 12.7). Whenever features are mentioned, they should be strongly linked to benefits.

Features	Benefits
This tax cut will effectively put $15 dollars per week back into the average pay packet.	It will help struggling families save more, and buy more of the little luxuries that make life worthwhile.
This model won the 2011 Sahara Economy run.	With this model, you'll cut your petrol bills — perhaps by as much as 70 per cent.
The new Superchill ice-cube facility means that the Chillout 6000 refrigerator can produce 60 ice-cubes in an hour.	You need never run out of ice-cubes at a party again! The new ice-cube facility can produce 60 ice-cubes in an hour.
We've worked for months to design this eye-catching new form.	This new form is colour-coded and written in plain English, so that you will be able to complete it with minimum hassle.
We use SPSS to create meaningful decision models.	Some number-crunching techniques can help reveal behaviour patterns of your customers you may not have seen before — for example, using SPSS software, we can produce graphs like these.

FIGURE 12.7 Features and benefits

Proofs

Features tend to relate to the objective properties of what it is you are trying to be persuasive about. Another objective approach is that of providing various kinds of proof. Proofs are verifiable and/or tangible concepts or things that have been shown to make people more amenable to persuasion (table 12.2).

TABLE 12.2 Examples of proofs

Type of proof	Example
Testimonials	Mrs CR of Yourtown says: 'It's the best I've ever tried'.
Statistics	Nine out of ten dentists use and recommend . . .
Independent research	Government tests show that . . .
Samples	Try this no-obligation sample pack.
Trial offers	Try it out, with no obligation, for a month.
Guarantees	Guaranteed for 12 months.
Comparative analysis	Ours is 40 per cent faster than theirs.

Language

The very words that we use can transform the meaning of our messages. One person's 'terrorist' is another person's 'freedom fighter'. Entire sentences can appear to be neutrally describing the same phenomenon, but the word choices (or register) indicate otherwise (figures 12.8 and 12.9) (see online chapter 'Writing skills 3: style').

Article	Adjective	Noun	Adverb	Verb	Article	Adjective	Noun
The	aggressive	terrorists	coldly	brainwashed	the	free-thinking	modernists.
The	bold	freedom-fighters	calmly	converted	the	deluded	heretics.

FIGURE 12.8 Two descriptions of the one situation

Language style 1	Language style 2
Shampoo #6 had a light-reflective index 12 per cent higher than the mean and an elasticity-inducing index eight per cent higher than the mean.	New, improved Satin Lox will make your hair shine like diamonds, and it will put bounce and spring back into tired, lifeless hair.

FIGURE 12.9 Two language styles

We tend to characterise our own views, values and behaviour as correct, and are less charitable in our perceptions of the views of others. Figure 12.10 demonstrates this in the form of the word game of 'conjugations'.

Loaded or biased language, euphemisms, jargon and other problematic and manipulative uses of words can dramatically alter the content of a message for the worse, just as inspiring and heart-warming words, and the imaginative revelation of new perspectives and points of view, can alter the content of a message for the better (bearing in mind, of course, that what is worse and what is better may be a matter of opinion) (see also online chapter 'Writing skills 4: plain English').

First person	Second person	Third person
I am firm.	You are obstinate.	She is a pig-headed fool.
I am nostalgic.	You are old-fashioned.	He is living in the past.
I am sparkling.	You are unusually talkative.	She is drunk.
I dream.	You escape.	He needs help.
I am casual.	You are informal.	He is an unshaven slob.
I am in charge of public relations.	You exaggerate.	She is a liar.
I am beautiful.	You have quite good features.	She isn't bad looking, if you like that type.
I am righteously indignant.	You are annoyed.	He is making a fuss about nothing.
I am influencing her.	You are pressuring her.	He is manipulating her.

FIGURE 12.10 Conjugations word game

Sending the message

What is the best way to send a message? This is partly a matter of technology and channel choice, but it is also a matter of communicative technique relating to:

- the manner in which the persuader opens up the attempt at persuasion
- the emphasis placed in the message by the persuader in order to trigger a type of response from the persuadee
- the sequence of gambits or ploys used by the persuader.

Foot-in-the-door versus door-in-the-face

The manner in which the persuader opens up the attempt at persuasion can be critical. For example, if a salesperson came to your front door, which approach do you think would be more successful in getting you to buy something?

- *Approach A:* 'Would you like to buy $400 worth of new, improved Junko? No? Well, okay, then, how about $18 worth?'
- *Approach B:* 'Would you like to buy $18 worth of new, improved Junko? I'm sure that you won't regret it. By the way, do you know that if you were to get an even bigger portion of Junko – say, $500 worth – I could let you have it at a discount for $400?'

Approach A is referred to by social psychologists as the **door-in-the-face** technique, whereas approach B is referred to as the **foot-in-the-door** technique (Aronson, Wilson & Akert 2010).

Both terms refer to the actual ritual of door-to-door selling, but are applied to the wider context of the analysis of attitudes and persuasion. The foot-in-the-door technique means that the persuader starts out asking for a small response from the other person. Once trust is gained and the ice is broken, the persuader then attempts to elicit an even stronger response. The door-in-the-face technique depends on the persuader making an unrealistic opening claim and then backing off, trying for a smaller gain. These approaches have much in common with negotiation tactics such as 'fait accompli' and 'nibble' (see 'Strategies and tactics' in chapter 13).

Door-in-the-face: a persuasion method that depends on first trying to effect an unrealistically large attitude change, and then promoting a smaller attitude change

Foot-in-the-door: a persuasion method that depends on trying to effect a small attitude change, and then building on that to effect a larger attitude change

Central versus peripheral processing

Central processing: the process of evaluating a persuasive message according to its objective content

Peripheral processing: the process of evaluating a persuasive message according to nonobjective factors

The emphasis placed in the message by the persuader in order to trigger a type of response from the persuadee can also be critical. We can draw a distinction between **central processing** and **peripheral processing** of messages (Stiff & Mongeau 2003; Aronson, Wilson & Akert 2010). When central processing of a message takes place, then the persuadee is concentrating on the core arguments being presented by the persuader.

Central processing occurs when:

- the arguments are presented in clear and logical style
- the subject matter of the argument has direct relevance to the audience or persuadee
- there are no distractions, such as noise and an uncomfortable environment
- the audience or persuadee has a high need for cognition – that is, the enjoyment of the mental process of thinking issues through
- the audience or persuadee does not give high priority to factors such as the attractiveness or prestige of the persuader
- the audience or persuadee has the ability and motivation to listen carefully.

Peripheral processing occurs when:

- the arguments are not presented in clear and logical style
- the subject matter of the argument does not have direct relevance to the audience or persuadee
- there are distractions, such as noise and an uncomfortable environment
- the audience or persuadee does not have a high need for cognition
- the audience or persuadee gives high priority to factors such as the attractiveness or prestige of the persuader
- the audience or persuadee does not have the ability or motivation to listen carefully.

Generally speaking, if a message is processed centrally, then it has a good chance of leading to long-term attitude change – of being an example of successful persuasion. If a message is peripherally processed, then it has a weaker chance of leading to long-term attitude change (but note the use of distraction in persuasion–propaganda sequences; see the next section).

Persuasion–propaganda sequences

The sequence of gambits or ploys used by the persuader can have a major impact on the persuasion process. For example, in their analysis of propaganda methods, Pratkanis and Aronson (2001) identified a chain of techniques that may lead to attitude change or persuasion.

- Create a pre-persuasion climate of similarity between persuader and persuadee by defining things that 'everybody knows or agrees on'.
- Classify or label ideas and proponents of ideas in extreme ways, polarising the terms of debate.
- Use strong generalisations, rumours and gossip.
- Build credibility in the eyes of the audience or persuadees.
- Communicate arguments when audiences or persuadees are distracted, do not have time to think about issues or are overloaded with information.
- Use emotional appeals, such as those that tap into fear and guilt.
- Create obligation and indebtedness in the audience or persuadees, and then make a claim on those feelings.

The message recipient

So much for the message sender, the message itself and the message process. What about the message recipient or the target – the persuadee? What motivates such a person, and how could such motivational patterns be enlisted to help you persuade that person to your point of view? We need to consider some models of motivation, and then examine the social context that individuals find themselves in.

Maslow's model

Hierarchy of needs: a model of motivation that arranges human needs and motivations in a sequence

A useful model of human motivation is the **hierarchy of needs**, developed by psychologist Abraham Maslow. He argued that human needs could be arranged in a sequence or hierarchy (figure 12.11). At the bottom of the hierarchy are physiological needs, such as the needs for food, water, shelter, clothing and reproduction. Next come safety and security needs — the needs for self-protection. After that are the social and belonging needs — the needs for the company of others. Next come esteem and status needs — the needs to have one's competence recognised by others, and to be granted approval by others. Finally comes the need for self-actualisation — to be all that one can be, the need to achieve one's ultimate human potential (Maslow 1999).

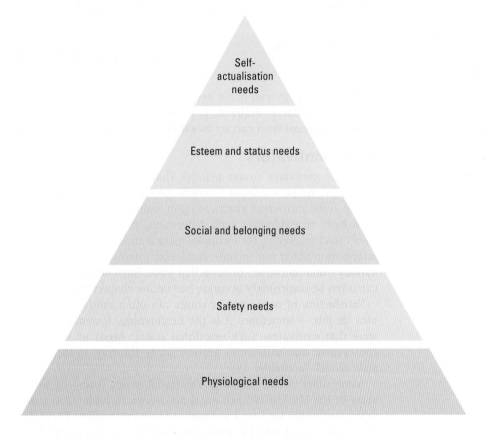

FIGURE 12.11 Maslow's hierarchy of needs

Maslow argued that we satisfy our needs in a sequence or hierarchy, starting with physiological needs and proceeding through each higher level. He argued that a satisfied need no longer motivates — that is, once we have satisfied our physiological and safety needs, for example, then and only then do we proceed to satisfying our social and other higher needs. While our lower needs remain satisfied, new opportunities to satisfy those needs will not motivate us.

Even though the hierarchy of needs model has been around for half a century, it is still not clear whether people are motivated in a hierarchical or sequential manner (Wachter 2003). It is also not always clear just what is a *need* and what is a *want*. Nevertheless, the various needs or wants described by Maslow — irrespective of their relationship with each other — accord with common sense, and almost certainly do exist.

It is possible to present different types of persuasive messages, each one aimed at the needs described by Maslow. For example, an ecotourism company promoting a new adventure holiday may use the needs concept to highlight a particular aspect or feature of the holiday in their advertising campaign (table 12.3).

TABLE 12.3 Maslow's five levels of human needs applied to an advertising campaign for an ecotourism company's adventure tours

Human needs	Wording in advertising campaign
Self-actualisation needs	Get away from civilisation, and rediscover the inner you.
Esteem needs	All of your friends and colleagues will be impressed that you are taking this trip.
Social needs	You'll meet new people, with an approach to the wilderness similar to yours.
Safety needs	A paramedic accompanies each group, and we are in continual radio contact with home base.
Physiological needs	We haven't forgotten your creature comforts — all tents have light and heating/cooling facilities.

This is a strategy you might keep in mind when creating a persuasive message. It may not always be possible, or desirable, to try and address all five levels of needs in your message, but the needs concept itself can act as a useful stimulus to differentiate or fine-tune your message.

Other motivators

What else motivates human beings? That, to say the least, is not a simple question. What motivates one person from a certain group, religion, culture or class may not motivate a person from a different group, religion, culture or class. Indeed, an enormous industry has been built on exploiting such differences, the better to facilitate the persuasive process. Direct mail marketers, for example, make it their business to construct databases containing information about our income, residence, interests and behaviour patterns, and then target various communications to us on that basis. Such demographic or psychographic approaches can often be surprisingly accurate (see online chapter 'Media and communication').

Satisfaction of needs and/or wants can often motivate, but sometimes it is not as complex as this — sometimes it is the heightening, lessening or elimination of an emotional state that motivates. Such emotional states, needs or wants are sometimes experienced consciously, and sometimes unconsciously (Murray 1938: see also 'Aronoff and Wilson's style model' in chapter 13).

Some other needs, wants or emotional states (some of which obviously overlap with some of the Maslow-defined ones) are shown in table 12.4, together with persuasive messages that might be aimed at tapping those motivators. These needs, wants and emotional states are tapped into by others but also by ourselves with internal dialogue or self-talk (see 'Intrapersonal communication: self-talk' in chapter 9).

TABLE 12.4 Some human needs, wants and emotional states

Need, want or emotional state	Possibly satisfied or controlled by	Typical persuasive message
Greed	Discounts, giveaways, prizes	You'll be rich beyond your dreams!
Thrift	Discounts, giveaways, prizes	Think of the money you'll save with these at-cost prices!
Vanity	Products that purport to beautify	There'll be a new, lovelier you minutes after you smooth it into your skin.

Need, want or emotional state	Possibly satisfied or controlled by	Typical persuasive message
Fear	Removal, reduction of threat; for example, loss of credit rating, legal action	How will your family survive if you have an accident?
Compassion	Helping others; for example, a donation	You can help little Izulo by giving just $5 a week.
Guilt	Helping others; for example, a donation	That kid will go to bed hungry unless I can give just a miserable $5 a week.
Conformity	Doing what everyone else is doing; getting on the bandwagon	All the best-dressed women will be wearing it this season.
Boredom	Excitement, novelty, distraction, danger	Get out of that rut and into the adventure of a lifetime.
Purposelessness	Definition of role; excitement, novelty, distraction, danger	I was going nowhere until I joined the armed forces.
Curiosity	Excitement, novelty, distraction, danger	Haven't you always wondered just what the mysterious East is really like?
Justice	Compensation, satisfaction, fair play	Do the right thing.
Sexuality or sensuality	Reality or illusion of being loved, of being attractive	The passion, the touch of that special one, can be yours tonight.
Punishment	Losing money, possessions; confirmation of perceived inadequacy	That's twice I've won. Should I quit? No, I'll just keep going. Probably won't keep it all anyway.
Envy	Obtaining an object identical to or better than someone else's	Stay ahead of the common herd with the new Elite Special Edition.
Spirituality	Sense of other-worldliness, of transcendence	Step out of the rat race and just sit in silence, meditate or pray.

Such motivators raise the question that should be at the heart of all persuasion: Is it ethical? It is ethical to enlist some of these needs, wants or emotional states when we attempt to persuade someone of something, while it would be quite unethical and/or counterproductive to enlist others.

The message recipient

The extent to which people are persuaded by messages from others depends on a number of factors, including **conformity**, especially when we are in groups. Factors that are important in determining whether people will conform to the will of, or pressure imposed by, others include (Aronson, Wilson & Akert 2010; Eunson 1987):

Conformity: going along with the values and actions of others

- *Age.* Children tend to be more conforming than adults; persons aged 18–25 tend to be more susceptible to attitude change than those who are 25 and over.
- *Gender.* Women, sometimes due to traditional social conditioning, are sometimes more conforming than men.
- *Intelligence, creativity.* People with low IQ and low creativity tend to conform more easily to group norms.
- *Ignorance.* If a person does not understand what is going on in a group setting, then he or she is more likely to follow the lead of someone who seems to know what is going on.
- *Personality.* People with certain personality characteristics (submissiveness or passivity, low self-esteem, high need for acceptance and strong fear of rejection) will tend to conform.

Conforming means being persuaded, or at least giving the impression of being persuaded. In the past 60 years, a number of social psychologists and writers have made some disturbing observations about the tendencies of people to conform. For example, Solomon Asch (1987) conducted experiments in social psychology to determine to what extent group pressure and context could get people to conform and to accept opinions that would normally be unacceptable. Naive subjects (i.e. volunteers in experiments who did not know that they were the true subjects of the experiments) found themselves in groups sitting around a table, the other people in fact having been briefed by Asch to behave atypically. All people in the group were shown sets of cards. Each set was comprised of one card with one line drawn on it, and the other card with three lines drawn on it. On the three-line card, one line obviously matched in length the line on the other card, and the other two lines did not. All participants were asked to identify which of the three lines matched the single line on the other card. Asch's accomplices gave the wrong answer, thus putting pressure on the naïve subject to either challenge the judgement of the others, or to simply and meekly go along with the others. Over a series of experiments, only an average of one in four refused to conform — that is, there was a 75 per cent chance that people would agree with a proposition that was obviously wrong.

Obedience, rationalising and true believers

Another psychologist, Stanley Milgram (Milgram 2010), created a series of experiments that were also based upon the deception of naive subjects to determine to what extent people might conform or obey authority. Naïve subjects showed up at a psychological testing laboratory expecting to be involved in an experiment on learning. Each subject was paired with another person: an actor briefed on how to behave. Lots were drawn (in a fixed draw), with the actor becoming the 'learner' and the subject becoming the 'teacher'. The learner was connected to a voltage generator, a fearsome looking device with 30 switches labelled from 15 volts to 450 volts. The teacher read a series of word pairs to the learner, and then started to read the series again, but this time only giving the first word in the pair.

As part of an experiment, two groups of students took on the roles of prisoners and warders in a simulated prison environment. The 'warders' began to victimise the 'prisoners' so quickly that the experimenters had to stop the test within a week. This experiment offers insights into how quickly conformity and obedience to authority can be achieved.

The psychologist running the experiment instructed the teacher to administer 'punishment' to the learner if a wrong response was given. The actor/learner gave numerous wrong responses, and then the teachers in the various experiments were confronted with a dilemma: should they administer electric shocks to another human being, or should they challenge the whole set-up of the experiment and the authority of the psychologist? The situation was made all the worse by the actor/learner showing increasing distress, and then appearing to have a heart attack. The ethics of this experiment, conducted in the 1960s, are still controversial to this day, as are the results. In various versions of this experiment, up to 80 per cent of the teachers in fact continued to give shocks. The teachers came from a variety of socioeconomic backgrounds and were not overtly aggressive, and yet, when placed in the right (or wrong) circumstances, appeared to be willing to hurt (and perhaps kill) another human being.

A similar experiment was conducted by Philip Zimbardo at Stanford University, in which two groups of students took on the roles of prisoners and warders. The role-playing in a simulated prison environment took over so completely that the 'warders' began to victimise the 'prisoners' in reality, and the experiment had to be stopped after less than a week. Zimbardo and others have since developed the idea of 'violence workers', speculating that roles and environments can themselves produce violence, brutalisation, torture and murder — from Brazilian prisons in 1964–85 to North American soldiers operating more recently in Iraqi jails (Zimbardo, Weber & Johnson 2003; Huggins, Haritos-Fatouros & Zimbardo 2002; www.prisonexp.org).

Leon Festinger (1996) coined the term **cognitive dissonance** to describe the uncomfortable feelings that a person experiences when a person holds two or more inconsistent beliefs and then behaves in a way that is inconsistent with the way that that person has behaved before. Therefore people confronted with dissonance in certain situations can either change their behaviour, or they can rationalise their refusal to change their behaviour (figure 12.12).

Cognitive dissonance: the stress experienced when a person behaves in a way inconsistent with that person's self-concept

Dissonant state	Behaviour change	Rationalisation involving no change
Smoking is bad for you — I am still smoking.	Give up smoking.	You're going to die anyway. I need it to handle stress. Look at my grandfather — he's still smoking.
Being overweight is bad for you — I am still overweight.	Lose weight.	There's no point — I have bad genes. This food tastes so good.

FIGURE 12.12 Cognitive dissonance and responses to it

Hoffer (2002) attempted to explain why so many people who had followed left-wing causes in the 1920s and 1930s later took up right-wing causes like fascism. He developed the idea of what he called the 'true believer': someone who has such a strong need to believe in something that they will believe in anything, and may swing wildly between apparently opposed belief systems. In a similar vein, Fromm (1995) argued that some people preferred living under authoritarian rule rather than in a democracy because they found the responsibilities of freedom too much to bear.

The work of these writers and researchers — Asch, Milgram, Festinger, Hoffer and Fromm — suggests that people can be persuaded to believe, or to act as if they do believe, in the most absurd and dangerous things, if the pre-conditions are right. Authoritarian governments and manipulators of ideas throughout history have, of course, been all too willing to ensure that conditions are right in all too many circumstances.

Responses to the message

We have just seen that responses to persuasive messages are sometimes not all that desirable. But not all messages are undesirable, and neither are all responses. Responses to messages can include:

- applause
- voting
- agreeing
- saying yes
- saying no
- throwing rotten eggs
- buying something
- telephoning
- returning a form
- going out on strike
- coming back from a strike.

Influence

Influence is a close relative of persuasion and logic. The distinction between influence on the one hand and persuasion and logic on the other may well be a distinction without a difference. Nevertheless, the study of influence styles and tactics, particularly within organisations, has produced some interesting findings in the past few years.

Principles of influence

Some research (Goldstein, Martin & Cialdini 2010; Cialdini & Goldstein 2002) indicates that there are relatively few basic principles that govern how one person might influence another. These include:

- *Liking.* People can influence us when they:
  - are physically attractive
  - are similar to us in appearance and manner
  - cooperate with us to achieve mutual goals
  - show liking for us.
- *Reciprocity.* People can influence us when we feel obligated to them in some way — for example, door-in-the-face dynamics (see also 'Foot-in-the-door versus door-in-the-face' earlier in this chapter).
- *Consistency.* People can influence us if they can show consistency and commitment in their behaviour and if they manage to get us to do the same (e.g. if we are persuaded to put down a deposit on a purchase, or when someone asks us to look after their belongings). This characteristic includes the tendency not to rationalise away doubts and inconsistencies of the cognitive dissonance type.
- *Scarcity.* People can influence us when they seem to be able to diminish scarcity, such as a bouncer who lets us into an exclusive nightclub, or a person who can put us in touch with high-status individuals or has access to other scarce resources and/or information ('inside knowledge').
- *Social validation.* People can influence us when they show us how to do things and how to win approval, as exemplified by:
  - celebrity endorsements of products
  - 'salting' or putting money in receptacles to show that other people have already given, so it's okay to give (e.g. a busker's hat, a bartender's tip jar or a church collection plate)
  - witnessing — for example, when evangelical preachers have accomplices in the audience to come forward and make a religious commitment
  - observation — for example, children may lose phobias (e.g. fear of dogs) simply by observing people without phobias being unstressed by situations
  - canned laughter on TV shows.
- *Authority.* People can influence us by having, or appearing to have, authority and/or expertise. Therefore, in an experiment involving an actor committing acts of jaywalking, three times more people copied the actor's actions when he was wearing a business suit than when he was wearing casual clothes (Argyle 1999).

Tactics of influence

Various tactics can be used to attempt to exert influence, both in professional and personal settings (Lambert 1996; Higgins, Judge & Ferris 2003; Fu & Yukl 2000; Lee & Sweeney 2001; Kipnis & Schmidt 2003; Cable & Judge 2003; Seta, Paulus & Baron 2000; Harvard Business School Press 2009). These include:

- *assertiveness* — using confrontational and nonconfrontational directness of speech and action to express wishes and needs to others

- *ingratiation* – using behaviours designed to increase others' liking of us or to make us appear friendly in order to get what we want
- *rationality* – using logical arguments to build a case and get what we want
- *sanctions* – using punishment or the threat of punishment to get what we want
- *exchange* – offering to do something for someone in exchange for their doing something
- *blocking* – attempting to stop others from carrying out actions by impeding their progress
- *coalitions* – mobilising others to help put pressure on the target individual
- *upward appeal* – relying on the chain of command, calling in superiors to help get our way, going over someone's head.
- *impression management* – look good and look confident in what you are doing (even if you are feel that you do not and are not).

It is also possible to use verbal and nonverbal tactics of negative politeness and positive politeness (Morand 2000) in order to exert influence over others (figure 12.13).

NEGATIVE POLITENESS		POSITIVE POLITENESS	
Tactic	**Example**	**Tactic**	**Example**
Use indirect questions such as enquiries into the hearer's ability or willingness to comply.	*Can you tell me what time it is?*	Notice hearer's admirable qualities or possessions, show interest, exaggerate.	*Nice to see you. Hey, really love your new car! Can I borrow it sometime?*
Use hedges: words or phrases that diminish the force of a speech act.	*Can I* perhaps *trouble you?*	Employ phonological slurring to convey in-group membership.	Heya, gimme *a hand* willya*?*
Use the subjunctive to express pessimism about hearer's ability or willingness to comply.	Could *I ask you a question?*	Use colloquialisms or slang to convey in-group membership.	*I know I seem like a stick-in-the-mud, but* what the hell.
Use words or phrases that minimise the imposition.	*I need* just a little *of your time.*	Use ellipsis (omission) to communicate tacit understandings.	[Do you] *Mind if I smoke?*
Give deference by using an honorific such as sir or Mr.	*Can I help you,* sir?	Use first names or in-group name to insinuate familiarity.	*Hey,* Bud, *have you got a minute?*
Use formal word choices to indicate seriousness and to establish social distance.	*Could you tolerate a slight imposition on my part?*	Claim common point of view: speaker asserts knowledge of hearer's wants or asserts that hearer has knowledge of speaker's wants.	*You know how the caretakers don't like it when …*
Apologise: admit the impingement, express reluctance.	I am sorry *to bother you, but …*	Give reasons: assert reflexivity by making activity seem reasonable to the hearer.	*I'm really late for an important appointment, so …*

FIGURE 12.13 Tactics of negative and positive politeness

(continued)

 **FIGURE 12.13** *(continued)*

NEGATIVE POLITENESS		POSITIVE POLITENESS	
Tactic	**Example**	**Tactic**	**Example**
Impersonalise the speaker and hearer by avoiding the pronouns 'I' and 'you'.	*Is it possible to ask a favour?*	Use inclusive forms such as 'we' or 'let's' to include both speaker and hearer in the activity.	We're *not feeling well, are* we?
Use the past tense to create distance in time.	*I* had *been wondering if I could ask a favour.*	Assert reciprocal exchange or tit for tat.	*Do me this favour, and I'll make it up to you.*
State the face-threatening act as a general rule.	*Regulations* require *that I ask you to leave.*	Give something desired: gifts, sympathy, understanding.	*You look like you've had a rough week.*

Source: Adapted from Morand (2000, p. 238).

Principles and tactics of influence, when combined with what we now know about logic and persuasion, may help us to become more effective when we engage in argument with others. Words of caution may be needed, however. There may be negative effects of trying too hard to influence and persuade others (Seta, Paulus & Baron 2000), such as:

- *The slime effect.* When an individual uses ingratiation or sycophancy to superiors but is not so positive towards subordinates; the hypocrisy is seen and undermines the credibility of the person doing the **sliming**.
- *Reactance.* Those who are the targets or persuadees may simply recognise persuasive/ influencing approaches and become less, not more, pliable.
- *Metamorphic effects.* Those actively pursuing persuasion/influence tactics may come to see targets or persuadees merely as objects to be manipulated, which will not only impoverish relationships between people but may make the would-be influencers less socially competent.

Sliming: when a person tries to use influence and persuasion in such a manipulative and transparent way that his or her actions and words elicit contempt from others

STUDENT STUDY GUIDE

SUMMARY

In this chapter we considered different aspects of argument, paying particular attention to logic, persuasion and influence. We first examined the different meanings of the word 'argument', and discussed the nature of facts and paradigms and their role in explaining reality. We considered the tools and limitations of logic, including inductive and deductive logic and logical fallacies. We looked at the roles played by persuasive message senders and receivers, and examined the nature of persuasive messages and the process of sending, including factors such as the credibility of the message sender, the nature of the message itself, the rhetorical mix, the features–benefits mix, proofs and language, foot-in-the-door versus door-in-the-face processes, central versus peripheral message processing, persuasion and propaganda sequences, and motivational patterns. Looking at the broader aspects of the persuasion process, we considered how social contexts sometimes induce conformity, producing potentially unhealthy patterns of persuasion via mechanisms such as group pressure, obedience to authority, cognitive dissonance, the true believer phenomenon and the creation of the fear of freedom. Finally, we examined persuasion and influence, and considered differing principles and tactics of influence.

KEY TERMS

benefits *p. 389*
central processing *p. 392*
cognitive dissonance *p. 397*
conclusion *p. 380*
conformity *p. 395*
deductive logic *p. 380*
distinction of degree *p. 381*
distinction of kind *p. 381*
door-in-the-face *p. 391*

ethos *p. 388*
excuse *p. 382*
explanation *p. 382*
fallacy *p. 382*
features *p. 389*
foot-in-the-door *p. 391*
hierarchy of needs *p. 393*
inductive logic *p. 380*
logos *p. 388*

necessary condition *p. 382*
paradigm *p. 379*
pathos *p. 388*
peripheral processing
   p. 392
premise *p. 380*
sliming *p. 400*
sufficient condition *p. 382*
syllogism *p. 380*

REVIEW QUESTIONS

1. What is the difference between inductive logic and deductive logic?
2. Give three examples of logical fallacies.
3. What is the difference between logos, pathos and ethos in argument?
4. Why is a benefit usually more persuasive than a feature?
5. What is the difference between a foot-in-the-door strategy of persuasion and a door-in-the-face strategy?
6. Why are some people more rather than less likely to conform to the wishes and values of others?
7. Give three examples of tactics of influence.
8. What is the slime effect, and why is it to be avoided?

APPLIED ACTIVITIES

1. Using print and/or internet sources, find out more about syllogisms. Use this information to write at least three valid syllogisms and three invalid ones.
2. Evaluate a written or spoken text (e.g. a politician's speech or a television commercial) in terms of its logos–pathos–ethos mix.
3. Using print and/or internet sources, find out more about Edward de Bono's concepts of lateral thinking versus vertical thinking (PO, thinking hats).

4. Evaluate a written or spoken text in terms of its use of language and motivational patterns.
5. Create at least two examples of two descriptions of one situation (figure 12.8).
6. Devise at least three examples of cognitive dissonance and the responses to them.
7. Identify examples of at least three principles of influencing.

WHAT WOULD YOU DO?

Rachel is the president of your industry union local branch, and you are the secretary. She also acts as treasurer, and you have suspected for some time that she has been embezzling official funds, but cannot prove it so far. The union head office has called a strike tomorrow, and if it goes on, then funds will have to be tapped to provide strike pay. You believe that the strike is vital; indeed, you believe that not to strike now would permanently damage the union and workers' conditions and wages.

Rachel is addressing a team meeting with two other branch leaders, and you are in a dilemma. It is well known that you two don't get on, and she has accused you of being jealous of her and her abilities. There is no doubt about the effect Rachel has on people: she is charismatic and well spoken, whereas you do not fare well in the charisma stakes, and become quite nervous when speaking. In an act that only mildly surprises you, Rachel has started speaking out against the strike, using every persuasive tool at her disposal. She starts out using ad hominem and flattery tactics ('those idiots at head office wouldn't know what it's like out here at the sharp end') and proceeds through another ten logical fallacies and manipulative persuasion strategies. You can see what she is doing – she is trying to avoid having the financial situation exposed. She is also beginning to win the other two branch leaders over.

What should you do or say now?

SUGGESTED READING

Copi, Irving M & Cohen, Carl 2004, *Essentials of logic*, Prentice Hall, Upper Saddle River, NJ.
Crosby, Richard 2010, *Persuasion and influence for dummies*, John Wiley & Sons, Hoboken, NJ.
Heinrichs, Jay 2007, *Thank you for arguing: what Aristotle, Lincoln and Homer Simpson can teach us about the art of persuasion*, Three Rivers Press, New York, NY.
Weston, Anthony 2010, *A rulebook for arguments*, 4th rev.edn, Hackett Publishing, Indianapolis, IN.

REFERENCES

Aristotle 1992, *The art of rhetoric*, trans. Hugh Lawson-Tancred, Penguin, London.

Aronson, Elliot, Wilson, Timothy D & Akert, Robin M 2010, *Social psychology*, 7th edn, Prentice Hall, Upper Saddle River, NJ.

Asch, Solomon 1987, *Social psychology*, Oxford University Press, New York.

Cable, Daniel M & Judge, Timothy A 2003, 'Managers' upward influence tactic strategies: the role of manager personality and supervisor leadership style', *Journal of Organizational Behavior*, vol. 24, pp. 197–214.

Carey, Stephen S 2000, *The uses and abuses of argument: critical thinking and fallacious reasoning*, Mayfield, Mountain View, CA.

Carnegie, Dale 1990, *How to win friends and influence people*, rev. edn, Arthur R Pell (ed.), Pocket Books, New York.

Chen, Jie-Qi, Moran, Seana, and Gardner, Howard (eds.) 2009, *Multiple intelligences around the world*, Jossey-Bass, San Francisco.

Cialdini, Robert B & Goldstein, Noah J 2002, 'The science and practice of persuasion', *Cornell Hotel and Restaurant Administration Quarterly*, vol. 43, no. 2, pp. 40–50.

Cooper, Sheila & Patton, Rosemary 1993, *Ergo: thinking critically and writing logically*, HarperCollins, New York.

De Bono, Edward 1990a, *Lateral thinking: a textbook of creativity*, Penguin, London.

—— 2010 *Think! Before it's too late*, Random House, London.

Der Derian, James 2005, 'Imaging terror: logos, pathos and ethos', *Third World Quarterly*, vol. 26, no. 1, pp. 23–37.

Drucker, Peter F 2002, *The effective executive*, rev. edn, HarperBusiness, New York.

Eunson, Baden 1987, *Behaving: managing yourself and others*, McGraw-Hill, Sydney.

Eysenck, Hans & Eysenck, Sybil 2007, *The structure and measurement of intelligence*, Transaction Publishers, Somerset, NJ.

Festinger, R Leon 1996, *Retrospections of social psychology*, Oxford University Press, New York.

Fromm, Erich 1995, *Escape from freedom*, Henry Holt and Company, New York.

Fu, Ping Ping & Yukl, Gary 2000, 'Perceived effectiveness of influence tactics in the United States and China', *Leadership Quarterly*, vol. 11, no. 2, pp. 251–66.

Gardner, Howard 2001, *Intelligence reframed: multiple intelligences for the 21st century*, Basic Books, New York.

—— 2004, *Changing minds: the art and science of changing our own and other people's minds*, Harvard University Press, Boston, MA.

Goldstein, Noah J., Martin, Steve J., and Cialdini, Robert B. 2010, *Yes! 50 scientifically proven ways to be persuasive*, Free Press, New York.

Harvard Business School Press 2009, *Tactics of influence: three ways to project influence*, press chapter, 3 May, Harvard Business School Press, Boston, MA.

Higgins, Chad A, Judge, Timothy A & Ferris, Gerald R 2003, 'Influence tactics and work outcomes: a meta-analysis', *Journal of Organizational Behavior*, vol. 24, pp. 89–106.

Hoffer, Eric 2002, *The true believer: thoughts on the nature of mass movements*, Harper Perennial, New York.

Huggins, Martha K, Haritos-Fatouros, Mika & Zimbardo, Philip G 2002, *Violence workers: police torturers and murderers reconstruct Brazilian Atrocities*, University of California Press, Berkeley, CA.

Kipnis, David M & Schmidt, Stuart M 2003, 'Upward influence styles: relationship with performance evaluations, salary and stress', in Lyman W Porter, Harold L Angle, & Robert W Allen (eds), *Organizational influence processes*, 2nd edn, M. E. Sharpe, Armonk, NY.

Kuhn Thomas S 2003, in James Conant & John Haugeland (eds), *The road since structure*, University of Chicago Press, Chicago.

Lambert, Tom E 1996, *The power of influence: intensive influencing skills in business*, Nicholas Brealey, London.

Lee, David R & Sweeney, Patrick J 2001, 'An assessment of influence tactics used by project managers', *Engineering Management Journal*, vol. 13, no. 2, pp. 16–24.

Maslow, Abraham 1999, *Towards a psychology of being*, 3rd edn, John Wiley & Sons, New York.

Mayo, Edward & Jarvis, Lance P 1992, 'The power of persuasion: lessons in personal selling from the White House', *The Journal of Personal Selling & Sales Management*, vol. 12, no. 4, pp. 56–81.

Milgram, Stanley 2010, *The individual in a social world: essays and experiments*, 3rd edn, Pinter and Martin Ltd., London.

Morand, David A 2000, 'Language and power: an empirical analysis of linguistic strategies used in superior–subordinate-communication', *Journal of Organizational Behavior*, vol. 21, pp. 235–48.

Murray, HA 1938, *Explorations in personality*, Oxford University Press, New York.

Myers, Marshall 2007, 'The use of pathos in charity letters: some notes towards a theory and analysis', *Journal of Technical Writing and Communication*, vol. 37, no. 1, pp. 3–16.

Nisbett, Richard E 2008, *The geography of thought: how Asians and Westerners think differently ... and why*, Nicholas Brealey, London.

Pratkanis, Anthony R & Aronson, Elliot A 2001, *Age of propaganda: the everyday use and abuse of persuasion*, W.H. Freeman, New York.

Rushkoff, Douglas 1999, *Coercion: why we listen to what 'they' say*, Riverhead/Penguin Putnam, New York.

Seta, Catherine E, Paulus, Paul B & Baron, Robert A 2000, *Effective human relations: a guide to people at work*, 4th edn, Allyn & Bacon, Boston, MA.

Stiff, James B & Mongeau, Paul A 2003, *Persuasive communication*, 2nd edn, Guildford Press, New York.

Tannen, Deborah 1998, *The argument culture: changing the way we argue and debate*, Virago, London.

Wachter, Kathy 2003, 'Rethinking Maslow's needs', *Journal of Family and Consumer Sciences*, vol. 95, no. 3, pp. 68–9.

Winn, Wendy & Beck, Kati 2002, 'The persuasive power of design elements on an e-commerce web site', *Technical Communication*, vol. 49, pp. 17–35.

Zimbardo, Phillip G, Weber, Ann L & Johnson, Robert L 2003, *Psychology: core concepts*, 4th edn, Pearson/Allyn & Bacon, Boston, MA.

13

Negotiation skills

LEARNING OBJECTIVES

After studying this chapter you should be able to:

- Explain why negotiation is not always the preferred mode for resolving a situation of conflict or disagreement
- Explain the nature of win–lose and win–win dynamics in conflicts
- Understand the value of research
- Define goals and bottom lines, and concessions, positions and interests
- Determine whether territory and time scarcity or abundance is relevant in negotiation
- Assess the role of publics or stakeholders in negotiation
- Understand how to package offers in negotiation
- Work better as an individual or as a member of a team in a negotiation situation
- Understand the role of nonverbal communication and signalling in negotiation
- Use listening skills, questioning skills and persuasive skills in negotiations
- Understand the role of culture and gender in negotiations
- Understand the importance of personal styles in negotiation
- Identify and use strategies and tactics in negotiations
- Identify and effectively use communication channels in negotiation situations
- Create an effective plan for a variety of negotiation situations

What is negotiation?

Our professional and personal lives might well be more satisfying and successful if we could only improve our negotiation skills. What do we mean by negotiation? Dictionary definitions of the concept include:

- to confer with another or others in order to come to terms or reach an agreement
- mutual discussion and arrangement of the terms of a transaction or agreement
- to settle by discussion and bargaining.

Other terms for negotiation include haggling, bargaining, making deals, transacting, higgling, dickering and horse-trading. (The English word, incidentally, comes from the Latin *neg* [not] + *otium* [leisure], i.e. 'not at leisure', or simply 'business'.) In the eyes of many, it is a specialised skill used by diplomats, businesspeople and union leaders — interesting, but not that relevant to everyday life. In reality, it could be argued without too much exaggeration that negotiation *is* everyday life.

Everyone negotiates in all kinds of situations:

- A child tries to convince a parent to buy sweets in the supermarket.
- You try to persuade your flatmate to do the dishes, even though it is your turn, so you can go out.
- A union representative sits down with management for an annual review of wages and conditions.
- You are running late on an assignment and are thinking of approaching your lecturer for an extension.
- You are thinking of trading in a car and upgrading to a better one.
- A mother tries to get her young daughter to eat her vegetables or clean up her room.
- Friends try to decide which movie they will see tonight.
- An employee asks for a raise in salary.
- A consumer tries to get a better deal on a refrigerator from a salesperson.
- New acquaintances try to determine whether they will become friends or lovers.
- The representatives of two countries sit down to discuss border tensions and the threat of war.

All of these situations, along with countless others, involve negotiation.

As political leaders, US President Barack Obama and Chinese Premier Wen Jiabao engage in negotiation on behalf of the nations and the people that they represent. An employee asking for a pay increase at work, a person trading in a vehicle at a car dealership, and even a girl pleading with her father to buy her something are all examples of situations that involve varying levels of negotiation.

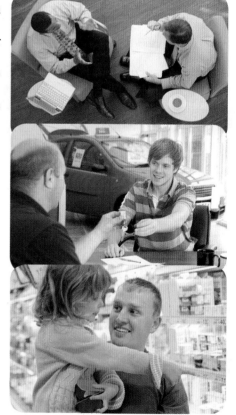

Negotiation is a communication and problem-solving process built on a broad foundation of skills and knowledge. It is also one of the most popular and effective means of resolving conflicts and misunderstandings (figure 13.1). In this context, negotiation tends to be used when:

- conflicts are relatively simple
- conflicts are of a low intensity
- both parties are relatively equal in power (Bercovitch & Jackson 2001).

Of course, this covers a very wide range of situations, so it makes sense to learn all we can about negotiation processes, theory and skills. In this chapter we will be exposed to, and perhaps initially bemused by, the jargon of negotiation – buzz words, acronyms and slang seem to litter the field. All this terminology, however, means very little unless we apply common sense in our approach to negotiation.

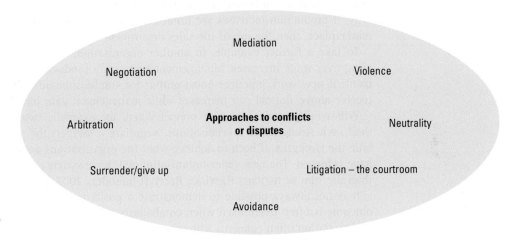

FIGURE 13.1 Approaches to conflicts or disputes

Winning and losing: games and pies

Conflict has differing outcomes. These outcomes can be classified according to the jargon of a branch of mathematics called *game theory* (Schelling 1960; Kydd 1997; Geckil & Anderson 2009) (figure 13.2).

	I win	I lose
You win	(+) Positive sum	(0) Zero sum
You lose	(0) Zero sum	(–) Negative sum

FIGURE 13.2 Win–lose dynamics of conflict

Source: Eunson (2002 [1997], p. 5).

If you and I are in a contest or a conflict situation, and one of us wins and one loses, then this is said to be a **zero-sum outcome**: my losses arithmetically cancel out your gains, producing zero. Sporting contests are typical zero-sum situations in which there can be only one winner (except in the case of a draw, which is usually perceived to be an unsatisfactory and temporary resolution). If we both lose (e.g. if we are both injured, or die, or lose something of value), this is called a **negative-sum outcome**. If we both win (if, say, we both gain something we want), this is called a **positive-sum outcome**, a **win–win situation**. Let's look at an example.

In an organisation, the sales department and the production department may fight over a limited source of funding in a given year. The conflict indicates that both sides see the situation as having a zero-sum outcome in which there can be only one winner and one loser. Yet if it can be shown that one department can help rather than hinder the other, then the situation changes: for example, if funds are allocated immediately to sales and new orders from customers arrive, then this could help fund production increases. Similarly, if production increases are funded and a high-quality product can be put out in the marketplace, then the job of the sales department is made easier.

To take a further example, in another organisation, management and labour are haggling over wage increases. Management proposes a productivity and profit-sharing agreement: if new work practices boost output for similar amounts of input, then workers will receive above-normal pay increases while management gain increased profits.

Win–win dynamics can also prevail when, for example, two organisations, each with their own strengths or specialisations, negotiate a merger: the merged identity will combine the strengths of both to achieve what the organisations acting separately could never have achieved. The new super-organisation will have synergy, with its whole being greater than the sum of its parts (Lewicki, Barry & Saunders 2007, pp. 11–12).

It is not always possible to demonstrate a positive-sum outcome, but such a potential outcome is often overlooked when combatants are trapped in a zero-sum mindset.

Negotiation often concerns who gets what, or who gets what share. The metaphor of a pie or cake is often used. We normally conceive of a pie as a fixed resource – the size will not change. So the carve-up of the pie necessarily involves a zero-sum calculation: what you don't get, I get. Sometimes, however, it is possible to increase the size of the pie by creating new resources – for example, when different departments in an organisation help each other to maximise growth, or when cooperation instead of competition opens up new opportunities. Thus, 15 per cent of a bigger pie may be better than 25 per cent of a smaller pie (figure 13.3).

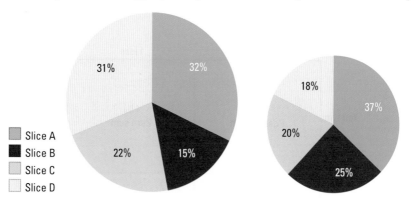

FIGURE 13.3 Who gets what: pies and slices

Slice A
Slice B
Slice C
Slice D

'Win–win': not just a cliché

A 'win–win outcome' has become almost a cliché these days; for some people the term sounds like a 'feel good' piece of nonsense that has no place in the harsh world of winners and losers. Yet in negotiation, where there is a need for a resolution that has some chance of lasting, at least in the short or medium term, a Win–win or positive-sum outcome is not simply an ethical ideal, but a hard-nosed, 'must have' goal. No-one likes to lose, and losers, whether real or apparent, will have little incentive to honour any agreement that damages their interests. Consider how you feel when you lose: Do you like it? Do you want to change things so you can get out of a losing position?

One of the most difficult lessons we will have to learn in negotiation is that, in order for a lasting agreement to be reached, we may need to concede valuable things to people whom we do not necessarily like. This is not simply because of the power exerted by those people, or because they would have been able to extract those concessions from us anyway.

That is, we may have to give in order to get. This is because unless the people we are negotiating with feel that they 'own' the result, and that they have not lost face or suffered a defeat, we can be sure that the agreement is unlikely to last. Both parties need to take something away from a negotiation, otherwise one party will leave feeling aggrieved, and a lasting resolution is unlikely to have been achieved. As a negotiating party, you need to put yourself in the other side's shoes: what's in it for them? If, for example, they lose face in front of the folks back home — their principals or constituency (a board of management, a union rank and file, a spouse or partner) — then they will resist. In other words, in order to win, we may have to lose a little or give to get.

For example, one side of a negotiation may attack so viciously that they win a great battle, but lose the war. They might need to negotiate with the other side (product suppliers, housemates, spouses, countries) down the track, at which time the other side might wish to return the win–lose favour. Unless you specifically wish to humiliate the other side, always allow them to save face, for you may need to cash in the favour one day. The wheel of fortune always turns — try not to be under it.

Figure 13.4 illustrates a simple model of the negotiation process.

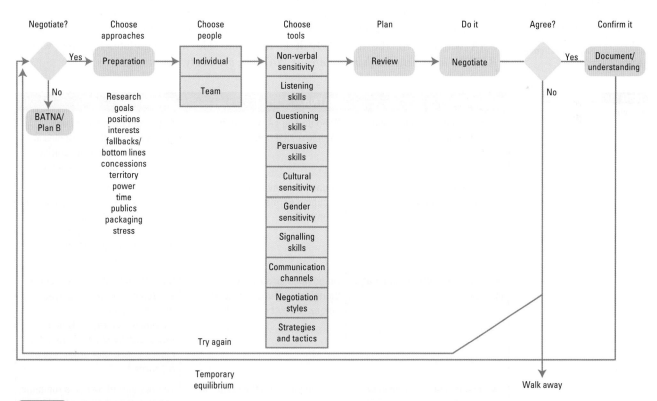

FIGURE 13.4 A model of negotiation

Source: Adapted from Eunson (2002 [1994], p. 3).

WATNAS, BATNAS and Plan Bs

Our model begins with the simple decision point: should we negotiate or not? Negotiation usually takes place between two individuals, or groups of individuals — that is, two sides. As we're going to continually refer to the two sides in our exploration of the issues, we will use the abbreviations OS (our side) and TOS (the other side).

Negotiation is usually about giving something to get something:

- 'We won't pay you $1.3 million for the business, but will you accept $1.27 million?'
- '*If* you eat your cabbage, *then* you can watch *Destructo man and Cuddles*.'

It also implies that neither side has absolute power, because if it did, the absolutely powerful side could simply demand and get what it wanted without giving anything in return.

Negotiation, however, may not be the only way to achieve your aim. People negotiate only when they believe they will fare worse if they adopt other approaches. In spite of this, they may choose not to negotiate, and instead choose other approaches. It might be better — or at least seem to be better — to try to resolve a dispute by punching someone on the nose, or by going on strike, or by going to court, or by going to war, or by simply walking away. Such an alternative course of action is referred to as an ATNA (Alternative to a Negotiated Agreement).

A **BATNA** (Best Alternative to a Negotiated Agreement) is another choice or substitute action that may produce an outcome superior to any outcome we might gain from a negotiation process. A **WATNA** (Worst Alternative to a Negotiated Agreement) is another choice or substitute action that may produce an outcome inferior to any outcome we might gain from a negotiation process.

We win with BATNAs and lose with WATNAs. BATNAs are a source of power, while WATNAs are a source of weakness (see table 13.1). The more likely that a side's WATNA will happen, the *more* likely it is that that side will negotiate. The more likely that a side's BATNA will happen, the *less* likely it is that that side will negotiate. In other words: *if BATNAs are likely, don't negotiate; if WATNAs are likely, negotiate.*

BATNA: (for Best Alternative To a Negotiated Agreement) another choice or substitute action that may produce an outcome superior to any outcome we might gain from a negotiation process

WATNA: (for Worst Alternative To a Negotiated Agreement) another choice or substitute action that may produce an outcome inferior to any outcome we might gain from a negotiation process

TABLE 13.1 BATNAs and WATNAs

Situation	WATNA	BATNA
A person is thinking of buying a used car from a car yard.	Keep driving current faulty vehicle until it breaks down.	Buy direct from other owners who advertise their vehicles in newspapers or online, cutting out the cost of the middleman.
Country A receives military threats from country B.	Country A is invaded and occupied permanently by country B.	Country B depends on oil revenues to wage war. The price of oil declines dramatically, as country A's intelligence predicted. Country B stops making threats.
Union wants a 30 per cent wage increase.	Union goes on strike, even though strike fund has been embezzled by corrupt official.	Market value of company stock suddenly rises. All employees have stock, so become wealthier as a result. Union representatives decide to defer claims until better organised and resourced.
Two lovers cannot agree over who is to pay a restaurant bill.	No-one pays and the restaurant owner calls the police.	The restaurant owner, a romantic at heart, tells them the food is on the house.

Plan B: alternative course of action that can give you flexibility in negotiations

When planning for negotiation, you should try to brainstorm as many BATNAs as possible, just as you should try to brainstorm as many different alternative negotiation approaches as possible. The more **Plan B**s you have, the greater your flexibility and the lower your stress levels will be in the negotiation itself. The fewer Plan Bs you have, the more vulnerable and therefore stressed you will be.

Do not despair, however, for there are likely to be more Plan Bs than you initially believe is the case. The various factors we are about to consider in the negotiating process are fertile sources of Plan Bs through to Plan Zs. Always strive to create options and alternative courses of action, rather than locking yourself into one or a limited range of plans.

Above all else, be realistic in your assessment of the possible outcome of any negotiation. Because so many people are unrealistic (often because they have not done enough research), we may need to compromise so that we may end up with one or more of the other conflict resolution strategies of figure 13.1. Some negotiation researchers have, therefore, suggested we also bear in mind a **MLATNA** (Most Likely Alternative to a Negotiated Agreement) (Guasco and Robinson 2007) or **PATNA** (Probable Alternative to a Negotiated Agreement) (Wade 2008).

MLATNA: (Most Likely Alternative to a Negotiated Agreement) another choice or substitute action that may produce an outcome superior to any outcome we might gain from a negotiation process — usually less extreme and more realistic than some BATNAs and WATNAs

PATNA: (Probable Alternative to a Negotiated Agreement) — same as MLATNA

ASSESS YOURSELF

Using the table that follows (or a copy), analyse at least two real or imaginary situations in terms of BATNAs and WATNAs.

Situation	WATNA	BATNA

Avoidance

A strong BATNA allows one side in a negotiation to refuse even to start negotiating. But the other side may not wish to negotiate for other reasons. For example, consider the following situations (adapted from Wallihan 1998; Spector 1998):

- A country is intent on developing nuclear weapons, but it is under pressure from other nations not to do so. The country plays for time by entering into negotiations, giving the public impression of bargaining on outcomes but in reality having no intention of negotiating.
- A person on a job selection panel sees the outstanding candidate as a potential threat to his position. Rather than state the true position, or be seen as unreasonably rejecting the candidate, he instead offers the candidate an insultingly low starting salary and package, which is duly rejected.
- A prosecutor perceives that an upcoming jury trial will give her much media exposure, and will thus boost her career. Because of this, she only goes through the motions of negotiating a settlement before the case goes to court, and she finally rejects such a settlement.
- Party A rejects negotiating with party B because party A says that party B is a villain who should never be negotiated with.

Refusal to negotiate, or 'phoney bargaining', constitutes a major blockage to the negotiation process. Some counters are (Wallihan 1998):

- Name the game: identify the tactics being used; accuse the other side of not being serious – of going through the motions and only being interested in making offers that must be refused.
- Appeal to those behind the other side (e.g. the union rank and file, the board and shareholders, the car yard owner, the other parent).
- Bring in a third party.
- Shift the negotiation to issues on which real bargaining is more likely to take place.

Choosing approaches

Once we choose – or are forced – to negotiate, we need to avoid just wading in unthinkingly. If we do not want to lose, we need to plan.

Research or sniffing around

The essence of all good negotiation is preparation, and the essence of all good preparation is research. You will need to try to predict the behaviour of TOS, and you can do that by constructing theories about them. First, though, you need facts. As Sherlock Holmes said to Dr Watson, 'I have no data yet. It is a capital mistake to theorise before one has data. Insensibly one begins to twist facts to suit theories instead of theories to suit facts'. Of course, we can never predict other people's behaviour with certainty, but it still usually helps to try. What do you really know about TOS? Research can sometimes be quite uncomplicated: it may mean simply sitting quietly and thinking, and not allowing your understanding of the situation to be clouded by wishful thinking or distorted perceptions. For example, if you want to try to persuade your flatmate to do the dishes when it's actually your turn, you will need to think about what you might offer in return in order to make this happen, but you will also need to think carefully about what you know of your flatmate's character, not to mention your own track record of reliability.

In more complex negotiation situations, research is commensurately more complex. In an industrial relations setting, for example, you will need to consider a wide range of points: Is the other side in a growth phase or in decline? Are they flush with funds or verging on bankruptcy? What is their industrial relations record like? What is their position within the wider industry? Do the people you are likely to face across the table have the personal health and stamina to stand up to the stresses of a protracted negotiation? Are they liked or disliked within their own organisation? Why, or why not? What about the other 'other sides' (i.e. your competitors, who also want to sell or buy)? What do you know about them, and what they are offering or demanding?

In these more complex negotiation situations, such data can be obtained from company reports, government documents, the media, the grapevines or rumour mills within TOS, or in the wider industry or community, and from people within your own organisation who have had prior experience dealing with TOS. You can also formally ask TOS for data: so long as it is not self-incriminating, there should be no overwhelming reason why they cannot provide you with information, particularly if the gesture is reciprocated.

Goals

Once we have our basic data, we can begin to plan. We need to clarify things about our own side too, and make some informed guesses about how each side's position relates to the other's. What are both sides trying to achieve? What motivates me? What will I be happy with? What exactly are we trying to achieve in this negotiation? These are fundamental questions, but they are not asked as often as they should be, and they should always be asked *before* negotiations rather than during or after them.

Remember the old saying, 'Don't wish too hard for something, because you might end up getting it'. In other words, we sometimes lose by winning, and win by losing. A person may use brilliant negotiation skills to secure a new job and a salary increase – and be dead from the stress within a year. Another person may successfully negotiate a switch in shifts with a workmate – and as a result miss meeting his dream partner. Negotiating success is not proof against life's ironies.

Positions, fallbacks and bottom lines

Let's now look at another model of negotiation (figure 13.5). Here the two sides in a negotiation (OS and TOS) are like ships in the night, moving in opposite directions. If there is to be any trade or transaction between them, the negotiators need to understand the structure of motivations and needs of both sides.

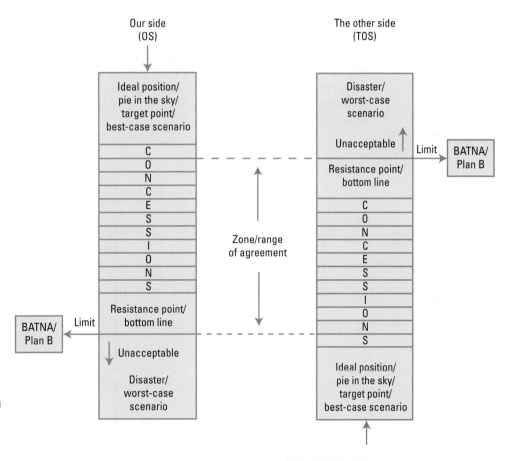

FIGURE 13.5 Two sides trying to reach agreement

Source: Eunson (2002 [1994], p. 7)

What will the opening positions be? Will OS open high ('We won't take a penny less than $4000?') or low ('We think $3000 is a reasonable figure. What do you say?')? Will TOS concentrate on price, or will they try to put together a package that involves price, service, spare parts and training?

In considering people's positions, we need to know, or speculate on, their fallback position, **bottom line**, limit or resistance point. This is the irreducible minimum point beyond which a negotiator will not or cannot go, because to do so would spell failure. A negotiator will often try to conceal information about this point, although there may be a tactical advantage in deliberately announcing what it is.

Bottom line: point beyond which no more concessions can be made to the other side without damaging our side's assets and position (also known as *fallback position, limit* or *resistance point*)

How does one reach the bottom line? One reaches it, with varying degrees of unwilling-ness, by making concessions to TOS.

Concessions

Concessions, or tradeables, are things or assets that you can give to the other side:

- I will do the dishes for you.
- You can watch the TV program you want to watch.
- You can have my dessert.
- You can have a $20/week wage increase for your union members.
- We will work overtime at reduced rates.
- You can have the disputed section of land.

A fair trade usually means that each side concedes or yields a number of things to the other. An unfair trade means that one side concedes more than the other side. Generally speaking, the less power or leverage a side has, the more that side will concede. The more you have to sacrifice in the way of concessions or tradeables, the more painful and dam-aging it will be to your situation.

Concessions can be cheap or expensive, but they may be perceived differently by each side. Ideally, what is of little importance to you (a cheap concession) may be highly desir-able to TOS. By conceding it, you want something in return and are now in a position to ask for it (figure 13.6). The worst case situation, of course, is where you attempt to trade something that is expensive or valuable for you, but is not desirable or valuable for the other side.

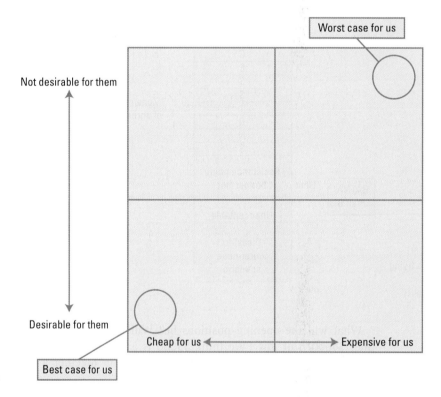

FIGURE 13.6 Analysing concessions or tradeables

In trading concessions with the other side, remember these guidelines:

- Trade what's cheap for you and what is valuable for the other side.
- Never make a concession without getting something in return (Kennedy, Benson & Macmillan 1984).

Situation 1

Freddy is furious with himself. His favourite band, Rama, is coming to town, but through his own procrastination he has missed out on tickets for their only show. 'My life is chaotic. I've got to get organised', he tells himself, and in a frenzy of self-punishment, he begins to clean up his flat. The housework is interrupted by the arrival of his friend Joe. They chat aimlessly for a while, then Joe pulls out two front-row seats for the Rama concert, crowing about his success in getting them. Freddy is about to abuse Joe for having the tickets, but then thinks better of it.

'Oh, they're an OK band, I suppose', he concedes, moving to block Joe's view of the collection of Rama records on his shelves.

'Hey, look at this!', says Joe, picking up some magazines that Freddy was going to throw out: *Cold (The Super-Cool Magazine)*, *Yob (For Men of the World)* and *Ghoul (For Connoisseurs of Road Accidents)*. 'Hey, could you sell me some of these? I've been after these numbers for years!', says Joe.

Freddy thinks quickly. 'Well, they are part of my special collection, of course . . . I'd hate to see them go . . . Tell you what, though . . . my girl Marie is a big fan of Rama, even though I can take 'em or leave 'em . . . how about four issues of whatever you want for your tickets?'

Joe looks confused, then annoyed, then looks back at the magazines. He smiles slowly. 'OK, it's a deal!'

Situation 2

Soula, the union rep, knows that the Despatch section of the office can perform much better than they currently are. In fact, most of the staff in that section are bored with their work. Barry, the manager, has told Soula in no uncertain terms that he wants greater productivity out of the Processing section, where Soula knows there is not much room for improvement, and where a much-loved older worker is ill but is being protected by her peers. In a productivity meeting with Barry and other management staff, Soula moves quickly to offer productivity improvements in the Despatch section in return for a pay increase, and a promise to look at the Processing section after a trial period to see how the Despatch section deal works out.

Situation 3

Two countries, Freedonia and Tyrannia, are haggling over a disputed tract of land. The chief negotiator for Freedonia doesn't think much of the land; the Central Lands Department has already used Freedonia's 'special friendship' with superpower Vespuccia to get satellite surveys of the land done, and these surveys have revealed no mineral deposits of value, even though the landscape looks like classic oil country. Freedonia is in urgent need of water, which Tyrannia has in abundance. Freedonia's negotiator notes the body language of the Tyrannian negotiators; they really want this land. He decides to 'reluctantly' relinquish control over the Freedonian section of the land on the condition that Tyrannia provides water through a pipeline for 20 years for free.

Positions versus interests

Distributive bargaining: a negotiating process in which the two sides try to concede as little as possible and to gain as much as they can — a zero-sum approach, using a positions-based approach rather than an interests-based approach

Integrative bargaining: a bargaining approach in which the negotiators try to move from a positions-based approach to an interests-based approach

The 'ships in the night' model of negotiation presented in figure 13.5 can be very useful when planning for a negotiation. It helps us to see that bottom lines, opening positions and concessions are vital to the horse-trading that takes place in many negotiations. This model accurately describes what is sometimes called **distributive bargaining** — that is, a negotiating process in which the two sides try to concede as little as possible and to gain as much as they can, using a zero-sum model of whatever it is that is being haggled over.

We should also be aware, however, of another model of negotiation, which is called **integrative bargaining**. The integrative bargaining approach means moving beyond a least–worst outcome for one or both sides, or from a *positions-based* approach to an *interests-based* approach. It may be, that is, that what people *say* they want is not what they need. The position they assume (and will not budge from, or can only be persuaded from with concessions) may not correspond to their interests. In other words, negotiation may not be a simple linear process, a tug of war, but something more multidimensional (Fisher, Ury & Patton 1991; Wheeler & Waters 2006; Da Conceição-Heldt 2006; Lewicki, Barry & Saunders 2007.

Consider, for example, these circumstances:

1. Two sisters argue over an orange. Both want it, but upon discussion they discover that one wants it for the juice, and the other wants the peel for a cake.
2. Two students are working in the library. One wants the window open, and the other wants it shut. Upon discussion they discover that one wants fresh air, while the other wants to lay out papers without having them blown about by the draft. The solution is to open a window in the adjacent room.
3. Two tribes go to war over access to a river. During a truce they discover that one side wants water for irrigation of crops, while the other side wants access to the best fishing spot.
4. Two managers feud over who is to get a corner office. Upon discussion they find that one really likes the view, while the other perceives that a corner office would confer prestige. A solution may be to give the office to the manager who simply wants the view, and give the other manager another office along with — resources permitting — a new title and real or symbolic extra responsibilities.

In all these situations, if both sides in the dispute dig in on positions, then settlement may be difficult and will probably entail a win–lose resolution. As very few of us like losing, and we usually resolve to right wrongs by reversing any agreement reached, win–lose outcomes are notoriously unstable and short-lived. If mutually beneficial outcomes can be created that satisfy both sides' underlying interests, however, then integrative, win–win solutions are possible (table 13.2).

TABLE 13.2 Integrative bargaining: some solutions

Position	Interest	Mutually satisfactory solution (win–win)	Interest	Position
I want ...	because ...	Common ground	because ...	I want ...
Orange	I want juice	One gets peel, the other gets fruit	I want peel	Orange
Window open	I want fresh air	Open window in adjacent room	Papers will get blown around if windows are open	Windows closed
Access to river	I want irrigation water	One gets irrigation runoff, one gets fishing spot	I want fish	Access to river
Corner office	I like view	One gets office, one gets new title/responsibilities	I like prestige	Corner office

In each of these cases, both sides win 100 per cent — a statistical impossibility if we are talking about limited resources, but not necessarily so if we redefine what a resource is. A 50–50, distributive or straight compromise outcome (e.g. each sister gets half of the unpeeled orange) would be unsatisfactory to both sides.

Is win–win always possible? No, but it is certainly highly desirable, because it satisfies natural justice and has a good chance of providing a permanent resolution.

Investing time in uncovering interests

People are not always aware that positions are not the same as interests, and indeed they may not have thought through the question of just what their interests are. We can't read minds; then how can we know what the other side is thinking so we can move beyond positions to uncover common interests? In negotiations, as in most human interactions, the other side is a partial mystery to us, just as we are a partial mystery to the other side. Using the Johari window model (see Luft 1969), let's now develop some models (figures 13.7–13.9) of how we might explore these situations.

We can find out a good deal about the other side by research, but that can still yield only a limited amount of knowledge. If we are to uncover common interests, we have to slow down the pace and use listening, questioning, feedback and other communication skills to open up the area of common understanding between the sides. If we do not do this — for example, if one or both sides is impatient, or if one or both sides thinks negotiation is only about shouting out some or all of the opening positions — then not much real negotiation will take place (figure 13.7).

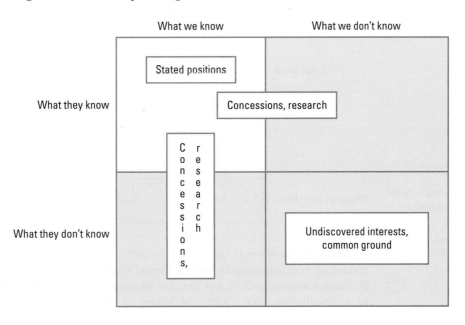

FIGURE 13.7 A matrix model of negotiation

We have to be patient, and often we will need to set aside some of our feelings (e.g. when we are negotiating with people we do not like). By doing these things we increase our chances of opening up areas of communication and discovering areas of common interest (figures 13.8 and 13.9). Otherwise, we might find ourselves afflicted with the '**winner's curse**' — paying too much for something because we did not have as much information as TOS to bid accurately — 'buyer, beware'. The more quickly TOS accepts our offer, the more likely we are to suspect we are victims of the curse (Freshman & Guthrie 2009; Grosskopf & Bazerman 2007).

Winner's curse: the perception that we have got the bad part of a deal; usually because we were full of enthusiasm but short on information

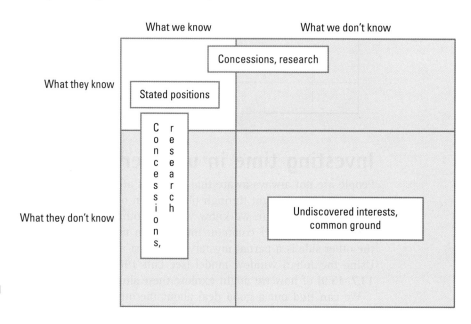

FIGURE 13.8 A matrix model of an unhealthy negotiation

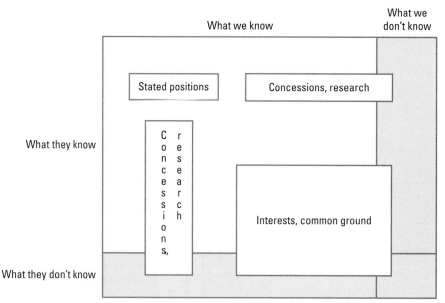

FIGURE 13.9 A matrix model of a healthy negotiation situation

The positions/interests distinction is undoubtedly a useful one, and can be useful in managing real negotiations (see McKersie, Eaton & Kochan 2004). Nevertheless, we must be careful not to push it too far. For example, Provis suggests that the distinction can be misleading in some cases and wrong in others, in that it may lead to a confusion in meaning, it may be divisive, and it may ignore other functions of positions, such as negotiating team discipline:

> The suggestion that one attends to interests rather than positions is rather like an injunction to attend to people's meanings rather than to the words they actually use. It is normally an error to attend to the words to the exclusion of their meaning, but that does not imply that we can concentrate on meaning without attending to the words. To concentrate on interests rather than positions implies that we ought to concentrate on what people really want, rather than on what they say they want. That is reasonable, but what people say they want may be a major source of information about what they really want ...
>
> Encouraging people to turn away from positions to concentrate on interests may encourage attention to individual interests at the expense of collective interests. To that extent, (the positions/interests distinction) may unintentionally serve a strong and long-established vein of anti-union sentiment in United States business and legal culture ... a position [may be] important for group cohesion ... In general, labour unions rely more strongly on a common position than business firms do, because the unity of the latter is more strongly sustained by institutional and legal structures. (Provis 1996, pp. 313–16)

Note also Hofstede's (2001) critique of the positions/interests model.

Territory and negotiation

The factors we have considered so far help us identify *what* we are negotiating about and *how* we will negotiate. But what about *where*? Should it be on our own territory, on their territory or on neutral ground? Sometimes it doesn't matter, but sometimes the issue is a complex one, and the fate of a negotiation process may be determined by the apparently trivial question of venue: history here is determined by geography. For example, consider the following situations:

- Two lovers are arguing on the telephone. After a heated exchange, they agree that they should try to deal with these relationship issues face to face. 'OK, you come over here', says one. 'No, you come over here', says the other.
- Two countries are at war. They decide to hold truce talks, but elect to meet in a third country, thousands of kilometres away.
- Two companies are planning a merger, but there is still considerable mistrust on both sides. The CEOs decide that they will take both sets of staff to an island resort to continue the discussions.
- Social welfare workers note that their clients often seem intimidated by the formal surroundings of the department's offices. The welfare workers decide that they will try to put their clients at ease by visiting them in their homes. This solves some problems but seems to create new ones.

Let's now look at the pros and cons of negotiating in different territories (table 13.3).

TABLE 13.3 Territory and negotiations

	For	Against
Our place	<ul><li>Familiarity</li><li>Control of environment (furniture, timing of breaks, security, access of media)</li><li>Access to experts, support personnel, superiors/principals for consultation, authorisation</li><li>Access to resources (e.g. for quickly writing up agreement documents)</li><li>Can do 'show and tell' (e.g. tour of plant/office)</li><li>Can do other work when not at the table</li></ul>	<ul><li>Obligation to behave in generous fashion</li><li>Greater pressure from constituents, internal opponents and local media</li><li>Proximity to principals a two-edged sword – harder to create delays</li><li>More difficult to walk out</li><li>TOS might be shown and told too much</li></ul>

(continued)

TABLE 13.3 *(continued)*

	For	Against
Their place	■ Can deviate from instructions, be flexible, bend the rules — 'difficulties' in communicating with home ■ Can delay, pleading necessity to consult, get other information ■ Easier to use limited authority tactic ■ Easier to walk out ■ Gives visitors chance to find out about TOS ■ Can be seen as a magnanimous gesture, which places obligation on TOS ■ Easier to appeal over head of TOS to their principals ■ Can conduct other business while there ■ Can concentrate fully without interruptions from home or housekeeping problems ■ Can use deadline tactic	■ Unfamiliarity with surroundings ■ Possibly higher stress, lowered performance ■ Greater distance from advisers and superiors/principals ■ High cost — travel, accommodation ■ TOS can still perform many normal work functions; OS cannot ■ Delays can be created, putting pressure on OS to agree — deadline tactic used against OS ■ Reliance on good will of TOS may create obligation ■ May weaken OS — symbolism of TOS's ownership of site may make transaction seem unequal
Another place	■ Neither side has special advantages ■ If hostility is high, may be only place — symbolism ■ May be more conducive to reaching agreement (e.g. combining business with pleasure) ■ When a third party has a vested interest	■ May be difficult to check with principals ■ May lack resources ■ Complicates process by introducing a third party ■ Host may have ulterior motives — bias, seeking kudos

Source: Adapted with permission from Salacuse and Rubin (1990).

Our place: what's good

There are obvious 'home ground' advantages, of course: the surroundings are familiar to you but not to TOS; you know where everything is. You have control of the environment: you decide everything – from the location of furniture in the negotiating room to the timing of breaks, the security and access of the media to the event. Just down the corridor, or up a flight or two, you have a resource base of experts and support personnel, and you can consult quickly with your principals or constituency, and get additional authorisation from them if needed. You have the resources to quickly write up agreement documentation. This means documentation can be prepared according to your house style – a subtle form of ownership or influence. It may also confer a tactical advantage if you are trying to speed up the process or if you plan to write the documentation in such a way as to gain an edge.

Being on your home ground can also have advantages if you are trying to impress TOS with your capabilities; for example, your ability to meet commitments to produce a commodity. You can lead a tour of your facilities – you will, of course, have briefed your people in advance. Such 'show and tell' can be a useful piece of theatre.

Finally, you can conduct normal business when you are not actually sitting at the negotiating table; and even then you may, if the occasion presents itself, see to other work, either openly or surreptitiously.

Our place: what's not so good

There are home ground disadvantages, however. Being a host can place you in a role of power over your guests, but it also gives them power over you: you must look after their needs; you will be expected to behave in a generous manner, and this expectation may filter down to the pattern of concession making that is integral to all negotiations.

You are also exposed directly to pressure from your constituency, who may cramp your style by 'looking over your shoulder' too often for your liking. All organisations are pluralistic, political structures, so it would not be surprising if there were insiders opposed to what you are trying to achieve in the negotiation process. These opponents will be uncomfortably close. If the negotiations are of interest to the media, you will have the local media to contend with: while foreign media in another place may be easy to fool and shake off, local media may prove to be more interested in and informed about what's going on, and persistent. They may be more adept and/or devious in dealing with you than would be the case if you were dealing with foreign media in another place.

Because you are on home ground, you are also prevented from using certain tactics. A theatrical but sometimes effective tactic is to walk out, either temporarily or permanently; if you are on home ground, however, you are placed in the same position as the party host with obnoxious guests – the host simply cannot walk out in disgust.

A number of other negotiating tactics are now suddenly unavailable to you. You can't call for a prolonged delay to consult with your principals, because they're just down the hall (and the purpose of the tactic is to maximise delay while you think things through, or perhaps simply to exasperate TOS). You can't say you don't have the authority to negotiate beyond a certain point, because that authority problem can be solved instantly by inviting your principals in (and in all probability they don't want to be invited in, because they want you to use your limited authority to create delays, and therefore have instructed you to use the limited authority tactic in the first place).

The visitors, on the other hand, can nose around, see things as they actually are, and evaluate your actual capacities. Can you really deliver on the promises you are making in the artificial environment of the negotiation room? If you have something to hide, then a 'show and tell' tour may be one the dumbest things you could do, and even without such a circus TOS will still gather a lot of intelligence just by keeping their eyes and ears open.

Their place: what's good

Travelling to TOS's turf can have a number of advantages. Principals, constituencies or publics can cramp a negotiator's style by their presence on the home ground – the *back-seat driver effect* – but when the negotiator is free of their immediate oversight, then he or she has much more flexibility to operate. After making a prudent evaluation of the risks of doing so, the negotiator can depart from the script and operate in a more flexible way, bending the rules where necessary. If challenged on this on returning home, the negotiator can cite 'difficulties' in communicating with home about every little detail.

Being away from home also makes it easier for the negotiator to delay, pleading the necessity to consult with home and/or get further information. It is also easier to use the authority and walk-out tactics. If TOS has something to hide, you may detect it when you are on their turf. The most potent forms of industrial espionage are often undertaken quite openly: you just have to look and listen. What you discover may convince you that your hosts are honourable and capable, but it may also convince you of the opposite.

Travelling to alien territory can sometimes be seen as a sign of weakness – the supplicant travelling to the master – but, depending on the situation and the way you choose to play it, the reverse perception can occur. Travelling may be seen as a sign of strength – a magnanimous gesture that obligates TOS (e.g. US President Richard Nixon's visit to China in 1972, or Egyptian President Anwar Sadat's trip to Jerusalem in 1978 to negotiate with Israel).

Just as it is easier for you to use the limited authority tactic on alien ground, it is harder for TOS to use it. In fact, you may have the option of appealing over the heads of the negotiators you are dealing with by walking down the corridor to talk to the power people yourself. They may not want to see you for tactical reasons, but if you believe that TOS is obstructing things, and is not operating in the principals' best interests, the principals may be interested in hearing this.

While you're in town or in the neighbourhood, you may be able to transact other business, renew contacts, plug into other networks, or simply gossip to maintain old relationships. Further, while your hosts have the advantage of not being far from their routine milieu, this can also be a millstone for them: there may be interruptions, and the interrupters may not understand the importance of the negotiation proceedings. Then there are the normal housekeeping problems of running a negotiation (the lunch hasn't shown up, the VCR has broken down), and this eats into TOS's time and concentration. None of these problems besets the visitor, who can concentrate totally on the substance of the negotiation.

Finally, when visiting, you can use the deadline or stampede tactic: I've got to leave by this hour or that day, so hurry up and settle (on terms that favour me).

Their place: what's not so good

What are the negative aspects of operating on their turf? Your relative unfamiliarity with the environment can be unsettling. Being away from home can be a lonely and stressful experience, and this may impair your performance; it may, for instance, motivate you to get out quicker and settle for terms that are less favourable than you would have otherwise preferred. Distance means it is more difficult, if not impossible, to draw on the advice of experts and superiors, and to get additional authority to proceed. It is also expensive to travel and to use accommodation, especially where teams of negotiators are concerned.

Although you can use the deadline tactic against TOS, it is quite possible to have the tables turned on you: if TOS creates delays, then it is you, not they, who are up against the deadline, under pressure to concede more than you would 'had [you] but world enough and time'.

Hospitality is a ritual of mutual obligation: while the host is obligated to behave generously to the guest, guests are also beholden to the host for inviting them in the first place. This may translate into the expectation of concessions to TOS.

Finally, there is the symbolism of ownership of territory: it may appear (and may in fact be) that by travelling to another site OS has already relinquished an advantage to TOS, and has therefore taken on an inferior role.

Another place: what's good

What is the best way of circumventing the problem of our place versus their place? One solution is to alternate venues for each meeting. Another is to meet at a third, neutral site where neither side has special advantages. If hostility between the negotiating parties is strong, a neutral site may be unavoidable: the symbolic overtones of one side approaching the other might simply prove unacceptable.

Neutral ground may also have the advantage of offering a pleasant environment — architecture, climate, facilities — more conducive to reaching agreement. Both sides may be in a better frame of mind when business and pleasure are agreeably combined. Third parties (e.g. financiers or investors in the deal) are often involved in negotiations and may request or even demand that the proceedings take place on their territory.

Another place: what's not so good

Some of the downsides to negotiating at a third venue are similar to the downsides of negotiating at TOS's place. It may be difficult to check with your principals, for example, or the site may lack resources. Further, introducing a third party may unduly complicate matters. Third parties may have ulterior motives: rather than being genuinely neutral, they may be secretly partial to one side and seek to influence the outcome accordingly. There is often kudos and prestige attached to the role of the disinterested mediator, and the host may try to garner public relations benefits from this role.

Time and negotiation

Is time a significant factor? Is time abundant or scarce? Can one side stampede the other by the use of deadlines? Does TOS operate within a culture that perceives time differently from OS? Is there a need to invest time in the process, so that rapport and empathy (Planken 2005; Martinovsky, Traum & Marsella 2007) can be built, trust developed and positions uncovered? The real or perceived scarcity or abundance of time during a negotiation can be vital in securing (or destroying) a positive outcome (Alon & Brett 2007; Crump 2007). McDuff argues that the effect of time on negotiations can be broken down into three categories:

Punctuality can affect the success of a negotiation.

1. Punctuality and timeliness – the importance or lack of importance placed on being 'on time' and getting the negotiations under way
2. The use of time – the overall length of the negotiation and how such activities as relationship building, story telling, etc. are prioritised in terms of how much time is allotted to them
3. Time as an issue within the negotiation – how far back in history does the discussion of relevant events, conflicts, grievances, etc. go? How far into the future do possible remedies extend? (McDuff 2006, p. 40).

We also need to be aware of behavioural patterns (on all sides) of procrastination and crisis management that will bear directly on all aspects of the negotiation process, but particularly the preparation phases.

Publics and negotiation

The publics or stakeholders surrounding the negotiation also need to be factored into our consideration. What impacts will flow from a given outcome, and who will those impacts affect? For example, a negotiation involving unions and management at a factory may result in an impasse or deadlock, which is resolved only by increasing wages and profits at the expense of increased prices: the community and consumer watchdogs may denounce the cosy agreement of the two sides, leading to negative public relations outcomes for all who work at the factory. Stakeholders in any decision are usually more numerous and less apparent than a first glance might suggest.

A key public for negotiators is the principals. Most negotiators are operating as agents representing others, such as the board of directors, or the union membership, or the electorate, or the client selling the house or car or antique. These principals, or main constituencies, rarely grant the negotiators complete authority to close a deal without some kind of consultation (in fact, withholding that authority may be a conscious tactic, and a tactic that the negotiator is sometimes happy to employ).

In planning, the negotiator and the principal may work out approaches together. In some circumstances, the negotiator may need to develop a strategy for working around the principal, perhaps even keeping the principal in the dark, if it is believed that a 'back-seat driver' could do more harm than good. In simple negotiating situations, of course, agents are often not involved. When you sell your car to me, we are both acting as principals, not agents (although we might experience principal-like pressure from spouses, friends and bank managers).

Stress and negotiation

Negotiations can be stressful, not least because some negotiators deliberately try to create stress as a tactic. In negotiation, as in public speaking, one of the best means of stress management is preparation: the more you know about negotiation, and the more you have prepared for it, the less likely it is you will experience stress. *Fail to plan, plan to fail; succeed in planning, plan to succeed.*

Packaging and negotiation

These days, when people apply for new positions, their main concern is not simply the salary, but rather the *package*: salary plus extras (which for professionals can often be more substantial than the salary itself). So, too, with negotiation: what may be most important is not the immediately quantifiable factors (e.g. the price or wage increase, or settlement), but other factors.

Ferris (2001), for example, notes:

> Unfortunately, for the amateur negotiator, (a) single-minded focus on price is just what the experienced bargainer wants to see when looking across the table. Like the magician, the bargaining pro often counts on the other side to focus on one thing, so that he or she can do so much more in the negotiation, just out of the line of sight. So, to really know the tricks of the bargaining table trade, you have to look beyond the raw price and pay attention to the When, How and Who of the Money deal.

To negotiate effectively, especially over money in its various disguises, you need to uncover more, not fewer, options, and an understanding of packaging offers (as presented by your side or TOS) gives you many more options. Table 13.4 outlines some examples of packaging.

TABLE 13.4 Packaging deals in negotiation

When do they get the money?	
Upon signing a contract	Money and other rewards as a signing bonus can cover start-up costs (e.g. debts), can help moderate long-term salary demands elsewhere in the negotiation, and can protect the buyer from competitors luring away talent (by requiring full or partial repayment of the bonus if the employee wants to move on).
After the freebies	Free goods and services are offered as incentives to close a deal. For example, a landlord may offer 'free rent' to close a deal: the tenant can use the money that would have been spent on rent to cover debts and to invest elsewhere, while the landlord may derive the benefit of getting cash flow in a new tax year, and use the guarantee of cash flow as collateral on loans.
In response to market indexes	Money is sometimes linked to performance, but sometimes to other factors, too: workers may negotiate a cost-of-living allowance, linked to inflation rates, while a builder may cut a deal with a customer that links the final price of a building to an index of building and/or labour costs.
How do they get the money?	
In cash	Cash is usually very appealing, but not always: for example, the tax penalties of a sudden boost in cash can be a disincentive, and cash offers made to shareholders in takeover bids have sometimes not proved effective because shareholders believed there were few good places to invest cash in an already saturated market.
To play the tax angle	An offer in a wage bargaining situation might be for nontaxable benefits, such as health fund payments, or payable at a later date, or deferred in segments, to maximise tax advantages.

How do they get the money? *(continued)*	
Guaranteed future earnings	Instead of offering cash in wage increases, an employer may offer locked-in job security for a specific period.
Who gets the money?	
Third parties	In a US airlines negotiation, salary was linked to the size of aeroplanes being flown, with older pilots flying the bigger craft. The airline paid the older pilots retirement packages so that younger pilots could move to bigger aircraft and be eligible for bigger salaries. A logging company avoided issues of blame and responsibility in a lawsuit by donating money to a university forestry program.
Related entities	If corporate tax rates are lower than individual taxes, it may make sense to make payments to a person's company than to that person.
Creditors	A negotiator may offer to take on debt and then renegotiate the terms of that debt with the creditor, or exchange something of value for that debt.

Source: Based on and adapted from Ferris (2001, pp. 47–58).

Choosing people

Once we have done our research and planning, we need to choose our people. The main decision to make is whether to use a single negotiator or a team. This can be a complex decision. If we are simply negotiating for ourselves, the question doesn't arise. Teams of negotiators experience the advantages and disadvantages of teams in all situations. Members of negotiating teams can back each other up, each providing specialised knowledge and skills the others lack; they can cooperate in implementing particular tactics; and can provide moral support and strength in numbers. On the other hand, members of negotiating teams may undermine each other, accidentally or deliberately, and may prolong the negotiation, making it unwieldy and chaotic.

Choosing tools

The numerous tools the negotiator can bring to bear on the negotiation process include nonverbal sensitivity; listening, questioning and persuasive and signalling skills; strategies and tactics; cultural and gender sensitivity; and familiarity with communication channels.

Nonverbal sensitivity

The complete negotiator is the complete communicator. A negotiator has to be aware not only of what is being said, but also of what is unsaid – in other words, the many aspects of nonverbal communication, such as posture, gesture, eye contact, clothing and so forth (not to mention deliberately false nonverbal communication or body language when used as a tactic).

Listening and questioning skills

A good negotiator needs to be a good listener, alert for hidden meanings and able simply to concentrate on what is said, setting aside all else. Importantly, as the following two quotations illustrate, the good negotiator also knows how to ask questions:

> Statements generate resistance, whereas questions generate answers. Questions allow the other side to get their points across and let you understand them. They pose challenges and can be used to lead the other side to confront the problem. Questions offer them no target to strike at, no position to attack. Questions do not criticize, they educate. (Fisher & Ury 1991, p. 117)

We [Americans] don't teach our students how to ask questions, how to get information, how to listen, or how to use questioning as a powerful persuasive tactic. Yet these latter skills are critical at the international negotiating table. Few of us realize that, in most places in the world, the one who asks the questions controls the process of negotiation and thereby accomplishes more in a bargaining situation. (Graham & Herberger 1983, p. 160)

Persuasive skills

Part of the essence of the negotiating process is persuasion, and detecting persuasive tactics when used by other actors in the process. The art and science of persuasion will therefore figure strongly in the way we negotiate.

Signalling skills

In the negotiation process, we need to pay attention to signals. Signals are verbal and nonverbal messages that tend to contradict or differ slightly from what is said. Why don't people just come right out and say what they mean? Sometimes they do, but sometimes they prefer not to: they are trying to probe without committing themselves, to find out just how far you will go. Some of these signals are illustrated in table 13.5.

TABLE 13.5 Signals in negotiation

Signal type	'Example'	Meaning	'Possible response'
Qualifier	'*As it stands*, the offer is just ridiculous.'	Why don't you change it slightly, and we'll fall for it.	'If you give us an idea of what you're looking for, we'll give it serious consideration.'
	'We don't *normally* give discounts . . . '	But we might this time if the price is right, or if you can do something for us . . .	'I would be able to take 5 per cent more than my normal purchase, and I might be able to do better next month.'
	'There's *no way* we could look at 8 per cent at this time.'	Lower it and we will, or break it up into phased increments, or link it to productivity gains, or come back next month . . .	'Why don't we settle on 6 per cent now [code for 'but you can beat me down to 5'], with 3 per cent next year?'
	'I'm not going to sign an agreement *in that form*.'	Show me a more interesting agreement.	'Let's discuss which paragraphs you take exception to, and I'll take it up with my boss.'
Mixed absolute/ qualifier	'We don't give discounts, and *even if we did* they wouldn't be as large as 14 per cent.'	I'll give you 4 per cent.	'If you did discounts, would you give 5 per cent?'
Grandstanding	'*It's board policy* that wage increases should not be higher than the national average.'	This is a like-to-have, not a must-have objective.	'I'm sure the board will be pleased to see dividends rise, as they will when productivity goes up after staff get this modest rise.'
	'*Our people* would like to see wage justice.'	Double dilution: they 'would like to' rather than 'demand'.	'Times are tough. Off the record, what are you looking for?'

Signal type	'Example'	Meaning	'Possible response'
Concealed appeal	'*If only you'd listened* to us last year!'	We'd like some sort of ritual apology and chest beating, and then we can get on with it. Post-mortems won't get either side anywhere, but if you want one, just try disagreeing!	'Yes, we made an error of judgement. It's a mess. We can still prevent disaster, though. Look at these figures and tell us what you think.'
Hypothetical	'*Let's assume* for the sake of argument that it is possible to do it before that date. What terms would you be able to offer a vendor?'	We're interested, but we don't want to be seen committing ourselves yet.	'Just for the sake of argument, we'd be looking at $100 000 down and the rest in 90 days.'
False refusal	'We won't be letting this contract until tomorrow. *However*, you've put so much trouble into preparing your bid, we thought it only fair to let you know that your offer wasn't competitive.'	There's still a chance — try harder. We won't risk appearing to be giving you an unfair advantage over the competition, so you take the initiative.	'Thanks for telling me. I'll see if I can't twist a few arms around here to come up with something better for a last-minute bid.'
	'I won't negotiate under duress.'	If you remove the threats, I'm willing to deal. Leave them in, and you've got a fight on your hands.	'If we lift our sanctions for 48 hours, are you willing to at least discuss preliminaries?'
Emphasis prompt	'*Our major concern* is that our people won't be able to run such sophisticated equipment.'	Price is not a problem for us — don't waste our time talking about it. Reassure us about training.	'This equipment will give you market leadership. We will supply training for free if you take four units.'
Cornering	'We present this offer to you, which we consider to be *most fair and reasonable*.'	If you reject this, you will show yourself to be unfair and unreasonable.	'Well, much of life is unfair, isn't it? Let's look at it on its merits.'

Sources: Adapted from Kennedy, Benson, and Macmillan (1984); Margerison (2000); Thorn (2001); Ma, Showail, Campagna and Parks (2006).

A *Qualifier* signal, then, may be attached to what sounds like an absolute negative statement, which makes TOS look strong and resolute: 'As it stands, the offer is just ridiculous', the last word spat out, perhaps accompanied by a dismissive gesture. But the real, hidden message rests in the qualifying 'As it stands' – which, decoded, suggests that TOS are not as hostile as they choose to sound.

The *Mixed absolute/qualifier* is attached to a statement that sounds even more negative, but again the qualification suggests a different signal is actually being sent. *Grandstanding* signals are for public consumption. Again, the real message may not be quite so hostile. *Concealed appeal* seems to invite post-mortems of past sins, but in fact it may be a signal to get on with things – if OS is willing to grovel a little to satisfy TOS's honour (we may choose not to grovel, but it can be quicker and cheaper than fighting).

Hypothetical is a signal that TOS is willing to move on the problem but can't commit itself yet until it knows approximately how OS will respond. *False refusal* appears to present a definite rebuff, but really it is only a definite maybe, which could become a definite yes under different circumstances (and it lies within the power of OS to change the circumstances). *Emphasis prompt* is a cue to what TOS really wants to talk about; it is a fairly obvious agenda-setting signal that is nonetheless often missed. *Cornering* is a 'loaded language' signal – TOS deliberately uses certain 'hurray' and 'boo' words, and dares us to challenge them (or they hope we don't notice).

Cultural and gender sensitivity

Effective negotiators are sensitive to cultural differences. Such sensitivity is important when negotiating formally with people from other countries but is also becoming important in day-to-day transactions with 'non-negotiators' in our increasingly multicultural workplaces and global enterprises (Brett & Gelfand 2005; Salacuse 1998; Graham & Hernandez 2008).

Gender may also be significant as a factor in certain negotiations. Men and women may have real or perceived differences (and similarities) when it comes to attitudes and values and verbal and nonverbal communication, and we ignore these at our peril (Florea et al. 2003; Karakowsky & Miller 2006; Babcock & Laschever 2009). From another point of view, we can see gender and cultural factors as aspects of negotiation styles (see online chapter 7 'Gender and communication').

Communication channels

The good negotiator is aware of the advantages and disadvantages of negotiating via different channels of communication – whether face to face (in formal or informal meetings, behind-the-scenes encounters (Wanis-St John 2006) or interactions through third parties) or mediated (via telephone, teleconference, fax, letter and email).

Negotiation styles

The process of negotiation can also be understood in terms of the personal styles used by those negotiating. In negotiation and conflict resolution, gender and cultural factors can be understood as styles (see previous section). The Jungian model (Jung 1923 [1976]) of 16 different psychological types, popularised through the Myers-Briggs Type Inventory, can be a useful guide to the dynamics of negotiation and conflict resolution (Reynolds 2006; Myers 1999; Eunson 2002 [1997]), pp. 147–50). The Thomas-Kilmann Conflict Mode model allows us to analyse and plan negotiations and conflicts by considering five styles of conflict handling (competing, collaborating, compromising, avoiding and accommodating). Hiam (1997) uses a model of negotiation process based on eight styles (compete, con, borrow, collaborate, compromise, rob, accommodate, withdraw).

Warner's style model

Warner (2000) has developed a model of negotiation styles that is based on differing values of empathy and energy (figure 13.10). Empathy is the ability to emotionally connect with others, and energy relates to verbal energy (does the negotiator use a louder voice, speak faster and more enthusiastically?) and nonverbal energy (does the negotiator give very direct eye contact, lean forward, position the hands high in aggressive gestures, such as pointing?). This gives rise to four styles: Pushy bullying, Confident promoting, Quietly manipulating and Carefully suggesting. Typical phrases used by negotiators using such styles are:

- Could you please just let me finish? (Pushy bullying)
- I can appreciate your position on this. (Confident promoting)
- What motivates you to say this? (Quietly manipulating)
- Let me summarise what I am suggesting. (Carefully suggesting)

Powerful

Pushy bullying	**Confident promoting**
Pros • Loudly commands attention on a key point • Draws negotiations to a rapid close **Cons** • May adopt a 'take it or leave it' attitude • Is often insensitive and misses subtle points	**Pros** • Quickly focuses on the major issues • Wins people over with enthusiasm • Usually adapts flexibly to reach a deal **Cons** • Can be too aggressive • Can fail to listen fully

Coercive — Level of empathy — Level of energy — **Persuasive**

Quietly manipulating	**Carefully suggesting**
Pros • Quickly draws attention to real threats to agreement • Can subtly focus a debate **Cons** • May distort information or the truth • Exploits other party's weaknesses openly	**Pros** • Keeps the negotiation calm • Good at drawing attention to the 'deeper' issues **Cons** • Can fail to commit to convincing the other side • May enjoy the negotiation process more than reaching the outcome

Gentle

FIGURE 13.10 Warner's styles of negotiation

Source: Warner (2000, p. 35).

Each negotiator may favour a particular style, but it may be possible for an individual negotiator to use two, three or all four styles in any given negotiation. While each style has strengths as well as weaknesses, coercion is not, in the final analysis, so productive, if only because it represents an aggressive win–lose orientation and thus may draw forth opposition and undermining of any agreements reached under such duress. Warner suggests that the most effective style is a super-style that involves elements of all four styles, with an emphasis on persuasiveness: this most effective super-style can be seen in the right-facing diamond shape overlaid on figure 13.10.

Aronoff and Wilson's style model

Aronoff and Wilson (1985) developed a theory of styles of negotiation based on 11 personality variables:

- Abasement – self-blaming, surrendering, apologising, confessing, atoning, complying, accepting punishment; establishing control and prediction of others' actions by self-deprecating manoeuvres
- Dependency – seeking aid, protection, sympathy or help; fearing the loss of a powerful protector
- Approval – admiring, emulating, cooperating with, yielding eagerly to, and willingly serve a leader
- Authoritarianism – holding to conventional values, being hostile towards others, stereotyping of others, holding antidemocratic attitudes, being submissive and uncritical towards authority
- Order – careful structuring of events by directly imposing order on interpersonal relationships, the self or the world; organising tasks and social transactions in precise and detailed ways

- Affiliation – interacting with others, establishing intimate equal involvements with others in mutually satisfying social transactions
- Machiavellianism – manipulating and opportunistically exploiting relationships (see online chapter 9 'Leadership and communication')
- Dominance – establishing self-worth through demonstrations of directing, influencing and persuading others
- Nurturance – establishing self-worth by responsibly caring for the successful development of persons, generations and institutions, as well as the quality and significance of achievements and products
- Recognition – establishing self-worth through personal displays that gain admiration, respect, praise and prestige from others; drawing attention to one's actions, through the seeking of honours, or by succeeding at extremely difficult feats
- Achievement – establishing self-worth through successful competition with standards of excellence in the pursuit of task-oriented activity; being competitive in meeting standards of excellence across a wide range of transactions with the world (adapted from Aronoff & Wilson 1985, pp. 38–64).

This model, based in part on the personality theories of Murray (1938), allows Aronoff and Wilson to analyse the approaches different individuals will have to negotiation situations. For example, different individuals will have different approaches to bargaining, not only in relation to those who are on the other side of a negotiation, but also to those on their own side who are part of a negotiating team: will they be capable of yielding to pressure from others, or will they be firm and not ready to move? Similarly, different individuals will have different approaches to information use, which means approaches to problem solving, framing arguments and responding to new data and events in the negotiating process: will they be rigid or flexible in such situations? These two variables – bargaining stance and techniques of information use – can be combined to map the 11 different personality variables (figure 13.11).

Techniques of information use	Bargaining stance: Firm	Bargaining stance: Yielding
Rigid	Abasement Order Dominance	Dependency Approval Authoritarianism Recognition
Flexible	Machiavellianism Achievement Nurturance	Affiliation

FIGURE 13.11 Bargaining versus information-using approaches in negotiation

Source: Adapted from Aronoff and Wilson (1985, pp. 81–2, 108, 269–91).

Also, it is possible to analyse the personality variables in terms of negotiating styles based on whether individual negotiators choose to maximise their own or joint outcomes – to stress competition or cooperation; and also on the degree to which individual negotiators are frank or guarded in sharing their purposes with others – whether they are more prone to reveal or conceal facts and emotions. The combinations of these factors help produce a map of four different negotiating styles – integrative, adversarial, ingratiating and exploitative (figure 13.12).

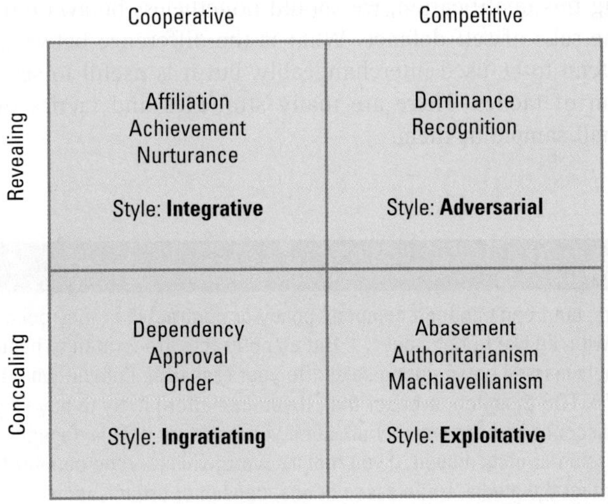

	Cooperative	Competitive
Revealing	Affiliation Achievement Nurturance Style: **Integrative**	Dominance Recognition Style: **Adversarial**
Concealing	Dependency Approval Order Style: **Ingratiating**	Abasement Authoritarianism Machiavellianism Style: **Exploitative**

FIGURE 13.12 Aronoff and Wilson's negotiation styles model

Source: Adapted from Aronoff and Wilson (1985, pp. 81–2, 108, 269–91).

The model may help us when in the middle of practical negotiations. For example, if we are not ready to move towards some type of compromise with the other side, or try to develop mutually satisfactory outcomes on common ground, or if we find that we are not responding as effectively as we might to new circumstances and information, perhaps the problem lies within ourselves rather than with objective conditions. We may need to consider to what extent our own personalities are working against our own best interests.

The model also gives other insights into the 'dark side' of human motivations:

- the authoritarian personality, while notoriously rigid in problem solving and coping with new circumstances, can be surprisingly yielding in negotiations, especially when confronted with opposing negotiators who seem to have higher status or rank
- the abasement personality may be self-sabotaging as a negotiator, working in a variety of conscious and unconscious ways to evoke dissatisfaction and irritation from others – in effect, by being as exploitative as the Machiavellians and authoritarians
- the nurturance personality, while being ready to consider new information, may not be open enough to move within the dynamics of the negotiation process – for example, from a distributive to an integrative mode of thinking; this means that they are just like achievement personalities, but also just like the more unpleasant Machiavellians.

Strategies and tactics

What about strategies and tactics? How can we use them ourselves, how can we identify when TOS uses them, and what counters might there be? For many people, this is the heart of negotiation, while for others (such as Calero and Oskam), the topic is somewhat over-rated and perhaps misses the point:

> There's no question that strategy and tactics are basic elements in any negotiation, but we think they're often over-emphasized. Somehow the impression develops that negotiation is nothing more than working a variety of ploys to manoeuvre an opposite into a desired commitment. More fundamental considerations are slighted in favour of a kind of 'game' theory that concentrates attention on techniques for 'playing' the opposition rather than on understanding the nature and psychology of the negotiation process itself. Unless you understand the art of persuasion, the importance of listening, the essentials of building trust and maintaining good will, you can't negotiate effectively, no matter what your line of strategy or arsenal of tactics includes. (Calero & Oskam 1988, p. 127)

Accepting this qualification, we should nonetheless be aware of strategies and tactics, if only for the sake of self-defence. What is the difference between a strategy and a tactic? The terms tend to be used interchangeably, but it is useful to see a strategy as a particular combination of tactics. There are many strategies and tactics in negotiation. Table 13.6 offers a small sample of them.

TABLE 13.6 Some tactics used in negotiation

Tactic	Brief description
1. It's official	TOS says 'Sorry, but I can't change company policy or contracts', or may point to the price tag. Often accompanied with 'I'd like to help, but ... ' But all contracts are written to benefit the seller, and price tags are routinely marked down during sales. Do your research: find out what rival other sides are offering, and ask TOS to match or better that. If you can afford it, try to buy several of the desired objects, and ask for a discount, threatening to walk out if you can't get it. This depends on what is more important to TOS: commission or units moved. If you feel it's worthwhile, try the counter tactic of smearing: threaten to contact the media, trade associations, consumer organisations, your local Consumer Affairs department and everyone at your workplace.
2. Grab the power seat	Symbolism is often silly, but many believe that if a negotiation or discussion is to take place at a rectangular table, then the person who sits at the narrow end (farthest from the door, in front of a window), has most power in a meeting or negotiation. The seat at the other end is often also perceived to have power, although not quite so much. Arrive early and grab what you want.
3. Record and facilitate	Negotiations can often be influenced by the way the agenda is set out (e.g. 'What comes first? Last? What is not there? What can be read between the lines? What is the hidden agenda?'). The same can be said for the minutes: no-one wants to write them; but volunteer, perhaps changing a few things to benefit OS. This requires some skill, if the wording or outcome is not to be challenged. Similar to writing the agenda and/or minutes and grabbing the power seat is volunteering to record ideas, and brainstorming on flipcharts or whiteboards. Rather than being a passive functionary, however, gradually assume the role of a facilitator — suggesting, questioning, and becoming, in fact, the de facto chair.
4. You owe me one	In negotiations over price, time, quality, salary, promotion — or, in fact, anything — TOS expects a battle from us. But what if we exercise strategic restraint? For example, your sales are up, but you know budgets are tight. Instead of asking for a raise, try something like saying (while smiling): 'I know things are bad on the cash flow front, so even though I would like to see some recognition of my sales, I'll bite my tongue and that might free up some resources for you. Maybe we can talk about it during our next three-monthly session, and maybe things won't be so tight then.' Try to have a witness present and or/ send a confirming email, creating a document trail. It doesn't always work, especially with nasty bosses, but it often does: you've helped them out with money and time, and now they're obligated. You're smiling now, but he/she knows that if things don't improve (especially if your sales keep going up), then the organisational grapevine will go wild, characterising him/her as an exploiter and a bad people and resources manager, and overall sales performance will probably go down, as other salespeople will realise that virtue will not be rewarded. This is a lose–lose situation for TOS. This is cashable restraint, and obligation, reputation, trust and fairness are very powerful tools in negotiation in both eastern and western societies. Untrustworthy negotiators may win the battle, but lose the war.
5. Getting the opposition to set limits	Negotiations in adversarial situations are usually about both sides opening up with extreme opening bids. The haggling and us-versus-them approach can sometimes be negated by this tactic. Give TOS an extreme case — more extreme than their opening bid (industrial sabotage as grounds for dismissal, eight pizzas for four moderate eaters, wedding guests numbers, ultra-high salaries after audited copies of a weak budget are distributed ['open-book management'] — and ask them if they think that is reasonable. Nonverbals are crucial here: don't be smug; be sincere, and show that you want a win–win situation. TOS will almost certainly (grudgingly) concede that the ridiculous is just that, and so you can begin to work backwards to something that will satisfy both parties. Know every detail of your case. What you are doing with this tactic is converting differences of kind into differences of degree. Both sides can thus move backwards, incrementally or bit-by-bit, from an extreme position to a more reasonable one. TOS will have participated in setting limits, and so may be more committed to the final deal.

Tactic	Brief description
6. Save face	If TOS's dignity is assaulted — for example, in a humiliating defeat — they won't forget it: your cheap victory may prove to be very expensive. Remember TOS's position vis-à-vis their principals or constituency. To be ethical, you should respect their dignity and competence. To be brutally cynical, it is wiser to give some crumbs to pushovers — and let them take the credit for it — than to have pushovers pushed over and replaced by much tougher operators. Classic Chinese military and strategic texts counsel restraint when thinking about annihilating TOS ('Build them a golden bridge for retreat' — Sun Tzu). You should do likewise.
	Remember, saving face is a phenomenon unique to all peoples on the planet, but it has specific resonances in certain cultures that you should be aware of if you are negotiating with representatives from those cultures. This is similar to getting the opposition to set limits: you come across as the good guys, and it creates obligation — a form of you owe me one. There is no guarantee that you will always be the winner, and TOS may feel obligated to return the favour.
7. Nibble	Nibbling is a tactic in which a negotiator will ask for a last-minute, relatively small (but still expensive) concession. Nibbling depends on the amount of time and effort that has been invested in the negotiation, and the hope that TOS will reluctantly go along with it (but still be irritated at your nerve). A classic nibble would be spending a lot of time on buying an expensive suit, and as the sales clerk writes up the sales docket (dreaming of the commission from the sale), you ask her/him to throw in a free tie or belt. Counter tactics to nibbles include playing it's official, anticipating a nibble by including it in your original time, and simply refusing it (otherwise, you may get known as a soft touch for this sneaky tactic from the nibbler).
8. Fait accompli	Fait accompli means 'accomplished fact' in French. It means that one side has no intention of negotiating or of giving to get, and probably believes that forgiveness is easier to get than permission. It has a 'take it or leave it' dynamic. It's substantially, but not totally, a matter of the respective power bases of the two sides. The more powerful are more inclined to try this on. Like the nibble, fait accompli may involve suddenly announcing additional costs, deliveries, services or repairs, or an unequal prenuptial agreement — the applicability of the tactic is endless. Of course, it destroys trust. Responses include accepting it meekly (which may be a strategic retreat, but may also lead TOS to think that you are weak, and they can try this on again); and going along but asking for a cooling-off period (if this is not legislated) and then renegotiating — that is, challenging the rationale of the demands, one by one.
	You can capitulate, but suddenly find reasons for going very slow and/or badly on carrying out your side of the deal (playing dumb all the while, of course). You can also threaten to go elsewhere, threaten to smear (as with it's official), threaten to destroy TOS's reputation — so that they win the battle but not the war (no-one else will want to work with treacherous bullies) — or walk away.
	This tactic demonstrates the necessity of clarifying guidelines for a negotiation before it has begun.
9. Volume control	This can be played loud or soft. The loud version involves one side staging tantrums, yelling and engaging in histrionics to disorient you (in the same way that police and anti-terror units yell to disorient suspects). This is all designed to frighten, bully and confuse. If it can be engineered, now's the time to take a break. You can counter with volume, but beware of being dragged into the conflict spiral. Remain cool and consider this example: In 1960, when giving a speech at the United Nations, British Prime Minister Harold Macmillan, who was renowned for his 'unflappability', or cool, was interrupted by the Soviet Premier Nikita Kruschev, who was pounding his desk with his shoe and yelling in Russian. Unfazed, Macmillan continued, asking for a translation; and in doing so, transforming Kruschev from frightening to ridiculous. Threaten to smear — after all, who wants to haggle with a sociopath?
	The soft version is when TOS simply goes silent. This is normal among people from some cultures, but it is sometimes used to disconcert other people, who may then, perhaps, fall into the 'pause pit' and say and sign things that they may later regret. Counters include saying 'Please continue thinking it over', and starting to work on your own (e.g. on a computer); taking a break; or talking nonstop (filibuster) about procedural matters until TOS becomes frustrated and re-joins the game.
10. Verify, verify, verify	Budget time in your negotiations to verify; that is, to clarify just what has been agreed to. Better yet, get it in writing: for example, a memorandum of understanding or contract written by lawyers on both sides or by a professional mediator, or a roster on housework taped onto the fridge or on a separate noticeboard. Memory is treacherous, and it is not to be relied upon. If you can confirm a negotiation with a handshake, and make it stick, consider yourself to be very lucky. Social norms — underpinned by a fear of being smeared — strengthen such agreements.

Source: Adopted from Mills (2005), Gosselin (2007), Lewicki and Hiam (1998), Eunson (2002 [1994]), Lewicki (2010).

Planning

We have now progressed a long way through our original model of the negotiation process. All the knowledge and skills in the world will do us no good, however, unless we have some kind of plan. *Fail to plan, plan to fail.* It doesn't matter whether we are to negotiate the borders between two countries, the price of a car or the end of a lovers' spat: we need to think about it beforehand. We should resist the temptation to jump straight into things simply because we have a bias towards action over thought, or because we imagine that time pressure leaves us no opportunity for planning.

If you feel that you have a reasonable grasp of the factors involved in the negotiating situation you have ahead of you, now is the time to work with the negotiation planning grid (see figure 13.13). Work with this copy of the grid or make as large a copy of it as you can. Notice that it addresses both sides in the negotiation — OS and TOS. For the most part we will be guessing about the relevant factors for TOS, but chance favours the prepared mind. The same applies to our own side. Don't think you can do without planning: one side is enough to guess about. (Note also that not all factors or panels in the grid may be relevant to any given negotiation situation.)

Factor	Our side	The other side
BATNA		
WATNA		
Goals (rated from top to bottom priority)		
Positions		
Mutual interests		
Bottom lines		
Concessions		
Territory		
Time constraints/opportunities		
Publics/stakeholders		
Packaging		
Strategies and tactics		
Team roles		
Stress factors		
Gender aspects		
Signals		
Listening/questioning/persuading factors		
Cultural aspects		
Communication channels		
Negotiation styles		

FIGURE 13.13 A negotiation planning grid

Role-play: be smart, not shy or cynical

Once you have made some notes on a copy of the grid, you might consider some role-plays, either with someone else taking the part of TOS or with you taking this role. Many people feel uncomfortable with role-playing, but it makes sense to overcome any inhibitions and at least try the experience. You may find that the pressures involved allow you to think of new approaches. You may also find that playing the role of TOS gives you insights into their motivation and approaches, and as a result you may begin to see a way to develop what is perhaps the most important panel in the whole grid, the one labelled 'Mutual interests'. Note that this panel is not divided into two sides.

Agreement

As we have noted, negotiation varies widely in scale and significance. It may comprise no more than a silent exchange of gestures between two individuals in a room, or it may involve an elaborate series of meetings between large teams of individuals over years.

Some problems have no solution, and agreement is not always possible. When this is recognised, people may opt to exercise their BATNAs, to submit to humiliating defeat and sign the paper, or merely to give a tearful nod. Alternately, both sides may celebrate a mutually satisfactory outcome, in which a win–win resolution is achieved: both sides win, there are no losers, and the agreement marks the beginning of a long, highly productive partnership. Still another alternative is for both sides to wearily return to the beginning of the negotiating process and start again.

Always be ready to walk away, either as a temporary tactic or to disengage permanently from the process. Remember, if you are so locked into the process that you can't walk away, or believe you can't walk away, then this constitutes crucial leverage that TOS has over you. Be ready to bluff on this, or at least do everything you can to avoid sending out nonverbal signals to the other side that you are locked in.

Confirming it

Confirmation of agreement can be validated by a simple handshake or nod of the head, or by signing a thousand-page contract. The form will vary considerably from situation to situation, and indeed from culture to culture. Wherever possible (and you should try to make it possible as often as you can), write it down and get all parties to endorse it. At the very least this will minimise post-negotiation controversies of the 'But I thought we agreed to ...' variety.

Negotiation: not a line but a circle

Now that confirmation has been made, the negotiation is over. Or is it? It may, in fact, simply be a beginning, rather than an end. You may have negotiated a temporary equilibrium that will soon become unstable again; it may have been a battle within a larger war. TOS may perceive the negotiations as ongoing, as never really ending. Depending on the culture, the negotiation process may be a ritualised aspect of an ongoing relationship that needs to be constantly maintained and nurtured. Whatever the situation, you will probably find yourself – whether in two or three hours, or two or three years – returning to the beginning of negotiation model. In other words, the model is circular, not linear (refer back to figure 13.4 on p. 409).

STUDENT STUDY GUIDE

SUMMARY

Negotiation is a communication and problem-solving process built on a wide foundation of skills and bodies of knowledge. It is also one of the most popular and effective methods of solving conflicts. It may not be appropriate in every situation, however. In deciding whether we want to negotiate, we need to consider BATNAs (best alternatives to a negotiated agreement), WATNAs (worst alternatives to a negotiated agreement), the virtues of avoidance and the necessity for Plan Bs.

Conflict is often perceived in terms of the dynamics of winning and losing, but a win–win outcome is a practical necessity if a negotiated agreement is to have lasting value. In preparing for a negotiation, we must first research the other side, then identify clearly our goals, our bottom lines and the concessions we are willing to make. Effective negotiators are aware of the dynamics of the exchange of concessions in negotiations. They understand the difference between positions and interests, the role of territory and time, and of publics or stakeholders in negotiation. They are also aware of how packaging techniques can offer greater flexibility when discussing outcomes.

Sometimes culture and gender are relevant, even vital factors in managing negotiations. In team negotiations individuals can play different roles. We need to grasp the value of nonverbal communication, and listening, questioning and persuading skills, and to understand the functions and expressions of signals.

As negotiators, we should be aware of the effectiveness and limitations of strategies and tactics, and how different channels of communication can help or hinder negotiation processes. Finally, we must ensure that we plan the negotiation process in order to maximise our options, minimise our stress and provide a solid foundation for a lasting, fair and creative agreement between negotiating parties.

KEY TERMS

BATNA *p. 410*

bottom line *p. 413*

concession *p. 414*

distributive bargaining *p. 415*

integrative bargaining *p. 415*

MLATNA *p. 411*

negative-sum outcome *p. 408*

PATNA *p. 411*

Plan B *p. 411*

positive-sum outcome *p. 408*

WATNA *p. 410*

win–win situation *p. 408*

winner's curse *p. 418*

zero-sum outcome *p. 408*

REVIEW QUESTIONS

1. Why is the term 'win–win' more than simply a cliché in most negotiations?
2. Why should we bother to save the face of our opponents in situations when we can clearly dominate them and impose a win–lose outcome on them?
3. What is the difference between a WATNA and a BATNA?
4. When trading concessions, what is the ideal strategy to follow?
5. What is the main difference between a position and an interest?
6. List three points in favour of and three points against negotiating on your home ground.
7. What is the winner's curse, and how can it be avoided or minimised?
8. Identify at least three different types of signals.
9. Identify at least four different negotiation tactics.
10. Why is it important always to have the option of walking away from a negotiation rather than automatically settling?
11. What does the phrase 'negotiation – not a line but a circle' mean?
12. Compare two different models of negotiation.
13. Compare two negotiation styles.

1. Use the planning grid to plan an actual negotiation. Role-play it, using video if possible.
2. Using print and online sources, create a master list of negotiation strategies and tactics. Write brief notes on each, identifying strengths and weaknesses. Speculate on what strategies and tactics could be usefully combined, and what strategies and tactics would not work well together. If you wish to go further, answer the question: What is the difference between a negotiation strategy and a negotiation tactic?
3. Pick a situation, even one that does not apparently involve conflict, such as: Where will families meet to celebrate a ritual or festival like Christmas? Where should a meeting between separate departments take place? Where should students meet to study together? Where should band members meet to practise? Where should one meet with a client or customer?. Analyse the situation in terms of territorial dynamics. Does it matter where the encounter takes place? Why? Why not?
4. Write a dialogue in which two or more negotiators use different signals to send different messages. As a variation, write it twice – once in which both sides successfully decode the signals, and once in which one or both sides fails to decode the signals.
5. Consider a personal or professional situation that ended badly, with hurt feelings on both sides. Analyse the situation in terms of what concessions or tradeables could have been exchanged to achieve a more positive outcome.
6. Interview someone who works in a field involving money (e.g. an accountant, a lawyer, a human resources/personnel specialist or a banking specialist). Brief them on the idea of packaging in negotiation, and then ask them what packaging options they are aware of in their field.
7. Review the material on communication channels (see chapter 1). How might the outcome of a negotiation be affected by the use of one or several channels? What is the relationship of channels to territory in negotiations?
8. When resources are created, the pie becomes bigger, and parties to a negotiation are likely to be more satisfied. How can resources be created?

WHAT WOULD YOU DO?

You are the leader of the Red Party in federal Parliament. You would like to have a clear majority over your major opponents, the Blue Party, but can't, having instead to depend on the votes of seven members of the Orange Party. The support of the Orange Party is not always guaranteed, and they have proven to be tough negotiators to get some of their policies up in the past.

Two big issues are coming up in the Parliament: euthanasia and nuclear power. In terms of legalising euthanasia, it has been proposed that there be a free or conscience vote on the issue. However, your Red Party's secret survey data back from some recent state elections shows that a large conservative element is against the concept. It would therefore be politically risky to be seen to be supporting its introduction, though both the Blue and Orange Parties have indicated they are in favour of legalising euthanasia in appropriate circumstances. Regarding the second issue, most of the members of Parliament were treated to a demonstration of a new fusion plant recently, which puts out very little radioactivity and provides significantly cheaper electricity than that provided by alternative sources, not to mention putting out low carbon emissions (the Blue Party has been pro-nuclear for some time). The demonstration has changed the minds of many members of the Red Party, who have been stridently anti-nuclear for some time (as have the Orange Party). Further, you know for a fact that at least two members of the Orange Party – albeit reluctantly – support such a power system.

You invite these two Orange Party members, and an additional two of their parliamentary colleagues, along to a meeting. You ask them all to support the construction of a test reactor, offering a ministry position to any one of them as an inducement for this. You also show them your Party's survey data on euthanasia, which suggests that politicians seen to be supporting legislation to introduce it might lose many votes (and quite possibly their seats) at the upcoming election. You suggest to the four Orange Party members that they exercise their conscience vote against it, which is your Red Party's official stance on the issue.

You can see that they have strongly held mixed emotions on these issues, taking into account long-held policies, personal ambitions and beliefs. You also see the chance to split their party four to three on both issues, and in doing so, possibly destroy it.

What options are there for all players in this situation?

SUGGESTED READING

Babcock, Linda & Laschever, Sara 2009, *Ask for it: how women can use the power of negotiation to get what they really want*, Bantam, New York.

Bates, Christopher 2011, 'Lessons from another world: an emic perspective on concepts useful to negotiation derived from martial arts', *Negotiation Journal*, vol. 27, no. 1, pp. 95–102.

Bazerman, Max & Malhotra, Deepak 2008, *Negotiation genius: how to overcome obstacles and achieve brilliant results at the bargaining table and beyond*, Bantam, New York.

Billings-Yun, Melanie 2010, *Beyond dealmaking: five steps to negotiating profitable relationships*, Jossey-Bass, San Francisco.

Brown, David 2010, *Negotiating secrets*, Collins, New York.

Buskirk, Richard 1989, *Frontal attack, divide and conquer, the fait accompli, and 118 other tactics managers must know*, John Wiley & Sons, New York.

Cohen, Herb 1989, *You can negotiate anything*, Bantam, New York.

—— 2002, 'Genre analysis of business letters of negotiation', *English for Specific Purposes*, vol. 21, pp. 167–99.

—— 2005, *Negotiating the Middle East*, Reed Press, New York.

Donaldson, Michael C 2007, *Negotiating for dummies*, 2nd edn, John Wiley & Sons, New York.

Druckman, Daniel & Olekalns 2008, 'Emotions in negotiation', *Group Decision and Negotiation*, vol 17, no 1, pp. 31–49.

Elliott, Sinnikka & Umberson, Debra 2008, 'The performance of desire: gender and sexual negotiation in long-term marriages', *Journal of Marriage and Family*, vol 70, no 2, pp 391–406.

Gates, Steve 2011, *The negotiation book: your definitive guide to successful negotiating*, John Wiley & Sons, New York.

Ilich, John 2000, *The complete idiot's guide to winning through negotiation*, 2nd edn, Pearson, New York.

Khan, Mohammad, Marcue, Felipe & Chisholm, Donald 2011, *The basics of international negotiation: a student handbook*, VDM Verlag Dr. Müller, Saarbrücken, Germany.

Koren, Leonard & Goodman, Peter 1991, *The haggler's handbook*, Century Business, London.

Lewicki, Roy J 2010, *Negotiation: readings, exercises and cases*, McGraw-Hill, 6th rev. edn, New York.

Noesner, Gary 2010, *Stalling for time: my life as an FBI hostage negotiator*, Random House, New York.

Oliver, David 2011, *How to negotiate effectively: improve your success rate; get the best deal; achieve win–win results*, Kogan Page, 3rd. revised edn, Kogan Page, London.

Reardon, Kathleen 2005, *The skilled negotiator: mastering the language of engagement*, Jossey-Bass, San Francisco, CA.

Salacuse, Jeswald W 2004, *The global negotiator: making, managing and mending deals around the world in the twenty-first century*, Palgrave Macmillan, New York.

—— 2008, *Seven secrets for negotiating with government: how to deal with local, state, national, or foreign governments – and come out ahead*, Amacom, New York.

Shapiro, Ronald M & Jankowski, Mark A 2001, *The power of nice: how to negotiate so everybody wins – especially you!*, rev. edn, John Wiley & Sons, New York.

Tinsley, Catherine H, Cheledin, Sandra I, Schneider, Andrea Kupfer & Amanatullah, Emily T 2009, 'Women at the bargaining table: pitfalls and prospects', *Negotiation Journal*, vol 25, no 2, pp. 233–48.

REFERENCES

Alon, Ilai & Brett, Jeanne M 2007, 'Perceptions of time and their impact on negotiations in the Arabic-speaking Islamic world', *Negotiation Journal*, vol. 23, no. 1, pp. 55–73.

Aronoff, Joel & Wilson, John P 1985, *Personality in the social process*, Lawrence Erlbaum Associates, Hillsdale, NJ.

Babcock, Linda & Laschever, Sara 2009, *Ask for it: how women can use the power of negotiation to get what they really want*, Bantam, New York.

Bercovitch, Jacob & Jackson, Richard 2001, 'Negotiation or mediation? An exploration of factors affecting the choice of conflict management in international conflict', *Negotiation Journal*, vol. 17, no. 1, pp. 59–71.

Brett, Jeanne M & Gelfand, Michele J 2005, 'Lessons from abroad: when culture affects negotiating style', *Negotiation*, January, pp. 3–5.

Brown, David 2010, *Negotiating secrets*, Collins, New York/London.

Calero, Henry & Oskam, Bob 1988, *Negotiate for what you want*, Thorsons Publishing, Wellingborough, UK.

Camp, Jim 2002, *Start with NO ... the negotiating tools that the pros don't want you to know*, Crown Business, New York.

Clarke, GR & Davies, IT 1992, 'Mediation: when is it not an appropriate dispute resolution process?' *Australian Dispute Resolution Journal*, May.

Crump, Larry 2007, 'A temporal model of negotiation linkages', *Negotiation Journal*, vol. 23, no. 2, pp. 117–53.

Da Conceição-Heldt, Eugenia 2006, 'Integrative and distributive bargaining situations in the European Union: what difference does it make?', *Negotiation Journal*, vol. 22, no. 2, pp. 145–65.

Eunson, Baden 2002 [1994], *Negotiation skills*, Ebooks.com, Boston, MA.

—— 2002 [1997], *Dealing with conflict*, Ebooks.com, Boston, MA.

Ferris, Frank D 2001, 'The things negotiators do with money', *Negotiation Journal*, vol. 17, no. 1, pp. 47–58.

Fisher, Roger, Ury, William & Patton, Bruce 1991, *Getting to yes: negotiating an agreement without giving in*, rev. edn, Business Books, London.

Florea, Natalie B, Boyer, Mark A, Brown, Scott W, Butler, Michael J, Hernandez, Magnolia, Mayall, Hayley J, Clarisse, Lima, Johnson, Paula R, Meng, Lin & Weir, Kimberley 2003, 'Negotiating from Mars to Venus: gender in simulated international negotiations', *Simulation & Gaming*, vol. 34, pp. 226–48.

Folger, JP, Poole, MS & Stutman, RK 2008, *Working through conflict: strategies for relationships*, groups and organisations, 6th edn. HarperCollins, New York.

Freshman, Clark & Guthrie, Chris 2009, 'Managing the goal-setting paradox: how to get better results from high goals and be happy', *Negotiation Journal*, vol. 25, no. 2, pp. 217–31.

Geckil, Ilhan K & Anderson, Patrick L 2009, *Applied game theory and strategic behavior*, Chapman and Hall/CRC, Boca Raton, FLA.

Graham, John L & Herberger, Roy A Jr 1983, 'Negotiators abroad – don't shoot from the hip', *Harvard Business Review*, vol. 83, no. 3, pp. 160–8.

Graham, John & Requejo, William Hernandez 2008, *The rules of engagement: a global negotiation protocol*, Palgrave Macmillan, New York/London.

Guasco, Matthew P & Robinson, Peter R 2007, *Principles of negotiation: strategies, tactics and techniques to reach agreement*, Entrepreneur Press, Irvine, CA.

Grosskopf, Brit, Bereby-Meyer, Yoella & Bazerman, Max 2007, 'On the robustness of the winner's curse phenomenon', *Journal of Theory and Decision*, vol 63, no 4, pp. 389–418.

Hiam, Alexander 1997, *Flex style negotiating instructor's manual*, HRD Press, Amherst, MD.

Hofstede, Geert 2001, *Culture's consequences: comparing values, behaviors, institutions and organizations across nations*, 2nd edn, Sage, Thousand Oaks, CA/London.

Jung, CG 1976 [1923], *Psychological types*, Princeton University Press, Princeton, NJ.

Karakowsky, Leonard & Miller, Diane L 2006, 'Negotiator style and influence in multi-party negotiations: exploring the role of gender', *Leadership and Organization Development Journal*, vol. 27, no. 1, pp. 50–65.

Karrass, Chester 1993, *The negotiating game*, HarperCollins, New York.

Kennedy, Gavin, Benson, John & McMillan, John 1984, *Managing negotiations*, 2nd edn, Business Books, London.

Kydd, Andrew 1997, 'Game theory and the spiral model', *World Politics*, vol. 49, no. 3, pp. 371–400.

Lewicki, Roy J 2010, *Negotiation: readings, exercises and cases*, 6th rev. edn, McGraw-Hill, New York.

Lewicki, Roy J & Hiam, Alezander 1998, *The fast forward MBA in negotiating and deal making*, John Wiley & Sons, New York.

Lewicki, Roy J, Barry, Bruce & Saunders, David M 2007, *Essentials of negotiation*, 4th edn, McGraw-Hill Irwin, New York.

Luft, Joseph 1969, *Of human interaction*, National Press, Palo Alto, CA.

Ma, Li, Showail, Sammy, Campagna, Rachel & Parks, Judi McLean 2006, 'Concessions in negotiations: the roles of initial assessment and signaling on outcomes of a negotiated agreement', paper presented at the International Association for Conflict Management 19th conference, Montreal, Canada, June, http://papers.ssrn.com.

McDuff, Ian 2006, 'Your place or mine? Culture, time and negotiation', *Negotiation Journal*, vol. 22, no. 1, pp. 31–45.

McKersie, Robert B, Eaton, Susan C & Kochan, Thomas A 2004, 'Kaiser permanente: using interest-based negotiations to craft a new collective bargaining agreement', *Negotiation Journal*, vol. 20, no. 1, pp. 13–36.

Margerison, Charles J 2000, *If only I had said ... conversation control skills for managers*, Management Books 2000, Cirencester, UK.

Martinovsky, Bilyana, Traum, David & Marsella, Stacy 2007, 'Rejection of empathy in negotiation', *Group Decision and Negotiation*, vol. 16, no. 1, pp. 61–76.

Murray, HA 1938, *Explorations in personality*, Oxford University Press, New York.

Myers, Isabel Briggs 1999, *Introduction to type: a guide to understanding your results on the Myers-Briggs Type Indicator*, Center for Applications of Psychological Type, Gainesville, FLA.

Planken, Brigitte 2005, 'Managing rapport in lingua franca sales negotiations: a comparison of professional and aspiring negotiators', *English for Special Purposes*, vol. 24, pp. 381–400.

Provis, Chris 1996, 'Interests vs. positions: a critique of the distinction', *Negotiation Journal*, vol. 12, no. 4, pp. 307–23.

Reynolds, Andrea 2006, 'Bargaining positions', *Supply Management*, vol. 11, no. 2, pp. 30–1.

Rubin, JZ & Zartman, IW 1995, 'Asymmetrical negotiations: some survey results that may surprise', *Negotiation Journal*, vol. 11, no. 4 , pp. 349–64.

Salacuse, Jeswald W 1998, 'Ten ways that culture affects negotiating style: some survey results', *Negotiation Journal*, vol. 14, no. 3, pp. 221–40.

Salacuse, Jeswald W & Rubin, Jeffrey Z 1990, '"Your place or mine": site location and negotiation', *Negotiation Journal*, vol. 6, no. 1, pp. 5–10.

Schelling, TC 1960, *The strategy of conflict*, Oxford University Press, Oxford, UK.

Spector, Bertram J 1998, 'Deciding to negotiate with villains', *Negotiation Journal*, vol. 14, no. 1, pp. 43–59.

Susskind, Lawrence 2006, 'Negotiating with a 900-pound gorilla', *Negotiation Journal*, vol. 22, no. 2, pp. 3–5.

Thorn, Jeremy G 2001, *How to negotiate better deals*, Management Books 2000, Cirencester, UK.

Wade, John 2008, 'Persuasion in negotiation and mediation', *QUT Law and Justice Journal*, vol. 8, no. 1, pp. 253–78, www.law. qut.edu.au/ljj/.

Wallihan, James 1998, 'Negotiating to avoid agreement', *Negotiation Journal*, vol. 14, no. 3, pp. 257–68.

Wanis-St John, A 2006, 'Back-channel negotiation: international bargaining in the shadows', *Negotiation Journal*, vol. 22, no. 2, pp. 119–45.

Warner, Jon 2000, *Negotiating skills*, Team Publications, Varsity Lakes, Queensland.

Wheeler, Michael & Waters, Nancy J 2006, 'The origins of a classic: *Getting to Yes* turns twenty-five', *Negotiation Journal*, vol. 22, no. 4, pp. 475, 481.

14

conflict management

14

Conflict management

LEARNING OBJECTIVES

After studying this chapter you should be able to:

- Describe the pros and cons of conflict
- Explain the causes of conflict
- List different approaches to conflict
- Explain five different styles of conflict handling
- Describe the phases of a conflict spiral
- Give an account of the causes of organisational conflict
- Explain various solutions to conflict situations
- Describe the nature of the stalemate, impasse or deadlock, and explain why such static processes can sometimes be useful
- Explain why conflict sometimes needs to be created
- Explain the difference between dysfunctional and functional conflict

Conflict: not always a bad thing

Why can't people just get along? Why is there conflict in the world? We see conflict in the kindergarten, in marriages, in friendships, in the workplace, in courtrooms and between nations – the phenomenon seems universal. We usually think of conflict as a negative, stressful experience, leading to verbal violence and, all too often, to physical violence. Conflict, as we all know from bitter experience, can be nasty.

Conflict can lead to:

■ negative emotions
■ blocked communication
■ increased negative stereotyping of those we are in conflict with
■ reduced coordination between people who have to work and live together
■ a shift towards autocratic leadership when discussion-based decision making breaks down
■ reduced ability to view other perspectives; a breakdown in empathy and vision (Seta, Paulus & Baron 2000).

Surprisingly enough, however, conflict can sometimes produce positive payoffs (see table 14.1).

TABLE 14.1 Positive payoffs of conflict

Payoff	Explanation
Pressures and frustrations are released	When unexpressed conflicts are finally expressed, combatants sometimes experience a sense of relief, and can calm down and consider the situation with less heat and more light — for example, 'I was just letting off steam', and 'At least I got it out of my system'.
New perspectives and information can be gathered about the other side.	Combatants can become aware of each other's point of view, and may see some merit in opposing views. Empathy increases, and better decisions can be made.
New perspectives can be gained about our side.	We may not even be aware of our own views until a conflict situation forces the expression of those views. Also, we may become aware of weaknesses and inconsistencies in our own views. Conflict energises us to do and think new things.
Better decision making and problem solving can take place.	New information and perspectives are created as a result of the conflict, which allow us to see things more clearly and take appropriate action.
Cohesiveness can increase.	Groups, teams, couples and organisations may find that members are closer after the stress of conflict (and the release that comes with a successful resolution of that conflict) than they were before — the bonds between them are stronger, not weaker (see 'Stages of group development' in chapter 18).
Complacency can be challenged.	Lack of, or suppression of, conflict in some situations may mean that various unhealthy things are happening — there may be opposition to new ideas, as well as paralysing timidity and myopic denial of unresolved tensions. Conflict may challenge all of these things.
Change can take place.	Conflict is often the engine of change. Charles Darwin argued that conflict between organisms produced the survival of the fittest, so that evolution was dependent on conflict. Karl Marx argued that human progress depended on conflicts between social classes. George Bernard Shaw put it another way: 'The reasonable man adapts himself to the world: the unreasonable one persists in trying to adapt the world to himself. Therefore all progress depends on the unreasonable man.'
Differences can be appreciated.	If differences between partners in a conflict are not perceived to be insurmountable, then a new synthesis, a combination of the energies of differing people (synergy) can take place.
Intrapersonal conflicts can be resolved.	We can have conflicts within ourselves as well as conflicts with others. Sometimes engaging in and resolving conflicts with others can resolve inner conflicts (see 'Intrapersonal communication: self-talk' in chapter 9).

Resolving and managing conflict

If conflict can have its uses, then it is conceivable that we might try to increase, rather than decrease, conflict in certain situations. We will look at *conflict creation* later in this chapter.

Given this rather novel (and perhaps disconcerting) approach to conflict, we will have to be careful about the terms we use. It is common, for example, for the terms 'conflict resolution' and 'conflict management' to be used interchangeably. But **conflict resolution** might be the wrong approach to take in situations that call for the presence of, or an increase in, conflict, rather than an absence of conflict.

Conflict resolution: an approach to conflict that usually involves the reduction or elimination of conflict

Absence of conflict means that conflict has been 'resolved' or 'solved' into nothingness, but even then that state would probably be only a temporary one. If the removal of the symptoms of conflict does not remove the causes of conflict, then the 'solution' reached is an illusory one. It may be better, therefore, to engage in **conflict management** rather than to simply solve or resolve it, allowing us to exercise the option of getting rid of conflict, but also preserving the option of increasing conflict where necessary.

Conflict management: an approach to conflict that may involve reduction or elimination of, or an increase in, conflict

By the same token, we need to be wary of unthinkingly talking about conflict management if this means that we underestimate the power and irrationality of conflict dynamics. We may delude ourselves into thinking that technical tinkering with human behaviour will fix a situation, when in fact the situation may be much more out of control and potentially dangerous. We might just as well delude ourselves by calling a brawl 'punch management' or nuclear war 'weapons management' – the terms are simply too tame and misleading. The best way to mismanage conflict is to think that it can always be merely 'managed'.

What causes conflict?

There are many possible causes of conflict, some of which are also causes of aggression. Some of the major ones may be:

- *Scarce resources.* Two parties want the same thing – a coat in a shop, a window view, an inheritance, a parking space, access to a river, a broadcasting licence, land, the affections of a third person, political control of a nation-state. When such a thing or resource cannot be shared, or is perceived to be unshareable, then conflict may ensue.
- *Adversity.* Economic hardship can increase stress. Tough times may (not will) predispose some individuals, groups and nations to conflict, reducing internal group cohesion. (Tough times may, of course, increase group cohesion if group members see that only cooperation will alleviate the situation, and if they find adversity to be more challenging than enervating: 'when the going gets tough, the tough get going'.) An economic recession, for example, when combined with external conflict, can exacerbate internal conflicts at the national level (Blomberg & Hess 2002).
- *Faulty communication.* A person may misinterpret a remark, taking it as an insult where none was given. Silence may be misinterpreted as hostility, when in fact it is simply silence. The ability to resolve conflict may be linked to communication skills: the fewer skills a person has, the more likely that person may become involved in verbal and physical conflict (Huffman 2009).
- *Perceived differences.* Throughout history, people have perceived others from different races, religions, classes, areas and belief systems as being 'the other', and as being threats as well as potential allies.
- *Biology.* Aggression may be part of our biological program, a predisposition to seek out conflict and then to resolve it via verbal or physical violence. For example, writers from fields such as evolutionary psychology and sociobiology argue that our human ancestors needed aggression to survive in a hostile environment and against wild animals.

Such aggression was also directed against other humans in competition for scarce resources such as food and territory (see online chapter 7 'Gender and communication'). These writers argue that we still have these impulses, even though we now live in allegedly more civilised surroundings, where resources may not be so scarce. Unfortunately, we now also have access to a variety of 'violence amplifiers', such as cars, guns and bombs, in addition to nuclear, chemical and biological weapons. Instinctual theories such as these, which are by no means universally accepted, suggest that we are not as rational as we think we are, and that we are not as in control of ourselves as we think we are (Hampton 2010; Wilson 2000; Brizendine 2010; Rizzuto, Buie & Meissner 2004; Barrett 2010). The opposing view – that we are not aggressive by nature (Ury 2000, 2001; Richardson 2010) – needs to be kept in mind when we are trying to understand human behaviour.

- *Environment.* Heat and crowding appear to predispose people to get involved in conflicts (Kassin, Fein & Markus 2010).
- *Health.* It is often the case that the more tired and/or ill people are, the less tolerance they have for dispute, ambiguity, differences and variation from routine. They may thus be more prone to engage in conflict in such circumstances.

Not all conflicts are the same. The more we can differentiate between conflicts, the greater the chance of detecting patterns and understanding the underlying causes, and the greater the chance of reaching some solutions. Therefore, particular types of conflict can call forth different responses or approaches, such as those shown in table 14.2.

TABLE 14.2 Approaches to conflict

Approach	Examples
Avoidance or inaction	■ Do nothing; adopt a wait and see attitude: useful when conflict dies a natural death; not so useful when conflict continues ■ Ignoring insults, ultimatums
Withdrawal	■ Two nations withdraw diplomatic recognition ■ A spouse walks out of the house in a huff ■ A person becomes ill through the stress of a workplace conflict and stays home
Domination	■ One individual abusing another ■ Bullying ■ War ■ Driving the competition out of business

Capitulation	■ Giving in to the other side, either because defeat seems total, or in the expectation that this can be traded for another concession later, for example:
	  – someone says, 'You win'
	  – a defeated nation signs a peace treaty, even though it dislikes the terms of the treaty

Unilateral power play	■ Involves physical violence, strikes, civil disobedience, behind-the-scenes manoeuvres
Referral up the chain of command	■ Let the bosses, senior officers, or parents take care of it
Negotiation	■ Two parties sit down and try and reach agreement, usually by seeking common ground and trading concessions (e.g. 'if you do this, then I'll do that')
Mediation	■ A third party is brought in to help disputing parties; can advise, but cannot compel
Arbitration	■ A third party is brought in to help and has some power to compel a decision
Other alternative dispute resolution techniques	■ Ombudsman ■ Private judge ■ Expert evaluation
Litigation	■ Courtroom, with judge having substantial power to compel decisions; with or without jury

Diagnosing conflict

Let's begin to examine the dynamics of conflict in greater detail. Greenhalgh (1986, 2002) has analysed conflict into various dimensions or variables, and he suggests that the dimensions of a conflict determine whether it is easy to resolve or difficult to resolve (table 14.3).

TABLE 14.3 Conflict diagnostic model

	Viewpoint continuum	
Dimension	**Difficult to resolve**	**Easy to resolve**
Issue in question	Matter of principle	Divisible issue
Size of stakes	Large	Small
Interdependence of the parties	Zero sum	Positive sum
Continuity of interaction	Single transaction	Long-term relationship
Structure of the parties	Amorphous or fractionalised, with weak leadership	Cohesive, with strong leadership
Involvement of third parties	No neutral third party available	Trusted, powerful, prestigious and neutral
Perceived progress of the conflict	Unbalanced: one party feeling the more harmed	Parties having done equal harm to each other

Source: Greenhalgh, L. (1986, p. 47). 'Managing conflict', *Sloan Management Review*, Summer. © Sloan Management Review Association. Reproduced with permission of the publisher. All rights reserved.

If the *issue in question* in the conflict is divisible in some way, then the conflict becomes easier to solve. The parties can decide to take equal shares of a disputed resource, or the issue can be broken up into sequences or subissues, with the parties concentrating on the high priority ones and/or conceding on the low priority ones. If, however, the issue is a matter of principle, then resolution becomes much harder: principles by definition cannot be subdivided, and parties tend to polarise – taking extreme stands to defend their different principles, and making the (usually futile) attempt to convince the other side.

If the *size of the stakes* is small, then the parties will not waste much time disputing over them. When the stakes get bigger, people get more serious. The heat of the moment sometimes distorts perceptions, so that stakes which are objectively not all that high may appear to be very big indeed. Sometimes a cooling-off period can help remove such distortions. A relatively small stake can take on a big appearance when it is seen to be establishing a precedent. A method of neutralising this effect may be to stress that no precedent will be created, and that this is indeed just a one-off situation.

The *interdependence of the parties* is also critical. It is useful to classify outcomes in conflict situations according to the jargon of a branch of mathematics called *game theory*. This involves a strange world of zero-sum, negative sum, and positive-sum or win–win outcomes, and is looked at in chapter 13 (see 'Winning and losing: games and pies'). Take a minute to read that section.

Let's now look at the *continuity of interaction*. When two sides deal with each other over a prolonged period of time, a number of things happen. Interpersonal chemistry begins to develop, with both sides becoming familiar with – and possibly comfortable with – each other's communication style. Trust and goodwill build up, as does long-term reciprocity: we'll allow you to have this concession now, because we'll be meeting again soon, and we'll expect you to grant us something similar. These relationship factors can help smooth the path of interactions. If the interaction is episodic, or one-shot, however, most of these relationship factors are not present, and neither side has the incentive to accommodate each other. This can result in a 'no-holds-barred' situation, where the past and future interactions of the parties are seen as irrelevant.

The *structure of the parties* needs to be looked at. If leadership of a party is weak, then any decisions reached may be overturned or undermined by rebellious factions or subgroups. Thus, a management group may dislike dealing with a union with a strong leadership, because that strong leadership may drive a hard bargain; yet the management group may decide to be thankful it is dealing with a strong union leadership, as a weak leadership may lead to the still more expensive bargain of wildcat strikes and resistance to change.

The presence or absence of *third parties* can also help or hinder in a conflict. A third party, acting as a mediator, can help to develop options among and build bridges between warring parties, particularly if the third party is seen as being prestigious, powerful, trusted and neutral. The sheer presence of a third party can sometimes act as a brake on the behaviour of the parties, who otherwise might behave in a far less civilised manner. The absence of such a third party in some situations will be a serious barrier to resolving conflict.

Finally, the *perceived progress* of the conflict is an important factor. One of the most basic mechanisms of conflict is 'tit for tat' or 'we owe you one'. If an asymmetry or imbalance is perceived by one side, then conflict will not stop until revenge is gained/honour is restored/things are evened up, and so on. Such escalation can go on permanently, of course, when one or neither side perceives that a balance has finally been achieved. It is usually only when a side has sustained a lot of damage, and perceives that the other side has sustained equal damage, that resolution can begin. Figure 14.1 is a conflict analysis chart that gives a visual representation of the continuum introduced in table 14.3.

CONFLICT NO._____		DESCRIPTION OF CONFLICT: _____				
DIFFICULT TO RESOLVE						
Issue in question	**Size of stakes**	**Interdependence of the parties**	**Continuity of interaction**	**Structure of the parties**	**Involvement of third parties**	**Perceived progress of the conflict**
Matter of principle	Large	Zero sum	Single transaction	Amorphous or fractionalised, with weak leadership	No neutral third party available	Unbalanced: one party feeling the more harmed
|	|	|	|	|	|	|
|	|	|	|	|	|	|
Divisible issue	Small	Positive sum	Long-term relationship	Cohesive, with strong leadership	Trusted, poweful, prestigious and neutral	Parties having done equal harm to each other
Issue in question	**Size of stakes**	**Interdependence of the parties**	**Continuity of interaction**	**Structure of the parties**	**Involvement of third parties**	**Perceived progress of the conflict**
EASY TO RESOLVE						

FIGURE 14.1 Conflict analysis chart

Source: Greenhalgh, L. (1986). Adapted with permission of the publisher.

Conflict-handling styles

Just as there are different approaches to conflict, so too are there different personal styles of reaction to conflict (and the two are not unrelated). An understanding of personal styles of reaction to conflict can help us to understand whether our reactions help or hinder solutions to any given conflict situation.

Thomas and Kilmann have developed a useful model of people's reactions to conflict (Thomas 1976, 1992; Thomas, Thomas & Schaubert 2008; Ogunyemi, Fong, Elmore, Korwin & Azziz 2010). They argue that people tend to have one dominant style of conflict handling, out of a possible five styles:

1. competing
2. collaborating
3. compromising
4. avoiding
5. accommodating.

This model (figure 14.2) is based on different mixes of assertive/unassertive and cooperative/uncooperative behaviour. Assertive and unassertive behaviour (see 'Assertiveness' in chapter 9) tell us about a party's desire to satisfy his/her/their own concerns, whereas cooperative and uncooperative behaviour tell us about a party's desire to satisfy the concerns of others.

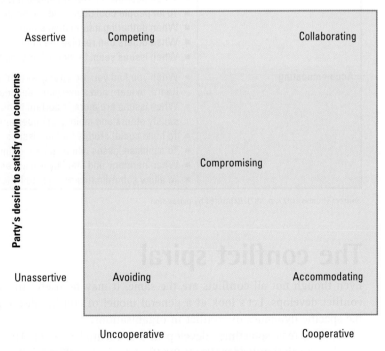

FIGURE 14.2 Conflict-handling styles
Source: Dunnette (1976, p. 900).

One style is not necessarily better than another. Each style has something to offer, depending on the situation (table 14.4; see overleaf). We may use one style in one situation and one in another. We may be happy with the style we tend to use most, or we may be quite unhappy about it. Different departments, organisations, families, professions and nations may have a preferred conflict-handling style.

TABLE 14.4 Analysis of conflict-handling styles

Conflict-handling style	When to use
Competing	▪ When quick, decisive action is vital (e.g. in emergencies) ▪ On important issues where unpopular actions need implementing (e.g. cost cutting, enforcing unpopular rules, discipline) ▪ On issues vital to company welfare when you know you're right ▪ Against people who take advantage of noncompetitive behaviour
Collaborating	▪ To find an integrative solution when both sets of concerns are too important to be compromised ▪ When your objective is to learn ▪ To merge insights from people with different perspectives ▪ To gain commitment by incorporating concerns into a consensus ▪ To work through feelings which have interfered with a relationship
Compromising	▪ When goals are important, but not worth the effort or potential disruption of more assertive modes ▪ When opponents with equal power are committed to mutually exclusive goals ▪ To achieve temporary settlements to complex issues ▪ To arrive at expedient solutions under time pressure ▪ As a backup when collaboration or competition is unsuccessful
Avoiding	▪ When an issue is trivial, or more important issues are pressing ▪ When you perceive no chance of satisfying your concerns ▪ When potential disruption outweighs the benefits of resolution ▪ To let people cool down and regain perspective ▪ When gathering information supersedes immediate decision ▪ When others can resolve the conflict more effectively ▪ When issues seem tangential or symptomatic of other issues
Accommodating	▪ When you find you are wrong — to allow a better position to be heard, to learn and show your reasonableness ▪ When issues are more important to others than to yourself, to satisfy others and maintain cooperation ▪ To build social credits for later issues ▪ To minimise losses when you are outmatched and losing ▪ When harmony and stability are especially important ▪ To allow subordinates to develop by learning from mistakes

Source: Thomas (1977, p. 487). Reprinted by permission.

The conflict spiral

Even though not all conflicts are the same, it may be useful to examine how a particular conflict develops. Let's look at a general model of conflict development, and then look at the specific dynamics of conflict in organisations.

Conflicts may sometimes develop in a sequential manner. The sequence is known as a spiral or escalation ladder (Pruitt 2009). A typical **conflict spiral** is seen in figure 14.3.

Conflict spiral: a fairly predictable developmental sequence of conflict events and perceptions

Not all conflicts develop in exactly this sequence – certain phases of the spiral may be skipped, or may occur in different orders, or entirely different phases may occur (Glaser 2000; Kydd 1997). How similar is this spiral to conflicts you have known? How might it be possible to reverse the spiral, so that the intensity of conflict might be lowered? How might it be possible to get out of the spiral, and to find a positive resolution of the conflict? How might we alert ourselves to the dangers of avoidance? Are there any circumstances where we might want to stay on the spiral, rather than get off?

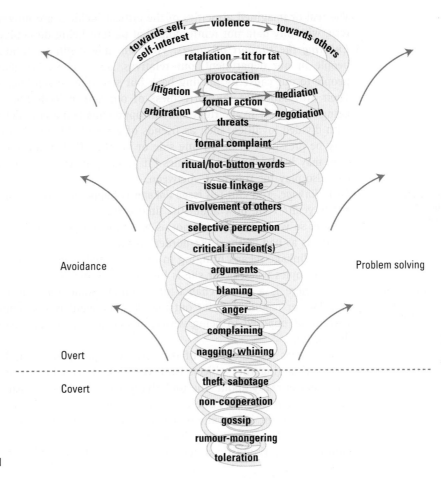

towards self, self-interest ← violence → towards others

retaliation – tit for tat

provocation

litigation → mediation

formal action

arbitration ↔ negotiation

threats

formal complaint

ritual/hot-button words

issue linkage

involvement of others

selective perception

critical incident(s)

arguments

blaming

anger

complaining

nagging, whining

Avoidance

Problem solving

Overt

Covert

theft, sabotage

non-cooperation

gossip

rumour-mongering

toleration

FIGURE 14.3 A conflict spiral

The spiral has two main zones: the overt and the covert. The covert zone is where the conflict has not yet emerged or erupted into public view. The overt zone is where the conflict does become public and direct. The sequence is as follows:

1. *Toleration.* At the very bottom of the spiral is toleration. The outcome of the conflict is accepted, but the acceptance is guarded, and not total.
2. *Covert resistance.* Moving up the spiral, we begin to see more resistance, albeit still of the covert variety. Patterns of employee resistance to conflict in organisations include gossip, noncooperation, theft and sabotage (Tucker 1993).
3. *Overt resistance.* We move now not only from the covert to the overt zone, but also from passivity to action. Once reaction to conflict is out in the open, the spiral moves through nagging and whining, through to complaining, to anger and then to arguments.
4. *Critical incidents.* Somewhere along the line, something happens that causes further polarisation. Such a **critical incident** can be an accident or part of an ongoing series of events. It may even be a provocation. Whatever the motivation, the incident or incidents become crystallising events that seem to reveal a pattern of ill feeling or hostility. Perception and labelling are vital here: a misunderstanding, a communication breakdown, a physical bump or nudge can be ignored or interpreted in the worst possible way.
5. *Selective perception.* **Selective perception** means that we tend to concentrate on the faults of our opponents, ignoring any virtues they or their arguments might have. We also concentrate on our virtues and our arguments, ignoring any shortcomings. In other words, we begin to filter or distort reality so that we can polarise the argument, with all evil on the other side, and all virtue on our own side (Pruitt & Kim 2004).

Critical incident: an event that is, or is perceived to be, significant in the escalation of a conflict

Selective perception: distorting or filtering reality so that conflict is polarised

The real or imagined atrocities of the critical incident are now definitely seen as a pattern, with any data not reinforcing that pattern being downplayed or ignored.

6. *Enlisting the support of others*. We then may begin to build a coalition of support: people in our department, our relatives, our friends. We may have recruited these people to our cause by playing back our selective perceptions or propaganda to them. Their affirmation of the correctness of our stance feeds back into our self-image of being completely in the right and our opponents being completely in the wrong. People with divided loyalties, such as friends of a couple involved in a divorce or separation, may be pressured to be on one side or another. If they do not accede to this pressure, they may be redefined as enemies ('if you're not with us, you're against us'), but they can also play the role of go-between.

7. *Issue linkage*. You can tell **issue linkage** is happening when you hear:
   - Oh, yeah? Well, how about the time you ...
   - Well, so what if I did? It's not as bad as when you ...
   - This is as bad as the 1987 border dispute.

   Issue linkage means bringing in other, related topics. Sometimes a person will bring in such topics when he or she is losing an argument and wants to shift it to an arena where there is a better chance of winning. Sometimes the linker is **building a case**, as a lawyer might, to point out that the opponent is systematically wrong or evil or corrupt, as opposed to being wrong or evil or corrupt on just the issue that is under discussion.

   Sometimes the relevance of the linkage is problematic, and the linker seems to be simply changing the subject. However, linkage can be a way of exposing what the argument is *really* about: the underlying conflict. This exposure may be done deliberately, to bring the real issue out into the open. It may also happen accidentally — by talking about the issues, the opposing sides stumble on the real issue.

8. *Ritual or hot-button words*. Ritual words are words or phrases indicating that the conflict has a ritualistic aspect to it, that we have been here before — perhaps too many times:
   - Don't start this again
   - That's so typical of you/men/accountants
   - Here we go again.

   Hot-button words are words that are charged with a particular emotion, value or prejudice that may trigger off rapid, unthinking responses on one or both sides
   - dismissal
   - industrial action
   - walking out
   - idiocy
   - white devil
   - bloody feminist
   - close down.

   Sometimes hot-button words sum up a situation succinctly; but otherwise, they can be real killers of coolheaded and creative problem solving (Evans & Cohen 2001).

9. *Threats*. Threats can be of violent or nonviolent action, but at this stage deeds do not match words. Threats can be letting off steam, empty posturing, face-saving or a real warning. Threats cost nothing if the threat does not have to be carried out. Brute force often fails because it may call forth a response, but threats may be adequate to secure compliance.

   Threats can be more effective in the short run than promises, because people are more motivated to avoid losses than to get rewards. Threateners can appear more powerful than promisors, because threats often contain more information about what is likely to happen — in other words, threats tend to be specific in terms of time frame

---

Issue linkage: linking issues that may or may not be connected, to strengthen a case

Building a case: developing an argument in a valid or invalid way to achieve persuasion

Hot-button words: words that are charged with a particular emotion, value or prejudice that may trigger off rapid, unthinking responses on one or both sides

and consequence, whereas promises are often more vague. Threateners can often win when they lose — that is, even when the threatener reneges on a threat, he or she may sometimes be seen as simply being humane and forgiving, powerful but compassionate, rather than weak and inconsistent. Promisors do not have this fall-back position.

The downside of threats is that they tend to elicit counter-threats, and we are off on the conflict spiral again. They tend to lead to compliance ('we'll have to do it') but rarely to commitment ('yes, let's do it!'). Those threatened tend to avoid the threatener and the arena in which the threats were made. This means a breakdown in communication, and in workplace settings this could mean a loss in productivity (Pruitt & Kim 2004).

10. *Action*. Formal action involves deliberate and structured routines, such as:
   - sitting down at a negotiating table
   - bringing in a third party or mediator
   - going into an industrial court for arbitration
   - going into a civil or criminal court for litigation
   - a couple taking time out from their pressured routines to sit down and talk.

   These approaches can be symbols of failure in the conflict resolution process, or they can lead to successful and permanent resolutions.

11. *Provocation*. **Provocation** — also known as coat-trailing, winding up or incitement — is deliberately teasing or needling someone, sometimes with a view to evoking a physically violent response. Provocations might be:
   - pushing, jostling, invading personal space
   - jeering, abuse
   - vandalism (car or house defaced)
   - departments in an organisation overloading each other with work
   - parking in someone else's spot, once only or repeatedly
   - conducting war games near another country's territory.

   Children, particularly siblings, are past masters of provocation, but children of all ages do it. Provocation may be accompanied by sarcastic or disingenuous protestations of innocence, particularly if it evokes retaliation ('He started it!' 'No, she started it!').

12. *Retaliation*. **Retaliation** initiates a cycle of tit-for-tat exchange, which is also the dynamic of revenge — like for like, an eye for an eye, a tooth for a tooth. Sometimes, however, the level of retaliation may be more than equal to what was dished out, or at least perceived to be. When the response is seen as disproportionate, this may call forth claims of unfairness, or conflict about conflict, or fighting about fighting.

13. *Violence*. Violence is sometimes justified; but more often than not, it's not. Violence in some circumstances can be further differentiated into violence towards others and violence towards self or self-interest. Violence towards oneself (or one's side, or to one's self-interest), if it happens at all, usually happens after violence towards others. It may take the form of an honourable or spiteful destruction of one's own resources to prevent others getting hold of them, to individual suicide with no further consequences, to catastrophic violence (everyone gets destroyed — a lose–lose situation (see 'Winning and losing: games and pies' in chapter 13).

Challenging the spiral

If it makes sense to get off the spiral (and it doesn't always), then critical reactions to different phases or levels of the spiral may help. Bear in mind that such critical reactions are easier if we are assertive and logical — refusing to blindly follow and resisting group pressures — and if those around us are the same. The second condition is harder to guarantee than the first, which may make the first condition all the harder to achieve.

Provocation: deliberately teasing or needling someone, sometimes with a view to evoking a physically violent response

Retaliation: reciprocal action in a conflict, where a real or perceived offence by one side is matched or surpassed by a real offence by the other side

When both conditions are achieved, then the wider situation – the group, the family, the workplace, the nation – is usually a pleasant place to be. When only one condition is achieved, then the world is an uncomfortable place for at least one person. Where neither condition is achieved, the world may still appear to be a pleasant place, but it is almost certainly heading, sooner or later, for a collision with reality. Table 14.5 shows some strategies appropriate to different parts of the conflict spiral.

TABLE 14.5 Strategies for getting off the conflict spiral

Spiral phase	Critical reaction
Covert resistance	Challenge the development of gossip, noncooperation, theft and sabotage
Overt resistance	Challenge nagging, whining, complaining, anger and arguments
Critical incidents	Challenge the unthinkingly negative interpretation of events and words
Selective perception	Challenge filtering or distorting perceptions of events and words
Enlisting support of others	Resist being recruited to an unthinking in-group; challenge those who wish to recruit
Issue linkage	Challenge whether issues really are linked
Ritual or hot-button words	Challenge the unthinking use of words and labels
Threats	Challenge the use of intimidation, pressure and bullying
Action	Encourage healthy structured actions; monitor to ensure transparency and effectiveness
Provocation	Challenge interpretation of events and words; resist or ignore incitement, hassling, needling and goading
Retaliation	Refuse to retaliate; or retaliate at a less intense level than might be otherwise expected; counsel others to do the same
Violence	Refuse to be violent towards self or self-interests; deflect or arrest violence of others by bringing in authorised third parties, such as respected elders, friends or police

ASSESS YOURSELF

Think back to a conflict situation you have been involved in, or are familiar with. Does the spiral model help explain what happened? Pick one or several of the strategies listed, and try to apply these to that situation. How effective might they have been?

Conflict in organisations

Let's now turn from the general dynamics of conflict spirals to the specific dynamics of conflict in organisations. Conflict in organisations occurs in four major patterns (Schermerhorn 2010):

1. **Vertical conflict** occurs between hierarchical levels, often between top management and middle management, middle managers and supervisors, and supervisors and subordinates. Conflicts are usually over resources, goals, deadlines or performance results.
2. **Horizontal conflict** occurs between people working at the same hierarchical level within an organisation. Conflicts are usually over incompatible goals, real or perceived scarcity of resources and territory, and interpersonal chemistry.
3. **Staff–line conflict** occurs between people performing different types of tasks. Line personnel are front-line staff, directly involved in the production of goods and services, such

Vertical conflict: conflict that occurs in organisations between people at different hierarchical levels

Horizontal conflict: conflict that occurs in organisations between people at the same hierarchical level

Staff–line conflict: conflict that occurs in organisations between people doing front-line and backup tasks

as assembly-line workers and supervisors, and clerks and analysts. Staff personnel are specialist staff who are there to back up line personnel. Staff jobs would include human resources, data processing and legal advisers. Conflicts might arise over issues such as promotion and appraisal, and access to specialised computer hardware and software.

4. **Role conflict** might occur when misunderstandings arise over just what it is that a person is meant to be doing. These intrapersonal and interpersonal conflicts can be caused by employees having incomplete, out-of-date or nonexistent job descriptions, reporting to more than one manager or supervisor, or receiving multiple and conflicting requests and orders.

These types of organisational conflict are shown in figure 14.4.

Role conflict: conflict that occurs in organisations when there are misunderstandings about what duties and behaviour are expected from persons

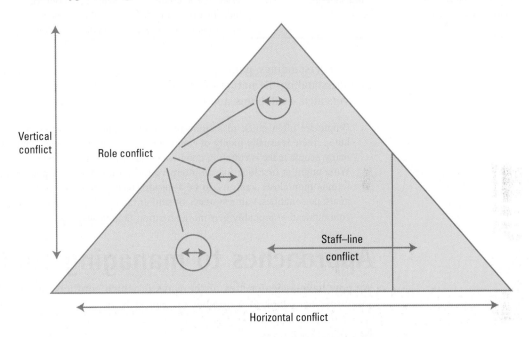

FIGURE 14.4 Some types of organisational conflict

There are also other factors which, when operating in organisations, may lead to conflict situations.

Resource scarcity: conflict that occurs in organisations when resources are, or are perceived to be, scarce

Workflow interdependence: conflict that occurs in organisations when the output of one section is the input of another, and mismatches occur

Power/value asymmetry: conflict that occurs in organisations between people with differing values and/or status

Goal incompatibility: conflict that occurs in organisations when the specific goals of different sections do not match

- **Resource scarcity.** When organisational resources are scarce (or perceived to be scarce), conflict will occur, as surely as animals will fight over scarce food. This may be exacerbated in hard times, when the resource pool is seen to be shrinking.

- **Workflow interdependence.** When the workflow is tightly coupled or closely interdependent, then all sections depend on each other. This means that all sections benefit from the efficiencies of other sections, but are vulnerable to and suffer from the inefficiencies of others. Buffering mechanisms, such as stockpiles, are less prevalent today with total quality practices, such as just-in-time manufacturing and processing (whereby one sector works on the raw materials or partly-processed product needed by the 'internal customer' in the next sector, and delivers it with a minimal amount of leeway or tolerance of delay).

- **Power and/or value asymmetry.** When a high-status person works with a low-status person, and is uncomfortable about it, or when people holding radically different values are required to work together, conflict may occur. This conflict also occurs when a person with high power refuses to help a person with low power.

- **Goal incompatibility.** When specific goals of differing departments, sections and divisions of the one organisation clash, even though they share the overall goal of the organisation, conflict may occur. Examples are shown in figure 14.5.

Department	Department's goal	Department's goal	Department
Purchasing	Seek efficiencies by buying in large quantities to minimise purchase frequencies	Want small inventories to keep costs down	Finance
Production	Want a limited number of products, few production disruptions	Want a variety of products to attract more customers	Marketing
Marketing	Want liberal credit policies in order to sell to marginal customers	Want conservative credit policies to minimise bad debts	Credit

FIGURE 14.5 Clashing goals within organisations

Source: Adapted from Robbins, Bergman, Stagg and Coulter (2009).

Misunderstandings, game-playing and a range of other communication patterns are vital to understanding the nature of organisational conflict. Yet the role of communication can be overstated, as Robbins and Coulter (2004, p. 551) have observed:

People are often quick to assume that most conflicts are caused by lack of communication, but ... there is usually plenty of communication going on in most conflicts ... The mistake that many people make is equating good communication with having others agree with their views. What might at first look like an interpersonal conflict based on poor communication is usually found, upon closer analysis, to be a disagreement caused by different role requirements, unit goals, personalities, value systems, or similar factors. As a source of conflict for managers, poor communication probably gets more attention than it deserves.

Approaches to managing conflict

We now have a clearer idea of the ways in which conflicts can develop. What, then, of the solutions? Let's look at a number of approaches.

Negotiation

Negotiation means different things to different people, but generally it is taken to mean interaction between two sets of individuals, groups or nations to settle disagreements through compromises and concessions (see chapter 13). Behavioural ploys, known as strategies and tactics, are sometimes important parts of the negotiation process. Negotiation tends to be used when (Bercovitch & Jackson 2001):

- conflicts are relatively simple
- conflicts are of a low intensity
- both parties are relatively equal in power.

Interpersonal skills

Interpersonal skills, used either singly or in combination, can do much to reduce tension and build bridges between people in conflict. Such skills include assertiveness, listening, questioning, framing or problem defining, and influencing skills.

Cultural and gender differences

Conflicts can sometimes be understood in terms of the gender and the culture of the people involved. Our understanding of these factors is still in its early stages, but what we do know should be used to shed light on just what is going on in a conflict situation (see chapter 15).

Group dynamics

Group dynamics can help us understand much about conflict. Groups, teams or meetings are often the crucibles of conflict – they can help conflict be managed in healthy ways, or they can exacerbate conflict by imposing a crippling conformity and creating the pre-conditions for bad decision making and problem solving.

Contact and communication

Usually it helps to simply get the sides to a conflict together. When they at least start talking to and listening to each other, then there is a chance that both sides will understand the motivations, fears and needs of the other side. Antagonists may even get to like, or at least respect, each other. Contact and communication does not always work: antagonists may use contacts to simply reiterate threats or to trick the other side.

Superordinate goals

Superordinate goal: a goal that can be worked towards by all parties to a conflict

A **superordinate goal** is something that both sides in a conflict can work on together – indeed, it may be that such a goal can be achieved *only* if both sides work together (Putnam, Burgess & Royer 2003; Richter, Scully & West 2005). Sometimes fear and self-interest are the only things that will motivate people to cooperate. If a threat can be created, or an existing threat can be made to appear more real, then conflict may be redirected towards that threat. It is a sign of an organisation in trouble, for example, when warring factions prefer to fight each other rather than the common enemy.

Superordinate goals can be thought of for virtually every occasion. When Russia and the United States realised that nuclear weapons made nuclear war unwinnable, the doctrine of Mutually Assured Destruction (MAD) was developed. This type of war could not be win–lose in outcome, only lose–lose. Therefore both sides had incentives to move towards a détente or partial disarmament. Similarly, Britain and the United States had been hostile towards Russia in the 1930s, but formed an alliance with that country against the Axis powers (Germany, Italy and Japan) in World War II. Science-fiction writers and political analysts sometimes speculate that the only way to stop countries fighting each other is to create or encounter a superordinate goal that will involve the complete effort of all against a common enemy, such as an alien invasion, or a meteorite shower that could damage or eliminate life from the planet. Uniting against a common enemy means united we stand, divided we fall.

At the interpersonal level, a superordinate goal strategy for couples in conflict may be to have a child (although this may not mean success). Within organisations, it is all too common to see territorial and demarcation disputes between departments, teams, divisions, buildings, offices and regions. Perhaps the only thing that can motivate the disputants to bury their differences is the threat of them all being 'buried' commercially by a new player in the marketplace who threatens everyone's job by offering superior goods and services.

Superordinate goals do not work when one party thinks that it can still achieve a win–lose outcome – for example, by a sneak attack or pre-emptive strike against the other party. They also do not work when the other side does not see the rationality of shared survival.

Tit for tat

One of the most basic strategies of human interaction, as we have seen with the conflict spiral, is that of tit for tat: if you do that, then I will do it back to you. It is the basis of much hostility and violence, such as paybacks, an eye for an eye, and vengeance. If both sides could agree on who started the interchange, then it may be possible to put an end to tit for tat: 'now, we're even'. Just who started it is, however, often a matter of perception.

Tit for tat can, however, work with cooperation as well as hostility. An act of kindness or love may be returned or reciprocated. In fact, hesitation in reciprocating – hostility as

GRIT: acronym for graduated and reciprocated initiatives in tension reduction, a conflict resolution method

well as positive regard — may induce further cooperation, because it shows that the hesitating party is thinking about a response rather than simply acting on reflex.

A related strategy is that of **GRIT** — graduated and reciprocated initiatives in tension reduction. Developed in the 1950s as an approach to deal with the Cold War, it has applications in a variety of situations. GRIT works by managing the conflict through a number of phases (Folger, Poole & Stutman 2008; Lindskold 1979; Morgan 2006):

1. Set the climate for conciliatory initiatives by making a general statement of intention to reduce tension through subsequent acts, indicating the advantages to the other of reciprocating.
2. Announce publicly each unilateral move prior to making it and indicate that it is part of a general strategy.
3. Each announcement should invite reciprocation from the other. Reciprocation needn't come in the form of the same move but should be a conciliatory step of some sort.
4. Each initiative must be carried out as announced without any requirement of reciprocation by the other.
5. Initiatives should be continued for some time even if the other does not reciprocate. This gives the other a chance to test the party's sincerity and also puts pressure on the other.
6. Initiatives must be unambiguous and permit verification.
7. Initiatives must be risky and vulnerable to exploitation, but they also must not expose the party to a serious and damaging attack.
8. Moves should be graded in degree of risk to match the reciprocation of the other. Once the other begins to reciprocate, the initiator should reciprocate with at least as risky or slightly more risky moves.

GRIT obviously involves risk, but it can be used by one side to break deadlocks without appearing weak or appearing to give in. Kudos can also go to the first side to initiate GRIT because it may appear magnanimous and statesmanlike.

De-escalation thresholds

As a conflict can escalate or spiral, so too can it de-escalate. The study of many conflicts in different situations reveals that there may be certain thresholds in de-escalation processes. Not all of these thresholds apply to each conflict we may encounter, but some of them might. Typical de-escalation thresholds include (Mitchell 1999):

- Opening a new channel of communication
- Change in rhetoric to describe the conflict system
- Suspension or alteration of a coercive ban, limitation or sanction
- Where disputants have been imprisoned, a change in the status of the captives (e.g. imprisoning them in 'home' zones or areas, or exiling them as an alternative to trial and/or imprisonment)
- Change of office-holders or leaders
- Public acknowledgement of some responsibility for existence and continuation of conflict
- Informal recognition of adversary's existence and the leader's right of representation
- Modifying or abandoning aspects of the ideology that justifies initiation of contentious goals or coercive actions
- Temporary cessation of violent coercion in a limited area
- Permission for, or participation in, informal discussion about solutions.

Apology

If one side simply decides to apologise to the other, then that may be all that is needed to settle a conflict, especially if the other side is suffering from wounded pride and loss of face. The party making the apology has to determine whether:

- the apology is too humiliating a move to make

- the other side has the good grace to simply and quietly accept the apology
- the other side may even reciprocate an apology
- the other side sees the apology as a sign of weakness, defeat and admission of complete responsibility, and then crows about it, wishing to rub it in still further (causing a further loss of face).

Forgiveness

If an apology is sometimes seen as a strategy of weakness, then forgiveness is usually seen as a strategy of strength. Often motivated by religious or ethical beliefs, forgiveness is another way of wiping the slate clean, of abandoning tit for tat. This may sometimes be the only solution in situations where guilt for past misdeeds is so distributed throughout the community or nation (such as in post-apartheid South Africa) that an impartial and neutral application of the law might be impossible or might lead to more people being inside jails than outside.

Praise

Another strategy of strength is praise. Everyone likes praise, and in breaking deadlocks, praise can be particularly effective in that it can take the edge off any perceived backdown. In the Cuban missile crisis of 1962, the North American side was quick to publicly praise the statesmanlike behaviour of the Russians, after the Russians were constrained to remove their missiles from Cuba. *Public* praise is the key factor: the witnessing world is asked to applaud a dignified retreat, and the retreater therefore gains considerable kudos and minimises loss of face.

Sacrifice

Sacrifice simply means giving in, and giving till it hurts. The sacrificing party may be seen to be in a position of weakness, but from another point of view may be seen to be in a position of moral or ethical superiority.

New resources

If a conflict is over limited resources, try to create new ones. These might be real or symbolic, such as new locations, markets, jobs, job titles, rewards, perks, productivity-linked bonuses or reclaimed wasteland for territory.

Decoupling and buffering

The terms 'decoupling' and 'buffering' here simply mean physically separating the warring factions so that interdependence is minimised or eliminated. For example, a demilitarised zone may be created between warring nations or regions; two children squabbling may be sent to different rooms; two departments feuding with each other may have their workflow patterns changed, with inventories of stock being built up so that one cannot easily deprive the other of critical inputs (Hallett & Ventresca 2006).

Formal authority

The traditional method of using authority has much to recommend it. Conflicted parties must, of course, recognise the authority: be it the police, the United Nations, a workplace boss with power over feuding departments or a parent dealing with squabbling children. The threat of sanctions – coercion, arrest, violence, dismissal, no food, cancellation of allowances or withdrawal of privileges – needs to be credible for this to work.

Planning

Use technically clean, authoritative and neutral means of sequencing tasks to be performed by different areas, and allocate resources among contesting parties. In organisations, for example, rational techniques – such as the critical path method, Gantt charts and other project management tools – can perform this function.

Scale

Match the scale of the solution to the nature of the situation. A small-scale pilot program or test is preferable if the consequences of the solution are small. If the pilot fails, it fails; but if it succeeds, it creates a model that can then be copied. In this way, the solution spreads to all.

However, if the consequences for the participants are great – that is, they risk being discriminated against, victimised or made the target of violence – then they need to be protected, and protection may exist in large-scale operations. Blalock (1989) notes that in any given side of a conflict, those who hold extremist views are likely to be hostile to those who hold moderate views and who would, therefore, be more likely to compromise (or 'collaborate') with the other side and bring the conflict to an end. (Indeed, extremists may find it more beneficial to keep conflict going than to end it – the paradox may be that extremists on both sides have more in common with each other than with the moderates on their own sides, and leaders are thus part of the problem rather than part of the solution.)

Any pilot or small-scale programs that encourage cooperation, compromise and problem solving between moderates on either side are probably doomed to failure if the consequences are great – extremists will ostracise, ridicule, pressure, victimise or kill the cooperators. This targeting behaviour can only work on a small scale, however. If extremists attack their own moderates on a large scale, then the legitimacy of the extremists collapses. Therefore, conflict may (not will) be settled if there is a large enough resource pool to motivate a large number of real and potential moderates on both sides to cooperate. For example, if a fund of one million dollars was set aside to fund cooperative ventures between potential cooperators in a conflict (e.g. Palestinians/Israelis, Rwandan Hutus/Tutsis, Cypriot Greeks/Turks, Irish Catholics/Protestants), then such a pilot scheme would probably fail, as cooperators would be too obvious and would not benefit from any safety in numbers. If a fund of several orders of magnitude greater (one billion, ten billion) was available, however, then the dynamics might well change, as the safety in numbers phenomenon might be used to undercut the motives and ability of extremists to prolong the conflict.

Stalemates

Pruitt and Kim (2004) suggest that escalation of conflict usually stops for one of five possible reasons:

1. One side overwhelms the other (e.g. one child takes a bicycle away from the other)
2. One side takes unilateral advantage of the other (e.g. one child takes the bicycle and rides off with it)
3. One side yields (e.g. one child hands the bicycle over to the other)
4. One side avoids the conflict (e.g. one child surrenders the bicycle because of lack of interest or some other reason, turning to other things)
5. Both sides reach a **stalemate** (e.g. neither child can beat the other).

A stalemate (impasse or deadlock) occurs because of one or all of four reasons (Pruitt & Kim 2004):

1. Contentious tactics have failed – each side knows the other too well, and can counter any move in advance.

Stalemate: the phase in a conflict when all parties seem unable to move to a solution; also known as a deadlock or impasse

2. Resources have become exhausted. Energy, money and time are not as plentiful as they were at the outset of the conflict.
3. Social support is diminishing. Backers, principals, allies, friends, cheer squads are not as enthusiastic, and may withdraw emotional and material support.
4. Costs have become unacceptable. Physical damage and/or haemorrhaging bank balances demonstrate that the current level of conflict is unsustainable.

Therefore, a stalemate need not be a 'bad thing' and can, in fact, be beneficial in certain situations. It may be sound strategy, in some circumstances, to try and *create* or *increase* the four factors that lead to stalemate in order to force de-escalation. Mayer (2000) proposes the following constructive approaches to stalemates or impasses:

- Accept impasses as normal, and don't presume that the fault must lie with the behaviour or personalities of one or both or all involved in a conflict. This distracts attention from the problem itself, and leads people to think that the impasse is the problem.
- People have good reasons for being at an impasse. A person may feel that there is no other choice at a particular stage of a conflict but that of impasse. Learn to respect this perception.
- Disputants have to find their own way through an impasse. Third parties such as mediators need to be careful about stepping in to break a deadlock or impasse, because this may relieve those in conflict of the responsibility of finding a way out of the impasse themselves.
- An impasse is a natural and often helpful part of the conflict process. It is often only the threat of impasse that forces people to see the conflict in a more realistic way. Indeed, some may not even see that a conflict exists until an impasse is reached.
- In an impasse, slower is usually faster. Deadlines sometimes have to be met, but it is often a mistake to apply pressure by imposing artificial deadlines. When time seems abundant, and not scarce, then people can become more flexible, imaginative and realistic. When pressure is applied, those inside the process may feel that compromise is in fact capitulation rather than a reasonable outcome.

Compromise

Compromise, or 'splitting the difference', is perhaps the most commonly used form of conflict resolution (see '8. Workable compromise' in chapter 9). Its intuitive appeal is powerful, but its weaknesses are not so apparent.

Splitting the difference works fairly well in situations involving quantitative things that can be meaningfully divided, where the difference between the two sides is not large, and where there is time pressure to settle. As a tactic, however, it can cause a lot of problems. People will tend to ask for much more than they would normally, mainly because they expect the final outcome to be about halfway between what one side says it wants and what the other side says it wants. In negotiation situations, splitting the difference is sometimes also used by experienced negotiators who are trying to conceal their own weak position, and by inexperienced negotiators who do not know what they are doing, prepare badly and open with a ridiculous position.

Fisher and Ury (1991, pp. 6–7) suggest that this approach doesn't work very well because:

- it produces unwise agreements. The more you defend your position, the more committed you become to it. Your ego becomes involved and you can't back down because to do so would mean a loss of face. Energy is now spent reconciling future actions with past positions.
- it is inefficient. By taking extreme opening positions, deceiving the other side as to true intents, and making small concessions, both sides set themselves up for a long, drawn-out process. The more extreme the opening positions and the smaller the

concessions, the more time and effort it will take to discover whether or not agreement is possible. Both sides have incentives to stall and engage in theatrics such as threatening to walk out.

- it endangers an ongoing relationship. It sets up conflicts as battles of will, and generates stress and bitterness.

Splitting the difference can therefore be lowest-common-denominator decision making. It may create more problems than it solves.

Mediation

Mediation involves a third party taking an active role in seeking solutions to a conflict between two parties. Mediation can be conducted informally by amateur mediators, or formally by professional mediators (Herrman 2006; Boulle & Nesic 2010).

Disputing parties may choose a mediator themselves, or may be instructed or compelled to seek mediation as an option to be explored before pursuing more structured action, such as arbitration or litigation. A mediator typically will conduct a number of sessions with both or all disputants present. The mediator may also find it useful to conduct private meetings, or caucuses, with individual disputants. Sometimes the mediator may practise 'shuttle diplomacy' — moving back and forth between private meetings, developing options with one party, and then offering those options to the other party.

Mediators may provide some type of structure for discussions, by generating options and issues on a board or on paper. They may even try and get informal agreement from disputants, or get them to sign a written agreement about just what was agreed to. Such an agreement will probably not have legal force, but can be a useful ritual, emphasising the commitment disputants need to make, and may in fact be referred to should the dispute still continue beyond the mediation process. Mediators may work for free or for a fee, and may require disputants to sign a contract prior to the commencement of the process.

Mediators

Mediators come from all walks of life. Some are lawyers, some are counsellors, some are psychologists, and some are lay people with little or no training or who have undergone specific mediation skills training. The ideal mediator should be:

- neutral and impartial
- appropriately assertive
- skilled in various interpersonal and communication skills, such as active listening, questioning, reframing and presentation
- skilled in generating options, alternatives, solving problems
- familiar with processes such as negotiation
- knowledgeable about appropriate legal and procedural factors
- comfortable with others expressing strong emotions
- accepting of disputants who may sometimes make the mediator a scapegoat or focus for frustration or aggression
- aware that some disputants will try to manipulate the process to achieve a favoured position.

A weak approach?

Some people might view the fact that a mediator has no power to compel an agreement — to force the disputants to settle, one way or another — as proof that mediation is then a weak and flawed approach. However, mediation's weakness can be its strength — when things are not going terribly well, a mediator can point out to the disputants that if they cannot reach settlement of their own free will, then the conflict may shift to arenas where they will have much less control, much less confidentiality, and perhaps considerably more expense – such as arbitration or litigation (Phillips 2006–2007). In other words, there are strong incentives to stay within a 'weak' process.

Mediation will probably fail in situations where:

- one party wants to delay the dispute for as long as possible
- one party is unwilling to honour basic guidelines (e.g. by attempting to intimidate the other party)
- one or both parties are dealing in bad faith, and misrepresenting facts or a commitment to mediate
- the dispute involves a question of law, where one or both parties need to set a precedent
- domestic violence or fear of violence is suspected; or where a party indicates agreement, not out of a free will, but out of fear of the other party
- there is suspicion or proof of child abuse or sexual abuse
- there is evidence of a party having serious psychological problems
- the parties are so bitter and conflict ridden that they are unable to separate their own emotions and feelings from the actual dispute – the 'all-or-nothing' dispute
- parties reach illegal agreements (e.g. tax evasion, breach of health and safety standards)
- parties reach a 'sweetheart deal' in which an unsuspecting third party or the community in general is disadvantaged
- the actual dynamics of the process inflames conflict rather than healing it. (Wade 1994; Lim 2002).

Conflict creation

If we find ourselves on a conflict spiral, do we necessarily want to get off? In most circumstances, we probably do, because the conflict building before our eyes appears to be primarily negative in tone and in potential outcome. In some situations, however, we may make a judgement that the conflict may well do more good than bad – for example, in a just war, or in a workplace situation where a confrontation is unavoidable, or in a personal relationship where a showdown may be required to clear the air. Where *more*, rather than *less*, conflict is needed, then it makes sense to sit back and let the explosion occur, or to help it along. For example, Robbins (1978) has suggested that organisations that are stagnating and not performing well may be in need of more, not less, conflict (figure 14.6).

---

1. Are you surrounded by 'yes' people?
2. Are subordinates afraid to admit ignorance and uncertainties to you?
3. Is there so much concentration by decision makers on reaching a compromise that they may lose sight of values, long-term objectives or the organisation's welfare?
4. Do managers believe that it is in their best interest to maintain the impression of peace and cooperation in their unit, regardless of the price?
5. Is there an excessive concern by decision makers for not hurting the feelings of others?
6. Do managers believe that popularity is more important for obtaining rewards than competence and high performance?
7. Are managers unduly enamoured of obtaining consensus in their decisions?
8. Do employees show unusually high resistance to change?
9. Is there a lack of new ideas?
10. Is there an unusually low level of employee turnover?

FIGURE 14.6 Is conflict stimulation needed?

Source: Robbins (1978, p. 71). Copyright 1978 by The Regents of the University of California. Reprinted from the *California Management Review*, vol. 21, no. 2. By permission of The Regents.

Robbins and Coulter (2007) distinguish between *functional conflict* (conflict that sweeps stagnation away, allowing creativity to flow) and *dysfunctional conflict* (conflict that explodes out of control, destroying all creativity). To distinguish between the two is obviously tricky, yet Robbins and Coulter suggest that managers have to make the effort, and create or stimulate conflict if the organisation is to flourish and not stagnate (figure 14.7). These approaches to conflict resolution and creation can be quite effective within organisations, and they are generally applicable to international politics and interpersonal relationships.

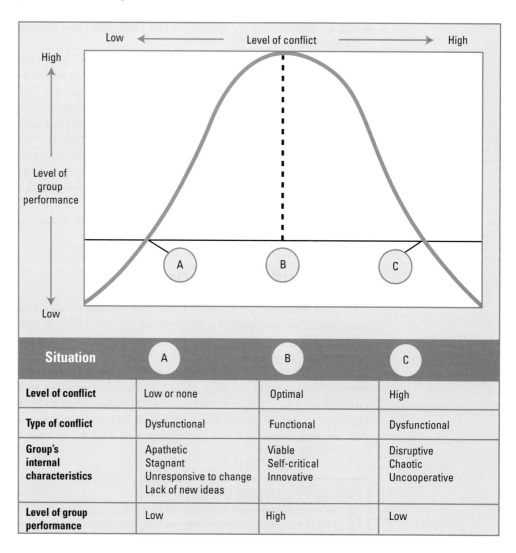

FIGURE 14.7 Conflict and organisational performance

Source: Robbins and Coulter (2007, p. 436).

Situation	A	B	C
Level of conflict	Low or none	Optimal	High
Type of conflict	Dysfunctional	Functional	Dysfunctional
Group's internal characteristics	Apathetic Stagnant Unresponsive to change Lack of new ideas	Viable Self-critical Innovative	Disruptive Chaotic Uncooperative
Level of group performance	Low	High	Low

STUDENT STUDY GUIDE

SUMMARY

Conflict can be a very destructive force, but it can also prove to be a creative and positive one if managed correctly. There are multiple causes of conflict, numerous ways of approaching conflicts and different styles of reacting to or managing conflict. Conflict can sometimes be understood as a spiral, or ladder of escalation, with distinct phases. Within organisations, conflict can also be understood in terms of a number of underlying dynamics. Conflict management solutions include negotiation, interpersonal skills, gender and cultural dynamics, group dynamics, contact and communication, superordinate goals, tit for tat, de-escalation thresholds, apology, forgiveness, praise, sacrifice, creation of new resources, decoupling and buffering, formal authority, planning, appropriate scale, stalemates, compromise and mediation. Conflict can be dysfunctional or functional — dysfunctional conflict needs to be minimised or eliminated and functional conflict may need to be increased or created.

KEY TERMS

building a case *p. 452*

conflict management *p. 445*

conflict resolution *p. 445*

conflict spiral *p. 450*

critical incident *p. 451*

goal incompatibility *p. 455*

GRIT *p. 458*

horizontal conflict *p. 454*

hot-button words *p. 452*

issue linkage *p. 452*

power/value asymmetry *p. 455*

provocation *p. 453*

resource scarcity *p. 455*

retaliation *p. 453*

role conflict *p. 455*

selective perception *p. 451*

staff–line conflict *p. 454*

stalemate *p. 460*

superordinate goal *p. 457*

vertical conflict *p. 454*

workflow interdependence *p. 455*

REVIEW QUESTIONS

1. Identify at least three positive payoffs or consequences of conflict.
2. List at least three causes of conflict.
3. Explain the differences between five conflict-handling styles.
4. Describe at least four consecutive levels on the conflict spiral.
5. Identify at least two causes of conflict in organisations.
6. Identify at least four different approaches to conflict.
7. Explain the differences and similarities between conflict management and negotiation.
8. Under what circumstances might conflict creation be needed?

APPLIED ACTIVITIES

1. Consider the pros and cons of conflict. Try to think of at least one other pro and one other con.
2. Refer back to figure 14.1, and make two copies of this figure. You can graphically analyse a conflict with this chart by first drawing crosses or checkpoints at the appropriate points (e.g. *Size of stakes* – large; *Interdependence of the parties* – positive sum), and then connecting up these crosses or checkpoints. This should result in a profile of the conflict. Some of the dimensions can only have extreme values (e.g. *issue in question*), but some can have partial values (e.g. *size of stakes*). Some dimensions may not be appropriate for all conflicts. Compare the profiles of the two conflicts. How do they differ? How are they similar? What is needed to shift the conflict profiles from the *difficult to resolve* side to the *easy to resolve* side?

3. What problems might there be in using terms like 'conflict resolution' and 'conflict management'?
4. Consider the Thomas–Kilmann conflict styles (table 14.4). Discuss what styles you feel that you, your friends, colleagues and family members might have.
5. Working in groups, write scripts for critical reactions to conflict spiral phases.
6. Think of an organisation you are familiar with. What types of conflict patterns are present there?
7. Is this organisation in need of conflict stimulation? If so, how could this best be achieved?
8. Analyse a conflict you are familiar with using the analysis chart. Jot down some approaches that might work, bearing in mind that not all approaches will be applicable to all situations. Try to devise as many different solutions to the situation as you can think of. Might any of the solutions be mutually exclusive (i.e. in conflict with each other)? Might any of the solutions be meaningfully combined?

Describe the conflict situation:	The people involved are:
APPROACH	**WHAT MIGHT WORK**
Negotiation	
Interpersonal skills	
Gender and cultural differences	
Group dynamics	
Contact and communication	
Superordinate goals	
Tit for tat	
De-escalation thresholds	
Apology	
Forgiveness	
Praise	
Sacrifice	
New resources	
Decoupling and buffering	
Formal authority	
Planning	
Scale	
Stalemates	
Compromise	
Mediation	
Conflict creation	

There appear to be a number of underlying tensions and hostilities within your workgroup at a leading graphic design studio. As a recent recruit, you feel it is the right thing to do

to point this out to Julie, the group supervisor. You enthusiastically suggest that perhaps she should talk individually to each of the members to find out what the issues are. She isn't sympathetic to this suggestion, and says, 'Look, conflict is just part of life. "If you can't stand the heat, get out of the kitchen" – that's my motto. I don't want to intervene; I want to let things boil, and see who comes out on top. That's the way you identify people with real potential – the leaders of tomorrow. Survival of the fittest, right? I got to where I am now by not chickening out when the pressure was on. I suggest you do the same if you want to get on around here!'

What will you say to Julie?

SUGGESTED READING

Astor, Hilary & Chinkin, Christine M 2002, *Dispute resolution in Australia*, 2nd edn, LexisNexis Butterworths, Sydney.

Eunson, Baden 1997, *Dealing with conflict*, John Wiley & Sons, Brisbane.

Keddy, Jackie and Johnson, Clive 2011, *Managing conflict at work: understanding and resolving conflict for productive working relationships*, Kogan Page, London.

Savage, Sara, and Boyd-Macmillan, Eolene 2011, *Conflict in relationships: understand it, overcome it: at home, at work, at play*, Lion Books, Oxford.

Tagar, Michal Reifen, Federico, Christopher M & Halperin, Eran 2011, 'The positive effect of negative emotions in protracted conflict: the case of anger', *Journal of Experimental Social Psychology*, vol. 47, no. 1, pp. 157–64.

REFERENCES

Barrett, Deidre 2010, *Supernormal stimuli: how primal urges overran their evolutionary purpose*, W.W. Norton and Company, New York.

Bercovitch, Jacob & Jackson, Richard 2001, 'Negotiation or mediation? An exploration of factors affecting the choice of conflict management in international conflict', *Negotiation Journal*, vol. 17, no. 1, pp. 59–77.

Blalock, Hubert M 1989, *Power and conflict: toward a general theory*, Sage, Newbury Park, CA.

Blomberg, S Brock & Hess, Gregory D 2002, 'The temporal links between conflict and economic activity', *Journal of Conflict Resolution*, vol. 46, no. 1, pp. 74–91.

Boulle, Laurence & Nesic, Miryana 2010, *Mediator skills and techniques: the triangle of influence*, Bloomsbury, London.

Brizendine, Louann 2010, *The male brain*, Broadway Books, New York.

Dunnette, Marvin D 1976, *Handbook of industrial and organizational psychology*, Rand McNally, Chicago.

Evans, Sybil & Cohen, Sherry Suib 2001, *Hot buttons: how to resolve conflict and cool everyone down*, HarperCollins, New York.

Fisher, Roger & Ury, William 1991, *Getting to yes: negotiating an agreement without giving in*, 2nd edn, Penguin, New York.

Folger, Joseph P, Poole, Marshall Scott & Stutman, Randall K 2008, *Working through conflict: strategies for relationships, groups and organizations*, 6th edn, HarperCollins, New York.

Greenhalgh, Leonard 1986, 'Managing conflict', *Sloan Management Review*, vol. 27, no.4, pp. 45–51.

—— 2002, 'Managing anxiety in negotiated decision-making', *Social Science Electronic Publishing*, http://papers.ssrn.com.

Hallett, Tim & Ventresca, Marc J 2006, 'How institutions form: loose coupling as mechanism in Gouldner's patterns of industrial bureaucracy', *The American Behavioral Scientist*, vol. 49, no. 7, pp. 908–4.

Hampton, Simon J 2010, *Essential evolutionary psychology*, Sage, Los Angeles/London/ New Delhi.

Herrman, Margaret S (ed.) 2006, *Blackwell handbook of mediation: bridging theory, research and practice*, Blackwell, Malden, MA.

Hollier, Fiona, Murray, Kerrie & Cornelius, Helena 2008, *CR trainer's manual*, 2nd edn, Conflict Resolution Network, Chatswood, NSW.

Huffman, Karen 2009, *Psychology in action*, 9th edn, John Wiley & Sons, New York.

Glaser, Charles L 2000, 'The causes and consequences of arms races', *Annual Review of Political Science*, vol. 3, pp. 251–76.

Kassin, Saul, Fein, Steven & Markus, Hazel Rose 2010, *Social psychology*, 8th edn, Wadsworth/Cengage, Belmont, CA.

Kydd, Andrew 1997, 'Game theory and the spiral model', *World Politics*, vol. 49, no. 3, pp. 371–400.

Lim, Lan Yuan 2002, 'Resolving conflicts in neighbourhood contexts', *Australasian Dispute Resolution Journal*, vol. 13, no. 1, February.

Lindskold, Svenn 1979, 'Managing conflict through announced conciliatory initiative backed by retaliatory capacity', in William G Austin & Stephen Worchel (eds.), *The social psychology of intergroup relations*, Wadsworth, Belmont, CA.

Mayer, Bernard 2000, *The dynamics of conflict resolution: a practitioner's guide*, Jossey-Bass, San Francisco, CA.

Mitchell, Christopher 1999, 'The anatomy of de-escalation', in Ho-Won Jeong (ed.), *Conflict resolution: dynamics, process and structure*, Ashgate, Aldershot, UK.

Morgan, Patrick M 2006, 'Deterrence and system management: the case of North Korea', *Conflict Management and Peace Science*, vol. 23, no. 2, pp. 121–38.

Ogunyemi, Dotun, Fong, Susie, Elmore, Geoff, Korwin, Devra & Azziz, Ricardo 2010, 'The associations between residents' behavior and the Thomas-Kilmann Conflict MODE instrument', *Journal of Graduate Medical Education*, vol. 2, no. 1, pp. 118–125.

Phillips, Gerald F 2006–2007, 'May arbitrators suggest mediation?', *Dispute Resolution Journal*, vol. 61, no. 4, pp. 28–36.

Pruitt, Dean G 2009, 'Escalation and de-escalation in asymmetric conflict', *Dynamics of Asymmetric Conflict*, vol. 2, no. 1, pp. 23–31.

Pruitt, Dean & Kim, Sung Hee 2004, *Social conflict: escalation, stalemate and settlement*, 3rd edn, McGraw-Hill, New York.

Putnam, Linda L, Burgess, Guy & Royer, Rebecca 2003, 'We can't go on like this: frame changes in intractable conflicts', *Environmental Practice*, vol. 5, no. 1, pp. 247–55.

Richardson, Robert C 2010, *Evolutionary psychology as maladapted psychology*, MIT Press.

Richter, Andreas W, Scully, Judy & West, Michael A 2005, 'Intergroup conflict and intergroup effectiveness in organizations: theory and scale development', *European Journal of Work and Organizational Psychology*, vol. 14. no. 2, pp. 177–203.

Rizzuto, Ana-Maria, Buie, Dan H & Meissner, WW 2004, *The dynamics of human aggression*, Taylor & Francis, London.

Robbins, Stephen 1978, '"Conflict management" and "conflict resolution" are not synonymous terms', *California Management Review*, vol. 21, no. 2, pp. 67–79.

Robbins, Stephen P & Coulter, Mary K 2007, *Management*, 9th edn, Prentice Hall, Englewood Cliffs, NJ.

Robbins, Stephen P, Bergman, Rolf, Stagg, Ian & Coulter, Mary 2009, *Management*, 5th revised edn, Pearson Education Australia, Sydney.

Schermerhorn, John R 2010, *Management*, 10th edn, John Wiley & Sons, New York.

Seta, Catherine E, Paulus, Paul, B & Baron, Robert A 2000, *Effective human relations: a guide to people at work*, 4th edn, Allyn & Bacon, Needham Heights, MA.

Thomas, KW 1976, 'Conflict and conflict management', in MD Dunnette (ed.), *Handbook of industrial and organizational psychology*, vol. II, Rand McNally, Chicago.

—— 1977, 'Towards multi-dimensional values in teaching: the example of conflict behaviors', *Academy of Management Review*, vol. 2, p. 487.

—— 1992, 'Conflict and conflict management: reflections and update', *Journal of Organizational Behavior*, May, vol. 13, no. 3, pp. 265–74.

Thomas, K W, Thomas, Gail Fann & Schaubert, Nancy 2008, 'Conflict styles of men and women at six organizational levels', *International Journal of Conflict Resolution*, vol. 19, no. 2, pp. 148–88, https://www.cpp.com.

Tucker, James 1993, 'Everyday forms of employee resistance', *Sociological Forum*, vol. 8, no. 1, pp. 25–45.

Ury, William 2000, *The third side: why we fight and how we can stop*, Penguin, New York.

—— 2001, *Must we fight? From the battlefield to the schoolyard – a new perspective on violent conflict and its prevention*, John Wiley & Sons, New York.

Wade, John 1994, 'Strategic interventions used by mediators, facilitators and conciliators', *Australian Dispute Resolution Journal*, vol. 1, pp. 292–304.

Wilson, Edward O 2000, *Sociobiology: the new synthesis. Twenty-fifth anniversary edition*, Harvard University Press, Cambridge, MA.

15

Intercultural communication

LEARNING OBJECTIVES

After reading this chapter you should be able to:

- Explain basic processes of acculturation
- Discuss Hofstede's model of culture
- Apply the GLOBE model of culture to your own and other cultures
- Use the context model of culture to explain intercultural agreements and disagreements
- Assess the validity of the clash of civilisations model
- Understand the relationship between multiculturalism at the macro-cultural level and diversity at the micro-cultural level
- Apply theories of intercultural communication to encounters with people from other cultures
- Apply aspects of intercultural communication to explain processes of negotiation and conflict resolution

Culture and cultures — some definitions

We saw in chapter 1 that it can be useful to visualise a continuum of communication using a concentric circles model (figure 15.1).

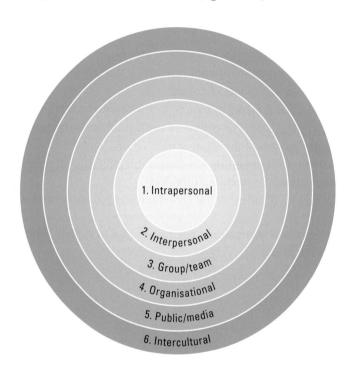

FIGURE 15.1 A concentric model of fields of communication

1. Intrapersonal
2. Interpersonal
3. Group/team
4. Organisational
5. Public/media
6. Intercultural

But what is 'culture'? How well do we understand communication processes generally, let alone those between cultures? We also raised the question of whether communication is always a good thing. Perhaps we should ask whether intercultural communication is always a good thing. On balance, it is, but in order for it to work well, we need to understand the pitfalls and limitations associated with intercultural communication, as well as the delights and opportunities.

If we turn to the dictionary to define culture, we see an almost bewildering array of meanings, such as:

- the cultivation of micro-organisms, as bacteria, or of tissues, for scientific study, medicinal use
- the action or practice of cultivating the soil; tillage (*Macquarie dictionary*)
- the quality in a person or society that arises from a concern for what is regarded as excellent in arts, letters, manners, scholarly pursuits, etc
- a particular form or stage of civilisation, as that of a certain nation or period: Greek culture
- the behaviours and beliefs characteristic of a particular social, ethnic or age group: the youth culture; the drug culture (*Random House unabridged dictionary* 2006)
- all the arts, beliefs, social institutions, etc. characteristic of a community, race etc. (*Oxford advanced learner's dictionary of current English* 1974)
- advanced development of the human powers; development of the body, mind and spirit by training and experience (*Oxford advanced learner's dictionary of current English* 1974)

Macro-culture: all the arts, beliefs, social institutions, etc. characteristic of a community, race, etc.

Micro-culture: the predominating attitudes and behaviour that characterise the functioning of a group or organisation

■ the predominating attitudes and behaviour that characterise the functioning of a group or organisation (*American heritage dictionary*)

Let's focus on two meanings — *all the arts, beliefs, social institutions, etc. characteristic of a community, race, etc.* and *the predominating attitudes and behaviour that characterise the functioning of a group or organisation*, and categorise them as being either **macro-culture** or **micro-culture** (figure 15.2)

Macro-culture	Micro-culture
All the arts, beliefs, social institutions etc. characteristic of a community, race etc.	The predominating attitudes and behaviour that characterise the functioning of a group or organisation

FIGURE 15.2 Two meanings of culture

We will look more closely at organisational culture in chapter 16, but we will also consider it later in this chapter when we discuss workplace diversity. Indeed, one of the most interesting aspects of intercultural communication is that, as nation-states become more multicultural in ethnic makeup, the issues of communicating 'over there' or elsewhere are also becoming the issues of 'here', and the dividing line between 'communities' and 'groups or organisations' becomes blurred. For example, Wiseman (2005) suggested that US foreign policy in the Middle East in the 2000s was in conflict with the 'culture' of diplomacy, with diplomacy understood as an international community.

People from different cultural groups often interact together in contemporary business settings.

Perhaps at no time in history has there been more contact between peoples of different cultures, ranging from refugees to asylum seekers to migrants to student 'sojourners' (Brown 2009; Sam & Berry 2006; Arnold 2011) to businesspeople to professional diasporas (people working in other countries on a semi-permanent basis) to tourists (and, some would say, terrorists). Indeed, the movement in and out of countries is now at a level where some are suggesting that the concept of migration be replaced with that of 'people flow' (Veenkamp, Bentley & Buonfino 2003; Button 2006). Within cultures or nation-states, there is an unparalleled degree of ethnic and cultural change, and within workplaces, increases in the levels of diversity. Perhaps at no time in history has there been a greater need for intercultural communication.

Let's therefore now focus on the macro-cultural dynamics of communication.

Intercultural communication: an overview

Nothing could appear to be more obvious than the fact that people from different nations communicate in different ways. Throughout history, one of the most fundamental ways in which cultures have interacted with each other is in trade, or in conflict situations over resources such as hunting and fishing rights. Today, tourists buy souvenirs or artefacts when in foreign lands, and businesspeople from different countries reach agreements and do deals to create products and services. All of these situations involved and involve what we would now call negotiation techniques.

In negotiations, for example, there can be dramatic differences in the way people define their opening positions, use tactics, persuade and listen (see chapter 13). Even the practice of 'haggling' over a price is an integral part of some cultures — which many revel in and consider the very stuff of life – whereas it is alien in other cultures, where the price on the tag is the price, and that's all there is to it.

Another major difference between cultures occurs when payment of money or goods (or the exchange of gifts) is considered a normal part of conducting a deal. Such payments would be seen as 'lubrication', 'dash', 'backhanders', 'favours' or 'baksheesh' in some cultures, but as 'bribery', 'graft' or 'corruption' in others. Similarly, gift-giving is a more honourable, but not less complex, system of interaction (Narlikar 2011).

Differences also occur in the use of time in negotiations and other encounters. People from culture A may think that they are using time effectively by sticking to schedules and norms of punctuality and dispensing with meaningless socialising, despairing at what they see as sloppy and procrastinating behaviour on the part of the culture B people they are negotiating with; those culture B people, however, may feel that they are the ones who are using the natural rhythms of time to build long-term relationships, and in turn see the culture A people they are negotiating with as abrupt, rude and untrustworthy. For culture B people, tasks are accomplished *because* of personal relationships, not in spite of them (Martin & Nakayama 2007, p. 243).

What is perhaps less obvious is that similarities between nations sometimes outweigh differences, and that 'nationality' or 'culture' is not always a helpful concept in trying to understand what is going on in a negotiation or any type of communication process. In fact, when talking about 'national' styles of negotiating and communicating, we have to be careful not to lurch into racist stereotypes about 'the Russian style of communicating' or 'the Australian style of negotiating'. It might be very difficult to generalise about what is a national communication style. It might be more useful to understand a person's behaviour in terms of other allegiances – to a state or region; to a cultural, religious, ethnic or language grouping; to a tribe; to a profession; to a sex; to a caste; to a class. For example, a French farmer may have less in common with a French factory worker than he does with a German farmer, where occupational and social statuses, rather than nationality, would here be the key variables in understanding motivation and vested interests (Haviland et al. 2010, p. 231).

People from a particular country may use differing negotiation styles when engaged in diplomacy or commerce, or simply when being tourists. Even then, a person may not behave 'typically' in the sense that one would expect. People tend to be themselves, and not fit the pigeonholes we would, for the sake of tidiness, prefer to keep them in.

Paradoxes of intercultural communication

When we are trying to generalise about the specific communication characteristics of a culture, we may need to specify which generation of that culture we are talking about (Yu & Miller 2003). This goes to the heart of the paradox inherent in the study of intercultural communication: just as the study of intercultural communication is becoming a large-scale and systematic endeavour, the very nature of cultures is changing before our eyes.

Some other paradoxes of intercultural communication include:

- As one set of conflicts seems to dissolve (e.g. the post-World War II battle between communism and capitalism), another set of conflicts seems to be on the rise (e.g. the processes of globalisation, ethnicity and religion) (Fukuyma 1993; Barber 2001; Brown 2009; Sparke 2011; Ali 2010).
- As processes of multiculturalism, ethnic diversity, immigration and tourism appear to offer opportunities for greater understanding and harmony between cultures, new divisive forces based on cultural differences seem to be emerging (e.g. among the United States, China, a resurgent Russia and radical Islam [Buchanan 2009]).
- As the plurality of cultures becomes more widely recognised, the apparent ascendance of the English language continues (Thumboo 2003; Bennett 2007; Ho & Chen 2010).
- As the growth of greater understanding and the shrinking of ignorance and xenophobia promises the end of global conflicts, the reality is that familiarity all too often breeds

contempt and violence – that the most violent wars are often not intercultural ones but *intracultural* or civil ones, and that some cultures (e.g. in Ireland and the Middle East) may know each other too well (Harries 2004).

■ As market economies and democracy are foisted on some societies, the result is not so much freedom and peace as the stirring of ethnic tensions (because some intranational ethnic groups are more successful in business than others) and global instability (Chua 2004).

In this chapter, we will explore some aspects of this enormous field of intercultural communication. We will begin by looking at the general processes of acculturation, and then at the specific approaches of 'the four Hs' – the cultural models proposed by Hofstede, House, Hall and Huntington. We will consider the impact of greater cultural diversity within organisations and within nations. We will then try to apply our knowledge of intercultural communication by creating a checklist of communication strategies, and will go on to look at a particular arena of applied communication – negotiation and conflict resolution.

Acculturation: coming to terms with 'the other'

The other: any group of people perceived as different in terms of nationality, ethnicity, religion, political alignment, class or caste, or gender

Throughout history, humans have experienced both fascination with and trepidation towards '**the other**' – understood as 'different nationalities, but also [as] any group of people perceived as different – perhaps in terms of so-called ethnicity, religion, political alignment, class or caste, or gender' (Holliday, Hyde & Kullman 2004, p. 23).

Acculturation: the process of the meeting of cultures and the changes which result from such meetings

The process by which we interact with 'the other' – in modes of varying peacefulness, aggression, understanding and confusion – is sometimes referred to as **acculturation**:

> Contact between peoples of different cultures is not a new phenomenon. Throughout human history, mankind has travelled around the world for various reasons, either in search of greener pastures, fleeing from persecution and catastrophe, to trade or to conquer and colonize, or in search of adventure or fun. These activities have resulted in the meeting of peoples of diverse backgrounds. This process has led to changes in the original patterns of life and cultures of the people concerned, as well as the formation of new societies. The meeting of cultures and the resulting changes are what collectively has come to be known as acculturation. (Sam & Berry 2006, p. 1)

Bennett (Hammer, Bennett & Wiseman 2003) suggests that when people interact with others from other cultures, they may acquire intercultural sensitivity (the ability to discriminate and experience relevant cultural differences), which may then allow them to develop intercultural competence (the ability to think and act in interculturally appropriate ways). This process can best be understood as a continuum of different phases (figure 15.3).

FIGURE 15.3 Bennett's developmental model of intercultural sensitivity

Source: Hammer, Bennett and Wiseman (2003, p. 424).

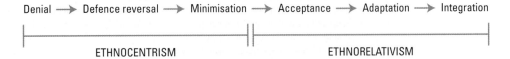

The phases identified by Bennett are denial, defence reversal and minimisation, which are part of an ethnocentric worldview; and acceptance, adaptation and integration, which are part of an ethnorelative worldview:

■ *Denial* is the default condition for most people, who are socialised into the one culture with little experience of other cultures. In this condition, all those outside the home culture are 'the other', and may be treated with indifference or aggression.

■ *Defense reversal* occurs when a person of one culture perceives another culture not to be inferior, but superior, and pays tribute to that culture by 'going native' or 'passing'. Like Denial, however, it still involves an 'us versus them' outlook.

- *Minimisation* occurs when a person moves beyond the fear of the Denial stage and instead begins to perceive – or attempts to perceive – universals or similarities between 'us and them', but only at a superficial level, and usually only in terms of 'our' values and norms.
- *Acceptance* is the first of the three 'ethnorelative' phases, with ethnorelativity meaning that one's own culture is now experienced in the context of other cultures. People in this phase can experience others as different from themselves, but as equally human. Acceptance, however, does not mean agreement.
- *Adaptation* occurs when a person can experience empathy with another culture – it is the state in which the experience of another culture yields perception and behaviour appropriate to that culture.
- *Integration* occurs when an individual begins to define their identity as being at the margin of two or more cultures and central to none. This can either take a negative or encapsulated form, where the separation from a culture is experienced as alienation; or a positive or constructive form, where movements in and out of cultures are seen as a necessary and positive part of one's identity.

Deardorff (2006) has also developed a model of intercultural competence (figure 15.4).

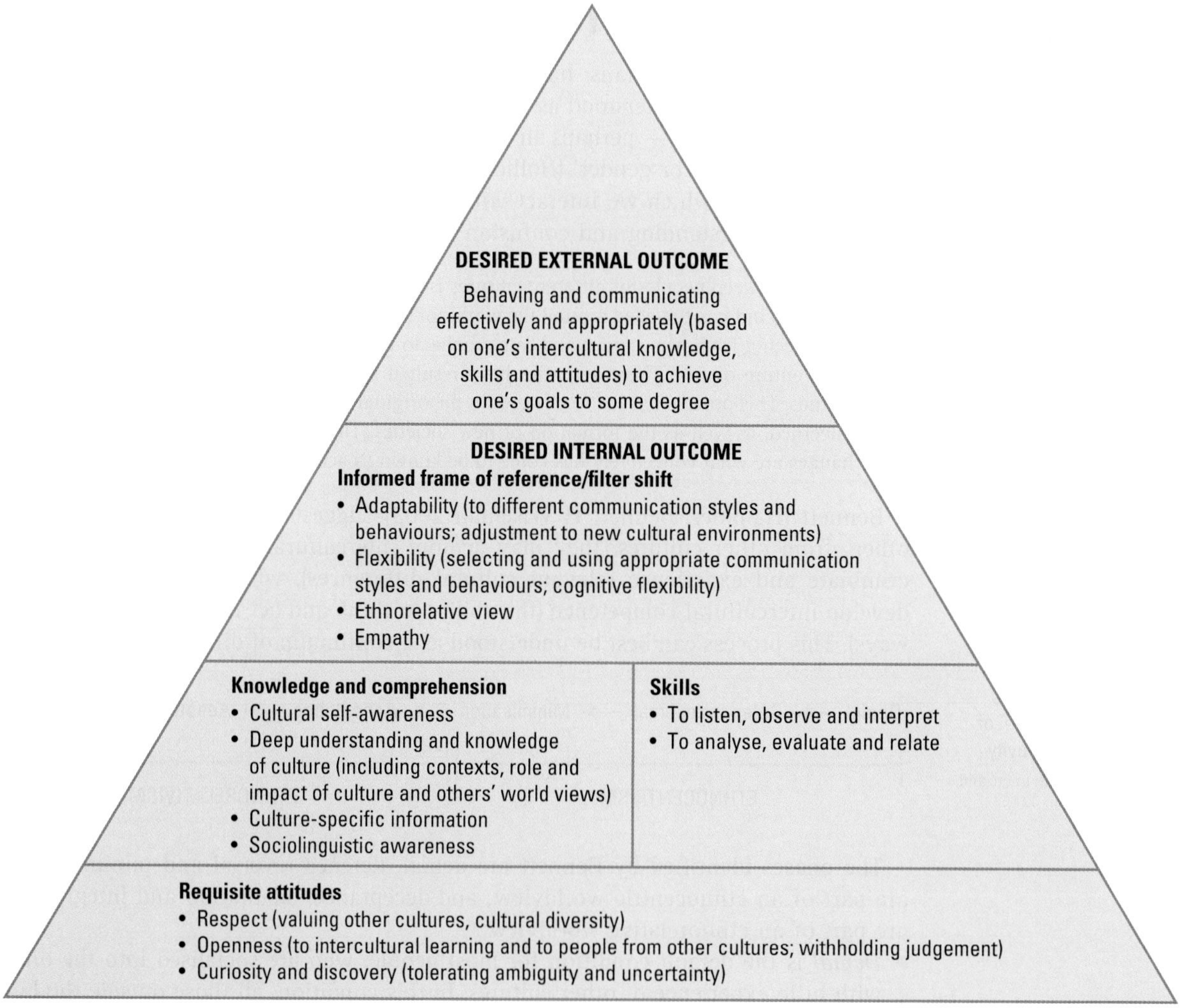

DESIRED EXTERNAL OUTCOME
Behaving and communicating effectively and appropriately (based on one's intercultural knowledge, skills and attitudes) to achieve one's goals to some degree

DESIRED INTERNAL OUTCOME
Informed frame of reference/filter shift
- Adaptability (to different communication styles and behaviours; adjustment to new cultural environments)
- Flexibility (selecting and using appropriate communication styles and behaviours; cognitive flexibility)
- Ethnorelative view
- Empathy

Knowledge and comprehension
- Cultural self-awareness
- Deep understanding and knowledge of culture (including contexts, role and impact of culture and others' world views)
- Culture-specific information
- Sociolinguistic awareness

Skills
- To listen, observe and interpret
- To analyse, evaluate and relate

Requisite attitudes
- Respect (valuing other cultures, cultural diversity)
- Openness (to intercultural learning and to people from other cultures; withholding judgement)
- Curiosity and discovery (tolerating ambiguity and uncertainty)

- *Move from personal level (attitude) to interpersonal/interactive level (outcomes).*
- *Degree of intercultural competence depends on acquired degree of underlying elements.*

FIGURE 15.4 Deardorff's pyramid model of intercultural competence

Source: Deardorff (2006, p. 254).

This model builds on a number of specific abilities and behaviours, such as:

- ability to communicate effectively and appropriately in intercultural situations based on one's intercultural knowledge, skills and attitudes
- ability to shift frame of reference appropriately and adapt behaviour to cultural context; adaptability, expandability and flexibility of one's frame of reference/filter
- behaving appropriately and effectively in intercultural situations based on one's knowledge, skills and motivation
- good interpersonal skills exercised interculturally; the sending and receiving of messages that are accurate and appropriate.

The model is hierarchical or pyramidal in structure, with attitudes forming a basis for knowledge and comprehension, which in turn form a basis for internal outcomes, which in turn form a basis for the desired external outcome of behaving to achieve maximum intercultural competence.

The dynamic of Bennett's and Deardorff's models are considered in more detail later in the chapter. Both models have an implicit optimism for better intercultural communication within them (pyramid, arrow line dynamics). Brown (2009), however, is not quite so optimistic. Working with a group of Asian and European postgraduate students in England, she found that many Asian students naturally felt loneliness and homesickness. There were host national friends who acted as cultural informants and were an important source of host culture and learning. Other mono-national friendships were not so successful, and paradoxically led back to the formation of ghetto patterns. With little cultural learning taking place, they pointed to a tension between the desire to improve intercultural competence and to maintain ethnic links. She concluded:

> (My study) also challenges the oft-claimed automatic link between the international sojourn and intercultural competence. Indeed, interaction across national and cultural boundaries was not the norm; it was noted only among those individuals who were determined to realize the universally stated aim of increasing intercultural knowledge. It is widely claimed that the international sojourn carries the power to produce the intercultural mediator, but my study found that this potential was fulfilled by only a handful of exceptionally motivated students. This finding has important implications for the understanding of multicultural society. (Brown 2009, p. 255)

While the sample used by Brown is small, her contrarian views on cultures working together automatically producing harmony is thought-provoking.

Berry suggests that there are different dimensions of cultural variation that help to explain acculturation processes, such as diversity (how many different positions, roles, and institutions are there?), equality (are differences horizontal [egalitarian] or vertical [hierarchical]?), conformity (how much are individuals enmeshed in the social order?), wealth (what is the average gross domestic product per person?), space (how does interpersonal space help explain non-verbal communication between individuals?), and time (how concerned are people with promptness and schedules?). Berry also suggests that religion is emerging as another important dimension in cultural variation, so that the combination of affluence and religion may help to explain some conflicts: cultures which are furthest apart in these characteristics (e.g. Afghanistan and the United States; Israel and Palestine) are often in conflict (Berry 2006, pp. 32–3).

We now have a good general basis for considering how intercultural communication might occur. Let's turn to four specific models of culture, and see how they can be applied to intercultural communication.

Hofstede's model of culture

Is 'culture' the same as 'nationality'? Hofstede (2001, p. 9) defines culture as 'the collective programming of the mind which distinguishes the members of one group or category of people from another'. He describes cultures in terms of five dimensions.

1. *Power distance* refers to the different solutions to the basic problem of human inequality.
2. *Uncertainty avoidance* refers to the level of stress in a society in the face of an unknown future.
3. *Individualism versus collectivism* refers to the integration of individuals into primary groups.
4. *Masculinity versus femininity* refers to the division of emotional roles between men and women.
5. *Long-term versus short-term orientation* refers to the choice of focus for people's efforts: the future or the present.

Using survey methods, Hofstede was able to produce number scores for each of these dimensions for many countries. The dimensions are continuums – that is, a particular culture that is associated with a particular nation-state may score at the extremes of a particular dimension or somewhere between those extremes. Similarly, the dimensions average-out data, which means that a culture may score high on certain aspects of a particular dimension but these particular scores may be masked by scores on other surveyed items and values. It may also be that values and cultures change over time – a particular society in this current year may not score the same in twenty or fifty years into the future, or twenty or fifty years into the past (although it may if underlying values persist over very long time periods).

Power distance was a term originally used to describe organisational settings. In high power-distance settings, the organisation was quite hierarchical, employees feared disagreeing with superiors, and superiors tended to have more authoritarian decision-making styles. The concept was then broadened to look at cultures, examining attitudes to power in education, society and the workplace. High power-distance cultures tend to have a fair amount of inequality, and obedience and submissiveness are favoured. Typical characteristics of low and high power-distance cultures are shown in figure 15.5.

Power distance: a measure of the inequality and equality within a culture

Low power-distance culture	High power-distance culture
▪ Students put value on independence	▪ Students put value on conformity
▪ Students initiate some communication in class	▪ Teachers initiate all communication in class
▪ Freedom more important than equality	▪ Equality more important than freedom
▪ Flat organisation pyramids	▪ Tall organisation pyramids
▪ Stress on reward, legitimate and expert power	▪ Stress on coercive and referent power
▪ Subordinates expect to be consulted	▪ Subordinates expect to be told
▪ Consultative leadership leads to satisfaction, performance and productivity	▪ Authoritative leadership and close supervision lead to satisfaction, performance and productivity

FIGURE 15.5 Power distance and culture

Source: Adapted from Hofstede (2001, pp. 96–108).

Uncertainty avoidance: a concept that helps explain how cultures respond to the uncertain nature of future events

Uncertainty avoidance helps explain how individuals, groups, organisations and cultures respond to the uncertain nature of future events. Organisations respond to uncertain events by creating rules, standard operating procedures, rituals and technology; and cultures, in turn, respond to uncertainty by using technology, law and religion. Uncertainty avoidance is not the same as risk avoidance – uncertainty avoidance is all about intolerance of ambiguity, and the search for structure, security and predictability. A high uncertainty-avoidance individual or culture may, for example, indulge in risky behaviour such as starting a fight or war rather than sitting back and waiting to see what the future will bring. Typical characteristics of low and high uncertainty-avoidance cultures are shown in figure 15.6.

Low uncertainty-avoidance culture	High uncertainty-avoidance culture
■ Facial expressions of sadness and fear easily readable by others	■ Nature of emotions less accurately readable by others
■ Individual decisions, authoritative management and competition among employees acceptable	■ Ideological preference for group decisions, consultative management; against competition among employees
■ Favourable attitude towards younger people; smaller generation gap	■ Critical attitudes towards younger people; larger generation gap
■ Independence for female students important	■ Traditional role models for female students
■ Innovators feel independent of rules	■ Innovators feel constrained by rules
■ Appeal of transformational leader role	■ Appeal of hierarchical control role
■ Belief in generalists and common sense	■ Belief in specialists and expertise

FIGURE 15.6 Uncertainty avoidance and culture

Source: Adapted from Hofstede (2001, pp. 160–70).

Individualism: the extent to which a culture tolerates individual expression and provides support

Individualism versus collectivism refers to the extent to which a person defines his or her identity according to group or separate and private values. Both concepts have positive and negative connotations. For example, person A may enjoy living in a country town because everyone knows everyone else and there is a lot of community support; the same person may move to a city and find it alienating and lonely. Person B, however, may find the same country town suffocating, full of busybodies and parochial hicks; this same person may move to the city and revel in the freedom of anonymity and the ability to make friends.

Collectivist sentiments may help bind a country together so that everyone feels part of one big family, but equally such sentiments may be used by authoritarian governments to impose conformity and stifle dissent. Typical characteristics of individualist and collectivist cultures are shown in figure 15.7.

Individualist culture	Collectivist culture
■ Individual decisions are better	■ Group decisions are better
■ 'Guilt' cultures	■ 'Shame' cultures
■ Hedonism	■ Survival
■ Weak family ties, rare contacts	■ Strong family ties, frequent contacts
■ Women express emotions more strongly than men	■ Women express emotions less strongly than men
■ Relationship with union calculative	■ Potential emotional commitment to union
■ Incentives to be given to individuals	■ Incentives to be given to work in groups
■ Media main source of information	■ Social network main source of information
■ More invention patents granted	■ Fewer invention patents granted
■ Moderate to cold climates	■ Tropical and subtropical climates

FIGURE 15.7 Individualistic and collectivist culture

Source: Adapted from Hofstede (2001, pp. 226–45).

Masculine: describes a culture in which traditional sex roles are observed

Feminine: describes a culture in which non-traditional sex roles are observed

Masculine and **feminine** are terms used by Hofstede to describe approaches to sex roles within a culture. His use of the terms, however, suggests that by 'feminine' he means 'androgenous' or non-traditional; whereas, by 'masculine' he means the traditional values of sex role specialisation that have typified most societies until the twentieth century.

Traditional sex or gender roles have meant that males have been associated with assertiveness and females with nurturance, with implications for family structure, leadership, organisational design and social norms. Typical characteristics of masculine and feminine cultures are shown in figure 15.8. Again, it needs to be stressed that Hofstede's dimensions are continuums – that is, a country may score at the extreme masculine end of the continuum or at the extreme feminine end or somewhere in between, and the same country might score as masculine on some characteristics and as feminine on other characteristics (Hofstede 2010).

Masculine culture	Feminine culture
■ Challenge and recognition in jobs important	■ Cooperation at work and relationship with boss important
■ Belief in individual decisions	■ Belief in group decisions
■ Men should be tough and take care of performance; women should be tender and take care of relationships	■ Men should be tender and take care of both performance and relationships; women should be the same
■ Sympathy for the strong	■ Sympathy for the weak
■ Live in order to work	■ Work in order to live
■ Fewer women in management positions	■ More women in management positions
■ Resolution of conflicts through denying them or fighting until the best 'man' wins	■ Resolution of conflicts through problem solving, compromise and negotiation
■ Less sickness absence	■ More sickness absence
■ Competitive advantage in manufacturing industries, price competition, heavy products and bulk chemistry	■ Competitive advantage in service industries, consulting, live products and biochemistry

FIGURE 15.8 Masculine and feminine cultures
Source: Adapted from Hofstede (2001, pp. 298–318).

The fifth dimension in Hofstede's model of cultures is that of long-term orientation. Long-term orientation refers to the time frames that a culture operates in, specifically the time frames of the near-to-distant future. Cultures that score low on this dimension typically tend to operate on close time horizons and may be more fixed in the 'here and now' than in the 'there and then'. Hofstede notes that East Asian societies score high on long-term orientation and suggests that this orientation or value set has been instrumental in the strong economic growth of these societies in the past few decades. Typical characteristics of low and high long-term orientation cultures are shown in figure 15.9.

Low long-term orientation culture	High long-term orientation culture
■ Quick results expected	■ Perseverance, persistence
■ Leisure time important	■ Leisure time not so important
■ Small share of additional income saved	■ Large share of additional income saved
■ In business, short-term results — 'the bottom line'	■ In business, building of relationships and a strong market position

FIGURE 15.9 Long-term orientation and culture
Source: Adapted from Hofstede (2001, pp. 360–7).

Low long-term orientation culture	High long-term orientation culture
▪ Lower performance in basic mathematics tasks	▪ Higher performance in basic mathematics tasks
▪ Meritocracy — economic and social life to be ordered by abilities	▪ People should live more equally
▪ Old age is seen as coming later	▪ Old age seen as coming sooner but as a satisfying life period

Limitations of Hofstede's model

Hofstede's five-dimensional model of culture has been very influential since the first versions of it appeared in the 1980s (Kirkman, Lowe & Gibson 2006; Soares, Farhangmehr & Shoham 2007). The insights it gives into culture are considerable, and it has substantial potential not only for understanding individual cultures but also for comparing cultures. For example, figure 15.10 shows data for all five dimensions for selected countries, and the trends revealed are an interesting starting point for discussion.

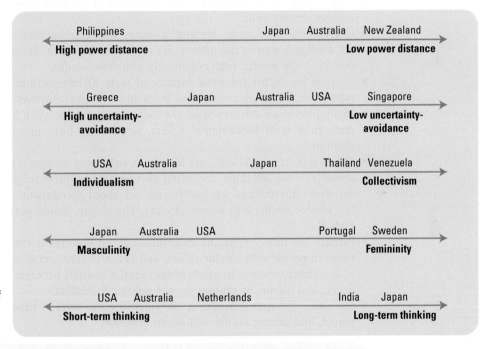

FIGURE 15.10 How selected countries compare on Hofstede's five dimensions of culture

Source: Adapted from Hofstede (2001).

There are limitations, however, in Hofstede's approach. Most of his data is based on surveys conducted from 1967 to 1973 of 116 000 employees of one US multinational (IBM), the employees being situated in 72 countries; and from a 1985 survey of students from 23 countries (50 males and females from each country). The questions to ask with this approach are:

▪ Is the data still relevant? Have things changed since the survey periods, or have value-sets remained robust over time?
▪ Might the earlier organisational culture of IBM not be so relevant anymore?
▪ Might IBM's internal micro-culture overwhelm the truth about the macro-culture of the countries outside the IBM buildings)?
▪ Do people respond truthfully to surveys? Do people describe the way things really are, or the way they would like them to be?

- Would the organisational culture of the one employer swamp or mask the true broader national cultural values of survey respondents? In other words, is the sample for the survey too narrow?
- What other variables might exist beyond Hofstede's five, and what individual attributes (e.g., cognitions) might better explain employee feelings or actions than cultural values? (Kirkman, Lowe & Gibson 2006)

Bearing these reservations in mind, it remains true that Hofstede's work is a considerable achievement and provides an insight into the things that separate and unite cultures. Some implications of this work for intercultural communication include:

- In intercultural encounters, such as negotiations, people from high power-distance cultures will prefer to work with high-status negotiators or principals rather than representatives.
- People from high uncertainty-avoidance cultures may prefer the reassurance of structure and ritual.
- People from collectivist cultures like to build relationships over a long period of time.
- People from high masculine cultures may tend to try and resolve conflicts by force, whereas those from feminine cultures may be more likely to resolve conflicts through compromise and consensus.
- People from long-term orientation cultures may persevere longer, and sacrifice more, to achieve desired ends.
- Intercultural encounters demand language and communication skills to guarantee that the messages sent to the other party or parties will be understood in the way they were meant by the sender, both cognitively and emotionally.
- Tourism represents the most superficial form of intercultural encounter, but may help raise intercultural awareness and boost business opportunities.
- Many people are threatened by the idea of cultural variation because it seems to undermine their most fundamental beliefs, which they have presumed to be universal and absolute.
- The slogan 'think globally, act locally' is naïve and arrogant, because no-one can think globally — we all think according to our own cultural programming or local mental software. Intercultural encounters are all about recognising that we think differently but resolve common problems anyway. The slogan should perhaps be 'think locally, act globally'.
- Perhaps his most important observation about cultures is that conflicts can still occur between people with similar values, and peaceful coexistence can prevail between people with different values. In other words, similar profiles between nations do not guarantee peace, and dissimilar profiles do not guarantee conflict.
- The same dynamic pertains at the interpersonal level — between individual and individual, and among family and group members.

ASSESS YOURSELF

How would you rate yourself personally on each of Hofstede's five dimensions?

House's GLOBE model of cultures

A larger and more complex study than Hofstede's is the global leadership and organisational behaviour effectiveness (GLOBE) model developed by House and his associates (House 1998; House et al. 2004; Ashkanasy, Trevor-Roberts & Earnshaw 2002; Gupta, Hanges & Dorfman 2002; Gupta et al. 2002; Javidan & House 2001, 2002; Kabasakal & Bodur 2002; Szabo et al. 2002; Hofstede 2006; Javidan et al. 2006; Smith 2006; House, Quigley &

Sully, 2010). The GLOBE survey draws on data from approximately 17 000 questionnaires completed by middle managers from approximately 825 organisations in 62 societies. As with the Hofstede model, the GLOBE approach draws more on management and leadership studies rather than broader disciplines like sociology, anthropology, economics, history, geography and psychology – an approach that creates strengths but may also induce weaknesses in the search for the meaning of culture.

The GLOBE project broke up the 62 societies surveyed into ten clusters (or groups) based on geography, common language, religion and historical accounts (figure 15.11).

Anglo	Latin Europe	Nordic Europe	Germanic Europe	Eastern Europe
England Australia South Africa 　(white sample) Canada New Zealand Ireland United States	Israel Italy Portugal Spain France Switzerland 　(French 　speaking)	Finland Sweden Denmark	Austria Switzerland The Netherlands Germany 　(formerly East) Germany 　(formerly 　West)	Hungary Russia Kazakhstan Albania Poland Greece Slovenia Georgia
Latin America	Sub-Saharan Africa	Arab	Southern Asia	Confucian Asia
Costa Rica Venezuela Ecuador Mexico El Salvador Colombia Guatemala Bolivia Brazil Argentina	Namibia Zambia Zimbabwe South Africa 　(black sample) Nigeria	Qatar Morocco Turkey Egypt Kuwait	India Indonesia Philippines Malaysia Thailand Iran	Taiwan Singapore Hong Kong South Korea China Japan

FIGURE 15.11 The ten GLOBE clusters

Source: Adapted from Gupta, Hanges and Dorfman (2002, p. 13).

The GLOBE study builds on the work of Hofstede and others and examines cultures in terms of nine cultural dimensions or attributes. These are shown in table 15.1.

TABLE 15.1 GLOBE cultural dimensions

Globe dimension	Definition	Examples
1. Assertiveness	The extent to which a society encourages people to be tough, confrontational, assertive and competitive versus modest and tender	High-scoring countries (e.g. United States, Austria) tend to have a 'can do' attitude and tend to value competition. They have sympathy for the strong and the winner. Low-scoring countries (e.g. Sweden, New Zealand) tend to prefer warm and cooperative relations and harmony. They have sympathy for the weak and emphasise loyalty and solidarity.
2. Future orientation	The extent to which a society encourages and rewards future-oriented behaviours such as planning, investing in the future and delaying gratification	High-scoring countries (e.g. Singapore, Switzerland, the Netherlands) tend to have a higher propensity to save for the future and longer thinking and decision-making time frames. Low-scoring countries (e.g. Russia, Argentina, Italy) tend to have shorter thinking and planning horizons and greater emphasis on instant gratification.

(continued)

TABLE 15.1 *(continued)*

Globe dimension	Definition	Examples
3. Gender differentiation	The extent to which a society maximises gender role differences	High-scoring countries (e.g. South Korea, Egypt, China) tend to have high degrees of gender differentiation. They tend to accord men higher social status and have relatively few women in positions of authority.
		Low-scoring countries (e.g. Hungary, Poland, Denmark) tend to have the least gender-differentiated practices. Such societies tend to accord women a higher status and a stronger role in decision making.
4. Uncertainty avoidance	The society's reliance on social norms and procedures to alleviate the unpredictability of future events	High-scoring countries (e.g. Switzerland, Sweden, Germany) tend towards orderliness and consistency, structured lifestyles, clear specification of social expectations, and rules and laws to cover situations.
		Low-scoring countries (e.g. Russia, Greece, Venezuela) tend to have a strong tolerance of ambiguity and uncertainty. People are used to less structure in their lives and are not as concerned about following rules and procedures.
5. Power distance	The degree to which members of a society expect power to be unequally shared.	High-scoring countries (e.g. Russia, Thailand, Spain) tend to expect obedience towards superiors, and clearly distinguish between those with status and power and those without it.
		Low-scoring countries (e.g. Denmark, the Netherlands) tend to be more egalitarian and favour stronger participation in decision making.
6. Institutional emphasis on collectivism versus individualism	The degree to which individuals are encouraged by societal institutions to be integrated into groups within organisations and the society	High-individualism-scoring countries (e.g. Greece, Italy, Argentina) tend to value autonomy and individual freedom. Rewards are based on individual performance because self-interest is more strongly valued than the collective good.
		High-collectivism-scoring countries (e.g. Sweden, South Korea, Japan) tend to prefer similarity to others rather than distinctiveness. They are motivated by other members' satisfaction and cooperation rather than individual autonomy and achievement.
7. In-group collectivism	The extent to which members of a society take pride in membership in small groups, such as their family and circle of close friends, and the organisations in which they are employed	High-scoring countries (e.g. Iran, India, China) tend to highly value being a member of a family and of a close group of friends – an in-group. It is not unusual to forgo due diligence, or equal employment opportunity, and to favour a close friend or family member in recruiting or in allocating rewards and promotions.
		Low-scoring countries (e.g. Denmark, Sweden, New Zealand) tend not to favour in-groups; people do not feel an obligation to ignore rules or procedures to take care of close friends or relatives.
8. Performance orientation	The degree to which a society encourages and rewards group members for performance improvement and excellence	High-scoring countries (e.g. Singapore, Hong Kong, United States) tend to have a 'can-do' attitude and believe in taking initiative. They prefer a direct and explicit style of communication and tend to have a sense of urgency.
		Low-scoring countries (e.g. Russia, Italy, Argentina) tend to emphasise loyalty and belonging, view feedback as discomforting, emphasise tradition and paying attention to one's family and background rather than performance. They associate competition with defeat and value sympathy.
9. Humane orientation	The degree to which a society encourages and rewards individuals for being fair, altruistic, generous, caring and kind to others	High-scoring countries (e.g. Malaysia, Ireland, the Philippines) tend to value human relations, sympathy, and support for others – especially the weak and the vulnerable.
		Low-scoring countries (e.g. former West Germany, France, Singapore) tend to see power and material possessions as motivators. Assertive styles of conflict resolution are preferred. People are expected to solve their own problems, and children are expected to be independent.

Source: Adapted from Javidan and House (2001, pp. 293–302).

GLOBE and communication

There are numerous implications for intercultural communication flowing from these findings:

> Effective communication requires the ability to listen, to frame the message in a way that is understandable to the receiver, and to accept and use feedback. Effective cross-cultural communication involves finding integrated solutions, or at least compromises, that allow decisions to be implemented by members of diverse cultures. While this sounds simple, it can be quite complicated in cross-cultural situations.
>
> The United States is among the high performance-oriented countries. To a typical North American manager, effective communication means direct and explicit language. Facts and figures and rational thinking are important pillars of communication. Economic rationale and expected outcomes are the key criteria in decision making. To a North American manager, communication is a means to an end. The end is the deliverable results.
>
> But people from other cultures do not necessarily share these attributes. People from lower performance-oriented cultures like Russia or Greece tend to prefer indirect and vague language. They are not too comfortable with strong results-driven and explicit communication. Hard facts and figures are hard to come by and not taken as seriously even when they are available. To a typical Greek manager, effective communication does not necessarily mean a clear agreement on facts and expectations. It may mean a discussion and exploration of issues without any commitments and explicit results.
>
> Others from less assertive countries such as Sweden may find it too aggressive, impolite, and unfriendly to speak of explicit and ambitious expectations. They would prefer a communication process that is two-way rather than one-way from the manager. They prefer a highly involved dialogue with much discussion about the subject. The end of the communication process to people from such countries is not just deliverable results but better relations among the parties ...
>
> A culture's level of uncertainty avoidance also influences the communication process. In countries with high levels of uncertainty avoidance, such as Switzerland and Austria, the communication needs to be clear and explicit, based on facts. The message needs to contain rules and procedures about how to get things done. The process of communication is highly structured and formal. Meetings are planned in advance, with a clear agenda. In contrast, in low uncertainty-avoidance countries like Greece or Russia, people are not used to structured or organized communication. Meetings are not planned in advance. They tend to have no agenda or a set time. They can go for hours and finish the meeting without any clear conclusions. (Javidan & House 2001, pp. 302–3)

Thus far, not all countries have been sampled in the GLOBE model, and there will always be controversies about classifying countries into clusters. (Do America and Britain really belong in the same cluster? Or in terms of the 'Anglosphere' idea, are the similar curves of Britain, the United States and Australia pure chance? Does Israel really belong in the Latin Europe cluster? Does Iran fit comfortably into the Southern Asia cluster? Does Turkey fit comfortably into the Arab cluster? How valid is it to split South Africa on racial lines, or Switzerland on language lines? How 'Confucian' is Japan?) Is GLOBE, in fact, insufficiently 'global'? That is, is it too focused on North American values and approaches (Hofstede 2006)? In spite of these limitations, GLOBE is a systematic and solid project that provides new perspectives on culture, conflict and communication.

Hofstede came first, with House building on that model. The researchers have had intellectual disagreements, at times, since the appearance of GLOBE. For example, Hofstede (2010, p. 1342) quotes another intercultural researcher: 'As an experienced cross-cultural researcher, he (Peter Smith) wondered about GLOBE's way of aggregating data from the individual to the nation level. Finally, he pointed to the dilemma of whether or not to control for differences in national wealth: GLOBE does not, I do.'

House has criticised Hofstede for arguing that GLOBE was too US-centred, pointing out that the original research work was commissioned by IBM, a US-centric company that would be interested primarily in a US-based model. Hofstede's fifth dimension, long-term orientation versus short-term orientation, was only added later, based on the work of others, and does not fit perfectly with the original four-dimension research design: 'Such an incremental approach of adding to the list of dimensions is due to the limitations of his original design and begs the question: what other dimensions are missing because IBM was not interested in them?' (Javidan et al. 2006, p. 898)

ASSESS YOURSELF

Using the GLOBE model, consider a cultural cluster you are familiar with. Do the similarities of the cluster members outweigh the differences? Why or why not?

Hall's context model

One of the most interesting schemas to classify cultures has been that developed by anthropologist Edward T Hall. Hall (1977) argues that communication and culture are about not only words and what is immediately tangible and visible, but also the context in which these things occur – not just text, but context. If context is real, then it can be measured, and it will vary from situation to situation and from culture to culture. Therefore, it is possible to argue that cultures can be understood in terms of two extreme types of context: low and high (table 15.2).

TABLE 15.2 High-context and low-context cultures

	High context	Low context
Association	How things get done depends on relationships with people and attention to group processes.	Things get done by following procedures and paying attention to a goal.
Interaction	High use of non-verbal elements; voice, tone, facial expression, gestures and eye movements carry significant parts of conversation.	Low use of non-verbal elements. Message is carried more by words than by non-verbal means.
Territoriality	Space is communal; people stand close to each other, share the same space.	Space is compartmentalised and privately owned; privacy is important, so people are further apart.
Temporality	Everything has its own time. Time is not easily scheduled; needs of people may interfere with keeping to a set time. What is important is that activity gets done.	Things are scheduled to be done at particular times, one thing at a time. What is important is that activity is done efficiently.
Learning	Knowledge is embedded in situation; things are connected, synthesised and global. Multiple sources of information are used. Thinking is deductive, proceeds from general to specific.	Reality is fragmented and compartmentalised. One source of information is used to develop knowledge. Thinking is inductive, proceeds from specific to general. Focus is on detail.

Source: Adapted from Halverson (1993); Usunier (2010); Livermore (2010).

Polychronic: literally, many times; an approach or cultural mindset that sees time as having multiple dimensions and experiences, with the practical upshot of emphasising slow pacing and multitasking

Monochronic: literally, one time; an approach or cultural mindset that sees time as linear and measurable, with the practical upshot of emphasising punctuality, detailed scheduling of activities, and doing only one task at a time

Low context: describes a culture in which the context of communicated messages is not as important as the communicated message itself

High context: describes a culture in which the context of communicated messages is as important as the communicated message

High context cultures, for example, tend to be **polychronic** – that is, they embody the view that there are multiple time frames and experiences, that time is not necessarily a linear and measurable thing, that things proceed at their own pace, and multitasking is possible and even desirable. Low context cultures, by contrast, tend to be **monochronic** – that is, they embody the view that there is only one experience of time, and norms like punctuality, scheduling and doing one thing at a time are important. Thus considered, time use can even be seen as a form of non-verbal communication. Cultures that are now monochronic may have been polychronic in the past: for example, westernised industrial cultures one or two centuries ago were controlled more by agricultural rhythms than machine pacing. Even today, small towns or country regions may be more polychronic than big towns and industrial regions. Even within the one culture, dominantly monochronic, females may be more polychronic than males in approaches to time scheduling and shopping behaviours (Lindquist & Kaufman-Scarborough 2004). People within polychronic cultures, however, can acquire monochronic behaviours such as time management practices (scheduling, goal setting) and even be more effective than monochronic individuals (Nonis, Teng & Ford 2005).

In terms of Hofstede's model, high-context societies tend to be more collectivist than individual, tend to have higher rather than lower power distances, and tend to have long-term rather than short-term orientation. The correlations with masculine–feminine and uncertainty avoidance are not so clear.

The two extremes of **low context** and **high context** make it possible to establish a continuum of context and classify cultures according to where they fall on the continuum (figure 15.12).

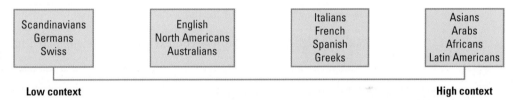

FIGURE 15.12 Cultural context continuum

Sources: Adapted from Hall (1977); Halverson (1993).

Context, understanding and misunderstanding

The context idea, though fascinating and suggestive, is still relatively undeveloped from a research point of view, and there are many exceptions to the rules. For example, the initiating of touching behaviour is a feature of some cultures that can be classified as high context (e.g. in Arab countries), but it is not a feature of some other cultures classified as high context (e.g. Japan). Context also depends on what generation within a culture we are talking about – a younger generation from a non-western culture may be taking on behaviour from western cultures, and western cultures, particularly the Anglo-American ones, tend to be low context. It also depends on the gender of the persons involved: the rules of same-sex touching are quite different from those for different-sex touching in virtually all cultures, regardless of context.

Nevertheless, the context idea can perhaps suggest why communication works and does not work when people from different cultures get together (Pekerti 2005; Hallenbeck 2006; Würtz 2005). The differing unspoken rules of cultures might lead to communication breakdowns, and therefore it may make sense for us to at least try to analyse intercultural situations to see whether the low context – high context model has something to offer. For example, table 15.3 (see overleaf) shows some of the 'rules' operating for people from differing cultures.

TABLE 15.3 Context rules of engagement

	Low context (British, North American)	High context (Arab)
Interpersonal distance – territoriality	Fingertips: I am most comfortable talking to someone at 80–100 cm distance, the distance of my arm to my fingertips touching the other person's shoulder. People who get closer are pushy, and need to be retreated from.	Elbows: I am most comfortable talking to someone at 20–40 cm distance, the distance from my elbow to my fingertips touching the other person's body. People who move away are cold or are getting away, and need to be advanced upon.
Touching	Touching another person's body for emphasis of points when talking is not likely, especially when I do not know the other person well.	Touching another person's body for emphasis of points when talking is likely, irrespective of whether I know the person or not.
Breath, smell	Body odours, especially breath odours, are taboo.	Sometimes I need to be able to breathe on someone when talking to them, and smell their breath.
Voice	If another person lowers the volume of their voice when talking, then I will increase the volume of mine to try to get them to do likewise.	I will sometimes lower my voice when talking to show respect; if a person talking to me increases the volume of their speech, perhaps they are angry, so I will need to make my voice even softer.
Time sense, chronicity	Punctuality, scheduling and sequence are all important. Time is to be managed.	Things happen at their own pace. Time is to be experienced.
Status roles	Informality (especially with North Americans) is desirable; hierarchy is a problem.	Formality is desirable; hierarchy is a solution.

Sources: Adapted from Morris (2002); Hall (1977).

Some high-context and low-context cultures are compared in the next figure.

HIGH-CONTEXT AND LOW-CONTEXT CULTURES

Foster (2002b) has used the context concept to analyse different cultures, although he admits his analysis will inevitably be caught up in 'the anthropologist's dilemma' — that is, the impossibility of describing a culture objectively, due to the fact that the 'describer' is always viewing the culture being observed in reference to his or her own culture (in his case, the United States). See what you think of his analysis of these five cultures.

Saudi Arabia

Arabs are very context-driven communicators. They will speak in metaphors, and use stories or codified phrases; they will employ analogies, Islamic precedent, and much non-verbal behaviour to convey true meaning. They generally avoid confrontation, and are honour-bound to do everything possible to make strangers like and honour them (they are lavish hosts). They will avoid unpleasant discussions as long as possible, and it is precisely because they shun unpleasantness in discussions that anger, often expressed as an insult to pride, can blow fast and hard when disagreements can no longer be avoided.

Germany

The German language and methodical, detail-oriented aspects of German culture combine to create a form of speech that is often very direct and low context. Words are used to mean exactly what they are meant to say (it is therefore very important not to interrupt German speakers, and particularly not to end their statements for them). This blunt, precise way of speaking can sound harsh and too controlling to the North American ear; it is usually not meant in this way, but results from the preoccupation with limiting oneself to statements of fact. This is especially the case in business, while in social situations, Germans can be more subtle and playful in their communication styles.

Indonesia

Indonesians are very high-context communicators. They avoid confrontation, and will speak in terms that maintain harmony at all costs, even if this results in speech that is indirect, evasive or contradictory. Because circumstances rather than universal truths or laws determine action, sensitivity to the context is critical if you want accurate information on what is really being meant or done. The use of the word *yes*, even though *no* is meant; the avoidance of explanations and statements that even gently criticise or make someone look bad; the eternal smile, even when things are not going very well; the failure to provide bad news or important negative information; all of these are common characteristics in Indonesia, which can be ultimately understood and precluded if one develops the ability to read between the lines. Read the context, not the words.

Brazil

Most Brazilians are high-context communicators; depending upon the situation at the moment in which the communication takes place, Brazilians can alternately be careful about what they say and how they say it, and very direct and honest. Of course, Brazilians, like most Latinos, want smooth interpersonal working relationships, especially with outsiders, and will go the distance to reassure you that everything is okay and that all is in order — even when it may not be. This is not based on a desire to deceive but rather a need to appear capable and competent, and not to lose face in the eyes of others, particularly when it may be in one's interests to cultivate a relationship. It is critical, therefore, to always confirm information; to have multiple and independent sources 'on the ground' to confirm for you what you are being told; and to be able to read between the lines without directly challenging the veracity of what the Brazilian is saying. There is a strong tolerance for, in fact a dependence on, the subjective interpretation of events and reality.

Australia

Nothing will get Australians to tell you what's on their minds faster than if you try to tell them what's on your mind first. Australians are usually very direct, and have no problem telling you what they think of just about anything, including you and your country. They do not shy away from confrontation, but react to these things with positive good humour, acknowledging that this stuff can make some people pretty uncomfortable. In fact, a common Australian complaint about North Americans is that they don't tell you what's on their mind. Most of the time, Australian directness will take the form of good-natured ribbing or kidding around over a 'shout' (that's a round of beers) or two. If you don't get the point that way, however, Australians can also tell you more straightforwardly.

Sources: Saudi Arabia — Foster (2002b, p. 16); Germany — Foster (2000a, pp. 74–5); Brazil — Foster (2002a, p. 142); Indonesia — Foster (2000b, p. 136); Australia — Foster (2000b, p. 190).

Mintu-Wimsatt (2002), after analysing negotiations between people from a low-context culture (North Americans) and a high-context culture (the Philippines), suggests that persons from high-context and collectivist cultures may be less confrontational, and tend to place greater emphasis on interpersonal interactions compared to those from low-context and individualist countries; whereas the persons from low-context individualist countries may tend to be more (self-defeatingly) aggressive, hurried and win–lose in orientation.

Cultural context may also help to explain communication styles. Du-Babcock (1999) analysed the structure of discussions in a high-context language (Cantonese) and a low-context language (English) and found that the structure of topic management and turn taking was more spiral in pattern in the high-context language and more linear in pattern in the low-context language. This may be evidence that members of high-context cultures view the world in synthetic, spiral logical terms (a circular pattern), and members from low-context cultures may view the world in analytical, logical terms (a linear pattern).

ASSESS YOURSELF

Consider the context continuum that follows. Where on the continuum would you place:
(a) yourself?
(b) your home culture?
(c) a friend or acquaintance from another culture?

Low context   High context

Give reasons for your choices.

Huntington's clash of civilisations model

Huntington (Huntington 1996; Berger & Huntington 2002; Huntington 2004) looks at cultural change and communication both within nations and between nations, and the pictures he paints are not necessarily rosy. He argues that the post–World War II situation of a polarised world – balanced in a battle primarily between the superpowers, the Soviet Union and the United States – has changed, particularly with the collapse of the Soviet Union. Under that system, nation-states were superpowers, allies, satellites, clients, neutrals or non-aligned. Now, in a post-Cold War world, countries relate to civilisations (Huntington 1996, pp. 21, 26):

> In the post–Cold War world, the most important distinctions among peoples are not ideological, political or economic. They are cultural. People and nations are attempting to answer the most basic question humans can face: Who are we? And they are answering that question in the traditional way human beings have answered it, by reference to the things that mean most to them. People define themselves in terms of ancestry, religion, language, history, values, customs and institutions. They identify with cultural groups: tribes, ethnic groups, religious communities, nations, and, at the broadest levels, civilizations. People use politics not just to advance their interests but also to define their identity. We know who we are only when we know who we are not and often only when we know whom we are against.

> Nation-states remain the principal actors in world affairs. Their behavior is shaped as in the past by the pursuit of power and wealth, but it is also shaped by cultural preferences, commonalities and differences. The most important groupings of states are no longer the three blocs of the Cold War [The Free World, The Communist Bloc, the Unaligned Nations or the Third World] but rather the world's seven or eight [sic] major civilizations [Western, Latin American, African, Orthodox, Islamic, Sinic, Hindu, Buddhist and Japanese].

This alignment of people in terms of civilisations has, he suggests, considerable potential for conflict, particularly conflict between the western and Islamic civilisations, and western and Sinic (primarily Chinese) civilisations. This is, then, the **clash of civilisations** that might become more prominent in the next few decades.

In this world, Huntington suggests, nation-states can be classified in different ways (table 15.4).

Clash of civilisations: the idea (developed by North American political scientists) that cultures now may be the basis of conflicts between nations

TABLE 15.4 Huntington's model of states within civilisations

State type	Example	Analysis
Member state	Italy	A country fully identified with European–western civilisation
	Egypt	A country fully identified with Arab–Islamic civilisation
Core state	China	Most powerful and central state of Sinic civilisation, with influence over a large diaspora of overseas Chinese
	United States and Franco-German core of Europe	Most powerful and central states of western civilisation, with Britain an additional power adrift between them
Lone countries	Japan	Lacks cultural commonality with other Asian societies
	Ethiopia	Lacks cultural commonality with other African societies
	Haiti	Lacks cultural commonality with other Caribbean societies
Cleft countries	Sudan, Nigeria	Different regions with different religious affiliations (Christian, Muslim) are in conflict
	Czechoslovakia	Different cultures lead to split of nation-state
	Canada	Different cultures threaten to lead to split of nation-state

State type	Example	Analysis
Torn countries	Turkey	Has a single predominant culture (Islamic) but its leaders want it to shift to another culture (western)
	Russia	Has a single predominant culture (Orthodox) but its leaders want it to shift to another culture (western)
	Mexico	Has a single predominant culture (Latin) but its leaders want it to shift to another culture (western)
	Australia	Has a single predominant culture (western) but its leaders want it to shift to another culture (Asian)

Source: Adapted from Huntington (1996).

Torn countries are a particularly interesting part of the Huntington model. Turkey, for example, is an Islamic country seeking entry into the European Union, but there is ambivalence (secular versus religious) within the country about this historical path. There appears to be considerable debate within the European Union about granting full membership rights – such as free movement of citizens between European Union countries – to an Islamic country, and also an ambivalence based on cultural, security and migration concerns. As of 2010, the earliest next date that Turkey could enter the European Union was 2013.

Huntington also sees Australia as a torn country – torn between its history of European affiliation and its geography in the Asian area. He argues that the attempt to integrate Australia into Asian cultures under Prime Minister Paul Keating in the 1990s might be regarded by future historians as a major marker in the 'decline of the West'.

Intercultural and intracultural clashes

Huntington also investigated changes within nations, particularly the rise of multiculturalism, diversity and large-scale ethnic or racial change. For example, he notes that white North Americans will be in a minority in parts of the United States within a few decades, with a combination of Black, Asian, Native American and Hispanic subpopulations comprising a majority. He postulates that this may make the United States a cleft country, riven with internal dissensions and tensions. Huntington (1996, p. 318) links this to the global level by stating opposition to the forces of globalisation and westernisation leading to the imposition of a homogeneous US-style civilisation across the planet:

> Multiculturalism at home threatens the United States and the West; universalism abroad threatens the West and the world. Both deny the uniqueness of Western culture. The global monoculturalists want to make the world like America. The domestic multiculturalists want to make America like the world. A multicultural America is impossible because a non-Western America is not American. A multicultural world is unavoidable because global empire is impossible. The preservation of the United States and the West requires the renewal of Western identity. The security of the world requires acceptance of global multiculturality.

Huntington argues that the way to maintain global peace is for civilisations not to interfere in the running of other civilisations. His work has, predictably, evoked strong reactions, especially after the terrorist attacks on New York and Washington on 11 September 2001. Abrahamian (2003) argues that the 'clash of civilisations' idea is in fact quite weak, and the waves of emotion unleashed by the horrors of 9/11 have given a flawed idea a spurious authenticity, and have also made it all but impossible to mention 'the P word' – Palestine – or the ongoing conflict between Israel and Islamic forces in the Middle East, the real source of so much acrimony between the western and Islamic civilisations. Aysha (2003) suggests that Huntington's real concern is not with the clash between cultures but the clash within the US culture itself – a concern with multiculturalism, immigration, the threat of ethnic separatism and 'declinism', reflected by commentators such as Schlesinger (1998), Steyn (2007), Blankley (2006), Buchanan (2002, 2006), Ferguson (2006), Phillips (2007) and Fallows (2010).

Others, however, either accept or modify the basic clash thesis. For example, Inglehart & Norris (2003) contend that the real clash between Islam and the West is not about democracy, but about sex. Fundamental differences in attitudes towards divorce, abortion, gender equality and gay rights seem to exist between Islamic and western countries, and this may prove to be another source of crisis and conflict. Still others contend that such clashes might be about economics, energy and oil, neocolonialism, and the emotions of fear, humiliation and hope (Imai 2006; Marsh 2007; Jan & Winter 2007; Moïsi 2007; see also Capetillo-Ponce 2007; Bottici & Challend 2006).

ASSESS YOURSELF

Discuss the idea of a 'clash of civilisations' with a person from another culture. What insights emerge?

Diverse planet, diverse nation, diverse organisation?

We have now considered aspects of communication within macro- or large-scale cultures. Now let's turn our attention to micro-cultures, or organisations. Many countries have become much more multicultural in composition in the past few decades, which in effect means that much of what we are learning about *inter*cultural communication can also be applied to *intra*cultural communication.

Ethnic diversity has been one of the main drivers behind diversity in the work-place. **Diversity** means different things to different people, but it usually means greater representation within organisations of people from differing ethnic or racial background, sex, age, disability, national origin, religion and sexual orientation (gay/lesbian) (Edelman, Fuller & Riggs 2001). Socioeconomic class may also be a factor that needs to be taken into account (Valdata 2005).

Diversity: greater representation within organisations of people from differing ethnic or racial background, sex, age, disability, national origin, religion and sexual orientation

'Inclusion' is now also emerging as a term to encompass a broader base for organisational composition. Robertson (2006, p. 230), for example, gives instances of definitions of these terms used by some organisations:

- *Diversity:* 'Diversity encompasses the many ways people may differ, including gender, race, nationality, education, sexual orientation, style, functional expertise, and a wide array of other characteristics and backgrounds that make a person unique.'
- *Inclusion:* 'A competitive business advantage that we build and maintain by leveraging the awareness, understanding and appreciation of differences in the workplace to enable individuals, teams and businesses to perform at their full potential.'

The case for greater diversity is primarily based upon the assumption that organisations should directly reflect the make-up of the broader community. This is an equity argument, but also an efficiency argument. Joshi (2006), for example, has merged macro- and micro-cultural concepts so that organisations can be understood in terms of 'organisational demography', (figure 15.13). He argues that multicultural organisations may be more effective than organisations with lower or non-existent levels of diversity because multicultural teams will have more external networks and personal connections, allowing for greater flow of information and opportunities (see chapter 16 for a discussion of networking).

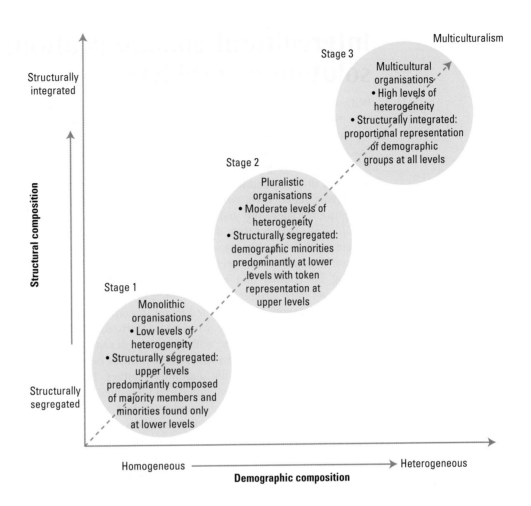

FIGURE 15.13 Joshi's three-stage model of organisational demography

Source: Joshi (2006, p. 586).

Within the figure:

Multiculturalism

Stage 3
Multicultural organisations
• High levels of heterogeneity
• Structurally integrated: proportional representation of demographic groups at all levels

Stage 2
Pluralistic organisations
• Moderate levels of heterogeneity
• Structurally segregated: demographic minorities predominantly at lower levels with token representation at upper levels

Stage 1
Monolithic organisations
• Low levels of heterogeneity
• Structurally segregated: upper levels predominantly composed of majority members and minorities found only at lower levels

Structurally integrated

Structural composition

Structurally segregated

Homogeneous — Heterogeneous

Demographic composition

There are, then, powerful arguments in favour of organisations becoming more diverse, just as there are for societies becoming more multicultural (Miller & Katz 2003; Cox 2001; Etzioni 2003; Jupp 1997, 2000–2001; Härtel 2004).

Multiculturalism as a concept, however, has sometimes been the subject of critique in the past decade, and to a certain extent, that critique has flowed on to the concepts of diversity and inclusion. Multiculturalism has come to be seen by some as a source of divisiveness in society, with individuals and groups from different cultural backgrounds sometimes perceived to be either opting out of participating in the mainstream culture, or in fact as being actively hostile towards the mainstream culture (Auster 2004; *BBC news* 2004; Schmidt 1997; Fukuyama 2005; Okin 1999; Farrar 2006; Sniderman 2007; Beck 2011). At the organisational level, it has been found that diversity does not always correlate with efficiency and effectiveness (Kochan et al. 2003; *Knight Ridder Tribune Business News* 2003), while others (Lasch-Quinn 2003; Lynch 2002; Wood 2003) have argued that diversity or inclusion, paradoxically, may be divisive, and may in fact undermine equality (e.g. beneficiaries of equal opportunity programs may be perceived to have been given positions because of diversity considerations rather than merit), and that 'diversity fatigue' may be setting in at some workplaces (Gordon 2003; Bronson & Merryman 2006; Benson 2005).

These issues involve deeply-held values and strong emotions, and feature strongly in discourse about diversity, multiculturalism, intercultural communication and intracultural communication.

Intercultural communication: solution or problem?

With all of the conflicts between nations and within nations these days, it may well be that the more we learn about intercultural communication, the less conflict there will be, and that has to be a good thing. There is much food for thought in what we have discovered so far, and research into intercultural communication in the next few years will undoubtedly produce still newer and more powerful insights. We need to be aware, however, that communication does not always solve problems, and indeed can sometimes exacerbate them. Thus, while the communication models of Bennett, Deardorff and Joshi are powerful tools for understanding human interaction, they are, to a certain extent, teleological. That is, they seem to suggest that a final goal of understanding between people of different cultures will always be reached, and that will be good thing (see online chapter 6 'Scientific and technical writing' for a discussion of teleology). In fact, the forces making for conflict and non-communication between cultures are strong, and perhaps have never been stronger. Better intercultural communication is probably a necessary, but not sufficient, condition for a reduction in conflict between cultures.

Yet we must not forget the warnings of Hoftstede (2001). Conflicts can still occur between people with similar values, and peaceful coexistence can prevail between people with different values. In other words, similar profiles between nations do not guarantee peace, and dissimilar profiles do not guarantee conflict. The same dynamic pertains at the interpersonal level – between individual and individual, and among family and group members.

Just as the growth of greater understanding and the shrinking of ignorance and xenophobia promises the end of global conflicts, the reality is that familiarity all too often breeds contempt and violence. The most violent wars are often not intercultural ones but intra-cultural or civil ones. Perhaps for people from some cultural groups (e.g. different cultural groups in Ireland and the Middle East) familiarity may very well contribute to ongoing tensions.

From theory to practice: communicating across cultures

We have now considered processes of acculturation, four separate models of culture, and the ideas of diversity and inclusion. How do we then put all of these ideas into practice? How do we communicate better with people from other cultures, either in their own country, or in our own country? In some respects, this is related to the question of just how well (or how badly) we communicate with people from our own primary culture.

It is impossible, and undesirable, to produce lists of 'tips and tricks' of how to communicate with people from other cultures – in fact, given that the writer of this book lives in a low-context culture, such lists could be seen as a classic low-context thing to create. Nevertheless, knowledge of other cultures is possible, so long as such lists are seen to be as important for what they leave out as for what they leave in. When communicating with peoples from other cultures, then, focus your energies on two phases – preparation and delivery:

Preparation: research the culture

Find out more about the culture before going there or before interacting with others from that culture. What are 'the rules'? Read, use the internet, talk to those who have visited before, and operate on the principle of assuming that at least 50 per cent of what you see and hear is wrong – sometimes diametrically so. Focus your attention on the categories in table 15.5.

TABLE 15.5 'Rules' of different cultures

'Rules' relating to …	Example
Time	■ Are norms of punctuality strictly observed, sometimes observed, or ignored? ■ How important are scheduling and sequences of activities, diary-keeping, use of watches and clocks? ■ Is time to be managed, or to be experienced? ■ In professional and personal lives, do people have long time horizons (focusing on one or ten or fifty years from now) or short time horizons (tomorrow, next week, quarterly financial statements)? ■ Is it expected that desires will be gratified immediately, or is it expected that gratification will be deferred?
Space	■ In personal and professional settings, is private space valued or ignored? ■ What is the population density? ■ How large are offices and dwellings?
Non-verbal communication	■ How close do people stand when they are talking to each other? ■ What are the rules for touching other people of the same or opposite sex in personal and professional settings? ■ What are the rules for eye contact with others? Do people avert gaze to show respect? Is direct eye contact correlated with honesty? Is it polite to stare? ■ What vocal volume do people use when speaking? ■ Are any gestures or mannerisms considered to be taboo or in bad taste? ■ What clothing is considered appropriate for differing situations? ■ What adornment (hair styling, jewellery, body marking, etc.) is considered acceptable/unacceptable?
Socioeconomic, political milieu	■ What is the per-capita income? ■ How much socioeconomic mobility is there? ■ How much socioeconomic equality is there? ■ What are the levels of wealth and savings? ■ What is the per-capita rate of energy consumption? ■ What is the average life expectancy for males and females? ■ What resources are present/lacking? ■ What is the nature of political power? ■ Are leaders elected? ■ Does every adult have a vote? ■ Is there optimism about leaders being able to solve large-scale problems? ■ How stable is the political situation? ■ Is ethnic diversity high or low? ■ What is the rate of change of ethnic diversity? ■ Is there separation of church and state? ■ How independent is the media? ■ How independent is the judiciary? ■ What online ratings are given by organisations such as Transparency International, Amnesty International, Freedom House, Global Witness, Nation Master, WorldWatch? ■ Do people work to live, or live to work? ■ Which is given more importance – seniority or merit? ■ What is the usage of computers, the internet and mobile/cell phones? ■ Are the prices of everyday commodities fixed or can they be bargained/haggled over? ■ How high is the level of trust in the police? ■ When agreements on medium- to large-scale enterprises are reached, is extensive legal documentation required, or are verbal agreements preferred? ■ Do subordinates expect to be consulted on decision making, or told? ■ Are organisational pyramids flat or tall? ■ Is nepotism (giving preference to relatives) acceptable? ■ Is it acceptable or expected to give gifts or money as an inducement in a transaction?

(continued)

TABLE 15.5 *(continued)*

'Rules' relating to ...	Example
Values and beliefs	■ What rituals and protocol are involved in meeting a person or group? What rituals and protocol are involved when you depart? ■ How important is religious ritual in everyday life? ■ Do females have the same rights as males? ■ What are dominant attitudes towards homosexuality? ■ Is there more sympathy for the strong than for the weak? ■ Is risk taking admired or frowned on? ■ Are strangers welcomed or are they viewed with suspicion? ■ What are the attitudes towards processes of globalisation? ■ How much tolerance is there of ambiguity and uncertainty? ■ Is competition or cooperation more important? ■ If an individual achieves success and wealth, is the expectation that the wealth should be kept by the individual or shared communally? ■ How is the year structured in terms of holidays (holy days) and festivals? ■ What differences in values and beliefs are there between different generations?
Roles	■ How are tasks and responsibilities allocated in households? ■ Are old people given respect and power? ■ In relationships, is formality or informality more important? ■ How do people primarily identify themselves – according to neighbourhood, state/province, family, clan, tribe, caste, class, ethnic group, religion, nationality? ■ How is status displayed?
Communication and conflict	■ Is it acceptable to express strong emotions in public? ■ What languages are spoken? ■ How many people speak more than one language? ■ What is the literacy level? ■ Which is more important – direct, explicit messages or indirect, implicit messages? ■ Is it more important to fight for an issue, no matter what the cost, or to compromise? ■ Do individuals or groups make decisions? ■ Is self-disclosure of weaknesses and problems admirable or contemptible? ■ What constraints are there on violent actions and words? ■ Are verbal and non-verbal messages always congruent? ■ What levels of tolerance are shown towards those of other classes, religions, nationalities?

Delivery: interact with the culture

Once you have some information about these categories (and you will never have all of the information you need), consider using these communication strategies:

1. Don't operate from the position of believing that your culture is superior to that of the person you are interacting with.
2. Don't operate from the position of believing that your culture is inferior to that of the person you are interacting with.
3. Try to ensure that your verbal and non-verbal communication reinforce, not contradict, each other.
4. Demonstrate and model respect for the other person, and expect respect in return.
5. Strive to present a calm and politely assertive demeanour – don't come across as aggressive or submissive.
6. Try to find common ground and mutual interests.
7. If working with a translator, try to break up your ideas into relatively short but sequential segments.
8. Monitor the other person's non-verbal communication to check how your messages are getting across.

9. Be willing to invest time in building rapport rather than always jumping into task-oriented specifics.
10. Speak clearly, and avoid using jargon and slang.
11. Try not to be disoriented by new sights, sounds, tastes and smells.
12. Participate in rituals of greeting and farewells.
13. Consider investing time and resources in learning the language of the area, or at least 20–30 words and phrases of that language. Only do this if you feel confident in doing so.
14. Try to ascertain what the optimal mix of communication channels is and will be for those you are interacting with.
15. Defer judgement and don't rush to conclusions – gather information by listening and by respectfully questioning; don't spend more time talking than listening.
16. Pay attention, but continually monitor your performance by refreshing your memories of what you have learnt about the culture's rules of time, space, non-verbal communication, the socioeconomic and political milieu, values and beliefs, roles, and communication and conflict.
17. Say what you mean, and mean what you say.
18. Pace yourself – this may be the first of numerous interactions, so take it easy, and be comfortable with adjourning to another time and place.
19. Be absolutely clear in your own mind what your objectives and goals are, and communicate these with clarity.
20. If you are part of a team or group, ensure beforehand that all others share objectives and goals, and understand their roles within the interaction.
21. Don't joke about the sounds of the names of people from other cultures, which may sound humorous or obscene in your own language: it's incredibly rude and potentially offensive. Consider your own name in the thousands of languages on the planet – maybe there's something to laugh about there, and you perhaps wouldn't necessarily see the joke.
22. Be ready to ruthlessly abandon any or all of these strategies if they are not working, and try something else.

Applied intercultural communication

Let's now consider two very different nations or cultures, the Chinese and the North Americans, and examine them within the specific communications arena of negotiation and conflict to see what insights emerge.

The Chinese

Much has been made of the economic, political and military rise of China (and India and Brazil) in recent times (Jacques 2010; Gupta & Wang, 2009). To better understand

the dynamics of this new world, Lee (2003, p. 5) suggests that outsiders like North Americans can best understand the Chinese by considering cultural backgrounds. North Americans, he suggests, are 'cowboys' (individualistic, profit-driven and ruled by law), whereas the Chinese are 'dragons' (group oriented, harmony-driven and ruled by hierarchical authority). This is also borne out by the research of Hofstede and the GLOBE team, and Hall's idea of Asians as high-context people.

Yu and Miller (2003) suggest that the Chinese business style is influenced by Buddhism (with its emphasis on obedience, trust, morals and stable mentality), Taoism (with its emphasis on control, collectivism and hierarchy), and Confucianism (with its emphasis on friendship, networks and loyalty). Graham and Lam (2003) suggest that four cultural threads have bound the Chinese people together for some 5000 years (agrarianism, morality, the Chinese pictographic language, and wariness of strangers), and these show through in Chinese business negotiations.

Mainland China, or the People's Republic of China, has been consciously engaging more with the rest of the world for some time. Under Communist control, particularly before the 'Four Modernisations' policy of 1978 (agriculture, industry, defence, and science and technology), this was not always so. The massacre in Tiananmen Square in 1989 arrested this engagement, or at least arrested the West's reciprocal engagement, but this appears to be improving, with the possibility of China emerging as a superpower.

The Chinese are apt to see issues, and begin negotiations, by looking at the big picture. Confucian holism portrays the world as a synthesis of differing parts, of yin and yang (Kirkbride & Tang 1990, pp. 5–6). In practical terms, this may mean that Chinese negotiators begin proceedings not by addressing specifics, but by considering general principles, by constructing a framework for all that is to follow. This can often make more pragmatic, issue-oriented westerners impatient. The slow opening is not only a reflection of a worldview; it is partly because the Chinese do not see negotiations as an adversarial process (even though they can be formidable adversaries), but rather as an occasion for building a relationship to work together (Seligman 2009, p. 156). It is also partly because at the opening of the negotiation, the Chinese are not yet negotiating — they are still doing research and preparation, sizing up the other side to determine their negotiating position, their trustworthiness and sincerity, and their vulnerabilities (Hendon, Hendon & Herbig 1999, p. 37):

> Confucianism, honesty, integrity, and sincerity in dealmaking are greatly appreciated ... Many cultures are holistic, especially in the Far East, where all issues are to be discussed at once and no decisions made until the end. Especially in the Far East, the negotiating session is less a forum for working out issues than it is a formal and public expression of what has already been worked out beforehand. Asians may use cooperative styles when negotiating among themselves but can be ruthless with outsiders.

> The Asian negotiation process is as much a ceremony and courtship as it is a form of business communication. The negotiation style in the Asian context is often described as relationship-oriented, and concentrates on a long-term, single-source arrangement. The implication of this style is that it is collaborative and will lead to some mutual satisfaction. The form is often more important than the functional. In contrast the American style of negotiation is to concentrate on the results (the ends) as an outcome. This focus on results is very characteristic of Western cultures ...

> Asians value details in formulating their business decisions; they consider information gathering to be the heart of a negotiation. However, what they call a 'know-how exchange' often becomes 'information rape', with the Asian side planning to reverse-engineer a Western product from the outset of collaboration with the firm. The Asians' objective of sharing in a company's know-how without paying for it may be partially cultural in origin. In Asia, no notion of proprietary know-how took root; new technology was shared by all. Knowledge was kept public, and to imitate or adopt someone else's methodology was considered virtuous, and a great compliment to the person who created it. Borrowing another person's know-how was considered to be neither thievery nor unethical. Knowledge is to be transmitted to the country as a whole, not hidden away.

In spite of a new openness to outsiders, China is still remarkably centralised, bureaucratic and secretive. It is unusual, for example, for an outside organisation to make contact with an end user — say, a company or collective that wants to purchase machine tools or educational services — and then negotiate totally with that end user. It is more likely that approaches will need to be made via official government agencies, and then negotiations will be concluded with those agencies. China, however, is not so centralised that successfully concluding an agreement with one agency means that you have an officially sanctioned and locked-up deal; other agencies may need to approve, and in fact may be hostile to the deal (Seligman 1999, p. 152).

The notion of 'closing a deal' needs to be treated with caution. In western countries, operating within a low-context mentality, one seals the deal and then walks away to begin another one. High-context countries, however, tend to see a deal as a part of an ongoing relationship, requiring much more emotional investment. In the case of Chinese negotiators, this is taken further so that everything is negotiable at all times: issues apparently settled early in the negotiation may be brought up towards the close, and bargaining may still take place as a low-context westerner is driven to the airport, or even after he or she has departed. Thus for the Chinese, a start may not really be a start, and a finish may not really be a finish (Hendon, Hendon & Herbig 1999, p. 38):

> The Chinese are quick to probe for, and then exploit in jujitsu fashion, any compelling interests of the other party. In particular they feel they have the advantage whenever the other party exudes enthusiasm and seems to be single-mindedly pursuing a particular objective. For the Chinese, working to a common goal is the most important feature of the negotiations. This means the development of a long-term relationship. The Chinese prefer an instrumental and competitive approach to bargaining. [They] conduct negotiations in a linear manner of discrete stages and in a distinctive (but not unique) style. They pursue their objectives through a variety of stratagems designed to manipulate feelings of friendship, obligation and guilt: the games of guanxi (Chinese communication networks). The Chinese tend to stress at the outset their commitment to abstract principles and will make concessions only at the eleventh hour after they have fully assessed the limits of the other side's flexibility. After protracted exchanges, when a deadlock seems to have been reached, concessions may be made to consummate an agreement. And while the end-game phase may produce a signed agreement, the Chinese negotiator will continue to press for his objective in the post-agreement phase (implementation stage), giving negotiations with the Chinese the quality of continuous bargaining in which closure is never fully reached. To the Chinese (and most East Asian cultures), a contract is relative to the conditions: if the conditions change, the contract should likewise be altered.

In spite of profound differences between Western countries and China, however, there are remarkable similarities between West and East. Kirkbride and Tang (1990, pp. 2–3) analysed a number of western books on negotiation, and found that these general 'rules' for successful negotiation (followed by Chinese and westerners) were usually proposed:

- Always set explicit limits or ranges for the negotiation process.
- Always seek to establish 'general principles' early in the negotiation.
- Always focus on potential areas of agreement and seek to expand them.
- Avoid taking the negotiation issues in sequence.
- Avoid excessive hostility, confrontation and emotion.
- Always give the other party something to 'take home'.
- Always prepare to negotiate as a team.

Chinese negotiation behaviour can be understood within a framework of strategies and tactics used all over the world (Seligman 1999; Kirkbride & Tang 1990; Brahm 2004; Eunson 2004), such as:

- *Invoking the competition*, and playing competitors off against each other – for example, by inviting rivals to a venue on Chinese soil and conducting parallel negotiations, using confidential information gained in one negotiation to pressure other negotiators in another negotiation.
- *Using time.* Negotiations with the Chinese often take a lot of time to set up, and they may ask for detailed technical presentations and detailed commercial negotiations that may take weeks. Other negotiators therefore have a massive time investment in the negotiations, and may be loath to cut their losses and walk away. With the Chinese

playing host on their own soil, they will have knowledge of when the other side is booked to leave the country, and may play the deadline tactic: leaving important matters till last, and attempting to stampede them into a better deal.

- *Good guy, bad guy* – for example, having a lower level negotiator test the other side's position and drive a hard bargain, or even appear hostile, and then allowing a higher level person to step in to effect a compromise.
- *Attrition*, or persevering with military precision: Chinese negotiators may have been influenced by historical military classics such as Sun Tzu's *The art of war* ('Strike hard, retreat, seize a position, reject compromise, and strike again.')

Western-style tactics that do not appear to work in China are ones such as 'lowballing' and 'splitting the difference'. ('Lowballing' is cutting one's prices to the bone and below, in expectation of better things later, and 'splitting the difference' is a 50–50 compromise between two opposed bottom lines.)

Non-verbal alert

The following list includes some insights into Chinese non-verbal behaviour (Seligman 2009; Axtell 1998):

- Chinese people operate at a close interpersonal distance.
- In spite of this, they are not touch-oriented, or may be selectively so; members of the same sex may touch each other, but members of the opposite sex may rarely touch each other in public (this is changing with younger Chinese).
- If you request something that will be difficult and/or embarrassing to satisfy, a Chinese may audibly suck in air through the teeth. This is a frustration and embarrassment signal. Change the request.
- Present business cards with both hands – a sign of respect.
- Chinese people may applaud as an approval sign – return it.
- It is not considered rude to stare at people, especially foreigners, in public.
- Silence is quite normal in conversations or negotiation.
- Age is venerated; white-haired negotiators have a hidden advantage, whereas young hot-shots may be seen as non-credible.

The North Americans

The United States currently possesses the largest economy on the planet, and produces more goods and services (and books on negotiation) than any other country. In terms of Hall's model of cultures, the United States is a classic low-context culture: individualistic; not group-oriented; lower sensory involvement in terms of interpersonal space and touching; more verbally than non-verbally oriented; monochronic rather than polychronic in time orientation.

The individualism of North Americans flows from their historical experience of revolution against tyranny, Protestantism, frontier resourcefulness and capitalist entrepreneurialism (stimulated by an enormous natural resource base). There has been an abiding suspicion throughout North American history of collectivist action and hierarchy, expressed as aristocracy or bureaucracy. Generally, these traits have made North Americans 'admirable'; and certainly, even though many non-North Americans are ambivalent about or hostile towards them, it is the image (as perhaps distinct from the reality) of the North American dream that has motivated and mesmerised hundreds of millions of people thirsting for freedom and/or material wealth.

North Americans, however, often have difficulty communicating with the outside world. Their strengths are sometimes their weaknesses, and this is particularly true of their negotiating style. As North American humorist Will Rogers observed in the 1930s: 'America has never lost a war and never won a conference' (in Graham & Herberger 1990). For many, North Americans are still 'ugly Americans', and this image can be understood in terms of low-context characteristics.

Individualism is a fine thing, but Japanese negotiators have noted, and been embarrassed by, the way members of North American negotiating teams will openly disagree with one another, rather than maintain a united front and settle their differences in private (Foster 1995, p. 81). Graham and Herberger (1990) suggest that the frontier image of the 'lone cowpuncher' or the macho John Wayne figure sometimes predisposes North American negotiators to enter another culture with some counterproductive, 'shoot first and ask questions later' types of behaviour, such as:

- North Americans who are influenced by the frontier hero 'outnumbered, and loving it' ethos may try to go it alone, to negotiate solo with a more skilled team from another, more group-oriented culture.
- North Americans may try to act independently, when in fact the essence of the negotiation process is interdependence.
- As relatively low power-distance people, they may prefer informality ('Call me John'), when in fact, in much of the world, formality is preferred.
- North Americans are mainly monolingual, only speaking English or at best, speaking other languages poorly.
- They may act as if winning is everything and that the adversarial approach is best, when in fact the best bargaining approaches relate to communication skills: 'in most places in the world, the one who asks the questions controls the process of negotiation and thereby accomplishes more in a bargaining situation' (Graham & Herberger 1990, p. 59).
- Sometimes, North Americans may not be aggressive enough. Chu (1991, p. 259) says that 'Asians know that 'the marketplace is a battlefield'. To the Americans, it is more like a football game'.

Other low-context characteristics that may present problems for North Americans in negotiations with, say, the Chinese are their monochronic time orientation and dependence on verbal, explicit communication. 'Time is money' for many North Americans. Often negotiations in America are quick, effective and pragmatic transactions; but in other cultures, more time is spent in building rapport and in finding out about the other side. This is primarily because negotiation is seen as a prelude to a long-term association, and thus negotiation never really ends. High-context cultures, with their networks of interconnecting relationships, provide a situation where people expect to see business partners face to face over long periods of time. This facilitates communication and builds trust. Many North Americans seem, to people of other cultures, in too much of a hurry to build this trust. As a Hong Kong businessman put it, North Americans are 'McDonaldised': 'Whatever they want to do, they want results right away' (quoted in Engholm 1993, p. 85).

Modes of communication and of chronicity are interconnected. North Americans are quite verbal and explicit rather than non-verbal and implicit in the way they communicate. Low-context cultures place great faith in the spoken and written word to regulate behaviour. Therefore North American negotiators are often uncomfortable with silence, and may say things just to fill up the voids: that may cost them in bargaining terms. They also tend to depend heavily on legalities, expressed in contracts. In other cultures, there is not so great a need for legal sanctions, because your partner is not going to hop on a jet and fly out in five minutes, never to be seen again. Some cultures find the North American insistence on getting legal staff to review deals offensive for this reason.

This behaviour can have consequences reaching far beyond the negotiating table. North Americans can be a very litigious people, and a litigious economic environment is a risk-averse, un-entrepreneurial culture (Kennedy 1985, p. 85). The Japanese, in contrast, seem to have more implicit, group-oriented mechanisms for solving conflict. The downside of this may be too much conformity; but the upside clearly is greater productivity and less risk-averse behaviour. Similarly, the short-term time orientation of North Americans in their negotiating style is merely a reflection of their business dealings generally, and this has led to an undue concern with quarterly profits rather than the long term – the reverse of high-context cultures where five-, ten- and hundred-year plans seem to be paying off (Foster 1995, p. 273; Mamman & Saffu 1998).

The egalitarianism of North Americans also leads many to believe in principle-based negotiation: 'Tell me your underlying principle'. This is at odds with other less egalitarian cultures, which tend to be more situation-based, more pragmatic in their negotiating style. For example, Hofstede has this to say about one of the world's best selling books on negotiation – *Getting to yes* (Fisher, Ury & Patton 1992):

> A well-known U.S. approach to negotiation training ... has stated four principles for 'coming to mutually acceptable agreements':
> 1. Separate the people from the problem
> 2. Focus on interests, not positions
> 3. Invent options for mutual gain
> 4. Insist on using objective criteria.
>
> All four of these principles contain hidden cultural assumptions:
>
> 1. Separating the people from the problem assumes an individualist value set. In collectivist cultures, where relationships prevail over tasks, this is an impossible demand. People are the first problem.
> 2. Focusing on interests, not positions, assumes a not-too-large power distance. In high PDI (power-distance index) cultures negotiation positions are often linked to power issues, which are of primary importance; vital interests are sacrificed to the maintenance of power positions.
> 3. Inventing options for mutual gain assumes a tolerance for new solutions – that is, a not-too-large uncertainty avoidance. In high UAI (uncertainty-avoidance index) cultures, where 'what is different is dangerous', some options are emotionally unthinkable for reasons that seem mysterious to the other party.
> 4. Insisting on using objective criteria assumes that there is a shared objectivity between the parties. Cultural values ... include attributions of rationality. What is objective to one party is subjective from a cross-cultural point of view. (Hofstede 2001, p. 436)

In spite of these considerations, North Americans are formidable negotiators, and should never be underestimated.

Non-verbal alert

The characteristics of North American non-verbal behaviour include the following:
- North Americans need a fair amount of interpersonal space.
- They are not too keen on being touched, but are more tactile than, say, the English – another low-context culture.
- A firm handshake and direct eye contact are considered to be tokens of honesty and directness.
- North Americans are among the most multiculturally diverse of peoples – generalisations about 'typical' behaviour are risky for any culture, but particularly for this one.
- North American behaviour – from the 'high five' to sporting triumph displays, to casual posture and clothing – continues via the global impact of its powerful media to be the most imitated in the world.

STUDENT STUDY GUIDE

SUMMARY

In this chapter, we have considered the process of acculturation, including Bennett's model of intercultural sensitivity with its six phases: denial, defence reversal, minimisation, acceptance, adaptation and integration. We looked at Deardorff's model of intercultural competence, which develops a hierarchy of specific skills, abilities and attitudes to achieve the desired behaviour (effective intercultural communication). We then examined the Hofstede model of culture, discussing power distance, uncertainty avoidance, individualism/collectivism, masculinity/femininity and short-term versus long-term time orientation. We looked at the GLOBE model of culture, which compared assertiveness, future orientation, gender differentiation, uncertainty avoidance, institutional collectivism versus individualism, in-group collectivism, performance orientation and humane orientation. We also considered Hall's model of low-context cultures and high-context cultures, and we examined the validity of Huntington's 'clash of civilisation' model. We then looked at Joshi's model of diversity and integration at an organisational level, and examined some strategies for implementing our knowledge in our communications with other cultures. We then applied these models to our understanding of intercultural communication between Chinese and North Americans in negotiation situations.

KEY TERMS

acculturation *p. 475*

clash of civilisations *p. 490*

diversity *p. 492*

feminine *p. 479*

high context *p. 487*

individualism *p. 479*

low context *p. 487*

macro-culture *p. 473*

masculine *p. 479*

micro-culture *p. 473*

monochronic *p. 487*

polychronic *p. 487*

power distance *p. 478*

the other *p. 475*

uncertainty avoidance *p. 478*

REVIEW QUESTIONS

1. Identify the six phases of Bennett's model of intercultural communication.
2. Identify at least four characteristics of masculine and feminine cultures in Hofstede's model.
3. Identify at least four of the cultural dimensions or attributes of the GLOBE model.
4. Identify at least two characteristics that distinguish high-context cultures from low-context cultures.
5. 'Context also depends on what generation within a culture we are talking about.' What does this mean?
6. Name at least two nations described by Huntington as being 'torn countries'.
7. What possible strengths and weaknesses might there be in a workplace diversity program?
8. Name at least three 'rules' relating to values and beliefs.
9. Identify at least four 'rules of negotiation' that apply equally to western and Chinese negotiators.
10. Why might time be a problem for a North American negotiator negotiating with people from other cultures?

APPLIED ACTIVITIES

1. Consider the integration phase of Bennett's model (p. 475). How might it be possible to help a person move from the encapsulated form of this phase to the constructive form?
2. 'Nationality and culture are the same thing.' Discuss.

3. Talk to someone from another culture who is familiar with the Hofstede model. How do they rate themselves on each of the five dimensions? How do they rate you? How do you rate them?
4. 'Hofstede's model of culture is completely useless because it depends on out-of-date data taken from too narrow a sample.' Discuss.
5. Imagine a situation in which two people from different cultures marry. Use the GLOBE model dimensions to explain how communication between the two might be enhanced or damaged.
6. 'The whole world will soon be low context.' Discuss.
7. 'There is no new clash of civilisations, only the same old national wars.' Discuss.
8. Consider the list of communication strategies (pp. 496–7). Working by yourself or with others, try to think of at least another three strategies.
9. Find a person who is a current or former Chinese or North American citizen. Give them a brief summary of the relevant section of this chapter. Ask them for their views.

WHAT WOULD YOU DO?

You are an Australian flying home from an overseas holiday. You find yourself next to a Japanese businessman, who is coming out to manage the Australian and New Zealand branch office of a company. He tells you that he has prepared thoroughly for this job, and has studied both Australian and New Zealand culture as much as possible through pop music, movies, TV soap operas and talkback radio (via the internet). He asks you for some tips on how to communicate effectively with Australians and New Zealanders, both in and out of the workplace.

Based on what you have read in this chapter on culture and intercultural communication, what would you say to him?

SUGGESTED READING

Beamer, Linda and Varner, Iris 2010, *Intercultural communication in the global workplace*, McGraw-Hill, New York.

Comfort, Jeremy, and Franklin, Peter 2010, *The mindful international manager: how to work effectively across cultures*, Kogan Page, London/New York.

Flammia, Madelyn and Sadri, Houman A. 2011, *Intercultural communication: a new approach to international relations and global challenges*, Continuum, New York.

REFERENCES

Abrahamian, Ervand 2003, 'The US media, Huntington and September 11', *Third World Quarterly*, vol. 24, no. 3, pp. 529–44.

Arnold, Guy 2011, *Migration: Changing the World*, Pluto Press, London.

Ashkanasy, Neal M, Trevor-Roberts, Edwin & Earnshaw, Louise 2002, 'The Anglo cluster: legacy of the British Empire', *Journal of World Business*, vol. 37, no.1, pp. 28–39.

Auster, Lawrence 2004, 'How multiculturalism took over America', *Frontpagemag.com*, 9 July, www.frontpagemag.com.

Axtell, Roger 1998, *Gestures: the do's and taboos of body language around the world*, rev. edn, John Wiley & Sons, New York.

Aysha, Emad El-Din 2003, 'Samuel Huntington and the geopolitics of American identity: the functions of foreign policy in America's domestic clash of civilizations', *International Studies Perspectives*, vol. 4, pp. 113–32.

Barber, Benjamin R 2001, *Jihad vs McWorld: terrorism's challenge to democracy*, Ballantine Books, New York.

BBC news 2004, 'Race chief wants integration push', BBC Television, 3 April, http://news.bbc.co.uk.

Beck, Jerome 2011, *How multiculturalism fails*, Kindle edn, Amazon Digital Services, seattle, WA.

Bennett, James C 2007, *The Anglosphere challenge: why the English-speaking nations will lead the way in the twenty-first century*, Rowman and Littlefield, Lanham, MD.

Benson, Rodney 2005, 'American journalism and the politics of diversity', *Media, Culture & Society*, vol. 27, no. 1, pp. 5–20.

Berger, Peter L & Huntingdon, Samuel P (eds.) 2002, *Many globalizations: cultural diversity in the contemporary world*, Oxford University Press, New York.

Berry, John W 2006, 'Contexts of acculturation', ch. 3 in David L Sam and John W Berry (eds), The *Cambridge handbook of acculturation psychology*, Cambridge University Press, Cambridge.

Blankley, Tony 2006, *The west's last chance: will we win the clash of civilizations?*, Regnery, Washington, DC.

Bottici, Chiara & Challend, Beno't 2006, 'Rethinking political myth: the clash of civilizations as a self-fulfilling prophecy', *European Journal of Social Theory*, vol. 9, no. 3, pp. 315–36.

Brahm, Laurence J 2004, *Doing business in China: the Sun Tzu way*, Charles E Tuttle, Boston, MA.

Bronson, Po & Merryman, Ashley 2006, 'Are Americans suffering diversity fatigue?', *Time*, 31 May. p. 17, also at www.time.com.

Brown, Lorraine 2009, 'Worlds apart: The barrier between east and west,' *Journal of International and Intercultural Communication*, Vol. 2, No. 3, pp. 240–259.

Buchanan, Patrick 2002, *The death of the West: how dying populations and immigrant invasions imperil our country and civilization*, St Martin's Press, New York.

—— 2006, *State of emergency: the third world invasion and conquest of America*, St Martin's Press, New York.

—— 2009, Day of reckoning: how hubris, ideology, and greed are tearing America apart, St Martin's press, New York.

Button, James 2006, 'Migrants are coming and going', *The Age*, 28 August, p. 12.

Capetillo-Ponce, Jorge 2007, 'From 'A clash of civilizations' to 'Internal colonialism': reactions to the theoretical bases of Samuel Huntington's 'The Hispanic challenge' ', *Ethnicities*, vol. 7, no. 1, pp. 116–34.

Chu, Chin-Ning 1991, *The Asian mind game: unlocking the hidden agenda of the Asian business culture. A Westerner's survival manual*, Scribners, New York.

Chua, Amy 2004, *World on fire: how exporting market democracy breeds ethnic hatred and global instability*, Anchor, New York.

Cox, Taylor 2001, *Creating the multicultural organization: a strategy for capturing the power of diversity*, Jossey-Bass, San Francisco.

Deardorff, Darla K 2006, 'Identification and assessment of intercultural competence as a student outcome of internationalization', *Journal of Studies in International Education*, vol. 10, no. 3, pp. 241–66.

Dougherty, Debbie, Mobley, Sacheen & Smith, Siobhan 2010, 'Language convergence and meaning divergence: A theory of intercultural communication,' *Journal of International & Intercultural Communication*; vol. 3 no. 2, pp. 164–86.

Du-Babcock, Bertha 1999, 'Topic management and turn taking in professional communication', *Management Communication Quarterly*, vol. 12, no. 4, pp. 544–75.

Edelman, Lauren B, Fuller, Sally Riggs & Mara-Drita, Iona 2001, 'Diversity, rhetoric and the managerialization of law', *American Journal of Sociology*, vol. 106, pp. 1589–1641.

Engholm, Christopher 1993, *When business East meets business West: the guide to practice and protocol in the Pacific Rim*, John Wiley & Sons, New York.

Etzioni, Amitai 2003, *The monochrome society*, Princeton University Press, Princeton.

Eunson, Baden 2004, *Negotiation Skills*, John Wiley & Sons, Brisbane.

Fallows, James 2010, 'How America can rise again', *The Atlantic*, January–February, www.theatlantic.com.

Farrar, Max 2006, 'When alienation turns to nihilism: the dilemmas posed for diversity post 7/7', *Conversations in Religion and Theology*, vol. 4, no. 1, pp. 98–123.

Ferguson, Niall 2006, *The war of the world: twentieth century conflict and the descent of the west*, Penguin, New York.

Fisher, Roger, Ury, William L & Patton, Bruce M 1992, *Getting to yes: negotiating agreement without giving in*, Penguin, New York.

Foster, Dean 2000a, *The global etiquette guide to Europe*, John Wiley & Sons, New York.

—— 2000b, *The global etiquette guide to Asia*, John Wiley & Sons, New York.

—— 2002a, *The global etiquette guide to Mexico and Latin America*, John Wiley & Sons, New York.

—— 2002b, *The global etiquette guide to Africa and the Middle East*, John Wiley & Sons, New York.

Foster, Dean Allen 1995, *Bargaining across borders: how to negotiate business successfully anywhere in the world*, McGraw-Hill, New York.

Fukuyama, Francis 1993, *The end of history and the last man*, Avon, New York.

—— 2005, 'A year of living dangerously', *The Wall Street Journal*, 2 November, p. A14.

Gordon, J Cunyon 2003, 'Diversity fatigue: sick and tired of being sick and tired', *Goal IX*, vol. 9, no. 2, pp. 1, 4–5, 8.

Graham, John L & Herberger, Roy A Jr 1990, 'Negotiators abroad: don't shoot from the hip', *Harvard Business Review*, vol. 68, no. 8, pp. 45–61.

Graham, John L & Lam, N Mark 2003, 'The Chinese negotiation', *Harvard Business Review*, vol. 81, no. 10, pp. 21–33.

Gupta, Vipin, Hanges, Paul J & Dorfman, Peter 2002, 'Cultural clusters: methodology and findings', *Journal of World Business*, vol. 37, no. 1, pp. 11–15.

Gupta, Vipin, Surie, Gita, Javidan, Mansour & Chhokar, Jagdeep 2002, 'Southern Asia cluster: where the old meets the new?', *Journal of World Business*, vol. 37, no. 1, pp. 16–27.

Hall, Edward T 1977, *Beyond culture*, Avon, New York.

Hallenbeck, James 2006, 'High context illness and dying in a low context medical world', *American Journal of Hospice and Palliative Medicine*, vol. 23, no. 2, pp. 113–18.

Halverson, Claire B 1993, 'Cultural context inventory', in J William Pfeiffer (ed.), *The 1993 annual: developing human resources*, Jossey-Bass/Pfeiffer, San Francisco.

Hammer, Mitchell R, Bennett, Milton J & Wiseman, Richard 2003, 'Measuring intercultural sensitivity: the intercultural development inventory', *International Journal of Intercultural Relations*, vol. 27, pp. 421–43.

Harries, Owen 2004, Benign or imperial? *Reflections on American hegemony—the 2003 Boyer lectures*, ABC Books, Sydney.

Härtel, Charmaine EJ 2004, 'Towards a multicultural world: identifying work systems, practices and employee attitudes that embrace diversity', *Australian Journal of Management*, vol. 29, no. 2, pp. 189–200.

Haviland, William A 2010, Prins, Harald E.L., Walrath, Dana, and McBride, Bunny *Cultural anthropology: the human challenge*, 13th edn, Wadsworth, Belmont, CA.

Hendon, Donald W, Hendon, Rebecca Angeles & Herbig, Paul 1999, *Cross-cultural business negotiations*, Praeger, Westport, CT.

Hofstede, Geert 2001, *Culture's consequences: comparing values, behaviors, institutions and organizations across nations*, 2nd edn, Sage, Thousand Oaks, CA/London.

—— 2006, 'What did GLOBE really measure? Researchers' minds versus respondents' minds', *Journal of International Business Studies*, vol. 37, pp. 882–96.

—— 2010 'The GLOBE debate: Back to relevance,' *Journal of International Business Studies*, vol. 41, pp. 1339–1346.

Holliday, Adrian, Hyde, Martin & Kullman, John 2004, *Intercultural communication: an advanced resource book*, Routledge, New York.

House, Robert J 1998, 'A brief history of GLOBE', *Journal of Managerial Psychology*, vol. 13, nos 3–4, pp. 230–40.

House, Robert J, Hanges, Paul J, Javidan, Mansour, Dorfman, Peter W & Gupta, Vipin 2004, *Culture, leadership and organizations: The GLOBE study of 62 societies*, Sage, Thousand Oaks, CA/London.

House, Robert J, Quigley, Narda, Sully, Mary 2010, 'Insights from Project Globe,' *International Journal of Advertising*, vol. 29, no. 1, pp. 111–39.

Huntington, Samuel P 1996, *The clash of civilizations and the remaking of the world order*, Simon & Schuster, New York.

—— 2004, *Who are we: the cultural core of American national identity*, Simon & Schuster, New York.

Imai, Kunihiko 2006, 'Culture, civilization, or economy? Test of the clash of civilizations thesis', *International Journal on World Peace*, vol. 23, no. 3, pp. 3–32.

Inglehart, Ronald & Norris, Pippa 2003, 'The true clash of civilizations', *Foreign Policy*, March–April, pp. 63–70.

Jan, Abid Ullan & Winter, Rory 2007, *The ultimate tragedy: colonialists rushing to global war to save the crumbling empire*, BookSurge, Charleston, SC.

Jacques, Martin 2010, *When China rules the world: the end of the Western World and the birth of a new global order*, Penguin Press, New York.

Javidan, Mansour & House, Robert J 2001, 'Cultural acumen for the global manager: lessons from Project GLOBE', *Organizational Dynamics*, vol. 29, no. 4, pp. 289–305.

—— 2002, 'Leadership and cultures around the world: findings from GLOBE. An introduction to the special issue', *Journal of World Business*, vol. 37, no. 1, pp. 1–2.

Javidan, Mansour, House, Robert J, Dorfman, Peter W, Hanges, Paul J & de Luque, Mary Sully 2006, 'Conceptualizing and measuring cultures and their consequences: a comparative review of GLOBE's and Hofstede's approaches', *Journal of International Business Studies*, vol. 37, pp. 897–914.

Joshi, Arpana 2006, 'The influence of organizational demography on the external networking behavior of teams', *Academy of Management Review*, vol. 31. no. 3, pp. 583–95.

Jupp, James 1997, 'An anxious society fears the worst', *Journal of Australian Studies*, nos. 54–5, pp. 1–11.

—— 2000–2001, 'Multiculturalism: maturing or dying?', *Dissent*, no. 4, pp. 30–1.

Kabasakal, Hayat & Bodur, Muzaffer 2002, 'Arabic cluster: a bridge between East and West', *Journal of World Business*, vol. 37, no. 1, pp. 40–54.

Kennedy, Gavin 1985, *Negotiate anywhere! Doing business abroad*, Business Books, London.

Kirkbride, Paul S & Tang, Sara FY 1990, 'Negotiation: lessons from behind the bamboo curtain', *Journal of General Management*, vol. 16, no. 1, pp. 1–13.

Kirkman, Bradley L, Lowe, Kevin B & Gibson, Cristina B 2006, 'A quarter century of culture's consequences: a review of empirical research incorporating Hofstede's Cultural Values Framework', *Journal of International Business Studies*, vol. 37, no. 3, pp. 285–321.

Knight Ridder Tribune Business News, 6 August 2003, 'Data show little gain in attempts to make workplace look more like society', p. 1.

Kochan, Thomas, Bezrukova, Katerina, Ely, Robin, Jackson, Susan, Joshi, Aparna, Jehn, Karen, Leonard, Jonathan, Levine, David & Thomas, David 2003, 'The effects of diversity on business performance: report of the Diversity Research Network', *Human Resource Management*, vol. 42, no. 1, pp. 3–21.

Lasch-Quinn, Elizabeth 2003, *Race experts: how racial etiquette, sensitivity training, and new age therapy hijacked the civil rights movement*, Rowman & Littlefield, Lanham, MD.

Lee, Charles 2003, *Cowboys and dragons: shattering cultural myths to advance Chinese–American business*, Dearborn Trade Publishing, Chicago.

Lindquist, Jay D & Kaufman-Scarborough, Carol F 2004, 'Polychronic tendency analysis: a new approach to understanding women's shopping behaviours', *The Journal of Consumer Marketing*, vol. 21, nos. 4/5, pp. 332–43.

Livermore, David 2010, *Leading with cultural intelligence: the new secret to success*, AMACOM, New York.

Lynch, Frederick 2002, *The diversity machine: the drive to change the 'White Male Workplace'*, Transaction Publishers, Piscataway, NJ.

Mamman, Aminu & Saffu, Kojo 1998, 'Short-termism, control, quick-fix and bottom-line: toward explaining the Western approach to management', *Journal of Managerial Psychology*, vol. 13, nos 5–6, pp. 291–308.

Marsh, Gerald E 2007, 'Can the clash of civilizations produce alternate energy sources?', *USA Today*, vol. 135, no. 2740, pp. 10–13.

Martin, Judith N & Nakayama, Thomas K 2007, *Intercultural communication in contexts*, 4th edn, McGraw-Hill, New York.

Miller, Frederick A & Katz, Judith H 2003, *The inclusion breakthrough: unleashing the real power of diversity*, Berrett-Koehler, San Francisco.

Mintu-Wimsatt, Alma 2002, 'Personality and negotiation style: the moderating effects of cultural context', *Thunderbird International Business Review*, vol. 44, no. 6, pp. 729–48.

Moïsi, Dominique 2007, 'The clash of emotions', *Foreign Affairs*, vol. 86, no. 1, pp. 8–10.

Morris, Desmond 2002, *People watching: the Desmond Morris guide to body language*, Vintage, London.

Narlikar, Amrita 2011, *Bargaining with the strong: negotiation processes in international regimes*, World Scientific Publishing, New Jersey.

Nonis, SA, Teng, JK & Ford, CW 2005, 'A cross-cultural investigation of time management practices and job outcomes', *International Journal of Intercultural Relations*, vol. 29, no. 4, pp. 409–28.

Okin, Susan Muller 1999, *Is multiculturalism bad for women?*, Princeton University Press, Princeton.

Pekerti, Andre A 2005, 'Cross-cultural perceptions in the leadership process: theoretical perspective on the influence of culture on self-concepts and manager-worker attributions', *Thunderbird International Business Review*, vol. 47, no. 6, pp. 711–35.

Phillips, Kevin 2007, *American theocracy: the peril and politics of radical religion, oil, and borrowed money in the 21st century*, Penguin, New York/London.

Robertson, Quinetta M 2006, 'Disentangling the meanings of diversity and inclusion in organizations', *Group & Organization Management*, vol. 31, no. 2, pp. 212–36.

Sam, David L & Berry, John W 2006, 'Introduction', in David L Sam and John W Berry (eds.), *The Cambridge handbook of acculturation psychology*, Cambridge University Press, Cambridge.

Sparke, Matthew 2011, *Introducing globalization: the ties that bind*, Wiley-Blackwell, New York/London.

Schlesinger, Arthur M Jr 1998, *The disuniting of America: reflections on a multicultural society*, rev. edn, W.W. Norton, New York.

Schmidt, Alvin J 1997, *The menace of multiculturalism: Trojan horse in America*, Praeger Publishers, New York.

Seligman, Scott D. 2009, *Chinese business etiquette: a guide to protocol, manners, and culture in the People's Republic of China*, Grand Central Publishing, New York.

Smith, Peter B 2006, 'When elephants fight, the grass gets trampled: the GLOBE and Hofstede projects', *Journal of International Business Studies*, vol. 37, pp. 915–21.

Sniderman, Paul M 2007, *When ways of life collide: multiculturalism and its discontents in the Netherlands*, Princeton University Press, Princeton.

Soares, Ana Maria, Farhangmehr, Minoo & Shoham, Aviv 2007, 'Hofstede's dimensions of culture in international marketing studies', *Journal of Business Research*, vol. 60, pp. 277–84.

Steyn, Mark 2007, *America alone: the end of the world as we know it*, Regnery, Washington, DC.

Szabo, Erna, Brodbeck, Felix C, Den Hartog, Deanne N, Reber, Gerhard, Weibler, Jürgen & Wunderer, Rolf 2002, 'The Germanic European cluster: where employees have a voice', *Journal of World Business*, vol. 37, no. 1, pp. 55–68.

Thumboo, Edwin 2003, 'Closed and open attitudes to globalised English: notes on issues', *World Englishes*, vol. 22, no. 3, pp. 233–43.

Usunier, Jean-Claude 2010 'The influence of high- and low-context communication styles on the design, content, and language of business-to-business web sites,' *Journal of Business Communication* vol. 47 no. 2 pp. 189–227.

Valdata, Patricia 2005, 'Class matters', *Diverse*, 3 November, pp. 20–3.

Veenkamp, Theo, Bentley, Tom & Buonfino, Alessandra 2003, *People flow: managing migration in a new European commonwealth*, Demos, London.

Wiseman, Geoffrey 2005, 'Pax Americana: bumping into diplomatic culture', *International Studies Perspectives*, vol. 6, pp. 409–30.

Wood, Peter 2003, *Diversity: the invention of a concept*, Encounter Books, New York.

Würtz, Elizabeth 2005, 'A cross-cultural analysis of websites from high-context cultures and low-context cultures', *Journal of Computer-Mediated Communication*, vol. 11, no. 1, article 13, http://jcmc.indiana.edu/.

Yu, Hui-Chun & Miller, Peter 2003, 'The generation gap and cultural influence—a Taiwan empirical investigation', *Cross-Cultural Management*, vol. 10, no. 3, pp. 23–41.

16

Organisational communication

LEARNING OBJECTIVES

After studying this chapter you should be able to:

- Explain the different types of channels that can be used in organisational communication
- Describe the nature of upward, downward and horizontal communication patterns
- Explain how organisational design factors (flat versus tall, centralised versus decentralised, mechanistic versus organic) affect organisational communication
- Explain network organisations, network roles and networking strategies
- Describe aspects of the informal organisation and communication system
- Identify different aspects of organisational culture, including silos and silence
- Explain the relationship between knowledge management and organisational communication

Organisations: systems of communication effectiveness and communication breakdown

In chapter 1, we saw that different areas of communication could be meaningfully analysed as a series of concentric circles (see figure 16.1). As we shall see, there are numerous interconnections between this chapter – dealing with communication in organisations – and nearly every chapter in this book, especially those dealing with interpersonal communication.

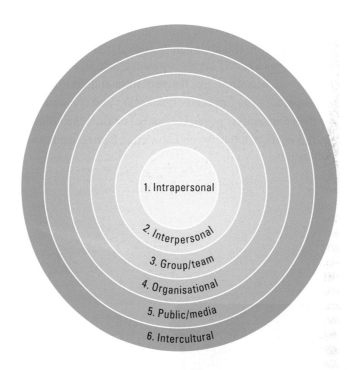

FIGURE 16.1 A concentric model of fields of communication

1. Intrapersonal
2. Interpersonal
3. Group/team
4. Organisational
5. Public/media
6. Intercultural

This means that, increasingly, there is no clear line of demarcation between where the organisation ends and where the outside world begins. Argenti and Haley (2006) point out, for example, that organisations need to align their communication messages to external and internal audiences, not only because it is professional and systematic to do so, but because all audiences, through a variety of formal and informal communication channels have unprecedented access to what has been said to the other audiences. Communicating with external audiences or publics, such as customers and/or the community and/or the media, needs thus to be consistent – to be aligned with – communication with the audiences or publics internal to the organisation. If there is no **alignment strategy** – if this is not done – the managers of an organisation may be seen at best as inconsistent and at worst as hypocritical and manipulative.

An **organisation** consists of a group of people who work together to achieve a common purpose. It can consist of two people or two million people, and can be structured as a small business or an army, corporation, government or church. An organisation is bigger than the individuals and groups that comprise it, but smaller than the society that gives it its context and environment.

Alignment strategy: ensuring that all messages communicated to audiences within an organisation are consistent with messages communicated to audiences outside the organisation

Organisation: a group of people who work together to achieve a common purpose

What is organisational communication?

Organisational communication is difficult to define. Richmond and McCroskey (2009) describe it as 'the process by which individuals stimulate meaning in the minds of other individuals, by means of verbal and nonverbal messages in the context of a formal organisation'. Pace and Faules (1994, p. 20) suggest it is 'the display and interpretation of messages among communication units who are part of a particular organisation. An organisation is comprised of communication units in hierarchical relations to each other and functioning in an environment'. Miller (2006, p. 1) has this to say:

> Most scholars would agree that an organisation involves a social collectivity (or a group of people) in which activities are coordinated in order to achieve both individual and collective goals. By coordinating activities, some degree of organisational structure is created to assist individuals in dealing with each other and with others in the larger organisational environment. With regard to communication, most scholars would agree that communication is a process that is transactional (i.e., it involves two or more people interacting within an environment) and symbolic (i.e., communication transactions 'stand for' other things, at various levels of abstraction). To study 'organisational communication', then, involves understanding how the context of the organisation influences communication processes and how the symbolic nature of communication differentiates it from other forms of organisational behaviour.

In this chapter we will examine what makes communication work within an organisation, and what prevents or distorts communication within an organisation. You may note the links to discussions elsewhere in this book on group or team communication, feedback, intercultural communication, gender communication, leadership, influencing and persuasion, and dealing with conflict. Because the organisation is not sealed off from the outer world, we may also see overlaps in content and approach between this chapter and the coverage on customer communication, public communication and mass communication.

Here we will consider a number of different aspects of organisational communication, including structures, channels, culture, roles, and the management of information, data, knowledge and learning.

Choosing the most appropriate channel for your message will help it reach the right audience.

Communication channels

Numerous pathways, channels or media can be used to convey messages within organisations.

In chapter 1, for example, we considered the strengths and weaknesses of workplace communication channels such as memos, email, voicemail, instant messaging, formal and informal meetings, noticeboards, suggestion boxes, 360° feedback, focus groups, plenary briefings, supervisor or team leader briefings, closed-circuit telecasts, video recordings, newsletters, charts and posters, management by walking around (MBWA), the grapevine or rumour mill, position papers, ombudsmen, blogs and websites. We learned how different channels, pathways or media can offer one-way, two-way or multidirectional communication that may be mediated or nonmediated, **synchronous** or **asynchronous**, involving individuals or groups.

Synchronous communication: communication that is sent and received at virtually the same time

Asynchronous communication: communication that is sent at one time and received at another time

When we want to send a message within an organisation, we need to consider channel, message type and audience or target. Choosing the right channel to get a certain message through to a certain audience can be more difficult than is first apparent. Clampitt (2000, p. 108), for example, notes:

- A *memo* is a poor choice whereas a small group meeting is a better choice in a situation where a midsize construction firm wants to announce a new employee benefit program (because the memo does not offer synchronous two-way or feedback potential to explain what may be seen as arcane information; some employees may have literacy problems).
- The *phone* is a poor choice whereas *email or voicemail* is a better choice in a situation where a manager wishes to confirm a meeting time with ten employees (because there is no need to use a rich and synchronous medium for a simple message).

Lewis (1999, p. 75) makes the following observations about channel choice:

- *Interpersonal channels* are more likely to meet specific needs of organisational members in overcoming risk and complexity associated with a change. When high risk or complexity are not major factors, *mediated channels* are more effective in providing general information.
- Most *mediated communications* (e.g. reports, newspapers, videos, posters, chief executive officer's (CEO's) presentations, closed-circuit TV shows) are centred on the CEO's message, which can be counter-productive: much research suggests that employees will change only if they receive rationales for change from their *immediate supervisor* rather than others further up the food chain of the organisation.
- Following from this, not enough organisations take advantage of the credibility that *lower-level supervisors* have: they are not briefed adequately, possibly because they are not trusted, or because the lower-level details of change programs have been insufficiently well thought out.

Thomas et al. (2006) note in relation to *email* that:

- It has become the channel of choice for many people in organisations, irrespective of the status or position of those people, with messages not being read once and deleted but rather filed and used as work tools.
- It threatens many with information overload, because:
  - inherent in the discourse or word patterns used in many emails is the expectation of immediate response: thus, while email is asynchronous in one sense, in another it is synchronous with a vengeance
  - when email is often copied to more than one person, duplication of tasks may occur when more than one person 'drops everything' to respond to the request or command in the text
  - the portability of computers and hand-held devices may entice some to do emailing while involved in other tasks (e.g. participating in meetings); such multitasking is often futile, dissipating concentration from one task to several
  - universal access to computers may generate an expectation that people will respond to email anytime, anywhere (weekends, holidays, out-of-work hours).

It has been said that the main cause of problems are solutions. The 'solution' to quick and widespread communication by email has led to some organisations implementing a 'no email Friday' policy to partially overcome the overcommunication caused by email (see chapter 6).

The best channel through which to convey information will depend on the situation. Effective organisational communicators use a number of channels, taking care to ensure that messages are repeated and reinforced in different ways.

We also need to take account of our own communication style, to ensure both that we choose channels we can work with and that we do not reject effective channels with which we are less comfortable. Practice in the use of new channels should help eliminate any shortcomings in delivery.

As we saw in chapter 1, using channels effectively therefore depends on four strategies. These four strategies are outlined in greater detail in figure 16.2.

Strategy 1:	Match the channel to the message and the audience or target.
Strategy 2:	Repeat and vary the message via different channels to reinforce the message.
Strategy 3:	Be ready to step outside our comfort zone to use the channels we are not necessarily comfortable with.
Strategy 4:	Be aware that the channel chosen may transform the content of the message.

FIGURE 16.2 Four strategies for effective organisational communication

ASSESS YOURSELF

Think of an organisation you are familiar with — perhaps a workplace, an educational institution, or a public transport or recreational facility. What channels of communication does this organisation use? How effective or ineffective are these channel choices?

Structures: organisational design

Organisational design: the structure of an organisation

Hierarchy: a system of organisation involving ranks or levels, with each level having power or influence over the level immediately below it

Chain of command: the system of power, communication and decision making within hierarchies, with people at different levels staying in rigid roles, deferring to those in the next level above them

Organisations, like the buildings in which most of them are housed, have structures. Organisational structure is sometimes referred to as **organisational design**, although some organisations are not so much designed as evolve in logical or not-so-logical ways over time. In order to understand why communication works or why it breaks down in organisations, we need to review a few basic ideas about organisational design.

Most organisations are **hierarchies** — that is, they are structured in ranks or levels, with each level having power or influence over the level immediately below it.

Most hierarchies resemble pyramids, with a few people at the top and many at the bottom (figure 16.3). Generally speaking, the people at the top of the pyramid have more power and are better rewarded than those at the bottom of the pyramid. The process of power and control flowing between the different levels of a hierarchy is sometimes known as the **chain of command**. The term has a military flavour, and it means that each level in a hierarchy is less powerful than the one immediately above it, and that information, decisions and authority or delegation of authority tend to flow downwards, with accountability flowing upwards. People within the chain of command usually stay in rigid, protocol-driven hierarchical roles, deferring to those in the next level above them. The chain of command is violated when someone 'goes above the boss's head' and communicates directly with others at least one level directly above their immediate superior. Reference to the chain of command can be a conflict resolution strategy.

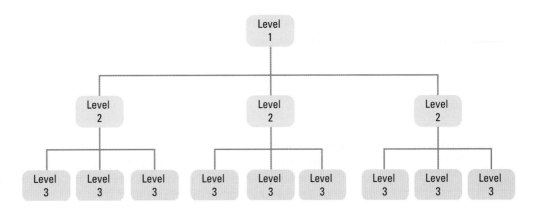

FIGURE 16.3 The pyramid hierarchy of organisations: the formal organisation

The pyramid or hierarchy, we need to remember, is the image of the **formal organisation** — what the world thinks the organisation is really shaped like. Before we truly understand organisational communication, however, we need to consider the **informal organisation** (see 'The informal organisation: I heard it through the grapevine' later in this chapter) to see whether the formal and informal organisations work with each other or against each other.

Communication flows

In understanding organisations and the patterns of communication within them, one of the critical concepts is directionality. **Vertical communication** refers to sending and receiving messages between the levels of a hierarchy, whether downward or upward. **Horizontal communication** refers to sending and receiving messages between individuals at the same level of a hierarchy.

Downward communication, used mainly to communicate messages from the more powerful to the less powerful, is perhaps the most common form of communication in organisations. Such communication involves instructions, budget approvals or nonapprovals, policy statements, variations in standard operating procedures and notification of other changes, general announcements, briefings, and expression of goals, objectives and mission statements. These messages may be transmitted via memos, email, notices and other individual-to-group or individual-to-individual channels; or they may be conveyed indirectly, passed on by others in the hierarchy. During the transfer, the original message may be edited, augmented, reduced, explained or distorted.

Time and again, however, top-down communication attempts fail, and that failure is often not grasped by those at the top of the hierarchy. Figure 16.4, which presents responses from two surveys of personnel in US organisations, shows how a top management perception of getting messages through to lower ranks was wildly at variance with perceptions held by those in the lower ranks.

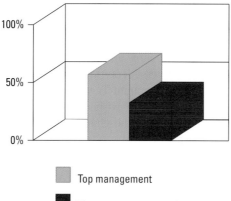

FIGURE 16.4 People operating in different layers of a hierarchy may have very different views on the effectiveness of top-down communication

☐ Top management

■ Non-management employees

SURVEY 1 'Management communicates frequently with employees' — *agree* responses

Source: Adapted from data cited in Seta, Paulus and Baron (2000, p. 149).

☐ Top management

■ Non-management employees

SURVEY 2 'Managers understand employees' problems' — *agree* responses

Source: Adapted from data cited in Crampton, Hodge and Mishra (1998, p. 571).

Upward communication may in some circumstances be even more important than downward communication. Upward communication channels convey data about and from customers, data about production of goods and services, and the intelligence that is needed in the day-to-day operation of an organisation.

This intelligence can be gathered if those at upper levels of an organisation are skilled in listening and gathering feedback (see chapter 10), and are committed to 'strategic listening' to customers and to organisational transparency. If there is no commitment to such approaches, then a 'culture of silence' and/or a 'culture of silos' will probably prevail, which may well have serious consequences for the organisation: with no early warnings of impending disaster, it may even result in large-scale crisis. In such situations, no news is definitely bad news, and bad news is no news: staff at lower levels will be loath to give bad news – which may be vital to the organisation's survival. If it will not be listened to, or worse, will attract criticism – a 'shoot-the-messenger' culture or ethos in which those who point out truths are punished for their efforts will develop.

Upward communication can also be a fertile source of new ideas and creative problem solving, primarily because people in the lower parts of a hierarchy are closer to specific problems and may be more aware of practical solutions than people further up the hierarchy.

Lateral or horizontal communication takes place primarily at one level of the organisation – for example, within teams, among heads of department, among others in coordination and liaison roles, or among virtually everyone at the lower levels of the pyramid (Adams 2007). As Richmond and McCroskey (2009: 30) point out:

> There is much more horizontal communication in organisations on a daily basis than there is vertical. This is a function of two things: (1) there are more employees than managers, and (2) employees at the same level feel more comfortable talking with each other than with people at different authority levels ... it is through the horizontal channels that you are likely to increase your knowledge, communication skills, and socialization skills. This is often where you can establish long-lasting interpersonal relationships that can assist you in becoming a better employee with a better chance of survival in the organisation.

It is sometimes quicker and more effective for messages to travel horizontally than upward, downward or across an organisation. Nevertheless, good horizontal communication is often impaired by rivalry, territorial behaviour and over-specialisation of job functions, which erects barriers leading to in-group/out-group exclusion, the use of jargon and other excluding codes, and a reluctance to share information.

Diagonal communication: communication that cuts across existing vertical and horizontal channels

Diagonal communication cuts across vertical and horizontal dimensions. For example, a junior staff member may 'go over the head' of his or her immediate superior and telephone, email or visit a senior technical expert in another area to get information (note in particular these interactions in the informal organisation). Wilson (1992) found that in low-performing organisations, staff used diagonal communication to seek information on the proper application of existing job procedures, while in high-performing organisations, staff used diagonal communication to seek information needed to solve complex and difficult work-related problems. While diagonal communication may be a sign of flexibility – for example, in organic organisations – it will obviously cause problems and perhaps chaos if taken to extremes.

In chapter 17 we will consider public communication, but here let's note that people working for an organisation routinely communicate with the outside world, and that these communications are often part of what is – and is not – communicated within organisations. Such external communication can be official, such as press releases, letters or boundary spanning, or unofficial, such as whistle-blowing (making public the details of unethical practices), industrial espionage or websites run by disaffected ex-employees (see figure 16.5 overleaf).

Let's now turn to some different aspects of organisational design. As we learn to distinguish between flat versus tall and centralised versus decentralised structures, remember that these are not mutually exclusive categories: for example, a flat organisation may also be decentralised.

↓ DOWNWARD COMMUNICATION	UPWARD COMMUNICATION ↑
■ Job instructions and descriptions ■ Policies and procedures manuals ■ Appraisal and performance feedback ■ Official briefings ■ Orders and directives ■ Meetings (face-to-face, electronic) ■ New employee induction programs ■ Memos and emails ■ Telephone ■ Intercom and public address systems ■ Notice boards and intranets ■ Newsletters ■ Annual reports ■ Posters, calendars/planners ■ Training programs ■ Nonverbal communication of culture (open plan/democratic work space, segregated 'mahogany row'; presence of/lack of status indicators — parking spots, privileges, secretaries etc.) ■ Social activities (in-house sports teams, exercise programs, water cooler and cafeteria, end-of-week party) ■ Blogs ■ Podcasts ■ Wikis	■ Meetings (face-to-face, electronic) ■ Participative decision making (teams, projects) ■ 'Captain's table' lunches — executives meet staff ■ Upward appraisal/360° feedback ■ Suggestion systems ■ Anonymous graffiti boards/intranets ■ Email ■ Telephone ■ Ombudsman/ombudswoman ■ Counsellors ■ Grievance procedures ■ Union newsletters ■ Training programs ■ Grapevine ■ Social activities (in-house sports teams, exercise programs, water cooler and cafeteria, end-of-week party) ■ Open-door policies ■ Opinion surveys and communication audits ■ Exit interviews
→ HORIZONTAL COMMUNICATION	DIAGONAL COMMUNICATION ↑↓
■ Meetings (face-to-face, electronic) ■ Grapevine ■ Cross-departmental, cross-divisional, cross-site projects ■ Telephone ■ Email ■ Social activities (in-house sports teams, exercise programs, water cooler and cafeteria, end-of-week party) ■ Training programs ■ Staff personnel (legal, IT, training/human resources) communicating with line (mainstream workflow) personnel ■ Messages defining territorial rivalries/silos ■ Instant messaging ■ Texting ■ Blogs ■ Wikis	■ Telephone, email ■ 'Going over the head of those immediately in chain of command' ■ Social activities (in-house sports teams, exercise programs, water cooler and cafeteria, end-of-week party) ■ Informal organisation — personal contacts ■ Staff personnel (legal, IT, training/human resources) communicating with line (mainstream workflow) personnel ■ Expertise-to-expertise communication — 'authority of knowledge' instead of 'authority of position' — internal networkers, boundary spanners
← EXTERNAL/PUBLIC COMMUNICATION (OFFICIAL)	EXTERNAL/PUBLIC COMMUNICATION → (UNOFFICIAL)
■ Press releases, conferences ■ Speeches ■ Advertising, marketing ■ Letters, email ■ Meetings with community and other stakeholders — boundary spanning ■ Blogs	■ Whistleblowers, media leaks ■ External grapevine ■ Insider trading ■ Industrial espionage/intellectual property theft ■ Blogs, complaints/'flaming' websites

FIGURE 16.5 Organisational communication networks and channels

Source: Adapted from Harris and Nelson (2007); Hodgetts and Hegar (2008); Goldhaber (1990); Pace and Faules (1989); Wilson (1992); Tourish and Robson (2006); Aamodt (2010).

Flat versus tall organisations

Span of control: the number of people who report directly to the person immediately above them in the hierarchy

We have considered directionality of message sending in organisations. Related to this factor is the concept of **span of control**. Span of control simply means the number of people who report directly to the person immediately above them in the hierarchy. If only three people report to the supervisor immediately above them in the hierarchy, then that supervisor has a narrow span of control; if 50 people reported to one person immediately above them, he or she could be said to have a wide span of control. Figure 16.6 shows spans of control of five and 25. Both organisations have 625 staff at the lowest level, but the organisations have different shapes: one is a tall and narrow pyramid, while the other is a flatter pyramid; one has two layers, while the other has four.

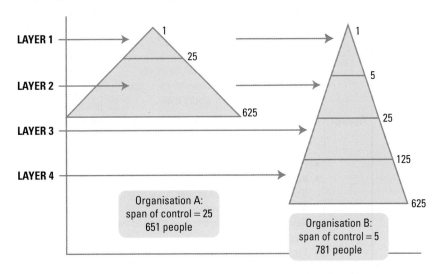

FIGURE 16.6 Wide span (flat) and narrow span (tall) organisational designs

The past few years have seen a tendency in some organisations to 'flatten the pyramid' in order to create a '**flat organisation**' (Dive 2003; Daft 2006). This has led to a number of developments, including:

Flat organisation: an organisational structure characterised by fewer middle layers, a shift in decision-making power to groups or teams, and increased worker empowerment

- a reduction in the number of levels or layers within organisations — a process sometimes referred to as **de-layering**

De-layering: reducing the number of layers or levels in an organisation, especially the middle levels

- a reduction in staff numbers, especially at the middle levels, driven by the belief that if the prime task of middle managers was to move information up and down the hierarchy, and if computerisation could now automate that information flow, then many middle management positions were redundant and could be dispensed with — a process sometimes called **downsizing**

Downsizing: reducing staff numbers in an organisation, especially in the middle levels

- a real or perceived shift of decision-making power to groups or teams to reduce the decision load on supervisors with wide spans of control — a process known as **empowerment**.

Empowerment: transferring decision-making power to others, especially teams

Tall organisations with narrow spans of control are not all bad, of course (see table 16.1 overleaf). If a manager, supervisor or team leader has only a few staff to supervise, those staff members may benefit from greater personal attention, just as a low student–teacher ratio may provide a better learning environment for students.

Tall organisation: an organisational structure characterised by more layers, narrower spans of control and more centralised decision making

Tall organisational design may also encourage centralisation, which can mean more control and uniformity over work outputs, rather than less control and more inconsistency. Having a tall organisation may mean that paths of communication, especially up and down the hierarchy, are more clearly delineated. This also helps decision making. Close supervision can be particularly helpful where the work being undertaken is nonroutine, and where subordinates are inexperienced or in training. Always having a boss around can be useful too, when mistakes are potentially expensive. Organisational scholars sometimes distinguish between placid and turbulent environments: in a **placid environment** the rate

Placid environment: a situation, society or market in which the rate of change is low and the future is fairly predictable

of change is low and the future is fairly predictable; in a **turbulent environment** the rate of change is high and the future is uncertain (see 'Organic vs mechanistic organisations' later in the chapter).

TABLE 16.1 Pros and cons of tall and flat organisations

	Tall organisations (narrow span of control)	Flat organisations (wide span of control)
For	▪ Close supervision can be supportive, permitting more intimate communication ▪ Encourages centralisation ▪ Establishes clear lines of communications, especially vertical communication ▪ Decision-making channels clearly understood ▪ Useful where work is nonroutine ▪ Useful where subordinates are inexperienced or in training ▪ Useful where mistakes will be costly ▪ Good in placid environments: clear task roles, specialisation works well	▪ Encourages decentralisation ▪ Encourages self-control, autonomy ▪ Simplifies vertical communication by stripping out layers ▪ Allows greater horizontal communication ▪ Useful where work is routine ▪ Useful where subordinates are experienced, needing minimal supervision ▪ Good in turbulent environments: task roles are fluid and specialisation does not work well
Against	▪ Close supervision can be intrusive: back-seat driver bosses can dampen initiative, autonomy ▪ Encourages centralisation ▪ Vertical communication can become distorted because messages have to go through so many levels ▪ Decision making can become clogged with a veto at every level ▪ Promotion can be slow	▪ Encourages decentralisation ▪ Difficult when people want/need control from above ▪ Horizontal communication is often more inefficient than vertical communication ▪ Greater demands placed on supervisors as more people report to one boss — possibility of increased bottlenecks ▪ Reduced promotion opportunities (fewer levels)

Sources: Adapted from Eunson (1987); Daft (2011).

Tall organisations operate more effectively in placid environments, where clear task roles and specialisation work well. There are many disadvantages to tall organisations, however. Close supervision can sometimes be intrusive, discouraging initiative and independent thought. Tall organisations tend to encourage centralisation, which can sometimes lead to excessive head office control and an insensitivity about local conditions far from the centre. Communication and decision making can become bogged down because so many levels have to be passed through, with an increased chance that the relayed messages are distorted. With so many levels, promotion may be slow too.

Flat organisations have a number of virtues. Flattening the pyramid or hierarchy encourages decentralisation, which may mean that local outposts can respond more flexibly to the changing local scene. This means an increase in self-control and autonomy, which can be very motivating for most people. Flatter organisations, with fewer layers to contribute to message distortion, may thus encourage quicker and more accurate communication. Better horizontal communication may also result, allowing empowered teams. Flat organisational design works well where work is routine, and where subordinates are experienced and can operate with minimal supervision and maximum empowerment. They also may cope well in turbulent environments, where task roles may need to be fluid and flexible, and where role specialisation may not be effective.

Although decentralisation can be a virtue, it can also cause difficulties in some circumstances, leading to inconsistent policy interpretation and product creation. To the extent that flat organisations lead to decentralisation, this can be a problem. Not every employee necessarily wants empowerment and freedom to make decisions: some can feel under-supervised in flat organisations. Flat organisations tend to stimulate horizontal

The conflict between the US government and the Al Qaeda terrorist network has been described as a battle between a tall organisation (the United States) and a flat one (Al Qaeda), with the flat organisation having an advantage.

communication, but horizontal communication is not always as efficient as vertical communication. Supervisors, managers and team leaders, with so many people reporting to them, sometimes experience task and role overload, and this can lead to decision-making and communication bottlenecks. Finally, because there are so many people at each level, and because the number of levels has been reduced, there may be reduced opportunities for promotion.

Toffler and Toffler (2004) have argued that current world conflicts can be partly understood in terms of flat and tall organisations (see also Friedman 2006). They suggest that the conflict between the US government and the Al Qaeda terrorist network is the battle between a tall organisation (the United States) and a flat one (Al Qaeda), and that in such a conflict, the flatter organisation has the advantage (but see 'Networking: group process and interpersonal strategies' later in the chapter):

> The United States and Al Qaeda are seen as unevenly matched, which is why think-tank experts and TV pundits call the conflict 'asymmetric'. In fact, Al Qaeda's strength derives precisely from the fact that it is small, fast, flexible and pancake-flat, while the North American government is huge, slow, sclerotic and pyramidal.

> Huge and pyramidal worked for World War II. It worked in the Cold War when the United States opposed an even more bureaucratic foe. But attempting to fight the deadly, fast-flitting, flea-sized terrorist enemy with yet another pyramidal bureaucracy, as the White House proposes, is a blueprint for failure. (Toffler & Toffler 2004)

Centralised versus decentralised organisations

Centralisation/decentralisation is another aspect of organisational design. Extreme decentralisation can occur when the organisation becomes 'virtual'. The main advantage of centralising an organisation's communication, decision making and production is that it becomes easier to impose uniformity (table 16.2). Close control and coordination become simpler. Wasteful duplication of resources can be eliminated, and economies of scale become possible. Some functions of an organisation, such as industrial relations, and financial and legal matters, benefit from being consolidated at a central point. Centralisation also works well when a 'big picture' or strategic approach to planning is needed.

TABLE 16.2 Pros and cons of centralised versus decentralised organisations

	Centralisation	Decentralisation
For	■ Produces uniformity of message communication ■ Produces uniformity of policy, action and standards ■ Enables closer control and coordination ■ Maximises economies of scale: eliminates duplication ■ Some functions (financial, legal, labour/management negotiations on wages/conditions etc.) better handled from central point ■ Best when 'big picture' perceptions and planning needed	■ Shortens lines of intra-unit communication ■ Increases participation in decision making, delegation ■ Increases morale, reduces feelings of alienation ('we're just cogs in the machine') ■ Allows top management to concentrate on policy issues ■ Allows flexible, quick response to local issues ■ Suited to fast change, dynamic growth ■ Accountability clear ■ May promote healthy competition among units ■ Eggs in many baskets — creative redundancy built in

(continued)

TABLE 16.2 *(continued)*

	Centralisation	**Decentralisation**
Against	■ Communication breakdowns may occur — distortion of messages ■ Upward communication may be impeded ■ 'Head office propaganda' perception ■ May increase sense of alienation ('we're just cogs in the machine') among non-elite ■ May overstress top management ■ Central elite may be insensitive to local conditions ■ 'One bomb effect' — all eggs in one basket, system vulnerable to improbable but destructive events	■ Lengthens lines of inter-unit communication ■ May cause problems of coordination and quick response ■ May result in lack of uniformity of policies, actions, standards ■ Jurisdictional and priority conflicts may arise ■ Economies of scale may be lost (e.g. access to computer, lab, duplication of resources) ■ Competition between decentralised units may be harmful ■ Not good when decentralised workers are not self-motivated, self-directing, self-controlling

Sources: Adapted from Eunson (1987); Daft (2011).

Centralisation has its disadvantages, however. Without alternative channels through which to transmit messages, communication breakdowns may occur, with messages being distorted. Upward communication may become distorted, with those on the periphery, away from the centre, feeling disempowered and tending to discount even valid messages from the centre as 'just more head office propaganda'. Top management may have too heavy a load to bear, and may be insensitive to local conditions. Because so many resources are concentrated in the one area, with little redundancy built in, the system may be vulnerable to unlikely but destructive events such as sabotage or the breakdown of a central computer.

Decentralisation shortens lines of communication within units and is more conducive to increased delegation of tasks and participation in decision making, which may improve morale. No longer preoccupied by operational details, top management can concentrate on policy issues. Decentralised organisations can respond more flexibly and quickly to changing local conditions and adapt more readily to rapid change and dynamic growth. Accountability can be clearer in decentralised organisations. Healthy competition may develop among decentralised units. Also, in the event of a disastrous event, all the organisation's eggs are not in one basket — creative or protective redundancy is built in.

While decentralisation can shorten the lines of intra-unit communication, it may also lengthen the lines of inter-unit communication. This can lead to problems such as slow response and lack of coordination in situations that spread over many areas.

Decentralisation may lead to jurisdictional or territorial battles, and may cause conflicts over priorities. Economies of scale (e.g. general access to one big computer or one big laboratory) may be lost. Budgets may be squandered on needless duplication of resources. Competition between different decentralised units can be good, but it can also be wasteful. Finally, decentralisation creates a work style that most benefits workers who are self-motivated and desire empowerment, but not all workers share these drives, and such individuals may feel cast adrift and directionless.

Mechanistic: organisational design or structure that depends on tall and centralised structure, with mainly downward vertical communication; flourishes in placid environments

Organic: organisational design or structure that depends on flat and decentralised structure, with mainly all-directional communication; flourishes in turbulent environments

Organic versus mechanistic organisations

Another way of looking at organisations is to classify them into having what Burns and Stalker (1961) called **mechanistic** and **organic** organisational designs or structures. Characteristics of these organisations are shown in figure 16.7. Burns and Stalker argued that mechanistic or bureaucratic organisations operated fairly well in placid environments, but that when the environment became turbulent, another form of organisational design — the organic model — became more effective, as it was able to cope more flexibly with such an environment. The mechanistic/organic model has had a profound impact on thinking about organisations and the experience of the world of work, not least because it seems to suggest that work environments that do not depend upon fear, control and rigid procedures are not only pleasant places to be in, but may also be more effective than bureaucratic organisations. In reference to the perceived flexibility of organic structures, some analysts have renamed it the 'adhocracy' (Bennis 1973; Robbins & Barnwell 2007).

	Mechanistic	Organic
Profile	Tall	Flat
Control	Centralised	Decentralised
Rules and procedures	Many, specified	Few, broad
Communication	Mainly vertical, mainly downwards	All directions, flows either way
Standards	Rigid	Flexible
Roles	Specific	Broad
Delegation	Little	Much
Leadership style	More autocratic; legitimate, coercive, reward power bases	More democratic, expert, referent power bases; team-based
Job specification	Stress skills	Stress potential
Source of motivation	Extrinsic (money, promotion)	Intrinsic (the job itself)
Check on performance	Frequent	Infrequent
Management of risk	Not so good; inflexible responses	Good; flexible responses
Optimal environment	Placid	Turbulent

FIGURE 16.7 Organic versus mechanistic organisations

Sources: Adapted from Burns and Stalker (1961); Dessler (2009); Kimbrough and Componation (2009).

Nevertheless, as we have seen, flat and decentralised organisations are not utopias, and have problems which seem intrinsic to their very structure, and organic organisations are flatter and more decentralised. There may also be a problem with terminology here: 'mechanistic' and 'bureaucratic' have negative connotations for most of us, while 'organic' sounds wonderfully utopian and problem-free.

Following from this, there may also be a teleology problem here. Teleology means that final goals or developments proceed and reveal themselves inevitably (see online chapter 6 'Scientific and technical writing'), and some discussions of the mechanistic/organic model may lead us to believe that mechanistic organisations are really the 'dark, Satanic mills' of the crude and violent past of industrialism, while organic utopias await all of us in the future.

Yet mechanistic organisations or bureaucracies have not ended up on the scrapheap of history, and are still very much with us. Not only have they survived, but they may be flourishing, suggesting that – in some circumstances at least – bureaucracies may not be such bad places to be:

- Like elephants being able to dance, they may in fact respond flexibly to turbulent environments (Kanter 1990; Gerstner 2004).
- They may be able to bring role clarification, useful formalisation and greater communication efficiency than is the case in organic organisations (Sine, Mitsuhashi & Kirsch 2006).
- They may present a more natural way of structuring workflow and allow clearer accountability (Jaques 1990).

- They may be more secure places for employees who do not wish to participate in decision making (Eunson 1987).
- There is also the possibility that most organisations start out small and organic, but as they grow larger, may need to become more mechanistic simply to get things done.

The trick is, perhaps, to try and create workplaces and organisations that are creative syntheses of the best of the mechanistic and organic models – to see the mechanistic–organic distinction not as comprised of polar opposites, but in fact as the extreme points on a continuum.

Networking: group process and interpersonal strategies

We have begun to understand the effects different organisational designs can have on communication. Again, we need to note that these are not mutually exclusive categories, and that one organisation may have different mixes of span of control and centralisation at differing phases of its development. We will now consider what happens when an organisation becomes thoroughly decentralised, so that it resembles a dispersed network rather than a monolithic hierarchy. We will also consider another network pattern – the network roles played by individuals predominantly at the intra-organisational levels. We will then consider the concept of networking – a set of interpersonal strategies that can benefit the organisation and the individual who deploys them. All these variations on the theme of networks touch on the interconnectedness of people, sometimes in the most surprising way. According to the **small world phenomenon**, for example, any person on the globe may be separated from any other person by no more than 'six degrees of separation' (Watts 2004).

Small world phenomenon: the idea that any person on the globe may be separated from any other person by no more than six steps, or 'six degrees of separation', and we are only now becoming aware that there may be patterns or networks of interconnection

Network, boundaryless, telecommuting and virtual organisations

An organisation can be described as a network. The demands of technology and globalisation, and the lifestyle preferences of employees, are driving changes in the structure or design of many organisations, some of whose employees are increasingly working at a geographic distance from one another. Employing different mixes of communication channels, increasing numbers of people now work in 'virtual teams' within a boundaryless or networked **virtual organisation**. Such **telecommuters** work out of their homes, connected to a central workplace via computer, phone and video links (Clarke & Nichols 2002; Illegams & Verbeke 2004; Stephenson 1999; Ashkenas et al. 2002). These working patterns can involve fragmentation in time as well as in space, with employees working across time zones and in temporary project constellations of individuals, as the following excerpts illustrate:

Virtual organisation: an organisation comprising a network of geographically dispersed workers connected to one another, and sometimes to a central workplace, via computer, phone, video and other links

Telecommuting: working from home using computer, phone, video and other links to communicate with fellow workers and/or a central workplace

> Virtual teams are an ad hoc collection of geographically dispersed individuals from different functions, specialties, or even organisations (inter-institutional virtual teams are becoming more common) constituted to complete a specific, complex task. Advanced computer and telecommunication technologies provide the primary media for interaction between and among team members. Aside from the commonality that organisational culture can provide, these individuals initially have little in common except a shared purpose or tasking and the interdependencies that purpose creates. Since these teams are project or task focused, they are transient; they disband or are significantly modified once the team's job is completed. (Suchan & Hayzak 2001, p. 175)

Virtual organisations and working provide new challenges, not least of which is working out the optimal mix of human and mediated communication experiences that units or teams need to function. Thus, virtual teams or telecommuters may rely on email, voicemail, instant messaging, social media, fax and videoconferencing, but may still crave and need human contact in project commencement meetings, quarterly liaison or update meetings, and annual retreats (Suchan & Hayzak 2001).

Critical commentators such as Thorne (2005) see nothing new or infallible in virtual organisations. However, they note that criminal and terrorist organisations, such as the Mafia and Al Qaeda, use flat organisational structures, communication networks and information technology to create toxic and unacceptable outcomes, and that – on the other side of the ledger – US intelligence agencies may have failed to detect terrorist activity, culminating in the 9/11 atrocity, because they are *too* virtual; too dependent on web and digital surveillance and simulation technology rather than human intelligence agents in the field, acting as part of a physical organisation. Thorne also notes that existing business organisations might well use virtual technologies to disempower, rather than empower, virtual employees working in teams. The central contradiction of virtual teams, he suggests, is that the ideal of knowledge workers moving from one project to another connected to each other via cyberspace means that the virtual organisation sees people as both essential and disposable, and the central norm which binds organisations together, and makes any type of output possible – trust – becomes compromised.

Network roles

Let's now look at another variation on the network theme – the roles people play within (and sometimes outside) organisations.

Research has established that basic networks of communication, power and problem solving can be classified into different types of interaction (figure 16.8) (Bavelas 1950; Leavitt 1951; Freeman 1978–1979; Mantei 1981).

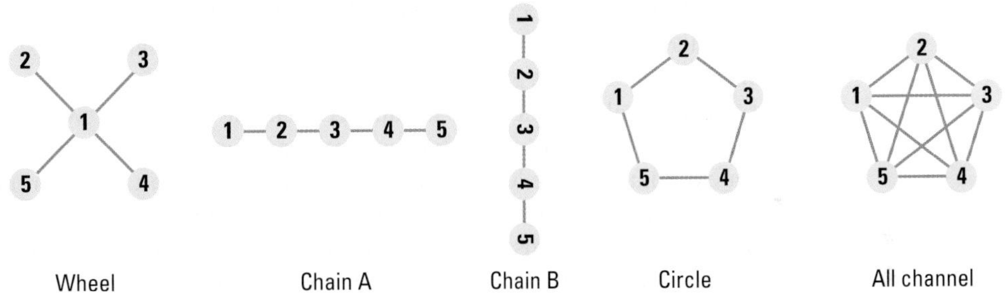

FIGURE 16.8 Types of communication networks

Source: Adapted from Bavelas (1950); Leavitt (1951); Freeman (1978–1979).

Wheel   Chain A   Chain B   Circle   All channel

The *wheel* or *star* network has an individual at the hub of the wheel. All individuals subordinate to that hub person have the role of channelling information and opinions to the hub. The flow of information and opinion is sometimes one-way and sometimes two-way. As Mears (1974) points out, however, the wheel could simply be part of the pyramid of the traditional hierarchy, with the number of spokes in the wheel merely being another way of viewing span of control.

The *chain* network can take two forms: a vertical one and a horizontal one. The vertical chain is in fact the traditional chain of command in a hierarchy, and again, the vertical chain could simply be the traditional hierarchy, with a very narrow span of control, or a even a span of control of one. The horizontal chain could be simply a work group in which the two outer individuals are so introverted that they only speak to the person next to them, while those in the middle may be prone to interact with each other (Mears 1974).

The *circle* network is a leaderless group in which each individual only communicates with the two others immediately adjacent. When all members of a circle network can communicate with each other, then the circle becomes a free circle or all-channel network.

All-channel networks have the advantage of multiple interactions between all members of a group, whether actual or virtual: in effect, the all-channel network is a leaderless group. The potential for brainstorming and maximum interchange of information is greatest in this model, but so too are the possibilities of information overload, paralysis by analysis, and difficulty in reconciling differences by consensus or other decision-making methods. McAllister, in analysing all-channel dynamics of terrorist groups, points out that the leaderless nature of this model makes it very hard to destroy. (While conventional armies become dysfunctional after 30 per cent losses, networks of terrorist cells will need to sustain losses of 70 per cent.) However, it also makes the network prone to loss of control and coordination, damage sustained by incompetent cells, and interception of coordinating messages transmitted by various technologies (McAllister 2004). Jones (2007) has noted the use of asymmetrical warfare, or conflict between two sides with one side having a massive conventional weaponry advantage and the other needing to improvise, using command structures that are both 'acephalous' (headless) and 'polycephalous' (multi- or Hydra-headed). Jones noted Israeli tactics against Palestinian combatants in 2002 led to the Israelis realising that the only way to fight a network is with another network. This involved decentralising decision making to junior officers in the field, with the entire armed force becoming a 'learning organisation'.

Thus, while the wheel network may appear to be unduly restrictive, Nemiro points out that 'creativity' in teams may in fact simply be an aggregation of creative interactions or brainstorming between isolated individuals and the hub or manager, and that creativity may be equal to or superior to all-channel or wheel interaction (Nemiro 2002). Also, new communication technology using computer networks may also mean that the wheel can be more effective than the circle (Belanger 1999).

Circle and chain, and sometimes wheel networks, also have the disadvantage of being prone to message distortion – as a message is passed from one individual to another, and sometimes from one level to another, the message is edited or mangled by the message sender in each interaction. Free circle or all-channel networks at least have the opportunity to correct distortions emerging in collective message formation – except of course if distorting mechanisms such as groupthink, conformity and cognitive dissonance are in operation.

There is also sometimes a gap between the official view of what communication networks are operating and what networks are actually operating. Thus, when participants in an experiment were led to believe that participation in decision making would be high, but in fact were excluded from decision making, their productivity dropped dramatically. They were, in other words, promised an all-channel network, but were in fact given a wheel (and performed worse than not only those participants working in an all-channel situation, but those in a conventional wheel situation) (Boggs et al. 2005).

Network analysis

Network analysis has revealed much about how people within work organisations interact with others in groups. Sometimes these groups are formally sanctioned; sometimes they are informal. One type of group is called a **clique**. A clique is a group of individuals at least half of whose work-day contacts are with each other. Clique members will probably work closely with one another, like one another and find these close contacts satisfying (Pace & Faules 1994).

Within cliques, people tend to play the following roles:

- *Bridge.* Bridges are members of cliques who create connections with other cliques.
- *Liaison.* Liaisons link cliques but are not members of cliques. Liaisons are often gregarious and influential, and have been with the organisation for some time (Goldhaber 1993). If a liaison is a bottleneck for data and workflow, however, the whole organisation can suffer (Pace & Faules 1994).
- *Gatekeeper.* Gatekeepers are people who ration access to other members of the clique and to resources. A typical gatekeeper is an executive secretary who has considerable say on who sees the executive, when and under what conditions, and who may also control the flow of communication through certain channels – for example, by screening mail.

Network analysis: a technique for mapping communication roles played by people within organisations

Clique: a group of individuals at least half of whose work-day contacts are with each other

- *Isolate.* Isolates are positioned outside the main interaction of cliques and the wider organisation. Isolates tend to be younger and less experienced, have less power, are often dissatisfied with the organisation and tend to withhold information rather than pass it on (Goldhaber 1993).
- *Opinion leader.* Opinion leaders, or stars, are influential people who interact a lot with others. They are not necessarily in official leadership positions, but may exercise expert and referent power bases.
- *Cosmopolite.* Cosmopolites are also known as boundary spanners. They are often the main link between the organisation and the outside world (see the following boundary spanners feature).
- *Power behind the throne.* These people often do not interact much with the rest of the clique, but exert influence over the opinion leaders or stars.

Figure 16.9 shows how these roles can be mapped to help us better understand the patterns of organisational communication.

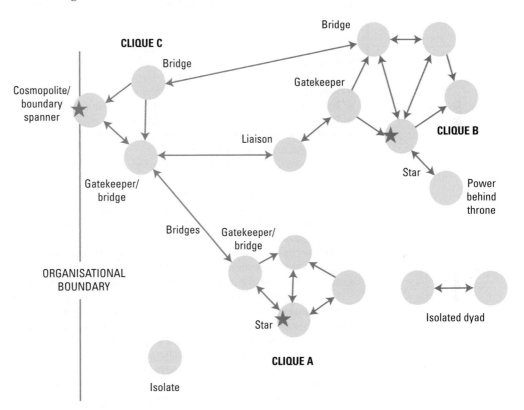

FIGURE 16.9 Network roles played in organisational communication

Are such roles permanent? Not necessarily. For example, anyone can become a gatekeeper by choosing to pass on or not to pass on information. An opinion leader or star in one set of circumstances, dealing with one set of work processes, may be an isolate in another set of circumstances, dealing with another set of work processes. Gatekeepers, liaisons or bridges may restrict information merely to demonstrate their power, or perhaps through incompetence, and may be challenged and either replaced or persuaded to perform more effectively.

The applications of network analysis are many. For example, Ennett et al. (2006) used network analysis to determine whether group pressure would be likely to induce members of a network or group to engage in substance abuse. They found that isolates were the group members most likely to abuse substances, and that group 'embeddedness' was more rather than less likely to lead to individuals abusing (see also 'Norms' in chapter 18). Wilson (1997) found that many African Americans found it hard to find employment because the culture of ghettoes lacked the informal network connections that transmit information about job availability beyond the boundary of the ghettoes.

Boundary spanner: an employee of the organisation who routinely moves between the organisation and the external environment

---

BOUNDARY SPANNERS

A **boundary spanner** or cosmopolite is someone who operates at the interface of the organisation and the society or environment of stakeholders surrounding it (Manev & Stevenson 2001; Miller 2008).
Boundary spanners tend to comprise:

- salespeople, public relations people
- customer support staff
- people who have ongoing and close liaison with stakeholders, and who often leave the internal territory of the organisation to travel to the external territory of stakeholders and the wider environment
- people who liaise on an ongoing basis with peers in the same profession outside the organisation
- people who have a specific brief, caseload or job role that places them in contact with clients and others; they sometimes spend more time with people outside the organisation than those within it
- people who are the public face of multinational organisations working in other cultures.
Boundary spanners fulfill the following specific functions:
- They gather strategic information about inputs and outputs of the organisation — they are its eyes and ears, or 'strategic listeners'.
- They gather managerial and technical information.
- They control the flow of information back to the organisation.
- They absorb some of the uncertainty of the external environment.
- They protect people inside the organisation by acting as a buffer from forces that might influence the behaviour of the organisation.
- They represent the organisation and influence how the organisation is perceived in the external environment.
- They act as a reality check when the organisation is tending to become too internally focused.
Boundary spanners can also operate inside an organisation by working for much of the time out of their home base with others in different parts of the organisation. They thus tend to be 'cosmopolitans' rather than 'locals'.
Boundary spanners are ideally situated to be the eyes and ears of the organisation because they are able to plug into external grapevines and networks. Much of the information they bring back is anecdotal, however, and may not be acted on by organisational managers.
In order to maximise the quality and quantity of information provided by boundary spanners, effective organisations tend to formalise this process, asking their boundary spanners to document their findings, or at least to report orally. In effect, boundary spanners fall somewhere between reporters and spies, although without the negative and manipulative sense that the latter role implies.
Boundary spanners tend to have a different set of experiences from other staff in an organisation. For example, they often experience divided loyalties or role conflict; do they completely identify with the organisation, or do they identify with others? This conflict can take several forms, such as:
- spanners taking on an advocacy role for clients, even when the best interests of the organisation may be compromised
- spanners being 'pirated' by other organisations, who view their talents as eminently transferable
- clients moving with spanners to another organisation; a client's loyalty, in other words, often lies with the spanner as a person rather than with the organisation.

Networkers

Networking: deliberately cultivating contact with others in your own organisation and in other organisations in order to create an informal system of relationships and to develop your career

Networking has become something of a buzz word in the past few years (Fisher 2001; Kahn 2002; Cope 2003; Crainer & Dearlove 2002; Warner 2004; Bjorseth 2009). The term commonly refers to people communicating with others outside the organisation in order to cultivate contacts and tap into information sources that would otherwise not be available to them.

Networking can take many forms, including:

- establishing communication links with other people at formally structured social gatherings at which 'shoptalk' is the primary focus
- relationship-building behaviour at formal gatherings such as conferences, professional association meetings, and social activities associated with lectures and presentations and similar gatherings
- relationship-building behaviour within organisations such as service clubs, religious groups and lodges that often bind members together with rituals for the purpose of fellowship and, sometimes, creating systems of reciprocal preference for professional opportunities or the sharing of confidential information
- relationship-building at social occasions such as luncheons, dinner parties and golf matches that provide circumstances for professional payoffs
- loose coalitions of organisation representatives that meet on an ongoing basis to exchange information and work towards unofficial, and sometimes official, cooperation.

The idea of such networks has been around for a long time. People sometimes speak derisively of 'old boys' networks', referring to informal networks whose members attended the same private school or association, and who, in the view of some, use such affiliations to give unfair preference, access, opportunities and information to fellow members of that in-crowd or clique. Some groups, such as women and ethnic minority groups, have deliberately set out to create their own networks to counter the influence of such exclusionist associations (Fraser 2004; Tung 2002; Huffman & Torres 2002; Whitely, Duckworth & Elliott 2004).

Effective networking involves a mix of communication skills such as assertiveness, listening, feedback and questioning. Would-be networkers who see networking solely in terms of personal gain without reciprocation – that is, as 'all take and no give' – will be seen (correctly) as self-serving manipulators who fail to grasp the cooperative dynamic of networking. Warner (2004) suggests that effective networkers are notable for:

- being able to initiate conversations with complete strangers
- being able to listen attentively and empathically
- thanking others when they offer support
- offering support to others
- maintaining a manual or computerised database of all contacts
- thinking carefully about who could assist them when they are faced with a major task
- demonstrating complete integrity in personal interactions.

Anand and Conger (2007) identify four capabilities or skills of consummate networkers. These are:

1. *Seeking out the kingpin.* This entails finding a person who seems to be in charge. This person is, or these persons are, not necessarily officially in charge, like the CEO (chief executive officer) in a corporation. They may well be a person who is particularly well informed and is respected and trusted within informal networks of friendship and solidarity.
2. *Matchmaking people to get the right things done.* People who are good at this are like marital matchmakers or gifted dinner party hosts – they seek to build synergy in the wider organisation by acting as a bridge between different areas, introducing people to each other and acting as a facilitator of communication and internal boundary spanners.
3. *Proactively enhancing network access.* People who are good at this work tirelessly to cultivate connections that will give them maximum flow of information. This may mean not only talking to immediate subordinates but also drivers and catering staff, taking the dog for a walk so that a mobile phone call can be made to another time zone, playing golf with others, and building friendships with colleagues on one board of management to make it easier to get nominated to other boards of management. People who are good at this are often fairly extroverted and like social situations and social media.

4. *Interacting amiably with others to build positive relationships.* People who are good at this work hard at conveying positive emotions and interpersonal support. They are astute at soft, or communication, skills such as reading nonverbal communication or body language, and resist pressures (work deadlines, temperamental inclinations to be unapproachable, arrogant or haughty) to be anything less.

The role demands and intended outcomes of each of these capabilities are shown in figure 16.10.

NETWORKING CAPABILITY	ROLE DEMANDS	INTENDED OUTCOMES
Seeking the kingpin	■ Gather information in uncertain situations ■ Obtain multiple interpretations of ambiguous events ■ Generate accurate knowledge of how power is distributed ■ Recognise pivotal decision makers and understand their perspectives, concerns and needs	■ Greater influence across and upwards in your organisation ■ More favorable decisions ■ Getting your tasks done more effectively and efficiently
Matchmaking	■ Build deeper relationships between departments or business units, or between vendors, suppliers and customers ■ Explore the possibility of mutual interests, benefits and common ground between unfamiliar parties ■ Spark creative joint outcomes from two parties that normally do not interact with each other	■ Achieving better coordination of cross-organisational tasks and cross-departmental activity ■ Obtaining access to information, ideas, resources and talent that are not accessible through normal channels ■ Creating synergy between individuals and groups ■ Deepening connections within and across your business community
Increasing access	■ Connect with a large and diverse audience ■ Spend time 'in the field' or engaging in 'face time' ■ Model trustworthiness, candor and openness to all forms of information	■ Strengthening decision quality with more up-to-date and accurate information ■ Accessing information from the 'front lines' and social media ■ Enhancing your public reputation as a leader
Amiability	■ Focus on relationship building ■ Ability to read body language ■ Comfort with discussing personal issues ■ Need to be plugged into the informal or gossip network ■ Need to obtain social support from friends and well-wishers	■ Fostering the sharing of sensitive and personal information ■ Strengthening the morale of a team or organisation ■ Increasing the number of individuals that can turn to you for support during stressful or sensitive times

FIGURE 16.10 Networking role demands and intended outcomes

Source: Anand and Conger (2007, p. 13). Reproduced with permission.

Networking, at least in its more reputable forms, benefits networkers in two ways. At the organisational level, it is a legitimate way to develop contacts in the world outside the organisation, and a source of valuable information that can be useful to the organisation. At the personal or individual level, it can open up connections and career opportunities.

These areas are not always in harmony with each other: a person networking on behalf of an organisation may be offered an alternative career path that would lead to severing ties with the organisation.

The informal organisation: I heard it through the grapevine

We have seen that the formal organisational structure, most clearly seen on an organisation chart (figure 16.3), helps to give us a framework for understanding just how communication works – or breaks down – in organisations.

Now, after having considered networks, let's go further, and consider the 'unofficial' organisation – the informal organisation.

Organisation charts and diagrams such as those we have looked at so far show us the official structures, but often conceal as much as they reveal (Mintzberg & Van Der Heyden 1999; Rosner 2001; Rummler & Brache 1995). For example, they do not show customers or other stakeholders, the patterns of power and influence, or the pathways of unofficial communication. Figure 16.11, for example, gives us another view of figure 16.3, showing what are almost certainly only several of the unofficial pathways of communication that deviate from the top-down chain-of-command model of information and power implicit in the official structure. The informal organisation can in fact be a 'shadow' organisation, a site of countervailing power and resistance – a shadow with a lot of substance, an anti-empire within an empire (see also the discussion of organisational silence to follow) (Gossett & Kilker 2006; Thomas & Davies 2005; De Maria 2006; Brown & Coupland 2005; Groat, 1997; Katzenbach & Khan, 2010).

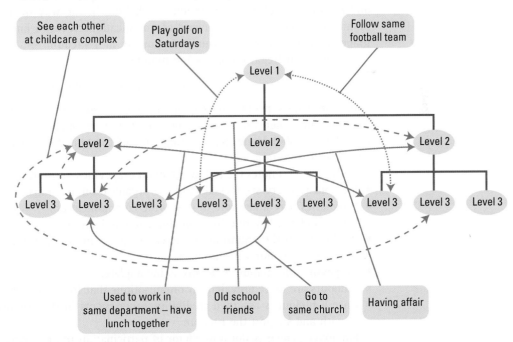

FIGURE 16.11 The informal organisation

The informal organisation differs in a number of different ways from the formal organisation. Formal and information organisations are compared in table 16.3.

The major part of the informal organisation is the informal communication system, sometimes called **the grapevine** or 'the rumour mill'. It's interesting to look at the derivation of some of the words that describe informal communication channels.

The grapevine: informal communication system; flourishes in a knowledge vacuum

TABLE 16.3 Formal and informal organisations compared

	Formal organisation	Informal organisation
Communication pace	Slow	Fast
Communication focus	Deliberate	Spontaneous
Communication channel	Mainly written	Mainly oral
Communication status	On the record	Off the record
Communication orientation	Towards things	Towards people
Control of communication	By management	By employees
Power bases used in communication	Legitimate, coercive, reward, expert	Expert, referent, informational, connectional
Norms present	Formal	Informal

Source: Adapted from Hodgetts and Hegar (2008); Andrews and Baird (2005).

Grapevine. This term is said to have been first used for the temporary telegraph wires, often strung from trees, used during the North American Civil War. The information carried via this system was not always accurate.

Scuttlebutt. The scuttlebutt is a drinking-water barrel on board sailing ships where sailors would congregate and pass on information and rumour.

Furphy. The water cart (first produced by Victorian, John Furphy) was a centre of gossip for Australian soldiers in World War I. The term came to be used to describe an unreliable rumour.

The three situations embodied in these terms capture the context for so much of gossip and rumour – high-stress situations, with little in the way of accurate downward communication. The lack of downward communication creates a knowledge vacuum, and the grapevine is the only plant known to flourish in a vacuum.

Hodgetts and Hegar (2008) define rumour thus:

$$\text{Rumour} = \text{interest} \times \text{ambiguity}$$

In other words, people will engage in rumour-mongering when they have an interest in the topic and when information about that topic is inadequate or ambiguous. Michelson and Mouly (2004) argue that the functions of rumour and gossip are to inform, to influence and to entertain.

Hellweg (1987) notes the following about grapevines or informal organisational networks:

- Five out of every six messages in the organisation are transmitted by the grapevine.
- Secretaries play a key role in grapevine communication.
- Liaisons play a key role in grapevine communication.
- As the size of the organisation increases, grapevine activity increases.
- Grapevine communication is fast.
- Grapevine information generally is incomplete.
- Rumours are more prevalent in organisations that foster secrecy.
- Once a rumour is assigned credibility, other events in the organisation are altered to fit in with and support the rumour.
- Employee gender is not a predictor of participation in grapevine communication.

Gossip, or the exchange of anecdotal information, appears to be a deeply ingrained human behaviour that fulfils the needs of reinforcing group solidarity, extending influence, and managing anxiety and uncertainty (Bordia et al. 2006; Dunbar 1997; DiFonzo & Bordia 2002; Michelson & Mouly 2002; Greengard 2001). Some of the different types of rumours or gossip are shown in figure 16.12.

Rumour/gossip type	Background	Example
'Bogey'/anxiety	Primarily driven by fear — create unease among recipients	Move towards privatisation of sanitation services in a local borough or council and the prospect of layoffs
Anticipatory	Often precipitated by situations of ambiguity	Will a new chief executive officer come from within the organisation or be appointed from elsewhere?
Aggressive	May damage reputation of individuals	Are nurses in an acute hospital ward romantically involved with doctors so that they can advance careers?
'Pipe dream'/wish fulfillment	Express the hopes of those who circulate them	Possible solution to a work problem that an employee wants changed

FIGURE 16.12 Some types of rumour/gossip in organisations

Source: Adapted from Michelson and Mouly (2004).

Nevertheless, the grapevine can do much harm if not controlled or at least influenced in some ways. There are no certain ways to manage the grapevine, because it has a life of its own, but Crampton, Hodge and Mishra (1998) suggest the following approaches can work:

- Increase the levels of participation in decision making, so that an information vacuum will be less likely to form. Likert (1976) suggests that in truly participatory organisations the informal organisation will simply wither or merge with the formal one.
- Reduce or eliminate secretive communication, and abolish information vacuums.
- Be aware of unclear communication (vague words) that may lead to misinterpretation; encourage two-way communication and ensure that information exchanged is accurate.
- Send out messages using more than one channel.
- Resist the temptation to hide bad news from employees. Don't censor reality and thus sacrifice credibility.

The informal organisation goes beyond the grapevine, however, to:

- work as a sounding board, allowing staff to let off steam and reduce stress
- create a socialisation milieu in which new staff learn about informal group norms
- give a sense of belonging to staff who may feel alienated in a bureaucratic environment
- process information not handled by formal channels
- help to get work done, when official channels and chains of command are too bureaucratic and slow, by using connections, influence and 'quick and dirty' methods and other types of knowledge
- demonstrate that staff are actually interested in their jobs and shoptalk
- act as a countervailing restraint on management, who may take extra pains in planning for fear the informal organisation would passively resist ill-considered initiatives (Hodgetts & Hegar 2008; Davis & Newstrom 1989).

We earlier considered the idea of alignment, or the notion of ensuring that all messages communicated to audiences within an organisation are consistent with messages communicated to audiences outside the organisation. Chan (2002), in looking at means of aligning information technology and business strategies, quotes Nadler and Gerstein (1992) on an approach that may help both such types of alignment: 'We "engineer" and "build" the formal organisation; we "plant" and "cultivate" the informal organisation'.

ASSESS YOURSELF

Think of a current or past learning situation you have been in. What formal and informal norms were present in the classroom? How were informal norms and behaviour used to challenge the formal norms of the classroom? How successful or unsuccessful were these tactics of challenge?

Organisational culture and communication

Macro-culture: all the arts, beliefs, social institutions, etc. characteristic of a community, race, etc.

Micro-culture: the predominating attitudes and behaviour that characterise the functioning of a group or organisation

In chapter 15, a distinction was drawn between macro-cultures and micro-cultures. **Macro-culture** was defined as the all the arts, beliefs and social institutions of a community or race, while **micro-culture** was defined as the predominating attitudes and behaviour that characterise the functioning of a group or organisation.

Let's now explore the idea of organisations having cultures, and what impact this might have upon communication within those organisations, and indeed in the communication of organisation to organisation.

In the past few decades researchers have suggested that organisations do indeed have their own cultures, and that these have a dramatic effect on communication patterns and practices. An organisation's culture is its 'personality', its feel, what distinguishes it from other organisations, a coding of 'the way things get done around here'. An organisation's culture is most apparent to an outsider interacting with the organisation for the first time, or when two organisations merge or experience a takeover.

Robbins and Barnwell (2007) suggest that the following are key characteristics of organisational culture:

1. *Individual initiative.* The degree of responsibility, freedom and independence that individuals have
2. *Risk tolerance.* The degree to which employees are encouraged to be aggressive, innovative and risk seeking
3. *Direction.* The degree to which the organisation creates clear objectives and performance expectations
4. *Integration.* The degree to which units within the organisation are encouraged to operate in a coordinated manner

5. *Management contact.* The degree to which managers provide clear communication, assistance and support to their subordinates

6. *Control.* The degree to which rules and regulations, and direct supervision, are used to oversee and control employee behaviour

7. *Identity.* The degree to which members identify with the organisation as a whole, rather than with their particular work group or field of professional expertise

8. *Reward system.* The degree to which reward allocations (i.e. salary increases, promotions) are based on employee performance criteria

9. *Conflict tolerance.* The degree to which employees are encouraged to air conflicts and criticisms openly

10. *Communication patterns.* The degree to which organisational communications are restricted to the formal line hierarchy of command.

Culture is also transmitted in other ways, such as:

- *rituals:* recognition and reward ceremonies, Friday afternoon or after-hours socialising, annual company picnics, contests, initiations
- *stories:* myths, gossip, jokes, anecdotes, narratives about people, events and things
- *material symbols:* the nonverbal communication of clothing, grooming, furniture, vehicles, parking, perks
- *language:* specialised language, jargon, nicknames and so on.

Some of these expressions are initiated and maintained by the formal organisational system, while some are also initiated and maintained by the informal organisational system.

Artefacts, or tangible and manufactured objects, and espoused values convey culture; all have basic underlying assumptions. Some examples of these assumptions are outlined in table 16.4.

TABLE 16.4 Expressions of culture and basic underlying assumptions

Artefact/espoused value	Basic underlying assumption
All the cars in the parking lot are oriented exactly the same way.	Conformity and order are important, extending even to the parking lot.
No visitor parking is available in the parking lot.	No special effort is made to take care of customers and suppliers.
The reception office is closed in, at the end of a long, dirty hallway, and is also unfriendly.	Visitors and customers are not welcome.
'If only those production people weren't so lazy.'	A 'we/they' mentality prevails on production floor.

Source: Adapted from Buch and Wetzel (2001).

Culture can also be expressed in other ways, such as:

- status/formality rituals, such as the use of first names or of formal titles (Morand 1996)
- the structure of buildings and the nature of workspace layout (Parker & Hildebrand 1996; Adams 2002; Baldry 1999)
- casual or formal dress codes (Wood & Benitez 2003)
- values and conformity pressures that repress individuality and diversity and act to disempower rather than empower (Ogbor 2001).
- attitudes and mindsets (blokey: dominated by male interests such as sport and male banter; hubris: proud and dismissive of other organisations; complacent, sluggish and inward-looking: uncaring of the organisation's environment and not prepared to change) (Robbins & Barnwell 2007).

Culture in itself is neither good nor bad; there can be negative as well as positive expressions of culture. Aspects of an organisation's culture may indeed be its biggest problem, causing enormous damage, and even becoming the main cause of that organisation's demise. Equally, the culture of an organisation may be the 'glue' that holds it

Dress codes, such as a uniform, are an expression of workplace culture. The characteristic white hat worn by chefs, known as a toque blanche (French for 'white hat'), has been around for hundreds of years. In addition to keeping hair away from food, the hat is a traditional indicator of status, with the number of pleats showing a chef's experience level.

together, the secret of the organisation's success and what makes it an enjoyable place to work. Thus, a mismatch between the culture of an organisation and the values and work styles of an individual (Del-Campo 2006) may lead to the individual leaving because 'I just feel I don't belong here'. On the other hand, it may well be that a person who does not share the dominant paradigms and worldviews of the organisation's culture may just be the very person that that organisation needs to shake it out of its complacency and its over-homogeneous culture.

Cameron and Quinn (2006; see also Yu & Wu 2009) have developed a model of culture based on competing values, in which they distinguish four different micro-cultures – clans, adhocracies, hierarchies and markets (see figure 16.13).

Culture type	Features	External focus and differentiation (EFD)/internal focus and differentiation (IFI)	Flexibility and discretion (FD)/ stability and control (SC)
Clan	■ emphasis on loyalty, mutual trust, commitment ■ like an extended family ■ leaders are mentors, parent figures ■ flexible operating procedures	IFI	FD
Adhocracy	■ emphasis on innovation and development ■ risk-taking valued ■ leaders are visionary and innovative ■ focus on unique and new products or services	EFD	FD
Hierarchy	■ emphasis on formal rules and policies ■ focus on smooth scheduling, low cost ■ leaders need to be good coordinators and toe the party line ■ focus on economy, formality, rationality, order	IFI	SC
Market	■ emphasis on achievement, goal accomplishment ■ focus on market share and penetration ■ leaders are hard drivers, competitors ■ aggressiveness, personal initiative favoured	EFD	SD

FIGURE 16.13 Cameron and Quinn's culture model

Sources: Adapted from Cameron and Quinn (2006); Igo and Skitmore (2006); Dani, Burns, Backhouse and Kochhar (2006).

The OCAI (Organisational Culture Assessment Instrument) developed by Cameron and Quinn asks respondents to analyse the culture of their organisation according to a number of variables, and according to the way it is now as perhaps distinct from the way respondents would like it to be. Igo and Skitmore (2006) surveyed 113 staff in an Australian engineering consultancy using the OCAI model, with some of the data being shown in figure 16.14.

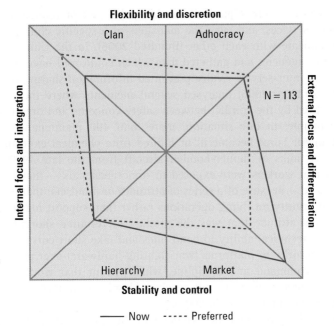

Figure 16.14 Overall 'now' and 'preferred' culture profile

Source: Igo and Skitmore (2006, p. 130).

In the figure: **Flexibility and discretion** (top), **Stability and control** (bottom), **Internal focus and integration** (left), **External focus and differentiation** (right). Quadrants labelled Clan, Adhocracy, Hierarchy, Market. N = 113. Legend: —— Now, - - - - Preferred.

Such data shows, in this instance, that while the organisation is currently perceived to have hard-driving market culture, staff would prefer the culture to be more that of a clan.

Cultures are sometimes determined or affected by the nature of the industry the organisation is in. In this case, that of engineering/construction, the nature of that work is project-driven and ad hoc. In these circumstances, the clan model might be better than the other three, or at least better than the market model, where the adversarial and competitive dynamics might not suit project teams that might benefit more from cooperation and consensus (Ito & Skitmore 2006). The alignment – or misalignment – of an organisation's culture with, on the one hand, its external environment, and on the other hand, the values and perceptions of its employees, will give us clues as to whether the organisation's culture is functional or dysfunctional.

Let's now see how cultures can be dysfunctional when looked at from the perspective of organisational communication. We will look at two 'bad cultures' – the culture of silos and the culture of silence – that have much in common with each other and are both bad news for organisations that suffer from one or both.

Bad culture 1: silos

In World War II, posters in allied countries advised people that 'Loose Lips Sink Ships' – that is, talk about sensitive military intelligence could be overheard by enemy spies. In today's world, the opposite – tight lips sink ships, or kill or injure people – could also become a motto for those dysfunctional organisations with what is sometimes called **silo culture** (Lencioni 2006; Bundred 2006; Hopkins 2005, 2006; Segal, Dalziel & Mortimer 2009). The term is a metaphor for over-compartmentalised and over-territorial organisations whose sections, departments or divisions stand aloof and apart from other sections, departments or divisions, like monolithic grain silos. The 'us versus them' climate means that communication between areas that should be communicating is minimal, or does not take place at all. Nobody talks, nobody listens and everybody pays.

Silo cultures are characterised by communication breakdowns, turf-war territorial behaviour and energy-sapping politicking between areas that should be cooperating rather than competing. Thus, in the UK, two schoolgirls were murdered by a man who had a previous history of sex offences, and a girl was tortured and abused (and subsequently

Silo culture: a culture of noncommunication between separate parts of one organisation

died), because different parts of the UK public sector (police, local government, hospitals, social services, and even the managers of a specific child protection database) failed to communicate with each other (Bundred 2006). In the United States in 2001, different intelligence agencies had gathered data which could well have prevented the 9/11 terrorist attacks, but inter-service rivalry prevented information sharing (Gottschalk 2006).

Hopkins (2005, 2006) analysed several incidents where there were serious injuries or deaths caused by the conflict between safety concerns and organisational culture.

For example, in one situation, more than 400 maintenance personnel in the Royal Australian Air Force became ill or injured from chemical exposure after working on and in the fuel tanks of fighter-bomber aircraft from the late 1970s to 2000. Investigation revealed that workers were exposed to toxic chemicals – that is, normal safety routines were ignored – because of a series of attitudes or mindsets; that is, culture. These included:

- placing priority on flying operations rather than support logistics
- a 'can-do' attitude that was the product of resource shortages and pride in the professional technical ability to bend rules and take short cuts to make things happen
- placing priority of platforms (war-fighting hardware) over people
- military command and discipline, which meant that workers might face disciplinary action if objectives were not reached (despite resources and safety procedures being inadequate) (Hopkins 2005, 2006).

Hopkins also examined the dynamics of the Glenbrook train crash of 1999, in which a New South Wales commuter train smashed into the *Indian Pacific* interstate train, resulting in the loss of seven lives. Hopkins found that a silo culture was prevalent within the system.

This silo culture was characterised by:

- Public pressures to make trains run on time, even at the expense of safety considerations (the culture of OTR, or on-time running). Train drivers would face direct pressure from supervisors if a train ran late, and this predisposed drivers to perhaps take risks that they would otherwise not have taken – a risk-blind culture (similar dynamics prevailed in the Ladbroke Grove rail crash in London in 1999).
- A culture of disempowerment and overly-restrictive rules, wherein drivers were discouraged from taking initiative, in a manner similar to the way in which the US space shuttles *Challenger* and *Columbia* sustained catastrophe because engineers close to the problems were overridden by rule-bound NASA administrators. This is a contrast to the culture of other organisations, such as the 'stop and think' and 'take time, take charge' protocols prevailing in the Western Mining Corporation or even on board US nuclear aircraft carriers, where routine tasks are controlled centrally but in emergency situations lower-level personnel are allowed to make decisions. The disempowerment leads to a sense of fatalism, a psychological defence mechanism developed by some occupations, such as miners, to deal with a 'culture of danger' in which accidents are seen as unavoidable.
- Evolution of a communication style among workers that was notable for carelessness and informality – a style completely in contrast to that of other professions, such as air-traffic control. The use of 'buddy' and 'mate' in radio transactions between drivers and signal controllers may have led them to believe that: 'It's a code for saying, we know that sometimes this doesn't mean what it says … that we are sharing the same sort of understanding about the ambiguity of the sign' (Thomas 2000).
- A culture of blame, based on inadequate documentation making rules difficult to apply (a critical rule, Rule 245 – passing an automatic signal at stop – was four pages long), combined with a tendency of inspectors to turn a blind eye to violations, leading to the suspicion of some staff that some rules were set up primarily to allocate blame and punishment.
- Absence or failure of communication systems and on-board control systems.
- Organisational restructuring and disaggregation of rail bureaucracies, resulting in a silo culture of noncommunication between different groups of transport managers.

Hopkins argues that for cultures of organisations whose operations involve risk, new practices need to be put in place, such as:

- a culture of reporting, in which all staff feel confident and competent to document problems, near-misses and other issues
- a just culture, in which people are not punished for reporting problems (see 'shoot-the-messenger' ethos)
- a learning culture, in which reports are taken seriously
- a flexible culture, in which lower-level personnel are empowered to respond rapidly to problems.

Bad culture 2: the culture of silence

It is vital that there is sufficient trust and transparency within the organisation to allow the upward communication of bad news, for example about customers or production. If the organisation has a **shoot-the-messenger ethos** or culture or climate, punishing individuals who point out bad news, then — logically enough — little or no bad news will move up through the hierarchy, and rather than an organisational 'voice', there will be a culture or climate of **organisational 'silence'** (Milliken, Morrison & Hewlin 2003; Perlow & Williams 2003; Tourish & Robson 2006; Gergen & Thatchenkery 1996; Edmonson & Munchus 2007) or a 'spiral of silence' (Bowen & Blackmon 2003). These concepts have much in common with the 'groupthink' phenomenon and organisational transparency.

Morrison and Milliken have developed a model of organisational silence (figure 16.15).

Shoot-the-messenger ethos: the tendency to punish people for communicating bad news about the organisation

Organisational silence: the tendency of lower levels of staff not to speak out on significant issues

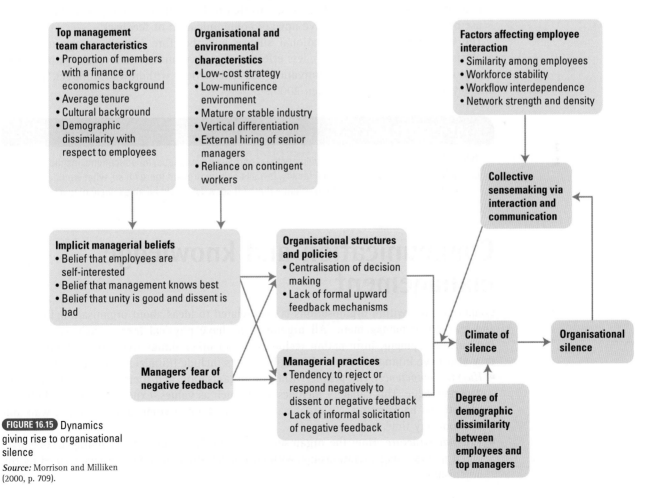

FIGURE 16.15 Dynamics giving rise to organisational silence

Source: Morrison and Milliken (2000, p. 709).

Morrison and Milliken suggest that a culture of silence is more, rather than less, likely to prevail in a given organisation if certain background conditions exist, such as:

- dominance of the senior management team by individuals with economic or financial backgrounds (who may be more prone to believe in Theory X rather than Theory Y, and therefore may be prone to distrust subordinates)
- members of senior management having been together for a long time, and thus perhaps having evolved a homogeneous set of beliefs (compare the groupthink phenomenon)
- staff at all levels coming from high power distance and collectivist cultures (compare Hofstede's model of cultural communication)
- top management and lower-level employees being dissimilar in terms of gender, race, ethnicity and age
- a commitment to cutting costs, and the presence of a reduced resource base ('low munificence'), which may exert pressures on senior managers, making them less likely to tolerate dissent and consider new ideas welling up from lower levels
- a mature and stable industry setting, which may make the need for innovative ideas less pressing
- tall organisational structures, the tendency to bring in top managers from outside rather than hiring from within, and the tendency to hire contingent or temporary workers, who may have less loyalty, commitment and self-interest than longer-term employees
- the tendency of upper-level staff not to seek feedback from lower-level staff
- lower-level staff who are similar to each other, who work in stable work roles, who are interdependent with each other, and who have strong network connections, all of which may predispose them to reach a consensus that it does not do much good to have and to use organisational voices to give upward communication or feedback.

The end products of organisational silence will therefore include a lack of critical analysis of ideas and alternatives, less effective organisational decision making, poor error detection and correction, low motivation and satisfaction, withdrawal, turnover, sabotage and deviance (Morrison & Milliken 2000).

ASSESS YOURSELF

Think of an organisation you are familiar with — perhaps a workplace, an educational institution, or a public transport or recreational facility. Is a silo culture present there? If so, what would be an example of this? Is there a culture of silence there? If so, what would be an example of this?

Communication and knowledge management

Communication within organisations is also related to ideas about organisational learning and knowledge management. All organisations have physical assets, such as buildings, furniture, equipment, information technology and other things that can be touched, but they also have intangible assets. Intangible assets include (Rumizen 2002, p. 242):

- *Human competence.* The people within an organisation and their capacity for action to generate value. This capacity includes assets such as values, experience, social skills and educational background. No organisation 'owns' human competence — it can walk out the door any time.
- *External structure.* How the organisation is regarded externally, including trademarks, brand names, image, relationships with customers, suppliers and partners. Owned by the organisation.

- *Internal structure.* What is left at work when the people go home, including databases, processes, models, documentation, patents, trade secrets and other intellectual property. Owned by the organisation.

In knowledge-based economies, it is becoming increasingly apparent that intangible assets are the key drivers of organisational success. This comes as a surprise to many managers, who in the past tended to concentrate on tangible assets. While lip service is usually paid to clichés such as 'our people are our most important asset', in practice such sentiments are rarely acted on. It seems much easier to manage tangible assets than intangible ones.

Organisations strive to create new products and improve old ones, to reach old and new customers, and to manage processes. Enormous resources are invested in finding out why things are or are not running well. When things go wrong, enormous resources are put into undoing the damage and ensuring it doesn't happen again. Time and again, however, employees observing such efforts will remark:

- 'We could have told them that, but no-one ever bothered to ask.'
- 'What's the point in trying to tell them? Nobody ever listens anyway.'
- 'There's an easier way of doing that, but I doubt they'd consider that.'
- 'I could tell you how to do it in half the time at a quarter of the cost, but if we made that public they'd probably just lay ten good people off.'
- 'We predicted that would happen, but the report was ignored.'
- 'Joe showed them how to do that, and they made millions from it. And what did Joe get out of it? A few measly bucks.'
- 'Nobody told us.'

Most employees within organisations already know how to do things better than they are currently being done, but for a variety of reasons that experience is not tapped into. As Lew Platt, former chief executive officer of Hewlett-Packard put it, 'If H-P knew what it knows, we'd be three times as profitable' (quoted in Dearlove 2000, p. 152).

Knowledge management: tapping into an organisation's intangible assets to systematically organise the knowledge of all its members so that it can be more effectively used for the organisation's benefit

Knowledge management is concerned with reversing this trend and tapping into the vast intangible assets of the organisation to systematically collect, categorise, fuse and disseminate the pool of perceptions, insights, experiences and skills of the people who are already there – in other words, to avoid the need to reinvent the wheel (unnecessarily repeating ourselves) by determining just what knowledge about 'wheels' already exists (Asllani & Luthans 2003). An organisation may be awash with data, but unless that data can be organised into information, and unless human minds can synthesise and learn from that information to create knowledge, then very little advantage is made of it. An example of this is captured in technology analyst Bill French's observation, 'email is where knowledge goes to die' (quoted in Venolia 2005, in her analysis of silos). See chapter 3 for a discussion on the distinction between data, information, knowledge and wisdom.

Following are some examples of knowledge management strategies that appear to be paying off for organisations:

- Xerox has a database known as Eureka to which all service technicians can contribute. When technicians discover a problem or situation that has not been anticipated in product design and recorded in documentation such as manuals and instructions, they enter a description and analysis of the problem or situation into the database via laptop computer. The knowledge-sharing system has more than 25 000 items, which are tapped into by 25 000 representatives worldwide. As a result of Eureka, Xerox now saves between 5 per cent and 10 per cent on labour and parts costs (Kermally 2002, pp. 162–3).
- Information technology company EMC is using 'social media' technologies to share knowledge: recently it had 10 000 wiki-based documents and 3000 blogs across 150 topical communities (Parise 2009).
- Over three days in May 2001, IBM held WorldJam, a global in-house brainstorming session. About 52 000 of a total of 320 000 employees contributed more than 6000 ideas,

which went into an online archive that has since been tapped into by many staff (Figallo & Rhine 2002, pp. 56–7).

- An Australian employee of Accenture, a consulting and technology firm, trained in the Malaysian branch to acquire technology consulting skills, and then went on to create a blog upon returning, sharing learning by posting a summary of the skills. The information was widely shared and other employees began to contribute to the blog, giving examples of solutions to problems they had encountered with clients. As the employee sees it, 'blogging (is) a positive cycle of learning that goes on and on' (Zhang, Zhu & Hildebrandt 2009, p. 117).
- A British company set up a 'what's hot and what's not' interactive voicemail system. Sales representatives dropped in 'hot news' in the form of 'micro stories' about customers, technology and products. Each story was less than one minute long, and representatives tapped into it via mobile phones (Cook 1999, p. 103).
- A small printing company consisted of three founding partners and four managers, who work with many associates and contract staff. Because the central decision-making group was so close-knit, there seemed no need to document anything about processes and products. Then one manager with a key client base died, and another left hurriedly. Knowledge was 'walking out the door', and the remaining group members found it difficult to conduct effective induction for two new staff members. The company is now documenting its key processes and achievements at the end of each project to build up a knowledge databank (Kermally 2002, p. 55).

Knowledge management thus understood has much in common with the idea of the 'learning organisation' developed by Argyris (1999) and Senge et al. (1999), in which intellectual capital is the key driver of growth, and the ability to learn from the past is the main predictor of how it will fare in the future (Frahm & Brown 2006).

How does knowledge management work, and what relationship does it have to organisational communication? Let's consider two models of knowledge management and see what relationships there might be.

Knowledge management model 1: the knowledge spiral

Takeuchi and Nonaka (2004) have developed a spiral model of knowledge acquisition, which moves through a SECI (Socialisation–Externalisation–Combination–Internalisation) sequence (figure 16.16). The sequence draws a distinction between explicit knowledge – knowledge in the public domain that 'everyone knows' – and tacit knowledge, or knowledge that has become second nature to those who hold it, but that they initially might find hard to explain to others (Nezafati, Afrazeh & Jalali 2009).

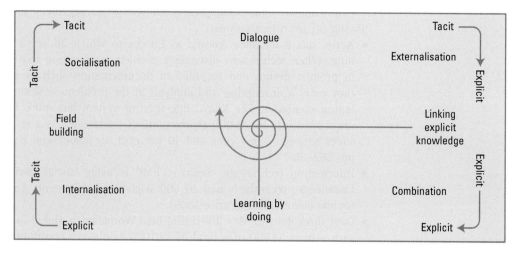

FIGURE 16.16 The SECI knowledge spiral

Source: Rumizen (2002, p. 21).

In this system the first phase of knowledge acquisition is socialisation. Here knowledge transfer is *tacit-to-tacit*. An example is Matsushita's efforts to create an automatic bread-making machine. The software engineers at the company were not expert bread makers, but the head baker at a hotel was, so the engineers worked with the baker to see how he stretched and twisted dough to achieve success. The engineers were then able to transfer this knowledge into the design of the bread-making machine. In the socialisation phase, tacit-to-tacit transfer of knowledge can be made systematic through brainstorming, informal meetings, discussions, dialogues, observation, on-the-job training, customer interaction, coaching, mentoring and learning groups (Kermally 2002, p. 61).

In the second phase, externalisation, the transfer process is *tacit-to-explicit*. For example, Canon engineers were trying to work out how to reduce costs on a new mini-copier. Engineers were discussing the issue over some beers, when peripheral data — the beer cans in their hands — became their central data: they thought of a way to use aluminium to produce disposable copier drums, and thus solved the problem. In the externalisation phase, tacit-to-external knowledge transfer can be put on a systematic basis through meetings, building hypotheses and models, cartoons to communicate, after-action reviews, workshops, master classes, assignment databases and best practice exchange.

In the third phase, combination, the transfer process is *explicit-to-explicit*. For example, Kraft Foods uses data from supermarket electronic point-of-sale transactions not only to find out what sells well but also to plan new ways of marketing products to customers. In the combination phase, explicit-to-explicit knowledge transfer can be put on a systematic basis by exploiting virtual libraries, publications and conferences.

In the final phase of the SECI sequence, internalisation, the circle is completed (and the cycle is set up for another iteration) by *explicit-to-tacit* transfer of knowledge. General Electric compiled a database of customer complaints, which design engineers were able to tap when creating the next generation of products (for a discussion of complaints, feedback and strategic listening). In the internalisation phase, explicit-to-tacit knowledge transfer can be put on a systematic basis by exploiting the potentials of facilitation skills, client–customer feedback reviews and development counselling (Kermally 2002, p. 61). While it has not always proven to be universally applicable (see Tong and Mitra 2009), the SECI model remains a powerful concept when discussing and applying knowledge management concepts.

Knowledge management model 2: the knowledge management technology stage model

Gottschalk (2006; 2009) suggests that knowledge management can best be understood in terms of four different stages or phases, namely:

1. *Person-to-technology stage.* In this stage, tools for end users are made available to knowledge workers in the simplest form. This means a capable networked PC on every desk or in every briefcase, with standardised personal productivity tools such as word processing, spreadsheets, legal databases, presentation software and scheduling programs. The dominating strategy is a tool strategy, while the predominant attitude towards the value of information technology in knowledge management processes is that of scepticism.

2. *Person-to-person stage.* In this stage, information about who knows what is made available to all people in the organisation and to selected outside partners. What people know in any given organisation is mapped into a directory or 'Yellow Pages', which might live on an intranet. This is 'metadata', or knowledge about knowledge, allowing individuals to contact other individuals to tap into their knowledge, which might just as easily be tacit knowledge as explicit knowledge. The dominating strategy at this stage is a flow strategy, while the skeptics of stage 1 might become conservatives.

3. *Person-to-information stage.* In this stage, information created by knowledge workers is stored and made available in the form of documents to those inside and some outside the organisation. Such documents might be contracts and agreements, reports, manuals and handbooks, business forms, letters, memos, articles, drawings, blueprints, photographs, email and voicemail messages, video clips, script and visuals from presentations, policy statements, computer printouts, and transcripts from meetings. Lawyers in a law firm might write up case notes in databases, while police forces might use relational databases for crime-specific cases (the Tucson Police Department keeps approximately 1.5 million incident record sets, which can be used to track approximately 1200 individuals suspected of being responsible for a majority of major crimes). The dominating strategy at this stage is a stock strategy, while the conservatives of stage 2 might now become early adopters of information technology in knowledge management.
4. *Person-to-system stage.* At this final stage, information systems solving knowledge problems are made available to knowledge workers and solution seekers. Artificial intelligence approaches such as neural networks, data mining, expert systems and business intelligence now come into play. The knowledge that was codified in stage 3 is now explicated and formalised (although tacit knowledge is difficult to codify). The dominating strategy at this stage is a growth strategy, while the early adopters of stage 3 might now become innovators in information technology in knowledge management.

The application of this model to police investigations is shown in figure 16.17.

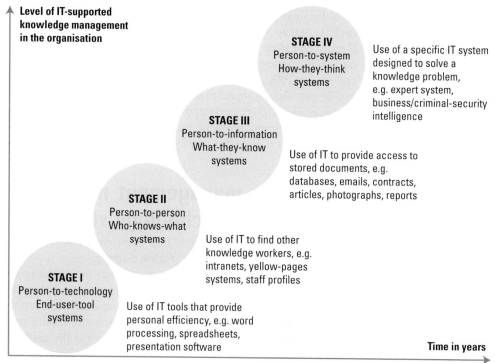

FIGURE 16.17 Stage of growth model for police investigations

Source: Gottschalk (2006, p. 626).

Knowledge management: the new and the old

Knowledge management thus conceived has enormous potential to facilitate development of any organisation, and creates exciting new perspectives. Expert power becomes the primary power base, and mentoring and coaching are vital. Listening and feedback skills are central to tapping the knowledge pool that already exists before any new knowledge is created. But knowledge management is not an entirely new concept; rather, it revives the decades-old debate about motivation, compensation, job security and natural justice in the workplace, along with the idea of an organisational culture in which the 'soft skills' of listening to people may be more important than the 'hard skills' involved in setting up a technology network to capture this knowledge. These dilemmas are crystallised in the following viewpoints:

- Companies install email or collaborative software and expect knowledge to flow freely through the electronic pipeline. When it doesn't happen, they are more likely to blame the software or inadequate training than to face a fact of life: people rarely give away valuable possessions (including knowledge) without expecting something in return (Davenport & Prusak 2000, p. 26).
- While technology can facilitate the exchange of ideas, sometimes it can block such exchanges. Many people prefer face-to-face interaction, but this may be ignored if there is too much emphasis on technological systems (Tong & Mitra 2009).
- Modern technology makes transmitting information easy, but companies have to create the right environment and incentives to persuade individuals to share what they know. The trouble is that knowledge, as the old adage tells us, is power. One of the greatest barriers to effective knowledge management lies in the basic insecurity and fear that prevails in many companies.
- The real issue for companies is: how do you persuade individuals to hand over their know-how when it is the source of their power and the only guarantee of their continuing employment? Until companies address this, for most, knowledge management will remain a pipe dream (Dearlove 2000, p. 155).
- The inescapable conclusion of this analysis of the 'knowledge management' idea is that it is, in large part, a management fad, promulgated mainly by certain consultancy companies, and the probability is that it will fade away like previous fads. Whatever businesses claim about people being their most important resource, they are never reluctant to rid themselves of that resource (and the knowledge it possesses) when market conditions decline. We have to ask, 'If getting promotion, or holding your job, or finding a new one is based on the knowledge you possess — what incentive is there to reveal that knowledge and share it?' (Wilson 2002; see also p. 628).

In other words, the problem is not the human-to-machine or machine-to-machine communication systems, but rather the human-to-human communication systems. Unless these are properly addressed, then the promise of knowledge management will remain unfulfilled.

STUDENT STUDY GUIDE

SUMMARY

In this chapter we considered how communication channels can help or impede the flow of messages through organisations. We looked at the strengths and weaknesses of, and the interconnections between, upward, downward and horizontal communication. We examined organisational design factors such as flatness and tallness, centralisation and decentralisation, and mechanistic versus organic, and speculated on how these factors affect communication patterns and behaviour. We looked at network organisations, network roles and networking strategies, and assessed the importance of the informal organisation and the grapevine. We considered the idea of organisational culture and its impact on communication, noting the concepts of organisational silence and organisational silos. Finally, we focused on the idea of knowledge management and its dependence on the soft or interpersonal skills involved in effective organisational communication.

KEY TERMS

alignment strategy *p. 510*

asynchronous communication *p. 511*

boundary spanner *p. 526*

chain of command *p. 513*

clique *p. 524*

de-layering *p. 517*

diagonal communication *p. 515*

downsizing *p. 517*

downward communication *p. 514*

empowerment *p. 517*

flat organisation *p. 517*

formal organisation *p. 514*

hierarchy *p. 513*

horizontal communication *p. 514*

informal organisation *p. 514*

knowledge management *p. 539*

macro-culture *p. 532*

mechanistic *p. 520*

micro-culture *p. 532*

network analysis *p. 524*

networking *p. 526*

organic *p. 520*

organisation *p. 510*

organisational design *p. 513*

organisational silence *p. 537*

placid environment *p. 517*

shoot-the-messenger ethos *p. 537*

silo culture *p. 535*

small world phenomenon *p. 522*

span of control *p. 517*

synchronous communication *p. 511*

tall organisation *p. 517*

telecommuting *p. 522*

the grapevine *p. 529*

turbulent environment *p. 518*

upward communication *p. 514*

vertical communication *p. 514*

virtual organisation *p. 522*

REVIEW QUESTIONS

1. Name at least five organisational communication channels.
2. 'Horizontal communication is always more effective than vertical communication.' Discuss.
3. What is the relationship between span of control and the 'height' of an organisation?
4. Is it possible to have a flat and centralised organisation?
5. 'Organic organisations are the future; mechanistic organisations are the past.' Discuss.
6. Name at least two functions performed by a boundary spanner.
7. 'The informal organisation is just another term for the grapevine.' True or false?
8. What is the relationship between organisational silence and organisational silos?
9. How do artefacts give insights into an organisation's culture?
10. What are the four phases of the knowledge spiral?
11. What are the four stages of the knowledge management technology stage model?

1. Draw a formal organisation chart for an organisation you are familiar with. How would you classify it in terms of flat/tall and centralised/decentralised? What impact does this organisational design have on communication within the organisation?
2. Re-draw the formal chart to show informal relationships that you are aware of. If possible, get at least one other person to do the same. Compare results.
3. Consider an organisation, part of an organisation or a friendship group you are familiar with. Analyse communication patterns in terms of cliques and roles (gatekeepers, liaisons, bridges, isolates, opinion leaders/stars, cosmopolites/boundary spanners, powers behind the throne). Create a diagram of the communication system, and discuss it with others. (Such an exercise can elicit strong reactions from those being 'analysed', so approach the task with foresight, sensitivity and tact.) Allow those 'analysed' to return the favour.
4. Compare two organisations you are familiar with. How do their cultures differ, and in what ways are their cultures similar?
5. Using the knowledge management spiral model, analyse how you gained (or did not gain) certain aspects of knowledge in your personal or private life, and how you then passed on (or did not pass on) that knowledge.
6. Using print and online resources, research the topic of communication audits. What value might such an audit have in analysing communication patterns in an organisation?
7. Using print and online resources, research the topics of departmental, divisional, matrix and staff/line organisational structuring. What impact might these structures have on analysing communication patterns in an organisation?

WHAT WOULD YOU DO?

You run the information technology section of your organisation. Your previous boss, John, asked you six months ago to set up The Grapevine, a chat-room section on the organisation intranet where employees can post anonymous comments. Anyone could enter anything they liked on the site, on a completely anonymous basis. Some of the material was nonsense, and some of it was offensive, but a number of things emerged that were more positive: industrial action was averted when chatters started complaining about the air quality down in the basement, and action was taken to clean it up; some of the best salespeople were kept on after complaints about commission rates were noted; intervention by government health officers was averted when gossip about the café food was acted on; the loss of one of your biggest customers was avoided when a number of its complaints were identified by chatters (complaints that were quickly attended to); and improvements in two product lines were made after faults in design were discussed by chatters.

John left two weeks ago, and his replacement, Jane, has just walked in. She has a cold expression on her face, and is visibly irate. 'Have you seen the quality of the information that is being put up on the site? I could sue over a number of the things they've said about me, and about the C-600 — I designed that myself. And it's all wasting too much time — they need to get off this site and back to work! I want you to set up a program that will identify all chatters, and get it to me by the end of the week. If people want to communicate with each other, they can just reacquaint themselves with the phone. And if they want to whine, they can do that with the others down at the employment agency!'

What will you say to Jane?

SUGGESTED READING

Bargiela-Chiappini, Francesca 2009, *The handbook of business discourse*, Edinburgh University Press, Edinburgh, SCO.

DiFonzo, Nicholas & Bordia, Prashant 2007, *Rumor psychology: social and organizational approaches*, American Psychological Association, Washington, DC.

Hargie, Owen D and Tourish, Dennis (eds) 2009, *Auditing organizational communication: a handbook of research, theory and practice*, 2nd edn, Routlede, London/New York.

Keyton, Joann & Shockley-Zalabek, Pamela 2009, *Case studies for organisational communication: understanding communication processes*, 3rd edn, Oxford University Press, New York, NY.

Mann, Monroe & Levinson, Jay Conrad 2008, *Guerilla networking: a proven battle plan to attract the very people you want to meet*, Morgan James Publishing, Garden City, NY.

Marlow, Eugene 1997, *The breakdown of hierarchy: communicating in the evolving workplace*, Butterworth-Heinemann, Boston, MA.

Modaff, Daniel P, Butler, Jennifer A & Dewine, Sue 2011, *Organizational communication: foundations, challenges and misunderstandings*, 3rd edn, Allyn & Bacon, Boston, MA.

Schein, Edgar H 2009, *The corporate culture survival guide*, revised new edn., Jossey-Bass, San Francisco, CA.

REFERENCES

Aamodt, Michael G 2010, *Industrial/organizational psychology: an applied approach*, 6th edn, Wadsworth/Cengage, Belmont, CA.

Adams, Scott 2002, *Another day in cubicle paradise: a Dilbert book*, Andrews McMeel Publishing, Kansas City, MO.

Adams, Terry 2007, 'Producers, directors, and horizontal communication in television news', *Journal of Broadcasting & Electronic Media*, vol. 51, no. 2, pp 337–54.

Anand, N & Conger, Jay A 2007, 'Capabilities of the consummate networker', *Organizational Dynamics*, vol. 36, no. 1, pp. 13–27.

Andrews, Patricia H & Baird, John E Jr 2005, *Communication for business and the professions*, Waveland Press, Long Grove, ILL.

Argenti, Paul A & Haley, Thea S 2006, 'Get your act together', *Harvard Business Review*, vol. 84, no. 10, p. 26.

Argyris, Chris 1999, *On organisational learning*, 2nd edn, Blackwell Business, Malden, MA.

Ashkenas, Ron, Ulrich, Dave, Jick, Todd & Kerr, Steve 2002, *The boundaryless organisation: breaking the chains of organisation structure*, rev. and updated edn, Jossey-Bass, San Francisco, CA.

Asllani, Arben & Luthans, Fred 2003, 'What knowledge managers really do: an empirical and comparative analysis', *Journal of Knowledge Management*, vol. 7, no. 3, pp. 53–66.

Baldry, Chris 1999, 'Space – the final frontier', *Sociology: The Journal of the British Sociological Association*, vol. 33, no. 3, pp. 535–49.

Bavelas, Alex 1950, 'Communication patterns in task-oriented groups', *The Journal of the Acoustical Society of America*, vol. 22, no. 6, pp. 725–30.

Belanger, France 1999, 'Communication patterns in distributed work groups: a network analysis', *IEEE Transactions on Professional Communication*, vol. 42, no. 4, pp. 261–75.

Bennis, Warren G 1973, *Beyond bureaucracy: essays on the development and evolution of human organisation*, McGraw-Hill, New York.

Bjorseth, Lillian 2009, *Breakthrough networking: building relationships that last*, 3rd edn, Duoforce Enterprises, Lisle IL.

Boggs, Leanne, Carr, Stuart C, Fletcher, Richard B & Clarke, David E 2005, 'Pseudoparticipation in communication networks: the social psychology of broken promises', *The Journal of Social Psychology*, vol. 145, no. 5, pp. 621–4.

Bordia, Prashant, Jones, Elizabeth, Gallois, Cindy, Callan, Victor J & Di Fonzo, Nicholas 2006, 'Management are aliens! Rumors and stress during organizational change', *Group & Organization Management*, vol. 11, no. 5, pp. 601–21.

Bowen, Frances & Blackmon, Kate 2003, 'Spirals of silence: the dynamic effects of diversity on organisational voice', *Journal of Management Studies*, vol. 40, no. 6, pp. 1393–1417.

Brown, Andrew D & Coupland, Christine 2005, 'Sounds of silence: graduate trainees, hegemony and resistance', *Organisation Studies*, vol. 26, pp. 1049–69.

Buch, Kimberly & Wetzel, David K 2001, 'Analyzing and realigning organisational culture', *Leadership and Organisation Development Journal*, vol. 22, no. 1, pp. 40–3.

Bundred, Steve 2006, 'Solutions to silos: joining up knowledge', *Public Money & Management*, vol. 26, no. 2, pp. 125–30.

Burns, T & Stalker, GM 1961, *The management of innovation*, Tavistock, London.

Cameron, KS & Quinn, RE 2006, *Diagnosing and changing organisational culture: based on the competing values framework*, rev. edn, Jossey-Bass, San Francisco.

Chan, Yolande E 2002, 'Why haven't we mastered alignment? The importance of the informal organisation structure', *MIS Quarterly Executive*, vol. 1, no. 2, pp. 97–112.

Clampitt, Phillip G 2000, *Communicating for managerial effectiveness*, Sage, Thousand Oaks, CA.

Clarke, Jane & Nichols, Laura 2002, *Wired working: thriving in a connected world*, Spiro Press, London.

Cook, Peter 1999, 'I heard it through the grapevine: making knowledge management work by learning to share knowledge, skills and experience', *Industrial and Commercial Training*, vol. 31, no. 3, pp. 101–5.

Cope, Mick 2003, *Personal networking: how to make your connections count*, Financial Times, London.

Crainer, Stuart & Dearlove, Des 2002, 'For new "old boys" only', *Across the Board*, vol. 39, no. 6, pp. 29–36.

Crampton, Suzanne M, Hodge, John W & Mishra, Jitendra M 1998, 'The informal communication network: factors influencing grapevine activity', *Public Personnel Management*, vol. 27, no. 4, pp. 569–84.

Daft, Richard L 2011, *Organisation theory and design*, 10th edn, South-Western Publishing, Mason, OH.

Dani, SS, Burns, ND, Backhouse, CJ & Kochhar, AK 2006, 'The implications of organisational culture and trust in the workings of virtual teams', *Proceedings of the Institution of Mechanical Engineers*, June, pp. 951–9.

Davenport, Thomas H & Prusak, Laurence 2000, *Working knowledge: how organisations manage what they know*, Harvard Business School Press, Boston, MA.

Davis, Keith & Newstrom, John W 1989, *Human behavior at work: organisational behavior*, 8th edn, McGraw-Hill, New York.

Dearlove, Des 2000, *The ultimate book of business thinking*, Capstone, Oxford, UK.

DelCampo, Robert G 2006, 'The influence of culture strength on person–organisation fit and turnover', *International Journal of Management*, vol. 23, no. 3, pp. 465–70.

De Maria, William 2006, 'Brother secret, sister silence: sibling conspiracies against managerial integrity', *Journal of Business Ethics*, vol. 65, pp. 219–34.

Dessler, Gary 2009, *Framework for Human Resource Management*, 5th edn, Prentice Hall, Upper Saddle River, NJ.

DiFonzo, Nicholas & Bordia, Prashant 2002, 'Corporate rumour, belief and accuracy', *Public Relations Review*, vol. 28, no. 1, pp. 1–19.

Dive, Brian 2003, 'When is an organisation too flat?', *Across the Board*, vol. 40, no. 4, pp. 2–23.

Dunbar, Robin 1997, *Gossip, grooming and the evolution of language*, Harvard University Press, Harvard, MA.

Edmondson, Vicki Cox & Munchus, George 2007, 'Managing the unwanted truth: a framework for dissent strategy', *Journal of Organizational Change Management*, vol. 20, no. 6, pp. 747–60.

Ennett, Susan T, Bauman, Karl E, Hussong, Andrea, Faris, Robert, Foshee, Vangie A, Cai, Li & DuRant, Robert H 2006, 'The peer context of adolescent substance use: findings from social network analysis', *Journal of Research on Adolescence*, vol. 16, no. 2, pp. 159–351.

Eunson, Baden 1987, *Behaving: managing yourself and others*, McGraw-Hill, Sydney.

Figallo, Cliff & Rhine, Nancy 2002, *Building the knowledge management network*, John Wiley & Sons, New York.

Fisher, Donna 2001, *Professional networking for dummies*, John Wiley & Sons, New York.

Frahm, Jennifer & Brown, Kerry 2006, 'Developing communicative competencies for a learning organization', *Journal of Management Development*, vol. 25, no. 3, pp. 201–12.

Fraser, George C 2004, *Success runs in our race: the complete guide to networking in the black community*, Amistad Press, New York.

Freeman, Linton C 1978–1979, 'Centrality in social networks: conceptual clarification', *Social Networks*, vol. 1, pp. 215–39.

Friedman, Thomas L 2006. *The world is flat: a brief history of the twenty-first century*, updated and expanded edn, Farrar, Straus and Giroux, New York.

Gergen, Kenneth J & Thatchenkery, Tojo Joseph 1996, 'Organisation science as social construction: postmodern potentials', *The Journal of Applied Behavioral Science*, vol. 32, no. 4, pp. 356–77.

Gerster, Lou 2004, *Who says elephants can't dance? Leading a great enterprise through dramatic change*, Collins, New York.

Goldhaber, Gerald M 1990, *Organizational communication*, 5th edn, Wm. C. Brown, Dubuque, IA.

—— 1993, *Organisational communication*, 6th edn, McGraw-Hill, New York.

Gossett, Loril M & Kilker, Julian 2006, 'My job sucks: examining counter institutional web sites as locations for organisational member voice, dissent and resistance', *Management Communication Quarterly*, vol. 20. no. 1, pp. 63–90.

Gottschalk, Petter 2006, 'Expert systems at stage IV of the Knowledge Management Technology Stage Model: the case of police investigations', *Expert Systems with Applications*, vol. 31, pp. 617–28.

—— 2009, 'Maturity levels for interoperability in digital government', *Government Information Quarterly*, vol. 26, pp. 75–81.

Greengard, Samuel 2001, 'Gossip poisons business: HR can stop it', *Workforce*, vol. 80, no. 7, pp. 24–8.

Groat, Malcolm 1997, 'The informal organisation', *Management Accounting*, vol. 75, no. 4, pp. 40–2.

Harris, Thomas E 2002, *Applied organisational communication: principles and pragmatics for future practice*, 2nd edn, Lawrence Erlbaum Associates, Mahwah, NJ.

Harris, Thomas E & Nelson, Mark D 2007, *Applied organizational communication*, 3rd edn, Lawrence Erlbaum Associates, Mahwah, NJ.

Hellweg, Susan 1987, 'Organisational grapevines: a state of the art review', in Brenda Dervin and Melvyn J Voight (eds), *Progress in the communication sciences*, vol. 8, Ablex, Norwood, NJ.

Hodgetts, Richard M & Hegar, Kathryn M 2008, *Modern Human Relations at work*, 10th edn, Cengage/South-Western College Publishing, Cincinnatti, OH.

Hopkins, Andrew 2005, *Safety, culture and risk: the organisational cause of disasters*, CCH, Sydney.

—— 2006, 'Studying organisational cultures and their effects on safety', *Safety Science*, vol. 44, issue 10, pp. 875–89.

Huffman, Matt L & Torres, Lisa 2002, 'It's not only "who you know" that matters', *Gender & Society*, vol. 16, no. 6, pp. 793–813.

Igo, Tony & Skitmore, Martin 2006, 'Diagnosing the organisational culture of an Australian engineering consultancy using the Competing Values Framework', *Construction Innovation*, vol. 6, pp. 121–39.

Illegams, Viviane & Verbeke, Alain 2004, *Moving towards the virtual workplace: managerial and societal perspectives on telework*, Edward Elgar Publishing, London.

Jaques, Elliott 1990, 'In praise of hierarchy', *Harvard Business Review*, January–February, vol. 68, no. 1, pp. 127–33.

Jones, Seth G 2007, 'Fighting networked terrorist groups: lessons from Israel', *Studies in Conflict & Terrorism*, vol. 30, no. 3, pp. 281–302.

Kahn, Gabriel 2002, 'Schmooze fest', *Far Eastern Economic Review*, vol. 165, no. 24, pp. 40–2.

Kanter, Rosabeth Moss 1990, *When giants learn to dance: mastering the challenges of strategy, management, and careers in the 1990s*, Random House, New York.

Katzenbach, Jon R & Khan, Zhia 2010, *Leading outside the lines: how to mobilize the informal organisation, energise your team, and get better results*, Jossey-Bass, San Francisco.

Kermally, Sultan 2002, *Effective knowledge management: a best practice blueprint*, John Wiley & Sons, London.

Kimbrough, RL & Componation, PJ 2009, 'The relationship between organizational culture and enterprise risk management', *Engineering Management Journal*, vol. 21, no. 2, pp. 18–27.

Leavitt, HJ 1951, 'Some effects of communication patterns on group performance', *Journal of Abnormal and Social Psychology*, vol. 46, pp. 38–50.

Lencioni, Patrick 2006, *Silos, politics and turf wars: a leadership fable about destroying the barriers that turn colleagues into competitors*, Jossey-Bass, San Francisco.

Lewis, Laurie K 1999, 'Disseminating information and soliciting input during planned organisational change: implementers' targets, sources, and channels for communicating', *Management Communication Quarterly*, vol. 13, no. 1, pp. 43–76.

Likert, Rensis 1976, *New ways of managing conflict*, McGraw-Hill, New York.

McAllister, Brad 2004, 'Al Qaeda and the innovative firm: demythologizing the network', *Studies in Conflict & Terrorism*, vol. 27, pp. 297–319.

McFarland, Daniel A. 2001, 'Student resistance: how the formal and informal organisation of classrooms facilitate everyday forms of student defiance', *American Journal of Sociology*, vol. 107, no. 3, pp. 612–78.

Manev, Ivan F & Stevenson, William B 2001, 'Balancing ties: boundary spanning and influence in the organisation's network of communication', *Journal of Business Communication*, vol. 38, no. 2, pp. 183–205.

Mantei, Marilyn 1981, 'The effect of programming team structures on programming tasks', *Communications of the ACM (Association for Computing Machinery)*, vol. 24, no. 3, pp. 106–13.

Mears, Peter 1974, 'Structuring communication in a working group', *Journal of Communication*, vol. 24, no. 1, pp. 71–80.

Michelson, Grant & Mouly, V Suchitra 2002, ' "You didn't hear it from us, but …": towards an understanding of rumour and gossip in organisations', *Australian Journal of Management*, vol. 27, pp. 57–65.

—— 2004, 'Do loose lips sink ships? The meaning, antecedents and consequences of rumour and gossip in organisations', *Corporate Communications*, vol. 9, no. 3, pp. 189–201.

Miller, Katherine 2009, *Organisational communication: approaches and processes*, 5th edn, Cengage/Wadsworth, Belmont, CA.

Miller, Peter Michael 2008, 'Examining the work of boundary spanning leaders in community contexts', *International Journal of Leadership in Education*, vol. 11, no. 4, pp. 353–77.

Milliken, Frances J, Morrison, Elizabeth W & Hewlin, Patricia 2003, 'An exploratory study of employee silence: issues that employees don't communicate upward and why', *Journal of Management Studies*, vol. 40, no. 6, pp. 1453–77.

Mintzberg, Henry & Van Der Heyden, Ludo 1999, 'Organigraphs: drawing how companies really work', *Harvard Business Review*, vol. 77, no. 5, pp. 87–95.

Morand, David A 1996, 'What's in a name? An exploration of the social dynamics of forms of address in organisations', *Management Communication Quarterly*, vol. 9, no. 4, pp. 422–51.

Morrison, Elizabeth Wolfe & Milliken, Frances J 2000, 'Organisational silence: a barrier to change and development in a pluralistic world', *The Academy of Management Review*, vol. 25, no. 4, pp. 706–25.

Nadler, D & Gerstein, M 1992, 'Designing high-performance work systems: organizing people, work, technology, and information', in D Nadler and M Gerstein (eds), *Organisational architecture: designs for changing organisations*, Jossey-Bass, San Francisco.

Nemiro, Jill E 2002, 'The creative process in virtual teams', *Creativity Research Journal*, vol. 14, no. 1, pp. 69–83.

Nezafati, Navid, Afrazeh, Abbas & Jalali, S. Mohammed J. 2009, 'A dynamic model for measuring knowledge level of organizations based on Nonaka and Takeuchi Model (SECI)', *Scientific Research and Essays*, vol. 4, no. 5, pp. 531–42.

Ogbor, John O 2001, 'Critical theory and the hegemony of corporate culture', *Journal of Organisational Change Management*, vol. 14, no. 6, pp. 590–609.

Pace, R Wayne & Faules, Don F 1989, *Organizational communication*, 2nd edn, Prentice Hall, Englewood Cliffs, NJ.

—— 1994, *Organisational communication*, 3rd edn, Allyn & Bacon, Boston, MA.

Parise, Salvatore 2009, 'Social media networks: what do they mean for knowledge management?' *Journal of Information Technology Case and Application Research*, vol. 11, no, 2, pp. 1–11.

Parker, Rodney D & Hildebrandt, Herbert W 1996, 'Business communication and architecture: is there parallel?', *Management Communication Quarterly*, vol. 10, no. 2, pp. 227–42.

Perlow, Leslie & Williams, Stephanie 2003, 'Is silence killing your company?', *Harvard Business Review*, vol. 81, no. 5, pp. 52–62.

Richmond, Virginia Peck, and McCroskey, James C, 2009, *Organizational communication for survival: making work, work*, Pearson/Allyn & Bacon, Boston, MA.

Robbins, Stephen P & Barnwell, Neil 2007, *Organisation theory: concepts and cases*, 5th edn, Pearson/Prentice Hall, Frenchs Forest, NSW.

Rosner, Bob 2001, 'Studying the world beneath the org chart', *Workforce*, vol. 80, no. 9, pp. 64–6.

Rumizen, Melissie Clemmons 2002, *The complete idiot's guide to knowledge management*, Alpha Books, Indianapolis, IN.

Rummler, Geary A & Brache, Alan P 1995, *Improving performance: how to manage the white space in the organisation chart*, Jossey-Bass, San Francisco, CA.

Segal, Leonie, Dalziel, Kim & Mortimer, Duncan 2009, 'Fixing the game: are between-silo differences in funding arrangements handicapping some interventions and giving others a head-start?' *Health Economics*, vol. 19, no. 4, pp. 449–65.

Senge, Peter M, Kleiner, Art, Roberts, Charlotte, Roth, George, Ross, Rick & Smith, Bryan 1999, *The dance of change: the challenges to sustaining momentum in learning organisations*, Doubleday, New York.

Seta, Catherine E, Paulus, Paul B & Baron, Robert A 2000, *Effective human relations: a guide to people at work*, Allyn & Bacon, Boston, MA.

Sine, Wesley D, Mitsuhashi, Hitoshi & Kirsch, David 2006, 'Revisiting Burns and Stalker: formal structure and new venture performance in emerging economic sectors', *Academy of Management Journal*, vol. 49, no. 1, pp. 121–32.

Stephenson, Karen 1999, *Networks: the deep structure of organisation*, CRC Press, Boca Raton, FL.

Suchan, Jim & Hayzak, Greg 2001, 'The communication characteristics of virtual teams: a case study', *IEEE Transactions on Professional Communication*, vol. 44, no. 3, pp. 174–86.

Takeuchi, Hirotaka & Nonaka, Ikujiro 2004, *Hitotsubashi on knowledge management*, John Wiley & Sons, New York.

Thomas, Gail Fann, King, Cynthia L with Baroni, Brian, Cook, Linda, Keitelman, Marian, Miller, Steve & Wardle, Adelia 2006, 'Reconceptualizing e-mail overload', *Journal of Business and Technical Communication*, vol. 20, no. 3, pp. 252–87.

Thomas, R 2000, 'Getting the safety message', *OHS Alert*, vol. 1, no. 7, p. 2.

Thomas, Robyn & Davies, Annette 2005, 'Theorizing the micro-politics of resistance: new public management and managerial identities in the UK public service', *Organisation Studies*, vol. 26, pp. 683–706.

Thorne, Kym 2005, 'Designing virtual organisations? Themes and trends in political and organisational discourses', *The Journal of Management Development*, vol. 24, nos 7/8, pp. 580–607.

Toffler, Alvin & Toffler, Heidi 2004, 'The war of pyramid vs. pancakes and how it will shape the future', Toffler Associates Publications: Alvin Toffler Articles, www.toffler.com.

Tong, Jin & Mitra, Amit 2009, 'Chinese cultural influences on knowledge management practice', *Journal of Knowledge Management*, vol. 13, no. 2, pp. 49–62.

Tourish, Dennis & Robson, Paul 2006, 'Sensemaking and the distortion of critical upward communication in organisations', *Journal of Management Studies*, vol. 43, no. 4, pp. 711–30.

Tung, Rosalie 2002, 'Building effective networks', *Journal of Management Enquiry*, vol. 11, no. 2, pp. 94–103.

Venolia, Gina 2005, 'Bridges between silos: a Microsoft research project', *Microsoft Research*, January, http://research.microsoft.com

Warner, Jon 2004, *The networking pocketbook*, Stylus, London.

Warner, Malcolm & Witzel, Morgen 2003, *The virtual organisation*, International Thomson Publishing, London.

Watts, Duncan J 2004, *Six degrees: the science of a connected age*, W.W. Norton, New York.

Whitely, Sharon, Duckworth, Connie & Elliott, Kathy 2004, *The old girls' network: insider advice for women building businesses in a man's world*, Perseus Books, Boulder, CO.

Wilson, Donald O 1992, 'Diagonal communication links within organizations', *Journal of Business Communication*, vol. 29, no. 2, pp. 129–43.

Wilson, TD 2002, 'The nonsense of "knowledge management"', *Information Research*, vol. 18, no. 1, http://informationr.net.

Wilson, William J 1997, *When work disappears: the world of the new urban poor*, Vintage, New York.

Wood, Nora & Benitez, Tina 2003, 'Does the suit fit?', *Incentive*, vol. 177, no. 4, pp. 31–4.

Yu, Tianyuan & Wu, Nengquan 2009, 'A review of study on the competing values framework', *International Journal of Business and Management*, vol. 4, no. 7, pp 37–42.

Zhang, M. Allee, Zhu, Yunxia & Hildebrandt, Herbert 2009, 'Enterprise networking websites and organizational communication in Australia', *Business Communication Quarterly*, vol. 72, pp. 114–19.

17

Public communication

LEARNING OBJECTIVES

After studying this chapter you should be able to:

- Explain different models of public relations
- Understand situation analysis, communication strategies, channels and tools, and publics and stakeholders
- Demonstrate techniques for writing media releases, backgrounders, fact sheets and position papers
- Explain transparency in organisations, and the way in which internal and external communications are linked
- Demonstrate the use of concise, clear, cool, concrete and concerned language in crisis communication

Context of public relations communication

'Public communication is the communication of ideas to the broader public.' That's perilously close to a circular definition, so we need to go further. Public communication is the communication of ideas by organisations to the broader public. It is similar to, but different from, other areas of communication, such as customer communication, organisational communication and media communication (see online chapter 'Media and communication').

There are, in fact, interesting overlaps and synergies emerging between these areas, just as there are interesting overlaps and synergies between public communication on the one hand and advertising, marketing and consumer behaviour on the other. And just as in other chapters we look at audiences rather than *the* audience for documents and spoken communication, and demographic segments rather than monolithic markets for media, so too we will look at *publics* rather than a monolithic public.

Public communication is most directly associated with the field of public relations, and in this chapter we will explore different aspects of public relations techniques, such as writing news releases and crisis communication. Before we begin looking at techniques, however, we should explore the context of public relations and public communication.

Detractors of public relations see it as a field (or profession) that is economical with the truth – that is, in plain English, it is about lying and **spin** (Isikoff & Corn 2007; Moore 2007; Stauber & Rampton 2002; Kurtz 1998; Pitcher 2004; L'Etang 1997; Baggini 2010; Ewen 1999). In effect, these critics are saying that PR has a 'PR problem' (Callison 2001). For example, Turner, Bonner and Marshall (2000, pp. 29–30) in their analysis of 'the production of celebrity' in the media have noted the impact and growth of the public relations industry:

> It has become commonplace today for discussions of contemporary culture to emphasise the cultural and economic centrality of various forms of publicity: advertising, promotion, marketing and public relations. Within the academic literature, Andrew Wernick's phrase – 'promotional culture' – provides a handy means of referencing the full range of activities performed by what John Hartley has sardonically called 'the smiling professions' ...

> A more widely understood but, lately, less strictly accurate label for a similar range of activities, still conventionally used in most public and media commentary, is that of 'public relations'. Bob Franklin, in his 1997 critique of contemporary journalism in Britain, refers to the growth of 'public relations', including 'government, party and industry-group press offices, agency and in-house corporate communications, and ... the public relations staff which even charities and voluntary organizations now employ'. Like many media commentators, within the academy and elsewhere, he criticises the degree to which the practice of journalism is being contaminated from outside. The 'fourth estate' [the press] is in danger of being overwhelmed by the 'fifth estate', the growing number of 'PR merchants and spin doctors' influencing the news agenda ... In his account of the contemporary situation, Franklin cites the editor of the British magazine *PR Week* who estimates that over 50% of the content of every section (except sport) of every broadsheet newspaper would be PR-generated.

This penetration of PR releases into the mainstream media appears to be quite substantial (Turner 2006, p. 232):

> A government-funded study which tracked the takeup rate of press releases emanating from government departments in Queensland ... established that an alarming amount of press release material is run without corroboration and in some cases without any significant changes in wording. In [this] study, 279 press releases from government were traced; 200 were taken up by

Spin: the angle, emphasis or distortion put on an event or person in order to influence public opinion

The penetration of press releases into the media is quite high, with many press releases being reused largely 'as is'.

Publicity model: characterised by one-way communication in which truth is not essential; press agentry

Pseudo-event: an event staged primarily to attract media coverage

Public information model: characterised by one-way communication in which truth is essential

TABLE 17.1 Four models of public relations

newspapers, 140 of them without significant changes in wording. Clara Zawawi's (1994) study of public relations activities in newspapers (i.e. stories which could be identified as being sourced through press releases) found levels up to 65 per cent of total content in *The Sydney Morning Herald* and up to 93 per cent in the business section of *The Australian*. The business press is particularly culpable in this regard, and the evidence suggests it is virtually in the capture of its sources …

The defenders of public relations argue that while there is some truth in this view, it plays a small part only. Grunig and Hunt (1984), for example, put forward four models of public relations communication (table 17.1). These four models can be understood as being either one-way or two-way, being concerned or not concerned with truth, and being symmetric or strategic (with public relations campaigns feeding back into policy making) or asymmetric (with public relations campaigns being primarily concerned with maintaining the status quo).

The **publicity model** (or press agentry) was pioneered by PT Barnum, the nineteenth-century circus impresario, who said 'there's no such thing as bad publicity'. He was a pioneer in creating what Boorstin (1992) called **'pseudo-events'**, or events staged primarily to attract media coverage: mock marriages between celebrities, press conferences, political debates and photo opportunities. (Boorstin defined a celebrity as someone 'famous for being famous'.)

This is the world of the 'celebrity industry', which encompasses not only entertainers but increasingly also athletes and politicians (Gamson 1994; Andrews & Jackson 2001; Wilson 2001; Summers and Morgan 2008). Within press agentry, communication is one-way (from creator to the public), truth is not essential, and the primary purpose is propaganda.

The **public information model** is also a one-way process, but here truth is essential. This is the largest area of public relations by output and personnel, and is primarily concerned with disseminating information. Information is never purely neutral, of course, and contains significant persuasive content.

	Publicity (press agentry)	Public information	Two-way asymmetric	Two-way symmetric
Purpose	Propaganda	Dissemination of information	Scientific persuasion	Mutual understanding
Nature of communication	One-way; truth not essential	One-way; truth important	Two-way; imbalanced	Two-way; balanced
Where practised	Sports, theatre, product promotion	Government, nonprofit organisations, structured companies	Competitive	Regulated business and modern flat-structure companies
Examples	Celebrity coverage, photo opportunities, pseudo-events	Media releases on government policy, position papers, background articles on websites	Public health campaigns, political campaigns	Food retailers against GM foods, political parties' use of market research for policy re-design
Percentage of market	15%	50%	20%	15%

Sources: Adapted from Grunig and Hunt (1984); Grunig and Grunig (2002); Tymson, Lazar and Lazar (2002); Philips and Young (2009).

Two-way asymmetric communication includes campaigns to change public behaviour, as well as political campaigns. **Two-way symmetric** communication means the organisation sending out the messages is not simply an unchanging entity wishing to change others; it also responds to feedback from the outside world to change its own policies. Examples of this would be a supermarket chain that picks up on public concern about genetically modified foods, changes its policy ('we won't stock GM foods any more'), and then communicates that change to the public ('we're not stocking GM foods'); and political parties that use market research and public relations techniques to assess public attitudes, and then change policies accordingly (Theaker 2001). This last model of public relations is strategic – that is, it does not simply employ superior communication skills to express management policy, but in fact feeds back into and changes management policy (see chapter 10). Grunig and Grunig (2002, pp. 37–39) note:

> PR is [not just] a technical support function for other management functions ... PR is a unique management function that helps an organisation interact with the social and political components of its environment. These components make up the institutional environment of an organisation which consists of publics who affect the ability of the organisation to accomplish its goals and who expect organisations to help them accomplish their own goals. Organisations solve problems for society, but they also create problems for society. As a result, organisations are not autonomous units free to make money or to accomplish other goals they set for themselves. They are interdependent with stakeholders. They have relationships with individuals and groups that help set the goals they choose, define what the organisation is and does, and affect the success of its strategic decisions and behaviours ...

> Excellent PR units do not de-emphasise the traditional technical skills of PR, such as writing and preparing materials for the media and for publications, writing speeches, working with the media or developing audio-visual materials and websites ... They integrate this technical knowledge into a framework of managerial knowledge. They conduct formative research to develop programmes and evaluative research to measure the results ...

> Excellent PR professionals do not just adapt themselves to the organisational conditions that affect PR, conditions such as organisational culture, structure, the system of internal communication and the situation for women and employees with diverse backgrounds. Rather they help to shape these underlying conditions of organisational excellence. Excellent PR departments do not flourish in authoritarian cultures, mechanical structures, asymmetrical communication systems and organisational conditions that devalue women and minorities.

In this model, the PR practitioner takes on the role of an organisational activist, someone who is willing to challenge the paradigms of the organisation (Holtzhausen & Voto 2002) and who acts as the early warning system to help the organisation avoid crises.

The PR model used in an organisation depends on a mix of factors, including:

- management policy and objectives
- internal politics and empire building
- prevailing combinations of idealism, realism and cynicism
- attitudes of those inside the organisation towards those outside the organisation
- the willingness (or unwillingness) of those inside the organisation to perceive just what is going on outside the organisation.

Hutton (1999) suggests that the Grunig and Hunt models are too narrow to adequately describe the field of public relations, suggesting instead that public relations is really about managing strategic relationships, which can be understood in the following terms:

- *Interest.* To what degree is the public relations function focused on the client's interests rather than the public interest? (At one extreme lies a philosophy of 'the public be damned'; at the other extreme lies a belief that the public's interest should supersede the client's interests.)

- *Initiative.* To what extent is the public relations function reactive versus proactive? (Proactive practitioner techniques include stakeholder surveys, communication audits, crisis planning, issues management and strategic communications planning.)
- *Image.* To what extent is the organisation focused on perception versus reality, or image versus substance? (US President Richard Nixon's strategy during the Watergate scandal – 'let's PR it' – might be one end of this continuum while an anonymous corporate gift to a charitable organisation might represent the other end.)

Other writers, such as Guth and Marsh (2003, p. 10), suggest that public relations is more meaningfully understood as one element of a three-part entity called 'integrated marketing communications' that embraces:

- Public relations – the management of relationships between an organisation and its publics
- Advertising – the use of controlled media (media in which one pays for the privilege of dictating message content, placement and frequency) in an attempt to influence the actions of targeted publics
- Marketing – the process of researching, creating, refining and promoting a product or service and distributing that product or service to targeted consumers.

What do PR practitioners actually do?

Public relations practitioners can work within organisations, as freelancers or part of specialised public relations companies that provide services to other organisations. Typical duties of a practitioner today include (Tymson, Lazar & Lazar 2002, p. 56):

PR practitioners perform a variety of roles. In addition to organising events and advising the media of interview opportunities, PR practitioners work to ensure that news conferences run as smoothly as possible. They can, at times, also be actively involved in crisis management.

- advising management on strategy and policy issues
- developing a company's or an organisation's public relations program
- answering public and media enquiries
- conducting internal communication courses, public relations workshops and media training
- advising the media of newsworthy events and arranging coverage
- issuing news releases and statements
- organising special events such as open days, tours and exhibitions
- writing and publishing newsletters, house magazines, annual reports, pamphlets and other publications
- monitoring public opinion and the organisation's image and suggesting action where necessary
- assisting in editing and production of organisation documents and submissions
- assisting the media at organisation meetings and news conferences
- overseeing and coordinating production of film or audiovisual material
- writing speeches
- speaking to the public
- designing and preparing content for websites
- managing stakeholder communication during an issue or crisis incident
- preparing internal communication materials.

Who are PR practitioners communicating with?

In other parts of this book, we talk about message receivers, persuadees, customers (external and internal) and audiences (see online chapter 'Media and communication') – people who are the targets of the messages we are trying to convey. With public communication, we are concerned with the broader community outside the organisation's boundaries, so it makes sense to talk about 'the public' as a monolithic audience. PR practitioners sometimes go further than this and talk about 'stakeholders', 'constituencies' and 'publics'.

These terms suggest that people outside the organisation are not simply passive targets of messages, but may in fact be more directly and actively involved in the organisation via two-way symmetric communication. Consider, for example, the **publics** (note the plural), also known as stakeholders or constituencies. These are individuals or groups interested in what it is that an organisation does, but even more so, which also either affect or are affected by the activities of that organisation (Mitchell, Agle & Wood 1997; Seitel 2010). A public may have a stake in an organisation, but it is not necessarily consciously aware that it has that stake.

This movement away from the idea of a monolithic public to specialised publics is further complicated by demographic, psychographic and market segmentation categories (Okigbo & Nelson 2003). Within publics, of particular interest are opinion leaders – or persons whose knowledge, prestige and status are particularly powerful in leading opinion and value formation within publics (Chaney 2001).

Typical publics of an organisation include:

- *Shareholders* – large or small, individual or corporate; people who may invest in the organisation for a variety of reasons and a variety of terms
  - Future shareholders
- *Investors* – different from shareholders, and can include banks and various others
  - Future investors
- *Staff and management*
  - Current – since the assets of companies now consist of people who share in the processes of making, selling and then servicing the needs of customers, it is of course vital that the best staff are recruited, trained and then retained. A major part in this is played by superior communication.
  - Future – organisations with poor awareness and/or poor reputations find it hard to attract, as well as retain, the right staff
  - Past – increasingly valuable, this group provides a strong reference for an organisation's reputation
- *Customers*
  - Current – those acquiring goods and/or services from the organisation (consumers, equipment users, clients, students, congregations)
  - Future – those who might acquire goods and/or services from the organisation
  - Past – those who have acquired goods and/or services from the organisation (persons using older equipment, graduates)
- *Suppliers* – those who provide raw materials, components, inputs. Often put into the background by businesses, this is a very important stakeholder group, and to fail to keep in close touch with them can risk severe consequences.
- *Governments* – at all levels and in most countries comprising local, state and federal constituencies, including both elected politicians and the large numbers of public servants that advise and support them. Organisations and government are often interdependent, with an organisation providing a stream of taxes, rates and employment opportunities, whereas governments have the power to reciprocate with an extensive

Public: an individual or group outside an organisation interested in what goes on inside that organisation and in the outputs of that organisation; also known as a constituency or stakeholder; targets of public communication messages

array of regulations and laws, as well as tax concessions, relief and exemptions, grants, subsidies and export assistance.

- *Media* – local, metropolitan, national, international; separated into print and electronic; daily, weekly, monthly, quarterly publications
- *Unions and labour*
- *Secondary customers* – organisations and businesses dependent on business from an organisation's staff (e.g. sandwich shop, local banks, schools)
- *Neighbours* – organisations and households that are geographically close to an organisation
- *Partners in joint ventures.*

Stakeholders, publics and constituencies also include opponents, critics, rivals and enemies – an organisation may not like them, but they may provide invaluable insights and feedback that an organisation's friends and staff cannot, or will not, give. These include 'limiter' publics, such as:

- competitors
- pressure groups
- watchdog organisations
- hostile bloggers (Eunson & Warner 2000; Hendrix 2007; Whitaker, Ramsay & Smith 2009).

PR campaigns

Campaign: an organised public relations communication exercise of significant scale

An organised public relations communication exercise of significant scale is called a **campaign**. Typically, a campaign involves a number of aspects or phases (figure 17.1).

FIGURE 17.1 A public communication campaign structure

Situation analysis

A situation analysis sets the scene. It is designed for audiences such as clients who might be paying for or allocating resources for the campaign, but it should also compel its writers (PR practitioners) to clarify just what it is that the campaign is meant to achieve. Analysis includes (Tucker, Derelian & Rouner 1997, p. 15):

- a focus statement describing the issue in terms of its potential as an organisational threat or opportunity

- an assessment of groups involved (and likely to be affected by the issue) and their perceptions, probable position on the issue and behavioural inclinations
- an analysis of factors working for and against the focus statement
- an analysis of the direction in which the issues appear to be headed.

Typical situation analyses, and some of the strategies used, include those listed in table 17.2.

TABLE 17.2 Situation analyses, with matching strategies

SITUATION ANALYSIS	STRATEGIES
A British tea company was losing market share to its main competitor, which used its charismatic founder to visit Australia every six months and promote his cheaper brand. Supermarkets were currently introducing their own home brands, limiting shelf space.	The company concerned was coming up to its 300th anniversary, so a year-long campaign was planned, focused on the current British manager, the tenth generation of tea makers for the brand. The focus was to be on expertise and quality.
A western Sydney council noted that many of its citizens had lower than average incomes and higher than average levels of lifestyle-related poor health. With insufficient public transport, local residents also had a high reliance on cars.	The council had been developing a cycle-way network and decided to promote it via a free bicycle lending scheme, which meant that for a one-off fee of $25 (which covered the cost of a helmet to keep) residents could borrow a bicycle for free for a period of up to two months, which could be extended after a mechanical service and check at headquarters.
A vegetarian products company wanted to boost sales of its products, which were hampered by low awareness and limited demand for vegetarian dishes.	A vegetarian radio personality was enlisted to promote vegetarian cooking on all media, and a vegetarian cookbook, featuring her on the cover at a barbeque, handling tongs, was printed. The issue was linked to global warming, demonstrating that vegetarian fare was 'Better for you, better for the planet'.

Source: Adapted from UTS: Library (nd).

Goals and objectives

Just what is the campaign meant to achieve? To be successful, a campaign needs to answer this question; and the answer lies in the development of goals and objectives. These typically include communication of a message, message retention by the audience, message acceptance by the audience, attitude formation or change, and overt behaviour change (Grunig & Hunt 1984) (table 17.3).

TABLE 17.3 Five types of content for public relations objectives

Content for public relations objectives	Example
Communication	To generate campaign message exposure with 20 per cent of the target public by 31 January
Message retention	To generate campaign message retention by 20 per cent of the target public by 31 January
Message acceptance	To generate acceptance of campaign message by 20 per cent of the target public by 31 January
Attitude formation or change	To increase numbers of the target audience who intend to change behaviour by 20 per cent by 31 January
Overt behaviour change	To increase numbers of the target public who change or begin a new behaviour by 20 per cent by 31 January

Source: Adapted from Grunig and Hunt (1984, p. 134).

Research

A good definition of research would be 'getting the facts before the facts get you' (see chapter 3). Research methods involved in a campaign might include (Daymon 2010; Stacks 2002):

- identifying and analysing existing data relevant to the target publics (secondary data search)
- creating new data via quantitative and qualitative methods, and then analysing them (primary data search)
- market research
- questionnaires
- interviews
- focus groups (face to face and online) – groups selected by random or nonrandom means participating in structured discussions, led by a facilitator
- observation – observing groups and individuals from publics (e.g. meetings of consumer activist groups, annual general meetings)
- document analysis (e.g. reading meeting minutes, reports, correspondence).

Communication strategy

After situation analysis, the setting of goals and objectives, research and the identification of target audiences or publics, comes the task of sending messages through the most effective channels. This is the phase of devising a communication strategy. How strategy can be linked to publics via messages, tools and channels is shown in figure 17.2. Examples of channels and tools are given overleaf.

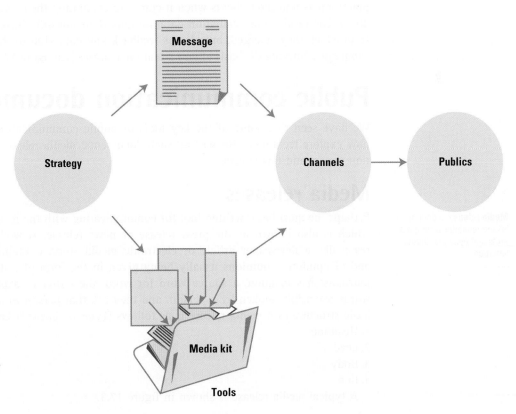

FIGURE 17.2 Linking strategy to publics via messages, tools and channels

The key part of a communication strategy is creating the optimal mix of channels, media or approaches. Different channels include:

- radio
- television
- print media (mass-circulation newspapers, magazines, trade/industry journals)
- internet
- direct mail, email
- exhibits (trade show displays, campaign buttons/badges)
- social media (blogs, Facebook, MySpace, Twitter, YouTube)
- briefings, speeches, presentations (Newsom & Carroll 2010).

Tools: the means of getting messages to channels

It may also be useful to talk of different **tools** being used to target channels. Such tools might include (Shin & Cameron 2003):

- print documents, such as media releases, backgrounders, positions papers, fact sheets
- media/press kits, which might be folders containing documents and also marketing artefacts, such as stickers, T-shirts, badges, video recordings, audio recordings, CD-ROMs, DVDs, posters, pens, mouse pads
- press tours, entertaining, golf, presents.

The line between channels and tools can become blurred, but the main thing to note is that communication strategy depends on matching messages with tools and channels in order to most effectively target publics (refer back to figure 17.2).

Budget, results and evaluation

The final sections of a campaign relate to numbers: how much it will cost (considered before the campaign) and how it went (considered after the campaign). The budget is the crucial factor in determining the quantity and quality of tools and channels used, and it may also restrict the number of publics that can be targeted. It is certainly an essential factor for PR practitioners and their clients when it comes to evaluating the campaign (Kates & Scholem 2001). The results and evaluation data are important not only in relation to the campaign from which they emerged, but also as feedback and data vital to the preparation of future campaigns, forming the basis of new situation analyses (see figure 17.1 earlier in the chapter).

Public communication documents

We have seen that some of the key tools of public communication are documents. Let's now explore techniques for writing such documents: media releases, backgrounders, position papers and fact sheets.

Media releases

Media release: a document issued to media setting out facts and opinions about a situation

Perhaps the most basic written tool for communicating with the media is the **media release**, which is also known as the press release or news release. A well-written media release reads like a newspaper article or electronic media story, containing statements of fact and of opinion – opinions usually being given in the form of a direct quote. Whereas a journalist has to quote a source word for word, the writer of a press release can create words ostensibly spoken by a person, and then ask that person to approve the words. The basic structure of a media release is as follows (Tymson, Lazar & Lazar 2002, p. 503):

1. Headline
2. Lead
3. Body
4. End.

A typical media release is shown in figure 17.3.

1. *Headline.* The headline in a media release should be catchy and informative.

2. *Lead.* The lead in a media release needs to convey the central message of the release clearly. It should not be too long, and it should encourage the reader to keep reading the release.

3. *Body.* The majority of the information in the release is contained in the body. This section of a media release should be laid out clearly (e.g. a numbered list is used in this particular release) and often includes quotes from a spokesperson and other relevant information (e.g. statistics).

4. *End.* Details about how to obtain further information, including contact details for a public relations officer/spokesperson, are included at the end of a media release. A link to a website is also included here for this purpose.

5. *Publication date.* The issue date for a media release is always included. Some media releases include a press embargo. The information in such releases cannot be published until a certain date, or until certain conditions are met.

Australian Competition & Consumer Commission

GPO Box 3131 Canberra ACT 2601
23 Marcus Clarke Street Canberra ACT
tel: (02) 6243 1111 fax: (02) 6243 1199
www.accc.gov.au

NEWS RELEASE

Beware: the 10 scams of Christmas[1]

Christmas is a busy time for most people – including scammers looking for a festive bonus by creaming money or personal details off unsuspecting consumers.[2]

'Although scammers are always around, they have greater opportunity at Christmas to sneak under the radar of consumers who are busy with trying to buy the perfect present or arrange their summer holidays,' warned Australian Competition and Consumer Commission deputy chair Peter Kell.

'That's why the ACCC has launched a Christmas SCAMwatch alert reminding consumers to bolster their defences.'

Scams around at this time of the year include:

1. Holiday scams: scammers approach victims on their holidays offering expensive memberships to scam travel clubs and fake discount hotel vouchers
2. Flight booking scams: where consumers think they have booked flights online but the website they booked through is fake and so are their bookings
3. Online shopping scams: the perfect gift is purchased online, but never arrives
4. Romance scams: if someone you have met online asks you for money as a result of some misfortune it may be a scam
5. Charity scams: charities often seek donations at this time of year – scammers try to camouflage themselves as genuine charities sites and capitalise on consumers' generosity
6. Telephone scams: particularly prevalent and varied this year including cold calls claiming computers infected by viruses, offering fake government grants or seeking bank details in order to 'process' a bank fee or tax refund
7. Weight loss scams: for those anxious to shed Christmas kilos, 'miracle' weight loss scams may be attractive – be wary
8. Door to door scams: an easy way to shop or lose money? Some traders are legitimate but others may sell poor quality products with no guarantees
9. Visa scams: when trying to help a friend or family member to visit from overseas in time for Christmas, these 'guaranteed services' may not be all the seem
10. Lottery scams: out of the blue winnings from a lottery you never entered? Scammers ask for money to 'process' your win but you will never receive the money.[3]

Full details about how these scams operate and how to protect yourself are available from the SCAMwatch website.[4]

Media inquiries
- Ms Lin Enright, Media, (02) 6243 1108 or 0414 613 520

General enquiries
- Infocentre 1300 302 502
Release # NR 266/10
Issued: 8th December 2010[5]

Links
- SCAMwatch radar — http://www.scamwatch.gov.au/content/index.phtml?itemId=814140

FIGURE 17.3 Sample media release

Source: Adapted from Australian Competition and Consumer Commission (2010), 'Beware: the 10 scams of Christmas', media release, 8 December, www.accc.gov.au.

Media releases are usually no longer than one page, and it is wise not to let them go beyond two pages. When writing a media release, you need to ask yourself questions such as the following:

- *Is it really news you are talking about?* Why should the media bother to read your release, or to act on it? Just because you think that the content is important is not enough. You've got to ask yourself: what's in it for them?
- *Does it have an angle?* That is, is there a 'hook' or feature that will interest readers, listeners and viewers of media? Does it have a local angle? You may end up writing more than one release relating to the same event or item, with each version targeted to a different audience.
- *Is it written in plain language?* The text should be free of jargon and specialised references.
- *Is it addressed to the real audience?* Your audience is not your boss, but an editor (Newsom & Haynes 2010) who acts as a media gatekeeper. This very busy person will probably give your release consideration for about ten seconds before moving on to the rest of the pile (figure 17.4).
- Does it meet (or come close to) meeting the journalist's criteria for a good story? That is, does it answer the 5W and H questions of what, why, when, who, where and how? (Mahoney 2008).

<figure>

What gatekeepers like in a media release	What gatekeepers don't like in a media release
■ A clear, concise statement ■ Exclusives ■ Their readers and viewers ■ Professional behaviour ■ Celebrities ■ Honesty ■ Hooks ■ Local angles ■ Strong visuals ■ Real news	■ People who won't take no for an answer ■ Hype in the place of news ■ Gimmicks ■ Interruption at a deadline ■ Explaining the business to neophytes ■ Being second. They *hate* being third. ■ Story ideas that have no audience hook ■ Being bypassed ■ Interruptions at the start of the day ■ 'Think pieces'

FIGURE 17.4 Media editors as gatekeepers

Source: Adapted from Levine and Gendron (2002, pp. 118–25); Truin (2007, pp 163–77).
</figure>

To reach your publics, you have to go through these publics of one. Therefore, don't kill or bury the lead with something that will stroke the ego of a client or superior (an internal public), but instead write for someone who cares about the news and not about the internal dynamics of your organisation. In fact, one of your greatest challenges in writing a release may be to convince some of your internal publics that the purpose of the exercise is to get coverage, not to stroke their vanity (see figure 17.5).

<figure>

Don't write a lead like this	Write a lead like this
The Chief General Manager, South-Eastern Region Division of Float8 Industries, Pty Ltd (incorporated in Australia and Singapore), Dr Ralph Hoskings, PhD, MSci., today announced the launch of a new Float8 product, the SuperLife Preserver. 'This is a great day for Float8', said Mr Hoskings. 'We have developed and patented a new system in this preserver, whereby we have created high viscosity photoelectric cells integrated into the structure of the preserver.'	A new Australian invention that may save lives this summer was launched in Perth today. The SuperLife Preserver (worn by model Cyndi, left) has a unique patented solar pump. This pump draws its energy from the sun, running off solar cells that continually re-inflate the preserver. Ralph Hoskings of Float8's office in Perth said: 'Summer is a time of fun, but it's also a time when people, many of them kids, drown. The SuperLife may help to save a few lives.'

FIGURE 17.5 Bad and good news leads in a media release
</figure>

When writing releases, also consider the functionality of the document design (see chapter 2). For example, if you are going to fax, mail, email or courier the release, use double-spaced text. This allows editors to actually work on it, to mark up changes they want to make. If you need to go to a second or third page, indicate that there is more to come (with 'more' at the end of each page). Also indicate where the release ends.

Media releases need to contain enough detail to inform and intrigue, but not to overwhelm. Provide full contact details, so that the media can get back to you or another spokesperson at any time (including after hours). If the release's information has no time constraints, write 'For immediate release' at the top. If information should not be released until a later time for whatever reason, write 'Embargo (date, time)' at the top.

Consider the style in which you write. You may choose to vary the style to match that of the target channel. Tabloid and broadsheet print media use different styles, the broadsheet style normally being more complex, with higher readability scores (see online chapters 'Writing skills 3: style' and 'Media and communication'). Similar considerations apply to magazines and electronic media. The closer your style is to that of the target channel, the less work a time-strapped editor will need to spend on cutting it for final use. Structure your text using the inverted pyramid model (see online chapter 'Media and communication'). Ten classic news release mistakes are listed in figure 17.6.

Ten classic news release mistakes

1. *Failure to provide a headline.* It's a news story and headlines articulate the theme. Subheadlines, too, are useful.
2. *Boiler-plate.* A first paragraph that jams in the client's name, their title, the company, its location etc., while ignoring the primary theme of the release, kills it.
3. *Spelling and grammatical errors.* Very harmful to any release because it suggests its writer is either uneducated or the release was not proofread.
4. *Punctuation errors.* Because editors and reporters, as well as broadcast news personnel, make their living writing, these mistakes are 'red flags', raising doubts about the source of the release.
5. *Hyperbole.* The word from which we get the term 'hype', in which ordinary things are given extraordinary qualities. It's instantaneously recognisable, creating barriers to credibility.
6. *Documentation.* Failure to attribute data to verifiable, independent sources diminishes credibility.
7. *Contacts.* Failure to provide the names, phones and/or fax numbers of informed, articulate spokesperson(s) renders a release useless.
8. *Too long.* The best releases are the briefest. Too much initial data can be a turn-off. If more is wanted, it will be requested.
9. *Localise.* Whenever possible, 'localise' the release.
10. *Be accessible at all times.* The best news release makes the media come to you. Opportunity ceases after the third ring of your phone.

FIGURE 17.6 Ten classic news release mistakes

Source: The Caruba Organization. Reproduced with permission of Alan Caruba.

Don't try to include too much in a single release. It's better simply to cover the basics in the release, and give additional material in other documents, such as fact sheets, backgrounders, media kits and position papers.

Backgrounders

Backgrounder: a document setting out the context of a situation; sometimes issued with a media release

A **backgrounder** is a multipage document giving detailed treatment of a story or situation, usually in narrative rather than point-form layout. As the name suggests, it fills in the background of a story, and there are not as many constraints on space as there are with the media release.

This is not, of course, an excuse to waffle or to indulge in self-serving hype and propaganda. Bivins (2010) suggests the following approach to backgrounders:

- Open with a concise statement of the issue or subject on which the accompanying news release is based. Try to make it as interesting as possible. This opening statement should lead logically into the next section.

- Follow the opening with a historical overview of the issue. You should trace its evolution (how it came to be) and the major events leading up to it. It is permissible here to use outside information.
- Work your way to the present. This is the meat of your backgrounder. You want to explain the issue you opened with and its significance. Be factual. Remember: a backgrounder is an information piece, not an advertisement or the place to sell your company's philosophy.
- Present the implications of the issue being discussed and point out the direction for future applications. Even though a backgrounder is a public relations piece, it needs to be carefully couched in fact-based information.
- Use subheads where appropriate. Subheads negate the need for elaborate transitions and allow you to order your information logically. Subheads need to be carefully chosen and should contribute to understanding.

Most backgrounders are four or five pages in length. Let your information dictate your length; however, don't become long-winded or pad your document. Editors will recognise fluff immediately. The object of a backgrounder is to provide information and answer anticipated questions, nothing more.

Position papers

A **position paper** is a document (sometimes brief, sometimes longer) in which a position, standpoint or policy on a particular issue or set of circumstances is developed. Position papers rarely contain quotes of direct speech and they have a longer 'shelf life' than media releases – that is, they don't go out of date so quickly. These papers can be produced and distributed, or else kept on hand should anyone request detailed information about where an organisation stands on a particular issue. Position papers are increasingly being posted on the internet. Rhody and Hackley (2006, p. 105) point out that the audience or public for position papers is usually small, but influential. They suggest a structure similar to this:

1. Start with a statement of the issue or problem, framing it as fairly as you can manage. If you skew this, you'll lose credibility immediately.
2. Present your case, arguing reasonably. Find ways to tie your objectives to the interests of the target public.
3. Summarise and end with a strong statement of the action or conclusion justified by the argument you have presented.

A position paper can be a lot of work to write (Newsom & Haynes 2010, pp. 172):

> Like the backgrounder, the position paper requires extensive research. Much of the information you need will be found in the backgrounder, so new research should be minimal. At this stage, however, you will need to solicit the input of management, which must scrutinize salient information, sort out the pros and cons of alternative positions and then make a policy decision. Research on a problem may produce a backgrounder that results in a management decision to offer or support a solution. Then you may be asked to write a position paper.

> Once that decision has been made, you can write a thorough position paper representing the company's point of view. If PR professionals in the company are held in high esteem, management may ask that a proposed position be written and used as a basis for discussion. After modifications are completed and approved, a final version is prepared for distribution to management and other publics.

> Whenever a new issue surfaces, the public relations department should alert management to the need for a position paper. Recognizing an issue constitutes the first step in writing a position paper.

Position papers, by their very nature, sometimes raise questions about fundamental policy that may not always occur with releases and backgrounders. Papers, like much of the better aspects of crisis communication can be two-way symmetric communication – they may lead to strategic reconsideration and feedback, which may in turn change the way the organisation commissioning the paper operates.

Fact sheets

Fact sheet: a short document setting out basic facts about a situation

A **fact sheet** (or data sheet) summarises data that helps give more depth to the basic release, often using point-form layout. More than one fact sheet relevant to one release may be created. Its simple construction sometimes means that it is the document in any media kit or press pack that is most looked at and used.

Profiles

Profile: a biographical sketch of a person within the organisation that is often accompanied by photographs

Profiles are about people in the organisation. A curriculum vitae or resume can be attached, but don't neglect personal interests (only release these with the person's approval, of course). Journalists and editors are often looking for new angles or hooks to base a story on, preferably without yet another boring photo of a person at a desk answering a phone or writing. For example, if a profile mentions that the person likes to sail, and the accompanying release is about how the person is taking over as CEO, an editor might decide to budget for a photographer to take a shot of the person at the wheel of a vessel. The headline might be 'New hands at the helm of Company X', with the journalist using themes of sensing winds of change and being ready to outrun the storm. It can be corny, but it can also be less boring, and give insights into the person that readers might find interesting. Attach high-resolution photos in hard copy or on a CD. On a grimmer note, profiles can also be used as material for obituaries (Mahoney 2008).

Media kits

Media kit: a package of informational and persuasive materials issued to the media

If a lot of information is to be given out to the target publics, perhaps a **media kit** or press kit could be considered. Such a kit contains print and other matter, usually packaged in a folder. These can be expensive, but in the right circumstances may be worth the expense. Kits are sometimes given out at press or media conferences. A kit might contain:

This Greenpeace media kit includes materials that might be issued to the media at a press conference.

- the basic release
- fact sheets
- backgrounders
- position papers
- photographs of people involved, objects, sites
- CD-ROMs, DVDs or other digital materials
- contact details, profiles of personnel
- giveaway objects (e.g. bumper stickers, buttons, caps, posters, mouse pads, pens)
- details of photo opportunities (e.g. people doing things such as cutting ribbons or demonstrating a product).

ASSESS YOURSELF

Using print and online resources, try to find samples of releases, backgrounders, position papers, fact sheets and media kits.

Crisis communication

In Grunig and Hunt's model (table 17.1), two-way symmetric communication involves public relations writing and strategies feeding back into an organisation's policy and decision making. This type of feedback becomes especially important when an organisation is involved in a crisis (Mitroff, Pearson & Harrington 1996; Eunson & Warner 2000; Cohn 2008; Sapriel 2003; Elliott & Smith 2004; Coombs & Holladay, 2010).

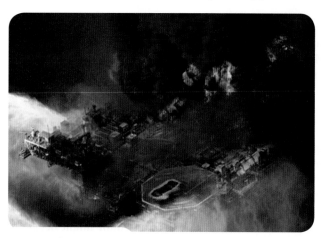

Crises can be many and varied, but they usually involve high stress and potential damage for an organisation because, suddenly, unwanted public attention is being focused on that organisation. For example, BP was forced into a public relations 'crisis control mode' after one of its oil rigs exploded in the Gulf of Mexico in 2010, creating the largest marine oil spill in history. In the first 16 weeks after the disaster, the company paid nearly $400 million in compensation payments (BP 2010). Such claims and the associated clean up operation is ongoing, with the environmental impact of the spill likely to be felt for years to come.

Let's look at causes and solutions for crises, and see how **crisis communication** can help manage the short-term crisis and ensure that future crises do not happen, or do not happen so frequently[1].

BP was forced to engage in crisis communication following the damaging Gulf of Mexico oil spill in recent times.

Crisis communication: techniques and approaches that can help an organisation to better manage an emergency situation

Issue: something that is a concern or preoccupation of one of your stakeholders or publics

Issue definition

Crises are linked to issues. Generally speaking, an **issue** is something that is a concern or preoccupation of one of your stakeholders or publics (figure 17.7).

FIGURE 17.7 Issues and nonissues

An issue is:	A nonissue is:
▪ controversial ▪ often difficult to predict ▪ capable of stimulating strong opinions ▪ capable of having major impact on the organisation's products and people ▪ likely to draw attention to the organisation	▪ uncontroversial ▪ easy to predict ▪ a routine event or process ▪ unlikely to have a major impact on the organisation's products and people ▪ unlikely to draw attention to the organisation

In an ideal organisation, issues are anticipated and then built into the planning process. In actual organisations, of course, issues are often unanticipated and often not built into the planning process. You know that issues are surfacing when you hear trigger phrases like these:

- *What are we going to do about ...?*
- *I've noticed a trend towards ... Do you see it too?*
- *How on earth did we let ... sneak up on us?*
- *This ... matter is becoming a major issue for us.*
- *We need an urgent meeting on ... to consider our options.*
- *The major challenges facing this industry in the next five years are ...*

Issues are not always nasty surprises – they can benefit the organisation, for example, when:

- new markets open up

---

1. Some of the material in this section is adapted from Eunson and Warner (2000).

- old, complacent ways of seeing things are turned upside down
- everyone in the organisation pulls together and new levels of achievement are reached in meeting a challenge.

Issues are not always things 'out there' – in the environment, beyond our control. Sometimes an organisation can create issues or be the agenda setter, the trendsetter, the market leader, the one to beat.

Environmental scanning and crisis control

Environmental scanning: processes for detecting trends on the horizon

Identifying issues sometimes goes by the jargon **environmental scanning**. The environment can be scanned, and issues identified, through the following means:

- Reading mainstream newspapers, magazines, trade journals
- Reading fringe literature, such as magazines put out by nonmainstream political, lifestyle, advocacy, futurist and environmental groups
- Reading books by trend predictors and 'futurologists'
- Clipping, photocopying, filing and cross-referencing research
- Subscribing to commercial clipping services
- Subscribing to electronic media monitoring services
- Searching the internet for keywords and phrases
- Gathering competitor intelligence (via general advertisements, job advertisements, annual reports and trade shows, and by the purchase and analysis of competitor products)
- Creating scenarios or 'what-if' projections
- Running brainstorming groups for those inside the organisation, and focus groups for those outside the organisation
- Listening to 'boundary spanners' (people within the organisation with strong formal and informal connections to the outside world, such as sales staff, purchasing staff, members of professional associations, people plugged into the community grapevine) (see 'Boundary spanners' feature in chapter 16)
- Strategically listening to stakeholders
- Creating a climate of feedback within and outside the organisation (see 'Feedback' in chapter 10).

Transparency and communication

Completely effective issue identification depends on:

- perfect information
- high levels of effectiveness and frankness within the organisational culture (see 'Organisational culture and communication' in chapter 16).

Truly perfect information does not exist, but what about the second factor? Do people feel that they can speak with complete frankness about the state of things within the organisation? Or do they feel that there is a **shoot-the-messenger climate** or culture or ethos, where anyone who reveals bad news about a situation will get punished for it (see 'Bad culture 2: the culture of silence' in chapter 16)?

Shoot-the-messenger climate: a situation in organisations where those who point out bad news are punished, even if it is not their fault

After a situation has been identified, do people believe that impartial, unemotional problem solving will occur, or will there be a witch-hunt, a search for a scapegoat? When a crisis occurs in an organisation, and the media and stakeholders subject the organisation to scrutiny, it may well be that skeletons will be discovered in various closets. Such skeletons might include:

- unsafe work practices
- accidents just waiting to happen
- serious malfunctions that do not appear to have been detected by decision makers
- suspect, unprofessional or corrupt practices
- anything which, when discovered, will cause a scandal or uproar.

Then people within organisations may be heard to say:

- *Why didn't we know about this sooner?*
- *Nobody told us.*
- *We knew about it, but no-one would listen.*
- *We knew about it, but it doesn't pay to shoot your mouth off around here.*
- *How could this have possibly happened without my knowing about it?*

Skeletons only get hidden in closets if people feel that they had better not speak out. Truth-talkers and whistle-blowers may be punished or praised, and this uncertainty is not healthy for the day-to-day running of an organisation. And if skeletons in closets go undiscovered, so too may the 'angels' in the closets — the good news stories, the information about achievements and positive situations. This means that decision makers not only do not get the bad news, but also may not get the good news either.

A shoot-the-messenger climate, then, is a major barrier to an organisation being transparent. A **high-transparency organisation** has a free flow of information, and a proactive, get-the-crisis-before-it-gets-us approach. A **low-transparency organisation** lacks such problem-solving approaches (figure 17.8) (Jahansoozi 2006; Welch & Rothberg 2006).

High-transparency organisation: an organisation with excellent internal and external communication processes; tends not to be crisis-prone

Low-transparency organisation: an organisation with poor internal and external communication processes; tends to be crisis-prone

High-transparency organisations:	Low-transparency organisations:
■ Have high levels of trust ■ Have effective flows of information — upwards, downwards, horizontally ■ Are often creative and innovative because of this free flow of information ■ Have weak internal and external grapevines (because truth drives out rumours) ■ Have few skeletons in closets ■ Have nothing to be ashamed of ■ Have few crises of their own making ■ Suffer few crises caused by outside events and issues ■ Are able to cope with such crises as might arise because of high trust levels and rapid information and communication flows ■ See mistakes as learning opportunities ■ Solve problems by looking for causes, not symptoms ■ Encourage feedback ■ Welcome scrutiny by stakeholders and media ■ Initiate communication with stakeholders and media ■ Are rarely vulnerable to damage caused by crises and bad news	■ Have low levels of trust ■ Have ineffective flows of information — upwards, downwards, horizontally ■ Are rarely creative and innovative, due to blocked free flow of information ■ Have strong internal and external grapevines (because rumour fills a truth vacuum) ■ Have many skeletons in closets ■ Have numerous things to be ashamed of ■ Have numerous crises of their own making ■ Suffer numerous crises caused by outside events and issues ■ Are rarely able to cope with crises that arise because of low trust levels and slow or blocked information and communication flows ■ See mistakes as excuses for punishment ■ Solve problems by looking for symptoms, not causes ■ Have a shoot-the-messenger culture ■ Fear scrutiny by stakeholders and media ■ Rarely initiate communication with stakeholders and media ■ Are vulnerable to damage caused by crises and bad news

FIGURE 17.8 Transparency in organisations

ASSESS YOURSELF

Consider at least one organisation you are familiar with. Where would you place it on the transparency continuum? Justify your answer.

Low transparency ⟷ High transparency

Communicating with the media in a crisis

Even high-transparency organisations have crises, however. A crisis is an issue threatening to get out of control. In crisis or noncrisis situations, the essence of good public communication is communicating differentially — that is, knowing what strategy will work with one particular target public, and what strategy will be disastrously counterproductive. Typical mismatchings of strategy to situation are:

- calling a press conference to announce something relatively minor (a press release would be more effective, and less likely to irritate media representatives)
- having staff with poor communication skills escort a group of VIPs on a plant tour
- issuing the same generic press release to all media outlets, without customising the releases to highlight different angles
- having a relatively junior spokesperson be the only person available for comment at the site of a major crisis
- threatening editors with removal of advertising if they don't kill a story unfavourable to your organisation (it only makes them more determined, and they may publicise your threat)
- issuing only glossy general brochures to specialist technical journalists
- expecting treatment from a metropolitan daily to be the same as the service you have been receiving from a local paper
- sending a document (annual report, newsletter) to an individual representing a major stakeholder with an impersonal covering letter
- filling the in-house newsletter with absurdly optimistic propaganda during a crisis, or not mentioning the crisis at all
- making clumsy attempts to get staff to masquerade as neutral parties by writing letters and ringing talkback radio with scripted responses.

By contrast, effective communication with the media and your publics will be based on the creation of a sensible mix of media releases, backgrounders, fact sheets, position papers and media kits, together with running media conferences, being interviewed, and talking to the media in a variety of formal and informal settings.

Communication language

When communicating with the media — written documents, face to face or via electronic means — it is wise to choose your words carefully, and use the five Cs. That is, ensure that your communication is concise, clear, cool, concrete and concerned.

Concise language

Time is scarce on television and radio, but it is also scarce with print journalists who have deadlines and need a succinct snapshot of what an event or crisis is about. There is a great need to get your message across without waffle or technical detail. Broadcast journalists sometimes speak of 'grabs' — short, succinct phrases that an editor can 'grab' or easily identify and select from an interview recording (figure 17.9). People who can communicate succinctly and with style are sometimes referred to by media professionals as good 'talent'.

Good grab	Bad grab
The report is not a threat to us. In fact, we think it's not all that good. Quite a few of the facts and figures are out of date, and you have to wonder how they reached some conclusions. We have issued a fact sheet where we rebut the claims one by one, and that will also appear in tomorrow's press.	The report is somewhat worrying for us, in that some sections appear to reflect negatively upon some of our products, and we have reservations about the currency of some of the data used and the validity of some of the conclusions reached.

FIGURE 17.9 Grabs — good and bad

Good talent give good grabs; they speak fluent **grabspeak**. A good grab is characterised by:

- short sentences
- fairly short words
- colourful, imaginative language, including perhaps an analogy, a metaphor, a figure of speech or even slang or humour
- a personal feel
- vocabulary and expression that summarise a complex situation
- variety of pitch and tone
- confident delivery.

Journalists are often looking for good 'grabs' — short, succinct phrases that an editor can easily select from an interview recording. Politicians are aware of this, and often use short, 'catchy' phrases in interviews, press conferences and debates.

Another aspect of the scarcity of media time is that, even in extended interview situations, you will not have time to get across all of the points you want. In an interview lasting a few minutes, you will be lucky to get three brief major points across, even though you may have more that might require explanations. If you don't learn to edit yourself, then someone else will, and you may feel that your words have been distorted or that you have been mis-represented.

A good way to prepare for a media interview, or a discussion with a stakeholder or public is to determine what you would like to say, what you must say and what can be said in other ways. Figure 17.10 demonstrates an example of an executive preparing for a radio interview about a chemical spill at a plant.

This is a priority-setting exercise. Our executive would not get a chance to get all of this information across in a 12-second grab on a radio bulletin, or a 25-second grab on the evening television news, or a 30-word direct quote and paraphrase in an article in tomorrow's newspapers.

When communicating with the media, therefore, you need to plan your:

- first priority – your 2–4 'must' says
- second priority – your 2–6 'like to' says
- third priority – any number of points you can get across using other means. You might circulate your most meaningful communication using other means.

Be warned: grabspeak can be overdone. If done all the time, it can sound gimmicky, super-slick and insincere. In longer interviews, mix pace and delivery, switching from grabs to longer sentences and longer words.

Must say	Like to say	Other channels
1. The spill is under control. 2. No-one has been hurt. 3. A full investigation is under way.	1. The chemical concerned is a new fully biodegradable one. 2. The chemical is used in a wide variety of medical and therapeutic applications, such as forming the medium for anaesthetic gases. 3. The plant has recently installed new safety procedures, which worked extremely effectively during the crisis.	1. Issue a press release, including fact sheets on the plant and the chemical. 2. Place advertisements in local and metropolitan newspapers outlining the facts. 3. Send out personally signed letters of reassurance by priority mail or courier to all residents living near the plant. 4. Have panel of experts ready to be interviewed on the safety of plant and chemical. 5. Issue press release, fact sheets and other information on company website.

FIGURE 17.10 Priorities in response

Clear language

Clear language has a minimum number of nominalisations, tautologies and clichés (see online chapter 4 'Writing skills: plain English'). But there is more to it than that. Every organisation tends to have its own specialised language, using technical terms, abbreviations, acronyms, slang, idioms and figures of speech. It's quite common for departments within organisations to have their own jargon, and perhaps sections of departments also have their own jargon. Jargon can be a very useful way of speeding up communication, but it can also be a way in which an organisation, department, section or even profession defends itself against outsiders. Therefore, jargon can be a major barrier to communication and transparency.

When communicating with the outside world, we need to engage in continual self-editing to ensure that we are not using a private language in a public communication situation. For example, consider a situation in which a representative of a toy manufacturer is asked: Is your product a danger to children? A bad response is loaded with jargon, which probably makes eminent sense among the speaker's professional, technical colleagues. But in an interview situation, that group is not the audience being communicated with (figure 17.11).

Unclear response	Clear response
Our A912 toy has passed rigorous ISO9000 testing with respect to its voltage parameters, and intensive sampling and statistical control reduces error to 0.001 per cent, and thus the chances of humans being injured in any way is commensurately remote. There may be confusion in the minds of the ill-informed about conversion from US to Australian earthing, and the voltage versus the wattage or amperage of the unit, but these are all within industrial standard tolerances.	The Rocker Quokka is a very safe toy [*holds up toy*]. My own kids play with it, and the same goes for our 190 employees — all of their kids play with it too, and have done since it came out in 1989. We won't put dangerous toys on the market. The SupaToy brand means safety, style and fun at affordable prices, and that's the way we're going to keep it. Any production process will create a few duds, but we catch those before they get out the door.

FIGURE 17.11 Clear versus unclear language

Cool language

Cool language shows that the speaker has not lost control of the situation. When communicating with the media and with stakeholders or publics, it is important to use language that cannot be misconstrued and taken out of context. This is particularly true when dealing with the media, where hundreds or thousands of words can be edited (because of space or time) to create an impression that is vastly different to the one that the speaker believed he or she was conveying.

It is also important not to respond to loaded language, or at least not to respond by merely repeating the words and without challenging the attitudes behind them (often provocation to elicit a response). If a spokesperson for an organisation does not appear to be cool and in control — in other words, appears panicked — then a sequence of panics may ensue, thus making the situation worse. Panics may result in a loss of share values, customer accounts, goodwill and reputation and even a loss of life.

Panic language is obviously conveyed through words, yet it also can be conveyed through verbal inflection and volume. Figure 17.12 (see overleaf) has some examples of panic language and cool language.

Panic language	Cool language
We don't know what's going on.	The situation is not clear at the moment.
God knows how many people are dead in there.	Yes, we do hold grave fears for some of our people in there.
It's just out of control!	We are having difficulty controlling it.
Get out while you can!	Please evacuate the area now.

FIGURE 17.12 Cool versus panic language

This is not to say that spokespersons should always express themselves like unfeeling robots. It is ethical human communication, not to say believable communication, to sincerely express certain emotions and states of mind (particularly sympathy, regret and urgency) in crisis situations. In situations where life or limb is threatened, it makes sense to communicate directly and loudly.

Nevertheless, a spokesperson is regarded as the public face and voice of an organisation during a crisis, and as such is performing a vital leadership role. Cool language acts as an antidote to panic, and thus helps the situation, rather than hinders it.

Concrete language

Concrete language is language that relates to the real world, rather than a world of abstractions. Abstract language is similar to jargon and style features (such as nominalisation) in that it conveys a bureaucratic, unreal feel to the communication process. Abstraction can be detected in certain word usage patterns, and should wherever possible be replaced with more concrete, plain English terms.

Concreteness can also be aided by the use of analogies, metaphors, proportions, percentages and figures of speech (figure 17.13).

Abstract expression	Concrete expression
The amount spilled is approximately 50 000 litres.	We think the amount spilled is about 50 000 litres. That's about enough to fill three average backyard swimming pools; but in the bay itself, it's roughly equivalent to half a teaspoon in a swimming pool.
We are re-examining our archives to see if there is any substance in the applicant's claim, but this is a time-intensive process.	We've put four of our best analysts onto looking at Mrs Martin's claim, but it takes time. Each file is this thick [*shows file*], and our back files contain over 18 000 files. That's enough to fill up this room to the ceiling and the walls.

FIGURE 17.13 Concrete versus abstract language

Concerned language

Concerned language shows that you are emotionally in tune with what is happening in the world outside the organisation. It's about seeing things from the point of view of others. This can be done by using direct, compassionate real-world language, rather than cold bureaucratic gobbledegook (figure 17.14).

Gobbledegook	Concerned language
It is not the company's policy to indicate our position vis-a-vis anyone involved in this situation.	We regret what has happened to the men working in that section, and will do everything in our power to help them.
I am unable to comment on that at the present moment.	I'm sorry. We made a mistake, and now we will try to create a better situation.

FIGURE 17.14 Concerned language versus gobbledegook

There can sometimes be legal problems with using concerned and compassionate language, as it can suggest liability, and thus can be used as a basis for legal prosecution of your organisation at a later stage. It is always wise to seek legal advice before issuing any type of public communication.

Feeding back: from crisis tactics to organisational strategy

Crises should lead to organisational learning. In other words, two-way symmetrical communication should take place so that the factors and policies that led to a crisis are removed or modified, and replaced with factors and policies that reflect a more proactive and transparent approach. In low-transparency organisations, public relations and crisis communication will be seen simply as window dressing and a fancier way to lie. This is not only unethical, but also incompetent – those who do not learn from history are condemned to repeat it.

STUDENT STUDY GUIDE

SUMMARY

In this chapter we considered different models of public relations. We saw that public relations is a type of applied communication, and that practitioners of public relations perform numerous functions, including advising management on strategy and policy issues; developing an organisation's public relations program; answering public and media enquiries; issuing news releases and statements; writing and publishing newsletters, house magazines, annual reports, pamphlets and other publications; monitoring public opinion and the organisation's image and suggesting action where necessary; and managing stakeholder communication during an issue or crisis incident. We saw that such practitioners communicate with stakeholders, who might include shareholders, investors, staff and management, customers, suppliers, governments, media, unions and labour, secondary customers, neighbours and partners in joint ventures. We looked at concepts such as situation analysis, communication strategies, channels and tools, and publics. We considered techniques involved in the production of media releases, backgrounders, fact sheets, profiles and position papers. We discussed transparency in organisations, and the way in which internal and external communication are linked. Finally, we considered what is involved in crisis communication, and how communicating with publics can be helped by the use of concise, clear, cool, concrete and concerned language – noting that lessons learned in crises need to be fed back into organisational strategy if transparency and effectiveness are to be valued.

KEY TERMS

backgrounder *p. 563*
campaign *p. 557*
crisis communication *p. 566*
environmental scanning *p. 567*
fact sheet *p. 565*
grabspeak *p. 570*
high-transparency organisation *p. 568*
issue *p. 566*

low-transparency organisation *p. 568*
media kit *p. 565*
media release *p. 560*
position paper *p. 564*
profile *p. 565*
pseudo-event *p. 553*
public information model *p. 553*
publicity model *p. 553*

public *p. 556*
shoot-the-messenger climate *p. 567*
spin *p. 552*
tools *p. 560*
two-way asymmetric model *p. 554*
two-way symmetric model *p. 554*

REVIEW QUESTIONS

1. Reference is made to the press as the 'fourth estate' and public relations as the 'fifth estate'. What historical model is this based on, and is it still relevant? Can you think of any 'sixth estates'?
2. What are the four models of public relations?
3. Identify at least four different publics.
4. List at least three things that public relations practitioners do.
5. What differences and similarities are there between media releases, backgrounders, fact sheets, profiles and position papers?
6. List at least three faults in some media releases.
7. Identify at least three methods of environmental scanning.
8. List at least three characteristics of nontransparent organisations.
9. What are the five Cs of crisis communication?

APPLIED ACTIVITIES

1. Using print and online sources, find examples of media releases, backgrounders, profiles, fact sheets and position papers.
2. Evaluate the documents located. Are they successful or unsuccessful? Why?
3. Locate a backgrounder, position paper or release, and create a fact sheet from the text(s).
4. Using print and online sources, track the use of media releases in media stories.
5. Locate copies of complete public relations campaigns (e.g. the Public Relations Institute of Australia Golden Target Awards, issued yearly; see table 17.2). Evaluate at least two campaigns.
6. Create good and bad examples of concise, clear, cool, concrete and concerned language.
7. Draw up a plan for environmental scanning for an organisation you are familiar with.
8. Identify an organisation that is currently receiving negative publicity. Monitor the organisation through its print and online documents. Evaluate the effectiveness of its crisis communication.

WHAT WOULD YOU DO?

Masha Tolenko rushed into the Hyperoil managing director's office. About ten people were watching a widescreen display, and none of them had happy expressions. The screen was split four ways. Each of the four television sources focused on the same event: the massive spill of oil from the Aphrodite oil rig; Hyperoil's biggest. The Aphrodite was the main source of oil for the Caribbean nation of La Planta. It was also responsible for driving a thriving and critical export trade. Everyone in the room lived in Esperanza, a small city populated by chemical engineers, drivers, drillers, pilots and divers, as well as a support network of shop owners, families and teachers. Esperanza was 80 kilometres away.

Raoul Spinks, head of public communications, moved to the shoulder of Jack Williams, the managing director. 'What do you want me to do? We can spin it. I've already located a marine ecologist at Central University who's willing to go on camera and say harmless chemical dispersants will solve the problem, and I've also lined up a weather guy who's willing to say that there's a powerful storm heading this way, which will break up the surface slick!'

'Yeah, and a storm like that could be the final straw for the bits of drill still intact underwater, not to mention the rig itself!' snapped Williams.

'Ah, Jack', said operations manager Kate Messenger. 'I've already had unofficial offers of help from Five Star oil and PB gas/oil. I think we should take it.'

'Oh yeah', retorted Raoul, 'and let them see our new drill heads! Great! We can get out of this ourselves, thanks! You do realise, Jack, that protest groups are already campaigning with "Shut down Aphrodite NOW!" signs with oil-soaked seals. It is very touching. This could wipe us out, not to mention Esperanza! Listen. Let me wheel out this ecology guy — I've already got him talking to a PR company in La Planta, briefing them on cute colour graphics of how the dispersants will fix it ... They probably will, you know; and how the drill break is only a temporary one. I can roll the whole thing out, with Jack doing a media conference with all that, in 24 hours!'

'Masha', said Jack, 'you've got the freshest set of eyes here. What's your take on this?'

Masha, somewhat overwhelmed (and a bit naïve, perhaps) stuttered a reply: 'Well, in the PR course I'm studying, the new emphasis is on transparency, which I suppose would mean a big conference with Jack apologising for the break. Run with the ecologist and the graphics, but line up a counter view from a rival ecologist. Everyone's got a rival! And then accept the help from Five Star and PB, and we'll fly the three general managers out to the safe parts of the rig, looking at the dispersant tanks, talking to the guys still out there, and back on solid ground, commiserating with the widows, giving them one million dollars each, and offering good wages to volunteers to help clean up the birds, seals and fish that have got this gunk on them – all on TV! I've talked with Matty Briars, in engineering, and he says that other companies have known about our drill bits for years, so there's no security problem! Make Jack the big man, saying Hyperoil takes full responsibility for the spill, and that we will do everything to compensate for damage!'

'Hmmm', said Jack. 'It's a bit upfront, but it might work!'

'Just a minute', said Shelley Hack, a tough assistant general manager with extensive legal and financial experience. 'If we do this, we accept legal responsibility for everything, and we'll be tied up in legal suits for years, which could break us – which wouldn't be too hard, if you've seen my urgent email about low cashflow! It will wipe us out, not to mention Esperanza. Everyone in this room lives there, and Hyperoil and La Planta will be condemned as environmental criminals!'

Questions

1. This case study scenario is hypothetical and features fictitious characters. Go online and research how BP handled its public communication efforts in relation to their massive oil spill off the Gulf of Mexico in 2010. Analyse BP's subsequent media releases in terms of language and transparency, and the general effectiveness of their crisis communication.

2. In terms of this fictitious case study, is Raoul a villain, or in fact the realist in the group? Justify your answer.

3. Is Masha's plan too unrealistic? Justify your answer.

4. If Jack does follow Masha's plan, what should he do about announcing an investigation to ensure this never happens again?

5. Following the guidelines for communication language, write a speech for Jack's media conference.

6. Looking at figure 17.8, analyse why this fiasco happened.

SUGGESTED READING

Johnston, Jane & Zawawi, Clara (eds) 2009, *Public relations: theory and practice*, 3rd edn, Allen & Unwin, Crows Nest, NSW.

Kent, Michael L 2010, *Public relations writing: a rhetorical approach*, Allyn & Bacon, Boston, MA.

Mizrahi, Janet 2010, *Fundamentals of writing for marketing and public relations*, Business Expert Press, Singapore.

Scholem, Peter & Mavondo 2003, 'Stakeholders and gender: a new phenomenon?', *Proceedings of the Australian and New Zealand Marketing Academy 2003 Conference*, Australian & New Zealand Marketing Academy, Adelaide, SA.

Scott, David Meerman 2009, *The new rules of marketing and PR: how to use news releases, blogs, podcasting, viral marketing and online media to reach buyers directly*, John Wiley & Sons, Hoboken, NJ.

Ward, Ian 2003, 'An Australian PR state?', *Australian Journal of Communication*, vol. 30, no. 1, pp. 25–42.

REFERENCES

Andrews, David L & Jackson, Steven J 2001, *Sport stars: the cultural politics of sporting celebrity*, Routledge, London.

Baggini, Julian 2010, *Do They Think You're Stupid?: 100 Ways of Spotting Spin and Nonsense Form the Media, Celebrities and Politicians*, 2nd rev. edn, Granta Books, London.

Bivins, Thomas H 2010, *Public relations writing: the essentials of style and format*, 7th edn, McGraw-Hill, New York.

Boorstin, Daniel 1992, *The image: a guide to pseudo-events in America*, reissue edn, Vintage, New York.

BP website 2010, www.bp.com.

Callison, Coy 2001, 'Do PR practitioners have a PR problem? The effect of associating a source with public relations and client-negative news on audience perception of credibility', *Journal of Public Relations Research*, vol. 13, no. 3, pp. 219–34.

Chaney, Isabella M 2001, 'Opinion leaders as a segment for marketing communications', *Marketing Intelligence and Planning*, vol. 19, no. 5, pp. 302–10.

Cohn, Robin 2008, *The PR crisis bible: how to take charge of the media when all hell breaks loose*, St Martin's Press, New York.

Coombs, W Timothy and Holladay, Sherry J 2010, *The handbook of crisis communication*, Wiley-Blackwell, New York, London.

Daymon, Christine 2010, *Qualitative research methods in public relations and marketing communications*, 2nd edn, Routledge, London.

Elliott, Dominic & Smith, Denis (eds.) 2004, *Crisis management: theory, systems and practice*, Routledge, London.

Eunson, Baden & Warner, Jon 2000, *Dealing with the media and external stakeholders*, Team Publications, Brisbane.

Ewen, Stuart 1999, *PR! A social history of spin*, Basic Books, New York.

Gamson, Joshua 1994, *Claims to fame: celebrity in contemporary America*, University of California Press, Los Angeles.

Grunig, James E & Grunig, Larissa A 2002, 'Implications of the IABC excellence study for PR education', *Journal of Communication Management*, vol. 7, no. 1, pp. 34–44.

Grunig, James E & Hunt, Todd 1984, *Managing public relations*, International Thomson, London.

Guth, David W & Marsh, Charles 2003, *Public relations: a values-driven approach*, 2nd edn, Pearson Allyn & Bacon, Boston, MA.

Hendrix, Jerry A 2007, *Public relations cases*, 7th edn, Wadsworth, Belmont, CA.

Holtzhausen, Derina R & Voto, Rosina 2002, 'Resistance from the margins: the postmodern public relations practitioner as organisational activist', *Journal of Public Relations Research*, vol. 14, no. 1, pp. 57–84.

Hutton, James 1999, 'The definitions, dimensions, and domain of public relations', *Public Relations Review*, vol. 25, no. 2, pp. 199–214.

Isikoff, Michael & Corn, David 2007, *Hubris: the inside story of spin, scandal, and the selling of the Iraq War*, Three Rivers Press, New York.

Jahansoozi, Julia 2006, 'Organization–stakeholder relationships: exploring trust and transparency', *Journal of Management Development*, vol. 25, no. 10, pp. 942–55.

Kates, S & Scholem, Peter 2001, 'Conceptualising and developing reflective practice in public relations', *Asia Pacific Public Relations Journal*, vol. 3, no. 1, pp. 23–31.

Kurtz, Howard 1998, *Spin cycle: inside the Clinton propaganda machine*, Simon and Schuster, New York.

L'Etang, Jacquie 1997, 'Public relations and the rhetorical dilemma: legitimate 'perspectives', persuasion, or pandering?', *Australian Journal of Communication*, vol. 24, no. 2, pp. 33–53.

Levine, Michael & Gendron, George 2002, *Guerilla PR wired: waging a successful publicity campaign on-line, off-line, and everywhere in between*, McGraw-Hill, New York.

Mahoney, James 2008, *Public Relations Writing in Australia*, Oxford, South Melbourne, Victoria.

Mitchell, RK, Agle, BR & Wood, DJ 1997, 'Toward a theory of stakeholder identification and salience; defining the principle of who and what really counts', *Academy of Management Review*, vol. 22, no. 4, pp. 853–87.

Mitroff, Ian I, Pearson, Christine M & Harrington, L Katharine 1996, *The essential guide to managing corporate crises: a step-by-step handbook for surviving major catastrophes*, Oxford University Press, Oxford.

Moore, Martin 2007, *The origins of modern spin: democratic government and the media in Britain 1945–51*, Palgrave Macmillan, London.

Newsom, Doug & Haynes, Jim 2010, *Public relations writing: form and style*, 9th edn, Wadsworth, Belmont, CA.

Okigbo, Charles & Nelson, Sonya 2003, 'Precision public relations: facing the demographic challenge', *Public Relations Quarterly*, vol. 48, no. 2, pp. 29–40.

Pitcher, George 2004, *The death of spin*, Halsted Press, New York.

Rhody, Ron & Hackley, Carol Ann 2006, *Wordsmithing: The art & craft of writing for public relations*, Pearson Custom Pulishing, Boston, MA.

Sapriel, Caroline 2003, 'Effective crisis management: tools and best practice for the new millennium', *Journal of Communication Management*, vol. 7, no. 4, pp. 348–55.

Seitel, Fraser P 2010, *The Practice of Public Relations*, 11th edn, Prentice Hall, Upper Saddle River, NJ.

Shin, Jae-Hwa & Cameron, Glen T 2003, 'Informal relations: a look at personal influence in media relations', *Journal of Communication Management*, vol. 7, no. 3, pp. 239–54.

Stacks, Don W 2002, *Primer of public relations research*, Guilford, New York.

Summers, Jane, and Morgan, Melissa Johnson 2008, 'More than just the media: Considering the role of public relations in the creation of sporting celebrity and the management of fan expectations', *Public Relations Review*, vol. 34, no. 2, pp. 176–82.

Stauber, John & Rampton, Sheldon 2002, *Toxic sludge is good for you! Lies, damned lies, and the public relations industry*, Common Courage Press, Monroe, ME.

Theaker, Alison 2001, *The public relations handbook*, Routledge, London.

Tucker, Kerry, Derelian, Doris & Rouner, Donna 1997, *Public relations writing: an issue-driven behavioral approach*, 3rd edn, Prentice Hall, Upper Saddle River, NJ.

Turner, Graeme 2006, 'Public relations', in Stuart Cunningham & Graeme Turner (eds) *The media and communications in Australia*, Allen & Unwin, Crows Nest, NSW.

Turner, Graeme, Bonner, Frances & Marshall, P David 2000, *Fame games: the production of celebrity in Australia*, Cambridge University Press, Cambridge.

Tymson, Candy, Lazar, Peter & Lazar, Richard 2002, *The new Australian and New Zealand public relations manual*, Tymson Communications, Chatswood, NSW.

UTS: Library, 'Golden Target Awards collection', University of Technology, Sydney, www.lib.uts.edu.au.

Welch, Theodora & Rothberg, Eugene H 2006, 'Transparency: panacea or Pandora's box?', *Journal of Management Development*, vol. 25, no. 10, pp. 937–41.

Whitaker, W. Richard, Ramsey, Janet E. & Smith, Ronald D. 2009, *Media writing: print, broadcast and public relations*, 3rd edn, Routledge, New York/London.

Wilson, Cintra 2001, *A massive swelling: celebrity re-examined as a grotesque, crippling disease and other cultural revelations*, Penguin, New York.

Zawawi, Clara 1994, 'Sources of news — who feeds the watchdogs', *Australian Journalism Review*, vol. 16, no. 1, pp. 67–71.

18

Team communication

LEARNING OBJECTIVES

After studying this chapter you should be able to:

- Identify the reasons why people join and leave groups
- Explain the concepts of synergy and social loafing
- Explain the dynamics of roles and norms within groups
- Identify different phases or stages of group development
- Define real and perceived differences between groups and teams
- Explain the similarities and differences between sports teams and work teams
- Explain the strengths and weaknesses of work teams
- Explain the strengths and weaknesses of virtual teams
- Explain the types of communication skills that can best be deployed in groups and teams

Groups, teams and leaders

In chapter 1, we saw that different areas of communication could be meaningfully analysed as a series of concentric circles. There are numerous interconnections between this chapter, dealing with communication in teams or groups, and communication theory, especially channels of communication. You may also note connections with interpersonal and intrapersonal communication ideas (see figure 18.1), particularly feedback (chapters 9 and 10), as well as intercultural, organisational, public and media communication (chapters 15, 16, 17 and online chapter 8). In fact, almost all of the chapters in this book that relate to direct communication are relevant to group interactions.

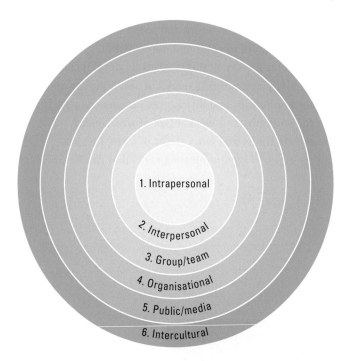

FIGURE 18.1 A concentric model of fields of communication

1. Intrapersonal
2. Interpersonal
3. Group/team
4. Organisational
5. Public/media
6. Intercultural

Groups or teams consist of people who feel they belong together and are united in a common purpose. Groups can be small or large, official or unofficial, permanent or temporary, task-oriented or relationship-oriented (or both), strongly or weakly cohesive, physically concentrated or dispersed, effective or ineffective, and so on.

Are groups and teams the same thing, or are they different? Teams can be seen as a particular type of group, and we will consider team dynamics in this chapter. When we examine groups and teams, we might also consider leaders. Do all groups and teams need leaders, or can they do without them? The issues we explore in this chapter are, in some respects, the mirror image of the ones surrounding the questions of leadership and of meetings as problem-solving tools.

Groups and teams have assumed greater prominence in organisations in the past few decades because of changes that have taken place in the workplace, including:

- a 'flattening' of organisation structure – a reduction in the number of administrative or decision-making levels in the hierarchy of the typical large organisation
- an increase in real or apparent delegation of power or empowerment from top leadership to workgroup members – a move towards organisational democracy
- an increase in the complexity of decision making, so that in some circumstances individuals acting alone no longer have enough technical knowledge and skills to make decisions without the help of others.

In this chapter, we look at the broader dynamics that help, and hinder, group communication. Meetings are a particular arena in which groups and teams flourish or founder, and these are covered in more detail in chapter 19.

Group dynamics: how do groups work?

Groups can come in all shapes and sizes, and include the following:

- committees
- families
- sporting teams
- supporters of sporting teams
- criminal gangs
- juries
- musicians
- fan clubs
- members of a commune
- combat units
- multidisciplinary problem-solving teams
- construction gangs
- Porsche owners
- followers of a particular religion.

These Buddhist monks, who together are preparing for a ceremony in Brisbane, Australia, are members of a group in society. AFL team supporters, business colleagues and family members are all also examples of groups.

Of such a list, which is by no means exhaustive, it might well be said: 'If groups are everything, perhaps they are nothing'. What possible connection could all of these collections of people have?

A **group** is distinguished from a **social aggregate** or a category. Examples of social aggregates are:

- all people earning the same income
- all people with the same height
- all people in the same occupation.

Members of groups act together to achieve common aims or goals. Mostly, members of social aggregates or categories do not act in this way, although an aggregate such as people in a lift who did not know each other might become a group if the lift broke down and people began to talk and act together.

Group: two or more people who act together to achieve common aims or goals

Social aggregate: a class or order of people who share certain characteristics but do not necessarily share goals

Group membership

Every individual is usually a member of many groups. For example, at work, Mary is a member of at least three groups (figure 18.2), although she is the only person who is a member of all three groups shown.

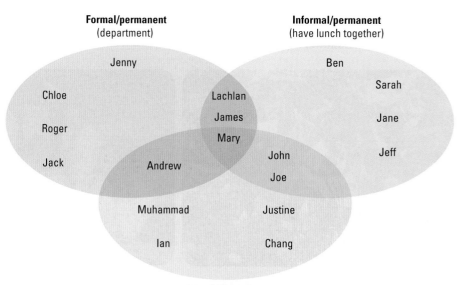

FIGURE 18.2 Group membership patterns

Source: Based on and adapted from Hodgetts and Hegar (2007).

Why should people try to achieve aims or goals in concert with others? Why is the world not composed of lone individuals pursuing their own particular aims and goals? In other words, why do people join groups in the first place? And having joined, will they stay, or leave? There are (at least) five reasons why people join, stay in or leave groups. These are security, task complexity, social interaction, proximity and exchange.

ASSESS YOURSELF

1. What social aggregates do you belong to?
2. What groups do you belong to?
3. Create at least one diagram similar to figure 18.2, to show your membership of at least two groups.

Security

There is safety in numbers. Being a member of a group may make us feel more secure in a hostile environment and therefore satisfy our **security** needs. United we stand, divided we fall.

Task complexity

Primitive humans joined together in groups or bands not only to satisfy security needs but also to handle **task complexity**. An individual might be able to trap a small animal or gather a small number of plants, but to trap a big animal or gather a large amount of plants required the coordinated efforts of a group.

In modern work environments, groups are almost totally unavoidable — there are very few jobs that can be done by one isolated individual (e.g. a lighthouse keeper) and even then, such an individual is dependent on a network of individuals and groups in the outside world to support the solitary role.

Social interaction

Groups can also satisfy the **social interaction** needs of humans. For many people, work does not simply satisfy economic or survival needs, it provides a social aspect as well. It is for this reason that some people would not quit work tomorrow if, say, they won a substantial lottery tonight. They may not be passionately enthusiastic about the people they work with, but it is their work peers, and the physical environment where the work takes place, that provides a structure for interaction among people. Some people find that this structure gives a sense of meaning to their lives, and when it is taken away — on retirement, for example — it is such a stressful life change their health suffers as a result.

Proximity

Why do we choose to become members of one group, or set of groups, rather than others? Often, there is no reason in particular: we would possibly be just as happy in one group, or set of groups, or culture, as another. Practically, the first reason why we choose one particular group is **proximity**: geographical or spatial nearness. This means that students sitting together are more likely to form into a group than a number of students scattered throughout the room, and it also means that a number of workers or managers who work in the same area are more likely to develop a group identity than those who are not physically located close together.

Exchange

The **exchange** theory of group membership could best be summed up by the expression 'what's in it for me?'. In other words, exchange theorists argue that we all — consciously or unconsciously — weigh up the costs and benefits of being in a group. If a person decides that the costs involved in being in a group (time, effort, putting up with others' idiosyncrasies, stress) exceed the benefits (companionship, economic gain, networking communication), then that person may well leave the group.

Now that we are aware of the five factors that determine whether we join, stay in or leave groups, we can visually analyse our membership in different groups. Using a pie chart, we can give approximate proportions or weight to the segments showing the differing factors. For example, figure 18.3 (see overleaf) shows how Mary could show the patterns of her membership of two groups.

The factors are different for each group. If people or circumstances changed in either group, the diagram for that group would be different.

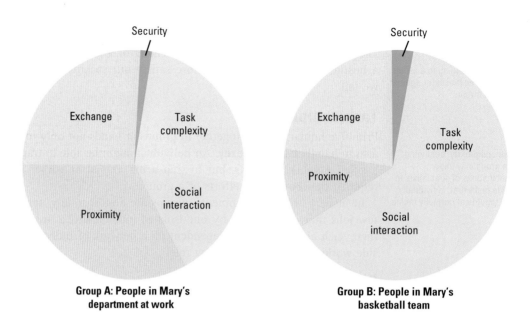

FIGURE 18.3 Five-factor analysis of two of Mary's groups

Group A: People in Mary's department at work

Group B: People in Mary's basketball team

Group versus individual performance

The next issue to consider is who is better at getting things done — groups or individuals? It's clear that when many complex tasks have to be performed simultaneously, then groups will perform better than individuals. When many complex tasks can be performed nonsimultaneously (e.g. in a sequence) groups may be more effective than individuals, but not necessarily.

When tasks can be performed by individuals independently of others, the presence of others may still have an effect — often beneficial — on an individual's performance. Individuals can be motivated by the presence of others because of:

- the sheer stimulating effect of other people
- self-presentation, or the desire to show others how good you are (which may take the form of competition).

Nevertheless, the presence of others is not always a blessing. We have all probably had the experience of doing something badly because others were watching. In fact, the presence of others makes good individual performance more likely only when tasks are familiar; when tasks are unfamiliar, the presence of others tends to lower performance.

Synergy and social loafing

Synergy: the whole group's performance is greater than the sum of its equal parts

We use groups when we believe that two plus two will equal five — that is, when **synergy** occurs. This means that group productivity is greater than the sum of its individual members' performances. Two plus two, however, sometimes might equal one, when not only does synergy not take place, but also the group's performance is worse than that of the sum of its individual members' performances. This may mean, for example, that:

- participants in a tug of war expend less effort as the team size grows
- members of an audience clap less enthusiastically as the audience size grows
- workers slack off when their computer use is not monitored, and indulge in 'cyberloafing' such as playing games instead of working.

Social loafing: the tendency of some group members to put in less effort if they believe that their underperformance will not be noted — the phenomenon of one group member getting a 'free ride' while others do the work

This phenomenon is known as **social loafing** (Goren, Kurzban & Rapoport 2003; Lim 2002; Høiagaard, Säfvenbom & Tønnesen 2006, Aggarwal & O'Brien 2009), and can occur in situations where a number of factors are present, such as a lack of obvious supervision (figure 18.4).

Factors that increase loafing	Factors that reduce loafing
■ Lack of identifiability ■ No individual evaluation ■ No individual or group standards of evaluation ■ Task is easy, boring or the same as others ■ Individual contributions not necessary ■ No individual or group incentives ■ Large group ■ Unfamiliar group	■ Individual identifiability ■ Individual or group evaluation ■ Individual or group standards of evaluation ■ Task is difficult, interesting or different from others ■ Individual contributions essential ■ Individual or group incentives ■ Small group ■ Familiar group

FIGURE 18.4 Factors that affect social loafing

Source: Seta, Paulus and Baron (2000, p. 218).

Social loafing can be overcome when group members become more accountable for their actions, when the activities of the group become more interesting, and when group pride is present – that is, when a group is competing with another group and group members wish to perform well and win the contest (Seta, Paulus & Baron 2000). A study of student project teams found that social loafing/free riding could be overcome to a certain extent by all team members participating in an online interactive activity log and peer review system – a software solution to making all group participants' efforts transparent, and thus perhaps keeping all members honest and hard-working (Brandyberry & Bakke 2006).

Aggarwal and O'Brien (2009) found that team assignments set for students often provided opportunities for social loafing, with the result that many students felt cheated in so far as they only got the same mark as the loafer or loafers. Their suggestions for controlling loafing more include:

■ *Limiting the scope of the project.* This is appropriate if students are to work in teams on projects. Instead of a big, semester-long project, break workload up into a smaller project and some other graded work.

■ *Reducing group size.* This makes it harder for loafers to hide behind the shield of anonymity. Group members in a small group setting can also get to know each other better, which will increase socio-emotional norms (discussed in more detail shortly) to get potential loafers to work.

■ *Running peer evaluations.* Peer evaluations send messages to group members that there will be consequences for nonparticipation, and allow actual or potential loafers to change their behaviour.

These suggestions should work as well in the world of work as they might in academic institutions.

Roles people play

Newcomb (1950) defined a group as consisting 'of people with shared norms and interlocking roles'. In this chapter, we will explore the model of roles and norms shown in figure 18.5 (see overleaf).

Strictly speaking, some informal and formal norms can also be destructive, as can some task and socio-emotional roles, but the model – with its separate categories – will be useful enough for our purposes.

We will look at norms shortly, but for now let's examine roles.

NORMS

ROLES		Formal	Informal	Destructive
	Task			
	Socio-emotional		Teams/groups	
	Destructive			

FIGURE 18.5 The roles/
norms model of group/team
formation

Role: an expected behaviour

A **role** is an expected behaviour (Hodgetts & Hegar 2007). An actor plays a role on stage or in front of the camera, but we all play roles in our day-to-day lives. Roles can also be thought of as ways of thinking, perceiving and acting. Perhaps these roles are inborn, or perhaps we acquire them along the way. The concept of a role helps explain others and ourselves. De Bono (2009) suggests that group members should improve their problem-solving abilities by consciously role-playing, or 'wearing different hats'. De Bono's hats include:

- the *white hat* for rational thinking
- the *red hat* for emotions and intuition
- the *black hat* for looking at things cautiously, pessimistically and defensively
- the *yellow hat* for positive thinking
- the *green hat* for creativity.

Process control is used by a chairperson or a group leader to use authority to 'change hats' when needed (see also 'Is logic enough?' in chapter 12).

In analysing many groups — the management task force, the counter staff in a bank, the group of friends in a car, the voluntary charity committee, the car assembly plant team, the sporting team — it is useful to distinguish between three types of roles:

- Task roles
- Socio-emotional roles
- Destructive roles.

Task role: relates to the functional or technical nature of work

Socio-emotional role: relates to the interpersonal aspects of work

Destructive role: causes conflict and ineffectiveness in work situations

Task roles are played by people when they are concerned solely with getting the job done. When we say that a particular person is adopting a particular task role, then we are considering this person and his or her work from a functional viewpoint. We are more concerned with the quality and the quantity of the output than we are with his or her feelings, values and perceptions. Belbin (2010), for example, discusses task roles played in groups (resource investigator, monitor–evaluator, implementer, completer–finisher and so on). **Socio-emotional roles** (or maintenance roles) are played by people when they are communicating feelings, values and opinions about the task, and about the world beyond the task. **Destructive roles** are played by people when they — consciously or unconsciously — wish to sabotage the efforts of the group. All destructive roles have a foundation in reality — sometimes it pays to shelve problems, sometimes other group members are victimising an individual — but destructive role-players move way beyond a rational assessment of what is really going on as they wreak havoc.

Figure 18.6 shows some task, socio-emotional and destructive roles played in groups, and a detailed analysis of these roles is given in table 18.1. (Note that some of these roles appear in different guises in other areas of this book.)

Task roles	Socio-emotional roles	Destructive roles
■ Brainstormer ■ Expert ■ Judge ■ Devil's advocate ■ Representative ■ Implementer ■ Ringmaster ■ Memory	■ Encourager ■ Peacemaker ■ Tension reliever ■ Confronter	■ Husher ■ Personaliser ■ Recognition seeker ■ Victim ■ Blocker ■ Shelver ■ Distractor ■ Aggressor ■ Shadow ■ Special-interest pleader

FIGURE 18.6 Roles played in groups

We need to bear in mind the following aspects of role formation and execution in groups:

- Sometimes people play only one type of role in both work and personal situations; sometimes people play the same type of multiple roles in both work and personal situations; and sometimes people play quite different roles in work and personal situations.
- Effective groups show a healthy mix of task and socio-emotional role-playing, and a minimal amount of destructive role-playing.
- Effective groups understand that all roles have strengths and weaknesses, and that maximum synergy is created when the mix of strengths is brought to the fore and the mix of weaknesses is kept under control.
- Sometimes groups can solve problems more effectively by letting people who are playing different roles assume dominance or leadership in a sequence or in phases – for example, a Brainstormer–Expert–Judge–Devil's advocate–Representative–Implementer sequence.
- Too much emphasis on task roles may lead to an over-emphasis on facts, and not enough weight given to opinion and feeling (which can be as important, and sometimes more important, than facts).
- Too much emphasis on socio-emotional roles may lead to a lack of emphasis on facts and not enough concern with producing real outcomes from the group.
- There should be a good mix of roles played, otherwise too many group members playing the one role may lead to a group having blind spots, and thus making bad decisions.

TABLE 18.1 Analysis of roles played in groups

Task roles			
Role	**Verbal behaviour**	**Nonverbal behaviour**	**Analysis**
Brainstormer	■ *Hey, what about …* ■ *I'm really excited about …* ■ *No, don't judge; not yet anyway.* ■ *We've possibly got ourselves into this mess because we're too conventional.* ■ *We're too close to it. We need lateral thinking here, not vertical.*	■ Jumps up, writes on board or flip chart ■ Jerky, explosive movements ■ Animated face, eyes ■ Touches others	■ Invaluable when team needs new ideas (i.e. all the time) ■ Not necessarily good at execution (i.e. a starter, not a finisher) ■ Possibly a short concentration span ■ Might be disorganised ■ Good at finding things and concepts; good at losing them too ■ Might need to have creativity channelled via structure, goals; ask for ideas in writing where possible ■ May need to be protected from more 'practical' members of team

(continued)

TABLE 18.1 *(continued)*

Task roles			
Role	**Verbal behaviour**	**Nonverbal behaviour**	**Analysis**
Expert	■ *Here are the facts/data.* ■ *My presentation begins with …* ■ *I presume you've all read my report/ memo on …*	■ Serious, methodical, restrained ■ Precise hand gestures; folds hands, points at diagrams, charts ■ Slightly impatient, waiting to be asked to go into action	■ Not emotional ■ Thinks that the pure beauty of ideas is obvious to everyone ■ Impatient with politics; doesn't understand compromise, lobbying or the necessity to repeat a good idea over and over ■ May be intolerant of Brainstormer's 'messiness' or emotional communication
Judge	■ *We've got conflicting opinions here.* ■ *Let's weigh up the pros and cons.* ■ *What's the practicality/logic?* ■ *Maybe we should sleep on it, and look at it later. It might benefit from some benign neglect.* ■ *Maybe we should put together a compromise package of parts of all proposals.*	■ Evaluative (e.g. biting glasses arm or pen, narrowing of eyes, chin-stroking) ■ Laying-down-the-law-type hand-chop ■ Counting on fingers in discussing alternatives ■ Gestures with one hand, then the other ('on the one hand and on the other')	■ Can work with Experts from differing fields ■ Might be an enemy of Brainstormer by forcing premature closure on decisions
Devil's advocate	■ *I can see a lot of good here, but let's look at it from the opposition's point of view.* ■ *Do we have any blind spots here?* ■ *What's the worst-case scenario? What can go horribly wrong? Let's not forget Murphy's Law.*	■ Sits back in chair; remains restrained even when ideas are flying and enthusiasm is high ■ Takes notes	■ Necessary to prevent groupthink syndrome ■ Vital that this role be rotated, otherwise there is the danger of Devil's advocate simply becoming a Blocker
Representative	■ *The union/management won't like parts of this.* ■ *I'll make a few calls.* ■ *I'll do some press releases, take X and Y to lunch and give them some background.*	■ Shares some behaviour of Judge, Devil's advocate and Implementer (evaluation, detachment, alertness)	■ A liaison with outside interests and stakeholders ■ A boundary spanner ■ A negotiator, a fixer ■ Might have divided loyalties
Implementer	■ *Can do.* ■ *Sure!* ■ *Okay!* ■ *I'll have a draft back to this group in a week.* ■ *There are ways and means.* ■ *Leave it to me.*	■ Alert ■ Shuffles, arranges papers ■ Makes notations ■ Looks at watch ■ Writes in diary ■ Uses calculator/laptop computer	■ A master of details ■ A fixer ■ Can become impatient, however, and might force team to premature closure
Ringmaster	■ *That's quite interesting, X, but I think we'll handle it as a separate item under 'general business' on the agenda.* ■ *We seem to have reached an impasse. Let me see if I can summarise the differing viewpoints we've heard so far.* ■ *That's out of line, Y. Please stick to discussing item 6, otherwise A and B can have the floor.*	■ Works through agenda papers with pen ■ May have hand over mouth while others are speaking ■ Looks around table to watch for cues indicating who would like to speak ■ Confers with secretary/note-taker	■ Can act as chairperson in meetings ■ Ideally, should have no strong opinions on matters under discussion (perfect neutrality is, of course, impossible) ■ It is useful to know his/her real opinions in case a casting vote is needed

Task roles			
Role	**Verbal behaviour**	**Nonverbal behaviour**	**Analysis**
Memory	■ *Excuse me, Y, how do you spell that?* ■ *[Silence]*	■ Head down	■ Can act as secretary in meetings ■ The collective memory and handler of mechanics: minutes, agendas, setting of agendas, checking up to see that people have followed through on items covered in the last agenda

Socio-emotional roles			
Role	**Verbal behaviour**	**Nonverbal behaviour**	**Analysis**
Encourager	■ *Before we go any further, I think we should hear from X. She's been telling me her opinions, and I think there's a lot in them. X? The floor is yours.* ■ *No, no, I don't think that's what X meant at all. I think she was saying … Have I got that right, X, or have I missed your point?*	■ Smile, nod ■ Head tilted to one side, listening ■ Open palms	■ Draws out reticent, protects the weak ■ Supports Ringmaster ■ A good listener
Peacemaker	■ *Let's go back a few steps, J. You agree that … right? And, S, you also agree that … right?* ■ *Yes, I understand that you disagree with … but my notes show that you agree with … Okay?*	■ Orients towards person with hot temper ■ Gestures with palms open or up ■ Eyebrows up (questioning)	■ Consensus-seeker, diplomat; knows that there may be no permanent solution to the problem under discussion ■ Knows that tempers may cool if team takes a break; may thus propose adjournment when conflict peaks
Tension reliever	■ *Time for coffee/lunch, I think.* ■ *Hey, I didn't know World War III had been declared!* ■ *[Uses puns/jokes]*	■ Pulls faces ■ Smiles, laughs ■ Animated face, body ■ Expansive gestures ■ Plays with pens, cups ■ Doodles	■ Good at breaking the ice in initial phases of meetings ■ Good at defusing conflict with humour ■ Needs to know how not to go too far in going too far; otherwise clowning will irritate people, and will be counterproductive ■ Similar to Brainstormer, but not as creative in transforming facts into ideas
Confronter	■ *No, we can't smooth this over.* ■ *There's a hidden agenda here; there are too many undercurrents in this group. We need to get this out in the open before we go any further.* ■ *No, I disagree. We shouldn't just stick to the facts. Facts can be twisted to suit any opinion. We need opinions, and we need honest opinions. No more playing games.*	■ Assertive/aggressive manner ■ Palm out in 'stop' gesture ■ Negative cross-fanning of hands	■ More assertive than aggressive ■ Not all conflict is bad; the Confronter is useful when conflict is being avoided, when group pussyfoots around hard decisions ■ Enemy of 'weak' consensus (i.e. taking the path of least resistance) ■ Similar to Devil's advocate, except that Confronter is more concerned with opinions and feelings than facts

(continued)

TABLE 18.1 *(continued)*

Destructive roles			
Role	**Verbal behaviour**	**Nonverbal behaviour**	**Analysis**
Husher	<ul><li>*Tsk, tsk.*</li><li>*Shh . . .*</li><li>*Let's not have any more of this unpleasantness.*</li><li>*I'm getting a headache*</li></ul>	<ul><li>Rapid head nods</li><li>Palms out, palms down; calming, hushing, placating gestures</li><li>Nervous posture; squirms</li><li>Sickly smile</li><li>Head-shaking</li><li>Index finger to lips, and in reprimanding, negating gestures</li><li>Blushing</li></ul>	<ul><li>Wishes to avoid conflict at all costs</li><li>The appearance of harmony is all-important to the Husher</li><li>Unwittingly aids other, more manipulative types in suppressing real discussion</li></ul>
Personaliser	<ul><li>*This is a roundabout way of attacking me, isn't it?*</li><li>*Why are you always attacking stuff from my area?*</li><li>*Humphh!*</li></ul>	<ul><li>Hands to chest, thumb to chest</li><li>Higher pitch in voice</li><li>Wide open, staring eyes</li><li>Crossed arms, orientation away from group after outburst</li></ul>	<ul><li>Alternates between aggressive/fight and submissive/flight behaviour</li><li>Feels that world is out to get him/her: the most innocent remarks from others are seen as an attack on the Personaliser's self</li><li>If this is continued long enough, the perceived will become the real; paranoia will become objective, and people will perceive such a person in a different way, and therefore will behave differently towards them</li></ul>
Recognition seeker	<ul><li>*It's funny that this should come up, you know. Something similar, well, not quite similar, happened to me about two years ago. I wrote about it in my half-yearly report. I'm sure you all remember?*</li><li>*[Loud laughter, drawing people's attention and stopping discussion]*</li><li>*You know, we've been working on this for quite some time in my section. Let me fill you in on the details.*</li></ul>	<ul><li>Self-confident, smug</li><li>Suddenly leans forward at point of interruption</li><li>Fidgets</li><li>May be flamboyant in dress</li></ul>	<ul><li>Has a short concentration span; is bored with most things, especially when he/she is not the centre of attention</li><li>Similar to the Personaliser, in that he/she insists on relating the most unrelated matters back to self; unlike the Personaliser, however, the Recognition seeker is quite happy about this</li></ul>
Victim	<ul><li>*I've really mucked this one up. Anyone got any bright ideas?*</li><li>*Sorry. I guess I've let the team down again.*</li><li>*We're just crumpling under pressure down in my section. We can't cope.*</li><li>*It's a no-win situation, again.*</li></ul>	<ul><li>Drooping, slumped posture</li><li>Peaked eyebrows, wrinkled brow</li><li>Shakes head</li><li>Entwines, disentwines legs</li><li>Appealing to others with eyes, hands</li></ul>	<ul><li>Everyone fails from time to time; at least a mistake indicates that someone stopped talking long enough to do something. The Victim, however, fails all the time, apparently having made the life decision that if praise is not available, then disapproval, or even punishment, is okay. Victims eventually get their wish.</li><li>A type of masochistic Recognition seeker</li></ul>
Blocker	<ul><li>*It'll never work.*</li><li>*What a mess.*</li><li>*I don't know why we bother.*</li><li>*It's never been done before.*</li></ul>	<ul><li>Crossed arms</li><li>Theatrical sighs</li><li>Contemptuous looks</li></ul>	<ul><li>Has one way to say yes, and a million ways to say no</li><li>Negative and destructive in approach; everything is a problem</li></ul>

Destructive roles			
Role	**Verbal behaviour**	**Nonverbal behaviour**	**Analysis**
Blocker (continued)	▪ *We tried that before, and it didn't work.* ▪ *It can't happen under the 1963 standing orders, and therefore it's not gonna happen.*	▪ Rolls eyes ▪ Shakes head ▪ Orientates body away	▪ Enamoured of red tape ▪ Confronter or Devil's advocate gone wrong
Shelver	▪ *Shouldn't we defer this?* ▪ *Is this the best place to discuss this?* ▪ *I don't know, I still think we need more information.*	▪ Whining voice ▪ Looks very worried ▪ Looks at watch/clock ▪ Looks as though he/she wants to be somewhere else	▪ A procrastinator and an avoider ▪ Sometimes delaying things can be wise, but the Shelver always wants to put things off ▪ Less aggressive than the Blocker, but just as effective in frustrating action
Distractor	▪ *[Whispers a lot]* ▪ *Psst!* ▪ *Anyway, she said ... he said ...*	▪ Passes notes ▪ Winks ▪ Nudges ▪ Yawns ▪ Looks everywhere but at agenda	▪ Short concentration span ▪ Treats all meetings as social occasions ▪ Doesn't necessarily want to be elsewhere, because a lot of gossip items may come up here ▪ Similar to Recognition seeker in producing terminally trivial and silly behaviour but does not want so high a profile
Aggressor	▪ *God! What a lot of garbage you're talking!* ▪ *That's typical of the gutless, incompetent nonsense we've come to expect of you!* ▪ *What kickback are you going to get from this?* ▪ *Tsk, tsk, tsk.*	▪ Glares ▪ Bares teeth ▪ Points ▪ Shakes fist ▪ Crosses arms ▪ Shakes head ▪ Broad, dismissive gestures ▪ Loud exhalation of air; expressing disgust	▪ Very hostile ▪ Suspicious of people's motives ▪ Dominates, and often wins
Shadow	▪ *[Says nothing]*	▪ Sits back from table ▪ Frightened or impassive	▪ Never says anything ▪ Is not quite clear why he/she is there ▪ May have some good things to say, but is dominated by others ▪ Needs an Encourager, or needs to be taken out of the group ▪ May in fact be acting rationally; may be an example of organisational silence — one shadow can suggest that she/he has a problem; more than one may suggest that the group or organisation has a problem
Special-interest pleader	▪ *Yes, all very well, but what about the small businessman/poor/housewives/ big companies staggering under the tax burden/data-processing department?*	▪ Sermonising tone of voice ▪ Looks around table at others while talking intently	▪ Draws all topics back to special interest, no matter how irrelevant the connection may be ▪ A Representative gone wrong ▪ The Personaliser operating at a collective level

1. What are the strengths and weaknesses of the various roles?
2. What is the ideal balance of task and socio-emotional roles?
3. To what extent should a Ringmaster play some or all of the socio-emotional roles?
4. Are the roles that people play an expression of deep-seated and unchangeable character, or are roles more superficial than this?
5. Do people play more than one role in the same group? Do they play different roles in different groups?
6. What other roles might there be?

Norms

You may recall that our definition of a group is that it consists of people with shared norms and interlocking roles. Norms are standards of customary behaviour and can be translated as 'rules' (Flynn & Chatman 2003; Mannix & Jehn 2004; Hogg & Reid 2006; Dydejcsyk, Kułakowski & Ryback 2009). Therefore one way to define groups is: Roles + Rules (Norms) = Groups.

Formal norm: an explicit rule-governing behaviour

Informal norm: an implicit rule-governing behaviour

We can distinguish between **formal norms** and **informal norms** in groups. Formal norms are those rules that are explicit in the way they define the group's behaviour; whereas informal norms are implicit in the way they define the group's behaviour. Figure 18.7 shows samples of a factory work group's formal and informal norms.

FIGURE 18.7 Formal and informal norms

Sources: Adapted from Grasha (1997); Hepner (1979).

Formal norms	Informal norms
Workers show up at the factory on time.	Workers often refer to each other by nicknames.
Workers must observe safety regulations.	Some workers engage in practical jokes and horseplay.
Workers in this group have lunch in the cafeteria from 12.45 to 1.30 pm.	Workers in this group always sit at the one table and always drink three cups of coffee.

In work situations, formal norms are usually laid down by management and represent the formal organisation (depicted on an organisation chart); whereas informal norms are usually laid down by the group of nonmanagement employees and represent the informal organisation. Both organisations coexist, often uneasily, and sometimes in a state of open conflict. The system of communication for the informal organisation is known as the grapevine.

Rules, whether formal or informal, have to be enforced. Enforcement of formal norms is straightforward, whereas enforcement of informal norms is usually more subtle. The conflict between informal and formal group norms, and the means by which one is enforced at the expense of the other, are complex phenomena. Work groups often have clearly defined informal norms, such as:

■ You don't dob on (report on) your mates to your superiors
■ A fair day's work around here is x amount of output.
■ We trust each other a lot, and we can try out weird and wonderful ideas on the group without getting laughed at.
■ We don't express too much emotion when discussing things.

- This group's output is a cut above what the others deliver, and we like it like that.
- We don't like working with women (men).

Such norms can be negative and punitive, or positive and rewarding. All have the unstated function of preserving the group and its collective self-esteem. If anyone deviates from these norms, they may be punished by various group behavioural mechanisms, such as ostracism ('sent to Coventry', 'freeze out') or ridicule ('Ratebuster!', 'Conch!' for overachievers; 'Goldbricker!', 'Bludger!' for underachievers).

In 1948 a classic study was done of group norm behaviour in a North American pyjama manufacturing plant (Coch & French 1948). At this plant, the informal group norm for productivity in a group of pressers was about 50 items a day. A new worker entered the group and, after a few days' learning, began to exceed the group norm (figure 18.8).

The rest of the group began to scapegoat or punish the newcomer deviating from the norm, so that after some days, the deviant conformed, and in fact over-conformed by producing slightly less than the group norm. After 20 days the group had to be split up, and even though all other workers were transferred elsewhere, the scapegoated worker remained. Her output rate increased dramatically, freed as she was from the restrictive group norm.

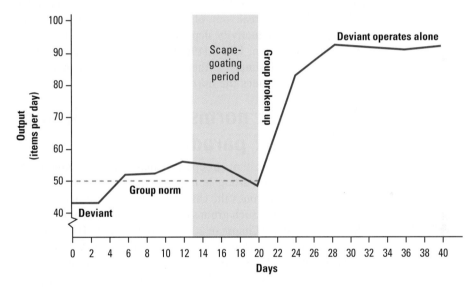

FIGURE 18.8 Group norms and deviant performance in a pyjama factory

Sources: Adapted from Coch and French (1948); Hepner (1979).

Similar dynamics of exclusion were observed in a German workplace in the 1990s, where a group member had higher qualifications and received a higher pay rate. The group expressed displeasure, and the woman considered returning to her former workstation. She didn't, but another woman was discouraged from seeking higher qualifications (Minssen 2005).

Informal group norms

The Coch and French findings have fascinating implications for the design of jobs, motivation, piecework and group dynamics concepts such as conformity and cohesiveness. It is sometimes concluded that:

- Data like that of the pyjama factory study prove that informal group norms are dangerous things, ruining organisational productivity and providing resistance to change.
- If managements could only destroy informal groups by getting workers to participate more in the running of the organisation — for example, by setting up semi-autonomous workgroups, or teams — then things would be better all round, for both management and workers.

However, when groups preserve informal norms that conflict with formal ones, group members are not being altogether dumb, nor are they necessarily neurotic or just plain cranky. If a work group were to lift its production norm to the maximum, will there be guarantees that additional profits generated will be shared proportionately among management and labour, and that the higher than normal output won't lead to staff being laid off? If such guarantees were given, then labour and management could work in more harmonious alliance.

Unfortunately, many work restructuring schemes have, in fact, led to staff being laid off (Kelly 1981), rather than the organisation increasing its marketing of its new high output, or retraining workers for other jobs. Viewed in this light, informal group norms that hold down output seem to be rational, counter-punching behaviour.

Managements within organisations also have their own formal and informal norms, some of which lead to what one would hope for and expect – high productivity – but some of which lead to the opposite outcome. A group of manufacturers may cause production to be artificially low because of cartelisation, administered prices, vertical and horizontal integration, a 'why should we bother, we're okay' culture, and so on. Professional groups may also have norms of holding down outputs – what peer-group pressures would there be on a doctor or a lawyer if they began to cut their prices, for example?

The trick is to break out of such a dilemma, and see that the formal and informal norms of high productivity depend on the formal and informal norms of high trust and open communication. Likert (1967), for example, suggests that the informal organisation or grapevine will simply wither away if genuine participation in decision making and empowerment becomes the norm in an organisation.

Destructive norms: groupthink and the Abilene paradox

We sometimes think that groups can make bad decisions because of conflicts within the group – that is, the group is not cohesive and is lacking in supportive socio-emotional norms. This is sometimes the case, but it is also true that sometimes highly cohesive groups make bad decisions. Such groups often make bad decisions because of **groupthink** (Janis 1982, 1989; Kowert 2002; Chapman 2006; Solomon 2006; Halbesleben, Wheeler & Buckley 2007).

Groupthink: a pattern of defective decision making seen in groups

Janis argued that groupthink occurs in five stages (figure 18.9).

The paradox with groupthink is that the groups it afflicts are usually quite pleasant company to work with: the 'we' feeling is very high, and group members often like each other a lot. In fact, the more cohesive the group, the greater the chance of groupthink occurring. The groupthink model was originally used to explain US foreign policy decision making under Presidents Roosevelt (Pearl Harbor), Kennedy (Bay of Pigs, Cuban missile crisis) and Johnson (Vietnam) (Janis 1982), but has subsequently been used to analyse a much broader range of areas. It has also been applied in analyses of:

- the 1972–73 Watergate crisis under President Nixon (Raven & Rubin 1983)
- the invasion of Iraq in 2003 led by President George W. Bush (Yetiv 2004; Kemper 2004; Woodward 2006; Fitsimmons 2008; Mackenzie 2010; Post & Panis 2011).
- the psychological mechanisms that could trigger a third world war (Thompson 1985)
- the space shuttle *Challenger* disaster of 1986 (Moorhead, Ference & Neck 1991)
- the performance of self-managing teams and organisational projects (Moorhead, Neck & West 1998; Haslam et al. 2006; Halbesleben, Wheeler & Buckley 2007; Hede 2007)
- the overmedication of 'difficult' patients in hospitals (Degnin 2009)
- the global financial crisis that began in 2008 (Schiller 2008).

In 1961, for example, President Kennedy and his group of advisers unwisely decided to support a CIA-planned invasion of Cuba by anti-Castro rebels. The Bay of Pigs invasion was a disaster. All the mechanisms of groupthink contributed to this negative outcome – the perception that the enemy was weak and incompetent; the norm of suppressing feelings, intuitions and criticism; the fear of being seen as weak if expressing criticism of the military option; the dominance of forceful, aggressive personalities such as Robert Kennedy; the exclusion of alternative data, and so on.

Similar dynamics were observed in the 2003 decision of US President George W. Bush to invade Iraq (the illusion of invulnerability, critics being excluded from important meetings). Schiller, in predicting what was to become the global financial crisis beginning in 2008, was a policy insider, but could not go along with the groupthink feeling that the financial system was stable, and almost succumbed to self-censorship, a groupthink symptom: 'I distinctly remember that, while writing this (a warning that catastrophic collapses of stock and housing markets was on its way), I feared criticism for gratuitous alarmism. And indeed, such criticism came.' (Schiller 2008)

	Stage	Characteristics
I	Antecedents	1. High levels of cohesiveness. 2. Structural defects — insulation, lack of leader impartiality, lack of procedural norms, and member homogeneity (everyone is like everyone else in values, cognitive style). 3. Provocative situational contexts — group efficacy, high stress.
II	Concurrence seeking	Group members openly agree with the perceived group position even if a group member privately disagrees — there is a need to be seen to 'be a team player', or not to 'rock the boat' or cause disruption.
III	Symptoms	1. *Illusion of invulnerability.* The group believes it is invulnerable, which leads to excessive optimism and risk taking. 2. *Rationalisation.* Group members rationalise away warnings or threats. 3. *Belief in inherent morality.* Group members believe that their decisions are inherently moral, brushing away thoughts of unethical behaviour by saying 'How could we do anything wrong?' 4. *Stereotyping.* Opponents of the group are stereotyped as being too evil, stupid or weak to be taken seriously. 5. *Direct pressure.* Anyone foolhardy enough to question the status quo within the group has direct pressure applied to conform. 6. *Self-censorship.* Group members with doubts censor themselves to preserve the appearance of consent. 7. *Illusion of unanimity.* Because silence is interpreted as consent, there is an illusion of unanimity. 8. *Mindguards.* Just as bodyguards protect us from physical harm, so some people set themselves as mindguards (censors or gatekeepers) in order to prevent challenging or threatening information available outside the group from appearing before the group.
IV	Decision-making defects	1. Incomplete survey of alternatives. 2. Incomplete survey of objectives. 3. Failure to examine risks associated with the preferred choice. 4. Poor information search. 5. Selective bias in processing information. 6. Failure to reappraise alternatives. 7. Failure to provide contingency plans.
V	Poor decision outcomes	Groupthink occurs. Almost certainly, a bad decision will be made when all previous factors are present. Sometimes groups in the grip of groupthink will still make a decision, especially when a leader advocates a good decision, but this is infrequent.

FIGURE 18.9 Stages in the groupthink process

Source: Adapted from Janis (1982, 1989).

The same group made better decisions the following year at the time of the Cuban missile crisis, employing a number of anti-groupthink techniques (see table 18.2 opposite and overleaf): other decision makers were invited to provide fresh perspectives; and Kennedy deliberately excluded himself from some meetings so that his presence would not lead to suppression of ideas or self-censorship (emphasising the role of power and status in discouraging others from speaking out; see Islam & Zyphur 2005). Interestingly, each person was further sanctioned by the President to be a critical evaluator or 'devil's advocate' of all presented ideas.

Eaton (2001) has noted groupthink dynamics in the tendency of organisations to treat competitors and even customers as idiots (the British store chain Marks and Spencer underestimating its 'downmarket' rival Tesco's; British Airways underestimating its rival Virgin airlines; IBM underestimating the power of the personal computer versus its 'big iron' or mainframe computers; Daimler-Benz dismissing concerns about the stability of its A-Class car after it failed the 'moose test').

Ko (2005) has analysed specific Chinese cultural patterns in Hong Kong businesses, such as status, face, trust, friendship and Guanxi (networks), and has found a correlation between groupthink and status of individuals in decision-making groups (note the remarks about US President Kennedy deliberately absenting himself from meetings so that his status would not swamp objective discussion and decision making).

All groups – whether political cabinets and ministries, ameteur or professional sporting teams, charity fundraising committees, teenage gangs or work groups – can be susceptible to groupthink.

The Abilene paradox

A variation on the groupthink model has been developed by Jerry Harvey, which he calls the **Abilene paradox** (Harvey 1996; Kim 2001; McManus 2006; Halbesleben, Wheeler & Buckley 2007; McAvoy & Butler 2009). The name comes from a journey Harvey and his family took through blistering heat to go to the town of Abilene, Texas, to eat at a restaurant. Upon returning home, all four family members discovered that none of them had really wanted to go, but each went along, presuming that everyone else wanted to go.

In such circumstances, we make bad decisions, not so much due to actual group tyranny and conformity pressures as to our own perceptions or anxiety about being alone – and about being separated from others by exclusion or ostracism. Harvey notes, for example, that a number of President Nixon's staff who participated in the Watergate hotel break-in in 1972 didn't really want to do it, but thought that everyone else did. As one participant said, '[I] ... drifted along ... because of the fear of the group pressure that would ensue, of not being a team player'.

The Abilene paradox then is: 'Organisations frequently take actions in contradiction to what they really want to do and therefore defeat the very purposes they are trying to achieve' (Harvey 1988).

The essential symptom that defines organisations caught in the paradox is that they are unable to *manage agreement*, rather than unable to *manage conflict* – because most agree with each other, rather than disagree, but all are operating in a fog of pluralistic ignorance. While the groupthink and Abilene paradox models vary in different ways (see figure 18.10 in the next section), they both create the same result: bad, sometimes disastrous, decisions made by people in groups.

So, how can groupthink and the Abilene paradox be avoided? There are numerous ways, most of which will be uncomfortable for group members, but some or all of which may be necessary. They are all concerned with expanding the focus of decision making, reducing or modifying the cohesiveness of the group, and reducing the risk of speaking out within the group. These approaches are summarised in table 18.2.

TABLE 18.2 Reducing the effects of groupthink and the Abilene paradox

Approach	Rationale
Examine alternatives, generate contingency plans	Don't be trapped into thinking that there's only one solution. Insist that multiple solutions be proposed for problems. Always have a plan B and, preferably, a plan C and plan D.
Appoint devil's advocate	A devil's advocate is empowered by the group to always present a critical, worst-case scenario without the group thinking any the worse of that person. Role needs to be rotated.
Increase group size, heterogeneity	Break the cosy dynamics of the group by making it bigger, and introduce people who are from different backgrounds, with differing opinions and problem-solving styles and who may challenge the consensus and expose the blind spots of an over-homogeneous group.
Remove physical isolation	Physically reintegrate the group with the rest of the organisation. Break down over-territorial 'us-and-them' or 'silo' mentality.
Do external reality checking	Stay in touch with suppliers, dealers, stakeholders and customers; use boundary spanners within organisation to bring back intelligence, rumours.
Facilitate organisational graffiti	Officially sanction space on organisational computer system for a graffiti bulletin board or intranet where people may anonymously input unpopular ideas and heresies for all to consider. Possibly dangerous, but less dangerous than trying to suppress the grapevine.
Eliminate competition with other groups	Break down 'us-and-them' mentality by social occasions, forcing groups to work together, exchanging and rotating personnel between groups.
Make confronters into heroes	Going beyond the devil's advocate. Instead of shooting messengers, reward them. Very painful, but less painful than the alternative, usually arrived at when someone says, 'How did we get into this mess?' If assertively confronting role models exist, and are rewarded (or at the very least, are not punished) then there will be more assertive confrontation. See Roberto (2009) with his view that great managers 'Don't take yes for an answer.'
Create multiple affiliations	Have group members report to more than one boss and interact with other areas, departments and teams. Expose them to other views and give them other supports they could fall back on if they fall out of favour with the main group.
Use special techniques (e.g. nominal group techniques)	Nominal group techniques reduce group pressures to conform by allowing members to anonymously contribute ideas in writing.
Provide training for group members	Boost group members' confidence and ability through training in technical skills, self-leadership and interpersonal skills such as feedback, questioning, listening and reframing.

(continued)

TABLE 18.2 *(continued)*

Approach	Rationale
Defer finality in decisions	Have a second-chance meeting, where decisions can be reviewed before committing to them.
Manage impact of high-status members	The presence of high-status group members can impair decision making when others feel intimidated or try to impress. It may help if such people absent themselves from some meetings.
Give higher priority to socio-emotional factors	Change the group norm so that it becomes more acceptable to express intuitions, hunches, gut feelings, vibes and misgivings.
Recruit young people with a broad perspective	Immerse them for the first six months in interdepartmental networking while they still have the protection given to newcomers.

Sources: Adapted from Janis (1982); Manz and Neck (1997); Moorhead, Neck and West (1998); Kim (2001); Schütz and Block (2006); Post and Panis (2011).

Silos: the clash of stereotypes

The in-group versus out-group dynamic present inside many organisations means that many subsections or silos of an organisation – departments, teams, divisions, units, colleges and centres – may focus more aggression, hostility and competition to those inside the organisation than to those outside the organisation. These dynamics are often aided and abetted by the groupthink and Abilene paradox phenomena. The organisation is a group of groups, and thus groupthink/Abilene may occur between groups.

These types of turf wars or territory spats are often driven by the gap between the self-perception of any one area or unit and the perceptions of that area or unit by other areas or units. These perceptions are often stereotypes (see table 18.3). If communication between different areas or silos does not occur, these stereotypes or clichés may turn into self-fulfilling prophecies (Schütz & Block 2006).

TABLE 18.3 Double vision in the silos: self-images and the perceptions of others

Area	Research	Production	Sales	Marketing
Self-perception	■ Project-oriented and systematic ■ The future of the enterprise depends on our innovation	■ Cool, calculating engineers ■ Because of us, production processes are stable, error-free	■ Relationship managers ■ Our performance is measurable and performance orientated	■ Innovative; representative of clients ■ Conceptual thinkers ■ We nurture the enterprise's greatest asset: its brand
Perception of area by others	■ Arrogant scientific types more interested in Nobel prizes and patents than profits ■ Enemy of sales ■ Techno freaks	■ Machinists who are stuck in old ways of thinking ■ Innovation blockers ■ Quantity kings ■ Dr No	■ Wafflers ■ Customer's buddies ■ Price killers ■ Incentive hunters ■ Likely to promise the world but not deliver	■ A lifeguard who never touches water ■ Sprinkle unrealistic fantasies from their ivory tower over the sales troops ■ Snooty verbal acrobat; obfuscator ■ Cash burner ■ PowerPoint artist

Source: Adapted from Schütz and Block (2006).

A reflection on destructive norms

So, considering what we have learned, especially about silos in an organisation and how the dynamics at play in the workplace can be characterised by groupthink and the Abilene paradox, what can we now take away? Take the time to consider figure 18.10, which compares the Abilene paradox with groupthink.

	Abilene paradox	Groupthink
Consciousness of participants	■ Individuals want to do one thing but willingly — though in despair — do the opposite ■ Absurdity of situation apparent from outset ■ Makes people feel bad about good private decisions withheld from the group	■ Group members often euphoric, enjoying high morale and sense of efficacy ■ Absurdity not obvious until fog lifts ■ Makes people feel good about bad public decisions
Immediate post-decision response	■ Conflict, malaise	■ Esprit de corps, optimistic views of the future, loyalty to organisation
Relevant unit of analysis	■ Individual ■ Group is less than sum of parts ■ Individuals feel guilty	■ Group ■ Individuals become immersed in collective identity ■ Group is more than the sum of parts ■ Members may feel exonerated from individual responsibility
Presence of external threats	■ No	■ Often — induces stress and feelings of urgency which may impair rational examination of procedures and alternatives
Perception of coercion	■ Yes — perception that to disagree would 'rock the boat'	■ Not always — members may feel that they are deciding of their own free will
Individuals' attitude	■ Passive	■ Active

FIGURE 18.10 Groupthink and the Abilene paradox compared

Sources: Adapted from Taras (1991); Kim (2001); Harvey et al. (2004).

As we have explained, both of these models create the same result: bad, sometimes disastrous decisions made by people in groups. By self-reflection, employees can strive to identify if and when these norms occur in the workplace, and if there are inconsistencies or 'double vision' in the silos (refer back to table 18.3). Then, they can look to use some of the approaches outlined in table 18.2 to challenge the status quo and reduce the effects of these norms.

Stages of group development

Individuals develop through discernible stages or phases, and products and organisations are sometimes described as having life cycles. It may well be that groups develop, change and/or die in similar ways. It is possible to see patterns or stages in team development, and this can help us to determine just what is going on inside a team – particularly if things don't appear to be going all that well. For example, table 18.4 (overleaf) shows that groups may move through five stages or phases (Tuckman 1965; Tuckman & Jensen 1977; Miller 2003).

Tuckman's is perhaps the most famous of the stage, phase or sequence models, and has been widely used (Wheelan Davidson & Tilin 2003; Akan 2005; Akrivou & Boyatzis 2006; Birchmeier, Joinson & Dietz-Uhler 2005; Fall & Wejnert 2005; Mannix & Jehn 2004; Miller 2003; Chang, Duck & Bordia 2006).

Phase	What happens
1. Forming	▪ Getting to know you, ice-breaking stage ▪ Group members attempt to identify what tasks they should be working on ▪ Members also begin to develop a sense of the group's independence
2. Storming	▪ Socio-emotional responses to task demands come to the fore ▪ Conflicts over leadership, control and influence — who will be the 'star', and who is in charge? (See Overbeck, Correll & Park 2005.) ▪ Misunderstandings about role and style behaviour and norms, conflicting goals, poor feedback and listening, ineffective group decision-making and problem-solving processes
3. Norming	▪ Formal and informal norms emerge ▪ Cohesion begins to develop ▪ Opinions are now stated more readily and are received in a less defensive manner
4. Performing	▪ Balance of rules (norms) and roles emerge ▪ Synergy develops via positive role-playing (optimal mix of task and socio-emotional roles, with destructive role-playing under control) ▪ Group begins to produce solutions to the problems it is focusing on
5. Adjourning	▪ Group reaches closure on tasks ▪ Members may leave for a variety of reasons ▪ Destructive role-playing may become more prevalent

TABLE 18.4 Stages of group development

There are other stage, sequence or phase models, however, such as:
▪ Bales and Strodtbeck (1951): orientation, evaluation, control
▪ Hunt (1979): orientation, deliberation, conflict, emergence, trust, reinforcement
▪ Wheelan (1994): dependency and inclusion, counterdependence and flight, trust and structure, work, termination
▪ Jassawalla and Sashittal (2006): at-stakeness, transparency, mindfulness, synergy.
Groups don't always behave in such systematic ways, of course. For example:
▪ Many groups are 'immortal' – that is, the group lives on, even though membership may change. Some groups may never reach Tuckman's stage 5, or may be in stage 5 and not know it.
▪ Groups may in fact move back and forth between different stages.
▪ Sometimes groups self-destruct before reaching Tuckman's stages 3–5.
▪ Sometimes groups have no storming phase at all. That is, there is little or no conflict because cooperative spirit is greater than adversarial behaviour and/or rules/norms are already in place to regulate behaviour (White, McMillen & Baker 2001).

But do stages only go forward? What about groups or teams that fail, or dissolve, often in predictable stages? McGrew, Bilotta and Deeney (1999) argue for three possible extra stages or phases – de-norming, de-storming, and de-forming. De-norming occurs when drift sets in: 'changes in the team environment, in changes in project scope, size, or personnel' (McGrew, Bilotta & Deeney 1991, p. 231). The original storming phase begins with conflict, and proceeds to a gradual acceptance of new norms of co-operation. De-storming, paradoxically, means the return of the storm – the breaking down of positive norms and the re-emergence of negative norms and of conflict. De-forming begins when individuals argue over who should get credit for which unit of work or innovation. Individuals set up communication barriers between themselves, leaders and the rest of the organisation, with anger, apathy and disillusionment prevailing; leading to a dramatic drop in the team's performance. Other models of group development have been proposed which do not depend upon stages, sequences or phases, or at least not critically.

Poole and Roth (1989), for example, argue that many groups do not develop through tidy stages or phases, and in fact their actions are often characterised by disorganisation, and taking action in different ways in different situations rather than simply reacting to an external environment (see also Arrow et al. 2004).

Gersick (1989) suggested that there are long periods in task group activity where nothing much happens, and then at the halfway point, inertia is overcome. She bases this on the evolutionary theory of punctuated equilibrium, which suggests that evolution is not a smooth upward curve progressing through discrete and universal phases, but rather is a series of plateaus punctuated by steep curves.

McGrath suggests that groups have modes of activity rather than stages or phases. Modes include goal choice (inception and acceptance of project), means choice (technical solution), policy choice (conflict resolution) and goal attainment (execution of performance) (McGrath 1991; McGrath, Arrow & Berdahl 2000), although these can form a sequence.

MYTHS ABOUT TEAMWORK
Amanda Sinclair

Look at any of the popular strategies for boosting organisational performance and you will find that using teams is in there somewhere ... Better-quality teamwork is seen as crucial to organisational effectiveness. But wishful thinking has jeopardised our capacity to create it. Aggressively marketed organisational solutions have overstated the healing properties and success rates of teams. The evidence about their effectiveness is nowhere near so clear-cut. Of course, no-one wants to advertise the failures — the time and resources wasted in teams which are the vehicles for personal agendas, or where they deteriorate into exercises for avoiding accountability. Even worse are the teams that tyrannise their members and severely impair individual work capacity. They can have high fall-out costs in personal and bottom-line terms.

The most important requirement in making teams work is to abandon our illusions, to scrutinise and learn from past mistakes. Only by owning up will we be able to evaluate what teams do best and how. Only then will we have a good chance of designing and participating in teams that work. There are five common illusions about teams.

Illusion 1: teams can do anything

Lingering from the 1960s and 1970s infatuation with human relations is the illusion that teams can do anything. The reality is that teams do some things very well and some things badly. Prospective team builders need to take a cold, hard look at what they really want a team to do. If it is to cover tracks, bury an issue under interminable meetings or give an appearance of consultation, then forget it.

Teams are not magic. They must have tasks that are achievable within a specified time frame. The team charged with 'management' has an impossible brief and will surely fail unless effort is spent spelling out what the management task involves and what constitutes success.

Neither are teams a cheap option. They inevitably consume resources and time. Teams rarely resolve conflict. More often, they pressure-cook it.

If an individual has the skills to do the job with the requisite creativity, then the individual, not the team, should do the job.

Teams should be considered only where there is a widely agreed case for their use. Teams are excellent devices for sharing skills and information creatively and they can coordinate big projects if the right people are team members.

Team tasks should also be relevant to present and future interests and skills of team members. If you want people to be committed to a team then it should have a personal career pay-off and not be seen as an onerous duty.

Illusion 2: good teams are purely task-oriented

A second illusion is that good teams focus only on the task.

Teams are there to get a job done. However, their existence as a group means that they have an emotional agenda as well as a task agenda.

(continued)

(continued)

They have a life cycle and momentum which determines when and under what circumstances the group will be likely to perform best and when it is vulnerable to diversion or disruption.

The emotional agenda is as powerful, if not more so, in determining how well the group does its job.

Teams need understanding of the emotional events that help and hinder performance, such as turnover of membership or lack of leadership.

They also need to experience achievement. An open-ended existence or indeterminate task can be offset by designing opportunities for feedback, ritual events and reporting schedules which enhance, not thwart, the team's momentum.

Illusion 3: teams don't need leaders

A third illusion is that leaders are not necessary in good teams.

Leadership is back in fashion. But people in teams often argue that good teamwork makes leadership redundant. Explicit or strong leadership behaviour is seen as contrary to the notional equality of teams.

This illusion and the lack of leadership it produces is one of the worst things that can happen to a team. It ensures an obsession with internal power relations and a team without a champion. A leader is the team's link with the wider organisation and the vital conduit for resources, support and credibility. Teams need help to understand how their leadership requirements change and how to make the most of the leadership resources distributed among members.

Illusion 4: everybody belongs in a team

Another illusory belief is that everyone can find a place in a team. Team mythology has it that everyone can find a productive role and that, with enough skill building, people can play many different roles, depending upon what is required. This is to deny all the psychological evidence that many personality types do their best work alone.

As with [sporting teams], no amounts of edicts from the coaches that 'you will be a team' will convert individualists into team players.

Illusion 5: teams are accountable

A final and controversial illusion is that teams can be held accountable. There is increasing attention to business ethics and the need to establish accountability for management actions. But how do you hold a team responsible? Teams are a time-honoured device for displacing responsibility and avoiding clear accountability. Bad decisions are put down to the members of the team who fall from favour.

Alternatively, if all the team members are to be held equally responsible, do you demand that they all resign or suffer penalties? This is hardly a practical solution, but it is frequently a political one.

Teams need to be designed with explicit recognition of where responsibility for their decisions and impacts lie. Teams have a better chance of being effective if they are a well-considered and well-resourced response to specific organisational requirements.

Source: This article appeared in full in *The Weekend Australian.*

Group or team?

We now have some basic ideas about the way in which groups develop. In many modern organisations, however, groups of workers are more likely to be called teams. Are 'group' and 'team' the same thing? Not necessarily. A team is probably (and the matter is still open for debate) a special case of a group:

- A team is a collection of people who must work interdependently to achieve a common goal or output, whereas a group is a collection of people who work together, but individual members may achieve individual goals while another member may not.
- Team members may differ from group members in that they are empowered or self-managing — that is, they may have decision-making power delegated to them, and thus not need leadership in the conventional sense.

- Team members may differ from group members in that they may experience more open and honest communication, they may have a greater sense of trust, they may accept conflict as normal, and they may feel more of a sense of ownership for their jobs and unit because they are committed to goals they helped establish (Maddux 1992).

We can very easily get stuck in wordplay here. 'Teams' has a very emotional, positive ring. Yet the 'empowered teams' and 'self-managing teams' of the 1990s and 2000s are not all that different from job design innovations in the 1960s and 1970s, such as the 'semi-autonomous work groups' pioneered in Scandinavia in the sociotechnical job design experiments, and the 'quality circle' movements developed in Japan, both of which involved (or in some cases only appeared to involve) a transfer of decision-making power from managers and supervisors to work group members (Grenier 1989; Pruijt 2003).

'Team building' is a distracting term. Strictly speaking, you can build a house, but how do you build a collection of human beings? 'Group development' might be a more accurate term for a process of unifying a collection of people so that they pursue goals with effectiveness, but it certainly sounds less exciting. (Team-building exercises, such as outdoor survival and cooperation training, are commonplace in many workplaces today, and yet the success rate of such activities is still problematic (Williams, Graham & Baker 2003; Keller & Olson 2000; Robbins & Finley 2001; Schütz & Bloch 2006). As Mieszkowski (2000) observed of a particularly painful US team-building exercise:

> But it was the night wandering around the mountain that led Damon, the executive recruiter with the painfully fractured shoulder, to what he described as an epiphany about the intersection of athletic team building and business. It seemed in the darkest hour, three teams, including Keen and Spencer Stuart, gave up the competition and worked together in their exhaustion and night blindness to find their way around. It made the whole experience more bearable and, yes, more fun. 'Sometimes it's better not to compete, but to cooperate even with your competitors, because the end result is better', Damon mused.

What people may mean when they use the term 'team' is simply 'effective group'. If they wish to use exciting terms like 'teams' and 'team building', and that excitement helps to motivate people to greater levels of effectiveness, then that should be okay. Groups and teams are sometimes seen as being more motivating, productive and emotionally healthy than the more traditional ways of organising human beings, but remember this is not always the case.

Organisational teams and sporting teams: the same or very different things?

When talking about work teams, the temptation to use sporting analogies or metaphors is almost irresistible (Keidel 1985; Torres & Spiegel 1990; Liu, Srivastava & Woo 1998; Smith 2006; Blanchard, Randolph & Grazier 2007).

Most of us first encounter the word 'team' in a sporting setting, and it is only logical we should project our experience and perception of sporting teams onto work teams. While there are undoubtedly some illuminating comparisons to be drawn, we should be careful about extending the analogy or metaphor, because the dissimilarities between work teams and sporting teams tend to outweigh the similarities (table 18.5; see overleaf).

TABLE 18.5 Comparison between work and sporting teams

Similarities	Dissimilarities
■ Need for training and preparation ■ Need for coordination and communication ■ Goal setting needed for motivation and planning ■ Exhortation can produce excitement, which can lead to better performance ■ Working in unison, and synergy effects, can be very gratifying	■ Goals are clear in sports teams; not always clear or may be multiple/contradictory in work teams ■ In sport, it is unlikely that an individual can pursue goals separate from team; at work, it is possible (albeit undesirable) ■ Rules are known in sport; rules can be official and unofficial at work ■ Exhortation can wear a bit thin in work situations ■ Time frames limited in sport; sometimes open-ended, multiple at work ■ Stable information environment in sport: future is reasonably predictable; turbulent information environment at work: future is not always predictable ■ Physical effort is crucial in sport; at work, mental effort only or mainly is increasingly the case ■ Aggression is channeled in sport; at work, overt aggression is usually inappropriate ■ Sports teams are an end in themselves (entertainment); work teams are a means to an end (products, services) ■ Sports teams are collectively competitive; work teams are collaborative with other work teams ■ Sports teams are usually culturally homogenous; work teams are usually culturally heterogeneous ■ Members of sports teams are compensated differentially (superstars get super salaries); ideally, members of work teams get the same pay as everyone else

Sources: Adapted from Eunson (1987); Collier (1992); Robbins and Finley (2001).

Sports teams, work teams: the similarities

Let's talk about similarities first.

■ Work teams and sporting teams are similar in that they both share needs to train and prepare before going into action, and they also share needs to coordinate and communicate when action is underway.

■ Both types of teams can benefit from goal setting, which can not only lay a logical basis for planning, but can also be a motivator ('Why are we trying so hard? That's why we're trying so hard!').

■ A coach can use exhortation to lift the morale of a sports team with a rallying speech, psyching the players up so that they will try just that much harder. A leader or manager of a work team can, under the right circumstances, obtain similar improvements in performance with the right kind of inspirational or visionary speech or conversation or memo.

■ Finally, being within a team – sporting or working – where everyone is working together harmoniously, in unison, can be a very pleasant experience, and that experience is enhanced further when the team experiences synergy, or that state where the collective output jumps above the mere sum of the individual outputs.

Sports teams, work teams: the dissimilarities

There are, by contrast, many more dissimilarities than similarities when comparing sport teams to work teams.

- While goals are clear in sporting teams (sometimes they are literally goals), goals are not always clear in working teams, and indeed there may be multiple and contradictory goals within and between work teams.
- In sporting teams, it is quite difficult for an individual to have goals different from the team and to remain inside that team; in work teams, however, people's actions and intentions are less transparent, and it is possible for a nonconforming individual to have separate goals and yet stay inside the team. This is not always a good thing, although it sometimes can be. Organisations are rarely unitary structures where everyone pulls together, laudable as that end might be. It is more realistic to see organisations as pluralistic coalitions of forces and empires, or as a double structure comprising the formal organisation on the one hand, which communicates through official channels, and the informal organisation on the other hand, which communicates through the grapevine. The goals of these suborganisations coincide sometimes — sometimes often, but rarely always.
- 'Get out there and kill 'em — I know you can do it!' is fine in the locker room, and sometimes fine in the office or on the factory floor, but unless it is backed up with resources to do the job and rewards upon completion of the job, exhortation is not enough, and wears thin very quickly.
- In the workplace, time frames, rules and the information environment can be complex, ambiguous and unpredictable — unlike the tidy realities of the playing field.
- While the psychological game is increasingly important in sport, it is only so as a means to the end of improving physical performance. Yet the industrial revolutions of the past few centuries have meant that, in many workplaces, physical labour is irrelevant: it has been substantially replaced in many jobs by mental or intellectual labour, and it is quite difficult to know if the brain is sweating.
- Similarly, aggression is normal within sport, and is usually kept under control within ritualised channels; in the workplace, however, aggression is usually inappropriate and its crudity as a force can be disastrously counter-productive, even when focused on outsiders like competitors. As Collier (1992, p. 10) remarks:

    > Also, talk about sports teams often conjures up an image which focuses on physical strength and physical aggression. To use this image as being analogous to the business environment may result in an unspoken message that power plays and aggression are appropriate. This message could undermine the participative management style required especially for interdepartmental teams.

- Sports teams are an end in themselves — they are primarily about entertainment, and it is not always vital that they win. Work teams, in contrast, are merely a means to an end; namely, the production of products and services, and the consequences of 'losing' much or all of the time are far more serious.
- Aggression and competition are closely linked. Sports teams are collectively competitive, in that they compete with other teams in the same league or table or system. The name of the game for work teams, however, is to be collaborative, not competitive with other teams in their organisation.

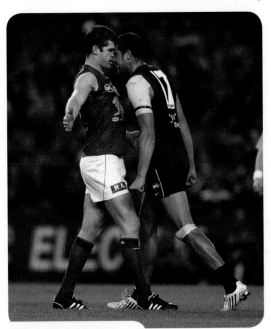

Aggression is normal in some sports, such as in AFL, boxing and rugby league, but physically aggressive behaviour is obviously inappropriate in team settings in the workplace.

- It is fairly common for sports teams to be culturally homogenous in terms of gender, age and race. Such homogeneity is seen less and less in the real world of work, where cultural and/or gender heterogeneity or diversity is more likely.
- Finally, to ensure equity and cooperation, it is probably wise to ensure that all work team members are paid the same, and in some circumstances, the pay may depend upon the collective group output. In the world of sport, by contrast, it is common for superstar players to get superstar salaries, so that there may be a wide range of pay within the sports team. This, of course, may be a source of grievance in sports teams, and in fact undermine the performance of a sports team, but it is nevertheless a reality (Robbins & Finley 2001).

Teams: strengths and weaknesses

The way in which teams make decisions and solve problems lies at the very heart of understanding effectiveness in teams. Are teams or groups effective or ineffective at making decisions and solving problems? Do 'too many cooks spoil the broth' (teams or groups are ineffective), or do 'many hands make light work' (teams and groups are effective)? Let's consider the good and the bad of teams.

Teams: the good news

There are many arguments for teams, including (and see table 18.6):
- Teams are good at generating many new ideas.
- They are also good at recalling information accurately. It would appear that the more minds there are present, the more ideas and memories can issue from them.
- Teams can deploy a multiplicity of task and socio-emotional roles that an individual would be hard-pressed to match (so long as destructive roles do not overwhelm the 'good' roles).
- Teams can make available a wide range of skills, contributions and experiences. They can present a wide range of cognitive styles, ensuring that blind spots (such as those an individual might have) do not distort perceptions. Of course, groups can have blind spots too, particularly if the group is over-homogeneous and lacking in alternative points of view.
- Teams can represent the advent of democracy in the workplace. If teams are genuinely empowered, then they can exercise the power formerly wielded by managers in autocratic organisations. This is not only ethically desirable, some would argue, but also practical – it is commonplace that team members know how to do their jobs better than most of their managers. Therefore teams can represent a benign revolution in the workplace – a utopia of power sharing, where everyone can participate in decision making – rather than a Darwinian, dog-eat-dog jungle of power-seeking managers desperate to control and subjugate workers (Kuipers & de Witte 2006).
- The exercise of authoritarian power by individuals may become much harder when groups act as a countervailing power, providing a structure of checks and balances via committees and executives. Even individuals within groups – such as dominant power figures – may change their behaviour if they cannot simply bulldoze the group.
- If all relevant decision makers are present in a group, then obviously it can be much easier to coordinate operations. Any clashes, overlaps or bottlenecks can be made transparent simply by the group sharing plans, and appropriate measures to forestall disaster can be put into place.
- Teams represent a form of organisational re-design – that is, they are increasingly seen in organisations that have been downsized, with numerous layers of middle management stripped out. In this new, flatter organisational design, there are fewer layers between the top and the bottom of the pyramid structure, which can mean faster communication and a reduction in middle management costs.

- Decisions and solutions of teams can be more creative than those produced by individuals if synergy takes place. The sheer stimulus of others' ideas can produce creativity in some team members, particularly if the team has deliberately undertaken brainstorming and lateral thinking exercises in structured creativity (see 'Meeting decision making and problem solving' in chapter 19).

- Risks can sometimes be managed more competently within teams. A high-risk decision for an individual can often be a moderate-risk decision for a team because risk is a function of knowledge, and team deliberations may increase knowledge about a particular situation.

- Motivation can be increased through participation (Ugboro 2006). No matter how high the quality of a decision, it has to be accepted by those who are going to implement that decision. If people have not been consulted or involved in the decision-making process, there is no mandate for change, and people may either implement the decision in an apathetic fashion or may actively work against it — they don't own it, they are not stakeholders in it, so why should they try for it? Team involvement means team commitment. Team input means team output — more input, more output; less input, less output.

- Teams are often criticised for being responsible for delays, when compared to individual processing of solutions and decisions. However, it is not often considered that delays might be a good thing. What if, for example, someone or some group decides that a problem could benefit from some benign neglect, or even better, suffer the death of a thousand subcommittees and attempts to get more data? This is not very honest, but such things do happen. This 'strength' of team decision making and problem solving can also be a weakness.

TABLE 18.6 The pros and cons of teams

Pros: teams can . . .	Cons: teams can . . .
- Generate many new ideas	- Impede decision making (not needed for routine decisions; individuals may generate more ideas)
- Recall information accurately	- Impede problem solving (not always good at solving problems which require long chains of decisions and solutions)
- Present multiplicity of roles (task, socio-emotional)	- Allow destructive role-playing to crowd out benign task/socio-emotional role-playing
- Present wide range of skills, contributions, experiences, and styles of decision making and problem solving	- Create pressures towards homogeneity of styles, roles, skills, experiences and contributions — can produce groupthink-type distortions
- Be ethically desirable — brings democracy to workplace	- Give people false expectations about workplace democracy (hierarchy inevitable?)
- Represent a benign revolution in the way people work together	- Be merely 'ideological hype' — inequality increases, not decreases
- Allow everyone to participate	- Crush individuality: not everyone is a team player
- Check authoritarian tyranny	- Create minority tyranny (dominant/authoritarian individual[s], cliques, factions, consensus holdouts — hidden agendas) - Create majority tyranny — enforcement of conformity may stifle creative individuals, produce faulty decisions
- Make coordination easier	- Make coordination harder if team is dominated by competition, empire-building
- Speed up communication and reduce middle management costs by flattening organisation design	- Induce 'corporate anorexia' and 'management by stress'

(continued)

TABLE 18.6 *(continued)*

Pros: teams can ...	Cons: teams can ...
■ Help induce more creative decisions and solutions — synergy	■ Help induce conservative, lowest-common-denominator decisions
■ Permit more competent risk management	■ Permit more risky behaviours (risky shift, dilution of responsibility)
■ Increase motivation through participation (quality/acceptance, mandate, input = output)	■ Decrease motivation ■ Allow group inertia to develop ■ Allow accountability to decline — free riding/social loafing
■ Bring about useful delays	■ Often be slow and costly

Teams: the bad news

There are also many arguments against teams, including:

■ Teams are not needed for routine decisions of most types: there is no need to agonise over which option to use when there is a standard operating procedure laid down and accepted by all. Also, it is by no means clear that teams are always better than individuals in generating numbers of new ideas. Some research indicates that individuals can generate more new ideas than groups or teams in certain circumstances (Ferris & Wagner 1985) and that claims of the superiority of group productivity are misguided (Nijstad, Stroebe & Lodewijkx 2006).

■ Teams are not always so good at solving problems that require long chains of decisions and solutions. Therefore groups or teams are fine at playing concertos, but not composing them; or solving crossword puzzles but not writing them; or making films, but not novels.

■ Ineffective teams allow destructive role-playing to become significant and even dominant.

■ In ineffective teams, the homogeneity of members' outlooks is so high, it might as well be an individual; and, in fact, a broad-minded individual could easily be more effective than a narrow-minded group. Group members may conform to narrow group norms and produce groupthink-type distortions in their decisions and solutions.

■ The rhetoric of 'workplace democracy' may sound good, but there may be problems with the idea. What if, for example, hierarchy and inequality are inevitable in all human affairs (Leavitt 2003)? As Jaques (1990, p. 128) observes (and see also Leavitt 2003; Overbeck, Correll & Park 2005):

> Solutions that concentrate on groups ... fail to take into account the real nature of employment systems. People are not employed in groups. They are employed individually, and their employment contracts – real or implied – are individual. Group members may insist in moments of great esprit de corps that the group as such is the author of some particular accomplishment, but once the work is completed, the members of the group look for individual recognition and individual progression in their careers. And it is not groups but individuals whom the company will hold accountable. The only true group is the board of directors, with its corporate liability.

■ Ideally, teams are the product of stable organisations, with members highly skilled and loyal to one another, but trends in the workplace (e.g. loss of job security) militate against this ideal state (Rabey 2001).

■ In teams, members are expected to be 'team players', but not everyone is a team player. It is not uncommon for supervisors or team members to criticise, or even remove, other members who do not fit into the team model. Apart from the fact that teams are not always the ideal solution to all problems and situations, this is not the best way to deal with some individuals (e.g. those who may be remarkably creative and productive rather than simply wilfully deviant) (Sinclair 1992).

- Team members' personal needs for power, influence and playing politics may overwhelm the collective good of the team (Watt, Thomas & Hochwarter 2001). In addition to the formal agenda of the team, there may be one or several hidden agendas with which individuals or subgroups may try to manipulate others.
- Cliques, factions or teams-within-the-team may dominate the team, and may choose to paralyse and perhaps destroy the group rather than see their opponents win. Minority tyranny may occur when the team seeks consensus, and those who hold out from unanimity can block with a power of leverage way beyond what their numbers would suggest. In fact, such a minority can be a minority of one – operating, of course, as an effective majority. An individual may simply dominate the team because his or her power base is so overwhelming. This power may be based on the ability to reward and punish; on expertise, personality or charisma; or because of position within the organisation. In these circumstances, the team is there to advise and consent only or, even worse, to be a mere rubber stamp for the leader's wishes (see 'Support of individual or leader' in chapter 19).
- Teams can also tyrannise using majorities, or force of numbers, producing authoritarian pressures that conventional managers would not dare apply:

  > There is often nothing inherently more 'democratic' about certain decisions because they were made by teams rather than by individual managers ... The benign 'tyranny' of peers can substitute for the benign 'tyranny' of managers, with conformity pressures as strong and sanctions for deviance as impelling. In one highly participative factory, workers complained that they felt too dependent on their teams for evaluation and job security and feared being ostracised by a clique. Members of autonomous work teams in a Cummins Engine plant were likely to be harder on absent members, according to a former plant manager, than management would have dared to be; they would often appear at the doorstep to drag a person in to work if the claimed illness did not satisfy members (of course, they relied on each other's contributions more than in a conventional work situation). Indeed, management often counts on this peer pressure to stay in line as a side benefit of participation. (Kanter 1983, p. 260; see also Sinclair 1990; Fambrough & Comerford 2006)

- Such intra-group squabbling, involving minorities or majorities, can also erode one of the potentially great strengths of teams: namely the ability to coordinate complex tasks. If the team is dominated by competition and empire building, its activities will become less coordinated than would be the case if, for example, one dominant individual with total power (and average or better-than-average competence) was running the same set of operations.
- Teams are often associated with downsized organisations, and this can lead to 'corporate anorexia' (Kanter 1983; Willams 2004; Mickhail & Ostrovsky 2005). Downsizing often does more damage than good (Roach 1996), and part of that damage is that 'survivors' tend to be reassigned to overloaded job roles (Ugboro 2006). Some critics of teams in the US car industry, for example, argued that teamwork organisation produced a 'management by stress' situation where workers were asked to assume supervisory responsibilities (without necessarily more authority or pay), by removing necessary slack from the system with 'just-in-time' inventory systems and by increasing harmful peer pressure in teams by introducing group bonus plans (Parker & Slaughter 1988).
- A mediocre or disastrous team will produce low-quality, high-risk decisions and solutions. Majority tyranny, for example, can often lead to stodginess and conservatism, with teams producing lowest-common-denominator decisions and solutions. The purity and strength of any original ideas entertained by the team become diluted by endless compromises and gestures of appeasement towards powerful vested interests outside the team.

Risky shift: a tendency of groups to make decisions that are riskier than those that would have been made by any of the group's members acting individually

- Alternatively, teams sometimes produce unstable, radical decisions. Group decision making and problem solving is sometimes characterised by the **risky shift**, whereby groups make decisions that are riskier than those that would have been made by any of the group's members acting individually. Even though this is not always a bad thing, it can be bad and indeed disastrous if members of a team feel that membership entails dilution of responsibility (what belongs to everyone belongs to no-one) and hence that normal procedures of risk evaluation are not relevant.

- Following on from such behaviour is the phenomenon of team inertia, wherein team members come to rely on others to think and act for them. In such cases, an individual leader or an elite may emerge as the real force within the team, with the rest of the team acting merely a rubber stamp, and thus being effectively redundant.

- Accountability is a major problem with teams as well. How do you hold a team responsible? Sinclair (1990) suggests that teams displace responsibility, and that it is not often practical to penalise all team members equally when things go wrong. With a reduction in accountability sometimes comes an increase in social loafing or free riding behaviour among team members.

- Teams can be slow and costly. Slowness is often related to team size: if team size increases arithmetically (1, 2, 3, 4), then interactions between team members increase geometrically (1, 2, 4, 16), and for everyone to talk to everyone else in a large team is time-consuming and cash-consuming. (Avoidance or delay of action may, of course, be a deliberate strategy.)

- What if much work is simply boring, and not amenable to team restructuring? (Baldrey & Hallier 2010). What if teams are just a dream? What if people perceive 'team building' as an invasive and presumptuous attempt to create a synthetic family atmosphere where there is none? Leheney (2008) notes that many workers relate strongly to dysfunctional workplaces as depicted in the Dilbert comic strip and *The Office* television shows (UK and US versions), while Krueger and Kilham (2006) note that one quarter of the US workforce is so disengaged and disgruntled that they would actively undermine the work of other team members.

Many employees relate strongly to the dysfunctional workplace depicted in the television show *The Office*. In the US version of the show, actor Steve Carell played a fictitious boss who was notorious for undermining his employees. Research suggests many employees would undermine the work of others in a team.

- What if all the talk of teams is just 'ideological hype' (Parker & Slaughter 1988)? That is, what if the more things change in the world of teams, the more things stay the same? Inequality within an organisation might increase, not decrease, with teams. Teams are empowered to a certain extent (but not necessarily financially rewarded) while upper management may be even more empowered – and richly rewarded financially (Sennett 1998; Pruijt 2003). Teams need to be based on equality and trust, but inequality may be built into organisations. Perhaps we cannot escape hierarchies? (See Leavitt [2003] and Jacques [2002] in online chapter 9.)

Symbolism of equality is important here. According to Denton (1991), it is not to be taken lightly:

> Workplace equity and work-force trust are enhanced when perks and status symbols and, most important, true power distributions between organizational levels are reduced. Perks reward – they also distract and punish. Oriental rugs, private parking, corner offices, mahogany desks, even office sizes based on rank are destructive because they focus everyone's efforts on securing the trappings of status rather than teamwork.

George (1987) agrees, saying:

> Several obvious signs of hierarchical inequality also doom any team-building effort. Reserved parking spaces, privileged office locations and many other signs of status may reinforce the efforts of the few, but they undermine the morale of the many who are denied. Most companies that work at day-to-day team-building downplay or eliminate such unpopular signals that say that some are more equal than others.

Even more potent than symbolism is cash, salary, pay — call it what you will. Various writers have deplored the cult of the chief executive officer (CEO), leading to a situation between 1982 and 2002 in which the average US chief executive officer's pay went from 42 to 400 times that of the average US production worker. At the same time, some executives were actually paid bonuses despite performing badly.

This trend of inequality exploded in the period following the global financial crisis, when governments around the world subsidised the stability of financial institutions with massive influxes of taxpayers' money, only to see some of those who had been rescued rewarding themselves with very high bonuses within months. As US President Obama remarked, 'The American people understand that we've got a big hole that we've got to dig ourselves out of, but they don't like the idea that people are digging a bigger hole even as they're asked to fill it up' (Goldman & Runningen 2009). Such displays of inequality make team building so much harder, if not impossible, to implement.

Virtual teams

Teams or groups have traditionally operated on a face-to-face basis, but increasingly teams are virtual — that is, team members may be dispersed geographically and will thus need to communicate via technology.

Virtual team communication can present specific challenges, such as:

- How comfortable are team members communicating in a mediated or technology-dependent way (see Van der Klein, Schraagen & Werkhoven 2009)? Johnson, Betting-hausen and Gibbons (2009) found that team effectiveness declined when teams used virtual channels 90 per cent or more of the time.
- Are there specific problems relating to different cultures and different time zones? (Timmerman & Scott 2006; Gareis 2006)
- Does the possibility of communication breakdown motivate virtual workers to over-communicate, sending messages through more than one channel, and thus in turn exacerbating message overload? (Bélanger & Watson-Manheim 2006)
- Is the team self-managed, or will some type of leadership be necessary? (Carte, Chidambaram & Becker 2006)
- Does virtuality enrich or impoverish human communication and social interaction?

Virtuality, of course, can be a matter of degree — there may be multiple types of virtual communication (Timmerman & Scott 2006). Much communication within the one physical workplace, for example, may take place via technology such as email and voicemail.

Also, even though it may appear to be expensive in terms of travel and accommodation costs, it might be cheaper in the long run for virtual team members to meet face to face physically at least once to establish communication norms. In a study of virtual teams in a multinational organisation, researchers (Lee-Kelley, Crossman & Cannings 2004, p. 654) noted that:

> The longer but less frequent face-to-face meetings were considered important by the virtual teams when dealing with both relationship and task issues. The longer co-presence allowed the negotiation and acceptance of the team's perceived goals and outcomes. In addition, the ability

Virtual team: a work group whose individual members are located in widely dispersed locations

to make eye contact and to use verbal and paraverbal cues helps context setting and role or status definitions, thus enabling the team to settle down very quickly and to move on to the performing stage.

In fact, it may make sense for a virtual team's members to meet face to face at least three times during the duration of its existence:

1. At commencement: to create buy-in; establish social relationships; build trust and commitment – more than a one-hour meeting.
2. At the intermediate stage: to deal with persistent misunderstanding – usually a full workshop event, not a brief meeting.
3. At winding-up: to tie up unresolved items; generate commitment to output; recognition by celebrating success (Lee-Kelley, Crossman & Cannings 2004, p. 656).

Yauch (2007) argues that if manufacturing organisations are to cope with turbulent environments, or environments characterised by constant and unpredictable change, then they need to use teams more often in order to become 'agile' or adaptive. Such teams, he argues, need to have the attributes of being multifunctional (team members have multiple skills), dynamic (teams will be temporary, project-based structures), cooperative (teams will need to manage conflict effectively) and virtual. We need, however, to understand the negative as well as positive aspects of these attributes to ensure that such teams can operate successfully and harmoniously (summarised in table 18.7).

TABLE 18.7 Positive and negative impacts associated with agile teams

Team attribute	Multifunctional	Dynamic	Cooperative	Virtual
Positive impacts	■ Learn new things; develop new skills ■ Greater task identity; broader perspective ■ Greater autonomy ■ Better feedback ■ Decreased repetitive motions	■ Learn new things; develop new skills ■ Greater task identity; broader perspective ■ Greater autonomy ■ Better feedback ■ Increased organisational commitment	■ Learn new things; develop new skills ■ Avoid creating winners and losers ■ Supportive work environment (positive interpersonal relationships) ■ Promotes higher individual achievement	■ Learn new things; develop new skills ■ Less wasted time (increased meaningfulness) ■ Reduced uncertainty and confusion
Negative impacts	■ Potential for underload or overload ■ Excessive responsibility ■ Increased fear of failure ■ Increased pressure ■ Need to police others ■ Social loafing ■ More difficulty solving problems	■ Excessive conflict ■ Insufficient time to establish group norms ■ Continually changing group dynamics ■ Boundary management more difficult	■ Groupthink ■ Loss of flexibility ■ Loss of creativity	■ Loss of richness of interaction ■ Loss of social contact ■ New skill demands (IT) ■ Difficulty in achieving cooperation ■ Higher dependence on technology

Source: Yauch (2007, p. 24).

Communicating with others in the group/team

We have seen in this chapter that there are many advantages to working with others in groups or teams, and when things go well there, work can be a pleasant experience. We have also seen that there are many disadvantages to working in groups or teams, and when such disadvantages inflict real outcomes, then working in groups or teams can be an unpleasant experience.

Nevertheless, much of life consists of living and working with others, so it makes sense to take what we have learnt in this chapter (and other chapters) and apply it to ensure that the pleasant experiences outweigh the unpleasant ones. Here are some suggestions for doing just that:

- Become aware of the reasons why people join and leave groups (security, task complexity, social interaction, proximity and exchange). Enjoy the company of others, but be ready to assertively challenge unacceptable situations. For example, might you be staying unnecessarily with a group because your membership is based largely on proximity, coincidence, inertia and complacency?
- Be aware of the preconditions for social loafing, and strive to change things to reverse those preconditions.
- Strive for an ideal balance of task and socio-emotional role-playing behaviours in your groups and teams. Expect such a balance from others, but set an example yourself. Pay attention to not only the verbal behaviour of others but also the nonverbal behaviour.
- Act and speak to reinforce healthy formal and informal norms, and challenge unhealthy ones.
- Be on the alert for groupthink effects in groups and teams, and assertively speak out against such causes of bad decisions.
- Be aware of the stages of group/team development, and work actively to move your group/team to the performing stage.
- Be aware of the strengths and weaknesses of teams, and be ready to speak out when weaknesses surface. For example, if you feel that some viewpoints or values are not being properly considered, and someone tries to silence you by accusing you of 'not being a team player', be ready to rebut the charge and explain why.
- When communicating with team members via technology rather than face to face, be aware of the pitfalls as well as the advantages of virtual team communication.
- Learn and practise communication skills such as assertiveness, feedback, questioning, listening and reframing (see chapters 9 and 10).
- Learn and practise the verbal skills of speaking (see chapter 11).
- Learn and practise negotiation and conflict resolution skills (see chapters 13 and 14).
- Learn and practise leadership skills.
- Learn and practise meeting and group skills such as brainstorming and nominal group technique (see chapter 19).
- Learn and practise sensitivity to intercultural and gender communication styles (see chapter 15 and online chapter 7 'Gender and communication').
- Learn and practise logical, persuasive and influential skills (see chapter 12)
- If you are serious about teams working, remember they are based on trust, flatter organisations, and the perception (and reality) of not too much inequality, especially in pay and nonverbal symbolism of power and wealth (see chapter 16).

STUDENT STUDY GUIDE

SUMMARY

In this chapter, we have explored the differences between groups, social aggregates and teams. We saw that there are (at least) five reasons why people join, stay in or leave groups (security, task complexity, social interaction, proximity and exchange).

We have looked at the concepts of synergy and social loafing and examined task roles (Brainstormer, Expert, Judge, Devil's advocate, Representative, Implementer, Ringmaster and Memory), socio-emotional roles (Encourager, Peacemaker, Tension reliever and Confronter) and destructive roles (Husher, Personaliser, Recognition seeker, Victim, Blocker, Shelver, Distractor, Aggressor, Shadow and Special-interest pleader).

We have examined formal and informal norms in groups, and noted destructive norms such as groupthink and the Abilene paradox. We have considered stage and nonstage models of group development (including Tuckman's Forming, Storming, Norming, Performing and Adjourning model). We have considered myths surrounding teamwork, and have examined the similarities and dissimilarities of work teams and sporting teams.

We have considered the strengths of teams: they can generate many new ideas and recall information accurately; can deploy a multiplicity of task and socio-emotional roles; can make available a wide range of skills, contributions and experiences; can represent the advent of democracy in the workplace; can restrain exercise of authoritarian power by individuals; can help coordinate operations; can help speed up communication and help lower middle management costs; can provide synergy in group decisions and solutions; can help manage risk; can motivate through participation; and can help create useful delays in decision making.

We have also considered the weaknesses of teams: they are not needed for routine decisions; not necessarily more creative than individuals; not so good at solving problems that require long chains of decisions and solutions; they can act as an arena for destructive role-playing; can lead to over-conformity; can be ineffective if human inequality is inevitable; can be just 'ideological hype'; can be bad for individuals who are not team players; can allow manipulative members to prevail; can facilitate minority tyranny; can restrict coordination of work flow; can be part of 'corporate anorexia'; can dilute idea generation; can facilitate high-risk decision making; can cause team inertia; can present accountability problems; can be slow and costly; may not be wanted by workers; and may be undermined by gross inequalities in pay and rewards.

We have considered virtual teams as part of virtual organisations. We have considered under what circumstances it might be better to attempt a task individually rather than as part of a team. Finally, we considered what communication skills would help team members become more effective.

KEY TERMS

Abilene paradox *p. 596*

destructive role *p. 586*

exchange *p. 583*

formal norm *p. 592*

group *p. 582*

groupthink *p. 594*

informal norm *p. 592*

proximity *p. 583*

risky shift *p. 610*

role *p. 586*

security *p. 583*

social aggregate *p. 582*

social interaction *p. 583*

social loafing *p. 585*

socio-emotional role *p. 586*

synergy *p. 584*

task complexity *p. 583*

task role *p. 586*

virtual team *p. 611*

REVIEW QUESTIONS

1. What differences are there between groups and social aggregates?
2. List at least three reasons why people join, stay in or leave groups.
3. List three factors that may predispose group members to engage in social loafing.
4. List four possible approaches to preventing groupthink.
5. List at least three differences between groupthink and the Abilene paradox.
6. What are Tuckman's five phases of team development, and why is this sequence not always followed in all teams/groups?
7. Identify five advantages of teams.
8. Identify five disadvantages of teams.
9. Identify three problems associated with virtual teams.
10. Identify four different types of communication skills that we may need to deploy in group/team settings.

APPLIED ACTIVITIES

1. Consider the five-factor model for group membership (security, task complexity, social interaction, proximity and exchange). Using figure 18.3 as a model, create pie charts for at least two groups of which you are a member, showing your motivational patterns as a member.
2. Create a list of strategies and points that might be useful in controlling destructive role-players.
3. How might task and socio-emotional roles take on destructive qualities?
4. How might formal and informal norms take on destructive qualities?
5. Discuss groupthink and/or the Abilene paradox with others. Has anyone experienced one or both? What value might the approaches to them suggested in this chapter have had in those actual situations?
6. Think of another three advantages and another three disadvantages of teams.
7. Someone accuses you of 'not being a team player', which you feel is inappropriate and wrong. Devise at least one response to the charge.
8. What is the relationship of leadership to team dynamics?
9. Read chapter 19. What is the relationship between meeting procedures and group problem-solving techniques on the one hand and team dynamics on the other?

WHAT WOULD YOU DO?

By Monday noon Julia Stoner was feeling stressed. Even though she had hoped to direct the conversation in a meeting, she watched most of the other managers conversing with some alarm. She had wanted to generate enthusiasm, but she had not anticipated the discussion would go in this direction.

As the newly appointed human resources manager of Western Technologies Corporation (WTC), she had just completed a presentation to the Monday morning heads of department meeting on the subject of boosting productivity by changing group norms on the shop floor and in the accounts department.

The start of the presentation had been delayed while a loud and humorous discussion about Saturday's football match had taken place. The managing director, Mike Johannson, was an ex-player in the main league, and he often invited a small group of other executives over to his house to watch the match on his big LCD screen, and then brought DVDs of the same matches along, playing them before the start of the meeting, while people were drinking their first coffee of the day.

Football bored Julia, and she knew it bored at least two of the other managers present, but they certainly revealed a detailed knowledge in this morning's banter. Most of the managers were concerned with the production of WTC's main products: microprocessor-controlled gauges and monitoring equipment. Industrial relations between management and workers had not been good for quite some time. Indeed, a number of the managers referred to parts of the shop floor as 'sheltered workshops', and the standing joke aimed at Julia was that she was the 'inhuman' resources manager.

When Julia started talking, she was aware that not everyone was concentrating. There were winks and raised eyebrows from some of her male colleagues. How childish, she thought. But after about five minutes, she noticed that Mike was looking less bored, and was beginning to take notes. Others began to do likewise.

Julia proposed that productivity levels could be raised by at least 15 per cent if she could get the go-ahead to start a team-building program, linked in with group bonuses of 1 per cent per 1.5 per cent productivity rise. Her brief, potted history of research in the area (not too much jargon, she hoped) gave evidence that it could be done.

'So we could lift our market share and/or lower prices, as well as motivate staff more. It's a win–win situation', she concluded, and sat down.

Silence. There was some uncomfortable shifting in seats, and numerous unhappy faces. Max Rinter, the marketing manager, was the first to speak, and stood up to get the attention of the team. 'That's good stuff, Julia, but ... I don't know about lowering prices. Our major client is the government, and they might start asking some embarrassing questions

about why we couldn't have done this years ago. We could end up with egg on our faces.' Heads nodded around the table.

'What about increasing our output, Max?' asked Claire.

'That could be tricky, too', said Max. 'The quota is pre-set, and if we try to move more, they might think we're being pushy. Inventory costs will go up if we try to stockpile in this part of the seasonal cycle.'

Jack Tuttle, the production manager, jumped in. 'That motivation stuff is interesting, Julia, but I'd need to re-jig the machines to get them working in groups. But I can see a lot of sense putting people onto piece rates to boost production.'

'What about the surplus goods, Jack?' Max said sarcastically.

'Surplus goods or surplus people?' responded Jack. 'If Julia's figures are correct, then according to the calculations I've just done, we could stay at our current level of output and get rid of 23 or 24 staff. That's about $700 000 in salaries and costs saved. Not bad, eh?'

'But ... ', said Julia.

'Not bad at all', said Claire, cutting her off. 'I don't think we'll get any flak from the union. They've been pretty gutless in my last few run-ins with them. We'll sell it as a downsizing exercise – everybody's doing it – the lean, mean organisation, doing more with less; that kind of thing.'

'That's right! They'd just go to water if we present this as a fait accompli. And the shareholders should be pretty happy at the cost saving', said Max. 'Jack, how could we re-do the layout if we had that number fewer staff?'

'Well, let's see', said Jack, taking some plans from the shelf behind him and spreading them on the table. 'Now, these lads here – the volleyball crowd that's always late back from lunch – they could go, and their machines could be shifted to ...'

As the conversation became more animated, Julia slumped in her chair, and wondered how things had got this far out of control.

What dynamics are at work in this group? What should Julia do?

SUGGESTED READING

Behfar, Kristin, Kern, Mary & Brett, Jeanne 2006, 'Managing challenges in multicultural teams', *Research on Managing Groups and Teams*, vol. 9, pp. 233–62.

Butterfield, Jeff 2010, *Teamwork and team-building: soft skills for a digital workplace*, Cengage, Florence, KY.

Chism, Marlene 2011, *Stop workplace drama: train your team to have no complaints, no excuses, and no regrets*. John Wiley & Sons, New York.

Diamond, Linda 2008, *Perfect phrases for building strong teams: hundreds of ready-to-use phrases for fostering collaboration, encouraging communication, and growing a winning team*, McGraw-Hill, New York.

DuFrene, Debbie & Lehman, Carol M 2010, *Building high-performance teams*, 4th edn, South-Western Cengage Learning, Boston, MA.

Erdem, F 2003, 'Optimal trust and teamwork: from groupthink to teamthink', *Work Study*, vol. 52, no. 5, pp. 229–33.

Eunson, Baden 1994, *Communicating for team building*, John Wiley & Sons, Brisbane.

Fraser, Kym 2010, 'Effective teamworking: can functional flexibility act as an enhancing factor? An Australian case study', *Team Performance Management*, vol. 16, no. 1, pp. 74–94.

Graham, Charles R 2003, 'A model of norm development for computer-mediated teamwork', *Small Group Research*, vol. 34, no. 3, pp. 322–52.

Hilton, H 2011, *Expanding your home business and inspiring others to work: team development for your business and life*, Kindle edn, Amazon Digital Services, Seattle, WA.

Islam, Gazi & Zyphur, Michael J 2005, 'Power, voice and hierarchy: exploring the antecedents of speaking up in groups', *Group Dynamics: Theory, Research and Practice*, vol. 9, no. 2, pp. 93–103.

Nicopoulou, Katerina, Koùs-tomaj, Mitja & Campos, Andre 2006, 'How to address group dynamics in virtual worlds', *AI & Society*, vol. 20, pp. 351–71.

Schafer, Mark & Crichlow, Scott 2010, *Groupthink versus high-quality decision-making in international relations*, Columbia University Press, New York.

Sesil, James C 2006, 'Sharing decision-making and group incentives: the impact on performance', *Economic and Industrial Democracy*, vol. 27, no. 4, pp. 587–607.

Zhong, Chen-Bo, Magee, Joe C, Maddux, William W & Galinsky, Adam D 2006, 'Power, culture and action: considerations in the expression and enactment of power in East Asian and Western societies', *Research on Managing Groups and Teams*, vol. 9, pp. 53–73.

REFERENCES

Aggarwal, Praveen 2009, 'Social loafing on group projects: structural antecedents and effects on student satisfaction', *Journal of Marketing Education*, vol 30, no. 3, pp. 255–64.

Akan, Obasi Haki 2005, 'The role of concrescent conversation in the performing stage of work groups', *Team Performance Management*, vol. 11, nos 1/2, pp. 51–62.

Akrivou, Kleio & Boyatzis, Richard E 2006, 'The evolving group: towards a prescriptive theory of intentional group development', *Journal of Management Development*, vol. 25, no. 7, pp. 689–706.

Arrow, Holly, Poole, Marshall Scott, Henry, Kelly Bouas, Wheelan, Susan & Moreland, Richard 2004, 'Time, change and development: the temporal perspective on groups', *Small Group Research*, vol. 35, no. 1, pp. 73–105.

Baldry, Chris & Hallier, Jerry 2010, 'Welcome to the house of fun: work space and social identity', *Economic and Industrial Democracy*, vol. 31, no.1, pp. 150–72.

Bales, RF & Strodtbeck, FL 1951, 'Phases in group problem solving', *Journal of Abnormal and Social Psychology*, vol. 46, pp. 485–95.

Bélanger, France & Watson-Manheim, Mary Beth 2006, 'Virtual teams and multiple media: structuring media use to attain strategic goals', *Group Decision and Negotiation*, vol. 15, pp. 299–321.

Belbin, Meredith 2010, *Management teams: Why they succeed or fail*, 3rd edn, Butterworth-Heinemann, London.

Birchmeier, Zachary, Joinson, Adam N & Dietz-Uhler, Beth 2005, 'Storming and forming a normative response to a deception revealed online', *Social Science Computer Review*, vol. 23, no. 1, pp. 108–21.

Blanchard, Kenneth, Randolph, Alan & Grazier, Peter 2007, *Go team! Take your team to the next level*, Berrett-Koehler, San Francisco.

Brandyberry, Alan A & Bakke, Sharen A 2006, 'Mitigating negative behaviors in student project teams: an information technology solution', *Journal of Information Systems Education*, vol. 17, no. 2, pp. 195–209.

Carte, Traci A, Chidambaram, Laku & Becker, Aaron 2006, 'Emergent leadership in self-managed virtual teams', *Group Decision and Negotiation*, vol. 15, pp. 323–43.

Chang, Artemis, Duck, Julie & Bordia, Prashant 2006, 'Understanding the multidimensionality of group development', *Small Group Research*, vol. 37, no. 4, pp. 327–50.

Chapman, Judith 2006, 'Anxiety and defective decision-making: an elaboration of the groupthink model', *Management Decision*, vol. 44, no. 10, pp. 1391–1404.

Coch, L & French, J 1948, 'Overcoming resistance to change', *Human Relations*, vol. 2, no. 4, pp. 512–32.

Collier, Marilyn R 1992, 'Team building may not be appropriate for groups', *OD Practitioner*, June, pp. 6–10.

De Bono, Edward 2009, *Six thinking hats: an essential approach to business management*, Penguin, London.

Degnin, Francis Dominic 2009, 'Difficult patients, overmedication, and groupthink', *Journal of Clinical Ethics*, vol. 20. no. 1, pp. 66–74.

Denton, D Keith 1991, *Horizontal management: beyond total customer satisfaction*, Lexington Books, New York.

Dydejcsyk, Antoni, Kułakowski, Krzysztof & Ryback, Marcin 2009, 'The norm game – how a norm fails', *Lecture Notes in Computer Science*, vol. 5545, pp. 835–44.

Eunson, Baden 1987, *Behaving: managing yourself and others*, McGraw-Hill, Sydney.

Fall, Kevin A & Wejnert, Tamara J 2005, 'Co-leader stages of development: an application of Tuckman and Jensen', *The Journal for Specialists in Group Work*, vol. 30, no. 4, pp. 309–27.

Fambrough, Mary J & Comerford, Susan A 2006, 'The changing epistemological assumptions of group theory', *The Journal of Applied Behavioral Science*, vol. 42, no. 3, pp. 330–49.

Ferris, Gerald F & Wagner, John A 1985, 'Quality circles in the United States: a conceptual re-evaluation', *Journal of Applied Behavioral Science*, vol. 21, no. 2, pp. 155–64.

Fitzsimmons, Dan 2008, 'Coherence in crisis: groupthink, the news media and the Iraq War', *Journal of Military and Strategic Studies*, vol. 10, no. 4, pp. 1–52.

Flynn, Francis J & Chatman, Jennifer A 2003, '"What's the norm here?" Social categorization as a basis for group norm development', *Research on Managing Groups and Teams*, vol. 5, pp. 135–60.

Gareis, Elisabeth 2006, 'Virtual teams: a comparison of online communication channels', *The Journal of Language for International Business*, vol. 17, no. 2, pp. 6–22.

George, Paul S 1987, 'Team building without tears', *Personnel Journal*, vol. 66, no. 11, pp. 122–9.

Gersick, CJ 1989, 'Marking time: predictable transitions in task groups', *Academy of Management Journal*, vol. 32, pp. 274–309.

Goldman, Julianna & Runningen, Roger 2009, 'Obama calls Wall Street bonuses in crisis "shameful"', *Bloomberg.com*, www.bloomberg.com.

Goren, Harel, Kurzban, Robert & Rapoport, Amnon 2003, 'Social loafing vs. social enhancement: public goods provisioning in real-time with irrevocable commitments', *Organizational Behavior and Human Decision Processes*, vol. 90, no. 2, pp. 277–90.

Grasha, Anthony 1997, *Practical applications of psychology*, 4th edn, Prentice Hall, Englewood Cliffs, NJ.

Grenier, Guilermo J 1989, *Inhuman relations: quality circles and anti-unionism in American industry*, Temple University Press, Philadelphia, PA.

Halbesleben, Jonathan RB, Wheeler, Anthony R & Buckley, M Ronald 2007, 'Understanding pluralistic ignorance in organizations: application and theory', *Journal of Managerial Psychology*, vol. 22, no. 1, pp. 65–83.

Harvey, Jerry B 1988, 'The Abilene paradox: the management of agreement', *Organizational Dynamics*, vol. 3, no. 1, pp. 63–80.

—— 1996, *The Abilene paradox and other meditations on management*, Jossey-Bass, San Francisco.

Harvey, Michal, Novicevic, Milorad M, Buckley, M Ronald & Halbersleben, Jonathan RB 2004, 'The Abilene Paradox after 30 years: a global perspective', *Organizational Dynamics*, vol. 33, no. 2, pp. 215–26.

Haslam, S Alexander, Ryan, Michelle K, Postmes, Tom, Spears, Russell, Jetten, Jolanda & Webley, Paul 2006, 'Sticking to our guns: social identity as a basis for the maintenance of commitment to faltering organizational projects', *Journal of Organizational Behavior*, vol. 27, no. 5, pp. 607–28.

Hede, Andrew 2007, 'The shadow group: towards an explanation of interpersonal conflict in work groups', *Journal of Managerial Psychology*, vol. 22, no. 1, pp. 25–39.

Henningsen, David Dryden, Henningsen, Mary Lynn Miller & Eden, Jennifer 2006, 'Examining the symptoms of groupthink and retrospective sensemaking', *Small Group Research*, vol. 37, no. 1, pp. 36–64.

Hepner, Harry Walker 1979, *Psychology applied to life and work*, 6th edn, Prentice Hall, Englewood Cliffs, NJ.

Hodgetts, Richard M & Hegar, Kathryn W 2007, *Modern human relations at work*, 10th edn, Thomson/South-Western, Mason, OH.

Hogg, Michael A & Reid, Scott A 2006, 'Social identity, self-categorization, and the communication of group norms', *Communication Theory*, vol. 16, pp. 7–30.

Høiagaard, Rune, Säfvenbom, Reidar & Tønnesen, Finn Egil 2006, 'The relationship between group cohesion, group norms, and perceived social loafing in soccer teams', *Small Group Research*, vol. 37, no. 3, pp. 217–32.

Hunt, John 1979, *Managing people at work: a manager's guide to behaviour in organizations*, Pan, London.

Janis, Irving 1982, *Groupthink: psychological studies of policy decisions and fiascoes*, 2nd edn, Houghton Mifflin, Boston.

—— 1989, *Crucial decisions: leadership in policymaking and crisis management*, Free Press, New York.

Jaques, Elliott 1990, 'In praise of hierarchy', *Harvard Business Review*, January–February, vol. 68, no. 1, pp. 127–33.

Jassawalla, Avan R & Sashittal, Hemant C 2006, 'Collaborating in cross-functional product innovation teams', *Advances in Interdisciplinary Studies of Work Teams*, vol. 12, pp. 1–25.

Johnson, Stefanie K, Bettenhausen, Kenneth & Gibbons, Ellie 2009 'Realities of working in virtual teams: affective and attitudinal outcomes of using computer-mediated communication', *Small Group Research*, vol. 40, no. 6, pp. 623–49.

Kanter, Rosabeth Moss 1983, *The change masters: innovation for productivity in the American corporation*, Simon & Schuster, New York.

Keidel, Robert 1985, *Game plans: sports strategies for business*, E.P. Dutton, New York.

Keller, Tiffany & Olson, William 2000, 'The advisability of outdoor leadership training: caveat emptor', *Review of Business*, vol. 21, nos 1–2, pp. 4–8.

Kelly, John E 1981, *Scientific management, job redesign and work performance*, Academic Press, New York.

Kemper, Vicki 2004, 'Groupthink viewed as culprit in move to war', *Los Angeles Times*, 10 July, p. 1.

Kim, Yoonho 2001, 'A comparative study of the "Abilene paradox" and "groupthink"', *Public Administration Quarterly*, vol. 25, no. 2, pp. 168–91.

Ko, Andrew Sai On 2005, 'Organizational communications in Hong Kong: a cultural approach to groupthink', *Corporate Communications*, vol. 10, no. 4, pp. 351–7.

Koerber, Charles P & Neck, Christopher P 2003, 'Groupthink and sports: an application of Whyte's model', *International Journal of Contemporary Hospitality Management*, vol. 15, no. 1, pp. 20–8.

Kowert, Paul A 2002, 'Groupthink or deadlock: when do leaders learn from their advisors?', State University of New York Press, New York.

Kuipers, Ben S & de Witte, Marco C 2006, 'The control structure of team-based organizations: a diagnostic model of empowerment', *Economic and Industrial Democracy*, vol. 25, no. 4, pp. 621–43.

Krueger, Jerry & Kilham, Emily 2006 'Why Dilbert is right – uncomfortable work environments make for disgruntled employees – just like the cartoon says', *Gallup Management Journal*, 9 March, http://gmj.gallup.com.

Leavitt, Harold J 2003, 'Why hierarchies thrive', *Harvard Business Review*, vol. 81, no. 3, pp. 96–102.

Lee-Kelley, Liz, Crossman, Alf & Cannings, Ann 2004, 'A social interaction approach to managing the "invisibles" of virtual teams', *Industrial Management & Data Systems*, vol. 104, no. 8, pp. 650–7.

Leheny, Mark 2008, *The five commitments of a leader*, Management Concepts, Vienna, VA.

Likert, Rensis 1967, *The human organization: its management and value*, McGraw-Hill, New York.

Lim, Vivien G 2002, 'The IT way of loafing on the job: cyberloafing, neutralizing and organizational justice', *Journal of Organizational Behavior*, vol. 23, pp. 675–94.

Liu, Jonathan, Srivastava, Ashok & Woo, Hong Sengg 1998, 'Transference of skills between sports and business', *Journal of European Industrial Training*, vol. 22, no. 3, pp. 93–112.

McAvoy, John & Butler, Tom 2009, 'Project post-mortems: mindless mismanagement of agreement', *Journal of Decision Systems*, vol. 18, pp. 53–73.

McGrath, JE 1991, 'Time, interaction and performance (TIP): a theory of groups', *Small Group Research*, vol. 22, pp. 147–74.

McGrath, Joseph E, Arrow, Holly & Berdahl, Jennifer L 2000, 'The study of groups: past, present and future', *Personality and Social Psychology Review*, vol. 4, no. 1, pp. 95–105.

McGrew, John F, Bilotta, John G & Deeney, Janet M 1999, 'Software team formation and decay: extending the standard model for small groups', *Small Group Research*, vol. 30, no.2, pp. 209–34.

Mackenzie, Deborah L 2010, *Hope, groupthink and the decision to invade Iraq: group hope and risky decision-making*, Lambert Academic Publishing, Saarbrücken, Germany.

McManus, Kevin 2006, 'Have you been to Abilene?', *Industrial Engineer*, vol. 38, no. 8, p. 20.

Maddux, Robert B 1992, *Team building: an exercise in leadership*, rev. edn, Crisp Publications, Los Altos, CA.

Mannix, Elizabeth & Jehn, Karen A 2004, 'Let's norm and storm, but not right now: integrating models of team performance', *Research on Managing Groups and Teams*, vol. 6, pp. 11–37.

Manz, Charles C & Neck, Christopher P 1997, 'Teamthink: beyond the groupthink syndrome in self-managing teams', *Team Performance Management*, vol. 3, no. 1, pp. 18–28.

Mickhail, George & Ostrovsky, Arsen 2005, 'The metacapitalism quest', *Journal of the American Academy of Business*, vol. 6, no. 1, pp. 290–8.

Mieszkowski, Katharine 2000, 'Corporate bonding unto death', *Salon*, 26 October, www.salon.com.

Miller, Diane L 2003, 'The stages of group development: a retrospective study of dynamic team processes', *Canadian Journal of Administrative Science*, vol. 20, no. 3, pp. 121–35.

Minssen, Heiner 2005, 'Challenges of teamwork in production: demands of communication', *Organization Studies*, vol. 27, no. 1, pp. 103–24.

Moorhead, Gregory, Ference, Richard J & Neck, Chris P 1991, 'Group decision fiascoes continue: space shuttle Challenger and a revised groupthink framework', *Human Relations*, vol. 44, no. 6, pp. 539–52.

Moorhead, Gregory, Neck, Christopher P & West, Mindy S 1998, 'The tendency towards defective decision making within self-managing teams: the relevance of groupthink for the 21st century', *Organizational Behavior and Human Decision Processes*, vol. 73, nos 2–3, pp. 327–51.

Newcomb, TM 1950, *Social psychology*, Dryden, New York.

Nijstad, Bernard A, Stroebe, Wolfgang & Lodewijkx, Hein FM 2006, 'The illusion of group productivity: a reduction of failures explanation', *European Journal of Social Psychology*, vol. 36, pp. 31–48.

Overbeck, Jennifer R, Correll, Joshua & Park, Bernadette 2005, 'Internal status sorting in groups: the problem of too many stars', *Research on Managing Groups and Teams*, vol. 7, pp. 169–99.

Parker, Mike & Slaughter, Jane 1988, *Choosing sides: unions and the team concept*, South End Press, Boston.

Poole, Marshall Scott & Roth, Jonelle 1989, 'Decision development in small groups V: test of a contingency model', *Human Communication Research*, vol. 15, no. 4, pp. 549–89.

Post, Jerrold M & Panis, Lara K 2011, 'Crimes of obedience: "groupthink" at Abu Ghraib', *International Journal of Group Psychotherapy*, vol. 61, no. 1, pp. 48–66.

Pruijt, Hans 2003, 'Teams between neo-Taylorism and anti-Taylorism', *Economic and Industrial Democracy*, vol. 24, no. 1, pp. 77–102.

Rabey, Gordon 2001, 'Is the team building industry nearing the apex of its S curve?', *Team Performance Management*, vol. 7, nos 7–8, pp. 112–18.

Raven, Bertram H & Rubin, Jeffrey Z 1983, *Social psychology: people in groups*, John Wiley & Sons, New York.

Roach, Stephen S 1996, 'The hollow ring of the productivity revival', *Harvard Business Review*, vol. 74, no. 6, pp. 81–90.

Roberto, Michael A 2009, *Why great leaders don't take yes for an answer: managing for conflict and consensus*, Wharton School Publishing, University of Pennsylvania, PA.

Robbins, Harvey A & Finley, Michael 2001, *The new why teams don't work: what goes wrong, and how to make it right*, Texere, Mason, OH.

Schiller, Robert J 2008, 'Challenging the crowd in whispers, not shouts', *The New York Times*, 1 November.

Schütz, Peter & Bloch, Brian 2006, 'The "Silo-virus": diagnosing and curing departmental groupthink', *Team Performance Management*, vol. 12, no. 1, pp. 31–43.

Sennett, Richard 1998, *The corrosion of character: the personal consequences of work in the new capitalism*, W.W. Norton, New York.

Seta, Catherine E, Paulus, Paul B & Baron, Robert A 2000, *Effective human relations: a guide to people at work*, 4th edn, Allyn & Bacon, Boston.

Sims, Henry P & Manz, Charles C 1995, *Company of heroes: unleashing the power of self-leadership*, John Wiley & Sons, New York.

Sinclair, Amanda 1992, 'The tyranny of a team ideology', *Organisation Studies*, vol. 14, no. 4, pp. 611–26.

Smith, Larry 2006, 'Some soccer lessons for litigators', *Of Counsel*, vol. 25, no. 8, pp. 12–15.

Solomon, Miriam 2006, 'Groupthink versus the wisdom of crowds: the social epistemology of deliberation and dissent', *The Southern Journal of Philosophy*, vol. 44, pp. 28–43.

Taras, Daphne Gottlieb 1991, 'Breaking the silence: differentiating crises of agreement', *Public Administration Quarterly*, vol. 14, no. 4, pp. 401–18.

Thompson, James 1985, *Psychological aspects of nuclear war*, British Psychological Society/John Wiley & Sons, Chichester.

Timmerman, C Erik & Scott, Craig R 2006, 'Virtually working: communicative and structural predictors of media use and key outcomes in virtual work teams', *Communication Monographs*, vol. 73, no. 1, pp. 108–36.

Torres, Crescencio & Spiegel, Jerry 1990, *Self-directed work teams: a primer*, Pfeiffer, San Diego, CA.

Tuckman, Bruce W 1965, 'Developmental sequence in small groups', *Psychological Bulletin*, vol. 63, pp. 384–99.

Tuckman, B & Jensen, M 1977, 'Stages of small group development revisited', *Group and Organizational Studies*, vol. 2, no. 4, pp. 419–27.

Ugboro, Isaiah O 2006, 'Organizational commitment, job redesign, employee empowerment and intent to quit among survivors of restructuring and downsizing', *Journal of Behavioral and Applied Management*, vol. 17, no. 3, pp. 232–51.

Van der Klein, Rick, Schraagen, Peter Maarten & Werkhoven, Peter 2009, 'How conversations change over time in face-to-face and video-mediated communication', *Small Group Research*, vol. 40, no. 4, pp. 355–81.

Wheelan, Susan A 1994, *Group processes: a developmental perspective*, Allyn & Bacon, Boston.

Wheelan, Susan A, Davidson, Barbara & Tilin, Felice 2003, 'Group development across time: reality or illusion?', *Small Group Research*, vol. 34, no. 2, pp. 223–45.

Watt, LA, Hilton, Thomas F & Hochwarter, Wayne A 2001, 'Addressing politics in matrix teams', *Group and Organization Management*, vol. 26, no. 2, pp. 230–48.

White, Judith, McMillen, M Cecilia & Baker, Ann C 2001, 'Challenging traditional models: towards an inclusive model of group development', *Journal of Management Inquiry*, vol. 10, no. 1, pp. 40–58.

Williams, S Mitchell 2004, 'Downsizing – intellectual capital performance anorexia or enhancement?', *The Learning Organization*, vol. 11, nos 4/5, pp. 368–80.

Williams, Scott D, Graham, T Scott & Baker, Bud 2003, 'Evaluating outdoor experiential training for leadership and team building', *Journal of Management Development*, vol. 22, no. 3, pp. 45–59.

Woodward, Bob 2006, *State of denial: Bush at war, Part III*, Simon & Schuster, New York.

Yauch, Charlene A 2007, 'Team-based work and work system balance in the context of agile manufacturing', *Applied Ergonomics*, vol. 38, pp. 19–27.

Yetiv, Steve A 2004, *Explaining foreign policy: U.S. decision-making and the Persian Gulf*, Johns Hopkins University Press, Baltimore, MD.

19

Communicating in meetings

LEARNING OBJECTIVES

After studying this chapter you should be able to:

- Identify different types of meetings
- Explain the interplay of structure and power in meetings
- Identify the advantages and disadvantages of virtual meetings when compared with face-to-face meetings
- Explain the use (and abuse) of formal meeting procedures
- Explain the role of the meeting chairperson and secretary
- Explain the effect that seating and table layout can have on meeting dynamics
- Discuss the pros and cons of different methods of decision making and problem solving in meetings
- Identify strategies that will help you become a more effective meeting participant

Meetings: the good news and the bad news

Meetings are formal or informal gatherings of people. They may be subject to elaborate systems of rules and conventions, or completely without ceremony. A meeting takes place whenever two or more people assemble to communicate.

When properly managed, meetings can be dynamic arenas in which:

- problems are solved
- decisions are made
- actions are planned and taken
- information is shared
- group morale is boosted
- communication quality and quantity are maximised
- satisfaction, rapport, synergy (the whole being greater than the sum of its parts) and effectiveness are experienced by all present.

Equally, however, meetings can produce none of these outcomes. Meetings have developed a mythology of their own, summed up in the following gems of cynical folk wisdom.

Meetings are places where minutes are kept and hours are lost.

A camel is a horse designed by a committee.

A committee is a group of the unfit, appointed by the unwilling to do the unnecessary.

A committee is a group that succeeds in getting something done only when it consists of three members, one of whom happens to be sick and another absent.

If you have enough meetings over a long enough period of time, the meetings become more important than the problem they were intended to solve.

The time spent on any item on the agenda will be in inverse proportion to the sum of money involved.

The possibility of avoiding decisions increases in proportion to the square of the number of members of the committee.

Sources: Dickson (1999); Fletcher (1983).

We should take note of these negative views of meetings, because there are elements of truth in all of them. Meetings are nevertheless an inevitable part of our lives, so we really should learn how best to make them work. In this chapter we consider the structures, levels of formality and different roles encountered in meetings. The review should be considered in the context of other chapters in this book, particularly those examining team communication, leadership, oral communication, negotiation skills, dealing with conflict, argument, persuasion and influence, nonverbal communication, organisational communication and interpersonal skills.

Meetings: how do they work?

Table 19.1 outlines some common types of meetings; however, it by no means exhausts the range of ways in which humans interact. Some work teams (e.g. aircraft crew, tank crew, graphic artists) are in constant close proximity to each other – their 'meeting' never ends. 'Virtual meetings', on the other hand, bring together participants who are physically remote from one another, using technology such as teleconferencing, videoconferencing or online computers (Chapman 2003; Thompson 2011).

TABLE 19.1 Types of meetings

Meeting type	What happens?	Who runs it?	Who else attends?
Public meeting	■ Issues of public concern are discussed ■ A forum is provided to hear information	■ Public action/pressure groups ■ Commercial companies ■ Local councils	■ Members of the public ■ Shareholders
Private meeting	■ Issues of concern to a particular group, association or organisation are discussed	■ Executives or committees of service clubs (Rotary, Lions), unions, hobby groups	■ Members of associations, unions, clubs
Briefing meeting	■ Information is given out about new policies, procedures, daily routines ■ Downward flow of information	■ Managers, team leaders in private and public sector organisations	■ Staff of teams, departments
Feedback meeting	■ Information and opinions are sought ■ Upward flow of information	■ Managers, team leaders in private and public sector organisations	■ Staff of teams, departments
Board meeting	■ Company directors monitor developments within an organisation (often monthly)	■ Board chairperson	■ Board members
Annual general meeting (AGM)	■ Company directors report on developments (usually annual) ■ Shareholders get chance to question directors	■ Company directors/board members	■ Shareholders
Extraordinary general meeting (EGM)	■ Same as an AGM, except held between normal AGMs ■ May be in response to a crisis ■ May be in response to shareholder initiative	■ Company directors/board members	■ Shareholders
Team/departmental meeting	■ Routine and nonroutine goals and objectives are discussed ■ Decisions made, problems solved	■ Managers, team leaders in private and public sector organisations	■ Staff of teams, departments
Standing committee	■ Permanent offshoot of a larger meeting ■ Focuses on a specific set of issues (finances, welfare, production)	■ Chairpersons with authority delegated from larger body	■ Board members, union members, staff
Ad hoc committee	■ Temporary offshoot of a larger meeting ■ Focuses on one particular issue	■ Chairpersons with authority delegated from larger body	■ Board members, union members, staff
Executive committee	■ Permanent offshoot of larger meeting ■ Meets more frequently than larger meeting to consider ongoing issues	■ Chairpersons with authority delegated from larger body	■ Board members, union members, staff
Negotiation meeting	■ Resolution of conflicts over goals, objectives and resources is sought	■ Leaders of contending parties	■ Other interested parties
Problem-solving meeting	■ Focuses on solving particular problems, using methods such as brainstorming	■ Facilitator	■ Interested parties
Informal meeting	■ Members meet by accident, or decide to kick issues around without constraints of formal structure	■ Nobody ■ Facilitator	■ Anyone relevant

Meetings: structure versus power

One of the key differences between types of meetings is their relative level of formality – that is, whether or not they are highly structured. High structure indicates formal procedures such as a meeting constitution with standing orders and voting or other decision-making procedures that are binding on all present. Low structure indicates the absence of formal procedures, either because members haven't got around to developing them, or because they have consciously avoided them, perhaps because interpersonal relationships are particularly trusting and/or members prefer informal approaches to decision making and problem solving.

When seeking to understand what goes on in meetings, we need to consider not only structure but also power. High power concentration means decision-making power is held by one or a few individuals; low power concentration means that power is distributed widely – for example, among an organisation's staff, board members or stockholders. Figure 19.1 gives us a means of mapping different types of meetings.

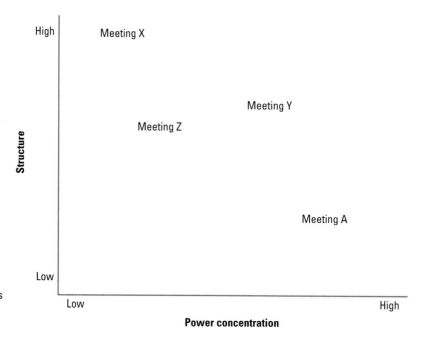

FIGURE 19.1 Structure versus power concentration in meetings

The varying relationships between power and structure can produce a surprising range of permutations and combinations in meetings (see table 19.2), although the one relationship will not necessarily always produce the same outcome – situational variables of motivation, trust/distrust and honesty/manipulativeness can see to that.

TABLE 19.2 Different structure/power mixes produce different types of meetings and meeting outcomes

Structure/power concentration mix	Situation	What happens
Low structure/high power concentration	Small business	Owner has built up business from scratch, and runs meetings with staff on an open basis with no formal agenda or minutes, encouraging brainstorming and input. Staff have good rapport with owner, and owner realises the need to train successors and hire specialists with knowledge she/he doesn't have.

Structure/power concentration mix	Situation	What happens
Low structure/high power concentration	Small business	Owner may have staff present at a meeting, but may prefer not to seek their advice either verbally or through voting, and indeed may choose to dismiss staff who disagree, even when they are right.
High structure/medium– low power concentration	Company annual general meeting	Board of directors is able to get actions approved by shareholders because a majority of shareholders approve of board policy.
High structure/medium– low power concentration	Company annual general meeting	Board of directors is able to get actions approved in spite of widespread shareholder disapproval because insufficient shareholders are present to express disapproval through a vote.
High structure/medium– low power concentration	Company annual general meeting	Organised shareholders move a vote of no confidence in the board of directors, and succeed in having the entire board dismissed.
Medium–high structure/ medium–low power concentration	Local community action group	Meeting rules are used to provide a safe and democratic arena in which members inexperienced in meeting procedures can express their views.
Medium–high structure/ medium–low power concentration	Local community action group	Meeting rules are used by a corrupt leadership group to confuse members inexperienced in meeting procedures, denying them a safe and democratic arena in which to express their views.
Low structure/low power concentration	Union executive	High-trust, collegial atmosphere allows meeting to do away with formal procedures and solve problems in a creative way.
Low structure/low power concentration	Union executive	Low-trust atmosphere and general incompetence means that meetings are a shambles where real decisions are rarely made (and those made are often bad ones).

Meeting structure

What are 'standing orders' and 'constitutions'? This terminology relates to systems of rules that have developed, literally over centuries, substantially from British Westminster parliamentary traditions, although there are significant variations on the rules as applied in different organisations and different national cultures (Puregger 1998; Brett 2001). When handled well, formal rules and regulations can facilitate creativity, flexibility, communication and problem solving; when handled badly, they can constitute a straitjacket that constrains creativity, flexibility, communication and problem solving (Susskind 2006; Susskind & Cruikshank 2007). When such negative outcomes occur, it may be time to consider other approaches to problem solving and eliciting feedback from groups, such as brainstorming, consensus and nominal group technique (discussed in more detail later in the chapter).

Constitutions, standing orders, by-laws, memoranda, motions: the dull and not so dull

Constitution: document setting out broad structures and requirements of an organisation

Formally structured groups often have a **constitution**. This document establishes formal characteristics and conventions such as the organisation's name, the criteria for membership, the time structure for meetings (e.g. annual general meetings, executive meetings once a month), the way in which finances will be structured and monitored, the office bearers or positions within the organisation, rules for election and other procedures. In some US organisations, by-laws may take the place of constitutions.

Standing orders: document setting out specific procedures for conducting business in meetings

Standing orders tend to focus on operational aspects of meetings, setting out procedures for rules of debate and the putting of motions, and detailing factors such as the duties and powers of office bearers, and what constitutes a quorum (the minimum number of people required in order to transact business).

In many countries, the law requires that every new commercial company sets up a memorandum and articles of association. The content of these types of documents can overlap with those of constitutions, standing orders and by-laws. In order to avoid confusion in such matters, it is usually preferable to engage a legal professional either to initiate such documents or, at least, to review existing documentation.

Many organisations flourish without such documentation, and yet formal documentation and structures – dull topics though they are – constitute an important means of imposing accountability and effective systems of feedback in organisations. For example, the knowledge that they will have to face shareholders at a legally mandated annual general meeting helps keep managers and board members honest, or relatively honest.

Dullness, of course, can have its uses, at least for some. Much of the quasi-legal detail of meeting procedure is simply too dull to master for many meeting participants. While this is understandable, it may well leave the meeting at the mercy of pedants (who are usually harmless) or manipulative individuals and elites (who may be anything but harmless). For ethical people, the advice is clear, if unexciting: master the details, or the details will master you.

Going through the motions: voting procedure

The simplest way of making up the group mind in a meeting is through a vote. Issues and proposals for action are expressed as **motions**, which are put forward or proposed by a mover. Conventionally, motions are put in writing and passed to the meeting secretary and/or chair of the meeting. For most motions, a seconder is needed – that is, the mover of the motion is supported by a second person who feels the issue or proposal worth debating. General debate then ensues. One of the duties of the chairperson is to ensure the debate is thorough and balanced: the chairperson may decide, for example, that the meeting hear from one speaker for the motion, then one opposed and so on.

Motion: a formal proposal for action or change put to a meeting that calls for those present to vote for or against it

Once a motion is open for discussion, others may attempt to introduce **amendments** to the motion (figure 19.2).

Amendment: a formal proposal for change to a motion; an amendment may qualify, but not negate, the intent of the original motion

Original motion	Possible amendment
'That this association seek out and hire a research director to be appointed for five years.'	'Replace the words "to be appointed for five years" with the words "for a trial period of six months".'

FIGURE 19.2 Sample motion and amendment

Amendments must be in the spirit of the original motion. For example, it would not be acceptable to move an amendment 'that the word "not" be placed after "association"'. Amendments are voted on and, if successful, added to the original motion. When a motion or amended motion is passed, it becomes a resolution, or binding policy for the organisation (figure 19.3). Any attempt to overturn or rescind the resolution could normally be made only at a later meeting.

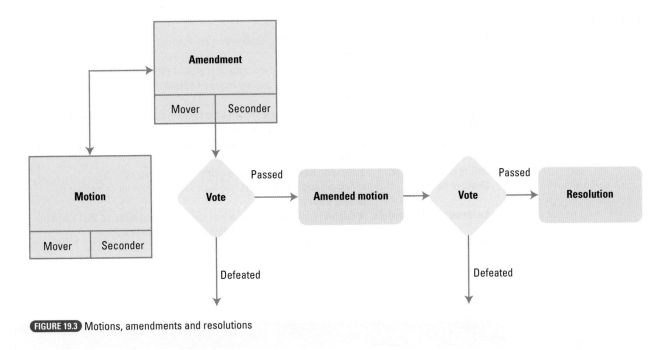

Motions, amendments and resolutions

Figure 19.4 lists some of the terms commonly encountered in a formally run meeting.

Abstention:	the act of not voting one way or another on an issue or motion
Acclamation:	voting by clapping or cheering
Adjourn:	to temporarily halt a meeting, to continue at a later time
Apologies:	messages of regret from those unable to attend
Ayes and noes:	words used for yes (in support of the motion) and no (against the motion) when voting
Carried:	the motion or amendment is passed, having received a majority of votes
Casting vote:	vote used to break a deadlock (when votes for and against are equal in number), often held by the chair. It is conventional in many meetings for the chair to make a casting vote in favour of the status quo.
Caucus:	a meeting before the main meeting, at which subgroups or factions decide on how they will vote (also used as a verb)
Closure:	a procedural gag motion (e.g. 'I move that the question be put') that forces the chair to take a vote on whether the motion currently being discussed should be voted on without further discussion
Defeated:	when a motion or amendment does not receive a majority of votes
Division:	a system of voting by which people in favour of a position show their commitment by walking to an agreed part of the meeting room
Foreshadow:	to give advance notice of action or intention
Gag:	closure motion
Hidden agenda:	implies that the meeting is being manipulated in some way for some undisclosed purpose
In camera:	closed or confidential sitting of meeting (visitors are required to leave)
Move into committee:	or 'move into committee of the whole'. Meaning varies with circumstances, but generally indicates that the meeting moves into more informal discussion, with no motions passed or minutes kept. The chair sometimes steps down in favour of someone else.
No confidence:	a motion challenging the authority of the chair

FIGURE 19.4 Meeting-speak — some terms encountered in meetings

(continued)

FIGURE 19.4 *(continued)*

Point of order:	a procedural motion, challenging the manner in which debate is being conducted
Proxy:	authorisation to cast the vote of someone not present
Quorum:	minimum number of people required before a meeting can be seen to be legitimate
Rescind:	to negate or reverse a motion or resolution passed at a previous meeting
Rescission:	a motion to rescind a resolution
Right of reply:	right granted to mover of motion to have the last word before a vote on the motion
Ruling from the chair:	a decision from the chair on a matter of controversy
Show of hands:	voting procedure where people indicate their vote for or against by raising a hand
Suspend standing orders:	to depart temporarily from normal meeting procedures so that certain things may happen, such as debate without time limits
Terms of reference:	guidelines created for ad hoc committees
Veto:	power to reject or prohibit an action

ASSESS YOURSELF

1. Conduct an internet search of strings such as 'meeting + standing orders', 'meeting + rules of debate', 'meeting + constitution' and 'meeting + by-laws'. Note the variation in interpretation between organisations and between national cultures.
2. Are you a member of a club or association, or do you work for a company? Enquire (diplomatically) whether there is a constitution, standing orders, by-laws, or memorandum and articles of association, and ask to see them. If possible, compare one set of documents with another.

Meetings: making them happen

Perhaps the two most significant people at a meeting are the chairperson and the secretary. The two most important tools they work with are the agenda and the minutes. Let's look at these roles and tools now.

The chairperson

Chairperson: office-holder who presides over a meeting according to established rules and conventions; also known as the chair

The **chairperson**, or chair, is the person who presides over, controls or leads a meeting or other group, such as a committee, board, commission, association, assembly, congress, convention, tribunal, panel, club or jury. The chairperson may or may not be the most powerful person in the group, but carries most influence in matters of procedure. The role may be held for a set time (such as a year) or for life, or may be shared with or rotated among others. The chairperson may be elected or appointed.

What does a chairperson do?

The chairperson acts in the role of ringmaster (see chapter 18), working with the participants of a meeting to achieve agreed outcomes, make decisions and solve problems. Depending on the nature or phase of the meeting, the chairperson may act to:

■ *brief:* impart information to members about policy, developments, facts and other matters
■ *clarify:* interpret and elucidate matters of procedure, such as the meeting's constitution, by-laws or standing orders

- *challenge:* act as the meeting's conscience, and confront it when complacency, mediocrity or tunnel vision threaten
- *control:* maintain order to ensure that procedures are followed, and give rulings on questions of procedure
- *facilitate:* manage group dynamics and communication, control tendencies towards groupthink, harmonise socio-emotional and task role-playing, and minimise destructive role-playing
- *focus:* make sure debate does not deviate from the point under consideration
- *reduce conflict:* smooth over differences between meeting members
- *increase conflict:* bring matters to a head when necessary to clear the air
- *draw out:* elicit contributions from members who have not contributed out of fear or laziness
- *suppress:* discourage unhelpful contributions from meeting members
- *police:* warn meeting members who cause unreasonable disruption, if necessary overseeing their removal (by any of a variety of means)
- *balance:* ensure that all sides of a debate are heard
- *provoke:* introduce new ideas to the group via the agenda
- *pace:* keep meeting members aware of the passage of time and the need to make effective use of time, but also ensure that decisions are not rushed
- *observe:* give feedback to meeting members on how he or she perceives what is happening
- *monitor:* watch members' nonverbal communication in order to anticipate problems, identify members who may be displaying doubts about decisions to be taken, and draw out their doubts by asking for input from these members
- *summarise:* sum up the views represented or conclusions reached in the debate
- *lead:* keep the debate on track so that decisions can be made and problems solved
- *provide an example:* create a role model of attentive listening, concentration, impartiality, courtesy, empathy and dignity.

Of course, to perform all these roles successfully is a tall order, and it is rare to find a chairperson who can do everything well. Again, the role of a chairperson is critically determined by the degree of structure or formality and the power mix within the meeting group. In groups with high degrees of formality and structure, for example, it is often considered inappropriate for the chairperson to enter the debate and express opinions, because the norm of impartiality is perceived as taking priority over the chairperson's direct input. (It is possible in formal meetings for the chairperson to vacate the chair temporarily, to 'switch hats' in order to contribute as a normal meeting member to avoid such role conflict.) In contrast, in a meeting with low formal structure, an individual or team leader may freely switch roles between contributing and chairing without drawing criticism.

Chairpersons are completely unnecessary for a large proportion of informal, ad hoc meetings that involve only two or three people. For other situations, however, the chairperson fulfils an invaluable role in facilitating the business of the meeting.

Chairing: the formal side

Chairpersons perform a number of functions in formal meeting settings. They:
- work with the meeting secretary on handling the logistics of the meeting (e.g. location, refreshments)
- work with the secretary on the paperwork of meetings: constructing an agenda, or list of business, and checking to see that the minutes, or record of the previous meeting, have been prepared accurately

- work with the secretary to canvass meeting members for matters to be included in the agenda
- work with the secretary on sending out appropriate paperwork (agenda, background material on agenda items, minutes of the previous meeting) to all meeting participants at least a few days before the scheduled meeting
- work with the secretary to create and send out correspondence on behalf of the group or meeting
- check that the meeting has a quorum
- normally open the meeting
- control the order of business of the meeting
- sign the minutes, once they are approved by the meeting
- provide leadership by working through the agenda
- manage the business of motions and amendments according to standing orders
- decide whether some items need to be deferred to the next meeting because of time constraints, because critical people are absent, or because certain information is lacking
- assign the tasks of taking action or gathering information (as agreed to in the meeting) to one or several meeting members, and ensure this responsibility is recorded in the minutes
- follow up on these matters at the next meeting
- rule on points of order
- close the meeting.

Are chairpersons all-powerful? Not at all. The authority of the chairperson can be challenged through a point of order, a motion of dissent from the chair's ruling or a vote of no confidence in the chair. Again, the power dynamics need to be explored here. An intransigent chairperson may simply refuse to acknowledge such challenges, in which case legal action may be necessary. A meeting may move a vote of no confidence in the chair, but if the chair is also the employer of all meeting members, then he or she could conceivably threaten them with dismissal.

The secretary or note-taker

Secretary: keeps written records of the meeting and works with the chairperson on managing the meeting process

The **secretary** or note-taker acts as the memory and the executive of the meeting group (see chapter 18). She or he will act together with the chair to ensure that logistics and documentation of the meeting are attended to. The ideal secretary should:
- be organised and disciplined
- be good with paperwork, scheduling and people management
- be content not to actively contribute to debate in meetings but instead to concentrate on procedural matters such as taking minutes
- manage all correspondence coming into the meeting and going out of the meeting
- take a roll of those attending, and accept and note apologies from those who cannot attend
- have the chairperson sign the minutes of the previous meeting if they are accepted by the meeting
- keep detailed minutes of proceedings in a minutes book, including specific motions, movers and seconders of motions, voting outcomes, and of responsibilities of individual members for actions to be undertaken and reported back at the next meeting
- ask for written copies and record details of motions without notice
- ask members for clarification of terms, spelling and other details to ensure that minutes are accurate.

Agendas and minutes

An agenda is a plan for a meeting. The minutes comprise the account of what actually went on in the meeting. Agendas and minutes form an important part of an organisation's corporate memory. The minutes, in particular, are defined by some as being legal documents (Zinski 2006), so care needs to be taken in creating such documents. Figure 19.5 presents a sample of a meeting agenda, and figure 19.6 shows the minutes taken as a record of that meeting.

Agenda

Coast City Amateur Rail Society
September Meeting — Friday, 5 September 2011
Coast City Municipal Chambers, Meeting Room B
8.00–10.00 pm

1. Opening of meeting
2. Apologies
3. Minutes of previous meeting
4. Business arising from minutes
5. Correspondence
6. Business arising from correspondence
7. Treasurer's report
8. Secretary's report
9. Adjourned business
10. Motion on notice 1:
    'That the erection of a 15-inch × 1.5 km track on the Fingleton estate begin immediately.'
    Moved: J. Baxter. Seconded: H. Young
    Motion on notice 2:
    'That Coast Technical Institute, Coast City Municipal Council and the State Department of Tourism be formally approached for development assistance.'
    Moved: K. Wheelham. Seconded: L. Venuti
11. General business
12. Closing of meeting

FIGURE 19.5 Agenda for a meeting

An agenda sets out a program for the business to be conducted by a group. The meeting needs to be formally opened by the chair. If there are visitors present, the chair may choose to welcome them. The minutes of the previous meeting need to be accepted, but only if members feel that this record gives a true and accurate reflection of the last meeting. The meeting as a group may have correspondence directed to it, and in turn may send correspondence out. All such correspondence needs to be reported by the secretary.

Reports are important for some meetings. If financial matters are involved, a financial officer or treasurer may need to report (in some meetings, the treasurer moves adoption of her or his own report). If the meeting has subcommittees, they may also need to report back. Any business adjourned from the previous meeting should be addressed before new business is raised. New business, often in the form of motions, is then dealt with before miscellaneous, general or any other business is taken care of.

Minutes can be kept in any number of styles. The traditional style uses past tense and passive voice. Meeting participants are identified by full name or by initials, or the secretary may choose simply to summarise the general outline of the debate. Sometimes details of votes and full information on amendments and their success or failure are noted.

Hidden agenda: unstated purpose or intention pursued covertly by one or a few members of a meeting to manipulate the outcome of the meeting

Note that meetings sometimes have a '**hidden agenda**' – that is, an individual or a group may be trying to manipulate the outcome of the meeting by pushing debate and decision making in a particular way.

Minutes of Coast City Amateur Rail Society September meeting — Friday, 5 September 2011 held at Coast City Municipal Chambers, Meeting Room B

PRESENT: Paula Skolnicki, Peter Balham, Winston Bao, John Baxter (Chair), Ian Benson, Martin Chekriss, Bill Felton (Secretary), Jerry Harris, Charles Manton, Harry Milligan, Christine Palance (Treasurer), Laurie Venuti, Keith Wheelham, Hilda Young.
APOLOGIES: Pat McClintock, Eric Williams

Meeting was opened by chair (JB) at 8.02 pm.

Apologies: Pat McClintock, Eric Williams

Minutes of the previous meeting

> MOTION: That the minutes of the previous meeting be accepted. Moved: JH. Seconded: LV. CARRIED

BUSINESS ARISING FROM MINUTES — nil

CORRESPONDENCE: Email to JB from Marni Charlton, reporter on Northern Echo, for story on Fingleton bequest and plans for miniature railway

BUSINESS ARISING FROM CORRESPONDENCE: JB will invite reporter to next month's meeting. ACTION: JB to email

TREASURER'S REPORT: CP reported that Salston's, the lawyer looking after Ben Fingleton's estate, has electronically deposited the bequest amount of $91 000 in the Society's account at the Coast City Megabank branch. MOTION: That the Treasurer's report be adopted. Moved: CP. Seconded: PS. CARRIED

SECRETARY'S REPORT: BF reported that title deeds for the Fingleton south paddock have been transferred to the Society. MOTION: That the secretary's report be adopted. Moved: WB. Seconded: KW

ADJOURNED BUSINESS — nil

MOTION on notice 1:

> 'That the erection of a 15-inch x 1.5 km track on the Fingleton estate begin immediately.' Moved: JB. Seconded: HY
> A prolonged debate ensued. Those opposing pointed out that the mid-August flood had significantly eroded parts of the paddock. Those in favour felt that a working bee would fix any problems. There seemed to be a consensus, however, that members may not have the skills to undertake major land works, and that it might be preferable to delay, pending expert advice. DEFEATED

MOTION: 'That the society seek technical advice on landfill management from the Coast City Engineering Department, the cost of such advice not to exceed $1000, and to be paid out of the bequest fund.' Moved: CM. Seconded: HY: CARRIED. ACTION: JB and BF to write to Council on Society letterhead, proposing survey.

MOTION on notice 2: 'That Coast Technical Institute, Coast City Municipal Council and the State Department of Tourism be formally approached for development assistance.' Moved: KW. Seconded: LV.

> There was extended debate on this. Some expressed the view that, in spite of the late Ben Fingleton's wonderful donation of money and land, the Society might be getting out of its depth by moving from a hobby-based model rail group to a potential commercial miniature rail group, attracting tourists. While all shared some misgivings, 'going miniature' was an option that had been discussed for years, and of course there are numerous precedents both here and overseas. CARRIED. ACTION: JB and BF to write to CTI, CCMC and SDT on Society letterhead, explaining proposal and seeking assistance.

GENERAL BUSINESS

> General discussion on our stand/display at this year's national convention. Specific recommendations to be considered in detail at next meeting.

Meeting closed: 9.58 pm. Date of next meeting: Friday, 3 October 2011.

Chairperson's signature: Secretary's signature:

Date: Date:

FIGURE 19.6 Minutes of a meeting

The meeting planning process

The agenda and the minutes are mirror-image documents; both are part of the meeting planning process (figure 19.7).

Meetings need to be well planned; when they are not, certain negative consequences are likely to occur:

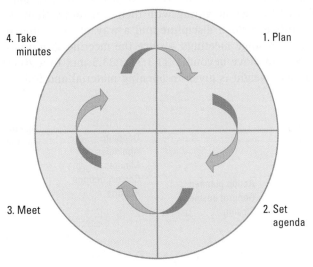

FIGURE 19.7 The meeting planning process

- Time is wasted or poorly allocated, with insufficient time spent on important items, and too much time spent on unimportant items.
- Members are unclear about what should happen next – that is, what action outcomes will follow.
- The meeting may, in fact, be action averse, having become little better than a talking shop.
- Even when action outcomes are agreed on, responsibility for implementing those actions is often unclear.
- There is no follow-through from meeting to meeting: instead of seeing one meeting as the input for the next, meetings are seen as disconnected events that happen mysteriously and independently.
- Complex issues are presented to the group in insufficient detail, so that decisions need to be delayed.
- Certain questions are never asked: What is this meeting for? Is this meeting really necessary? What alternatives might there be?

To ensure that meetings are as effective as possible and that these negative consequences are minimised, the chair and the secretary need to plan them carefully. They might, for example, adopt these approaches:

- Place time limits on agenda items and on the agenda itself.
- Develop a minutes style of recording action outcomes and accountabilities, noting the individuals responsible and following up on this at the next meeting.
- Send out with the agenda any background information others may need to grasp the context of the issues raised in the agenda.
- Invite participants to suggest agenda items.
- Suggest that agenda item suppliers nominate at least two alternative decisions that the meeting could adopt, and (briefly) explain why. Those who would waste the meeting's time will be put off by such constraints, while those who genuinely want to make the meeting a forum for informed decisions may decide that the hard work will be worth it.

Other meeting controls have been suggested by Tropman (2003):

- *The rule of halves.* Get all items to be discussed at the meeting to the agenda-maker by the midpoint between meetings (e.g. by the second week of a four-week cycle).

- *The rule of three-quarters.* At the three-quarter point between meetings, all relevant material should be sent to group members.
- *The rule of thirds.* Schedule the 'heavy' items for the middle third of the meeting (figure 19.8). This is when people are freshest, their concentration optimal, and both latecomers and early-leavers are present. This avoids the tendency in some meetings of saving the most important items to last, leading to maximum time pressure and irritation, and to people voting with their feet rather than with their hands. While the rule of thirds is a good discipline and a way of managing time and effort, it may be more useful in some meetings – once the meeting group has developed the discipline of process – to move beyond a 33.3:33.3:33.3 mix to a 20:60:20 or 10:80:10 mix, but only if proper weight is given to opening material and follow-up and general business.

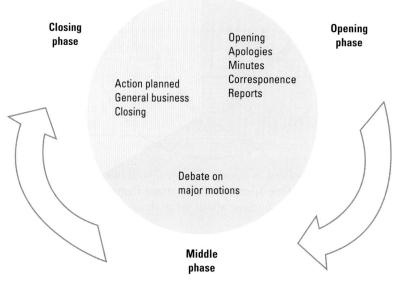

FIGURE 19.8 Scheduling the most important matters for the middle of the meeting

Source: Adapted from Tropman (2003).

Schümmer and Tandler (2008) have created a checklist of what goes wrong in meetings (figure 19.9). Do you recognise any of them?

FIGURE 19.9 Why do many meetings fail?

Source: Schümmer and Tandler (2008).

> **Why do many meetings fail?**
> 1. *Motivation and reliability.* The participants do not take the meeting seriously. Meetings are not considered as work. The participants arrive late or leave early and start to doodle.
> 2. *Clear goals.* The meeting lacks an agenda and there is no concrete vision for an output or result of the meeting.
> 3. *Information.* Important information is not available in a meeting. Participants did not prepare in advance and thus lack important background information. As a result, no decisions can be made.
> 4. *Context.* The environment in which the meeting is held is inappropriate for the subject matter. The meeting is scheduled at the wrong point in time.
> 5. *Focus and efficiency.* The participants gradually shift topics until they discuss issues that are totally unrelated to the agenda. They perform other tasks in parallel, which takes most of their attention.
> 6. *Trust and openness.* Participants tell lies in the meeting. There are long discussions, but no honest contributions. Conflict is avoided instead of being resolved.
> 7. *Respect.* Participants personally attack other participants. They start to look for mistakes made by others to make them lose their face.
> 8. *Communication.* Participants do not listen to one another. Too many participants speak at the same time.
> 9. *Participation.* Participants do not participate (which means that we should not call them participants, but rather attendees). Only few people engage in a discussion.
> 10. *Results.* There is no action after the meeting. The participants do not manage to implement decisions made. At a next meeting, resolved issues are discussed again.

Questions that need to be asked about meetings

If you are planning a meeting, consider asking some penetrating questions about the why, the who, the where and the when of the meeting.

The 'why' of meetings: is this meeting really necessary?

Sometimes there is simply not enough material to warrant having a full meeting of those who normally attend, and when that happens, maybe the meeting should just be cancelled. (Maybe or maybe not; the meeting with nothing much on the agenda may be a good place to have a discussion about broader, more strategic matters – subject to good chairing, of course.)

Do all agenda items concern everyone, or could some of them be better handled by just two or three people meeting face to face, by telephone or email, or by a 'virtual meeting' through computer teleconferencing? Have other channels of communication been fully considered before a meeting is actually called?

The 'who' of meetings: who should be there?

People often grumble about going to meetings, but they can grumble even more if they're not invited. If people expect to be there ex officio (as a function of their role), then they have to be there. At the very least, a quorum must be made up. Nevertheless, if a culture has developed of clear agendas and thorough minutes, some people may feel that they can skip the meeting and still stay in the loop of information and accountability. In some circumstances, this may be a good thing.

In the case of more nonroutine meetings, Hindle (1998) suggests that you should consider inviting those who can:

- *provide information.* An individual from one part of an organisation, such as sales, may be invited to inform other members about progress in their department.
- *offer advice.* A person's current involvement with a particular issue, or their past experience, may qualify them to offer helpful advice to other participants.
- *offer specialised expertise.* The presence of a person with specialised skills, either from inside or outside an organisation, may facilitate discussion.
- *authorise action.* Financial decisions in particular, such as signing or negotiating a new contract, may require the presence of a financial director to authorise the action.

The 'when' of meetings: when should they take place?

The timing of meetings depends on the organisation. Community and public meetings can really only take place at night or on weekends. Within organisations, it pays to take note of basic human needs – if it is held too early, then perhaps no-one will be awake enough to contribute or be creative; if it is held too late, perhaps people will be too tired. If it is just after lunch, people may be feeling contented and ready to concentrate, but they might also be in pre-siesta mode. Scheduling a meeting before lunch or before the formal end of the day may give attendees incentives to finish on time or even before time. Have a very good reason for calling a meeting that goes for more than 90 minutes. For example, an all-day meeting may in fact be needed to thrash out issues, or an all-morning or all-afternoon one (each one being approximately three hours) may also be justifiable. Be wary, however, of allocating large blocks of time for a meeting and remember that:

- the agenda can become over-stacked with items of low priority to the group at large, but which may be the hobbyhorse of individual members (You need to question whether a meeting is the best arena to discuss such issues.)
- the chair and secretary may not have been vigilant in keeping trivial matters off the agenda
- complacent attitudes can have an influence ('we always have a three-hour meeting')
- careless chairing can allow discussions to wander and eat up time ('talk expands to fill the time available')
- some people consider meetings a good way to avoid going back to real work.

The 'where' of meetings: where will they take place?

The territorial and nonverbal aspects of where meetings take place is important. A meeting in the boss's office may be convenient for the boss, but it may also be inhibiting for everyone else. Perhaps other rooms might be more 'neutral'. What would happen to the weekly meeting of a group if it took place in different venues? Such a 'trivial' variation should not change the outcome of more substantive matters, but sometimes it appears to do so. It is common, for example, for organisations to hold conferences or retreats away from the main workplace, and the change of scene sometimes does seem to change the dynamics of things (see 'Territory and negotiation' in chapter 13). Amer (2006) suggests that at least 50 per cent of business, networking and information sharing takes place outside a meeting room, before and after the formal meeting time in the formal meeting place.

Within the arena of the meeting room itself, however, there may be dynamics at work concerning apparently mundane matters, such as the shape of the meeting table, which might have direct and profound consequences for meeting outcomes. Let's consider this now.

Please be seated: chairs, tables and the curious habits of human beings

Can apparently trivial things like seating arrangements in meetings affect the results of a meeting? In chapter 8, we considered the idea of proxemics, or the study of personal space or territoriality, and proxemics sometimes exercises influence in curious ways:

- In 1973, the Vietnam war was still under way. Negotiations began in Paris to try to end the war, but before substantial negotiation could begin much time was spent on negotiating the shape of the table: should it be rectangular (perhaps emphasising or over-emphasising the differences of the multiple parties) or should it be round (perhaps emphasising equality and de-emphasising differences) (Kornienko 2003)?
- Legend has it that King Arthur introduced a round table to minimise conflict among his knights. Such conflict was based upon who had greater precedence or closeness or proximity to where Arthur sat at a rectangular table – in a hierarchical mediaeval society, a sure bone of contention regarding status hierarchy or pecking order. The innovation of the round shape meant to suggest equality (although an informal norm began to develop that whoever sat closer to Arthur was more favoured) (Sears 2005).
- A study of students in lecture theatres found that students who sat further back – away from the front – received lower grades or marks and had more absenteeism than students who sat at the front (Brooks & Rebeta 1991).

- Members of the European Social Forum – a group committed to 'open meeting places' – held a meeting in London, with all seating in circles; upon returning from a break, members were incensed to find that all chairs had been rearranged in rows, facing the chairing panel on a raised stage (Salusbury 2004).
- Practitioners of the Chinese art of feng shui sometimes argue against meetings around square or rectangular tables (because the sharp corners send out 'poison arrows' or negative environmental elements), instead recommending round tables (McCandless 2002).
- A study revealed that males and females with high testosterone levels entered meeting rooms more quickly, were more business-like or task-oriented and forward in their manner, focused directly on others, and displayed low levels of nervousness. This was in contrast to males and females with low testosterone levels, who tended to be more responsive, attentive and friendly or socio-emotional in orientation, but also more nervous (Hargie 2010).
- A study of doctor/patient interactions found that the doctor's desk was not only a physical barrier, but also a barrier to communication: when the doctor sat behind the desk, only 10 per cent of the patients were perceived at ease, whereas when the desk was removed, this figure increased to 55 per cent (Hayes 2002).
- In 2001 a survey showed that there had been a dramatic shift away from traditional row seating in US classrooms and towards U-shaped layouts or cluster layouts – changes which usually led to more teacher–student verbal interaction and more collaborative learning (Pappano 2002).
- Analysts of meeting dynamics have been known to conclude that: 'The success of a gathering of any kind is largely determined, not by speaker, subject matter or participation, but by size, comfort, number and location of chairs' (Stone & Stone 1974).
- Group members sometimes use control strategies based on proxemics and territorial claiming, because informal norms have developed that way.
- Organisers of christenings, weddings and funerals, dinner parties, business conferences and diplomatic conclaves often spend more time planning seating arrangements than other, apparently more important, aspects of occasions.

Hargie (2010) has argued that all social encounters can be analysed in terms of four phases:
1. Meeting
2. Greeting
3. Seating
4. Treating (talk and/or work).

(Compare these with the Tuckman sequence of group dynamics – Forming, Norming, Storming, Performing and Adjourning – discussed in 'Stages of group development' in chapter 18). Let's look at that third phase – seating.

Meeting geometries

So is there anything in the nature of seating and table shape that helps explain meeting dynamics? Yes, there is, but you have to continually test these ideas against your own gut feelings and common sense. It is interesting to note that much of the history of table shape development, and modern views on the same topic, emerged initially not from meeting or business interactions but social ones, particularly where people ate meals. Of course, with some ostensibly purely social occasions, much of the talk is shop talk, and some would say that more business agreements and communication take place in restaurants, at dinner parties, and on the golf course than in the task-focused meeting room (just as surely as the funeral of an internationally famous politician often provides many opportunities for informal communication and meetings to take place between politicians and other movers and shakers who come to mourn).

Let's start by considering the most conventional table shape – the rectangle. The rectangle makes a lot of functional sense as a chairperson or meeting coordinator or controller can sit at one end, while other meeting attendees can distribute themselves in space around the rest of the table.

However, in analysing what goes on in meetings, we need to consider not only physical factors such as sight lines (can everyone see everyone else?) and acoustics (can everyone hear everyone else?) but also the symbolism of power dynamics. If mediaeval knights and contemporary negotiators can get upset about table shape, perhaps there is something in it (or perhaps human beings can just be silly).

Hayes (2002), Pease and Pease (2007) and others, for example, have suggested that the most powerful person sits at the short end of the rectangle, usually the one furthest away from a doorway or access point ('the head of the table'). Behind the power person may be an artefact like a painting or window (figure 19.10). People closest to that power person may be allies. Power and precedence may also diminish the further away a person sits from the power person. The person sitting at the other narrow end of the rectangle may in fact be in a challenging position – a counter-power person. There may be a tendency for persons far away from the power person to engage in side-meetings, especially as seeing and hearing the power person becomes more difficult as the rectangle becomes longer.

Chairpersons or power people interested in breaking such dynamics might consider taking a seat half way down a side of the rectangle.

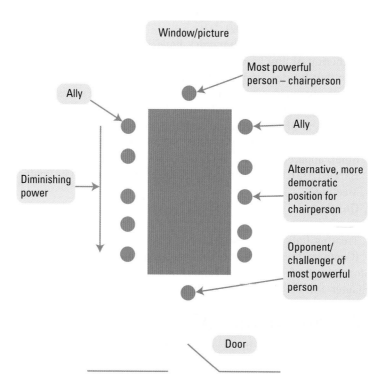

FIGURE 19.10 Possible symbolic dynamics of rectangular meeting tables and their environments

Sources: Adapted from; Hayes (2002); Pease and Pease (2007).

FIGURE 19.11 Circular or round table layout

What about other shapes? Other possible shapes for meeting tables are now considered.

The circle or round table is often cited as an ideal table shape (figure 19.11). Round tables can be hollow or solid. There is a message of equality sent out by the round shape, but considerations of hierarchy and precedence and power can still raise their ugly heads if proximity or closeness to the chairperson becomes a factor in some attendees' minds. Round tables can also be quite expensive to construct, and may take up a lot of room if not comprised of modular sections or wedges. Hearing and visibility are usually quite good, but if the table gets too big (some of the King Arthur legends have it that 150 knights sat at the Camelot round table!) then hearing and visibility can be a problem.

In very large groups, multiple round tables might be arranged in a large room in what conference organisers usually call 'banquet' layout (discussed in more detail shortly).

A variant of the round table is the oval shape (figure 19.12). The oval layout is particularly popular in the United States (e.g. consider the oval table at which the President and cabinet officers meet). The oval shape is midway between a rectangular and a circular shape. Unlike the rectangular shape, however, the end positions of the oval layout are not always seen as prestigious or powerful, and it is more usual for the chair or power person to sit in the middle position on one of the sides. The end positions of the oval table are somewhat like the corner positions of a square table – cramped, and usually lacking in desirability or prestige. If the table is not too big, then sight lines and audibility can be quite good. To a certain extent, the oval shape allows attendees to be closer to each other like those on either side of a rectangle, but also can send out messages of equality because of the quasi-round shape (bearing in mind, of course, that some attendees may be more equal than others). The prestige of the oval table relates partly to the fact that the shape was fashionable several centuries ago, and partly to the sheer expense of construction and complexity of craftmanship involved in making such an item of furniture.

Square tables are also, in shape, mid-way between round and rectangular tables (figure 19.13).

They can be solid or hollow in construction, and in fact can be easily formed in a modular way from a series of rectangular tables or desks. There is a symbolic aspect of equality to this layout. As with round tables, hearing and visibility can be good if the number of people present is not too large. It can be a problem if there are a lot of people present and some attendees need to sit at a corner, which will give them little personal space at the table.

U-shaped or horseshoe layouts (figure 19.14) are like rectangular layouts, with one of the short ends missing (although the horseshoe sometimes is created from a modular circular or round table, simply removing one or two modules or segments). There may be a tendency for the power person or chair to sit at the one narrow end. Such a layout is useful for focusing on the open end of the U or horseshoe shape, which can be useful for presentations and teleconferencing.

T-shaped table layouts (figure 19.15) are sometimes used, especially if the occasion is a social one (where some work is usually transacted). Attendees sitting along the column of the T may need to sit sideways to look at those seated across the bar of the T, which can be a problem for some in terms of postural

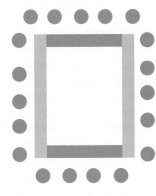

FIGURE 19.12 Oval table layout

FIGURE 19.13 Square table layout

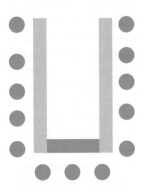

FIGURE 19.14 U-shaped or horseshoe layout

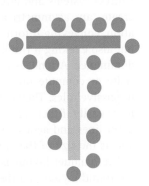

FIGURE 19.15 T-shaped table layout

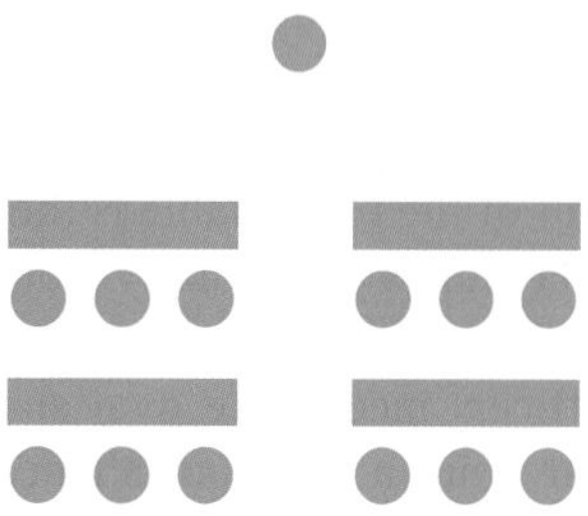

FIGURE 19.16 Classroom layout

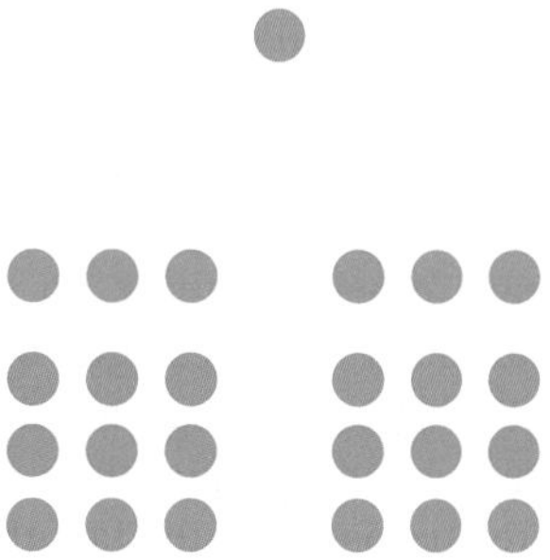

FIGURE 19.17 Theatre layout

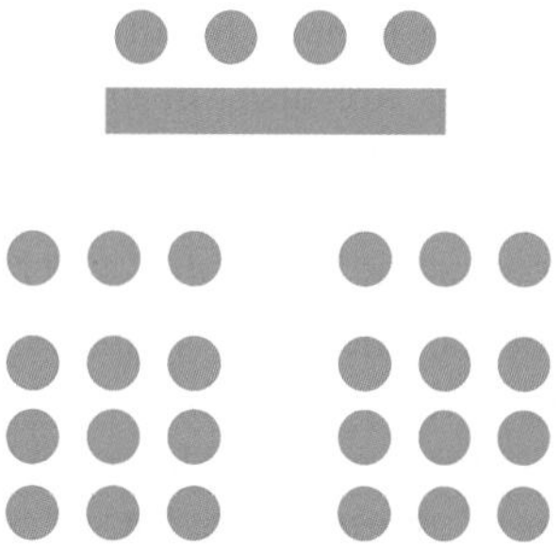

FIGURE 19.18 Panel/dais/rostrum layout

FIGURE 19.19 Banquet layout

comfort, sight lines and audibility (Lawren 1989), but — if the T and the group is not too large — may be helpful in sharing dialogue. There may be a symbolic focusing of power and prestige attached to seats across the bar of the T.

The classroom layout (figure 19.16) for meetings is excellent for getting large quantities of information across. Attendees can work like students on smaller tables, taking notes, looking at documents, and so on. While interaction can still take place in such a setup, it tends to be on a teacher–student basis, with individual attendees interacting with the central figure at the front of the room. Subgroups at individual tables can achieve some significant interaction (compare the way teams confer on quiz shows), with a spokesperson conveying the table group's views to the plenary or larger group and to the leader. Sight lines and acoustics may not be ideal for all-way interaction, with communication being primarily one way, or two-way individual-to-individual. This may evoke some uncomfortable role feelings for some about school experiences, and may be favoured by more authoritarian leaders — who might see meetings as briefings or presentations, rather than as collaborative problem-solving situations.

The theatre or presentation layout of meetings (figure 19.17) is perhaps even more one-way in communication flow than that of the classroom layout. Whereas with the classroom layout, at least attendees have table surface area to work on, attendees here have none. The theatre layout is quite good for briefings or presentations to large groups of people, but the larger the group, the weaker the sight lines and acoustics will be, and the fewer the chances for all-way communication.

The panel layout (figure 19.18) is a variant of the theatre and T-shaped layouts, and usually occurs in large to very large meetings. Those who are most likely to take a disproportionate amount of 'air time' or speaking time are at a high table or dais or podium, often vertically elevated above those who are listening 'on the floor'. Those on the panel might be chosen because of expertise, or because of their role (e.g. the board of directors at an annual general meeting) and will speak to the group in turn, either from their panel seat, or from a rostrum or podium. The technology of microphones, public address systems and large projection screens can create an asymmetrical communication situation, conveying information at the factual level, but also evoking a ritual of overwhelming power dominance. Attendees do not have work areas to write or compute on, and may find themselves in passive roles. They can interact with the panel more easily if there are microphones on the floor. Sight lines and acoustics become more problematic as the size of the group grows.

The banquet layout is a compromise between the round layout and the theatre or panel layout (figure 19.19). Multiple tables, usually round, accommodate most of the attendees, but there is usually a central area on a stage or dais to carry a leadership group. There are opportunities for attendees around the individual tables to interact with each other, and then it may be that a spokesperson will convey the views of that table to a leadership group. However, the bigger the complete group, the worse the sight lines and audibility will be.

Finally, let's consider a meeting without a table – the stand-up meeting (figure 19.20). As Fletcher (1983) observes, many people have ulterior or perhaps unconscious motives for attending meetings, such as feeling lonely working on their own, being scared of decisions being taken in their absence and being able to get a rest from real work. These are not the most noble of motives, and when combined with the 'death of the meeting' syndrome – the tendency of attendees not to want to finish the meeting because they have become physically comfortable in the room, and are not overly motivated to return to their real work – then sometimes radical thinking is needed to make meetings more productive. Stand-up meetings are simply meetings conducted without tables and chairs. This may sound bizarre at first, but they can be surprisingly effective, sometimes even more so than conventional sit-down meetings (Bluedorn Turbank & Love 1999). Stand-up meetings are very task-oriented, although there can be considerable socio-emotional interaction. The incentive is obviously to finish meeting business before everyone gets too tired. The downsides of stand-up meetings are fairly obvious – difficulty of handling paperwork like agendas and minutes, difficulty of finding a venue, and difficulty in tackling problem solving and decision making, which might benefit from extended discussion and from processes such as brainstorming and nominal group technique.

FIGURE 19.20 Stand-up/no table layout

We have now considered 11 different types of meeting layouts, and they can all help or hinder meeting communication in different ways. Figure 19.21 shows a continuum of the degrees of interaction that might take place in the different ways. Interaction is not always desirable, of course – for example, if all that is required is simply a briefing to a very large group or, to put it bluntly, if some, most or all of meeting attendees have bad process skills and don't have much to say in the first instance. Nevertheless, the waste of talent and ideas in meetings is a phenomenon we ignore at our peril, and maximum, rather than minimum interaction is usually the better way to go.

| Stand-up | Circle | Oval | Square | U-shape | T-shape | Rectangle | Classroom | Banquet | Theatre | Panel |

Maximum interaction   Minimum interaction

FIGURE 19.21 A continuum of interaction of meeting geometries

ASSESS YOURSELF

1. Think of a past or present situation in which you are or were a group member (student in a class some years back, or right now; member of an ongoing group or team — a work group, a personal interest/hobby group — which meets frequently). Where did people sit if their places were not allocated by the meeting organisers? Why?
2. Consider the continuum in figure 19.21. Now attempt to rearrange the order of meeting types on the continuum. Give reasons why you think this makes sense.

These considerations of proxemics and power are important, even though they sometimes seem silly. Perception, however, is reality, and if other people think that such non-verbal factors are real, then we need to respect that and – if necessary – make it work in our favour.

We need to apply some common sense to such situations. The reality is that, if a work group has good rapport and good process skills, as discussed in this chapter and in chapter 18 (such as awareness of differing methods of group problem-solving and decision-making methods, and avoidance of groupthink, free riding, bad structure/power mixes, destructive role playing and other dynamics), and its members are motivated to work together cooperatively and with mutual respect, then the physical layout details of a meeting – who sits where, what table shape prevails, what colour the walls are – are immaterial, or not greatly important. Good work can be done in rooms with poor acoustics and sight lines, and with people sitting wherever they like – if the will is present to do good work.

Thus, even though the continuum in figure 19.21 is approximately accurate, it is quite conceivable that a stand-up meeting or a meeting at a round table might be ineffective because of faulty process (e.g. poor procedure, bad structure/power mixes, groupthink or destructive role-playing). It is also conceivable that a panel situation might be highly interactive – for example, an annual general meeting of a company, where assertive and organised stockholders work from the floor of the meeting, using microphone/public address system technology and knowledge of meeting procedures and constitutions to stage a successful motion of no confidence in the board of management, resulting in the board's dismissal.

Meeting decision making and problem solving

Let's now turn our attention to types of meetings, employing different types of decision-making and problem-solving processes. Meetings are a form of the **basic interacting group (BIG)**, which simply means that most of them tend to involve people meeting face to face and voting publicly on issues that are debated. BIGs are different to meetings that use techniques such as consensus, brainstorming, nominal group technique, and virtual or electronic technology, all of which we examine shortly (Graefea & Armstrong 2011).

We have seen that meeting procedure or structure can help or inhibit true effectiveness of such BIGs. It is also true that broader dynamic features of groups, such as work teams, can have similar negative or positive impacts on effectiveness. For example, groupthink dynamics may impose oppressive conformity; and extroverts and high-status individuals may predominate in some meetings and teams, sometimes effectively silencing others who may have something to contribute but feel inhibited from doing so.

When groups, teams or meetings try to make up their minds, there is a range of approaches that they may choose from (or be forced to choose from), including:

- Support of individual or leader (used in BIGs)
- Voting (used in BIGs)
- Consensus
- Brainstorming
- Delphi
- Nominal group technique
- Improved nominal group technique.

Members of truly effective groups, teams or meetings need to know about the strengths and weaknesses of all of these processes. For example, it may be possible for more flexible BIGs to decide to use alternative methods of decision making and problem solving for part of the meeting, returning to more conventional procedures later in the meeting. The processes of support, voting and consensus are visually summarised in figure 19.22.

Basic interacting group (BIG): a group that meets and uses the authority of the leader and/or voting to make decisions and solve problems, rather than using special techniques such as consensus, brainstorming and nominal group technique

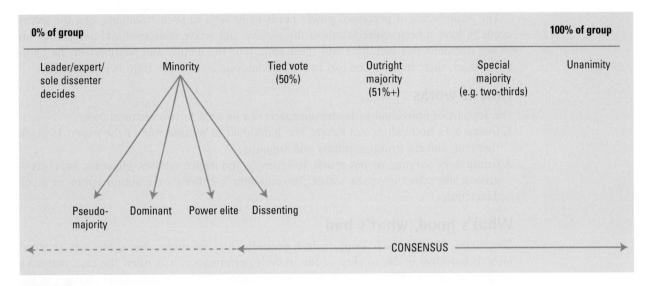

FIGURE 19.22 Methods of reaching decisions and solutions in groups

Source: Eunson (1987, p. 357).

Let's have a look at these seven meeting approaches now.

Support of individual or leader

Support of individual or leader: a situation where most power resides with one person, and the group or meeting works primarily to support that person

Support of individual or leader is concerned with the majority of the group deferring to one person. This one person might be an individual in a not-very-powerful position simply carrying out a routine procedure — so long as it is done competently, the rest of the group is happy to delegate authority and responsibility to that person to get on with the job.

Another example is where this person does not have legitimate power (is not a 'boss' in the formal sense of the word) but instead has expert power — the individual is presumed to have special expertise in the area, and the group knows that it makes sense in terms of specialisation and division of labour to go along with what that individual wants to do. It is dangerous, of course, for groups to have blind faith in experts or nonpowerful individuals simply doing routine jobs; group members should, however, monitor and support (Graefea & Armstrong 2011).

Finally, there is the support of leaders or individuals with legitimate power: 'bosses'. This support comprises nonleaders witnessing the exercise of power, giving advice and consent to the leader, or even just being a rubber stamp. This process embodies a paradox: it comprises what is almost a nonrole, and yet throughout most of recorded history this has been the traditional role of the group. Were such decisions and solutions necessarily inferior to group-based ones? Not at all. Great leaders, and even some not-so-great ones, have done just fine throughout history exercising sole authority (keeping in mind, of course, that there was little basis for comparison with alternatives).

In modern organisations, such dynamics still exist, sometimes explicitly, sometimes implicitly. Sometimes the leader's power is so great that decisions and solutions are announced, and the group (an advisory panel, the totality of subordinates) has to 'like it or lump it' or grudgingly accept it. There is no participation, there are no teams, there are no standing orders or constitutions or motions (let alone ones of no confidence); there is no industrial democracy. Sometimes the situation is more subtle, yet all the more insidious. That is, the leader and the group mouth the rhetoric of participation, but the reality is that you'd better vote the right way (or the 'consensus' you reach had better be the right one) or else! (This is a low structure, high power situation shown in figure 19.1.)

The leader's real or perceived power needs to be high in such situations, and the leader needs to have a keen appreciation of the passive and active resistance and acceptance his or her decisions and solutions will meet with. (For the heroic, and possibly for the paranoid leader, there may be comfort in the maxim 'one man in the right is a majority'.)

How it works

The support of individual or leader approach can be seen in two circumstances:
1. Group does nothing, or not much. The individual in routine role or the expert is given free rein, and the group monitors and supports.
2. Group does nothing, or not much. It listens to the leader, advises, consents, supports – gives leader what he or she wants. The situation is either purely authoritarian, or mock democratic.

What's good, what's bad

Sometimes this approach leads to bad decisions and solutions, but sometimes to good ones. Irrespective of the quality of the leader's performance, it is often the case that such exercise of autocratic power profoundly demotivates others. Organisational changes in the twentieth and twenty-first centuries have been largely bound up with eroding such autocracy and strengthening democracy.

Yet the tension between the exercise of power by individuals and the exercise of power by groups remains an unresolved – and perhaps unresolvable – one. Certainly, even though the move away from autocracy is to be applauded, sometimes inequality is not a disaster; sometimes the input from the leader, individual expert or dominant extrovert is simply the best thing to happen to a team, and asking the individual to 'hold back' in the interests of team or meeting participation may be seriously counterproductive (Kanter 1983).

Voting

The basic interacting group is the main arena for voting, although brainstorming and the nominal group technique also use some form of **voting**.

We have already considered voting in the context of motions and amendments, but now let's consider the process in greater detail. Voting can be either private (e.g. secret ballot) or public (e.g. show of hands). Groups choose one of these methods because they value privacy over public demonstration of belief or public demonstration of belief over privacy, or because they simply haven't thought about the pros and cons of the method they use.

Public voting can be quick; it can be convenient in small groups; and it forces people to publicly commit themselves to a decision. It can, however, force people to conform to the pressure from articulate and assertive individuals who dismiss attempts to have secret ballots with remarks like 'what have you got to hide?' and 'all right-thinking people know that there's only one way to vote on this one'.

Secret ballots have the virtue of protecting privacy and preventing pressure to conform in public settings, but they can be inconvenient in small groups and may allow people to vote in a particular way without demonstrating overt commitment to a belief. This, in turn, may lead to hypocrisy (i.e. saying one thing and voting for another).

Various constellations of minorities and majorities are revealed by voting patterns, including:

- *Veto.* A veto is the right exercised by an individual or a representative of a group to reject or forbid something. It is a 'super vote', the presence of which stops an entire process of decision making. Effectively, it is a minority of one acting as a majority. Sometimes the veto is an official one (e.g. the vote of a chief executive officer who has powers of veto under the standing orders of the board of directors) and sometimes it is an unofficial one (e.g. the vote of a person who wields power and/or expertise).

Voting: the expression of preferences through voices, show of hands or ballots

- *Pseudo-majority.* A pseudo-majority can exist when a minority exercises power via inequalities in votes. For example, a political party exercising a gerrymander, shareholders in a company having different classes of shares and voting rights, and a minority using proxy votes of people outside the group currently meeting all use this approach.
- *Dominant minority.* A dominant minority is one that rules when its opponents cannot agree enough to form a majority. For example, if group A with 30 per cent of power and group B with 30 per cent of power loathe each other so much that they cannot form a coalition, then group C, with 40 per cent, effectively controls the wider group.
- *Power elite.* A power elite may control the group in much the same way as a strong individual leader does, either officially or unofficially. An elite may make decisions and not be challenged by others, or the elite may influence or control the votes of others.
- *Dissenting minority.* A dissenting minority may occur, for example, in a panel or bench of judges. Here the majority may give a verdict or decision, but a minority of one or several judges may, rather than remain silent or give the impression of unanimity, issue a statement of dissent or a minority report.
- *Tied votes.* Tied votes occur when two subgroups each have 50 per cent of power. (Tied votes could also occur with, say, three subgroups each with 33 per cent, and so on.) Groups sometimes have mechanisms for resolving such ties – for example, the chair has the casting vote; tied votes on a motion mean that the motion is lost; the casting vote is drawn from a hat; the chair votes for the status quo (no change).
- *Straight majorities.* These are usually anything over 50 per cent. Some straight majorities are, in fact, pseudo-unanimous: government ministries or cabinets usually operate on the principle of cabinet solidarity. That is, decisions made by a straight majority (or perhaps by a powerful leader or power elite) must be defended by all ministers in public, with (officially) no breaches attributable to dissenting minorities or 'leakers'. In the democratic tradition, the majority is always right: vox populi, vox Dei (the voice of the people is the voice of God). This may not always be the case, of course: quantity does not always equal quality. For example, in Hendrik Ibsen's play, *An enemy of the people*, the hero Stockmann argues that the majority is always wrong: majorities, by definition, says Stockmann, are mediocre and conservative, and cannot discern current realities and future trends as well as perceptive individuals and elites. In this case, majorities are merely instances of '**pooled ignorance**', where the whole is definitely less than the sum of the parts.

Pooled ignorance: a situation in which a majority of people believe something, but their belief is wrong

- *Special majorities.* Special majorities are often required on extremely important decisions – for example, two-thirds majority rather than simply 50 per cent.
- *Unanimity.* Unanimity, or 100 per cent agreement, is unusual, but sometimes it is required for some decisions. For example, in some parts of the world, a unanimous verdict is required of juries in murder trials; whereas, in other parts of the world, a straight or special majority is required. The group dynamics of juries changes considerably according to what type of majority verdict is required. A single individual blocking a unanimous decision can have as much power as a consensus holdout (see the section on consensus) or a leader with veto.

How it works

The voting procedure is as follows:

1. Determine which type of voting is required and what it will achieve. For example, will the voting (a) preserve the anonymity of voters, (b) be a public demonstration of belief, (c) be performed for speed or convenience, (d) establish a clear or unambiguous mandate for important decisions, or (e) preserve the reserve power of the chief executive?
2. Establish rules and conventions. For example, a tied vote will be lost.
3. Arrange for special resources, such as ballot papers, tally sheets, whiteboards and electronic voting equipment.
4. Vote.

What's good, what's bad

Voting, in all its various forms, is possibly as old as giving support to an individual or leader as a group process. It can provide a clear quantitative view of what people's opinions really are. With public display voting, accountability is possible; unlike the situation with secret ballots in basic interacting groups and the various nominal groups, and unlike the situation of the public 'voting' in brainstorming and consensus (where, in worst-case situations, it is possible to mumble assent and no-one is the wiser as to where you really stand). Private voting, nevertheless, preserves anonymity and neutralises the potentially oppressive dynamics of personality and status in groups.

It is public voting (e.g. a show of hands) that presents problems for many people. It can induce conformity because of group pressure. It takes a lot of courage to be in a minority, or even to be a minority of one. Also, voting can encourage a win–lose mentality, which can be divisive in a group trying to find common areas of agreement between disputing parties (Saaty & Shang 2007).

Consensus

Consensus is a method of reaching agreement without taking a vote. Some response from all group members is required, of course, either positive or negative and either verbal or nonverbal. The pros and cons of issues are thrashed out at length, with someone such as the chair or a facilitator trying to find common areas of agreement between disputing parties (Schyns 2010). Schein (1988, p. 112) has said that elimination of dissent may not be the aim of consensus – a consensus decision is reached when a dissenting group member can say 'I understand what most of you would like to do. I personally would not do that, but I feel that you understand what my alternatives would be. I have had sufficient opportunity to sway you to my point of view, but clearly have not been able to do so. Therefore I will gladly go along with what most of you wish to do.'

Consensus is not always the ideal tool for meetings or teams to use, but it is particularly useful when all participants or members need to be committed to the decision or solution in order to implement it.

How it works

Consensus can be achieved using the following guidelines:
1. Appoint a leader.
2. Leader announces that decision will not be reached by voting. The leader will instead periodically test for consensus by asking 'Can you support this decision?'.
3. Members will respond verbally and need to consider whether they are at the point of minimal agreement, where they can say: 'I understand what most of you would like to do. I personally would not do that, but I feel that you understand what my alternative would be. I have had sufficient opportunity to sway you to my point of view, but clearly have not been able to do so. Therefore I will gladly go along with what most of you wish to do.'
4. Avoid bargaining. ('I'll vote for this if you vote for that.')
5. Avoid abdicating, giving in or changing minds merely to reach agreement and reduce conflict.
6. Avoid chance mechanisms, such as flipping a coin.
7. Encourage differences of opinions. See differences as chances to generate more options for the group, not as causes of conflict.
8. Encourage the participation of all – listen and observe nonverbal reactions.
9. Avoid a win–lose mentality; strive for win–win solutions.
10. Don't expect a quick fix – this is a time-intensive process.

What's good, what's bad

Consensus has recently gained importance as a method of making decisions and producing solutions within groups and teams. The spectacular improvements in the quality of Japanese manufactured goods since the 1960s is sometimes attributed to the extreme effectiveness of work-based teams known as quality circles, and their use of the consensus method. Other effects of the process, such as improved motivation and job satisfaction, have also been observed. Attempts (some successful, some not so successful) have been made to implement quality circles in western countries.

Although consensus is a time-consuming decision-making and problem-solving method, if all meeting participants feel as though they 'own' the decision or solution, they will probably be more committed to implementing it. This may save time in the long run, minimising misunderstandings and hostility from such participants who feel as though they are the losers in a win–lose situation (Susskind & Cruikshank 2007).

Critics of the consensus method suggest that cultures such as the Japanese are very group-oriented and cooperation-focused, whereas western cultures are more individual-oriented and competition-focused; and that Japanese 'cooperation' may in fact simply be conformism by members of the groups and manipulation of the groups by paternalistic managements. Clearly then, consensus is not simply a small-scale process that occurs in groups and has no wider repercussions. It, and the other methods of group decision making and problem solving we are analysing here, may have national, cultural and historical dimensions to consider.

Consensus, even though it can be an effective tool in some situations, can go wrong in a number of ways (Davis 1981, p. 62; Sinclair 1992, p. 619):

- It can be used by manipulative chairs and/or lazy group members to lower, rather than increase, participation. ('We all agree on this, don't we?' resulting in nods and/or mumbled replies.)
- It may become the paramount goal, causing people to suppress their opposition or to say they agree when they honestly do not.
- It is frustrating to all members to have to keep discussing a subject long after their minds are made up, simply because they are hoping to convince honest dissenters. (Considered a waste of time and an embarrassment to the dissenters.)
- While blocking consensus can have its uses, the consensus process may permit one dissenter to make the decision for the whole group, which destroys the basic purpose for which the group was convened (Bressen 2004).
- It can distort and mask normal patterns of conflict and power, giving a false impression of harmony.
- It can be the wrong approach when strong leadership is called for. One of the strongest opponents of consensus decision making was former British Prime Minister Margaret Thatcher, who said: 'To me, consensus seems to be the process of abandoning all beliefs, principles, values and policies. So it is something in which no one believes and to which no one objects'.

Brainstorming

Brainstorming: a method of creating ideas by deferring premature judgement and concentrating initially on quantity rather than quality of ideas

Brainstorming is a way of trying to break the dynamics (or more accurately, the statics) of groups that are conformist and that have become stuck in a rut of logical, analytical thinking and cannot make the jump to imaginative, creative thinking (Van Gundy 2007).

Creativity, or getting new perspectives, cannot be programmed or commanded – it usually happens only when group members can step outside their task roles, relax and have fun. This does not normally happen in task-oriented situations. So much of what we do is concerned with making sure that existing processes are operating, and that like things and ideas are tidily pigeon-holed together; yet so much creativity is about the relating of things and ideas that were previously unrelated.

Brainstorming as a process depends on deferring judgement and on quantity breeding quality. Normally, we judge our own and others' ideas immediately. Alex Osborn (the inventor of 'brainstorming') suggests that this is often a bad thing because many good ideas strike people as being too 'way out' or impractical, when in fact they may be simply ahead of their time. How 'practical' would aeroplanes or automobiles have been to a citizen of the eighteenth, or even very early twentieth, century? Quantity can breed quality, Osborn argues, if an enormous amount of poor or weak ideas nevertheless contain one good idea (quoted in Rawlinson 1981, p. 23).

How it works

The process of brainstorming involves the following steps, which can be varied as necessary:

1. Select one problem that is specific, and where novel and multiple solutions are possible.
2. Select a brainstorming group, limited to 6–12 participants.
3. Try to have participants who are of roughly equal status (the presence of superiors and subordinates tends to inhibit creativity).
4. Inform the group of the problem several days before the session.
5. Appoint a leader/facilitator, and a secretary who records all suggestions.
6. Try to heighten stimuli with enthusiastic encouragement from leader, bright lighting and music.
7. Encourage participants to suggest as many far-out solutions as possible.
8. Encourage building on other people's ideas (hitchhiking, piggy-backing, cross-fertilising).
9. Brainstorm for 30–45 minutes.
10. Appoint an evaluation group of 3–5 (odd number to avoid tied votes), either from the brainstorming group or from outside.
11. Organise solutions into categories. Assign priorities, based on practicality.

What's good, what's bad

Solutions emerging from brainstorming are often zany and impractical, but occasionally illuminating – that is, after all, what the process is meant to achieve. Brainstorming, however, should be used only when problems can be stated specifically, when there is a possibility of multiple solutions, and when the solution or concept or thing being sought is genuinely new (e.g. inventing a new product, rather than developing a marketing strategy for an existing product). Group cohesiveness can be built into brainstorming, especially when extroverts can give full rein to their sense of play and their desire to outdazzle peers with their ideas.

Brainstorming has been criticised, however (Van Gundy 2007; Furnham 2000; Teschler 2006; Nijstad, Stroebe & Lodewijkx 2006), because of the following apparent weaknesses:

- Its usefulness is limited to relatively simple problems.
- Creativity can collapse into anarchy.
- Dominant individuals can have too much influence.
- It is often inferior to nominal groups or individuals working alone in terms of output of creative ideas.
- It is prone to 'production blocking', or getting a word in edgewise – the flow of ideas is interrupted and sometimes choked off by the need to let others finish.
- Sometimes the process is just a charade to approve ideas that have already been arrived at by group leaders and upper management.

Delphi

Delphi: a method of group decision making and problem solving, involving polling geographically dispersed experts using questionnaires to quantify opinions and predictions

Delphi is a town in Greece where, in ancient times, priests and priestesses called upon the god Apollo to give them insight into the future. Hence, the group decision-making technique first used in the United States in the 1950s to predict the impacts of Russian atomic bomb attacks on US industry came to be known as **Delphi** (Chinyio and Olomolaiye [eds] 2010).

How it works

The Delphi process involves the following steps:

1. Select a problem, or problems. Usually, these relate to possible future events, where it is meaningful to give a quantitative probability as to the likelihood (or unlikelihood) of such events ever occurring.
2. Devise first-round questionnaire. Items should relate to estimating probabilities of events A, B, C ...
3. Select a panel of experts. Such experts should preferably be geographically separate from each other, preferably unknown to each other, and not in communication with each other.
4. Send out questionnaires as hard copies or online.
5. Collect questionnaires.
6. Analyse questionnaires for trends, convergences, patterns.
7. Devise next-round questionnaire. Items should now be more specific, asking for estimates of probabilities of events based upon trends, convergences and patterns observed in first-round responses.
8. Repeat steps 4–7 until sufficient trends are clear to base forecasts on.

The technique therefore consists of polling or administering a series of questionnaires to experts in one given field (Rowe & Wright 1999; Van Gundy 2007). The experts are usually geographically distant from one another, do not meet face to face, and have no direct or written communication with each other. They are asked to make a series of predictions in a particular area. Their responses are gathered and analysed for trends, convergences and similarities. These patterns form the basis of the next round of questionnaires sent out, the experts this time being asked to be more precise in their responses. This process can occur several times, until the analysts running the Delphi process decide that enough significant trends have emerged to base forecasts upon. Delphi has been used in various areas, such as military, education, medical, marketing, manufacturing, energy policy and local government planning (Linstone & Turoff 1975; Kadam, Jordan & Croft 2006; Howze & Dalrymple 2004; Alberts 2007; Jung-Erceg et al. 2007; Van Teijlingen et al. 2006; Graefea & Armstrong 2011).

What's good, what's bad

Researchers such as Asch and Janis have noted how group pressure can strongly influence, and in fact distort, the decision making of individuals (see 'Obedience, rationalising and true believers' in chapter 12 and 'Destructive norms: groupthink and the Abilene paradox' in chapter 18), and Delphi can help remove such potentially harmful group pressure to conform, which is often present in brainstorming and conventional decision-making groups (Mitroff & Linstone 2003). Anonymous experts are free to make up their own minds in a quiet, reflective environment, and each participant has an equal opportunity to contribute, with all ideas given equal consideration. A large quantity of ideas can be generated, and some precision can be given ('What is the probability of x happening in the next seven years?').

Delphi is also useful when it is impractical to bring together people who are widely separated by geography.

However, Delphi can lead to perhaps too much detachment on the part of the participants. Because others are not close at hand to clarify their ideas or terms, confusion can arise. Any conflicts in predictions of the future are 'solved' by simple majority vote, which may mean that the correct prediction will be swamped by pooled ignorance. Related to this is the fact that Delphi panels are usually made up of experts in a given field, who may be too close to the problem, or more bluntly, just plain wrong:

> The specialist is not necessarily the best forecaster. He focuses on a subsystem and frequently takes no account of the larger system ... These experts concentrate on a single logistic curve rather than on the envelope of a series of such curves ... A dogmatic drive for conformity, the

'tyranny of the majority', sometimes threatens to swamp the single maverick who may actually have better insight than the rest of the 'experts' who all agree with each other. This is not unknown in science; it is, in fact, a normal situation in the arduous process of creating new paradigms; i.e., scientific revolutions. In short, a consensus of experts does not assure good judgement or superior estimates. (Linstone 1975, pp. 581–2)

The apparent precision of the predictions ('54 per cent of the panel think that this has an 86 per cent chance of happening.') may trick people into half-believing that the future can be predicted scientifically.

Finally, Delphi can be very time-consuming, particularly if not completed online: a three-round process may take over 45 days to complete, which presupposes very high levels of organisation on the part of the organisers and very high levels of motivation on the part of the participants.

Nominal group technique (NGT)

Nominal group technique (NGT): a method of group decision making and problem solving involving minimal verbal interaction

Nominal group technique (NGT), like Delphi, can be used when normal group dynamics of conformity and pressure might possibly distort decision making and problem solving in groups (Silber & Foshay 2010; Van Gundy 2007; Graefea & Armstrong 2011). It involves individuals making written responses to problems; but like brainstorming and basic interacting groups, there is some group discussion. However, in some parts of the process the members might as well be separate individuals in different places – hence the group is 'nominal' or a group in name only.

How it works

Nominal group technique can be achieved by following these steps:
1. Select a problem.
2. Select a group of 5–9 people.
3. Convene the meeting in a normal venue.
4. Appoint a leader who presents the problem to the group.
5. Writing phase (10–20 minutes). Group members begin, silently and individually, to write out possible solutions to the problem.
6. Idea recording phase (5–10 minutes). Leader asks each member in turn to give an idea, recording these on a chart or board. Leader continues to ask for further contributions from members, keeping to the original sequence ('round-robin reporting') until all ideas have been recorded. No discussion at this stage. All ideas are numbered.
7. Discussion phase (10–30 minutes). All ideas are clarified and discussed, but not to the stage where passionate differences are allowed to emerge.
8. Voting stage (10–30 minutes). Each individual selects a number (e.g. 5–9) of ideas as being better than the rest, ranking each idea according to a weighting system (e.g. 5 = excellent, 1 = just all right). These votes are written on separate cards, with idea number at top right and ranking number at bottom right (clearly identified to avoid confusion with the idea number). The leader collects these cards, shuffles them (to preserve anonymity) and then records the votes for the various ideas.
9. If no clear preferences emerge, continue discussion and hold second ballot.

What's good, what's bad

Nominal group technique relieves individuals of pressures to conform, allowing individuality to emerge. There is less pressure than in basic interacting groups or brainstorming groups from other group members who might be more articulate or of higher or lower status (Paulus & Yang 2000). Because there is more anonymity in the process, attention can be switched away from personalities to the ideas themselves. This is not to say that the group is exclusively task-role oriented – the discussion period or periods allows socio-emotional role orientation, as well. Nominal group technique often produces a lot of ideas, and the outcome of the group (expressed as quantified priorities) is often much clearer than in basic interacting groups.

Nominal group technique, of course, has its drawbacks, such as:

- It can only be used to solve one problem at a time.
- True anonymity cannot be guaranteed because of verbal 'inputting'.
- Spontaneity and freewheeling enthusiasm can be inhibited.
- It requires a skilled leader.
- Group size must be small (nine or fewer), otherwise the process takes too long.
- It sometimes makes people uncomfortable because of its controlled or ritualistic sequencing.

Improved nominal group technique (INGT)

Improved nominal group technique (INGT) is similar to NGT, as the names would suggest, except that ideas are 'input' prior to the meeting. Participants write on cards and submit them. The cards are analysed to see if the meeting might be improved by bringing along other people or specialised resources (Fox 1989; Jacobson 2010).

Improved nominal group technique (INGT): a method of group decision making and problem solving involving minimal verbal interaction, and ideas submitted to a meeting prior to the meeting

How it works

1. Select problem to be solved.
2. Announce meeting time, venue. Distribute multiple copies of blank cards to members beforehand. Ask members to write down one solution per card. Members should not identify themselves on the cards. Specify a deadline, say, three days before meeting, when cards must be submitted. Allow for anonymous submission; e.g. via a drop or suggestion box.
3. Collect cards. Analyse to see if meeting would benefit by bringing along other people or specialised resources. Arrange to bring these if needed.
4. Publish list of ideas before meeting. Number and list – do not change in any way. Provide more cards in case this list stimulates further idea generation; members may bring these along to meeting and submit anonymously.
5. Hold meeting. Leader asks for submission of further cards. Anonymity is maintained via members with no new ideas submitting blank cards.
6. Continue with normal NGT procedure of discussion and voting.

What's good, what's bad

INGT allows true anonymity in the idea generation phase as well as the voting phase. Any inhibitions based on personality and status experienced by members should thus be non-existent. Meeting times can be reduced, because many or all ideas would be already known and would have been transcribed onto a board or flip chart before the meeting. Because the bottleneck of one-person-per-turn transcribing of ideas is reduced or eliminated, it is more practical to run bigger meetings if necessary. Also, the leader and the people doing the transcribing/recording can have creative input, at least in the idea generation before the meeting. This is in contrast to their neutral role in other group settings like NGT (and brainstorming and consensus).

On the down side, INGT shares some of the drawbacks of NGT – it requires a skilled leader, it can only be used to process one idea at a time, it can inhibit spontaneity, and participants might feel uncomfortable with the 'artificial' dynamics of the process.

The pros and cons of the various methods of group decision making and problem solving are listed in table 19.3 (see overleaf).

TABLE 19.3 Pros and cons of group problem-solving and decision-making methods

Method	Pros	Cons
Support of individual or leader	■ Individual in routine role or expert can get on with job ■ Leader can act quickly ■ Leader may produce good solutions and decisions	■ Individuals doing routine tasks and experts can be wrong ■ Leader may miss vital perceptions, opinions, information ■ Followers may become de-motivated and hostile or apathetic
Voting	■ Can provide a clear, quantitative view of opinions ■ Can preserve anonymity, and thus neutralise negative group pressures ■ Can ensure accountability	■ Can lead to negative group pressure ■ Can lead to hypocrisy, lack of accountability ■ Can lead to win–lose mentality
Consensus	■ Can avoid win–lose mentality ■ Can build commitment to decisions and solutions ■ Can lead to improvements in product quality, motivation, job satisfaction	■ Can reduce participation ■ Can cause delays ■ Holdouts can effectively decide for whole group ■ May mask conflict and power dynamics ■ May be excuse for poor leadership
Brainstorming	■ Many ideas generated — often quantity does mean quality ■ Group cohesiveness can be built ■ Extroverts' energy can be harnessed to group's purpose ■ Premature judging or closure avoided ■ Fun, zaniness, creativity given legitimate role (socio-emotional needs satisfied)	■ Usefulness limited to relatively simple problems ■ Creativity can collapse into anarchy ■ Dominant individuals can have too much influence ■ Often inferior to nominal group technique or individuals working alone in producing solutions
Delphi	■ Removes group pressure to conform ■ All ideas given equal consideration ■ Anonymity allows group to focus on issues rather than on personalities ■ Large quantity of ideas generated ■ Ideas can be quantified easily ■ Useful even when/especially if group is geographically dispersed or 'virtual' ■ Task needs satisfied	■ Participants can become overly detached — 'too much' task orientation ■ Confusion can arise because clarification is difficult (less so in online, real-time Delphi) ■ Conflicts are 'solved' by brute force of majority vote ■ Experts are not always right — 'pooled ignorance' effect ■ Apparent precision of predictions may be spurious ■ Time consuming (less so with real-time online Delphi) ■ Requires lots of organisation ■ Requires high level of motivation of participants
Nominal group technique	■ Removes group pressure to conform ■ All ideas given equal consideration ■ Anonymity allows group to focus on issues rather than on personalities ■ Task and socio-emotional needs satisfied ■ Many ideas generated ■ Voting priorities give precise basis for decision making and problem solving	■ Can only be used for one problem at a time ■ Can inhibit spontaneity, freewheeling, enthusiasm ■ Can make people uncomfortable because of degree of control required ■ Requires a skilled leader ■ True anonymity not guaranteed ■ Suitable only for small groups
Improved nominal group technique	■ Guarantees anonymity ■ Allows for provision of special resources, other people ■ Can shorten meetings ■ Allows leader, recorders to participate creatively ■ Suitable for large groups	■ Can only be used for one problem at a time ■ Can inhibit spontaneity, freewheeling, creativity ■ Can make people uncomfortable because of degree of control required ■ Requires a skilled leader

Sources: Adapted from Silber and Foshay (2010); Delbecq, Van De Ven and Gustafson (1975); Van Gundy (2007); Furnham (2000); Paulus and Yang (2000); Fox (1989); Rietzschel, Nijstad and Stroebe (2006); Tseng et al. (2006); Graefea and Armstrong (2011).

All of these techniques have much to offer. All of them can be used to substantially improve the effectiveness of some or all meetings. Meeting planners should perhaps consider experimenting with some of them to see if they make a difference.

Virtual meetings: audio-, video- and web conferencing

Technology is changing the ways in which we communicate, particularly in relation to so-called **virtual meetings**, which are situations in which people communicate with each other using technology rather than via **FTF (face-to-face interaction)**.

The concept of virtual communication is also covered in the discussions of virtual teams (in the previous chapter) and virtual organisations (see chapter 16).

Such situations might include:

- problem-solving meetings of people in geographically dispersed branches of an organisation
- ongoing monitoring of tasks and projects by members of 'virtual teams' – groups of workers physically remote from each other
- broadcasting of policy statements to members of an organisation
- training or e-learning programs for in-house human resource development and education purposes
- negotiation between parties physically remote from each other
- remote medical consultations
- delivery of speeches and sermons
- business and presentations
- interviews (Jaatinen, Forsstršm & Loula 2002; Bunt 2000; Bélanger & Watson-Manheim 2006; Carte, Chidambaram & Becker 2006; Lee-Kelley & Crossman 2004; Timmerman & Scott 2006; Sadowski-Rasters, Duysters & Sadowski 2007; Zimmerman 2011).

Brake (2006) suggests that 'virtual' is perhaps not the greatest term to describe mediated communication, as it also conveys the meanings of nearly, close to or not perfect. ('As one wit said, "If you want virtual results, create a virtual team".')

There are three main modes of virtual meetings. These are:

- **Audioconferencing**. Audioconferencing is achieved using telephone technology, specifically by exploiting conference call facilities, which permit more than two parties to conduct a conversation in real time. Audioconferencing technology is increasingly focused on table-top two-way/microphone speakerphone units. Despite technological development over four decades, videophone technology remains quite primitive, so existing telephone technology does not include a visual component or channel.
- **Videoconferencing**. Videoconferencing is achieved by using video cameras and private broadcast or narrowcast distribution of signals via cable or satellite. Participants can see as well as talk to each other. Videoconferencing normally has more complex equipment requirements, such as meeting rooms set up as studios.
- **Web conferencing**. Web conferencing is achieved using the internet to convey a variety of signals and messages in an online meeting environment. Participants are usually seated in front of their desktop computers. Web conferencing may consist simply of email or instant messaging technologies, combined with the ability to use 'whiteboards', or common areas on computer screens where meeting participants can sketch or notate ideas via word processing, database or spreadsheet files, and slide technology (such as Microsoft's PowerPoint). More advanced web conferencing technologies allow meeting members to participate in polls, ballots or votes, or samples of opinions (which can be published or viewed confidentially by the meeting facilitator). 'Persistent meeting rooms' allow all content – video, audio and data – to be stored until the next time the participants meet. The most advanced web conferencing technologies now allow videoconferencing, whereby all meeting participants have miniature cameras, usually on or near their computers, and may also wear headsets. Video images of all participants may then be displayed on computer screens.

Virtual meeting: situation in which people communicate with each other using technology rather than face-to-face interaction (FTF)

FTF (face-to-face interaction): meeting of people physically present in the one spot, not using technology to facilitate communication

Audioconferencing: using telephone technology to conduct meetings via conference calls

Videoconferencing: using video technology to conduct meetings

Web conferencing: using internet and sometimes video technology to conduct online meetings

Videoconferencing provides another way for colleagues from around the world to stay in regular contact.

Of the three technologies, audioconferencing is the cheapest, while videoconferencing is the most expensive. There are always trade-offs in terms of costs, and costs not just of the technology. Thus, while web conferencing has been described as providing only one-quarter of the picture and sound quality of videoconferencing, it can currently work out to be about one-thousandth of the cost (Doyle 2006). On the other hand, videoconferencing has been described as providing 95 per cent of the experience of face-to-face meetings at 25 per cent of the cost – the cost, that is, of travel and accommodation and the time spent in those activities when compared to simply staying home, videoconferencing, and then returning to normal workplace activities (Lee 2006).

Virtual technologies can be used for conferencing (two-way synchronous communication), casting or broadcasting (one-way synchronous communication), or caching (one-way asynchronous communication of data, video and audio to participants who will access it at a later time). Such technologies can be lean or rich in content (Spielman & Winfield 2003).

Virtual meetings: the upside

Virtual meetings have a number of advantages over real or FTF meetings. Virtual meetings can be cheaper and less environmentally damaging than an actual meeting, which may entail a number of participants travelling across states or countries and using accommodation and other resources at the meeting location, while also – in the view of some – contributing unnecessarily to global warming (Arnfalk & Kogg 2003; Doyle 2006). Travel can also be very stressful, particularly in a world in which security threats may encroach on routine travel (Spielman & Winfield 2003).

Facilitators or chairpersons of virtual meetings may be able to use techniques such as polling (getting participants to cast votes) and online collaboration (having participants notate files) to get higher levels of participation and retention or recall of meeting content from meeting members (Converse 2004).

Online meetings may act as a hierarchical leveller, putting all participants on an equal footing and thus increasing participation, and may act to stimulate participants into giving more effective feedback on proceedings.

Online or virtual meetings may, paradoxically enough, elicit higher productivity from participants *because* they are remote or working at a distance, and *because* the technology – file notation, whiteboards, polling, presentations – allows them to collaborate and problem-solve more intensely than they might have done in a face-to-face meeting (Spielman & Winfield 2003).

Distance, paradoxically, may help some meeting interactions because face-to-face meetings may be too 'hot' or conflict-charged, as opposed to the 'cool' interaction of virtuality (Brake 2006).

The focused nature of the virtual meeting may actually encourage meeting organisers to be better organised – to have prepared agendas and content in greater depth than they might have done for a face-to-face meeting. Virtual meeting technology at the group level may also accelerate the growth of the virtual organisation (i.e. organisations that are decentralised in space and centralised in time, operating across the globe because 'all the walls have been blown away in the world' (Friedman 2004; Rutkowski et al. 2007).

Finally, virtual meetings may be the technological trailblazer that makes it possible for communication via moving video images plus sound to become routine, existing on platforms such as computers, mobile telephones and landline telephones – a true communications revolution.

Virtual meetings: the downside

Virtual meetings also have downsides, of course. They can never replace direct contact, such as through the handshake – the tactile presence of others in a face-to-face situation. No matter how 'rich' the content, there is a 'social presence' – the whole panoply of nonverbal communication or body language – as well as patterns of influence, power, trust, deception and hidden agenda behaviour that operate in face-to-face meetings, but which are obscured, distorted or concealed in virtual meeting situations (Andres 2002; Carlson & Joey 2004; Credé & Sniezek 2003; Beard 2004). Owen (2010, pp. 94–5) goes even further with this line of critique:

> In many of these organisations there is huge frustration in working in global, virtual teams. There is plenty of research on how to organize global firms, (but) there is very little knowledge about the practice of running a global team. The team can have the protocols, goals, roles and responsibilities and communication in place, and it still does not work. The challenge is about people and power. Teams are built on trust: video conferencing does not build trust. Trust takes time and personal contact: these are expensive activities. The frustration comes because power is uneven: decisions, promotions, resource allocation and priorities are not decided democratically. For managers who are not at the power centre of the global team, this is hugely frustrating: they will have to double-guess what will happen; they find their priorities being arbitrarily changed and they feel out of the power loop. Few firms are able to transcend geography.

Shareholders have also expressed concern that online annual general meetings will allow management boards to fix the agenda and proceedings, effectively railroading shareholders (Thomson 2011).

Virtual meeting technology is still expensive, although becoming less so. This is particularly true of web conferencing. Nevertheless, there is a variety of software and hardware vying for market dominance in all types of conferencing, and not all are mutually compatible.

Also, some find the artificiality of the experience disconcerting. Participants may behave as if they are in an on-stage performance, and may exaggerate gestures and behaviour. They may not be aware that they are still 'on stage' or on camera after they have finished contributing (Fayard 2006). The normal nonverbal cues of conversation (see chapter 8), such as eye contact and turn-taking behaviour, may be distorted if participants look at a screen rather than a camera, and slow technical processing of signals may suggest hesitation or dishonesty (Bekkering & Shim 2006).

This artificiality of the process, combined with the content-rich nature of some virtual technologies, may force the pace of decision making, trapping meetings into premature decisions. The content richness of visual media may in fact distract from effective decision making, making audioconferencing sometimes preferable over video- or web conferencing (Yuan, Head & Du 2003).

The technology is also in its early stages, with system failure a danger, while slow or distorted moving images and acoustic problems are common (Werkhoven, Schraagen & Punte 2001; Spielman & Winfield 2003). Saffer (2008) has coined the term **topless meetings** as a sexual pun describing meetings in which all laptops, handheld devices and phones are banned so that 'attention-sucking devices' allow meeting members to really concentrate on what is going on. Similar bans are now appearing in some academic settings, such as in lectures.

Topless meeting: meeting in which laptop computers and other technological devices are banned because they may distract from real work getting done in the meeting

Nevertheless, if you think that virtual meetings may have something to offer as a communication tool, keep in mind the following pointers:

- If participants are in different time zones, all should 'share the pain' of early or late (local time) meetings.
- Have participants work 'asynchronously' between meetings by participating in discussion threads and by annotating documents held in a collective repository; these can often help generate goals and agenda items on an ongoing basis (Malhotra, Majchrzak & Rosen 2007).
- Only use virtual meetings in situations where the technology's strengths outweigh its weaknesses. Virtual technology may be most effective in groups that already know each other and need to process relatively routine matters on an agenda. Face-to-face meetings may be much more effective for 'kick-off and kick-out' meetings — that is, meetings that occur at the beginning of a problem-solving process, with participants who do not know each other; and meetings that conclude a problem-solving process, with participants who now know each other but who may benefit from a face-to-face debriefing experience (Arnfalk & Kogg 2003; Lee-Kelley & Crossman 2004).
- Make decisions to 'go virtual' based on real costs. Research vendors of hardware and software intensively. Consider training costs as well.
- Take pains to prepare for virtual meetings. Ensure both agendas and content — computer files and presentations — are ready.
- Expect participants to take a while to get used to the process.
- Pay attention to the nonverbal communication of participants.
- Don't be intimidated by the technology: allow people to participate or not to participate, if they so choose. Don't allow the pace of decision making to be forced, and don't be overwhelmed by content presented.

The pros and cons of virtual meetings are summarised in table 19.4.

TABLE 19.4 Pros and cons of virtual meetings

Virtual meetings: pros	Virtual meetings: cons
- Can be cheaper, less environmentally damaging - Can be less stressful, safer if security threats are present - Technology may allow higher levels of participation, concentration and retention of meeting content - Can be hierarchical leveller, thus increasing participation - May help to cool down face-to-face conflict - May force meeting organisers to be more organised - May accelerate growth of virtual organisations - May lead technological revolution in communications	- Can never replace direct FTF contact - Much nonverbal behaviour will not be as detectable - Travel can be beneficial - Expensive, although becoming less so - Technologies not always compatible - Artificiality of experience can be disconcerting — participants are 'on-stage' - Decision making may be too rushed - Technology failures still common

ASSESS YOURSELF

Conduct an internet search on *virtual meeting*, *audioconferencing*, *videoconferencing* and *web conferencing*. Find out as much about these processes as you can. Bear in mind that most of the web pages you view will be in the business of selling particular products, and therefore may not provide an objective assessment of the downside of the technologies.

Getting the most out of meetings: surviving and flourishing as a participant

The chairperson and the secretary play important roles, but the majority of persons at a meeting — and that may include you — are neither the chair nor the secretary. So how can you get the most out of meetings? Consider these guidelines:

- Prepare well. Read the agenda, minutes of the previous meeting, and any supporting materials for the upcoming meeting.
- If you are new to a meeting, read old agendas and minutes. Just as a secretary is the 'living memory' of a group, documents are its inanimate memory, and it is possible that you, as the newest member, may end up knowing more than longer serving members. (Be careful how you display your knowledge, of course.)
- Read the constitution and standing orders of the meeting if they exist. If a formal meeting procedure is used, be familiar with it. Of course, use the procedure to stimulate, not strangle, creativity.
- Note any listed motions or major items for discussion and decision making, and do some homework on those as well, especially if they will have a direct impact on your work.
- If you have been asked to speak on any issue, make sure that you are well prepared. Consider which audiovisual tools you should use, and apply your briefing and pitching skills. Rehearse, rehearse and rehearse — it won't be time wasted.
- Show up, and if you can't show up, make sure that your apologies are recorded in the minutes.
- Stay awake and concentrate. Pay attention to the printed agenda, and try to determine if there are any hidden agendas being pushed as well.
- Listen and learn, and ask questions. Listening is so much more than hearing, and questions are powerful tools for uncovering facts, for getting others to open up, for stalling and for general illumination.
- Contribute, especially if it makes sense in terms of your expertise. Don't make sweeping statements or promises you can't keep, but try to demonstrate modesty and competence.
- Be aware of task, socio-emotional and destructive role-playing, and be alert for groupthink-type dynamics within the meeting.
- Be aware of variations on the basic interacting group, such as brainstorming, Delphi or nominal group technique. If the time is right (e.g. if the meeting is in a rut and is not producing many good ideas, or if a few individuals are dominating to the detriment of broader participation), suggest that perhaps one of these methods might provide some variety and productivity in the meeting's output.
- If it makes sense, volunteer. Action outcomes only make sense when there is someone who can take action. If you feel that you can handle the workload, take it on, and then make sure that you do it. Your success (or failure) will live on in the minutes for this and for subsequent meetings. If you do it well, then the meeting will provide an arena for other people to take note of you as someone who not only talks but also acts. Meetings are one of the few places where you may encounter people from a broad spectrum, and if you perform well in their eyes, that may do you some good.
- Consider using virtual meeting technologies if cost and opportunity permit.

STUDENT STUDY GUIDE

SUMMARY

In this chapter we considered different types of meetings. We saw that the interplay of structure and power can critically determine just what goes on (or doesn't go on) in meetings. We examined formal meeting procedures such as motions and amendments, and noted how these emerge from a context of standing orders, by-laws, memoranda and constitutions. We explored the roles of chairperson and secretary not only in the running of the actual meeting, but also in the planning before and the following up after the meeting (including agendas and minutes), as well as the meeting planning process. We identified questions that need to be asked about meetings to ensure their effectiveness (Why is this meeting really necessary? Who should be there? Where will this meeting take place? When will this meeting take place?). We considered how the geometry of meeting seating might change the dynamics of meetings. We looked at the structure of the basic interacting group (BIG), using mechanisms such as power exerted by the sole leader and power exercised by voting. We considered alternatives to the BIG, such as meetings that employ methods of decision making and problem solving including consensus, Delphi, brainstorming, nominal group technique and improved nominal group technique. We considered the pros and cons of virtual meetings. We also considered strategies for individuals to become more effective in participating in face-to-face and virtual meetings.

KEY TERMS

amendment *p. 628*
audioconferencing *p. 655*
basic interacting group (BIG) *p. 644*
brainstorming *p. 649*
chairperson *p. 630*
consensus *p. 648*
constitution *p. 628*
Delphi *p. 650*

FTF (face-to-face interaction) *p. 655*
hidden agenda *p. 633*
improved nominal group technique (INGT) *p. 653*
motion *p. 628*
nominal group technique (NGT) *p. 652*
pooled ignorance *p. 647*

secretary *p. 632*
standing orders *p. 628*
support of individual or leader *p. 645*
topless meeting *p. 657*
videoconferencing *p. 655*
virtual meeting *p. 655*
voting *p. 646*
web conferencing *p. 655*

REVIEW QUESTIONS

1. Who is in charge of an informal meeting?
2. What does it mean to rescind a resolution?
3. List four of the tasks undertaken by a meeting secretary.
4. What is the rule of thirds?
5. What is a veto?
6. Identify two strengths and two weaknesses of the consensus process.
7. Identify two strengths and two weaknesses of the nominal group technique.
8. Identify two pros and two cons of virtual meetings.
9. List four things that you can do to become a more effective meeting participant.

APPLIED ACTIVITIES

1. Visit a public meeting – for example, a local council, a student union, a company annual general meeting – and observe meeting procedures.
2. Using print or internet resources, study different sets of meeting minutes. Compare and contrast at least two meetings.

3. Study meeting procedures and devise two tactics that could be used to manipulate a meeting. Then devise countertactics for these.
4. Working with others, think of a simple technical problem — for example, inventing a new pizza flavour, improving fuel economy in cars or saving water. Now, have one subgroup work on solutions using brainstorming, and have another subgroup work on the same problem using nominal group technique. This might take 20–40 minutes. Make sure the subgroups operate at some distance from each other. At the end of the process, compare solutions. Does one process produce better results? What are people's experiences of working through the processes?
5. Using print and internet sources, investigate the technology available to facilitate virtual meetings via telephone and computer–internet systems.
6. Using print and internet sources, evaluate the concept of 'topless meetings'. What are the pros and cons of the concept?

WHAT WOULD YOU DO?

Your department has something of a reputation for being wild and way out, but you and your colleagues are also famous as brainstormers who can come up with novel and practical (if sometimes unorthodox) solutions to problems. The chemistry between the 12 department members is very positive, with all members being very supportive of each other. Each day is like a long rambling meeting, with subgroups forming and disengaging, chatting and bouncing ideas off each other. Vance is the department head, and while he often has his hands full trying to keep the crew together, he appears to see that sometimes you have to let people run with things to make changes happen.

One Monday morning, Vance calls the department together. He seems nervous and excited. 'Well, our exploits have apparently travelled far and wide. It seems that we are going to be featured in the company magazine, and the big chief from Central is coming along to sit in on one of our meetings for the photo shoot. Now, I think that outsiders might be a bit perplexed by the way we operate, so what I suggest is that we run our meetings formally, at least until this is over. I've got a copy here of a meeting rule book for each of us, and I'd like you all to swot up on it. It is 150 pages long. They're all coming Thursday, so I suggest that we have a dry run on Wednesday. If we play this right, we could get another 20 or 30 staff in here. Wouldn't that be great?'

With two other colleagues, you open the meeting rule book. You all forge enthusiasm because you like your department head, but you are very concerned this is a bad idea. After all, isn't the culture of creative thinking that Vance has fostered exactly what has made the group a success? How should you best respond to Vance?

SUGGESTED READING

Dressler, Larry & Schwartz, Roger 2010, *Standing in the fire: leading high-heat meetings with clarity, calm and courage*, Berrett-Koehler, New York.

Gutmann, Joanna 2010, *Taking minutes of meetings*, Kogan Page, London.

Harris, Thomas E. & Sherblom, John C 2010, *Small group and team communication*, 5th edn, Allyn and Bacon, Boston, MA.

Haynes, Elvin 2010, *Meeting skills for leaders: make meetings more productive*, 4th edn, Crisp Publications, Menlo Park, CA.

REFERENCES

Alberts, Daniel J 2007, 'Stakeholders or subject matter experts: who should be consulted?', *Energy Policy*, vol. 35, no. 4, pp. 2336–46.

Amer, Suzie 2006, 'Hustle and flow', *Successful Meetings*, vol. 55, no. 3, pp. 44–5.

Andres, Hayward P 2002, 'A comparison of face-to-face and virtual software development teams', *Team Performance Management*, vol. 8, no. 1/2, pp. 39–48.

Arnfalk, P & Kogg, B 2003, 'Service transformation: managing a shift from business travel to virtual meetings', *Journal of Cleaner Production*, vol. 11, pp. 859–72.

Beard, Jon W (ed.) 2004, *Managing impressions with information technology*, Praeger, New York.

Bekkering, Ernst & Shim, JP 2006, 'i2i trust in videoconferencing', *Communications of the Association for Computer Machinery (ACM)*, vol. 49. no. 7, pp. 103–7.

Bélanger, France & Watson-Manheim, Mary Beth 2006, 'Virtual teams and multiple media: structuring media use to attain strategic goals', *Group Decision and Negotiation*, vol. 15, pp. 299–321.

Bluedorn, Allen C, Turbank Daniel B & Love, Mary Sue 1999, 'The effects of stand-up and sit-down meeting formats on meeting outcomes', *Journal of Applied Psychology*, vol. 84, no. 2, pp. 277–85.

Brake, Terence 2006, 'Leading global virtual teams', *Industrial and Commercial Training*, vol. 38, no. 3, pp. 116–21.

Bressen, Tree 2004, 'When and why to block consensus', *Communities*, Spring, pp. 14–16.

Brett, Judith 2001, 'Meetings, parliament and civil society: Reid oration 2001', Institute of Public Administration, IPAA knowledge centre: Orations, www.ipaa.org.au.

Brooks, Charles I & Rebeta, James L 1991, 'College classroom ecology: the relation of sex of student to classroom performance and seating preference', *Environment and Behavior*, vol. 23, no. 3, pp. 305–13.

Bunt, Gary R 2000, *Virtually Islamic: computer-mediated communication and cyber-Islamic environments*, University of Wales Press, Cardiff.

Carlson, John R & Joey, George F 2004, 'Media appropriateness in the conduct and discovery of deceptive communication: the relative influence of richness and synchronicity', *Group Decision and Negotiation*, vol. 13, no. 2, pp. 191–206.

Carte, Traci A, Chidambaram, Laku & Becker, Aaron 2006, 'Emergent leadership in self-managed virtual teams', *Group Decision and Negotiation*, vol. 15, pp. 323–43.

Chapman, Ben 2003, 'The best damn guide to meeting technology, period', *Successful Meetings*, vol. 52, no. 6, pp. 39–49.

Chinyio, Ezekiel, and Olomolaiye, Paul (eds.) 2010, *Construction stakeholder management*, Wiley-Blackwell, Chichester, UK.

Converse, Lance 2004, 'Make the most of online meetings', *Pharmaceutical Executive*, April, p. 42.

Credé, Marcus & Sniezek, Janet A 2003, 'Group judgement processes and outcomes in video-conferencing versus face-to-face groups', *International Journal of Human-Computer Studies*, vol. 59, pp. 875–97.

Davis, Keith 1981, *Human behavior at work: organizational behavior*, McGraw-Hill, New York.

Delbecq, Andre L, Van de Ven, Andrew H & Gustafson, David H 1975, *Group techniques for program planning: a guide to nominal group and delphi processes*, Scott, Foresman, Glenview, IL.

Dickson, Paul 1999, *The official rules and explanations: the original guide to surviving the electronic age with wit, wisdom and laughter*, Federal Street Press, Darien, CT.

Doyle, Eric 2006, 'Videoconferencing gets a new image', *Computer Weekly*, 11 July, pp. 26–8.

Eunson, Baden 1987, *Behaving: managing yourself and others*, McGraw-Hill, Sydney.

Fayard, Anne-Laure 2006, 'Interacting on a video-mediated stage: the collaborative construction of an interactional setting', *Information Technology & People*, vol. 19, no. 2, pp. 152–69.

Fletcher, Winston 1983, *Meetings, meetings: how to manipulate them and have more fun*, Michael Joseph, London.

Fox, William M 1989, 'The improved nominal group technique (INGT)', *Journal of Management Development*, vol. 18, no. 1, pp. 20–7.

Friedman, Thomas L 2004, 'Technology and terror: two responses to globalization', *New York Times*, 15 March, p. 10.

Graefea, Andreas & Armstrong, Scott 2011, 'Comparing face-to-face meetings, nominal groups, Delphi and prediction markets on an estimation task', *International Journal of Forecasting*, vol. 27, no. 1, pp. 183–95.

Hargie, Owen 2010, *Skilled interpersonal communication: research, theory and practice*, 5th edn, Routledge, London.

Hayes, John 2002, *Interpersonal skills at work*, Routledge, New York.

Hindle, Tim 1998, *Managing meetings*, Dorling Kindersley, London.

Howze, Philip C & Dalrymple, Connie 2004, 'Consensus without all the meetings: using the Delphi method to determine course content for library instruction', *Reference Services Review*, vol. 32, no. 2, pp. 174–84.

Jaatinen, PT, Forsstrŝm, J & Loula, P 2002, 'Teleconsultations: who uses them and how?', *Journal of Telemedicine and Telecare*, vol. 8, no. 6, pp. 324–30.

Jacobson, Susan Kay 2010, *Communication skills for conservation professionals*, 2nd edn, Island Press, Washington D.C.

Jung-Erceg, Petra, Pandza, Krsto, Armbruster, Heidi & Dreher, Carsten 2007, 'Absorptive capacity in European manufacturing: a Delphi study', *Industrial Management & Data Systems*, vol. 107, no. 1, pp. 37–51.

Kadam, Umesh T, Jordan, Kelvin & Croft, Peter R 2006, 'A comparison of two consensus methods for classifying morbidities in a single professional group showed the same outcomes', *Journal of Clinical Epidemiology*, vol. 59, pp. 1169–73.

Kanter, Rosabeth Moss 1983, *The change masters: innovation for productivity in the American corporation*, Simon & Schuster, New York.

Kornienko, Georgii 2003, 'An episode of U.S.–Vietnamese negotiations in 1973', *International Affairs*, vol. 49, no. 1, pp. 155–7.

Lawren, Bill 1989, 'Seating for success', *Psychology Today*, vol. 23, no. 9, pp. 16–17.

Lee, Louise 2006, 'Are you ready for your close-up?', *Business Week*, 6 November, p. 13.

Lee-Kelley, Liz & Crossman, Alf 2004, 'A social interaction approach to managing the "invisibles" of virtual teams', *Industrial Management & Data Systems*, vol. 104, no. 8, pp. 650–7.

Linstone, Harold A 1975, 'Eight basic pitfalls: a checklist', in Harold A Linstone, and Murray Turoff (eds), *The Delphi method: techniques and applications*, Addison-Wesley, Reading, MA.

McCandless, Cathleen 2002, 'Sweet harmony: use the Chinese practice of feng shui to arrange a great meeting', *Successful Meetings*, vol. 51, no. 12, pp. 42–3.

Malhotra, Arvind, Majchrzak, Ann & Rosen, Benson 2007, 'Leading virtual teams', *Academy of Management Perspectives*, vol. 21, no. 1, pp. 60–70.

Mitroff, Ian I & Linstone, Harold A 2003, *The unbounded mind: breaking the chains of traditional business thinking*, Oxford University Press, New York/London.

Nijstad, Bernard A, Stroebe, Wolfgang & Lodewijkx, Hein FM 2006, 'The illusion of group productivity: a reduction of failures explanation', *European Journal of Social Psychology*, vol. 36, pp. 31–48.

Owen, Jo 2010, *The death of modern management: how to lead in the new world disorder*, John Wiley & Sons, Chichester, UK.

Pappano, Laura 2002, 'Seating moves up in the classroom scheme', *Boston Globe*, 16 February, p. C1.

Paulus, Paul B & Yang, Huei-Chuan 2000, 'Idea generation in groups: a basis for creativity in organizations', *Organizational Behavior and Human Decision Processes*, vol. 80, no. 1, pp. 74–87.

Pease, Allen & Pease, Barbarra 2007, *The definitive book of body language: the hidden message behind people's gestures and expressions*, Bantam, New York.

Puregger, Marjorie 1998, *The Australian guide to chairing meetings*, University of Queensland Press, St Lucia, Qld.

Ramsey, Lydia, 'Meeting seating – where to sit for your best career moves', article directory: career planning, www.employment360.com.

Rawlinson, J Geoffrey 1981, *Creative thinking and brainstorming*, Gower, Wetmead, Farnborough, UK.

Rowe, Gene & Wright, George 1999, 'The Delphi technique as a forecasting tool: issues and analysis', *International Journal of Forecasting*, vol.15, no. 4, pp. 353–76.

Rutkowski, Anne-Francoise, Saunders, Carol, Vogel, Douglas & van Genuchten, Michiel 2007, '"Is it already 4 a.m. in your time zone?" Focus immersion and temporal dissociation in virtual teams', *Small Group Research*, vol. 38, no. 1, pp. 98–129.

Saaty, Thomas L & Shang, Jen S 2007, 'Group decision-making: head-count versus intensity of preference', *Socio-Economic Planning Sciences*, vol. 41, no. 1, pp. 22–37.

Sadowski-Rasters, Gaby, Duysters, Geert & Sadowski, Bert 2007, *Communication and cooperation in the virtual workplace: teamwork in computer-mediated communication*, Edward Elgar Publishing, Camberley, Surrey.

Saffer, Dan 2008, 'Rules for topless meetings', blog, *adaptive path*, www.adaptivepath.com.

Salusbury, Matt 2004, 'Unsocial seating arrangements', *New Statesman*, 1 March, pp. 18–19.

Schein, Edgar A 1988, *Process consultation*, 2nd edn, Addison-Wesley, Reading, MA.

Schümmer, Till & Tandler, Peter 2008, 'Patterns for technology advanced meetings', in Hvatuma, L. and Schümmer, T. (eds.), *Proc. of EuroPLoP 2007*, UVK: Konstanz, Germany, pp. 97–119, http://living-agendas.de.

Schyns, Birgit (ed.) 2010, 'Do I see us like you see us? Consensus, agreement, and the context of leadership relationships', *European Journal of Work and Organizational Psychology*, vol. 19, no. 3.

Sears, Theresa Ann 2005, 'Squaring the Round Table: time, hierarchy, and the fall of Camelot', *The Romanic Review*, vol. 96, no. 1, pp. 3–14.

Silber, Kenneth & Foshay, Wellesly R. 2010, Handbook of improving performance in the workplace: Instructional design and training delivery, vol. 1, Pfeiffer, San Francisco, CA.

Sinclair, Amanda 1992, 'The tyranny of a team ideology', *Organisation Studies*, vol. 14, no. 4, pp. 611–26.

Spielman, Sue & Winfield, Liz 2003, *The web conferencing handbook: understand the technology, choose the right vendors, software and equipment, start saving time and money today!*, Amacom, New York.

Stone, Donald & Stone, Alice 1974, 'The administration of chairs', *Public Administration Review*, vol. 34, no. 1, pp. 71–7.

Susskind, Lawrence E & Cruikshank, Jeffrey L 2007, *Breaking Robert's rules: the new way to run your meeting, build consensus, and get results*, Oxford University Press, New York.

Teschler, Leland 2006, 'Brainstorming or just hot air?', *Machine Design*, 10 August, p. 8.

Thompson, Louis, Jr. 2011, 'Behind the resistance to virtual meetings', *Compliance Week*, vol. 8, no. 84, pp 60–1.

Timmerman, C Erik & Scott, Craig R 2006, 'Virtually working: communicative and structural predictors of media use and key outcomes in virtual work teams', *Communication Monographs*, vol. 73, no. 1, pp. 108–36.

Tropman, John E 2003, *Making meetings work: achieving high quality group decisions*, 2nd edn, Sage, Thousand Oaks, CA.

Van Gundy, Arthur B. 2007 *How asking the right questions generates the great ideas your company needs*, Amacom, New York, NY.

Werkhoven, Peter J, Schraagen, Maarten, Jan & Punte, Patrick AJ 2001, 'Seeing is believing: communication performance under isotropic teleconferencing conditions', *Displays*, vol. 22, pp. 137–49.

Yuan, Yufei, Head, Milena & Du, Mei 2003, 'The effects of multimedia communication on web-based negotiation', *Group Decisions and Negotiation*, vol. 12, no. 1, pp. 89–109.

Zimmerman, Angelika 2011, 'Interpersonal relationships in transnational, virtual teams: towards a configurational perspective', *International Journal of Management Reviews*, vol. 13, no. 1, pp. 59–78.

Zinski, Christopher J 2006, 'Choose your words carefully: board minutes matter', *ABA Banking Journal*, vol. 98, no. 10, pp. 22, 24, 26, 32.

20

Employment communication

LEARNING OBJECTIVES

After studying this chapter you should be able to:

- Explain the different types of career choices open to job seekers
- Explain different strategies relating to jobs that are, and are not, advertised
- Discuss the relevance of transferable skills
- Give an example of a personal brand statement
- Write effective documents, such as cover letters and résumés
- Prepare for job interviews
- Explain the role of testing in job seeking

Employment: the bigger picture

For many of us, a job is crucial to economic survival, but it also helps first to define just who we are. Job seeking is not simply a matter of people leaving secondary or tertiary education and then trying to get into the workforce. Today, there are many individuals trying to get into — and out of — the workforce, including:

- people already in a job who are seeking a change
- people who have previously been in the workforce, and now want to voluntarily re-enter, such as those who have been caring for children and running a household full-time
- people who have retired but want to return to the workforce
- people who are contemplating retirement but do not want to give up work altogether
- people who want to 'downshift' or adopt a less hectic form of employment
- people who want to work for themselves
- people who want to build a portfolio career of various part-time and 'temp' jobs
- people who want to telecommute or work from home.

There have been many changes in the nature of employment in recent decades, and we can expect there will be even more change in the future. Borchard (1995) relates the experience of being in a job, looking for a job or leaving a job to a wider historical context, contrasting the way it was in the era of mass production (1865–1980s) to the more recent knowledge-service era (table 20.1) (Borchard 1995, p. 10).

TABLE 20.1 Career development — then and now

Structural characteristics	Mass production era (1865–1980s)	Knowledge-service era (1980s and beyond)
Economic reality: job-creating forces	Huge manufacturing industries oriented to the national economy	Knowledge-service enterprises, competing in a global market
Job-market structure or dominant job types	Two-tiered factory: ■ blue collar ■ white collar	Multi-tiered (no tiered); mixed technical, service, professional, executive
Occupational characteristics	A few stable, clearly classifiable types	Many rapidly evolving and amorphous types
Career preparation	Complete your education and then get a job	Continue working, learning, keeping pace with information technology growth
Career choice: how you enter and pursue a career	Luck, happenstance, what you happened to know about or fall into	Decision making aided by a professional and ongoing attention
How you get jobs	■ Blue collar: family work ties ■ White collar: résumés, classified ads, placement services	Skill or competency based on self-definition and ongoing networking
Primary employment targets	Large corporations	Small companies, skill-contracting agencies
Who controls your career	The organisation	The individual (with the aid of professionals)
Career development objective	Climbing prescribed organisational ladders	Personal development in areas of expertise
Employment source	One organisation for entire career	Series of organisations and contracting agents
Primary employment concerns (rewards)	Salary, benefits, leave, promotion, titles	Developing potentials, pursuing work interests
Major career limitations	Restrictions based on sex, race, age, religion	Skills, knowledge and job development savvy
Retirement financing	Company retirement and government pension	Portable, personal retirement programs
Retirement considerations	40 years — gold watch and never work again. Relax, play, travel, die	Ongoing balance in self; developing work, leisure and learning

Job takers and job makers

Most of the discussion in this chapter is concerned with using communication skills to improve the chances of getting a job. But what if the solution to the economic problem of life is not employment, but self-employment? What if we become 'job makers' instead of 'job takers' (Ellyard 2001)? There has been considerable growth in recent years in self-employment, or running a business from premises separate from the owner's dwelling, or even from the dwelling (home-based businesses). There are variations, such as completely running your own organisation or working for others as a contractor or subcontractor, temping or running a franchise operation. Some workers choose these roles because of the freedom and independence they bring, whereas others have no choice but to offer their services on a contract basis. (This is usually cheaper for employers, as they may not have to pay certain overheads such as superannuation contributions and leave entitlements.)

Career paths

Let's say that a person enters the full-time workforce in 2010 and leaves it in 2060. In the past, this person would probably have had a career path that included long tenures at only a few, or maybe just one, company, with different amounts of part-time work along the way to supplement income and to provide broader experiences. Today, it is more likely that such a person would face a series of different work experiences, as illustrated in figure 20.1. These might involve a number of changes between careers, between full-time and part-time, contract or consulting work, between nonworking phases by choice and not by choice, between being employed by others and being self-employed, between employment and retirement, between being retrained and being on paid leave, and volunteering in differing social situations.

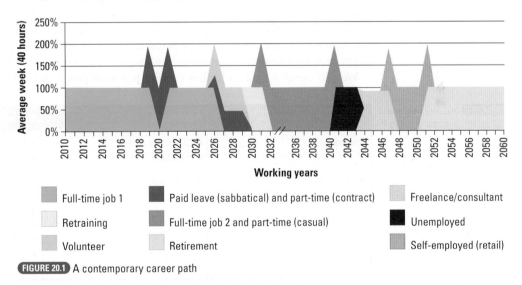

FIGURE 20.1 A contemporary career path

Where are the jobs?

In this chapter we will consider the communication techniques needed to get a job in the conventional fashion, such as by writing a job application letter and sending it, together with a résumé, in response to an advertisement in a newspaper or on an internet employment site. For example, figure 20.2 (see overleaf) shows the steps job seekers took to obtain employment over a recent period (obviously, figures add up to more than 100 per cent because seekers employed more than one strategy).

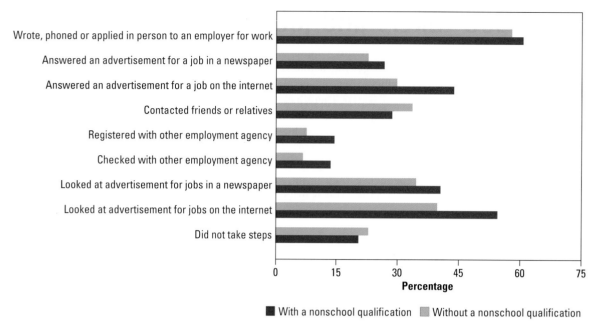

Wrote, phoned or applied in person to an employer for work
Answered an advertisement for a job in a newspaper
Answered an advertisement for a job on the internet
Contacted friends or relatives
Registered with other employment agency
Checked with other employment agency
Looked at advertisement for jobs in a newspaper
Looked at advertisement for jobs on the internet
Did not take steps

0   15   30   45   60   75
Percentage

■ With a nonschool qualification   ■ Without a nonschool qualification

Note: Figure refers to all steps taken to obtain a job; people may appear in more than one category.

FIGURE 20.2 Employee (excluding owner–manager of incorporated enterprises) job starters: selected steps taken to attain a job by holders of nonschool [post-secondary] qualification versus those without a nonschool qualification.

Source: Australian Bureau of Statistics (2010). Reproduced with permission.

It appears that those holding post-school qualifications are more assertive in seeking jobs (with the exception of contacted friends and relatives). This pattern is also notable in those who have been in work, as opposed to those seeking work for the first time. Online job searching is becoming more popular. In fact, it is taking so much revenue from newspaper classified revenues that some newspapers have closed down.

We can use this data to further explore just how people get jobs (table 20.2).

TABLE 20.2 Job seeking and placement: a model

	Advertised	**Not advertised**
Contest	■ Open contest ■ Election	■ Unsolicited approaches ■ Networking, contacts
No contest	■ Put-up job	■ Appointment from within ■ Incumbent by default ■ Agencies, headhunters ■ Stand-by pool ■ Internships, holiday jobs ■ Nepotism ■ Corruption

The most obvious way to find employment is to apply for advertised jobs. Application is usually made by sending in a cover letter and a résumé or CV. In ethical and transparent situations, this usually means that the best person for the job gets the job. Some people also get jobs not through selection, but through election.

However, in the real world, sometimes all is not as it seems. Merely because a job is advertised does not mean that there is a fair and open contest for that job. Sometimes a job is advertised to give the appearance of transparency and fairness — and sometimes to meet legal obligations to advertise. The brutal reality, however, may be that there is no job. Instead, there may be a put-up job: in effect, a conspiracy to ensure that a certain individual – usually someone already inside the organisation – gets the job. It doesn't happen all that often, and it's completely unethical, but you should be aware of this possibility.

This is a bad process, and often produces mediocre placements. In a few cases, however, it may produce reasonably effective placements, but only because other methods of selection – evaluation of résumés, interviews and testing – are not always successful in identifying competent candidates who intend to stay around long enough to repay the investment of time and resources in hiring them in the first place.

As we have seen, many jobs are filled even though they are not advertised. Some of these are filled in a competitive or semi-competitive situation by job seekers making unsolicited applications and by having networks of contacts who let them know that positions are available. Other positions are filled, in ethical and not-so-ethical ways, without any competitive dynamics. For example, an organisation may simply decide that it wishes to appoint from within its own staff, or perhaps a person occupying the role in a temporary capacity becomes a permanent employee by default. Generally speaking, private sector organisations have much more freedom to operate in this way than public sector organisations.

Jobs may be filled by candidates recommended by job agencies or executive recruitment (headhunter) agencies. There may also be a standby pool: this is a reserve of résumés on file from candidates who were unsuccessful in previous applications or who have expressed interest on an unsolicited basis. Even though you may be unsuccessful in one attempt at getting a job with an organisation, it is possible that you might be contacted at a later date. Sometimes part-time staff are taken on in apprentice or experience-gaining roles, such as students doing internships or holiday jobs. Sometimes these people perform so well that they are offered full-time employment. In family-based organisations, it may be considered normal to appoint relatives because they are 'family' (nepotism). Finally, the process of employing at an organisation may simply be corrupt, with rules bent to put someone into a position because that's the way powerful people want it to be.

What do employers really want?

When preparing for a career, people tend to study a core of technical skills and knowledge – for example, electronics, physics, hairdressing, journalism, sales, information technology. The list of areas of technical competence is almost endless. Technical skills and knowledge are indispensable because they give us the practical and specific competencies we need to operate in any given area. Technical skills and knowledge, however, can have their limitations. For example:

- they may become obsolete fairly quickly
- they may not be transferable to a second or subsequent career
- they may not give us the 'soft skills' we need to deal with people
- they may predispose us to use narrowly conventional, technical and tactical approaches to problems and decisions, rather than novel, systematic and strategic ones
- they may infect us with a 'tribe' mentality, so that we come to (erroneously) see our profession or trade as an in-group with a monopoly on wisdom, as opposed to the out-groups who do not.

Recent research in numerous countries has shown that nontechnical skills and knowledge are as important as, and sometimes more important than, technical skills and knowledge. Such skills and knowledge are known as **transferable skills**, or employability, generic graduate, or soft skills (figure 20.3; see overleaf) (DEST 2002).

Transferable skills: skills that are relevant to more than one area of technical expertise

Australia key competencies (Mayer Key Competencies)	United Kingdom core skills (National Centre for Vocational Qualifications)	Canada employability skills profile	United States workplace know-how (Secretary's Commission on Achieving Necessary Skills)
■ Collecting, analysing and organising information	■ Communication	■ Thinking skills	■ Information ■ Foundation skills: basic skills
■ Communicating ideas and information	■ Communication ■ Personal skills: improving own performance and learning	■ Communication skills	■ Information ■ Foundation skills: basic skills
■ Planning and organising activities	■ Personal skills: improving own performance and learning	■ Responsibility skills ■ Thinking skills	■ Resources ■ Foundation skills: personal qualities
■ Working with others and in teams	■ Personal skills: working with others	■ Positive attitudes and behaviour ■ Work with others ■ Adaptability	■ Interpersonal skills
■ Using mathematical ideas and techniques	■ Numeracy: application of number	■ Understand and solve problems using mathematics	■ Foundation skills: basic skills
■ Solving problems	■ Problem solving	■ Problem-solving and decision-making skills ■ Learning skills	■ Foundation skills: thinking
■ Using technology	■ Information technology	■ Use technology ■ Communication skills	■ Technology ■ Systems
■ Post-Mayer additions ■ Cultural understandings	■ Modern foreign language	■ Manage information ■ Use numbers ■ Work safely ■ Participate in projects and tasks	

FIGURE 20.3 Generic employability skills identified by four countries

In the communication area in particular, the following skills have been identified as contributing to employability (DEST 2002, p. 8):
- Listening and understanding
- Speaking clearly and directly
- Writing to the needs of the audience
- Negotiating responsively
- Reading independently
- Empathising
- Using numeracy effectively
- Understanding the needs of internal and external customers
- Persuading effectively
- Establishing and using networks
- Being assertive
- Sharing information
- Speaking and writing in languages other than English.

These trends were confirmed with other reports on what employers look for when selecting new employees. Figure 20.4, for example, shows that academic qualifications are not considered to be nearly as important as interpersonal and communication skills (see also the Preface to this book). Other areas looked at in depth in this book – team skills, leadership skills, emotional intelligence, critical reasoning and lateral thinking, and fit with organisational culture – have assumed high priority, whereas they were not mentioned as recently as a decade ago (see also Australian Association of Graduate Employers, 2007). Truly, soft skills have hard impact as far as employers are concerned.

FIGURE 20.4 The top ten selection criteria for recruiting graduates

Source: Graduate Careers Australia (2010), 'What employer's want', www.graduatecareers.com.au.

1. Interpersonal and communication skills (written and oral)
2. Passion, knowledge of the industry, drive, commitment and attitude
3. Critical reasoning and analytical skills, problem solving, lateral thinking and technical skills
4. Calibre of academic results
5. Teamwork skills
6. Work experience
7. Cultural alignment, values fit
8. Emotional intelligence (including self-awareness, strength of character and confidence motivation)
9. Leadership skills
10. Intra and extracurricular activities.

These trends and preferences are not new. Other older research has singled out written communication as a transferable (graduate) skill that employers particularly seek (but do not often find) (e.g. DEST 1998). Interpersonal and communication skills have ranked as the most important selection criteria used in recruiting graduates in recent years (Graduate Careers Australia, 2010).

Academic institutions are often reluctant to run subjects, modules, courses or electives dealing specifically with soft/generic/graduate/transferable/communication skills – sometimes arguing that these skills and knowledge sets are already 'embedded' in existing courses. This is a debatable point. Some commentators have argued that 'embedding' is meaningless, as it implies that a large body of learning about human behaviour can be absorbed by osmosis or telepathy while students learn 'real' content, with such content best reflected in academic results and prowess in the technicalities of a particular field (Eunson 2004, 2005). Employers, apparently, feel otherwise (see, for example, figure 20.4). All other things being equal, a communication and/or writing subject or module listed on your academic record and résumé may be the point of differentiation – a point in your favour – that employers are looking for when considering your job application along with those of many others.

How to prepare for the job market

If we look at the matters covered in the previous sections, a number of things become apparent about how we can better prepare for finding work in the future.

Become more flexible

Because of the increased rate of change in the workplace, it makes sense to adopt a more flexible and resilient mindset. As Moses (2001) observes:

> no matter what our official employment status, we are all temporary workers. Whether we have conventional full-time jobs or are contingent, contract or freelance workers, we are all living and working in TempWorld. In TempWorld, everything shifts rapidly. Nothing is forever, everything is temporary: where you work, what you do there, the skills you use, the people you work with.

One way in which you can build your flexibility is to create a company for yourself. This will give you the opportunity of taking work as a contractor or consultant (bearing in mind that contractors or consultants may not be able to benefit from the 'extras' that full-time employees have, such as superannuation contributions, workers compensation and holiday and sick leave). Setting yourself up as a company means that you should consider the following:

- company registration
- business number or code
- stationery, such as business cards and a letterhead
- basic communications and work equipment (a computer, a telephone, a fax, a smartphone)
- business email address and a website.

You should also consider seeking the advice of a private business consultant or government small business agency before you set up, and it would be useful to obtain initial and ongoing services of an accountant to help out with tax and other matters.

Become more organised

Even if you do not intend to create your own company, you can be organised with some type of business card, or at least a card with personal contact details on it (it's cheaper than you might think, and an ideal tool for networking). You might consider a separate email account and social media accounts for your professional or job-seeking identity.

If you are actively engaged in a job search and have put one or several phone numbers down as contacts, answer the phone in a professional manner, and ensure that any greetings you put on answering machines are professional in tone.

Prepare a database or spreadsheet of potential employers, and record details of contacts made and information gained.

Think big and think small

If you are going to put some effort into finding a job, then you need to think about scale. Bolles (2011) suggests that you need to devote 20–30 hours a week to your campaign, and you should seriously be planning to contact up to 200 potential employers. At the same time, he suggests, focus should not be exclusively on big employers – small businesses have created the greatest number of jobs in the past few decades, and that is where most of your energies should be concentrated.

Become a job researcher

Systematically search online, newspaper and trade magazine sources of job ads; researching potential employers and recording details of your research. Obtain copies of annual reports and brochures; learn the names and roles of key personnel from the organisation chart; look at websites; join professional social networking websites, such as LinkedIn, and make contact with employees at the organisation and in the industry; trawl through industry journals; and talk to people who work at the target organisation or in the wider industry. What does the grapevine or rumour mill say about the target organisation?

It is possible that a reasonable effort at research will, in fact, make you more informed about the target organisation than many people within that organisation. The reality of any organisation is, of course, only partially revealed by print and online data, but even partial revelations are a good start. Researching like this helps you in a number of ways:

- It helps you to decide whether you want to get involved in the target organisation.
- It helps you to more specifically target your job application or cover letter and résumé.
- It helps reduce any performance stress you might feel in a job interview because the stress of unfamiliarity has been partially reduced.

- It may impress selection interviewers if you have taken the trouble to find out about the organisation. It shows that you are motivated and organised, and are a self-starter with transferable skills. It suggests that if you get the job, you may take less time to settle in than other candidates.

Not all the details of a position can be published on a website or in a newspaper ad. There may be a more extensive job or position description, where the role is described in greater detail, and where **key selection criteria** are provided.

If there is no position description, make a point of telephoning the organisation and asking about the position. If there is a position description, obtain it, and then telephone and ask further questions about it. If the organisation welcomes telephone enquiries, you should prepare for a 'mini-interview' — and your performance in conversation may possibly do you a lot of good, or a lot of harm. This is because the person on the other end of the line may have influence on the entire selection process, either officially or unofficially, and will naturally form an impression of you from the way you come across on the telephone. So you should prepare. Write down key points you want information about. Research the organisation and weave that into your enquiry. Use a professional voice. If necessary, rehearse the entire exercise.

Key selection criteria: standards or benchmarks of performance, ability, qualifications and experience that employers have set in relation to a job position

Become a networker

Modern career seekers have a number of mini-careers with different employers, and thus have 'boundaryless careers'. The hallmarks of those who are successful in the marketplace are:
- portable skills, knowledge and abilities across multiple firms
- personal identification with meaningful work
- on-the-job action learning
- development of multiple networks and peer-learning relationships
- individual responsibility for career management (Sullivan, 2001).

Of these, the ability to network may in fact be essential before even entering the job market for the first time. Consider, for example, the number of people who obtained employment through personal networks and connections (figure 20.2).

Networking involves making contacts with people who may be instrumental in getting you a job. A discussion of networking philosophies and techniques can be found in chapter 16. Don't be shy about it — the more you get to know a particular industry or line of work, the more you will realise that there may be many people employed there with abilities considerably below yours. So why shouldn't you do what you can to raise your profile and increase your chances of employment? But where are these networks? They're out there, and they include:
- professional associations, such as industry associations or general management associations that may run seminars or meetings on various topics. (Locate these through advertisements in industry publications and in the Yellow Pages. Take out a student or associate membership.)
- online social networks with a business focus, such as LinkedIn

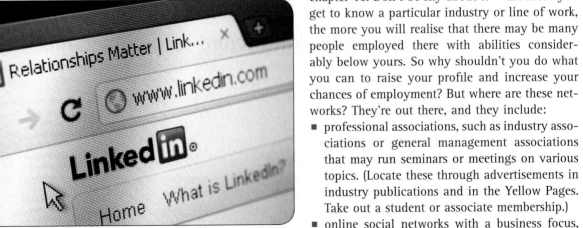

Millions of professionals around the world use online social networks that have a business focus, such as LinkedIn, to network with potential employers.

- trade fairs, exhibitions, industry conferences and seminars
- volunteer and community organisations
- service clubs
- on-campus employer interviews.

When you are networking, be professionally dressed and groomed. Consider carrying your business or personal card, copies of your résumé and a portfolio of your work. Don't be too pushy, but don't be too shy. Don't be sycophantic or manipulative in the way you go about this – if you do, it will be obvious, and will do you more damage than good. By the same token, don't feel that you have to demean or ingratiate yourself in this process. If the price of a job involves sacrificing your self-esteem, then think carefully before taking such a job.

Build a personal brand

Think of famous brands of shoes, soft drink and clothing. The brand, consisting of the name, the logo and the attention it draws from the public, is what gives certain products and services their profile. Sampson (2002) and others suggest that you need to market yourself to employers by creating a **personal brand** for yourself. Your personal brand is also known as your unique selling proposition (USP), which is what differentiates you from other candidates.

Personal brand: the set of characteristics and skills that sets one person apart from another; also known as unique selling proposition (USP)

Define your personal brand or USP in 2–3 sentences. You can then use this brand statement in employment correspondence and conversation, or keep it as a private statement that will motivate you. When writing the statement, analyse yourself and seek feedback from others about your strengths and weaknesses (see Karseras 2007; McNally & Speak 2011). Some examples of personal brand statements are shown in figure 20.5.

Brand statement 1 (full sentences)	Brand statement 2 (partial sentences)
I am a social worker with good interpersonal skills and a total commitment to everything I do. I have street-smart knowledge of the bureaucracy and the regulatory background, and I can work well with my subordinates, peers and superiors to deliver the best possible outcomes for our clients.	Skilled laboratory technician. Fully qualified, with additional training conducted at own expense. Methodical, with a good eye for detail. Provide good back-up for others. Enjoy working with researchers with varying temperaments and styles. A good listener and team player. Disciplined, and a self-starter. Enjoy working with and for those researchers at the cutting edge of knowledge creation.

FIGURE 20.5 Examples of personal brand statements

Build a skills–knowledge–experience mix

In a knowledge-based economy and society, the more knowledge, skills and experience you can deploy, the more employable you will be, and the stronger your personal brand or USP will be. Gladwell (2008) argues that to succeed in any field, you have to practice for 10 000 hours in it.

Technical skills

Consider your own cognitive style, and then consider whether it might not be useful to take on some skills and knowledge outside that style to broaden your frame of reference (and to make yourself more employable). For example, you may be undertaking (or planning to undertake) studies in a technical field, with a base qualification such as a degree, diploma or certificate. If, in the base qualification, you are focusing on foundation technical skills – such as engineering, law, science, carpentry or medicine – then perhaps you should consider taking a 'soft skill' subject or sequence of subjects, in fields such as writing or management and supervision. If you are undertaking (or planning to undertake) studies in a generalist or arts field, consider taking a 'hard skill' subject or sequence of subjects in fields such as accounting, information technology or statistics.

Consider combining sequences so that you not only have more than one string to your bow, but are in a position to exploit emerging synergistic areas, such as chemistry and law; textiles and home economics; plumbing and electrical; information technology and writing ... the possibilities are endless! Choose one field for your heart (what gives you pleasure now and in the future), and one field for your head (what gives you money and survival now and in the future).

Transferable skills

Transferable skills are obviously highly desirable for employers, but are often difficult to prove and/or document. Depending on your budget and time, consider taking single subjects or short courses from educational institutions and training organisations in:

- communication
- professional writing
- interpersonal skills
- negotiation and conflict resolution
- public speaking
- team building
- time management and stress management
- decision making and problem solving
- research skills
- software programs (word processing, spreadsheets, databases, presentation, project management, website creation).

National governments and private companies are now devising test instruments for a range of transferable skills. In Australia, for example, post-secondary students can sit for the Graduate Skills Assessment test, which will give them a qualification showing potential employers that a set of transferable skills has been acquired in a period of formal study. The Australian Association of Graduate Employers (AAGE), agreeing with Graduate Careers Australia (see figure 20.4) has affirmed the preferences of employers for these 'soft skills', rather than for technical skills in areas from electronics to law and everything in between (AAGE, 2009).

Postgraduate study

Again, depending upon your budget and time, consider doing postgraduate study in your base field. There are risks in becoming overqualified for certain jobs, but such risks tend to be outweighed by the dynamics of **credentialism** and the prestige attached to higher qualifications.

Credentialism: the process of restricting access to professions by setting higher and higher entrance standards

Postgraduate studies – in law, plumbing, communications, child care or space engineering – can be done immediately after completion of the base qualification, or some years after that. Postgraduate work can help expand on the core knowledge and skills acquired in the base qualification and/or can bring the learner up to speed on new developments.

Self-directed learning

Institutions of learning sometimes do not do the best job possible in making courses of study relevant to the workplace, or indeed of telling us about workplaces. Sometimes the research and generalist skills that are picked up along the way in a course of study are completely transferable to a wide range of job situations, but sometimes they are not, and sometimes – for example, in a job interview – it would be helpful to be able to demonstrate succinctly and persuasively the concrete relevance of the fields we have studied (this is particularly true of arts/generalist areas). There are no set ways to do this, but it may help you to pursue your own studies by searching library catalogues and websites for books and other materials that tell you about the practical applications of the fields you have studied and the practical dynamics of organisations, business and workplace culture.

Experience

Experience, by definition, is not something that can be purchased off the shelf – you have to live it. The basic dilemma that confronts many job seekers is shown in figure 20.6.

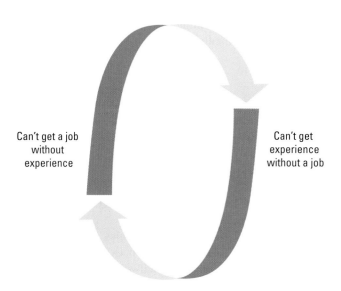

Can't get a job without experience

Can't get experience without a job

FIGURE 20.6 The employment–experience paradox

Employment–experience paradox: the situation that occurs when you can't get a job without experience, and you can't get experience without a job

Many students need to take on part-time employment to pay for their education and to cover living costs. This work, over and above the work of study, can be interesting and motivating, but equally, it can be exhausting and demotivating. There is, however, an upside: it *is* work experience and it helps to break the **employment–experience paradox**.

Part-time work, particularly when it involves an increase in responsibility and task variety, not only builds your skill mix, but also makes it more likely that you can approach your employer to be a referee. Indeed, if your performance in your part-time work is satisfactory, then your part-time employer might well become your full-time employer.

Money to live on and to pay for education, as well as experience and contacts, can also be gained from working through holidays and by doing industry placement work as part of a qualification.

Putting it all together

These five factors – the technical skills of your base qualification, postgraduate qualifications, transferable skills, self-directed learning and experience – can be used to plan your future employability. If you can obtain and combine these five factors, you can be a 'multiple threat' and increase your chances with potential employers.

The earlier you start planning your job search, the more likely you will be able to create an effective personal brand that will prove attractive to employers. You may find it useful to develop a five-year plan for your career moves, no matter where you are on your career path. Mobilise your time, money, energy and resources to build that personal brand.

Job application evaluation

As we have seen (figure 20.2), employers use advertisements and agencies to fill jobs. In turn, job seekers may make contact with organisations, even though no jobs are advertised, and may also use contacts to find out if there are 'hidden jobs' or unadvertised jobs in the offing. Employers evaluate job seekers through job application letters, résumés and the document mix, interviews, reference checks and tests. Be aware that an increasing number of employers are checking out social media websites like Facebook, YouTube, Twitter and MySpace, and search engines like Google, to view you in your social and other settings. This is sneaky but true, and can be potentially embarrassing. It can even be the cause of a job not being offered to you (Smith & Kidder, 2010). Job selectors should, of course, be aware that this is a two-way street: they may find their images and words posted where they never expected them to be.

The document mix

Documents are the beginning of the employment application process. When you apply for a job, there are certain documents you should send (figure 20.7; see overleaf). The most obvious ones are a cover letter and a résumé, but under certain circumstances, you might also include a completed application form, results or a transcript of results from accredited education/training institutions, copies of qualifications from accredited education/training institutions, written references or letters of recommendation, and a portfolio or samples of work.

The documents you write are not an end in themselves, but a means to an end. They comprise a request from you to give a performance in an interview. Such documents are also examples of your work: employers will assume that the quality of your written communication with them will be similar to that you would use with their most valued clients, so it is important that you give your potential employers reasons to feel confident in this. This means that you set aside time to draft, redraft, lay out and proofread such documents. If you do not, you are giving the employer an excuse to cull your application from the list of applicants.

The tone, style and design you use in employment communication should be of a standard professional type for most situations, but some flexibility can be used, depending on how you read the employment situation. For example, if you are applying for a job in advertising or graphic design and the employers say they are looking for people with 'new bright ideas, the ability to think outside the box and a strong track record in creativity', then it might make sense to design documents in bold formats, use humour in your wording, and attach a copy of graphic art samples (or perhaps even send a résumé in multimedia format). The same approach, however, would not be very smart when responding to a position for an auditor in a highly conservative bank.

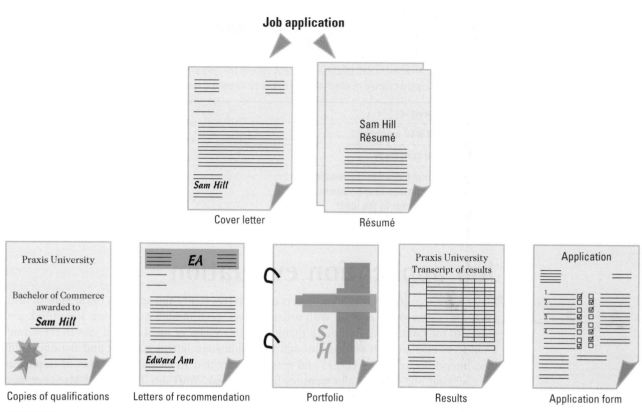

FIGURE 20.7 The document mix in employment communication

Be careful how you 'edit reality' when creating a picture of yourself. If there are unfavourable things about you that you do not want brought to light, use common sense to ensure that editing does not bring you into conflict with a potential employer or the law. Lying about qualifications, in particular, has become a problem, and elaborate detection measures are now available to track these (Wood et al. 2007). Be as honest as you can, and resist the temptation to edit or embroider (see 'Ethics and rationalisation' in chapter 1).

Of course, you should never forget the 'you' attitude: what's in it for them? Employers are not waiting humbly for the privilege of offering you a job. They need to be convinced that you will 'value add' to their operations. Don't presume, don't demand. *Persuade.*

Job application cover letters

Beatty (2003, p. 3) suggests that the application or cover letter is in fact three letters in one:

1. *A business transmittal letter*, explaining to the prospective employer what the accompanying document (the résumé) is all about
2. *A letter of introduction*, introducing you and your background to the prospective employer
3. *A sales letter*, seeking to convince the prospective employer that you have something valuable to contribute and that it will be worth their time to grant you an interview.

The job application or cover letter is usually sent with a résumé. These two documents *complement* each other (figure 20.8) — one should not take the place of the other.

Letter	Résumé
First in sequence/package	Second in sequence/package
Sometimes read first	Sometimes read first
Not easy to skim in order to get quick impression	Easy to skim in order to get quick impression
More personal style	Less personal style
More specific approach: identifies which job is being sought	More general: could be used for a number of jobs
More persuasive in tone	More informative in tone
Needs to be fairly short; say, two pages	Can be fairly long, but be careful of going beyond four pages for most positions
Used to make assertions about capability	Used to provide evidence for assertions about capability
Used to reinforce some points in résumé, but not to repeat all of them	Used to provide reference point for readers of letter
Used to respond to job description criteria	Not directly involved in responding to criteria

FIGURE 20.8 Letters and résumés

Note that some employers specify a handwritten cover letter (obviously not suitable for an online application). Why is this? The most commonly cited reason is that employers are employing the dark art of graphology, or attempting to determine a person's capabilities and personality from their writing (Greasley, 2000); while others may be using equally dubious techniques, such as astrology and numerology (Ryan et al., 1999).

Bangerter et al. (2009) rebut this interpretation, pointing out that graphology is in fact rarely used (and in fact is quite ineffectual, even though as of 2011, there are over 500 books in print on the topic), suggesting that human resource officers or personnel selectors are using handwriting for variety of reasons. Recruiters profess using them as a filter, hoping that the extra effort involved will discourage unmotivated individuals from applying. Some recruiters use them as an initial screening tool (e.g. screening out letters with coffee stains or too many visible erasures). Additionally, some recruiters use them to gain a first impression of applicants (e.g. whether they have understood the application instructions). Handwriting also shows your real abilities in grammar, spelling and punctuation without any help from software checkers, so beware and prepare.

Your cover letter may be difficult to write, especially as it should be as short as possible (two pages at most, and preferably one page only), and yet it needs to cover a lot of ground:

- It should refer to the job in question – for example, by name and/or reference number. (It is possible that there is more than one job advertised.)
- It should contain your responses to the key selection criteria as stated in the job advertisement or in the full position description document.
- It should paraphrase and expand on the information contained in your résumé.
- It should contain a statement about why you are applying and why you believe that you would perform well in the position.

Solicited and unsolicited letters

A **solicited application letter** (figure 20.10) is written in response to an actual advertisement (figure 20.9) or notice of a job vacancy. An **unsolicited application letter** is written when no advertisement or notice has been placed in the hope that it might attract interest from a potential employer. Sometimes making an unsolicited approach is a waste of your time, but sometimes it isn't — the success rate of applying for nonadvertised jobs is too high to ignore (figure 20.2).

MANAGEMENT TRAINEE
$40 000

POSITION J2311

JUGGERNAUT MANUFACTURING INC. We are a rapidly growing international company that is looking for new blood. We need fifteen new management trainees.

Are you good enough to be one of them? We are looking for self-starters who are highly motivated. You will have a bachelor's degree, although the field of the degree is not vital. If you do not have a degree, maybe you can persuade us that your qualifications and experience make you a candidate.

You will have excellent writing, speaking and interpersonal skills. You will be a team player with excellent time and pressure management skills. You will already have begun to demonstrate exceptional problem-solving and leadership abilities. You will be the kind of person who can research any field or problem quickly and thoroughly, and present a professional briefing paper and presentation to a top-level executive audience. You will have first-rate computer skills, and be able to communicate effectively with internal and external customers.

Does this sound like you? Write to us and enclose a résumé. This could be the start of something big!

Contact:
Ms Tanya Hemmings
Human Resources
Juggernaut International
1255 Pacific Highway
GONDWANA 9251

FIGURE 20.9 Sample job advertisement

The key to an unsolicited letter is to convey an air of polite enquiry and attractive professionalism without coming across as cheeky or presumptuous. You need to hold your reader's attention for long enough so that you can pitch your case and outline your capabilities. Some sample openings of unsolicited letters are now shown, and a sample unsolicited letter is shown in figure 20.11.

- *I am writing to you to express an interest in working for* [organisation] *at some time in the future. While I appreciate that you may have no positions vacant at the moment, I believe that I could make a real contribution to* [organisation] *and would be grateful if you could keep this letter and résumé on file.*

- *I will be graduating with a* [qualification] *in* [field of study] *from* [learning institution] *in* [weeks or months]. *With my qualifications and some experience in the field, I think that I could add to the effectiveness and productivity of* [organisation] *if given a chance. I am writing to you to ask for a meeting or interview where I could demonstrate my capabilities in person.*

- *I note in this week's Business Express that* [organisation] *is proposing to substantially expand its operations at the Greenfields site. If you are looking for able and motivated staff to make this happen, please keep me in mind. I have* [years] *experience in* [experience] *and I have a* [qualification] *in* [field of study] *from* [learning institution].

21 January 2012

Ms Tanya Hemmings
Human Resources
Juggernaut International
1255 Pacific Highway
GONDWANA 9251

24 Stone Avenue
Moonee Ponds 3039

Tel: 03 9666 6666
Mobile: 0411 966 666
Email: jh21@telstra.net

Dear Ms Hemmings

Management Trainee position: Your ref. J2311

I wish to apply for this position, advertised in *The Australian*, Saturday 15 January 2012. I believe that my qualifications and experience could help me make a significant contribution to Juggernaut International.

I have recently completed an honours degree in Business, with a minor in Professional Writing, from Praxis University. My grades in both major and minor were in the distinction to high distinction range, and I also received strong grades in critical thinking, problem solving, interpersonal understandings and written communication in the Graduate Skills Assessment Test conducted by the Australian Council for Educational Research.

I have developed a fair degree of practical experience over the past few years by working at MDB Accounting, Parnell Smythe, Inc., and Asda and Woolworths supermarkets.

In academic and practical situations, I believe that I have developed excellent writing, speaking and interpersonal skills. I am confident that you would see that any documents I might be called on to write for Juggernaut would be grammatically perfect and professionally laid out. Presentations done in academic and professional settings, together with my debating experience, have strengthened my speaking skills.

I work well in team situations, and have experience in teams as a shift supervisor at supermarkets, part of an accountancy unit working on company tax returns, as editor of the Praxis student newspaper, as a member of the Praxis squash team, and as a volunteer with St John's Ambulance. All of these situations have also honed my time and pressure management skills, and my leadership and problem-solving abilities.

I believe that I have developed strong research skills in work I have done for accounting firms and also in my academic work, especially in my honours thesis 'Applications of data mining software packages in accounting projects'.

In my various workplace and academic experiences I have developed strong skills in dealing with internal and external customers, and I have attained a high degree of proficiency in a number of general and specialised software packages.

I would welcome the opportunity to have my capabilities tested in an interview. I attach a résumé and an academic transcript, and look forward to hearing from you.

Yours sincerely,

Joshua Humphries

Joshua Humphries

Encs

FIGURE 20.10 Sample solicited letter

6 June 2012

202 Barnes Street

WELLINGTON 6008

Tel: 04 7999 9999

Email: marie@aslanis.net

Mr Jasper Stewart

Manager

Mellow Dramas Corporate Theatre

112 Kari Street

AUCKLAND 1001

Dear Mr Stewart

I read with great interest the story about Mellow Dramas in last week's Arts pages of *The New Zealand Herald*. Congratulations on your plans to expand further into the areas of national and international corporate theatre and convention entertainment.

If you need management staff to make this expansion happen, please keep me in mind.

I have substantial experience in Theatre Management not only locally but also nationally and internationally. Two of my most recent appointments were with the 2008 Dunedin Fringe Festival and the Breakout Theater, Boston, USA.

I have considerable knowledge of and experience in the Auckland theatre scene, and have substantial experience of the scenes in Wellington and Dunedin.

I have worked in numerous roles behind the scenes and built up a large array of skills ranging from front of house to having a solid command of the latest ticketing and cash management software packages. I think that I have good rapport with a wide range of artistic and technical personnel, and this has been aided by my actually having experience of being on the stage as well as backstage.

I think that I am a good negotiator, communicator and problem-solver, and I have a good track record as a fundraiser and resource-getter. I am motivated, focused and energetic.

I have an advanced qualification in arts management from Otago Polytechnic and advanced software skills training from the University of Auckland.

I would relish the challenge of being involved in an expanding operation such as yours. I enclose a résumé for your interest.

Please contact me if you would like to assess my capabilities face to face.

Yours sincerely,

Eleni Aslanis

Eleni Aslanis

Encs

FIGURE 20.11 Sample unsolicited letter

Résumés

A résumé (pronounced *rez-oo-may*) or curriculum vitae (CV) is a summary of your abilities, experience and qualifications. There are many different ways of constructing and laying out résumés. The two major formats of résumés are the chronological and the functional.

Chronological versus functional format

Chronological format résumé: a résumé with personal information laid out in time sequence

A **chronological format résumé** lays out personal information in a time sequence. It is conventional to use a reverse sequence, with the most recent dates first. An example of a chronological format résumé is shown in figure 20.12.

FIGURE 20.12 Chronological format résumé

Name	Joshua Humphries
Address	24 Stone Avenue, Moonee Ponds, 3039 Australia
Home phone	03 9666 6666
Mobile	0411 966 666
Personal email	jh21@telstra.net
Tertiary education 2008–2012	■ Bachelor of Business (Hons), Praxis University ■ Completed 2012 ■ Major in Accounting ■ Minor in Professional Writing ■ Distinction average in major and minor
Secondary education 2002–2007	■ International Baccalaureate, Hillside Secondary College ■ Completed 2007 ■ IB score 33, corresponding to 2003 Equivalent National Tertiary Entrance Rank (ENTER) score of 94.1
Work experience 2005–2012	■ Holiday internship at MDB Accounting — general company accounting, business activity statements (Dec 2011 – Feb 2012) ■ Work experience at Parnell Smythe Inc — equipment depreciation estimation, international taxation (Jul–Aug 2010) ■ Part-time shift supervisor at Moonee Ponds Asda supermarket — cash/credit/EFTPOS management, electronic/paper bookkeeping, general supervision, stock/inventory control, roster management (2010–2012) ■ Checkout clerk and shelf stacker at Moonee Ponds Woolworths supermarket (2002–2006)
Professional memberships	■ Passport, CPA Australia ■ Student member, Australian Institute of Management
Professional development	■ Managing your time — one-day course, Global Training Seminars ■ Managing stress and pressure — one-day course, Global Training Seminars ■ Quicken/QuickBooks master class — short course, Deakin University ■ Interpersonal skills — short course, RMIT ■ General thinking skills — online course, Edward de Bono (http://www.edwdebono.com) ■ Advanced first aid certificate, St John's Ambulance
Software skills	■ Microsoft Word, PowerPoint, Access, Excel, Publisher, FrontPage; Macromedia Dreamweaver; Corel Office, Ventura; OpenOffice; Linux Red Hat; Quark Xpress; Adobe InDesign; StyleWriter; Quicken; MYOB; AdvancePro; Job Cost; LoadLedger; iPad app developer

FIGURE 20.12 *(continued)*

Extracurricular	■ Member, Praxis University Debating Team (2010–2012)
	■ Editor, *Praxos,* student newspaper, Praxis University (2011)
	■ Squash team member, Praxis University (intervarsity champions, 2011)
	■ Volunteer, St John's Ambulance, sporting/entertainment venues

| Other skills | ■ Fluent in Spanish and Bahasa Indonesia |

Referees	■ Professor Amanda Charlton
	Accountancy Department
	Faculty of Business
	Praxis University
	Southbank
	Melbourne 3400
	Tel: 03 9100 0009
	Fax: 03 9100 2311
	Email: ac@praxis.edu
	■ Mr Selwyn Choate
	Human Resources Manager
	MDB Accounting
	1432 Collins Street
	Melbourne 3000
	Tel: 03 3299 9990
	Fax: 03 3299 9102
	Email: selch@mdb.biz
	■ Ms Molly Finster
	Manager
	Asda Supermarket
	1622 Puckle Street
	Moonee Ponds 3039
	Tel: 03 1220 9578
	Fax: 03 1220 9579
	Email: finster@asda.net

Functional format résumé: a résumé with personal information arranged in categories

A **functional format résumé** arranges personal information into categories (figure 20.13). Typical categories in functional résumés include:

■ experience
■ interpersonal skills
■ track record
■ evidence of problem-solving abilities
■ field experience
■ technology know-how
■ leadership.

The functional format tends to be persuasive as well as informative because the writer arranges pieces of information to create an impression for the reader. Functional résumés can work well when:

■ you don't have much experience
■ a chronological exposition might mask key patterns in what you have to offer
■ you are attempting to change careers, and the technical experience of one job will not be so relevant for the job you are going after
■ you have gaps in your employment history you can't explain or don't want to explain.

Eleni Aslanis
202 Barnes Street
Thordon
Wellington,
New Zealand, 6008
Tel: 04 7999 9999
Email: marie@aslanis.net

Employment objectives

To work with emerging and experimental theatre groups in developing and staging new theatre experiences. To provide management and background support to creative individuals.

Profile

Well-rounded professional who can work under pressure and with a variety of temperaments. Entrepreneur who thrives on providing back-up and balanced critique to playwrights, actors, directors and producers. Expertise in backstage coordination, liaison with lighting, set, costume, makeup and sound specialists. Known for competent front-of-house management. Versatile, diplomatic, assertive. Good listener and problem-solver.

Professional experience

- Theatre Arts Liaison Officer, Dunedin Fringe Festival 2012 — coordinated resourcing and staging management of 22 productions
- Office Manager, Breakout Theater, Boston, USA, 2010–2011 — streamlined online bookings system; assisted in negotiating new labour award conditions with lighting, staging, sound staff
- Front of house, Agora playhouse, Dunedin, 2009
- Organiser, 'Meet the Players' social events/fundraisers, Agora playhouse, Dunedin — liaised with patrons, customers, critics/media, 2008
- Responsible for raising $46 000 from costume/prop auctions, patron donations, Agora playhouse, Dunedin, 2008
- Actor/Assistant producer, 'Under Milk Wood', New Edge Drama Company, Wellington 2007
- Wrote successful National Arts Council submission ($76 500) for new sound system and costume workshop, New Edge Drama Company, Wellington, 2006
- Actor, 'Mourning Becomes Electra', 'Phaedra', 'Two Gentlemen of Verona', 'Tooth of Crime', Morningside Players, Auckland, 2005
- Assistant Manager, Dunedin Players — coordinated booking systems, installation of new lighting grid, development of set construction workshop 2004
- Costume maker, Dunedin Players, Dunedin Community Centre 2003
- Domestic manager 1999–2002

Key skills

- In-depth experience with handling subscriptions, mailing lists, group sales, marketing
- Proven ability to work with technical and artistic professionals in a wide variety of settings
- Proven ability to raise funds via grants, patrons, auction-fundraisers
- Ability to keep calm in pressure situations
- Good negotiator and conflict manager
- Intermediate to advanced skills in Provenue, Ticketmaker, Retriever Venue ticketing, concession management, cash control and inventory software

Education and training

- Toi Whakaari Graduate, New Zealand Drama School (2008)
- Advanced Diploma in Arts Management, Otago Polytechnic (2007)
- Microsoft Office Specialist, Master Certificate, University of Auckland (2007)
  (Microsoft Word, Access, Excel, PowerPoint, Outlook, Publisher, FrontPage, ProjectManager)

References

Available on request

FIGURE 20.13 Functional format résumé

Employers sometimes view functional résumés with suspicion, however, because they may like to see continuity and real data on the roles and responsibilities had up until now (Messmer 1999, p. 70).

Chronological résumés can work well when:

- your track record speaks for itself
- clear layout shows career progress
- job changes show logical steps in building a hierarchy of skills and experiences, rather than job-hopping.

Mixed format

You can mix functional and chronological formats, depending on the application or situation. For example, in the sample functional format résumé shown (figure 20.13) the 'experience' section could have shown dates. It may also be useful to present a résumé using categories. For example, if you have had experience at different organisations, or in different industries, you may choose to categorise this information under subheadings, using a chronological listing or a functional synthesis of concepts.

Some writers of résumés also choose to put a 'career objective' or 'summary' section at the beginning of the document (figure 20.14).

Career objectives	Summary
■ A floor supervisory position in nursing at a leading hospital, allowing me to work with new techniques in intensive care ■ A senior position in an emerging telecommunications company that will allow me to take my technical and interpersonal skills to a new level	■ Lawyer specialising in patents and intellectual property. Emphasis on international communication, legal and contractual problem solving, and liaising with innovators and funding managements ■ Specialist in data and electrical systems seeking new opportunities in the emerging home-network installation industry

FIGURE 20.14 Sample wording for résumé objective statements and summary statements

References

A referee is someone who is willing to write something complimentary about you and/or be contacted to discuss your abilities. Before nominating a referee, always check with the person concerned. Here are some things to consider with organising references:

- Some job seekers prefer not to provide details of referees on their résumés or cover letters, choosing instead to present them at an interview or to send them on after an interview. When in doubt, see what the employer prefers.
- A written reference or letter of recommendation usually begins with the nonspecific heading 'To whom it may concern' (which means you can use it more than once) and may be on company letterhead (figure 20.15).
- A written reference from a credible referee can be persuasive, although this is not always the case. Some referees are loath to say anything critical out of politeness, and may give good references just to get rid of someone; others are loath to give references at all (perhaps because of legal implications).
- Employers often prefer to talk directly to referees to get opinions that may be more forthcoming than if they were recorded in writing.
- Even if you don't like your job, it may be worthwhile for you to consider delaying applying for other roles. By putting in an excellent performance at work, you will put yourself in the best position to receive strong references in the future.

LETTER OF RECOMMENDATION: CYNTHIA PARRY

To whom it may concern

Cynthia Parry worked with us at the Eastern Regional Offices of Megabank from June 2010 to July 2012.

In that time, she showed herself to be a professional worker with outstanding interpersonal skills. She has considerable expertise in double-entry bookkeeping and Quicken and Excel software.

She worked very well with her co-workers, and demonstrated good problem-solving abilities on several notable occasions. She has proven to be a motivated person who can meet and beat deadlines.

I unreservedly recommend her to any employer who might wish to retain her services, and I can be contacted at the number below if you would like further details.

FIGURE 20.15 Sample letter of recommendation

Transcripts and qualifications

Transcripts (or results sheets) and qualification documents (degrees, diplomas, certificates) are proof that you have achieved certain levels in education and training. There is no guarantee that excellence in learning will translate to excellence on the job, but such documents can be useful.

Results sheets or printouts can be useful if the details of subjects or modules undertaken are interesting in themselves and attest to specific competencies, and are obviously also interesting if your grades or marks are good (see figure 20.16 overleaf). Copies of qualifications may be called for if they were earned in another country or area, or if they are not well known to the employer.

Are results and qualifications persuasive? It's not always clear. Some employers will be impressed, others will be unimpressed; some will be annoyed and some will be resentful and envious. The only real virtues they have are that they can document in detail what you have to offer and they can give you an additional boost in the credentialism race.

Portfolios

Work portfolios also demonstrate what competencies you have to offer. Portfolios can be quite important in certain professions (graphic arts, online writing and design, architecture, writing), but they can be adapted to any profession if you feel that presentation of your work may help your prospects. Your portfolio may be presented in hard copy format, on DVD, or online – via a file transfer protocol hyperlink or on a professional social networking website. Ensure that you do not violate copyright, privacy or confidentiality when putting work you have done for others in the public domain.

Application forms

Sometimes employers will ask you to complete an application form to include with other employment communication documents. This may be a hard-copy or an online document. Getting you to do this fulfils a number of functions:

- It allows employers to standardise application data from many candidates so that data can be more easily manipulated and searched.
- It allows them to see if you can follow instructions.
- It allows them to see if you can produce tidy, accurate and thorough work under pressure and without the aid of technology such as computers or spellcheckers.

PRAXIS UNIVERSITY
TRANSCRIPT OF ACADEMIC RESULTS
GRADUATE: JOSHUA ALEXANDER HUMPHRIES

Year	Subject	Semester	Mark	Grade
2012	B411 - Money and Capital Markets	1	74	D
	B408 - Investments and Portfolio Management	1	89	HD
	B313 - Management Accounting	2	72	D
	B400 - Short Thesis: Applications of Data Mining Software Packages in Accounting Projects	2	90	HD
2011	B319 - Company Reporting	1	67	C
	B322 - Data Mining and Knowledge Management	1	72	D
	B354 - Strategic Management	1	92	HD
	B322 - Advanced Financial Accounting Methods	2	81	HD
	B342 - Auditing	2	71	D
	B212 - Human Resource Management 1	2	71	D
2010	B231 - Corporation Laws and Trusts	1	67	C
	A299 - Document Editing and Production	1	68	C
	A298 - Document Design	1	92	HD
	B254 - Cost Accounting	2	73	D
	B201 - Financial Modelling	2	78	HD
	A291 - Professional and Technical Writing 2	2	71	D
2009	B101 - Managing People and Organisations	1	71	D
	B103 - Accounting 1A	1	65	C
	B104 - Communication	1	70	D
	B105 - Accounting 1B	2	72	D
	A191 - Professional and Technical Writing 1	2	67	C
	A198 - Lessons of History	2	78	D
2012	Graduate Skills Assessment Test (External Assessment: Australian Council for Educational Research)			
	ACER2112 - Critical Thinking			82
	ACER2113 - Problem Solving			91
	ACER2114 - Interpersonal Understandings			78
	ACER2115 - Written Communication			95

KEY: HD = High distinction   D = Distinction   C = Credit   P = Pass   N = Fail

Dr May Lin
Academic Registrar
Praxis University
Southbank
Melbourne 3400

FIGURE 20.16 Sample transcript or results sheet

Job seeking: the funny side

Résumés or CVs are a critical part of the job seeking process — they are proof of our competence as well as samples of our work. Therefore, they need to be well written and scrupulously proofread and edited. Some applicants, however, do not always put enough time and thought into their résumés. The Resumania.com website has numerous examples of extracts from actual résumés, and these examples can give us a laugh as well as motivate us to try harder with our real résumés (figure 20.17).

- Education: attended collage courses
- Cover letter: for more details, Google me
- EXPERIENCE: 'Detailed-oriented saleman.'
- SKILLS: 'I can type without looking at the keyboard.'
- JOB DUTIES: 'Answer phones, file papers, respond to customer e-mails, take odors.'
- EXPERIENCE: 'I am a very capapable proofreader.'
- Skills: 'Grate communication skills.'
- Qualifications: 'I have guts, drive, ambition and heart, which is probably more than a lot of the drones that you have working for you.'

Similarly, writing references for someone is a pleasant experience when you like the person being written about and feel that they are truly competent. But what happens when someone you don't like asks for a reference? And what about the legal implications you might expose yourself to by writing a bad reference? Thornton (1988) suggests (only half-seriously) that a solution to this dilemma may be to write a deliberately ambiguous recommendation or reference, such as:

- He's a man of many convictions.
- Waste no time in making this man an offer of employment.
- A man like him is hard to find.
- Once you hire him, you'll see how important it is to have more qualified people.
- I recommend this man with no qualifications whatsoever.
- It's been a good two years since he left our employment . . .
- I can assure you that no one would be better for this job.

FIGURE 20.17 Job seeking: the funny side

Sources: www.resumania.com; Thornton (1988).

Online technologies

New computer software and hardware technologies are changing the way jobs are advertised and filled. These systems, sometimes referred to by the term '**e-cruitment**', include:

- online job advertisements on specialised job-search or job-board websites
- online job advertisements on specific company websites
- online submission of résumés via websites or via email with attached files
- automatic responses to correspondence
- analysis, screening/filtering and storage of online, emailed and scanned print résumés and matching content with vacant positions
- scheduling of interviews
- online assessment and testing.

A tip when responding online (not all systems allow this): write and edit your information in a word processor, making it perfect, and then copy and paste it into the 'black hole' of the website. Yours will be perfect, while the others will be well short of perfect.

E-cruitment: automated system used to advertise jobs; input résumés from web, email and print sources; analyse and filter résumé data; reply to correspondence; set up selection interviews; and conduct applicant testing

Readers: human and machine

A person looking at your job application — for example, a clerk or manager in a human resources or personnel department — will always be working under time and resource constraints. (It is not unusual for one advertised job to attract several hundred applications.)

Realistically, this means that a person reviewing the applications might only be able to allow sixty seconds per application. The reader is looking for reasons to reject applications to get down to a short list. Therefore, it makes sense to have applications that:

- are clearly and professionally laid out
- show perfect grammar, punctuation and spelling
- answer the selection criteria.

New technology means that an increasing number of employers are automating this vetting process by using résumé scanners. Scanning and data mining software can record information into a relational database, which can then match what you are offering against what they need. This may be part of an e-cruitment or **applicant tracking system**, which may also integrate online résumé data entered by jobseekers.

Scanning technology is still somewhat limited in what it can do, and thus has trouble with: bullet points; graphics (lines, borders, shading); colour; bold, underline and italic and fancy fonts; fonts under ten point and above 14 point; printing on both sides of the paper; documents printed from low-grade printers; and verbs instead of nouns. Therefore, you might consider sending two versions of your résumé: one formatted for humans with a pleasing but complex document design, and a stripped-down version suitable for scanning with one very basic font and layout, and perhaps a separate keyword section of nouns.

Keywords and phrases are useful if your document is going to be scanned. Prepare a list of keywords and/or phrases to include, and you will find that this list might keep you on track and ensure that you don't neglect to mention everything that you have to offer (and which may also be on the employer's shopping list). Sample text for two professions is shown in figure 20.18.

Applicant tracking system: automated system used by employers to gather and analyse data from online and paper résumés

Keywords and phrases: wording likely to be scanned from résumés and used as criteria for selection

Research project manager	Electronics technician
<ul><li>Led team</li><li>Coordinated major project</li><li>Statistics</li><li>Wrote reports</li><li>Conflict management</li><li>Budget management</li><li>Data mining</li><li>Good interpersonal skills</li><li>Designed questionnaires</li><li>Problem solving</li><li>Master's degree</li><li>Analytical ability</li><li>Database management</li><li>Knowledge management</li><li>Communication</li><li>Clients</li><li>Motivated</li><li>Quantitative</li><li>Qualitative</li><li>Stakeholders</li><li>Provided advice</li><li>Submissions</li><li>Briefs</li><li>Liaison</li><li>Policy development</li><li>Prepared position papers</li></ul>	<ul><li>Certificate of technology in electronic engineering</li><li>Associate diploma electronic engineering</li><li>Fault finding</li><li>Diagnosis and repair</li><li>Analog electronics</li><li>Digital electronics</li><li>Communication skills</li><li>Microprocessors</li><li>Problem-solver</li><li>Assembly language programming</li><li>High-level language programming</li><li>PCB layout (Protel)</li><li>Circuit design and testing</li><li>Consumer electronics fault finding and repair</li><li>Team player</li><li>Hardware diagnostic tools</li><li>Software diagnostic tools</li><li>Software simulation packages (Spice)</li><li>Customer service</li><li>Troubleshoot</li></ul>

FIGURE 20.18 Sample keywords and phrases for two professions

The interview process

If your job application makes it through to the short list, then you may be interviewed for the position. As mentioned earlier, the documents you include with your application don't necessarily get you the job; rather, they comprise a request from you to participate in a performance, and that performance is the interview.

Preparing for the interview

Interviews can be stressful, but that stress can be managed, or at least reduced. There are a number of stress management strategies that you can follow, but perhaps the best strategies relate to preparation. The more prepared you are, chances are the less stressed you will feel. Review the documents you have sent in. If there are some documents you have not submitted, such as educational or training results, copies of qualifications, references and portfolios, consider taking them along (make multiple copies if you are going to be interviewed by a panel). Look at them now with fresh eyes: Are there any shortcomings? Any proofreading errors you missed the first time around? Also consider working with a friend or colleague to role-play an interview scenario in which you respond to a variety of questions.

Make sure that you are dressed and groomed appropriately for the job you are going for. Try to look as relaxed and confident as possible, and try to create a positive impression with a firm and confident voice and handshake. It's a cliché, but first impressions of voice and appearance do count, and are sometimes critical (Parton et al. 2002).

Thinkbox: brains, brawn or both? Which is best?

The overwhelming emphasis in this chapter has been geared towards tertiary education – working with our heads rather than our hands. This is partly a by-product of the automation of agricultural and manufacturing industries, and partly a socioeconomic class factor. Getting a degree and working with your head has got to be better and pay better, right? Not necessarily, says Matthew Crawford, author of *The case for working with your hands: why office work is bad for you and fixing things feels good* (2010). Crawford has a PhD in political philosophy and has worked in a prestigious Washington think tank. Crawford (quoted in Brooks, 2010, p. 11) observes, counter to all mainstream thinking at the moment, that:

> For many youngsters there is absolutely no point studying for some liberal arts degree, even which then might not get them a job unless it is very badly paid and often boring, or even a no-pay job, such as some now in publishing or the arts ... It's long been thought that if the work is dirty, then you must be stupid to do it. But working with your hands is by far the cleverest thing you can do. If you get a trade qualification, it always leads to a reliable job that will almost certainly be in demand. Not many plumbers are out of work. You may not get super-rich as a mechanic, but you will be comfortable and content.

Then again, you may be relatively super-rich: urban myths abound about doctors and lawyers still on relatively low pay, with enormous student debts to pay, while trade professionals, with almost no (or no) student debt can charge what the market will bear, and – dare it be said – have greater access to the black market of cash payments without tax. Flintoff (2010) also makes the point:

> Manual trades are embedded in a particular location. Those that have not already been outsourced overseas are probably safe, because if pipes are blocked in the UK, a Chinese plumber

is no use. White collar jobs are more vulnerable. So, even if you don't feel mentally mutilated in your office, have no interest in dipsticks, and aren't lured by manual work, just ask yourself: how safe is your office job?

A Princeton economist, Alan Blinder (cited in Agger 2009), has speculated that levels of education may not be as crucial in the future as we have been led to believe:

> The critical divide in the future may instead be between those types of work that are easily deliverable through a wire (or via wireless connections) with little or no diminution in quality and those that are not.

Agger (2009) adds:

> Learning a trade is not limiting but, rather, liberating. If you are in possession of a skill that cannot be exported overseas, done with an algorithm, or downloaded, you will always stand a decent chance of finding work. Even rarer, you will probably be a master of your own domain, something the thousands of employed but bored people in the service industries can only dream of.

Crawford (1999c) sees too many young people going into 'ghost work' in cubicles, which he describes as part of a 'rising sea of clerkdom'.

The nature of interviews

Interviews can be conducted by one person or a panel of people. They may take place in an office or a conference room, although they can also take place over a meal, on a tour of a building, at a job fair or convention, at a campus, over the telephone or via a videoconference.

The protocol for most interview sequences goes like this:

1. The interviewee is notified of an appointment time and arrives at the specified time.
2. The interviewee is shown into the interview area and is introduced to those who will do the interviewing.
3. The interviewer explains the sequence of events.
4. The interviewer may make small talk to break the ice and put the interviewee at ease.
5. The interviewer works through a series of questions.
6. The interviewee will be asked if he or she has any questions.
7. The interview is terminated, and then the post-interview phase begins. This can mean that the interviewee is notified of the outcome by mail, telephone or email within several weeks, or further interviews may be arranged.
8. The interviewee may choose to write a follow-up or thank-you letter to the interviewer, perhaps enclosing other employment communication documents.

Questioning techniques

Interviewers will sometimes use a mix of **open questions** and **closed questions** — for example:

- *How did you feel working with that version of the software?* (Open question — requires a discursive response)
- *Did you like having to work with that version of the software when the new version was being used by your competitors?* (Closed question — requires a specific answer).

There may also be a mixture of directive and behavioural questions (Tullier 1999). **Directive questions** are targeted to specific aspects of your résumé and your performance and capabilities; **behavioural questions** are case-study or scenario-type questions, designed

Open question: a question that requires a general and discursive response

Closed question: a question that requires a specific and short response

Directive question: a question that is targeted to specific aspects of a candidate's résumé, performance and capabilities

Behavioural question: a question designed to draw a candidate out, to describe what actually happened in a situation or what might happen in a hypothetical situation

Forced-choice question: a question designed to see if a candidate gives priority to one set of skills or values over another

Creativity question: a question designed to see if a candidate could cope with unexpected or bizarre situations and concepts

Interviewers use a variety of different questioning techniques in interviews.

to draw you out and describe what you actually did in specific circumstances or might do in hypothetical circumstances. For example:

- *Can you handle conflict well?* (Directive question)
- *There is an ongoing and simmering dispute between two members of your team. It seems to be based on a personality conflict. How do you handle it?* (Behavioural question).

Other interview techniques include **forced-choice questions** (or dilemma-type questions) – designed to see if you give priority to one set of skills or values over another – and **creativity questions** (or brainstorming questions) – designed to see if you can cope with the unexpected or the bizarre.

Question types

There are many types of questions that can be asked in interview situations (Lee 2006; Allen 2004; Hodgson 2002; Martin 2004; Poundstone 2003; De Luca & De Luca, 2010; Yate 2011). Let's look, however, at just some of them (table 20.3). Some opening responses are suggested, but there are many possibilities that you will be able to think up for yourself.

TABLE 20.3 Interview questions

Question	Rationale	Opening response
1. Why do you want this job?	Designed to reveal your motivation and whether you will fit in. An open question, it's designed to get you to open up. However, you need to align your goals with the goals of the organisation — don't go on an ego trip.	*I want it because I really enjoy this type of work, and I find it challenging. In this field, and possibly in others, I think that I could make a positive contribution to the program here at . . .*
2. Why do you want to leave your current situation?	A tricky one. Are you a malcontent or troublemaker? Are you a problem or a solution? Be upfront about real problems, but be dignified and not slanderous or full of hate. Accentuate the positive if possible.	*It is okay there, but I think I've gone about as far as I can go. I want some new horizons, and they appear to be here, not there.*
3. Tell me about yourself.	An opportunity for you to divulge your brand statement, but also an opportunity to shoot yourself in the foot. This isn't therapy, remember, but an attempt to see how you will fit in. Keep it short and sweet: 60–120 seconds.	*Without any false modesty, I think that I am an energetic and resourceful person. I'm a bit frustrated in my current position, and I need room to grow. I think that I can get that here, and give something back.*
4. What is your greatest weakness?	Beware: this is an interview, not a confession. Concentrate on technical skills, which can be easily upgraded, and say you're working on it. In the interpersonal area, pick a minor sin, and say you're working on it.	*I'm not up to speed with my Excel skills, but I start a night class on that next week. I think that you have to confront your weaknesses. On the people side, I think I'm sometimes too judgemental when other people don't share my standards. I'll compromise on that partly, but not totally.*
5. Give me an example where you have taken the initiative on something.	A question to see whether you are energetic and resourceful, but also to see whether you are a rule bender or breaker, and possibly a loose cannon.	*I worked on the . . . project. I couldn't get a clear decision on it out of my boss, so I worked back late three nights doing research, which I then used to persuade . . .*

(continued)

TABLE 20.3 (continued)

Question	Rationale	Opening response
6. How would you compare your interpersonal skills to your technical skills?	This is a choice trap. If you say that one is stronger than the other, then you are admitting a flaw. Try to give a balanced response; you can say that one area is weaker, but also say that you are working on it.	*I think that I have now got them at about the same level, and they reinforce each other anyway. I have seen problems caused when one is emphasised to the detriment of the other.*
7. Tell me about a time when you have shown leadership.	A behavioural or case-study question. They want the short version, so give it to them. Set the scenario up, put yourself in the picture as the hero, and lead to a plausible happy ending. Stress logic and persuasion rather than orders and shouting.	*Several months back, the team I am currently with got blocked on a problem. I researched the issue and produced a demo solution, and they liked it. I got to be the first author of the report on it, and the management team liked it.*
8. How would you do …?	A technique question. How good are you? Show, but don't show off. Show that you are a problem-solver and are on top of the latest methods and tools. Don't, however, neglect the personal dimension.	*I tend to go by the book for the most part, tackling … first, and then … There's a new software package out that may speed that up, and I hope to try it soon. If I were doing this here, I would check with others to see what angles and local knowledge they have.*
9. What do you think your referees would say about you?	A mind-reader question. Redefine the question and remain confidently modest.	*I don't know what they will say. I hope that they will give me credit where credit's due, and focus on the things I have actually done. I enjoyed working with them, and I put them down as references because I thought they could give you the real story.*
10. Do you prefer to work alone or in a group?	Another choice trap. Give an 'it all depends' response.	*I prefer both, depending on the problem to hand. Sometimes many hands make light work, and that's when it's great to work with others. Sometimes it makes more sense for me to work alone to produce results. You've got to be flexible.*
11. What goals do you want to achieve in the next five years?	This is partly a test to see if you are a planner, but also to see if you are a job-hopper. Stress goal alignment and synergy: what's good for you is good for them too.	*I want to go to the next level in my speciality, but I also want to broaden out. As I see it, this company seems to be the best place to do that. I'll benefit from being here, but I think I'll put back more than I take out.*
12. Tell me about the time you failed at something.	Some selective editing might be wise here. Avoid unmitigated disasters, but stress what you learned.	*About six months ago, I was under a lot of pressure to deliver on a project. I delivered, but it wasn't my best work. I should have resisted the pressure a bit more assertively, and managed my time better. If I met the same situation now, I think I'd do better.*
13. How would you handle a complaint from a client or customer?	A front-line and interpersonal skills question. Stress problem solving, sensitivity and systems knowledge.	*I would listen — really listen — to the customer, and get all the information. I would analyse what had gone wrong without blaming individuals. I would try to learn how the system had worked and how it had failed, and build that learning into the system. I would make sure that the customer was kept in the loop, and was given a solution that works. Customers are not always right, but in the long run we have to be.*

Question	Rationale	Opening response
14. **What do you think is more important: work or personal life?**	Still another choice or false dilemma trap. Refuse the dilemma and recast the question from an 'either/or' to a 'both/and'.	*I think they are both equally important because they balance each other. If it's all work, then your work suffers, as does your personal life. If your personal life is all-encompassing, then you lose perspective on your loved ones, and your work suffers, of course.*
15. **How did you prepare for this interview?**	How good are you? How much effort have you put into this? Prove it, but don't go over the top.	*I read the position description, of course, and then I rang up … and talked about it, to get a better feel for it. I got the last three annual reports, and I worked my way through most of the pages on the website. All of that, of course, can't replace inside knowledge, but it gave me a better picture, and it motivated me to apply rather than walk away.*
16. **How do you handle stress?**	Can you handle pressure and crises, and how do you manage your time? The question is self-referential, of course. They want someone who won't panic under pressure and who is practical, rather than overly dramatic, in responding to stressful situations.	*I try to keep perspective on things, and I always get back to others for a reality check. You meet a crisis with concentration, planning and leading the team. I push myself when required, but I still try to stay objective. Adrenalin can be positive, at times, in a work setting.*
17. **Tell us about a time when you had a personality conflict with another person.**	A behavioural or case-study question. Set the scene, don't settle scores. Tell it reasonably fairly, and acknowledge how you could have tried a bit harder, and what you have learned from it. They want to predict the future from your past, so give them reasons to think that the future would be bright, rather than dark.	*I remember a time working with a colleague on a project, and we always seemed to be disagreeing about technical procedures. All the staff did some personality tests months later, and I realised that we had different approaches to detail. I still feel that this person was unreasonable on some aspects, but I would be better able to handle that now.*
18. **What makes you better than all of the other people we are talking to?**	Another mind-reader question, only more provocative. Don't take it personally. Patiently proving, not blustering, will win the day.	*I can't answer that — only you can. I applied for this position because I think that I have achieved a fair amount, and now I'm ready to achieve more. I hope the best person is offered this position. I only hope that, on balance, you consider that I am this person.*

The other side of the table

In order for interviews to be as successful as possible, a number of guidelines need to be followed.

- The job description should be carefully constructed to describe the real situation.
- The search process should be conducted in an ethical manner.
- If using nonhuman systems to scan documents and match criteria, check for quality and accuracy.
- The interviewers should be chosen for their expertise and/or the likelihood that they will be working with the successful candidate.
- The interviewers should read the job description and all documents from all candidates.
- The interviewers should determine a routine of questions that will stay the same for all candidates to ensure fairness and comparability of data.
- The interview environment should be quiet, comfortable and professional.
- The interviewers should be objective.

- The interviewers should be fully aware of broader issues (such as equal opportunity, anti-discrimination policy, and health and safety).
- The interviewers should take notes where appropriate.
- The interviewers should behave in a courteous, cordial and professional manner, and not resort to pressure tactics or mind games.
- When the interviews are completed, the interviewers should conduct a patient and scrupulous evaluation of the candidates.

Testing, testing … assessment of applicants

Screening of candidates can occur through interviewing, but some employers also use testing or assessment procedures as another method of screening. Testing can occur on a number of areas, such as:
- numerical reasoning and verbal reasoning
- problem solving and creativity
- situation simulation
- emotional intelligence and personality
- honesty and integrity
- handwriting.

Testing sometimes occurs as a replacement for interviews, and sometimes as a complement. It may be conducted on or off site, and even online. There is not much controversy about the more straightforward aptitude tests, such as numerical and verbal reasoning. Accounting firms, for example, might note an applicant's degree in mathematics but still insist on testing for numerical reasoning (because skill in mathematics does not automatically correlate with numeracy) and verbal reasoning (because emerging role demands mean that staff need to be able to interact with clients, write reports and analyse information) (Keelan 2003).

Tests on problem solving and creativity are becoming popular. The rationale here is that such tests might be able to identify future employees who are able to think laterally, who can cope with fluid and chaotic situations, and who might have interesting answers to unusual questions that are designed to catch interviewees off guard (Poundstone 2003).

In situation simulation tests, job applicants are presented with hypothetical job-related situations or participate in a problem-solving simulation game (Tolley & Wood 2009). Some organisations are also testing for emotional intelligence, personality, honesty and integrity, and even handwriting (as a possible insight into personality) (Daniels 2001; Perry & Kleiner 2002; Kwiatkowski 2003; Healy 2008).

This 'soft skills' testing has a number of advantages over résumés and interviewing as a selection mechanism (Daniels 2001). For example:
- Interviews can be notoriously ineffective at detecting incompetent or unethical employees because of possible subjective decision making by selectors, whereas testing is objective.
- Testing takes selection out of the hands of part-time amateurs (those sitting on selection panels) and puts it in the hands of full-time professionals (psychologists).
- Well-written tests may reveal unconscious patterns of motivation that might not emerge in interviews.
- Testing can take into account the culture or values of the organisation and help select potential employees who will most closely match such values and culture.
- Test data, because of its objectivity, can be used to compare employees over space and time.

- Testing may be an enjoyable experience that helps candidates discover insights about themselves.

  However, there are significant problems with behavioural testing, such as:
- The predictive validity of a number of tests is quite low, depending on emerging or unfounded concepts such as emotional intelligence and handwriting as a surrogate for behavioural self-revelation and honesty; much 'objectivity' may be spurious (Perry & Kleiner 2002; National Workrights Institute 2010; Spillane & Martin 2005).
- Applicants can prepare for such tests, which undercuts any notion that what is being tested for is innate, and gives test-wise applicants an unfair advantage (Bryon 2011a, 2011b; Australian Council for Educational Research 2002; Cohen 1995; Hoffman 2002; Keelan 2003; Parkinson 2000, 2001; Hart & Sheldon 2007).
- Developments in organisations, such as working in teams, empowerment and flatter hierarchies, may mean that some tests are no longer relevant – they test for the wrong things ('Psychobabble' 2004).
- Applicants may be able to fake results, cheat and/or have others take tests for them (Rees & Metcalfe 2003; Kwiatkowski 2003; Rothstein & Goffin 2006).
- The key concepts of testing may be culturally biased (Kwiatkowski 2003).
- Testing may only admit those candidates who most closely match the existing culture and values of the organisation ('cloning'), when what is most urgently needed is fresh blood to challenge that very culture and set of values (Brannan & Hawkins 2007; Keelan 2003).
- Testing may discourage excellent candidates from even applying (*Training* 2000). This may be because of a fear of the process, a fear of clinical psychological concepts, or perceiving that any organisation that would use testing is not worth working for (Daniels 2001; Briggs 1995).
- Testing may invade civil rights and provide grounds for legal action (National Workrights Institute 2010).
- Testing often leads to higher turnover rates, not lower, because testing may select in high-flyers who see the position as merely transitional and screen out those who might have grown into stable and productive employees (Perry & Kleiner 2002).
- The validity of testing is asserted primarily by professional psychologists who have a vested interest in the process; thus, it may be biased (National Workrights Institute 2010).

STUDENT STUDY GUIDE

SUMMARY

In this chapter we considered the larger historical context of job searching, noting that economic and social changes mean that modern employers are looking for candidates with particular skill-sets. We saw that job seekers might have to undergo a role change and be job makers as well as job takers, and might also choose or be compelled to choose alternative career paths. We saw that to prepare for the job market we need to become more flexible and more organised; think big and think small; research, network and build a personal brand; and build a skills–knowledge–experience mix. We explored the different strategies to adopt when pursuing jobs that are, and are not, advertised. We looked at the relevance of transferable skills for the job market and at the notion of a personal brand statement. We considered the approaches to writing effective employment communication documents (such as various types of cover letters and résumés), and we considered including transcripts, qualifications, portfolios and application forms. The interview process (including responses to questions and the testing of applicants) was also investigated.

KEY TERMS

applicant tracking
  system *p. 690*
behavioural question
  p. 692
chronological format
  résumé *p. 683*
closed question *p. 692*
creativity question *p. 692*
credentialism *p. 675*

directive question *p. 692*
e-cruitment *p. 689*
employment–experience
  paradox *p. 676*
forced-choice question
  p. 692
functional format résumé
  p. 684
key selection criteria *p. 673*

keywords and phrases
  p. 690
open question *p. 692*
personal brand *p. 674*
solicited application letter
  p. 680
transferable skills *p. 669*
unsolicited application
  letter *p. 680*

REVIEW QUESTIONS

1. What are the three most popular approaches for attaining a job for nonschool and post-secondary qualification holders?
2. What is meant by the phrase 'put-up job'?
3. What is a transferable skill?
4. What similarities and differences are there between a personal brand statement, a résumé objective statement and a résumé summary statement?
5. Identify three differences between a cover letter and a résumé.
6. In what circumstances might a chronological format résumé be preferable to a functional format résumé?
7. Under what circumstances might a job applicant consider presenting a portfolio?
8. Why might a job seeker, using an online employment site, compose a letter of application and a résumé in a word processor and then copy that text into the website?
9. How does behavioural interviewing differ from directive interviewing?
10. What would be the point of a selection interviewer asking a behavioural or creativity question in an interview?
11. List three things for and three things against psychological testing as a means of employee selection.

1. Find a job advertised in a newspaper, magazine or on a website. Set up a folder for that job and the organisation advertising it. Now research the organisation, and find out everything you can about it and the job advertised. How useful would this information be in creating a job application or cover letter and a résumé?

2. Using the Yellow Pages (either the online or print format), advertisements in industry journals, advice from your teachers or lecturers, and whatever contacts you have, locate at least one professional organisation and at least one upcoming conference, seminar or meeting in your field of study.

3. Using internet or print sources, or by simply browsing through bookshops, find at least two books that might help you (through self-directed study) strengthen the relevance of your major fields of study.

4. Visit two online employment sites and compare them. Do either or both of them use a preset application form approach? Do either or both of them allow posting of attachments, such as a résumé file?

5. Create a résumé for yourself in chronological format. Now redo it as a functional format résumé. Which do you prefer? How might you combine them?

6. Prepare a list of keywords and phrases for a profession you are familiar with.

7. Using the questions list in this chapter, role-play an interview with a colleague, responding to at least ten questions. Write down your responses. Are they good, or could they be improved?

8. Using print or online sources, find at least another ten questions that might be used in job interviewing situations.

9. Using print or online sources, find examples of different types of testing used in job selection. What do you think of them?

10. If you use social media websites (e.g. Facebook and LinkedIn), check out your pages. Do you wish to edit them, or are they ok? Google yourself as well to see what impression is conveyed.

WHAT WOULD YOU DO?

It hadn't been a great year for Joe Smithers. Earlier this year he had turned 56. He had been called into his boss' office, only to be told he was being made redundant. The company was restructuring its operations, and a layer of middle managers, including Joe, were being removed. Joe wasn't ready to retire, and still had significant financial commitments to meet. The global financial crisis had also significantly dented his superannuation savings. He had intended to work until the standard retirement age of 65. He was worried about the future for himself and his wife, and he still had two children in high school, as well as a son, Quentin, aged 22, living at home.

In the months after he was made redundant, Joe applied for 64 jobs – all with no luck. Employers and governments were talking incessantly about hiring older workers because they had excellent knowledge and experience, a strong work ethic, took low or no sick leave and were loyal employees; however, the reality was different. Joe recalled the faces on so many interview panels – and the inevitable 'we'll be in touch' message that concluded the interviews he participated in. 'Being in touch' merely consisted of rejection letters and emails.

'Though they don't openly admit it, companies only want to hire younger people these days', Joe mused to his son Quentin.

Quentin spoke of his own issues. He had graduated in the middle of the year with a degree in computer science, but had been unable to find work in his chosen field. 'Companies only want to hire people with experience Dad', he said ruefully. 'But how do you get experience if you can't get a job in the first place?' The irony of his comments was not lost on Joe.

Based on what you have read in the chapter, what advice would you give Joe and Quentin?

SUGGESTED READING

Barrett, Jim 2011, *Aptitude test workbook: discover your potential and improve your career options with practice psychometric tests*, Kogan Page, London/New York.

Kleiman, Jessica & Cooper, Meryl Weinsaft 2011, *Be your own best publicist: how to use PR techniques to get noticed, hired, and rewarded at work*, Career Press, Pompton Plains, NJ.

Maltby, Lewis 2010, *Can they do that? Retaking our fundamental rights in the workplace*, Portfolio/Penguin, New York.

Taylor, Denise 2009, *How to get a job in a recession*, Brook House Press, Dartmouth, NS, Canada.

REFERENCES

Agger, Michael 2009, 'Heidegger and the art of motorcycle maintenance – get out of your cubicle, and get those cuticles dirty!' May 19, *Slate,* www.slate.com.

Allen, Jeffrey G 2004, *How to turn an interview into a job*, rev. edn, Fireside, New York.

Australian Association of Graduate Employers 2007, *AAGE graduate recruitment survey 2007*, Mitcham, Vic.

—— 2010, *AAGE graduate recruitment survey 2009*, Mitcham, Vic.

Australian Council for Educational Research 2002, *Practice now! How to prepare for recruitment and selection tests*, ACER Press, Camberwell, Vic.

Bangerter, Adrian, König, Cornelius J, Blatti, Sandrine, and Salvisberg, Alexander 2009, 'How widespread is Graphology in personnel selection practice? A case study of a job market myth', *International Journal of Selection and Assessment*, vol. 17, no. 2, p. 222.

Beatty, Richard H 2003, *The perfect cover letter*, 3rd edn, John Wiley & Sons, New York.

Bolles, Richard Nelson 2011, *What color is your parachute 2011?: a practical manual for job-hunters and career changers*, Ten Speed Press, Berkeley, CA.

Borchard, David 1995, 'Planning for career and life: job surfing and the tidal waves of change', *The Futurist*, vol. 29, no. 1, pp. 8–12.

Brannan, Matthew J & Hawkins, Beverley 2007, 'London calling: selection as pre-emptive strategy for cultural control', *Employee Relations*, vol. 29, no. 2, pp. 178–91.

Briggs, Susan 1995, 'Taking the test and wondering why', *Best's Review*, vol. 96, no. 6, p. 55.

Bryon, Mike 2011a, *The graduate psychometric test book*, Kogan Page, London.

—— 2011b, *How to pass graduate psychometric tests: essential preparation for numerical and verbal ability tests plus personality questionnaires*, 4th edn, Kogan Page, London.

Cohen, David 1995, *How to succeed in psychometric tests: understanding job selection tests and how to prepare for them*, Wrightbooks, North Brighton, Vic.

Crawford, Matthew B 1999a, Shop class as soulcraft: an inquiry into the value of work, Penguin, New York/London.

—— 2009b, 'The case for working with your hands', *The New York Times*, May 24, www.nytimes.com.

—— 2009c, 'Real men don't eat quiche, they ride hogs over it', *The New York Times*, May 28 www.nytimes.com.

—— 2010, *The case for working with your hands: why office work is bad for us and fixing things feels good*, Penguin, London/New York.

Daniels, Cora 2001, 'Does this man need a shrink?', *Fortune*, vol. 143, no. 3, pp. 205–8.

De Luca, Nanette & DeLuca, Matthew 2010, *Best answers to the 201 most frequently asked interview questions*, 2nd edn, McGraw-Hill, New York.

Department of Education, Science and Training 1998, *Employer satisfaction with graduate skills*, Executive Summary, Canberra.

—— 2002, *Employability skills for the future*, Canberra.

DEST, *see* Department of Education, Science and Training.

Ellyard, Peter 2001, *Ideas for a new millennium*, 2nd edn, Melbourne University Publishing, Melbourne.

Eunson, Baden 2004, 'Are soft skills merely a fad?', *Campus Review*, 29 September, p. 8.

—— 2005, 'They must know how to put it', *The Australian Higher Education Supplement*, 3 August, p. 29.

Flintoff, John-Paul 2010, review of Matthew Crawford's *The case for working with your hands: why office work is bad for us and fixing things feels good*, *Financial Times*, May 10, www.ft.com.

Gengler, Barbara 2002, 'Online track of résumé cheats', *The Australian*, 15 October, p. 34.

Gladwell, Malcolm 2008, *Outliers: the story of success*, Penguin, London/New York.

Graduate Careers Australia 2006, *Graduate Outlook 2006: a snapshot*, Parkville, Vic.

—— 2010, *Snapshot: Graduate Outlook 2010*, www.graduatecareers.com.au.

Greasley, Peter 2000, 'Handwriting analysis and personality assessment: the creative use of analogy, symbolism, and metaphor', *European Psychologist*, vol. 5, no.1, pp. 44–51.

Hart, Anne & Sheldon, George 2007, *Employment personality tests decoded*, Career Press, Franklin Lakes, NJ.

Healy, Liam 2008, *Psychometric tests for dummies*, John Wiley & Sons, Brisbane.

Hodgson, Susan 2002, *Brilliant answers to tough interview questions: smart responses to whatever they throw at you*, Prentice Hall, Upper Saddle River, NJ.

Hoffman, Edward 2002, *Psychological testing at work: how to use, interpret, and get the most out of the newest tests in personality, learning style, aptitudes, interests and more*, McGraw-Hill, New York.

Karseras, Hugh 2007, *From new recruit to high flyer: no-nonsense advice on how to fast track your career*, Kogan Page, London.

Keelan, Emma 2003, 'Psychometric tests – psychokiller?', *Accountancy*, 1 May.

Lee, John 2006, *You're hired: the essential guide to successful job seeking*, Trafford, Oxford.

McNally, David & Speak, Karl D 2011, *Be your own brand: achieve more of what you want by being more of who you are*, Berrett-Koehler, San Francisco.

Martin, Carole 2004, *Boost your interview IQ: the best answers to the toughest questions you'll be asked*, McGraw-Hill, New York.

Martin, Yate 2011, *Knock 'em dead 2011: the ultimate job search guide*, Adams Media Corporation, Avon, MA.

Messmer, Max 1999, *Job hunting for dummies*, 2nd edn, IDG Books, Foster City, CA.

Moses, Barbara 2001, 'Recession-proofing your career: 12 strategies for bad times and good', *The Futurist*, vol. 35, no. 4, pp. 18–24.

National Workrights Institute 2010 'Other pertinent issues', www.workrights.org

Parkinson, Mark 2000, *How to master psychometric tests*, Kogan Page, London.

—— 2001, *How to master personality questionnaires*, 2nd edn, Kogan Page, London.

Parton, SR, Siltanen, SA, Hosman, LA & Langenderfer, J 2002, 'Employment interview outcomes and speech style effects', *Journal of Language and Social Psychology*, vol. 21, no. 2, pp. 143–61.

Perry, Amity & Kleiner, Brian H 2002, 'How to hire employees effectively', *Management Research News*, vol. 25, no. 5, pp. 3–11.

Poundstone, William 2003, *How would you move Mount Fuji? Microsoft's cult of the puzzle – how the world's smartest company selects the most creative thinkers*, Little, Brown, New York.

'Psychobabble' 2004, *International Journal of Productivity and Performance Management*, vol. 53, no. 6, p. 564.

Rees, Christopher J & Metcalfe, Beverley 2003, 'The faking of personality questionnaire results', *Journal of Managerial Psychology*, vol. 18, no. 2, pp. 156–65.

Rothstein, Mitchell G & Goffin, Richard D 2006, 'The use of personality measures in personnel selection: what does current research support?', *Human Resource Management Review*, vol. 16, no. 2, pp. 155–80.

Ryan, Ann Marie, McFarland, Lynn, Baron, Helen & Page, Ron 1999, 'An international look at selection processes: nations and culture as explanations for variability in practice', *Personnel Psychology*, vol. 52, p. 261.

Sampson, Eleri 2002, *Build your personal brand*, 3rd edn, Kogan Page, London.

Smith, William P & Kidder, Deborah L 2010, 'You've been tagged! (then again, maybe not): employers and Facebook', *Business Horizons*, doi: 10.1016/j.bushor.2010.0.004

Spillane, Robert & Martin, John 2005, *Personality and performance: foundations for managerial psychology*, University of New South Wales Press, Sydney.

Sullivan, Sherry E 2001, 'Careers in the 21st century', *Group and Organization Management*, vol. 26, no. 3, pp. 252–4.

Thornton, Robert 1988, *LIAR: lexicon of intentionally ambiguous recommendations*, Meadowbrook/Simon and Schuster, New York.

Tolley, Harry & Wood, Robert 2009, *How to succeed at an assessment centre: essential preparation for psychometric tests, group and role-play exercises, panel interviews and presentations*, 3rd edn, Kogan Page, London.

Training 'Job seekers squeamish about psychological tests', 2000, vol. 37, no. 12, p. 30.

Tullier, Michelle 1999, *The unofficial guide to acing the interview*, Macmillan, New York.

Wood, Jennifer, Schmidtke, L, James M & Decker, Diane L 2007, 'Experience lying on job applications: the effects of job relevance, commission, and human resource management', *Journal of Business and Psychology*, vol. 22, no.1, pp. 1–9.

21

Social media

LEARNING OBJECTIVES

After studying this chapter you should be able to:

- Outline the key differences between old (or traditional) and new (or social) media
- Explain the basics of social media sites and tools such as blogs, Twitter, Facebook, MySpace, wikis and Wikipedia, YouTube, podcasting and RSS
- Provide an overview of social media issues relating to marketing and monetisation, as well as how individuals use social networking sites
- Summarise the pros and cons of social media

What is social media?

As we saw in chapter 1, there are numerous channels of communication we can use, and big media (TV, radio, newspapers and magazines) are vital tools for communication. In the past decade or so, however, still newer channels or media have emerged – some of them with wild and mysterious names such as blogs, Facebook, MySpace, Google Wave, wikis, YouTube, Twitter, RSS (really simple syndication), Flickr, Second Life (a virtual reality game/experience), Wikipedia and podcasting. These have come to be grouped under the heading of social media.

Social media has quickly become a popular style of communication.

The growth of these media has been facilitated by the arrival of new media hardware, such as smartphones that can not only receive pictures but take them (including moving ones) (e.g. the Apple iPhone) and handheld microcomputers or Personal Digital Assistants or palmtop computers (e.g. Black-berries and PalmPilots), as well as by the wireless connectivity of laptop computers.

Shih (2009) refers to social media as 'the fourth revolution', giving the following sequence:

- 1970s – mainframe computers as the dominant mode
- 1980s – personal computing as the dominant mode
- 1990s – internet as the dominant mode
- 2000s – social networking as the dominant mode.

Web 2.0: a term probably characterised by user-generated content and mobility (not needing to be at a desk to log on to the net)

Social networking is also often referred to as part of **Web 2.0**, a term still in the process of definition, but most probably characterised by mobility (not needing to be at a desk to log on to the net), as well as by user-generated content: consumers become active producers, instead of being passive consumers of professional creators (e.g. newspaper editors, disc jockeys, television producers and books publishers) (Toffler 1981; Shirky 2000; Bruns 2009).

Previously, the content of websites and emails were naturally created by the writers of the same, and the recipients or users reacted to them accordingly. Now, the new media depends on user-generated content, and thus the old electronic media has come to be collectively called Web 1.0 while the new media have come to be collectively called Web.2.0.

Kaplan and Heinlen (2010) point out that Web 2.0 is not a technical upgrade of Web 1.0. It needed a number of things, primarily software innovations, to make it happen. Key innovations are outlined in table 21.1.

TABLE 21.1 Some of the tools needed to make Web 2.0 happen

Innovation	Features
Adobe Flash	A popular method for adding animation, interactivity, and audio/video streams to web pages
RSS	Really Simple Syndication, a family of web feed formats used to publish frequently updated content, such as blog entries or news headlines, in a standardised format (see discussion of RSS that follows)
AJAX	Asynchronous Java Script, a technique to retrieve data from web servers asynchronously, allowing the update of web content without interfering with the display and behaviour of the whole page).

Source: Adapted from Kaplan and Heinlen (2010).

So how do most of the social media differ from the old media? Table 21.2 scratches the surface of the situation.

TABLE 21.2 Old media versus new media

Feature	Old media	Social media
Communication flow	One-way (partial exception — talkback radio)	Two-way
Participant roles	Producers (but sometimes consumers, e.g. when newsroom journalists monitor personal networks for breaking stories)	Producers of straight content, but also sampling, mashups, remixing (also consumers of existing media for entertainment, but may also legally/illegally download content)
Intellectual property	High respect for copyright, original format of artefact	Often low respect for copyright
Technical skills needed	High	Low–medium
Set-up costs	High	Low
Recording and disseminating events, views	Slow	Fast, not so slow
Permanency of artefacts	Permanent (except where editing is done for malicious effect)	Not necessarily permanent: other creators may change content: 'it never ends'; process, not product
Editorial control of content	Strong — centralised	Weak — decentralised (but some controller may act on legal grounds to censor)
Financial viability	Once invincible, but some newspapers have closed as advertising revenues have migrated to websites	Some producers produce for the love of it. Others accepts ads, bringing in some cash flow

But surely this mix of characteristics means that new or social media will never be able to match the production values of TV, radio and film? Pesce (2006) calls this 'the Big Lie of the media: if it isn't professionally produced, the audience won't watch it. No statement could be more mendacious; no assertion could be further from the truth'. People will tolerate less than professional standards, if the content is good, particularly if it is produced by themselves. As we shall see, this is not always the case, but it's a provocative point of view.

The new media: what are they?

Let's turn our attention to some of these new social media. Here, we will only consider Blogs, Twitter, Facebook, MySpace, wikis and Wikipedia, YouTube, podcasting and RSS. Figure 21.1 (see overleaf) outlines the pros of social media.

Sent an email lately? You're a publisher. Posted a photo, video, a comment or a vote on a website? You're a publisher. Keyed in a text message to friends on your cell phone? You're a publisher . . .

Something is changing in the way everyday people look at themselves and the world. We are creating new and strengthened relationships and allegiances. We are beginning to look upon institutions that we used to rely on for providing us with cohesion and value in our lives as less valuable in the face of publishing technologies that allow us to organise ourselves and our lives more to our suiting. We are creating and participating in new markets for goods and services that do not require traditional suppliers and brokers. We are doing our jobs differently. We are living our lives differently.

Blossom 2009

Social media captures collective intelligence. Through them, we can work seamlessly in teams, no matter how geographically dispersed . . .

Social media is accessible, easy to use and understand. There are low barriers to entry. Social media tools are both versatile and flexible . . .

With social media, an individual can shift easily between the role of audience and the role of author. With easy-to-use software, ordinary individuals can create their own content and seamlessly share it with others.

Lincoln 2009

Dr John Grohol, an U.S. psychologist and expert on online behaviour and internet addiction, said people share online for hundreds of reasons, from wanting to keep in touch with colleagues and friends to expanding their horizons in a hobby or profession. 'If there's a core reason, it is mainly to stay and feel connected with one another. It is simply socialising on a vast, unheard of scale,' he says. This desire for recognition is easy to ridicule, but it is part of the human condition. It is nothing new.

Martin 2009

We are already seeing the economic potential of social media in its ability to reduce inefficient marketing and middlemen. Million dollar television advertisements are no longer the king influencer of purchase intent. People referring products and services via social media tools are the new king. It is the world's largest referral program in history. There is also less need to subscribe to costly newspapers when consumers are pushed more relevant and timely free content from their peers via social media. The news finds us. All of this can be done easily from the comfort of home or while on the go with mobile devices.

Qualman 2009

The social web will become the primary centre of activity for whatever you do when you shop, plan, learn or communicate. It may not take over your entire life (one hopes), but it will be the first place you turn for news, information, entertainment, diversion — all of the things the older media supplied. In fact, according to a Forrester Research Report, young people (18–22) spend more time using a PC at home — 10.7 hours a week — than they spend watching TV — 10–12 hours a week — an important point for businesses looking to build early brand loyalty.

Weber 2009

FIGURE 21.1 Social media — the pros

There is healthy debate about social media. Consider figure 21.2 (opposite), which includes quotes that highlight some of the cons of social media.

I would rather have a prostate exam on live television by a guy with very cold hands than have a Facebook page.

George Clooney (cited in Green and Meeser 2009)

The problem with Twitter is there a lot of marketers and spam, and not a lot of controls there to stop that — and that's turning people off. It will remain popular with a hardcore group of users who can use it for research and business purposes. But there's not much value on Twitter for younger people.

Dr Ross Monaghan, Deakin University (cited in Munro 2009)

Some ex-users seemed shaken, even heartbroken, by their breakups with Facebook. 'I primarily left Facebook because I was wasting so much time on it', my friend Caroline Harting told me by e-mail. 'I felt fairly detached from my Facebook buddies because I rarely directly contacted them.' Instead, she felt as if she stalked them, spending hours a day looking at their pages without actually saying hello.

Heffernan 2009

In the Web hype-o-sphere, things matter hugely until, very suddenly, they don't matter at all. Thanks to the unprecedented growth of MySpace and Facebook, 'social media' matters hugely right now, but it is likely only another in a long string of putatively disruptive, massively hyped technologies that prove just one more step in the long march. Like 'push', 'social media' is a functional advance pimped out as a revolution. *Web 2.0*, a term used somewhat interchangeably with *social media*, carries the not-so-veiled suggestion that everything else is merely 1.0 — that is to say, Cro-Magnon. Really cool people now like to talk about *Web 3.0*.

The social media sites are touting their expertly tended, notably fecund, but still fenced-in offerings. And to be fair, they are free, unlike the old subscription-based AOL (*America Online*). But, as with the dial-ups, the distinctions in and among these offerings will become less interesting. Instant messaging, in yet another example of the Web's buzz-to-blah dynamic, was once a unique and compelling reason to subscribe to AOL, not to mention hyped as a revolutionary application that would render e-mail fogeyish and vestigial. It is now a commodity function.

Hirschorn 2007

FIGURE 21.2 Social media — the cons

Social media in detail

We need to know that they may not all survive, or indeed may be overtaken by still newer media. But first, some brief context before we begin. Most social media started out as exercises or hobbies by young people – often at educational institutions. Their motivations were primarily **hedonic** – it was fun, and an end in itself rather than a means to an end, like profits (Sledgianowsk & Kulviwat 2009). As they have grown dramatically in size, with some being **mashups** the general market has become very interested: not only those newspaper proprietors losing advertising revenue to websites on the internet, but media proprietors interested in reaching younger and smaller audiences who are sometimes hostile to most advertising and marketing.

Hedonic: pleasure seeking; inventing something as an end in itself, not as a means to an end

Mashup: a digital mixing of various sources, such as music, images and animation

Meanwhile, entrepreneurs are trying to figure out how to **monetise** their product: that is, make money out of it – a task that is difficult, and may well be counterproductive if by so doing they alienate their original audiences (Clemons 2009). But this is not an age war: already, users of social media are getting older; into their 30s, 40s and 50s. Figure 21.3 (see overleaf) roughly maps out the terrain we will now explore.

Monetise: a jargon term used in information industries — it simply means to enable a product to make money, particularly when the product has been free up until now

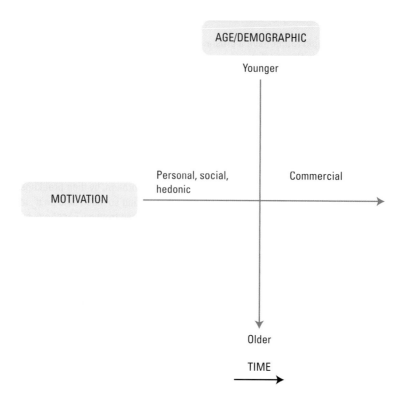

AGE/DEMOGRAPHIC

Younger

Personal, social, hedonic

Commercial

MOTIVATION

Older

TIME

FIGURE 21.3 The terrain of social media

Next is a discussion of actual social media – blogs, Twitter, Facebook, MySpace, wikis and Wikipedia, YouTube, podcasting and RSS.

Social medium 1: blogs

Blog: a log or record or diary on the web

A **blog** is a log or record or diary on the web. The term was first coined in 1999 (Safko & Brake 2009). Scott (2009, p. 46) defines it thus:

> A blog is just a Web site. But it is a special kind of site that is created and maintained by a person who is passionate about a subject and wants to tell the world about his or her area of expertise. A blog is almost always written by one person who has a fire in the belly and wants to communicate with the world. There are also group bogs (written by several people) and even corporate blogs produced by a department or entire company (without individual personalities at all), but these are less common. The most popular form by far is the individual blog.

So what do people write about? Gardner and Burley (2008, p. 134) list the most popular topics:

- children
- personal hobbies or interests
- technology
- politics
- weird news (oddities, quirks; using posts and hyperlinks)
- specialised news (sites collected or aggregated together)
- personal diaries.

If you want to locate blogs on particular areas, try sites like Technorati, Google Blogs, Blogsearch, blogs.com.au and blogs.nz. If you would like to create a blog, but are unsure of your software proficiency, there are software packages you can use, such as Moveable Type, Expression Engine, Word Press, Type Pad and many, many more.

How big is the blogging phenomenon? Safko and Brake (2009) explain that:

> The Gartner Research Group expects that the novelty value of the blog will wear off eventually, since so many people who were interested in the phenomenon create a blog just to see what it's like. Gartner further expects that new bloggers will outnumber those bloggers who abandon their blogs out of boredom, and estimates that more than 200 million former bloggers have already ceased posting to their blogs ...
>
> Safko & Brake 2009, p. 169

McGovern (2004) lists the advantages and disadvantages of corporate blogs (see table 21.3). Most of the principles hold true for individuals and groups (see also Cashone 2009).

TABLE 21.3 The advantages and disadvantages of blogs

Advantages	Disadvantages
1. The consumer and citizen are potentially better informed and this can only be good for the long-term health of our societies and economies.	1. Most people don't have very much [that is] interesting to say and/or are unable to write down their ideas in a compelling and clear manner.
2. Blogs have potential to help the organisation develop stronger relationships and brand loyalty with their customers, as they interact with the 'human face' of the organisation through blogs.	2. I have often found that the people who have most time to write have least to say, and the people who have most to say don't have enough time to write it. Thus, the real expertise within the organisation lays hidden, as you get drowned in trivia.
3. Blogs, in an intranet environment, can be an excellent way of sharing knowledge within the organisation.	3. Like practically everything else on the web, blogs are easy to start and hard to maintain. Writing coherently is one of the most difficult and time-consuming tasks for a person to undertake. So, far from blogs being a cheap strategy, they are a very expensive one. As a result, many blogs are not updated, thus damaging, rather than enhancing, the reputation of the organisation.
4. Blogs can be a positive way for getting feedback, and keeping your finger on the pulse, as readers react to certain pieces and suggest story ideas.	4. Organisations are not democracies. The web makes many organisations look like disorganisations, with multiple tones and opinions. Contrary to what some might think, the average customer likes that the organisation they are about to purchase a product from is at least somewhat coherent.
5. Blogs can build the profile of the writer, showcasing the organisation as having talent and expertise.	

So, what is finally the value of blogs? *The Wall Street Journal*, in 1997 (calling that year the tenth anniversary of blogging), interviewed a number of authors, celebrities/actors and journalists. Perhaps the two extremes of attitudes are best summed up by actor Mia Farrow and writer Tom Wolfe:

> Unfiltered publishing was once the exclusive domain of media moguls, but today, who needs Rupert Murdoch? Blogging has become a publishing equalizer that was scarcely dreamed of years ago. It's free, you don't need editors or publishers, you don't even need to be able to write well.

Last year, I followed my own advice. I started www.miafarrow.org. I am my own toughest critic, and I can't say the acceptance rate for my pieces is vastly improved, but the only person I have to convince that an article is worth publishing is the editor in chief: me. (When a piece is posted, the entire staff is elated.)

It is through this experience that I've come to appreciate the purity and power of blogging. I have appeared in more than 40 movies, written a book and given countless interviews on TV, radio and in print. Yet none of this has allowed me to spotlight issues important to me as completely as my blog.

Mia Farrow (cited in Varadarajan 2007)

Favorite blogs: Mr. Wolfe, 'weary of narcissistic shrieks and baseless "information"', says he no longer reads blogs.

Tom Wolfe (cited in Varadarajan 2007)

Keep in mind that what you see is not always what you get. The person who signs the blogging is not always the person who wrote it. Ghostwriters for blogs and even emails are becoming as numerous as ghostwriters for celebrities (Kernohan 2010, p. 17).

Blogs as citizen journalism?

Citizen journalism: the idea that anyone can be a journalist by using social media tools and hardware to record, and perhaps comment on, events

The concept of **citizen journalism** has come to the fore in the past few years — not surprising, perhaps, when you can use your phone as a video camera and sell the footage to an old-media TV station. But some journalists dismiss the idea out of hand.

Foster (2001), a journalist, is not impressed by the concept. He says that webloggers prioritise their individual views and appreciate their right to give them publicly. However, he argues that webloggers lack professional integrity and risk damaging the reputation of weblogs as a credible source of journalism. Additionally, he contends that once a weblogger adds their 'voice' that their content shifts from news to opinion. He explains:

Basically, if you have a Blogger site, you have yourself a homepage. A page about you, with your personal info and thoughts, has been called a homepage since 1992 or so, and no one was ever all that impressed with them.

Foster 2001

Social medium 2: microblogging with Twitter

Another new social medium is called Twitter (http://twitter.com). It's like blogging, only with much greater space restrictions: the messages you send can only be 140 characters (not letters) long. Twitter messages can be sent from desktop/laptop computers, but also from smartphones, so they can be sent from anywhere, anytime. Messages are known as **tweets**. By searching, you can be a 'follower' or be 'followed'. You can put up (and change) a photo of yourself, known as an **avatar**. As with blogs, what started out as an experimental tool mainly used by young people now is taking on a commercial/workplace role (Zhao & Rosson 2009; Sagolla 2009; Fitton, Gruen & Poston 2009; Micek & Whitlock 2009; Comm, 2009; Hardin & Heyman 2009). Consider the words of Silver (2009):

Tweet: a message sent or received via the Twitter microblogging system
Avatar: a pictorial representation of yourself on Twitter

Twitter, at first a place to tell everyone what you ate for breakfast, is now a place to promote yourself, your company or your product.

Table 21.4 lists some typical tweets.

Tweet	Sender	Analysis
Want to work in health? The Gillard Govt is funding training for the professions in highest demand. See here http://tinyurl.com/35hmpyx JG 2:09 PM Oct 14th via Twitter for iPad	Australian Prime Minister, Julia Gillard, October, 2010	Notice hyperlink at end promoting health scheme; public sector marketing
I get to do the interviewing for once for @VirginBlue 10th birthday celebrations, and even try a spot of dancing! http://bit.ly/bwdgQt Tuesday, 14 September 2010 1:43:03 AM via web	Sir Richard Branson	Hyperlink at the end of the message links to a video and blog about Virgin Blue's tenth anniversary staff celebrations, which Sir Richard Branson attended. A good public relations exercise for both Branson and Virgin Blue.
RT @timryan House passes historic reform to provide health care for every American. Congratulating my colleagues on the floor. 8:25 PM Nov 7th from web	US President Barak Obama responds to supporter Tim Ryan regarding the Health Bill	RT mean re-tweet, like forwarding an email. All Obama's followers now get this tweet.
@barackobama Thank you for the RT, Mr. President. This is a great day for the country. 8:35 PM Nov 7th from TwitterBerry	Obama supporter Tim Ryan responds to the US President ten minutes later	

TABLE 21.4 Examples of Twitter use in government and business

Images using the Twitpic photo site of Twitter have been used by conventional media because they are available minutes after crucial events, such as terrorist bombings. In Australia, *News.com* editor-in-chief David Higgins, commenting on this facility, observed, 'Twitter has become the de facto global news network' (Canning 2009).

Writing on Twitter

Writing in 140 characters represents a real challenge. Sagolla (2009) recommends these writing tips:

- The best advice is from old Strunk and White themselves. Omit needless words.
- Be short, blunt, vigorous and concise. Minimise adverbs and articles. Commas are a favour to the reader, they are not always necessary. Eliminate personal pronouns.
- Lead with a verb.
- Restrict the message to one tweet: resist the desire to send a long message, chopped up into individual tweets. There is no guarantee in what order they will arrive, and confusion might follow.
- When all else fails, use a hashtag (#), which will act a target for someone searching for a tweet.

Twitter: not all a happy story

Even though many are talking about and trying Twitter, Nielsen Online, which measures internet traffic, has found that a high percentage of initial users have dropped it within a month (Martin 2009). What of the typical Twitter user? Pemberton (2009) reports a gloomy prognosis:

> The clinical psychologist Oliver James has his reservations. 'Twittering stems from a lack of identity. It's a constant update of who you are, what you are, where you are. Nobody would Twitter if they had a strong sense of identity.'

'We are the most narcissistic age ever,' agrees Dr David Lewis, a cognitive neuropsychologist and director of research based at the University of Sussex. 'Using Twitter suggests a level of insecurity whereby, unless people recognise you, you cease to exist. It may stave off insecurity in the short term, but it won't cure it.'

As with all social media, there are security concerns. The British insurance firm Legal and General worked with a burglar to see what security breaches, particularly in households, social media made people prone to (and of course, there is no reason why these techniques could not be used to target businesses).

According to the report (Woollacott 2009):

- 38 per cent of people on sites such as Facebook and Twitter have posted status updates detailing their holiday plans, and a third have posted updates saying that they are away for the weekend
- Younger people are even more likely to give away their whereabouts, with 64 per cent of 16–24 year olds sharing their holiday plans
- Reformed burglar Michael Fraser said: 'I call it "internet shopping for burglars". It is incredibly easy to use social networking sites to target people, and then scope out more information on their actual home using other internet sites like Google Street View, all from the comfort of the sofa.'
- Another quote was: 'It scares me to see how many people are prepared to give away valuable information about themselves, to people they simply don't know well enough — if at all.'

Social medium 3: Facebook

Facebook (www.facebook.com) is a social networking site, founded in 2004, that within six years had more than 500 million users (Evans 2010). In a few short years, the modest project has become a giant networking machine, linking hundreds of millions of people. If Facebook were a country, it would be the third biggest one on the planet. Its users tend to be urban and affluent, more so than on rival products such as MySpace (Gaudin 2009a). Australians are among the website's biggest fans. Among the 14 million Australians who use the internet in any given month, around 8.8 million (63 per cent) are Facebook users (Evans 2010, p. 11).

Facebook was originally designed in 2004 by Harvard University students with the modest aim of letting new students get to know other faces. Mark Zuckerberg has been identified in the public eye (particularly after the release of the film *The Social Network* in 2010) as the genius who created Facebook while at university. There were several skilled software designers working on the project, and many of these designers have either sued (successfully) or are still suing (Mezrick 2010) for Zuckerberg claiming sole patent rights. Intellectual property disputes are likely to become increasingly common in the years to come.

Users of Facebook first establish a profile, which is like a resume. Different aspects of your profile can be revealed to different people according to what settings you put in place. Facebook has a 'wall' on which you can place photographs, messages and videos. Safko and Brake note that:

> [Facebook] can be used in business environments for networking, locating business leads, as a method of intercompany communication, as a platform to organize and track events, and as a medium to provide updates between organizations and departments. Due to its popularity, Facebook could be used to promote a new product, service or performer by word of mouth through 'friends' within a social network. In academic environments, Facebook can be used to promote or enhance course communication, organize school functions, and as a platform to organize and track intramural and extracurricular events.
>
> Safko & Brake 2009, p. 452

Facebook: controversies and criticisms

One of the features of Facebook is that you can 'poke' another person, providing a stimulus to get their attention. This irritates some people, and has even led to legal action in the United States, with the poke being seen as a form of assault (Suarez 2009). There have been security concerns expressed about just how effective the privacy controls on Facebook are. In the US, marines have been banned from using Twitter, MySpace and Facebook, especially in combat situations, due to concerns that information could be extracted by an enemy force (Schachtman 2009). In South Australia, police have been warned off using such sites for similar reasons, with the Police Association president warning that an exchange of personal information could be used by criminals obtaining that information, and also that interstate and overseas lawyers had planted wrong information on sites to discredit police (Rodrigues 2009).

The Control Your Info direct action group took over 289 Facebook groups (groups sharing similar interests) in November 2009, to make the point that security was not tight enough (Choney 2009). One of Facebook's chief security advisors has no photo of himself on his Facebook page, nor any indication of how many friends he has, nor any montage of photos typically seen on such pages (Farrer 2009). The US Director of the FBI has no profile on Facebook, and warns people about putting too much personal information on Facebook and similar sites (Mills 2009).

In a recent year, the wife of the new director of MI6 put personal photographs of her husband on her Facebook page, causing a security scare (Bingham 2009). This raises the question of where one's work life ends and where does one's private life begin, or are they becoming blurred in a 24/7 'always in touch' world?

There is also the vexed issue of something being too much of a good thing. While advertisers and friends might be happy that a student is online on Facebook, that student might be getting lower grades or scores by being online instead of studying (Gaudin 2009b; Heffernan 2009).

These are some of the 'counterpublics' of Facebook – those who question its use, efficacy, security and alienation of users from the real world (Milioni 2009). For example, Google had almost four million entries under 'I hate Facebook' in early 2011.

Street-Porter (2009) conveys one idea about why the site may be so successful:

> Facebook has been a runaway success because it allows people to create their own profile and welcome new 'friends' with whom they can share their every waking thought. This, in turn, allows them to feel important and individual, no matter how humdrum their existence might be – by designing a far more interesting version of themselves online.

Tim Berners-Lee, a British scientist sometimes called 'the father of the web', has reservations about the website. Kelleher (2010) explains:

> Social network sites like Facebook, Berners-Lee says, are silos, connecting data and content only within its walled gardens. Apple's iTunes traps people into a proprietary store. Even Google, whose search revenue is dependent on an open web, is chided for abandoning its support of net neutrality. All lead to a fragmented web, damaging the 'single, universal information space' that made it work in the first place. They can also breed monopolies, which the web was initially designed to resist.

Social medium 4: MySpace

MySpace is the major rival of Facebook, and once had market dominance – but no more (Angwin 2009; Gorkjazi, Rejaie & Willinger 2009; Fixmer & Rabil 2011). It provides similar services to those of Facebook, although computer-literate users are able to customise the look of their site much more than a Facebook site (Hupfer, Maxson & Williams 2008).

It still has several hundred million users (Levinson 2009; Brake 2008). MySpace has a younger demographic than Facebook, and has played to this strength by promoting new music (Brake 2008; Gauvin et al. 2010).

In 2006, in a sign that the old media was recognising the power of the new, News Corporation paid US$580 million for MySpace (Safko & Brake 2009). However, it has been losing market share since, and has had to lay off staff. In early 2011, MySpace announced that it was cutting 47 percent of its workforce, and firing about 500 staff across its broad operations. The news followed reports that News Corporation planned to sell off the website (Fixmer & Rabil 2011).

Social medium 5: wikis and Wikipedia

A wiki is a document with multiple collaborating authors. It can be a relatively simple document on a private intranet of an organisation, or it can be one of the most commonly used sites on the internet today, Wikipedia. 'Wiki' is in fact the Hawaiian word for 'quick', and Ward Cunningham, in naming the concept and who uploaded the first wiki in 1995, remembered this from a time when he was at Honolulu International Airport where the shuttle buses were called 'wiki-wikis' (Safko & Brake 2009). In internal or closed wikis, they are used as knowledge management tools, building up collective expertise:

> Many companies today are utilizing the wiki to create knowledge management systems for retaining corporate information for collaboration and training. By incorporating a company wiki, many firms can gather the collective knowledge of their employees on subjects such as policies and procedures, manufacturing and sales, company history, products — and even how to fix the fax machine's paper jams.
>
> Safko & Brake 2009, p. 181

Wikipedia (www.wikipedia.org) was developed by Jimmy Wales and Larry Sanger, who launched it on the internet in 2001. By December 2010, it hosted more than 3.5 million articles in English, and more than 22 million pages (Wikipedia 2010). Wikipedia has always been fraught with controversy because of the bottom-up, collaborative approach which accepts all 'experts' and 'nonexperts'. In other words, because it was and remains free, it presented a threat to existing encyclopaedias such as the Britannica, which partly in response has moved from a book-based product to a CD-ROM/DVD model and online model (which obviously are not free).

The critical question was, and remains, the reliability of Wikipedia, and academic institutions all over the world have usually taken a dim view of Wikipedia because of this. Content on Wikipedia is monitored, and 'trolls' — those who maliciously change entries — are banned. Jimmy Wales' radical defence of almost total access and the defence of the amateur against the professional led to a philosophical split with his co-founder, Larry Sanger, who is creating a rival online free encyclopaedia called 'Citizendium' (www.citizendium.org). Sanger wants articles written only by professionals in order to maintain higher standards. Pesce (2006) sums up the dilemma over standards, accuracy and speed:

> Citizendium is proactive and presumes too much; Wikipedia is reactive (and for this reason will occasionally suffer malicious damage) but only modifies its access policies when a clear threat to the stability of the community has been demonstrated. Wikipedia is an anarchic horde, moving by consensus, unlike Citizendium, which is a recapitulation of the top-down hierarchy of the academy. While some will no doubt treasure the heavy moderation of Citizendium, the vast majority will prefer the noise and vitality of Wikipedia. A heavy hand versus an invisible one; this is the central paradox of community.
>
> Pesce 2006

In 2009, Wales caused more controversy in the Wikipedia camp when he announced that there would be much more editorial oversight on articles. Some felt this went against the egalitarian spirit of the original concept (Johnson 2009). Meanwhile, Britannica has retaliated by announcing that it will allow its users to submit their own updates to entries (Johnson 2009). Citizendium is building slowly, but its task is obviously a huge one.

In a way, the controversy sums up some of the central dilemmas of all social media: can we trust it? What does it mean to have 'professional standards', and are they necessarily accurate? What are the legal implications of putting content on the web that is incorrect? (see Bruns 2009).

There remains the worrying question of whether Wikipedia is just another gatekeeper, keeping us from things we know. Thus, Jimmy Wales, the founder, writes:

> Administrators, commonly known as admins or sysops (system operators), are Wikipedia editors trusted with access to restricted technical features ('tools'). For example, administrators can protect, delete and restore pages, move pages over redirects, hide and delete page revisions, and block other editors. See Wikipedia:Administrators/Tools.
>
> Administrators assume these responsibilities as volunteers; they are not acting as employees of the Wikimedia Foundation. They are never required to use their tools, and must never use them to gain an advantage in a dispute in which they are involved.
>
> Wales 2010

At the other extreme of openness is Wikileaks, a website with no gatekeeper. This site was founded by Australian Julian Assange, who believes in full disclosure of uncensored documents, no matter what the consequences. Documents posted to the site have usually been leaked by anonymous sources. This site polarises opinion. Supporters argue that it promotes freedom of speech, transparency and accountability, helping to expose corruption or wrongdoing by governments, corporations and individuals. Critics argue that the publication of sensitive information can potentially endanger lives. An ethical question with Wikileaks is: 'Could the release of information lead to the identification, torture and execution of undercover agents?' (Lee 2010)

More divergent views on social media are shown in figure 21.4.

ANTI-SOCIAL MEDIA	PRO-SOCIAL MEDIA
British neuroscientist Susan Greenfield said those who were over-reliant on smartphones could become addicted to short, shallow interactions and become uncomfortable face-to-face. She said those who used phones to constantly access Twitter and Facebook had a 'dodgy sense of identity' and were seeking constant reassurance and feedback for everyday experiences.	Deloitte Digital's chief executive officer, Peter Williams, said such technologies were better than reading because they were less passive, stimulated wider parts of the brain and allowed quick access to useful information. 'These technologies create a whole new world of knowledge, learning and opportunity', he said.

FIGURE 21.4 More divergent views on social media
Source: Adapted from Dobbin (2010, p. 3).

Social medium 6: YouTube

YouTube (www.youtube.com) was launched in November 2005, with its logo — 'broadcast yourself' (Levinson 2009). Anyone can upload a video for free onto the system, and such videos can played back on computers, blogs, email or mobile devices such as smartphones. The majority of content on YouTube is music videos, but the copyright situation regarding these is still a matter for contention: thus, you may see a video you like

YouTube is a hugely successful social media forum that provides people with the opportunity to broadcast video content online.

one day, and go back the next, with the intention of downloading it, and it is missing: the music company has spoken to YouTube, and they are not happy.

One might think, therefore, that the primary audience for YouTube is teenagers and young adults who want to see music clips, but in fact, that is not so:, for example, research in the United States found that the demographic of users was 52 per cent male and 48 per cent female, with the main age groups being 45–50 year olds and people over 55 years of age (Safko & Brake 2009).

Other content includes advertisements, movie trailers, amateur footage of people just being silly or attempting stunts, sporting event highlights, newscasts and homemade movies (Safko & Brake 2009).

YouTube, like other social media we have considered, needs to monetise. Large companies are spending substantial budgets on advertisements such as H&R Block (tax consultants), Intuit, Levi's, Mountain dew soft drink, MTV, Smirnoff, and Warner Brothers (Miller 2009). Miller warns that boring will not make it on YouTube-uploaded content needs to be quirky or striking (such as the Smirnoff commercial, using expensive computer-generated imagery [CGI]), but it can be low-budget quirky or striking as well (as in Blendtec's 'Will it Blend?' series, in which various things considered un-destroyable [such as iPhones, magnets, guitars, Rubik's Cube, remote controls, computer game DVDs] are blended). Often these low-budget videos become cult objects, or are heard about by word of mouth or their URLs are emailed to others. As such, they qualify to be classified as **viral marketing**, a term which is rather vague and has been given many meanings, but basically means attracting customers via social networks or word of mouth rather than through conventional marketing (Cruz & Fill 2008; Silver 2009).

Viral marketing: sending commercial messages to potential customers via social networks, rather than by conventional advertising

Miller also suggests other low budget approaches, such as how-to videos, such as how to build a bookcase or change a flat tire (Miller 2009). This aspect taps into another feature of social media – activity rather than passivity. Miller notes a US survey that found that online viewing led to 82 per cent brand awareness and 77 per cent product recall, in contrast to 54 per cent brand awareness and 18 per cent product recall for similar television ads. 'Experts believe this is because online viewers are more engaged than television viewers; the web is a more interactive medium than the passive viewing inherent with television' (Miller 2009).

YouTube is also the site for embarrassing moments, where one's mistakes can be played over and over by millions. For example, in 2006, US senator George Allen, while on a speaking tour, referred to an audience member as 'macaca', which has racist connotations in some parts of the world. The clip was played many times on YouTube, and Allen lost his bid for re-election and a possible nomination for president in 2008 (Burroughs 2007; Levinson 2009). Michael Richards (the Kramer character on the television comedy *Seinfeld*) was heckled at a nightclub while performing in 2006. Richards used the term 'nigger' several times to refer to the heckler, and his performance was recorded on a video-enabled phone and uploaded to YouTube. This did enormous damage to his career (Levinson 2009).

Social medium 7: podcasting

The Apple iPod has received widespread acclaim. Initially, it was launched as a music player, but it is now also used as a device to play back audio files and video podcasts.

MP3 or mpeg3: a digital audio format devised by the Moving Pictures Expert Group in 1991 compresses original file size

In Stanley Kubrick's 1968 film, *2001: A Space Odyssey*, the main spacecraft has several small pods or spacecraft attached to it so that astronauts can make small journeys away from the mother ship. The mother ship is controlled by a computer called HAL, who decides to kill all on-board. One of the astronauts returns to the ship in a pod and says some of the most famous words in film: 'Open the pod bay door, HAL!' HAL, needless to say, has no intention of doing so.

When Apple computer was about to launch its portable music player in 2001, it had no name. A copywriter hired to name it immediately thought of a phrase about a pod in the movie *2001: A Space Odyssey*, and called it the internet pod or iPod (Safko & Brake 2009). The iPod's main use initially was as a music player, but some soon began to use it as a device to play back audio files of talks, speeches, training seminars, educational lectures, share market advice, interviews, school subject revision, sermons, samples of professional musicians' new songs, playbacks of radio programs ... there is a lot of audio content out there, and — perhaps surprisingly — people want to listen to it (as the growth in sales of audio books — books usually ready by famous actors — attests) (Levinson 2009). Some devices can also receive video podcasts. Most of it is free, while you need to subscribe to some services. Some have the impression that podcasting requires Apple hardware and software: this is not so. Audio files, usually in **MP3** format, can be played on non-Apple equipment and software.

The internet will give you lists of Apple, Windows and Linux software to choose from (e.g. buzzmaven) — yes, you will need special software to record, but increasingly these are being built into hardware/software combinations, such as Apple's Garage Band or Windows Zune. Some of this software will also help you upload your podcast to the net. You will need a microphone and ideas — and a lack of perfectionism when recording (in fact, the 'unprofessionalism' of some podcasts are what listeners find attractive.) Be aware of the size of your audio files — a 30 megabyte file could take more than an hour to download for users of dial-up modems (Safko & Brake 2009).

To give you some inspiration, go to a web browser and type in 'podcasts' — you will be amazed at how many are out there, from different countries, from amateur musicians, from professional interviewers on a broadcasting site. Increasingly, car manufacturers are making their vehicle dashboards podcast-friendly. As with YouTube, 'broadcast yourself'.

Social medium 8: RSS

You may have noticed on an increasing number of sites an orange logo with 'Get RSS' or similar words. What does it all mean? RSS as an acronym has several translations, such as 'rich site summary' or 'really simple syndication'. It is the youngest social medium we have looked at yet, as it was only launched in 2006 (Safko & Brake 2009).

Why should you care? What's in it for you? Let's say you spend quite a lot of time online pursuing news, hobbies or other interests, visiting one site at a time (how else?). RSS aggregates or collects sites, blogs, audio, video and photographs and delivers them to your computer in one compact passage. It saves one of your time problems, because you can browse a lot of content relevant to one area, but creates another time problem — there are so many RSS feeds out there, all covering the most fascinating topics.You need software to 'catch' the RSS feeds as they come in (e.g. Google reader, Newsgator, My Yahoo!). This installs easily, and will start delivering the aggregated content that you have chosen from websites.

That's content coming in. You can also use RSS to send out content to people who you want to see/hear what it is you have to say.

Social media: marketing, monetisation and user feedback

Businesses are increasingly making use of social media, sometimes effectively, sometimes not. There are many books and websites advising on how to incorporate social media into a business's marketing efforts. Stewart (2010), for example, is full of ideas for businesses, such as:

- adding Facebook Widget/plugins to a website or blog
- showing a Twitter stream on a website
- adding Share/Like/Tweet buttons on products and content on a website
- including Facebook/Twitter information on invoices and receipts
- incorporating Facebook/Twitter in advertising material.

Not all marketing uses of social media, however, seem upfront and ethical. Sweet (2009) notes that the pharmaceutical industries do not have a great record in this regard: Pfizer, for example, sends questionnaires out to doctors regarding medical products, with a provision to rank postings that may be used to shape future company marketing efforts. Sermo hosts a site where doctors can anonymously chat about products. On its own, the website would not generate revenue. However, Sermo subsequently makes this data available to hedge funds that can then use it to predict future patterns.

As mentioned earlier in the chapter, entrepreneurs are trying to figure out how to 'monetise' their online product; that is, how to make money out of it. This is a difficult task. The question abides: How do you make a buck out of Web 2.0? This dilemma can best be explained using an 'old world' media example. Why would I pay for a newspaper when I could go to that newspaper's website and get much (but not all) of the content of the print version for nothing, let alone go to Google and probably get the lot? Google, Yahoo and other search engines are now known as news **aggregators**. Their search mechanisms locate most content and publish it free.

Aggregator: a search engine that collects news from multiple sources, both print and online, and makes it available for free

A bold (some would say desperate) move has been taken by News International, headed by Rupert Murdoch and James Murdoch, to head off the aggregators by creating a two-class system for their print media (e.g. *The Times*, *The Sunday Times* and *News of the World*). They have created pay walls on their online versions, putting premium content in a restricted zone that consumers need to pay for. All links to aggregators have been cut. The idea has had its critics and supporters, but as one entertainment publicist complained, how could he get his UK clients to consent to interviews that might only be read by a minority of people, given that the whole purpose of publicity is to promote something – for example, a film, a record or a book (Wolff, 2010). And if that logic applies to entertainers, then it applies to advertisers and anyone else who would pay money to appear in a newspaper.

Even though the internet is vast, as we have seen, the fortunes of those who use it can vary dramatically. Social media is about user-generated content. This means that the old media acted as gatekeepers (Shoemaker & Vos 2009), or editorial controllers of content, and that therefore we were dependent on them – as consumers – for truth in news and quality and variety in entertainment. Social media holds out the prospect of us becoming producers as well as consumers, but the rules are still not clear.

The changes proposed at Wikipedia over editorial control touch upon this, and the split between Wikipedia and Citizendium touch upon the reliability of what we find on the net: can we believe it? The debate about monetisation continues: will we pay for what we formerly have had for free? That's us speaking as consumers. But if we speak as producers, we might say 'why shouldn't they pay? I've worked hard for this, and I can plough the money back in to give them a better product anyway.'

Masum and Yang have proposed that credibility at least is being approached in non-traditional ways, building trust and reputation in those who want to look, to quote, and perhaps to buy:

> The process of filtering information to distill a smaller yet more refined set of usable, verified, trustworthy judgements is not easy. But it is doable. And it is both more feasible and more necessary now than ever before, due to information proliferation, technological advances, and pressing socio–economic problems. Indeed, we already see many types of reputation systems emerging, especially online.
>
> Masum & Yang 2004

The authors argue that Amazon has grown to be a 'juggernaut' that offers a 'gold mine' of tips that consumers may find useful. They highlight that reputation is at the heart of eBay's auction system — a factor that has surely influenced the success of the shopping website. Masum and Yang (2004) also discuss how BizRate and ePinions have taken a creative approach to establishing credibility: these sites provide business ratings, and, like eBay, rely heavily on consumer feedback as a means of influencing future purchasing decisions.

Krieger (2008) surveyed samples of users of social media — Facebook, Twitter, Wikipedia and Google (although the Google remarks may be more suitable to Facebook/MySpace's Google competitor, Google Wave). Tables 21.5, 21.6, 21.7 and 21.8 show what they have to say. Some you may find surprising (in ethical terms, at least). How much do you agree/disagree with the opinions expressed?

TABLE 21.5 Public opinion on Facebook

WORK	I was looking for the contact details of a consultant. A Google search resulted in finding her French tax number on Facebook. With the tax number I was able to go to the appropriate government site and come up with her contact details.
	I first saw and used Facebook for work! Yes, we were asked to sign up for Facebook and check out what this social networking deal was all about. Then we got to spend several days at work checking out all the different apps and games available, to get ideas for writing our own app to advertise for the company we work for. I actually got paid to play around for several days on the internet.
(RE:) FINDING PEOPLE	It was actually through Facebook that I found a sister that I never knew. My parents had given her up for adoption when she was born because they were not yet married and (had) no means of caring for her. I searched and searched for her, but it wasn't until I discovered Facebook that I discovered her :)
KEEPING TABS ON EXES, DAUGHTERS	I use it to spy on my 13 year old daughter and see that she is not doing anything bad.
	I use Facebook to spy on my fiancé. I sometimes make fake profiles and add him to see if he is cheating on me.
STAYING IN TOUCH	I've used it to reconnect with old classmates that I haven't seen in years.
	I'm coming up on my ten-year high school class reunion. Our class president decided to send out all of the details on Facebook, so everyone who wants to go the reunion and actually know the times and dates of the events has to sign up for a Facebook account. I currently have no other use for it. I think she just wanted to use it to brag about her advanced chemistry degree.
GETTING SMARTER AND TEACHING	I'm a young faculty member at a university. I use Facebook to keep up with my friends and colleagues — and to get important information out to my classes! When there is an announcement that people need to see quickly, I'll write a Facebook note and tag all of the members of the class concerned. That way, everyone who needs to know gets notified as soon as they check Facebook — usually much faster than email!!! I also used MySpace (I don't even have a profile there myself) to gather evidence on my cheating husband. He set the profile to 'private', but it didn't occur to him that many of his friends would not approve of his behaviour. One of his friends gave me access to all of the information!
DATING + NEW FRIENDSHIPS	I have had a renewed communication with my daughter using Facebook. She is 26 and I am 50, so this is really wonderful! Every couple of days we chat through Facebook, and we can see significant details of each other's lives. This is very helpful, since we live 2000 miles apart.

Now, consider the views expressed regarding the social medium of Twitter.

TABLE 21.6 Public opinion on Twitter

NARROWCASTING	I live-blogged via Twitter during the birth of my son! It gave family and friends moment-by-moment updates and delivery without having to deal with multiple telephone calls.
	I let my friends know I was arrested and needed bail money. Better than the one phone allowed me.
	Several of our friends who live far away use Twitter, and my partner and I tweeted our wedding vows to one another so our friends who were unable to attend could still share our experiences virtually.
WORK	I'm a member of DynamIT Technologies LLC, a Columbus Ohio based web engineering group and development group. We recently sponsored Startup Weekend Columbus. I've been 'following' some of the reporters at NBC4 on Twitter for the last few months. One day, they 'tweeted', saying they were looking for a great story for the news. Long story short? We spoke at 5 PM on Twitter, by 6 PM the news truck was here, and we were on the 11 PM news talking about our company and the event. The power of Twitter!
	If only my work would allow me to use Twitter in the way I want to use it. I would like to use Twitter as a daily way to let people know the daily status of swimming beaches in my state. I would like to daily update a feed to tell people where to go or not to go.
NEWS DISSEMINATION	Letting my friends know when an impromptu concert happened. People were there in 15 minutes.
ALTRUISM	I created an account where I did not connect with my friends or make business contacts but only to send out positive, happy, comforting messages to strangers to give them a smile or feel someone was thinking of them.
CHECKING ON OTHERS	I found out my sister-in-law was using Twitter. I was curious what she was writing about and although she mentioned just about every minor detail of her boring life on the site, she made no mention whatsoever of attending an evening recently with my husband and I. I figured we were low on her list, but there's the proof.
OTHER CULTURES	I've used various messaging services, and my favourite thing to do with them is to talk to people in different countries. I use the social network site italki.com to make new friends, and instead of communicating with just people I know, I enjoy making friends from all over the world. I have talked to people from Morocco, Hungary, Mexico, India and Puerto Rico. It is great to learn different cultures and languages.
MISCHIEF, MISINFORMATION AND ENTERTAINMENT	I have used Twitter to give away codes for use on Microsoft's XBox Live Marketplace.

Now, consider the views expressed regarding the popular search engine Google.

TABLE 21.7 Public opinion on Google

LOOKING UP INFORMATION	I use Google mostly to search about ANYTHING, and it's really effective. My 8 and 5 year old sons use Google Earth to explore and learn about the world. They think it's really cool. Sometimes I'll use Google Earth to check out the houses and neighbourhoods of friends, relatives or people I'm just interested in.
SEARCH OURSELVES	Out of curiosity I Googled myself only to find that there was about 100 items with my name/email that came up. Not only did I find stuff that was legit, there was someone who had stolen my identity and was using my name online. Suffice it to say, not only was it stupid of him, but he was easily tracked down and apprehended.
PREVENTING FRAUDS AND SCAMS	It's amazing to students that I have access to the very same internet that they do! They copy and paste entire pages or articles into their papers and then pretend that they wrote them on their own. And this is AFTER I have told them not to do this because they cannot outsmart me!
	Type in phone numbers of annoying telemarketers and find out who they are.

EXES, INFIDELITY AND SIGNIFICANT OTHERS	I use Google to spy on my ex-girlfriends and see if their name pops up on anything.
	I've used Google to do detective work. To find information out about the girl my boyfriend cheated on me with. It was very helpful, as to I found her address and phone numbers listed.
FINDING LONG LOST PEOPLE	I used Google to find my mother whom I have not seen in 15 years. The search was easy and quick.
MEDICAL	To learn how to pierce my own belly button or someone else's!
AS A FRIEND OR CO-CONSPIRATOR	I've used GoogleMaps to see if my boyfriend is home or not to surprise him without him knowing I was coming over.
WORK	I use it to find out about everything. I even used multiple companies to determine which job would best fit for me.
AS PART OF A CONVERSATION	My boyfriend and I use Google to solve arguments we have just about everything. One time in particular we couldn't agree over which light in the sky was Mars and which was a star...so we Googled it and of course it came out that I was right.
SEARCHING OTHERS	I use Google to find out things about people I work with. One of our managers is actually on the sexual offenders registry. So naturally I emailed it to everybody from his computer.
	Whenever I plan a meeting with a new business networking contact, I always Google them. That's pretty standard, but I look for more than the standard material (bio, resume, checking for anything embarrassing. I look for the person's hobbies or special interests whenever possible. I'll make a mental note about something in the person's life that aligns with my own interests or is especially intriguing. Although I don't say 'I Googled you' when meeting the new contact over lunch, I find ways to work any shared interests into the conversation — as a way of establishing rapport and standing out from other people in the business world.

Now, consider the views expressed regarding the social medium of Wikipedia.

TABLE 21.8 Public opinion on Wikipedia

EDUCATION	Wikipedia is like the god of dictionaries. I've used it on 98 per cent of my homework and projects; it really is a good way to get answers. Universities are starting to ban Wikipedia, luckily they haven't got here yet.
	Instead of circulating his essays by email for the rest of the class to read, a friend of mine put it up on Wikipedia and we tracked how it was edited.
LANGUAGE + WORDS	I often use Wikipedia in conjunction with the thesaurus features of Word. Given the limitations of the thesaurus, I find I can grasp a better understanding and make my writing and communications more succinct by using both features.
RESOLVING DISPUTES	At work, whenever someone has a general question about something, or there's a disagreement, the running joke is to 'Wiki it!' That means, one of us goes to Wikipedia to figure out the answer.
SOURCES	I use Wikipedia not so much for the information but as a way to find the original sources.
	I am a freelance writer. I use Wikipedia not just as a reference but also for the links it provides to other web pages that I am not overly familiar with. I also use this to debunk erroneous information on Wikipedia as well. I have found that there is a lot of info on there that is not accurate.
SEARCHING FOR ONESELF/ FOR OTHERS	I used Wikipedia to see the historical events that happen on my birthdate. I also used to track my family tree which was not available anywhere else but surprisingly was there on Wikipedia.
MISCHIEF, MISINFORMATION AND ENTERTAINMENT	Yes. I bet a friend that there was a permanent dock on the moon. I then changed the Wikipedia article and added the false statement about a space station being docked on the moon. I then showed him the article and he believed me.
	I had learned that you could alter or edit Wiki pages so I sent a page link to my husband as a gag. The page I made up was one of Lance Armstrong. I listed my husband as a son of one of Lance's relatives.

(continued)

GENERAL LEARNINGS	I've actually used Wikipedia to look up the identities of various inventors. Like the one that invented the throw away cell phone. And I've also used it to find other inventors/ astronomy regions. Somewhere on there is where to find that the Little Dipper is also known as Ursa Minor, also what means in Latin (Little Bear). Then it also has a map so that you can find them outside at night!
NO-JUDGEMENT INFORMATION	To figure out what my nephew is talking about.
	I have used Wikipedia to ask questions that I would normally not ask family or friends. Sometimes it is something that I probably should have known already by my age. People are usually nice on Wikipedia and I can remain anonymous.

Social media: strengths and weaknesses

So what's good and what's bad in social media? Which of them will survive, perhaps to earn billions? Which will die – the victims of the boredom of former enthusiasts?

To answer such questions, we need to look at models which integrate a vast range of social media, and such models are few given the newness of the social media scene. Kaplan and Haeinlein (2010) have bravely attempted this in figure 21.5 (included later in this section).

First, some background. In other chapters in this book, we look at the Johari Window, which attempts to classify human behaviour into how much information we wish to disclose (or not disclose) to others. Related to this concept is that of self-presentation, or wishing to present ourselves to the world in a particular way. Kaplan and Haeinlein (2010, p. 61) also use the concept of social presence, which partly overlaps with the previous ideas:

> Social presence is influenced by the intimacy (interpersonal vs. mediated) and immediacy (asynchronous vs. synchronous) of the medium, and can be expected to be lower for mediated (e.g., telephone conversation) than interpersonal (e.g., face-to-face discussion) and for asynchronous (e.g., e-mail) than synchronous (e.g., live chat) communications. The higher the social presence, the larger the social influence that the communication partners have on each other's behavior. Closely related to the idea of social presence is the concept of media richness.

Kaplan and Haenlein's ideas are illustrated in figure 21.5. This model is, in effect, synthesising personality types with preferences for types of social media.

FIGURE 21.5 A classification model for social media

Source: Kaplan and Haenlein (2010, p. 62).

		Social presence/media richness		
		Low	**Medium**	**High**
Self-presentation/ self-disclosure	**High**	Blogs	Social networking sites (e.g. Facebook)	Virtual social worlds (e.g. Second Life)
	Low	Collaborative projects (e.g. Wikipedia)	Content communities (e.g. YouTube)	Virtual game worlds (e.g. World of Warcraft)

What's good?

In spite of the enthusiasm of the most ardent social media advocates, it seems unlikely that old media is going to go away. Nevertheless, social media has achieved much, and promises more:

- It has given people a chance to have more control over their lives.
- It has given them opportunities to express themselves and report on the world that was unthinkable until quite recently.
- It has led to a proliferation of points of view and fact that was denied us before.
- It has made people more confident in the use of technology.
- Despite the warnings that social media may lead to more isolation, in fact some media messages are 'let's meet up' messages – social contact may increase, not decrease.

Following on from this, social media may help individuals lacking in confidence in social situations to launch out, meeting friends and contacts:

- It enhances **phatic** communication (Miller 2008).
- It reinforces group solidarity in a manner similar to primates grooming each other Zeynepi (2008).
- It enhances **homophily** between like-minded individuals (Thelwall 2009).
- It has helped overcome the 'tyranny of distance' in communication; for example, family members thousands of kilometres away from each other.
- It can help communication among democratic forces in authoritarian countries in the same way that illegal **samizdat** publications (typed, printed and photocopied pamphlets and books) helped break up the Soviet Union (Srebeny & Khiabany 2010; Kulikova & Perlmutter 2007).

What's bad?

The security of new media cannot be guaranteed. **Hacking** and **phishing** are becoming more common (Mills 2009; Schachtman 2009; Fogel & Nehmad 2009; George 2006; Luscombe 2009; Heffernan 2009; McDowell 2009; Zhao & Rosson 2009). Wireless or **wi-fi** transmission of signals can be tapped into, raising a range of security concerns. Security settings on some media appear to be not as powerful as those on other software, and many people do not even apply them. Some insurance companies are now charging higher premiums for users of social media because of the risk that criminals will have hacked into their systems and know when the users will be away (Marceau 2009).

Related to this is the tendency of some users of social media to disclose personal information – sometimes more than they would in face to face encounters (George 2006; Moreno et al. 2009; De Souza &

Australian swimmer Stephanie Rice is one of several popular identities to have made the mistake of publishing a careless message on a social media site.

Dick 2009). This can create unforeseen issues for the user. For example, employers are increasingly checking social media websites as well as resumes to see if they can glean further information about a candidate for hiring; thus, your resume and your appearance may be excellent and professional, but digital photos on your or someone else's social medium looking less than excellent and professional may lead to your not getting the job.

In 2009, 45 per cent of employers were doing this (Grasz 2009). On a related note, with employers checking websites (and for that matter, people fearful for their jobs and working on weekends, not to mention the ability of mobile phones to be used for business purposes in 'leisure' time), social media may be breaking down the walls between our personal and professional lives. This is not necessarily a good thing.

Following from this, it is wise to keep in mind that 'the internet is forever'. Just as surely as most of the material you have deleted on your computer can be recovered, all material you put out on the net is exceptionally difficult – some say impossible – to get rid of. Social media provides ample opportunities for user indiscretion. Many people (including famous sportspeople), seem prone with social media to what was called 'flaming' on email; that is, saying the best things they will ever live to regret. Swimmer Stephanie Rice (@ItsStephRice), for instance, was publicly castigated and stripped of her Jaguar sponsorship for posting a highly derogatory tweet about South African rugby union players. She posted the tweet immediately after the Wallabies had won a Test Match in which her boyfriend had been playing. The comment was subsequently plastered all over the media, with Rice apologising – and wiping away tears – via a press conference several days later. In the United States, basketball and football players are now banned from tweeting immediately before and after games. A 'cooling off' solution has been adopted after several embarrassing social media 'incidents' (Jackson 2010).

Social media may, in fact, be anti-social media if users become more attached to virtual reality rather than reality itself: as Greenfield (2008, p. 147) observes, speaking of sex and love:

> Perhaps it would not be too extreme to imagine a time, not so far off, when the whole idea of messy, face-to-face interaction, with its pheromones, body language, immediacy and above all unpredictability, may have become an unpalatable alternative to a remote, online and sanitized and far more onanistic cyber-persona and life.

The use of social media may also be leading to shorter attention spans (Greenfield 2008; Bauerlein 2008) and a decline in academic performance: an *America Online* (AOL) page of celebrity photos has the subtitle 'Because it's better than homework' (Gaudin 2009b; Bauerlein 2008, p. 133). This may be related to the concept of multitasking, or doing more than one thing at once. Many social media users will use social and traditional media at the same time. Unfortunately, the evidence we have is that multitasking does not work, and in fact produces inferior performance (see online chapter 5 'How to write').

In addition, the user-generated nature of social media may mean a narrowing of experience and a lack of exposure to alternative points of view, leading to a narcissistic 'Daily Me'. As Bauerlein (2008, pp. 137–8) notes:

> A 16-year-old panellist at the 2006 Online News Association convention summed it up perfectly. When a journalist in the audience asked if sticking solely to RSS feeds made her miss 'the broader picture,' she snapped, 'I'm not trying to get a broader picture. I'm trying to get what I want.'

Demassification: the process of transforming a few traditional outlets into many nontraditional ones

This may be a case of over-homophily. Toffler (1981) predicted this **demassification** of media, whereby a world that consumed a few large, general format magazines and electronic media now found itself flooded with hundreds, if not thousands, of magazines, television channels and radio stations.

While working on social media can be satisfying, it also takes up a fair amount of time, and some people get bored with it, thinking of the prospect of maintaining it for months? Years? Decades?

Following from this, we need to exercise caution about just how many people are using Web 1.0 or Web 2.0 (and eventually Web 3.0, whatever shape that is). Data collection methods in this area are still fairly primitive, and some social media have a vested interest in blowing up their figures. Remember the words attributed to writer Mark Twain about 'lies, damned lies and statistics'. In spite of the user-friendliness of the technology of social media, many are still daunted by it, and may never try it.

Social media is also not necessarily intrinsically democratic: terrorist groups and hate groups use blogs and other media to send messages to the world (Mandari 2009; Parsons 2009). In addition, bullying – sometimes known as **cyber bullying** – can occur on social networking sites (e.g. insulting comments left, unflattering digital photos uploaded, insulting text messages), and this has emerged as a significant issue in the contemporary environment for school children.

Cyber bullying: bullying a person by using technology to convey aggressive and demeaning messages

Keen (2008), in his book *The cult of the amateur: how blogs, MySpace, YouTube and the rest of today's user-generated media are destroying our economy, our culture and our values*, wages a major attack on social media – not to mention other practices like downloading film and music piracy. He argues that intellectual property laws are routinely flouted by users who are really just plagiarisers, and amateurs to boot. In a way, his critique is similar to that of those trying to monetise content on the web: if everything can be stolen, why pay? In a reality TV environment of cheap (and, at times, manipulative, humiliating and disingenuous) programs, why bother with quality? As the North American artist Andy Warhol once said, 'In the future, everyone will be famous for fifteen minutes'. The minute count may vary, but his cynical view of modern culture is obvious, especially when related to social media.

Although the larger part of scientific research so far supports the safety of social media and its tools (mobile phone technology and the supporting phone tower infrastructure, and wireless support for mobile computing), there are some worrying doubts: Lakehead University in Canada has banned wi-fi networking for its computer systems. President Fred Gilbert, a zoologist and environmentalist, states the policy thus:

> The scientific evidence continues to mount showing long-term exposure to wireless communications technologies affects human health. Health providers and even the World Health Organization are suggesting cause–effect relationships that minimally require the use of the precautionary principle and the lowering of standard values for exposure.
>
> Researchers in the field have passed the Catania Resolution (2002), the Benevento Resolution (2004) and most recently the Venice Resolution (2008). The latest resolution attests to 'electrosensitivity, blood brain barrier changes, learning and behavioral effects, changes in anti-oxidant enzyme activities [and] DNA damage' as consequences of exposure to non-ionizing electromagnetic fields at intensities below where thermal effects occur. Long term use and/or exposure consequences include cancer. Users of social media should be aware of these facts
>
> Gilbert 2009

In 2009, France banned the use of mobile phones in primary schools (Bremner 2009). Kapdi, Hoskote and Joshi (2008) have discovered a decline in sperm counts and mobility in even light mobile phone users, and rats subjected to radiation from mobile phones were found to have damaged DNA and low sperm count, leading to infertility and reduction in testis size. The researchers also noted the exposure to electromagnetic frequencies may also alter DNA, which would make it possible for transmission of genetic diseases to the offspring (see also Khuranam et al, 2008; Sage and Carpenter, 2009; Davis, 2010).

These moves fly in the face of large-scale marketing campaigns by telecommunications and equipment manufacturers, but the brutal truth may be that there is a dark side to social media – they may make us ill, and may in some cases kill us. The tools – wi-fi computers, mobile phones with new models that have different features apparently every few months, handheld devices and even cordless phones – are beautiful examples of industrial design, but they may potentially harm us in spite of that. It may well be that much of our own self-image – of being cool, of being techno-savvy – is part of the problem: we may be reluctant to give them up or cut back on them, despite whatever research turns up in the next few years. Clearly, we need some definitive answers here.

And so we come to the end of our exploration of social media. For some, it is an exciting transformation in the way we live and will live in the future, while for others it is a non-event, having no impact on their lives at all. Whatever our views, we will probably see interesting hybrids of old media and new media in the next few years (perhaps the most poignant/bizarre of which might be printers advertising to reproduce all your blogs or tweets in colour in a bound volume – as a book). This may give us information nirvana, or information overload. Whatever happens, it will be an interesting journey.

STUDENT STUDY GUIDE

SUMMARY

We have examined the differences between so-called old (or traditional) and new (or social) media. We have then considered eight social media: Blogs, Twitter, Facebook, MySpace, wikis and Wikipedia, YouTube, podcasting and RSS. We have seen opinions pro and con social media, and we have seen the views of users of four social media. We have considered the questions of gatekeepers, monetisation, trust and reputation. Finally, we have considered the pros and cons of social media.

KEY TERMS

aggregator, *p. 718*
avatar *p. 710*
blog *p. 708*
citizen journalism *p. 710*
cyber bullying *p. 725*
demassification *p. 724*
hacking *p. 723*

hedonic *p. 707*
homophily *p. 723*
MP3 or mpeg3 *p. 717*
mashup *p. 707*
monetise *p. 707*
phatic *p. 723*

phishing *p. 723*
samizdat *p. 723*
tweet *p. 710*
viral marketing *p. 716*
Web 2.0 *p. 704*
wi-fi *p. 723*

REVIEW QUESTIONS

1. Explain at least three differences between old and social media.
2. Summarise at least three pro and three con opinions on social media.
3. How many people have tried blogging but abandoned it?
4. What is 'citizen journalism'?
5. What are the chief problems experienced by online encyclopaedias?
6. 'Most users of social media tend to be teenagers.' Is this true?
7. What does the term RSS mean, and what function does it perform?
8. Summarise at least three strengths and weaknesses of social media.

APPLIED ACTIVITIES

1. Go to the internet sites of Slashdot, Digg, Wired, Bebo and Reddit. Speculate on what audiences they are aimed at. Are some or all of the audiences the same? Comment on the design of the sites and the values they project.
2. Go to the networking sites Boardex and LinkedIn. What similarities and differences do they have to more general sites like MySpace and Facebook?
3. Work with a partner on this. You will need a fair amount of paper and pens. Restricting yourself to 140 characters, conduct a conversation in writing, with each of you writing at least three messages. Discuss your conversation with your partner afterwards. What does it say about communication processes generally, and what does it say about Twitter as a communication medium?
4. Consider what you have learned, and review it in light of Priestley's Paradox (see chapter 1). ('The more we elaborate our means of communication, the less we actually communicate.') What is your view?
5. Revisiting chapter 1 again, if you found out that a technology or technologies presented a threat to your health, would you
   - avoid using it/them
   - reduce your use of it/them
   - continue using it/them at the level you have been using them at
   - increase your level of the use of it/them?

WHAT WOULD YOU DO?

You are about to graduate from university and have just sent applications for several positions that you have found online that match your qualifications and interests. You are looking forward to embarking on the first stages of your professional career. However, at a family barbecue, your uncle tells a story about a Google search that his company recently

did on a prospective employee. The search revealed 'more than they cared to know' about an applicant that they had interviewed. The end result was that his company didn't hire the (otherwise suitable) applicant, and gave the position to a candidate who was their (initial) second choice.

You are mildly concerned about some of your social media use over the past few years. That night, when you arrive home, you do a Google search on your own name. As expected, a plethora of social media links are revealed (such as blogs, YouTube videos, and various Facebook and Twitter accounts). Not all of these links paint you in the best possible light from a potential employer's perspective.

What would (or can) you do?

SUGGESTED READING

Baker, Stephen 2009, 'Beware social media snake oil', *Business Week*, 14 November, pp. 48–51.

Brown, Rob 2009, *Public relations and the social web: how to use social media and web 2.0 in communications*, Kogan Page, London/Philadelphia.

Bruns, Axel & Adams, Debra 2009, 'Mapping the Australian blogosphere', in Rusell, Adrienne & Echchaibi, Nabil (eds.) *International blogging: identity, politics and networked publics*, Peter Lang, New York.

Cass, John 2007, *Strategies and tools for corporate blogging*, Butterworth-Heinemann, Burlington, MA/ Oxford, UK.

Falkner, Xristine & Culwin, Fintan 2005, 'When fingers do the talking: a study of text messaging', *Interacting with Computers*, vol. 17, 167–85.

Fortunati. Leopoldina 2005, 'Mobile telephones and the presentation of self', Ling, Richard & Pedersen, Per E (eds.). *Mobile Communications: Re-negotiation of the social sphere*, Springer, London.

Hay, Deltina 2009, *A survival guide to social media and web 2.0 optimization: strategies, tactics and tools for succeeding in the social web*, Wiggy Press/ Dalton Publishing, Austin, Texas.

Kraynak, Joe & Belicove, Mikal E 2010, *The complete idiot's guide to Facebook*, Indianapolis, IN: Alpha Books/Pearson.

Li, Charlene & Bernoff 2008, *Groundswell: winning in a world transformed by social technologies*, Harvard Business School Press.

Licoppe, Christian 2004, 'Connected presence: the emergence of a new repertoire for managing social relationships in a changing communications technoscape', *Environment and Planning: Society and Space*, vol. 22, pp. 135–56.

Ling, Rich & Donner, Jonathan 2009, *Mobile communication*, Polity Press, Cambridge UK/Malden MA.

MacArthur, Amber 2010, *Power friending: demystifying social media to grow your business*, Portfolio/ Penguin, New York.

Mahar, Sue Martin & Mahar, Jay 2009, *The unofficial guide to building your business in the Second Life® virtual world: marketing and selling your product, services and brand in-world, 2009*, Amacom, New York.

Marshall, Michael 2009, 'Facebook is good for you', *New Scientist*, 7 March, pp. 22–3.

Myers, Greg 2010, *Discourse of blogs and wikis*, Continuum, London/New York.

Parsons, Claudia 2009, 'Hate goes viral on social networking sites', *The Australian*, 15 May, www.news.com.au.

Pesce, Mark, 'Hypercasting', Lab, *no. 0.5*, http://lab-zine.com.

'The revolution will be shared: social media and innovation' 2011, *Research–Technology Management*, vol. 54, no. 1, pp. 64–8.

Schwartz, Heather E. 2009, *Yourspace: questioning new media*, Capstone Press, Mankato, Minnesota.

Shirky, Clay 2009, *Here comes everybody: the power of organizing without organizations*, Penguin, New York.

Solis, Brian & Livingston, Geoff 2008, *Now is gone: a primer on new media for executives and entrepreneurs*, Bartleby Press, Savage, MD.

Tapscott, Don 2009, *Grown up digital: how the net generation is changing your world*, McGraw-Hill, New York.

Zhang, Allee M., Zhu, Yunxia & Hildebrandt, Herbert 2009, 'Enterprise Networking Websites and Organizational Communication in Australia', *Business Communication Quarterly*, vol. 72, no. 1, pp. 114–19.

REFERENCES

Abaya, Eleanor & Gilbert, Fred 2008, 'Lakehead says no to WiFi: Lakehead University takes a precautionary approach to the widespread application of WiFi technology', *Lakehead University Magazine*, http://magazine.lakeheadu.ca.

Abram, Carolyn & Pearlman, Leah 2008, *Facebook for dummies*, John Wiley & Sons, New York.

Anderson, Paul 2011, *Web 2.0: principles and technologies*, Chapman and Hall, United Kingdom.

Angwin, Julia 2009, *Stealing MySpace: the battle control the most popular website in America*, Random House, New York.

Bauerlein, Mark 2009, *The dumbest generation: how the digital age stupefies young Americans and jeopardizes our future*, Tarcher/Penguin, New York.

Bingham, John 2009, 'MI6's chief's security 'compromised' by wife's Facebook postings', *The Telegraph*, 6 July, www. telegraph.co.uk.

Blossom, John 2009, *Content nation: surviving and thriving as social media changes our work, our lives, and our future*, John Wiley & Sons, Indianapolis, IN.

Brake, David 2008, 'Shaping the "me" in MySpace: the framing of profiles on a social network site', in Lundby, Knut (ed.) *Digital storytelling, mediatized stories: self-representations in the new media*, Peter Lang, New York.

Burroughs, Benjamin 2007, 'Kissing Macaca': blogs, narrative and political discourse', *Journal for Cultural Research*, vol. 11 no. 4, pp. 319–35.

Bruns, Axel 2009, *Blogs, Wikipedia, Second Life, and beyond: from production to produsage*, Peter Lang, New York.

Canning, Simon 2009, 'Social websites help to broadcast news', *The Australian*, 3 August, p. 38.

Cashone, Josh 2009, 'Top 5 business mistakes and how to avoid them', *Open Forum*, 17 September, www.openforum.com.

Choney, Suzanne 2009, 'Facebook hit by 'Control Your Info' intruder', *MSNBC*, 10 November, www.msnbc.msn.com.

Clemons, Erik K 2009, 'The complex problem of monetizing virtual electronic social networks', *Decision Support Systems*, vol. 48 no.1, pp. 46–56.

Comm, Joel & Burge, Ken 2009, *Twitter power: how to dominate your market one tweet at a time*, John Wiley & Sons, New York.

Cruz, Danilo & Fill, Chris 2008, 'Evaluating viral marketing: isolating the key criteria', *Marketing Intelligence & Planning*, vol. 26 no. 7, pp. 743–58.

Davis, Devra 2010, *Disconnect: the truth about cell phone radiation, what the industry has done to hide it, and how to protect your family*, Dutton, New York.

De Souza, Zaineb & Dick, Geoffrey N 2009, 'Disclosure of information by children in social networking – not just a case of 'you show me yours, and I'll show you mine', *International Journal of Information Management*, vol. 29 pp. 255–61.

Dobbin, Marika 2010, '$78,000 to tweet for city council', *The Age*, 18 November, p. 3.

Dudley-Nicholson, Jennifer 2009, 'Facebook, MySpace social networking bigger than email', *The Courier Mail*, 10 March, www.news.com.au.

Evans, Kathy 2010, 'This is our life', *The Sunday Age*, 28 November, p. 11.

Facebook 2009. *Facebook phishing scam awareness*, www.facebook.com.

Fitton, Laura, Gruen, Michael, & Poston, Leslie 2009, *Twitter for dummies*, John Wiley & Sons, Hoboken, NY.

Fixmer, A & Rabil, S 2011, 'News Corp.'s MySpace cuts staff by 47% amid reports website may be sold', *Bloomberg*, 12 January.

Fogel, Joshua & Nehmad, Elham 2009, 'Internet social network communities: risk-taking, trust, and privacy concerns', *Computers in human behavior*, vol. 25 pp. 153–60.

Foster, Rusty 2001, 'The utter failure of weblogs as journalism', *Kuro5hin*, 11 Oct, www.kuro5hin.org.

Gardner, Susannah & Birley, Shane 2008, *Blogging for dummies*, 2nd edn, John Wiley & Sons, Hoboken, NJ.

Gaudin, Sharon 2009a, 'Facebook, Twitter users are affluent and urban, study shows', *Computerworld*, 28 September, p. 7.

—— 2009b, 'Study: Facebook linked to lower grades in college', *Macworld*, 14 April, p. 4.

Gauvin, W. et al. 2010, 'Measurement and gender-specific analysis of user publishing characteristics on MySpace', *IEEE*, vol. 24 no. 5, pp. 38–43.

George, Alison 2006, 'Things you wouldn't tell your mother', *New Scientist*, 16 September, pp. 50–1.

Gilbert, Fred 2009, personal communication, 4 November.

Giles, Jim 2005, 'Internet encyclopedias go head to head', *Nature*, vol. 438 no.7070, pp. 900–1.

Goldsmith, Belinda 2009, 'Many Twitters are quick quitters: study', *Reuters*, 29 April, www.reuters.com.

Gorkjazi, Mojtaba, Rejaie, Reza & Willinger, Walter 2009, 'Hot today, gone tomorrow: on the migration of MySpace users', in *Proceedings of the 2nd ACM workshop on Online social networks*, ACM Digital Library, Washington, DC.

Grasz, Jennifer 2009, '45% Employers use Facebook-Twitter to screen job candidates, 19 August, *Wall Street Journal*, http://online.wsj.com.

Green, Mary & Meeser, Lesley 2009 'George Clooney prefers prostate exams over Facebook', *People*, 16 September, www.people.com.

Greenfield, Susan 2008, *I.D.: the quest for identity in the 21st century*, Sceptre, London.

Harden, Leland & Heyman, Bob 2009, *Digital engagement: internet marketing that captures customers and builds intense brand loyalty*, Amacom, New York.

Harfoush, Rahaf 2009, *Yes, we did: an inside look at how social media built the Obama brand*, New Riders, Berkeley, CA.

Hassan Masum & Yi-Chen Zhang 2004, 'Manifesto for the reputation society', *First Monday*, July, http://firstmonday.org.

Heffernan, Virginia, 2009, 'Facebook exodus', *The New York Times*, 30 August, www.nytimes.com.

Hirschorn, Michacl 2007, 'The Web 2.0 bubble: why the social media will go out with a whimper', *The Atlantic*, www.theatlantic.com.

Hodkinson, Tom 2008, 'Why you should beware of Facebook', *The Age*, 20 January, www.theage.com.au.

Hupfer, Ryan, Maxson, Mitch & Williams, Ryan 2008, *MySpace for dummies*, 2nd edn, John Wiley & Sons, Hoboken, NY.

Jackson, Sally 2010, 'Sportspeople oft excel at being twits onsite', *The Australian,* 13 September, www.theaustralian.com.au.

Johnson, Bobbie 2009, 'Wikipedia editors may approve all changes', *Guardian.co.uk*, 27 January, www.guardian.co.uk.

Kapdi, Mukta, Hoskote, SS & Joshi SR 2008, 'Health hazards of mobile phones: an Indian perspective', *Journal of Association of Physicians of India*, vol. 56 pp. 893–97.

Kaplan, Andreas M & Haenlin, Michael 2010, 'Users of the world, unite! The challenges and opportunities of social media', *Business Horizons*, vol. 53 pp. 59–68.

Keen, Andrew 2008, *The cult of the amateur: how blogs, MySpace, YouTube, and the rest of today's user-generated media are destroying our economy, our culture, and our values*, Crown Business, New York.

Keller, Kevin 2010, 'Berners-Lee: Apple, Facebook are enemies of the web', *Reuters Online*, 22 October, http://blogs.reuters.com.

Kernohan, Kathryn 2010, 'Ghost writing: the other side of the story', *Melbourne Weekly*, 24 November, p. 17.

Khuranam Vini G. 2008, 'Mobile phone-brain tumour public health advisory', *www.brain-surgery.us*, www.der-mast-muss-weg.de.

Krieger, Mike 2008, 'Two dollars, two hundred stories', *Crowdlog*, July, http://mkrieger.org.

Kulikova, Svetlana V & Perlmutter, David D 2007, 'Blogging down the dictator? The Kyrgyz revolution and samizdat websites', *International Communication Gazette*, vol. 69 no. 1, pp. 29–50.

Lee, Matthew 2010, 'US asks WikiLeaks to halt document release', *The Associated Press*, 28 November, http://news.yahoo.com.

Levinson, Paul 2009, *New new media*, Pearson, Boston.

Lincoln, Susan Rice 2009, *Mastering web 2.0: transform your business using key website and social media tools*, Kogan Page, London/Philadelphia.

Luscombe, Belinda 2009, 'Facebook and divorce: airing the dirty laundry', *Time*, 22 June, www.time.com.

McDowell, Mindi 2009, 'Avoiding social engineering and phishing attacks', *US Cert: United States Computer Emergency Readiness Team*, National cyber alter system/Carnegie Mellon University, 22 October, www.us-cert.gov.

McGovern, Gerry 2004, 'Web content guru Gerry McGovern on blogging', at Wackå, Frederick, 'Your guide to corporate blogging' *CorporateBlogging.Info: Archive*, www.corporateblogging.info.

—— 2008, *Killer web content: make the sale, deliver the service, build the brand*, A & C Black, Soho, London.

Mandari, Presi 2009, 'Al-Qaeda blog claims Jakarta hotel bombings', *Mail&Guardian Online*, 29 July, www.mg.co.za.

Mann, Mike 2009, 'Graham Linehan's we love the NHS campaign shows political power of Twitter', *The First Post*, 14 August, www.thefirstpost.co.uk.

Marceau, Alexandra 2009, 'Facebook, Twitter users face higher insurance premiums', *The Herald Sun*, 28 August, www.heraldsun.com.au.

Martin, David 2009, 'Twitter quitters post roadblock to long-term growth', Nielsen Wire, blog, http://blog.nielsen.com/nielsenwire.

Martin, Lorna 2009, 'Too much information! From Facebook to Twitter, why do so many think we care about the minutiae of their tedious lives?', *Mail Online*, www.dailymail.co.uk.

Masum, Hassan & Zhang, Y-Chen 2004, 'Manifesto for the reputation society', *First Monday*, vol. 9. no. 7, http://firstmonday.org.

Mezrich, Ben 2010, *The accidental billionaires: the founding of Facebook: a tale of sex, money, genius and betrayal*, Anchor, New York.

Micek, Deborah & Whitlock, Warren 2008, *Twitter revolution: how social media and mobile marketing is changing the way we do business and market online*, Xeno Press, Las Vegas, NV.

Milioni, Dimitra L 2009, 'Probing the online counterpublic sphere: the case of Indymedia Athens', *Media, Culture & Society*, vol. 31 no. 2, pp. 4099–431.

Miller, Michael 2009, *YouTube for business: online video marketing for any business*, Que, Indianapolis, in Miller, Vincent 2008, 'New media, networking and phatic culture', *Convergence*, vol.14, no. 4, pp. 387–400.

Mills, Elinor 2009, 'Wife bans FBI head from online banking', *CNet News*, 7 October, http://news.cnet.com.

Moreno, Megan A, Marks, MR, Zimmerman, FJ, Brito, TE & Christakis, DA 2009, 'Display of health risk behaviors on MySpace by adolescents', *Archives of Pediatrics and Adolescent Medicine*, vol. 163 no. 1, pp. 27–34.

Morris, Tee, Tomasi, Chuck & Terra, Evo 2008, *Podcasting for dummies*, 2nd edn, John Wiley & Sons, New York.

Munro, Peter, 2009, 'As Twitter finds, it's hard to stay perched on the cutting edge', *Sunday Age*, 18 October, p. 13.

Pemberton, Andy 2009, 'A load of Twitter', *TimesOnline*, 22 February, http://women.timesonline.co.uk.

Pesce, Mark 2006, 'Herding cats', *The human network: what happens after we're all connected?* 20 October, http://blog.futurestreetconsulting.com.

Porter, Liz 2008, 'Malice in wonderland: today's youth may live to regret sharing their intimate moments on the internet', *The Sunday Age*, 10 August, p. 18.

Qualman, Eric 2009, *Socialnomics: how social media transforms the way we live and do business*, John Wiley & Sons, Hoboken, NJ.

Rodrigues, Sam 2009, 'Police warned on social sites', *Adelaide Now*, 6 November, http://www.news.com.au.

Rolling Stone 2009, 'Kanye West rages against Twitter imposters in blog rant', 13 May, www.rollingstone.com.

Ruggiero, TE 2000, 'Uses and gratification theory in the 21st century', *Mass Communication and Society*, vol. 3 no. 1, pp. 3–37.

Safko, Lon & Brake, David K. 2009, *The social media bible: tactics, tools and strategies for business success*, John Wiley & Sons, Hoboken, NY.

Sage, Cindy & Carpenter, David O. 2009, 'Public health implications of wireless technologies', *Pathophysiology*, vol. 16 nos. 2–3, pp. 233–46.

Sagolla, Dom 2009, *140 characters: a style guide for the short form*, John Wiley & Sons, Hoboken, NY.

Schachtman, Noah 2009, 'Marines ban Twitter, My Space, Facebook', *Wired*, 3 August, www.wired.com.

Scott, David Meerman 2009, *The new rules of marketing and PR: how to use news releases, blogs, podcasting, viral marketing & online media to reach buyers directly*, John Wiley & Sons, Hoboken, NY.

Shih, Clara 2009, *The Facebook era: tapping online social networks to build better products, reach new audiences, and sell more stuff*, Prentice-Hall./Pearson, Boston MA.

Shirky, Clay 2000, 'RIP the consumer, 1900–1999', *Clay Shirky's writings about the Internet*, www.shirky.com.

Shoemaker, Pamela J & Vos, Tim P 2009, *Gatekeeping theory*, Routledge, New York and London.

Siapera, Eugenia 2009. 'Theorizing the Muslim blogosphere: blogs, rationality, publicness and individuality', in Rusell, Adrienne & Echchaibi, Nabil (eds) *International blogging: identity, politics and networked publics*, Peter Lang, New York.

Silver, Curtis 2009, 'Organized chaos: viral marketing, meet social media', *Wired*, 29 October, www.wired.com.

Sledgianowski, Deb & Kulviwat, Songpol 2009, 'Using social network sites: the effects of playfulness, critical mass and trust in hedonic context', *Journal of Computer Information Systems*, vol. 49 no. 4, pp. 74–83.

Srebeny, A & Khiabany, G. 2010, *Blogistan: The internet and politics in Iran*, I.B. Tauris, London.

Stewart, Patsy 2010, '23 ways to integrate Facebook and Twitter with traditional advertising', *SocialMediaToday*, 7 November, www.socialmediatoday.com.

Suarez, Paul 2009, 'On Facebook, don't get too pokey', *The Industry Standard*, 10 September, www.thestandard.com.

Thelwell, Mike 2009, 'Homophily in MySpace', *Journal of the American Society for Information Science and Technology*, vol. 60 no.2, pp. 219–31.

Toffler, Alvin 1981, *The third wave*, Bantam, New York.

Varadarajan, Tunku 2007, 'Happy blogiversary', *The Wall Street Journal*, 14 July, http://online.wsj.com.

Wales, Jimmy 2010, 'Wikipedia: administrators', 9 December, http://en.wikipedia.org.

Weber, Larry 2009, *Marketing to the social web: how digital communities build your business*, 2nd edn, John Wiley & Sons, Hoboken, NY.

Wikipedia 2010, 'Wikipedia: size of wikipedia', www.wikipedia.org.

Woolff, Michael 2010, 'Peering through the cracks of Murdoch's paywall', *Crikey*, 16 July, www.crikey.com.au.

Woollacott, Emma 2009, 'Social media users invite burglars in', *TG Daily*, 27 August, www.tgdaily.com.

Young, Trevor 2010, 'It's good to tweet with customers', by Louis White, Weekend Professional, *The Age*, November 6–7, p. 1.

Zeynep, Tufekci 2008, 'Grooming, gossip, Facebook and MySpace', *Information, Communication and Society*, vol. 11 no. 4, pp. 544–64.

Zhao, Dejin & Rosson, Mary Beth 2009, 'How and why people Twitter: the role that micro-blogging plays in informal communication at work', Proceedings of the ACM 2009 International Conference on Supporting Group Work, ACM Digital Library, Washington, DC.

GLOSSARY

Abilene paradox: The behavioural effect which occurs when organisations and individuals frequently take actions in contradiction to what they really want to do and therefore defeat the very purposes they are trying to achieve (page 596)

Acculturation: the process of the meeting of cultures and the changes which result from such meetings (page 475)

Active listening: a communication skill that requires concentration, attention and a minimal verbal response to help the speaker articulate his or her thoughts (page 319)

Aggregator: a search engine that collects news from multiple sources, both print and online, and makes it available for free (page 718)

Aggressive listening: patient listening with the primary purpose of spurring speakers to say things they might later regret (page 313)

AIDA sequence: an approach to structuring persuasive documents (acronym for Attention–Interest–Desire–Action) (page 138)

Alignment: the positioning of text lines in relation to the left and right margins of a page (page 50)

Alignment strategy: ensuring that all messages communicated to audiences within an organisation are consistent with messages communicated to audiences outside the organisation (page 510)

Amendment: a formal proposal for change to a motion; an amendment may qualify, but not negate, the intent of the original motion (page 628)

Announcement email: an email sent to all persons in an organisation. A reply is usually not called for, and thus it is usually a one-way communication (page 144)

Appendix: supplementary material placed after the body of a report, where it is available for the reader to consult, without disturbing the flow of the argument in the main body section (page 169)

Applicant tracking system: automated system used by employers to gather and analyse data from online and paper résumés (page 690)

Articulateness and articulation: articulateness (the ability to say meaningful words) can be helped considerably by articulation (the ability to say those words clearly) (page 365)

Assertions: a specific line of reasoning, using specific arguments or claims (page 227)

Asynchronous communication: communication that is sent at one time and received at another time (pages 18, 511)

Attachment: a data file electronically attached to an email. It can contain text, graphics, video or audio in a compressed or uncompressed format (page 206)

Audience: the reader(s) of the report; the audience may be larger than you expect, including both official and unofficial components (page 159)

Audioconferencing: using telephone technology to conduct meetings via conference calls (page 655)

Audiovisual aids: objects and mechanical and electronic systems used to communicate information (page 367)

Authorial voice: the style most favoured in a discipline, area or publication, usually involving use or non-use of first-person pronouns and use or non-use of passive voice, nominalisations and hedging (page 237)

Avatar: a pictorial representation of yourself on Twitter (page 710)

Backchanneling: in conversation, responding to a speaker with nonverbal and paraverbal feedback, such as nodding, smiling and 'friendly grunts' (page 261)

Backgrounder: a document setting out the context of a situation; sometimes issued with a media release (page 563)

Bad news letter: a letter in which the writer conveys news that the reader will probably not be happy to read (page 121)

Bad news sandwich: embedding a bad news message within more positive information (page 127)

Balanced approach: an even-handed writing approach that avoids bias in what is presented or omitted (page 167)

Basic interacting group (BIG): a group that meets and uses the authority of the leader and/or voting to make decisions and solve problems, rather than using special techniques such as consensus, brainstorming and nominal group technique (page 644)

BATNA: (for Best Alternative To a Negotiated Agreement) another choice or substitute action that may produce an outcome superior to any outcome we might gain from a negotiation process (page 410)

Behavioural question: a question designed to draw a candidate out, to describe what actually happened in a situation or what might happen in a hypothetical situation (page 692)

Benefits: the advantages to, or relevance of, a feature (page 389)

Bias: a tendency in argument to ignore opposing opinion by using sources selectively or deceptively and/or by giving disproportionate weight to sources that support only one point of view (page 229)

Biblio-dumping: the unprofessional practice of simply listing your sources in the bibliography, but not citing them directly even though the sources have been quoted from or paraphrased (page 97)

Blog: a log or record or diary on the web (page 708)

Boosterism: a characteristic of reports that focus only on positive aspects of a situation, unrealistically ignoring negative aspects (page 168)

Boosting: assertion of statements or claims (page 236)

Bottom line: point beyond which no more concessions can be made to the other side without damaging our side's assets and position (also known as *fallback position*, *limit* or *resistance point*) (page 413)

Boundary spanner: an employee of the organisation who routinely moves between the organisation and the external environment (page 526)

Brainstorming: a method of creating ideas by deferring premature judgement and concentrating initially on quantity rather than quality of ideas (page 649)

Broadband: high-capacity transmission channels that can carry multiple simultaneous transmissions (page 199)

Building a case: developing an argument in a valid or invalid way to achieve persuasion (page 452)

Campaign: an organised public relations communication exercise of significant scale (page 557)

Central processing: the process of evaluating a persuasive message according to its objective content (page 392)

Chain of command: the system of power, communication and decision making within hierarchies, with people at different levels staying in rigid roles, deferring to those in the next level above them (page 513)

Chairperson: office-holder who presides over a meeting according to established rules and conventions; also known as the chair (page 630)

Channel: the medium or means of sending messages (page 18)

Channel suitability: matching the channel to the message and the receiver, audience or target (page 25)

Chartjunk: unnecessary and distracting graphics (page 56)

Chronemics: the study of time use behaviour in relation to communication (page 271)

Chronological format résumé: a résumé with personal information laid out in time sequence (page 683)

Citizen journalism: the idea that anyone can be a journalist by using social media tools and hardware to record, and perhaps comment on, events (page 710)

Clash of civilisations: the idea (developed by North American political scientists) that cultures now may be the basis of conflicts between nations (page 490)

Clique: a group of individuals at least half of whose work-day contacts are with each other (page 524)

Closed question: a question that requires a specific and short response (page 692)

Closed search strategies: approaches to creating primary data that restrict respondents to a limited range of responses (page 101)

Cluster: in relation to nonverbal communication, a group of different types of nonverbal behaviours or tells. (page 256)

Cognitive dissonance: the stress experienced when a person behaves in a way inconsistent with that person's self-concept (page 397)

Collection letter: a document sent to an organisation or individual seeking overdue payment for goods or services (page 141)

Column: vertical layout of text in blocks (page 52)

Communication: the study of the transfer of meaning (page 4)

Communication breakdown: a misunderstanding or failure to communicate (page 9)

Communication success: achievement of understanding between interacting individuals and groups (page 9)

Communications: the study of the transfer of data (page 4)

Complex sentence technique: a way of de-emphasising bad news by placing it in a subordinate clause of a complex sentence (page 129)

Concession: something that can be given to the other side, usually in return for something else (also known as *tradeables*) (page 414)

Conclusion: an outcome flowing from a premise or initial proposition (page 380)

Conclusions: section of a report in which writers set out their opinions about the facts presented in the report body (page 168)

Conflict management: an approach to conflict that may involve reduction or elimination of, or an increase in, conflict (page 445)

Conflict resolution: an approach to conflict that usually involves the reduction or elimination of conflict (page 445)

Conflict spiral: a fairly predictable developmental sequence of conflict events and perceptions (page 450)

Conformity: going along with the values and actions of others (page 395)

Congruence: the extent to which verbal and nonverbal messages reinforce or contradict each other (page 257)

Consensus: a method of reaching agreement without voting (page 648)

Constitution: document setting out broad structures and requirements of an organisation (page 628)

Convenience sampling: asking questions of whoever happens to be available when data is required, with no guarantee that those asked will be typical of the broader population (page 106)

Creative doubt: process in which study and synthesis of research may help a writer detect shortcomings in the literature and thus come up with original perspectives (page 230)

Creativity question: a question designed to see if a candidate could cope with unexpected or bizarre situations and concepts (page 692)

Credentialism: the process of restricting access to professions by setting higher and higher entrance standards (page 675)

Crisis communication: techniques and approaches that can help an organisation to better manage an emergency situation (page 566)

Critical incident: an event that is, or is perceived to be, significant in the escalation of a conflict (page 451)

Cumulative method: the construction of one argument upon another, creating momentum and building up a persuasive sequence of reasoning (page 228)

Cyber bullying: bullying a person by using technology to convey aggressive and demeaning messages (page 725)

Databases: large collection of information stored electronically and organised in categories for ease of retrieval (page 84)

Dataholic: a person who is emotionally dependent on communications systems such as mobile phones and the internet (page 7)

Decision avoidance: the behaviour of those who commission reports in order to avoid solving a problem (page 168)

Decoding: qualitatively transforming or converting a message from a coded form into a plain form (page 14)

Deductive logic: logic that moves from the general to the specific (page 380)

De-layering: reducing the number of layers or levels in an organisation, especially the middle levels (page 517)

Delphi: a method of group decision making and problem solving, involving polling geographically dispersed experts using questionnaires to quantify opinions and predictions (page 650)

Demassification: the process of transforming a few traditional outlets into many nontraditional ones (page 724)

Destructive role: causes conflict and ineffectiveness in work situations (page 586)

Dewey decimal classification system: a numeric system of classifying published materials into subject-classes and divisions (page 80)

Diagonal communication: communication that cuts across existing vertical and horizontal channels (page 515)

Direct structure: used to deliver a 'good news' message in a straightforward manner at the beginning of the report (page 164)

Directive question: a question that is targeted to specific aspects of a candidate's résumé, performance and capabilities (page 692)

Distinction of degree: a difference between two things of the same kind or class, measured solely by extent or quantity (page 381)

Distinction of kind: a difference between two things of unlike or distinct kind or class, measured by identity or quality (page 381)

Distributive bargaining: a negotiating process in which the two sides try to concede as little as possible and to gain as much as they can – a zero-sum approach, using a positions-based approach rather than an interests-based approach (page 415)

Diversity: greater representation within organisations of people from differing ethnic or racial background, sex, age, disability, national origin, religion and sexual orientation (page 492)

Document design: a process focusing on the appearance and navigability of documents (page 40)

Documentary-note system: referencing system using in-text superscript numbers or symbols rather than author name and year of publication (page 94)

Door-in-the-face: a persuasion method that depends on first trying to effect an unrealistically large attitude change, and then promoting a smaller attitude change (page 391)

Downsizing: reducing staff numbers in an organisation, especially in the middle levels (page 517)

Downward communication: sending messages from upper levels to lower levels of a hierarchy (page 514)

DRAFS: an email management system (acronym for Delete, Reply, Act, Forward, Save) (page 208)

Drafting: writing multiple versions of a document, allowing time to reconsider, reconceptualise and re-edit each version until a final draft is achieved (page 163)

Dyad: a group of two people (page 19)

Dyssemia: the condition of having difficulties in understanding or sending nonverbal information (page 275)

E-book: electronic book, or book that can be read and/or interacted with on computers (page 216)

E-cruitment: automated system used to advertise jobs; input résumés from web, email and print sources; analyse and filter résumé data; reply to correspondence; set up selection interviews; and conduct applicant testing (page 689)

Editing: consciously or unconsciously choosing to quantitatively transform or limit the content of a message after it is received (page 16)

Effective questioning: knowing the different types of questions that can be asked, and matching them to the situations we find ourselves in and the personalities with whom we interact (page 321)

Email: electronic text messages sent over a communications network between computers (page 202)

Email addiction: the apparently compulsive behaviour of people who check their email far more frequently than is necessary. (page 210)

Emotional competency: describes the personal and social skills that lead to superior performance in the world of work (page 285)

Emotional intelligence: a person's basic underlying capability to recognise and use emotion to better communicate with others (page 285)

Employment–experience paradox: the situation that occurs when you can't get a job without experience, and you can't get experience without a job (page 676)

Empowerment: transferring decision-making power to others, especially teams (page 517)

Encoding: qualitatively transforming or masking a message in some way (page 14)

Environmental scanning: processes for detecting trends on the horizon (page 567)

Essay: a document type that is concerned primarily with analysis rather than problem solving, and which rarely contains recommendations (page 157)

Ethos: appeal to credibility (page 388)

Exchange: belonging to a group sometimes depends on a cost-benefit calculation made continually by members (page 583)

Excuse: a defence or justification of something, sometimes expressed from a self-interested perspective and sometimes in persuasive and/or biased language (page 382)

Expert user review: a process in which a draft document is appraised by experts (page 47)

Explanation: a factual account of a situation without any values or opinions attached, usually expressed from a disinterested perspective and in neutral language (page 382)

Expositional technique: the development of a structure of propositions that can be easily followed by a reader (page 227)

Extranet: a linked system of intranets that facilitates B2B (business-to-business) communication (page 198)

Eye candy: visual material designed to reinforce the meaning of spoken or written messages (page 44)

Fact sheet: a short document setting out basic facts about a situation (page 565)

Fallacy: a false statement or belief (page 382)

Features: the characteristics of an idea, product or process (page 389)

Feedback: advice, support and critique provided in response by one person to another (page 323)

Feedback: response from message recipient, turning one-way into two-way communication (page 18)

Feminine: describes a culture in which non-traditional sex roles are observed (page 479)

File transfer protocol (FTP): a process that allows uploading and downloading of files on a network (page 206)

Flag-waving: a characteristic of reports that overemphasise the value of the writers' own department, team or section (page 168)

Flat organisation: an organisational structure characterised by fewer middle layers, a shift in decision-making power to groups or teams, and increased worker empowerment (page 517)

Font: the complete assortment of letters, numerals, punctuation marks and other characters of a specific typeface (page 49)

Footer: text at the bottom of the page set off from the main body of text and containing details about the document (page 52)

Foot-in-the-door: a persuasion method that depends on trying to effect a small attitude change, and then building on that to effect a larger attitude change (page 391)

Forced-choice question: a question designed to see if a candidate gives priority to one set of skills or values over another (page 692)

Formal norm: an explicit rule-governing behaviour (page 592)

Formal organisation: the 'official' structure of an organisation, usually represented in an organisational chart; most communication occurs through formally sanctioned channels, and reflects the legitimate or sanctioned chain of command (page 514)

FTF (face-to-face interaction): meeting of people physically present in the one spot, not using technology to facilitate communication (page 655)

Full block format: layout style in which all elements of a letter are justified to the left margin (page 119)

Functional format résumé: a résumé with personal information arranged in categories (page 684)

Goal incompatibility: conflict that occurs in organisations when the specific goals of different sections do not match (page 455)

Good news letter: a letter in which the writer conveys news that the reader will probably be happy to read (page 121)

Grabspeak: succinct expression of a situation (page 570)

GRIT: acronym for graduated and reciprocated initiatives in tension reduction, a conflict resolution method (page 458)

Group: two or more people who act together to achieve common aims or goals (page 582)

Groupthink: a pattern of defective decision making seen in groups (page 594)

Hacking: the activity of illegally breaking into other people's computers and electronic equipment (page 723)

Haptics: the study of touch as a form of communication (page 267)

Harvard system: system for citing sources using author names and the year of publication (page 92)

HATS: an acronym standing for headings, access, typography and spacing (page 48)

Header: text at the top of the page set off from the main body of text and containing details about the document (page 52)

Hedging: qualification of statements or claims (page 236)

Hedonic: pleasure seeking; inventing something as an end in itself, not as a means to an end (page 707)

Hidden agenda: unstated purpose or intention pursued covertly by one or a few members of a meeting to manipulate the outcome of the meeting (page 633)

Hierarchy: a system of organisation involving ranks or levels, with each level having power or influence over the level immediately below it (page 513)

Hierarchy of needs: a model of motivation that arranges human needs and motivations in a sequence (page 393)

High context: describes a culture in which the context of communicated messages is as important as the communicated message (page 487)

High-transparency organisation: an organisation with excellent internal and external communication processes; tends not to be crisis-prone (page 568)

Hobby horse: a pet project or idea given undue prominence in a report (page 168)

Homophily: the tendency for friendships and many other interpersonal relationships to occur between similar people (page 723)

Horizontal communication: sending and receiving messages between individuals at the same level or layer of a hierarchy (page 514)

Horizontal conflict: conflict that occurs in organisations between people at the same hierarchical level (page 454)

Hot-button words: words that are charged with a particular emotion, value or prejudice that may trigger off rapid, unthinking responses on one or both sides (page 452)

Improved nominal group technique (INGT): a method of group decision making and problem solving involving minimal verbal interaction, and ideas submitted to a meeting prior to the meeting (page 653)

Indirect structure: used to defer the major impact of a 'bad news' message until later in the report (page 164)

Indiscreet insiderism: a characteristic of reports full of in-group jargon and often unjustified hostility to out-group others (page 168)

Individualism: the extent to which a culture tolerates individual expression and provides support (page 479)

Inductive logic: logic that moves from the specific to the general (page 380)

Inflection: modulation of voice, changing pitch and/or loudness (page 367)

Informal norm: an implicit rule-governing behaviour (page 592)

Informal organisation: the 'unofficial' structure of an organisation, rarely if ever represented on an organisational chart; most communication occurs through unofficial channels, and can reinforce the norms and goals of the official organisation or can work against the norms and goals of the official organisation (page 514)

Information architecture: a process focusing on the structure of content, especially that of websites (page 40)

Information design: a process focusing on the fusion of content, structure and appearance of documents (page 40)

Information/persuasion mix: the synthesis of fact and opinion in a report; information is concerned with fact; persuasion is concerned with opinion (page 155)

Instruction email: a document, sent within an organisation, setting out information about procedures or operating routines (page 145)

Integrative bargaining: a bargaining approach in which the negotiators try to move from a positions-based approach to an interests-based approach (page 415)

Internet: a network of computer networks allowing the transfer of data and information between remote computer users (page 198)

Interpersonal communication skills: processes that help, distort or block communication of messages between individuals (page 284)

Intranet: a private computer network operating within an organisation (page 198)

Intrapersonal communication skills: processes that help, distort or block communication messages within an individual (page 284)

Issue: something that is a concern or preoccupation of one of your stakeholders or publics (page 566)

Issue linkage: linking issues that may or may not be connected, to strengthen a case (page 452)

Job creationism: the process by which researcher/writers present the outcome of a report in such a way that they become the most likely candidates to implement its recommendations (page 168)

Johari window: model for understanding communication interactions with others in terms of the extent to which we seek or solicit feedback (our capacity to listen) and the extent to which we are willing to give feedback about ourselves (our capacity to disclose) (page 330)

Judgement sampling: asking questions of experts rather than people who have been randomly sampled (page 106)

Justification: the equal spacing of words and lines according to a given measure (page 51)

Key selection criteria: standards or benchmarks of performance, ability, qualifications and experience that employers have set in relation to a job position (page 673)

Keyword: a word or phrase, highlighted by a meta-tag, used by search engines to identify and classify web pages (page 215)

Keywords and phrases: wording likely to be scanned from résumés and used as criteria for selection (page 690)

Kinesics: the study of nonlinguistic body movement in relation to communication (page 267)

Knowledge management: tapping into an organisation's intangible assets to systematically organise the knowledge of all its members so that it can be more effectively used for the organisation's benefit (page 539)

Landscape: a text block, page or image having a width greater than its height (page 51)

Lean medium: a medium that conveys little detailed information beyond the main message (page 19)

Learning and manipulation problem: knowledge of human nature may be used equally to enhance communication and as a tool of manipulation (page 287)

Letter of transmittal: introductory or covering document for a report, used when the audience is outside the organisation (page 165)

Library of Congress classification system: a library classification system using both numbers and letters (page 80)

List: vertical array of related ideas (page 52)

Literature search or survey: review of published work in a given field (page 79)

Logos: appeal to logic (page 388)

Low context: describes a culture in which the context of communicated messages is not as important as the communicated message itself (page 487)

Low-transparency organisation: an organisation with poor internal and external communication processes; tends to be crisis-prone (page 568)

Macro-culture: all the arts, beliefs, social institutions, etc. characteristic of a community, race, etc. (pages 473, 532)

MADE: formula for structuring emails (acronym for Message, Action, Details, Evidence) (page 204)

Management by listening: allowing others to reach their own solutions by talking through their problems (page 312)

Margin: the point at which white space ends and text begins (page 50)

Masculine: describes a culture in which traditional sex roles are observed (page 479)

Mashup: a digital mixing of various sources, such as music, images and animation (page 707)

Mechanistic: organisational design or structure that depends on tall and centralised structure, with mainly downward vertical communication; flourishes in placid environments (page 520)

Media kit: a package of informational and persuasive materials issued to the media (page 565)

Media release: a document issued to media setting out facts and opinions about a situation (page 560)

Mediated communication: communication that takes place by means of a technological channel (page 18)

Memo of transmittal: introductory or covering document for a report, used when the audience for your document is within the organisation (page 165)

Memo/memorandum: paper or email document sent to one or more recipients within an organisation (page 142)

Message: information conveyed by any means from one person or group to another person or group (page 13)

Message termination and failure: when messages are terminal and when there is no reciprocal response from the message receiver switching into the role of a message sender (page 26)

Meta-communication: communication about communication and communications (page 6)

Metacrawler: a search engine, or a software program, that displays results from multiple search engines (page 86)

Meta-tag: a few lines of HTML code that identify keywords and make it easier for search engines to search and classify web pages (page 215)

Micro-culture: the predominating attitudes and behaviour that characterise the functioning of a group or organisation (pages 473, 532)

Mirroring: consciously or unconsciously copying the nonverbal behaviour of someone admired (page 267)

MLATNA: (Most Likely Alternative to a Negotiated Agreement) another choice or substitute action that may produce an outcome superior to any outcome we might gain from a negotiation process – usually less extreme and more realistic than some BATNAs and WATNAs (page 411)

Modem: a device that allows computers to talk to each other in the same way that a telephone allows humans to talk to each other (page 199)

Monetise: a jargon term used in information industries – it simply means to enable a product to make money, particularly when the product has been free up until now (page 707)

Monochronic: literally, one time; an approach or cultural mindset that sees time as linear and measurable, with the practical upshot of emphasising punctuality, detailed scheduling of activities, and doing only one task at a time (page 487)

Mosaic form: a nonlinear approach to information design facilitated by hyperlinking around and between web pages (page 200)

Motion: a formal proposal for action or change put to a meeting that calls for those present to vote for or against it (page 628)

MP3 or mpeg3: a digital audio format devised by the Moving Pictures Expert Group in 1991 compresses original file size (page 717)

Naïve user review: a process in which a draft document is appraised by individuals who have no specific expertise in the area (page 47)

Necessary condition: a condition or situation that provides a basis for something, but by itself is not adequate to make that something happen (page 382)

Negative-sum outcome: a situation in which both parties lose (page 408)

Network analysis: a technique for mapping communication roles played by people within organisations (page 524)

Networking: deliberately cultivating contact with others in your own organisation and in other organisations in order to create an informal system of relationships and to develop your career (page 526)

No-email Fridays: policy of some organisations to cut down on too many emails and promote face-to-face communication (page 209)

Noise: anything that interferes with or distorts a message, or creates barriers to communication (page 17)

Nominal group technique (NGT): a method of group decision making and problem solving involving minimal verbal interaction (page 652)

Open question: a question that requires a general and discursive response (page 692)

Open search strategies: approaches to creating primary data that provide for an unlimited range of responses from respondents (page 100)

Organic: organisational design or structure that depends on flat and decentralised structure, with mainly all-directional communication; flourishes in turbulent environments (page 520)

Organisation: a group of people who work together to achieve a common purpose (page 510)

Organisational design: the structure of an organisation (page 513)

Organisational silence: the tendency of lower levels of staff not to speak out on significant issues (page 537)

Orphan: the first line of a paragraph at the bottom of a column or page, which then spills onto the next column or page (page 52)

Paradigm: the most popular current view of an aspect of reality (page 379)

Paragraph: block of text dealing with one topic (page 52)

Paralinguistics: the properties of voices, separate from the words being spoken, that can convey meanings (page 263)

Paraphrasing: recasting someone else's words in your own (page 98)

Pathos: appeal to emotions (page 388)

PATNA: (Probable Alternative to a Negotiated Agreement) – same as MLATNA (page 411)

Performance stress: anxiety related to performance; also known as *speaker anxiety* or *stage fright* (page 355)

Peripheral processing: the process of evaluating a persuasive message according to nonobjective factors (page 392)

Personal brand: the set of characteristics and skills that sets one person apart from another; also known as unique selling proposition (USP) (page 674)

Persuasive letter: a document sent to an organisation or individual to influence or effect a change in behaviour (page 138)

Phatic: a type of communication that is neither informational nor dialogic, which reinforces social bonds by the sharing of feelings and establishing a mood of sociability (page 723)

Phishing: the activity of sending out fake, but realistic-looking, messages from trustworthy sources, asking for the receiver's details (passwords, user names) in order to steal from that receiver (page 723)

Placid environment: a situation, society or market in which the rate of change is low and the future is fairly predictable (page 517)

Plagiarism: passing off someone else's ideas, and the way in which they are expressed, as your own (page 96)

Plan B: alternative course of action that can give you flexibility in negotiations (page 411)

Point of view: a stance or position; the expression of an opinion and the backing up of that opinion (page 227)

Polychronic: literally, many times; an approach or cultural mindset that sees time as having multiple dimensions and experiences, with the practical upshot of emphasising slow pacing and multitasking (page 487)

Pooled ignorance: a situation in which a majority of people believe something, but their belief is wrong (page 647)

Portrait: a text block, page or image having a height greater than its width (page 51)

Position paper: document setting out position, standpoint or policy on a particular issue or set of circumstances; sometimes issued with a media release (page 564)

Positive-sum outcome: a situation in which both parties win (page 408)

Power distance: a measure of the inequality and equality within a culture (page 478)

Power/value asymmetry: conflict that occurs in organisations between people with differing values and/or status (page 455)

Pre-editing: consciously or unconsciously choosing to quantitatively transform or limit the content of a message before it is sent (page 14)

Preferences: the inclination or bias towards one particular communication channel rather than another (page 25)

Premise: a proposition or claim on which an argument is based, or from which a conclusion is drawn (page 380)

Priestley's paradox: the more we elaborate our means of communication, the less we actually communicate (page 7)

Primary data: original unpublished material or material published in an original form (page 78)

Profile: a biographical sketch of a person within the organisation that is often accompanied by photographs (page 565)

Pronunciation: the act of producing the sounds of speech (page 365)

Proofs and examples: evidence to substantiate assertions (page 227)

Proposals, tenders, submissions, bids, grants and quotations: persuasive documents often used in situations of competitive bidding for scarce resources (page 190)

Provocation: deliberately teasing or needling someone, sometimes with a view to evoking a physically violent response (page 453)

Proxemics: the study of the spatial relationships between individuals (page 270)

Proximity: belonging to a group sometimes happens simply because members find themselves located physically near each other (page 583)

Pseudo-event: an event staged primarily to attract media coverage (page 553)

Psychobabble: superficial and banal treatments of psychological theory (page 285)

Public: an individual or group outside an organisation interested in what goes on inside that organisation and in the outputs of that organisation; also known as a constituency or stakeholder; targets of public communication messages (page 556)

Public information model: characterised by one-way communication in which truth is essential (page 553)

Publicity model: characterised by one-way communication in which truth is not essential; press agentry (page 553)

Reactivity: a characteristic of reports that focus only on the past (page 168)

Recommendations: final section of a report consisting of suggestions for action based on conclusions reached (page 169)

Reinforcement: sending the same message through different channels (page 25)

Request email: a document, sent within an organisation, asking for solutions and action (page 144)

Resource scarcity: conflict that occurs in organisations when resources are, or are perceived to be, scarce (page 455)

Retaliation: reciprocal action in a conflict, where a real or perceived offence by one side is matched or surpassed by a real offence by the other side (page 453)

Rich medium: a medium that conveys a range of verbal and nonverbal information, including colour, auditory and visual elements (page 19)

Risky shift: a tendency of groups to make decisions that are riskier than those that would have been made by any of the group's members acting individually (page 610)

Role: an expected behaviour (page 586)

Role conflict: conflict that occurs in organisations when there are misunderstandings about what duties and behaviour are expected from persons (page 455)

Samizdat: Russian term for illegal self-publications created on basic technology that produced literature whose messages helped break up the Soviet Union (page 723)

Scope: the terms of reference of a report; what the document is about, and what it is not about (page 161)

Secondary data: material that interprets primary material, published after primary data is published (page 78)

Secretary: keeps written records of the meeting and works with the chairperson on managing the meeting process (page 632)

Security: belonging to a group may make us feel safer against external threats (page 583)

Selective perception: distorting or filtering reality so that conflict is polarised (page 451)

Self-talk: internal conversations we have with ourselves; a form of intrapersonal communication (page 290)

Sender–Message–Receiver (SMR) model: a model showing a one-way path or pattern of communication (page 9)

Shoot-the-messenger climate: a situation in organisations where those who point out bad news are punished, even if it is not their fault (page 567)

Shoot-the-messenger ethos: the tendency to punish people for communicating bad news about the organisation (page 537)

Silo culture: a culture of noncommunication between separate parts of one organisation (page 535)

Sliming: when a person tries to use influence and persuasion in such a manipulative and transparent way that his or her actions and words elicit contempt from others (page 400)

Sloppiness: a characteristic of reports written in a superficial and unprofessional manner (page 168)

Small world phenomenon: the idea that any person on the globe may be separated from any other person by no more than six steps, or 'six degrees of separation', and we are only now becoming aware that there may be patterns or networks of interconnection (page 522)

Social aggregate: a class or order of people who share certain characteristics but do not necessarily share goals (page 582)

Social interaction: belonging to a group may help satisfy a need for human company (page 583)

Social loafing: the tendency of some group members to put in less effort if they believe that their underperformance will not be noted – the phenomenon of one group member getting a 'free ride' while others do the work (page 585)

Socio-emotional role: relates to the interpersonal aspects of work (page 586)

Solicited application letter: a cover or application letter written in response to an actual advertisement or notice of a job vacancy (page 680)

Spacing: the vertical distance between lines of text on a page (page 50)

Span of control: the number of people who report directly to the person immediately above them in the hierarchy (page 517)

Spice: variety added to a presentation, such as quotations, statistics, anecdotes, analogies or metaphors, dramatic visuals, demonstrations or humour (page 351)

Spin: the angle, emphasis or distortion put on an event or person in order to influence public opinion (page 552)

Staff–line conflict: conflict that occurs in organisations between people doing front-line and backup tasks (page 454)

Stalemate: the phase in a conflict when all parties seem unable to move to a solution; also known as a deadlock or impasse (page 460)

Standing orders: document setting out specific procedures for conducting business in meetings (page 628)

Sufficient condition: one possible cause of a result, although not necessarily the only one (page 382)

Summary: briefly sums up the content of the document; sometimes the only part of a report that is properly read (page 166)

Superordinate goal: a goal that can be worked towards by all parties to a conflict (page 457)

Support of individual or leader: a situation where most power resides with one person, and the group or meeting works primarily to support that person (page 645)

Syllogism: a sequence of statements composed of premises leading to a conclusion (page 380)

Synchronous communication: communication that is sent and received at virtually the same time (pages 18, 511)

Synergy: the whole group's performance is greater than the sum of its equal parts (page 584)

Tactile thinking: the process by which the physical activity of writing by hand (as opposed to using a keyboard) can trigger thought patterns (page 89)

Tall organisation: an organisational structure characterised by more layers, narrower spans of control and more centralised decision making (page 517)

Task complexity: belonging to a group may allow combinations of specialists to tackle tasks that, individually, they would not normally tackle (page 583)

Task role: relates to the functional or technical nature of work (page 586)

Technologically mediated communication: human communication that uses mechanical or electronic means to transfer meaning (page 5)

Telecommuting: working from home using computer, phone, video and other links to communicate with fellow workers and/or a central workplace (page 522)

Tell: a nonverbal behaviour that reveals a person's true state of mind (page 256)

Tertiary data: material that synthesises and summarises primary and secondary material, usually published well after primary and secondary sources (page 78)

The grapevine: informal communication system; flourishes in a knowledge vacuum (page 529)

The other: any group of people perceived as different in terms of nationality, ethnicity, religion, political alignment, class or caste, or gender (page 475)

Thesis statement: sentence or sentences, usually positioned at the beginning of an essay, that sum up the writer's argument and purpose in the discussion to follow (page 233)

Thesis statement: statement of research goal (page 77)

Three-part talk structure: Tell them what you are going to tell them; tell them; tell them what you have told them. (page 353)

Timidity: a characteristic of reports that do not confront or tackle the real issues of a situation (page 168)

Tools: the means of getting messages to channels (page 560)

Topic loyalty or capture: the process by which researcher/writers become so involved with an idea they are reporting on that they lose objectivity and recommend implementation even when some of the evidence suggests this would be inadvisable (page 168)

Topic sentence: usually the first sentence in a paragraph; introduces the main idea of the paragraph (page 234)

Topless meeting: meeting in which laptop computers and other technological devices are banned because they may distract from real work getting done in the meeting (page 657)

Transferable skills: skills that are relevant to more than one area of technical expertise (page 669)

Turbulent environment: a situation, society or market in which the rate of change is high and the future is uncertain (page 518)

Tweet: a message sent or received via the Twitter microblogging system (page 710)

Two-way asymmetric model: characterised by two-way communication, but with little chance of feedback into the sending organisation (page 554)

Two-way symmetric model: characterised by two-way communication, with messages feeding back into sending organisation to change that organisation (page 554)

Uncertainty avoidance: a concept that helps explain how cultures respond to the uncertain nature of future events (page 478)

Unsolicited application letter: a cover or application letter that is written when no advertisement or notice has been placed, in the hope that it might attract interest from a potential employer (page 680)

Upward communication: sending messages from lower levels to upper levels of a hierarchy (page 514)

Usability: the extent to which a document or process or product can be understood and used (page 42)

Vancouver: system for citing sources using superscript numbers instead of names and dates, and often grouping several cross-reference numbers at the same point in the text (page 94)

Variation: the possible tendency of media or message processes to vary or transform or change the content of a message (page 25)

Vendetta: a characteristic of reports that unfairly ascribe blame to innocent parties (page 168)

Verbal headlining: using words like print headlines to give cues to content (page 353)

Vertical communication: sending and receiving messages between the levels or layers of a hierarchy (page 514)

Vertical conflict: conflict that occurs in organisations between people at different hierarchical levels (page 454)

Videoconferencing: using video technology to conduct meetings (page 655)

Viral marketing: sending commercial messages to potential customers via social networks, rather than by conventional advertising (page 716)

Virtual meeting: situation in which people communicate with each other using technology rather than face-to-face interaction (FTF) (page 655)

Virtual organisation: an organisation comprising a network of geographically dispersed workers connected to one another, and sometimes to a central workplace, via computer, phone, video and other links (page 522)

Virtual team: a work group whose individual members are located in widely dispersed locations (page 611)

Voice pitch: height or depth of voice (page 367)

Voting: the expression of preferences through voices, show of hands or ballots (page 646)

Waffle: to pad out a piece of writing with meaningless or redundant words (page 235)

Warning memo: a document sent when there is a perception that someone is not doing the right thing (page 146)

WATNA: (for Worst Alternative To a Negotiated Agreement) another choice or substitute action that may produce an outcome inferior to any outcome we might gain from a negotiation process (page 410)

Web conferencing: using internet and sometimes video technology to conduct online meetings (page 655)

Web page: a document on the world wide web consisting of an HTML file and associated graphics and script files; a website may comprise a number of web pages (page 212)

Web 2.0: a term probably characterised by user-generated content and mobility (not needing to be at a desk to log on to the net) (page 704)

Whitewash: a characteristic of reports that avoid apportioning blame where it is due (page 168)

Widow: the last line of a paragraph at the top of a column or page (page 52)

Wi-fi: a term back-formed from hi-fi, or high fidelity audio; wireless transmission of the internet and other signals (page 723)

Winner's curse: the perception that we have got the bad part of a deal; usually because we were full of enthusiasm but short on information (page 418)

Win–win situation: a positive-sum outcome (page 408)

Wireless transmission: transmitting data as a broadcast signal in the electromagnetic spectrum (page 199)

Workflow interdependence: conflict that occurs in organisations when the output of one section is the input of another, and mismatches occur (page 455)

'You' attitude: approach to writing that prioritises the needs and interests of the reader (page 113)

Zero-sum outcome: a situation in which one person's gains equal another person's losses (page 408)

INDEX